ENGLISH LAW

Cavendish
Publishing
Limited

London • Sydney

ENGLISH LAW

Gary Slapper, LLB, LLM, PhD, PGCE (Law)
Director of the Law Programme, The Open University

David Kelly, BA, BA (Law), PhD
Principal Lecturer in Law, Staffordshire University

Cavendish
Publishing
Limited

London • Sydney

First published in Great Britain 2000 by Cavendish Publishing Limited,
The Glass House, Wharton Street, London WC1X 9PX, United Kingdom
Telephone: +44 (0) 20 7278 8000   Facsimile: +44 (0) 20 7278 8080
E-mail: info@cavendishpublishing.com
Visit our Home Page on http://www.cavendishpublishing.com

British Library Cataloguing in Publication Data

Slapper, G
English Law
1 Law – England 2 Law – Wales
I Title II Kelly, David, 1950 Aug 16–
349.4'2

ISBN   1 85941 558 X

Printed and bound in Great Britain

PREFACE

As we begin this millennium, English law probably exercises more influence, for better or worse, over people's lives across the world than any other set of legal principles and procedures. This is certainly so in most of the 54 members of the Commonwealth, including the considerable jurisdictions of places like Canada, Pakistan, India and Australia. It is also worthy of note that the original law and legal systems in North America were largely based on the principles of English law.

We have aimed in this text to provide the reader with a clear and accurate explanation of how the English legal system currently works, and the actual content of English law in all of its key areas of operation. Where we have deemed it appropriate, we have aimed to put a legal rule or principle in its social, historical or economic context. We have also put several areas of law into some legal theory settings. Given a little depth in another dimension, a plain legal rule will often be not just easier to understand but also more interesting.

Few people go through life without, at various stages, developing strong opinions about the desirability or otherwise of some aspect of law. Moreover, lawyers represent the single largest occupational grouping in the British Parliament, and it is clear that many debates about law are very important because the way the debates are resolved ultimately has a substantial effect upon the way we live. We have, therefore, in this text allowed a critical element into our explanations and discussions. We have thought it helpful to present the legal theory underlying policies and law in many of the chapters of this book. At the end of the last century, a great many major changes were made to the English legal system and several areas of English law. In the Woolf reforms, we saw a fundamental redesign of the whole of civil procedure – the most fundamental changes in 150 years to the way the civil courts work. The Access to Justice Act 1999 fundamentally changed the way legal services are provided to those with limited means; it established the Legal Services Commission, the Community Legal Service, and the Criminal Defence Service, and introduced changes to conditional fee arrangements, the magistrates' court system, rights of audience and appeals; and the Human Rights Act 1998 is set to have what will probably be the greatest impact upon public law and criminal law for over 100 years. Major changes in European law, criminal law, contract law, employment law, tort and commercial law will also have a substantial impact. All this new law is incorporated into the text, and we have, where we have thought appropriate, commented upon the types of challenge and issue that will be likely to follow as a consequence of this new law.

Gary Slapper
David Kelly
March 2000

ACKNOWLEDGMENTS

We are very grateful to many people for the work and expertise that contributed to this book. We owe a particular debt to Suzanne, Hannah, Emily, Charlotte, Jane and Michael for their patience and support while we researched, read and wrote.

We greatly benefited from the encouragement, guidance, and the unstinting dedication to the project of Jo Reddy, Sonny Leong and Cara Annett at Cavendish. We are very grateful to Marilyn Lannigan for her conscientious research, and to Denis Lanser, MA Ramjohn, and Ann Holmes for their excellent contributions on criminal law, trusts and negligence and employment law. Professor Hazel Genn, Liz Rodgers, Michael Fealy, Steve Greenfield, David Stott, Mlcèal Barden and Janice Richardson made very valuable comments on draft chapters.

Many others have given encouragement, observations and assistance or have stimulated our thoughts in a helpful way. Thanks are thus due to Doreen and Ivor Slapper, Raie Schwartz, David and Julie Whight, Hugh McLaughlan, Alison Morris, Frances Gibb at *The Times*, and Professor Roland Kaye for his ribald good humour on the law and lawyers.

ONLINE SUBSCRIPTION

This book is supported by an online subscription to give you access to periodic updates.

English Law has been written to comprehensively cover all the main subjects of English law, and is fully up to date as at 1 March 2000. You do not need to have a computer to use any part of this book, as it stands entirely independent as a text. The website pages you are entitled to visit by virtue of the password purchased with this book additionally gives you 12 months' free access to periodic updates. If you want to use these, but do not possess a computer, you need only go to a public library, internet café, or your local college in order to print off any updating pages you require.

FOR TEACHERS, the website pages draw your attention to websites that are helpful and to any developments that English law teachers may wish to focus on in various contexts, including schools, colleges, universities, and those preparing students for organisational exams like those for the police, company secretaries, banking and so forth. Questions and model answers are also periodically posted on these website pages.

FOR STUDENTS, the website pages include updates to keep you informed of the most important recent developments across all of the subject areas covered in the book. Model answers to examination questions are periodically posted on these website pages.

There is also a question and answer section in the website pages which will allow users to share information relevant to the book.

To gain access to the website pages, you need to enter the unique password (printed on the card inside the front of the book) at our website at:

http://www.cavendishpublishing.com

The password is protected and your subscription to the site is free for 12 months from the date of registration.

Follow the instructions printed on the card to activate your subscription today.

CONTENTS

Contents

13 THE CRIMINAL PROCESS: (1) THE INVESTIGATION OF CRIME 691

TABLE OF CASES

Table of Cases

Table of Cases

TABLE OF STATUTES

TABLE OF STATUTORY INSTRUMENTS

TABLE OF EC LEGISLATION

TABLE OF ABBREVIATIONS

AA	Arbitration Act 1950/1979/1996
ABWOR	Assistance by way of representation
ACLEC	Advisory Committee on Legal Education and Conduct
ADR	Alternative dispute resolution
AJA	Administration of Justice Act 1985
BA	Bail Act 1976
BIS	Bail Information Schemes
Br J Crim	British Journal of Criminology
British JLS	British Journal of Law and Society
CA	Children Act 1989
CAA	Criminal Appeal Act 1968/1995
CCR	County Court Rules
CCRC	Criminal Cases Review Commission
CDS	Criminal Defence Service
CEO	Civilian enforcement officers
CJA	Criminal Justice Act 1967/1972/1982/1987/1988/1991/1994
CJPOA	Criminal Justice and Public Order Act 1964/1984/1994
CJR	Civil Justice Review
CLC	Citizens' Law Centre
CLS	Community Legal Service
CLSP	Community Legal Service Partnership
CLSA	Courts and Legal Services Act 1990
CPIA	Criminal Procedure and Investigations Act 1996
CPR	Civil Procedure Rules 1998
CPS	Crown Prosecution Service
Crim LR	Criminal Law Review
CSA	Child Support Agency
DCOA	Deregulation and Contracting Out Act 1994
DGFT	Director General of Fair Trading
DPMCA	Domestic Proceedings and Magistrates' Courts Act 1978
DPP	Director of Public Prosecutions

EAT	Employment Appeal Tribunal
EC	European Community
ECHR	European Court of Human Rights
ECJ	European Court of Justice
EEC	European Economic Community
EL Rev	European Law Review
EMS	European Monetary System
EMU	European Monetary Union
EP(C)A	Employment Protection (Consolidation) Act 1978
ERA	Employment Rights Act
EU	European Union
Howard J	Howard Journal
Howard J of Criminal Justice	Howard Journal of Criminal Justice
HRA	Human Rights Act 1998
JA	Juries Act 1974
JCE	Justices' chief executive
JdA	Judicature Act 1873
JLS	Journal of Law and Society
JP	Justice of the Peace
JPA	Justices of the Peace Act 1979
JSB	Judicial Studies Board
JSPTL	Journal of Society of Public Teachers of Law
LAA	Legal Advice and Assistance
LAdA	Legal Aid Act 1988
LAG	Legal Action Group
Law Soc Gazette	Law Society Gazette
LCD	Lord Chancellor's Department
LPC	Legal Practice Course
LQR	Law Quarterly Review
LSO	Legal Services Ombudsman
MA	Misrepresentation Act 1967
MCA	Magistrates' Courts Act 1980

Table of Abbreviations

MCC	Magistrates' Courts Committee
MDP	Multi-disciplinary partnerships
MLR	Modern Law Review
MNP	Multi-national partnerships
NCC	National Consumer Council
NILQ	Northern Ireland Legal Quarterly
NLJ	New Law Journal
OSS	Office for the Supervision of Solicitors
PACE	Police and Criminal Evidence Act 1984/1994
PAP	Pre-action protocol
PCA	Parliamentary Commissioner for Administration
PCCC	Professional Conduct and Complaints Committee
POA	Prosecution of Offences Act 1985
QBD	Queen's Bench Division
QC	Queen's Counsel
RSC	Rules of the Supreme Court
SJ	Solicitors Journal
SLR	Student Law Review
SFO	Serious Fraud Office
SEA	Single European Act 1986/1987
SGSA	Supply of Goods and Services Act
SoGA	Sale of Goods Act 1979
SSGA	Sale and Supply of Goods Act 1994
TLATA	Trusts of Land and Appointment of Trustees Act 1996
UCTA	Unfair Contract Terms Act 1977
UNICTRAL	United Nations Commission on International Trade Law

CHAPTER 1

INTRODUCTION TO LAW

1.1 The nature of law

One of the most obvious and most central characteristics of all societies is that they must possess some degree of order to permit the members to interact over a sustained period of time. Different societies, however, have different forms of order. Some societies are highly regimented with strictly enforced social rules whereas others continue to function in what outsiders might consider a very unstructured manner with apparently few strict rules being enforced.

Order is therefore necessary, but the form through which order is maintained is certainly not universal as many anthropological studies have shown (see Mansell and Meteyard, *A Critical Introduction to Law*, 1999).

In our society, law plays an important part in the creation and maintenance of social order. We must be aware, however, that law, as we know it, is not the only means of creating order. Even in our society, order is not solely dependent on law, but also involves questions of a more general moral and political character. This book is not concerned with providing a general explanation of the form of order. It is concerned, more particularly, with describing and explaining the key institutional aspects of that particular form of order that is legal order.

The most obvious way in which law contributes to the maintenance of social order is the way in which it deals with disorder or conflict. This book, therefore, is particularly concerned with the institutions and procedures, both civil and criminal, through which law operates to ensure a particular form of social order by dealing with various conflicts when they arise.

Law is a formal mechanism of social control and as such it is essential that the student of law be fully aware of the nature of that formal structure. There are, however, other aspects to law that are less immediately apparent, but of no less importance, such as the inescapable political nature of law. Some textbooks focus more on this particular aspect of law than others and these differences become evident in the particular approach adopted by the authors. The approach favoured by the authors of this book is to recognise that studying English law is not just about learning legal rules but is also about considering a social institution of fundamental importance.

1.2   Categories of law

There are various ways of categorising law which initially tend to confuse the non-lawyer and the new student of law. What follows will set out these categorisations in their usual dual form whilst at the same time trying to overcome the confusion inherent in such duality. It is impossible to avoid the confusing repetition of the same terms to mean different things and indeed the purpose of this section is to make sure that students are aware of the fact that the same words can have different meanings depending upon the context in which they are used.

1.2.1   Common law and civil law

In this particular juxtaposition, these terms are used to distinguish two distinct legal systems and approaches to law. The use of the term common law in this context refers to all those legal systems which have adopted the historic English legal system. Foremost amongst these is, of course, the US but many other Commonwealth, and former Commonwealth, countries retain a common law system. The term civil law refers to those other jurisdictions which have adopted the European continental system of law derived essentially from ancient Roman law, but owing much to the Germanic tradition.

The usual distinction to be made between the two systems is that the former, common law system, tends to be case centred and hence judge centred, allowing scope for a discretionary, *ad hoc*, pragmatic approach to the particular problems that appear before the courts; whereas the latter, civil law system, tends to be a codified body of general abstract principles which control the exercise of judicial discretion. In reality, both of these views are extremes, with the former over-emphasising the extent to which the common law judge can impose his discretion and the latter under-estimating the extent to which continental judges have the power to exercise judicial discretion. It is perhaps worth mentioning at this point that the European Court of Justice (ECJ), established, in theory, on civil law principles, is, in practice, increasingly recognising the benefits of establishing a body of case law.

It has to be recognised, and indeed the English courts do so, that, although the ECJ is not bound by the operation of the doctrine of *stare decisis* (see 2.3), it still does not decide individual cases on an *ad hoc* basis and, therefore, in the light of a perfectly clear decision of the European Court, national courts will be reluctant to refer similar cases to its jurisdiction. Thus, after the ECJ decided, in *Grant v South West Trains Ltd* (1998), that Community law did not cover discrimination on grounds of sexual orientation, the High Court withdrew a similar reference in *R v Secretary of State for Defence ex p Perkins (No 2)* (1998) (see 2.7.2 for a detailed consideration of the ECJ).

1.2.2 Common law and equity

In this particular juxtaposition, the terms refer to a particular division within the English legal system.

The common law has been romantically and inaccurately described as the law of the common people of England. In fact, the common law emerged as the product of a particular struggle for political power. Prior to the Norman Conquest of England in 1066, there was no unitary, national legal system. The emergence of the common law represents the imposition of such a unitary system under the auspices and control of a centralised power in the form of a sovereign king; and, in that respect, it represented the assertion and affirmation of that central sovereign power.

Traditionally, much play is made about the circuit of judges travelling round the country establishing the King's peace and, in so doing, selecting the best local customs and making them the basis of the law of England in a piecemeal but totally altruistic procedure. The reality of this process was that the judges were asserting the authority of the central State and its legal forms and institutions, over the disparate and fragmented State and legal forms of the earlier feudal period. Hence, the common law was common to all in application but certainly was not common from all. By the end of the 13th century, the central authority had established its precedence at least partly through the establishment of the common law. Originally, courts had been no more than an adjunct of the King's Council, the *Curia Regis*, but gradually the common law courts began to take on a distinct institutional existence in the form of the courts of Exchequer, Common Pleas and King's Bench. With this institutional autonomy, however, there developed an institutional sclerosis, typified by a reluctance to deal with matters that were not or could not be processed in the proper form of action. Such a refusal to deal with substantive injustices, because they did not fall within the particular parameters of procedural and formal constraints, by necessity led to injustice and the need to remedy the perceived weaknesses in the common law system. The response was the development of equity.

Plaintiffs unable to gain access to the three common law courts might directly appeal to the sovereign, and such pleas would be passed for consideration and decision to the Lord Chancellor who acted as the King's conscience. As the common law courts became more formalistic and more inaccessible, pleas to the Chancellor correspondingly increased and eventually this resulted in the emergence of a specific court constituted to deliver equitable or fair decisions in cases which the common law courts declined to deal with. As had happened with the common law, the decisions of the Courts of Equity established principles which were used to decide later cases, so it should not be thought that the use of equity meant that judges had discretion to decide cases on the basis of their personal idea of what was just in each case.

The division between the common law courts and the Courts of Equity continued until they were eventually combined by the Judicature Acts (JdA) 1873–75. Prior to this legislation, it was essential for a party to raise their action in the appropriate court, for example, the courts of law would not implement equitable principles; the Acts, however, provided that every court had the power and the duty to decide cases in line with common law and equity, with the latter being paramount in the final analysis.

Some would say that, as equity was never anything other than a gloss on common law, it is perhaps appropriate, if not ironic, that now both systems have been effectively subsumed under the one term: common law.

Common law remedies are available as of right. Remedies in equity are discretionary, in other words, they are awarded at the will of the court, and depend on the behaviour, and situation, of the party claiming such remedies This means that, in effect, the court does not have to award an equitable remedy where it considers the conduct of the party seeking such an award does not deserve such an award (*D and C Builders v Rees* (1965)). The usual equitable remedies are:

- *injunction*: this is a court order requiring someone to do something or, alternatively, to stop doing something (*Warner Bros v Nelson* (1937));

- *specific performance*: this is a court order requiring one of the parties to a contractual agreement to complete their part of the contract. It is usually only awarded in respect of contracts relating to specific individual articles, such as land, and will not be awarded where the court cannot supervise the operation of its order (*Ryan v Mutual Tontine Westminster Chambers Association* (1893));

- *rectification*: this order relates to the alteration, under extremely limited circumstances, of contractual documents (*Jocscelyne v Nissen* (1970));

- *rescission*: this order returns parties to a contractual agreement to the position they were in before the agreement was entered into. It is essential to distinguish this award from the common law award of damages, which is intended to place the parties in the position they would have been in had the contract been completed.

1.2.3 Common law and statute law

This particular conjunction follows on from the immediately preceding section in that the common law here refers to the substantive law and procedural rules that have been created by the judiciary through the decisions in the cases they have heard. Statute law, on the other hand, refers to law that has been created by Parliament in the form of legislation. Although there has been a significant increase in statute law in the 20th century, the courts still have an important role to play in creating and operating law generally and in determining the operation of legislation in particular. The relationship of this pair of concepts is of central importance and is considered in more detail in Chapters 2 and 4.

1.2.4 Private law and public law

There are two different ways of understanding the division between private and public law.

At one level, the division relates specifically to actions of the State and its functionaries vis à vis the individual citizen, and the legal manner in which, and form of law through which, such relationships are regulated: that is, public law. In the 19th century, it was at least possible to claim as AV Dicey did that there was no such thing as public law, in this distinct administrative sense, and that the powers of the State with regard to individuals was governed by the ordinary law of the land, operating through the normal courts. Whether such a claim was accurate or not when it was made, and it is unlikely, there certainly can be no doubt now that public law constitutes a distinct, and growing, area of law in its own right. The growth of public law, in this sense, has mirrored the growth and increased activity of the contemporary State, and has seen its role as seeking to regulate such activity. The crucial role of judicial review in relation to public law will be considered in some detail in Chapter 4.

There is, however, a second aspect to the division between private and public law. One corollary of the divide is that matters located within the private sphere are seen as purely a matter for individuals themselves to regulate, without the interference of the State, whose role is limited to the provision of the forum for deciding contentious issues and mechanisms for the enforcement of such decisions. Matters within the public sphere, however, are seen as issues relating to the interest of the State and general public, and, as such, to be protected and prosecuted by the State. It can be seen, therefore, that the category to which any dispute is allocated is of crucial importance to how it is dealt with. Contract may be thought of as the classic example of private law, but the extent to which this purely private legal area has been subjected to the regulation of public law, in such areas as consumer protection, should not be underestimated. Equally, the most obvious example of public law in this context would be criminal law. Feminists have argued, however, that the allocation of domestic matters to the sphere of private law has led to a denial of a general interest in the treatment and protection of women. By defining domestic matters as private, the State, and its functionaries, have denied women access to its power to protect themselves from abuse. In doing so, it is suggested that, in fact, such categorisation has reflected and maintained the social domination of men over women.

1.2.5 Civil law and criminal law

Civil law is a form of private law and involves the relationships between individual citizens. It is the legal mechanism through which individuals can assert claims against others and have those rights adjudicated and enforced. The purpose of civil law is to settle disputes between individuals and to provide remedies; it is not concerned with punishment as such. The role of the State in relation to civil law is to establish the general framework of legal rules and to provide the legal institutions for operating those rights, but the activation of the civil law is strictly a matter for the individuals concerned. Contract, tort and property law are generally aspects of civil law.

Criminal law, on the other hand, is an aspect of public law and relates to conduct which the State considers with disapproval and which it seeks to control and/or eradicate. Criminal law involves the enforcement of particular forms of behaviour, and the State, as the representative of society, acts positively to ensure compliance. Thus, criminal cases are brought by the State in the name of the Crown and cases are reported in the form of *Regina v* (*Regina* is simply Latin for Queen and case references are usually abbreviated to *R v ...*), whereas civil cases are referred to by the names of the parties involved in the dispute, for example, *Smith v Jones*.

A crucial distinction between criminal and civil law is the level of proof required in the different types of cases. In the criminal case, the prosecution is required to prove that the defendant is guilty beyond reasonable doubt, whereas, in a civil case, the degree of proof is much lower, and has only to be on the balance of probabilities. This difference in the level of proof raises the possibility of someone being able to succeed in a civil case, although there may not be sufficient evidence for a criminal prosecution. And indeed, this strategy has been used successfully in a number of cases against the police where the Crown Prosecution Service has considered there to be insufficient evidence to support a criminal conviction for assault.

It should also be noted that the distinction between civil and criminal responsibility is further blurred in cases involving what may be described as hybrid offences. These are situations where a court awards a civil order against an individual, on the balance of probabilities, but with the attached sanction that any breach of the order will be subject to punishment as a criminal offence. As examples of this procedure may be cited the Protection from Harassment Act 1997 and the new provision for the making of Anti-Social Behaviour Orders available under s 1(i) of the Crime and Disorder Act 1998. Both of these provisions are of considerable interest and deserve some attention in their own right. The Protection from Harassment Act was introduced as a measure to deal with stalking, the harassment of individuals by people continuously following them, and allowed the victim of harassment to get a court order to prevent the stalking. Whereas stalking may have been the high profile source of the Act, it is possible, however, that its most useful provision, if it is used appropriately, may actually lie in providing more protection for women, who are subject to assault and harassment from their partners, than is available under alternative criminal or civil law procedures. The newly instituted Anti-Social Behaviour Orders, available against individuals aged 10 or over on the application of the police or local authority, may be made in situations where there has been: intimidation through threats, violence and a mixture of unpleasant actions; persistent unruly behaviour by a small group on an estate; families who resort to abuse when complaints are made to them; vandalism; serious and persistent organised bullying of children; persistent racial or homophobic harassment; persistent anti-social behaviour as a result of drug or alcohol abuse (Home Office Guidance Document (1999)). The first person to be imprisoned for breaching an anti-social behaviour order was a 14 year old boy called Declan Madigan who was given a 12 month custodial sentence in March 2000.

Whereas these Acts may seem initially to offer a welcome additional protection to the innocent individual, it has to be recognised that such advantage is achieved, in effect, by criminalising what was, and remains, in other circumstances, non-criminal behaviour, and deciding its applicability on the basis of the lower civil law burden of proof.

Nor should it be forgotten that, although prosecution of criminal offences is usually the prerogative of the State, it remains open to the private individual to initiate a private prosecution in relation to a criminal offence. It has to be remembered, however, that, even in the private prosecution, the test of the burden of proof remains the criminal one requiring the facts to be proved beyond reasonable doubt. An example of the problems inherent in such private actions can be seen in the case of Stephen Lawrence, the young black man who was gratuitously stabbed to death by a gang of white racists whilst standing at a bus stop in London. Although there was strong suspicion, and indeed evidence, against particular individuals, the Crown Prosecution Service declined to press the charges against them on the basis of insufficiency of evidence. When the lawyers of the Lawrence family mounted a private prosecution against the suspects, the action failed for want of sufficient evidence to convict. As a consequence of the failure of the private prosecution, the rule against double jeopardy meant that the accused could not be re-tried for the same offence at any time in the future, even if the police subsequently acquired sufficient new evidence to support a conviction. (The Macpherson Inquiry, into the manner in which the police dealt with the Stephen Lawrence case, recommended the removal of the double jeopardy rule, but this particular recommendation is not likely to be implemented on grounds of civil liberties.) To conclude at this stage, however, it has been reported that the Lawrence family were considering initiating a private law action against the suspects – the point for now being that the burden of proof would be lower.

In considering the relationship between civil law and criminal law, it is sometimes thought that criminal law is the more important in maintaining social order, but it is at least arguable that, in reality, the reverse is the case. For the most part, people come into contact with the criminal law infrequently, whereas everyone is continuously involved with civil law, even if it is only the use of contract law to make some purchase. The criminal law of theft, for example, may be seen as simply the cutting edge of the wider and more fundamental rights established by general property law. In any case, there remains the fact that civil and criminal law each has its own distinct legal system. The nature of these systems is considered in detail in later chapters.

1.3   The separation of powers

Although the idea of the separation of powers can be traced back to ancient Greek philosophy, it was advocated in early modern times by the English philosopher John Locke and the later French philosopher Montesquieu and found its practical expression in the constitution of the US. The idea of the separation of powers is posited on the existence of three distinct functions of government, the legislative, executive and judicial functions, and the conviction that these functions should be kept apart in order to prevent the centralisation of too much power. Establishing the appropriate relationship between the actions of the State and the legal control over those actions crucially involves a consideration of whether there is any absolute limit on the authority of the government of the day. Answering that question inevitably involves an examination of the general constitutional structure of the UK, and, in particular, the inter-relationship of two doctrines: parliamentary sovereignty; and judicial independence.

1.3.1   Parliamentary sovereignty

As a consequence of the victory of the parliamentary forces in the English revolutionary struggles of the 17th century, Parliament became the sovereign power in the land. The independence of the judiciary was secured, however, in the Act of Settlement 1701. The centrality of the independence of the judges and the legal system from direct control or interference from the State in the newly established constitution was emphasised in the writing of Locke who saw it as one of the essential reasons for, and justifications of, the Social Contract on which the social structure was assumed to be based. It is generally accepted that the inspiration for Montesquieu's *Spirit of Law* (*De l'Esprit des Lois*) was the English constitution but, if that is truly the case, then his doctrine of the separation of powers was based on a misunderstanding of that constitution as it failed to take account of the express superiority of Parliament in all matters, including its relationship with the judiciary and the legal system.

It is interesting that some Conservative thinkers have recently suggested that the whole notion of parliamentary sovereignty is itself a product of the self-denying ordinance of the common law. Consequently, they have suggested that it is open to a subsequent, more robust, judiciary, confident in its own position and powers within the developing constitution, to re-assert its equality with the other two elements. When, however, it is recalled that when the Conservative Party was in power, it was to no little extent embarrassed by, and not too understanding of, the actions of recalcitrant judges, it is at least a moot point whether such a proposition reflects a real commitment to judicial equality with the executive, or merely represents the gall of a defeated executive, hoping to enlist the judges in their oppositional role. It does not require an uncritical commitment to the role of the judiciary to recognise that powerful executives, which exercise effective control over acquiescent legislatures, do not take too well to the interference of an active judiciary.

Given the existence of the doctrine of parliamentary sovereignty, which effectively means that Parliament, as the ultimate source of law, can make such law as it determines, the exact extent to which the doctrine of the separation of powers operates in the UK is a matter of some debate. For example, the position of the Lord Chancellor, who is at the same time a member of the government and the most senior judge in the land with control over judicial appointments, is not unproblematic (this will be considered in detail in Chapter 4). There is, however, high judicial authority for claiming that the separation of powers is an essential element in the constitution of the UK (see *R v Hinds* (1977) in which Lord Diplock, whilst considering the nature of different Commonwealth constitutions in a Privy Council case, stated that: 'It is taken for granted that the basic principle of the separation of powers will apply ...' (p 212)). In any case, the point of considering the doctrine at this juncture is simply to highlight the distinction, and relationship, between the executive and the judiciary and to indicate the possibility of conflict between the two elements of the constitution. This relationship assumes crucial importance if one accepts, as some have suggested, that it is no longer possible to distinguish the executive from the legislature as, through its control of its majority in the House of Commons, the executive, that is, the government, can legislate as it wishes, and, in so doing, can provide the most arbitrary of party political decisions with the form of legality. The question to be considered here is to what extent the judiciary can legitimately oppose the wishes of the government expressed in the form of legislation, or the extent to which it can interfere with the pursuit of those wishes.

1.3.2 Judicial independence

The exact meaning of judicial independence became a matter of debate when some members and ex-members of the senior judiciary suggested that the former Lord Chancellor, Lord Mackay of Clashfern, had adopted a too restrictive interpretation of the term which had reduced it to the mere absence of interference by the executive in the trial of individual cases. They asserted the right of the legal system to operate independently, as an autonomous system apart from the general control of the State, with the judiciary controlling its operation, or at least being free from the dictates and strictures of central control.

According to Lord Mackay, in the first of his series of Hamlyn Lectures entitled *The Administration of Justice* (1994):

> The fact that the executive and judiciary meet in the person of the Lord Chancellor should symbolise what I believe is necessary for the administration of justice in a country like ours, namely, a realisation that both the judiciary and the executive are parts of the total government of the country with functions that are distinct but which must work together in a proper relationship if the country is to be properly governed ... It seems more likely that the interests of the judiciary in matters within the concerns covered by the Treasury are more likely to be advanced if they can be pursued within government by a person with a lifetime of work in law and an understanding of the needs and concerns of the judiciary and who has responsibility as Head of the Judiciary, than if they were to be left within government as the responsibility of a minister with no such connection with the judiciary.

There is, however, some concern within the judiciary as to whether the relationship between the executive and the judiciary is proper and doubts have been raised as to the Lord Chancellor's positioning between the two institutions. Fears have been expressed that rather than representing the interests of the judiciary within the government, the current Lord Chancellor, Lord Irvine of Lairg, is actually pursuing and implementing policies that are driven by the economic dictates of the Treasury and which are having a severely detrimental impact on the operation of the whole justice system. Rather than being the voice of the judiciary in Cabinet, he is suspected by some, as was his predecessor, of being the voice of the Cabinet in the judiciary.

In a paper presented to the Bar Conference and subsequently published in the *New Law Journal* ((1994) 144 NLJ 1306) Sir Francis Purchas claimed that the second half of the 20th century had seen the executive make substantial inroads into the independence of the judiciary and warned against the dangers of an executive-centred court system in which the judges have no effective protection against executive interference and in which the disposal of cases took priority over the attainment of justice. In his view:

> The quality and extent of justice available has been reduced, and the access to that justice has been curtailed. Generally speaking, this has arisen as a succession of legislative acts, orders or provisions brought into being by the executive, or a policy of inaction followed in pursuance of the Treasury ethos of market forces and competition policy

In relation to the situation of the Lord Chancellor, Sir Francis stated that:

> ... when the Lord Chancellor is an active member of the Cabinet charged with the introduction of measures which he knows will be opposed by the judges and in many respects by the professions, the inadequacy of the traditional structure is fatally exposed. In the present context of acute confrontation with an all-powerful executive pursuing a market-forces ethos which is wholly inapplicable to the provision of justice, the judiciary may well require a more

powerful and representative body through which their independence may be preserved so as to be an effective check on the executive.

Does this suggest that the Lord Chancellor should be replaced by a judicial trade union? If it does, it is ironic, coming from the body who have traditionally been the enemies of trade unions, although always ready to defend the closed-shop interests of the Bar from which they came.

The tension inherent in the relationship between the courts and the executive government has taken on an even more fundamental constitutional aspect in relation to the development of the process of judicial review by means of which the courts assert the right to subject the actions and operations of the executive to the gaze and control of the law in such a way as to prevent the executive from abusing its power. In the US, with its written constitution, the judiciary have the power to declare the Acts of the legislature to be unconstitutional and, therefore, unlawful.

As Roger Smith observed, in an article, 'Politics and the judiciary' ((1993) 143 NLJ 1486):

> Judicial review is pushing our political system towards a greater separation of powers. The judiciary is disengaging itself from its earlier subservience to the legislature and the executive. There are, doubtless, various strands to this which include the influence of the US of Europe. However, another important element must be the failure in recent years of the usual checks and balance of democracy. Britain is in danger of becoming a one-party State. Other parts of the constitution are forced into the opposition role, particularly when their interests and perceptions are offended.

It is of no little interest to note that Parliament, in the form of the House of Commons, re-asserted its ultimate authority in relation to the recommendations of the Committee on Standards in Public Life, which was established, under the chairmanship of the senior judge Lord Nolan. The committee was set up to consider, amongst other things, ways in which either actual or perceived corruption within the legislative body could be controlled. The committees recommendation that an independent Parliamentary Commissioner for Public Standards, an Ombudsman, should be appointed to enforce controls over the activities of MPs was resisted by some members of the Commons on the grounds that nobody outside of Parliament could be given the authority to regulate Parliament. The fact that such an assertion might be seen as protecting the right of particular members to engage in sleaze was portrayed as being of secondary importance to the constitutional question as to the sovereignty of Parliament. The fact that this argument was almost completely spurious, in that any such Ombudsman would be acting for Parliament and representing the authority of Parliament, was recognised and Sir Gordon Downey was appointed to fill the office of Commissioner for Public Standards, responsible to the Commons Committee on Standards and Privileges. Much of Sir Gordon's work has related to what has become known as the 'cash for questions' scandal. This affair refers to the fact that a number of MPs have been accused of, and some have admitted, being paid for asking questions in the House. The payment was made by Mohammed Al Fayed, the chairman of the House of Fraser group which owns Harrods, and was organised through the offices of the parliamentary lobbyist Ian Greer. In July 1997, Sir Gordon Downey issued a three volume report on the allegations of sleaze made against certain MPs ((1997) *The Times*, 4 July; (1997) *The Guardian*, 4 July). Although five MPs were censured in the report with a severity which would have required them to be expelled from the House of Commons, they were still MPs. In the event, however, all those condemned in the report had either not stood as candidates at the General Election on 1 May 1997 or were defeated on that occasion. Geoffrey Robertson QC, who acted in the Downey Inquiry, stated after publication of the report:

> The real lesson of the Downey Report is that never again should MPs be regarded or regard themselves as above the law ... Self-regulation is not enough: it is time to follow the lead of Parliaments in the Commonwealth which have established an independent commission against corruption headed by a judge, to investigate and report allegations against ministers, MPs and public servants [(1997) *The Guardian*, 4 July].

The sensitive relationship between the judiciary and Parliament was highlighted in two cases. In *R v Parliamentary Commissioner for Standards ex p Al Fayed* (1997), it was held that the operation of the Parliamentary Commissioner for Public Standards was not open to judicial review, as he dealt with matters relating to the internal operation of Parliament. The operation of the Parliamentary Commissioner for Administration (the Ombudsman, see 12.4) is subject to judicial review, however, because his is an external, rather than an internal, parliamentary role (*R v Parliamentary Commissioner for Administration ex p Balchin* (1997)).

Judicial review and its political implications will be considered in detail in Chapter 4, but at this point it should be noted that any general treatment of the relationship of the judiciary and executive must consider the particular meaning and scope of the doctrine known as the Rule of Law and its relationship to human rights.

1.4 The Rule of Law

The Rule of Law represents a symbolic ideal against which proponents of widely divergent political persuasions measure and criticise the shortcomings of contemporary State practice. This varied recourse to the Rule of Law is, of course, only possible because of the lack of precision in the actual meaning of the concept; its meaning tending to change over time and, as will be seen below, to change in direct correspondence with the beliefs of those who claim its support and claim, in turn, to support it. It is undeniable that the form and content of law and legal procedure have changed substantially in the course of the 20th century. It is usual to explain such changes as being a consequence of the way in which, and the increased extent to which, the modern State intervenes in everyday life, be it economic or social. As the State increasingly took over the regulation of many areas of social activity, it delegated wide ranging discretionary powers to various people and bodies in an attempt to ensure the successful implementation of its policies. The assumption and delegation of such power on the part of the State brought it into potential conflict with previous understandings of the Rule of Law which had entailed a strictly limited ambit of State activity.

1.4.1   Human rights discourse and the Rule of Law

In an article published in the *London Review of Books* and *The Guardian*, in May 1995, the High Court judge, as he then was, Sir Stephen Sedley, made explicit the links and tensions between the doctrine of the Rule of Law and the relationship of the courts and the executive, and the implications for the use of judicial review as a means of controlling the exercise of executive power. In his view:

> Our agenda for the 21st century is not necessarily confined to choice between a rights instrument interpreted by a judiciary with a long record of illiberal adjudication, and rejection of any rights instrument in favour of Parliamentary government. The better government becomes, the less scope there will be for judicial review of it.

> But, for the foreseeable future, we have a problem: how to ensure that as a society we are governed within a law which has internalised the notion of fundamental human rights. Although this means adopting the Rule of Law, like democracy, as a higher-order principle, we do have the social consensus which alone can accord it that primacy. And, if in our own society the Rule of Law is to mean much, it must at least mean that it is the obligation of the courts to articulate and uphold the ground rules of ethical social existence which we dignify as fundamental human rights. There is a potential tension between the principle of democratic government and the principle of equality before the law ... The notion that the prime function of human rights and indeed the Rule of Law is to protect the weak against the strong is not mere sentimentality. It is the child of an era of history in which equality of treatment and opportunity has become perceived ... as an unqualified good, and of a significant recognition that you do not achieve equality merely by proclaiming it fundamental human rights to be real, have to steer towards outcomes which invert those inequalities of power that mock the principle of equality before the law.

Such talk of fundamental human rights denies the absolute sovereignty of Parliament in its recognition of areas that are beyond the legitimate exercise of State power. It also recognises, however, that notions of the Rule of Law cannot be satisfied by the provision of merely formal equality as Dicey and Friedrich von Hayek would have it and previous legal safeguards would have provided. For Sedley, the Rule of Law clearly imports, and is based on, ideas of substantive equality, that market systems and legal formalism cannot provide and, in fact, undermine. His version of the Rule of Law clearly involves a reconsideration of the relationship of the executive and the judiciary and involve the latter in a further reconsideration of their own previous beliefs and functions.

1.5 The Human Rights Act 1998

As is evident in the previous quotation from Sedley, some judges, at least, saw their role in maintaining the Rule of Law as providing protection for fundamental human rights. In attempting to achieve this end, they faced a particular problem in relation to the way in which the unwritten English constitution was understood, and was understood to operate. The freedom of individual action in English law was not based on ideas of positive human rights, which could not be taken away, but on negative liberties: that is, individual subjects were entitled to do whatever was not forbidden by the law. This was particularly problematic when it was linked to the doctrine of the sovereignty of Parliament, which, in effect, meant that Parliament was free to restrict, or indeed remove, individual liberties at any time, merely by passing the necessary legislation.

It is generally accepted that the courts developed the procedure of judicial review, as an aspect of the Rule of Law, in an attempt to protect individuals from the excesses of an over-powerful executive (see 4.11 for a detailed consideration). But, in so doing, they were limited in what they could achieve by the very nature of the procedure available to them. They could not directly question the laws produced by Parliament on the basis of substance, as constitutional courts in other systems could, but were restricted, essentially, to questioning the formal or procedural proprieties of such legislation. There was, however, an alternative forum capable of challenging the substance of English law; and one that was based on the assumption of positive rights, rather than negative liberties. That forum was the European Court of Human Rights (ECHR).

It has to be established, and emphasised, from the outset that the substance of this section has absolutely nothing to do with the European Union (EU) as such; the Council of Europe is a completely distinct organisation and, although membership of the two organisations overlap, they are not the same. The Council of Europe is concerned not with economic matters but with the protection of civil rights and freedoms (the nature of these institutions and the operation of the ECHR will be considered in detail in Chapter 2).

The UK was one of the initial signatories to the European Convention on Human Rights in 1950, which was established in post-war Europe as a means of establishing and enforcing essential human rights. In 1966, it recognised the power of the European Commission on Human Rights to hear complaints from individual UK citizens, and, at the same time, recognised the authority of the

ECHR to adjudicate in such matters. It did not, however, at that time, incorporate the European Convention into UK law.

The consequences of non-incorporation was that the Convention could not be directly enforced in English courts. In *R v Secretary of State for the Home Department ex p Brind* (1991), the Court of Appeal decided that ministerial directives did not have to be construed in line with the European Convention on Human Rights as that would be tantamount to introducing the Convention into English law without the necessary legislation. UK citizens were, therefore, in the position of having to pursue rights, which the State endorsed, in an external forum rather than through their own court system; and, in addition, having to exhaust the domestic judicial procedure before they could gain access to that external forum. Such a situation was extremely unsatisfactory, and not just for complainants under the Convention. Many members of the judiciary, including the present Lord Chief Justice, Lord Bingham, were in favour of incorporation, not merely on general moral grounds, but equally on the ground that they resented having to make decisions, in line with UK law, which they knew full well would be overturned on appeal to the European Court. Equally, there was some discontent that the decisions in the European Court were being taken, and its general jurisprudence was being developed without the direct input of the UK legal system. The courts, however, were not completely bound to decide cases in presumed ignorance the Convention, and did what they could to decide cases in line with it. For example, where domestic statutes were enacted to fulfil Convention obligations, the courts could, of course, construe the meaning of the statute in the light of the Convention. It was also possible that, due to the relationship of the Convention to European Community law, the courts could find themselves applying the former in considering the latter. More indirectly, however, where the common law was uncertain, unclear or incomplete, the courts ruled, wherever possible, in a manner which conformed with the Convention. Or, where statute was found to be ambiguous, they presumed that Parliament intended to legislate in conformity with the UK's international obligations under the Convention. As Lord Bingham himself put it:

> In these ways, the Convention made a clandestine entry into British law by the back door, being forbidden to enter by the front [Earl Grey Memorial Lecture, 1998, http://webjcli.ncl.ac.uk/1998/issue1/bingham1.html].

But, even allowing for this degree of judicial manoeuvering, the situation still remained unsatisfactory. Pressure groups did agitate for the incorporation of the Convention into the UK legal system but, when, in 1995, a Private Member's Bill moving for incorporation was introduced in the House of Lords, the Home Office Minister, Lady Blatch, expressed the then government's view that such incorporation was undesirable and unnecessary, both in principle and practice. The Opposition (the Labour Party), however, was committed to the incorporation of the Convention into UK law and, when it gained office in 1997, it immediately set about the process of incorporation. This process resulted in the Human Rights Act (HRA) 1998.

The Articles incorporated into UK law, and listed in Sched 1 of the Act, cover the following matters:

- general commitment to human rights (Art 1);

- the right to life (Art 2);

- the prohibition of torture (Art 3);

- the prohibition of slavery and forced labour (Art 4);

- the right to liberty and security (Art 5);

- the right to a fair trial (Art 6);

- the general prohibition of the enactment of retrospective criminal offences (Art 7);

- the right to respect for private and family life (Art 8);

- freedom of thought, conscience and religion (Art 9);

- freedom of expression (Art 10);

- freedom of assembly and association (Art 11);

- the right to marry (Art 12);

- the prohibition of discrimination (Art 14);

- the freedom of aliens to enter into political activity, which may be restricted (Art 16).

The above list of rights are not all seen in the same way. Some are absolute and inalienable and cannot be interfered with by the State. Others are merely contingent and are subject to derogation, that is, Signatory States can opt out of them in particular circumstances. The absolute rights are those provided for in Arts 2, 3, 4, 7 and 14. All the others are subject to potential limitations; and, in particular, the rights provided for under Arts 8, 9, 10 and 11 are subject to legal restrictions, such as are:

> ... necessary in a democratic society in the interests of national security or public safety, for the prevention of crime, for the protection of health or morals or the protection of the rights and freedoms of others [Art 11(2)].

In deciding the legality of any derogation, courts are required not just to be convinced that there is a need for the derogation, but they must also be sure that the State's action has been proportionate to that need. In other words, the State must not overreact to a perceived problem by removing more rights than is necessary to effect the solution. With further regard to the possibility of derogation, s 19 of the Act requires a minister, responsible for the passage of any Bill through Parliament, either to make a written declaration that it is compatible with the Convention or, alternatively, to declare that, although it may not be compatible, it is still the government's wish to proceed with it.

The HRA has profound implications for the operation of the English legal system. Section 2 of the Act requires future courts to take into account any previous decision of the ECHR. This provision impacts on the operation of the doctrine of precedent within the English legal system, as it effectively sanctions the overruling of any pervious English authority that was in conflict with a decision of the ECHR. Also, s 3, requiring all legislation to be read so far as possible to give effect to the rights provided under the Convention, has the potential to invalidate previously accepted interpretations of statutes which were made, by necessity, without recourse to the Convention.

Section 6 declares it unlawful for any public authority to act in a way which is incompatible with the Convention, and s 7 allows the victim of the unlawful act to bring proceedings against the public authority in breach. Section 8 empowers the court to grant such relief or remedy against the public authority in breach of the Act as it considers just and appropriate.

To understand the structure of the HRA, it is essential to be aware of the nature of the changes introduced by the Act, especially in the apparent passing of such fundamental powers to the judiciary. Under the doctrine of parliamentary sovereignty, the legislature could pass such laws at it saw fit, even to the extent of removing the rights of its citizens. The new Act reflects a move towards the entrenchment of rights recognised under the Convention, but, given the sensitivity of the relationship between the elected Parliament and the unelected judiciary, it has been thought expedient to minimise the change in the constitutional relationship of Parliament and the judiciary. To that effect, the Act expressly states that the courts cannot invalidate any primary legislation, essentially Acts of Parliament, which are found to be incompatible with the Convention: they can only make a declaration of such incompatibility and leave it to the legislature to remedy the situation through new legislation (s 4). Where a public authority is acting under the instructions of some primary legislation which is itself incompatible with the Convention, the public authority will not be liable under s 6.

The Act does provide for the provision of remedial legislation through a fast track procedure which gives a Minister of the Crown the power to alter such primary legislation by way of statutory instrument. It is significant that legislation proceeding from the newly elected Scottish Parliament is not deemed to be primary legislation, and therefore is open to the full rigour of the HRA procedures, with its legislation being capable of being invalidated by the courts.

Reactions to the introduction of the HRA have been broadly welcoming, but some important criticisms have been raised. First, the Convention is a rather old document, and does not address some of the issues that contemporary citizens might consider as equally fundamental to those rights actually contained in the document. For example, it is silent on the rights to substantive equality relating to such issues as welfare and access to resources. Also, the actual provisions of the Convention are uncertain in the extent of their application, or perhaps more crucially in the area where they can be derogated from; and at least to a degree they are contradictory. The most obvious difficulty arises from the need to reconcile the right to privacy (Art 8) with freedom of expression (Art 10). Newspapers have already expressed their concern in relation to this particular issue, and fear the development, at the hands of the court, of an overly limiting law of privacy which would prevent investigative journalism. This leads to a further difficulty which is the potential politicisation, together with a significant enhancement in the power, of the judiciary. Although this factor has been significantly played down by those concerned, notably Lord Bingham (Earl Grey Lecture, 1998) and Lord Woolf (Neil Lecture, 1998), it is certainly true that it has not gone without criticism, especially from those on the Left of the political spectrum, who are concerned about what they see as the shift in power to an unelected, unrepresentative, and unaccountable judiciary (this issue is further discussed in Chapter 4).

Perhaps the most serious criticism of the HRA is the fact that the government has not seen fit to establish a Human Rights Commission, to publicise, and facilitate, the operation of its procedures. Many have seen the setting up of such a body as a necessary step in raising human rights awareness and assisting individuals, who might otherwise be unable to use the Act, to enforce their rights.

Apart from s 19, which is already in force, the bulk of the HRA 1998 will not be brought into effect until 3 October 2000. The reason for the substantial time delay is the need to train all members of the judiciary from the highest Law Lord to the humblest magistrate, and the Lord Chancellors Department has already allocated some £4.5 million for that purpose. However, even if the Act has not officially been brought into effect, it is already having an impact on decisions. Thus, in *R v DPP ex p Kebilene* (1999), Lord Bingham, with whom the other members of the Divisional Court concurred, declared that those sections of the Prevention of Terrorism Act 1989 which reversed the normal burden of proof in criminal trials were contrary to Art 6 of the Convention. Although the HRA was not yet in force, Lord Bingham held that the Director of Public Prosecutions should have taken into account the fact that any conviction against the defendant under the present law would in all likelihood be quashed when the HRA came into force. The Lord Chief Justice granted leave to appeal to the House of Lords, in recognition that the High Court's decision had such potentially far reaching implications; which it certainly has in respect of the 100 or so convictions gained in Northern Ireland under the same provisions. On October 1999, the House of Lords allowed the DPP's appeal and did not rule on the issue of compatibility between the powers under the Prevention of Terrorism Act and Art 6 of the Convention

INTRODUCTION TO LAW

The nature of law

Legal systems are particular ways of establishing and maintaining social order. Law is a formal mechanism of social control. Studying the English legal system involves considering a fundamental institution in our society.

Categories of law

Law can be categorised in a number of ways, although the various categories are not mutually exclusive.

Common law and civil law relate to distinct legal systems. The English legal system is a common law one as opposed to continental systems which are based on civil law.

Common law and equity distinguish the two historical sources and systems of English law. Common law emerged in the process of establishing a single legal system throughout the country. Equity was developed later to soften the formal rigour of the common law. The two systems are now united but in the final analysis equity should prevail.

Common law and statute relate to the source of law. Common law is judge made: statute law is produced by Parliament.

Private law and public law relate to whom the law is addressed. Private law relates to individual citizens whereas public law relates to institutions of government.

Civil law and criminal law distinguish between law whose purpose it is to facilitate the interaction of individuals and law that is aimed at enforcing particular standards of behaviour.

Separation of powers

The judges and the executive in the separation of powers have distinct but interrelated roles in the constitution. The question arises as to the extent to which the courts can act to control the activities of the executive through the operation of judicial review. The position of the present Lord Chancellor as judge and member of the government has been questioned by some.

The Rule of Law

The Rule of Law represents a symbolic ideal against which proponents of widely divergent political persuasions measure and criticise the shortcomings of contemporary State practice.

The Human Rights Act 1998

The Human Rights Act 1998 incorporates the European Convention on Human Rights into domestic UK law. The Articles of the Convention cover the following matters:

- the right to life (Art 1);

- the prohibition of torture (Art 3);

- the prohibition of slavery and forced labour (Art 4);

- the right to liberty and security (Art 5);

- the right to a fair trial (Art 6);

- the general prohibition of the enactment of retrospective criminal offences (Art 7);

- the right to respect for private and family life (Art 8);

- freedom of thought, conscience and religion (Art 9);

- freedom of expression (Art 10);

- freedom of assembly and association (Art 11);

- the right to marry (Art 12);

- the prohibition of discrimination (Art 14);

- freedom from restrictions on the political activity of aliens (Art 16).

The incorporation of the Convention into UK law means that UK courts can decide cases in line with the above Articles. This has the potential to create friction between the judiciary and the executive/legislature.

CHAPTER 2

SOURCES OF LAW

2.1 European Community

Ever since the UK joined the European Economic Community (EEC), now the European Community (Union in some legal contexts), it has progressively, but effectively, passed the power to create laws which have effect in this country to the wider European institutions. In effect, the UK's legislative, executive and judicial powers are now controlled by, and can only be operated within, the framework of European Community law. It is essential, therefore, even in a text that is primarily concerned with the English legal system, that the contemporary law student be aware of the operation of the legislative and judicial powers of the European Community. Later in this chapter (see 2.7), the European Community and its institutions will be examined in some detail, but first of all attention will be focused on internal sources of law.

2.2 Legislation

If the institutions of the European Community are sovereign within its boundaries, then within the more limited boundaries of the UK the sovereign power to make law lies with Parliament. Under UK constitutional law, it is recognised that Parliament has the power to enact, revoke or alter such, and any, law as it sees fit. Coupled to this wide power is the convention that no one Parliament can bind its successors in such a way as to limit their absolute legislative powers.

This absolute power is a consequence of the historical struggle between Parliament and the Stuart monarchy in the 17th century. In its struggle with the Crown, Parliament claimed the power of making law as its sole right. In so doing, Parliament curtailed the royal prerogative and limited the monarchy to a purely formal role in the legislative procedure. Prerogative powers still exist and remain important, but are now exercised by the government in the name of the Crown, rather than by the Crown itself. In this struggle for ultimate power, the courts sided with Parliament and, in return, Parliament recognised the independence of the courts from its control.

Although we still refer to our legal system as a common law one and although the courts still have an important role to play in the interpretation of statutes, it has to be recognised that legislation is the predominant method of law making in contemporary times. It is necessary, therefore, to have a knowledge of the workings of the legislative process.

2.2.1 The pre-parliamentary process

Any consideration of the legislative process must be placed in the context of the political nature of Parliament. Most statutes are the outcome of the policy decisions taken by government and the actual policies pursued will of course depend upon the political persuasion and imperatives of the government of the day. Thus, a great deal of law creation and reform can be seen as the implementation of party political policies. Examples of this type of legal reform are the changes in trade union law, or education law, or the financing of local services introduced by the previous Conservative administrations.

It also has to be recognised that the current Labour Government, elected in May 1997, has introduced considerable constitutional changes as proposed in its election manifesto. Thus, the Scottish Parliament and the Welsh Assembly have been instituted, and the first elections have taken place for both bodies; and moves are well afoot for the removal of the hereditary peerage from the House of Lords, although it is not as yet certain what is to replace that forum (this latter issue gives rise to a particular difficulty in relation to the judiciary in the House of Lords (see 4.1)).

As, by convention, the government is drawn from the party controlling a majority in the House of Commons, it can effectively decide what policies it wishes to implement and trust to its majority to ensure that its proposals become law. Accusations have been made that, when governments have substantial majorities, they are able to operate without taking into account the consideration of their own party members, let alone the views of opposition members. It is claimed that their control over the day to day procedure of the House of Commons backed with their majority voting power, effectively reduces the role of Parliament to that of merely rubber-stamping their proposals.

It is certainly true, as the experience of the previous Conservative administration in the UK demonstrated, that governments with small majorities, if not actually in a minority, have to be circumspect in the policies they pursue through Parliament. The fact that the May 1997 parliamentary elections returned the Labour Party to power, with a much larger majority than, even they, expected, has raised, once again, the prospect of an over-powerful executive forcing its will through a politically quiescent parliament.

The government generates most of the legislation that finds its way into the statute book but individual MPs may also propose legislation in the form of Private Members' Bills.

There are in fact three ways in which an individual MP can propose legislation:

(a) through the ballot procedure by means of which 20 backbench members get the right to propose legislation on the 10 or so Fridays in each parliamentary session specifically set aside to consider such proposals;

(b) under Standing Order 39 which permits any member to present a Bill after the 20 balloted Bills have been presented; and

(c) under Standing Rule 13, the 10-minute rule procedure, which allows a member to make a speech of up to 10 minutes in length in favour of introducing a particular piece of legislation.

Of these procedures, however, only the first has any real chance of success and even then success will depend on securing a high place in the ballot and on its not being too contentious. As examples of this can be cited the Abortion Act 1967 which was introduced as a Private Members' Bill to liberalise the provision of abortion; and the various attempts that have subsequently been made by Private Members' Bills to restrict the original provision. In relation to particular reforms, external pressure groups or interested parties may very often be the original moving force behind them; and, when individual MPs are fortunate enough to find themselves at the top of the ballot for Private Members' Bills, they may well find themselves the focus of attention from such pressure groups proffering pre-packaged law reform proposals in their own particular areas of interest.

The decision as to which Bills are to be placed before Parliament in any session is under the effective control of two cabinet committees:

• the Future Legislation Committee determines which Bills will be presented to Parliament in the following parliamentary session;

• the Legislation Committee is responsible for the legislative programme conducted in the immediate parliamentary session. It is the responsibility of this committee to draw up the legislative programme announced in the Queen's Speech delivered at the opening of the parliamentary session.

Green Papers are consultation documents issued by the government which set out and invite comments from interested parties on particular proposals for legislation. After considering any response, the government may publish a second document in the form of a White Paper in which it sets out its firm proposals for legislation.

2.2.2 The legislative process

Parliament consists of three distinct elements: the House of Commons, the House of Lords and the Monarch. Before any legislative proposal, known at that stage as a Bill, can become an Act of Parliament, it must proceed through and be approved by both Houses of Parliament and must receive the Royal Assent. The ultimate location of power, however, is the House of Commons which has the authority of being a democratically elected institution.

A Bill must be given three readings in both the House of Commons and the House of Lords before it can be presented for the Royal Assent. It is possible to commence the procedure in either House although Money Bills must be placed before the Commons in the first instance.

When a Bill is introduced in the Commons, it undergoes five distinct procedures:

- *First reading*. This is purely a formal procedure in which its title is read and a date set for its second reading.

- *Second reading*. At this stage, the general principles of the Bill are subject to extensive debate. The second reading is the critical point in the process of a Bill. At the end, a vote may be taken on its merits and, if it is approved, it is likely that it will eventually find a place in the statute book.

- *Committee stage*. After its second reading, the Bill is passed to a standing committee whose job is to consider the provisions of the Bill in detail, clause by clause. The committee has the power to amend it in such a way as to ensure that it conforms with the general approval given by the House at its second reading.

- *Report stage*. At this point, the standing committee reports the Bill back to the House for consideration of any amendments made during the committee stage.

- *Third reading*. Further debate may take place during this stage, but it is restricted to matters relating to the content of the Bill and questions relating to the general principles of the Bill cannot be raised.

When a Bill has passed all these stages, it is passed to the House of Lords for its consideration. After consideration by the Lords, the Bill is passed back to the Commons which must then consider any amendments to the Bill that might have been introduced by the Lords. Where one House refuses to agree to the amendments made by the other, Bills can be repeatedly passed between them but, as Bills must complete their process within the life of a particular parliamentary session, a failure to reach agreement within that period might lead to the total loss of the Bill.

Since the Parliament Acts of 1911 and 1949, the blocking power of the House of Lords has been restricted as follows:

- a Money Bill, that is, one containing only financial provisions, can be enacted without the approval of the House of Lords after a delay of one month;

- any other Bill can be delayed by one year by the House of Lords.

The House of Lords, no doubt, has used its reforming and delaying powers to good effect, but its inbuilt Conservative/conservative majority has also been deployed for less than totally praiseworthy campaigns. The latest of these involves the procedure of equalising the age of sexual consent between homosexuals at 16, as it is with heterosexuals. In 1998, the House of Lords managed to avoid an equalisation of the age of consent by threatening the government's major Criminal Justice Bill, subsequently, the Crime and Disorder Act 1998. In order to get the Bill through Parliament before the end of the session, the Home Secretary removed the provision. However, the House of Lords has maintained its resistance and has still refused to pass the proposal, now contained in the Sexual Offences (Amendment) Bill. The government has expressed the intention to use the Parliament Acts to ensure that this legislative provision reaches the statute book, in spite of the House of Lords objections.

The Royal Assent is required before any Bill can become law. There is no constitutional rule requiring the monarch to assent to any Act passed by Parliament. There is, however, a convention to that effect; and refusal to grant the Royal Assent to legislation passed by Parliament would place the constitutional position of the monarchy in jeopardy. The procedural nature of the Royal Assent was highlighted by the Royal Assent Act 1967 which reduced the process of acquiring Royal Assent to a formal reading out of the short title of any Act in both Houses of Parliament.

An Act of Parliament comes into effect on the date of the Royal Assent, unless there is any provision to the contrary in the Act itself.

2.2.3　The drafting of legislation

In 1975, in response to criticisms of the language and style of legislation, the Renton Committee (*Report on the Preparation of Legislation*, Cmnd 6053, 1975) examined the form in which legislation was presented. Representations were made to the Committee by a variety of people ranging from the judiciary to the lay public. The Committee divided complaints about statutes into four main headings relating to:

(a) obscurity of language used;

(b) over-elaboration of provisions;

(c) illogicality of structure;

(d) confusion arising from the amendment of existing provisions.

It was suggested that the drafters of legislation tended to adopt a stylised archaic legalism in their language and employed a grammatical structure that was too complex and convoluted to be clear, certainly to the layperson and even, on occasion, to legal experts. These criticisms, however, have to be considered in the context of the whole process of drafting legislation and weighed against the various other purposes to be achieved by statutes.

The actual drafting of legislation is the work of parliamentary counsel to the Treasury who specialise in this task. The first duty of the drafters must be to give effect to the intention of the department instructing them, and do so in as clear and precise a manner as is possible. These aims, however, have to be achieved under pressure, and sometimes extreme pressure, of time. An insight into the various difficulties faced in drafting legislation was provided by a former parliamentary draftsman, Francis Bennion in an article entitled, 'Statute law obscurity and drafting parameters' ((1978) 5 JLS 235). He listed nine specific parameters which the drafter of legislation had to take into account. These parameters are:

- *Legal effectiveness*. This is the need for the drafters to translate the political wishes of those instructing them into appropriate legal language and form.

- *Procedural legitimacy*. This refers to the fact that the legislation must conform with certain formal requirements if it is to be enacted. For example, it is a requirement that Acts be divided into clauses and Bills not assuming this form would not be considered by Parliament.

- *Timeliness*. This refers to the requirement for legislation to be drawn up within particularly pressing time constraints. The effect of such pressure can be poorly drafted and defective provisions.

- *Certainty*. It is of the utmost importance that the law be clearly set down so that individuals can know its scope and effect and can guide their actions within its provisions. The very nature of language, however, tends to act against this desire for certainty. In pursuit of certainty, the temptation is for the person drafting the legislation to produce extremely long and complex sentences, consisting of a series of limiting and refining subclauses. This process in turn, however, tends merely to increase the obscurity of meaning.

- *Comprehensibility*. Ideally, legislation should be comprehensible to the lay person, but given the complex nature of the situation that the legislature is dealing with such an ideal is probably beyond attainment in practice. Nonetheless, legislative provisions certainly should be open to the comprehension of the members of Parliament who are asked to vote on it and they certainly should not be beyond the comprehension of the legal profession who have to construe it for their clients. Unfortunately, some legislation fails on both these counts.

- *Acceptability*. This refers to the fact that legislation is expected to be couched in uncontentious language and using a traditional prose style.

- *Brevity*. This refers to the fact that legislative provisions should be as short as is compatible with the attainment of the legislative purpose. The search for brevity in legislation can run counter to the wish for certainty in, and acceptability of, the language used.

- *Debatability*. This refers to the fact that legislation is supposed to be structured in such a way as to permit it and the policies that lie behind it to be debated in Parliament.

- Legal compatibility. This refers to the need for any new provision to fit in with already existing provisions. Where the new provision alters or repeals existing provisions, it is expected that such effect should be clearly indicated.

A consideration of these various desired characteristics shows that they are not necessarily compatible and indeed some of them, such as the desire for clarity and brevity, may well be contradictory. The point remains that those people charged with the responsibility for drafting legislation should always bear the above factors in mind when producing draft legislation but if one principle is to be pursued above others it is surely the need for clarity of expression and meaning.

2.2.4 Types of legislation

Legislation can be categorised in a number of ways. For example, distinctions can be drawn between:

Public Acts which relate to matters affecting the general public. These can be further subdivided into either government Bills or Private Members' Bills.

Private Acts, on the other hand, relate to the powers and interests of particular individuals or institutions, although the provision of statutory powers to particular institutions can have a major effect on the general public. For example, companies may be given the power to appropriate private property through compulsory purchase orders.

Enabling legislation gives power to a particular person or body to oversee the production of the specific details required for the implementation of the general purposes stated in the parent Act. These specifics are achieved through the enactment of Statutory Instruments. (See 2.2.5 for a consideration of delegated legislation.)

Acts of Parliament can also be distinguished on the basis of the function they are designed to carry out. Some are unprecedented and cover new areas of activity previously not governed by legal rules, but other Acts are aimed at rationalising or amending existing legislative provisions.

Consolidating legislation is designed to bring together provisions previously contained in a number of different Acts, without actually altering them. The Companies Act of 1985 is an example of a consolidation Act. It brought together provisions contained in numerous amending Acts which had been introduced since the previous Consolidation Act of 1948.

Codifying legislation seeks not just to bring existing statutory provisions under one Act, but also looks to give statutory expression to common law rules.

The classic examples of such legislation are the Partnership Act of 1890 and the Sale of Goods Act 1893, now 1979.

Amending legislation is designed to alter some existing legal provision. Amendment of an existing legislative provision can take two forms:

- a textual amendment is one where the new provision substitutes new words for existing ones in a legislative text or introduces completely new words into that text. Altering legislation by means of textual amendment has one major drawback in that the new provisions make very little sense on their own without the contextual reference of the original provision it is designed to alter;

- non-textual amendments do not alter the actual wording of the existing text but alter the operation or effect of those words. Non-textual amendments may have more immediate meaning than textual alterations, but they too suffer from the problem that, because they do not alter the original provisions, the two provisions have to be read together to establish the legislative intention.

Neither method of amendment is completely satisfactory but the Renton Committee on the Preparation of Legislation favoured textual amendments over non-textual amendments.

2.2.5 Delegated legislation

Delegated legislation is of particular importance. Generally speaking, delegated legislation is law made by some person or body to whom Parliament has delegated its general law making power. A validly enacted piece of delegated legislation has the same legal force and effect as the Act of Parliament under which it is enacted; but equally it only has effect to the extent that its enabling Act authorises it.

The Deregulation and Contracting Out Act (DCOA) 1994 is an example of the wide ranging power that enabling legislation can extend to ministers. The Act gives ministers the authority to amend legislation by means of statutory instruments, where they consider such legislation to impose unnecessary burdens on any trade, business, or profession. Although the DCOA 1994 imposes the requirement that ministers should consult with interested parties to any proposed alteration, it nonetheless gives them extremely wide powers to alter primary legislation without the necessity of having to follow the same procedure as was required to enact that legislation in the first place. An example of the effect of the DCOA may be seen in the Deregulation (Resolutions of Private Companies) Order 1996 (SI 1996/1471), which simplifies the procedures which private companies have to comply with in passing resolutions. The effect of this statutory instrument was to introduce new sections into the Companies Act 1985 relaxing the previous provisions in the area in question. A second example is the Deregulation (Model Appeal Provisions) Order 1996 (SI 1996/1678), which set out a model structure for appeals against enforcement actions in business disputes.

The output of delegated legislation in any year greatly exceeds the output of Acts of Parliament as may be seen from the 1998 statistics which reveal that although just over 49 general public Acts were passed, no less than 3,321 statutory instruments were made.

In statistical terms, therefore, it is at least arguable that delegated legislation is actually more significant than primary Acts of Parliament.

There are various types of delegated legislation:

- Orders in Council permit the government through the Privy Council to make law. The Privy Council is nominally a non-party-political body of eminent parliamentarians but in effect it is simply a means through which the government, in the form of a committee of ministers, can introduce legislation without the need to go through the full parliamentary process. Although it is usual to cite situations of State emergency as exemplifying occasions when the government will resort to the use of Orders in Council, in actual fact, a great number of Acts are brought into operation through Orders in Council. Perhaps the widest scope for Orders in Council is to be found in relation to European Community law, for, under s 2(2) of the European Communities Act 1972, ministers can give effect to provisions of the Community which do not have direct effect.

- Statutory Instruments are the means through which government ministers introduce particular regulations under powers delegated to them by Parliament in enabling legislation. Examples have already been considered in relation to the DCOA.

- Bylaws are the means through which local authorities and other public bodies can make legally binding rules. Bylaws may be made by local authorities under such enabling legislation as the Local Government Act 1972.

- Court Rule Committees are empowered to make the rules which govern procedure in the particular courts over which they have delegated authority under such Acts as the Supreme Court Act 1981, the County Courts Act 1984, and the Magistrates' Courts Act 1980.

- Professional regulations governing particular occupations may be given the force of law under provisions delegating legislative authority to certain professional bodies who are empowered to regulate the conduct of their members. An example is the power given to The Law Society, under the Solicitors Act 1974, to control the conduct of practising solicitors.

2.2.6 Advantages in the use of delegated legislation

The advantages of delegated legislation include:

- *Time saving*

    Delegated legislation can be introduced quickly where necessary in particular cases and permits rules to be changed in response to emergencies or unforeseen problems.

    The use of delegated legislation, however, also saves parliamentary time generally. Given the pressure on debating time in Parliament and the highly detailed nature of typical delegated legislation, not to mention its sheer volume, Parliament would not have time to consider each individual piece of law that is enacted in the form of delegated legislation. It is considered of more benefit for Parliament to spend its time in a thorough consideration of the principles of the enabling Act, leaving the appropriate minister or body to establish the working detail under its authority.

- *Access to particular expertise*

    Related to the first advantage is the fact that the majority of members of Parliament simply do not have sufficient expertise to consider such provisions effectively. Given the highly specialised and extremely technical nature of many of the regulations that are introduced through delegated legislation, it is necessary that those authorised to introduce the legislation should have access to the necessary external expertise required to formulate such regulations. With regard to bylaws, it practically goes without saying that local and specialist knowledge should give rise to more appropriate rules than reliance on the general enactments of Parliament.

- *Flexibility*

    The use of delegated legislation permits ministers to respond on an ad hoc basis to particular problems as and when they arise and provides greater flexibility in the regulation of activity subject to the ministers overview.

2.2.7 Disadvantages in the prevalence of delegated legislation

The disadvantages in the use of delegated legislation include:

- *Accountability*

    A key issue involved in the use of delegated legislation concerns the question of accountability and erosion of the constitutional role of Parliament.

    Parliament is presumed to be the source of legislation but with respect to delegated legislation the individual members are not the source of the law. Certain people, notably government ministers and the civil servants who work under them to produce the detailed provisions of delegated legislation, are the real source of such regulations. Even allowing for the fact that they are, in effect, operating on powers delegated to them from Parliament, it is not beyond questioning whether this procedure does not give them more power than might be thought appropriate, or indeed constitutionally correct, whilst at the same time disempowering and discrediting Parliament as a body.

- *Scrutiny*

The question of general accountability raises the need for effective scrutiny, but the very form of delegated legislation makes it extremely difficult for ordinary MPs to fully understand what is being enacted and to monitor it effectively. This difficulty arises in part from the tendency for such regulations to be highly specific, detailed and technical. This problem of comprehension and control is compounded by the fact that regulations appear outside the context of their enabling legislation but only have any real meaning in that context.

- *Bulk*

The problems faced by ordinary MPs in effectively keeping abreast of delegated legislation is further increased by the sheer mass of such legislation. And, if parliamentarians cannot keep up with the flow of delegated legislation, how can the general public be expected to do so?

These difficulties and potential shortcomings in the use of delegated legislation are, at least to a degree, mitigated by the fact that specific controls have been established to oversee it.

- *Parliamentary control over delegated legislation*

Power to make delegated legislation is ultimately dependent upon the authority of Parliament and Parliament retains general control over the procedure for enacting such law.

New regulations in the form of delegated legislation are required to be laid before Parliament. This procedure takes two forms depending on the provision of the enabling legislation. Some regulations require a positive resolution of one or both of the Houses of Parliament before they become law. Most Acts, however, simply require that regulations made under their auspices be placed before Parliament. They automatically become law after a period of 40 days unless a resolution to annul them is passed.

The problem with the negative resolution procedure is that it relies on MPs being sufficiently aware of the content, meaning, and effect of the detailed provisions laid before them. Given the nature of such statutory legislation, such reliance is unlikely to prove secure.

Since 1973, there has been a Joint Select Committee on Statutory Instruments whose function it is to consider Statutory Instruments. This committee scrutinises Statutory Instruments from a technical point of view as regards drafting and has no power to question the substantive content or the policy implications of the regulation. Its effectiveness as a general control is therefore limited. European Community legislation is overseen by a specific committee and local authority bylaws are usually subject to the approval of the Department of the Environment.

- *Judicial control of delegated legislation*

It is possible for delegated legislation to be challenged, through the procedure of judicial review, on the basis that the person or body to whom Parliament has delegated its authority has acted in a way that exceeds the limited powers delegated to them. Any provision outside this authority is *ultra vires* and is void. Additionally, there is a presumption that any power delegated by Parliament is to be used in a reasonable manner and the courts may on occasion hold particular delegated legislation to be void on the basis that it is unreasonable. The process of judicial review will be considered in more detail in 4.11. However, an interesting example of this procedure may illuminate the point. In January 1997, the Lord Chancellor raised court fees and, at the same time, restricted the circumstances in which a litigant can be exempted from paying such fees. In March, a Mr John Witham, who previously would have been exempted from paying court fees, successfully challenged the Lord Chancellors action. In a judicial review, it was held that Lord Mackay had exceeded the statutory powers given to him by Parliament. One of the judges, Rose LJ, stated that there was nothing to suggest that Parliament ever intended a power for the Lord Chancellor to prescribe fees so as to preclude the poor from access to the courts.

2.3 Case law

Case law refers to the creation and refinement of law in the course of judicial decisions. The foregoing has highlighted the increased importance of legislation in its various guises in today's society but, even allowing for this, and the fact that case law can be overturned by legislation, the UK is still a common law system and the importance and effectiveness of judicial creativity and common law principles and practices cannot be discounted.

2.3.1 Precedent

The doctrine of binding precedent, or *stare decisis*, lies at the heart of the English legal system. The doctrine refers to the fact that, within the hierarchical structure of the English courts, a decision of a higher court will be binding on a court lower than it in that hierarchy. In general terms, this means that when judges try cases they will check to see if a similar situation has come before a court previously. If the precedent was set by a court of equal or higher status to the court deciding the new case, then the judge in the present case should follow the rule of law established in the earlier case. Where the precedent is from a lower court in the hierarchy, the judge in the new case may not follow but will certainly consider it. (The structure of the civil and criminal courts will be considered in detail in Chapter 3.)

It can be seen that the operation of the doctrine of binding precedent depends on the existence of an extensive reporting service to provide access to previous judicial decisions. The earliest summaries of cases appeared in the Year Books but, since 1865, cases have been reported by the Council of Law Reporting, established as a corporate body in 1870, which produces the authoritative reports of cases. Modern technology has resulted in the establishment of the Lexis computer based storage of cases. It should be noted, however, that whilst over 200,000 legal cases are dealt with in the courts each year, only about 25,000 get reported.

The most authoritative case reports are those provided in the law reports. These contain very useful summaries of the submissions made to the court by counsel in the case and also have the distinct advantage of the actual judgments being revised by the judges involved.

For reference purposes, the most commonly referenced law reports are cited as:

Law reports:

Appeal Cases	(AC)
Chancery Division	(Ch D)
Family Division	(Fam)
Kings/Queens Bench	(KB/QB)

Other general series of reports:

All England Law Reports	(All ER)
Weekly Law Reports	(WLR)
Solicitors Journal	(SJ or Sol Jo)
European Court Reports	(ECR)

Various series of private reports have been collected together in the 178 volume collection of English Reports. The last two volumes are indexes to enable researchers to find their way through the other 176 volumes of cases.

There are a number of specialist reports. Indeed, there are too many of these to list all of them but amongst the most important are:

Industrial Relations Law Reports	(IRLR)
Knights Local Government Reports	(LGR)

Lloyd's Law Reports	(Lloyd's Rep and Ll L Rep)
Reports on Tax Cases	(TC or Tax Cas)
Criminal Appeal Reports	(Cr App R and Cr App Rep)

2.3.2 The hierarchy of the courts

The structure of the court system is treated in more detail in Chapters 3 and 4. The House of Lords stands at the summit of the English court structure and its decisions are binding on all courts below it in the hierarchy. Up until 1966, the House of Lords regarded itself as bound by its previous decisions. In a Practice Statement of that year, however, *Practice Statement (Judicial Precedent)*, Lord Gardiner indicated that the House of Lords would in future regard itself as free to depart from its previous decisions where it appeared right to do so. Given the potentially destabilising effect on existing legal practice based on previous decisions of the House of Lords, this is not a discretion that the House of Lords exercises lightly. For example, in *Food Corp of India v Antclizo Shipping Corp* (1988), it was stated that the House of Lords would only review its previous decisions in cases where, not only was it of the opinion that there might be a general justification for reconsidering the accuracy of existing precedents, but such a consideration must also be necessary for and capable of deciding the particular case in point. In the *Food Corp of India* case, although the general point was made, the particular point failed on the facts of the case. There have been a number of cases, however, in which the House of Lords has overruled or amended its own earlier decisions. For example, in *Conway v Rimmer* (1968), the previous decision in *Duncan v Cammell Laird & Co* (1942), that an affidavit sworn by a government minister was sufficient to preclude the courts from examining documents on the ground of Crown privilege, was overturned to allow judges the final say in whether such documents should be considered or not. In *Herrington v British Rail Board* (1972), the House of Lords extended the previous ambit of occupier's liability to include non-intentional, non-reckless injury sustained by a child trespassing on property. In *Miliangos v George Frank (Textiles) Ltd* (1976), they decided, contrary to their own existing authority that damages could be paid in currency other that sterling and, in *R v Shivpuri* (1986), the House bravely, if surprisingly, took the decision to overrule a previous decision in relation to criminal attempts made only some 12 months previously.

In civil cases, the Court of Appeal is generally bound by previous decisions of the House of Lords. Although the Court of Appeal, notably under the aegis of Lord Denning, attempted, on a number of occasions, to escape from the constraints of *stare decisis*, the House of Lords repeatedly reasserted the binding nature of its decisions on the Court of Appeal.

Civil

Criminal

Rare leapfrog appeal to House of Lords

House of Lords

Court of Appeal

Civil Division

Criminal Division

High Court

Queen's Bench Division
Family Division
Chancery Division

Crown Court

county court

Including Small Claims Procedure

Occasional appeals on point of law

magistrates' court

Civil

Criminal

Fig 1. The hierarchy of the courts

The Court of Appeal generally is also bound by its own previous decisions in civil cases. There are, however, a number of exceptions to this general rule. Lord Greene MR listed these exceptions in *Young v Bristol Aeroplane Co Ltd* (1944). The exceptions arise where:

- there is a conflict between two previous decisions of the Court of Appeal. In this situation, the later court must decide which decision to follow and as a corollary which to overrule. Such a situation arose in *Tiverton Estates Ltd v Wearwell Ltd* (1974). In that case, which dealt with the meaning of s 40 of the Law of Property Act 1925 (subsequently repealed), the court elected to follow older precedents rather than follow the inconsistent decision in *Law v Jones* (1974);

- a previous decision of the Court of Appeal has been overruled, either expressly or impliedly, by the House of Lords. In this situation, the Court of Appeal is required to follow the decision of the House of Lords. Thus, in *Family Housing Association v Jones* (1990), the Court of Appeal felt obliged to ignore its own precedents on the distinction between a licence and a tenancy in property law where, although they had not been expressly overruled, they were implicitly in conflict with a later decisions of the House of Lords;

- the previous decision was given *per incuriam* or, in other words, that previous decision was taken in ignorance of some authority, either statutory or case law, that would have led to a different conclusion. In this situation, the later court can ignore the previous decision in question. An example of this may be seen in *Williams v Fawcett* (1985), in which the Court of Appeal found exceptional circumstances under which it could treat its previous decisions as having been made *per incuriam*. Of importance amongst these circumstances was the fact that the case would be unlikely to go to the House for their final determination of the legal situation.

There is also the possibility that, as a consequence of s 3 of the European Communities Act, the Court of Appeal can ignore a previous decision of its own which is inconsistent with Community law or with a later decision of the European Court.

Although, on the basis of *R v Spencer* (1985), it would appear that there is no difference in principle between the operation of the doctrine of *stare decisis* between the criminal and civil divisions of the Court of Appeal, it is generally accepted that, in practice, precedent is not followed as strictly in the former as it is in the latter. Courts in the criminal division are not bound to follow their own previous decisions which they subsequently consider to have been based on either a misunderstanding or a misapplication of the law. The reason for this is that the criminal courts deal with matters involving individual liberty and therefore require greater discretion to prevent injustice.

The Divisional Courts, each located within the three divisions of the High Court, hear appeals from courts and tribunals below them in the hierarchy. They are bound by the doctrine of *stare decisis* in the normal way and must follow decisions of the House of Lords and the Court of Appeal. It is also normally bound by its own previous decisions, although in civil cases it may make use of the exceptions open to the Court of Appeal in *Young v Bristol Aeroplane Co Ltd* (1944), and, in criminal appeal cases, the Queen's Bench Divisional Court may refuse to follow its own earlier decisions where it feels the earlier decision to have been made wrongly.

The High Court is also bound by the decisions of superior courts. Decisions by individual High Court judges are binding on courts inferior in the hierarchy, but such decisions are not binding on other High Court judges although they are of strong persuasive authority and tend to be followed in practice.

Crown Courts cannot create precedent and their decisions can never amount to more than persuasive authority.

County courts and magistrates' courts do not create precedents.

It has to be particularly noted that the HRA now requires courts in the UK to take into consideration all previous decisions of the ECHR, which now become precedents for the UK courts to follow. This is the case even where the ECHR decision was in conflict with previous UK law. Equally, any English precedent which was in conflict with a decision of the ECHR is now invalidated.

2.3.3 Binding precedent

Not everything in a case report sets a precedent. The contents of a report can be divided into two categories:

- *Ratio decidendi*. It is important to establish that it is not the actual decision in a case that sets the precedent; that is set by the rule of law on which the decision is founded. This rule, which is an abstraction from the facts of the case, is known as the *ratio decidendi* of the case. The *ratio decidendi* of a case may be understood as the statement of the law applied in deciding the legal problem raised by the concrete facts of the case.

- *Obiter dictum*. Any statement of law that is not an essential part of the *ratio decidendi* is, strictly speaking, superfluous; and any such statement is referred to as *obiter dictum* (*obiter dicta* in the plural), that is, said by the way. Although *obiter dicta* statements do not form part of the binding precedent, they are persuasive authority and can be taken into consideration in later cases, if the judge in the later case considers it appropriate to do so.

The division of cases into these two distinct parts is a theoretical procedure. Unfortunately, judges do not actually separate their judgments into the two clearly defined categories and it is up to the person reading the case to determine what the *ratio* is. In some cases, this is no easy matter, and it may be made even more difficult in appellate cases where each of the judges may deliver their own lengthy judgments with no clear single *ratio*. (The potential implications of the way in which later courts effectively determine the *ratio* in any particular case will be considered below and in 4.9.) Students should always read cases fully; although it is tempting to rely on the headnote at the start of the case report, it should be remembered that this is a summary provided by the case reporter and merely reflects what he or she thinks the *ratio* is. It is not unknown for headnotes to miss an essential point in a case.

Example

Carlill v Carbolic Smoke Ball Co Ltd (1892)

Facts

Mrs Carlill made a retail purchase of one of the defendants medicinal products: the Carbolic Smoke Ball. It was supposed to prevent people who used it in a specified way (three times a day for at least two weeks) from catching influenza. The company was very confident about its product and placed an advertisement in a paper, The *Pall Mall Gazette*, which praised the effectiveness of the Smoke Ball and promised to pay £100 (a huge sum of money at that time) to:

> ... any person who contracts the increasing epidemic influenza, colds, or any disease caused by taking cold, having used the ball three times daily for two weeks according to the printed directions supplied with each ball.

The advertisement went on to explain that the company had deposited £1,000 with the Alliance Bank, Regent Street, London, as a sign of its sincerity in the matter. Any proper claimants could get their payment from that sum. On the faith of the advertisement, Mrs Carlill bought one of the balls at the chemists and used it as directed but still caught the flu. She claimed £100 from the company but was refused it so she sued for breach of contract. The company said there was no contract for several reasons but mainly because:

(a) the advert was too vague to amount to the basis of a contract there was no time limit and no way of checking the way the customer used the ball;

(b) the plaintiff did not give any legally recognised value to the company;

(c) one cannot legally make an offer to the whole world so the advert was not a proper offer;

(d) even if the advert could be seen as an offer, Mrs Carlill had not given a legal acceptance of that offer because she had not notified the company that she was accepting;

(e) the advert was a mere puff, that is, a piece of insincere sales talk not meant to be taken seriously.

Decision

The Court of Appeal found that there was a legally enforceable agreement, a contract between Mrs Carlill and the company. The company would have to pay damages to the plaintiff.

Ratio decidendi

The three Lord Justices of Appeal who gave judgments in this case all decided in favour of Mrs Carlill. Each, however, uses slightly different reasoning, arguments and examples. The process, therefore, of distilling the reason for the decision of the court is quite a delicate art. The *ratio* of the case can be put as follows.

Offers must be sufficiently clear to allow the courts to enforce agreements that follow from them. The offer here was a distinct promise expressed in language which is perfectly unmistakable. It could not be a mere puff in view of the £1,000 deposited specially to show good faith. An offer may be made to the world at large and the advert was such an offer. It was accepted by any person, like Mrs Carlill, who bought the product and used it in the prescribed manner. Mrs Carlill had accepted the offer by her conduct when she did as she was invited to do and started to use the smoke ball. She had not been asked to let the company know that she was using it.

Obiter dictum

In the course of his reasoning, Bowen LJ gave the legal answer to a set of facts which were not in issue in this case. They are, thus, *obiter dicta*. He did this because it assisted him in clarifying the answer to Mrs Carlill's case. He said:

> If I advertise to the world that my dog is lost, and that anybody who brings the dog to a particular place will be paid some money, are all the police or other persons whose business it is to find lost dogs to be expected to sit down and write me a note saying that they have accepted my proposal? Why, of course, they at once look [for] the dog, and as soon as they find the dog they have performed the condition.

If such facts were ever subsequently in issue in a court case, then the words of Bowen LJ could be used by counsel as persuasive precedent.

This decision has affected the outcome of many cases. The information system LEXIS, for example, lists 70 cases in which *Carlill* is cited. It was applied in *Peck v Lateu* (1973), and distinguished in *AM Satterthwaite & Co v New Zealand Shipping Co* (1972).

2.3.4 Evaluation

The foregoing has set out the doctrine of binding precedent as it operates in theory to control and indeed limit the ambit of judicial discretion. It has to be recognised, however, that the doctrine does not operate as stringently as it appears at first sight and that there are particular shortcomings in the system that have to be addressed in weighing up the undoubted advantages with the equally undoubted disadvantages.

2.3.5 Advantages of case law

There are numerous perceived advantages of the doctrine of *stare decisis*; amongst which are:

- *Consistency*. This refers to the fact that like cases are decided on a like basis and are not apparently subject to the whim of the individual judge deciding the case in question. This aspect of formal justice is important in justifying the decisions taken in particular cases.

- *Certainty*. This follows from, and indeed is presupposed by, the previous item. Lawyers and their clients are able to predict what the likely outcome of a particular legal question is likely to be in the light of previous judicial decisions. Also, once the legal rule has been established in one case, individuals can orient their behaviour with regard to that rule relatively secure in the knowledge that it will not be changed by some later court.

- *Efficiency*. This refers to the fact that it saves the time of the judiciary, lawyers and their clients for the reason that cases do not have to be re-argued. In respect of potential litigants, it saves them money in court expenses because they can apply to their solicitor/barrister for guidance as to how their particular case is likely to be decided in the light of previous cases on the same or similar points. (It should, of course, be recognised that the vast bulk of cases are argued and decided on their facts rather than on principles of law, but that does not detract from the relevance of this issue, and is a point that will be taken up later in 4.9.)

- *Flexibility*. This refers to the fact that the various mechanisms by means of which the judges can manipulate the common law provide them with an opportunity to develop law in particular areas without waiting for Parliament to enact legislation.

  In practice, flexibility is achieved through the possibility of previous decisions being either overruled, or distinguished, or the possibility of a later court extending or modifying the effective ambit of a precedent. (It should be re-emphasised that it is not the decision in any case which is binding, but the *ratio decidendi*. It is correspondingly and equally incorrect to refer to a decision being overruled.)

This apparently small measure of discretion, in relationship to whether later judges are minded to accept the validity of *obiter* statements in precedent cases, opens up the possibility that judges in later cases have a much wider degree of discretion than is originally apparent in the traditional view of *stare decisis*. It is important in this respect to realise that it is the judges in the later cases who actually determine the *ratio decidendi* of previous cases.

Judges, as has been noted previously, in delivering judgments in cases, do not separate and highlight the *ratio decidendi* from the rest of their judgment and this can lead to a lack of certainty in determining the *ratio decidendi*. This uncertainty is compounded by the fact that reports of decisions in cases may run to considerable length; and, where there are a number of separate judgments, although the judges involved may agree on the decision of a case, they may not agree on the legal basis of the decision reached. This difficulty is further compounded where there are a number of dissenting judgments. In the final analysis, it is for the judge deciding the case in which a precedent has been cited to determine the *ratio* of the authority and thus to determine whether he is bound by the case or not. This factor provides later courts with a considerable degree of discretion in electing whether to be bound or not by a particular authority.

The main mechanisms through which judges alter or avoid precedents are:

- *Overruling*

  This is the procedure whereby a court higher up in the hierarchy sets aside a legal ruling established in a previous case.

  It is somewhat anomalous that, within the system of *stare decisis*, precedents gain increased authority with the passage of time. As a consequence, courts tend to be reluctant to overrule long standing authorities even though they may no longer accurately reflect contemporary practices or morals. In addition to the wish to maintain a high degree of certainty in the law, the main reason for judicial reluctance to overrule old decisions would appear to be the fact that overruling operates retrospectively with the effect that the principle of law being overruled is held never to have been law. Overruling a precedent might, therefore, have the consequence of disturbing important financial arrangements made in line with what were thought to be settled rules of law. It might even, in certain circumstances, lead to the imposition of criminal liability on previously lawful behaviour. It has to be emphasised, however, that the courts will not shrink from overruling authorities where they see them as no longer representing an appropriate statement of law.

  The decision in *R v R* (1992) to recognise the possibility of rape within marriage may be seen as an example of this, although, even here, the House of Lords felt constrained to state that they were not actually altering the law but were merely removing a misconception as to the true meaning and effect of the law. As this demonstrates, the courts are rarely ready to challenge the legislative prerogative of Parliament in an overt way. For example, in *Curry v DPP* (1994), the Court of Appeal attempted to remove the presumption that children between the ages of 10 and 14 who were charged with a criminal offence did not know that what they did was seriously wrong and that the prosecution had to provide evidence to rebut that presumption. Mann LJ justified reversing the presumption by claiming that, although it had often been assumed to be the law, it had never actually been specifically considered by earlier courts. On such reasoning, he felt justified in departing from previous decisions of the Court of Appeal which otherwise would have bound him. The House of Lords subsequently restored the previous presumption. Although they recognised the problem, and indeed appeared to sympathise with Mann LJ's view, they nonetheless thought that such a significant change was a matter for parliamentary action rather than judicial intervention. The doctrine of *doli incapax* was finally removed by s 34 of the Crime and Disorder Act 1998. Of perhaps even greater concern is the fact that s 35 extended s 35 of the Criminal Justice and Public Order Act (CJPOA) 1994 to cover all persons aged 10 or over. Thus, courts are now entitled to draw (adverse) inferences from the failure of such children to either give evidence or answer questions at their trial.

Overruling should not be confused with reversing which is the procedure whereby a superior court in the hierarchy reverses the decision of a lower court in the same case.

• *Distinguishing*

In comparison to the mechanism of overruling which is rarely used, the main device for avoiding binding precedents is that of distinguishing. As has been previously stated, the *ratio decidendi* of any case is an abstraction from, and is based upon, the material facts of the case. This opens up the possibility that a court may regard the facts of the case before it as significantly different from the facts of a cited precedent and thus consequentially it will not find itself bound to follow that precedent. Judges use the device of distinguishing where, for some reason, they are unwilling to follow a particular precedent and the law reports provide many examples of strained distinctions where a court has quite evidently not wanted to follow an authority that it would otherwise have been bound by.

2.3.6 Disadvantages of case law

It should be noted that the advantage of flexibility, at least, potentially contradicts the alternative advantage of certainty, but there are other disadvantages in the doctrine which have to be considered. Amongst these are:

• *Uncertainty*

This refers to the fact that the degree of certainty provided by the doctrine of *stare decisis* is undermined by the absolute number of cases that have been reported and can be cited as authorities. This uncertainty is increased by the ability of the judiciary to select which authority to follow through use of the mechanism of distinguishing cases on their facts. A further element leading to uncertainty has been highlighted by James Richardson, the editor of *Archbold* (1995), the leading practitioners' text on criminal law, who has claimed that the lack of practical experience of some judges in the Criminal Appeal Court is:

> ... compounded by an apparent willingness, on occasion, to set aside principle in order to do what the court feels to be right (either way) in the individual case.

As Richardson suggests:

> In the long run, this can only undermine a system which claims to operate on the basis of a hierarchy of binding precedent.

- *Fixity*

  This refers to the possibility that the law in relation to any particular area may become ossified on the basis of an unjust precedent with the consequence that previous injustices are perpetuated. An example of this is the long delay in the recognition of the possibility of rape within marriage, which has only relatively recently, given its long history, been recognised (*R v R* (1992)).

- *Unconstitutionality*

  This is a fundamental question that refers to the fact that the judiciary are overstepping their theoretical constitutional role by actually making law rather than restricting themselves to the role of simply applying it. This possibility requires a close examination of the role of the courts in the process of law making.

The traditional declaratory theory of law claims that judges do not make law, they simply state what it is. This view, however, gives rise to two particular conceptual difficulties:

- *Innovation*

  Legal rules, as social institutions and creations, cannot be subject to infinite regression: they must have had a beginning at some time in the past when some person or group of people made or recognised them. Every common law rule must have had an origin. To put this in a simpler way, if a particular law was not created by statute, it must have been created by a judge; even if the level of creative activity was no more than recognising the legitimacy, or otherwise, of the practice in question, as was the role of the original circuit judges. Where an issue arises before a court for the first time, it follows, as a matter of course, that there can be no precedent for the court to follow, and, given the rapid change in contemporary society, it can only be suggested that such innovations and potentially innovatory court cases, are increasingly likely. In such novel circumstances, courts are faced with the choice of either refusing to decide a case, or stating what the law should be. In earlier times, judges did not shirk from this task and, even in modern times, courts are required on occasion to consider situations for the first time. Such cases are described as cases of first impression and inevitably involve judges in the creation of new law.

- *Reform*

The question arises as to how the law is to develop and change to cater for changed circumstances if cases are always to be decided according to precedent.

These considerations raise the question that if the law, as represented in either common law or statute law, is out of line with current social beliefs and practices, then should it not be incumbent upon the judiciary to decide cases in line with the currently prevailing standards, even if this means ignoring previous decisions and interpretations? Not to do so leaves the judges open to the charge of being out of touch with social reality. To overtly change the law, however, opens them up to the alternative charge of acting beyond their powers and of usurping the role and function of the legislature. Opinions on this matter range from those that would deny completely the right of judges to make or change the law, to those that would grant the judges the right to mould the law in line with their conception of justice. Others would recognise the fact that the common law was judge made and restrict judicial creativity; to the development of established common law principles. There is an important corollary to this latter position which links it with those who limit judicial creativity, for the implicit assertion is that judges have no place in reforming statutory provisions. They may signal the ineffectiveness of such provisions and call for their repeal or reform, but it would be a usurpation of the legislatures function and power for the courts to engage in such general reform.

In any case, this question unavoidably raises the issue of the actual extent of judicial creativity. (Compare and contrast *R v R* and *Curry v DPP* (above) in this light.) The previous consideration of distinguishing has demonstrated how the doctrine of *stare decisis* can be avoided by the judiciary. A further way in which judges have a creative impact on the law is in the way in which they adapt and extend precedent in instant cases. In addition, judicial reasoning, which will be considered in detail later in Chapter 4, tends to be carried out on the basis of analogy and judges have a large degree of discretion in selecting what are to be considered as analogous cases. They also have a tendency to extend, continuously, existing precedents to fit new situations, as the history evolution of the tort of negligence will show.

It is now probably a commonplace of legal theory that judges do make law. Perhaps the more interesting question is not whether judges make law but why they deny that they do so. In spite of the protestations of the judiciary, law and judicial decision making is a political process to the extent that it is deciding about which values are to be given priority within society. Through their choice of values the judiciary sanction or prohibit particular forms of behaviour. Due to their position in the constitution, however, judges have to be circumspect in the way in which and the extent to which they use their powers to create law and impose values. To overtly assert or exercise the power would be to challenge the power of the legislature. For an unelected body to challenge a politically supreme Parliament would be unwise, to say the least. It is for that reason that the courts on occasion take refuge behind the cloak of a naïve declaratory theory of law. (The political nature of judicial action will be considered further in 4.11.7 and 4.12.)

2.4   Books of authority

When a court is unable to locate a precise or analogous precedent, it may refer to legal textbooks for guidance. Such books are subdivided, depending on when they were written. In strict terms, only certain works are actually treated as authoritative sources of law. Amongst the most important of these works are those by Glanville from the 12th century, Bracton from the 13th century, Coke from the 17th century and Blackstone from the 18th century. When cases such as *R v R* are borne in mind, then it might be claimed, with justification, that the authority of such ancient texts may be respected more in the breach than in the performance. Given the societal change that has occurred in the intervening time, one can only say that such a refusal to fetishise ancient texts is a positive, and indeed necessary, recognition of the need for law to change in order to keep up with its contemporary sphere of operation. Legal works produced after Blackstone's *Commentaries* of 1765 are considered to be of recent origin, and they cannot be treated as authoritative sources. The courts, however, will look at the most eminent works by accepted experts in particular fields in order to help determine what the law is or should be. For example, in the sphere of company law, the work of Professor LCB Gower has been referred to by the courts in order to help to elucidate some abstruse legal principles, as has Sir William Wade and Anthony Bradley's work in the sphere of public law. For a recent example, see the citation of Shetreet's, *Judges on Trial* (1976), and De Smith, Wolf and Jowell, *Judicial Review of Administrative Action* (1995), in Lord Browne-Wilkinson's decision in *Re Pinochet* (1999).

2.5 Custom

There is some academic debate about the exact relationship of custom and law. Some claim that law is simply the extension of custom and that with the passage of time customs develop into laws. From this point of view, law may be seen as the redefinition of custom for the purposes of clarity and enforcement by the legal institutions. The State institutions are seen as merely refining the existing customary behaviour of society. Others deny this evolutionary link and claim that law and custom are in fact contradictory, with law emerging in opposition to, and replacing, customary forms of behaviour. From this perspective, law is seen as being a new form of regulation handed down by the State rather than emerging from society as a whole.

The traditional view of the development of the common law tends to adopt the first of these views. This overly romantic view of the common law represents its emergence as no more than the crystallisation of common customs. This distillation is accomplished by the judiciary in the course of their historic travels round the land. This view, however, tends to play down the political process that gave rise to the procedure. The imposition of a common system of law represented the political victory of a State that had fought to establish and assert its central authority. Viewed in that light, the emergence of the common law can be seen actually to support the second of the two approaches suggested above.

Although some of the common law may have had its basis in general custom, a large proportion of these so called customs were invented by the judges themselves and represented what they wanted the law to be, rather than what people generally thought it was.

One source of customary practice that undoubtedly did find expression in the form of law was business and commercial practice. These customs and practices originally were constituted in the distinct form of the Law Merchant but gradually this became subsumed under the control of the common law courts and ceased to exist apart from the common law.

Notwithstanding the foregoing, it is still possible for specific local customs to operate as a source of law. In certain circumstances, parties may assert the existence of customary practices in order to support their case. Such local custom may run counter to the strict application of the common law and, where they are found to be legitimate, they will effectively replace the common law. Even in this respect, however, reliance on customary law as opposed to common law, although not impossible, is made unlikely by the stringent tests that have to be satisfied. The requirements that a local custom must satisfy in order to be recognised are that:

- it must have existed from time immemorial, that is, 1189;

- it must have been exercised continuously within that period;

- it must have been exercised peaceably without opposition;

- it must also have been felt as obligatory;

- it must be capable of precise definition;

- it must have been consistent with other customs; and

- it must be reasonable.

Given this list of requirements, it can be seen why local custom is not an important source of law. However, the courts will have recourse to custom where they see it as appropriate as may be seen in *Egerton v Harding* (1974), in which the courts upheld a customary duty to fence land against cattle straying from an area of common land.

2.6   Law reform

At one level, law reform is either a product of parliamentary or judicial activity as has been considered previously. Parliament tends, however, to be concerned with particularities of law reform and the judiciary are constitutionally and practically disbarred from reforming the law in other than an opportunistic and piecemeal basis. Therefore, there remains a need for the question of law reform to be considered generally and a requirement that such consideration be conducted in an informed but disinterested manner.

Reference has already been made to the use of consultative Green Papers by the government as a mechanism for gauging the opinions of interested parties to particular reforms. More formal advice may be provided through various advisory standing committees. Amongst these is the Law Reform Committee. The function of this Committee is to consider the desirability of changes to the civil law which the Lord Chancellor may refer to it. The Criminal Law Revision Committee performs similar functions in relation to criminal law.

Royal Commissions may be constituted to consider the need for law reform in specific areas. The Commission on Criminal Procedure (1980) led to the enactment of the Police and Criminal Evidence Act (PACE) 1984, and the recommendation of the 1993 Royal Commission on Criminal Justice (Runciman Commission) are still making their way into current legislation.

Committees may be set up in order to review the operation of particular areas of law. The most significant of these being the Woolf review of the operation of the civil justice system. Detailed analysis of the consequences flowing from the implementation of the recommendations of the Woolf Report will be considered subsequently.

If a criticism is to be levelled at these committees and commissions, it is that they are all *ad hoc* bodies. Their remit is limited and they do not have the power either to widen the ambit of their investigation or initiate reform proposals.

The Law Commission fulfils the need for some institution to concern itself more generally with the question of law reform. Its general function is to keep the law as a whole under review and to make recommendations for its systematic reform. The Commission continuously keeps under review the need to remove antiquated and/or anachronistic laws from the statute book, whose continued existence make it subject to derision if they do not bring it into disrepute. To that end, 14 Statute Law Repeal Acts have been enacted since 1969, and following a 1995 Law Commission Report (No 230), the Law Reform (Year and a Day Rule) Act was was introduced in 1996. This Act removed the ancient rule which prevented killers being convicted of murder or manslaughter if their victim survived for a year and a day after the original offence.

The Commission is a purely advisory body and its scope is limited to those areas set out in its current programme of law reform. It recommends reform after it has undertaken an extensive process of consultation with informed and/or interested parties. At the conclusion of a project, a report is submitted to the Lord Chancellor and Parliament for their consideration and action.

The annual report of the Law Commission for 1996 reveals that eight of its reports were, in whole or in part, implemented by Parliament. These reports related to family law, criminal law, property law amongst others and the notable legislation that the Law Commission could rightly claim credit for in the year in question were the Theft (Amendment) Act 1996 and the Family Law Act 1996. The report is, however, refreshingly if surprisingly open as to its disappointment in the lack of legislative action that has been taken in pursuance of its reports and recommendations. As its chair, Mrs Justice Arden, stated in the introduction to the annual report:

> It is a striking fact, worthy of repetition, that the public do not obtain the benefit of our work until it is implemented. There are nearly 20 Law Commission reports listed in this Report which the government has either accepted but not implemented, or to which it has not yet given its response ... Our widely welcomed *Report on Offences Against the Person* would modernise and rationalise an area of the criminal law in constant use. Yet this remains neither accepted, rejected nor implemented a public asset from which the public is not getting any benefit ... We hope that ... greater priority will be given by governments to implementing our law reform recommendations

The 1997 annual report evidences the continued activity of the Commission, but again its chair, still Mary Arden, had to report a lack of statutory outcome, this time due to the newly elected governments own heavy legislative programme. A new chair, the Honourable Mr Justice Carnwath, was appointed in February 1999.

Current judicial review procedures are very much the consequence of a 1976 Law Commission Report, *Remedies in Administrative Law*, Cmnd 6407, No

73 and a review of their operation and proposals for reform was issued in October 1994. This report and its recommendations will be considered in detail in 4.11.6.

The establishment within the Lord Chancellor's Department of a division, one of whose tasks is to promote law reform, may signal an increased recognition of the importance of the process of law reform; alternatively, it may signal a move to marginalise the role of the Law Commission by bringing the law reform process more directly under the control of the Lord Chancellor.

Mention should also be made of the relatively new Civil Justice Council, established under the Civil Procedure Act 1997. The remit of this committee, which is made up a variety of judges, lawyers, academics and those representing the interests of consumers and others, under the chair of Lord Woolf, is to:

- keep the civil justice system under review;

- consider how to make the civil justice system more accessible, fair and efficient;

- advise the Lord Chancellor and the judiciary on the development of the civil justice system;

- refer proposals for change to the civil justice system to the Lord Chancellor and the Civil Procedure Rule Committee;

- make proposals for research.

Given the massive upheaval that has resulted from the implementation of Lord Woolf's recent review of the civil justice system, it is to be hoped that this new committee will function effectively to bring about smaller alterations in the system as soon as they become necessary.

2.7   The European context

As was stated at the start of this chapter, it is unrealistic and, indeed, impossible for any student of English law and the English legal system, to ignore the UK's membership of the European Union and European Communities. Nor can the impact of the European Court of Human Rights be ignored, especially now that the HRA 1998 has made the Articles of the European Convention on Human Rights directly applicable in the UK. However, it has to be recognised that placing the English legal system in its European context does make some demands on the individual. For one thing, although the Treaty on European Union 1992 (the Maastricht Treaty) established the Union of its title, it did not dissolve its constituent communities which therefore continue in existence, distinct from that Union. There are said to be three pillars to the EU:

(a) European Community consisting of not only its treaties but wider aspects relating to citizenship and, indeed, economic and monetary union;

(b) common foreign and security policy;

(c) police and judicial co-operation in criminal matters.

It is particularly important to note, however, that the EU does not share the same legal institutional form as the European Community and that it is, therefore, still appropriate to talk about Community law rather than Union law.

It is also essential to distinguish between the two different courts that operate within the European context: the European Court of Justice (ECJ), which is the court of the European Community, sitting in Luxembourg; and the ECHR, which deals with cases relating to the European Convention on Human Rights and sits in Strasbourg.

The long term process leading to the, as yet still to be attained, establishment of an integrated European Community was a response to two factors: the disasters of the Second World War; and the emergence of the Soviet Bloc in Eastern Europe. The aim was to link the separate European countries, particularly France and Germany, together in such a manner as to prevent the outbreak of future armed hostilities. The first step in this process was the establishment a European Coal and Steel Community. The next step towards integration was the formation of the EEC under the Treaty of Rome in 1957. The UK joined the EEC in 1973. The Treaty of Rome has subsequently been amended in the further pursuit of integration as the Community has expanded. Thus, the Single European Act (SEA) 1986 established a single economic market within the European Community and widened the use of majority voting in the Council of Ministers. The Maastricht Treaty further accelerated the move towards a federal European supranational State in the extent to which it recognised Europe as a social and political as well as an economic community. Previous Conservative governments of the UK have resisted the emergence of the EU as anything other than an economic market and have objected to, and resiled from, various provisions aimed at social as opposed to economic affairs. Thus, the UK was able to opt out of the Social Chapter of the Treaty of Maastricht. The present Labour administration in the UK has had no such reservations and, as a consequence, the Treaty of Amsterdam 1997 incorporated the European Social Charter into the EC Treaty which, of course, applies to the UK. One of the consequences of the Amsterdam Treaty was a renumbering of all the Articles in the various EC Treaties. This book will adopt the new numbering, but list the old numbers in brackets.

As the establishment of the single market within the European Community progressed, it was suggested that its operation would be greatly facilitated by the adoption of a common currency, or at least a more closely integrated monetary system. Thus, in 1979, the European Monetary System (EMS) was established, under which individual national currencies were valued against a nominal currency called the ECU and allocated a fixed rate within which they were allowed to fluctuate to a limited extent. Britain was a member of the EMS until 1992, when financial speculation against the pound forced its withdrawal. Nonetheless, other members of the EC continued to pursue the policy of monetary union, now entitled European Monetary Union (EMU) and January 1999 saw the installation of the new European currency, the Euro, against which all currencies within the scheme are allocated fixed values. Thereafter, the newly created European Central Bank will oversee the replacement of national currencies by the Euro. The UK did not join the EMU at its inception and the question as to whether or not it should join is one of the most pressing of current political issues.

The general aim of the EU is set out in Art 2 (number unchanged) of the Treaty of Rome, as amended by the Maastricht Treaty, as follows.

The Community shall have as its task, by establishing a common market and an economic and monetary union and by implementing the common policies or activities referred to in Art 3, to promote throughout the Community a harmonious and balanced development of economic activities, sustainable and non-inflationary growth respecting the environment, a high degree of convergence of economic performance, a high level of employment and of social protection, the raising of the standard of living and quality of life, and economic and social cohesion and solidarity among Member States.

Amongst the policies originally detailed in Art 3 (number unchanged) were included:

- the elimination, between Member States, of custom duties and of quantitative restrictions on the import and export of goods;

- the establishment of a common custom tariff and a common commercial policy towards third countries;

- the abolition, between Member States, of obstacles to the freedom of movement for persons, services and capital;

- the adoption of a common agricultural policy;

- the adoption of a common transport policy;

- the harmonisation of laws of Member States to the extent required to facilitate the proper functioning of the single market;

- the creation of a European Social Fund in order to improve the employment opportunities of workers in the community and to improve their standard of living.

Article 3 has subsequently been extended to cover more social, as opposed to purely economic, matters and now incorporates policies relating to education, health, consumer protection, the environment and culture generally. In 1989, the Community adopted a Charter of Fundamental Social Rights of Workers, although the UK government under the leadership of the then Prime Minister, Margaret Thatcher, declined to sign it, seeing it as representing an unacceptable interference in the free operation of the market. The Treaty on European Union, the Maastricht Treaty, had originally contained a Social Chapter, based on the earlier Social Charter, and designed to further the promotion of employment, improved living and working conditions, proper social protection, dialogue between management and labour, the development of human resources with a view to lasting high employment and the combating of exclusion. Once again, the UK government, this time under the leadership of John Major, refused to accede to such provisions, and, in order to save the rest of the Treaty, the Social Chapter had to be removed and appended as a protocol binding on the then other 11 Members of the Community but not the UK. It is of perhaps signal importance that one of the very first measures taken by the new Labour administration, led by Prime Minister Tony Blair, was to declare its intention to sign up to the Social Chapter.

Consequent upon the agreement of the UK government, the Treaty of Amsterdam 1997 was able to incorporate the European Social Charter into the EC Treaty.

Article 10 (formerly, Art 5) requires:

Member States to take all appropriate measures, whether general or particular, to ensure fulfilment of the obligations arising out of this Treaty or resulting from action taken by the institutions of the Community. They shall facilitate the achievement of the Community's tasks. They shall abstain from any measure which could jeopardise the attainment of the objectives of this Treaty.

This Article effectively means that UK courts are now Community law courts and must be bound by, and give effect to, that law where it is operative. The reasons for the national courts acting in this manners are considered by John Temple Lang, Director in the Competition Directorate General, in an article entitled, 'The duties of national courts under Community constitutional law' ((1997) 22 EL Rev 3). As he writes:

National courts are needed to give companies and individuals remedies which are as prompt, as complete and as immediate as the combined legal system of the Community and of Member States can provide. Only national courts can give injunctions against private parties for breach of Community law rules on, for example, equal pay for men and women, or on restrictive practices. Private parties have no standing to claim injunctions in the Court of Justice against a Member State, they can do so only in a national court. In other words, only a national court could give remedies to individuals and companies for breach of Community law which are as effective as the remedies for breach of national law.

Before the UK joined the EU, its law was just as foreign as law made under any other jurisdiction. On joining the EU, however, the UK and its citizens accepted, and became subject to, European Community law. This subjection to European law remains the case even where the parties to any transaction are themselves both UK subjects. In other words, in areas where it is applicable, European law supersedes any existing UK law to the contrary.

An example of European Community law invalidating the operation of UK legislation can be found in the *Factortame* case (*Factortame Ltd v Secretary of State for Transport (No 1)* (1989)). The Common Fishing Policy established by the EEC had placed limits on the amount of fish that any member country's fishing fleet was permitted to catch. In order to gain access to British fish stocks and quotas, Spanish fishing boat owners formed British companies and re-registered their boats as British. In order to prevent what it saw as an abuse and an encroachment on the rights of indigenous fishermen, the UK government introduced the Merchant Shipping Act 1988, which provided that any fishing company seeking to register as British would have to have its principal place of business in the UK and at least 75% of its shareholders would have to be British nationals. This effectively debarred the Spanish boats from taking up any of the British fishing quota. Some 95 Spanish boat owners applied to the British courts for judicial review of the Merchant Shipping Act on the basis that it was contrary to Community law. The case went from the High Court, through the Court of Appeal, to the House of Lords who referred the case to the ECJ. There, it was decided that the Treaty of Rome required domestic courts to give effect to the directly enforceable provisions of Community law and, in doing so, such courts are required to ignore any national law that runs counter to Community law. The decision gave rise to some heated responses in the UK where it was attacked on the basis that it effectively undermined parliamentary sovereignty.

2.7.1 Sources of European Community law

Community law, depending on its nature and source, may have direct effect on the domestic laws of its various members; that is, it may be open to individuals to rely on it, without the need for their particular State to have enacted the law within its own legal system (see *Factortame*).

There are two types of direct effect. Vertical direct effect means that the individual can rely on Community law in any action in relation to their government, but cannot use it against other individuals. Horizontal direct effect allows the individual to use the EC provision in an action against other individuals. Other EC provisions only take effect when they have been specifically enacted within the various legal systems within the Community.

The sources of Community law are fourfold:

- internal treaties and protocols;

- international agreements;

- secondary legislation;

- decisions of the ECJ.

Internal treaties

Internal treaties govern the Member States of the EU and anything contained therein supersedes domestic legal provisions. The primary treaty is the Treaty of Rome as amended by such legislation as the SEA 1986; or the Maastricht Treaty on European Union and the Amsterdam Treaty. Upon its joining the Community, the Treaty of Rome was incorporated into UK law by the European Communities Act 1972.

As long as treaties are of a mandatory nature and are stated with sufficient clarity and precision, then they have both vertical and horizontal effect (*Van Gend en Loos* (1963)).

International treaties

International treaties are negotiated with other nations by the European Commission on behalf of the EU as a whole and are binding on the individual members of the EU.

Secondary legislation

Secondary legislation is provided for under Art 249 (formerly, Art 189) of the Treaty of Rome. It provides for three types of legislation to be introduced by the European Council and Commission. These are:

- Regulations apply to, and within, Member States generally without the need for those States to pass their own legislation. They are binding and enforceable from the time of their creation and individual States do not have to pass any legislation to give effect to regulations. Regulations must be published in the Official Journal of the EU. The decision as to whether or not a law should be enacted in the form of a regulation is usually left to the Commission, but there are areas where the Treaty of Rome requires that the regulation form must be used. These areas relate to: the rights of workers to remain in Member States of which they are not nationals; the provision of State aid to particular indigenous undertakings or industries; the regulation of EU accounts and budgetary procedures.

- Directives, on the other hand, state general goals and leave the precise implementation in the appropriate form to the individual Member States. Directives, however, tend to state the means as well as the ends to which they are aimed and the ECJ will give direct effect to directives which are sufficiently clear and complete. See *Van Duyn v Home Office* (1974).

Directives usually provide Member States with a time limit within which they are required to implement the provision within their own national laws. If they fail to do so or implement the directive incompletely, then individuals may be able to cite, and rely on, the directive in their dealings with the State in question. Further, *Francovich v Italy* (1991) has established that individuals who have suffered as a consequence of a Member State's failure to implement Community law may seek damages against that State.

The provisions in the Unfair Terms in Consumer Contracts Regulations 1994 is an example of UK law being introduced in response to EU directives.

- Decisions on the operation of European laws and policies are not intended to have general effect but are aimed at particular States or individuals. They have the force of law under Art 249 (formerly, Art 189).

- Additionally, Art 211 (formerly, Art 155) provides for the Commission to issue recommendations and opinions in relation to the operation of Community law. These have no binding force although they may be taken into account in trying to clarify any ambiguities in domestic law.

Judgments of the European Court of Justice

The ECJ is the judicial arm of the EU and, in the field of Community law, its judgments overrule those of national courts. Under Art 234 (formerly, Art 177), national courts have the right to apply to the ECJ for a preliminary ruling on a point of Community law before deciding a case.

The mechanism through which Community law becomes immediately and directly effective in the UK is provided by s 2(1) of the European Communities Act 1972. Section 2(2) gives power to designated ministers or departments to introduce Orders in Council to give effect to other non-directly effective Community law.

2.7.2 The institutions of the European Union

The major institutions of the EU are: the Council of Ministers; the European Parliament; the European Commission; the ECJ.

The Council of Ministers

The Council is made up of ministerial representatives of each of the 15 Member States of the EU. The actual composition of the Council varies depending on the nature of the matter to be considered. When considering economic matters, the various States will be represented by their finance ministers or, if the matter before the Council relates to agriculture, the various agricultural ministers will attend. The organisation of the various specialist councils falls to the President of the Council and that post is held for six monthly periods in rotation by the individual Member States of the EU. The Presidency of the Council is significant to the extent that the country holding the position can, to a large extent, control the agenda of the Council and thus can focus EU attention on areas that it considers to be of particular importance.

The Council of Ministers is the supreme decision making body of the EU and, as such, it has the final say in deciding upon EU legislation. Although it acts on recommendations and proposals made to it by the Commission, it does have the power to instruct the Commission to undertake particular investigations and to submit detailed proposals for its consideration.

Council decisions are taken on a mixture of voting procedures. Some measures only require a simple majority; in others, a procedure of qualified majority voting is used; and, in yet others, unanimity is required. Qualified majority voting is the procedure in which the votes of the 15 Member countries are weighted in proportion to their population from 10 down to two votes each. There are a total of 87 votes to be cast and, in order to pass a vote on the basis of a qualified majority, a minimum of 62 votes in favour is required. The corollary of this is that it requires a total of 26 votes to block any proposal that can be decided on by qualified majority voting. It can be seen, therefore, that even qualified majority voting requires a substantial degree of agreement across the EU.

Prior to approving the enlargement of the EU, by the accession of Austria, Finland and Sweden on 1 January 1995, both the UK and Spain insisted on what is known as the Ioannina Compromise. The Compromise states that:

> ... if members of the Council representing a total of 23 to 25 votes indicate their intention to oppose the adoption by the Council of a decision by qualified majority, the Council will do all in its power to reach within a reasonable time and without prejudicing obligatory time limits laid down in the Treaties and by secondary law, such as Arts 251 and 252 [formerly, Arts 189B and 189C] of the Treaty establishing the European Community, a satisfactory solution that could be adopted by at least 65 votes.

The effectiveness of this Compromise is a matter of some doubt, especially given the Commission's subsequent declaration that it would call for a vote on the new basis, as soon as it considered that a reasonable time had elapsed.

The SEA (a European Treaty legislated into UK law as the European Communities (Amendment) Act 1986) extended the use of qualified majority voting but unanimity is still required in what can be considered as the more politically sensitive areas, such as those relating to the harmonisation of indirect taxation, or the free movement of individuals. In addition to the need for unanimity in such sensitive areas, there is also the ultimate safeguard of what is known as the Luxembourg Compromise. This procedure, instituted at the behest of the French government in 1966, permits individual Member States to exercise a right of veto in relation to any proposals which they consider to be contrary to what they consider to be a very important interest of theirs.

As the format of particular council fluctuates, much of its day to day work is delegated to a committee of permanent representatives which operates under the title of COREPER.

Article 2 of the SEA 1986 provided that:

> The European Council shall bring together the Heads of State or of government of the Member States and the President of the Commission of the European Communities. They shall be assisted by the Ministers for Foreign Affairs and by a member of the Commission. The European Council shall meet at least twice a year.

The European Council, now known as the Council of the European Union, can be seen, therefore, as a form of EU summit meeting. It is chaired by the head of government currently holding the presidency of the Council. Although not originally recognised in the Treaty of Rome, the function of the European Council was clarified by Art D of the Treaty on European Union which stated that it shall provide the union with the necessary impetus for its development and shall define the general political guidelines thereof.

The European Parliament

The European Parliament is the directly elected European institution and, to that extent, it can be seen as the body which exercises democratic control over the operation on the EU. As in national Parliaments, members are elected to represent constituencies, the elections being held every five years. There are a total of 626 members divided amongst the 15 members approximately in proportion to the size of their various populations. Members of the European Parliament do not sit in national groups but operate within political groupings.

The European Parliament's general secretariat is based in Luxembourg and, although the Parliament sits in plenary session in Strasbourg for one week in each month, its detailed and preparatory work is carried out through 18 permanent committees which usually meet in Brussels. These permanent committees consider proposals from the Commission and provide the full Parliament with reports of such proposals for discussion.

Powers of the European Parliament

The powers of the European Parliament (the Parliament), however, should not be confused with those of national Parliaments, for the Parliament is not a legislative institution and, in that respect, it plays a subsidiary role to the Council of Ministers. Originally, its powers were merely advisory and supervisory.

In pursuance of its advisory function, the Parliament always had the right to comment on the proposals of the Commission and, since 1980, the Council has been required to wait for the Parliaments opinion before adopting any law. In its supervisory role, the Parliament scrutinises the activities of the Commission and has the power to remove the Commission by passing a motion of censure against it by a two-thirds majority.

The legislative powers of the Parliament were substantially enhanced by the SEA 1986. Since that enactment, it has had a more influential role to play particularly in relation to the completion of the internal market. It can now negotiate directly with the Council as to any alterations or amendments it wishes to see in proposed legislation. It can also intervene to question and indeed alter any joint position adopted by the Council on proposals put to it by the Commission. If the Council then insists on pursuing its original joint position, it can only do so on the basis of unanimity.

The SEA 1986 also required the assent of Parliament to any international agreements to be entered into by the EU. As a consequence, it has ultimate control, not just in relation to trade treaties, but also as regards any future expansion in the EU's membership.

The Parliament is, together with the Council of Ministers, the budgetary authority of the EU. The budget is drawn up by the Commission and is presented to both the Council and the Parliament. As regards what is known as obligatory expenditure, the Council has the final say but, in relation to non-obligatory expenditure, the Parliament has the final decision whether to approve the budget or not. Such budgetary control places the Parliament in an extremely powerful position to influence EC policy, but perhaps the most draconian power the Parliament wields is the ability to pass a vote of censure against the Commission, requiring it to resign en masse.

The events of 1998–99 saw a significant shift in the relationship between the Parliament and the Commission. In December 1998, as a result of sustained accusations of mismanagement, fraud and cover ups levelled against the Commission, the Parliament voted not to discharge the Commission's accounts for 1996. Such action was, in effect, a declaration that the Community's budget has not been properly handled and was tantamount to a vote of no confidence in the Commission. In January 1999, the Community's Court of Auditors delivered what can only be described as a devastating report on fraud, waste and mismanagement and maladministration on the part of the Commission. It was found that the Commission had understated its financial obligations by £3.3 billion, and was so lax in its control that it had not even noticed that its banks were not paying any interest on huge amounts of money they were holding. The report of the Court of Auditors led to a vote of no confidence in the Commission in early January 1999 and, although the Commission survived the vote by a majority of 293 to 232, it had to accept the setting up of a committee of wise persons to investigate and report on its operation. At the time, the appointment of this committee was thought to be a diplomatic fudge, allowing the Commission to carry on under warning as to its future conduct. However, when the committee submitted its report, it was so damning that it was immediately obvious that the Parliament would certainly use its power to remove the Commission. To forestall this event, the Commission resigned en masse. Somewhat ironically and certainly anti-climactically, however, as this book is being written, the previous President of the Commission, Jacques Santer, has actually gone, to be replaced by Romano Prodi; but the same commissioners, including the ones who were particularly picked out as the objects of blame, are still in place; on a temporary basis of course, simply ensuring the continuing smooth operation of the Commission.

The Europe wide selection of a new Parliament in June 1999 saw the election of a centre-right majority which will have a significant role to play in approving a new Commission.

As this book was being written, the previous President of the Commission, Jacques Santer, had gone, to be replaced by Romano Prodi; but the same commissioners, including the ones who were particularly picked out as the objects of blame, remained in place; on a temporary basis of course, simply ensuring the continuing smooth operation of the Commission. However, by the first week of July 1999, a new Commission had been proposed and gained the approval of the European Parliament in September of that year. In what President Prodi has said was to be a reforming Commission, the senior UK commissioner, Neil Kinnock, has been appointed as vice president with the specific remit of reforming the EU.

Economic and Social Committees

If the Parliament represents the directly elected arm of the EU, then the Economic and Social Committee represents a collection of unelected but, nonetheless, influential interest groups throughout the EU. This Committee is a consultative institution and its opinion must be sought prior to the adoption by the Council of any Commission proposal. The Economic and Social Committee represents the underlying corporatist nature of the EU to the extent that it seeks to locate and express a commonality of view and opinion on proposals from such divergent interests groups as employers, trade unions and consumers. It is perhaps symptomatic of the attitude of recent UK governments to this underlying corporatist, essentially Christian Democratic, strand within the EU that it dispensed with its own similar internal grouping, the National Economic Development Council in 1992.

The European Commission

The European Commission is the executive of the EU and, in that role, it is responsible for the administration of EU policies. There are 20 Commissioners chosen from the various Member States to serve for renewable terms of four years. Commissioners are appointed to head departments with specific responsibility for furthering particular areas of EU policy. Once appointed, Commissioners are expected to act in the general interest of the EU as a whole rather than in the partial interest of their own home country.

In pursuit of EU policy, the Commission is responsible for ensuring that Treaty obligations between the Member States are met, and that Community laws relating to individuals are enforced. In order to fulfil these functions, the Commission has been provided with extensive powers both in relation to the investigation of potential breaches of Community law and the subsequent punishment of offenders. The classic area in which these powers can be seen in operation is in the area of competition law. Under Arts 81 and 82 (formerly, Arts 85 and 86) of the Treaty of Rome, the Commission has substantial powers to investigate and control potential monopolies and anti-competitive behaviour and it has used these powers to levy what, in the case of private individuals, would amount to huge fines where breaches of Community competition law have been discovered. In February 1993, the Commission imposed fines totalling more than £80 million on 17 steel producers for what was described as a very serious, illegal price fixing cartel. The UK company British Steel suffered the greatest individual imposition of £26.4 million.

The Commission also acts, under instructions from the Council, as the negotiator between the EU and external countries.

In addition to these executive functions, the Commission also has a vital part to play in the EU's legislative process. The Council can only act on proposals put before it by the Commission. The Commission, therefore, has a duty to propose to the Council measures that will advance the achievement of the EU's general policies.

The European Court of Justice

The ECJ is the judicial arm of the EU and, in the field of Community law its judgments overrule those of national courts. It consists of 15 judges, assisted by nine advocates general, and sits in Luxembourg. The role of the advocate general is to investigate the matter submitted to the Court and to produce a report together with a recommendation for the consideration of the Court. The actual Court is free to accept the report or not as it sees fit.

The SEA 1986 provided for a new Court of First Instance to be attached to the existing Court of Justice. The jurisdiction of the Court of First Instance is limited mainly to internal claims by employees of the Community and to claims against fines made by the Commission under Community competition law. The aim is to reduce the burden of work on the Court of Justice but there is a right of appeal, on points of law only, to the full Court of Justice.

The ECJ performs two key functions:

(a) it decides whether any measures adopted, or rights denied, by the Commission, Council or any national government are compatible with treaty obligations. Such actions may be raised by any EU institution, government or individual. A Member State may fail to comply with its Treaty obligations in a number of ways. It might fail or, indeed, refuse to comply with a provision of the Treaty or a regulation; or, alternatively, it might refuse to implement a directive within the allotted time provided for. Under such circumstances, the State in question will be brought before the ECJ, either by the Commission or another Member State or, indeed, individuals within the State concerned;

(b) it provides authoritative rulings, at the request of national courts under Art 234 (formerly, Art 177) of the Treaty of Rome, on the interpretation of points of Community law. When an application is made under Art 234, the national proceedings are suspended until such time as the determination of the point in question is delivered by the ECJ. Whilst the case is being decided by the ECJ, the national court is expected to provide appropriate interim relief, even if this involves going against a domestic legal provision, as in the *Factortame* case).

This procedure can take the form of a preliminary ruling where the request precedes the actual determination of a case by the national court.

Article 234 (formerly, Art 177) provides that:

> The Court of Justice shall have jurisdiction to give preliminary rulings concerning:
>
> (a) the interpretation of treaties;
>
> (b) the validity and interpretation of acts of the institutions of the Union and of the European Central Bank;
>
> (c) the interpretation of the statutes of bodies established by an act of the Council, where those statutes so provide.
>
> Where such a question is raised before any court or tribunal of a Member State, that court or tribunal may, if it considers that a decision on the question is necessary to enable it to give judgment, request the Court of Justice to give a ruling thereon.
>
> Where any such question is raised in a case pending before a court or tribunal of a Member State against whose decision there is no judicial remedy under national law, that court or tribunal shall bring the matter before the Court of Justice.

It is clear that it is for the national court and not the individual parties concerned to make the reference. Where the national court or tribunal is not the final court or tribunal, the reference to the ECJ is discretionary. Where the national court or tribunal is the final court, then reference is obligatory. However, there are circumstances under which a final court need not make a reference under Art 234 (formerly, Art 177). These are:

- where the question of Community law is not truly relevant to the decision to be made by the national court;

- where there has been a previous interpretation of the provision in question by the ECJ so that its meaning has been clearly determined;

- where the interpretation of the provision is so obvious as to leave no scope for any reasonable doubt as to its meaning. This latter instance has to be used with caution given the nature of Community law; for example, the fact that it is expressed in several languages using legal terms which might have different connotations within different jurisdictions. However, it is apparent that, where the meaning is clear, no reference need be made.

In undertaking the task of interpreting Community law, the ECJ adopts a purposive and contextual approach, as against the more restrictive methods of interpretation favoured by UK courts in relation to domestic legislation. It should be noted, however, that UK courts themselves adopt a purposive approach in relation to Community law (this will be considered in more detail later in this chapter.) The clearest statement of this purposive contextualist approach adopted by the ECJ is contained in its judgment in *CILFIT Srl v Minister of Health* (1982):

> Every provision of Community law must be placed in its context and interpreted in the light of the provisions of Community law as a whole, regard being had to the objectives thereof and to its state of evolution at the date on which the provision in question is to be applied.

It can be appreciated that the reservations considered previously in regard to judicial creativity and intervention in policy matters in the UK courts apply *a fortiori* to the decisions of the ECJ.

Another major difference between the ECJ and the court within the English legal system is that the former is not bound by the doctrine of precedent in the same way as the latter is. It is always open to the ECJ to depart from its previous decisions where it considers it appropriate to do so. Although it will endeavour to maintain consistency, it has, on occasion, ignored its own previous decisions, as in *European Parliament v Council* (1990) where it recognised the right of the Parliament to institute an action against the Council.

The manner in which European law operates to control sex discrimination, through the Equal Treatment Directive, is of significant interest and, in *Marshall v Southampton and West Hampshire Area Health Authority* (1993), a number of the points that have been considered above were highlighted. Ms Marshall had originally been required to retire earlier than a man in her situation would have been required to do. She successfully argued before the ECJ that such a practice was discriminatory and contrary to Directive 76/207/EC on the equal treatment of men and women.

The present action related to the level of compensation she was entitled to as a consequence of this breach. UK legislation, the Sex Discrimination Act 1975, had set limits on the level of compensation that could be recovered for acts of sex discrimination. Marshall argued that the imposition of such limits was contrary to the Equal Opportunity Directive and that, in establishing such limits, the UK had failed to comply with the Directive.

The House of Lords referred the case to the ECJ under Art 234 (formerly, Art 177) and the latter determined that the rights set out in relation to compensation under Art 6 of the Directive were directly effective, and that, as the purpose of the Directive was to give effect to the principle of equal treatment, that could only be achieved by either reinstatement or the awarding of adequate compensation. The decision of the ECJ, therefore, overruled the financial limitations placed on sex discrimination awards and effectively overruled the domestic legislation.

P v S and Cornwall County Council (1996) extended the ambit of unlawful sex discrimination under the directive to cover people who have undergone surgical gender reorientation (sex change). However, in *Grant v South West Trains Ltd* (1998), the ECJ declined to extend the directive to cover discrimination on the grounds of sexual orientation (homosexuality), even though the Advocate General had initially supported the extension of the directive to same sex relationships. Whilst *Grant* was in the process of being decided in the ECJ, a second case, *R v Secretary of State for Defence ex p Perkins (No 2),* had been brought before the English courts arguing a similar point, that discrimination on grounds of sexual orientation was covered by the Equal Treatment Directive. Initially, the High Court had referred the matter, under Art 234 (formerly, Art 177), to the ECJ for decision, but, on the decision in Grant being declared, the referral was withdrawn. In withdrawing the reference, Lightman J considered the proposition of counsel for Perkins to the effect that:

> ... there have been a number of occasions where the ECJ has overruled its previous decisions; that the law is not static; and, accordingly, in a dynamic and developing field such as discrimination in employment there must be a prospect that a differently constituted ECJ may depart from the decision in *Grant* ... But, to justify a reference, the possibility that the ECJ will depart from its previous decision must be more than theoretical: it must be a realistic possibility. The decision in *Grant* was of the full Court; it is only some four months old; there has been no development in case law or otherwise since the decision which can give cause for the ECJ reconsidering that decision ... I can see no realistic prospect of any change of mind on the part of the ECJ.

It could be pointed out that there could be no change in case law if judges, such as Lightman J, refused to send similar cases to the ECJ; but there may well be sense, if not virtue, in his refusal to refer similar cases to the ECJ within such a short timescale.

The Court of Auditors

Given the part that the Court of Auditors played in the 1998–99 struggle between the Parliament and the Commission, the role of this body should not be underestimated.

As its name suggests, it is responsible for providing an external audit of the Communities finances. It examines the legality, regularity and soundness of the management of all the Communities revenue and expenditure. The following passage, from its statement of assurance relating to the budget for the year 1996–97, provides a flavour of its findings:

> ... as in previous years, the incidence of errors affecting the transactions underlying the Commissions payments is too high for the Court to provide assurance about their legality and regularity.
>
> Many of the errors found in the payments provide direct evidence of failure to implement the control mechanisms foreseen in the regulations or to apply requisite checks before payments are made ... there were, again, many formal errors affecting payments. These are, essentially, cases where there was a failure to comply with the applicable regulations ... in many cases, formal errors involve specific systems weaknesses, notably failure to implement the control procedure required to ensure the eligibility of the recipients and the accuracy of the amounts paid [www.eca.eu.int.EN/notinf/dasra97.htm].

From this passage may well be seen the reason why the Parliament sought to establish some control over the operation of the Commission.

2.7.3 The European Convention on Human Rights

It has to be established, and emphasised, from the outset that the substance of this section has absolutely nothing to do with the EU as such; the Council of Europe is a completely distinct organisation and, although membership of the two organisations overlap, they are not the same. The Council of Europe is concerned not with economic matters but with the protection of civil rights and freedoms.

It is gratifying, at least to a degree, to recognise that the Convention and its Court are no longer a matter of mysterious external control; the HRA 1998 having incorporated the European Convention on Human Rights into UK law and placing the ECHR as the supreme court in matters related to its jurisdiction. Much attention was paid to the Convention and the HRA in Chapter 1 (see 1.5), so it only remains to consider the structure and operation of the ECHR.

The Convention originally established two institutions:

(a) the European Commission of Human Rights. This body was charged with the task of examining, and if need be investigating the circumstances of, petitions submitted to it. If the Commission was unable to reach a negotiated solution between the parties concerned, it referred the matter to the Court of Human Rights;

(b) the European Court of Human Rights (ECHR). The European Convention on Human Rights provides that the judgment of the Court shall be final and that parties to it will abide by the decisions of the Court. This body, sitting in Strasbourg, was, and remains, responsible for all matters relating to the interpretation and application of the current Convention.

However, in the 1980s, as the Convention and its Court became more known and popular as a forum for asserting human rights, so its workload increased. This pressure was exacerbated by the break up of the old Communist Eastern Bloc and the fact that the newly independent countries, in both senses of the words, became signatories to the Convention. The statistics support the view of the incipient sclerosis of the original structure.

Applications registered with the Commission

Year	Number of applications registered
1981	404
1993	2,037
1997	4,750

Cases referred to the Court

Year	Number of cases referred
1981	7
1993	52
1997	119

As a consequence of such pressure, it became necessary to streamline the procedure by amalgamating the two previous institutions into one Court. In pursuit of this aim, Protocol 11 of the Convention was introduced in 1994. The new ECHR came into operation on 1 November 1998, although the Commission continued to deal with cases which had already been declared admissible for a further year.

The ECHR consists of 40 judges, representing the number of signatories to the Convention, although they do not have to be chosen from each State and, in any case, sit as individuals rather than representatives of their State. Judges are elected, by the Parliamentary Assembly of the Council of Europe, generally for six years, but arrangements have been put in place so that one half of the membership of the judicial panel will be required to seek renewal every three years.

It has to be recognised that the UK does not have a good record in relation to cases taken against it in the ECHR; in fact, currently, it comes second only to Turkey in the league of offenders. A number of case studies may highlight the way in which the ECHR deals with cases. It must not be forgotten, however, that these previous decisions of the ECHR are now binding precedents in UK law.

In *Malone v UK* (1984), the ECHR decided that telephone tapping by the police, authorised by the UK Government, and condoned under common law powers by the High Court, was in breach of Art 8 of the European Convention on Human Rights which guarantees the right to privacy. The Article holds:

> There shall be no interference by a public authority with the exercise of this right except such as is in accordance with the law and is necessary in a democratic society in the interests of national security ...

The ECHR held that the tapping was against the Convention because it was not in accordance with law but rather governed by an unregulated discretion. It could not be necessary in a democratic society as there were no constitutional safeguards against misuse of the power. The government reacted by introducing legislation to control telephone tapping by the police. The Interception of Communications Act 1985 limits telephone tapping to cases where the Home Secretary has issued a warrant and, to safeguard against arbitrary use, the warrant can only be issued in three specified circumstances, one of which is the prevention of serious crime. Further safeguards are provided by a tribunal to investigate complaints about the use of these powers and by the establishment of a commissioner to review annually how the Home Secretary has exercised his powers.

Another example of the way in which the system operates may be seen in the case of Earnest Saunders, one of the original defendants in the Guinness fraud trial of 1990, *R v Saunders* (1996). Prior to his trial, Saunders had been interviewed by Department of Trade and Industry inspectors and was required, under the provisions of the companies legislation, to answer questions without the right to silence. It was claimed that interviews under such conditions, and their subsequent use at the trial leading to his conviction, were in breach of the Convention on Human Rights. In October 1994, the Commission decided in Saunders favour, and the Court confirmed that decision in 1996, although Saunders was not awarded damages. As a result, the Government has recognised that the powers given to DTI inspectors, breach the Convention, and has declared an intention to alter them, but not in a retrospective way that would benefit Mr Saunders.

Nor should one forget the potentially crucially important decision in *McGonnell v UK* (1995), in which the Commission has placed the situation of the Lord Chancellor in doubt.

In deciding cases before it, the ECHR applies what is known as the margin of appreciation. This means that Member States have a measure of national discretion in the way they give effect to general standards set out in the Convention. An example of this may be seen in the 1996 decision on the ECHR in favour of the UK's decision to ban the film, *Visions of Ecstasy*, under its blasphemy law, in spite of the directors claim that the ban was contrary to his right to freedom of speech. The Court decided that such delicate decisions as those relating to issues such as blasphemy should be decided at the local level and should not be imposed centrally. This particular decision may have pleased the UK Government, but it has been less than pleased with a number of other controversial cases in which the decisions have gone against it. Notable amongst these was the decision that the rights of the suspected IRA terrorists had been violated by their summary execution in Gibraltar.

Equally, the concerns of the government cannot but have been strengthened by the recent decision of the High Court to effectively take the impact of the HRA into consideration immediately (see 1.5).

2.7.4   The European Convention and the European Union

Having started this section by stressing the fundamental distinction between the ECJ and the ECHR, it is necessary to finish it by blurring it and pointing out the various ways in which the European Community, and then Union, have expressly recognised the rights provided in the Convention and the decisions made by the ECHR. Thus, in a joint declaration delivered in 1997, the European Parliament, the Council, and the Commission emphasised the prime importance they attached to the protection of fundamental rights:

> ... as derived particularly from the constitution of the Member States and the European Convention for the Protection of Human Rights and Fundamental Freedoms [(1977) OJ C103].

Article 6 (formerly, Art F(2)), which was introduced by the Maastricht Treaty, expressly states that:

> The Union shall respect fundamental rights, as guaranteed by the European Convention for the Protection of Human Rights and Fundamental Freedoms ... as general principles of Community law.

The ECJ, in the same way as English courts, has equally been guided by the Convention where Community law is silent. It still remains possible, however, for cases to be brought to either or both judicial forums. Issues relating to discrimination are an ideal case in point by being potentially both in breach of employment law regulated by the EC, and fundamental human rights regulated by the ECHR. It is also an unfortunate fact that it is possible for at least a degree of incompatibility between the decisions of the two courts in relation to very similar matters (for example, see *SPUC v Grogan* (1991); and *Open Door and Well Women v Ireland* (1992)). Such possibilities would be precluded if, following the recent action of the UK, the EU, as a body, were formally to incorporate the Convention.

SOURCES OF LAW

Legislation

Legislation is law produced through the parliamentary system. Government is responsible for most Acts but individual members of Parliament do have a chance to sponsor Private Members' Bills. The passage of a Bill through each House of Parliament involves five distinct stages; first reading, second reading, committee stage, report stage, and third reading. Then it is given Royal Assent. The House of Lords only has limited scope to delay legislation.

Amongst the problems of drafting Acts is the need to reconcile such contradictory demands as brevity and precision. Legislation can be split into different categories: Public Acts affect the general public; Private Acts relate to particular individuals; Consolidation Acts bring various provisions together; Codification Acts give statutory form to common law principles; Amending Acts alter existing laws and amendments may be textual, which alters the actual wording of a statute or non-textual in which case the operation rather than the wording of the existing law is changed.

Delegated legislation

Delegated legislation appears in the form of: Orders in Council; Statutory Instruments; bylaws; professional regulations.

The main advantages of delegated legislation relate to: speed of implementation; the saving of parliamentary time; access to expertise; flexibility.

The main disadvantages relate to: the lack of accountability of those making such law; the lack of scrutiny of proposals for such legislation; the sheer amount of delegated legislation.

Controls over delegated legislation are: in Parliament, the Joint Select Committee on Statutory Instruments; and, in the courts, *ultra vires* provisions may be challenged through judicial review.

Case law

Case law is that law created by judges in the course of deciding cases. The doctrine of *stare decisis* or binding precedent refers to the fact that courts are bound by previous decisions of courts equal to or above them in the court hierarchy. The House of Lords can now overrule its own previous rules; the Court of Appeal cannot.

It is the reason for a decision, the *ratio decidendi*, that binds. Everything else is *obiter dictum* and not bound to be followed.

Judges avoid precedents through either overruling or distinguishing them.

The advantages of the doctrine relate to: saving the time of all parties concerned; certainty; flexibility; the meeting of the requirements of formal justice.

The disadvantages relate to: uncertainty; fixity; and unconstitutionality.

Custom

Custom is of arguable historic importance as a source of law and is of very limited importance as a contemporary source.

Law reform

Law reform in particular areas is considered by various standing committees particularly established for that purpose, and Royal Commissions may also be established for such purposes. The Law Commission, however, exists to consider the need for the general and systematic reform of the law.

The European Union

UK law is now subject to Community law in particular areas.

In practice, this has led to the curtailment of parliamentary sovereignty in those areas.

Sources of European Community law

The sources of EC law are:

- internal treaties and protocols;
- international agreements;
- secondary legislation; and
- decisions of the ECJ.

Secondary legislation takes three forms:

- regulations which are directly applicable;
- directives which have to be given statutory form;
- decisions are directly applicable.

Major institutions

The major institutions of the EU are:

- the Council of Ministers;
- the European Parliament;
- the Commission; and
- the ECJ.

The European Court of Human Rights

The European Council, the European Commission of Human Rights and the ECHR are distinct institutions whose purpose is to regulate the potential abuse of human rights. They are not part of the EU structure.

Since the enactment of the Human Rights Act 1998, the European Convention on Human Rights has been incorporated into UK law. It remains to see what effect this has on domestic UK law but it cannot but be significant.

CHAPTER 3

CIVIL AND CRIMINAL COURT STRUCTURES

The first part of this chapter looks at the structure of the civil courts. We look at which type of cases are heard in which trial courts; the rules relating to transfer of case from one level of court to another; the system of appeals and the criticisms which have been made of the various aspects of these systems. The second part of the chapter (3.13) looks at the criminal courts

What is the difference between a criminal and civil case? There are several key distinctions:

- Criminal cases are brought by the State against individual or corporate defendants whereas civil cases are brought by one citizen or body against another such party. The State here involves the police (or possibly Customs and Excise officers or tax inspectors) who investigate the crime and collect the evidence; and the Crown Prosecution Service which prepares the Crown's case. In civil cases, the State is not involved here except in so far as it provides the courts and personnel so that the litigation can be judged. If a party refuses, for example, to be bound by the order a court makes in a civil case then that party may be found in contempt of court and punished, that is, imprisoned or fined.

- The outcomes of civil and criminal cases are different. If a criminal case is successful from the point of view of the person bringing it (*the prosecutor*) because the magistrate or jury finds *the defendant* (sometimes called *the accused*) guilty as charged, then the result will be a sentence. There is a wide range of sentences available, from absolute or conditional discharges (where the convicted defendant is free to go without any conditions or with some requirement, for example, that the defendant undertakes never to visit a particular place), to life imprisonment. Criminal sentences, or 'sanctions', are to mark the State's disapproval of the defendant's crime. Sometimes, the State loses financially in imposing a punishment, for example, with custodial sentences: in 1999, the prison population rose to over 63,000 with very high costs to the State. It costs £34,000 to keep a prisoner in Brixton prison for one year and £32,000 to keep a woman in Holloway for one year. On the other hand, fines (the most common sentence or 'disposal') can often bring revenue to the State. In any event, however, the victim of a crime never gains from the sanction imposed on the criminal. A criminal court can order a convicted person to pay the victim compensation but this will be in addition to and separate from the sentence for the crime.

- If a civil case is successful from the point of view of the person bringing the action (*the claimant*), then the outcome will be one of a number of civil remedies which are designed to benefit the *claimant* and in which the State, or wider community, has no direct interest. Civil remedies include damages, and court orders like injunctions, orders of prohibition and specific performance. So, in civil proceedings, the *claimant* will sue the *defendant* and a successful action will result in *judgment for the claimant*. In matrimonial cases, the party who brings an action is called the *petitioner* and the other party is known as the *respondent*.

- Civil and criminal cases are processed differently by the English legal system. They use different procedures, vocabulary and they are dealt with, on the whole, by different courts. It is very important not to confuse the vocabularies of the different systems and speak, for example, about a claimant *prosecuting* a company for breach of contract. The law of contract is civil law so the defendant would be *sued* or *litigated against* or have *an action* taken against it by the plaintiff.

The question then arises: 'What is the difference between a crime and a civil wrong; how am I to tell into which category a particular wrong falls?' The answer is simply by building up a general legal knowledge. There is nothing inherent in any particular conduct which makes it criminal. One cannot say, for example, that serious wrongs are crimes and that lesser transgressions will be civil wrongs: some crimes are comparatively trivial, like some parking offences, whilst some civil wrongs can have enormously harmful consequences as where a company in breach of a contract causes financial harm to hundreds or thousands of people.

Sometimes, a single event can be both a crime and a civil wrong. If you drive at 50 mph in a 30 mph zone and crash into another vehicle, killing a passenger, you may be prosecuted by the State for causing death by dangerous driving and, if convicted, imprisoned or fined. Additionally, you may be sued for negligence (a tortious civil wrong) by a dependant of the killed passenger and the driver.

The organisation of the civil courts is currently undergoing a period of relatively rapid change. A highly detailed study of the business of the civil courts was undertaken by the Civil Justice Review (CJR) which was instituted by Lord Hailsham, then Lord Chancellor, in 1985. The purpose of the review was to improve the machinery of civil justice by means of reforms in jurisdiction, procedure and court administration. In particular, the review was concerned with ways of reducing delays, costs and complexity of process. The report of the review was based on a study of five areas of civil action: personal injury, small claims, the commercial court, the process of debt enforcement and housing cases. In each area, a fact finding research project was commissioned mostly from management consultants. The Lord Chancellor's

Department then published five discussion papers on these areas. A *General Issues Paper* was published in 1987 in which problems common to civil process were discussed. The Review's final report was published a year later and largely implemented in the Courts and Legal Services Act (CLSA) 1990.

'High quality justice' had been identified in the *General Issues Paper* as the main objective in all parts of the civil court process. This included fair procedures, methods of adjudication so that each party was given proper opportunity to present his case and to have it judged impartially within a setting of consistency of judicial decisions. The primary aim was not, however, to be paramount. It had to be balanced against the aim of keeping parties' costs, delay and the cost to the State in proportion to the subject matter in dispute. This aim of efficiency included time targets for the handling of cases by the courts; effective deployment of judges, court staff and court facilities; the appropriate matching of the complexity of case to the level of experience of the judge; the adoption of streamlined procedures for simple cases; limiting the costs to the parties and to the court service.

An additional aim was expressed as the need for the courts to be 'effective', that is, court locations and hours that were convenient to litigants, the use of simple rules regarding jurisdiction and procedure.

Generally, the Review recommended that much of the case work previously dealt with by the High Court should be moved to the county courts as they were more numerous, relatively cheap and used simpler procedure. This has been carried out by the CLSA and by Statutory Instruments, as we shall see later in this chapter.

Since the introduction of the Civil Procedure Act 1997 and the new Civil Procedure Rules (CPR) 1998, the operation of the civil courts has undergone yet another series of major changes. The implications of these changes are dealt with in Chapter 7.

3.1 The Court Service

From April 1995, a new executive agency was established to run all the courts except the magistrates' courts and the coroners' courts, both of which remain under the control of local authorities. The Court Service, which was previously controlled by the Lord Chancellor's Department, now has overall management responsibility for the law courts. Statements from the agency that it aims at 'reducing the unit cost of production per court hour' have attracted criticism that judges may thus be put under pressure to wind up cases more quickly. The agency is introducing court fees for litigants (for example, £200 per day for the county courts), and its longer term aim is to move to recovering the full costs of the civil courts, including the judges, from fees charged to litigants.

3.2   Magistrates' courts

Magistrates' courts have a significant civil jurisdiction. They hear family proceedings under the Domestic Proceedings and Magistrates' Courts Act (DPMCA) 1978 and the Children Act (CA) 1989. Here, the court is termed a 'family proceedings court'. A family proceedings court must normally be composed of not more than three justices, including, as far as is practicable, both a man and a woman. Justices who sit on such benches must be members of the 'family panel' which comprises people specially appointed to deal with family matters. The magistrates' court deals with adoption proceedings, applications for residence and contact orders (CA 1989) and maintenance relating to spouses and children. Under the DPMCA 1978, the court also has the power to make personal protection orders and exclusion orders in cases of matrimonial violence. They have powers of recovery in relation to the community charge and the council tax and charges for water, gas and electricity. Magistrates grant, renew and revoke licences for selling liquor.

3.3   County courts

The county courts were introduced in 1846 to provide local, accessible fora for the adjudication of relatively small scale litigation. There are 240 county courts. These courts are served by 539 circuit judges and 337 district judges, the latter appointed by the Lord Chancellor from persons who have a seven year qualification (s 71 of the CLSA 1990).

Before the 1999 civil justice reforms, jurisdiction of the county courts was separated from that of the High Court on a strict financial limit basis, for example, a district judge heard cases where the amount was £5,000 or less. The new CPR which we examine in Chapter 11, operate the same process irrespective of whether the case forum is the High Court or the county court. Broadly, county courts will hear small claims and fast track cases while the more challenging multi-track cases will be heard in the High Court.

The new civil justice reforms (see Chapter 11) are likely to put a considerable burden of work on the county courts. One question is, however, how much busier can the county courts become without a significant improvement in their resources? In 1990, whilst a combined total of 417,000 actions were commenced in the Queen's Bench and Chancery Courts of the High Court, 3.5 million cases were commenced in the county courts. The profile of county court work is changing. Whereas the number of full trials has been relatively constant during recent years, the number of small claims arbitrations has risen sharply. In 1989, there were 22,267 trials and 49,829 arbitrations, whereas, in 1994, the comparable figures were 24,219, and 87,885. This reflects the doubling of the small claims limit from £500 to £1,000 in 1989.

The trebling of this limit to £3,000 in 1996 resulted in the numbers of small claims rising to over 95,000 in 1998. The following complaints by practitioners working in the county courts are cited in Smith (ed), *Achieving Civil Justice* (1996):

- inconsistent practice between different courts;
- too many judges without specialist knowledge of relevant areas of law, like housing;
- inadequate use of new technology, lost files, and judges without access to computer assistance;
- overloading of case lists, for example, 40–50 housing possession cases listed for hearing within one hour.

In *Practice Direction (Transfer Between High Court and County Courts)* (1991) it is stated that certain types of actions set down for trial in the High Court are considered too important for transfer to a county court. These are cases involving:

- professional negligence;
- fatal accidents;
- allegations of fraud or undue influence;
- defamation;
- malicious prosecution or false imprisonment;
- claims against the police.

The county court jurisdiction also involves probate, property cases, tort, contract, bankruptcy, insolvency, and relations. Regarding remedies, the county court cannot grant the prerogative remedies of mandamus, prohibition and certiorari. (See 4.11.2.) They cannot grant Anton Piller orders (an interlocutory mandatory injunction, obtained ex parte to prevent the defendant from removing, concealing or destroying evidence in the form of documents or moveable property) and neither, generally, can they grant Mareva injunctions (as for an Anton Piller order but to prevent the defendant from removing his assets out of the jurisdiction of the English courts or dissipating them). For authoritative guidance of both of these orders, see *Practice Direction ex p Mareva Injunctions and Anton Piller Orders* (1994).

The nomenclature for cases beginning after April 1999 has altered under the CPR. Henceforward, *ex parte* actions are simply actions without notice (being given to the other side); an Anton Piller order becomes an order to search premises; and a Mareva injunction becomes an order to freeze a company's assets.

Lord Woolf's Interim Report in 1995 recommended that the limit claims in the small claims court should be raised from £1,000 to £3,000, and this was brought into effect for all claims except personal injury claims in 1996. The Final Report of Lord Woolf, *Access to Justice* (1996), recommended (Recommendation 274) that, except for personal injury claims, the financial limit of the small claims jurisdiction should be eventually extended to £5,000.

From April 1999, the small claims limit rose from £3,000 to £5,000, except for personal injury claims which will be limited to £1,000. The small claims procedure has been seen by many as a major success of the civil justice system. Over 90,000 cases are disposed of this way (known as 'arbitration') by small claims courts annually. The procedure's speed, simplicity and relative inexpensiveness makes it attractive to many users. In 1999, the average time between the issue of summons and the start of the hearing was 21 weeks.

The government believes that extension of the small claims regime to a wider band of cases will enable more people to benefit from this quick and effective means of securing their rights.

One problem with the system, however, is that a significant proportion of successful small claimants are unable to recover the monies awarded them by the court. Following a National Audit Office report in 1997, the Court Service has been working on proposals to improve the efficiency and effectiveness of county court bailiffs.

The main advantage to litigants using the small claims process is the fact that, if sued, they can defend without fear of incurring huge legal costs, since the costs that the winning party can claim are strictly limited. Although successful plaintiffs are unable to recover costs of legal representation, the small claims procedure does not exclude litigants from seeking legal advice or engaging such legal representation. If a litigant is unrepresented, the District Judge may assist him or her by putting questions to witnesses or to the other party, and by explaining any legal terms or expressions.

A litigant simply needs to complete a claim form, available from any county court, and send it to the court with the issue fee appropriate to the amount claimed (ranging from £10 to £80, depending on the value of the claim). If the case is defended, it will be dealt with at an informal hearing, sitting around a table in the district judge's office. This avoids the need for a trial in open court, which many litigants find daunting.

A successful claimant can reclaim the issue fee from the defendant, and the judge may also award up to £50 for loss of earnings in attending court, any reasonable travelling expenses incurred in getting to court, up to £200 towards the fees of an expert's report, and up to £260 for advice and assistance in preparing or defending a claim which includes a claim for an injunction or an order for specific performance or similar relief. Where the case involves a relatively complex matter of fact or law, the judge would be able to transfer it out of the small claims procedure and into the fast track.

The working of the small claims system is looked at in greater detail in Chapter 12.

3.4　The High Court of Justice

The High Court was created in 1873 as a part of the Supreme Court of Judicature. It now has three administrative divisions: the Court of Chancery, the Queen's Bench Division and the Family Division (Divorce and Admiralty and Exchequer and Common Pleas were merged with the Queen's Bench Division in 1880 and 1970). High Court judges sit mainly in the Courts of Justice in the Strand, London, although it is possible for the High Court to sit anywhere in England or Wales. Current directions from the Lord Chancellor mean that the court sits in 27 provincial cities and towns.

The High Court judiciary comprises the Lord Chancellor (who is technically president of the Chancery Division but never sits, the Vice Chancellor usually sits); the Lord Chief Justice who presides over the Queen's Bench Division; the President, who presides over the Family Division; the Senior Presiding Judge (s 72 of the CLSA 1990); and up to 96 High Court judges or '*puisne* judges' (pronounced 'pewnee' and meaning 'lesser').

To be qualified for appointment as a *puisne* judge, a person must have 10 years' qualification within the meaning of s 71 of the CLSA 1990 – essentially, someone who has had a general right of audience on all matters in that court for at least 10 years. (See Chapter 15.) These judges are appointed by the Queen on the advice of the Lord Chancellor. There is particular controversy about these appointments as they are made by invitation without any advertisement. The Lord Chancellor consults opinion he thinks relevant and reads a secret dossier on each possible appointee. Although the Lord Chancellor agreed in 1993 to appoint district judges using advertisements and conventional appointment procedures, he declined to use such methods in the appointment of High Court judges. High Court judges are appointed to a particular division although they can, if required by the Lord Chancellor, be asked to sit in another division when the volume of work dictates such transfer.

3.4.1　The Queen's Bench Division

The Queen's Bench Division, the main common law court, takes its name from the original judicial part of the general royal court which used to sit on a bench in the Palace of Westminster. It is the division with the largest workload and has some criminal jurisdiction (see 3.5.1 and 3.5.2 on criminal courts) and appellate jurisdiction. The main civil work of this court is in contract and tort cases. The Commercial Court is part of this division, being served by up to 10 judges with specialist experience in commercial law and presiding over cases concerning banking and insurance matters. The formal rules of evidence can be abandoned here, with the consent of the parties, to allow testimony and documentation which would normally be inadmissible. This informality can be of considerable benefit to the business keen to settle their dispute as quickly and easily as possible. The Queen's Bench Division also includes an Admiralty Court to deal with the often esoteric issues of law relating to shipping. Commercial Court judges are sometimes appointed as arbitrators.

The Restrictive Practices Court, established by the Restrictive Practices Act 1956, hears cases relating to the area of commercial law concerned with whether an agreement is unlawful owing to the extent to which it restricts the trading capabilities of one of the parties. One Queen's Bench Division judge sits with specialist lay persons to hear these cases. The Employment Appeal Tribunal is presided over by similar panels, hearing appeals from Industrial Tribunals. These courts are not part of the High Court but are termed superior courts of record.

It is important to remember that most civil actions are settled out of court; only about 1% of cases where writs are issued result in civil trials.

3.4.2 The Queen's Bench Divisional Court

The nomenclature can be puzzling here. This court, as distinct from the Queen's Bench Division, exercises appellate jurisdiction. Here, two, or sometimes three, judges sit to hear appeals in the following circumstances:

- appeals on a point of law by way of case stated from magistrates' courts, tribunals and the Crown Court;

- by exercising judicial review of the decisions made by governmental and public authorities, inferior courts and tribunals. Leave to apply for judicial review is granted or refused by a single judge. Civil judicial reviews can be heard by a single judge;

- applications for the writ of habeas corpus from persons who claim they are being unlawfully detained.

3.4.3 The Chancery Division

The Chancery Division is the modern successor to the old Court of Chancery, the Lord Chancellor's court from which equity was developed. Its jurisdiction includes matters relating to:

- the sale or partition of land and the raising of charges on land;

- the redemption or foreclosure of mortgages;

- the execution or declaration of trusts;

- the administration of the estates of the dead;

- bankruptcy;

- contentious probate business, for example, the validity and interpretation of wills;

- company law;

- partnerships;

- revenue law.

Like the QBD, Chancery contains specialist courts; these are the Patents Court and the Companies Court. The Chancery Division hears its cases in London or in one of eight designated provincial High Court centres. The work is very specialised and there is a Chancery Bar for barristers who practise in this area. Chancery judges are normally appointed from this Bar.

3.4.4 The Chancery Divisional Court

Comprising one or two Chancery judges, this appellate court hears appeals from the Commissioners of Inland Revenue on income tax cases, and from county courts on certain matters like bankruptcy.

3.4.5 The Family Division

The Family Division of the High Court was created by the Administration of Justice Act (AJA) 1970. It deals with:

- all matrimonial matters both first instance and on appeal;

- matters relating to minors, proceedings under the CA 1989;

- legitimacy;

- adoption;

- proceedings under the Domestic Violence and Matrimonial Proceedings Act 1976 and s 30 of the Human Fertilisation and Embryology Act 1990.

3.4.6 The Family Divisional Court

The Family Divisional Court, consisting of two High Court judges, hears appeals from decisions of magistrates' courts and county courts in family matters. Commonly these involve appeals against orders made about financial provision under the DPMCA 1978.

3.5 Appeals from the High Court

Appeals from decisions made by a judge in one of the three High Court Divisions will go to the Court of Appeal (Civil Division). An exception to this rule allows an appeal to miss out or 'leapfrog' a visit to the Court of Appeal and go straight to the House of Lords (ss 12–15 of the AJA 1969). In order for this to happen, the trial judge must grant a 'certificate of satisfaction' and the House of Lords must give leave to appeal. For the judge to grant a certificate he or she must be satisfied that the case involves a point of law of general public importance either concerned mainly with statutory interpretation or one where he or she was bound by a Court of Appeal or House of Lords' decision. Also, both parties must consent to the procedure. There are usually fewer than six leapfrog procedures a year.

3.6   The Court of Appeal (Civil Division)

The Court of Appeal was established by the Judicature Act (JdA) 1873. Together with the High Court of Justice, the Court of Appeal forms the Supreme Court of Judicature. Why is it called 'Supreme' if the House of Lords is a superior court? The answer is that the JdA 1873 abolished the House of Lords in its appellate capacity, hence the Court of Appeal became part of the Supreme Court but, after a change of government, the House of Lords was reinstated as the final Court of Appeal by the Appellate Jurisdiction Act 1876.

The Court of Appeal is served by senior judges, currently 35, termed Lords Justices of Appeal. Additionally, the Lord Chancellor, the President of the Family Division of the High Court, the Vice Chancellor of the Chancery Division, and High Court judges can sit. The court hears appeals from the three divisions of the High Court; the divisional courts; the county courts; the Employment Appeal Tribunal; the Lands Tribunal and the Transport Tribunal. The most senior judge is the Master of the Rolls. Usually, three judges will sit to hear an appeal although for very important cases five may sit. In the interests of business efficiency, some matters can be heard by two judges. These include:

- applications for leave to appeal;

- an appeal where all parties have consented to the matter being heard by just two judges;

- any appeal against an interlocutory order or judgment (that is, one which is provisional).

Where such a court is evenly divided, the case must be reheard by three or five judges before it can be further appealed to the House of Lords.

There may be four or five divisions of the court sitting on any given day. The court has a heavy workload dealing with about 1,000 cases a year in contrast to the 50 or so disposed of by the House of Lords. In cases of great urgency, this court is often *de facto* the final Court of Appeal so that a party can act in reliance on its decision without waiting to see the outcome of any possible appeal to the Lords. In *C v S and Others* (1987), a case concerning a putative father's right to prevent a prospective mother from having an abortion, the woman was between 18 and 21 weeks' pregnant and her termination, if it was to be carried out, had to be performed within days of the Court of Appeal's decision. The hospital concerned was reluctant to carry out the operation in case the father appealed to the Lords and they favoured his case. To have earlier terminated the pregnancy might then, the hospital believed, have been the crime of infanticide. Leave to appeal to the Lords was refused and the termination was performed but, in the Court of Appeal, Sir John Donaldson MR said:

> It is a fact that some thousand appeals are heard by this court every year, of which about 50 go to the House of Lords ... So, in practical terms, in the every day life of this country, this court is the final court of appeal and it must always be the final court of appeal in cases of real urgency. In those circumstances, no one could be blamed in any way, *a fortiori* could they as a practical matter be prosecuted, for acting on a judgment of this court. If that be wrong, which it is not, the life of the country in many respects would grind to a halt. The purpose of any supreme court, including the House of Lords, is to review historically and on a broad front; it is not to decide matters of great urgency which have to be decided once and for all.

3.6.1 The Bowman Report 1998

The Report of the Review of the Court of Appeal (Civil Division) undertaken by Sir Jeffrey Bowman was published in 1998. The report contains important recommendations for reducing the number of cases coming to the Court of Appeal and for improving practice and procedures in the Civil Appeals Office and in the court itself.

In 1995, the then Master of the Rolls said:

> The delay in hearing certain categories of appeal in the Civil Division of the Court of Appeal has reached a level which is inconsistent with the due administration of justice. On current projections, there is every reason to think that, over the next few years, the situation will (if nothing effective is done) get worse and not better.

Based on averages, the time between setting down and final disposal of 70% of appeals in 1996 was 14 months. Thirty per cent of appeals took over 14 months, and, at the end of 1996, there were some appeals that had been outstanding for over five years. This is even more disturbing when you take into account that the time between the end of the first instance trial and the setting down of the appeal in the Court of Appeal is not included in the periods mentioned above.

The Review's major recommendations included:

- that certain appeals which now reach the Court of Appeal Civil Division should be heard at a lower level – the largest category of such cases being appeals against decisions in fast track cases;

- that it should still be possible for appeals which would normally to be heard in a lower court to reach the Court of Appeal in certain circumstances. In particular, an appeal could be considered if it raises an important point of principle or practice or one which for some other special reason should be considered by the Court of Appeal;

- that the requirement for leave to appeal should be extended to all cases coming to the Court of Appeal except for adoption cases, child abduction cases; and appeals against committal orders or refusals to grant habeas corpus;

- that there should be an increasing role for appropriate judicial case management;

- that there should be more focused procedures: that cases should be better prepared at a much earlier stage in the process and realistic timetables should be set, which must be strictly observed;

- that the Court of Appeal should impose appropriate time limits on oral argument; on appeals the balance of judicial time should lean more towards reading and less towards sitting in court;

- that the courts should make greater use of information technology to support the other recommendations of this Review;

- information for litigants in person about the appeal process and what it can deliver must be available at an early stage. The information must be easily understandable and delivered in a range of different ways.

Some of the report's more controversial recommendations are concerned with the way the Court of Appeal is constituted. The following recommendations will doubtless draw much debate:

34   There should be a power to appoint lawyers of outstanding distinction as academics or practitioners to sit as members of the Court of Appeal on occasions.

35   There should be a discretion to list cases before a single member of the Court of Appeal ...

37   Where specialist knowledge of law, procedure or subject matter is an advantage: the constitution [of the Court of Appeal] should usually include one or two members with the appropriate specialist knowledge; but the constitution should not usually consist solely of specialist members.

38   Where a constitution contains specialist members, as many cases as possible within the particular specialist area should be listed before them.

In different ways, these proposals suggest radical departures from the accepted underlying principles of judicial justice, that is, that only practising lawyers can become senior judges, that judges are not appointed for their expertise in any given area of law, and, to hear a case, it is not necessary or preferred that a judge be an expert in the area of law of subject matter of the case.

The number of appeals set down has risen steadily over recent years. The latest set of *Judicial Statistics* (1996, HMSO) show 1,853 civil appeals were set down for a hearing in 1995. Unburdening the Court of Appeal of many of these cases will achieve the reformers aims of improved efficiency at this level but the question will then be: how will the lower courts which will have to deal with the extra cases cascading down to them cope without extra personnel and resources?

Sir Jeffrey Bowman states:

> We believe that the quality of justice will be improved by these changes. The elimination of delays in the Court of Appeal and the facility for simpler appeals to be heard more locally should yield substantial benefits to all litigants and will allow the Lords Justices of Appeal to devote their valuable time and skills to the most important issues.

The issue will be whether the full quantity of appeals is dealt with expeditiously, irrespective of how that number of cases is distributed between the Court of Appeal and other courts.

3.7 The Access to Justice Act 1999 – reforms to the appeal process

Part IV of the Access to Justice Act 1999 deals with aspects of reforms for the system for appeals in civil and family cases:

- it establishes the principles that should underlie the jurisdiction of the civil courts to hear appeals;

- it gives the Lord Chancellor power to define the venue for appeal in different categories of case;

- it changes the law relating to the constitution of the Civil Division of the Court of Appeal.

The intention is to ensure that the appellate system reflects the principle, which underlies the government's wider programme of civil justice reforms, that cases should be dealt with in a way that is proportionate to the issue at stake.

Background

In his 1994–95 *Annual Report on the Court of Appeal*, the then Master of the Rolls, Lord Bingham, stated that 'the delay in hearing certain categories of appeal in the Civil Division of the Court of Appeal has reached a level which is inconsistent with the due administration of justice'.

In his report, *Access to Justice*, Lord Woolf set out his proposals for the reform of the civil justice system. At the heart of his proposals was the allocation of civil cases to 'tracks', which would determine the degree of judicial case management. Broadly speaking, cases would be allocated to the small claims track, the fast track or to the multi-track, depending upon the value and complexity of the claim. Those proposals have now been implemented in the The Civil Procedure Act 1997 and the Civil Procedure Rules 1998 (see Chapter 11). The principle that underlies this system of tracks is the need to ensure that resources devoted to managing and hearing a case are proportional to the weight and substance of that case. In order that the benefits arising from these reforms should not be weakened on appeal, Lord Woolf recommended that an effective system of appeals should be based on similar principles.

In 1996, Sir Jeffery Bowman chaired a Review of the Civil Division of the Court of Appeal *(Review of the Court of Appeal (Civil Division) – Report to the Lord Chancellor*, September 1997). He identified a number of problems besetting the Court of Appeal. In particular, he noted that the court was being asked to consider numerous appeals which were not of sufficient weight or complexity for two or three of the country's most senior judges, and which had sometimes already been through one or more levels of appeal. Additionally, he concluded that existing provisions concerning the constitution of the court were too inflexible to deal appropriately with its workload. To redress this situation, Sir Jeffery Bowman's report included recommendations to alter the jurisdiction and constitution of the Court of Appeal. The Lord Chancellor consulted on proposals to effect certain of these changes (LCD, *Reform of the Court of Appeal (Civil Division): Proposals for Change to Constitution and Jurisdiction*, July 1998).

Due to the complex nature of routes of appeal in family matters, Sir Jeffery Bowman's report recommended that a specialist committee should examine this area with a view to rationalising the arrangements for appeals in family cases and bringing them in line with the underlying principles for civil appeals. The Family Appeal Review Group, chaired by Lord Justice Thorpe, published recommendations in July 1998 aimed at simplifying the current appeals procedure in family cases, applying the principles outlined in Sir Jeffery Bowman's Report.

The provisions enabling certain matters to be heard by a single High Court judge have the same objective of ensuring that the most appropriate use is made of judicial resources. The provision about the High Court's powers to deal with appeals by way of case stated from the Crown Court follows a recommendation by the Law Commission in its 1994 report *Administrative Law: Judicial Review and Statutory Appeals*.

Changes made by the Access to Justice Act 1999 (Pt IV)

In relation to civil appeals, the 1999 Act will make the following changes, which are expected to come into effect in 2000:

- provide for permission to appeal to be obtained at all levels in the system (s 54);

- provide that, in normal circumstances, there will be only one level of appeal to the courts (s 55);

- introduce an order making power to enable the Lord Chancellor to vary appeal routes in secondary legislation, with a view to ensuring that appeals generally go to the lowest appropriate level of judge (s 56);

- ensure that cases which merit the consideration of the Court of Appeal reach that court (s 57);

- give the Civil Division of the Court of Appeal flexibility to exercise its jurisdiction in courts of one, two or more judges (s 59).

Together, these proposals are intended to ensure that appeals are heard at the right level, and dealt with in a way which is proportionate to their weight and complexity; that the appeals system can adapt quickly to other developments in the civil justice system; and that existing resources are used efficiently, enabling the Court of Appeal (Civil Division) to tackle its workload more expeditiously.

The provisions relating to the High Court (ss 61–65):

- allow judicial review applications, appeals by way of case stated and applications for habeas corpus which are related to criminal matters, together with appeals from inferior courts and tribunals in contempt of court cases, to be routinely heard by a single judge in the High Court, rather than, as at present, by a Divisional Court of two or more judges;

- place on a statutory footing the powers of the High Court to deal with appeals by way of case stated coming from the Crown Court.

Right to appeal

The Act provides for rights of appeal to be exercised only with the permission of the court, as prescribed by rules of court. Previously, permission was required for most cases going to the Civil Division of the Court of Appeal, but not elsewhere. For the future, it is proposed that, with three exceptions, rules will require permission to appeal to be obtained in all appeals to the county courts, High Court or Civil Division of the Court of Appeal. The exceptions are appeals against committal to prison, appeals against a refusal to grant habeas corpus, and appeals against the making of secure accommodation orders under s 25 of the CA 1989 (a form of custodial 'sentence' for recalcitrant children). There will be no appeal against a decision of the court to give or refuse permission, but this does not affect any right under rules of court to make a further application for permission to the same or another court.

The Act provides that, where the county court or High Court has already reached a decision in a case brought on appeal, there will be no further possibility of an appeal of that decision to the Court of Appeal, unless (s 55) the Court of Appeal considers that the appeal would raise an important point of principle or practice, or there is some other compelling reason for the Court of Appeal to hear it.

Destination of appeals

Section 56 of the AJA 1999 enables the Lord Chancellor to vary, by order, the routes of appeal for appeals to and within the county courts, the High Court, and the Civil Division of the Court of Appeal. Before making an order, the Lord Chancellor will be required to consult the Heads of Division, and any order will be subject to the affirmative resolution procedure. The present intention of the government is that the following appeal routes will be specified by order:

- in fast track cases heard by a district judge, appeals will be to a circuit judge;

- in fast track cases heard by a circuit judge, appeals will be to a High Court judge;

- in multi-track cases, appeals of interlocutory decisions made at first instance by a district judge will be to a circuit judge, by a master or circuit judge to a High Court judge, and by a High Court judge to the Court of Appeal; and

- in multi-track cases, appeals of final orders regardless of the court of first instance, will be to the Court of Appeal;

- the Heads of Division are the Lord Chief Justice, the Master of the Rolls, the President of the Family Division, and the Vice Chancellor;

- a decision is interlocutory where it does not determine the final outcome of the case.

The legislation provides for the Master of the Rolls, or a lower court, to direct that an appeal that would normally be heard by a lower court be heard instead by the Court of Appeal. This power would be used where the appeal raises an important point of principle or practice, or is a case which for some other compelling reason should be considered by the Court of Appeal.

Civil Division of Court of Appeal

The Act makes flexible provision for the number of judges of which a court must be constituted in order for the Court of Appeal to be able to hear appeals. Section 54 of the Supreme Court Act 1981 provided that the Court of Appeal was constituted to exercise any of its jurisdiction if it consisted of an uneven number of judges not less than three. In limited circumstances, it provided that a court could be properly constituted with two judges. The 1999 Act allows the Master of the Rolls, with the concurrence of the Lord Chancellor, to give directions about the minimum number of judges of which a court must consist for given types of proceedings. Subject to any directions, the Act also allows the Master of the Rolls, or a Lord Justice of Appeal designated by him for the purpose, to determine the number of judges who will sit to hear any particular appeal.

Jurisdiction of single judge of High Court

The 1999 Act allows certain applications to be routinely heard by a single judge of the High Court. It does this by removing an obstacle that exists in the current legislation by which the route of appeal for these cases is to the House of Lords, but the Administration of Justice Act 1960 provides that the House of Lords will only hear appeals in these matters from a Divisional Court (that is, more than one judge) of the High Court. The 1999 Act amends the 1960 Act, so that the House of Lords can hear appeals from a single High Court judge. It will then be possible to make rules of court to provide for these cases to be heard by a single judge, while enabling the judge to refer particularly complex cases to a Divisional Court.

The cases in question are:

- judicial reviews and appeals by way of case stated in criminal causes and matters;

- appeals from inferior (civil and criminal) courts and tribunals in contempt of court cases;

- criminal applications for habeas corpus.

Another change made by the 1999 Act concerns appeals from the Crown Court for opinion of High Court. The Supreme Court Act 1981 gives the High Court specific powers of disposal over appeals by way of case stated coming from a magistrates' court. However, it does not do the same for cases coming from the Crown Court. Section 61 of the Access to Justice Act 1999 provides a statutory footing for the powers of the High Court to deal with appeals by way of case stated coming from the Crown Court.

3.8   The House of Lords

Acting in its judicial capacity, as opposed to its legislative one, the House of Lords is the final Court of Appeal in civil as well as criminal law. Its judgments govern the courts in England, Wales and Northern Ireland. They can also govern civil law in Scotland. Most appeals reaching the House of Lords come from English civil cases. In 1997, the Lords pronounced on 62 cases of which 44 came from England and only six were criminal. There is also a 'leapfrog' procedure, introduced by ss 12–15 of the AJA 1969, by which an appeal may go to the Lords direct from the High Court if the High Court judge certificates the case as being suitable for the Lords to hear and the House of Lords gives leave to appeal. All the parties must consent and the case must be one which involves a point of general public importance about a matter of statutory interpretation (sometimes called statutory 'construction' from the verb *to construe* meaning to interpret) or where the contentious issue is one on which the trial judge is bound by a precedent of the Court of Appeal or House of Lords.

The appeals are heard by Lords of Appeal in Ordinary of whom there are currently 12. Two of these must be from Scotland and one from Northern Ireland. Other senior judges like the Lord Chancellor sometimes sit to hear appeals. It is customary for only peers with distinguished legal and judicial careers to become Lords of Appeal in Ordinary. These judges are known journalistically as 'Law Lords'.

For most cases, five Lords will sit to hear the appeal but seven are sometimes convened to hear very important cases. The House of Lords' decision which abolished the 250 year old rule against convicting a husband for rape of his wife (*R v R* (1991)) is such a case. Cases are heard in relative informality in a committee room in the Palace of Westminster. The Appellate Committee of the House of Lords, as it is technically termed, sits with its members in suits, not judicial robes. Counsel, however, do wear wigs and robes. Unlike criminal cases (s 33 of the Criminal Appeal Act (CAA) 1968), there is no requirement that the appeal is on a point of law of general public importance. An appeal from the Court of Appeal to the House of Lords must have 'leave' (that is, permission) of either court.

The judges may deliver their judgments termed 'opinions' as speeches in the parliamentary chamber. A majority decides the case. Sometimes, however, where a case has been heard at three levels of the civil process, the final outcome is not determined, overall, by a majority of what could be described as senior judges. Consider the case of *Gillick v West Norfolk and Wisbech Area Health Authority* (1985), in which the plaintiff, Mrs Gillick, sought a ruling that the defendant's policy to allow contraceptive advice to be given to girls under 16 in some circumstances was illegal. Her argument was rejected by the judge hearing the case in the High Court; accepted unanimously by the three Lords Justice in the Court of Appeal and then rejected in the House of Lords by three votes to two. Thus, overall, a majority of the eight senior judges who heard her case accepted it (five out of eight) but she lost her case because she lost in the final court.

3.9 The European Court of Justice

As we shall see in detail in Chapter 17, the Treaty of Amsterdam 1997 introduced a completely new system for numbering the Articles of the European Community treaties. In order to try to avoid confusion when readers consult other, already existing authorities which will refer to the old numbering, this book will refer to both the new and the previous numbering.

The function of the ECJ, which sits in Luxembourg, is to 'ensure that in the interpretation and application of this Treaty [the EEC Treaty 1957] the law is observed' (Art 200, formerly, 164). The court is the ultimate authority on European law. As the Treaty is often composed in general terms, the court is often called upon to provide the necessary detail for European law to operate. By virtue of the European Communities Act 1972, European law has been enacted into English law so the decisions of the court have direct authority in the English jurisdiction.

The court hears disputes between nations and between nations and European institutions like the European Commission. An individual, however, can only bring an action if he is challenging a decision which affects him.

The Treaty states in Art 234 (formerly, 177) that any judicial or quasi-judicial body, however low ranking, may refer a question to the European Court if it considers that 'a decision on that question is necessary to enable it to give judgment' and that such a reference must be made in a national court from which there is no further appeal. So, the High Court would have a discretion as to whether to refer a point but the House of Lords would not. The system was installed to try and ensure uniformity of interpretation of European law across all the Member States. Without such a mechanism, it would be possible for the English courts to be interpreting a point of European law one way while the Spanish courts were treating it as meaning something different.

Lord Denning formulated guidelines in *Bulmer v Bollinger* (1974) as to when an inferior court should refer a case to the Court of Justice for a preliminary ruling. He offered four guidelines to determine whether the reference was 'necessary' within the meaning of Art 234 (formerly, 177):

- the decision on the point of European law must be conclusive of the case;

- the national court may choose to follow a previous ruling of the European Court on the same point of Community law, but it may choose to refer the same point of law to the court again in the hope that it will give a different ruling;

- the national court may not make a reference on the grounds of *acte clair* where the point is reasonably clear and free from doubt;

- in general, it is best to decide the facts first before determining whether it is necessary to refer the point of Community law.

If a national court decides that a reference is necessary, it still has the discretion (unlike the highest court) as to whether to refer the point. Lord Denning then listed some factors to help courts decide whether to refer; for example: bear in mind the expense to parties of a reference and do not send points unless they are difficult and important.

These guidelines have been influential in a number of subsequent cases. It is possible, however, for an appeal to be made against a decision of a court of first instance to refer a case to the European Court for a preliminary ruling under Art 234 (formerly, 177). The appellate court will interfere with the discretion of the trial judge who referred the case but only if the decision was 'plainly wrong': *Bulmer v Bollinger* (1974).

The language of Art 234 (formerly, 177) is imperative, saying that courts or tribunals against whose judgments there is no appeal *must* refer a point of Community law. This does not apply where the point has already been ruled on by the European Court. Equally, it does not apply where the national court has ruled that the issue in question is not one which requires the application of Community law. In *R v London Boroughs Transport Committee* (1992), the House of Lords decided that the case did not involve any community law issues because it concerned the regulation of local traffic, even though the Court of Appeal had held unanimously that UK legislation was in breach of certain community directives.

The ECJ is a court of reference: the ruling the Court makes is preliminary in the sense that the case is then remitted to the national court for it to apply the law to the facts. The Court only addresses itself to points arising from actual cases; it will not consider hypothetical problems.

Lord Diplock (*R v Henn* (1981)) has characterised the Court's work in the following way:

> The European Court, in contrast to English courts, applies teleological rather than historical methods to the interpretation of the Treaties and other Community legislation. It seeks to give effect to what it conceives to be the spirit rather than the letter of the Treaties; sometimes, indeed, to an English judge, it may seem to the exclusion of the letter. It views the Communities as living and expanding organisms and the interpretation of the provisions of the Treaties as changing to match their growth.

The Court is made up from senior judges from each Member State (15) and a President of the Court, assisted by nine Advocates General. The latter are 'persons whose independence is beyond doubt' (Art 223, formerly, 167) and their task is to give to the Court a detailed analysis of all the relevant legal and factual issues along with recommendations. The recommendations are not necessarily followed by the Court but they can be used on later occasions as persuasive precedent. The Court attempts to ensure consistency in its decisions but is not bound by precedent to the same extent as a court in England.

The Court of First Instance was set up to ease the mounting workload of the Court of Justice. It began work in 1989 and has a jurisdiction which is limited to hearing disputes between the community and its staff, cases involving EU competition law (excluding Art 234 (formerly, 177) references) and some matters involving the European Coal and Steel Community.

3.10 The European Court of Human Rights

The ECHR does not arise from the EU. It arises from the 1950 European Convention on Human Rights, signed by 21 European States including the United Kingdom, and deals with matters relating to human and political rights. The court sits in Strasbourg and comprises of a judge from each Member State. The signatory States undertook to ensure a range of human and political rights to the citizens within their jurisdictions.

See 17.4 for further treatment of the ECHR.

3.11 Judicial Committee of the Privy Council

The Judicial Committee of the Privy Council was created by the Judicial Committee Act 1833. Under the Act, a special committee of the Privy Council was set up to hear appeals from the dominions. The cases are heard by the judges (without wigs or robes) in a committee room in London. The committee's decision is not a judgment but an 'advice' to the monarch, who is counselled that the appeal be allowed or dismissed.

The Committee is the final court of appeal for certain Commonwealth countries which have retained this option and from some independent members and associate members of the Commonwealth. The Committee comprises Privy Councillors who hold (or have held) high judicial office. In most cases, which come from places such as the Cayman Islands and Jamaica, the Committee comprises five Lords of Appeal in Ordinary, sometimes assisted by a judge from the country concerned. The decisions of the Privy Council are very influential in English courts because they concern points of law that are applicable in this jurisdiction and they are pronounced upon by Lords of Appeal in Ordinary, in a way which is thus tantamount to a House of Lords' ruling. These decisions, however, are technically of persuasive precedent only although they are normally followed by English courts; see, for example, the tort case *The Wagon Mound* (1963), a case in which the Privy Council ruled, on an appeal from Australia, that, in negligence actions, a defendant is liable only for the reasonably foreseeable consequences of his tortious conduct. A total of 73 appeals were registered in 1997. The Committee is also the final appeal court for the Professional Conduct and Health Committees of the General Medical Council and the General Dental Council.

3.12   Civil court fees

As from 15 January 1997, a new scale of court fees for civil cases came into effect. The aim of the new fee scales is to raise £50 million and to make the civil courts self-financing. The fee for setting down a county court action doubles from £50 to £100. Filing a divorce petition, previously carrying an £80 cost has risen to £150. Issuing a High Court writ, previously requiring a £150 fee, will now cost £300 where the value of the claim is £50,000 to £100,000 and £500 where the value of the claim is over £100,000. The full court fee for pursuing a sizeable court fee could, henceforward, easily exceed £1,500. The principle of running the civil courts according to business principles is highly controversial. The innovation, announced by the Lord Chancellor, was denounced by Sir Richard Scott, head of the Chancery division of the High Court. He warned that justice should be reasonably accessible and without excessive cost. He stated that:

> The policy fails to recognise that the civil justice system is, like the criminal justice system, the bulwark of a civilised State and the maintenance of order within that State. People have to use the civil courts. They can't engage in self-help in a way which would lead to chaos.

Under the new scheme, people on legal aid would still have their court fees paid, but many unaided people can only just afford to litigate and the raised fees would be turn a difficult hurdle into an insurmountable barrier. The policy of making litigants pay for judges and courtrooms – for that is the essence of this new court fee structure – is a highly controversial policy. Many litigants would believe that they and others, as taxpayers, have already contributed to the funding of the legal system.

The cost of civil business in the courts (including judicial salaries, accommodation, staff, and administration) is over £335 million a year, of which £78 million is met by the taxpayer. The rest is recouped from court fees. In a debate in the House of Lords (Hansard, 1997 Vol 581 Cols 863–81), the Lord Chancellor revisited the theme of at what rate, if at all, citizens should be charged fees for using the civil courts. He stated that he did not accept that all citizens had a constitutional right to go to law in the civil courts freely at the point of use. To do that, he observed, it would be necessary to find the money currently supporting the system from court fees (£257 million paid by citizens) from somewhere else. He would have to cut that amount from somewhere else in his budget. He raised the possibilities of ending criminal legal aid, or ending legal aid for family proceedings. The Lord Chancellor said:

> Those who argue for free access to courts for all are really arguing that the government should charge taxpayers an additional £257 million and then increase my budget by that amount. The Secretary of State for Health might argue that with that money he could provide several new acute hospitals. The Secretary of State for Education might argue that with that money he could provide 30 extra secondary schools.

Many theoretical questions about 'justice' and the legal system quickly reduce to matters of political economy. The issue of court fees is a good illustration. Is the provision of free access to court services for all (including many who could easily afford to pay court fees) more important than the provision of schools and hospitals?

The Court Service has issued a consultation paper proposing that fees for taking cases to civil courts are updated to reflect more closely the costs that are involved.

The principle idea here is that, where people can afford to pay the costs involved in their bringing a legal action, the taxpayer should not be expected to pay for them.

Nonetheless, it seems likely there will be a subsidy for costs associated with some family proceedings. This would be to put as few barriers as possible in the way of people using the courts to protect themselves from violence or harassment, or trying to resolve disputes on the care of children.

Under the new proposals, people on low incomes would continue to be exempted from all court fees. Automatic exemptions to the fees would apply to people in receipt of Income Support, Family Credit, Disability Working Allowance and income based Jobseeker's Allowance.

Should fees be payable by those wishing to use the courts? Some observers point out that payments are not made by members of the public at the point of use in the education and health systems, and that justice can be seen as being just as important as those services. On the other hand, the Lord Chancellor has pointed out that were the courts to become free at the point of use, the money needed to pay for this would have to come from closing down large parts of the civil legal aid or shutting schools or hospitals. Thus, legal policy is inextricably bound up with social policy in general.

3.13   The criminal courts

The following sections look at the structure of the criminal courts. You need to know which type of cases are heard in which trial courts; the procedures of summary hearings, either way offences, transfers for trial, Crown Court trials and the rules governing the transfer of proceedings; the system of appeals and the criticisms which have been made of the various aspects of these systems.

3.14   Coroners' courts

The coroners' courts are one of the most ancient parts of the English legal system, dating back to at least 1194. They are not, in modern function, part of the criminal courts but because of historical associations, it makes more sense to classify them with the courts in this chapter than that dealing with civil courts. Coroners were originally appointed as *custos placitorum coronae*, keepers of the pleas of the Crown. They had responsibility for criminal cases in which the Crown had an interest, particularly a financial interest.

Today, there are 157 coroners' courts, of which 21 sit full time. Coroners are usually lawyers (with at least a five year qualification within s 71 of the CLSA 1990), although about 25% are medical doctors with a legal qualification. The main jurisdiction of the coroner today concerns unnatural and violent deaths, although treasure trove is also something occasionally dealt with in these courts.

The classifying of types of death is clearly of critical importance, not just to the State, politicians and policy makers, but also to the sort of campaign groups that exist in a constitutional democracy to monitor suicides, drug-related deaths, deaths in police custody and prison, accidental deaths, deaths in hospitals, and through industrial diseases.

In 1998, there were 600,000 registered deaths in England and Wales. Deaths must be reported to a coroner if they seem unnatural or violent; the coroner will order a postmortem and this may reveal a natural cause of death which can be duly registered. If not, or in certain other circumstances, such as where the death occurred in prison or police custody, or if the cause is unknown, then there will be an inquest. There were 196,000 deaths reported to coroners in 1998 resulting in 124,400 post-mortem examinations and 23,600 inquests (Government Statistical Service, *Statistics of Deaths Reported to Coroners in England and Wales*, April 1999).

Most inquests (96%) are held without juries but the State has been insistent that certain types of case must be heard by a jury in order to promote public faith in government. When, in 1926, legislation for the first time permitted inquests to be held without juries, certain types of death were deliberately marked off as still requiring jury scrutiny, and these included deaths in police custody, deaths resulting from the actions of a police officer on duty, and deaths in prison. This was seen as a very important way of fostering public trust in potentially oppressive aspects of the State. In 1971, the Brodrick Committee Report on the coronial system saw the coroner's jury as having a symbolic significance and thought that it was a useful way to legitimate the decision of the coroner.

The coroner's court is unique in using an inquisitorial process. There are no 'sides' in an inquest. There may be representation for people like the relatives of the deceased, insurance companies, prison officers, car drivers, companies (whose policies are possibly implicated in the death) and train drivers, etc, but all the witnesses are the coroner's witnesses. It is the coroner who decides who shall be summoned as witnesses and in what order they shall be called.

Historically, an inquest jury could decide that a deceased had been unlawfully killed and then commit a suspect for trial at the local assizes. When this power was taken away in 1926, the main bridge over to the criminal justice system was removed. There then followed, in stages, an attempt to prevent inquest verdicts from impinging on the jurisdictions of the ordinary civil and criminal courts. Now, an inquest jury is exclusively concerned with determining who the deceased was, and 'how, when and where he came by his death'. The court is forbidden to make any wider comment on the death and must not determine or appear to determine criminal liability 'on the part of a named person'.

Nevertheless, the jury may still now properly decide that a death was unlawful (that is, crime). The verdict 'unlawful killing' is on a list of options (including 'suicide', 'accidental death', and 'open verdict') made under legislation and approved by the Home Office.

3.15   The criminal trial courts

There are over 7,000 different criminal offences in English law. These offences can be classified in different ways. You could, for example, classify them according to whether they are offences against people or property; again, you could classify them according to the type of mental element (*mens rea*) required for the offence, for example, 'intention' or 'recklessness'. One other type of classification, and the one to concern us here, is whether the offence is triable *summarily* in a magistrates' court (for relatively trivial offences like traffic offences) or is an *indictable* offence (the more serious offences like murder and rape) triable in front of a judge and jury in a Crown Court.

From the mid-19th century, magistrates were empowered to hear some indictable cases in certain circumstances. Today, there is still a class of offence which is triable 'either way', that is summarily or in a jury trial. A typical example would be a potentially serious offence like theft but one which has been committed in a minor way as in the theft of a milk bottle. These offences now account for about 80% of those tried in Crown Courts. Most defendants, however, opt for summary trial. Where several defendants are charged together with either way offences, each defendant's choice can be exercised separately so if one elects for trial in the Crown Court the others may still be tried summarily if the magistrates agree (*R v Brentwood Justices ex p Nicholls* (1991)).

Which types of case should be dealt with in which courts? This question was investigated by the James Committee which reported in 1975 on *The Distribution of Business between the Crown Court and Magistrates' Courts*. It found that for similar cases, Crown Court trials were three times more expensive than summary hearings. It concluded that the division of work between the different levels of court should reflect the public view as to what are the more serious offences justifying full trials and those which should be dealt with by magistrates. The committee also proposed a category of cases triable either way.

In all offences triable either way, the defendant has the right of trial by jury. If the defendant elects for summary trial the magistrates (and, in some cases, the prosecution) still have the right to remit the case for trial at the Crown Court if they think trial there would be more suitable.

3.16   Magistrates' courts

The office of magistrate or Justice of the Peace (JP) dates from 1195 when Richard I first appointed 'keepers of the peace' to deal with those who were accused of breaking 'the King's peace'. The JPs originally acted as local administrators for the King in addition to their judicial responsibilities. Apart from the 29,000 lay justices who sit in some 700 courts, there are also 92 stipendiary magistrates who sit in cities and larger towns. They are qualified, experienced lawyers who are salaried justices. Where a magistrates' court commits a person for trial of offences in classes one to three (see 3.17), the most convenient location of the Crown Court where a High Court judge regularly sits should be specified, and for offences in class four, the most convenient location of the Crown Court. These matters are confirmed in the *Practice Direction on the Allocation of Crown Court Business* (1995).

3.16.1   Summary trial

Summary offences are created and defined by statute. There are thousands of different summary offences. They include traffic offences, common assault, taking a motor vehicle without consent and driving whilst disqualified. Ninety eight per cent of all criminal cases are dealt with by the courts summarily.

Cases are heard in the court for the district in which the offence is alleged to have been committed. In most cases, the defendant will be in court but it is possible for the accused in road traffic offences to plead guilty by post and not to attend court.

The cases will be heard by two or three magistrates whose powers of sentencing are limited by the Acts which govern the offences in question. A stipendiary magistrate may sit without lay magistrates. The maximum sentence that magistrates can impose, however, is a £5,000 fine and/or a six month prison sentence. The maximum sentences for many summary offences are much less than these limits. Where a defendant is convicted of two or more offences at the same hearing, consecutive sentences amounting to more than six months are not permitted although this can rise to 12 months in cases involving offences triable 'either way' (s 133 of the Magistrates' Courts Act (MCA) 1980). Many statutory offences are now given particular 'levels' according to their seriousness. This means that if a government minister wishes to raise fines (say to be in line with inflation) he or she does not have to go through hundreds of different offences altering the maximum fine in relation to each one separately;

the maxima for each level are simply altered. The current figures (from the Criminal Justice Act (CJA) 1991) are as follows: Level 5 up to £5,000; Level 4 up to £2,500; Level 3 up to £1,000; Level 2 up to £500; and Level 1 up to £200.

The CJA 1991 provided for a new system of fining in magistrates' courts: the 'unit fine' system. Under this system, fines were linked to the offender's income. The idea was that the rich should pay more than the poor for the same offence. Crimes were graded from one to 10 and the level of crime was then multiplied by the offender's weekly disposable income. The system's figures, however, resulted in many anomalies and it was eventually abolished. Nevertheless, in fixing the appropriate amount for a convicted defendant's fine, the magistrates will still take into account his or her income. Other sentences that the court may use include absolute discharge, conditional discharge, probation, community service orders and compensation orders. This latter order is enjoying progressively wider use and is designed to save the victim of the crime suing the defendant in a civil court for damages. Whereas a fine goes to the State, the compensation goes to the victim. This system is governed by s 35 of the Powers of the Criminal Courts Act 1973. Their use has been encouraged by the amendment made by the CJA 1988.

After a conviction, the magistrates will hear whether the defendant has a criminal record and if so for what offences. This is to enable them to pass an appropriate sentence. If, after hearing that record, they feel that their powers of sanction are insufficient to deal with the defendant then he or she may be sent to the Crown Court for sentencing.

A bench of lay magistrates is legally advised by a justices' clerk who is legally qualified and guides the justices on matters of law, sentencing and procedure. The justices' clerk may give advice even when not specifically invited to do so. It is an established principle of English law that 'justice should not only be done but manifestly and undoubtedly be seen to be done' (*R v Sussex Justices ex p McCarthy* (1924), *per* Lord Hewart CJ). The magistrates are independent of the clerks and, according to the principle, the clerks should not *instruct* the magistrates what decision to make on any point nor should they appear to be doing so. The clerk should not, therefore, normally retire with the justices when they go to consider their verdict in any case although he or she may be called by them to give advice on any point. The clerk should not give any judgment on matters of fact.

The court is required in certain cases to consider a compensation order and to give reasons if it decides not to make such an order. As amended, s 35 states that a court before which a person is convicted, in addition to dealing with him in any other way may make a compensation order. The order is to compensate personal injury, loss or damage resulting from the offence in question or any other one 'taken into consideration' (that is, admitted by the defendant) by the court. The defendant can also be ordered to make payments for funeral expenses or bereavement in respect of a death resulting from an offence committed by the defendant (other than a death due to a motor accident). The court, s 35(1) states, 'shall give reasons, on passing sentence, if it does not make such an order in a case where this section empowers it to do so'. In 1994, the Crown Court issued compensation orders in 9% of cases where the accused was sentenced – a total of 6,600 orders. The magistrates' courts issued over 88,000 orders.

A new system of funding the magistrates' courts was introduced in 1991. The system links the amount of money given to a court to the number of cases it processes. One survey (for *File on Four*) found that 74% of clerks felt these changes put justice at risk. Clerks have reported that the changes have put pressure on the courts to give priority to 'quick' cases such as television licence prosecutions and traffic offences. Courts are allocated points for each case processed but a complex case may attract the same points as a simple one. The government has contended that, under good management, 'efficiency is the handmaiden of justice'. Anthony Scrivener QC, Chairman of the Bar Council when the system was introduced, stated that courts were not 'canning factories, their most important function is to dispense justice and this cannot be measured statistically'. Cost-conscious courts could be pressured into making poor decisions.

3.16.2 Offences triable 'either way'

The procedure for determining the mode of trial in cases triable 'either way' is set out in ss 18–26 of the MCA 1980. The justices (although it can be just one for this function) must decide whether the offence is more suitable for summary trial or trial on indictment. The court must consider: (a) the nature of the case; (b) whether the circumstances make the offence one of a serious character; (c) whether the punishment that the magistrates' court could impose would be adequate; and (d) any representations made about the mode of trial made by the prosecution and defence. Further guidelines appear in a *Practice Note (Offences Triable Either Way: Mode of Trial)* (1990). The gist of this guidance is that 'either way' offences should be tried summarily unless a case has one or more aggravating features *and* the court considers that its sentencing powers are inadequate. Prosecutions conducted by the Attorney General, the Solicitor General or the Director of Public Prosecutions must be tried on indictment if so requested by the prosecutor. In 1995, these guidelines (the National Mode of Trial Guidelines) were revised by the Secretariat of the Criminal Justice Consultative Committee. The guidelines set out general principles. They explain features, for example, which would make trial on indictment appropriate for certain offences like burglary, criminal damage, dangerous driving, drugs offences, indecent assault, fraud and offences of violence. The guidelines say, for instance, that trial in the Crown Court is appropriate in the case of burglary where it has been committed in the daytime when the occupier or another person was at home; or where entry was at night into a house normally occupied; or where the offence has professional hallmarks.

If, after considering all the relevant matters, the court decides that summary trial is more suitable, it must explain its decision to the accused in ordinary language and then ask him whether he consents to such trial or wishes to be tried by a jury. The accused must also be told that if he is tried summarily and convicted, he may be committed for sentence to the Crown Court if the magistrates, having had information about his 'character and antecedents', think that greater punishment should be imposed than they have the power to use. Section 29 of the CJA 1991 amended the MCA and provided that an offence is not to be regarded as more serious for sentencing purposes by reason of a person's previous convictions or his failure to respond to previous sentences. During the first six months of this provision's operation (October 1992 to March 1993), there was widespread opposition to this rule from the magistracy, the judiciary and the police. Thirty magistrates resigned in protest, stating that it restricted their powers to give deterrent sentences on young offenders who continued to commit petty offences. Section 66 of the CJA 1993 restored the previous position. The court is now allowed to take into account any failures to respond to previous sentences when sentencing a defendant.

As amended by s 1(2) of the CJA 1993, s 1(2) of the CJA 1991 now provides that the court shall not pass a custodial sentence on an offender unless it is of the opinion that:

(a)   the offence or the combination of the offence and one or more offences associated with it, was so serious that only such a sentence can be justified for the offence; or

(b)   where the offence is a violent or sexual offence, that only such a sentence would be adequate to protect the public from serious harm from him.

The section's import is that if a non-custodial sentence can be 'justified' then custody should not be imposed. To be given as a sentence, custody must be seen as the only suitable option. In *Cox* (1992), it was suggested that a non-custodial sentence would not be justified if the offence was:

... the kind of offence ... which would make all right thinking members of the public, knowing all the facts, feel that justice had not been done by the passing of any sentence other than a custodial one.

When the court comes to assess the phrase 'so serious' in s 1, it must carry out a very similar test to the one it carried out before the CJA 1993 except that it may now consider the offence together with one or more associated offences. An 'associated offence' (s 31(2)) is one for which the offender is to be sentenced if he is convicted of it in the same proceedings, or sentenced for it at the same time, or one he asks to be taken into consideration.

If the accused consents to summary trial, then the magistrates proceed to summary trial. If he does not consent, the magistrates proceed as examining magistrates.

Where a magistrates' court has started to try an 'either way' case summarily, it may, before the conclusion of the prosecution evidence, change (without the consent of the accused) from a summary trial to transfer proceedings (under s 44 of the CJPOA 1994). If the bench finds that the evidence does not support the 'either way' offence with which the accused is charged but does allow for a conviction for a summary offence, they may proceed to try the lesser offence.

These procedures apply where the accused is 17 or older. Children (aged 10 to under 14) and young persons (aged 14–16) appearing before magistrates on an indictable charge must normally be tried summarily except: (a) where the charge is homicide; or (b) in the case of a young person, where the offence is one for which an adult could be sentenced to 14 years imprisonment or more; or (c) where a child or young person is charged jointly with an adult and the magistrates consider it necessary in the interests of justice that they be transferred for trial to the Crown Court (s 44 and Sched 4, Pt II, para 36 of the CJPOA 1994).

If the defendant does not consent to be tried summarily, then the magistrates proceed to initiate the transfer for trial procedure. If, though, after considering all the relevant matters, the court decides that trial on indictment is more suitable, this decision is final.

A defendant charged with an 'either way' offence who has elected for trial at the Crown Court will first have his case subject to committal proceedings. (A person charged with an indictable only offence now goes direct to the Crown Court: see 3.16.4.) These proceedings used to take the form of 'old style' committals (small trials) or 'new style' committals (or 'paper trials' where the evidence was just documentary). Following a recommendation by the Royal Commission on Criminal Justice (Cm 2263, 1993), committal proceedings were abolished by s 44 of the CJPOA 1994. The new system, however, of 'transfers for trial', which would have expedited the process of deciding whether a defendant should stand trial, encountered great difficulties in being implemented and was never brought into force. Section 44 of the Criminal Procedure and Investigations Act (CPIA) 1996 repeals s 44 of the CJPOA 1994, and, in effect, introduces a new, streamlined version of committal proceedings in which no oral evidence can be given.

The new system of committals is governed by s 47 and Sched 1 of the CPIA 1996. The effect of the new law is to abolish the 'old style' mini-trial committals and the right of the defendant to have witnesses called and cross-examined at the magistrates' court. Now, defendants may only use written evidence at committal stage like witness statements and depositions from the prosecution. Exhibits may also be considered. Both sides can make oral representations to the magistrates as to whether the defendant should be sent for trial or discharged.

The system thus remains largely unchanged with the exception of the exclusion of witness testimony. This will save witnesses from having to go through the ordeal of giving evidence twice. Time and money will also be saved. There can no longer be any unmeritorious requests for 'old style' committals made in the hope that witnesses will not turn up. Nevertheless, the new system also means that the defence will be deprived of the opportunity of testing the evidence and having the defendant discharged early during the proceedings if the witnesses do not come up to proof.

In a few limited circumstances, a case can reach the Crown Court without having passed through committal proceedings. This applies to serious fraud cases (s 4 of the CJA 1987) where the case complexity demands that it be managed from the outset by a Crown Court. The bypass procedure also exists for certain cases involving children where there has been alleged violence, cruelty or a sexual element (s 53 of the CJA 1991).

Old style committal proceedings were expensive, and the proportion of all committals that they occupied rose from 8% in 1981 to 13% in 1986. The effectiveness of the sifting procedure designed to weed out very weak cases was called into doubt by the high acquittal rate in jury trials. How far the new system will be an improvement upon the old remains to be seen.

Either way offences: venue for trial

There has been great debate about changing the rules in relation to who should choose the venue for trial (magistrates or defendants), and a government Consultation Paper, *Determining Mode of Trial in Either Way Cases* (August 1998), added further heat to the public discussion.

As noted above, the decision as to where an 'either way' case should be heard is made at a hearing before the magistrates. Where a defendant pleads guilty, the magistrates will proceed to convict, otherwise they will go on to determine the mode of trial. They may consider it is more appropriate for the case to be tried at the Crown Court, in which case they will decline jurisdiction and direct it there. If they decide to try it themselves, the defendant has the right to refuse and choose to be tried at the Crown Court.

Approximately 22,000 defendants charged with either way offences elected to be tried in the Crown Court in 1998. Crown Court trials cost the State about £8,000 per day, whereas a magistrates' court hearing costs less than £2,000.

In practice, a common problem is where the nature of the charge is very serious (for example, theft) so a conviction for it could be ruinous for a defendant, but the actual facts of the case are not so serious (for example, alleged theft of a milk bottle). Is such a case relatively trivial? Well, not, perhaps to the defendant! Now, the defendant can elect for trial at the Crown Court (which is much more expensive and prolonged).

In January 2000, the Criminal Justice (Mode of Trial) Bill was rejected by the House of Lords. The Bill sought to deprive defendants in either way cases of the right to jury trial where magistrates took the view that they should deal with the case. Many legal groups, including The Law Society and the Bar Council, opposed such a change. The Home Secretary tried to placate opponents of the Bill by inserting a clause permitting a defendant who had been denied a jury trial the right to appeal against the decision to try him in the magistrates' court. Even so, the Bill still fell in the Lords. Not daunted, however, the government insisted that it would re-introduce the Bill in the House of Commons and use the Parliament Acts 1911–49 to push through the legislation (see (2000) *The Times*, 21 January and, in February 2000, the government published the Criminal Justice (Mode of Trial) (No 2) Bill which would, in relation to 'either way offences', remove the defendant's right to elect for jury trial but would offer 'added safeguards to ensure fair treatment for defendants' (Home Office Statement 034/2000). However, Professor Lee Bridges of Warwick University ('Letter' (2000) *The Independent*, 29 February) argues that the Bill should be withdrawn and the issue should be put before the Auld Review in its systematic review of the criminal courts (see http://www.criminal-courts-review.org.uk).

The Consultation Paper presents four possible options for reform of the current system in triable either way cases, which allows defendants to elect for a jury trial at the Crown Court if they wish to do so, even after magistrates have indicated that they are happy to hear their case. The options are:

(1) maintaining the status quo defendants who are charged with offences that are triable either way can elect for trial by jury if they wish;

(2) reclassification of particular offences. Particular either way offences such as minor theft could be reclassified as triable only in the magistrates court;

(3) outright abolition of election for trial:

(i) if parties cannot agree on a venue for trial, magistrates would decide where the case should be heard. Following representations from the defence, they would have regard to such considerations as the complexity of the case and the effect of conviction on the defendant for example.

This approach was favoured by the Royal Commission on Criminal Justice which reported in 1993;

(ii) the decision on venue for trial should rest entirely with magistrates after having listened to representations from the prosecutor and the defence.

This approach was favoured by the Narey Review of Delay in the Criminal Justice System published in 1997;

(4) removal of the right to elect for jury trial in certain cases the right of a defendant to elect for a jury trial would be removed where they have been prosecuted for an offence which is similar in nature to an earlier conviction.

The Narey Review of Delay in the Criminal Justice System indicated that there is considerable support for a change to the current system, although the general public were not consulted about this, and it is a matter of speculation what response would be drawn by a plebiscite on the issue. In 1999, the Home Secretary, Jack Straw, announced the government's intention to legislate in accordance with point (3)(ii) (above). (See (1999) *The Times*, 19 May; see Chapter 14.)

3.16.3 Youth courts

Magistrates sit in these courts to try children and young persons. A child is someone who has not reached his 14th birthday. These private tribunals sit separately from the ordinary magistrates' court in order to protect the young defendants from publicity. There jurisdiction was enlarged by the CJA 1991, to include 17 year olds. There must be three justices to hear such a case, of whom a least one must be a man and one a woman. The public do not have access to such a court. The CJA 1991 allowed for parents to be required to attend in any case and it is mandatory in the case of a child or young person under the age of 16 unless such requirement would be unreasonable in the circumstances. The name or photograph of any person under 17 appearing in the case must not be printed in any newspaper or broadcast without the authority of the court or Home Secretary.

Apart from these arrangements which aim to keep young people out of the criminal environment of the ordinary courts, there are special provisions relating to punishments for this age group. The current maximum fine for a child is £250 and £1,000 for a young person. Members of both age groups may be made the subject of supervision orders and compensation orders. A sentence in a young offender institution is possible for anyone with a minimum age of 15 years. The minimum age for imprisonment is 21. No criminal prosecution can be brought against someone under 10. Such people are irrebuttably presumed to be incapable of committing crime. Such a child who committed a crime could be brought before a youth court.

3.16.4 Indictable offences – committal proceedings

Where the magistrates decide that an offence triable either way should be tried in the Crown Court, they hold committal proceedings (as described above).

Section 51 of the Crime and Disorder Act 1998

These proceedings were also held where the defendant was charged with, an indictable-only offence (for example, murder). If, having read the papers, the magistrates took the view that there was a *prima facie* case to answer, they had to transfer the defendant to the Crown Court for trial; if not, they had to discharge the defendant. Now, however, s 51 of the Crime and Disorder Act 1998 states that, where an adult is charged with an offence triable only on indictment, the court shall send him directly to the Crown Court for trial. Where he is also charged with an either way offence or a summary offence, he may be sent directly to trail for that as well, provided the magistrates believe that it is related to the indictable offence and, in the case of a summary offence, it is punishable with imprisonment or involves obligatory or discretionary disqualification from driving. This system is being piloted in some courts in 1999 with a view to extension nationally in due course.

- *Reporting committal proceedings*

In the old style committal proceedings, it was generally only the prosecution that would give evidence, with the defence reserving its arguments. Until 1967, this prosecution case was frequently reported on in the press so that it was virtually impossible to find an unbiased jury for the trial. A notorious instance of this was the case of Dr John Bodkin Adams in 1957. During the committal, deaths of patients other than the one for which he was to stand trial were referred to but were not afterwards part of the evidence at the trial. The law on reporting was eventually changed in the CJA 1967 and is now in the MCA 1980, as amended by the CJPOA 1994. There are restrictions now on any application for dismissal put in by the defence. It is thus an offence to report on any aspect of the case if reporting restrictions have not been lifted by the bench. The bare matters which may as a matter of course be reported are:

- the identity of the court and the names of the examining magistrates;
- the names, ages, addresses and occupations of the accused and witnesses;
- the offence charged;
- the names of the lawyers engaged in the case;
- the decision of the court whether to commit or not and, if so, details of the committal, for example, to which court;
- any arrangements for bail;
- whether legal aid was granted.

These restrictions, however, must be lifted by the magistrates if requested to do so by the accused. Where there are two or more accused and one objects to the reporting restrictions being lifted then the magistrates must not lift them unless they regard it to be in the interests of justice to do so.

- *Effectiveness*

Full committal proceedings were protracted and expensive. A government research project in 1987 found that their average duration was one hour and 15 minutes as opposed to 6.7 minutes for new style 'paper' committals. The overall cost for committals was about £4 million a year (excluding the costs of the CPS and legal aid) of which £2.7 million was spent on full committals. That this system does not effectively achieve what it aims to do – act as a filter against cases with insufficient evidence – is testified to by the high acquittal rate on the direction of the judge in the High Court: of all those acquitted in Crown Court trials after pleading not guilty in 1990, for example, 16% were acquitted on the direction of the judge (mainly because the prosecution case was inadequate) and 42% of those acquitted were discharged by the judge because, for instance, the prosecution offered no evidence. The lists for Crown Court cases are growing relentlessly and there has been strong criticism of magistrates that they are unnecessarily reluctant to refuse to commit defendants in old style committals. It now remains to be seen how effective the new system of transfers is.

- *Consistency of sentencing*

Concern is often expressed at the sometimes quite notable discrepancies in sentencing practices employed by different benches of magistrates. It might be that these variations are unavoidable in circumstances where the rigidity of fixed penalties is unacceptable for most offences and regional differences in types of prevalent crime prompt justices to have certain attitudes to particular offences. There are several research surveys which demonstrate the discrepancies in magistrates' sentencing. Tarling, for example (*Sentencing and Practice in Magistrates' Courts*, 1979, Home Office Study 98), showed that, in the 30 courts he surveyed, the use of probation varied between one and 12%, suspended sentences between four and 16%, and fines between 46 and 76%. There is a Home Office book, *The Sentence of the Court*, which explains desirable sentencing practice, but its guidance cannot form the basis of an appeal and it is rather outdated, the latest edition being one from 1986.

- *Independence*

Magistrates' courts were often called 'police courts' from the time when they were situated in the same building, or adjacent to the local police station. There is criticism that, as the magistrates still hear local police officers giving evidence so regularly, they become too credulous and trusting of the officers' evidence. There is also criticism that many magistrates are too suggestible under the influence of their clerks.

- *The future*

The current system has the twin advantages of being relatively inexpensive to run (as the 29,000 lay justices are unsalaried) and allows for lay participation (albeit from a narrow social band) in a crucially important part of the criminal justice system. Any change to a system involving fully paid, legally qualified inferior judges or inquisitors would entail great expense for the Exchequer.

3.16.5 The Access to Justice Act 1999 – magistrates' courts

Important changes to the magistrates' court system have been made by Pt V of the Access to Justice Act 1999.

Part V contains a range of provisions relating to magistrates and magistrates' courts:

- it provides for various changes to the organisation and management of magistrates' courts;

- it unifies the provincial and metropolitan stipendiary magistrates into a single bench;

- it removes the requirement for magistrates to sit on cases committed to the Crown Court for sentence and enables the Crown Court, rather than a magistrates' court, to deal with breaches of community sentences imposed by the Crown Court;

- it extends and clarifies the powers of civilians to execute warrants; this is intended to enable this function to be transferred from the police to the magistrates' courts.

The government's objective is to develop a magistrates' court service which is effectively and efficiently managed, at a local level by local people, within a consistent national framework. The government announced its plans for developing this new framework in statements to both Houses of Parliament on 29 October 1997 (*Hansard*, 1997 HL Col 1057–67; HC Col 901–14). As part of this programme of reform, the Act includes provisions to:

- Reform the organisation and management of the magistrates' courts by:

  o creating more flexible powers to alter the various territorial units that make up the magistrates' court service, and to allow summary cases to be heard outside the commission area in which they arose;

  o expanding the potential membership of magistrates' courts committees by removing the limit on co-opted members;

  o establishing a single authority to manage the magistrates' courts service in London;

  o removing the requirement for justices' chief executives to be qualified lawyers, and transferring responsibility for certain administrative functions from justices' clerks to justices' chief executives; and

  o giving the Lord Chancellor power to require all MCCs to procure common goods and services, where he considers this will lead to more effective or efficient administration.

- Unify the Provincial and Metropolitan stipendiary benches into a single bench of District Judge (Magistrates' Courts), able to sit in any magistrates' court in the country.

- Remove the requirement for lay magistrates to sit as judges in the Crown Court on committals for sentence.

- Extend and clarify the powers of civilians to execute warrants.

The new powers to change organisational units reflect the government's intention to develop a more coherent geographical structure for the criminal justice system as a whole. Common boundaries should enable the various criminal justice agencies to co-operate more effectively.

In a move in 1999 to open the appointment of magistrates to a wider section of society, the Lord Chancellor, Lord Irvine, launched an advertising campaign aimed at ordinary people, with the message: 'Have you ever thought about serving your community by becoming a magistrate?' Adverts appeared on posters and in a wide range of papers, but the aim seemed to be to get fewer middle class professionals into the judicial business and to enlarge the constituency of people with other interests (see (1999) *The Times*, 15 March). No adverts were placed in journals like *The New Statesman*, but one did go into *TV Quick*.

In some ways, it is self-evidently desirable that the legal system is operated on as open access a basis as is possible, and by as demotic a personnel as possible. There are, however, ways in which the new, 'people's justice' might bring unexpected results. As working class people are more likely to be victims of crimes like burglary than middle class people, and are possibly, therefore, more intolerant of such offending, it might be that sentencing becomes more severe over time as the middle class is edged out of its current hegemonic position in the magistracy.

The administration of the magistrates' courts service is based on three organisational units – the magistrates' courts committee (MCC) area, the commission area and the petty sessions area. The MCC area is the unit on which the administration and organisation of the courts is based. MCCs are the bodies responsible for the administration of the magistrates' courts service. There are currently 96 MCCs in England and Wales. Each MCC appoints a justices' chief executive to manage the courts in its area.

The Justices of the Peace Act 1997 already provides power to change the boundaries of MCC areas. The government believes that a structure with fewer and larger areas would be more efficient and effective. The number of MCCs has been reduced in recent years by a series of amalgamations; this trend is likely to continue in future, as part of the policy of a greater alignment of boundaries between criminal justice agencies. The commission area is the unit on which the appointment of magistrates and the jurisdiction of the magistrates' courts to hear summary cases is based. Magistrates are appointed to a particular commission area, on the basis of where they reside; and most summary offences must be tried in the commission area where the alleged offence took place.

Historically, MCC and commission areas have aligned with one another and with county and metropolitan county borders. However, most commission areas are defined in primary legislation, and can be changed by secondary legislation only to reflect changes in local government boundaries. Increasingly, there are MCCs which cover two or more commission areas. These MCCs cannot transfer magistrates or cases between areas. The ability to change commission area boundaries is intended to enable MCCs to allocate cases, and deploy magistrates, between the courts in their MCC area more effectively and efficiently.

Most MCC areas are broken down into smaller areas, called petty sessions areas. These are the benches, the basic unit of local court organisation. Petty sessions areas are defined in terms of local authority boundaries. This can limit an MCC's ability to organise its structure effectively, particularly where amalgamation has occurred. As a result, the full benefits of amalgamation may not be realised.

The Act redefines the basis of these units, to allow MCCs to decide the most appropriate and efficient structure for their area. The Act also removes the artificial distinction between a petty sessions area and a 'petty sessional division' – a distinction which currently exists solely for the purposes of geographical identification.

Constitution of MCCs

Each MCC comprises up to 12 members and is composed primarily of lay magistrates, appointed by their peers, who undertake the task in addition to their magisterial duties. Individuals are appointed to the MCC on the basis of their skills and experience.

Where an MCC believes that additional skills are required which cannot be found amongst the applicants for membership of the MCC, they may co-opt individuals, who need not be magistrates.

Currently, the number of co-options is limited to two. These may be in addition to the maximum membership of 12. In addition, the Lord Chancellor may appoint up to two individuals to an MCC.

Neither lay magistrates nor co-opted and appointed non-magistrates receive remuneration for their committee work. The Act removes the limit on the number of co-opted and appointed members, and provides power for MCCs to remunerate those members.

MCCs are the bodies responsible for the administration of the magistrates' court service. Local authorities are responsible for providing the accommodation needed by an MCC and for paying the expenses it incurs. Local authorities recoup 80% of the net cost from the Lord Chancellor's Department in the form of specific grant. In cases where an MCC area encompasses two or more authorities, the costs and accommodation are divided equitably between the authorities, but a 'lead' authority is appointed to receive the grant and pay the expenses.

A single authority for London

The Greater London area comprises a significantly larger number of MCCs (22) and local authorities (33) than any other area. The consequences of this, for issues such as funding and accommodation, are such that amalgamation under the provisions of the Justices of the Peace Act 1997 is not practical. The Act provides for the establishment of a Greater London Magistrates' Courts Authority, with special provision for its funding, accommodation, constitution and other necessary powers to enable the existing MCCs to be amalgamated effectively.

Justices' clerks and justices' chief executives

Most cases in magistrates' courts are heard by magistrates who are not qualified lawyers. They rely heavily on the legal advice of justices' clerks and their deputies, acting as court clerks. All justices' clerks are legally qualified and may have certain powers of a single magistrate delegated to them.

The post of justices' chief executive (JCE) was introduced in 1994, and every MCC has appointed a JCE. The JCE supports the MCC in planning and managing the efficient and effective administration of the courts within the area of the MCC. At present, however, justices' clerks continue to be responsible in statute for many administrative matters. In practice, many of these tasks are delegated to administrators. In 1998, the government published a consultation paper which considered the functions of justices' clerks (LCD, *The Future Role of Justices' Clerks*, September 1998).

The provisions in the Act relating to the qualifications and functions of justices' chief executives are intended to clarify the role of the JCE and the lines of responsibility and accountability between the JCE, the MCC and the other staff of the MCC; and to achieve a clearer distinction between the roles of JCEs and justices' clerks. The primary function of justices' clerks will continue to be the giving of legal advice to lay magistrates. Under the new management structure, JCE will be able to delegate any administrative function to any staff, including the justices' clerks, depending on local needs.

Unification of the stipendiary bench

The Act unifies the stipendiary bench, establishing the 92 stipendiary magistrates as a unified bench of professional judges with a new judicial title – District Judge (Magistrates' Courts). In April 1998, the government published a consultation paper about creating a unified stipendiary bench with national jurisdiction (LCD, *Unification of the Stipendiary Bench: Consultation Paper*, April 1998), with the intention of increasing the efficiency of the administration of justice at summary level.

The effect of this provision is to create a unified national bench, headed by a single judge, which can be deployed anywhere in the country to deal with fluctuations in workload as and when they occur, or with particularly complex cases that arise. The new District Judges (Magistrates' Courts) will be able to exercise jurisdiction in every commission area of England and Wales. The new title is intended to recognise more fully the status of stipendiaries as members of the professional judiciary. The new law has amended ss 11–22 of the Justices of the Peace Act 1997.

The main differences from the old law are as follows.

- appointments are to be made without reference to any specific Commission area within England and Wales. A District Judge (Magistrates' Courts) has jurisdiction for every commission area);

- a Senior District Judge (Chief Magistrate) will be appointed as a national head of all District Judges (Magistrates' Courts). Previously, there was a Chief Metropolitan Stipendiary Magistrate, but no equivalent head of the provincial stipendiary bench;

- the Lord Chancellor will be able to remove one of these judges from office on the grounds of 'incapacity or misbehaviour'. Previously, the Lord Chancellor could remove a metropolitan stipendiary from office on the grounds of 'inability or misbehaviour'. Provincial stipendiaries could only be removed from office on the Lord Chancellor's recommendation, but no criteria were specified in statute (s 11(3)(b) of the JPA 1997).

The test and procedure for removal have been unified to remove the inconsistency. 'Incapacity' has replaced 'inability' to reflect a similar change relating to Circuit Judges under the Courts Act 1971. The change of language brings these judicial posts into line;

- the Lord Chancellor may appoint Deputy District Judges (Magistrates' Courts) (new s 10B(1)). Unlike the appointment of acting stipendiary magistrates under the previous provisions, these appointments are not limited to three months duration, or solely permitted for the purpose of avoiding delays in the administration of justice:

  o s 10A(1): the 'seven year general qualification' is defined in the CLSA 1990 as 'a right of audience in any class of proceedings in the county courts or magistrates' courts';

  o s 10D(2): this provision maintains specific exclusions of the rule codified under the Stipendiary Magistrates Act 1858, which allowed a single stipendiary to exercise the jurisdiction of two lay justices. Any express provision to the contrary made after that Act came into force survives by virtue of this section;

  o s 10D(6): s 65 of the MCA 1980 defines family proceedings. A stipendiary magistrate may hear these cases, subject to any rules and statutes specific to family proceedings (for example, the Children Act 1989).

Committals for sentence

Currently, cases committed to the Crown Court for sentence must be heard in the Crown Court by a bench composed of a High Court Judge, Circuit Judge or Recorder sitting with between two and four JPs. In October 1997, a new procedure was implemented by which defendants are required to indicate whether they intend to plead guilty or not guilty, before the decision is made about whether the case should be heard in the magistrates' court or the Crown Court (s 17A of the MCA 1980, as amended by s 49 of the Criminal Procedure and Investigations Act 1996). This has led to a significant increase in the number of cases committed to the Crown Court solely for sentence, and an increase in the seriousness of the cases being committed for sentence. (Previously, all more serious cases were committed for trial, although many defendants subsequently pleaded guilty.)

The change in procedure has meant that magistrates are dealing in the Crown Court with cases which are outside their normal range of experience. In 1999, the government issued a consultation paper (LCD, *Magistrates Sitting as Judges in the Crown Court*, August 1998) which examined the role of magistrates in the Crown Court. The majority of responses agreed that the requirement for magistrates to sit on committals for sentence should be removed.

Warrant execution

Until now, the police have been primarily responsible for arresting fine defaulters and those in breach of community sentences. Increasingly, however, some police forces have given this work a low priority. The government therefore intends to transfer responsibility for the execution of warrants from the police to the magistrates' courts. The intention is to ensure that fines and community sentences are seen as credible and effective punishments, by ensuring that they can be effectively enforced.

A number of MCCs already employ civilian enforcement officers (CEOs), who work with the police under local arrangements. However, under current legislation, the powers of CEOs are unclear in a number of respects. In order to enable the courts to take on this new function effectively, the Act contains provisions to clarify and extend the powers of appropriate civilians to execute certain kinds of warrant issued by a magistrates' court.

The provisions relating to warrants are intended to enhance the credibility of fines and community sentences, by improving the effectiveness of their enforcement. This involves a transfer of resources from the police to magistrates' courts. The government has stated its intention to consult individual MCCs about the additional resources they require to implement the transfer, but no significant change in overall public expenditure on this function is expected. Over time, it is hoped to achieve an increase in the proportion of fines collected of at least 5%. (In 1996–97, the courts imposed over one million fines, worth £144 million in total. In the same period, unpaid fines to the value of £52 million, mostly imposed in previous years, had to be written off.)

The Act extends and clarifies the range of warrants issued by a magistrates' court which may be executed by civilian enforcement officers (CEOs), employed by MCCs, local authorities or police authorities.

The warrants in question will be listed in an order made jointly by the Lord Chancellor and the Home Secretary. It is intended that the list should include warrants of distress, commitment, arrest or detention in connection with the payment of any sum, and also warrants of arrest issued in connection with breaches of a range of non-financial penalties. A list of the warrants that the government intends CEOs to be able to execute includes warrants made under the Child Support Act 1991 and the Council Tax (Administration and Enforcement) Regulations 1992.

The Act allows MCCs to approve and appoint private enforcement agencies to execute certain kinds of warrant. Some MCCs already use private enforcement agencies or bailiffs to execute distress warrants. However, there is presently some uncertainty about whether a warrant can be 'directed' to such a person within the meaning of s 125(2) of the Magistrates' Courts Act 1980 unless it refers to him by name. The Act clarifies the law, so that warrants can be addressed to approved agencies for the area concerned, rather than just to an individual, named, bailiff. In future, the authorised employees of approved enforcement agencies will be able to execute the same range of warrants as CEOs anywhere in England and Wales.

These provisions significantly enlarge the use of private commercial agencies to perform what many would see as proper matters for only properly trained and accountable police officers or officials to perform. Is this enlargement of the private and for-profit sector within the criminal justice system a desirable development? It can be argued that, without it, the criminal justice system would come under unnecessary and severe strain as police officers, much-needed on patrol and responding to dangerous crime, would be occupied in chasing debtors. On the other hand, the entry of private commercial companies into the criminal justice system has been marked by periodic crises. In November 1998, for example, there was public scandal at the extent of injury to prison officers and trainers, and criminal damage at Britain's first private penal institution for young offenders. Riots at the Medway Secure Training Centre in Kent caused £100,000 of damage and the police were called in to deal with the rampaging 12–14 year olds ((1998) *The Times*, 13 November).

3.17 The Crown Court

Until 1971, the main criminal courts were the Assizes and the Quarter Sessions. These courts did not sit continuously and were not held in locations which corresponded with centres of population as had been the case when they developed. The system was very inefficient as circuit judges wasted much time simply travelling from one town on the circuit to the next and many defendants spent long periods in jail awaiting trial.

Change was made following the *Report of the Beeching Royal Commission on Assizes and Quarter Sessions* (1969). The Courts Act 1971 abolished the Assizes and Quarter Sessions. These were replaced by a single Crown Court, a part of the Supreme Court of Judicature. The Crown Court is not a local court like the magistrates' court but a single court which sits in over 90 centres. England and Wales are divided into six circuits each with its own headquarters and staff. The centres are divided into three tiers. In first-tier centres, High Court judges hear civil and criminal cases whereas circuit judges and recorders hear only criminal cases. Second-tier centres are served by the same types of judge but hear criminal cases only. At third-tier centres, recorders and circuit judges hear just criminal cases.

Criminal offences are divided into four classes according to their gravity. Class 1 offences are the most serious, including treason and murder and are usually tried by a High Court judge; exceptionally he may transfer a murder case (including attempts) to be heard by a circuit judge approved for this purpose by the Lord Chief Justice. Class 2 offences include manslaughter and rape and are subject to similar provisions. Class 3 offences include all remaining offences triable only on indictment and are usually tried by a High Court judge although releases of cases to circuit judges are more common here. Class 4 offences include robbery, grievous bodily harm and all offences triable 'either way' and are not normally tried by a High Court judge.

3.17.1 The judges

The High Court judges are usually from the Queen's Bench Division. Circuit judges are full time appointments made by the Queen on the advice of the Lord Chancellor. They are drawn from advocates with at least 10 years' experience of Crown Court practice (s 71 of the CLSA 1990) or lawyers who have been recorders. Appointment is also possible for someone who has had three years' experience in a number of other quasi-judicial offices like that of the stipendiary magistrate. Circuit judges retire at the age of 72, or 75 if the Lord Chancellor thinks it is in the public interest.

A circuit judge may be removed from office by the Lord Chancellor on the grounds of incapacity or misbehaviour (s 17(4) of the Courts Act 1971). This right has not been exercised since 1983 when Judge Bruce Campbell, an Old Bailey judge, was removed from office a week after being convicted of two charges of smuggling.

To qualify for appointment as a recorder, a person must have 10 years' experience of advocacy in the Crown or county courts. JPs may also sit in the Crown Court, provided they are with one of the types of judge mentioned above. It is mandatory for between two and four JPs to sit when the Crown Court is hearing an appeal or dealing with persons committed for sentence by a magistrates' court.

3.17.2 Jurisdiction

The Crown Court hears all cases involving trial on indictment. It also hears appeals from those convicted summarily in the magistrates' courts. At the conclusion of the hearing, it has the power to confirm, reverse or vary any part of the decision under appeal (s 48(2) of the Supreme Court Act 1981). If the appeal is decided against the accused, the Crown Court has the power to impose any sentence which the magistrates could have imposed, including one which is harsher than the one originally imposed on the defendant.

3.17.3 Delay

Defendants committed to the Crown Court to be tried will have to wait an average of three months for their case to come to trial. This wait is sometimes in custody. Ever since the Streatfield Committee recommended in 1961 that the maximum time a defendant should have to wait after committal for trial should be eight weeks, there have been many schemes to help achieve this aim but none has been particularly successful. Since 1985, for example, a person charged with an offence triable 'either way' can request the prosecution to furnish him with information (in the form of witness statements, a summary of the case, etc) of the case against him. This was aimed at increasing the number of guilty pleas by showing to the defendant at an early stage the strength of the prosecution's case.

The slowness of the trial procedure, the increasing number of annual trials and the relatively small number of judges to hear the cases all contribute to this problem. In 1990, the Crown Court dealt with 119,828 defendants, of whom 33,000 elected for trial before a jury on a plea of not guilty. These cases were to be heard by just 420 circuit judges and about 750 part time recorders. When one remembers that the average time to try a case on a plea of not guilty is about seven hours (one and a half court days), the burden of work on the courts becomes clear. The consequent delay has very serious repercussions on the criminal justice system: justice delayed is justice denied. The accuracy of testimony becomes less reliable the longer the gap between the original reception of the data by a witness and his or her account of it in court. Also important is the stress and pain for those innocent defendants who have to wait so long before their case can be put to a jury.

The largest ever study of Crown Court cases, undertaken by Zander and Henderson for the Runciman Commission, made some worrying findings. Their research was based on responses to questionnaires by more than 22,000 people involved in 3,000 Crown Court cases. The views of lawyers, judges, clerks, jurors, police and defendants were all canvassed. There were convictions in 8% of cases that defence lawyers thought weak, 6% that prosecution barristers thought weak and 4% that judges thought weak – suggesting that innocent people were still being convicted in significant numbers. Further, 31 defendants said that they had pleaded guilty to offences they had not committed. Their reasons were varied: to avoid a trial; to gain a less severe sentence or because they had been advised to do so by their lawyers.

Another worrying discovery, since poor defence lawyers have recently been cited as contributing to miscarriages of justice, is the large number of Crown Court cases (about one-third) that were being dealt with by clerks rather than by trained, qualified solicitors. Some defendants met with their barrister for the first time on the morning of their trial and for about one-third of these cases the conference lasted for just 15 minutes. In about one-third of all cases, the barristers only received their instructions the day before the trial.

3.17.4 Magistrates' courts v Crown Courts

For offences triable 'either way', there has been much debate about the merits of each venue. Each year, about 25,000 defendants elect for trial at the Crown Court only to enter a guilty plea at the last moment and this costs the Crown Prosecution Service about £7 million in wasted preparation. One of the reasons defendants do this is that prosecution cases often fall apart during the delay before a Crown Court hearing, allowing the defendant to go free (see 14.3.4). Another is that juries cannot be compelled to give reasons for convicting, unlike magistrates, who can be required to justify their reasons in writing for review in the High Court which can overturn convictions or acquittals. Thus, there is a greater chance with jury convictions that an appeal court will regard a conviction (should there be one) as unsafe and unsatisfactory because the jury's reasons for having convicted will not be known. Thus, a defendant who suspects that he might be convicted can reasonably prefer to be convicted by a jury than by a magistrate because the former do not and cannot give reasons for their verdicts and are therefore perhaps easier to appeal. Jury verdicts are arguably more likely to be regarded as unsafe on appeal because it will not be known whether some improper factor (like a judge's misdirection) had entered their deliberation. The reports of the Court of Appeal (Criminal Division) contain many cases where the court states that a conviction should be quashed because the jury might have been influenced by a misleading statement from the judge. It might be said that a defendant should prefer the magistrates' court as the sentencing is generally lower but when the defendants antecedents are known (after a conviction) he can still be committed to the Crown Court for sentence, so the magistrates' courts are not really preferable to a defendant with a criminal record who fears another conviction is likely.

3.18 Criminal appeals

The process of appeal depends upon how a case was originally tried, whether summarily or on indictment.

3.18.1 Appeals from magistrates' courts

Two routes of appeal are possible. The first route allows only a defendant to appeal. The appeal is to a judge and between two and four magistrates sitting in the Crown Court and can be (a) against conviction (only if the defendant pleaded not guilty) on points of fact or law, or (b) against sentence. Such an appeal will take the form of a new trial (a trial de novo).

Alternatively, the defendant can appeal 'by way of case stated' to the High Court (the Divisional Court of the Queen's Bench Division). This court consists of two or more judges (usually two) of whom one will be a Lord Justice of Appeal. Here, either the defence or the prosecution may appeal but the grounds are limited to: (a) a point of law; or (b) that the magistrates acted beyond their jurisdiction. If the prosecution succeeds on appeal the court can direct the magistrates to convict and pass the appropriate sentence. There is also an appeal by way of case stated from the Crown Court to the Divisional Court when the Crown Court has heard an appeal from the magistrates' court.

Appeal from the Divisional Court is to the House of Lords. Either side may appeal but only on a point of law and only if the Divisional Court certifies the point to be one of general public importance. Leave to appeal must also be granted either by the Court of Appeal or the House of Lords.

3.18.2 Appeals from the Crown Court

Appeals from the Crown Court lie to the Court of Appeal (Criminal Division) which hears appeals against conviction and sentence. This court, replacing the Court of Criminal Appeal, was established in 1966. The Division usually sits in at least two courts: one composed of the Lord Chief Justice sitting with two judges of the Queen's Bench Division and the other of a Lord Justice of Appeal and two Queen's Bench judges. The court hears about 8,000 criminal appeals and applications per year. In 1997, it heard 8,675 cases, 2,318 of which were appeals against conviction and 6,357 of which concerned sentence.

Until 1996, s 2 of the Criminal Appeal Act read:

2 (1) Except as provided by this Act, the Court of Appeal shall allow an appeal against conviction if they think:

(a)   that the verdict of the jury should be set aside on the ground that, under all the circumstances of the case, it is unsatisfactory or unsafe; or

(b)   that the judgment of the court of trial should be set aside on the ground of a wrong decision of any question of law; or

(c)   that there was a material irregularity in the course of the trial,

and in any other case shall dismiss the appeal:

provided that the court may, notwithstanding that they are of opinion that the point raised in the appeal might be decided in favour of the appellant, dismiss the appeal if they consider that no miscarriage of justice has actually occurred.

January 1996 saw the introduction of the many sections of the Criminal Appeal Act (CAA) 1995. The introduction of ss 1, 2 and 4 of the Act bring particularly significant changes to the criminal appeal system.

Section 1 amends the CAA 1968 so as to bring an appeal against conviction, an appeal against a verdict of not guilty by reason of insanity, and an appeal against a finding of disability, *on a question of law alone* into line with other appeals against conviction and sentence (that is, those involving questions of fact, or mixtures of law and fact). Now, all appeals against conviction and sentence must first have leave of the Court of Appeal or a certificate of fitness for appeal from the trial judge before the appeal can be taken. Before the new Act came into force, it was possible to appeal without the consent of the trial judge or Court of Appeal on a point of law alone. In Parliament, the reason for this change was given as the need to 'provide a filter mechanism for appeals on a ground of law alone which are wholly without merit' (HC Official Report, SC B (Criminal Appeal Bill) Col 6, 21 March 1995).

Section 2 changes the grounds for allowing an appeal under the CAA 1968. Under the old law, the Court of Appeal was required to allow an appeal where: (1) the conviction, verdict or finding should have been set aside on the ground that, under all the circumstances, it was unsafe or unsatisfactory; or (2) that the judgment of the court of trial or the order of the court giving effect to the verdict or finding should be set aside on the ground of a wrong decision of law; or (3) that there was a material irregularity in the course of the trial. In all three situations, the Court of Appeal was allowed to dismiss the appeal if it considered that no miscarriage of justice had actually occurred. The law now requires the Court of Appeal to allow an appeal against conviction under s 1 of the CAA 1968, an appeal against verdict under s 12 (insanity) or an appeal against a finding (disability) if it thinks that the conviction, verdict or finding is 'unsafe' (as opposed to the old law which used the 'unsafe *or unsatisfactory*' formula).

During the parliamentary passage of the Act, there was much heated debate about whether the new provisions were designed to narrow the grounds of appeal. That would amount to a tilt in favour of the State, in that it would make it harder for (wrongly) convicted people to appeal. Government ministers insisted that the effect of the new law was simply to restate or consolidate the practice of the Court of Appeal. One government spokesman said that:

> In dispensing with the word 'unsatisfactory', we agree with the Royal Commission on criminal justice that there is no real difference between 'unsafe' and 'unsatisfactory'; the Court of Appeal does not distinguish between the two. Retaining the word 'unsatisfactory' would imply that we thought there was a real difference and would only lead to confusion.

There were many attempts during the legislation's passage to insert the words 'or may be unsafe' after the word 'unsafe'. The Law Society, the Bar, Liberty, and JUSTICE called on the government to make such a change. Also opposed to the use of the single word 'unsafe' was the eminent criminal law expert Professor JC Smith. He has argued cogently that there are many cases where a conviction has been seen as 'unsatisfactory' rather than 'unsafe', so there is a need for both words. Sometimes, the Court of Appeal might be convinced that the defendant is guilty (so the conviction is 'safe') but still wish to allow the appeal because fair play according to the rules must be seen to be done. Accepting improperly extracted confessions (violating s 76 of Police and Criminal Evidence Act (PACE) 1984) simply because it might seem obvious that the confessor is guilty will promote undesirable interrogation practices because police officers would think that even if they break the rules any resulting confession will nevertheless be allowed as evidence.

Professor Smith has given the example ((1995) 145 NLJ 534) of where there has been a serious breach of the rules of evidence. In *Algar* (1954), the former wife of the defendant testified against him about matters during the marriage. The Court of Appeal allowed his appeal against conviction but Lord Goddard said: 'Do not think that we are doing this because we think that you are an innocent man. We do not. We think that you are a scoundrel.' The idea behind such remarks is that rules are rules, and the rules of evidence must be obeyed in order to ensure justice. Once you start to accept breaches of the rule as being justified by outcome (ends justifying means), then the whole law of evidence could begin to collapse.

The proposal to include 'or might be unsafe' was rejected for the reason probably best summarised by Lord Taylor, the then Lord Chief Justice, who argued in the Lords, that there was no merit in including the words 'or may be unsafe' as the implication of such doubt is already inherent in the word 'unsafe'.

Section 4 provides a unified test for the receipt of fresh evidence in the Court of Appeal. Under the old law, the Court of Appeal had a discretion under s 23(1)(c) of the CAA 1968 to receive fresh evidence of any witness if it was thought necessary or expedient in the interests of justice. Section 23(2) added a duty to receive new evidence which was relevant, credible, and admissible, and which could not reasonably have been adduced at the original trial. There was often much argument about whether new evidence should be received under the court's discretion or its duty. Gradually, the 'duty' principles came to be merged into the 'discretion' principles. The aim of the latest amendment is to reflect the current practice of the court. The general discretion under s 23(1) has been retained, but the 'duty' principle has been replaced with a set of criteria which the court must consider. They are:

- whether the evidence appears to the court to be capable of belief;

- whether it appears to the court that the evidence may afford any ground for allowing the appeal;

- whether the evidence would have been admissible at the trial on the issue under appeal; and

- whether there is a reasonable explanation for the failure to adduce the evidence at trial.

Only the accused may appeal. No permission to appeal is required if the appeal is against conviction on a point of law but it is needed for appeals on points of fact or mixed fact and law. Permission is also required for appeals against sentence.

Under s 36 of the CJA 1972, the Attorney General can refer a case which has resulted in an acquittal to the Court of Appeal where he believes the decision to have been questionably lenient on a point of law. The Court of Appeal deals just with the point of law and the defendant's acquittal is not affected even if the court decides the point against the defendant. It merely clarifies the law for future cases.

The CJA 1988 (ss 35–36) allows the Attorney General to refer indictable-only cases to the Court of Appeal where the sentence at trial is regarded as unduly lenient. The court can impose a harsher sentence.

Following the determination of an appeal by the Court of Appeal or by the Divisional Court, either the prosecution or the defence may appeal to the House of Lords. Leave from the court below or the House of Lords must be obtained and two other conditions fulfilled according to s 33 of the CAA 1968:

- the court below must certify that a point of law of general public importance is involved; and

- either the court below or the House of Lords must be satisfied that the point of law is one which ought to be considered by the House of Lords.

In the wake of a string of notorious miscarriages of justice coming to light in the late 1980s and early 1990s, and its remit to investigate how these occurred and how they could best be avoided, the Runciman Commission made a number of recommendations that are relevant to our discussion here. It suggested that s 2(1) of the CAA 1968 should be redrafted and the grounds of appeal should be reduced to a single broad ground which would give the court greater flexibility. The law, it states, should be made clear that the court can allow an appeal even if there is no new evidence and where the jury were properly directed by the trial judge if, after reviewing the case, the court concludes the verdict is or may be unsafe. Recommendation 320 of the Commission's report says that in considering whether to receive fresh evidence, the Court of Appeal should take a broad approach to the question whether the fresh evidence was available to the trial court. This, coupled with Recommendation 321, could afford a significant change to appellants who have been disadvantaged by poor defence lawyers. The latter recommendation says that where an appeal is based on an alleged error by trial lawyers, the test to be applied by the Court of Appeal should not be confined to whether there was 'flagrantly incompetent advocacy'. The test to be applied to fresh evidence is (Recommendation 322) 'whether it is capable of disbelief'.

The High Court can quash tainted acquittals under s 54 of the CPIA 1996. An acquittal is 'tainted' where someone has since been convicted of conspiring to pervert the course of justice in the case by interfering with the jury.

3.18.3 The Access to Justice Act 1999 – jurisdiction

Section 61 of the Access to Justice Act 1999 establishes the jurisdiction of the High Court to hear cases stated by the Crown Court for an opinion of the High Court. This part of the Act (Pt IV) enables these and certain other applications to the High Court to be listed before a single judge. It provides for the appointment of a Vice President of the Queen's Bench Division. It also prohibits the publication of material likely to identify a child involved in proceedings under the CA 1989 before the High Court or a county court; and allows for under 14 year olds to attend criminal trials.

Jurisdiction of single judge of High Court

The Act allows certain applications to be routinely heard by a single judge of the High Court. It does this by removing an obstacle that exists in the current legislation by which the route of appeal for these cases is to the House of Lords, but the Administration of Justice Act 1960 provides that the House of Lords will only hear appeals in these matters from a Divisional Court (that is, more than one judge) of the High Court. The 1999 Act (ss 63–65) amends the 1960 Act, so that the House of Lords can hear appeals from a single High Court judge. It will then be possible to make rules of court to provide for these cases to be heard by a single judge, while enabling the judge to refer particularly complex cases to a Divisional Court.

The cases in question include:

• appeals by way of case stated in criminal causes and matters;

- appeals from inferior (civil and criminal) courts and tribunals in contempt of court cases;

- criminal applications for habeas corpus.

3.18.4 The Judicial Committee of the Privy Council

The Judicial Committee of the Privy Council was created by the Judicial Committee Act 1833. Under the Act, a special committee of the Privy Council was set up to hear appeals from the dominions. The cases are heard by the judges (without wigs or robes) in a committee room in London. The committee's decision is not a judgment but an 'advice' to the monarch, who is counselled that the appeal be allowed or dismissed.

The Committee is the final court of appeal for certain Commonwealth countries which have retained this option and from some independent members and associate members of the Commonwealth. The committee comprises Privy Councillors who hold (or have held) high judicial office. In most cases, which come from places such as Hong Kong and Jamaica, the Committee comprises five Lords of Appeal in Ordinary, sometimes assisted by a judge from the country concerned.

Most of the appeals heard by the Committee are civil cases. In the rare criminal cases, it is only on matters involving legal questions that appeals are heard. The Committee does not hear appeals against criminal sentence.

The decisions of the Privy Council are very influential in English courts because they concern points of law that are applicable in this jurisdiction and they are pronounced upon by Lords of Appeal in Ordinary, in a way which is thus tantamount to a House of Lords' ruling. These decisions, however, are, technically, of persuasive precedent only although they are normally followed by English courts; see, for example, the Criminal Appeal case *Abbot v R* (1977). This was an appeal from Trinidad and Tobago. The Privy Council ruled that duress is no defence to the perpetrator of murder.

3.18.5 The Royal Commission on Criminal Justice

Research undertaken for the Royal Commission by Kate Malleson of the London School of Economics found that judges' mistakes are by far the most common ground for successful appeals against conviction. The research discovered that in about 80% of cases where convictions were quashed, there had been an error at the trial; in most instances it was judicial error.

Of 300 appeals in 1990, just over one-third were successful. Of those appealing, almost two-thirds of defendants appealed against conviction on the ground that the trial judge had made a crucial mistake and, of those, 43% succeeded in having their convictions quashed. Sixteen defendants were vindicated by the Court of Appeal in claims that the judge's summing up to the jury was biased or poor; a further 42 convictions were quashed because the judge was wrong about the law or evidence.

This research was critical of the way the Court of Appeal failed to consider cases where fresh evidence had emerged since the trial or where there was a 'lurking doubt' about the conviction. The *Report of the Royal Commission on Criminal Justice*, Cm 2263, 1993, urges that the court is given a new role allowing it to investigate the events leading up to a conviction.

The Royal Commission was set up, under the chairmanship of Viscount Runciman, in March 1991, after the release of the Birmingham Six (an important case in a series of notorious miscarriages of justice in which people were found to have been wrongly convicted and sentenced for serious crimes). It reported in July 1993 with 352 recommendations, largely designed to prevent wrongful conviction. Several of the recommendations are relevant to discussion of the criminal courts. The numbers here refer to those of the recommendations in the report.

The Commission recommended (331) that the Home Secretary's power to refer cases to the Court of Appeal under s 17 of the CAA 1968 should be removed and a new body, the Criminal Cases Review Authority, should be set up to consider allegations (332) that a miscarriage of justice might have occurred. The authority should have 'operational independence' (333) with a chairman appointed by the Queen on the advice of the Prime Minister. The authority should be independent of the court structure (336) and should refer meritorious cases directly to the Court of Appeal. There should be neither a right of appeal nor a right to judicial review (340) in relation to decisions reached by the authority. The authority should consist of both lawyers and lay people, should be supported by a staff of lawyers and (344) should devise its own rules and procedures. It should be able to discuss cases direct with applicants (345) and should have powers (347) to direct its own investigations. These recommendations were largely met by the terms of the CAA 1995.

The CAA 1995 legislates for the new Criminal Cases Review Commission (CCRC) which was established in 1997. The CCRC took over the Home Secretary's power (under s 17 of the CAA 1968) to reinvestigate already unsuccessfully appealed cases and refer back to Court of Appeal cases of suspected miscarriage of justice. The organisation JUSTICE has expressed doubts about the independence of the CCRC as its members are to be government appointees. The wide power to reinvestigate cases where there appears to be a 'real possibility' (s 13) of miscarriage has been generally greeted with approval but it is a matter of regret in some quarters that those reinvestigating cases will not be CCRC investigators but, usually, police officers (s 19). As many allegations of injustice involve accusations against the police, there is a school of thought suggesting that a manifestly impartial, outside body should be responsible for the reinvestigation. In *R v Secretary of State for the Home Department ex p Hickey* (1994), it was held that when the Home Secretary, on receiving a petition from somebody wishing to have his case referred back to the Court of Appeal, makes inquiries and thereby obtains fresh evidence, fairness requires that he must disclose this new evidence to the petitioner. It is assumed this principle of openness will now also apply to the CCRC.

3.18.6 The Criminal Cases Review Commission

The CCRC is an independent body set up under the CAA 1995. The CCRC came into being on 1 January 1997. It is responsible for investigating suspected miscarriages of criminal justice in England, Wales and Northern Ireland. This function was previously carried out through the office of the Home Secretary. He would make occasional referrals of cases back to the Court of Appeal when a unit of civil servants in the Home Office evaluated a case (which had otherwise exhausted the formal court appeal system) as warranting further consideration. Over 250 cases were transferred from the Home Office around 31 March 1997, when the Commission took over responsibility for casework.

There are 14 CCRC members from a wide variety of backgrounds. Any decision to refer a case to the relevant court of appeal (the Court of Appeal (Criminal Division) or the High Court) has to be taken by a committee of at least three members. The CCRC considers whether or not there is a real possibility that the conviction, finding, verdict or sentence would not be upheld were a reference to be made.

In order to establish that there is a real possibility of an appeal succeeding regarding a conviction, there has to be:

- an argument or evidence which has not been raised during the trial or at appeal; or

- exceptional circumstances.

In order to establish that there is a real possibility of an appeal succeeding against a sentence, there has to be a legal argument or information about the individual, or the offence, which was not raised in court during the trial or at appeal.

Other than in exceptional circumstances, the Commission can only consider cases in which an appeal through the ordinary judicial appeal process has failed and, once a decision is taken to refer a case to the relevant court of appeal, the Commission has no other involvement.

The CCRC referred the notorious case of Derek William Bentley to the Court of Appeal. Mr Bentley was convicted of the murder of PC Sidney Miles at the Central Criminal Court on 11 December 1952. Mr Bentley did not actually shoot the officer. The gun was fired by his accomplice in a failed burglary attempt but Mr Bentley was convicted under the principles of 'joint enterprise', even though he was being held by a police officer under arrest metres away from where his accomplice fired the pistol. An appeal against conviction was heard by the Court of Criminal Appeal on 13 January 1953 and dismissed. Mr Bentley was hanged on 28 January 1953.

Bentley's conviction and sentence were the subject of numerous representations to the Home Office. In July 1993, on the recommendation of the Home Secretary, Her Majesty The Queen, in the exercise of the Royal Prerogative of Mercy, granted to Mr Bentley a posthumous pardon limited to sentence.

Following submissions from the applicants' solicitors and the completion of its own inquiries, the CCRC concluded that Mr Bentley's conviction should be reconsidered by the Court of Appeal. The trial was seen as unfair in a number of respects, for example, the fact that, although 18, Bentley had a mental age of 11 was kept a secret from the jury, and the judge's summing up to the jury was astonishingly biased in favour of the police. In August 1998, on a momentous day in legal history, the Court of Appeal cleared Bentley of the murder for which he was hanged 46 years earlier. In giving judgment, the Lord Chief Justice, Lord Bingham, said: '... the summing up in this case was such as to deny the appellant that fair trial which is the birthright of every British citizen.'

The CCRC cannot overturn a conviction or change a sentence. In those cases where specific criteria are met (essentially where there is new evidence or new argument), the Commission can refer a case to the Court of Appeal (in the case of Crown Court convictions) or the Crown Court (in the case of magistrates' court convictions). Only about 5% of new cases received by the Commission since 1997 have been against summary convictions.

The CCRC Annual Report for 1999 notes that 44 cases had been referred to the Court of Appeal by 31 March 1999, of which 13 had been heard resulting in 10 convictions or sentences being quashed and three upheld. By July 1999, the CCRC had received a total of 2,605 applications of which 961 cases had been completed.

Assessing the success of the CCRC thus far is difficult. The volume of documents it has to deal with (albeit electronically) is formidable, averaging around 2,000 pages per case. In the 1999 Report, the Chairman of the CCRC warns that more staff are needed to reduce the accumulation of cases awaiting review and deal with the numbers of new cases received – currently around four every working day.

Ultimately, the test of success for the CCRC will be the same one as that which was apparently failed by its predecessor – carrying the confidence of the general public and of politicians – that it represents a safe, quick and impartial method of dealing with cases not given justice in the ordinary courts.

3.19 A miscarriage of justice

One of the English legal system's worst miscarriages of justice cases in recent history was exposed in the Court of Appeal in February 1998. In 1979, Vincent Hickey, Michael Hickey, Jimmy Robertson and Pat Molloy, who became known as the Bridgewater Four, were convicted of the murder of a 13 year old boy, Carl Bridgewater. Although the men were not angelic characters (and two had serious criminal records), they strenuously protested that they were not guilty of the horrific child murder.

Eighteen years later, and after two earlier failed visits to the Court of Appeal and seven police investigations, three of the men were released on 21 February on unconditional bail in anticipation of an appeal hearing in April. The fourth defendant, Mr Molloy, died in jail in 1981. The appeal was eventually allowed.

The Crown has conceded that the case against the men was 'flawed' by evidence falsified and fabricated by police officers. There has also come to light significant fingerprint evidence, tending to exonerate the four which was not disclosed to the defence by the prosecution. Mr Molloy was questioned for 10 days without access to a solicitor, and a fabricated statement from Vincent Hickey was used to persuade Mr Molloy to confess to the crime. Before he died, Mr Molloy claimed he had been beaten by police officers in the course of his interrogation.

The case was given extensive coverage in the print and broadcast media in February 1997 and made a significant impact upon public consciousness. How far it will negatively affect public confidence in the criminal justice system remains to be judged. This major case raises many points germane to the operation of the criminal justice system. The following are of particular importance:

- The case was originally investigated in 1978, before the PACE 1984 had been passed. The requirements under the PACE 1984 for suspects to be given access to legal advice (s 58, Code C) and for interviews to be recorded (s 60, Code E) may have reduced or eliminated the opportunity for police malpractice of the sort which occurred in the *Bridgewater* case.

- Although the criminal justice system ultimately corrected an injustice, this result was achieved primarily through the indefatigable efforts of a few dedicated family members, campaigning journalists and members of Parliament who would not let the issue disappear from the public forum. The case attracted attention because of the terrible nature of the crime – a child murder. It is quite possible that many other unjust convictions in cases with more mundane facts are never propelled into public discussion or overturned.

- Miscarriages of justice cases involve two types of insult to notions of legal fairness: (a) the wrongly imprisoned endure years of incarceration; (b) the real culprits (a child killer in the *Bridgewater* case) are never identified and could well go on to commit other offences.

- The men were released due to the discovery of evidence which had been fabricated and falsified, yet the CPIA 1996 will in future restrict defence access to prosecution evidence.

- The CCRC has been established to re-evaluate alleged cases of miscarriages of justice. One criticism of it has been that it does not have its own independent investigators but will rely on police officers to re-examine cases. How far this new body will be able to succeed in its mission statement, and carry public confidence, remains to be seen.

- The jury is only as good as the information and arguments put before it allow it to be. After the prosecution's case had been devastated by the discovery of new scientific evidence in 1993 (a forensic psychiatrist showed that Molloy's 'confession' used language the suspect would not have used), the foreman of the jury from the 1979 trial risked prosecution for contempt of court by issuing a statement to say that he thought that the men were not guilty. He, along with another juror, said they regretted that they had not been given all the evidence that was available at the time of the trial.

CIVIL AND CRIMINAL COURT STRUCTURES

The differences between civil and criminal law

There is no such thing as inherently criminal conduct. A crime is whatever the State has forbidden on pain of legal punishment. The conduct which attracts criminal sanctions changes over time and according to different social systems. The terminology and outcomes of the two systems are different. In criminal cases, the *prosecutor prosecutes the defendant* (or *accused*); in civil cases, the *claimant sues the defendant*.

The Court Service

The courts (except for the magistrates' courts and coroners' courts) are now run by the Court Service, an executive agency, formerly part of the Lord Chancellor's Department.

Magistrates' courts

Magistrates' courts have a significant civil jurisdiction, especially under the CA 1989 as 'family proceedings courts'.

County courts

There are about 240 county courts in England and Wales. They are presided over by district judges and circuit judges. County courts hear small claims, that is, those whose value is £5,000 or under, and fast track cases. The civil justice reforms are likely to put a considerable burden of work on the county courts under the new system. The main advantage to litigants using the small claims process is the fact that, if sued, they can defend without fear of incurring huge legal costs, since the costs the winning party can claim are strictly limited.

The High Court

The High Court's judicial composition should be noted and the meaning of the 10 year qualification according to s 71 of the CLSA 1990. The High Court is under considerable pressure of work, hence the CLSA 1990 provisions to ease its workload. The Queen's Bench Division deals with contract and tort, etc; its Divisional Court deals with judicial review and criminal appeals from magistrates' and Crown Courts. Chancery deals with cases involving land, mortgages and bankruptcy and probate, etc; its Divisional Court hears taxation appeals. The Family Division hears matrimonial and child-related matters and its Divisional Court hears appeals from magistrates' and county courts on these issues.

The Court of Appeal (Civil Division)

The Court of Appeal (Civil Division) usually has three judges whose decision is by majority. For many purposes it is the *de facto* final Appeal Court (*C v S and Others* (1987)).

The Bowman Report 1998

The Report contained important recommendations for reducing the number of cases coming to the Court of Appeal and for improving practice and procedures in the Civil Appeals Office. The review's major recommendations included:

Certain appeals which previously reached the Court of Appeal (Civil Division) should be heard at a low level, and that the requirement for leave to appeal should be extended to all cases coming to the Court of Appeal except for adoption cases, child abduction cases and appeals against committal orders or refusal to grant habeas corpus. The *Access to Justice Act 1999* reforms the appeal process by establishing the principle that there is the need for permission to appeal at all levels in the system. The Act provides that, in normal circumstances, there will be only one level of appeal to the courts and it gives to the Civil Division of the Court of Appeal flexibility to exercise its jurisdiction in courts of one, two or more judges. Taken together, these proposals are intended to ensure that appeals are heard at the right level and in a way which is proportionate to their weight and complexity.

Civil court fees

A new scale of court fees for people using the civil courts came into effect in 1997. The aim of the new fees is to make the civil court self-financing. This change raises matters of importance in legal, social and economic debates. There are those who argue, for example, that the courts should, like the National Health Service, be free to people at the point of use, and financed by general taxation. There are others who argue that some payments should be made at the point of use. The Lord Chancellor has pointed out that, were the courts to become free in this way, the money needed to pay for this would have to come from closing down large parts of the civil legal aid system or closing schools or hospitals.

The House of Lords

In most of its 50 or so cases, five Law Lords sit. They hear cases of general public importance concerning points of law, for example, *R v R* (1991) changing a 250 year old rule and allowing prosecutions for marital rape.

The European Court of Justice

The ECJ sits in Luxembourg to ensure that the interpretation and application of the EEC 'Treaty of Rome' is observed consistently by all Member States. Note the importance of Art 234, formerly 177, and the guidance provided by *Bulmer v Bollinger* (1974).

The European Court of Human Rights

The ECHR sits in Strasbourg and arose from the 1950 European Convention on Human Rights. It has no mechanism for enforcement other than of a political nature. Its effect can be illustrated by cases like *Malone v UK* (1984).

As a consequence of the Human Rights Act 1998, the decisions of the European Court of Human Rights are now precedents for, and binding on, domestic UK courts. In terms of human rights issues, therefore, it is superior to the House of Lords.

The Judicial Committee of the Privy Council

The Judicial Committee of the Privy Council acts as a final Appeal Court for some Commonwealth countries and, because it comprises senior judges from the English legal system, it gives decisions which are persuasive precedent in English law.

Criminal courts

The trial courts are the magistrates' courts and Crown Courts. In serious offences, known as *indictable offences*, the defendant is tried by a jury in a Crown Court, for *summary offences* he or she is tried by magistrates and for 'either way' offences the defendant can be tried by magistrates if they agree but he or she may elect for jury trial. Note the new 'transfer for trial' procedure, and the contention from some groups that this could facilitate miscarriages of justice.

The main issues here concern the distribution of business between the magistrates' court and Crown Courts: what are the advantages of trial in the magistrates' court: (a) for the State; and (b) for the defendant? Conversely, what are the disadvantages?

In 1999, the government announced its intention to introduce a change concerning the way decisions are made about where a defendant is to be tried. Under the new system proposed by the government, a defendant charged with an 'either way' offence would be able to make representations to magistrates that he or she wished to be tried in the Crown Court before a judge and jury, but the magistrates would have power to override the desire of the defendant and try the case themselves if they thought they were properly suited to this task, even against the wishes of the defendant.

Certain changes concerning the magistrates' courts have been made by the Access to Justice Act 1999. The 1999 Act provides for various changes to the organisation and management of the magistrates' courts. For example, the Act redefines the basis of the unit of Magistrates' Courts Committees (MCCs). The Act also unifies the provisional and metropolitan stipendiary magistrates into a single bench, and it removes the requirement for magistrates to sit on cases committed to the county court for sentence. The Act also makes some controversial changes in relation to warrant execution, by allowing MCCs to approve and appoint private enforcement agencies to execute certain kinds of warrant.

Criminal appeals from the magistrates go to the Crown Court or to the Queen's Bench Divisional Court 'by way of case stated' on a point of law or that the JPs went beyond their proper powers. If the prosecution succeeds on appeal, the court can direct the magistrates to convict and pass the appropriate sentence. There is also an appeal by way of case stated from the Crown Court to the Divisional Court when the Crown Court has heard an appeal from the magistrates' court. From the Crown Court, appeals against conviction and sentence lie to the Court of Appeal (Criminal Division). Note the powers of the Attorney Relational Justice General under s 36 of the CJA 1972; and his powers under ss 35 and 36 of the CJA 1988.

Part IV of the Access to Justice Act 1999 establishes the High Courts' jurisdiction to hear cases stated by the Crown Court for an opinion. It enables these cases stated to be heard by a single judge.

The Judicial Committee of the Privy Council hears final appeals from some Commonwealth countries and its decisions are of persuasive precedent in English law.

Runciman Royal Commission recommendations

The Runciman Royal Commission recommendations cover a wide range of issues. Note, in particular, the commission recommended:

- that the Home Secretary's power to refer cases to the Court of Appeal under s 17 of the CAA 1968 should be removed and a new body, the Criminal Cases Review Authority ('the authority'), should be set up to consider allegations that a miscarriage of justice might have occurred. The authority should have 'operational independence' with a chairman appointed by the Queen on the advice of the Prime Minister. The authority should be independent of the court structure and should refer meritorious cases directly to the Court of Appeal. The authority was established under the Criminal Appeal Act 1995: see 3.18;

- the abolition of committal proceedings (now abolished by s 44 of the CPIA 1996 – see above);

- the curtailment of the right to jury trial.

CHAPTER 4

THE JUDICIARY

4.1 The constitutional role of the judiciary

Central to the general idea of the Rule of Law is the specific proposition that it involves the rule of law rather than the rule of people. Judges hold a position of central importance in relation to the concept of the Rule of Law. They are expected to deliver judgment in a completely impartial manner through a strict application of the law, without allowing their personal preference, or fear or favour of any of the parties to the action, to affect their decision in any way.

This desire for impartiality is reflected in the constitutional position of the judges. In line with Montesquieu's classical exposition of the separation of powers, the judiciary occupy a situation apart from the legislative and executive arms of the State; and operate independently of them. Prior to the English revolutionary struggles of the 17th century between Parliament and the monarch, judges held office at the King's pleasure. Not only did this mean that judges could be dismissed when the Monarch so decided but it highlighted the lack of independence of the law from the State in the form, and person, of the monarch. With the victory of Parliament and the establishment of a State based on popular sovereignty, and limited in its powers, the independence of the judiciary was confirmed in the Act of Settlement 1701. The centrality of the independence of the judges and the legal system from direct control or interference from the State in the newly established constitution was emphasised in the writing of the English philosopher John Locke who saw it as one of the essential reasons for, and justifications of, the Social Contract on which the social structure was assumed to be based.

In order to buttress the independence of the judiciary, and remove them from the danger of being subjected to political pressure, it has been made particularly difficult to remove senior judges once they have been appointed. Their independence of thought and opinion is also protected by the doctrine of judicial immunity. Both of these principles will be considered in more detail below.

4.1.1 The constitutional role of the Lord Chancellor

It should be noted that the Lord Chancellor holds an anomalous position in respect of the separation of powers in the contemporary State, in that the holder of that position plays a key role in each of the three elements of the State. The Lord Chancellor is the most senior judge in the English court structure, sitting as he does in the House of Lords. At the same time, however, the Lord

Chancellorship is a party political appointment, and the occupant of the office owes his preferment to the Prime Minister of the day. Not only is the incumbent a member of the executive, having a seat in the Cabinet, but he is also responsible for the operation of his own government department. In addition to these roles, it should not be overlooked that the Chancellor is also the Speaker of the House of Lords in its general role as a legislative forum. The peculiar situation of the Lord Chancellor is also reflected in the fact that the incumbent can be dismissed, or persuaded to resign, by the Prime Minster and may cease to hold office on the election of a new government.

The present Lord Chancellor, Lord Irvine of Lairg and his immediate predecessor, Lord Mackay, have not gone without criticism from within the legal profession generally, and the judiciary in particular. The suggestion has been made that these Lord Chancellors have represented the interests of their political masters, at the expense of the interests of their legal colleagues. For some time, the legal professions have argued that economic imperatives have driven the machinery of the justice system, rather than the wish to provide the best possible service. Lord Mackay's motives and actions were continuously open to such suspicions. As Lord Steyn, one of the Lords of Appeal in Ordinary in the House of Lords, was quoted as saying:

> The Lord Chancellor is always a spokesman for the government in furtherance of its party political agenda [[1997] PL 84].

However, for the moment at least, a truce appears to have been declared between the judges and the (relatively) new Lord Chancellor as is evident from the words of the Master of the Rolls, Lord Woolf:

> I do not forget that there was a period of confrontation between some of the judiciary and the former Lord Chancellor, Lord Mackay, but that was primarily concerned with reforms relating to the professions, including rights of audience for solicitors, and not the role of the judiciary in the administration of the courts. There was also the concern over the shortage of judges in 1994–95. However, after powerful and frank speeches by the then Lord Chief Justice and Master of the Rolls, a much needed injection of additional judges was provided. The present Lord Chancellor, Lord Irvine of Lairg, is also proposing far reaching changes to the rights of audience, but these are unlikely to meet with the same hostility [(1998) 114 LQR 579, p 585].

Whether this truce survives Lord Irvine's proposals in the White Paper *Modernising Justice* (1998), and what many see as the ironically titled Access to Justice Act 1999, remains to be seen.

In addition to difficulties arising directly from their responsibility for implementing political policies in relation to the legal system, the question of the Lord Chancellor's judicial role has also come into question. As a consequence of the fact that the appointment of the Lord Chancellor is a purely political one, there is no requirement that the incumbent should have held any prior judicial office. Indeed, in the case of Lord Irvine, he has never served in any judicial capacity, making his reputation as a highly successful barrister, at one time having both the present Prime Minister and his wife in his chambers. Nonetheless, as Lord Chancellor, he is the most senior judge and is entitled to sit, as he deems appropriate (see 4.3.2 for further observations about the Lord Chancellor's residual powers).

There is, however, a much more fundamental issue relating to the manner in which the Lord Chancellor's multi-functional role may be seen as breaching the doctrine of the separation of powers. There cannot but be doubts as to the suitability, not to say propriety, of a member of the executive functioning as a member of the judiciary. Given the heightened sensitivity in relation to impartiality, generated by Lord Hoffman's participation in the *Pinochet* case (see below), the Lord Chancellor himself withdrew from sitting in a case in March 1999, in which he recognised the possibility of a conflict of interest. That case involved an action by the family of a man who had died in police custody. The suggestion was made that the Lord Chancellor's participation in the judicial panel raised doubts as to whether the case would be decided by an independent and impartial tribunal. Given his recent guidelines warning the judiciary about the need to be sensitive to issues of conflict of interest, the Lord Chancellor clearly felt himself required to stand down from hearing the case. Such action on his part, however, merely raises the question as to in which cases can a Lord Chancellor sit, without having a political interest? The Lord Chancellor's position with regard to this mixture of political and judicial functions has been further questioned by Lord Steyn, in a paper written for the Constitution Unit at University College London in May 1999.

In any event, considerations of this nature may be forestalled by the European Court of Human Rights decision relating to the operation of the constitution on the island of Guernsey (*McGonnell v UK* (1998)). The Bailiff of Guernsey has a similar mixture of administrative, legislative and judicial roles as has the Lord Chancellor. In a case brought by a Guernsey resident against a judicial decision of the Bailiff, the European Commission on Human Rights held that it was inappropriate for the Bailiff to take such decisions. In the view of the Commission:

> It is incompatible with the requisite appearances of independence and impartiality for a judge to have legislative and executive functions as substantial as those carried out by the Bailiff.

If the decision of the Commission is confirmed by the Court, as appropriate for the microcosm of Guernsey, it is equally applicable for the macrocosm of the UK. It is even possible that, under the Human Rights Act (HRA) 1998, the Lord Chancellor's judicial position will be invalidated by the other judges. It should of course be recognised, perhaps with no little degree of irony, that it was Lord Irvine who was instrumental in bringing the European Convention into UK law, through the HRA 1998.

It might be preferable if the position of the Lord Chancellor were considered afresh. To do so would require a complete reassessment of the present structure of the English legal system, but this possibility is not without merit, as will be considered below.

4.1.2 The constitution and the role of the House of Lords

A number of issues have come together to raise questions about the operation of the House of Lords as the final court of appeal in the English legal system. Amongst these are the devolution of parliamentary power to the new Scottish Parliament and Welsh Assembly; the proposed abolition of the rights of hereditary peers to vote in the House of Lords; the enactment of the HRA; and the role of the House of Lords itself in the *Pinochet* case (see below). It is almost incontrovertible that changes will be required in the future and perhaps this time of large constitutional change presents the best opportunity for a considered revision of the operation of the senior judiciary and their courts.

In other constitutional systems, both civil, as in France, or common law, as in the US, not only is there a clear separation of powers between the judiciary, the executive and the legislature, but there is also a distinct Constitutional Court, which deals with such issues. The English Constitution provides for neither of these. The anomalous position of the Lord Chancellor has already been commented on, as has the doctrine of the supremacy of Parliament (see 1.4) but it remains to to be considered whether either of these can continue to exist as they have, under the changed circumstances of the contemporary constitution. Equally, the potential role of the courts as Constitutional Courts, and the existing position of the House of Lords as a court within the legislative body, must come into issue.

It is a commonplace of politics that the devolution of power from the UK Parliament in London, particularly to the Scottish Parliament in Edinburgh, will give rise to disputes as to the relationship between the two bodies. Eventually, such issues will have to be resolved in the courts. Equally, the HRA will, for the first time, give the courts clear power to declare the UK Parliament's legislative provision to be contrary to essential human rights (see 1.5). Moreover, as a result of the secondary nature of the legislation produced by the Scottish Parliament, the courts will have the power to quash such Acts as invalid for lack of compatibility with the European Convention on Human Rights. Even allowing for the fact that the Human Rights Act has been introduced in such a way as to maintain the theory of parliamentary sovereignty, in practice, the courts will inevitably become involved in political/constitutional issues. Once the courts are required to act in constitutional matters, it is surely a mere matter of time before they become Constitutional Courts, as distinct from ordinary courts, with specialist judges with particular expertise in such matters. Once a Constitutional Court develops, the position of the Lord Chancellor will become untenable as a judge, as his political roles would automatically place him in a position of conflict of interest. He would have to give up his position as head of the judiciary, probably, as some have already proposed, to the Lord Chief Justice.

A further problematic consequence of such a development would be the continued location of the Constitutional Court within the House of Lords. If the existing House of Lords were to be replaced by an elected body, then questions would have to be asked about the situation of unelected members, such as bishops and judges; but, even if it were replaced by an appointed second chamber, the separation of powers would surely demand that the Constitutional Court be separate from it.

Membership of such a court could also be an issue. The present situation, where panels of five Law Lords, or seven as in the third *Pinochet* hearing, are selected from the full complement of 12, has been criticised as introducing an element of lottery into the judicial procedure. The question arises, would the decision in any case have been different, had a different body of judges been empanelled? In the *Pinochet* case (see below), the second panel of seven reached the same decision as the previous five member court, but for different reasons. The Pinochet proceedings brought the House of Lords, no doubt unwelcome, publicity, and may have revealed the need for its internal reform. Already, suggestions have been made that the court should sit as a full court, involving all its members; but that, in turn, must bring into question the actual appointment procedures of these most senior judges, especially if it were to develop into a Constitutional Court. For the question has to be asked as to what expertise in constitutional matters generally, and human rights in particular, do the commercial lawyers who make up a significant number of the highest judicial posts have? And, if expertise in such issues is to be seen as the criterion for appointment to the Constitutional Court, then should not membership of the court be open to non-practitioners, such as academics? For the moment, such issues remain purely hypothetical, but for how much longer can this remain the case?

In his May 1999 paper, Lord Steyn, in commenting on the fact that the current Royal Commission on Reform of the House of Lords will consider the position of the Law Lords, but will not be asked to consider the situation of the Lord Chancellor, expressed the view that:

> The strategic thinking behind this coyness may be that turning the searchlight
> on the Lord Chancellor's position may expose the fragility of the supposed
> pragmatic justifications for the present arrangement.

It is worth noting that the case set out in the above two sections for the reform of the Lord Chancellor's position and against the location of the most senior judges in the House of Lords was presented, in essence, to the commission examining the reform of the House of Lords by JUSTICE, the civil rights organisation. Both aspects of the challenges were strongly rejected by Lord Chancellor Irvine in a speech to the Third Worldwide Common Law Judiciary Conference in Edinburgh, delivered on 5 July 1999 (www.open.gov.uk/lcd/speeches/1999/5-7-99).

4.1.3 The case of General Pinochet

No consideration of the operation of the judiciary generally, and the House of Lords in particular, can be complete without a detailed consideration of what can only be called the *Pinochet* case (the various cases are actually cited as *R v Bow Street Metropolitan Magistrates ex p Pinochet Ugarte (No 1)* (1998) (House of Lords, first hearing); *(No 2)* (1999) (House of Lords, appeal against Lord Hoffman); *(No 3)* (1999) (final House of Lords decision). There will undoubtedly be other cases relating to the extradition of the ex-dictator, but the foregoing are the ones that established that his office as Head of State gave him no general immunity to extradition for offences against the United Nations Convention Against Torture, since the date it was incorporated into UK law by the Criminal Justice Act 1988.

In September 1973, the democratically elected government of Chile was overthrown in a violent army coup led by the then General Augusto Pinochet Ugarte; the President Salvador Allende, and many others were killed in the fighting. Subsequently, in the words of Lord Browne-Wilkinson, in the final House of Lords hearing:

> There is no doubt that, during the period of the Senator Pinochet regime, appalling acts of barbarism were committed in Chile and elsewhere in the world: torture, murder and the unexplained disappearance of individuals on a large scale.

Although it was not suggested that Pinochet had committed these acts personally, it was claimed that he was fully aware of them and conspired to have them undertaken.

In 1998, General Pinochet, by now Senator for life and recipient of a Chilean amnesty for his actions (extracted as the price for his returning his country to democracy), came to England for medical treatment. Although he was initially welcomed, he was subsequently arrested, on an extradition warrant issued in Spain, for the crimes of torture, murder and conspiracy to murder allegedly orchestrated by him in Chile during the 1970s. Spain issued the international warrants, but Pinochet was actually arrested on warrants issued by the metropolitan stipendiary magistrate under s 8(1)(b) of the Extradition Act 1989. The legal question for the English courts was whether General Pinochet, as Head of State at the time when the crimes were committed, enjoyed diplomatic immunity. In November 1998, the House of Lords rejected Pinochet's claim by a three to two majority, Lord Hoffman voting with the majority but declining to submit a reasoned judgment.

Prior to the hearing in the House of Lords, Amnesty International, which campaigns against such things as State mass murder, torture and political imprisonment, and in favour of general civil and political liberties, had been granted leave to intervene in the proceedings, and had made representations through its counsel, Geoffrey Bindman QC. After the *Pinochet* decision, it was revealed, although it was hardly a secret, that Lord Hoffman was an unpaid director of the Amnesty International Charitable Trust, and that his wife also worked for Amnesty. On that basis, Pinochet's lawyers initiated a very peculiar action: they petitioned the House of Lords, about a House of Lords decision: for the first time, the highest court in the land was to be subject to review, but to itself; only itself differently constituted. So, in January 1999, another panel of Law Lords set aside the decision of the earlier hearing on the basis that Lord Hoffman's involvement had invalidated the previous hearing. The decision as to whether Pinochet had immunity or not would have to be heard by a new, and differently constituted, committee of Law Lords.

It has to be stated in favour of this decision that the English legal system is famously rigorous in controlling conflicts of interest which might be seen to affect what should be a neutral decision making process. The rule, which applies across the board to trustees, company directors and other fiduciaries as well as judges, is so strict that the mere possibility of a conflict of interest is sufficient to invalidate any decision so made, even if in reality the individual concerned was completely unaffected by their own interest in coming to the decision. In the words of the famous *dictum* of Lord Hewart, it is of fundamental importance that justice must not only be done but should manifestly and undoubtedly be seen to be done (*R v Sussex Justices ex p McCarthy* (1924)). With regard to the judicial process, it has been a long established rule that no one may be a judge in his or her own cause, that is, they cannot judge a case in which they have an interest. This is sometimes known by the phrase *nemo judex in causa sua*. Thus, for example, judges who are shareholders in a company appearing before the court as a litigant must decline to hear the case (*Dimes v Grand Junction Canal* (1852)). It is, therefore, astonishing that Lord Hoffman did not withdraw from the case, or at least declare his interest in Amnesty when it was joined to the proceedings. The only possible justification is that Hoffman assumed that all of those involved in the case, including the Pinochet team of lawyers, were aware of the connection. Alternatively, he might have thought that his support for a charitable body aimed at promoting civil and political liberties was so worthy in itself as to be unimpeachable: could not, and indeed should not, every English judge subscribe, for example, to cl 3(c) of the Amnesty International Charitable Trust memorandum, which provides that one of its objects is to procure the abolition of torture, extra-judicial execution and disappearance?

In either case, Lord Hoffman was wrong.

Once it was shown that Lord Hoffman had a relevant interest in its subject matter, he was disqualified without any investigation into whether there was a likelihood or suspicion of bias. The mere fact of his interest was sufficient to disqualify him unless he had made sufficient disclosure. Hitherto, only pecuniary or proprietary interests had led to automatic disqualification. But, as Lord Browne-Wilkinson stated, Amnesty, and hence Lord Hoffman, plainly had a non-pecuniary interest, sufficient to give rise to an automatic disqualification for those involved with it.

It is important not to overstate what was decided in *Re Pinochet*. The facts of that case were exceptional and it is unlikely that it will lead to a mass withdrawal of judges from cases; however, there might well be other cases in which the judge would be well advised to disclose a possible interest. Finally, with regard to *Re Pinochet*, whatever ones views about the merits, sagacity or neutrality of the current judiciary, there is considerable evidence to support the proposition that, historically, judges have often been biased towards certain causes and social classes. For example, JAG Griffiths' book, *The Politics of the Judiciary* (1997) (see 4.12.1), is brimming with concrete examples of judges who have shown distinctly conservative and illiberal opinions in cases involving workers, trade unions, civil liberties, Northern Ireland, police powers, religion and other matters. Lord Hoffman was wrong, but it is nonetheless ironic that the first senior judge to have action taken against him for possible political bias is someone whose agenda was nothing more than being against torture and unjudicial killings. It will be very interesting now to see what other associations are declared by presiding judges in the wake of the Lords' decision.

The House of Lords, therefore, decided that Lord Hoffman had been wrong, but it remained for the House of Lords to extricate itself, with whatever dignity it could manage, from the situation it, through Lord Hoffman, had got itself into. This it endeavoured to do by reconstituting the original hearing with a specially extended committee of seven members. Political and legal speculation was rife before the decision of that court. It was suggested that the new committee could hardly go against the decision of the previous one, without bringing the whole House of Lords procedures into disrepute, yet the earlier court had actually contained the most liberal, and civil liberties minded, of the Lords. It was assumed that the new hearing would endorse the earlier decision, if with reluctance, but what was not expected was the way in which it would actually do so.

In reaching the decision that General Pinochet could be extradited, the House of Lords relied on, and established, Pinochet's potential responsibility for the alleged crimes, from the date on which the UK incorporated the United Nations Convention on Torture into its domestic law, through the CJA 1988, 29 September 1988. Consequently, he could not be held responsible for any crimes committed before then, but was potentially liable for any offences after that date. Thus, although the later House of Lords decision provided the same decision as the first one, it did so on significantly different, and much more limited, grounds to those on which Lords Steyn and Nicholls, with the support of Lord Hoffman, relied. Such a conclusion is neither satisfactory in law, nor political practice, and does nothing to deflect the unflattering glare of unwonted publicity that has been visited on the House of Lords.

The *Pinochet* case eventually ended in March 2000 when the Home Secretary, Jack Straw, used his discretion under the Extradition Act to release the General on medical grounds."

4.2 Judicial offices

Although not required to know the names of present incumbents, students should be at least aware of the various titles of judges and equally know which courts they operate in:

- *Lord Chancellor*. The peculiar nature of this office has already been commented on, but it should be pointed out that, as well as being the senior judge in the House of Lords, the Lord Chancellor is formally the most senior judge in the Court of Appeal, and holds the position of President of the Chancery Division. On the announcement of the general election of 1997, the serving Lord Chancellor, Lord Mackay, announced his intention to resign from office, and the incoming Labour administration appointed Lord Irvine in his place. The present Lord Chancellor, therefore, is Lord Irvine of Lairg and he is referred to in reports as Lord Irvine LC.

- *Lord Chief Justice*. The holder of this position is second only to the Lord Chancellor in eminence. The Lord Chief Justice is the President of the Criminal Division of the Court of Appeal and is formally the senior judge in the Queen's Bench Division of the High Court. The present incumbent is Lord Bingham CJ.

- *Master of the Rolls*. The holder of this office is President of the Civil Division of the Court of Appeal. At present, this position is held by Lord Woolf MR.

- *President of the Family Division of the High Court of Justice*. This person is the senior judge in the Family Division and is responsible for organising the operation of the court. The current President is Sir Stephen Brown P.

- *Vice Chancellor*. Although the Lord Chancellor is nominally the head of the Chancery Division of the High Court, the actual function of organising the Chancery Division falls to the Vice Chancellor. The current incumbent is Sir Richard Scott VC.

- *Senior Presiding Judge for England and Wales*. The Courts and Legal Services Act 1990 recognised the existing system and required that each of the six separate Crown Court circuits should operate under the administration of two Presiding Judges appointed from the High Court. In addition, a Senior Presiding Judge is appointed from the Lords Justices of Appeal (see 4.2.1).

4.2.1 Judicial hierarchy

The foregoing are specific judicial offices. In addition, the various judges who function at the various levels within the judicial hierarchy are referred to in the following terms:

- *Lords of Appeal in Ordinary.* These are the people who are normally referred to as the Law Lords for the simple reason that they sit in the House of Lords and are ennobled when they are appointed to their positions. There can be between seven and 12 Law Lords, although the maximum number is subject to alteration by Order in Council. The function of the House of Lords, as the highest domestic court in the UK, is considered elsewhere but the legislative role of the Law Lords deserves some mention. Although the claim that the Law Lords do not take part in the party political debate in the House of Lords is correct, it is no longer accurate, as is sometimes claimed, that the Law Lords refrain from controversy in their contributions to debate. A comparatively recent example can be cited in the controversial debate that took place with regard to the reform of the legal profession. In that particular situation, some of the Law Lords were not shy of engaging in the debate to express their disapprobation with the proposals in a fairly controversial manner. (The increased willingness of the judiciary generally, and the senior judiciary in particular, to engage in overt political criticism of the government will be considered in more detail below, see 4.9.)

  The qualifications for the position of Lord of Appeal in Ordinary will be considered later. They are referred to by their specific titles.

- *Lords Justices of Appeal.* This category, of which there may be up to 35 individuals, constitutes the majority of the judges in the Court of Appeal, although the other specific office holders considered previously may also sit in that court, as may High Court judges specifically requested so to do. They all used to be known as Lord Justice, even if they were female. The one present female member of the Court of Appeal, Elizabeth Butler-Sloss, had to be referred to by the male title because the Supreme Court Act 1981 had not considered the possibility of a woman holding such high judicial office. Now, however, the rules have been changed to permit her to be referred to as Lady Justice Butler-Sloss.

- *High Court judges.* These latter are sometimes referred to as *puisne* (pronounced pewnee) judges, in reference to their junior status in relation to those of superior status in the Supreme Court. There may be up to 98 such judges appointed. Judges are appointed to particular divisions depending on the amount of work needing to be conducted by that division, although they may be required to hear cases in different divisions and may be transferred from one division to another by the Lord Chancellor. Others, such as former High Court and Court of Appeal judges, or former circuit judges, or recorders, may be requested to sit as judges in the High Court. High Court judges are referred to by their name followed by the initial J.

- The Lord Chancellor may also appoint *deputy judges* of the High Court on a purely temporary basis in order to speed up the hearing of cases and to reduce any backlog that may have built up. The Heilbron Report on the operation of the civil justice system was critical of the use of deputy judges and recommended that more permanent High Court judges should be appointed if necessary. The maximum numbers were subsequently increased to their present level, but the use of deputy judges has continued to provide grounds for criticism of the operation of the legal system, and has led to suggestions that the use of second rate judges might eventually debase the whole judicial currency. This situation has to be considered within the context of the general arguments about the financial limitations within which the operation of the legal system is increasingly being required to operate, to the dismay and anger of many senior members of the judiciary.

- *Circuit judges*. Although there is only one Crown Court, it is divided into six distinct circuits which are serviced, in the main, by circuit judges who also sit as county court judges to hear civil cases. There are currently 562 circuit judges.

- *Recorders* are part time judges appointed to assist circuit judges in their functions in relation to criminal and civil law cases.

- *District judges*. This category of judge, previously referred to as registrars, are appointed on a full time and part time basis to hear civil cases in the county court.

- The situation of magistrates will be considered separately below and the situation of Chairmen of Tribunals will be considered in a later chapter.

4.2.2 Legal offices

In addition to these judicial positions, there are three legal offices which should be noted:

- *The Attorney General*, like the Lord Chancellor, is a political appointee whose role is to act as the legal adviser to the government. The Attorney General alone has the authority to prosecute in certain circumstances and appears for the Crown in important cases. The Solicitor General is the Attorney General's deputy.

- *The Director of Public Prosecutions* is the head of the national independent Crown Prosecution Service (CPS) established under the Prosecution of Offences Act 1985 to oversee the prosecution of criminal offences.

4.3　Appointment of judiciary

In the first of his Hamlyn Lectures of 1993, the then Lord Chancellor, Lord Mackay, stated that the pre-eminent qualities required by a judge are:

> ... good sound judgment based upon knowledge of the law, a willingness to study all sides of an argument with an acceptable degree of openness, and an ability to reach a firm conclusion and to articulate clearly the reasons for the conclusion.

Although the principal qualification for judicial office was experience of advocacy, Lord Mackay recognised that some people who have not practised advocacy may well have these necessary qualities to a great degree, as is reflected in the appointment of an academic and member of the Law Commission, Professor Brenda Hoggett, to the High Court in December 1993. Professor Hoggett, who sits as Mrs Justice Hale, is the first High Court judge not to have had a career as a practising barrister, although she qualified as a barrister in 1969 and was made Queen's Counsel in 1989.

The CLSA 1990 introduced major changes into the qualifications required for filling the positions of judges. Judicial appointment is still essentially dependent upon the rights of audience in the higher courts; but, at the same time as the CLSA effectively demolished the monopoly of the Bar to rights of audience in such courts, it opened up the possibility of achieving judicial office to legal practitioners other than barristers.

4.3.1　Qualifications

The main qualifications for appointment are as follows (the CLSA is dealt with in detail in 15.7):

- *Lord of Appeal in Ordinary*
  - o the holding of high judicial office for two years; or
  - o possession of a 15 year Supreme Court qualification under the CLSA.
- *Lord Justice of Appeal*
  - o the holding of a post as a High Court judge; or
  - o possession of a 10 year High Court qualification under the CLSA.
- *High Court judges*
  - o the holding of a post as a circuit judge for two years; or
  - o possession of a 10 year High Court qualification under the CLSA.

- *Deputy judges* must be qualified in the same way as permanent High Court judges.

- *Circuit judges*
  - the holding of a post as a recorder;
  - possession of either a 10 year Crown Court qualification or a 10 year county court qualification under the CLSA;
  - the holding of certain offices, such as district judge, Social Security Commissioner, chairman of an industrial tribunal, stipendiary magistrate for three years.

- *Recorders*
  - candidates must possess a 10 year Crown Court or county court qualification under the CLSA.

- *District judges*
  - require a seven year general qualification under the CLSA.

4.3.2   Selection of judges

The foregoing has concentrated on the specific requirements for those wishing to fulfil the role of judge; but it remains to consider the more general question relating to the general process whereby people are deemed suitable and selected for such office. All judicial appointments remain, theoretically, at the hands of the Crown. The Crown, however, is guided, if not actually dictated to, in regard to its appointment by the government of the day. Thus, as has been seen, the Lord Chancellor is a direct political appointment. The Prime Minister also advises the Crown on the appointment of other senior judicial office holders and the Law Lords, and Appeal Court judges. Such apparent scope for patronage in the hands of the Prime Minister has not gone without criticism. It has been suggested that the former Master of the Rolls, Sir John Donaldson, owed either his elevation or his previous failure to achieve such high office, at least in part, to his service in the Industrial Relations Court instituted by a former Conservative government in 1971 to pursue its trade union policies. It has also been suggested that Prime Ministers have vetoed recommendations made by Lord Chancellors.

Judges at the level of High Court judges and Circuit Bench are appointed by the Crown on the advice of the Lord Chancellor and the Lord Chancellor personally appoints district judges, lay magistrates and the members of some tribunals. This system has not gone without challenge either, the question being raised as to how the Chancellor actually reaches his decision to recommend or appoint individuals to judicial offices. It is accepted that the Lord Chancellor's recommendations are made on the basis of the opinions of the existing judiciary as to the suitability of the potential candidates. Although the Lord Chancellor's Department (LCD) published a guidance booklet entitled Judicial Appointments, the problem, or at least the suspicion shared by both the Bar and The Law Society, with the system is reflected in the widespread belief that it is over-secretive and leads to a highly conservative appointment policy. Judges are suspected, perhaps not unnaturally, of favouring those candidates who have not been troublesome in their previous cases and who have shown themselves to share the views and approaches of the existing office holders.

In his 1993 Hamlyn Lecture, Lord Mackay stated that the arrangements in the UK for the collection of data about candidates for the judiciary are comparatively well developed and provide those who have to take the decisions, essentially the Lord Chancellor himself, with fuller information than would otherwise be available to them. The reasoning behind this claim would appear to be that, because the procedure is secret and limited, people commenting on the suitability of candidates are willing to be more frank and open than would otherwise be the case were the references open to wider inspection. Such spurious justification is worrying in its complacency and its refusal to recognise that the secretive nature of the process might permit referees to make unsubstantiated derogatory comments that they would otherwise not feel free to make.

In 1994, advertisements were used, for the first time, to recruit likely candidates from the professions for the positions of assistant recorder, deputy district judge and circuit judge. In 1998, advertising was extended to appointments to the High Court Bench.

The first of such advertisements stated:

> The Lord Chancellor will recommend for appointment the candidates who appear to him to be best qualified regardless of ethnic origin, gender, marital status, sexual orientation, political affiliation, religion or (subject to the physical requirements of the office) disability.

This was seen as a practical step to address the matter of gender and race imbalance amongst the present judicial body. Currently, there are no women in the House of Lords, and only one in the Court of Appeal. In the High Court, the number is seven out of 98, and, of 562 circuit judges, 36 are women. At the level of recorders, there are 80 women from a total of 880; and, at district judge level, the number is 52 from 379 (www.open.gov.uk/lcd/judicial/senjud.htm) (February 1999).

Statistics relating to the ethnic origin of judges are more difficult to locate, but a survey carried out in 1997 estimated that only 1% of judges came from a non-white background, and all of those were sitting as circuit judges (Labour Research, July 1997).

Lord Irvine has continued this policy of encouraging women and people from ethnic backgrounds, or other minorities, to apply for judicial positions, encapsulated in his sound bite, 'Don't be shy! Apply!'. As he admitted:

Yes, it is true that many judges today are white, Oxbridge educated men. But, it is also true that they were appointed on merit, from the then available pool, at the time the vacancies arose ... It does not mean that the social composition of the judiciary is immutably fixed. For too long barristers were drawn from a narrow social background. As this changes over time, I would expect the composition of the Bench to change too. That is inherent in the merit principle. [Speech to the Association of Women Barristers, February 1998].

The 1997 Labour Research survey referred to previously, although admittedly carried out when Lord Irvine was only in his new job for two months, found that, in fact:

... even greater proportions of the judiciary attended Oxbridge universities than a decade earlier ...

Still, Lord Irvine remains optimistic, not to say bullish, about the way things are changing. As he points out:

... things are already on the move. In December 1994, 7.6% of the main tiers of the judiciary ... were women. It is now a little over 9%. Not a meteoric rise, true, but a steady one.

Accepting Lord Irvine's statistics, one certainly would have to agree that the change is not meteoric; in fact, at the rate he quotes, it would take 90 years for women to hold 50% of judicial offices.

A report on the judiciary carried out in 1992 by Justice, the British section of the International Commission of Jurists, recommended that a Judicial Commission should be established as the best way of reducing the strain on the administration of justice. It was suggested that such a commission should operate independently of the judiciary and should be responsible for: all judicial appointments, including lay magistrates and tribunals; all judicial training; the career development of all judges; the maintenance of levels of performance and dealing with complaints.

In September 1994, the Labour Party peer and spokesman on legal affairs, and former chairman of the Bar Council, Lord Williams of Mostyn, attacked the reforms introduced by Lord Mackay, categorising them as 'merely cosmetic tinkering to no lasting or sensible purpose ... offer[ing] nothing which is likely to improve either judicial performance or public confidence in the judiciary'. His article presented a powerful indictment of the system of judicial appointment, claiming that:

The present system, barely touched by the new changes, is secretive and ineffective. The first step is to apply to become an assistant recorder. That is, when the lock on the secret file creaks open. There is a file on every applicant. You cannot look at your file. You cannot ask who has commented on you. The cruellest error can remain unknown and uncorrected. The new system leaves all that firmly in place. The final decision about appointment remains in the hands of the Lord Chancellor.

Lord Williams maintained that a more fundamental reform of the judicial appointments procedure was called for and his preferred course of action would be for the Judicial Studies Board, which is currently responsible for training the judiciary, to be elevated to the level of a full judicial commission with responsibility for appointment as well as training.

Such proposals did not find favour with the then Lord Chancellor. In his Hamlyn Lecture, Lord Mackay indicated that he would not consider the introduction of an independent Judicial Appointments Commission, although he somewhat inconsistently admitted that:

> ... if one were to consider the establishment of a new system for the judiciary, such a body might be regarded as appropriate.

If such a body would be appropriate if a scheme were to be instituted *de novo*, then why should it not be introduced as a reform of the existing system? The answer could only lie in the Lord Chancellor's faith in, and conviction as to the success of, the operation of the existing procedure. It is suggested that such faith approached the level of wilful blindness and the conviction is unsafe, Somewhat surprisingly, Lord Irvine seems to have come round to a similar opinion. One of his earliest actions was to declare the governments intention to inquire into the merits of establishing a Judicial Appointments Commission, as Lord Mostyn had previously proposed. This now seems to have been dropped during the turbulent time when the highly contentious Access to Justice Act 1999 was being taken through Parliament.

As this book was being written, it looked as if secrecy surrounding the way in which judicial and other legal offices are filled was about to be opened up to scrutiny, to the dismay and discomfort of all of those involved. When the government appointed a new Treasury Devil in 1998, that is, their chief advocate in the civil courts, senior members of the judiciary were consulted about the suitability of the candidates on the usual secret basis. However, when the appointment went to a male member of the Lord Chancellor's ex-chambers, a woman candidate registered a claim for sex discrimination in relation to the appointment. As result of this action, the then Attorney General, John Morris, who made the appointment, would have been required to disclose details of the process leading to the decision, which included representations made by senior judges. The soundings were actually taken by the Attorney General's deputy, the Solicitor General, Lord Falconer at the time. Lord Falconer, however, was himself a close personal friend of the Prime Minister and his wife, who were both, once, members of the Lord Chancellor's chambers. It would at least appear, therefore, that there was a measure of the legitimate dubiety about the procedure, especially when it is alleged that all of the people sounded out were men, including the Lord Chancellor, and at least two others were intimates of the Blairs and the Lord Chancellor. This case merely compounded the Lord Chancellor's misfortune in his and/or his department's appointment policy, in that he had already been found to have appointed a member of staff in breach of the sex discrimination legislation. Fortunately for all those involved, although not for those who wished to see the appointment procedures opened up to scrutiny, the matter was resolved, and the case dropped, when the Attorney General agreed to pay £5,000 to a charity promoting the rights of women.

A different approach, following the example of the US, might be for the holders of the higher judicial offices to be subjected to confirmation hearings by, for example, a select committee of the House of Commons. Lord Mackay dismissed any such possibility as follows:

> The tendency of prior examination ... is to discover and analyse the previous opinions of the individual in detail. *I question whether the standing of the judiciary in our country, or the public's confidence in it, would be enhanced by such an inquiry,* or whether any wider public interest would be served by it [emphasis added].

It is perhaps unfortunate that the italicised words in the above passage can be interpreted in a way that no doubt Lord Mackay did not intend but which, nonetheless, could suggest a cover up of the dubious opinions of those appointed to judicial office.

An even more radical alternative would be to open judicial office holding to election as they also do in the US, although in this case one might well agree with Lord Mackay that:

> The British people would not feel that this was a very satisfactory method of appointing the professional judiciary.

Alternatively, and following Lord Mackay's emphasis on the professional nature of the judiciary, the UK could follow continental examples and provide the judiciary with a distinct professional career structure as an alternative to legal practice. (For a consideration of the way in which other jurisdictions appoint their judges, readers are referred to a 1991 Law Society Research Study No 5 entitled *Judicial Appointments* by Eleni Skordaki.)

Such alternative suggestions would not eradicate all questions of the judges impartiality but they would certainly be an improvement on the existing system. For, as things stand at present, the lack of transparency in the appointment procedure merely clouds a more fundamental question, which can be posed in two forms: first, whether the best people are being selected from the available pool of talent; or, alternatively, and more radically, whether the present procedure ensures the appointment of the wrong type of judge generally.

4.4   Training of the judiciary

All judicial training, from the induction of new magistrates (see 4.8.3) to the honing of the skills of the judges in the House of Lords, is the responsibility of the Judicial Studies Board (JSB). Prior to the establishment of the JSB, the training of judges in the UK was almost minimal; especially when considered in the light of the Continental practice, where being a judge, rather than practising as an advocate, is a specific, and early, career choice which leads to specialist and extensive training.

The JSB provides training and instruction to all part time and full time judges in judicial skills. An essential element of the philosophy of the JSB is that the training is provided by judges for judges. The training requirements of the different jurisdictions are the responsibility of five committees (Criminal, Civil, Tribunals, Family and Magisterial). Another committee, the Equal Treatment Advisory Committee, provides advice and support for all five committees. The JSB membership is drawn mainly from the judiciary, but also includes some leading academics and other professionals. The JSB enjoys considerable autonomy from its parent department, the LCD, in deciding the need for and nature of judicial training

Assistant recorders are required to attend seminars on procedure and sentencing before they can sit on their own in the Crown Court. Later, training takes the form of further, intermittent seminars focusing primarily on sentencing. Those sitting in the Crown Court benefit specifically from the advice contained in the *Crown Court Bench Book of Specimen Directions*, which, as Lord Bingham states in the foreword to the most recent edition, 1997, are likely to provide useful source material which will in turn assist in the resolution of the problem under consideration. The specific nature of the Specimen Directions is a delicate matter, as they do not, and indeed cannot, represent an unconditional statement of what the law, and judicial practice, is. They always have to be adapted by the judges to fit particular circumstances. Such a fact has to be recognised, and, indeed, it is enforced by an injunction not to reproduce the directions as a part of any commercial activity. Nonetheless, it is made available on the Internet at: www.cix.co.uk/~jsb/specdir/index.htm.

The topic of judicial training raises the related question of the general competence of judges to decide particular cases when they may have been appointed to courts having jurisdiction in areas where they have had no previous practical experience and very little knowledge. That such appointments are made is a common enough practice, but its deleterious effect was highlighted by PJ Richardson in the preface to the 1995 edition of *Archbold*, the leading work on criminal procedure, in which he claimed that:

> Some of those who sit hearing criminal appeals have little or no practical experience of criminal law ... [consequently] the judgments get longer; authorities of apparent relevance are not cited or are overlooked.

The seriousness of the situation is emphasised in Richardson's prescription to remedy the problem:

> ... the identification of a nucleus of judges with experience of practice in the criminal courts and a common understanding of the principles of criminal liability, the rules of procedure and evidence and the considerations relevant to sentencing discretion.

If those hearing criminal appeals do not presently have such basic understanding, then the situation is certainly grave and requires immediate remedial action.

Also, as has been pointed out earlier in this chapter, doubts have been raised as to the knowledge and competence of the senior judiciary with specific regard to issues relating to human rights and civil liberties. Such doubts become pressing, with the introduction of the HRA 1998, and the potential development of the House of Lords as a Constitutional Court.

It should be noted, however, that today judicial training has probably never been of greater public concern nor been executed with such rigour since the JSB was established in 1979. A number of factors have precipitated this change. As we note in the preface to this book, the machinery and processes of law have undergone great change during the last few years. Consequently, the judiciary has been subject to thorough re-training in the new civil procedure (see Chapter 11). This training has included residential seminars for all full time and part time judges dealing with civil work, local training, and conferences held at various national locations. Similarly, following the incorporation of the European Convention on Human Rights into English law by the HRA 1998, the government set aside £4.5 million for human rights judicial training during 1999–2000. This budget for this enormous project included £1.6 million for the JSB, and £1 million for the Court Service to provide cover for judges who were in training.

Another consideration here should be the growth of consumer awareness. Frances Gibb has argued this point (see 'Rude judges must mind their language' (1999) *The Times*, 29 June). She notes that we inhabit an era of litigants who know their rights and expect good service, and that judges are under greater scrutiny than in previous times. In April 1999, the LCD published figures showing that, from August 1998 (when data was first collected), 2,109 complaints were made against judges. Most, however, were against the actual judicial decision which the Lord Chancellor cannot investigate without violating the principle of the independence of the judiciary. Only 183 cases were investigated because they involved serious allegations about the conduct of the judge. Following that, five judges were sent letters by the LCD. The Director of Studies at the JSB, Judge Paul Collins, observes that, as there are over 5,000 full time and part time judges making hundreds of decisions, the number of complaints upheld is relatively small.

In 1988, there were 2,000 judicial training days (days when any one judge is training, not sitting). In 1999, the number will be more than 10,000 (*Judicial Studies Board Annual Report*, 1999, London: HMSO). In 1999, for the first time, JSB training will include new guidance for all judges on equal treatment issues such as disability, gender and sexual orientation, and litigants-in-person. Equal treatment training is now integral to all induction courses. Lord Justice Waller's (chairman of the JSB) attitude is encouraging:

> There is absolutely no room for complacency in these areas. And I am not going to say just because someone has been on our course, they will be perfect, but I hope that, as result, judges are better equipped to do their jobs [(1999) *The Times*, 13 July].

4.4.1 Runciman Commission's recommendations

The nature of the training undergone by barristers and judges was one of the issues considered by the Runciman Commission (1993). In relation to the judiciary, the Commission made several recommendations:

- that substantially more resources be allocated to judicial training in general;

- that training courses should involve a mixture of people from different agencies and disciplines within the criminal justice system and should not just be judge focused;

- that experienced judges should monitor the performance of those judges undergoing training;

- that judges should be required to attend refresher training courses every three years;

- that assistant recorders should receive their first refresher training two years after their initial training.

In particular, emphasis was placed on the need to ensure that judges were conscious of their situation in a multi-ethnic society, and it was specifically recommended:

- that there should be an increased effort to improve and extend the existing training of judges in the awareness of race issues;

- the question of judicial attitudes to women was apparently not as crucial in the view of the committee, as is evident in its recommendation that consideration should be given to extending such training to cover an awareness of gender issues;

- a further contentious suggestion of the committee was that judges should be subject to appraisal. Thus, it recommended that the Lord Chancellor should look to establishing a formal system of performance appraisal with presiding and resident judges having a leading role in the procedure; and

- that members of the Bar should be able to comment on the performance of judges.

It is gratifying to note that the JSB, in recognising the need for, and in implementing the provision of, necessary training, has gone a long way to accommodate the recommendations of Runciman.

4.4.2   Judicial reaction to race awareness training

The JSB has instituted seminars for training part time and circuit judges in racial awareness, for example, reminding them that, in a multi-cultural/multi-faith society, it is offensive to ask for peoples' Christian names, as well as warning them as to the dangers of even more crassly offensive language and racial stereotyping that appears to be so much a part of the English use of metaphor. It has been reported, however, that such training has met with resistance. Lincoln Crawford, a barrister, part time judge, Bar Council member and former member of the Commission for Racial Equality, has commented on the existence of such resistance, in *Counsel* (February 1994), the journal of the Bar. In his article, he lists a number of reasons why judges are opposed to the training. First, there is the belief that judges apply the law fairly and do not need to be trained in race awareness for the simple reason that they are not racist in their outlook or practice. Such an assertion sits uncomfortably, however, with the documented research that reveals that black defendants found guilty of offences are treated more harshly than equivalent white defendants. Secondly, this initial approach is supported by an attitude that considers it to be an affront to the independence of their judgments to require judges to try to take account of the different cultural backgrounds of those black and Asian people who come before them. (One white judge actually remarked that he had been called nigger at his school and that it had not caused him any harm.) Thirdly, Crawford claims, there is a bloody-mindedness amongst the judiciary, representing the view that they operate the British legal system and that anyone within the jurisdiction should take the law as they find it, even if it is partial and discriminatory in its lack of sympathy for other cultural values. The fourth justification for resistance to race awareness training is the view that it smacks of interference with the impartiality and independence of the judiciary, the implication being that judges should not be held to account even when they are operating in a questionable if not a patently discriminatory manner.

All of the foregoing supposed justifications are completely spurious and represent a denial of the cultural existence of a large section of British society. As Lincoln Crawford puts it:

A judiciary which fears and feels nervous about plurality and diversity runs the danger of becoming closed, narrow and brittle.

It also runs the danger of completely alienating large sections of the population over which it exercises its power and, when law is reduced to the level of mere power rather than legitimate authority, its effectiveness is correspondingly reduced.

There was a surge of public resentment when a truly shocking example of judicial insensitivity, not to say stupidity, came to light. At the annual dinner of the Criminal Bar Association, High Court Judge Graham Boal told a joke, much more offensive than it was funny, which was, at one and the same time, sexist, homophobic, racist and antagonistic to measures being taken to address such prejudices within the legal profession and the judiciary. When the circumstances were leaked to the newspapers by those at the dinner who were genuinely shocked by his behaviour, the consequent uproar resulted in the Lord Chancellor writing a strong letter of rebuke to Boal, warning him as to his future conduct. Lord Justice Waller, the chairman of the JSB, suggests that such incidents are becoming fewer as a result of judicial training.

He contends that remarks such as those of Judge Boal will be:

> ... picked up and brandished across the headlines and, in one sense, the judge deserves it. Yet, the rest of the judiciary is doing its job perfectly well. Most judges in this modern day are as courteous and sensitive as their predecessors were not [(1999) *The Times*, 13 July].

But, of continuing concern is the fact that some of the audience actually laughed at his attempt at humour. Following the finding of institutionalised racism within the police force by the Macpherson Inquiry into the murder of Stephen Lawrence, such behaviour cannot but raise questions as to the institutional culture of the bench, and the legal profession generally. The removal of rights to jury trial in relation to each way offences, in the light of contrary representations made by and on behalf of the black community, by such people as Courtney Griffiths QC, would seem merely to emphasise the perceived, even if unsubstantiated, doubts about the extent of racism within that culture.

4.5 Retirement of judges

All judges are now required to retire at 70, although they may continue in office at the discretion of the Lord Chancellor. The Judicial Pensions and Retirement Act 1993 reduced the retirement age from the previous 75 years for High Court judges and 72 years for other judges.

The reduction of the retirement age may have been designed to reduce the average age of the judiciary, but of perhaps even more significance in this respect is the change that was introduced at the same time in judicial pensions. The new provision requires judges to have served for 20 years, rather than the previous 15, before they qualify for full pension rights. This effectively means that, if judges are to benefit from full pension rights, they will have to take up their appointments by the time they are 50. Given that judges are predominantly appointed from the ranks of high earning QCs, this will either reduce their potential earnings at the Bar or reduce their pay package as judges by approximately 7.5%. This measure led to a great deal of resentment within both the Bar and the judiciary, Lord Chief Justice Taylor referring to its unfairness and meanness; and was one of the issues that fuelled the antagonism between Lord Mackay and the other members of the judiciary.

In any event, according to the statistics provided by the Lord Chancellor's Department, the average age for the Law Lords is 65.5, with Lord Slynn being the oldest at 69, and Lord Hope the youngest at 60. In the Court of Appeal, the average age is almost 62, with youngest being Sir John Laws at 53 and the oldest, Sir Alexander Beldam, at 74. Apart from Lord Irvine, who is a mere 58, the average age of the four other Heads of Division in the High Court is 67, this being considerably raised by Sir Stephen Brown who is 74.

4.6   Removal of judges

Reference has already been made to the need, with of course the exception of the Lord Chancellorship, to protect the independence of the judiciary, by making it difficult for a discomforted government to remove judges from their positions on merely political grounds. The actual provision is that judges of the House of Lords, the Court of Appeal and the High Court hold their office during good behaviour, subject to the proviso that they can be removed by the Crown on the presentation of an address by both Houses of Parliament. In actual fact, this procedure has never been used in relation to an English judge, although it was once used in 1830 to remove an Irish judge who was found guilty of misappropriating funds.

Judges below the level of the High Court do not share the same degree of security of tenure as their more senior colleagues, and can be removed, on grounds of misbehaviour or incapacity, by the action of the Lord Chancellor who does not require the sanction of Parliament. Although the famous/infamous Judge Pickles was notoriously the object of the displeasure of the Lord Chancellor in the mid- to late-1980s, he was never actually dismissed and, as yet, the only judge to be removed for misbehaviour remains the circuit judge who, in 1983, was found guilty of smuggling cigarettes and alcohol.

In a letter circulated in July 1994, Lord Mackay asked that judges inform him immediately if they are ever charged with any criminal offence, other than parking or speeding violations. The Lord Chancellor stated that he wished to make it clear that a conviction for drunk driving would amount, *prima facie*, to misbehaviour. Causing offence on racial or religious grounds could also be seen as misbehaviour, as could sexual harassment.

The discretionary power of the Lord Chancellor not to extend the appointment of a recorder, without the need to explain or justify his action, has previously provided grounds for criticism of, and accusations of political interference on the part of, the Lord Chancellor.

Stipendiary magistrates are subject to removal by the Crown on the recommendation of the Lord Chancellor and lay magistrates are subject to removal by the Lord Chancellor without cause or explanation.

4.7   Judicial immunity from suit

A fundamental measure to ensure the independence of the judiciary is the rule that they cannot be sued in relation to things said or acts done in their judicial capacity in good faith. The effect of this may be seen in *Sirros v Moore* (1975) in which a judge wrongly ordered someone's detention. It was subsequently held by the Court of Appeal that, although the detention had been unlawful, no action could be taken against the judge as he had acted in good faith in his judicial capacity. Although some judges, on occasion, may be accused of abusing this privilege, it is nonetheless essential if judges are to operate as independent representatives of the law, for it is unlikely that judges would be able to express their honest opinions of the law and the situations in which it is being applied, if they were to be subject to suits from disgruntled participants.

Given the increased use of the doctrine of *ultra vires* to justify legal action by way of judicial review against members of the executive, it is satisfyingly ironic that at least one judge, Stephen Sedley, sees the possibility of a similar *ultra vires* action providing grounds for an action against judges in spite of their previously assumed legal immunity. As he expresses the point, in the *London Review of Books* of April 1994:

> Judges have no authority to act maliciously or corruptly. It would be rational to hold that such acts take them outside their jurisdiction and so do not attract judicial immunity.

No doubt, such a suggestion would be anathema to the great majority of the judiciary, but the point remains: why should judges be at liberty to abuse their position of authority in a way that no other public servant can?

Before 1991, magistrates could be liable for damages for actions done in excess of their actual authority but the CLSA 1990 extended the existing immunity from the superior courts to cover the inferior courts, so magistrates now share the same protection as other judges.

It is worth stating at this point that this immunity during court proceedings also extends as far as advocates and witnesses, and of course jurors; although the controls of perjury and contempt of court are always available to control what is said or done in the course of court proceedings.

Related to, although distinct from, the principle of immunity from suit is the convention that individual judges should not be subject to criticism in parliamentary debate, unless subject to an address for their removal: legal principles and the law in general can be criticised but not judges.

4.8   Magistrates

The foregoing has concentrated attention on the professional and legally qualified judges. There are, however, some 30,000 unpaid part time lay magistrates and 92 full time professional stipendiary magistrates operating within some 700 or so magistrates courts in England. These magistrates are empowered to hear and decide a wide variety of legal matters and the amount and importance of the work they do should not be underestimated: 97% of all criminal cases are dealt with by the magistrates' court.

4.8.1   Powers

Magistrates' courts have considerable power in relation to both criminal and civil procedure.

- *Criminal law*

  Magistrates are empowered to try summary cases, that is, cases which are triable without a jury. Additionally, however, they may deal with cases triable either way, that is, cases which can either be tried summarily by the magistrates, or which can be tried on indictment before a jury in the Crown Court. (See 3.15 and 14.8.)

  In relation to summary offences, the maximum prison sentence magistrates can impose is six months, even in relation to consecutive sentences in relation to more than one offence (Magistrates Courts Act 1980). The maximum fine that can be imposed for a summary offence is £1,000 under the Criminal Justice Act 1991.

  The above represent general maxima and particular statutes may impose a lesser maximum penalty; nor should it be forgotten that magistrates can impose alternative sentences, such as community service orders, or probation orders. They can also discharge offenders either conditionally or absolutely.

  In relation to offences triable either way, magistrates courts have increased sentencing powers. In these circumstances, although the maximum prison sentence that can be awarded in relation to a single offence is still six months, they can, in cases where more than one offence is involved, impose consecutive prison sentences up to a maximum of 12 months. They may also impose a maximum fine of £5,000.

In addition to the foregoing sentences, magistrates can issue compensation orders. Such orders are not used as a means of punishing the offender but as a way of compensating the victims of the offender without them having to sue the offender in the civil courts. Compensation orders can, however, be issued without the imposition of any other sentence. The maximum payment under any such order is £5,000.

It should also be recalled (see 3.15.3) that the magistrates' court also sits as a youth court, with its members drawn from a special panel of Justices of the Peace, to hear criminal cases involving individuals below the age of 18.

- *Civil law*

Magistrates most significant area of civil law jurisdiction is in family law cases, particularly under the Children Act 1989 and the Domestic Proceedings and Magistrates' Courts Act 1978. In such cases, they sit as a Family Proceedings Court.

They also have powers relating to the collection of such civil debts as water, gas and electricity charges and for the council tax, the replacement for the former community charge or poll tax. They also sit as a licensing court and consider applications for the provision of liquor licences.

- *Crime and Disorder Act 1998*

Since April 1999, the magistrates' courts now have an important new role in awarding Anti-Social Behaviour Orders under the Crime and Disorder Act 1998 (see 1.2.5).

According to the Home Office guide to the Act, its intentions are to: introduce measures designed to reduce delays by bringing cases to court promptly, but, on closer examination, it looks suspiciously like another economy driven measure in relation to the criminal justice system. Section 48 allows metropolitan stipendiary magistrates to sit alone in youth courts. Section 49 allows specific powers of magistrates courts to be exercised by single magistrates or, indeed, and perhaps of even more concern, by magistrates clerks. Clerks, however, will not be allowed to remand accused into custody, or decide disputes in relation to bail. Section 53 provides that members of the CPS, who are not Crown Prosecutors, may be designated by the Director of Public Prosecutions to perform the functions of prosecutors in magistrates' courts. This power is only intended to be used in relation to straightforward guilty pleas and proof in absence in motoring cases. It specifically does not apply in relation to: contested trials; indictable only cases; and cases where the magistrates have declined jurisdiction or the defendant has elected for jury trial.

4.8.2   District Judges (Magistrates' Courts)

Stipendiary magistrates, so called because they are paid a salary, are legally qualified, being required under the Justices of the Peace Act 1979 to be barristers or solicitors of at least seven years standing. Following the Access to Justice Act 1999 (s 78), stipendiary magistrates are to be called District Judges (Magistrates' Courts).

There are currently 92 such magistrates sitting in London and other urban centres. The advantage of the stipendiaries over the lay magistrates, apart from the obvious fact that they are legally qualified, is that they are full time and sit alone. This allows for a potentially greater through-put of cases; but advantages in efficiency have to be weighed against corresponding professionalisation of the judicial process and the loss in terms of the democratising effect of the lay magistracy. However, given the apparent lack of confidence that exists in the lay magistracy, perhaps such increased professionalisation would be no bad thing, although it would only come at a price, and an expensive one at that. The Runciman Report made two specific recommendations in relation to stipendiary magistrates:

(a) that there should be a more systematic approach to the role of stipendiary magistrates in order to make best use of their special skills and qualifications;

(b) that the whole administration of the stipendiary magistrates system be overhauled.

The Access to Justice Act 1999 (s 78) amends the Justice of the Peace Act 1997, to unify the Metropolitan and Provincial salaried magistrates benches so that we now have just one bench of District Judges (Magistrates' Courts). This is not an entirely uncontroversial change because whereas local magistrates were once regarded (like police forces) as being intrinsically local and beyond the reach of central governmental powers, the new arrangement can be seen as increasing the potential influence of the LCD over local justice. Another viewpoint, however, and the reason advanced by the government for the change, is that a single bench will improve the geographic consistency of sentencing.

4.8.3   Qualifications and training

There is no requirement for lay magistrates to have any legal qualifications. On being accepted onto the bench, however, magistrates undertake a training process, under the auspices of the JSB. Magistrates are required to attend training courses, with a special emphasis being placed on Equal Treatment Training. The way in which the training programme seeks to overcome conceptions as to the politically limited nature of the magistracy is evident in the content of the extensive training materials produced for the magistrates.

These include modules on: raising awareness and challenging discrimination; discretion and decision making; prejudice and stereotype; so the overall emphasis may be seen to be on equality of people, and equality of treatment. There is, however, a new emphasis on the practical skills involved in performing the duties placed on magistrates, and, consequently, much of the training will actually be based on sitting as a magistrate, with the input of specially trained monitors to give guidance and advice on how the new magistrate performs their tasks, and fulfils their role.

The training course is designed to give new magistrates an understanding of the functions and powers of the bench generally and to locate that understanding within the context of national practice, particularly with regard to sentencing. On the topic of discretion and sentencing, Lord Irvine provided the magistrates with the following strong advice, not to say warning:

> You ... must exercise your discretion in individual cases with great care within a system that needs to secure continuing public confidence. This is what makes the sentencing guidelines produced by the Magistrates Association so important. They are guidelines they do not curtail your independent discretion to impose sentences you think are right, case by case. But the guidelines exist to help you in that process, to give you more information in reaching your decision. And they help to assist the magistracy, to maintain an overall consistency of approach ... I urge you to follow the guidelines, which are drawn up for your benefit and the magistracy as a whole [Speech to the Council of Magistrates Association, March 1999].

Although particular key legal issues may be considered in the course of the training, it is not the intention to provide the magistrate with a complete grasp of substantive law and legal practice. Indeed, to expect such would be to misunderstand both the role of the magistrates and the division of responsibility within the magistrates court. Every bench of magistrates has a legally qualified justices clerk, whose function it is to advise the bench on questions of law, practice, and procedure; leaving matters of fact to magistrates to decide upon (see 3.16.1).

4.8.4 Appointment

Under the JPA 1997, magistrates are appointed to, and indeed removed from, office by the Lord Chancellor, on behalf of the Queen, after consultation with local advisory committees. There are currently 111 such advisory committees, and 134 sub-committees within the UK. Section 50 of the Employment Rights Act 1996 provides that employers are obliged to release their employees, for such time as is reasonable, to permit them to serve as magistrates. In the event of an employer refusing to sanction absence from work to perform magistrates duties, the employee can take the matter before an employment tribunal. Understandably, there is no statutory requirement for the employer to pay their employees in their absence, but magistrates are entitled to claim expenses for loss of earnings in the exercise of their office.

Proposals for office tend to be generated by local interest groups, such as political parties, trade unions, chambers of commerce and such like bodies, and this limited constituency may give rise to the view that the magistracy only represents the attitudes of a limited section of society. In a multi-cultural, multi-racial society, it is essential that the magistrates court should reflect the composition of the wider society, and the rules relating to the appointment, and training, of magistrates do, at least in theory, support this conclusion. Nonetheless, there remains a lingering doubt, at least in the minds of particular constituencies, that the magistracy still represents the values, both moral and political, of a limited section of society. A further significant step towards opening up the whole procedure of appointing magistrates was taken when local advisory committees were granted the power to advertise for people to put themselves forward for selection. As the chairman of the Mid-Staffordshire Magistrates' Bench stated in a local newspaper, although previously rank and social position were the main qualifications, nowadays:

> ... it is important a bench has a balance of sexes, professions and political allegiances.

Given the current proposal to increase the cases to be decided by magistrates, it is to be hoped that the appointment and training procedures will give the general public more confidence in the much vaunted representational function of the magistrates' courts.

According to the former Lord Chancellor, Lord Mackay, in the first of his 1993 Hamlyn Lectures, magistrates should possess qualities of fairness, a judicial temperament and a willingness to hear both sides of a case. These desired attributes are supported by the current guidance notes to the application form for becoming a magistrate, which set out six key qualities to be looked for in an applicant:

(a) good character;

(b) understanding and communication;

(c) social awareness;

(d) maturity and sound temperament;

(e) sound judgment; and

(f) commitment and reliability.

Once candidates of a suitable quality have been identified, the local advisory committee is placed under the injunction to have regard to the need to ensure that the composition of the bench broadly reflects the community which it serves, in terms of gender, ethnic origin, geographical spread, occupation and political affiliation. It may even be that individuals, who are otherwise suitably qualified, may not be appointed, if their presence would exacerbate a perceived imbalance in the existing bench. However, in 1998, the LCD issued a consultation paper entitled *Political Balance in the Lay Magistracy*, relating to the political balance in the lay magistracy (www.open.gov.uk/lcd/consult/general/jp-pol.htm). The paper suggested that political affiliation is no longer a major issue, and therefore may not have to be controlled in relation to the make up of benches of magistrates. As support for its suggestion, the consultancy document makes three points. First, that actually ensuring a political balance on the bench raises:

> ... the danger of creating a perception that politics do play a part in the administration of justice, notwithstanding that it is agreed on all sides that, in a mature democracy, politics have no place in the court room.

Secondly, that advisory committees:

> ... have increasingly found that many magistrates have declined to provide the information [relating to their political allegiance] or classed themselves as uncommitted.

Thirdly, it claimed that, in any case, geodemographic classification schemes, based on an analysis of particular personal attributes, such as ethnicity, gender, marital status, occupation, home ownership, car owning status, are much more sensitive indicators for achieving social balance on benches than stated political allegiance.

This may well represent the emergence of the truly classless society. Alternatively, it might represent a worrying denial of the importance of political attitudes within law generally, and the magistrates' bench in particular.

The report of the Runciman Commission recommended that magistrates be given the power to decide more cases by taking away the defendants right to elect for a trial on indictment in certain situations. This recommendation was subsequently adopted by the current Home Secretary, Jack Straw. In support of its recommendation, the Commission referred to research that revealed that, for offences that could be tried either way, that is, by either the magistrates' court or before a jury in the Crown Court, the chances of acquittal are substantially higher in the Crown Court (57%) than in the magistrates' courts (30%). The report of the Commission stated that defendants should not be entitled to choose a particular mode of trial just because they thought it offered them a better chance of acquittal. The question that has to be asked in response to this is: why not? Because Crown Courts acquit more defendants than magistrates' courts does not necessarily mean that the Crown Court procedure is inappropriate. The problem may lie not with the Crown Court, but with the magistrates' courts. This matter will be considered in more detail in 14.8.5 and 14.8.6 but, for the present, it has to be recognised that the Runciman Report did nothing to address the fact that the magistrates' courts are more likely than the Crown Court to convict, and that this gives rise to, at least, the perception of the Crown Court being a fairer forum in which to decide cases; or, alternatively, the suspicion that the magistrates' courts are not as just as they might be.

4.9 Legal reasoning

There is a long running controversy as to the relationship of law and logic and the actual extent to which legal decisions are the outcome of, and limited by, logical processes. At times, lawyers have sought to reject what is seen as the rigid inflexibility inherent in logical reasoning in favour of flexibility and discretion. As the American Supreme Court Judge, eminent legal writer, and proponent of Legal Realism, Oliver Wendel Holmes, expressed it: 'The life of the law has not been logic, it has been experience' (*The Common Law* (1881)).

The implication of this position is that the law is no more than a mechanism for solving particular problems and that judges should operate in such a way as to ensure the best possible result, even if this means ignoring previously established legal rules.

At other times, however, the courts have appeared to base and justify their decisions on the working out of deterministic formal rules of law, categorised in such phrases as, 'The Law is the Law and the Law must run its course'. The suggestion behind such expressions of the Declaratory Theory of Law is that the judge is no more than the voice of an autonomous legal system that he, through his legal training, is able to gain access to but is in no way able to influence. If, as the declaratory theory of law maintains, judges do no more than give expression to already existing legal principles and rules, then the particular views, opinions, or prejudices of the judiciary are of absolutely no consequence. If such a representation were accurate, then the logical conclusion would be that judges could be replaced by a computerised expert system which could be programmed to make decisions on the basis of a strict application of general rules. It is doubtful, however, if anyone would actually accept such a suggestion. It cannot be denied that the bulk of cases are decided on the simple application of the legal rules to the particular facts of the case with little or no consideration of the legal principles. In other cases, however, the straightforward and automatic application of a legal rule might lead to the possibility of injustice.

(For those particularly interested in the possibility of developing computer models of judicial reasoning and decision making, see Allen, Aikenhead and Widdison, 'Computer simulation of judicial behaviour', www.webjcli.ncl.ac.uk/1998/issue3/allen3.html.)

Hard cases are decided on the basis of judicial reaction to the immediate facts of the case. Such a situation, however, is clearly antithetical to the declaratory theory of law.

These hard cases demand a consideration of the legal principles involved in order to achieve a just result. They may therefore be decided other than on the strict application of the law as it had been previously expressed. It should be pointed out that such cases are usually the province of the higher courts and of particularly active judges within those courts. The old maxim/cliché that hard cases make bad law should also be borne in mind. (The career of Lord Denning might be cited as an example of this procedure and its shortcomings. Reference should be made to material covered previously in 2.3 for a more detailed consideration of the problems inherent in judicial law making and reform.)

4.9.1 The syllogism in law

Some statutory provisions and also some common law rules can be expressed in the form of a logical syllogism. For example, the offence of theft may be reduced into such a formulation:

If A dishonestly appropriates B's property with the intention of permanently depriving B of it, then A is guilty of theft.

A has done this.

Therefore, A is guilty of theft.

This, however, represents an oversimplification of the structure of statute but, more importantly, the effect of concentrating on the logical form of the offence tends to marginalise the key issues in the relation to its actual application. As has been stated previously, the great majority of cases are decided on the truth of the premises rather than the formal validity of the argument used. In other words, argument will concentrate primarily on whether A actually did the act or not, and, secondly, on whether A appropriated the property either dishonestly or with the intention of permanently depriving B of it. Those are questions of fact not logic.

4.9.2 The logical form of precedent

The operation of the rules of precedent appears, at first sight, to involve a similar operation of deductive logic to that applied in statute law: the judge merely applies the legal principle established in the precedent to the facts in hand to determine the outcome of the case. Thus:

Precedent: in case X involving particular circumstances, legal principle Y was applied leading to conclusion Z.

Instant case: in case W similar circumstances to those in X have occurred.

Therefore: principle Y must be applied to reach a conclusion similar to Z.

A closer consideration of the actual procedure involved in precedent, however, will reveal that it is not totally accurate to categorise precedent as a form of deductive reasoning.

In looking for a precedent on which to base a decision, judges are faced with a large number of cases from which to select. It is extremely unlikely that judges will find an authority which corresponds precisely to the facts of the case before them. What they have to do is to find an analogous case and use its reasoning to decide the case before them. This use of analogy to decide cases is prone to the same shortcomings as were revealed in the previous consideration of reasoning from analogy in general. The major difficulty is the need to ensure the validity of the analogy made, if the conclusion drawn is to be valid. There is, no doubt, considerable merit in the wish for similar cases to be treated similarly but given the lack of precision that is inherent in the process of reasoning by analogy it is not altogether certain that such a wish will be met.

A further reason why the operation of precedent cannot simply be considered as an example of deductive reasoning relates to the process through which the precedent is actually determined once an analogous case has been selected. The binding element in any precedent is the *ratio decidendi* of the decision. In delivering his decision, the judge does not separate the *ratio* of the case from other *obiter* comments. As has been considered previously, the *ratio* is a legal abstraction from the concrete facts of the case in which it appears and, in practice, it is for judges in subsequent cases to determine the *ratio* of any authority. The determination of the *ratio* and thus the precedent in a previous case may be seen as a process of inductive reasoning, in that the judge in the present case derives the general principle of the *ratio* from the particular facts of the previous case. This move from the particular to the general is by its nature inductive. The point to be remembered here is that, as was considered in relation to reasoning in general, the use of inductive reasoning cannot claim the certainty inherent in the use of deductive reasoning. The introduction of this increased element of uncertainty is inescapable and unconscious but it is also appropriate to note that the determination of precedent by later courts gives the later judges scope to consciously manipulate precedents. This is achieved by the later judges formulating the *ratio* of a previous case in the light of their opinion as to what it should have been, rather than what it might actually have been. In other words, they have the scope to substitute their version of the *ratio* even if it contradicts what the original judge thought the *ratio* was.

Thus, the apparent deductive certainty of the use of precedent is revealed to be based on the much less certain use of inductive reasoning and reasoning by analogy, with even the possibility of personal views of the judges playing some part in deciding cases. This latter factor introduces the possibility that judges do not in fact use any form of logical reasoning to decide their cases but simply deliver decisions on the basis of an intuitive response to the facts of the case and the situation of the parties involved. The suggestion has been made that the judges decide the outcome of the case first of all, and only then seek some *post hoc* legal justification for their decision; and given the huge number of precedents from which they are able to choose, they have no great difficulty in finding such support as they require. The process of logical reasoning can be compared to the links in a chain, but a more fitting metaphor for judicial reasoning would be to compare it with the legs of a chair: forced into place to support the weight of a conclusion reached *a priori*. Some critics have even gone so far as to deny the existence of legal reasoning altogether as a method of determining decisions and have suggested that references to such is no more than a means of justifying the social and political decisions that judges are called upon to make.

In conclusion, however, it is not suggested that legal reasoning does not employ the use of logic but neither can it be asserted that it is only a matter of logic. Perhaps the only conclusion that can be reached is that legal reasoning as exercised by the judiciary is an amalgam; part deductive, part inductive, part reasoning by analogy with an added mixture of personal intuition not to say personal prejudice.

4.9.3 Statutory interpretation

A particular aspect of legal reasoning, and one which also raises questions as to the political persuasion of judges and the scope they have to exercise that persuasion in their decisions, relates specifically to the manner in which the judges interpret statutes when they are called upon to do so.

Problems in interpreting legislation

The accepted view is that the constitutional role of the judiciary is simply to apply the law. The function of creating law is the prerogative of Parliament. As has already been seen, such a view is simplistic to the extent that it ignores the potential for judicial creativity in relation to the operation of the common law and the doctrine of judicial precedent. Equally, however, it ignores the extent to which the judiciary have a measure of discretion and creative power in the manner in which they interpret the legislation that comes before them.

The general difficulties involved in drafting legislation from the point of view of the person carrying out the drafting has already been considered in 2.2.3; but equally, it has to be recognised that determining the actual meaning of legislation presents judges with a practical difficulty. In order to apply legislation, judges must ascertain the meaning of the legislation, and in order to ascertain the meaning they are faced with the difficulty of interpreting the legislation.

Before considering the way in which judges interpret legislation, it is pertinent to emphasise that, in spite of the best endeavours of those who draft legislation to be precise in communicating the meaning of what they produce, the process of interpretation is inescapable and arises from the nature of language itself. Legislation can be seen as a form of linguistic communication. It represents and passes on to the judiciary what Parliament has determined the law should be in relation to a particular situation. Legislation, therefore, shares the general problem of uncertainty inherent in any mode of communication. One of the essential attributes of language is its fluidity, the fact that words can have more than one meaning and that the meaning of a word can change depending on its context. In such circumstances, it is immediately apparent that understanding is an active process. Faced with ambiguity, the recipient of information has to decide which of various meanings to assign to specific words, depending upon the context in which they are used.

Legislation gives rise to additional problems in terms of communication. One of the essential requirements of legislation is generality of application, the need for it to be written in such a way as to ensure that it can be effectively applied in various circumstances without the need to detail those situations individually. This requirement, however, gives rise to particular problems of interpretation, for, as has been pointed out in 2.2.3, the need for generality can only really be achieved at the expense of clarity and precision of language. A further possibility, that is not as uncommon as it should be, is that the legislation under consideration is obscure, ambiguous, or indeed is meaningless or fails to achieve the end at which it is aimed, simply through being badly drafted. The task facing the judge in such circumstances is to provide the legislation with some effective meaning.

Legislation, therefore, involves an inescapable measure of uncertainty that can only be made certain through judicial interpretation. To the extent, however, that the interpretation of legislative provisions is an active process, it is equally a creative process; and inevitably it involves the judiciary in creating law through determining meaning and effect to be given to any particular piece of legislation. There is a further possibility that has to be considered: that judges might actually abuse their role as necessary interpreters of legislation in such a way as to insinuate their own particular personal views and prejudices into their interpretations, and in so doing misapply the legislation and subvert the wishes of the legislature.

Approaches to statutory interpretation

Having considered the problems of interpreting language generally and the difficulties in interpreting legislation in particular, it is appropriate to consider in detail the methods and mechanisms which judges bring to bear on legislation in order to determine its meaning. There are, essentially, two contrasting views as to how judges should go about determining the meaning of a statute; the restrictive, literal approach and the more permissive, purposive one:

(a) *The literal approach* is dominant in the English legal system, although it is not without critics and devices do exist for circumventing it when it is seen as too restrictive. This view of judicial interpretation holds that the judge should look primarily to the words of the legislation in order to construe its meaning and, except in the very limited circumstances considered below, should not look outside of, or behind, the legislation in an attempt to find its meaning.

(b) *The purposive approach* rejects the limitation of the judge's search for meaning to a literal construction of the words of legislation itself. It suggests that the interpretive role of the judge should include, where necessary, the power to look beyond the words of statute in pursuit of the reason for its enactment; and that meaning should be construed in the light of that purpose and so as to give it effect. This purposive approach is typical of civil law systems. In these jurisdictions, legislation tends to set out general principles and leaves the fine details to be filled in later by the judges, who are expected to make decisions in the furtherance of those general principles.

European Community legislation tends to be drafted in the continental manner. Its detailed effect, therefore, can only be determined on the basis of a purposive approach to its interpretation. This requirement, however, runs counter to the literal approach that is the dominant approach in the English system. The need to interpret such legislation, however, has forced a change in that approach in relation to Community legislation and even with respect to domestic legislation designed to implement Community legislation. Thus, in *Pickstone v Freemans plc* (1988), the House of Lords held that it was permissible, and indeed necessary, for the court to read words into inadequate domestic legislation in order to give effect to Community law in relation to provisions relating to equal pay for work of equal value. (For a similar approach, see, also, the House of Lords decision in *Litster v Forth Dry Dock* (1989) and the decision in *Three Rivers District Council v Bank of England (No 2)* (1996) considered in 4.9.4.)

The advent of purposive interpretation for Community law has not dislodged the primacy of literal interpretation for non-Community domestic legislation. It should be pointed out, however, that the traditional restrictive approach has not gone unchallenged and it should not be surprising to find that Lord Denning was involved in the attack. As in other areas, his unorthodox approach was rejected by the House of Lords (see *Nothman v London Borough of Barnet* (1988)).

In advocating the adoption of a purposive approach, Lord Denning was, in fact, merely expressing the earlier view of the Law Commission which, as early as 1969, had recommended such a change without success.

It is now clearly established that judges can only adopt the purposive approach where they can discover a clear statement of the purpose of the legislation expressed either in the statute itself, or in extrinsic material to which they may legitimately refer for guidance as to meaning (*Shah v Barnet LBC* (1983)). The effect of *Pepper v Hart* (1993), considered below, permitting access to Hansard remains to be seen but, for the moment, it is still the case that the judges remain subject to the established rules of interpretation of which there are three primary rules of statutory interpretation, together with a variety of other secondary aids to construction.

Rules of interpretation

What follows in this and the following two sections should be read within the context of the HRA 1998, which requires all legislation to be construed in such a way as, if at all possible, to bring it within the ambit of the European Convention on Human Rights.

The three rules of statutory interpretation are as follows:

- *The literal rule*

  Under this rule, the judge is required to consider what the legislation actually says rather than considering what it might mean. In order to achieve this end, the judge should give words in legislation their literal meaning that is, their plain, ordinary, everyday meaning even if the effect of this is to produce what might be considered an otherwise unjust or undesirable outcome. The literal rule appears at first sight to be the least problematic method of interpreting legislation. Under this rule, the courts most obviously appear to be recognising their limitations by following the wishes of Parliament as expressed in the words of the legislation under consideration. When, however, the difficulties of assigning a fixed and unchallengeable meaning to any word is recalled, the use of the literal rule becomes less uncontroversial and a consideration of the cases reveals examples where the literal rule has been used as a justification for what otherwise might appear as partial judgments on the part of the court concerned in the case.

  A classic example of this approach from the area of contract law is *Fisher v Bell* (1961) where, in line with the general contract law principles, it was decided that the placing of an article in a window did not amount to offering but was merely an invitation to treat, and thus the shopkeeper could not be charged with offering the goods for sale. In this case, the court chose to follow the contract law literal interpretation of the meaning of offer in the Act in question and declined to consider the usual non-legal literal interpretation of the word offer. (The executives attitude to the courts legal-literal interpretation in *Fisher v Bell* (1961), and the related case of *Partridge v Crittenden* (1968), can be surmised from the fact that later legislation, such as the Trade Descriptions Act 1968, has effectively legislated that invitations to treat are to be treated in the same way as offers for sale.)

A further problem in relation to the literal rule, relating to the difficulty judges face in determining the literal meaning of even the most common of terms, can be seen in *R v Maginnis* (1987). The defendant had been charged under the Misuse of Drugs Act 1971, with having drugs in his possession and with intent to supply them. He claimed that, as he had intended to return the drugs to a friend who had left them in his car, he could not be guilty of supplying as charged. In this case, the judges, from first instance, through the Court of Appeal, to the House of Lords, disagreed as to the literal meaning of the common word 'supply'. Even in the House of Lords, Lord Goff, in his dissenting judgment, was able to cite a dictionary definition to support his interpretation of the word. It is tempting to suggest that the majority of judges in the House of Lords operated in a totally disingenuous way by justifying their decision on the literal interpretation of the law whilst, at the same time, fixing on a non-literal meaning for the word under consideration. In actual fact, in *R v Maginnis*, each of the meanings for 'supply' proposed by the various judges could be supported by dictionary entries. That fact, however, only highlights the essential weakness of the literal rule, and that is that it wrongly assumes that there is such a thing as a single uncontentious literal understanding of words. *Bromley LBC v GLC* (1983) may be cited as an instance where the courts arguably took a covert political decision under the guise of applying the literal meaning of a particular word in a piece of legislation.

- *The golden rule*

This rule is generally considered to be an extension of the literal rule. In its general expression, it is applied in circumstances where the application of the literal rule is likely to result in what appears to the court to be an obviously absurd result. It should be emphasised, however, that the court is not at liberty to ignore, or replace, legislative provisions simply on the basis that it considers them absurd; it must find genuine difficulties before it declines to use the literal rule in favour of the golden one. How one determines or defines genuine difficulty is of course a matter of discretion, and therefore dispute.

It is sometimes stated that there are in fact two versions of the golden rule:

(a) *The narrow meaning*

This is used where there are two apparently contradictory meanings to a particular word used in a legislative provision or the provision is simply ambiguous in its effect. In such a situation, the golden rule operates to ensure that preference is given to the meaning which does not result in the provision being an absurdity. An example of the application of the golden rule in this narrow sense is *Adler v George* (1964). The defendant had been charged, under the Official Secrets Act 1920, with obstruction in the vicinity of a prohibited area whereas she had actually carried out the obstruction inside the area. The court preferred not to restrict itself to the literal wording of the Act and found the defendant guilty as charged.

(b) *The wider meaning*

This version of the golden rule is resorted to where, although there is only one possible meaning to a provision, the court is of the opinion that to adopt such a literal interpretation will result in an absurdity. The classic example of this approach is to be found in *Re Sigsworth* (1935) in which the court introduced common law rules into legislative provisions, which were silent on the matter, to prevent the estate of a murderer from benefiting from the property of the party he had murdered.

Another example of this approach is found in *R v National Insurance Commissioner ex p Connor* (1981) in which the court held, in spite of silence in the actual legislation, that Connor was not entitled to a widow's pension, on the grounds that she had been the actual cause of her widowed status by killing her husband.

If it is not irrefutable, it is almost unarguable that matters relating to public policy issues are involved in cases in which the golden rule is employed. Subsequent to the *Connor* case, for example, the Forfeiture Act 1982 was passed giving courts the discretionary power to ignore the rule of public policy which precludes a person who has unlawfully killed another from acquiring a benefit in consequence of the killing. This provision, however, merely serves to emphasise the extent to which such judicial decisions on points of law are based on wider considerations of public policy in the first place. In doing so, it immediately raises the question of the judges understanding of, and right to determine, public policy, which questions will be considered later in the next section of this chapter.

- *The mischief rule*

At one level, the mischief rule is clearly the most flexible rule of interpretation but in its traditional expression it is limited by being restricted to using previous common law rules in order to decide the operation of contemporary legislation. It is also, at least somewhat, paradoxical that this most venerable rule, originally set out in *Heydon's Case* (1584), is also the one which most obviously reveals the socio-political nature of judicial decisions.

In *Heydon's Case*, it was stated that in making use of the mischief rule the court should consider the following four things:

(a) what was the common law before the passing of the statute?;

(b) what was the mischief in the law which the common law did not adequately deal with?;

(c) what remedy for that mischief had Parliament intended to provide? and

(d) what was the reason for Parliament adopting that remedy?

It has to be remembered that, when *Heydon's Case* was decided, it was the practice to cite in the preamble of legislation the purpose for its enactment, including the mischief at which it was aimed. (An example where the preamble made more sense than the actual body of the legislation is the infamous Bubble Act of 1720.) Judges in this earlier time did not therefore have to go beyond the legislative provision itself to implement the mischief rule. With the disappearance of such explanatory preambles, the question arises as to the extent to which judges can make use of the rule in *Heydon's Case* to justify their examination of the policy issues that underlie particular legislative provisions. Contemporary practice is to go beyond the actual body of the legislation. This, however, raises the question as to what courts can legitimately consider in their endeavour to determine the purpose and meaning of legislation, which will be considered, separately, below.

The example usually cited of the use of the mischief rule is *Corkery v Carpenter* (1950), in which a man was found guilty of being drunk in charge of a carriage although he was in fact only in charge of a bicycle. A much more controversial application of the rule is to be found in *Royal College of Nursing v DHSS* (1981), where the courts had to decide whether the medical induction of premature labour to effect abortion, under the supervision of nursing staff, was lawful. In this particularly sensitive area, whether one agrees with the ultimate majority decision of the House of Lords, in favour of the legality of the procedure, or not, probably depends on ones view of abortion. This fact simply serves to highlight the socio-political nature of the question that was finally determined by the House of Lords under the guise of merely determining the legal meaning of a piece of legislation.

From one point of view, the mischief rule serves a very positive purpose by providing courts with the authority to go behind the actual wording of statutes in order to consider the problem that those statutes are aimed at remedying. Alternatively, it is possible to see the mischief rule as justifying the courts interference in the areas of public policy that are, strictly speaking, beyond the realm of their powers and competence.

It is equally relevant to point out that in cases such as *Royal College of Nursing v DHSS* such decisions are forced on the courts, whether they like it or not. It is only to be hoped that they make proper and socially acceptable decisions: but such questions remain to be considered below.

It is sometimes suggested that the rules of interpretation form a hierarchical order. On that basis, the first rule that should be applied is the literal rule, and that rule only cedes to the golden rule, in particular circumstances where ambiguity arises from the application of the literal rule. The third rule, the mischief rule, it is suggested, is only brought into use where there is a perceived failure of the other two rules to deliver an appropriate result. On consideration, however, it becomes obvious that no such hierarchy exists. The literal rule is supposed to be used unless it leads to a manifest absurdity in which case it will give way to the golden rule. The immediate question this supposition gives rise to is what is to be considered as an absurdity in any particular case, other than the view of the judge deciding the case. The three rules are contradictory, at least to a degree, and there is no way in which the outsider can determine in advance which of them the courts will make use of to decide the meaning of a particular statute. Perhaps it would be better if the 1969 recommendation of the Law Commission was given effect and judges were expressly permitted to adopt a purposive approach to statutory interpretation. At least, then, judicial creativity in this regard would be out in the open.

4.9.4 Aids to construction

In addition to the three main rules of interpretation, there are a number of secondary aids to construction. These can be categorised as either intrinsic or extrinsic in nature:

* *Intrinsic assistance*

   Intrinsic assistance is derived from the statute which is the object of interpretation; the judge uses the full statute to understand the meaning of a particular part of it.

   The title, either long or short, of the Act under consideration may be referred to for guidance (*Royal College of Nursing v DHSS* (1981)).

   It should be noted, however, that a general intention derived from the title cannot overrule a clear statement to the contrary in the text of the Act.

   It was a feature of older statutes that they contained a preamble, which was a statement, preceding the actual provisions of the Act, setting out its purposes in some detail, and to which reference could be made for purposes of interpretation. Again, however, any general intention derived from the preamble could not stand in the face of express provision to the contrary within the Act.

Whereas preambles preceded the main body of an Act, schedules appear as additions at the end of the main body of the legislation. They are, however, an essential part of the Act and may be referred to in order to make sense of the main text.

Some statutes contain section headings and yet others contain marginal notes relating to particular sections. The extent to which either of these may be used is uncertain although *DPP v Schildkamp* (1969) does provide authority for the use of the former as an aid to interpretation.

Finally, in regard to intrinsic aids to interpretation, it is now recognised that punctuation has an effect on the meaning of words and can be taken into account in determining the meaning of a provision.

- *Extrinsic assistance*

Extrinsic assistance, that is, reference to sources outside of the Act itself, may on occasion be resorted to in determining the meaning of legislation; but which sources? Some external sources are unproblematic. For example, judges have always been entitled to refer to dictionaries in order to find the meaning of non-legal words. They also have been able to look into textbooks for guidance in relation to particular points of law; and in using the mischief rule, they have been able to refer to earlier statutes to determine the precise mischief at which the statute they are trying to construe is aimed. The Interpretation Act 1978 is also available for consultation with regard to particular difficulties. Unfortunately, its title is somewhat misleading in that it does not give general instructions for interpreting legislation but simply defines particular terms that are found in various statutes.

Other extrinsic sources, however, are more controversial. In 2.2, the various processes involved in the production of legislation were considered. As was seen, there are many distinct stages in the preparation of legislation. Statutes may arise as a result of reports submitted by a variety of commissions. In addition, the preparation of the precise structure of legislation is subject to consideration in working papers, known as *travaux preparatoires*. Nor should it be forgotten that in its progress through Parliament a Bill is the object of discussion and debate in Parliament, both on the floor of the Houses of Parliament and in committee. Verbatim accounts of debates are recorded and published in *Hansard*.

Each of these procedures provides a potential source from which a judge might discover the specific purpose of a piece of legislation or the real meaning of any provision within it. The question is: which of these sources are the courts entitled to have access to?

Historically, English courts have adopted a restrictive approach to what they are entitled to take into consideration. This restrictive approach has been gradually relaxed, however, to the extent that judges are allowed to use extrinsic sources to determine the mischief at which particular legislation is aimed. Thus, they have been entitled to look at Law Commission reports, Royal Commission reports, and the reports of other official commissions. Until very recently, however, *Hansard* literally remained a closed book to the courts, but in the landmark decision in *Pepper v Hart* the House of Lords decided to overturn the previous rule. The issue in the case was the tax liability owed by teachers at Malvern College, a fee paying school. Employees were entitled to have their sons educated at the school whilst paying only 20% of the usual fees. The question was as to the precise level at which this benefit in kind was to be taxed. In a majority decision, it was held that, where the precise meaning of legislation was uncertain or ambiguous or where the literal meaning of an Act would lead to a manifest absurdity, the courts could refer to *Hansard*'s reports of parliamentary debates and proceedings as an aid to construing the meaning of the legislation.

The operation of the principle in *Pepper v Hart* was extended, in *Three Rivers District Council v Bank of England (No 2)* (1996), to cover situations where the legislation under question was not in itself ambiguous, but might be ineffective in its intention to give effect to some particular European Community directive. Applying the wider purposive powers of interpretation open to it in such circumstances (see 4.9.3), the court held that it was permissible to refer to *Hansard* in order to determine the actual purpose of the statute. The *Pepper v Hart* principle only applies to statements made by ministers at the time of the passage of legislation, and the courts have declined to extent it to cover situations where ministers subsequently make some statement as to what they consider the effect of a particular Act to be (*Melluish (Inspector of Taxes) v BMI (No 3) Ltd* (1995)).

It is essential to bear in mind that *Pepper v Hart* is not intended to introduce a general purposive approach to the interpretation of non-European Community legislation. Recourse to *Hansard* is to be made only in the context of the mischief rule, as a further method of finding out the mischief at which the particular legislation is aimed.

An additional restriction is that it is likely that only statements made by a government minister, or some other sponsor, responsible for the legislation will be considered as authoritative in setting out the mischief. It is of some interest to note that the dissenting judgment of the Lord Chancellor, Lord Mackay, considered that a relaxation of the previous procedure would merely serve to increase the expense of litigation.

4.9.5 Presumptions

In addition to the rules of interpretation, the courts may also make use of certain presumptions. As with all presumptions they are rebuttable. The presumptions operate:

- against the alteration of the common law. Parliament is sovereign and can alter the common law whenever it decides to do so. In order to do this, however, Parliament must expressly enact legislation to that end. If there is no express intention to that effect, it is assumed that statute does not make any fundamental change to the common law. With regard to particular provisions, if there are alternative interpretations, one of which will maintain the existing common law situation, then that interpretation will be preferred;

- in favour of the requirement that *mens rea* be a requirement in any criminal offence. The classic example of this presumption is *Sweet v Parsley* (1969) in which a school teacher had been found guilty of allowing her premises to be used for the purpose of taking drugs contrary to the Misuse of Drugs Act 1971. As she had no idea whatsoever of what her tenants were doing, the House of Lords decided that she could not be convicted. Her lack of knowledge meant she had no intention of committing the offence alleged and therefore did not possess the required *mens rea*. This presumption can be rebutted expressly by the wording of the legislation. Offences which do not require the presence of *mens rea* are referred to as strict liability offences, and they usually involve aspects relating to the enforcement of public policy issues, rather than offences of a truly criminal nature. The presumption as to the need for *mens rea* may also be impliedly rebutted, on the basis of the judges interpretation of the statute in question;

- against retrospective application. It is open to Parliament to expressly enact legislation contrary to this presumption. Although this is usually done in relation to areas such as tax law, the War Crimes Act 1990 shows that Parliament can impose criminal responsibility retrospectively, where particular and extremely unusual circumstances dictate the need to do so;

- against the deprivation of an individuals liberty, property or rights. Once again, the presumption can be rebutted by express provision and it is not uncommon for legislation to deprive people of their rights to enjoy particular benefits. Nor is it unusual for individuals to be deprived of their liberty under the Mental Health Act 1983;

- against application to the Crown. Unless the legislation contains a clear statement to the contrary, it is presumed not to apply to the Crown;

- against breaking international law. Where possible, legislation should be interpreted in such a way as to give effect to existing international legal obligations;

- in favour of words taking their meaning from the context in which they are used. This final presumption refers back to, and operates in conjunction with, the major rules for interpreting legislation considered previously. The general presumption appears as three distinct sub-rules, each of which carries a Latin tag. The *noscitur a sociis* rule is applied where statutory provisions include a list of examples of what is covered by the legislation. It is presumed that the words used have a related meaning and are to be interpreted in relation to each other. (See *IRC v Frere* (1965) in which the House of Lords decided which of two possible meanings of the word interest was to be preferred by reference to the words location within a statute.) The *ejusdem generis* rule applies in situations where general words are appended to the end of a list of specific examples. The presumption is that the general words have to be interpreted in line with the prior restrictive examples. Thus, a provision which referred to a list that included, horses, cattle, sheep and other animals would be unlikely to apply to domestic animals such as cats and dogs (see *Powell v Kempton Park Racecourse* (1899) in which it was held that, because a statute prohibited betting in a specified number of indoor places, it could not cover an outdoor location). The *expressio unius exclusio alterius* rule simply means that where a statute seeks to establish a list of what is covered by its provisions, then anything not expressly included in that list is specifically excluded (see *R v Inhabitants of Sedgley* (1831) where rates expressly stated to be payable on coal mines were held not to be payable in relation to limestone mines).

4.10 Politics and the judiciary

Law is an inherently and inescapably political process. Assertions as to the substantive autonomy of law merely disguise the fact that, in making legal decisions, judges decide where the weight of public approval is to be placed and which forms of behaviour are to be sanctioned (see *R v Brown* (1993) where the House of Lords criminalised the sexual activities of consenting sado-masochists, arguably without fully comprehending some aspects of what was going on).

There is, however, an increasingly apparent tendency for contemporary judges to become actively, directly and openly engaged in more overtly political activity. The 1955 Kilmuir Rules, named after the Lord Chancellor who introduced them, were designed to control the instances when the judiciary could express opinion in the media. The rules were abrogated in 1987 by Lord Mackay and, since then, the judiciary have been more forthcoming in expressing their views, not just on matters strictly related to their judicial functions but also in wider political matters.

An example of this process can be cited in the concerted action of the judiciary in response to the pronouncements of the then Home Secretary, Michael Howard, at the Conservative Party Conference in Autumn 1993 in which he asserted the success of prison as a means of dealing with crime and declared his commitment to sending more offenders to prison. First of all, Lord Woolf, architect of the governments prison reform programme and who was conducting an investigation into the operation of the whole civil law process, responded by making reference to:

> ... a fashion, not confined to the totally uninformed, to indulge in rhetoric advocating increased sentences across the board in a way which will be counter productive ...

and he was quoted in *The Guardian* newspaper as stating that such talk was shortsighted and irresponsible.

Perhaps the really surprising aspect of this difference of opinion was not that Lord Woolf disagreed with the Home Secretary but that he was supported in his views by seven other judges in a series of interviews in *The Observer*, 17 October 1993, including the then Law Lord, Lord Ackner, and the chairman of the Judicial Studies Board, Lord Justice Farquharson.

Lord Ackner was prominent in taking Lord Mackay to task for his various interventions in the operation of the legal system. He also warned the Home Secretary that he was in danger of acting illegally by introducing a new system of criminal injuries compensation (see 4.11.7), but he has not been alone. For example, in January 1994, Lord Taylor, the then Lord Chief Justice, made an outspoken attack on the then governments criminal justice policy both in the House of Lords and in a public lecture, suggesting that government legislation might tend to undermine judicial impartiality.

The Home Secretary's approach to sentencing policy, and particularly his wish to impose minimum sentences for criminals convicted of certain offences or repeat convictions, consistently came under attack from the judiciary. As early as October 1995, when Michael Howard announced his intention to introduce such policies, the then Lord Chief Justice Lord Taylor took a mere two hours to issue a withering challenge to the Home Secretary's policy statement. According to Lord Taylor:

> Judges apply the [sentencing] framework conscientiously, but must be free to fit the particular punishment to the particular crime if justice is to be done. Minimum sentences are inconsistent with doing justice according to the circumstances of each case. Instead of limiting judicial discretion by introducing unnecessary constraints on sentencing, the police should be provided with the resources they need to bring criminals before the courts in the first place.

When the proposals were eventually issued in a White Paper in April 1996, they were commented on with severe scorn by the former Master of the Rolls, Lord Donaldson, in an article in *The Guardian* newspaper. Lord Donaldson stated that the objectives of sentencing policy should have nothing to do with the election of particular politicians or particular parties and that the proposals would require the judge to pass what he believed to be an unjust sentence in any case in which, taking account of the circumstances of the crime and the offender, he would otherwise have passed a lighter sentence.

Lord Taylor's replacement as Lord Chief Justice, Lord Bingham, took the opportunity of a television interview in November 1996 to express his opinion that the problems with the Home Secretary's proposals would only be mitigated if judges were not obliged to give mandatory sentences where they considered it unjust to do so. In his view, that, at least, would enable him to give effect to his sense of the justice of the case.

Lord Ackner then took up the attack on the proposals, which then were contained in the Crime (Sentencing) Bill, in another article in *The Guardian* in November 1996 in which he compared the action of the government with the action of the government in the former Soviet Union.

In the event, the early dissolution of Parliament in advance of the General Election in May 1997 ensured that, in order to get the majority of the Bill through Parliament, the Home Secretary was required to reach a compromise and accept the retention of judicial discretion as proposed in an amendment to the Bill in the House of Lords.

However, perhaps the most vital area in which the judges play an active political role is in the relation to the operation of judicial review. As was stated in Chapter 1, judicial review subjects the executive arm of the State to the overview of the judges in such a way as to raise fundamental questions about the structure of the British Constitution and the role of the judges therein.

4.11   Judicial review

The recent growth in applications for judicial review is truly startling. The statistical records show that, in 1980, there were only 525 applications for judicial review; in 1996, 4,586; in 1997, 4,636 such applications; and, in 1998, 5,201. In recognition of the growth in applications for judicial review, 40% of which originate from outside London, the Heilbron Report recommended that such applications should not have to be made in London, but should be capable of being heard by circuit judges.

The remedies open to anyone challenging the decisions or actions of administrative institutions or public authorities can be divided into private or public law remedies.

4.11.1   Private law remedies

There are three private law remedies:

• *Declaration*

   This is a definitive statement, by the High Court or county court, of what the law is in a particular area. The procedure may be used by an individual or body to clarify a particular contentious situation. It is a common remedy in private law but it also has an important part to play in regard to individuals relations with administrative institutions, as can be seen, for example, in *Congreve v Home Office* (1976), where the Court of Appeal stated that it would be unlawful for the Home Office to revoke yearly television licences after only eight months because they had been bought in anticipation of an announced price rise but before the expiry of existing licences.

Declarations, however, cannot be enforced either directly or indirectly through the contempt of court procedure. Public authorities are, as a matter of course, expected to abide by them.

- *Injunctions*

Usually, an injunction seeks to restrain a person from breaking the law; alternatively, however, a mandatory injunction may instruct someone to undo what they have previously done, or alternatively to stop doing what they are doing. Both types of injunction may be sought against a public authority. See *Attorney General v Fulham Corporation* (1921) in which a local authority was ordered to stop running a laundry service where it only had the power to establish laundries for people to wash their own clothes.

- *Damages*

Damages cannot be awarded on their own in relation to administrative misconduct but may be claimed in addition where one of the other remedies, considered above, is sought, as, for example, in *Cooper v Wandsworth Board of Works* (1863). In this case, a builder had put up a building without informing the Board of Works as he was required to do. When the Board demolished the building, he nonetheless recovered damages against them on the basis that the Board had exceeded its powers by not allowing him to defend or explain his actions.

In order to seek one of these private law remedies, an individual merely had to issue a writ against a public authority in their own name. They did not require the approval of the court.

4.11.2 The prerogative orders

The prerogative orders are so called because they were originally the means whereby sovereigns controlled the operation of their officials. As a consequence, the prerogative orders cannot be used against the Crown, but they can be used against individual ministers of State and, since *R v Secretary of State for the Home Department ex p Fire Brigades Union* (1995), considered at 4.11.7, it is clear that ministers cannot avoid judicial review by hiding behind the cloak of prerogative powers:

- Certiorari is the mechanism by means of which decisions of inferior courts, tribunals and other authoritative bodies are brought before the High Court to have their validity examined. Where any such decision is found to be invalid, it may be set aside. An example of this can be seen in *Ridge v Baldwin* (1964). Here, the plaintiff had been dismissed from his position as Chief Constable without having had the opportunity to present any case for his defence. The House of Lords held that the committee which had taken the decision had acted in breach of the requirements of natural justice and granted a declaration that his dismissal was null and void.

- Prohibition is similar to certiorari in that it relates to invalid acts of public authorities, but it is different to the extent that it is pre-emptive and prescriptive in regard to any such activity and operates to prevent the authority from taking invalid decisions in the first place. An example of the use of the prohibition order arose in *R v Telford Justices ex p Badhan* (1991). In this case, an order was issued to stop committal proceedings in relation to an alleged rape that had not been reported until some 14 years after the alleged incident. The delay meant that the defendant would have been unable to prepare a proper defence against the charge.

- Mandamus may be seen as the obverse of prohibition, in that it is an order issued by the High Court instructing an inferior court or some other public authority to carry out a duty laid on them. Such an order is frequently issued in conjunction with an order of certiorari, to the effect that a public body is held to be using its powers improperly and is instructed to use them in a proper fashion. In *R v Poplar Borough Council (Nos 1 and 2)* (1922), the court ordered the borough council to pay over money due to the county council and to levy a rate to raise the money if necessary. Failure to comply with the order led to the imprisonment of some of the borough councillors.

Access to these public law remedies was not directly open to individuals. They had to apply to the court for judicial review under Ord 53 of the Rules of the Supreme Court (RSC).

The present procedure for applying for remedies against public authorities was established in 1977 when the old RSC were altered by a new Ord 53. (Subsequently, the procedural changes introduced in 1977 were given statutory effect by s 31 of the Supreme Court Act 1981.) In order to avail oneself of the prerogative orders, an application had to be made under the procedure established in RSC Ord 53; there was normally a time limit of three months for applications (*R v Aston University Senate ex p Roffey* (1969)). The non-prerogative orders, however, continued to exist as distinct remedies in private law, apart from Ord 53. The judicial review procedure was not compulsory in order to enforce private rights against public authorities, although Ord 53 permitted that procedure to be used.

Before the introduction of the present procedure, an applicant had to apply for a specific remedy or remedies. If, for some reason, they failed to obtain the remedy sought, the court was not at liberty to grant an alternative which would have been available had the applicant sought it in the first place. Under the present procedure, an applicant may seek more than one remedy, either jointly or alternatively, and may even seek the courts leave to amend their application at the hearing. Initially, it appeared that the new procedure had merely simplified the procedure for obtaining judicial review and, although it permitted the use of Ord 53 to get access to the private remedies, those remedies still could be sought by the issuing of a writ.

In *O'Reilly v Mackman* (1982), however, the House of Lords decided that issues relating to public rights could only be enforced by means of the judicial review procedure, and that it would be an abuse of process for an applicant to seek a declaration by writ in relation to an alleged breach of a public duty or responsibility by a public authority. In deciding the case in this way, the House of Lords did much to demarcate and emphasise the role of judicial review as the method of challenging public authorities in their performance of their powers and duties in public law.

4.11.3 *Locus standi* standing

The right to make an application for judicial review is not automatic. There is an initial stage which involves a party making an *ex parte* application to a judge stating the facts of the case, the remedy sought and the reason for the remedy. This initial stage is sometimes seen as a filtering process in which baseless causes are rejected. The party seeking judicial review must show that they have, at least, an arguable case and that judicial review is the appropriate mechanism for dealing with it.

They must also show that they have sufficient *locus standi* in the matter and are not just officious bystanders with no real interest. In order to show *locus standi*, they must have sufficient interest in the matter to which the application relates to justify their taking it on themselves to pursue it. Whether a person has such an interest or not is a matter for the court to determine as decided in *IRC v National Federation of Self-Employed and Small Businesses Ltd* (1981). (See 4.11.6.)

Standing to seek judicial review was extended to pressure groups with a particular interest in the matter at issue in *R v HM Inspector of Pollution ex p Greenpeace* (1994) and *R v Secretary of State for Foreign Affairs ex p World Development Movement* (1995), considered in detail below.

4.11.4 Grounds for application for judicial review

The grounds of application can be considered under two heads: procedural *ultra vires* and substantive *ultra vires*:

- Procedural *ultra vires*, as its name suggests, relates to the failure of a person or body, provided with specific authority, to follow the procedure established for using that power. It also covers instances where a body exercising a judicial function fails to follow the requirements of natural justice, by acting as prosecutor and judge in the same case or not permitting the accused person to make representations to the panel deciding the case.

- Substantive *ultra vires* occurs where someone does something that is not actually authorised by the enabling legislation. And, in *Associated Provincial Picture House v Wednesbury Corporation* (1947), Lord Greene MR established the possibility of challenging discretionary decisions on the basis of unreasonableness.

Lord Greene's approach was endorsed and refined by Lord Diplock in *Council of Civil Service Unions v Minister for the Civil Service* (1984) in which he set out the three recognised grounds for judicial review, namely:

(a) illegality;

(b) irrationality;

(c) procedural impropriety.

Lord Diplock, however, introduced the possibility of a much more wide ranging reason for challenging administrative decisions: namely, the doctrine of proportionality. Behind this doctrine is the requirement that there should be a reasonable relation between a decision, and its objectives. It requires the achievement of particular ends by means that are not more oppressive than they need be to attain those ends. The potentially innovative aspect of this doctrine is the extent to which it looks to the substance of the decisions rather than simply focusing on the way in which they are reached.

Lord Diplock's listing of proportionality within the grounds for judicial review was controversial, if not at the very least, arguably, mistaken. Proportionality, however, is a key principle within the jurisdiction of the European Court of Human Rights, and is used frequently to assess the validity of State action which interferes with individual rights protected under the Convention. Consequently, as the HRA 1998 has incorporated the European Convention into UK law, proportionality will be a part of UK jurisprudence and legal practice; at least, in cases which fall within the scope of the HRA. Although HRA cases and judicial review are different and distinct procedures, nonetheless, it is surely a mere matter of time before the doctrine of proportionality is applied by the judges in judicial review cases unrelated to the Convention.

4.11.5 The exclusion of judicial review

As will be considered in Chapter 8, one of the reasons for the setting up of extensive systems of administrative tribunals was precisely the wish to curb the power of the judges. It was felt that judges, and indeed the common law itself, tended to be more supportive of individual rights and freedoms as opposed to collective notions of welfare pursued by post-war governments, and that they would not administer such policies sympathetically. The judges, however, asserted their ultimate control over such tribunals generally, through the use of judicial review. There have been various attempts by parliamentary drafters to exclude the judiciary from certain areas by wording provisions in such a way as to deny the possibility of judicial review. These attempts, however, have mainly proved to be in vain and have been rendered ineffective by the refusal of the courts to recognise their declared effect. Examples are:

- *Finality or ouster clauses*

  There are a variety of possible wordings for these clauses. For example, the legislation might provide that the minister's (or the tribunal's) decision shall be final, or alternatively it might attempt to emphasise the point by stating that the decision in question shall be final and conclusive or it might even provide that it shall be final, conclusive and shall not be questioned in any legal proceedings whatsoever. Unfortunately for the drafter of the legislation and the minister or tribunal in question, all three formulations are equally likely to be ineffective. The courts have tended to interpret such phrases in a narrow way, so as to recognise the exclusion of an appeal procedure but to introduce the possibility of judicial review, as distinct from appeal. The classic case on this point is *R v Medical Appeal Tribunal ex p Gilmore* (1957), in which Lord Denning stated that: 'The word final ... does not mean without recourse to certiorari.' This, however, raised the point of provisions which expressly sought to exclude certiorari.

  In *South East Asia Fire Bricks Sdn Bhd v Non-Metallic Mineral Products Manufacturing Employees Union* (1980), the Privy Council decided that a Malaysian statute was sufficiently detailed in its wording to effectively exclude certiorari for an error of law on the face of the record. The Privy Council pointed out, however, that the exclusion could not be effective to prevent judicial review where the institution in question had acted *ultra vires* or in breach of natural justice.

- *Partial exclusion clauses*

  Where legislation has provided for a limited time period within which parties have to apply for judicial review, then applications outside of the period will not be successful. In *Smith v East Elloe Rural District Council* (1956), the House of Lords, although only by a three to two majority, recognised the effectiveness of a six week limitation clause in the Acquisition of Land (Authorisation Procedure) Act 1946. Although that case was subject to criticism in *Anisminic Ltd v Foreign Compensation*

Commission (1969), it was explained and followed in *R v Secretary of State for the Environment ex p Ostler* (1976).

In response to the Franks Committee's recommendation that judicial review should not be subject to exclusion, s 14(1) of the Tribunals and Inquiries Act 1971 was enacted to that end. Unfortunately, it only applies to pre-1958 legislation.

The current Immigration and Asylum Bill, whilst not in any way seeking to ban the possibility of judicial review in law, contains provisions which will, in effect, punish people who attempt to make use of it. The proposal in the Bill is that any asylum seeker who challenges a decision made by the Home Office, by way of judicial review, will automatically lose the right to State support.

4.11.6 Law Commissions Report on judicial review

In October 1994, the Law Commission published a report, *Administrative Law: Judicial Review and Statutory Appeals* (No 226), on the current operation of judicial review and made recommendations as to its future. The major proposals for the reform are:

- inappropriately commenced writ actions should be allowed to be converted into proceedings for judicial review;

- a preliminary consideration stage, to be conducted on paper, should be introduced and the test for whether a case should proceed should be whether there is a serious issue which ought to de determined rather than the present test which requires the case to be arguable;

- claims for restitution, debt and interest should be available in judicial review;

- the court should be able to grant interim relief before the conclusion of the preliminary consideration, and should be able to grant interim and advisory declarations;

- *locus standi* should be determined on the basis that the applicant has been or would be adversely affected by the action complained of or even more widely that it is in the public interest, and unincorporated associations such as pressure groups should be given standing. This latter recommendation follows the practice established in such cases as *R v HM Inspectorate of Pollution ex p Greenpeace* (1993) and *R v Secretary of State for Foreign Affairs ex p World Development Movement Ltd* (1995);

- legal aid should be available where an issue of general public interest is involved and costs should be available from central funds in such instances.

The Woolf Report has also had several implications for the operation of judicial review:

- judicial review should be seen as a last resort and parties are to be encouraged to use other mechanisms, such as ombudsmen, to resolve their difficulties;

- the first stage of the process, the currently named leave stage, is renamed the preliminary consideration stage;

- the preliminary consideration stage will be considered in writing;

- interim relief may be granted before the preliminary stage;

- right of action, standing, will be decided either, on the basis that the claimant will be adversely affected by the decision to be reviewed, or, on grounds of public interest;

- cases will be held outside London where appropriate; and

- judges from other than the Queen's Bench Divisional Court will be used where appropriate.

4.11.7 The politics of judicial review

The relationship of the executive and the judiciary and the role of judicial review in establishing that relationship has been highlighted in a number of cases.

In *M v Home Office* (1993), the House of Lords decided that the court has jurisdiction in judicial review proceedings to grant interim and final injunctions against officers of the Crown and to make a finding of contempt of court against a government department or a minister of the Crown in either his personal or his official capacity.

M v Home Office is of signal importance in establishing the powers of the courts in relation to the executive. It is also interesting to note that in delivering the leading speech Lord Woolf quoted extensively from, and clearly supported, Dicey's view of the Rule of Law as involving the subjection of all, including State officials, to the ordinary law of the land (see Chapter 1).

In November 1994, the government suffered two damaging blows from the judiciary. In *R v Secretary of State for Foreign Affairs ex p World Development Movement Ltd* (1995), the Queen's Bench Divisional Court held that the Secretary of State had acted beyond his powers in granting aid to the Malaysian Government in relation to the Pergau Dam project. The financial assistance was given not for the promotion of development *per se* as authorised by s 1 of the Overseas Development and Cooperation Act 1980, but in order to facilitate certain arms sales. As Rose LJ stated:

Whatever the Secretary of States intention or purpose may have been, it is, as it seems to me, a matter for the courts and not for the Secretary of State to determine whether, on the evidence before the court, the particular conduct was, or was not, within the statutory purpose.

In *R v Secretary of State for the Home Department ex p Fire Brigades Union*, the Court of Appeal held that the Home Secretary had committed an abuse of power in implementing a scheme designed to cut the level of payments made to the subjects of criminal injuries. The court held that he was under an obligation, under the CJA 1988, to put the previous non-statutory scheme on a statutory basis. It was not open for the Secretary of State to use his prerogative powers to introduce a completely new tariff scheme contrary to the intention of Parliament as expressed in the CJA 1988. The decision of the Court of Appeal was confirmed by a three to two majority in the House of Lords in April 1995, the majority holding that the Secretary of State had exceeded, or abused, powers granted to him by Parliament. It is of interest to note that in his minority judgment Lord Keith warned that to dismiss the Home Secretary's appeal would be:

... an unwarrantable intrusion into the political field and a usurpation of the function of Parliament.

In 1997, in *R v Secretary of State ex p Venables and Thompson*, the House of Lords decided that the Home Secretary had misused his powers in relation to two juveniles who had been sentenced to detention during Her Majesty's pleasure. The case, known generally as the Jamie Bulger case, related to the killing of a small child by two other children. The unusual nature of the case had caused a general furore and, when the two accused were found guilty, a tabloid newspaper started a public petition in an endeavour to ensure that they were locked up for life. In the light of such representations, the Home Secretary decided that the minimum period the two should spend in custody should be 15 years. On judicial review of the Home Secretary's decision, the House of Lords held that he should not have treated the children in this case in same way as adult prisoners sentenced to life imprisonment, and that he had a duty to review their sentence to ensure its continued appropriateness. The House of Lords also stated that, in acting in a quasi-judicial manner, the Home Secretary should not allow himself to be swayed by irrelevant considerations such as public petitions.

Even Lord Chancellors have not escaped the unwanted control of judicial review and, in March 1997, John Witham successfully argued that the Lord Chancellor had exceeded his statutory powers in removing exemptions from court fees for those in receipt of State income support. The exemptions had been removed as part of a wider measure to increase court income by raising fee levels, but Lord Justice Rose and Mr Justice Laws held that Lord Mackay had exceeded the statutory powers given to him by Parliament. Rose LJ stated that there was nothing to suggest that Parliament ever intended a power for the

Lord Chancellor to prescribe fees so as to preclude the poor from access to the courts. Mr Justice Laws on the other hand stated that:

> Access to the courts is a constitutional right; it can only be denied by the government if it persuades Parliament to pass legislation which specifically permits the executive to turn people away. That has not been done in this case [*R v Lord Chancellor ex p Witham* (1997)].

It can be seen from the foregoing that the judiciary have at their disposal the means for addressing the potential for abuse that has followed on from the growth of discretionary power in the hands of the modern State, through the mechanism of judicial review, particularly if it is operated on the basis of the doctrine of proportionality. There are also significant indications that the higher judiciary may well be attempting to assert just such a measure of control over the executive. For example, the former Master of the Rolls and now Lord Chief Justice, Sir Thomas Bingham, was quoted in (1993) *The Observer*, 9 May as saying that:

> Slowly, the constitutional balance is tilting towards the judiciary. The courts have reacted to the increase in powers claimed by the government by being more active themselves.

Judicial review is a delicate exercise and by necessity draws the judiciary into the political arena, using the word political in its widest, non-party sense. That the judges are aware of this, is evident from the words of Lord Woolf in the same article. As he recognised:

> Judicial review is all about balance: between the rights of the individual and his need to be treated fairly, and the rights of government at local and national level to do what it has been elected to do. There is a very sensitive and political decision to be made.

However, another current Law Lord, Lord Browne-Wilkinson, as observed, admirably before his elevation to the House of Lords, on a BBC radio programme, that a great void was apparent in the political system, deriving from the fact that no government had a true popular majority and yet all governments were able to carry Parliament in support of anything they wanted. He went on to express the view that Parliament was not a place where it was easy to get accountability for abuse or misuse of powers. According to Sir Nicholas, while judicial review could not overcome the will of Parliament, judges had a special role because democracy was defective. He then asked a rhetorical question as to who else but the judges could ensure that executive action is taken in accordance with law, and not abused by growingly polarised political stances.

Such thinking has continued amongst the judiciary as can be seen from Mr Justice, as he was then, Stephen Sedley's article in the May 1995 edition of the *London Review of Books* in which he asserted that, after decades of passivity, there is a new culture of judicial assertiveness to compensate for, and in places repair, dysfunctions in the democratic process, and that the last three decades of the 20th century may have seen the British Constitution being re-fashioned by judges with sufficient popular support to mute political opposition.

These manifestations of almost judicial triumphalism should at least give people cause for thought. The fact that the judges increasingly see it as incumbent upon them to use judicial review as the means of questioning and controlling what they see as the abuse of executive power does, at the very least, raise very serious questions in relation to their suitability for such a role. These doubts can be set out in terms of:

- *Competence*

  This refers to the question whether the judges are sufficiently competent to participate in deciding the substantive issues that they have been invited to consider under the guise of judicial review and may be entitled to consider under the HRA. Judges are experts in law; they are not experts in the various and highly specialised areas of policy that by definition tend to be involved in judicial review cases. They may disagree with particular decisions but it has to be, at least, doubted that they are qualified to take such policy decisions. A classic example of this difficulty were the fares fair cases (*Bromley LBC v GLC* (1983) and, later, *R v London Transport Executive ex p GLC* (1983)) in which the courts got involved in deciding issues relating to transport policy for London on the pretext that it was judicially defining the meaning of particular words in a statute. As was considered in 4.9, the apparently technocratic, and hence neutral, application of rules of interpretation simply serve to disguise a political procedure and, in these cases, the policy issue concerned was certainly beyond the scope of the judges to determine.

- *Constitutionality*

  This refers to the wider point that the separation of powers applies equally to the judiciary as it does to the executive. In interfering with substantive decisions and involving themselves in political matters, albeit in the pretence of merely deciding points of law, the judiciary may be seen to be exceeding their constitutional powers. It has to be remembered that judges are unelected and unaccountable.

- *Partiality*

  This refers to the possibility of individual and indeed corporate bias within the judiciary as will be considered in the following section.

The foregoing has indicated that the relationship between the State and the courts may, on occasion, involve a measure of tension, with the courts attempting to rein in the activities of the State. The relationship between the judiciary and the executive is well summed up in the words of Lord Justice Farquharson, again taken from an *Observer* article:

> We have to be very careful: the executive is elected. We have a role in the Constitution but, if we go too far, there will be a reaction. The Constitution only works if the different organs trust each other. If the judges start getting too frisky, there would be retaliation, renewed attempts to curb the judiciary.

It should also be borne in mind that many of the judicial statements above were made during the time of a large Conservative majority in the House of Commons pursuing policies that were seen by the judiciary as certainly inimical to its own interests and those of the Bar from whence they came; and which policies were portrayed as likely to undermine the whole justice system. The question remains to be asked whether this increased political activity on the part of the judiciary represented a truly disinterested pursuit of the rule of law or whether it is the product of a disgruntled judiciary intent on retaliating against an executive which has undermined its operation and situation?

The judicial statements above were made during the time of a large Conservative majority in the House of Commons pursuing policies that were seen by the judiciary as certainly inimical to its own interests, and those of the Bar from whence they came. A time characterised by Lord Woolf MR as a period when the other checks on government were not operating as effectively as they usually do (see 'Judicial review the tensions between the executive and the judiciary' (1998) 114 LQR 579).

That Conservative majority has now been replaced by a similarly large Labour majority. The number of judicial review cases continues to grow, and there have been judicial decisions against the government. For example, both the Home Secretary and the Secretary of State for Social Security have lost cases in some, although by no means the majority of, decisions in asylum cases (for example, *R v Secretary of State for Social Security ex p Joint Council for the Welfare of Immigrants* (1997), and the Health Secretary has been found wanting in his initial decision to limit supply of the impotency drug Viagra ((1999) *The Times*, 27 May)). It has to be said, however, that the judiciary do not appear as overtly antagonistic as they did during the previous administration.

As was suggested in the passage from Lord Woolf's article, quoted in Chapter 1, it appears that a truce has been called between the judiciary and the executive. Perhaps they are being more circumspect because they realise that changes in the constitution, such as the HRA, must have an impact on, and increase the importance of, the judge's role. Given these changes, and the fiasco that was the *Pinochet* case, perhaps a period of judicial quietness, and self-reflection, is more in keeping than suggestions of expansionism or triumphalism. Although no longer in force, the Kilmuir Rules did have a valid point to make:

... the overriding consideration ... is the importance of keeping the judiciary in this country isolated from the controversies of the day. So long as a judge keeps silent, his reputation for wisdom and impartiality remains unassailable; but every utterance which he makes in public ... must necessarily bring him within the focus of criticism.

4.12 Politics of the judiciary

When considering the role which the judiciary plays in the process of applying the law or indeed the process, already adverted to in Chapter 2, whereby the judiciary actually make the law, criticism is usually levelled at the particular race, class and gender position of the majority of the judges. It is an objective and well documented fact that the majority of judges are white, middle class, middle aged to elderly men: but the question that has to be considered is whether this necessarily leads to the conclusion that judges reach inherently biased decisions. It is always possible, indeed, the newspapers make it relatively easy, to provide anecdotal evidence which apparently confirms either the bias, or the lack of social awareness, of the judiciary; but the fundamental question remains as to whether these cases are exceptional or whether they represent the norm.

Why should judges' class/race/gender placement make them less objective arbiters of the law? It is worth considering the fact that unsupported general assertions as to the inherently partial approach of the judiciary is itself partial. Simon Lee, not totally fatuously, has highlighted the logical flaw in what he refers to as the Tony Benn Thesis (Benn is the Left Wing, Labour Party MP who created history by being the first hereditary peer to renounce his peerage in order to remain in the House of Commons). Just because judges are old, white, rich, upper middle class, educated at public school and Oxbridge does not mean that they all necessarily think the same way; after all, Benn was a product of the same social circumstances. There is, of course, the point that people from that particular background generally tend to be conservative in outlook, and the apparent validity of Lee's argument is clearly the product of logic-chopping that reverses the accepted relationship and uses the exception as the rule rather than seeing the exception as proving/testing the rule. Nevertheless, Lee's point remains true; that proof of judicial bias is needed.

As the previous chapter of this book pointed out, if law were completely beyond the scope of judges to manipulate to their own ends, then the race, class, and gender placement of individual judges would be immaterial, as they would not be in any position to influence the operation of the law. That chapter also demonstrated, however, that the way in which the doctrines which set the limits within which the judiciary operate are by no means as rigid and restrictive as they might first appear. It was seen that, although judges are supposed merely to apply, rather than create, law, they possess a large measure of discretion in determining which laws to apply, what those laws mean, and how they should be applied. In the light of this potential capacity to create law, it is essential to ensure that the judiciary satisfactorily represents society at large in relation to which it has so much power, and to ensure further that it does not merely represent the views and attitudes of a self-perpetuating élite.

The limited class background of the judiciary was confirmed in figures issued by the Lord Chancellor's office on 17 May 1995 which revealed that 80% of Lords of Appeal, Heads of Division, Lord Justices of Appeal and High Court judges were educated at Oxford or Cambridge. In justifying the figures, the Lord Chancellor's Permanent Secretary, Sir Thomas Legg, showing insouciance to the level of arrogance, simply stated that:

> It is not the function of the professional judiciary to be representative of the community. Such a response, if it is true, or even acceptable, must surely undermine the right of such an unrepresentative body to take action in the name of the majority, as the courts do in their use of judicial review.

Unfortunately, the continuing social imbalance amongst the senior judiciary was further confirmed in a report on judicial appointments by the Commons Home Affairs Committee presented in June 1996. It revealed that four-fifths of judges went to both public schools and Oxbridge colleges, that only seven out of 96 High Court judges were women, and that only five out of the 517 circuit judges were black or Asian. Nevertheless, the Committee rejected proposals for positive discrimination or even for the establishment of a judicial appointments committee to replace the present informal system under the control of the Lord Chancellor.

Instead of things improving, if one actually has the temerity to consider it an improvement to have fewer Oxbridge men on the bench, a Labour Research investigation found that things were actually getting worse in terms of the wider representational make up of the judiciary (as has been considered in 4.3.2). Still, Lord Irvine holds fast to appointment solely on merit, which appears wholly commendable; but, as has been stated before, who decides on merit, and what are they actually measuring?

4.12.1 Criticisms

Given the central position of judges in the operation of law and the legal system, particularly with regard to the growth in judicial review and their new role in relation to giving effect to the HRA, the question these reports raise is whether the social placement of the judiciary leads to any perceptible shortfall in the provision of justice. The pre-eminent critic of the way in which the judiciary permit their shared background, attitudes and prejudices to influence their understanding and statement of the law is Professor JAG Griffith. According to Griffith, bias can occur at two levels:

- *Personal bias*

Personal bias occurs where individual judges permit their own personal prejudices to influence their judgment and, thus, the effective application of the law. It is relatively easy to cite cases where judges give expression to their own attitudes and in so doing exhibit their own prejudices. As examples of this process, two cases can be cited which consider the rule of natural justice, that a person should not be both the accuser and judge in the same case. In *Hannam v Bradford Corp* (1970), the court held that it was contrary to natural justice for three school governors to sit as members of a local authority education disciplinary committee charged with deciding whether or not to uphold a previous decision of the governors to dismiss a teacher. This was so even though the three governors had not been present at the meeting where it was decided to dismiss the teacher. On the other hand, in *Ward v Bradford Corp* (1971), the Court of Appeal refused to interfere with a decision by governors of a teacher training college to confirm the expulsion of a student, although they had instituted the disciplinary proceedings, and three members of the governors sat on the original disciplinary committee. What possible explanation can there be for this discrepancy? The only tenable explanation is to be found in the latter courts disapproval of the plaintiffs behaviour in that case. The truly reprehensible judgment of Lord Denning concludes that the student lost nothing as she was not a fit person to teach children in any case. Can such a conclusion be justified on purely legal grounds or is it based on individual morality? Lord Denning did his best to buttress his judgment with spurious legal reasoning, but it could be suggested that, in so doing, he merely brought the process of legal reasoning into disrepute and revealed its fallaciousness.

Courts have also been notoriously unsympathetic to victims of rape and have been guilty of making the most obtuse of sexist comments in relation to such victims. Nor can it be claimed that depreciatory racist remarks have been totally lacking in court cases.

Such cases of bias are serious and reprehensible but the very fact that the prejudice they demonstrate appears as no more than the outcome of particular judges, who are simply out of touch with current standards of morality or acceptable behaviour, suggests that it might be eradicated by the Lord Chancellor exercising stricter control over such mavericks, and appointing more appropriate judges in the first place. Professor Griffith, however, suggests that there is a further type of bias that is actually beyond such relatively easy control.

- *Corporate bias*

Corporate bias involves the assertion that the judges as a body decide certain types of cases in a biased way. This accusation of corporate bias is much more serious than that of personal bias for the reason that it asserts that the problem of bias is systematic rather than merely limited to particular maverick judges. As a consequence, if such a claim is justified, it has to be concluded that the problem is not susceptible to treatment at the level of the individual judge, but requires a complete alteration of the whole judicial system.

Griffith claims that, as a consequence of their shared educational experience, their shared training and practical experience at the Bar and their shared social situation as members of the Establishment, judges have developed a common outlook. He maintains that they share homogeneous values, attitudes and beliefs as to how the law should operate and be administered. He further suggests that this shared outlook is inherently conservative, if not Conservative in a party political sense.

Griffith's argument is that the highest judges in the judicial hierarchy are frequently called upon to decide cases on the basis of a determination of what constitutes the public interest and that, in making that determination, they express their own corporate values, which are in turn a product of their position in society as part of the ruling Establishment. Griffith maintains that judges can be seen to operate in such a way as to maintain the status quo and resist challenges to the established authority. Underlying this argument is the implication that the celebrated independence of the judiciary is, in fact, a myth and that the courts will tend to decide cases in such a way as to buttress the position of the State, especially if it is under the control of a Conservative government.

In an attempt to substantiate his claims, Griffith examines cases relating to trade union law, personal rights, property rights and matters of national security where he claims to find judges consistently acting to support the interests of the State over the rights of the individual. Some of the concrete examples he cites are the withdrawal of trade union rights from GCHQ at Cheltenham (*Council of Civil Service Unions v Minister for Civil Service* (1984)); the banning of publishing any extracts from the *Spycatcher* book (*AG v Guardian Newspapers Ltd* (1987)); and the treatment of suspected terrorists.

Griffith, and other academics associated with the left, have expressed their reservations about the extent to which the HRA will hand power to an unelected, unaccountable, inherently conservative and unreformed body, as they claim the judiciary is. But, at the same time, they appear equally concerned that the government is delaying implementation of the Act to 3 October 2000, until the judiciary can be suitably trained: the concern would appear to be as to what is meant by the word suitably.

A notable, if somewhat complacent, response to Griffith's book was provided by Lord Devlin. Lord Devlin pointed that, in most cases, and on most issues, there tended to be plurality rather than unanimity of opinion and decision amongst judges. He also claimed that it would be just as possible for a more conservatively minded person that Griffith to go through the casebooks to provide a list of examples where the courts had operated in a over-liberal manner. Lord Devlin also adopted a different explanation of the judiciary's perceived reluctance to abandon the status quo. For him, any conservatism on the part of judges was to be seen as a product of age rather than class. In conclusion, he asserted that even if the judiciary were biased, its bias was well known and allowances could be made for it.

The issue of the way in which the criminal appeal procedure dealt with suspected terrorist cases is of particular relevance in the light of the Runciman Commission Report. General dissatisfaction with the trials and appeals involving suspected terrorists such as the Maguire Seven, the Birmingham Six, the Guildford Four, the Tottenham Three, Stefan Kiszko and Judith Ward helped to give rise to the widespread impression that the UK criminal justice system and, in particular, the British appeal system needed to be considered for reform.

In the light of the fact that the appeal system did not seem to be willing to consider the possibility of the accused's innocence once they had been convicted, the Runciman Commissions recommendation that a Criminal Case Review Authority be established independent of the Home Office were widely welcomed and resulted in the establishment of the Criminal Cases Review Commission (CCRC) in the Criminal Appeal Act 1995 (see 3.18.6). The question still remains, however, whether those earlier cases reflect an inherently and inescapably conservative judiciary or were they simply unfortunate instances of more general errors of the system which the implementation of the CCRC can overcome? And, perhaps more importantly, will the Court of Appeal give a fair hearing to the cases referred to it by the CCRC?

It is apparent from the statistics produced by the Lord Chancellor's Department cited previously that senior judges are still being appointed from the same limited social and educational élite as they always have been. This gives rise to the suspicion, if not the reality, that the decisions that this élite make merely represent values and interests of a limited and privileged segment of society, rather than society as a whole. Even if the accusations levelled by Professor Griffith are inaccurate, it is surely still necessary to remove even the possibility of those accusations.

THE JUDICIARY

The constitutional role of the judiciary

Judges play a central role in the English constitution. The doctrine of the separation of powers maintains that the judicial function be kept distinct from the legislative and executive functions of the State. The Lord Chancellor fills an anomalous situation in this respect.

The constitutional role of the Lord Chancellor

The Lord Chancellor holds an anomalous position in respect of the separation of powers within the UK Constitution, in that he is, at one and the same time; the most senior member of the judiciary and can hear cases in the House of Lords as a court; a member of the legislature as speaker of the House of Lords as a legislative assembly; and a member of the executive holding a position in the government. Although doubts have been raised about this situation, the present incumbent shows no desire to alter it, and indeed has gone on record as supporting the status quo.

The effect of the *Pinochet* case on the House of Lords

The recent case involving the previous dictator of Chile, General Augusto Pinochet, has brought the House of Lords into the glare of unlooked for publicity. It has raised questions as to its current role within the present constitution and even more concern has been expressed about its role under a reformed constitution with devolution and a non-hereditary House of Lords.

Judicial offices

The main judicial offices are the Lord Chancellor, the Lord Chief Justice, the Mater of the Rolls, the President of the Family Division, the Vice Chancellor and the Senior Presiding Judge. Law Lords are referred to as Lords of Appeal in Ordinary. Court of Appeal judges are referred to as Lords Justices of Appeal.

Appointment of judiciary

The CLSA 1990 has opened the possibility of judicial office, even in the higher courts, to non-barristers.

All judicial appointments remain, theoretically, at the hands of the Crown. The Prime Minister advises the Crown on the appointment of senior judicial office holders and the Law Lords, and Appeal Court judges. Judges at the level of High Court judges and below, including lay magistrates, are appointed on the advice of the Lord Chancellor.

Lord Chancellor Mackay's limited steps to open up appointment procedure have been followed up by Lord Irvine, but as yet the system remains secretive, not to say mysterious, and the establishment of an independent Judicial Appointments Commission remains unlikely.

Training of the judiciary

Training of English judges is undertaken under the auspices of the Judicial Studies Board. Judges for the highest Law Lord to the lowest magistrate are subject to training. It is gratifying to note that anti-discriminatory training is a priority, although some have continued to express doubt about judicial attitudes in this regard. Special training has been instituted in relation to the Woolf reforms and the introduction of the HRA. This being said, it remains arguable that the training undergone by UK judges is not as rigorous as the training of judges on the Continent.

Removal of judges

Senior judges hold office subject to good behaviour. They can be removed by an address by the two Houses of Parliament.

Judges below High Court status can be removed by the Lord Chancellor on grounds of misbehaviour or incapacity and he can remove magistrates without the need to show cause.

Judicial immunity

To ensure judicial integrity, it is provided that judges cannot be sued for actions done or words said in the course of their judicial function.

This immunity extends to trial lawyers, witnesses and juries.

Magistrates

Magistrates have powers in relation to both criminal and civil law.

Stipendiary magistrates, now District Judges (Magistrates' Courts) are professional and are legally qualified.

Lay magistrates are not paid and they are not legally qualified.

Magistrates are appointed by the Lord Chancellor.

Important issues relate to the representative nature of the magistracy.

Judicial review

Under the Constitution of the UK, and within the doctrine of the separation of powers, judges and the executive have distinct but interrelated roles.

Regarding the Rule of Law, various writers have various understandings, but see it essentially as involving a control of arbitrary power: Dicey; Hayek; Thompson; Raz; Unger; Weber.

Judicial review remedies are the prerogative remedies of certiorari, mandamus, prohibition, together with the private law remedies of declaration, injunction and damages. Private law remedies cannot be used in relation to public law complaints.

Increased judicial activity in relation to State programmes raises questions as to the competence and authority of judges to act as well as raising doubts as to their political views.

A recent Law Commission report has suggested various improvements to judicial review procedure to allow it operate effectively into the 21st century.

Judicial reasoning

Laws can be presented in the form of syllogisms but do not actually focus on questions of deductive reasoning.

The doctrine of judicial precedent appears at first sight to involve deductive reasoning but is in fact based on the much less certain use of inductive reasoning and reasoning by analogy.

Statutory interpretation

Communication is inherently uncertain, but legislation has particular problems that arise from the contradictory nature of the various ends it tries to achieve.

Judges have to interpret legislation to give it effect the question is do they give it the effect that Parliament intended?

Approaches to statutory interpretation

The literal approach, theoretically at least, limits judges to simply deciding the meaning of the words of the statute. It is the main approach in the English legal system, apart from cases involving European Community law.

The purposive approach allows judges to go behind the words of the statute to seek to give effect to its purpose but it is only recognised in relation to Community law.

The rules of interpretation

The literal rule gives words in legislation their plain, ordinary, everyday meaning, even if this leads to an apparent injustice.

The golden rule is used in circumstances where the application of the literal rule is likely to result in an obviously absurd result. In such circumstances, the court will not apply the literal meaning but will instead interpret the provision in such a way as to avoid the absurdity.

The mischief rule permits the court to go beyond the words of the statute in question to consider the mischief at which it was aimed. This is the nearest the English system comes to openly acknowledging the purposive approach to statutory interpretation but its ambit of operation is not nearly so wide.

Aids to construction

Intrinsic assistance relies on such internal evidence as the statute under consideration can provide through reference to the following: the title of the Act, any preamble, or any schedules to it.

Extrinsic assistance permits the judge to go beyond the Act in question in order to ascertain its meaning. Amongst possible sources are dictionaries, textbooks, other statutes including the Interpretation Act 1978, reports, other parliamentary papers, and, since *Pepper v Hart* (1993), *Hansard* may also be consulted.

Presumptions

In addition to the rules of interpretation, there are also various presumptions that will be applied, unless rebutted. The most important of these are presumptions against the alteration of the common law; against retrospective application; against the deprivation of an individuals liberty, property or rights; and against application to the Crown. In addition, there are presumptions in favour of the requirement for *mens rea* in relation to criminal offences; and deriving the meaning of words from their contexts.

Politics of the judiciary

Judges have a capacity to make law the question is do they exercise this power in a biased way?

Bias can take two forms: personal and corporate.

Accusations of corporate bias suggest that, as a group, judges represent the interest of the status quo and decide certain political cases in line with that interest.

CHAPTER 5

THE CRIMINAL LAW

5.1 The general principles of criminal liability

5.1.1 The nature and sources of criminal law

Criminal law obviously concerns crime, but what is a crime? There is a view that it is impossible to identify a universal definition of the nature of a crime because the essence of criminality changes with historical context. As Glanville Williams has observed:

> ... a crime (or offence) is a legal wrong that can be followed by criminal proceedings which may result in punishment [*Learning the Law*, 1983, p 27].

In other words, a crime is anything that the State has chosen to criminalise. A similar analysis was adopted by Lord Atkin:

> ... the domain of criminal jurisprudence can only be ascertained by examining what acts at any particular period are declared by the State to be crimes, and the only common nature they will be found to possess is that they are prohibited by the State and that those who commit them are punished [*Proprietary Articles Trade Association v AG for Canada* [1931] AC 324].

One way to escape the circularity of these definitions of crime is to refer to the seriousness of the wrongs. Thus, Williams eventually concedes that:

> ... a crime is an act that is condemned sufficiently strongly to have induced the authorities (legislature or judges) to declare it to be punishable before the ordinary courts [*Learning the Law*, 1983, p 29].

In an early edition of the leading theoretical text *Criminal Law* (1992), Smith and Hogan acknowledge the view of Sir Carleton Allen, who writes:

> ... crime is crime because it consists in wrongdoing which directly and in serious degree threatens the security or well being of society, and because it is not safe to leave it redressable only by compensation of the party injured [p 16].

At the outset of this new millennium, there are about 7,000 criminal offences in English law. They range from the most minor traffic offences (for example, driving a vehicle with one of the rear break lights not working) to genocide (criminalised under the Genocide Act 1969). These different criminal offences have no common denominator other than that they are things which the State has, for different reasons and at different times, decided are sufficiently serious to warrant being treated as crimes.

Much of the criminal law is now to be found in statutes, though there are a number of offences (murder and manslaughter, for example) and defences (such as automatism, intoxication and duress) which depend largely upon decisions of the courts and have not been reduced into statutory form. There is certainly no all-embracing code of criminal law, even though proposals for codification were made as long ago as the 19th century. The Law Commission has revived attempts to devise a Code and has been publishing proposals since 1989, but they have not yet been enacted.

5.1.2   Classification of crimes

There are a number of ways of classifying crimes. The more common ways of doing so include:

- by source – crimes may be treated as common law or as statutory offences, although today more and more crimes are regulated by statute;

- by method of trial – summary, indictable and triable either way;

- by reference to the powers of arrest – whether they are arrestable or non-arrestable;

- by whether they can be regarded as 'true' crimes or merely as 'regulatory' crimes – this classification may be of some value in considering whether a crime should be regarded as imposing strict liability.

5.1.3   The elements of criminal liability

It is generally argued that criminal liability consists of three components:

(1) the *actus reus* – some 'conduct' by D accompanied by the existence of legally relevant 'circumstances'. For many offences, it will also be necessary to show that the conduct 'caused' certain 'consequences'. These are the external elements of an offence and, in the traditional terminology, they comprise the *actus reus* of the offence. For example, D elbows V in the face. V is a police constable on duty. This is the *actus reus* of assaulting (meaning here a battery) a police constable in the execution of his duty. The conduct is the elbowing, the consequence is that force is inflicted on V, and the circumstances are that V was not just any person (which would have made it a common assault) but a police constable acting in the execution of his duty;

(2) the *mens rea* – a blameworthy state of mind in relation to the conduct, circumstances and consequences (that is, to the *actus reus* elements identified above). Traditionally, this blameworthy state of mind is referred to as *mens rea* and encompasses intention, knowledge, recklessness

(awareness of risk) and, in very limited cases, recklessness without awareness of risk. In the example above, if D was trying to elbow V in the face, he intended to inflict force. If he knew there was a risk that he would elbow V in the face (if, for instance, he had his back to V and swung his elbow back in V's direction to keep him away), he was reckless as to the infliction of force;

(3) the absence of any defence, whether general or specific, total or partial, which D could plead to avoid liability. In the example previously discussed, suppose that V was not wearing a uniform and that D thought V was an ordinary member of the public who was about to attack him. He would be entitled to use reasonable force to defend himself. So, D might avoid liability for elbowing V in the face (the issues of mistake and self-defence are discussed in 5.2).

The actus reus

It will be clear from the discussion above that the *actus reus* of a crime is not merely any act by D:

- criminal liability does not always require proof of an act. In some situations, an omission to act will suffice. This is why the broader term 'conduct' is used in discussing *actus reus*. For example, D will usually kill by an act such as beating, shooting or stabbing, but he may do so by withholding food from someone who is helpless. This is an omission;

- it is also usual to qualify 'conduct' by asserting that it must be 'voluntary', that is, it is at least in part the product of control by the conscious brain. So, 'voluntariness' is another element in the *actus reus* of crimes. If D is feeling a little unwell and clumsily breaks a vase on sale in a shop, he is probably still acting voluntarily because he has some conscious control of his movements. If, instead, he had received a severe blow to the head moments before he broke the vase, it may be that he was not acting voluntarily because he was concussed;

- it includes any elements appearing in the definition of the crime which are neither conduct nor consequences. These elements are generally termed 'circumstances'. As explained above, in the offence of assaulting a police constable in the execution of his duty, V must have two special characteristics: he must be a police constable; and he must be performing his duty. These are 'circumstances' to be proved, as required by the definition of the crime;

- the *actus reus* of many crimes will incorporate a required 'consequence' which must be 'caused' by D's conduct. If D kicks out at V, he will only commit the *actus reus* of inflicting grievous bodily harm if the kick lands on V and causes him serious injury. D may miss with his kick, or he may kick V and cause him only minor injury. In either case, there will be no offence of inflicting grievous bodily harm (though there may be an offence of attempt).

A general way of expressing all of this might be to say that the *actus reus* of a crime consists of all those elements which cannot be described as part of the *mens rea*.

Conduct

Criminal liability generally depends upon proof that D engaged in some act. If we think about crimes such as murder, causing grievous bodily harm with intent and theft, we envisage acts such as shooting, stabbing, kicking or punching V, or stealthily removing V's wallet from his pocket or taking items from a shop. Most of us grow up accepting the idea that we are forbidden from doing some things, however much we might want to do them. We absorb notions of prohibition and punishment from an early age and so are familiar with the general structure of criminal law and criminal justice. So, criminal liability based on the prohibition of acts creates no special problems.

By contrast, we find it difficult to envisage the factual situations in which the common crimes may be committed by failures to act (that is, omissions). How is it possible to say, for instance, that D killed V by not doing something? If D fails to help V who has been knocked down by a hit-and-run driver and is bleeding to death, how does that failure *cause* V's death? To believe that D could be responsible, we have to persuade ourselves that he ought to have intervened. But, however much we might feel morally obliged to help others, we are not accustomed to thinking that there is a general legal obligation to do so. In any case, what exactly would D be required to do, and would the same obligation be placed on every other bystander who was aware of V's injuries? Would all of them be prosecuted if they failed to help? If so, then the criminal justice system might be overwhelmed. If not, selective prosecution might bring the system into disrepute.

On the other hand, there are some situations in which we have no difficulty in regarding others as responsible for harmful consequences when they fail to act. A parent is expected to be vigilant for the health and safety of the child. A swimming pool supervisor is expected to act to ensure the safety of swimmers. The difference between the witness to the hit-and-run and the parent or supervisor is easy to see. Nothing marks out the witness to the accident from any other witness. The law would have to recognise a very broad obligation to help others, applicable to everyone, in order to impose liability on him (though some countries do recognise obligations of this kind). To impose liability on the parent or supervisor, however, is to recognise an obligation grounded in a pre-existing relationship between parent and child, or supervisor and swimmer, into which parent and supervisor have entered (more or less) freely. It does not imply that anyone else is under the obligation.

Liability for omissions to act, then, requires the following:

(a) The crime must be defined in such a way that it makes sense to say that an omission will suffice. For instance, though D will usually 'cause' grievous bodily harm by doing acts such as kicking and punching, he could also do so by failing to warn V that he is about to suffer the injury. Similarly, D could destroy or damage property by failing to put out a fire. Where a statute imposes an obligation to do something, then obviously the liability is defined in terms of an omission, for example, the obligation of a driver to stop and give certain information after being involved in an accident which resulted in personal injury or damage to property (s 170 of the Road Traffic Act 1988).

If the definition uses the word 'act', it is unlikely that an omission will suffice. So, an attempt to commit a crime requires proof of 'an act more than merely preparatory' to the commission of the full offence (s 1(1) of the Criminal Attempts Act 1981). In *Lowe* (1973), it was held that 'unlawful act manslaughter' can only be committed by an act.

In some instances, it remains unclear whether an act is required or an omission will suffice. An assault occurs when D causes V to fear the infliction of immediate personal injury. A battery is constituted by the infliction of the injury. In *Fagan v Metropolitan Police Commissioner* (1968), the court held unanimously that both assault and battery require proof of an act but, in *DPP v K* (1990), there were suggestions that an assault occasioning actual bodily harm could be committed by an omission.

(b) It must be proven that D was under a duty to do some positive act. A duty generally arises out of a relationship created, at least in part, by D's own conduct. The major examples are:

- *parental, family or equivalent.* Parents have statutory obligations to their children and there is a specific crime of neglect of a child (s 1 of the Children and Young Persons Act 1933). In *Gibbins and Proctor* (1918), D1 was convicted of the murder of his child, V, from whom food had been withheld by D2, D1's partner. In *Stone and Dobinson* (1977), even though D1 was 67 years old and V was 61, D1 was considered to be under a duty to care for V, partly because he was her brother (see below for a fuller account of this case);

- *contractual, especially employment.* Entering into a contract to perform a particular job can create a duty on the employee to both the employer and any other person who is at risk of injury or damage in the performance of that job. In *Pittwood* (1902), a level crossing keeper employed by a railway company to open and close the gates was guilty of manslaughter when he forgot to close the gates on the approach of a train and a person crossing the line was killed;

- *voluntary assumption of responsibility by D.* This is a rather controversial category, best illustrated by reference to *Stone and Dobinson*, already briefly mentioned above. V, who was anorexic, had become bedridden and had died from infected bedsores whilst living with D1 and D2. It was held that D1 and D2 had assumed responsibility for V by intervening to clean her at an earlier stage, and so were guilty of manslaughter for failing to get help for her when her condition deteriorated again;

- *the deliberate or accidental creation of a dangerous situation by D.* If D's conduct creates a danger to persons or property, he must do something to eliminate or reduce the danger. He is under this duty even if he was not initially at fault. In *Miller* (1983), D fell asleep whilst smoking a cigarette and set light to a mattress. When he woke up, he simply went off to another room and fell asleep again whilst the fire caused further damage. His initial conduct in falling asleep created the dangerous situation and thus imposed a duty on him to put the fire out or raise the alarm. His failure to do so made him guilty of criminal damage;

- *a public office.* There is a common law offence of misconduct in a public office. A police constable is the holder of a public office and he is under a duty, amongst other things, to preserve the Queen's peace, to prevent crime and to apprehend suspected offenders. The court in *Dytham* (1979) upheld the conviction of a police constable for this offence, on evidence that he had witnessed an attack outside a nightclub and had deliberately taken no action to stop V being beaten to death.

(c) The omission to act must amount to a breach of the duty.

(d) If the crime is a result crime, then it must be possible to argue that, if D had acted in fulfilment of his duty, the consequence might not have occurred. In that sense, the breach must be a legal cause of the consequence. For example, suppose that a carer did not seek help for a patient who had suddenly suffered a heart attack. If the evidence showed that the heart attack was so severe that the patient would have died no matter what treatment had been administered, then the failure to seek help did not cause the death.

Voluntariness

There can be no criminal liability in any offence requiring proof of conduct unless D's conduct was voluntary. Suppose that D slips on ice which he could not reasonably have known was there and slides into V, causing her injury. D's conduct was involuntary, and so he did not commit the *actus reus* of any personal injury offence. In this case, D was not suffering from any impaired consciousness, but issues of voluntariness more commonly arise where D asserts that his actions were not under the control of his conscious brain, such as where he is suffering from the effects of high or low blood sugar associated with diabetes. In these kinds of cases, the focus is not so much on 'voluntariness' as on 'involuntariness', and the plea is given the special name of automatism. D asserts automatism (that he was an automaton) when he asserts that he was not acting voluntarily. This plea is closely connected with the pleas of insanity and intoxication and is further explained in the analysis of the general defences in 5.2.

Causation

In any crime which requires the proof of a consequence, it will be necessary for the prosecution to prove a causal connection ('causation') between D's conduct and that consequence. In the vast majority of cases, this will present no problems and will be satisfied by proving that the consequence would not have happened 'but for' D's conduct. Suppose that D punches V and knocks him backwards towards a wall. V strikes his head on the wall and suffers a broken skull. If D had not punched V, V would not have suffered the injury, and nothing else can be said to have caused it.

But proof of causation will not be quite so straightforward in some cases, especially in those involving homicide, where there may be a significant gap between any attack by D and the occurrence of V's death (the consequence). The greater the gap, the greater the possibility that D may be able to claim that the true cause of V's death was something that occurred after the attack, such as another injury inflicted by someone else or some very poor medical treatment administered by incompetent doctors. Instead of trying to develop a comprehensive definition of causation, the courts have tended to concentrate on the commonly recurring problems. As a result, analysis has usually focused on the question of what kinds of actions and events break the chain of causation.

In broad terms, to establish that D's conduct caused a consequence, the prosecution must prove that the conduct:

- was a cause *in fact* of the consequence, that is, the consequence would not have occurred but for D's conduct; and
- was a cause *in law* of the consequence, that is, it made a significant contribution to the occurrence of the consequence (other phrases used to express this requirement include 'substantial', 'operating and substantial' and 'proximate').

Causation in fact

It is impossible to establish that D's conduct was a cause in law without first proving that it was a cause in fact. In *White* (1910), D did not cause his mother's death and so was not guilty of murder when the medical evidence showed that she had died of a heart attack rather than from the poison which D had put in her bedtime drink. It was not even established that she took any of the drink. In *Pagett* (1983), on the other hand, D's conduct in kidnapping V and using her as a human shield after he had shot at police officers was certainly a cause in fact of her death when she was killed by return fire from the police officers.

Causation in law

Evidently, there may be many 'causes in fact' of a consequence in the sense indicated above and some further test is necessary to distinguish those which are legally sufficient from those which are not. Expressions such as 'significant contribution' and 'operating and substantial' can do no more than suggest an idea of what is required. They are not formulae into which facts can be fed to unerringly produce the solution. The following points are important in understanding the approach adopted by the courts:

- whatever expression is used, the contribution of D's conduct to the occurrence of the consequence must reach a certain minimum level – it must be more than merely trivial;

- D's conduct need not be the sole cause. This may be particularly important where X's conduct later aggravates the consequences of D's original conduct. Far from breaking the chain of causation between D's conduct and the aggravated consequence, this may merely make both D and X guilty of causing the consequence. For example, there have been cases in which D has inflicted injury on V, who has then died after receiving poor or inadequate medical treatment by doctors. In such cases, it is possible that both D and the doctors can be said to have caused the death. However, it is a big step from that conclusion to the further conclusion that the doctors are actually guilty of a crime; quite rightly, the courts will not be too ready to attribute criminal liability to those who, however imperfectly, were seeking to assist V;

- in the case of death (or any other lesser consequence), if injuries inflicted by D are the immediate and sufficient cause of the consequence (the phrase 'operating and substantial' is often used in this context), then D causes that consequence no matter what has happened after D inflicted the injuries; at best, subsequent actions and events are merely additional causes. In *Smith* (1959), V was stabbed by D in a fight between several soldiers. Subsequently, his friend dragged him roughly to receive treatment from an overworked doctor, who failed to recognise the seriousness of his injuries and administered treatment which certainly did not help V and may have contributed to his death. Prompt and correct treatment, using equipment which was not available to the doctor, might have saved his life. D's act in stabbing V was held to be the 'operating and substantial' cause of his death since he died from the stab wounds, whatever the contribution made by the rough handling and poor treatment;

- if D's conduct has not caused injuries which are 'immediate and sufficient' (in the above sense) at the time that the consequence occurs, there are two possibilities. First, the immediate and sufficient cause may have been some conduct by another person, who may be either the victim or a third person. Secondly, injuries inflicted by D may be contributing to the consequence but may not be sufficient in themselves to bring it about. In the first case, D can only be said to have caused the consequence if some other principle can be invoked which will sufficiently connect D's conduct with the subsequent conduct of the victim or third person. In the second case, the tendency of the courts is to argue that D's conduct was a legal cause even though it would not have been sufficient in itself;

- the principle applied to connect D's conduct to that of the victim or a third person will often be reasonable foreseeability. Thus, in *Pagett*, D was held to have caused V's death, not only in fact (see above), but also in law. The acts of the police officers in returning fire were considered by the court to be reasonable acts in self-preservation and in performance of their legal duty. They were regarded as comparable with the reasonably foreseeable acts of a victim in attempting to escape from the violence of an attack by D (as in *Pitts* (1842)). However, free and voluntary action by a victim will usually prevent D from being liable for causing the consequence, even if that action was reasonably foreseeable.

It is now possible to examine the approach of the courts to some common instances where causation is in issue.

(a) Refusal of treatment and/or aggravation of injuries by V

If D injures V and V makes the injuries worse by neglect or maltreatment of himself, D will nonetheless be held to have caused the injuries. In *Holland* (1841), D was held to have caused V's death when V died from tetanus contracted as a result of a wound to his finger inflicted by D. V's refusal to have the finger amputated as a precaution against tetanus did not break the chain of causation. At that time, V's refusal might not have been unreasonable. Yet, in the more modern case of *Blaue* (1976), it was held that the reasonableness of a refusal of treatment is not relevant to the issue of causation. On account of her religious beliefs, V had refused a blood transfusion which might have saved her life after she had been stabbed by D. D's conviction for manslaughter was upheld. The court asserted that there would be no yardstick by which to measure reasonableness, but their reluctance to look for one might be attributable to the fact that V's refusal was neither malicious nor a mere whim but was grounded in sincerely held convictions.

(b) The especially susceptible victim (the 'thin skull' victim)

The general rule is that D must 'take his victim as he finds him'. This means that if, because of some special weakness in V, D causes greater injury to V than would normally have been expected, D will nevertheless be held to have caused the full extent of the injuries. If D hits V on the head in a way which would cause little more than bruising in most victims but V happens to have a weak skull and the blow kills him, D will be held to have caused his death. This rule was relied on in *Blaue*, where it was said that the rule extended to 'the whole man, not just the physical man'. Though V had no physical weakness, she was at special risk because of her religious beliefs.

(c) Injuries resulting from an attempted escape

If V tries to escape from an attack by D and in doing so suffers injury, D causes the injury unless V's actions were not reasonably foreseeable. In applying this rule, allowance has to be made for the fact that those in fear cannot be expected to behave entirely rationally. In *Roberts* (1971), D was held to have caused V's injuries when V jumped from D's car to avoid being sexually assaulted by him. Since the car was travelling at a moderate speed on a deserted road and V had every reason to fear a serious assault, V's actions were reasonably foreseeable. Similarly, in *Corbett* (1996), D caused V's death when V died as a result of stumbling into the path of a motor vehicle while trying to escape from an attack by D.

(d) Negligent, poor or inappropriate medical treatment

Suppose that D injures V, who then receives poor medical treatment. If V suffers more serious injury than might have been expected, or dies, some questions are raised about the medical treatment:

- does it break the chain of causation between D's conduct and V's more serious injury or death, and so free D from liability?

- does it mean that the medical staff caused the injury or death?

- if it does, are the medical staff guilty of a crime?

Generally, negligent, poor or inappropriate treatment does not break the chain of causation. The courts do not apply the rules to such treatment that they use for other intervening acts or events. The question is not about reasonable foreseeability or even whether or not there was negligent or otherwise inappropriate treatment. As was stressed in *Mellor* (1996), the question is whether D's conduct made a significant contribution to the consequence. Negligent or inappropriate treatment will cast doubt on the extent to which D's conduct amounts to a significant contribution *only* if it is of such a kind that the original wound was 'merely the setting in which another cause operates' or where 'the second cause is so overwhelming as to make the original wound merely part of the history' (*Smith* (1959)).

In *Cheshire* (1991), the rule was expressed in a slightly different way. It was asserted that negligent medical treatment would only break the chain of causation if it was '... so independent of D's acts, and in itself so potent in causing death ...' that the contribution made by D's acts in causing death was insignificant. So, even though V's death resulted from undetected complications some weeks after an operation, D was held to have caused his death. The operation and its complications were not causes independent of D's actions; V needed the operation because he had been shot by D. The only significant example of a successful argument that medical treatment broke the chain appears to have been in *Jordan* (1956). In that case, V had substantially recovered from injuries inflicted by D when a hospital doctor administered a drug to which he was known to be intolerant and made intravenous injections of excessive quantities of liquid, with the apparently predictable result that V died from bronchopneumonia.

Even if the chain of causation is not broken, it is possible that negligent or poor medical treatment might be regarded as an additional cause of the injury or death. Yet this would not necessarily mean that medical staff were guilty of an offence. As pointed out earlier, courts will not readily interpret the rules in such a way as to make criminals out of those who are striving to prevent injury or save life.

Circumstances

'Circumstances' is the term used to describe those elements in the definition of the *actus reus* of a crime which are neither conduct nor consequences. In the offence of murder, for instance, the required circumstances are that the victim must be a 'human being' and must be 'within the Queen's peace'.

Consequences

The meaning of 'consequences' will be apparent from earlier discussion. There is no crime of homicide unless V has died. There is no crime of assault occasioning actual bodily harm unless V has suffered some injury amounting to actual bodily harm. Of course, charges of attempt may be available in these cases if the consequence has not occurred. The requirement in many crimes for proof of a consequence inevitably means that there is an element of chance in much criminal liability. Where D beats V, intending serious injury, his liability for murder rather than the lesser offence of causing grievous bodily harm with intent depends upon the chance of V's death occurring, even though D's actions and intentions, and so arguably his blameworthiness, are the same, whatever the outcome.

The mens rea

In serious crimes of the kind discussed in this chapter, the prosecution will be required to prove that D had the necessary *mens rea*. Regardless of whether a crime is a statutory or a common law crime, the *mens rea* required consists of both the specific requirements of the crime itself and the general common law requirement that there must be proof of intention or recklessness in relation to the *actus reus* elements. In murder, common law prescribes that the unlawful killing must be done with malice aforethought, an intention either to kill or to cause grievous bodily harm. The intention requirement is an expression of the common law demand for proof of a sufficient mental element. So strong is this demand that there is a general common law presumption that all crimes require proof of *mens rea*. Even if no *mens rea* requirement is expressed in the statutory definition of a crime, a court will imply one unless persuaded that the presumption has been rebutted. Crimes which do not require proof of *mens rea* are known as crimes of strict liability.

When used in the sense of the common law presumption, *mens rea* means 'intention' or 'recklessness' as to the elements of the *actus reus*. The meaning of these terms is to be found only in case decisions, even though statutory definitions have been proposed on a number of occasions, most recently by the Law Commission as part of its codification project. These meanings are also applied when the terms are used in statutory crimes. So, at common law, *mens rea* requires proof that D either intended any consequence or knew of the existence of any circumstance, or that D was aware of the risk of causing the consequence or of the existence of the circumstance. Such requirements are generally said to impose a subjective test, because D can be guilty only if he intended or knew or was aware of the risk.

However, in some cases, D can be regarded as blameworthy even if he neither intended nor was reckless in the senses described above. If D does not realise that his car's brakes are not working properly though any reasonable driver would have done so, he may be liable for manslaughter if he crashes his car and kills V. In such a case, his liability will depend upon his failure to meet an objective standard, the standard of the reasonable man. This is liability for negligence, though the courts have also recognised a category of objective recklessness. Finally, if D can be liable even though he is not subjectively or objectively blameworthy, then the crime is one of strict liability, and D is sometimes described as liable even though he is blamelessly inadvertent.

Intention

Though most offences can be committed without proof of intention to bring about a particular consequence (recklessness suffices), there are significant exceptions, murder being an obvious example.

We all have a general idea of what it means to intend to cause a particular consequence, and we all have experience of occasions on which our intentions have been fulfilled or have been thwarted. If asked to define intention, we would probably use words and phrases such as 'aim', 'purpose', 'desire', 'wanting to' or 'acting in order to'. In the vast majority of cases, magistrates or juries need no special guidance to enable them to decide whether or not D intended a particular consequence. If, for example, D is charged with causing serious injury and the evidence shows that he repeatedly kicked V about the head whilst V was on the floor, there will be little difficulty in concluding that D intended such injury. D would need to come up with a very convincing story to put reasonable doubt into the mind of any magistrate or juror. In cases where the evidence clearly suggests that it was D's purpose to cause the consequence, the prosecution would not need to show that he foresaw it as likely or probable, only that he genuinely believed that he might be able to achieve it by his conduct.

Nevertheless, there are cases where the evidence may not lead to an unambiguous, common sense answer and guidance may be required. D may aim to cause a particular consequence, which may or may not be criminal, but be prepared to risk a different, prohibited consequence in order to achieve it. Typical examples of this kind are to be found in *Hyam v DPP* (1974) and *Nedrick* (1986), cases in which D set fire to a house in pursuit of a grudge and caused the death of one or more occupants whilst claiming to have intended merely to cause fear. In other examples, violence may be used or threatened as a means of conveying some political or other message, as in *Hancock and Shankland* (1986), where D1 and D2, miners involved in the 1984 miners' strike, sought to prevent another miner from going to work by pushing concrete objects from a motorway bridge into the path of a convoy of police vehicles escorting a taxi which was taking him to work. One of the objects smashed through the windscreen of the taxi and killed the driver. They argued that their only intention was to stop the convoy and so stop the miner from getting to work.

Other cases do not fit neatly into any category. In *Woollin* (1998), D experienced a fit of rage and frustration when his three month old baby, V, choked on his food. He threw V with some violence in the direction of his pram, which was standing close to the wall. V died from a broken skull. D's only explanation was that he 'just did not want to know' V because of the feeding problem. Clearly, D did not have any obvious other aim for which he was prepared to risk death or serious injury to V, but equally, it is not immediately obvious that he intended death or serious injury.

Faced with these examples, the courts could have taken the view that there is no significant difference in moral blameworthiness between a person whose purpose is to cause a consequence and one who knows ('foresees') that his conduct will cause the consequence unless something extraordinary happens (often described as 'foresight of virtual certainty'). Intention could have been defined to include both states of mind, consistent with a recognised philosophical distinction between direct and oblique intention:

- *direct intention* – D's purpose is to cause the consequence;
- *oblique intention* – it is not D's purpose to cause the consequence but he foresees that it is virtually certain to result from his conduct.

In this scheme, any other state of mind is not sufficient to amount to intention. So, if it was not D's purpose to cause the consequence but he foresaw it as probable (or even highly probable), that would not be enough. As the explanation below will show, that state of mind is recklessness. Obviously, it might be difficult for a jury to decide whether D foresaw a consequence as virtually certain or as highly probable or merely probable, but juries are frequently faced with difficult questions of fact and they have to do their best.

In cases such as *Hyam v DPP* and *Nedrick*, for instance, they would have to look at matters such as how the fire was started, what time of the day or night it occurred, D's knowledge of how many people were in the house, what their ages were, how easy it might be to escape, and so on.

Until the decision of the House of Lords in *Woollin*, however, there was considerable confusion about the meaning of intention and, in particular, about whether foresight of virtual certainty was intention or was merely evidence from which a jury was entitled to infer intention. In quashing D's conviction for murder in *Woollin*, the House of Lords acknowledged that 'a result foreseen as virtually certain is an intended result' and this ought to have cleared up the confusion. In the case itself, for example, it would not have been necessary for the prosecution to show that D's purpose was to kill the baby or to cause it serious injury. It would have been enough to show that D knew that it was virtually certain that he would kill him or (more likely) cause him serious injury by throwing him in the direction of the pram.

The decision in *Woollin* has not yet been subjected to interpretation by the Court of Appeal and its true implications remain a little uncertain. In particular, the House of Lords said that, in cases where there is no obvious purpose to cause the consequence, the jury is 'not entitled' to find intention unless they are satisfied that D foresaw the consequence as virtually certain to occur. This might imply that, even if they are satisfied that D foresaw the consequence as virtually certain, the jury are not obliged to find ('are entitled not to find') intention. Clearly, this would conflict with the proposition that foresight of virtual certainty is intention. Further, their Lordships said that the decision related only to the meaning of intention in the law of murder and that 'it does not follow that "intent" necessarily has precisely the same meaning in every context in criminal law'.

Before the decision in *Woollin*, the position was that foresight (of whatever degree of probability) was not intention in itself but was at best evidence of intention. In cases where it was not possible to establish that it was D's purpose to cause the consequence, the jury could be invited to infer intention if satisfied that D foresaw the consequence with virtual certainty. Yet the jury was not bound to do so and it remained within their discretion. Of course, to infer intention, the jury had to be satisfied that D did intend and that his foresight of virtual certainty was evidence of that intention. But it must be remembered that these were cases in which it did not appear to be D's purpose to cause the consequence. So, what exactly was this 'intention' which the jury were being invited to infer? The courts astutely avoided the obvious logical difficulty by adopting the simple expedient of refusing to define intention! The jury were told that they could infer it but they were not told what it was!

In both *Hancock and Shankland* and *Nedrick*, convictions for murder were quashed and convictions for manslaughter substituted because the trial judge was considered to have misdirected the jury on the intention issue. Had they been properly directed, the jury in each case could have concluded that the accused foresaw the virtual certainty of death or serious injury and yet have refused to infer intention, with the result that the offence would have been manslaughter and not murder. If *Woollin* actually decides that foresight of virtual certainty is intention, that discretion would no longer be available to the jury. In *Woollin* itself, it may have been possible to persuade a jury that D foresaw the virtual certainty of serious injury to his child, but it seems more likely that he gave little thought to the consequences and that it was a very serious case of manslaughter rather than murder.

Some commentators lament the removal of the jury's discretion (if that is what *Woollin* has achieved), seeing in that discretion a valuable mechanism for distinguishing between degrees of moral blameworthiness. This implies that there might be some instances in which D would not be regarded as having intended a consequence despite his knowledge of virtual certainty. It is not immediately obvious why the jury should be trusted with such a discretion, or on what basis they might validly exercise it in favour of one, but against another, accused. To take *Hancock and Shankland* as an example, if the jury decided that the accused foresaw death or serious injury as a virtual certainty, what factors could legitimately influence the jury to decide against convictions for murder? Surely not the defendants' avowed aim of stopping the miner from getting to work or what lay behind the aim, that is, the circumstances of the strike and the coal industry of the time. Wherever sympathies lay in the matter of the strike, it could hardly be a significant factor in the legal issues of criminal liability for murder. Yet, what other significant factors were there? Conversely, it has also been argued that confining the 'foresight' route to intention to *foresight of virtual certainty* means that the net is not cast sufficiently wide. On this argument, D's conviction for murder in *Hyam v DPP* (where foresight of high probability was deemed to be sufficient) was correct because it satisfied perceptions of moral blameworthiness. Yet, on the facts of *Hyam*, conviction for manslaughter would now be the more likely outcome of the application of the foresight of virtual certainty rule.

The difficulties which persist in the interpretation of the decisions on the meaning of intention suggest that a statutory definition is desirable. The Law Commission has proposed the following definition:

> ... a person acts ... intentionally with respect to a result when:
>
> (i) it is his purpose to cause it; or
>
> (ii) although it is not his purpose to cause that result, he is aware that it would occur in the ordinary course of events if he were to succeed in his purpose of causing some other result.

> [*Offences Against the Person and General Principles*, No 218, 1993.]

This definition, subsequently adopted in a 1997 Government consultation document on reform of the law on non-fatal offences against the person, is hardly very different from that which the House of Lords in *Woollin* appears to have adopted.

Recklessness

Proof of recklessness is generally sufficient to establish the *mens rea* for a criminal offence. Recklessness involves taking risks, and yet most aspects of our lives involve taking some risks. Crossing a road, driving a car and flying in an aeroplane all carry risks. Modern life would grind to a halt if it was not permissible to take such risks. Recklessness in the criminal sense consists of *unjustified* risk taking. Driving a car with defective brakes or steering creates a level of risk well beyond that associated with driving a car in general. It amounts to unjustified risk taking.

To 'take' a risk, D must know of the risk, and this suggests that recklessness involves knowledge or awareness. As indicated earlier, a legal rule which requires proof that D was aware of a risk is said to impose a subjective test. D is only liable if he was aware. Even so, recklessness is sometimes also thought of as describing a particularly blameworthy failure to meet the standard of behaviour expected of a reasonable person. In a way, it is an especially grave kind of negligence. Used in this sense, D may be reckless even though he gave no thought to any risk, because he *should* have given thought to the risks involved (any reasonable person would have done so). Again, as indicated earlier, a legal test which requires proof merely that D should have been aware of a risk is said to impose an objective test.

Subjective recklessness must be proved in almost all the offences where recklessness suffices, for example, assault, battery, inflicting grievous bodily harm or wounding. The only significant exception is the offence of criminal damage, where objective recklessness will suffice.

Subjective recklessness

It is convenient to regard the modern development of the meaning and application of subjective recklessness as dating from the case of *Cunningham* (1957), by which name this kind of recklessness is sometimes known. D fractured a gas pipe in pulling a gas meter from the wall whilst committing theft. Gas escaped and permeated through to the house next door where it affected the occupant, endangering her life. D was convicted of malicious infliction of a noxious substance (s 23 of the Offences Against the Person Act 1861) after a trial in which the judge said that 'malicious' meant 'wicked'. D's conviction was quashed on appeal, when it was held that 'malicious' means 'intentionally or recklessly' and that 'recklessly' requires proof, at the very least, that D knew that injury might be caused (in other words, was aware of the risk of injury). Whether D was aware of the risk is something we do not know, precisely because the jury was not asked to consider the matter.

Therefore, subjective recklessness is the conscious taking of an unjustified risk. D will have given thought to, and will have recognised, the risk but will have gone on to take it anyway. His reasons for doing so are irrelevant – it does not matter whether he simply could not care less or fervently hoped that no harm would result. Whether it is a risk that he was justified in taking is a question to be judged objectively. That is, would a reasonable person have taken it? The question is not whether D himself thought it was justifiable to take the risk. A reasonable person might run a low risk of causing some personal injury or damage to property in order, for instance, to save life or prevent serious injury. Yet, there are few cases in which it will be justifiable to run any risk of causing injury to the person or damage to property, and fewer still where it would be justifiable to run a high risk. Consequently, this objective component of subjective recklessness is rarely in issue.

If, for whatever reason, D did not think about or recognise any risk of a particular consequence occurring or of a particular circumstance existing, then he is not subjectively reckless with respect to that consequence or circumstance. This remains so, no matter how obvious the risk would have been to any other person. But if D 'turns a blind eye' to the risk or deliberately refrains from making further inquiries because he has a good idea of what he will discover, that will probably be sufficient evidence of subjective recklessness. If D knows that his bank account is overdrawn and is expecting a letter from his bank to tell him that he must not use his cheque guarantee card, his deliberate refusal to open a letter to that effect from the bank will probably not save him if he tries to say that he was not aware of the risk that his authority to use the card had been withdrawn.

Objective recklessness

Though notions of objective recklessness were already present in other crimes (such as reckless driving and manslaughter), the major development occurred in 1981 when the House of Lords in *Caldwell* applied objective recklessness to the offence of criminal damage. For a time afterwards, it seemed that the objective test of recklessness might be applied to a much greater range of offences, but, by 1994, it was clear that it would remain confined to criminal damage.

As Lord Diplock expressed it in his judgment in *Caldwell*, D will be reckless if his conduct:

(a) creates an obvious risk of destroying or damaging property; and

(b) either:

- D did not give any thought to the possibility of there being any such risk; or
- D recognised that there was some risk involved and nevertheless went on to take it.

This definition includes subjective recklessness, but goes beyond it. Recklessness is present if D recognised some risk and took it (subjective recklessness) but also if his conduct created an obvious risk but he gave no thought to it (objective recklessness). So, *Caldwell* recklessness is a 'package' comprising subjective and objective recklessness, though the extension into an objective definition is the crucial aspect of the decision. In the case itself, D's conviction for criminal damage endangering life was upheld. He had drunkenly set fire to a hotel owned by V, with whom he had had a dispute. The fire was quickly put out and there was little damage. His conduct created a risk that lives might be endangered and the risk would have been obvious to any reasonable person. If D gave no thought to the risk he was reckless, whether his failure to do so resulted from drink or from any other cause.

In the aftermath of *Caldwell*, the courts had to deal with three problems:

(1) If D is incapable of recognising a risk which would have been obvious to any reasonable person, is D reckless within Lord Diplock's test? The key to this question is the word 'obvious' in the first part of the test. The two possible interpretations were:

- the risk would have been obvious to the reasonable person; or
- the risk would have been obvious to D if he had thought about it.

The first interpretation would result in a purely objective test and ensure that D would be guilty even if essentially blameless. The second would allow a restricted subjective element into the test and absolve the essentially blameless from liability. Though Lord Diplock insisted in *Caldwell* that recklessness is a state of mind of D and said enough to make the second interpretation possible, in *Elliott v C* (1983), the Divisional Court felt bound to adopt the first interpretation. They directed the magistrates to convict D, a 14 year old girl, for destroying a garden shed by setting fire to white spirit which she had poured on the shed floor. The court had to deny any significance to her age, educational retardation, tiredness and hunger and the possibility that, because of those factors, she may have been incapable of understanding the probable consequences of her actions.

This interpretation was confirmed by the Court of Appeal in *Stephen Malcolm R* (1984), but some of their Lordships' judgments in the House of Lords' decision in *Reid* (1992) appeared to suggest that D might not be reckless if his 'capacity to appreciate risks' was adversely affected by some condition not involving fault on his part, including being 'afflicted by illness or shock'. The Court of Appeal in *Coles* (1995) did not adopt these suggestions but instead re-affirmed the purely objective nature of the test.

(2) If D gives thought to a possible risk and decides that none exists, is he reckless within Lord Diplock's test? This state of mind falls into neither category of Lord Diplock's definition of recklessness. This originally prompted the suggestion that there was a gap (a lacuna) in Lord Diplock's definition, though the view subsequently taken has been that Lord

Diplock never intended to include this state of mind. It was held in *Reid*, albeit *obiter*, that D is not reckless in these circumstances.

Even so, the law remains ambiguous and unsatisfactory:

- there is no clear answer to the question of whether D is reckless if, recognising that his conduct creates a risk, he changes it and believes that he has eliminated the risk, even though any reasonable person would recognise that a risk remains. In *Chief Constable of Avon and Somerset Police v Shimmen* (1986), D's conviction for recklessly breaking a shop window was upheld, despite his claim that he had merely intended to demonstrate his prowess in martial arts to his friends by stopping his kick close to the window and had deliberately allowed a bigger margin for error than he believed his skill required;

- it was held in *Merrick* (1996) that D is reckless if his conduct briefly creates a theoretical risk of which he is aware and which he has prepared himself immediately to eliminate. D exposed live electricity cables and immediately rendered them safe, the cable being exposed for about six minutes in total. It was held that knowingly creating a risk and then eliminating it is recklessness, whereas a belief that steps have been taken to avoid a risk arising is not.

(3) To which offences does the objective definition of recklessness apply? As explained in the earlier discussion of the development of the rules on recklessness, the objective test is applied only in the criminal damage offences.

Transferred malice

Suppose that D intends to inflict serious injury on X but unintentionally inflicts it on V. If he had succeeded in relation to X, he would have been guilty of causing grievous bodily harm with intent to cause such harm (s 18 of the Offences Against the Person Act 1861). Clearly, he had no such intention in relation to V and this might suggest that he is not guilty of the crime in relation to V. In fact, the prosecution is not required to prove that D had a separate intention against V. Provided that the *actus reus* is that of the crime intended against X, D's *mens rea* in relation to X can be transferred to the *actus reus* against V. D can be liable even if he had no idea that V was anywhere near the scene when he tried to inflict injury on X. In *Latimer* (1886), D aimed a blow with his belt at X, but the belt was deflected onto V and severely wounded him. D was taken to have the necessary *mens rea* for the wounding of V.

The doctrine applies also to recklessness and operates whether or not D succeeds in committing the *actus reus* against the intended target. In *Mitchell* (1983), D pushed or punched X, a 72 year old man who was trying to stop him pushing to the front of a post office queue. X fell back onto V, a frail 89 year old woman, who broke her femur. A few days later, a hip replacement operation had to be carried out on V, but she died two days later from pulmonary embolism caused by a blood clot resulting from the break. D's conviction for unlawful act manslaughter was upheld, partly on the grounds of transferred malice. Of course, D did succeed in causing injury to his intended target, X, but his intention to cause injury to X could also be transferred to the injury caused to V.

The only limitation on the doctrine is that D must cause the *actus reus* of the kind of crime for which he has *mens rea*. If he causes the *actus reus* of a different crime, he will be guilty of that crime only if it can be shown that he possessed the *mens rea* for that crime. Suppose that D throws a brick at V but misses. The brick breaks a window. D's intention to injure V cannot be transferred to the criminal damage in breaking the window and he will only be liable if, as well as intending injury to V, he also intended or was reckless as to the damage.

Coincidence of actus reus and mens rea

Actus reus and *mens rea* must be present together at the same time (they must 'coincide') if D is to be guilty of the offence. Therefore, where the *actus reus* of a crime is instantaneous and complete, D must possess the relevant *mens rea* at that very moment. If D punches V, intending or foreseeing only minor injury, he cannot be guilty of the offence of causing grievous bodily harm with intent to cause grievous bodily harm even if V suffers such harm and, a few moments after delivering the punch, D hopes that he *does* cause grievous bodily harm. But if the offence has an *actus reus* which continues for some time, D can be guilty if he has *mens rea* at some point during the *actus reus*, even if he does not have it at the start. A famous example of this point is supplied by the case of *Fagan v MPC* (1968), in which D accidentally drove his car onto the foot of V, a policeman, when directed to stop. When he realised what he had done, D refused for a short time to move the car. His conviction for assaulting a police constable in the execution of his duty was upheld because, though he did not initially have *mens rea* (a generous interpretation of the facts!), the *actus reus* continued during the time that D 'kept' the car on V's foot, and the subsequent presence of *mens rea* during this time was sufficient.

The case of *Thabo Meli* (1954) is an example of a variation on this principle. D and others, intending to kill V, lured him to a remote spot and beat him severely. Believing they had killed him, they then rolled him down a small hill. In truth, he was not dead but he later died from the effects of exposure. D argued that, believing V already to be dead, he could not have intended death or serious injury in rolling him down the hill and leaving his 'body'. The argument was rejected on the grounds that the beating and disposal were all part of the same 'transaction', so that presence of *mens rea* in relation to the beating was sufficient coincidence of *actus reus* and *mens rea* to establish liability for murder. So, where D engages in a number of acts designed to result in a particular consequence, it may be possible to treat the presence of *mens rea* at any point in the sequence of acts (the 'transaction') as sufficient for liability, even if there was no *mens rea* in relation to the act most proximate to the consequence. More questionably, this principle was applied to manslaughter in *Church* (1965), despite the fact that D had severely injured V in a spontaneous attack arising out of a dispute and had actually killed her when disposing of what he thought to be her dead body. In the absence of a 'plan', how were these acts welded into a single 'transaction'?

Liability *without* mens rea

On the definition of *mens rea* adopted above, crimes of negligence and strict liability do not require proof of *mens rea*. Liability for negligence might be justified on the grounds that D's conduct was blameworthy in failing to meet the standard expected of a reasonable person. This requires us to accept that such failure should be enough for some criminal offences, though it would never be enough for the most serious offences such as murder, grievous bodily harm, theft and deception. Strict liability invites conviction of those who may not be blameworthy at all and certainly requires justification. As explained below, justification is usually sought in the 'regulatory' nature of the offences and consequent lack of stigma in conviction for their breach, that is, it does not matter too much if it is easy to convict D for a strict liability offence as the conviction will not be a matter of shame.

Negligence

There is no general principle which imposes liability for negligence in English criminal law. The common law view of *mens rea* is that either intention or recklessness must be proved or the offence is one of strict liability. Thus, liability for negligence is imposed:

- by statute, either in a primary manner, as in the crimes of dangerous driving and driving without due care and attention under the Road Traffic Act 1988, or in a secondary manner, as in the Misuse of Drugs Act 1971, where the statute obliges the Crown to make out a *prima facie* case of possession but then gives D the opportunity to avoid liability by proving that he was not negligent;

- (very rarely) by the common law, a notable example being gross negligence manslaughter;

- by appearing as an element in some general defences, as in duress/duress of circumstances, where D's unreasonable mistake may deprive him of the defence.

Negligence is the failure to achieve the standard of conduct to be expected of the reasonable person. D will be negligent whether or not he is aware of the risk of his failure to achieve the standard, though, of course, if he is aware of it, his culpability will be greater and his state of mind will be recklessness or intention. Since D is being judged against the standard of the reasonable person, deficiencies in D's knowledge and capacity for understanding or for reasoning are irrelevant if they would not be shared by the reasonable person (the reasonable person is not intoxicated, for instance). By contrast, if D has specialist knowledge or expertise, then he will be expected to achieve the standard of the reasonable person possessed of such knowledge or expertise.

Strict liability

Strict liability offences are predominantly regulatory in nature and tend to deal with activities which are of general concern, perhaps because of danger to the safety of the public or possible widescale fraud on the public. Examples are offences dealing with pollution and general damage to the environment; adulteration of food and drink; evasion of health and safety regulations and planning and building construction requirements; and misdescriptions of the quality and price of goods and services. But they extend into many other areas, such as possession of drugs, road traffic offences and even assaults on police officers.

Justifications put forward for this remarkable form of liability include the following:

- it forces people to think actively about compliance – a butcher, for instance, is more likely to adopt measures to stop contamination of his products if he knows that even lack of negligence will not save him from liability if his products are contaminated;

- the offences are minor and conviction carries no social stigma, the penalty often being no more than a fine;

- proving fault would often be almost impossible and trying to do so would consume a lot of court time, leading to delays and inefficiency;

- the disparity between the minor nature of the offence and the considerable effort that would need to be expended in proving fault invites the obvious conclusion that proof of fault should not be required.

An offence is said to be one of strict liability where it is not necessary for the prosecution to prove intention, recklessness or negligence in relation to any one or more of the elements of the *actus reus*. For example, in *Pharmaceutical Society of Great Britain v Storkwain* (1986), D was a pharmacist who supplied prescription-only drugs when presented with a prescription which he did not realise was a forgery. Though he was 'blameless' (there was no reason for him to be suspicious of the prescription), he was convicted because the House of Lords held that it was unnecessary to prove any knowledge that the prescription was not valid.

In some offences, *mens rea* must be proved in relation to some *actus reus* elements but not in relation to others. For the offence of assaulting a police constable in the execution of his duty (s 89(1) of the Police Act 1996), it must be proved that D intended or was reckless as to the elements of the assault but, remarkably, not that he knew, suspected or even should have suspected that his victim was a police constable! The offence is a *mens rea* offence in relation to the assault but a strict liability offence in relation to the fact that the victim is a police constable and is acting in the execution of his duty.

Though most strict liability offences are statutory, they owe their status as strict liability offences not to Parliament, which has usually said nothing on the matter, but to judges who have decided to interpret them in that way. Since the House of Lords in *Sweet v Parsley* (1970) laid great stress on the importance of the general common law presumption that *mens rea* must be proved, the imposition of strict liability requires evidence to rebut that presumption. An approach frequently relied on is that suggested by Lord Scarman in *Gammon v AG for Hong Kong* (1985):

(a) there is a presumption that *mens rea* is required;

(b) it is particularly strong where the offence is 'truly criminal' – this is not a particularly helpful classification. It echoes the comments above about 'regulatory' and 'minor' offences. In *Blake* (1997), it was suggested that any offence for which a sentence of imprisonment may be imposed is 'truly criminal', though the court went on to hold that unlicensed broadcasting was an offence of strict liability even though it carried a sentence of imprisonment. In *Harrow London Borough v Shah* (1999), the offence of selling a national lottery ticket to a person under 16 years of age was held to be one of strict liability even though it carried a sentence of two years imprisonment. In that case, the court pointed out that the offence in *Gammon* itself carried a sentence of three years' imprisonment and yet was found to be one of strict liability. Nor can it be said that all of these offences are trivial in nature. Pollution offences or breaches of health and safety regulations may threaten the lives of scores of people. The 'truly criminal' offences are generally committed in relation only to a single victim;

(c) the presumption applies to statutory offences and can be displaced only if this is clearly or is by necessary implication the effect of the statute – evidence of this may be sought in:

- the words used – some words, such as 'knowingly', inevitably import *mens rea* notions, others, such as 'cause', are neutral;

- the relationship with other sections in the statute creating offences – if *mens rea* words appear in some sections but not others, this makes it easier for a judge to conclude that Parliament deliberately excluded *mens rea* in the latter. This was a strong factor in the *Storkwain*, where a number of other offences in the relevant statute required proof of *mens rea*;

(d) the only situation in which it can be displaced is where the statute deals with an issue of social concern – the nature of these issues has been indicated above;

(e) even then, the presumption stands unless it can be shown that the creation of strict liability will be effective to promote the objects of the statute by encouraging greater vigilance to prevent commission of the prohibited act – again, this is explained above.

The arguments in favour of the imposition of strict liability would, perhaps, be more credible if the choice were simply between liability requiring the Crown to prove fault and strict liability. In truth, there is a further possibility which Parliament has shown an increasing tendency to adopt. This is to create offences which can be interpreted as being *prima facie* of strict liability – that is, that the Crown merely has to prove that D engaged in some prohibited conduct – but which then give D the opportunity, and place on him the burden, to prove that he was not negligent.

5.2   General defences

5.2.1   Introduction

A general defence is one which may be raised to all, or at least to most, crimes, unlike a defence such as diminished responsibility, which relates only to the offence of murder. Where a general defence is successfully pleaded, the usual effect is that D avoids liability entirely. The basis of the defences varies. For instance, automatism is a denial that the prosecution has established one of the main elements of the *actus reus* (that D's conduct must be voluntary). Intoxication, on the other hand, is usually introduced to deny that the prosecution has established the *mens rea*. Insanity may operate as a denial of either or both (though recent cases suggest that it only operates to deny *mens rea*, and so cannot be used where the offence is one of strict liability), or simply as a claim to be excused from liability because of a failure to perceive that the conduct was 'wrong'. In pleading self-defence, however, D admits the *actus reus* and the *mens rea* but claims to be justified in what he did. Some commentators see such a justificatory defence as denying that the conduct was in any way 'unlawful' (some crimes expressly incorporate the word 'unlawful' in their definition, though it might be argued that all crimes impliedly incorporate the requirement). Similarly, in duress or duress of circumstances, D admits *actus reus* and *mens rea* but claims to be justified, or at any rate excused, because of the pressure applied to him by others or by the circumstances.

The burden of proof in these defences is generally on the prosecution; that is, once the defence has been introduced, the prosecution must disprove it. Even so, D usually has to present some credible evidence in support of the defence before the prosecution is put to the task of disproving it. The defence of insanity is an exception to this rule about burden of proof. The burden is on D to prove that he was insane at the time of the commission of the alleged offence.

5.2.2 Children

Before the enactment of the Crime and Disorder Act 1998, there were three key ages for the purposes of criminal liability, namely:

(a) *under 10* – by virtue of s 50 of the Children and Young Persons Act 1933, as amended by s 16 of the Children and Young Persons Act 1963, a child under 10 years cannot incur criminal liability. There is an irrebuttable presumption against such a child having responsibility for a crime;

(b) *10 years or over but not yet 14* – under a long standing rule, the law provided that such children could be held criminally liable, but only if they had a 'mischievous discretion', that is, they understood the distinction between right and wrong. Though the rule had been subjected to penetrating criticism in recent years, it was upheld by the House of Lords in *C v DPP* (1995) where it was asserted that, in addition to proving the *mens rea* for the offence, the prosecution must also prove that the child knew that it was a 'wrong act as distinct from an act of mere naughtiness or childish mischief'. The older the child and the more obviously wrong the act, the easier it would be to rebut the presumption;

(c) *14 years and over* – full criminal responsibility.

However, the doubts expressed about the rule in (b) led to proposals for its abolition and this was achieved in s 34 of the Crime and Disorder Act. Consequently, there are now only two significant ages as far as criminal liability is concerned:

(a) *under 10 years of age* – no criminal liability; and

(b) *10 years of age or above* – full criminal liability. Of course, different procedures and sentences continue to apply to young offenders.

5.2.3 Insanity

Insanity may be relevant to criminal liability in two very distinct ways:

(a) it may prevent D from being tried at all, since he may be unfit to plead;

(b) it may provide an actual defence to the crime if D can show that he was insane at the time he allegedly committed the crime.

Unfitness to plead

D's state of mind at the time of the offence is not the issue. The issue is whether his current state of mind makes it impossible for him to be tried because he cannot understand the nature of the proceedings and cannot instruct legal advisers. If D is awaiting trial, he may be ordered to be detained in a hospital because of his mental state. Alternatively, he may be found unfit to plead at his trial. In this case, to avoid the possibility of a person found unfit to plead having the prospect of prosecution and conviction hanging over him where the evidence may not be sufficient to establish that he was guilty, the Criminal Procedure (Insanity) Act 1964, as amended by the Criminal Procedure (Insanity and Unfitness to Plead) Act 1991, enables a determination to be made of whether he did in fact 'do the act or make the omission' (though the point is currently the subject of some dispute, this probably means 'did commit the *actus reus*') which amounts to the offence charged. If not, then clearly he is innocent and is outside the criminal justice system. If it is determined that he did do the act or make the omission, the court has power to impose any one of a number of orders:

• admission to a hospital specified by the Secretary of State (with or without direction as to restriction on release);

• guardianship;

• supervision and treatment;

• absolute discharge.

In the case of a murder charge, the order must be for detention in a hospital with a restriction on release.

Insanity at the time of the crime – the M'Naghten Rules

Suppose that D is arguing that he should be excused from liability because he was insane at the time of the offence. If D succeeds in establishing this claim, then, under the Trial of Lunatics Act 1883, as amended by the Criminal Procedure (Insanity) Act 1964, the jury will return 'the special verdict' of 'not guilty by reason of insanity'. Though technically an acquittal, D will not necessarily go completely free. The judge may impose any of the orders identified above where there was a finding of unfitness to plead and, again, must make an order for detention in a hospital with a restriction on release in the case of a murder charge.

Just as in the case of unfitness to plead, the jury must be satisfied that D 'did the act or made the omission charged' before determining whether D was insane so as to be entitled to the special verdict (s 2 of the Trial of Lunatics Act 1883). In *AG's Reference (No 3 of 1998)* (1999), the Court of Appeal rejected the argument that this meant that the prosecution must prove both *actus reus* and *mens rea*. Clearly, since the whole basis of D's claim of insanity is that he lacked mental capacity and therefore did not have *mens rea*, it makes little sense to require the prosecution to prove *mens rea* before the defence of insanity can be considered. In this context, according to *AG's Reference (No 3 of 1998)*, when considering whether D 'did the act or made the omission', the jury must take into account any possible defence not founded on the insanity itself.

In the past, the insanity defence has rarely been used in anything other than murder cases and, even there, its use declined markedly following the introduction of the defence of diminished responsibility in 1957. This was understandable in view of the fact that, prior to 1991, no matter what the offence charged, the judge had to direct that anyone found not guilty by reason of insanity be detained in a specified hospital. There is some evidence to suggest that the wider range of orders now available, including absolute discharge, have resulted in increased use of the defence, though the total number of successful pleas in any year is so small that it would be unwise to read too much into the statistics.

The definition of insanity is based upon the M'Naghten Rules derived from the *M'Naghten* (1843) case. These rules provide that, to succeed in a plea of insanity, D must establish (so, unusually, D bears the burden of proof) that he was suffering from:

- a defect of reason;

- arising from a disease of the mind;

- having the consequence that either he was unaware of the nature and quality of his act, or that he did not realise that he was doing what was wrong.

Defect of reason

This is established where D was incapable of exercising powers of reason, not by a mere failure to exercise such powers. In *Clarke* (1972), D changed her plea to guilty when the trial judge ruled that her defence to a charge of theft of a small number of items from a supermarket amounted to insanity. She had claimed that she had behaved absent-mindedly in putting the items in her bag before reaching the cashier and sought to support her claim by reference to medical evidence which showed that she had been suffering from mild depression. The Court of Appeal quashed her conviction, characterising D's state of mind not as a defect of reason but merely as one of temporary absent-mindedness, confusion and failure to concentrate.

Disease of the mind

This involves disorders of brain function (described in *Kemp* (1957) as 'affecting the powers of reason, memory and understanding'). In *Sullivan* (1983), the House of Lords asserted:

> ... it matters not whether the aetiology of the impairment is organic, as in epilepsy, or functional, or whether the impairment itself is permanent or is transient and intermittent, provided that it subsisted at the time of the act ...

unless it were a temporary impairment which:

> ... results from some external physical factor such as a blow on the head causing concussion or the administration of an anaesthetic for therapeutic purposes.

So, the key distinction appears to be that between internal and external factors. Provided that the defect of reason results from an internal factor, it does not matter whether it is clearly attributable to physical (organic) disease or is only recognisable by its effects on D's behaviour (functional). Nor does it matter whether it is of long or short duration, especially where it is recurrent.

Examples of organic diseases which can cause a defect of reason and so give rise to the defence of insanity are:

- *epilepsy* – in *Sullivan*, D, whilst undergoing a *petit mal* seizure (psychomotor epilepsy), repeatedly kicked, and caused serious injury to, V, who had tried to assist him. The House of Lords held that epilepsy was a disease of the mind which had caused a defect of reason in D;

- *arteriosclerosis* (narrowing of the arteries causing constriction of blood flow to the brain) – in *Kemp*, D had struck his wife with a hammer whilst allegedly suffering from this condition, which was characterised as a disease of the mind. Logically, a tumour having the same effect ought also to be treated as a disease of the mind, so the contrary decision in *Charlson* (1955) was almost certainly wrong;

- *diabetes* – diabetes is a disease in which the body does not produce enough insulin to break down blood sugar. If not reduced, increasing levels of blood sugar lead to the condition of hyperglycaemia, resulting progressively in confusion, disorientation, possible drunken-like behaviour and aggression, lack of consciousness, coma and death. Excessively low levels of blood sugar lead to the condition of hypoglycaemia and produce almost identical effects. The former condition results from lack of insulin, the latter from too much (usually because D has injected insulin and has not eaten appropriate food to correct an excessive reduction in blood sugar). The courts have categorised the defect of reason due to hyperglycaemia as being due to a disease of the mind (an internal factor, the disease itself), and so can form the basis of the defence of insanity (*Hennessy* (1989)). On the other hand, hypoglycaemia resulting from an injection of insulin has been categorised as a defect of reason due to an external factor (the taking of the insulin) and so does not amount to insanity because it is not due to a disease of the mind (*Quick* (1973));

- *degenerative changes to the brain or other organs* resulting from (usually) persistent use of intoxicants.

Examples of functional diseases are:

- *the major psychoses* – such as schizophrenia and clinical depression;

- *brain disorder* – which results in 'sleepwalking' and its very dramatic manifestation in 'night terrors' (though whether this is functional or organic is perhaps open to question). The broad approach adopted in *Sullivan* made it almost inevitable that sleepwalking would be classified as being due to disease of the mind. How else does the brain disorder occur except as something within the brain itself, something internal? So, in *Burgess* (1991), D and V fell asleep whilst watching television. D claimed that he was still asleep when he hit V on the head with a bottle and a video recorder and put his hands round her throat. His claim of 'sleepwalking' was held to be a plea of insanity because the disorder, albeit transitory, was due to an internal factor, had manifested itself in violence, and was likely to recur, even though a further instance of serious violence was unlikely.

D does not know nature and quality of his act or does not know that what he was doing was wrong

D must prove at least one or other of these effects:

- 'does not know the nature and quality of his act' – in *Codere* (1916), the Court of Appeal held that 'nature and quality' means physical nature and quality. This would refer to very fundamental defects in awareness and understanding, such as D's lack of consciousness whilst suffering an epileptic seizure or hyperglycaemic episode, or his belief that he is strangling an animal and not, as is actually the case, his girlfriend (see the example of *Lipman* (1970) in the discussion of automatism which follows in 5.2.4, but note that D's distorted perception resulted from taking a drug). It would extend equally to his belief that strangling does not kill or his lack of understanding of what death is;

- 'does not know that he was doing what was wrong' – in *Windle* (1952), it was held that D will only escape liability under this head if his defect of reason is such that he does not appreciate that what he is doing is legally wrong. For instance, if he is convinced that he is being attacked in circumstances where he could legally use deadly force in self-defence or believes that he has been given special legal dispensation to engage in otherwise prohibited conduct, he does not believe that what he is doing is legally wrong. On the other hand, if he appreciates that it is wrong in this sense but is convinced that it is morally acceptable, the defence would fail (the Australian case of *Stapleton* (1952) took the contrary view in suggesting that D *must know* that it is morally wrong). So, in *Windle*, D's defence failed because he knew that it was legally wrong to kill his wife, who had often talked of committing suicide, even if he might have thought that it was a kindly act, given her constant unhappy state of mind.

5.2.4 Automatism

The prosecution must prove that D's conduct was voluntary. This means that he must have been sufficiently in control of his bodily movements for the conduct to be said to be truly 'his' conduct. D's claim to have been acting involuntarily is called a plea of automatism. Though such a plea will inevitably imply an absence of *mens rea*, it goes further in denying that D has committed the *actus reus*. This is especially important where the crime does not require proof of *mens rea*, as in crimes of strict liability or negligence. If automatism was merely denial of *mens rea*, D would still be guilty of an offence of strict liability even if an automaton at the time. This has proved to be important in driving offences, a number of which are strict liability offences. If D can present sufficient evidence that he may have been an automaton, the Crown must then prove that he was not. If the Crown fails to do so, then D must be acquitted.

Claims of automatism result from two distinct kinds of factual circumstances:

(1) those where D asserts a physical incapacity to control movement which is not related to any kind of brain malfunction. Examples might include:

- being propelled by superior force – for example, X pushes D into V (*Mitchell* (1983)) or D is blown off his feet by a very strong gust of wind and is thrown against V;

- slipping or skidding on ice or oil (without any prior fault);

- suffering a muscular spasm when stung by bees (a hypothetical example given by the court in *Hill v Baxter* (1958));

- experiencing mechanical, electrical or other failure in a machine which makes control of the machine temporarily impossible – as in *Burns v Bidder* (1967), where D's conviction for failing to accord precedence to a pedestrian on a pedestrian crossing (he knocked the pedestrian down!) was quashed on appeal on the grounds that his brakes had unaccountably failed, rendering him an automaton (when subsequently tested, they worked perfectly);

(2) those where D asserts that the failure to control his movement resulted from some significant malfunction of the brain. In most of these cases, there is evidence of purposeful actions by D (for example, 'striking' V or 'driving' a car). So, D's claim is that any control of movement by his brain was not at a conscious level and that only such a level of control will suffice. Examples of these claims might be:

- conduct whilst concussed or semi-concussed from some blow to the head;

- conduct whilst under the influence of a drug taken under medical advice (for example, insulin taken by a diabetic) or involuntarily taken;

- conduct whilst under the influence of a substance which was not generally known to produce intoxicating effects, as in *Hardie* (1983), where D claimed to have been unconscious when behaving aggressively and destructively after having taken tranquiliser tablets prescribed some years previously for his girlfriend.

Whatever D's explanation for the failure to control movement, his plea will not be successful unless he can present evidence of a fundamental loss of control, not merely some partial loss as might occur when movements are poorly co-ordinated through tiredness, illness or drink. Consequently, it was held in *AG's Reference (No 2 of 1992)* (1993) that D's claim to have been 'driving without awareness' (an allegedly trance-like state caused by prolonged driving on featureless motorways) when he had collided with two vehicles on the hard shoulder of a motorway and had killed two people could not amount to automatism. There was no evidence of total absence of control, merely of impaired, reduced or partial control. More questionably, in *Broome and Perkins* (1983), D, a diabetic who had suffered a hypoglycaemic attack shortly after beginning his drive home from work, was held to be 'driving' for some parts of the journey and so was unable to plead automatism. The court reasoned that, if he had somehow 'driven' the car for a distance of five miles without serious incident, there must have been periods of control, even if D could remember nothing of what had happened (this decision fails to pay sufficient attention to the different levels at which the brain can function).

Even if it appears that D was an automaton at the time of the alleged crime, the Crown may still succeed in establishing guilt if it can show that D was at fault in a way which should deprive him of the defence. There are two relevant kinds of fault (see below).

Voluntary consumption of an intoxicant

In this case, D's liability falls to be determined by application of the rules on intoxication (see 5.2.5). Those rules are concerned purely with issues of *mens rea*. So, when D concedes that he became an automaton as a result of, say, taking drugs, he is not allowed to argue that he did not commit the *actus reus* of the offence, only that he did not have *mens rea*. Even then, he is not allowed to argue that he did not have *mens rea* unless he is seeking to avoid liability for an offence requiring proof of nothing less than intention (a specific intent offence). If the *mens rea* of the offence includes recklessness (a basic intent offence), D will simply not be allowed to introduce the explanation that he was an automaton because of intoxication and so will inevitably be convicted. In *Lipman*, D killed his girlfriend whilst suffering from an LSD-induced hallucination that he was fighting serpents at the centre of the earth. Clearly, he was an automaton at the time since his brain functions had been fundamentally disordered by the drug. However, since he had voluntarily taken the drug, he was acquitted of the specific intent offence of murder, but convicted of the basic intent offence of manslaughter.

Any other kind of fault in becoming an automaton

D cannot be in a worse position than if the fault was related to intoxication, so he must at least be able to plead the automatism as a defence to a specific intent offence (you can plead intoxication as a defence to a crime requiring a 'specific intent', see 5.2.5). However, it was held in *Bailey* (1983) that there are no obvious policy reasons, such as apply to intoxication, for restricting D's defence to specific intent offences. The defence can be pleaded to any offence and the question is then whether the Crown can prove that, at the time when D could have prevented himself becoming an automaton, he was aware that he might commit an offence of the kind in question. In other words, even though, as an automaton, he did not have the *mens rea* for the offence at the time of its alleged commission, does it appear that he had an equivalent *mens rea* at the earlier stage? Suppose that D, a diabetic, takes insulin and then allows himself to get into a hypoglycaemic state by subsequently not eating. In that state, he attacks and injures V. D will only be liable for the personal injury offence if, before he went into the hypoglycaemic state, he knew that he might attack someone if he did fall into such a state.

In an offence of objective recklessness (criminal damage) or negligence (for example, gross negligence manslaughter), it might be enough to prove that D ought to have been aware (a reasonable person would have been aware) before he became an automaton that he might commit an offence of the kind in question if he were to become an automaton. This is because both types of offence use an objective test of liability.

5.2.5 Intoxication

A plea of intoxication presents particular difficulties for the criminal law. On the one hand, it is generally acknowledged that a great deal of criminal behaviour, especially behaviour consisting of spontaneous acts of personal violence, aggression and damage to property, is associated with consumption of alcohol and drugs. There is also evidence to suggest that intoxication may be a factor in many instances of theft, robbery and burglary, which may be motivated by a need for funds to sustain drug taking habits. Why allow D to plead intoxication when intoxication may be the very root of the problem? On the other hand, the Crown must prove all the elements of an offence. If D is intoxicated, so that one of those elements might not be present (intention or recklessness, say), why should D be prevented from introducing evidence of the intoxication?

A first step in confronting this dilemma is to make two crucial distinctions:

- between substances which are regarded as intoxicants and substances which are not; and

- between intoxication for which D is responsible (is at fault) (voluntary intoxication) and intoxication for which he is not (involuntary intoxication).

Substances which are intoxicants

Put in simple terms, any substance which is commonly known to produce the kind of effects generally associated with intoxication can be regarded as an intoxicant. These effects include changes of mood, perception and consciousness, reduction in inhibitions, impaired ability for self-control, reduction in motor skills and ability to react and increased difficulty in forming judgments and assessing consequences of actions. They are characteristic of the consumption of alcohol and drugs (both medical and recreational), and also of other substances such as glues and solvents. As the earlier discussion (see 5.2.4) of *Hardie* indicates, a substance may be regarded as an intoxicant when it produces the effects which would be expected of it, but not when it produces entirely unexpected effects. So, the tranquiliser was not an intoxicant in relation to the wholly unexpected violent and aggressive behaviour, but would have been had the issue been about impaired perception and responses caused by the expected tranquilising effects.

Where D suffers intoxication effects from consumption of a substance which is not an intoxicant, he may introduce the explanation in evidence as he would introduce any other explanation to cast doubt on the Crown's case.

Voluntary and involuntary intoxication

D will be voluntarily intoxicated where he was consuming a substance which he knew or should have known (it is commonly known) to be an intoxicant. He will be held to be voluntarily intoxicated even if he makes a mistake about the strength of the intoxicant. In *Allen* (1988), D's claim to have underestimated the alcoholic content of the wine he was drinking, and so not to have been voluntarily intoxicated, was rejected. It was enough that he knew that he was drinking wine. If D consumes a medical drug which can be characterised as an intoxicant and either does not follow medical advice or the drug has not been prescribed for him, then this will probably be voluntary intoxication.

Conversely, D will be involuntarily intoxicated when he has consumed an intoxicant without knowing that he has consumed the substance at all or, perhaps, when he neither knew nor should have known that it was an intoxicant. The obvious examples are where D's non-alcoholic drink is 'spiked' without his knowledge with alcohol or some drug, and where he innocently eats food to which a drug has been added. A further example ought to be where, without D's knowledge, a different intoxicant is added to the intoxicating substance he knows himself to be consuming, as where a mildly alcoholic drink is spiked with stronger alcohol or a drug. Theoretically, this is significantly different from the situation in *Allen*, discussed above, though the practical distinction might be hard to make.

Liability where D is involuntarily intoxicated

In cases of involuntary intoxication, the rule is that D is entitled to introduce evidence of the intoxication to refute the Crown's allegation of *mens rea*, whether the offence requires proof of intention or recklessness. But the effect of the intoxication must be that D did not form the required *mens rea*. D cannot claim that, though he knew what he was doing, he would not have done it but for the intoxication. Even though D could claim that it was not his fault in such a case, the broader excuse thus created would be difficult to fit within the existing legal framework and would generate considerable problems of proof. The rules on involuntary intoxication were established by the House of Lords in *Kingston* (1994) when restoring D's conviction for indecently assaulting a youth after it had been quashed by the Court of Appeal. D had claimed that he had been drugged without his knowledge as part of a deliberate plot to exploit his suppressed homosexual paedophilic tendencies and had only given way to them because of the drug. The House of Lords held that the Crown was only required to prove *mens rea* in the conventional sense and did not have to prove some extra element of moral fault.

Liability where D is voluntarily intoxicated

The current rules on the effect of voluntary intoxication were established by the House of Lords in *DPP v Majewski* (1976). They provide that:

- offences are divided into two categories, specific intent on the one hand, basic intent on the other. Specific intent offences are satisfied by proof of nothing less than an intention. They include murder, causing grievous bodily harm with intent to cause such harm, theft and robbery. Basic intent offences are satisfied by proof of recklessness and include manslaughter, inflicting grievous bodily harm, assault occasioning actual bodily harm, assault, battery and criminal damage. Some offences are specific intent offences as to one element but basic intent as to another. Thus, rape requires proof of intention to have sexual intercourse but merely recklessness as to V's lack of consent;

- if D is charged with a specific intent offence, he may introduce evidence of intoxication in asserting that, at the time of the offence, he did not have the required intention. This does not mean that anyone who was drunk inevitably avoids liability for such an offence. The effect of the intoxication must be evaluated by the jury and D avoids liability if it tends to show that he did not form the intention. As is well known, intoxication often simply makes people more aggressive or less inhibited and, if this was the case, it would not assist D. On the other hand, the issue is whether D did or did not form the intention; it is not whether he was capable of forming any intention at all. This distinction is important because D may argue that he did not form the *particular* intention, whilst being prepared to concede that he had formed *some* intention. In *Brown and Stratton* (1998), the trial judge erred in directing the jury that a plea of intoxication would only be relevant if D was saying, 'I was so drunk on this occasion that I was almost unconscious and I was not capable of forming any intention at all'. D's conviction for causing grievous bodily harm with intent was quashed and a conviction for the lesser offence of inflicting grievous bodily harm (requiring proof only of intention or recklessness as to some harm and, as such, a basic intent offence) was substituted;

- if D is charged with a basic intent offence, he is not allowed simply to introduce evidence of intoxication to explain why he was not aware of a risk (was not reckless). Consequently, if he has no other independent argument to advance, it is almost certain that he will be convicted. Recently, the Court of Appeal has stated that the Crown must prove that D would have foreseen the risk had he not been intoxicated (*Richardson and Irwin* (1999)). A person who raises evidence of intoxication to avoid conviction for a specific intent offence will inevitably be convicted of any associated basic intent offence. The reader should recall that, in *Lipman*, D avoided liability for murder (specific intent) but was convicted of manslaughter (basic intent);

The House of Lords in *Majewski* sought to justify this approach to the effect of voluntary intoxication on criminal liability by suggesting that voluntary consumption of intoxicants is itself a reckless course of conduct which supplies the *mens rea* element that was apparently lacking at the time of commission of the offence. Clearly, this rather general recklessness has little in common with the awareness of particular risks usually necessary in proof of *mens rea*. It might be more realistic to accept that a policy decision has been made in which the courts have tried to strike a balance between practical and theoretical concerns. The balance depends upon the arbitrary division of offences into specific and basic intent, to which distinct rules of liability are then applied when intoxication is in issue.

It is unnecessary to apply the basic intent rule to offences which can be committed with objective recklessness or negligence. In such offences, D's conduct is judged against the standard of a reasonable sober person, so his excuse of intoxication cannot succeed (*Caldwell*). Strict liability offences do not require proof of *mens rea* and so intoxication would be irrelevant.

In some cases, D may seek to raise another defence, such as self-defence, but may need to rely on proof of his intoxication to render that defence credible. Suppose, for instance, that D thinks he is being attacked by V. In reality he is not, but he thinks he is because he is intoxicated. As the discussion of mistake (see 5.2.6) and of self-defence (see 5.2.8) will reveal, D is usually entitled to defend himself by using such force as is proportionate to the danger which he genuinely, even though mistakenly, believes to exist. Yet, where this 'genuine' mistaken belief is brought about by intoxication, the rule is that D cannot rely on the intoxication to explain his mistake. Consequently, his defence of self-defence will fail. This rule was proposed in *O'Grady* (1987), where D had killed V in the drunken and mistaken belief that he needed to use deadly force to protect himself from being killed. Curiously, the courts seem to be prepared to accept that D may rely on the intoxication to explain a mistake where he is arguing that he believed that V was consenting to the risk of injury (assuming that it was a situation in which genuine consent would have been a defence). This was the effect of the decision in *Richardson and Irwin* (1999).

5.2.6   Mistake

For the most part, D's plea of mistake is merely a denial of *mens rea*. In saying that he made a mistake, D means that he could not have intended or known of the risk of a consequence, or known, or have been aware of, the risk of the existence of a particular circumstance. If the offence requires proof of intention/knowledge or subjective recklessness, then an honest mistake is evidence of lack of *mens rea*. If the offence is satisfied by proof of objective recklessness or negligence, then only an honest and reasonable mistake will suffice. This approach to mistake was confirmed by the House of Lords in *DPP v Morgan* (1975), where it was held that D could not be guilty of rape if he genuinely, albeit mistakenly, believed that V was consenting. His belief did not have to be reasonable, though, of course, a reasonable mistake is more likely to be perceived as a genuine mistake. Despite the controversy generated by the ruling, D's conviction for rape was actually upheld because his belief that V was consenting was not credible. His argument had been that he genuinely believed her to be consenting, despite obvious evidence to the contrary, because V's husband had invited him to have sexual intercourse with V and had told him to expect some resistance because 'that was how [V] liked it'.

An alternative way in which mistake may be of relevance is where D pleads a defence which he cannot sustain on the actual facts but argues that it would have been available had the facts been as D mistakenly believed them to be (this is the same kind of situation as that discussed in 5.2.5). The courts have not applied a uniform rule to this kind of claim. In self-defence, for instance, D is entitled to be judged on the facts as he genuinely believed them to be. In *Beckford* (1987), D, a police officer, shot and killed a suspect, V, in the mistaken belief that V was armed and was about to shoot at D. The issue was not whether D's belief was reasonable but simply whether it was genuine. If so, was his response a use of proportionate force in the circumstances that he believed existed? By contrast, the courts have demanded that mistakes made in the context of the defence of duress must be reasonable (see 5.2.7). So, if D mistakenly believes that there is a threat of death or serious injury to himself or another, his defence will fail if the mistake is unreasonable (*Graham* (1982)).

5.2.7 Necessity, duress and duress of circumstances

The common basis of the defences

In these defences, D is claiming that he was faced with two possible courses of action: either to commit the offence alleged; or to allow some other harmful consequence to occur. In the case of necessity, it may be that D should be viewed as being in a position to choose between these courses of action. In duress and duress of circumstances, 'compulsion' may be a more appropriate expression than 'choice'. D is claiming that the nature of the harmful consequence was such that, in reality, his will was overborne. The broad concept, of which the other two are more restricted examples, is necessity, but the courts have been reluctant to accept any general defence of necessity and have been more prepared to develop the narrower forms of duress and duress of circumstances. If the defence succeeds, then D is entitled to be acquitted.

Necessity

In a general defence of necessity, D would be entitled to argue that his decision to commit any crime was excused or justified by the need to avoid an even more harmful consequence. For example, D might seek to argue that his decision to break a minor traffic regulation was justified by his desire to get V to a hospital so that V could receive medical treatment for a painful, though perhaps not serious, injury. Of course, it would be necessary to show that there was no other way of achieving this and that the other consequence would have been significantly more harmful than the commission of the offence itself. As indicated above, the judges have never quite been able to bring themselves to acknowledge this broad proposition. They rejected it in the very unusual case of *Dudley and Stephens* (1884), where D1 and D2 killed and ate the cabin boy while adrift at sea after a shipwreck. Ten days after killing the boy, D1 and D2 were rescued by a passing ship. They were charged with murder and, even after a special verdict, were found guilty (although the death sentence was commuted).

But the charge of murder is so grave that courts might be expected to balk at accepting a defence in these circumstances. There have been signs recently that the judges are beginning to accept a more general defence, as in *F v West Berkshire Health Authority* (1989), where a sterilisation operation on a patient who lacked capacity to consent was held to be lawful, as pregnancy was considered to pose risks of great psychiatric harm to the patient. Nevertheless, the development of the defence of duress of circumstances has reduced the scope for the application of the defence of necessity. Additionally, there are numerous examples of specific defences which are underpinned by the notion of necessity and which, therefore, further inhibit the development of the general defence. For example, s 5 of the Criminal Damage Act 1971 provides a defence to the charge of criminal damage where D caused the damage to protect property which he believed to be in immediate need of protection and where he believed that the measures adopted were reasonable.

Duress

In the defence of duress, D is claiming that pressure was applied to D by another to compel him to commit an offence. Examples could include the situation where terrorists kidnap members of D's family and threaten to kill them if D does not assist in the planting of a bomb, or where thieves carry out a kidnap of someone loved by D to force D to give them access to money and other valuables in a shop or bank of which D is the manager.

This defence cannot succeed if:

- *the crime is murder or attempted murder.* The House of Lords laid down this rule in *Howe* (1987) and in *Gotts* (1992), arguing that, in the case of murder, the sanctity of life must be protected and that severe anomalies would arise if duress were to be made available for a charge of attempted murder. No account was taken of the arguments that D might be saving the lives of many at the expense of the life of one, or that it may be unjust and impractical to expect D to risk the life of members of his family (rather than his own) in order to preserve the life of a stranger;

- *D has been at fault in associating himself with a person or group whom he knew might threaten him with death or serious injury to compel him to commit an offence.* This rule evolved in connection with membership of terrorist gangs but was applied to association with criminal gangs in general in the case of *Sharp* (1987), where D knew that he was joining a violent gang whose leader was willing to use firearms and would not permit him to withdraw from the armed robberies at post offices in which they were engaged. It was further extended to voluntary association with an individual in *Ali* (1995). It was held that D could not plead duress to a charge of robbery as the evidence showed that he knew that the drug dealer with whom he was involved was extremely violent and would be likely to threaten his life to compel him to commit crimes to pay money owing on a drugs deal. D may rely on this defence where he voluntarily participates in a criminal enterprise without knowing of any violent tendencies on the part of his associates (*Shepherd* (1988)).

If the offence is not murder or attempted murder and there is no voluntary association with violent criminals, then D's plea of duress must satisfy further tests.

First, his will must have been overborne by a threat of death or serious injury to himself or any other person, made with the purpose of compelling him to commit a particular crime, which he could only avert by committing the crime.

A threat of death or serious injury

Threats of serious psychological injury (*Baker and Wilkins* (1997)) or other unpleasant consequences, such as shame at being revealed as a homosexual (*R v Valderrama-Vega* (1985)), are insufficient. Where D acts for more than one reason, the threat of death or serious injury must be the overwhelming reason (in other words, he would not have done it if there had been no such threat: *R v Valderrama-Vega*).

... to himself or any other person

Family members would be the most obvious example, but there is no reason why D should not feel compelled to prevent injury to a stranger.

... which D could only avert by committing the crime

This suggests that the threat could have been implemented immediately and before D could realistically seek any help, as in a case where, though D is himself free, his family are being held and could be injured at any time if he does not comply. However, a liberal interpretation was adopted in *Hudson and Taylor* (1971), where convictions for perjury of D1 and D2, women aged 19 and 17, were quashed. Threats to cut them up if they gave evidence against X in his criminal trial had been made by Y. Y was present at the trial and D1 and D2, even though within the protection of the court, felt too intimidated to give truthful evidence. It was held that the threat was capable of being no less real and present if it could be carried out on the streets that night, even if it could not be carried out immediately.

The approach in *Hudson and Taylor* was followed in *Abdul-Hussain and Others* (1999), where it was suggested that the threat must be 'imminent' in the sense that it hangs over D in a sufficiently powerful way as to make the threat 'immediate'. That is, that the threat is operating at the relevant time to overbear D's will. The defence does not require that D should act virtually spontaneously in response to a threat that could be carried out in the next few minutes. On the other hand, an aspect of the immediacy of the threat is that D has no opportunity to avoid it except by committing the offence. A delay between the threat and its implementation may give D the opportunity to avoid committing the offence and might deprive him of the defence if he chose not to take it. This was exactly the view taken in *Heath* (1999), where it was held that D's defence of duress failed because he had had about three days in which he could have contacted the police and thus avoided delivering a consignment of cannabis which he had been ordered to collect.

This is the subjective aspect of the defence of duress (because we are asking whether D's will was overborne), but it contains objective elements. For example, any mistake made by D, for example, as to the existence or nature of the threat or as to a possible avenue of escape, must be reasonable, otherwise the defence will be lost (*Graham*).

The second requirement is that it must appear that a sober person of reasonable firmness, sharing D's characteristics, would have responded as D did – this introduces a still stronger objective element into the requirements for duress. Even if D's will was overborne by the threats, his defence will be unsuccessful if he did not display the courage and fortitude to be expected of the average person. However, in applying this test, a concession is granted. The reasonable person will be presumed to 'share D's characteristics'. In other words, we must ask: 'Would the will of a person of average courage and fortitude, possessing the relevant characteristics of D, have been overborne by the threats?' In *Bowen* (1996), it was held that:

- mere pliability, vulnerability, timidity, and undue susceptibility to threats are not characteristics shared by the person of reasonable firmness, and nor are characteristics due to self-induced abuse such as alcohol or drug abuse or glue-sniffing;

- on the other hand, D may be in a category of persons whom the jury may think are less able to resist pressure than those not within any such category (by reason of, for example, age, possibly sex, pregnancy (because of added fear for the unborn child), serious physical disability, recognised mental illness or psychiatric condition, such as post-traumatic stress disorder leading to learned helplessness). In such cases, the correct test will be how a reasonable person with such a characteristic would have responded.

These considerations led the court to suggest that in most cases, only D's age and sex would be relevant characteristics. The court rejected D's appeal against conviction for obtaining services by deception. He claimed that he had committed the offence because two men threatened to petrol bomb him and his family if he did not obtain the goods, and that he had not told police because he was worried about repercussions. It was held that D's vulnerability was irrelevant and his low IQ of 68 fell short of mental impairment or defect and could not be classified as a characteristic which made those who possessed it less courageous and less able to withstand threats and pressure.

Duress of circumstances

In duress of circumstances, the threat which compels D to commit an offence arises out of the 'circumstances'. These circumstances may include:

- deliberate conduct by another person. Just as in duress, the threat of injury to D or others may come from another person. Unlike duress, the threat is not made with the aim of compelling D to commit the offence;

- natural events, accidental conduct and so on. The threat may result from natural catastrophes such as flooding or fire, more personal events such as the sudden onset of illness, or from some accident which has befallen a person.

However, the circumstances must be in some way external to D's own thoughts and responses; they cannot be constituted entirely by those thoughts and responses. So, in *Rodger and Rose* (1998), D1 and D2, who were serving terms of life imprisonment for murder, were unable to rely on the defence. They alleged that they had tried to break out of prison because an increase in the original tariff recommended by the trial judge in each case had made them suicidal (and this constituted the threat of death). It was held that the circumstances allegedly imposing the duress were the suicidal thoughts, not the Home Secretary's decisions on raising the tariffs.

The defence of duress of circumstances was initially developed in a series of cases which all involved driving offences. A typical example is *Conway* (1989), in which D drove recklessly (as the offence then was) to escape from two men who had approached his car. He did so because, two weeks earlier, his passenger had narrowly escaped serious injury when he was the target of an attack on another vehicle, and D now feared that a further attack was about to be made. Though the two men later proved to be plain clothes police officers, it was held that there was a valid defence. Again, in *DPP v Bell* (1992), the defence was available to D when he drove with excess alcohol to escape from a gang of men intent on injuring him and stopped in a layby as soon as he believed himself to be out of danger. Until the case of *Pommell* (1995), some doubts persisted as to whether the defence was available only to driving offences. In that case, the Court of Appeal made it clear that the defence is not limited to any particular kind of offence but is of general application. Police had discovered D in possession of a firearm and the trial judge had ruled that D's claim that he was keeping it only to prevent his friend from using it to shoot someone could not found a defence. Holding that the defence of duress of circumstances should have been left to the jury, the court ordered a re-trial.

Though it is evidently a 'necessity' defence, duress of circumstances is much narrower than a true defence of necessity because its elements follow those of duress. So:

- it is not available where the charge is murder or attempted murder;
- it may not be available if D knowingly and voluntarily exposed himself to the risk of compulsion (this is merely speculation by analogy with duress, since there is no decision on the issue);
- the threat must be one of death or serious injury;
- D's will must be overborne by the threat;
- a sober person of reasonable firmness would have responded as D did.

A final important point to note is that the defence will not be available if there is a legislative provision which deals with the situation in which D finds himself. In *DPP v Harris* (1995), D was a police officer who drove across a junction against a red light and collided with another vehicle whilst following a gang believed to be intending to commit robbery. He could not use the defence of duress of circumstances because reg 34(1)(b) of the Traffic Signs Regulations and General Directions 1981 specified the circumstances in which the emergency and police services may proceed against a red light and this did not include the circumstances here.

5.2.8 Self-defence/prevention of crime

The rule that a person may use reasonable force to defend himself and his property is long established and is firmly rooted in our beliefs about our rights. Its application to particular facts, however, can often prove very difficult. In recent years, much controversy has been provoked by the criminal prosecution of ordinary people who allegedly used excessive force, usually involving a weapon, to protect themselves or their property from determined criminals. One of the most notorious examples was the case of *Revill v Newbery* (1996), in which a 76 year old man, tired of constant theft and vandalism at his allotment, had waited in his shed late at night and shot and injured V. A criminal prosecution against D failed but he was found guilty of negligence in a civil action brought by V and required to pay V compensation (even though V had himself been convicted of criminal offences in connection with the incident).

The rule provides that D may act not only in protection of himself and his property, but also in protection of the person and property of others and, more generally, to prevent the commission of any crime. In most cases, when D acts to protect his own person and property, or those of any other person, he will be acting in the prevention of crime, but the law formerly distinguished between self-defence and prevention of crime by applying different rules. Even today, when the rules are identical, self-defence still survives because not all cases of justifiable use of force can be described as prevention of crime if 'crime' means that all the elements of an offence are present. For instance, the person allegedly committing the crime which causes D's response may be under the age of criminal responsibility, or may not have *mens rea*, or may be insane.

The rule on force in the prevention of crime is expressed in s 3 of the Criminal Law Act 1967:

> A person may use such force as is reasonable in the circumstances in the prevention of crime, or in effecting or assisting in the lawful arrest of offenders or suspected offenders or of persons unlawfully at large.

The courts have gradually modified the common law defence of self-defence to bring its rules into line with the statutory requirement for prevention of crime.

In doing so, they have removed special rules dealing, for instance, with the duty to 'retreat' before striking a blow in self-defence.

So, in both defences, the use of force will be reasonable if two conditions are satisfied:

(1) *the use of some force is necessary* – whether in relation to the facts as they actually were or in relation to the facts as D believed them to be, even if he was mistaken. Any mistake as to the facts (which could be about whether any attack was taking place or about the amount of force being used in the attack, or both) merely has to be genuine. It does not have to be reasonable. So, in *Beckford* (1987), a police officer was able to use the defence when he shot dead a suspect whom he had gone to arrest and whom he mistakenly believed to have a gun which he was about to use against the police officer. The only exception to this rule is that D may not rely upon a mistake which is induced by intoxication, whether the offence is one of specific or basic intent (*O'Grady* (1987));

(2) *the actual force used must be proportionate* – an objective test is applied here, that is, would a reasonable person consider that an appropriate degree of force was used in view of the danger which existed or which D genuinely believed to exist? In applying this test, it must be remembered that D may well be experiencing a great deal of fear and will probably have little time to make careful judgments about the level of force which he should use. This explains the suggestion of Lord Morris in *Palmer v R* (1971) that a sympathetic view should taken of the level of force which D 'honestly and instinctively thought necessary' in 'a moment of unexpected anguish'. The requirement for proportion, therefore, permits the use of extreme (even deadly) force to counter a threat of death or serious injury, and the use of lesser force where less serious injury or, perhaps, damage to property, is threatened.

Unlike the defences of duress and duress of circumstances, there is no restriction to the offences to which self-defence/prevention of crime can be a defence. In particular, the defence can be, and often is, pleaded to a charge of murder. However, if D kills when using more force than is proportionate, even though some force was necessary, he will lose the defence entirely and will be convicted of murder, not merely of manslaughter. This proposition was starkly illustrated in the case of *Clegg* (1995), where a British soldier serving in Northern Ireland shot at a car which had broken through a checkpoint, killing a passenger. It subsequently emerged that the driver and passengers were joyriders, not terrorists. D was adjudged to have used excessive force, since the danger to other soldiers from the speeding car or anything its occupants might do had passed once the car had cleared the checkpoint. Accordingly, D's conviction for murder was upheld (later developments saw D's conviction quashed and his acquittal at a re-trial but his conviction for lesser offences arising out of the incident).

The old rules on self-defence required D to retreat if at all possible, at any rate before using deadly force. Evidence that D did retreat or did try to avoid a physical confrontation is certainly powerful evidence that he was not the aggressor and that what he did truly was done in self-defence. Even so, the modern rule is merely that it must be necessary to use force. If retreat or negotiation were possible, then force may not have been necessary. But retreat or attempts to talk may only delay the inevitable and, sometimes, striking the first blow may be the most effective form of defence. Indeed, in some cases, not to strike the first blow may be to invite inevitable disaster. These realities were recognised in *Bird* (1985), where the Court of Appeal held that there is no duty to seek to avoid a confrontation (whether by retreat or other means). The court therefore considered that, even if D had struck the first blow in lashing out at V with a glass whilst being restrained by him, that was not inconsistent with the notion of self-defence.

Equally, D will not lose the defence simply because he knowingly 'walked into trouble'. A person is not required to avoid going to places where he may lawfully go but where he knows that danger may await, as occurred in *Field* (1972). In that case, D went to a café despite having been warned that V and others were waiting for him there. Nor is evidence that D was unlawfully in possession of a weapon necessarily fatal to the defence. It would be absurd to suggest that force was necessary in self-defence but that, in using proportionate force, D should not be able to use whatever was to hand. In both cases, of course, such evidence may reduce the credibility of D's claim to have been acting in self-defence or in the prevention of crime.

5.2.9 Self-defence/prevention of crime and duress of circumstances

There is clearly a very close connection between these defences and it may sometimes be difficult to decide which is the correct one to argue. If the elements were essentially the same, it would make little difference. However, duress of circumstances is a much more limited defence than that of self-defence/prevention of crime:

- duress of circumstances cannot be pleaded to a charge of murder or attempted murder;

- duress of circumstances may not be available where D has voluntarily put himself in a position where he knows there is a risk of compulsion;

- duress of circumstances requires a threat of death or serious injury;

- any mistake made by D must be reasonable if he is to rely on the defence of duress of circumstances.

None of these restrictions apply to the defence of self-defence/prevention of crime.

Symonds (1998) provides an interesting example of the close connection between the defences. D was charged with both inflicting grievous bodily harm on V and dangerous driving. He had driven off in his car whilst V's arm was trapped in the door and V had been dragged for a distance, suffering injury. D and V gave conflicting accounts of how this occurred. V was a drunken pedestrian and his story was that D was racing another car and that he (V) was forced to jump out of the way of D's car. When D's car stopped, V put his hand into the driver's window to stop D driving off so that he could remonstrate with him, but D drove off. D said that V had lurched into his path, forcing him to stop, and had then tried to pull him from the car. D was very frightened and drove off to escape. The trial judge directed the jury on self-defence as a defence to the grievous bodily harm count but did not do so in relation to the driving offence or to the lesser offence of careless driving, which the judge left to the jury without consultation with counsel. D was acquitted of the counts charged but convicted of careless driving. The Court of Appeal allowed the appeal. Though it was difficult to think in terms of self-defence in offences where D did not use force on another (careless driving, in this instance), the elements relied on for self-defence in the grievous bodily harm offence were the same as those which would make out the defence of duress of circumstances for the driving offence and the judge should have directed the jury to this effect (of course, it is not really true to say that the elements of the two defences are the same!).

5.3   Offences against the person

5.3.1   Introduction

The protection of individuals against physical injury is traditionally seen as one of the most important functions of the criminal law. The offence of murder itself is usually regarded as the most serious offence in criminal law (save, perhaps, for treason in times of war). This is recognised by the almost unique provision of a mandatory sentence (life imprisonment) for its commission. Manslaughter, however, covers an enormous range of culpable killings, from those which are little short of murder to those which are barely more than accidental. Similarly, the non-fatal offences against the person encompass a range from the intentional infliction of very serious injury, in which it may be the merest chance that the victim survives and that the charge is not murder, to conduct which merely causes a person to fear violence without ever inflicting it. Murder and manslaughter are still almost entirely defined by the common law and have attracted criticism precisely because they have not been subjected to statutory reform. The non-fatal offences are largely defined in the Offences Against the Person Act 1861, a statute which has patently exceeded its useful life and the deficiencies of which have also prompted persistent calls for reform.

5.3.2 Unlawful homicide

The actus reus of unlawful homicide

The traditional definition of the *actus reus* of unlawful homicide requires proof that D:

(a) *causes death* – the difficult issues arising out of this requirement have already been considered when causation was examined in 5.1.3. The old rule that death must occur within a year and a day has been abolished by the Law Reform (Year and a Day Rule) Act 1996. However, the Attorney General must consent to any prosecution where the death occurred more than three years after the incident or where D has already been convicted of an offence committed in circumstances alleged to be connected with the death;

(b) *of a human being* – this means that aborting a foetus or damaging it in such a way that it is not born alive cannot be murder (separate offences of procuring miscarriage and child destruction exist to cover these kinds of injuries). However, as long as the baby is born alive, it may be the victim of homicide even where the conduct which eventually caused its death took place whilst the baby was unborn. In *AG's Reference (No 3 of 1994)* (1997), D caused serious injury to X whilst she was pregnant. Consequently, V was born prematurely and survived for only a few months. It was held that D could have been guilty of the manslaughter of V on these facts. The House of Lords rejected the claim that this was murder because it was not satisfied that an appropriate *mens rea* could be found, but it did not rule out the possibility of a murder conviction where D's acts are directed at the foetus itself, rather than at the mother.

There are two other important points here:

- a comatose person who has already suffered brain-stem death is dead, even though he may appear to be alive because vital functions are being performed by a machine. When the machine is switched off, this does not break the chain of causation between D's conduct and V's death, as D had already caused V's death. The only issue here is whether a proper diagnosis of brain-stem death has been made and the courts have insisted that they will not challenge the medical diagnosis except on the strongest of evidence (*Malcherek* (1981));

- different considerations apply in the case of comatose victims in a persistent vegetative state. Such victims are neither legally nor medically dead but the House of Lords ruled in *Airedale NHS Trust v Bland* (1992) that 'treatment' may be withdrawn or withheld if in the best interests of the patient. This does not permit acts with no purpose other than to bring about V's death (such as a lethal injection), but withholding or withdrawal of treatment can be viewed as an omission (and therefore permissible) in circumstances where the doctors are under no duty to act. The distinctions between acts and omissions and treatment and general feeding are subtle in such cases. In *Airedale NHS Trust v Bland*, it was impossible to feed V except by intrusive methods which were characterised as 'treatment', and this gave the House of Lords the opportunity to permit the course of action by the doctors' withdrawal of treatment which eventually resulted in V's death;

(c) *within the Queen's peace* – in practice, this includes everyone except enemy aliens killed in the heat of battle.

Murder

The *mens rea* of murder is traditionally called 'malice aforethought', but in truth requires neither malice nor forethought but simply an intention to cause death or grievous bodily harm. Most of the cases on the meaning of intention were cases arising out of murder charges (see the discussion of those cases in 5.1.3).

The other aspect of the definition of malice aforethought which remains controversial is its extension to an intention to cause 'grievous bodily harm'. There is no definition of such harm, beyond the assertion that it means 'really serious' harm. There is little complaint about this in cases where D's acts are aimed at causing injury which is obviously of a life-threatening nature, such as head injuries sustained in a punching or kicking assault. But the liability goes further than this. At present, D may be guilty of murder if he kills V by an act which he intends will cause serious injury but which he does not intend to be life-threatening serious injury (and which even a reasonable person would not have viewed as likely to cause life-threatening serious injury). For instance, he might deliberately break V's leg in circumstances where V will readily be able to get medical treatment but V dies because of complications which occur during surgery. The House of Lords has recently criticised this rule on two occasions (*AG's Reference (No 3 of 1994)* (1997) and *Powell and Daniels* (1997)), rejecting the views of its staunch proponent, Lord Hailsham in *Cunningham* (1981), and has called for legislative intervention to change the rule.

Voluntary manslaughter

Voluntary manslaughter covers those killings where D has the *mens rea* for murder but the law regards the killing as partly excused due to:

- diminished responsibility; or

- provocation.

(A further excuse is provided in cases where D kills V in the course of carrying out a suicide pact to which they are both parties.)

The effect of a successful plea is that D is acquitted of murder but convicted of manslaughter, which leaves the sentence at the discretion of the judge. The defences of diminished responsibility and provocation are only relevant if the evidence appears to show that D did have the *mens rea* of murder. If D did not have the *mens rea* then the crime can be no more than manslaughter anyway.

Diminished responsibility

This defence was created by s 2 of the Homicide Act 1957 with the aim of filling a gap left by the rules on the common law defence of insanity. As explained in 5.2.3, the defence of insanity only succeeds in cases where D either has no idea of the physical nature of what he is doing or is so disturbed that he does not realise that it is legally wrong. Yet there were obvious cases of reduced mental capacity or responsibility which would not fit within the defence and where, as a convicted murderer, D faced the death penalty. The new statutory defence enabled the law to take account of these other conditions.

Two preliminary points:

- the burden of proof lies on D unless the Crown seeks to show that D was suffering from diminished responsibility (for example, where D's state of mind is put in issue by a plea of insanity or automatism). If D does not raise the issue but it emerges through the evidence, the judge has no duty other than to point it out to D's counsel (*Campbell* (1997));

- there must be medical evidence to support the plea. Uncontradicted medical evidence entitles, but does not oblige, the judge to direct a conviction for manslaughter.

Section 2 of the Homicide Act 1957 defines diminished responsibility as:

> ... such abnormality of mind (whether arising from a condition of arrested or retarded development of mind or any inherent causes or induced by disease or injury) as substantially impaired his mental responsibility for his acts or omissions ...

It is clear from this definition that there are three requirements:

(1) An abnormality of mind

This was defined in the case of *Byrne* (1960) as requiring:

... a state of mind so different from that of ordinary human beings that the reasonable man would term it abnormal ...

In the case itself, D had killed and mutilated a young woman whilst suffering powerful urges which did not prevent him from knowing what he was doing but which he found impossible or very difficult to control. He was described as a sexual psychopath and his condition qualified as an abnormality of mind.

(2) *Arising from a condition of arrested or retarded development of mind or any inherent causes or induced by disease or injury*

It is not enough that there is an abnormality of mind. The abnormality has to result from a specified cause, though the causes are defined in such broad terms that this requirement is often relatively easy to satisfy. It is also clear that there is a great deal of overlap amongst the causes: 'arrested or retarded development of mind' would amply cover those whose so called 'mental age' remains far lower than their age in years; 'inherent causes' can be interpreted as including functional mental disorders and 'disease or injury' is self-explanatory. Action in the grip of powerful emotions such as jealousy would probably not qualify, unless the condition was extreme.

Pleas of diminished responsibility are often linked with intoxication. A person who is intoxicated may well be described as suffering from a temporary abnormality of mind but the intoxicant is not a specified cause within the statute. So:

- abnormality due only to intoxication is excluded. If there is evidence of intoxication as well as some other possible cause of the abnormality, the jury must ignore the intoxication and determine whether there was a sufficient abnormality due to any specified cause. This approach was established in *Fenton* (1975) and confirmed in *Gittens* (1984), where the trial judge had made the mistake of inviting the jury to examine the respective contributions of intoxication and mental illness to D's abnormality which had caused him to kill his wife and stepdaughter;

- abnormality due to disease or injury caused by the effects of drink or drugs is admissible. So, too, is abnormality due to intoxication where the drinking (or, presumably, drug taking) is involuntary in the sense that D cannot resist taking the drink. This rule emerged from *Tandy* (1987), in which D, an alcoholic, had strangled her 11 year old daughter after drinking a large amount of vodka, which was not her usual drink. However, because the evidence suggested that D could have resisted the first drink (though not subsequent drinks), her defence failed. The intoxication was not involuntary.

(3) Substantial impairment of mental responsibility

The courts have interpreted this provision as requiring an impairment which must be more than trivial but which need not be total. In the case where D is driven by an impulse, as in *Byrne*, his difficulty in controlling his impulse must merely be substantially greater than that experienced by an ordinary person.

Provocation

Provocation was, and remains, a common law defence, though its elements have been modified significantly by s 3 of the Homicide Act 1957. Its essence is that D, though *prima facie* guilty of murder, killed whilst suffering a sudden and temporary loss of self-control in response to something said and/or done by another person. Additionally, D's response must be such as might have been expected of a reasonable person in the same situation. So, the defence will succeed if the following elements were present:

- there was provocation;

- D lost self-control and killed on account of that provocation; and

- a reasonable person would have done as D did.

If any evidence that D was provoked to lose his self-control appears at the trial, whether the issue is expressly raised by D or not (even if D asserts that he did not kill V – *Cambridge* (1994)), then the judge must put the defence to the jury, which has the task of deciding both whether D did lose his self-control on account of the provocation (the subjective test) and whether a reasonable person would have done as D did (the objective test). The onus is on the Crown to disprove the defence beyond reasonable doubt. However, there must be some evidence on which the jury can deliberate. It is not enough that there may be a strong suspicion that, if D did attack V, it was because he lost self-control. Without some evidence, there would be nothing on which the jury could determine whether a reasonable man would have done as D did (*Acott* (1997)).

Nature of provocation

Section 3 of the Homicide Act makes it absolutely clear that D can be provoked by words or conduct ('whether by things done or by things said or by both together') but does not specify who must offer the provocation nor to who it must be directed. Subsequent interpretation now seems firmly to have established that it need not come from V, nor need it be directed at D. In *Davies* (1975), D immediately sought out and killed his estranged wife, V, upon seeing her lover walking in the direction of the place where she worked. Though his conviction was upheld, the Court of Appeal ruled that the trial judge had misdirected the jury in telling them that only the conduct of V was capable of being provocation. The conduct of her lover in walking to meet her was also capable of being provocation.

Implicit in the decision in *Davies* are two further rules. First, the conduct does not have to be directed at D, since the lover was totally unaware that he was being observed by D. Secondly, the provocation need not consist of unlawful conduct. *Doughty* (1986), where the crying of a small baby was held to be capable of being provocation, is a dramatic illustration of both of these rules.

Incidents which have occurred well before the time of the killing are unlikely to be capable of amounting to provocation in themselves. However, evidence of such incidents may be very important in explaining why the most immediate incident, which may in itself have seemed to be very trivial, should be regarded as provocation. In *Davies*, the lover's apparently innocent conduct in walking down the street took on a totally different meaning when viewed in the light of a number of incidents arising out of D's separation from V and which had taken place over the previous nine months. Similarly, in *Humphreys* (1995), there was a considerable history of violence, exploitation and emotional abuse in D's relationship with V, as well as evidence of more immediate provocation at the time of the killing. The Court of Appeal held that it was a misdirection by the judge not to analyse for the jury's benefit the 'several distinct and cumulative strands of potentially provocative conduct'.

Since the judge must allow the jury to consider the defence if there is any evidence of provocation, he cannot withdraw it from the jury merely because the provocative conduct was itself provoked by D, as where D picks a fight in the course of which he becomes enraged at V's response. This was recognised in *Johnson* (1989), where D had stabbed V after being assaulted and threatened with a glass by V. V's actions had been in response to unpleasant behaviour and violent threats from D.

D must have lost self-control on account of the provocation

The defence does not license controlled acts (of revenge, for example) nor those where there is merely a loss of self-restraint, as occurred in *Cocker* (1989), where D eventually gave way to the persistent requests of his terminally ill wife that he should end her life. However, though it is proper to describe the loss of self-control required as being such that D was 'no longer master of his mind' (as did Devlin J in *Duffy* (1949)), this does not require that D should have suffered a complete loss of control so that he does not know what he is doing (*Richens* (1994)).

Evidence that some time elapsed between the last provocative act and D's response ('cooling off' time) will cast doubt on D's assertion that he killed whilst suffering a loss of self-control. In the highly controversial case of *Thornton* (1992) (where the main defence was diminished responsibility), the Court of Appeal considered that, when directing the jury on provocation, the trial judge had been correct to emphasise the fact that the requirement for a sudden and temporary loss of self-control and D's behaviour indicated that, though she had suffered threats of violence a relatively short time before, she had cooled down by the time she killed her husband. However, it is important to recognise, as the Court of Appeal strongly emphasised in the cases of *Thornton, Ahluwalia* (1992) and, on a further and successful appeal, *Thornton (No 2)* (1995), that the only rule is that D must have suffered a sudden and temporary loss of self-control related to words or deeds capable of being regarded as provocation. There is no rule that the response must be immediate. Two examples of possible delayed response might be:

- D immediately begins to 'seethe' on being subjected to the provocation and this builds up until there is a loss of self-control. This must be distinguished from a 'slow burn' response, where there is either no actual loss of self-control or a loss of self-control too remote from any act of provocation (as is possibly the case with battered women who kill);

- D loses self-control immediately in response to the provocation and remains out of control for some time, during which time the killing takes place. In *Baillie* (1995), on being informed by his youngest son that the drug dealer (V) who supplied all his sons was intending to punish them for switching to a different dealer, D immediately went into a rage, armed himself with a shotgun and razor, and drove to V's house. There he seriously injured V with the razor and then, as V tried to escape, shot and killed him. It was held that there was sufficient evidence that D had remained out of control during the whole of this episode.

A reasonable person would have done as D did

The Homicide Act places the responsibility for deciding whether a reasonable person would have done as D did entirely in the hands of the jury. This means that there is no longer any scope for the judge to tell the jury how the reasonable person would respond. In particular, there is no longer any rule that D's response (the act of killing) must be proportionate to the provocation.

But the courts have retained some power to direct the jury about who the reasonable person is and about the general nature of his responses. The House of Lords in *Morhall* (1995) was anxious to make it clear that the reasonable person test invites comparison with the response of an ordinary person placed in the same situation as D, not with a person using powers of reason in the way that might be expected in the application, say, of the tort of negligence. Essentially, the test serves the policy of denying the defence to those who are perceived as too quick to lose their temper and/or to react excessively.

In *DPP v Camplin* (1978), the House of Lords had held that the reasonable person must be regarded as having the power of self-control to be expected of an ordinary person (not unusually pugnacious or excitable) of the age and sex of D, and bearing such other characteristics of D as are relevant to the gravity of the provocation. In *Newell* (1980), the Court of Appeal stressed that the characteristics should have some degree of permanence and be in some way unusual and that the characteristics would affect the gravity of the provocation by being the target of that provocation (so that D's characteristic of being an alcoholic was properly regarded as irrelevant because the provocation concerned insulting remarks made by V about D's girlfriend). However, the House of Lords in *Morhall* counselled against an emphasis on 'characteristics' and preferred to stress that the jury should consider a reasonable man placed in 'the entire factual situation' in which D found himself or subject to 'all those factors' which would affect the gravity of the provocation.

It may be possible to draw a distinction between:

- factors which affect the gravity of the provocation experienced by D; and

- factors which affect D's capacity for self-control.

The argument would then be that the reasonable person should be considered to have been exposed to all the factors (including possession of any of D's personal characteristics) which would determine the degree of provocation experienced by D, but would not share any lack of capacity for self-control which D might display. Put simply, if D, an extremely bad-tempered man, had killed V after V taunted him about his big nose, the reasonable person would have a big nose (relevant to the gravity of the provocation) but would not be bad-tempered (relevant only to D's capacity for self-control).

Factors affecting the gravity of the provocation might include:

- sex, age and (im)maturity – the latter two factors may obviously affect capacity for self-control. So, in *DPP v Camplin*, D's age (15) was regarded as relevant to his capacity for self-control when taunted by V about the sexual assault which V had just performed on him. Similarly, in *Humphreys*, D's immaturity was regarded as relevant where she had suffered an unhappy childhood including drug abuse and sexual promiscuity, had been exploited as a prostitute by V and had killed him when she was 17 years old. However, age was regarded as irrelevant in *Ali* (1989) where a 20 year old man had stabbed another in a disco. At that age, D was no more immature than anyone else. The relevance of sex as such is less obvious;

- characteristics (permanent or otherwise) which are the specific target of the provocation and therefore increase its gravity, for example, addiction to glue-sniffing (*Morhall*) and attention seeking traits (*Humphreys*);

- the general background of relevant events – for instance, the reasonable person must be assumed to have experienced any earlier instances of provocative conduct which may have produced a cumulative effect;

- other general conditions such as obsessiveness and eccentricity (*Dryden* (1995)) and battered woman syndrome (*Ahluwalia; Thornton (No 2)*, but see the comments below on *Luc Thiet Thuan v R* (1996)).

At present, there is some confusion about exactly how the courts should treat factors which merely affect D's capacity for self-control. In *Luc Thiet Thuan v R*, the Privy Council held that the reasonable person should not be invested with D's organic brain disorder which allegedly caused D to lose self-control more easily. The Privy Council stressed that characteristics which may merely have a general effect on powers of self-control may not be attributed to the reasonable person since, by definition, the reasonable person has the powers of self-control of an ordinary person and is not unusually short-tempered, aggressive or prone to lose self-control. This seems consistent with the House of Lords' decisions in *DPP v Camplin* and *Morhall* but it casts doubt on the suggestion in *Ahluwalia* and in *Thornton (No 2)* that account can be taken of the condition of 'learnt helplessness' arising from battered woman syndrome. This approach also places a question mark over the decision in *Dryden* regarding 'obsessiveness and eccentricity'.

The Court of Appeal has so far refused to be moved by the decision in *Luc Thiet Thuan*. In *Smith* (1998), evidence had been introduced at D's trial for murder (in relation to a plea of diminished responsibility) that D was suffering from a depressive illness which might have reduced his threshold for erupting with violence and might have disinhibited him. On the issue of provocation, the trial judge ruled that this characteristic was relevant only to the gravity of the provocation and not to the reasonable man's loss of self-control. On appeal against his conviction for murder, D successfully contended that the decisions in *Ahluwalia*, *Humphreys*, *Dryden* and *Thornton (No 2)* favoured a flexible approach to the reasonable man test, so that the trial judge's ruling was incorrect. The Court of Appeal considered that the defence of provocation was gradually increasing in scope and that there was nothing in *Camplin* to support the distinction between characteristics relevant only to gravity and characteristics relevant to loss of control. *Morhall* was not concerned with this distinction and there was nothing said in that case that was inconsistent with the Court of Appeal decisions in *Thornton (No 2)* and the other cases. *Luc Thiet Thuan* was not binding on the Court of Appeal; the earlier Court of Appeal decisions were. However, the court gave leave to appeal to the House of Lords, which should enable a resolution to be found.

Involuntary manslaughter

Involuntary manslaughter extends to all blameworthy killings in which D's *mens rea* is less than that required for murder. It may be established through two, or possibly three, different routes:

- proof that D killed in the course of committing an unlawful and dangerous act (unlawful act or constructive manslaughter);

- proof that D killed in the course of any conduct with gross negligence (gross negligence manslaughter). This was re-established in *Prentice* (1993) and affirmed in *Adomako* (1994);

- proof that D killed in the course of any conduct and was subjectively reckless as to serious (or, perhaps, some) injury (subjective reckless manslaughter). It is unclear whether the revival of gross negligence manslaughter has also revived this category.

Unlawful act manslaughter

Involuntary manslaughter by an unlawful act is also known as constructive manslaughter. Its essence is that D caused V's death whilst engaged in an act which was both a crime and created a risk of some personal injury. Typically, it occurs when D attacks V intending relatively minor injury (an act which is a crime and, self-evidently, creates a risk of some personal injury) and V sustains unexpectedly severe injuries from which death results – a very common cause is a broken skull suffered by V when falling backwards under a blow and striking his head on a wall or a kerb.

The Crown must prove the following elements.

An unlawful act ...

Though the courts insist on using this term, they actually mean a crime, despite one or two instances where they have been prepared to relax the demand. The implications are:

- that other kinds of wrongdoing, such as torts, are not enough. However, many torts are also crimes;

- that all the elements of the relevant crime must be proved, both *actus reus* and *mens rea*. In *Lamb* (1967), D shot and killed his friend when he pressed the trigger of a gun during a game. He knew there were bullets in the gun but, since he did not understand the operation of a revolver, he did not believe any bullet would be ejected. He was not guilty of unlawful act manslaughter because he did not have *mens rea* for an assault or for a battery. Ill considered comments by the House of Lords in *DPP v Newbury and Jones* (1976), that it was enough if D intentionally did an act which was unlawful but that he did not need to know that it was unlawful, have sometimes been thought to cast doubt on this proposition. Even so, it was clearly re-affirmed by the Court of Appeal in *Jennings* (1990), where D's brother, V, had been fatally but unintentionally stabbed whilst trying to take a knife from D to stop him from using it in a potential confrontation with others. It was held that the jury should have been directed to consider whether D might have had a lawful excuse for the possession of the knife. A lawful excuse would have meant that he was not guilty of the alleged crime of possession of an offensive weapon, and so not guilty of unlawful act manslaughter;

- that crimes of negligence are not enough (*Andrews v DPP* (1937)). This is because the whole liability would then be founded on negligence (the test of 'dangerousness' discussed in the following paragraph is also, essentially, one of negligence). If negligence is to be the basis of the liability, then it must satisfy the test of gross negligence which is explained below. For instance, driving without due care and attention is a crime of (minimal) negligence. D could not be guilty of unlawful act manslaughter if, whilst driving without due care and attention, he killed someone. If the driving was grossly negligent, then D might be guilty of gross negligence manslaughter;

- that it must involve an act – an omission will not suffice. This is the rule laid down in *Lowe* (1973), where D had neglected the health of his child and had been convicted of manslaughter on the basis that the crime was wilful neglect of a child under the Children and Young Persons Act 1933. The conviction was quashed because D had not engaged in any act but, rather, had made an omission. Though the decision is unsatisfactory (the court very obviously confused 'neglect' and 'negligence'), it has never been overruled.

... of a dangerous kind ...

In *Church* (1965), the court defined this as being:

> ... such as all sober and reasonable people would inevitably recognise must subject the other person to, at least, the risk of some harm resulting therefrom ...

In *AG's Reference (No 3 of 1994)* (1997), it was held that 'the other person' need not necessarily be V. In that case, the risk of injury was to V's mother, though it was V who eventually died.

The test will be easy to satisfy where the crime alleged is actually an offence against the person, such as assault or battery. In *Larkin* (1943), for instance, D was convicted of manslaughter when he confronted his girlfriend with a 'cut throat' razor in a confined space at a party and she, 'being groggy with drink', fell against it and cut her throat. D's threatening conduct with the razor was an assault and there was an obvious risk of injury, given the high emotions, confined space and V's condition. Yet other crimes can also create a risk of personal injury and so be 'dangerous', for example, criminal damage. In *DPP v Newbury*, the probable crime (the crime was never actually specified) was criminal damage, which occurred when D threw a paving slab into the path of a train and it smashed through the window of the cab, killing the guard. In *Goodfellow* (1986), D set fire to his council house in a complicated scheme to force the council to move him, but the plan went drastically wrong and his child, wife and a friend all died in the blaze. This was clearly a case of aggravated criminal damage (criminal damage where D intends to endanger life or is reckless as to doing so), the danger to life being all too obvious.

Nevertheless, the reasonable person must be taken to possess only the knowledge that D had and should have had at the time when he committed the offence (including knowledge gained during the commission of the offence), and if the risk of injury would not have been apparent with such knowledge, then D must be acquitted. In *Dawson* (1985), V suffered a fatal heart attack during a robbery committed by D and others. Though V was apparently healthy and D had no reason to suppose otherwise, in reality he suffered from a heart condition. Since this could not have been known to D, the test applied was whether a reasonable person ignorant of V's condition would have recognised a risk of that kind of injury. D's conviction was quashed. By contrast, in *Watson* (1989), D had ample opportunity to observe the condition of his very old victim during the burglary in which he was engaged. D's conviction was quashed only because of problems about causation.

... *which causes death*

By now, this should be a perfectly familiar proposition and it ought to be sufficient to return to the discussion of causation in 5.1.3. In unlawful act manslaughter, unfortunately, the issue is sometimes complicated by the need to prove that the unlawful act alleged was itself dangerous. This is best illustrated by the kind of case in which V has died after voluntarily consuming a drug supplied by D (contrast these facts with those in a case such as *Cato* (1976), in which D actually injected heroin into V, with V's consent). The Crown faces formidable hurdles in proving the offence. D will object that his act of supply was neither the direct cause of V's death nor in itself dangerous. Only when V voluntarily took the drug did the danger arise.

Substantially, these were the facts of *Dalby* (1982), with the additional complication that V took the tablets by way of injection of a solution, a significantly different form from that in which D had supplied them. The court quashed D's conviction but was induced to express its decision in terms of a requirement that the unlawful act must be 'directed at' V. This was inconsistent with the position adopted in other cases, such as *Pagett*, where the court had considered that D's act in firing at the police officers, though obviously not directed at V, was a sufficient unlawful act, and *Mitchell*, where D had attacked X, who had fallen onto V. It is now generally considered that there is no requirement that the act be 'directed at V'. For instance, in *Goodfellow* (another case in which D's act was definitely not aimed at the ultimate victims), the decision in *Dalby* was explained as being concerned purely with causation and not as imposing any restriction to acts 'directed at' V or anyone else.

The use of drugs is now so prevalent in society that this issue was certain to come before the courts again, as it did in the case of *Kennedy* (1999). There, D, a dealer, had himself prepared the solution of heroin and water with which V then fatally injected himself. Upholding D's conviction for manslaughter, the court held that D's conduct was unlawful either as an offence under s 23 of the Offences Against the Person Act 1861 (which makes it an offence to 'administer to or cause to be administered to or taken by any other person any poison or other destructive or noxious thing') or because D had assisted in and wilfully encouraged V's own unlawful act in injecting himself with a mixture of heroin and water which, at the time of the injection and for the purposes of the injection, V had unlawfully taken into his possession. This unsatisfactory decision was achieved by the tortuous route of identifying V's acts of taking possession of the heroin and injecting it as unlawful, and then arguing that D's act in wilfully encouraging those acts by V was itself unlawful and dangerous because the encouragement to inject carried with it the risk of some harm. In response to the crucial objection, founded on the decision in *Dalby*, that D did not cause V's death, the court returned to the significance of the preparation of the solution by D and the handing of it by him to V. Yet this appears to be nothing more than proof of causation in fact. V would not have died 'but for' the supply to him of the heroin by D, but his own decision to inject it surely broke any chain of causation. Much the same could be said in response to the argument that D committed the offence under s 23.

Gross negligence manslaughter

Until 1983, the other major form of involuntary manslaughter was gross negligence manslaughter. Though never clearly defined by the courts, it extended to any conduct, whether unlawful in itself or not (for example, driving a car) and was said to require that:

> ... the facts must be such that, in the opinion of the jury, the negligence of the accused went beyond a mere matter of compensation between subjects and showed such disregard for the life and safety of others as to amount to a crime against the State and conduct deserving of punishment [*Bateman* (1925)].

Development of this form of manslaughter was arrested in 1983 by the House of Lords' decision in *Seymour* that, henceforth, it would be defined as *Caldwell* reckless manslaughter. It was not altogether clear whether this represented merely a change in name or extended to a change in definition of the elements of such manslaughter. This change generated a good deal of controversy and was itself abandoned when, in 1993, the House of Lords restored gross negligence manslaughter in *Adomako*.

As now defined, gross negligence manslaughter requires proof of:

(a) *any conduct* – it does not have to be an act, so omissions will suffice (contrast unlawful act manslaughter). It does not have to be unlawful in itself, so it may arise out of any activity which poses a risk of injury, for example, employment, medical treatment, driving, installation of domestic appliances, manufacturing, sale and distribution of food and drink;

(b) *amounting to breach of a duty* – exactly what this involves remains unclear at present. In the opinion of Lord McKay in *Adomako*, 'ordinary principles of negligence apply to ascertain whether or not the defendant has been in breach of a duty of care towards the victim who has died', but it seems unlikely that he intended an enquiry into the conditions for criminal liability to be burdened with all the technicalities which surround the notion of duty of care in the civil law of negligence. In any case, by definition, D will have engaged in conduct which created an obvious risk of death to another and this, in itself, is a powerful reason to argue that a duty of care is created. In cases of liability for omission, it will in any case be necessary to establish an appropriate duty to act (recall the duties established in cases such as *Pittwood* and *Stone and Dobinson* discussed in 5.1.3. Equally, duties will arise out of the conduct of professions and business enterprises which carry with them risks to workers, clients, consumers and, more generally, members of the public. Examples include: medical treatment (*Adomako* (1994)); domestic electrical work (*Holloway* (1993)); installation of gas fires (*Singh* (1999)); the organisation of hazardous sports and recreational pursuits (*OLL Ltd* (1994)); and sailing a ship around potentially dangerous rocks (*Litchfield* (1998));

(c) *which creates a risk of death* (or, possibly, of serious injury). This was never a formal requirement before, but it was stressed by Lord MacKay in *Adomako*;

(d) *which causes death* according to the principles of causation considered earlier;

(e) *some further element*, whether described as a state of mind or not, which supplies the requisite degree of culpability; which makes it gross negligence. In *Adomako*, Lord MacKay stressed that this is entirely a matter for the jury to determine:

> The essence of the matter, which is *supremely a jury question*, is whether, having regard to the risk of death involved, the conduct of the defendant was so bad in all the circumstances as to amount in their judgment to a criminal act or omission ... [Emphasis supplied.]

There is some illogicality in requiring the conduct to be so bad as to amount to a 'criminal act or omission' if, in the first place, D's breach of duty amounted in itself to a criminal offence (that is, an offence other than manslaughter). Where this is the case, the culpability of D's conduct must lie in being something more than 'merely criminal'! Essentially, the culpability lies in its being conduct which the jury consider should amount not merely to a crime, but to the particularly grave crime of manslaughter. In *Litchfield*, D was the owner and master of a sailing ship which had foundered on rocks and smashed to pieces, with the loss of three lives. D's conduct in sailing the ship almost certainly disclosed breaches of duty which made him guilty of offences under the Merchant Shipping Act 1970. Yet the prosecution decided not to proceed with such charges, on the grounds that the penalties which could be imposed on conviction did not truly reflect D's culpability. Hence, the prosecution was prepared to show conduct which amounted not just to criminal rather than civil law negligence, but which was conduct deserving of punishment as manslaughter (and succeeded in doing so).

Reckless manslaughter

Before gross negligence manslaughter was abandoned in 1983 in favour of *Caldwell* reckless manslaughter, there was a strong belief that a category of subjective reckless manslaughter existed alongside gross negligence and unlawful act manslaughter. During the period that *Seymour* (*Caldwell* reckless manslaughter) prevailed, there was no scope for any such category, since it was subsumed within the much broader category of *Caldwell* reckless manslaughter. Now that the latter has been abandoned, the possible existence of a category of subjective reckless manslaughter arises again. Its required scope of application would be very limited:

- it would differ from unlawful act manslaughter in encompassing both unlawful and lawful conduct, and omissions as well as acts, in addition to requiring D to be aware of the risk;

- it would differ from gross negligence manslaughter in not requiring proof of any duty, but also in requiring awareness of risk.

What remains unclear is what risk D must be aware of. Is it a risk of death or serious injury, or will it be enough that D was aware of a risk of some injury? *Litchfield* is a good example of a case in which D's conduct might have been better expressed as subjective recklessness rather than gross negligence. D had plenty of opportunity to observe the prevailing weather conditions and the position of his ship in relation to the coast. He also knew that there was a serious doubt about whether the engines which might be needed to get the ship out of trouble would work, because he had been advised that the fuel was contaminated (in the event, they failed and the ship was unable to resist being drawn onto the rocks). Clearly, there was strong evidence to suggest that D knew that his conduct created a risk of death or serious injury.

5.3.3 Non-fatal offences against the person

Assault

Though the word 'assault' is popularly used to describe actual physical violence, it bears a much more technical meaning in criminal law. It consists of causing V to fear violence, whilst 'battery' is the term used for the infliction of violence itself. The distinction is easily obscured by the tendency of statutes to use 'assault' when the offence can be committed by either an assault or a battery, as in assault occasioning actual bodily harm (s 47 of the Offences Against the Person Act 1861) and indecent assault (ss 14 and 15 of the Sexual Offences Act 1956).

The *actus reus* of assault is that D causes V to apprehend immediate unlawful personal violence. Typically, it occurs where D raises his fist or a weapon or makes some other menacing gesture which leads V to think that he is about to be attacked. If V does not see the gesture (if, for example, D is behind V) or does not anticipate being struck, then there is no assault. But V is not required to be literally in fear. A courageous person who does not fear the anticipated blow may still be the victim of an assault. The offence has been subject to recent important re-evaluation by the courts and the following interpretations have emerged:

- the assault may consist of words alone. This was always in doubt until the decisions in *Ireland* (1997) (assault by means of silent telephone calls) and *Constanza* (1997) (assault by means of two letters). It was never doubted that words could operate to prevent an otherwise apparently aggressive act from being an assault, as in *Tuberville v Savage* (1669) (D's gesture of putting his hand on his sword was accompanied by words indicating an intention not to use it);

- the assault must cause fear of 'immediate' personal violence but, according to *Constanza*, this is satisfied by proof that V feared that violence would be inflicted 'at some time not excluding the immediate future'. This seems to mean that it would be sufficient to show that V had thought, 'it may happen now, very soon or happen later'. Thus, V was the victim of an assault where, on receiving two letters from D (who had pursued a campaign of harassment against her for 20 months), she believed that he had 'flipped' and that he might do something at any time of the day or night. It was especially important that D lived not far from V but there was no requirement that V must be able to see the potential perpetrator of the violence. Similarly, it was held in *Ireland* that receipt of silent telephone calls from D could give rise to an assault if V feared that D might seek her out as soon as the telephone call was ended. Obviously, where the threat is clearly to inflict violence at some later time, the 'immediacy' requirement will not be satisfied. Yet, even here, it will be a question of degree as to how much later that time is;

- an act (rather than an omission) may be necessary. There are conflicting cases on this issue (*Fagan v MPC* (1969) and *DPP v K* (1990)), as explained in 5.1.3 in the discussion of liability for omissions.

The *mens rea* of an assault is intention or recklessness in relation to causing apprehension of immediate unlawful personal violence. Recklessness here is subjective.

Battery

The *actus reus* of battery requires infliction of unlawful personal violence. Though 'violence' can consist of very little, such as pushing and shoving, there is a limit below which it will not be recognised by the law (this is sometimes expressed in the maxim *de minimis non curat lex* – the law takes no account of very trifling matters). We are all taken to give our implied consent to the trivial bumps and knocks encountered in everyday life, such as when we are in crowds, in shops, at sporting events and so on. So, the following are important in understanding the *actus reus*:

- battery typically consists of a direct application of force by D on V, whether with fists or feet, by a headbutt, by the use of a weapon held or thrown or by spitting. It could also be constituted by instructing a dog to bite the victim, as occurred in *Ramsell* (1999);

- though direct and immediate contact is usually involved, it may be possible to commit battery in less direct ways. In *DPP v K*, D left acid in a hand dryer and so created the circumstances in which V would be certain to suffer injury if he used the hand dryer in the expected way. *Martin* (1881) is a more questionable example, since D's actions (putting out the lights in a theatre and barring the exit doors) only resulted in injury because of the extreme panic generated, in the course of which theatre-goers trampled on each other;

- no hostility is required – if D tries to show his affections towards V by persistently kissing her against her will, this is a battery just as much as if he had punched her in anger;

- even though psychological injury is recognised as injury, it is not possible to commit a battery simply by causing V to suffer psychological injury. Violence must be inflicted (*Ireland* (1997));

- as in assault, an act may be required.

The *mens rea* of a battery is intention or recklessness in relation to infliction of unlawful personal violence. So, in *Venna* (1975), D was guilty of an assault (in the sense of a battery) occasioning actual bodily harm when he lashed out wildly with his feet after he realised that he had been arrested by police officers and broke a bone in the hand of one of the officers. In *Spratt* (1991), D's conviction for assault (again, in the sense of a battery) occasioning actual bodily harm was quashed when it appeared that, though he had pleaded guilty, he had not given any thought to the possibility that he might injure anyone by firing airgun pellets from a bedroom window in order to see how far they would go. Subjective recklessness had to be proved.

Since the infliction of violence must be unlawful, D will not be guilty if his intention is to inflict violence which he believes to be lawful. This may arise in two situations:

- where D believes that V expressly or impliedly consents;

- where D genuinely believes that he has a lawful excuse for inflicting violence, such as self-defence or prevention of crime. In this case, of course, D must intend to use force which is reasonably proportionate to the harm feared. In *Blackburn v Bowering* (1994), D was not guilty of battery where he defended himself against an attempt by court bailiffs to restrain him. Though the bailiffs were acting lawfully, D did not know who they were and believed that he was simply the victim of an attack.

Assault occasioning actual bodily harm

Assault occasioning actual bodily harm is a statutory offence by virtue of s 47 of the Offences Against the Person Act 1861. Its elements are entirely as for assault or battery (it is either an assault occasioning actual bodily harm or a battery occasioning actual bodily harm) but with the addition that actual bodily harm must result. Thus, as affirmed in *Ireland* (1997):

- D must cause V to apprehend immediate personal violence with the consequence that V suffers actual bodily harm (physical or psychological); or

- D must inflict violence upon V with the consequence that V suffers actual bodily harm (physical or psychological).

'Actual bodily harm' was formerly described as including 'any hurt or injury calculated to interfere with the health or comfort [of a person] ...' and so extended to mental injury (hysterical and nervous conditions) (*Miller* (1954)). However, this form of expression was disapproved of in *Chan-Fook* (1994) where, analysing all three ingredients of the offence under s 47, the Court of Appeal held that:

- 'harm' requires hurt or injury;

- 'actual' requires that it is not so trivial as to be wholly insignificant;

- 'bodily' is not limited to 'skin, flesh and bones' since the body includes organs, the nervous system and the brain. So it extends to psychiatric injury but not to mere emotions such as fear, distress or panic, nor to states of mind which are not themselves evidence of an identifiable clinical condition. To conclude that fear, distress or panic would in itself amount to actual bodily harm would be to risk equating the elements of assault with those of assault occasioning actual bodily harm, since an assault is itself constituted by fear of immediate violence.

The court warned against use of phrases such as 'injury to state of mind' or 'hysterical and nervous condition' and advised that expert evidence should be called in any case where psychiatric injury is relied upon and not admitted by the defence. This warning was ignored by the trial judge in *Morris* (1998) with the result that a new trial had to be ordered, since V's alleged injuries as a result of being 'stalked' appeared to be psychological and were unsupported by expert evidence. The inclusion of psychological/psychiatric injury within actual bodily harm (and grievous bodily harm) and the general approach adopted in *Chan-Fook* were approved by the House of Lords in *Ireland*.

The *mens rea* of the offence is purely that of the assault or battery, the actual bodily harm being entirely a matter of causation. So, an assault which causes a victim to seek to escape and in the course of which she suffers injury can satisfy the requirements of this offence (as in *Roberts* (1971), a case considered in 5.1.3 in the discussion of causation). An intentional battery accompanied by an 'accidental' act which results in actual bodily harm also suffices. In *Savage* (1991), D intentionally threw beer over V but 'accidentally' allowed the glass to slip from her hand, cutting V. Intentionally soaking V with the beer was a battery and the court was content that there was a sufficient causal connection between that act and the breaking of the glass which caused V's injuries.

Unlawful and malicious wounding or inflicting/causing grievous bodily harm

There are two different sets of offences involving wounding/grievous bodily harm. The less serious set is unlawful and malicious wounding or infliction of grievous bodily harm (s 20 of the Offences Against the Person Act 1861). The second set is unlawful and malicious wounding or causing of grievous bodily harm with intent to cause grievous bodily harm (s 18 of the 1861 Act) (a further version of this offence deals with the intent to resist arrest). In turn, each set can be committed in two distinct ways: by wounding or by bringing about grievous bodily harm. Since they have so many elements in common, it is convenient to examine them together.

The *actus reus*

- A wound requires that both layers of the skin (dermis and epidermis) be broken. In *JCC (A Minor) v Eisenhower* (1984), injury to V's eye caused by airgun pellets fired by D was not a wound. His eye was bruised just below the eyebrow and, for a time afterwards, the fluid in his eye abnormally contained red blood cells but there was no break in the layers of the skin.

- A bruise is not a wound because the outer layer of skin is not broken. A graze or scratch may not be a wound because the inner layer may not be broken.

- Wounds can be minor or serious. If serious then they may amount, in addition, to grievous bodily harm.

- Grievous bodily harm is nothing more than any really serious injury. It might be constituted by injuries such as broken bones, permanent disfigurement, serious loss of blood, significant loss of consciousness and severe psychological/psychiatric illness. In *Brown and Stratton* (1998), evidence of a broken nose, the loss of three teeth and a laceration over one eye (with other evidence available of gross facial swelling and widespread laceration and bruising) was sufficient to be left to the jury to determine whether it amounted to grievous bodily harm.

• The s 20 and s 18 offences differ in requiring grievous bodily harm to have been 'inflicted' and 'caused' respectively. Until recently, this distinction was viewed as significant and had caused much judicial and academic soul searching. The House of Lords has now put an end to the anguish by declaring that there is no significant difference and that 'inflict' under s 20 is just as broad as 'cause' under s 18. In particular, an infliction can take place without the application of force, direct or indirect. This enlightened approach was prompted by the need for a judicial response to conduct generally now described as 'stalking'. In cases such as *Burstow* (1997), where D had waged a lengthy campaign against V, a former friend, it would have been impossible to achieve a conviction on the law as it stood before the decision of the House of Lords, since D did not use force. Despite this, V had been reduced to a nervous wreck by his attentions and the severe depressive illness which she suffered was easily described as grievous bodily harm. This change in the law also opens up the possibility that a s 20 charge could be brought against a person infecting a victim with, say, HIV in the course of consensual sexual activity.

The *mens rea*

• Both sets of offences use the term 'malicious'. This simply means intention or subjective recklessness, as established in *Cunningham* (1957) (see the discussion of recklessness in 5.1.3).

• In the case of s 20, no further *mens rea* is required but it is well established that D does not have to intend or be reckless as to a wound or grievous bodily harm. It is enough that he intends or is reckless as to some personal injury (*Savage; Parmenter*). So, if D pushes V over, intending at the most that V will have a painful fall, D may be guilty of the s 20 offence if V falls awkwardly and breaks bones. Similarly, an intention to inflict a minor wound might become a case of grievous bodily harm if D causes more serious injury than intended.

• In s 20, an intention to frighten alone is not enough (contrast s 47). At the very least, D must be aware that physical injury might result. In *Flack v Hunt* (1979), D, a gamekeeper, unintentionally shot V, a poacher, whom he had tried to induce to come out of hiding by firing his shotgun into an area of bushes away from where he believed that V was hiding. In fact, V was in the line of fire. D's conviction for the s 20 offence was quashed because it had not occurred to him that he might cause any injury.

• In the case of s 18, the Crown must go on to prove that, when D wounded V or caused V grievous bodily harm, he had an intention to cause grievous bodily harm. Consequently, there is little significance in the requirement for recklessness imposed by the use of the term 'malicious' in the definition of the offence (in other forms of this offence, it does have a role to play). The definition of intention follows that already discussed in 5.1.3 and this requires account to be taken of the approach now indicated by the House of Lords in *Woollin*.

Harassment

Even though the courts responded admirably to the challenge posed by a sudden surge in stalking cases, changing the law in the areas of assault and infliction of grievous bodily harm, in particular, it was evident that the problem of stalking (or, to give it a less dramatic name, harassment) could not be addressed in such piecemeal fashion. Eventually, Parliament was driven to intervene and the result was the Protection from Harassment Act 1997.

The Act creates two criminal offences:

(1) s 2 – harassing another (which includes alarming a person or causing the person distress) by a course of conduct (which includes speech and requires conduct on at least two occasions). It must be proved that D knew or ought to have known (in other words, a reasonable person in possession of the same information as D would have known) that it amounted to harassment.

(2) s 4 – causing a victim to fear violence against himself on at least two occasions by a course of conduct (which includes speech and itself requires conduct on at least two occasions). It must be proved that D knew or ought to have known (in other words, a reasonable person in possession of the same information as D would have known) that his course of conduct would cause the other to fear such violence on each occasion.

In both cases, it is a defence for D to show:

• that he pursued the course of conduct for the purpose of preventing or detecting crime; or

• that it was pursued under any enactment or rule of law or to comply with any condition or requirement imposed by any person under any enactment; or

• (in the case of s 2) that, in the particular circumstances, the pursuit of the course of conduct was reasonable; or

• (in the case of s 4) that, in the particular circumstances, the pursuit of the course of conduct was reasonable for his own or another's protection or for the protection of his own or another's property.

These provisions are supplemented and supported by civil procedures. Thus, damages may be awarded in a civil action for actual or apprehended harassment and an injunction may be granted to restrain a person from engaging in such a course of conduct. Breach of the injunction entitles the plaintiff to apply for the issue of a warrant for D's arrest and is an offence.

Following D's conviction for an offence under s 4, the court may issue, in addition to any other measure, a restraining order to protect V or any other person mentioned from further conduct amounting to harassment or likely to cause a fear of violence and may prohibit D from doing anything specified. Breach of this order is also an offence.

Consent as a defence to offences of personal injury

Apart from those offences (such as rape) where the definition requires that the activity be non-consensual, consent may be a defence to other non-fatal offences. It is essential that any consent is genuine and this cannot possibly be so if V lacks capacity to understand, whether because of age or other mental disability, or is under duress. On the other hand, consent obtained by some trick or fraud will not be invalid unless it concerns fundamental matters such as the identity of the other person involved or the nature of the act. In *Clarence* (1888), for instance, V's consent to sexual intercourse with D, her husband, was not invalidated by his failure to tell her that he was suffering from venereal disease, despite the fact that she would not have consented had she known. Similarly, in *Richardson* (1998), consent given to D, a dentist who, unknown to her patients, was continuing to provide treatment after being suspended from practice, was not invalidated by her fraud. The patients knew what treatment was being administered, and by whom, and the fraud was irrelevant.

The basic rule is that V can only consent to suffer injury, or the risk of injury, where that injury is less than actual bodily harm. Given the relatively minor injuries that may constitute actual bodily harm, this leaves little scope for the application of the 'defence' in the ordinary case. So, as established in *AG's Reference (No 6 of 1980)* (1981), D will not be able to avoid liability for injuries amounting to actual bodily harm (or worse) inflicted in an ordinary fight in which V has agreed to participate. In *Donovan* (1934), D's convictions for assault and indecent assault where he beat V with a cane with her consent in circumstances of indecency were quashed only because the trial judge had not directed the jury to consider whether or not the blows were likely or intended to cause bodily harm. If they were, then the consent would have been irrelevant.

However, there are exceptions to this basic rule which are generally seen as grounded in public policy, though the precise policy is not always easy to discern. So, in the following cases, consent may enable D to avoid conviction within the limits explained, even where the injury intended or risked is serious:

- in surgery, both medically indicated and for cosmetic purposes;

- in the case of 'body adornment', such as body piercing (earrings, nose studs and rings, etc) and tattooing (subject to the statutory requirement that V must be at least 18 years of age). In *Wilson* (1996), D's crude attempt to carve his initials on his wife's buttocks (at her request) by use of a hot knife was equated with body adornment;

- in the case of properly regulated sports, where the injury is inflicted, broadly speaking, within the rules of the game and, except in the case of boxing, D does not intend to inflict injury. Boxing is exceptional, in that V can consent to intentionally inflicted serious injury;

- in the case of rough 'horseplay', as in *Jones* (1986), where two younger boys were subjected to 'bumps' (being thrown in the air) by older boys who believed (so it was alleged) that their victims were consenting. This exception was also applied in the case of *Aitken* (1992) to an RAF officer who had set fire to the flying suit being worn by one of his colleagues during celebratory horseplay and inflicted serious burns and, in the case of *Richardson and Irwin* (1999), it applied to two students who had unintentionally dropped their friend when holding him over a balcony during some horseplay after they had been out drinking;

- in the case of dangerous entertainments and displays (where the skill of the performer is vital if an assistant or member of the audience is not to suffer injury).

In *Brown and Others* (1993), the House of Lords refused to extend the scope of the exceptions to cover deliberately inflicted injury for the purposes of sexual gratification. Consequently, a group of homosexual sado-masochistic men were found guilty of various offences arising out of apparently extreme practices but which caused no permanent injuries. The majority of their Lordships considered that the injuries were *prima facie* within the statute and that public policy considerations were against allowing consent as a defence (for example, the dangers of serious injury from infected blood and of events getting out of control). The minority viewed it from the opposite perspective, arguing that the activity was primarily sexual and that there were no valid public policy reasons for bringing it within the offences contained in the statute. In *Laskey and Others v UK* (1997), the European Court of Human Rights rejected a complaint by those convicted in *Brown* that their convictions for the offences constituted an unjustifiable interference with their right to respect for private life under Art 8 of the European Convention on Human Rights. Their prosecution was held to be 'necessary in a democratic society ... for the protection of health' (Art 8(2)). Though explicable on the narrow grounds already discussed, the decision in *Wilson* offered some prospect that the courts would not adopt an extreme, unliberal interpretation of *Brown*, at least where more conventional relationships were involved. However, in *Emmett* (1999), the Court of Appeal was unmoved by the fact that D and V were heterosexual partners engaged in rather extreme consensual sexual activity in private. It was held that V could not consent to the risk of the injuries which actually occurred when D put a plastic bag over her head to increase sexual excitement and when he set fire to lighter fuel which he had poured onto her breasts.

Reform of the law on non-fatal offences against the person

The discussion of the non-fatal offences has revealed that there are many flaws in the structure and detail of the rules and that legislative reform is long overdue. The courts have struggled to adapt some of the offences to cope with modern developments, particularly the stalking phenomenon, but there is limited scope for change. A glaring anomaly, for example, is that there is no simple offence of causing injury which is not serious. The Crown must prove the elements of an assault or battery and then show that this caused the injury. So, persistent harassment which causes psychological injury is not an offence within the traditional offences against the person unless it causes V to fear immediate personal violence. By contrast, persistent harassment which causes serious psychological injury may be an offence of inflicting grievous bodily harm, which no longer requires proof of the application of force. Another recent example of the anomalies that keep being thrown up is revealed by *Ramsell* (1999), where D was convicted of wounding with intent to resist arrest under s 18, an offence which carries a maximum sentence of life imprisonment, when she instructed her dog to bite a police officer during a dispute with neighbours. This charge was selected because the police officer was trying to arrest her for a breach of the peace whilst the lesser, and apparently much more appropriate, offence under s 38 of assault with intent to resist arrest required that the police officer should be trying to arrest for an offence. The further alarming feature of the case was that, having been convicted under s 18, D was then at risk of incurring a mandatory sentence of life imprisonment under the Crime (Sentences) Act 1997 should she unfortunately commit another 'serious offence'.

In 1993, the Law Commission published a report in which it made proposals for such reform (No 219) and, in 1998, the government issued a consultation document on reform which closely follows those proposals. The major effect would be that the familiar Offences Against the Person Act 1861 offences (ss 18, 20 and 47) and the offences of assault and battery would disappear and be replaced by offences of:

- intentional serious injury;
- reckless serious injury;
- intentional or reckless injury;
- assault (defined as including applying force and causing V to believe force is imminent).

Law Commission definitions of intention and recklessness would be adopted. Liability for the transmission of diseases would be restricted to the offence of intentional serious injury, as would liability for an omission. 'Injury' would be defined to mean physical injury (including pain, unconsciousness and any other impairment of a person's physical condition, but excluding anything caused by disease) or mental injury (any impairment of mental health, excluding anything caused by disease). No definition of 'serious' injury would be provided.

THE CRIMINAL LAW

The rules of criminal law are derived from both common law and statute, though the latter is now much the more significant source. As well as by source, crimes may be classified in a number of ways, for instance, according to mode of trial, whether the crime is an arrestable offence, and whether it represents 'true crime' or is merely a 'regulatory' offence.

The general elements of liability

Criminal liability is generally said to require proof of an *actus reus*, accompanied by *mens rea*, in the absence of any defence (general or specific, complete or partial).

The *actus reus* of an offence is comprised of the external elements represented by the accused's conduct in the presence of any relevant circumstances and which may be required to result in prescribed consequences. In addition, the accused's conduct must be voluntary in the sense that it must be under the control of the conscious brain to a sufficient extent. Lack of voluntariness is often termed automatism, and may give rise to a defence. Conduct will usually involve an act but in many crimes liability may be based upon an omission to act. However, this will depend upon proof that the accused was under a duty to act and that the failure to do so made a significant contribution to the harmful consequence.

All crimes requiring proof of a harmful consequence require proof that the accused's conduct was the cause of that consequence. Proof of causation is established by showing that the accused's conduct was a cause in fact and a cause in law, though in most cases, proof of the former will lead inevitably to proof of the latter. The accused's conduct is a cause in fact when the consequence would not have occurred 'but for' that conduct. It is a cause in law when it makes a significant contribution to the consequence. Problems occur when the accused asserts that the consequence was attributable to the conduct of some other person (the victim or a third person) or to some natural event. It will be strongly arguable that the accused remains responsible if the conduct or natural event was reasonably foreseeable in consequence of the accused's actions. Yet such a test need not necessarily be satisfied. The accused must 'take his victim as he finds him' (the whole person, not just the physical person) and medical intervention, even if negligent, may not break the chain of causation.

Mens rea functions as a higher level fault requirement. It generally requires proof either of intention or of recklessness, though some offences are only committed if the accused intends the consequence. A clear definition of intention remains elusive despite the fact that the issue has been considered by the House of Lords on four occasions in the last 25 years. Whilst it certainly includes an aim or purpose, doubts persist about whether it extends to foresight of the virtual certainty of a consequence without aim or purpose. There are two different tests of recklessness, subjective and objective. Subjective recklessness must be proved in almost all offences, and certainly in the non-fatal offences against the person. Objective recklessness suffices only in offences of criminal damage. The accused is subjectively reckless when aware of a risk which it would be unreasonable to take. The accused is objectively reckless when his conduct creates an obvious risk (a risk which any reasonable person would recognise) to which he gives no thought, no matter what the reason for his failure to give thought, and even if he would not have recognised the risk had he given thought to it. An accused who gives thought and decides that no risk exists is probably not reckless.

In some instances, *mens rea* is not required. Negligence suffices in some common law and many statutory offences. Negligence is the failure to achieve the standard of conduct expected of a reasonable person. In yet other offences, neither *mens rea* nor negligence need be proved. These offences are termed strict liability offences and are of particular significance in the sphere of so-called regulatory crime.

General defences

Apart from the restriction on criminal liability to those who are at least 10 years of age, it may be possible for an accused to avoid liability by justifying or excusing his conduct.

The defence of insanity requires the accused to prove that he suffered from a defect of reason, due to disease of the mind in such a way that he did not understand what conduct he was engaged in (the 'nature and quality' of his act) or, if he did, that he did not understand that what he was doing was legally wrong. If the accused succeeds in proving these elements, he will be found not guilty by reason of insanity but may be ordered to be detained in a secure hospital. A similar condition which does not arise from a disease of the mind but which prevents awareness of the nature and quality of the act will be termed automatism. This will entitle the accused to an acquittal unless it can be shown that the accused was at fault in becoming an automaton and was aware that he might commit an offence of the kind in question if he did become an automaton. Automatism may also be pleaded in situations where the accused cannot control his movements because of the application of superior force.

Intoxication, which may result from drink or drugs, may be voluntary or involuntary. If voluntary, the accused may use it to suggest that he did not form the intention in a specific intent offence. He will be unable to rely on it in any offence requiring proof merely of recklessness (a basic intent offence). Involuntary intoxication (where the accused is unaware that he is ingesting the intoxicant) may be used in any offence to suggest that the accused neither formed any intention nor was reckless. Voluntary intoxication will usually be of no help to the accused in offences of objective recklessness, and will be irrelevant in offences of negligence and strict liability.

An accused may be able to justify or excuse his conduct by arguing that he chose to commit the 'offence' as the lesser of two evils or because he was subjected to such pressure by way of threats of death or serious injury that his will was overborne. In the first case, he will plead necessity, the existence of which as a defence still remains in doubt. In the second case, he will plead duress or duress of circumstances. A closely related defence is that of self-defence or prevention of crime. Here, the accused will be able to justify his conduct if the use of some force was necessary for either of those purposes and the force which he actually used was roughly proportionate to the harm threatened.

Offences against the person

Offences against the person may be divided into two categories, fatal and non-fatal. The fatal offences fall within the umbrella of unlawful homicide, which is comprised of murder and manslaughter. The *actus reus* of unlawful homicide involves proof that the accused caused the death of a human being, the differentiation between the offences being in the *mens rea* and other elements. Murder is distinguished by the requirement for proof of 'malice aforethought', which can be translated more simply as intention to kill or cause serious injury.

Manslaughter is customarily described as being voluntary or involuntary. Voluntary manslaughter consists of a *prima facie* case of murder reduced to the status of manslaughter by a successful plea of provocation or of diminished responsibility. The defence of provocation consists of a killing whilst the accused was experiencing a loss of self-control in response to something done or said by any other person and in such circumstances that a reasonable person might have responded as did the accused. Diminished responsibility is an abnormality of mind caused by one of a number of specified conditions such that the mental responsibility of the accused for his conduct was substantially impaired.

Involuntary manslaughter consists of killings where the accused is regarded as culpable but he never possessed the *mens rea* for murder. In unlawful act manslaughter, the accused kills whilst engaged in committing a crime which created an obvious risk of some injury to any person. In gross negligence manslaughter, the accused may be engaged in lawful or unlawful conduct which amounts to a breach of a duty of care, creates an obvious risk of death, and is of such a nature that a jury would consider that it merits punishment as a crime. Subjective recklessness manslaughter occurs where the accused is aware of a risk of (perhaps serious) injury when engaged in any lawful or unlawful conduct.

The whole structure of the non-fatal offences of assault, battery, assault occasioning actual bodily harm, and wounding or inflicting/causing grievous bodily harm has been subjected to frequent criticism and proposals for reform. Assault is the intentional or reckless causing of fear of immediate infliction of personal violence, whilst battery is the infliction of the violence itself. Assault occasioning actual bodily harm requires proof of the elements of either assault or battery and that it caused the victim to suffer actual bodily harm, whether physical or psychological. A wound is a break in both layers of skin and may or may not be grievous bodily harm, which itself can be physical or psychological. Both versions of the offence require proof of intention or recklessness as to some injury. The more serious versions require proof that the accused wounded or caused grievous bodily harm and intended grievous bodily harm. Consent by the victim may be a defence in limited circumstances. Recently, offences involving harassment have been introduced in response to the 'stalking' phenomenon.

CHAPTER 6

THE LAW OF CONTRACT

6.1 Introduction

The simplest possible description of a contract is a legally binding agreement. It should be noted, however, that, although all contracts are the outcome of agreements, not all agreements are contracts; that is, not all agreements are legally enforceable. In order to be in a position to determine whether a particular agreement will be enforced by the courts, one must have an understanding of the rules and principles of contract law.

The essential elements of a binding agreement, and the constituent elements of the classical model of contract, are as follows:

- offer;

- acceptance;

- consideration;

- privity;

- capacity;

- intention to create legal relations;

- there must be no vitiating factors present.

The first six of these elements must be present, and the seventh one absent, for there to be a legally enforceable contractual relationship (each of these elements will be considered in detail).

The emphasis placed on agreement highlights the consensual nature of contracts. It is sometimes said that contract is based on *consensus ad idem*, a meeting of minds. This is slightly misleading, however, for the reason that English contract law applies an objective test in determining whether or not a contract exists. It is not so much a matter of what the parties actually had in mind, as what their behaviour would lead others to conclude regarding their state of mind.

6.2   The legal effect of agreements

The legal effect of particular agreements may be distinguished as follows:

- *Valid contracts*

  These are agreements which the law recognises as binding in full. The court will enforce the contract by either insisting on performance or awarding damages to the innocent party.

- *Void contracts*

  This is actually a contradiction in terms, for this type of agreement does not constitute a contract: it has no legal effect. Agreements may be void for a number of reasons including mistake, illegality, public policy, or the lack of a necessary requirement such as consideration. The ownership of property exchanged does not pass under a void contract and remains with the original owner. The legal owner may recover it from the possession of the other party, or indeed any third party if it has been passed on to such a person. This is so even where the third party has acquired the property in good faith and has provided consideration for it.

- *Voidable contracts*

  These are agreements which may be avoided, that is, set aside, by one of the parties. If, however, no steps are taken to avoid the agreement then a valid contract ensues. Examples of contracts which may be voidable are those which have been entered into on the basis of fraud, misrepresentation or duress. Goods which have been exchanged under a voidable contract can be sold to an innocent third party, who will receive good title.

- *Unenforceable contracts*

  These are agreements which, although legal, cannot be sued upon for some reason. One example would be where the time limit for enforcing the contract has lapsed. The title to any goods exchanged under such a contract is treated as having been validly passed and cannot, therefore, be reclaimed.

6.3   Formalities

There is no general requirement that contracts be made in writing. They can be created by word of mouth, or by action, as well as in writing. Contracts made in any of these ways are known as parol or simple contracts, whereas those made by deed are referred to as speciality contracts. It is generally left to the parties to decide on the actual form that the contract has to take, but in certain circumstances formalities are required:

- *Contracts that must be made by deed*

Essentially, this requirement applies to conveyances of land and leases of property extending over a period of more than three years. Conveyance is the legal process of the transfer of land. It is distinct from a contract to sell land which is merely a legal agreement to transfer the land and not the actual process of transfer which comes later. Agreements, which would not otherwise be enforceable as contracts, will be implemented by the courts where they have been made by deed.

- *Contracts that must be in writing (but not necessarily by deed)*

Among this group are: bills of exchange, cheques and promissory notes (by virtue of the Bills of Exchange Act 1882); consumer credit agreements such as hire purchase agreements (by virtue of the Consumer Credit Act 1974); contracts of marine insurance (by virtue of the Marine Assurance Act 1906). The Law of Property (Miscellaneous Provisions) Act 1989 requires all contracts for the sale or disposition of land to be made in writing.

- *Contracts that must be evidenced in writing*

The sole remaining member of this category are contracts of guarantee, derived from s 4 of the Statute of Frauds Act 1677.

6.4 Offer

An offer is a promise which is capable of acceptance, to be bound on particular terms. The person who makes the offer is the offeror; the person who receives the offer is the offeree. The offer sets out the terms upon which the offeror is willing to enter into contractual relations with the offeree.

The offer must be capable of acceptance, thus it must not be too vague.

In *Scammel v Ouston* (1941), Ouston ordered a van from Scammel on the understanding that the balance of the purchase price could be paid on hire purchase terms over two years. Scammel used a number of different hire purchase terms and the actual terms of Ouston's agreement were never actually fixed. When Scammel failed to deliver the van, Ouston sued for breach of contract. It was held that the action failed on the basis that no contract could be established due to the uncertainty of the terms.

6.4.1 Distinguishing factors of an offer

An offer may, through acceptance by the offeree, result in a legally enforceable contract. It is important to be able to distinguish what the law will treat as an offer from other statements which will not form the basis of an enforceable contract. An offer must be distinguished from the following:

- *A mere statement of intention*

  Such a statement cannot form the basis of a contract even though the party to whom it was made acts on it. See, for example, *Re Fickus* (1900), where a father informed his prospective son-in-law that his daughter would inherit under his will. It was held that the fathers words were simply a statement of present intention which he could alter as he wished in the future. They were not an offer, and therefore the father could not be bound by them.

- *A mere supply of information*

  The case *Harvey v Facey* (1893) demonstrates this point. The plaintiff telegraphed the defendants: 'Will you sell us Bumper Hall Pen? Telegraph lowest cash price.' The defendant answered: 'Lowest price for Bumper Hall Pen £900.' The plaintiff then telegraphed: 'We agree to buy Bumper Hall Pen for £900', and sued for specific performance when the defendants declined to transfer the property. It was held that the defendants' telegram was not an offer capable of being accepted by the plaintiff. It was simply a statement of information.

- *An invitation to treat*

  This is an invitation to others to make offers. The person extending the invitation is not bound to accept any offers made to them. The following are examples of common situations involving invitations to treat:

  (a) *The display of goods in a shop window.* The classic case in this area is *Fisher v Bell* (1961) in which a shopkeeper was prosecuted for offering offensive weapons for sale, by having flick-knives on display in his window. It was held that the shopkeeper was not guilty as the display in the shop window was not an offer for sale but only an invitation to treat.

  (b) *The display of goods on the shelf of a self-service shop.* In this instance, the exemplary case is *Pharmaceutical Society of Great Britain v Boots Cash Chemists* (1953). The defendants were charged with breaking a law which provided that certain drugs could only be sold under the supervision of a qualified pharmacist. They had placed the drugs on open display in their self-service store and, although a qualified person was stationed at the cash desk, it was alleged that the contract of sale had been formed when the customer removed the goods from the shelf. It was held that Boots were not guilty. The display of goods on the shelf was only an invitation to treat. In law, the customer offered to buy the goods at the cash desk where the pharmacist was stationed. This decision is clearly practical, as the alternative would mean that once customers had placed goods in their shopping baskets they would be bound to accept them and could not change their minds and return the goods to the shelves.

(c) *A public advertisement.* Once again, this does not amount to an offer. This can be seen from *Partridge v Crittenden* (1968) in which a person was charged with offering a wild bird for sale contrary to Protection of Birds Act 1954, after he had placed an advert relating to the sale of such birds in a magazine. It was held that he could not be guilty of offering the bird for sale as the advert amounted to no more than an invitation to treat.

(d) *A share prospectus.* Contrary to common understanding, such a document is not an offer; it is merely an invitation to treat, inviting people to make offers to subscribe for shares in a company.

It can be seen that the decisions in both *Fisher v Bell* and *Partridge v Crittenden* run contrary to the common, non-legal, understanding of the word 'offer'. It is interesting to note that later legislation, such as the Trades Descriptions Act 1968, has specifically been worded in such a way as to ensure that invitations to treat are subject to the same legal regulation as offers.

6.4.2 Offers to particular people

An offer may be made to a particular person or to a group of people or to the world at large. If the offer is restricted, then only the people to whom it is addressed may accept it; but if the offer is made to the public at large, it can be accepted by anyone.

In *Carlill v Carbolic Smoke Ball Co* (1893), the company advertised that they would pay £100 to anyone who caught influenza after using their smoke ball as directed. Carlill used the smoke ball but still caught influenza and sued the company for the promised £100. Amongst the many defences argued for the company, it was suggested that the advert could not have been an offer as it was not addressed to Carlill. It was held that the advert was an offer to the whole world which Mrs Carlill had accepted by her conduct. There was, therefore, a valid contract between her and the company.

6.4.3 Acceptance of offers

A person cannot accept an offer that they do not know about. Thus, if a person offers a reward for the return of a lost watch and someone returns it without knowing about the offer, they cannot claim the reward. Motive for accepting is not important as long as the person accepting knows about the offer. See *Williams v Carwardine* (1883), where a person was held to be entitled to receive a reward although that was not the reason they provided the information requested. (Acceptance generally will be considered in detail in 6.5.)

6.4.4 Rejection of offers

Express rejection of an offer has the effect of terminating the offer. The offeree cannot subsequently accept the original offer. A counter-offer, where the offeree tries to change the terms of the offer has the same effect.

In *Hyde v Wrench* (1840), Wrench offered to sell his farm for £1,000. Hyde offered £950, which Wrench rejected. Hyde then informed Wrench that he accepted the original offer. It was held that there was no contract. Hyde's counter-offer had effectively ended the original offer and it was no longer open to him to accept it.

A counter-offer must not be confused with a request for information. Such a request does not end the offer, which can still be accepted after the new information has been elicited. See *Stevenson v McLean* (1880), where it was held that a request by the offeree as to the length of time the offeror would give for payment did not terminate the original offer, which he was entitled to accept prior to revocation.

6.4.5 Revocation of offers

Revocation, the technical term for cancellation, occurs when the offeror withdraws their offer. There are a number of points that have to be borne in mind in relation to revocation:

- *An offer may be revoked at any time before acceptance*

  Once revoked, it is no longer open to the offeree to accept the original offer.

  In *Routledge v Grant* (1828), Grant offered to buy Routledge's house and gave him six weeks to accept the offer. Within that period, however, he withdrew the offer. It was held that Grant was entitled to withdraw the offer at any time before acceptance and upon withdrawal Routledge could no longer create a contract by purporting to accept it.

- *Revocation is not effective until it is actually received by the offeree*

  This means that the offeror must make sure that the offeree is made aware of the withdrawal of the offer, otherwise it might still be open to the offeree to accept the offer.

  In *Byrne v Tienhoven* (1880), the defendant offerors carried out their business in Cardiff, the plaintiff offerees in New York. On 1 October, an offer was made by post. On 8 October, a letter of revocation was posted, seeking to withdraw the offer. On 11 October, the plaintiffs telegraphed their acceptance of the offer. On 20 October, the letter of revocation was received by the plaintiffs.

It was held that the revocation did not take effect until it arrived and the defendants were bound by the contract which had been formed by the plaintiff's acceptance. (See, also, the consideration of the postal rule in 6.5.2.)

- *Communication of revocation may be made through a reliable third party*

Where the offeree finds out about the withdrawal of the offer from a reliable third party, the revocation is effective and the offeree can no longer seek to accept the original offer.

In *Dickinson v Dodds* (1876), Dodds offered to sell property to Dickinson and told him that the offer would be left open until Friday. On the Thursday, the plaintiff was informed by a reliable third party, who was acting as an intermediary, that Dodds intended selling the property to someone else. Dickinson still attempted to accept the offer on the Friday, by which time the property had already been sold. It was held that the sale of the property amounted to revocation which had been effectively communicated by the third party.

- *A promise to keep an offer open is only binding where there is a separate contract to that effect*

This is known as an option contract, and the offeree/promisee must provide consideration for the promise to keep the offer open.

- *In relation to unilateral contracts, revocation is not permissible once the offeree has started performing the task requested*

A unilateral contract is one where one party promises something in return for some action on the part of another party. Reward cases are examples of such unilateral promises. There is no compulsion placed on the party undertaking the action but it would seem to be unfair if the promisor were entitled to revoke their offer just before the offeree was about to complete their part of the contract.

In *Errington v Errington* (1952), a father promised his son and daughter-in-law that he would convey a house to them when they had paid off the outstanding mortgage. After the father's death, his widow sought to revoke the promise. It was held that the promise could not be withdrawn as long as the mortgage payments continued to be met.

6.4.6 Lapsing of offers

Offers will lapse and will no longer be capable of acceptance in the following circumstances:

- *At the end of a stated period*

  It is possible for the parties to agree, or the offeror to set, a time limit within which acceptance has to take place. If the offeree has not accepted, the offer within that period the offer lapses and can no longer be accepted.

- *After a reasonable time*

  Where no set time limit is set, then an offer will lapse after the passage of a reasonable time. What amounts to a reasonable time is of course dependent upon the particular circumstances of each case.

- *Where the offeree dies*

  This automatically brings the offer to a close.

- *Where the offeror dies and the contract was one of a personal nature*

  In such circumstances, the offer automatically comes to an end but the outcome is less certain in relation to contracts that are not of a personal nature. See *Bradbury v Morgan* (1862) for an example of a case where it was held that the death of an offeror did not invalidate the offerees acceptance.

  It should be noted that the effect of death after acceptance also depends on whether the contract was one of a personal nature or not. In the case of a non-personal contract, the contract can be enforced by and against the representatives of the deceased. On the other hand, if performance of the contract depended upon the personal qualification or capacity of the deceased, then the contract will be frustrated (see 6.12.3).

6.5 Acceptance

Acceptance is necessary for the formation of a contract. Once the offeree has assented to the terms offered, a contract comes into effect. Both parties are bound: the offeror can no longer withdraw their offer, nor can the offeree withdraw their acceptance.

6.5.1 Form of acceptance

In order to form a binding agreement, the acceptance must correspond with the terms of the offer. Thus, the offeree must not seek to introduce new contractual terms into their acceptance.

In *Neale v Merrett* (1930), one party offered to sell property for £280. The other party purported to accept the offer by sending £80 and promising to pay the remainder by monthly instalments. It was held that this purported acceptance was ineffective as the offeree had not accepted the original offer as stated.

As was seen in *Hyde v Wrench*, a counter-offer does not constitute acceptance. Analogously, it may also be stated that a conditional acceptance cannot create a contract relationship. Thus, any agreement subject to contract is not binding but merely signifies the fact that the parties are in the process of finalising the terms on which they will be willing to be bound (*Winn v Bull* (1877)).

Acceptance may be in the form of express words, either oral or written; or it may be implied from conduct. Thus, in *Brogden v Metropolitan Railway Co* (1877), the plaintiff, having supplied the company with coal for a number of years, suggested that they should enter into a written contract. The company agreed and sent Brogden a draft contract. He altered some points and returned it marked approved. The company did nothing further about the document, but Brogden continued to deliver coal on the terms included in the draft contract. When a dispute arose, Brogden denied the existence of any contract. It was held that the draft became a full contract when both parties acted on it.

6.5.2 Communication of acceptance

The general rule is that acceptance must be communicated to the offeror. As a consequence of this rule, silence cannot amount to acceptance. The classic case in this regard is *Felthouse v Bindley* (1863), where an uncle had been negotiating the purchase of his nephew's horse and he eventually wrote offering to buy it at a particular price stating 'If I hear no more about him, I shall consider the horse mine'. When the horse was mistakenly sold by an auctioneer, the uncle sued the auctioneer in conversion. It was held that the uncle had no cause of action as the horse did not belong to him. Acceptance could not be imposed on the offeree on the basis of his silence.

There are, however, exceptions to the general rule that acceptance must be communicated which arise in the following cases:

- *Where the offeror has waived the right to receive communication*

  In unilateral contracts, such as *Carlill v Carbolic Smoke Ball Co* or general reward cases, acceptance occurs when the offeree performs the required act. Thus, in the *Carlill* case, Mrs Carlill did not have to inform the Smoke Ball Co that she had used their treatment. Nor, in reward cases, do those seeking to benefit have to inform the person offering the reward that they have begun to perform the task that will lead to the reward.

- *Where acceptance is through the postal service*

  In such circumstances, acceptance is complete as soon as the letter, properly addressed and stamped, is posted. The contract is concluded even if the letter subsequently fails to reach the offeror.

  In *Adams v Lindsell* (1818), on 2 September, the defendant made an offer to the plaintiff. Due to misdirection, the letter was delayed. It arrived on 5

September, and Adams immediately posted an acceptance. On 8 September, Lindsell sold the merchandise to a third party. On 9 September, the letter of acceptance from Adams arrived. It was held that valid acceptance occurred when Adams posted the letter and Lindsell was therefore liable for breach of contract.

As has already been seen in *Byrne v Van Tienhoven,* the postal rule applies equally to telegrams. It does not apply, however, when means of instantaneous communication are used (see *Entores v Miles Far East Corp* (1955) for a consideration of this point). It follows that, when acceptance is made by means of telephone, fax, or telex, the offeror must actually receive the acceptance.

It should be noted that the postal rule will only apply where it is in the contemplation of the parties that the post will be used as the means of acceptance. If the parties have negotiated either face to face, in a shop, for example, or over the telephone, then it might not be reasonable for the offeree to use the post as a means of communicating their acceptance and they would not gain the benefit of the postal rule.

In order to expressly exclude the operation of the postal rule, the offeror can insist that acceptance is only to be effective on receipt (see *Holwell Securities v Hughes* (1974)). The offeror can also require that acceptance be communicated in a particular manner. Where the offeror does not insist that acceptance can only be made in the stated manner, then acceptance is effective if it is communicated in a way no less advantageous to the offeror (see *Yates Building Co v J Pulleyn & Sons* (1975)).

6.5.3 Tenders

These arise where one party wishes particular work to be done and issues a statement asking interested parties to submit the terms on which they are willing to carry out the work. In the case of tenders, the person who invites the tender is simply making an invitation to treat. The person who submits a tender is the offeror and the other party is at liberty to accept or reject the offer as they please.

The effect of acceptance depends upon the wording of the invitation to tender. If the invitation states that the potential purchaser will require to be supplied with a certain quantity of goods, then acceptance of a tender will form a contract and they will be in breach if they fail to order the stated quantity of goods from the tenderer.

If, on the other hand, the invitation states only that the potential purchaser may require goods, acceptance gives rise only to a standing offer. There is no compulsion on the purchaser to take any goods but they must not deal with any other supplier. Each order given forms a separate contract and the supplier must deliver any goods required within the time stated in the tender. The supplier can revoke the standing offer but they must supply any goods already ordered.

In *Great Northern Railway v Witham* (1873), the defendant successfully tendered to supply the company with such quantities as the company may order from time to time. After fulfiling some orders, Witham refused to supply any more goods. It was held that he was in breach of contract in respect of the goods already ordered, but once those were supplied he was at liberty to revoke his standing order.

6.6 Consideration

English law does not enforce gratuitous promises unless they are made by deed. Consideration can be understood as the price paid for a promise. The element of bargain implicit in the idea of consideration is evident in the following definition by Sir Frederick Pollock, adopted by the House of Lords in *Dunlop v Selfridge* (1915) as:

> An act or forbearance of one party, or the promise thereof, is the price for which the promise of the other is bought, and the promise thus given for value is enforceable.

It is sometimes said that consideration consists of some benefit to the promisor or detriment to the promisee. It should be noted that both elements stated in that definition are not required to be present to support a legally enforceable agreement; although, in practice, they are usually present. If the promisee acts to their detriment, it is immaterial that the action does not directly benefit the promisor.

6.6.1 Forbearance

Forbearance involves non-action, or the relinquishing of some right. An example is forbearance to sue. If two parties, A and B, believe that A has a cause of legal action against B, then, if B promises to pay a sum of money to A if B will give up the right to pursue the action, there is a valid contract to that effect: A has provided consideration by giving up the recourse to law. Such action would not amount to consideration if A knew that the claim was either hopeless or invalid.

6.6.2 Types of consideration

Consideration can be divided into the following categories:

- *Executory consideration*

This is the promise to perform an action at some future time. A contract can be made on the basis of an exchange of promises as to future action. Such a contract is known as an executory contract.

- *Executed consideration*

In the case of unilateral contracts, where the offeror promises something in return for the offerees doing something, the promise only becomes enforceable when the offeree has actually performed the required act. If A offers a reward for the return of the lost watch, the reward only becomes enforceable once it has been found and returned.

- *Past consideration*

This category does not actually count as valid consideration sufficient to make any agreement based on it a binding contract. Normally, consideration is provided either at the time of the creation of a contract or at a later date. In the case of past consideration, however, the action is performed before the promise that it is supposed to be the consideration for. Such action is not sufficient to support a promise as consideration cannot consist of any action already wholly performed before the promise was made.

In *Re McArdle* (1951), a number of children were entitled to a house on the death of their mother. Whilst the mother was still alive, her son and his wife had lived with her, and the wife had made various improvements to the house. The children later promised that they would pay the wife £488 for the work she had done. It was held that as the work was completed when the promise was given, it was past consideration and the later promise could not be enforced.

There are exceptions to the rule that past consideration will not support a valid contract:

- under s 27 of the Bills of Exchange Act 1882, past consideration can create liability on a bill of exchange;
- under s 29 of the Limitation Act 1980, a time barred debt becomes enforceable again if it is acknowledged in writing;
- where the plaintiff performed the action at the request of the defendant and payment was expected, then any subsequent promise to pay will be enforceable.

In *Casey's Patents* (1892), the joint owners of patent rights asked Casey to find licensees to work the patents. After he had done as requested, they promised to reward him. When one of the patent holders died, his executors denied the enforceability of the promise made to Casey on the basis of past consideration. It was held that the promise made to Casey was enforceable. There had been an implied promise to reward him before he had performed his action and the later payment simply fixed the extent of that reward.

6.6.3 Rules relating to consideration

It has already been seen that consideration must not be past. But that is only one of the many rules that govern the legal definition and operation of consideration. Other rules are as follows:

* *Performance must be legal*

  The courts will not countenance a claim to enforce a promise to pay for any criminal act.

* *Performance must be possible*

  It is generally accepted that a promise to perform an impossible act cannot form the basis of a binding contractual agreement.

* *Consideration must move from the promisee*

  If A promises B £1,000 if B gives his or her car to C, then normally C cannot enforce B's promise, because C is not the party who has provided the consideration for the promise.

  In *Tweddle v Atkinson* (1861), on the occasion of the marriage of A and B their respective fathers entered into a contract to pay money to A. When one of the parents died without having made the payment, A tried to enforce the contract against his estate. It was held that A could not enforce the contract as he personally had provided no consideration for the promise. (This point should be considered in relation to privity of contract. See 6.7.)

* *Consideration must be sufficient but need not be adequate*

  It is up to the parties themselves to decide the terms of their contract. The court will not intervene to require equality in the value exchanged, as long as the agreement has been freely entered into.

  In *Thomas v Thomas* (1842), the executors of a man's will promised to let his widow live in his house in return for rent of £1 per year. It was held that £1 was sufficient consideration to validate the contract, although it did not represent an adequate rent in economic terms.

  In *Chappell & Co v Nestlé Co* (1959), it was held that a used chocolate wrapper was consideration sufficient to form a contract, even although it had no economic value whatsoever to Nestlé and was, in fact, thrown away after it was returned to them.

6.6.4 Performance of existing duties

Although it has generally been accepted that performance of an existing duty does not provide valid consideration, the recent authority of *Williams v Roffey Bros* (1990) has indicated a contrary possibility. The rules relating to existing duty are as follows:

• *The discharge of a public duty*

As a matter of public policy, to forestall the possibility of corruption or extortion, it has long been held that those required to perform certain public duties cannot claim the performance of those duties as consideration for a promised reward.

In *Collins v Godefroy* (1831), the plaintiff was served with a subpoena which meant that he was legally required to give evidence in the court case in question. Additionally, however, the defendant promised to pay him for giving his evidence. When the plaintiff tried to enforce the promised payment, it was held that there was no binding agreement as he had provided no consideration by simply fulfiling his existing duty.

Where, however, a promisee does more than their duty, they are entitled to claim on the promise. See, for example, *Glassbrook v Glamorgan CC* (1925), where the police authority provided more protection than their public duty required; and the similar case of *Harris v Sheffield United FC* (1987), where the football club was held liable to pay police costs for controlling crowds at their matches.

In cases where there is no possibility of corruption and no evidence of coercion, the courts have stretched the understanding of what is meant by consideration in order to fit the facts of the case in question within the framework of the classical model of contract. See, for example, *Ward v Byham* (1956) in which a mother was held to provide consideration by looking after her child well and *Williams v Williams* (1957) in which the consideration for a husbands promise of maintenance to his estranged wife seemed to be the fact of her staying away from him. In both of these cases, Lord Denning introduced *obiter dicta* which directly questioned the reason why the performance of an existing duty should not amount to consideration but the cases were ultimately decided on the basis that sufficient consideration was provided.

• *The performance of a contractual duty*

Lord Denning's challenge to the formalism of the classical model of contract is particularly pertinent when considered in the context of commercial contracts, where the mere performance of a contract may provide a benefit, or at least avoid a loss, for a promisor. The long established rule, however, was that the mere performance of a contractual duty already owed to the promisor cannot be consideration for a new promise.

In *Stilk v Myrick* (1809), when two members of his crew deserted, a ship's captain promised the remaining members of the crew that they would share the deserters wages if they completed the voyage. When the ship was returned to London, the owners refused to honour the promise and it was held that it could not be legally enforced since the sailors had only done what they were already obliged to do by their contracts of employment.

Although *Stilk v Myrick* is cited as an authority in relation to consideration, it would appear that the public policy issue in the perceived need to preclude even the possibility of sailors in distant parts exerting coercive pressure to increase their rewards was just as important. Thus, although the reason for the decision was a matter of public policy, its legal justification was in terms of consideration.

As in the case of a public duty, so performance of more than the existing contractual duty will be valid consideration for a new promise. Thus, in *Hartley v Ponsonby* (1857), the facts of which were somewhat similar to those in *Stilk and Myrick*, it was decided that the crew had done more than they previously had agreed to do because the number of deserters had been so great as to make the return of the ship unusually hazardous. On that basis, they were entitled to enforce the agreement to increase their wages. Once again, in this case, one finds a reluctance to deny the theoretical application of the classical model of contract whilst, at the same time, undermining its operation in practice.

The continued relevance and application of *Stilk v Myrick* in commercial cases has been placed in no little doubt in recent years by a potentially extremely important decision of the Court of Appeal.

In *Williams v Roffey Bros* (1990), Roffey Bros had entered into a contract to refurbish a block of flats and subcontracted with Williams to carry out carpentry work for a fixed price of £20,000. It became apparent that Williams was in such financial difficulties that he might not be able to complete his work on time with the consequence that Roffey Bros would be subject to a penalty clause in the main contract. As a result, Roffey Bros offered to pay Williams an additional £575 for each flat he completed. On that basis, Williams carried on working but, when it seemed that Roffey Bros were not going to pay him, he stopped work and sued for the additional payment in relation to the eight flats he had completed after the promise of additional payment. The Court of Appeal held that Roffey Bros had enjoyed practical benefits as a consequence of their promise to increase Williams' payment: the work would be completed on time; they would not have to pay any penalty; and they would not suffer the bother and expense of getting someone else to complete the work. These benefits were sufficient in the circumstances to provide consideration for the promise of extra money and Williams was held to be entitled to recover the extra money owed to him.

It should be emphasised that the Court of Appeal in *Williams v Roffey Bros* made it clear that they were not to be understood as disapproving the *ratio* in *Stilk v Myrick*. They distinguished the present case but, in so doing, they effectively limited the application of the *ratio* in *Stilk v Myrick*. As the owners in *Stilk v Myrick* would appear to have enjoyed similar practical benefits to those enjoyed by Roffey Bros, it would seem that the reason for distinguishing the cases rests on the clear absence of any fraud, economic duress or other improper pressure, as emphasised by the Court of Appeal in *Williams v Roffey*.

The legal situation would now seem to be that the performance of an existing contractual duty can amount to consideration for a new promise in circumstances where there is no question of fraud or duress, and where practical benefits accrue to the promisor. Such a conclusion not only concurs with the approach suggested earlier by Lord Denning in *Ward v Byham* and *Williams v Williams* but also reflects commercial practice where contracts are frequently renegotiated in the course of their performance.

The foregoing has considered the situation that operates between the parties to an existing contract. It has long been recognised that the performance of a contract duty owed to one person can amount to valid consideration for the promise made by another person.

In *Shadwell v Shadwell* (1860), the plaintiff had entered into a contract to marry. His uncle promised that, if he went ahead with his marriage, he would pay him £150 per year, until his earnings reached a certain sum. When the uncle died owing several years payment, the nephew successfully sued his estate for the outstanding money. It was held that going through with the marriage was sufficient consideration for the uncles promise, even although the nephew was already contractually bound to his fiancée.

6.6.5 Consideration in relation to the waiver of existing rights

At common law, if A owes B £10 but B agrees to accept £5 in full settlement of the debt, B's promise to give up existing rights must be supported by consideration on the part of A. In *Pinnel's Case* (1602), it was stated that a payment of a lesser sum cannot be any satisfaction for the whole. This opinion was approved in *Foakes v Beer* (1884) where Mrs Beer had obtained a judgment in debt against Dr Foakes for £2,091. She had agreed in writing to accept payment of this amount in instalments. When payment was finished, she claimed a further £360 as interest due on the judgment debt. It was held that Beer was entitled to the interest as her promise to accept the bare debt was not supported by any consideration from Foakes.

It can be appreciated that there are some similarities between the rule in *Foakes v Beer* and the rule in *Stilk v Myrick* in the way in which promisors escape subsequent liability for their promises. In the former case, however, the promisor was being asked to give up what she was legally entitled to insist on; whereas in the latter the promisors were being asked to provide more than they were legally required to.

As has been considered above, the rule in *Stilk v Myrick* has been subsequently modified and made less strict in its application by *Williams v Roffey Bros*. However, no corresponding modification has taken place in relation to *Foakes v Beer*; indeed, the Court of Appeal has recently rejected the argument that it should be so modified.

In *Re Selectmove Ltd* (1994), in negotiations relating to money owed to the Inland Revenue, the company had agreed with the collector of taxes that it would pay off the debt by instalments. The company started paying off the debt only to be faced with a demand from the Revenue that the total be paid off immediately on the threat of liquidation. It was argued for the company, on the basis of *Williams v Roffey*, that its payment of the debt was sufficient consideration for the promise of the Revenue to accept it in instalments. It was held that situations relating to the payment of debt were distinguishable from those relating to the supply of goods and services, and that, in the case of the former, the court was bound to follow the clear authority of the House of Lords in *Foakes v Beer*.

The practical validity of the distinction drawn by the Court of Appeal is, to say the least, arguable. It ignores the fact that payment by instalments, and indeed part payment, is substantially better than no payment at all, which is a possible, if not likely, outcome of liquidating businesses in an attempt to recover the full amount of a debt. It is surely unnecessarily harsh to deny legal enforceability to renegotiated agreements in relation to debt where the terms have been renegotiated freely without any suggestion of fraud, or coercion. Nonetheless, the Court of Appeal clearly felt itself constrained by the doctrine of binding precedent and had less scope to distinguish *Foakes v Beer* than it had with regard to *Stilk v Myrick*. It remains to be seen whether the House of Lords will be asked to reconsider the operation of *Foakes v Beer* in the light of current commercial practice.

In any case, there are a number of situations in which the rule in *Foakes v Beer* does not apply. The following will operate to fully discharge an outstanding debt:

- *Payment in kind*

Money's worth is just as capable of satisfying a debt as is money. So A may clear a debt if B agrees to accept something instead of money.

As considered previously, consideration does not have to be adequate, thus A can discharge a £10 debt by giving B £5 and a chocolate sweet. Payment by cheque is no longer treated as substitute payment in this respect (see *D and C Builders Ltd v Rees* (1966)).

- *Payment of a lesser sum before the due date of payment*

The early payment has, of course, to be acceptable to the party to whom the debt is owed.

- *Payment at a different place*

As in the previous case, this must be at the wish of the creditor.

- *Payment of a lesser sum by a third party*

See *Welby v Drake* (1825).

- *A composition arrangement*

This is an agreement between creditors to the effect that they will accept part payment of their debts. The individual creditors cannot subsequently seek to recover the unpaid element of the debt (see *Good v Cheesman* (1831)).

6.6.6 Promissory estoppel

It has been seen that English law generally will not enforce gratuitous promises, that is, promises not supported by consideration by the promisee. The equitable doctrine of promissory estoppel, however, can sometimes be relied upon to prevent promisors from going back on their promises. The doctrine first appeared in *Hughes v Metropolitan Railway Co* (1877) and was revived by Lord Denning in *Central London Property Trust Ltd v High Trees House Ltd* (1947).

In *Central London Property Trust Ltd v High Tress House Ltd,* the plaintiffs let a block of flats to the defendants, in 1937, at a fixed rent. Due to the war, it became difficult to let the flats and the parties renegotiated the rent to half the original amount. No consideration was provided for this agreement. By 1945, all the flats were let and the plaintiffs sought to return to the terms of the original agreement. They claimed they were entitled to the full rent in the future and enquired whether they were owed additional rent for the previous period. It was held that the plaintiffs were entitled to the full rent in the future but were estopped from claiming the full rent for the period from 1941 to 1945.

The precise scope of the doctrine of promissory estoppel is far from certain. There are a number of conflicting judgments on the point, with some judges adopting a wide understanding of its operation, whilst others prefer to keep its effect narrowly constrained. However, the following points may be made:

- *It arises from a promise made by a party to an existing contractual agreement*

The promise must have been made with the intention that it be acted upon and must actually have been acted on. It was once thought that the promisee must have acted to their detriment but such detriment is no longer considered necessary (see *WJ Alan & Co v El Nasr Export & Import Co* (1972)).

- *It only varies or discharges rights within a contract*

Promissory estoppel does not apply to the formation of contract and, therefore, it does not avoid the need for consideration to establish a contract in the first instance. This point is sometimes made by stating that promissory estoppel is a shield and not a sword (see *Combe v Combe* (1951)).

- *It normally only suspends rights*

It is usually open to the promisor, on the provision of reasonable notice, to retract the promise and revert to the original terms of the contract (see *Tool Metal Manufacturing Co v Tungsten Electric Co* (1955)). Rights may be extinguished, however, in the case of a non-continuing obligation, or where the parties cannot resume their original positions. (Consider *D and C Builders v Rees* (1966) below. It is clear that, had the builders been able to reply on promissory estoppel, the Rees family would have permanently lost their right to recover the full amount of the original debt.)

- *The promise relied upon must be given voluntarily*

As an equitable remedy, the benefit of promissory estoppel will not be extended to those who have behaved in an inequitable manner. Thus, if the promise has been extorted through fraud, duress, or any other inequitable manner, it will not be relied on and the common law rules will apply.

In *D and C Builders v Rees* (1966), the defendants owed the plaintiffs £482, but would agree to pay only £300. As the builders were in financial difficulties, they accepted the £300 in full settlement of the account. The plaintiffs later successfully claimed the outstanding balance on the grounds that they had been forced to accept the lesser sum. As the defendants themselves had not acted in an equitable manner, they were denied the protection of the equitable remedy and the case was decided on the basis of the rule in *Pinnel's Case* (1602).

6.6.7 Promissory estoppel after *Williams v Roffey*

It is likely that the decision in *Williams v Roffey* will reduce the need for reliance on promissory estoppel in cases involving the renegotiation of contracts for the supply of goods or services since performance of existing duties may now provide consideration for new promises. As was stated previously with regard to *Re Selectmove*, however, the same claim cannot be made in relation to partial payments of debts. Those situations are still subject to the rule in *Foakes v Beer* as, uncertainly, modified by the operation of promissory estoppel. As estoppel is generally only suspensory in effect, it is always open to the promisor, at least in the case of continuing debts, to reimpose the original terms by withdrawing their new promise. Although it is at least arguable that *Foakes v Beer* would itself be decided differently on the basis of promissory estoppel, on the grounds that it involved a one-off debt, it is unlikely that the same would be true in regard to *Re Selectmove* which involved a continuing debt.

6.7 Privity of contract

There is some debate as to whether privity is a principle in its own right, or whether it is simply a conclusion from the more general rules relating to consideration. In any case, it is a general rule that a contract can only impose rights or obligations on persons who are parties to it. This is the doctrine of privity and its operation may be seen in *Dunlop v Selfridge* (1915). In this case, Dunlop sold tyres to a distributor, Dew and Co, on terms that the distributor would not sell them at less than the manufacturers list price, and that they would extract a similar undertaking from anyone they supplied with tyres. Dew and Co resold the tyres to Selfridge who agreed to abide by the restrictions and to pay Dunlop £5 for each tyre they sold in breach of them. When Selfridge sold tyres at below Dunlop's list price, Dunlop sought to recover the promised £5 per tyre sold. It was held that Dunlop could not recover damages on the basis of the contract between Dew and Selfridge to which they were not a party.

There are, however, a number of ways in which consequences of the application of strict rule of privity may be avoided to allow a third party to enforce a contract. These occur where:

- *The beneficiary sues in some other capacity*

   Although an individual may not originally be party to a particular contract they may, nonetheless, acquire the power to enforce the contract where they are legally appointed to administer the affairs of one of the original parties. An example of this can be seen in *Beswick v Beswick* (1967) where a coal merchant sold his business to his nephew in return for a consultancy fee of £6.10s during his lifetime, and thereafter an annuity of £5 per week payable to his widow. After the uncle died, the nephew stopped paying the widow. When she became administratrix of her husband's estate, she sued the nephew for specific performance of the agreement in that capacity as well as in her personal capacity. It was held that, although she was not a party to the contract and therefore could not be granted specific performance in her personal capacity, such an order could be awarded to her as the administratrix of the deceased person's estate.

- *The situation involves a collateral contract*

A collateral contract arises where one party promises something to another party if that other party enters into a contract with a third party, for example, A promises to give B something if B enters into a contract with C. In such a situation, the second party can enforce the original promise, that is, B can insist on A complying with the original promise. It may be seen from this that, although treated as an exception to the privity rule, a collateral contract conforms with the requirements which relate to the establishment of any other contract: consideration for the original promise being the making of the second contract. An example of the operation of a collateral contract will demonstrate, however, the way in which the courts tend to construct collateral contracts in order to achieve what they see as fair dealing.

In *Shanklin Pier v Detel Products Ltd* (1951), the plaintiffs contracted to have their pier repainted. On the basis of promises as to its quality, the defendants persuaded the pier company to insist that a particular paint produced by Detel be used. The painters used the paint but it proved unsatisfactory. The plaintiffs sued for breach of the original promise as to the suitability of the paint. The defendants countered that the only contract they had entered into was between them and the painters to whom they had sold the paint, and that as the pier company were not a party to that contract they had no right of action against Detel. The pier company were successful. It was held that, in addition to the contract for the sale of paint, there was a second collateral contract between the plaintiffs and the defendants by which the latter guaranteed the suitability of the paint in return for the pier company specifying that the painters used it.

- *There is a valid assignment of the benefit of the contract*

A party to a contract can transfer the benefit of that contract to a third party through the formal process of assignment. The assignment must be in writing, and the assignee receives no better rights under the contract than the assignor possessed. The burden of a contract cannot be assigned without the consent of the other party to the contract.

- *Where it is foreseeable that damage caused by any breach of contract will cause a loss to a third party*

  In *Linden Gardens Trust Ltd v Lenesta Sludge Disposals Ltd* (1994), the original parties had entered into a contract for work to be carried out on property with the likelihood that it would subsequently be transferred to a third party. The defendant's poor work, amounting to a breach of contract, only became apparent after the property had been transferred. There had been no assignment of the original contract and, normally, under the doctrine of privity, the new owners would have no contractual rights against the defendants and the original owners of the property would have suffered only a nominal breach as they had sold it at no loss to themselves. Nonetheless, the House of Lords held that, under such circumstances, and within a commercial context, the original promisee should be able to claim full damages on behalf of the third party for the breach of contract.

- *One of the parties has entered the contract as a trustee for a third party*

  There exists the possibility that a party to a contract can create a contract specifically for the benefit of a third party. In such limited circumstances, the promisee is considered as a trustee of the contractual promise for the benefit of the third party. In order to enforce the contract, the third party must act through the promisee by making them a party to any action. For a consideration of this possibility, see *Les Affréteurs Réunis SA v Leopold Walford (London) Ltd* (1919).

The other main exception to the privity rule is agency, where the agent brings about contractual relations between two other parties even where the existence of the agency has not been disclosed.

In the area of motoring insurance, statute law has intervened to permit third parties to claim directly against insurers.

Significant inroads into the operation of the doctrine of privity has been made by the Contracts (Rights of Third Parties) Act 1999, which gives statutory effect to the recommendations of the 1996 Law Commission report into this aspect of contract law (No 242, 1996). The new Act establishes the circumstances in which third parties can enforce terms of contracts. Essentially, the requirement is that, in order for the third party to gain rights of enforcement, the contract in question must, either, expressly confer such a right on the third party or, alternatively, it must have been clearly made for their benefit (s 1). In order to benefit from the provision of the Act, it is required that the third party be expressly identified in the contract by name, or as a member of a class of persons, or answering a particular description. Interestingly, however, the third person need not be in existence when the contract was made, so it is possible for parties to make contracts for the benefit of, as yet, unborn children or a future marriage partner. This provision should also reduce the difficulties relating to pre-incorporation contracts in relation to registered companies. The third party may exercise the right to any remedy which would have been available had they been a party to the contract. Such rights are, however, subject to the terms and conditions contained in the contract and they can get no better right than the original promisee, and the actual parties to the contract can place conditions on the rights of the third party.

Section 2 of the Act provides that, where a third party has rights by virtue of the Act, the original parties to the contract cannot agree to rescind it or vary its terms without the consent of the third party; unless the original contract contained an express term to that effect.

Section 3 allows the promisor to make use of any defences or rights of set-off they might have against the promisee in any action by the third party. Additionally, the promisor can also rely on any such rights against the third party. Any such rights are subject to any express provision in the contract to the contrary.

Section 5 removes the possibility of the promisor suffering from double liability in relation to the promisor and the third party. It provides, therefore, that any damages awarded to a third party for a breach of the contract be reduced by the amount recovered by the promisee in any previous action relating to the contract.

Section 6 of the Act specifically states that it does not alter the existing law relating to, and confers no new rights on third parties in relation to, negotiable instruments, s 14 of the Companies Act 1985, contracts of employment, or contracts for the carriage of goods.

Although the Act came into force on 11 November 1999, it does not apply in relation to contracts entered into before the end of the period of six months beginning with that date, unless the contract in question specifically provides for its application (s 10).

6.8   Capacity

Capacity refers to a person's ability to enter into a contract. In general, all adults of sound mind have full capacity. The capacity of certain individuals, however, is limited.

6.8.1   Minors

A minor is a person under the age of 18 (the age of majority was reduced from 21 to 18 by the Family Reform Act 1969). The law tries to protect such persons by restricting their contractual capacity and thus preventing them from entering into disadvantageous agreements. The rules which apply are a mixture of common law and statute, and depend on when the contract was made. Contracts entered into after 9 June 1987 are subject to the Minors Contracts Act 1987 which replaced the Infants' Relief Act 1874. Agreements entered into by minors may be classified within three possible categories.

Valid contracts

Contracts can be enforced against minors where they relate to the following:

• *Contracts for necessaries*

A minor is bound to pay for necessaries, that is, things necessary to maintain the minor. Necessaries are defined in the s 3 of the Sale of Goods Act 1979 as goods suitable to the condition in life of the minor and their actual requirements at the time of sale. The operation of this section is demonstrated in *Nash v Inman* (1908), where a tailor sued a minor to whom he had supplied clothes, including 11 fancy waistcoats. The minor was an undergraduate at Cambridge University at the time. It was held that, although the clothes were suitable according to the minor's station in life, they were not necessary, as he already had sufficient clothing.

The minor is, in any case, only required to pay a reasonable price for any necessaries purchased.

• *Beneficial contracts of service*

A minor is bound by a contract of apprenticeship or employment, as long as it is, on the whole, for their benefit.

In *Doyle v White City Stadium* (1935), Doyle, a minor, obtained a professional boxer's licence, which was treated as a contract of apprenticeship. The licence provided that he would be bound by the rules of the Boxing Board of Control, who had the power to retain any prize money if he was ever disqualified in a fight. He claimed that the licence was void as it was not for his benefit; but it was held that the conditions of the licence were enforceable. In spite of the penal clause, it was held that, taken as whole, it was beneficial to him.

There has to be an element of education or training in the contract and ordinary trading contracts will not be enforced. See, for example, *Mercantile Union Guarantee Corp v Ball* (1937), where a minor, who operated a haulage business, was not held liable on a hire purchase contract he had entered into in relation to that business.

Voidable contracts

Voidable contracts are binding on the minor, unless they are repudiated during the period of minority or within a reasonable time after reaching the age of majority. These are generally transactions in which the minor acquires an interest of a permanent nature with continuing obligations. Examples are contracts for shares, leases of property or partnership agreements.

If the minor has made payments prior to repudiation of the contract, such payment cannot be recovered unless there is a total failure of consideration, and the minor has received no benefit whatsoever. An example is the case of *Steinberg v Scala (Leeds)* (1923). A Miss Steinberg, while still a minor, applied for, and was allotted, shares in the defendant company. After paying some money on the shares, she defaulted on payment and repudiated the contract. The company agreed that her name be removed from its register of members, but refused to return the money she had already paid. It was held that Steinberg was not entitled to the return of the money paid. She had benefited from membership rights and thus there had not been a complete failure of consideration.

Void contracts

Under the Infants' Relief Act (IRA) 1874, the following contracts were stated to be absolutely void:

- contracts for the repayment of loans;
- contracts for goods other than necessaries;
- accounts stated, that is, admissions of money owed.

In addition, no action could be brought on the basis of the ratification, made after the attainment of full age, of an otherwise void contract.

The main effect of the Minors Contracts Act 1987 was that the contracts set out in the IRA 1874 were no longer to be considered as absolutely void. As a consequence, unenforceable, as well as voidable, contracts may be ratified on the minor attaining the age of majority.

Although the IRA stated that such contracts were absolutely void, in effect, this simply meant that they could not be enforced against the minor. The other party could not normally recover goods or money transferred to the minor. Where, however, the goods had been obtained by fraud on the part of the minor, and where they were still in the minor's possession, the other party could rely on the doctrine of restitution to reclaim them. The minor, on the other hand, could enforce the agreement against the other party. Specific performance would not be available, however, on the grounds that it would be inequitable to grant such an order to minors while it could not be awarded against them.

The Minors Contracts Act has given the courts wider powers to order the restoration of property acquired by a minor. They are no longer restricted to cases where the minor has acquired the property through fraud but can order restitution where they think it just and equitable to do so.

Minor's liability in tort

As there is no minimum age limit in relation to actions in tort, minors may be liable under a tortious action. The courts, however, will not permit a party to enforce a contract indirectly by substituting an action in tort, or quasi-contract, for an action in contract.

In *Leslie v Shiell* (1914), Shiell, whilst a minor, obtained a loan from Leslie by lying about his age. Leslie sued to recover the money as damages in an action for the tort of deceit. It was held, however, that the action must fail as it was simply an indirect means of enforcing the otherwise void contract.

6.8.2   Mental incapacity and intoxication

A contract by a person who is of unsound mind or under the influence of drink or drugs is *prima facie* valid. In order to avoid a contract, such a person must show:

- that their mind was so affected at the time that they were incapable of understanding the nature of their actions; and

- that the other party either knew or ought to have known of their disability.

The person claiming such incapacity, nonetheless, must pay a reasonable price for necessaries sold and delivered to them. The Sale of Goods Act (SoGA) 1979 specifically applies the same rules to such people as applies to minors.

6.9   Intention to create legal relations

All of the aspects considered previously may well be present in a particular agreement, and yet there still may not be a contract. In order to limit the number of cases that might otherwise be brought, the courts will only enforce those agreements which the parties intended to have legal effect. Although expressed in terms of the parties intentions, the test for the presence of such intention is once again an objective, rather than a subjective, one. For the purposes of this topic, agreements can be divided into three categories, in which different presumptions apply.

6.9.1   Domestic and social agreements

In domestic and social agreements, there is a presumption that the parties do not intend to create legal relations.

In *Balfour v Balfour* (1919), a husband returned to Ceylon to take up his employment and he promised his wife, who could not return with him due to health problems, that he would pay her £30 per month as maintenance. When the marriage later ended in divorce, the wife sued for the promised maintenance. It was held that the parties had not intended the original promise to be binding and therefore it was not legally enforceable.

It is essential to realise that the intention not to create legal relations in such relationships is only a presumption and that, as with all presumptions, it may be rebutted by the actual facts and circumstances of a particular case. A case in point is *Merritt v Merritt* (1970). After a husband had left the matrimonial home, he met his wife and promised to pay her £40 per month, from which she undertook to pay the outstanding mortgage on their house. The husband, at the wife's insistence, signed a note agreeing to transfer the house into the wife's sole name when the mortgage was paid off. The wife paid off the mortgage but the husband refused to transfer the house. It was held that the agreement was enforceable as in the circumstances the parties had clearly intended to enter into a legally enforceable agreement.

6.9.2 Commercial agreements

In commercial situations, the strong presumption is that the parties intend to enter into a legally binding relationship in consequence of their dealings.

In *Edwards v Skyways* (1964), employers undertook to make an *ex gratia* payment to an employee whom they had made redundant. It was held that in such a situation the use of the term *ex gratia* was not sufficient to rebut the presumption that the establishment of legal relations had been intended. The former employee, therefore, was entitled to the payment promised.

As with other presumptions, this one is open to rebuttal. In commercial situations, however, the presumption is so strong that it will usually take express wording to the contrary to avoid its operation. An example can be found in *Rose and Frank Co v Crompton Bros* (1925) in which it was held that an express clause stating that no legal relations were to be created by a business transaction was effective. Another example is *Jones v Vernons Pools Ltd* (1938) where the plaintiff claimed to have submitted a correct pools forecast, but the defendants denied receiving it and relied on a clause in the coupon which stated that the transaction was binding in honour only. Under such circumstances, it was held that the plaintiff had no cause for an action in contract as no legal relations had been created.

6.9.3 Collective agreements

Agreements between employers and trade unions may be considered as a distinct category of agreement, for although they are commercial agreements, they are presumed not to give rise to legal relations, and, therefore, are not normally enforceable in the courts. Such was the outcome of *Ford Motor Co v AUEFW* (1969) in which it was held that Ford could not take legal action against the defendant trade union which had ignored previously negotiated terms of a collective agreement.

Once again, this presumption can be rebutted if the circumstances of the particular case make it clear that the parties intend legal relations to be created.

6.9.4 Letters of comfort

Such documents are generally used by parent companies to encourage potential lenders to extend credit to their subsidiary companies by stating their intention to provide financial backing for those subsidiaries. It is generally the case that such letters of comfort merely amount to statements of present intention on the part of the parent company and therefore they do not amount to offers that can be accepted by the creditors of any subsidiary companies. Given the operation of the doctrine of separate personality, this effectively leaves the creditors with no legal recourse against the parent company for any loans granted to the subsidiary (see 9.3.2).

In *Kleinwort Benson v Malaysian Mining Corp* (1989), the defendant company had issued a letter of comfort to the plaintiffs in respect of its subsidiary company MMC Metals. However, when MMC Metals went into liquidation, the defendants failed to make good its debts to the plaintiffs.

At first instance, the judge decided in favour of the plaintiffs, holding that in such commercial circumstances the defendants had failed to rebut the presumption that there had been an intention to create legal relations. On appeal, it was held that, in the circumstances of the instant case, the letter of comfort did not amount to an offer but a statement of intention which could not bind the defendants contractually. Malaysian Mining Corp, therefore, was not legally responsible for the debt of its subsidiary.

It is important to note that the *Kleinwort Benson* case opens up the possibility that, under different circumstances, letters of comfort might be considered to constitute offers capable of being accepted and leading to contractual relations. Under such circumstances, the presumption as to the intention to create legal relations as they normally apply in commercial situations will operate; although it is almost inconceivable that a court would decide that a letter of comfort amounted to an offer without also finding an intention to create legal relations.

6.10 Contents of contracts

Whereas the previous sections of this chapter have dealt with how a binding contractual agreement comes to be formed, this section will consider what the parties have actually agreed to do.

6.10.1 Contract terms and mere representations

As the parties will normally be bound to perform any promise that they have contracted to undertake, it is important to decide precisely what promises are included in the contract. Some statements do not form part of a contract, even though they might have induced the other party to enter into the contract. These pre-contractual statements are called representations. The consequences of such representations being false will be considered in 6.11.2, but for the moment it is sufficient to distinguish them from contractual terms, which are statements which do form part of the contract. There are four tests for distinguishing a contractual term from a mere representation:

- Where the statement is of such major importance that the promisee would not have entered into the agreement without it, then it will be construed as a term. In *Bannerman v White* (1861), as the defendant wanted to buy hops for brewing purposes, he asked the plaintiff if they had been treated with sulphur. On the basis of the plaintiff's false statement that they had not been so treated, he agreed to buy the hops. When he discovered later that they had been treated with sulphur, he refused to accept them. It was held that the plaintiffs statement about the sulphur was a fundamental term of the contract, and since it was not true, the defendant was entitled to repudiate the contract.

- Where there is a time gap between the statement and the making of the contract, then the statement will most likely be treated as a representation.

  In *Routledge v McKay* (1954), on 23 October, the defendant told the plaintiff that a motorcycle was a 1942 model. On 30 October, a written contract for the sale of the bike was made, without reference to its age. The bike was actually a 1930 model. It was held that the statement about the date was a pre-contractual representation, and the plaintiff could not sue for damages for breach of contract. However, this rule is not a hard and fast one. In *Schawell v Reade* (1913), the court held that a statement made three months before the final agreement was part of the contract.

- Where the statement is oral, and the agreement is subsequently drawn up in written form, then the exclusion from the written document will suggest that the statement was not meant to be a contractual term. *Routledge v McKay* may also be cited as authority for this proposition.

- Where one of the parties to an agreement has special knowledge or skill, then statements made by them will be terms, but statements made to them will not.

  In *Dick Bentley Productions Ltd v Harold Smith (Motors) Ltd* (1965), the plaintiff bought a Bentley car from the defendant after being assured that it had only travelled 20,000 miles since its engine and gearbox had been

Forms of representation

replaced. When this statement turned out to be untrue, the plaintiff sued for breach of contract. It was held that the statement was a term of the contract and the plaintiff was entitled to damages.

In *Oscar Chess Ltd v Williams* (1957), Williams traded in one car when buying another from the plaintiffs. He told them that his trade-in was a 1948 model; whereas it was actually a 1939 model. The company unsuccessfully sued for breach of contract. The statement as to the age of the car was merely a representation, and the right to sue for misrepresentation had been lost due to delay.

6.10.2 Conditions, warranties and innominate terms

Once it is decided that a statement is a term, rather than merely a pre-contractual representation, it is necessary to determine which type of term it is, in order to determine what remedies are available for its breach.

Terms can be classified as one of three types.

Conditions

A condition is a fundamental part of the agreement and is something which goes to the root of the contract. Breach of a condition gives the innocent party the right either to terminate the contract and refuse to perform their part of it, or to go through with the agreement and sue for damages.

Warranties

A warranty is a subsidiary obligation which is not vital to the overall agreement, and does not totally destroy its efficacy. Breach of a warranty does not give the right to terminate the agreement. The innocent party has to complete their part of the agreement, and can only sue for damages.

The difference between the two types of term can be seen in the following cases:

- In *Poussard v Spiers and Pond* (1876), the plaintiff had contracted with the defendants to sing in an opera they were producing. Due to illness, she was unable to appear on the first night, or for some nights thereafter. When Mme Poussard recovered, the defendants refused her services as they had hired a replacement for the whole run of the opera. It was held that her failure to appear on the opening night had been a breach of a condition, and the defendants were at liberty to treat the contract as discharged.

- In *Bettini v Gye* (1876), the plaintiff had contracted with the defendants to complete a number of engagements. He had also agreed to be in London for rehearsals six days before his opening performance. Due to illness, he only arrived three days before the opening night, and the defendants refused his services. On this occasion, it was held that there was only a breach of warranty. The defendants were entitled to damages, but could not treat the contract as discharged.

The distinction between the effects of a breach of condition as against the effects of a breach of warranty was enshrined in s 11 of the SoGA 1893 (now the SoGA 1979). For some time, it was thought that these were the only two types of term possible, the nature of the remedy available being prescribed by the particular type of term concerned. This simple classification has subsequently been rejected by the courts as too restrictive, and a third type of term has emerged: the innominate term.

Innominate terms

In this case, the remedy is not prescribed in advance simply by whether the term breached is a condition or a warranty, but depends on the consequence of the breach.

If the breach deprives the innocent party of substantially the whole benefit of the contract, then the right to repudiate will be permitted even if the term might otherwise appear to be a mere warranty.

If, however, the innocent party does not lose substantially the whole benefit of the contract, then they will not be permitted to repudiate but must settle for damages, even if the term might otherwise appear to be a condition.

In *Cehave v Bremer (The Hansa Nord)* (1976), a contract for the sale of a cargo of citrus pulp pellets, to be used as animal feed, provided that they were to be delivered in good condition. On delivery, the buyers rejected the cargo as not complying with this provision, and claimed back the price paid from the sellers. The buyers eventually obtained the pellets when the cargo was sold off, and used them for their original purpose. It was held that, since the breach had not been serious, the buyers had not been free to reject the cargo, and the sellers had acted lawfully in retaining the money paid.

6.10.3 Express and implied terms

So far, all the cases considered have involved express terms: statements actually made by one of the parties, either by word of mouth or in writing. Implied terms, however, are not actually stated, but are introduced into the contract by implication. Implied terms can be divided into three types.

Terms implied by statute

For example, under the SoGA 1979 and the Supply of Goods and Services Act (SGSA) 1982, terms relating to description, quality and fitness for purpose are all implied into sale of goods contracts. (For consideration of these implied terms, see 7.1.)

Terms implied by custom

An agreement may be subject to customary terms, not actually specified by the parties. For example, in *Hutton v Warren* (1836), it was held that customary usage permitted a farm tenant to claim an allowance for seed and labour on quitting his tenancy. It should be noted, however, that custom cannot override the express terms of an agreement (*Les Affréteurs v Walford* (1919)).

Terms implied by the courts

Generally, it is a matter for the parties concerned to decide the terms of a contract, but on occasion the court will presume that the parties intended to include a term which is not expressly stated. They will do so where it is necessary to give business efficacy to the contract.

Whether a term may be implied can be decided on the basis of the officious bystander test. Imagine two parties, A and B, negotiating a contract. A third party, C, interrupts to suggest a particular provision. A and B reply that that particular term is understood. In just such a way, the court will decide that a term should be implied into a contract.

In *The Moorcock* (1889), the appellants, owners of a wharf, contracted with the respondents to permit them to discharge their ship at the wharf. It was apparent to both parties that when the tide was out the ship would rest on the river bed. When the tide was out, the ship sustained damage by settling on a ridge. It was held that there was an implied warranty in the contract that the place of anchorage should be safe for the ship. As a consequence, the shipowner was entitled to damages for breach of that term.

6.10.4 The parol evidence rule

If all the terms of a contract are in writing, then there is a strong presumption that no evidence supporting a different oral agreement will be permitted to vary those terms.

In *Hutton v Watling* (1948), on the sale of a business together with its goodwill, a written agreement was drawn up and signed by the vendor. In an action to enforce one of the clauses in the agreement, the vendor claimed that it did not represent the whole contract. It was held that the vendor was not entitled to introduce evidence on this point as the written document represented a true record of the contract.

The presumption against introducing contrary oral evidence can be rebutted, however, where it is shown that the document was not intended to set out all of the terms agreed on by the parties.

In *Re SS Ardennes* (1951), a ship's bill of lading stated that it might proceed by any route 'directly or indirectly'. The defendants promised that the ship would proceed directly to London from Spain with its cargo of tangerines. However, the ship called at Antwerp before heading for London, and as a result the tangerines had to be sold at a reduced price. The shippers successfully sued for damages as it was held that the bill of lading did not constitute the contract between the parties, but merely evidenced their intentions. The verbal promise was part of the final contract.

The effect of the parol evidence rule has also been avoided by the willingness of the courts to find collateral contracts which import different, not to say contradictory, terms into the written contract. An example of this may be seen in *City and Westminster Properties (1934) Ltd v Mudd* (1959) where, although the written expressly provided that the defendant had no right to live on particular premises, the court recognised the contrary effect of a verbal collateral contract to allow him to do so. (See further 6.7 for the use of collateral contracts to avoid the strict operation of the doctrine of privity.)

City and Westminster v Mudd at least suggests that the courts will find justification for avoiding the strict application of the parol evidence rule where they wish to. On that basis, it has been suggested that it should be removed from contract law entirely. Interestingly, however, a Law Commission Report (No 154) took the opposite view, in deciding that there was no need to provide legislation to remove the rule as it was already a dead letter in practice.

6.10.5 Exemption or exclusion clauses

In a sense, an exemption clause is no different from any other clause, in that it seeks to define the rights and obligations of the parties to a contract. However, an exemption clause is a term in a contract which tries to exempt, or limit, the liability of a party in breach of the agreement. Exclusion clauses give rise to most concern when they are included in standard form contracts, in which one party, in a position of commercial dominance, imposes their terms on the other party, who has no choice (other than to take it or leave it) as far as the terms of the contract go. Such standard form contracts are contrary to the ideas of consensus and negotiation which underpin contract law; for this reason they have received particular attention from both the judiciary and the legislature, in an endeavour to counteract their perceived unfairness.

The actual law relating to exclusion clauses is complicated by the interplay of the common law, the Unfair Contract Terms Act (UCTA) 1977, and the various Acts which imply certain terms into particular contracts. However, the following questions should always be asked with regard to exclusion clauses:

- Has the exclusion clause been incorporated into the contract?

- Does the exclusion clause effectively cover the breach?

- What effect does the UCTA 1977 have on the exclusion clause?

Has the exclusion clause been incorporated into the contract?
An exclusion clause cannot be effective unless it is actually a term of a contract.

There are three ways in which such a term may be inserted into a contractual agreement:

(a) By signature

If a person signs a contractual document, then they are bound by its terms, even if they did not read it.

In *L'Estrange v Graucob* (1934), a café owner bought a vending machine, signing a contract without reading it, which took away all her rights under the SoGA 1893. When the machine proved faulty, she sought to take action against the vendors, but it was held that she had no cause of action as she had signified her consent to the terms of the contract by signing it.

The rule in *L'Estrange v Graucob* may be avoided where the party seeking to rely on the exclusion clause misled the other party into signing the contract (*Curtis v Chemical Cleaning and Dyeing Co* (1951)).

(b) By notice

Apart from the above, an exclusion clause will not be incorporated into a contract unless the party affected actually knew of it, or was given sufficient notice of it. In order for notice to be adequate, the document bearing the exclusion clause must be an integral part of the contract, and given at the time the contract is made.

In *Chapleton v Barry UDC* (1940), the plaintiff hired a deck-chair and received a ticket which stated on the back that the council would not be responsible for any injuries arising from the hire of the chairs. After he was injured because his chair collapsed, Chapleton successfully sued the council. It was held that the ticket was merely a receipt, and could not be used effectively to communicate the exclusion clause.

In *Olley v Marlborough Court Hotel Ltd* (1949), a couple arrived at a hotel and paid for a room in advance. On reaching their room, they found a notice purporting to exclude the hotel's liability in regard to thefts of goods not handed in to the manager. A thief later stole the wife's purse. It was held that the hotel could not escape liability since the disclaimer had only been made after the contract had been formed.

Whether the degree of notice given has been sufficient is a matter of fact, but, in *Thornton v Shoe Lane Parking Ltd* (1971), it was stated that the greater the exemption, the greater the degree of notice required.

In *Interfoto Picture Library Ltd v Stiletto Programmes Ltd* (1988), the Court of Appeal decided that a particular clause was not to be considered as imported into a contract even although it had been available for inspection before the contract was entered into. The clause in question sought to impose a charge of almost £4,000 liability for any delay in returning the photographic negatives which were the subject of the contract. It was held, following *Thornton v Shoe Lane Parking Ltd*, that this penalty was so severe that it could not have been fairly brought to the attention of the other party by indirect reference and required notification in the most explicit way.

(c) By custom

Where the parties have had previous dealings on the basis of an exclusion clause, that clause may be included in later contracts (*Spurling v Bradshaw* (1956)), but it has to be shown that the party affected had actual knowledge of the exclusion clause.

In *Hollier v Rambler Motors* (1972), on each of the previous occasions when the plaintiff had his car repaired at the defendant's garage, he had signed a form containing an exclusion clause. On the last occasion, he had not signed such a form. When the car was damaged by fire through negligence, the defendants sought to rely on the exclusion clause. It was held that there was no evidence that Hollier had been aware of the clause to which he had been agreeing and, therefore, it could not be considered a part of his last contract.

Does the exclusion clause effectively cover the breach?

As a consequence of the disfavour with which the judiciary have looked on exclusion clauses, they have developed a number of rules of construction which operate to restrict the effectiveness of exclusion clauses. These are:

*   *The* contra proferentem *rule*

    This requires that any uncertainties or ambiguities in the exclusion clause be interpreted against the meaning claimed for it by the person seeking to rely on it.

    In *Andrews v Singer* (1934), the plaintiffs contracted to buy some new Singer cars from the defendant. A clause excluded all conditions, warranties and liabilities implied by statute, common law, or otherwise. One car supplied was not new. It was held that the requirement that the cars be new was an express condition of the contract and therefore was not covered by the exclusion clause which only referred to implied clauses.

    In *Hollier v Rambler*, it was stated that as the exclusion clause in question could be interpreted as applying only to non-negligent accidental damage, or alternatively to include damage caused by negligence; it should be restricted to the former, narrower, interpretation. As a consequence, the plaintiff could recover for damages caused to his car by the defendants negligence.

    A more recent example of the operation of the *contra proferentem* rule may be seen in *Bovis Construction (Scotland) Ltd v Whatlings Construction Ltd* (1995). The details of the contract between the two parties were based on a standard form and a number of letters. One of the letters introduced a term which limited the defendants liability in relation to time related costs to £100,000. The plaintiffs terminated the contract on the basis of the defendants' lack of diligence in carrying out the contracted work. When they subsequently sued for £2,741,000 the defendant relied on the limitation clause. The House of Lords decided that as the defendant had introduced the limitation clause it had to be interpreted strictly, although not as strictly as a full exclusion clause. It was held that the term 'time-related costs' applied to losses arising as a consequence of delay in performance and not non-performance. The defendants had been guilty of the latter and therefore were fully liable for the consequence of their repudiatory breach.

- *The doctrine of fundamental breach*

  In a series of complicated and conflicting cases, ending with the House of Lords' decision in *Photo Production v Securicor Transport* (1980), some courts attempted to develop a rule that it was impossible to exclude liability for breach of contract if a fundamental breach of the contract had occurred, that is, the party in breach had failed altogether to perform the contract.

  In *Photo Production v Securicor Transport,* the defendants had entered into a contract with the plaintiffs to guard their factory. An exclusion clause exempted Securicor from liability even if one of their employees caused damage to the factory. One of the guards later deliberately set fire to the factory. Securicor claimed the protection of the exclusion clause. It was ultimately decided by the House of Lords that whether an exclusion clause could operate after a fundamental breach was a matter of construction. There was no absolute rule that total failure of performance rendered such clauses inoperative. The exclusion clause in this particular case was wide enough to cover the events that took place and so Photo Production's action failed.

What effect does the UCTA 1977 have on the exclusion clause?

This Act represents the statutory attempt to control exclusion clauses. In spite of its title, it is really aimed at unfair exemption clauses, rather than contract terms generally. It also covers non-contractual notices which purport to exclude liability under the Occupier's Liability Act 1957. The controls under the UCTA 1977 relate to two areas:

- *Negligence*

  There is an absolute prohibition on exemption clauses in relation to liability in negligence resulting in death or injury (ss 2 and 5). Exemption clauses relating to liability for other damage caused by negligence will only be enforced to the extent that they satisfy the requirement of reasonableness (s 5).

In *Smith v Bush* (1989), the plaintiff bought a house on the basis of a valuation report carried out for her building society by the defendant. The surveyor had included a disclaimer of liability for negligence in his report to the building society and sought to rely on that fact when the plaintiff sued after the chimneys of the property collapsed. The House of Lords held that the disclaimer was an exemption clause and that it failed the requirement that such terms should be reasonable.

- *Contract*

These provisions apply in consumer transactions. They also apply in non-consumer transactions, where one party deals on the other's standard terms. Any exclusion clause which seeks to avoid liability for breach of contract is only valid to the extent that it complies with the requirement of reasonableness (s 2). This test also applies where a clause seeks to permit a party to avoid performing the contract completely, or to permit performance less than reasonably expected.

The UCTA 1977 applies to business activity, but s 14 provides a wide enough definition of such activity as to include the professions, local and central government departments and public authorities. However, the implied term relating to title, under s 12 of the SoGA 1979, cannot be excluded in any contract (s 6(1)).

The other implied terms as to description, fitness, satisfactory quality and sample, cannot be excluded in a consumer contract (s 6(2)); and, in a non-consumer transaction, any restriction is subject to the requirement of reasonableness (s 6(3)).

A person deals as a consumer if they do not make the contract in the course of business, nor hold themselves out as so doing, and the other party does make the contract in the course of business, the goods being supplied normally for private consumption (s 12).

Indemnity clauses are covered by s 4 of the UCTA 1977. These are provisions in contracts by means of which one party agrees to compensate the other for any liability incurred by them in the course of carrying out the contract. Although these may be legitimate ways of allocating risk and insurance responsibilities in a commercial context, they are of more dubious effect in consumer transactions and are therefore required to satisfy the requirement of reasonableness.

The requirement of reasonableness means 'fair and reasonable ... having regard to the circumstances ...' (s 11). Schedule 2 to the UCTA provides guidelines for the application of the reasonableness test in regard to non-consumer transactions, but it is likely that similar considerations will be taken into account by the courts in consumer transactions. Amongst these considerations are:

- the relative strength of the parties bargaining power;
- whether any inducement was offered in return for the limitation on liability;
- whether the customer knew, or ought to have known, about the existence or extent of the exclusion;
- whether the goods were manufactured or adapted to the special order of the customer.

In *George Mitchell (Chesterhall) Ltd v Finney Lock Seeds Ltd* (1983), the respondents planted 63 acres with cabbage seed supplied by the appellants. The crop failed, due partly to the fact that the wrong type of seed had been supplied, and due partly to the fact that the seed supplied was of inferior quality. When the respondents claimed damages, the sellers relied on the protection of a clause in their standard conditions of sale limiting their liability to replacing the seeds supplied or refunding payment. It was held, however, that the respondents were entitled to compensation for the loss of the crop. The House of Lords decided that although the exemption clause was sufficiently clear and unambiguous to be effective at common law, it failed the test of reasonableness under the UCTA 1977.

It is likely that many of the situations in the cases considered under the common law prior to the UCTA would now be decided under the Act. It is still important, however, to understand the common law principles for the very good reason that the UCTA does not apply in many important situations. Amongst these are transactions relating to insurance, interests in land, patents and other intellectual property, the transfer of securities, and the formation of companies or partnerships.

6.10.6 The Unfair Terms in Consumer Contracts Regulations

The first Unfair Terms in Consumer Contracts Regulations were enacted in December 1994. The Regulations were introduced to implement the European Unfair Contract Terms Directive (93/13/EEC). Those original Regulations were repealed and replaced by the current Regulations (SI 1999/2083), which came into effect on 1 October 1999. The new Regulations are intended to reflect more closely the wording of the original, but they also introduce significant alterations to the old Regulations.

It has to be stated that there was some criticism that the previous regulations merely introduced the Directive without engaging in a comprehensive review of this area. Concern was expressed as to the precise way in which the UCTA and the Regulations impact on one another and how their interaction would affect consumer law generally. Unfortunately, the new Regulations have done nothing to improve this general problem and, in this particular respect, the criticisms of the previous Regulations are still relevant.

The Regulations apply to any term in a contract concluded between a seller or supplier and a consumer, which have not been individually negotiated. The Regulations are, therefore, wider in scope than the UCTA in that they cover all terms and not just exclusion clauses. However, reg 6(2) states that, apart from the requirement in respect of plain language, neither the core provisions of a consumer contract, which set out its main subject matter, nor the adequacy of the price paid are open to assessment in terms of fairness. The Regulations, therefore, would still appear to focus on the formal procedure through which contracts are made rather than the substantive contents of the contract in question.

By virtue of reg 5, a term is unfair 'if contrary to the requirements of good faith, it causes a significant imbalance in the parties' rights and obligations arising under the contract to the detriment of the consumer'. Schedule 2 sets out a long indicative, but non-exhaustive, list of terms which may be regarded as unfair. Examples of terms included in this list are: a term which excludes or limits liability in the event of the supplier or seller causing the death or injury of the consumer; inappropriately excluding or limiting the legal rights of the consumer in the event of total or partial non-performance or inadequate performance; requiring any consumer who fails to fulfil his obligations to pay a disproportionately high sum in compensation; enabling the seller or supplier to alter the terms of the contract unilaterally without a valid reason which is specified in the contract.

Any such term as outlined above will be assumed to be unfair and, under reg 8, if a term is found to be unfair, it will not be binding on the consumer, although the remainder of the contract will continue to operate if it can do so after the excision of the unfair term.

Two further provisions of the Regulations, worthy of mention, have been continued from the previous Regulations. First, there is the requirement for all contracts terms to be in 'plain intelligible language' and that, when there is any doubt as to the meaning of any term, it will be construed in favour of the consumer (reg 7). This is somewhat similar to the *contra proferentem* rule in English common law.

Secondly, although the Regulations will be most used by consumers to defeat particular unfair terms, regs 10–12 give the Director General of Fair Trading the power to take action against the use of unfair terms by obtaining an injunction to prohibit the use of such terms. However, the power of the Director General to seek injunctions to control unfair contract terms has been extended to other qualifying bodies. These qualifying bodies are listed in Sched 1 of the regulations and include the various regulatory bodies controlling the previous public utilities sector of the economy, the Data Protection Registrar and every weights and measures authority in Great Britain.

6.11 Vitiating factors

Vitiating factors are those elements which make an agreement either void, or voidable, depending on which vitiating factor is present. The vitiating factors are:

- mistake;

- misrepresentation;

- duress;

- undue influence;

- contracts void or illegal for reasons of public policy.

6.11.1 Mistake

Generally speaking, the parties to a contract will not be relieved from the burden of their agreement simply because they have made a mistake. If one party makes a bad bargain, that is no reason for setting the contract aside. Very few mistakes will affect the validity of a contract at common law, but where a mistake is operative, it will render the contract void. This has the effect that property transferred under operative mistake can be recovered, even where it has been transferred to an innocent third party.

It is usual to divide mistakes into the following three categories:

- common mistake;

- mutual mistake;

- unilateral mistake.

Common mistake

This is where both parties to an agreement share the same mistake about the circumstances surrounding the transaction. In order for the mistake to be operative, it must be of a fundamental nature.

In *Bell v Lever Bros Ltd* (1932), Bell had been employed as chairman of the company by Lever Bros. When he became redundant they paid off the remaining part of his service contract. Only then did they discover that Bell had been guilty of offences which would have permitted them to dismiss him without compensation. They claimed to have the payment set aside on the basis of the common mistake that neither party had considered the possibility of Bell's dismissal for breach of duty. It was held that the action must fail. The mistake was only as to quality and not sufficiently fundamental to render the contract void.

The cases suggest that a mistake as to quality can never render an agreement void for mistake, and that the doctrine of common mistake is restricted to the following two specific areas:

- *Res extincta*

  In this case, the mistake is as to the existence of the subject matter of the contract.

  In *Couturier v Hastie* (1856), a contract was made in London for the sale of corn being shipped from Salonica. Unknown to the parties, however, the corn had already been sold. It was held that the London contract was void, since the subject matter of the contract was no longer in existence.

  It should be recognised, however, that, in *Associated Japanese Bank v Credit du Nord* (1988), a contract was treated as void for common mistake on the basis of the non-existence of some gaming machines, although the agreement in point actually related to a contract of guarantee in relation to the non-existent machines.

- *Res sua*

  In this case, the mistake is that one of the parties to the contract already owns what they are contracting to receive.

  In *Cooper v Phibbs* (1867), Cooper agreed to lease a fishery from Phibbs. It later transpired that he actually owned the fishery. The court decided that the lease had to be set aside at common law. In equity, however, Phibbs was given a lien over the fishery in respect of the money he had spent on improving it, permitting him to hold the property against payment.

  Cooper v Phibbs is an example of one possible way in which equity may intervene in regard to common mistake, namely setting an agreement aside on particular terms. Alternatively, the agreement may even be set aside completely in equity.

In *Magee v Pennine Insurance Co Ltd* (1969), a proposal form for car insurance had been improperly filled in by the plaintiff. When the car was subsequently written off, the insurance company offered Magee £375 as a compromise on his claim. After he had accepted this offer, the defendants discovered the error in the proposal form, and sought to repudiate their agreement. It was held that, although not void at common law, the agreement could be set aside in equity.

Mutual mistake

This occurs where the parties are at cross-purposes. They have different views on the facts of the situation, but they do not realise it. However, an agreement will not necessarily be void simply because the parties to it are at cross-purposes. In order for mutual mistake to be operative, that is, to make the contract void, it must comply with an objective test. The court will try to decide which of the competing views of the situation a reasonable person would support, and the contract will be enforceable on such terms.

In *Smith v Hughes* (1871), the plaintiff offered to sell oats to the defendant. Hughes wrongly believed that the oats were old, and on discovering that they were new oats, he refused to complete the contract. It was held that the defendants mistake as to the age of the oats did not make the contract void.

In *Scriven Bros v Hindley and Co* (1913), at an auction, the defendants bid for two lots believing both to be hemp. In fact one of them was tow, an inferior and cheaper substance. Although the auctioneer had not induced the mistake, it was not normal practice to sell hemp and tow together. It was decided that in such circumstances, where one party thought he was buying hemp while the other thought he was selling tow, the contract was not enforceable.

If the court is unable to decide the outcome on the basis of an objective reasonable person test, then the contract will be void.

In *Raffles v Wichelhaus* (1864), the defendants agreed to buy cotton from the plaintiffs. The cotton was to arrive *ex Peerless* from Bombay. There were, however, two ships called Peerless sailing from Bombay; the first in October, the second in December. Wichelhaus thought he was buying from the first but Raffles thought he was selling from the second. Under the exceptional circumstances, it was impossible for the court to decide which party's view was the correct one. It was decided, therefore, that the agreement was void for mutual mistake.

In respect of mutual mistake, equity follows the common law.

In *Tamplin v James* (1880), James purchased a public house at auction. He had believed wrongly that the property for sale included a field which the previous publican had used. The sale particulars stated the property for sale correctly, but James did not refer to them. When he discovered his mistake, James refused to complete the transaction. It was held that, in spite of his mistake, an order of specific performance would be granted against James.

Unilateral mistake

This occurs where only one of the parties to the agreement is mistaken as to the circumstances of the contract, and the other party is aware of that fact.

Most cases of unilateral mistake also involve misrepresentation, although this need not necessarily be so. It is important to distinguish between these two elements whereas unilateral mistake makes a contract void, and thus prevents the passing of title in any property acquired under it, misrepresentation merely makes a contract voidable, and good title can be passed before the contract is avoided. This distinction will be seen in *Ingram v Little* and *Phillips v Brooks*.

The cases involving unilateral mistake mainly relate to mistakes as to identity. A contract will only be void for mistake where the seller intended to contract with a different person from the one with whom they did actually contract.

In *Cundy v Lindsay* (1878), a crook named Blenkarn ordered linen handkerchiefs from Lindsay & Co, a Belfast linen manufacturer. His order, from 37 Wood Street, was signed to look as if it were from Blenkiron & Co, a reputable firm known to Lindsay, who carried on business at 123 Wood Street. The goods were sent to Blenkarn, who sold them to Cundy. Lindsay successfully sued Cundy in the tort of conversion. It was held that Lindsay had intended only to deal with Blenkiron & Co. Since there was no contract with Blenkarn, he received no title whatsoever to the goods, and therefore could not pass title on to Cundy.

Although *Kings Norton Metal Company v Edridge, Merrit and Co* (1897) appears to be similar, it was decided differently on the grounds that the crook had made use of a completely fictitious company to carry out his fraud. The mistake, therefore, was with regard to the attributes of the company rather than its identity.

Where the parties enter into a contract face to face, it is generally presumed that the seller intends to deal with the person before the, and, therefore, they cannot rely on unilateral mistake to avoid the contract.

In *Phillips v Brooks* (1919), a crook selected a number of items in the plaintiff's jewellery shop, and proposed to pay by cheque. On being informed that the goods would have to be retained until the cheque was cleared, he told the jeweller that he was Sir George Bullough of St James's Square. On checking in a directory that such a person did indeed live at that address, the jeweller permitted him to take away a valuable ring. The crook later pawned the ring to the defendant. Phillips then sued the defendant in conversion. It was decided that the contract between Phillips and the crook was not void for mistake. There had not been a mistake as to identity, but only as to the creditworthiness of the buyer. The contract had been voidable for misrepresentation, but the crook had passed title before Phillips took steps to avoid the contract.

A similar decision was reached by the Court of Appeal in *Lewis v Avery* (1971), in which a crook obtained possession of a car by misrepresenting who he was to the seller. The court declined to follow its earlier decision in *Ingram v Little* (1960), a very similar case. It is generally accepted that *Lewis v Avery* represents the more accurate statement of the law.

Here, again, equity follows the common law, and considers contracts tainted by unilateral mistake to be void.

Mistake in respect of documents

There are two mechanisms for dealing with mistakes in written contracts.

- *Rectification*

  Where the written document fails to state the actual intentions of the parties, it may be altered under the equitable doctrine of rectification.

  In *Joscelyne v Nissen* (1970), the plaintiff agreed to transfer his car-hire business to his daughter in return for her agreeing to pay certain household expenses, although this was not stated in a later written contract. The father was entitled to have the agreement rectified to include the terms agreed.

- Non est factum

  Where a party signs a contract, they will usually be bound by the terms as set out. It is assumed that the signatory has read, understood and agreed to the terms as stated and the courts are generally reluctant to interfere in such circumstances.

  Where, however, someone signs a document under a misapprehension as to its true nature, the law may permit them to claim *non est factum*, that is, that the document is not their deed. Originally, the mistake relied on had to relate to the type of document signed, but now it is recognised that the defence is open to those who have made a fundamental mistake as to the content of the document they have signed. However, the person signing the document must not have been careless in regard to its content.

  In *Saunders v Anglia Building Society* (1970), Mrs Gallie, a 78 year old widow, signed a document without reading it whilst her glasses were broken. She had been told, by a person named Lee, that it was a deed of gift to her nephew, but in fact it was a deed of gift to Lee. Lee later mortgaged the property to the respondent building society. Mrs Gallie sought to repudiate the deed of gift on the basis of *non est factum*. Her action failed. Although it was accepted that she had not been careless, the document was not fundamentally different from what she expected to sign.

  This decision can be contrasted with a later successful reliance on the defence in *Lloyds Bank plc v Waterhouse* (1990) where the defendant, who was illiterate, intended to provide a guarantee in relation to his sons purchase of a farm. In actual fact the document he signed was a guarantee in relation to all of his sons liabilities. In the Court of Appeal, it was decided that the father could rely on *non est factum*. He had not been careless, he had questioned the extent of his liability; and the document was fundamentally different from what he expected to sign.

6.11.2 Misrepresentation

As was seen in 6.10.1, a statement which induces a person to enter into a contract, but which does not become a term of the contract, is a representation. A false statement of this kind is a misrepresentation, and renders the contract voidable. The innocent party may rescind the contract, or in some circumstances claim damages (see 6.12.5).

Misrepresentation can be defined as a false statement of fact, made by one party before or at the time of the contract, which induces the other party to enter into the contract. The following points follow from this definition.

There must be a statement

There is no general duty to disclose information, and silence does not generally amount to a representation. There are exceptions to this rule:

* Where the statement is a half-truth. It may be true, but misleading nonetheless.

  In *Notts Patent Brick and Tile Co v Butler* (1886), the buyer of land asked the sellers solicitor whether the land was subject to any restrictive covenants. The solicitor said that there were none that he knew of, but did not mention that he had not read the documents to find out. It was held that the solicitors statement was a misrepresentation, and the buyer could rescind the contract.

* Where the statement was true when made, but has subsequently become false before the contract is concluded.

  In *With v O'Flanagan* (1936), in January, the seller of a doctors practice told the prospective buyer that it was worth an income of £2,000 per annum. By the time the contract was concluded its value had dropped substantially to only £5 per week. The court held that the representation was of a continuing nature, and as it was false when it induced the contract, the buyer was entitled to rescind.

* Where the contract is *uberrimae fidei*, that is, it is based on utmost good faith. In contracts of this nature, such as those involving insurance, there is a duty to disclose all material facts.

The following statements will not amount to a representation:

* *Mere sales puffs*

  The statement must have some meaningful content. Thus, in *Dimmock v Hallett* (1866), it was held that a statement that land was fertile and improvable was not actionable as a misrepresentation.

- *Statements of law*

  Everyone is presumed to know the law and, therefore, in theory, no one can be misled as to what the law is.

- *Statements of opinion*

  These are not actionable, because they are not statements of fact.

  In *Bisset v Wilkinson* (1927), the vendor of previously ungrazed land in New Zealand stated that it would be able to support 2,000 sheep. This turned out to be untrue but it was held that the statement was only an expression of opinion and as such was not actionable.

  If, however, the person does not actually believe the truth of the opinion they express, then an action for misrepresentation will be possible (*Edgington v Fitzmaurice* (1884)).

The statement must actually induce the contract

That the statement must actually induce the contract means that:

- the statement must have been made by one party to the contract to the other, and not by a third party;

- the statement must have been addressed to the person claiming to have been misled;

- the person claiming to have been misled must have been aware of the statement;

- the person claiming to have been misled must have relied on the statement.

In *Horsfall v Thomas* (1962), Horsfall made and sold a gun to Thomas. He concealed a fault in it by means of a metal plug, but Thomas never even examined the gun. After short usage, the gun blew apart. Thomas claimed that he had been misled, by the plug, into buying the gun. It was held that the plug could not have misled him as he had not examined the gun at the time of purchase.

Whether the reliance was reasonable or not is not material once the party claiming misrepresentation shows that they did in fact rely on the statement. See *Museprime Properties Ltd v Adhill Properties Ltd* (1990), in which an inaccurate statement contained in auction particulars, and repeated by the auctioneer, was held to constitute a misrepresentation, in spite of the claims that it should have been unreasonable for anyone to allow themselves to be influenced by the statement.

Types of misrepresentation

Misrepresentation can be divided into three types, each of which involves distinct procedures and provides different remedies.

Fraudulent misrepresentation

In the case of fraudulent misrepresentation, the statement is made, knowing it to be false, or believing it to be false, or recklessly careless whether it is true or false. The difficulty with this type of misrepresentation is proving the necessary mental element; it is notoriously difficult to show the required *mens rea*, or guilty mind, to demonstrate fraud.

In *Derry v Peek* (1889), the directors of a company issued a prospectus, inviting the public to subscribe for shares. The prospectus stated that the company had the power to run trams by steam power, but in fact it only had power to operate horse-drawn trams; it required the permission of the Board of Trade to run steam trams. The directors assumed that permission would be granted, but in fact it was refused. When the company was wound up, the directors were sued for fraud. It was held that there was no fraud since the directors had honestly believed the statement in the prospectus. They may have been negligent but they were not fraudulent.

Negligent misrepresentation

With negligent misrepresentation, the false statement is made in the belief that it is true, but without reasonable grounds for that belief. (It follows that the directors in *Derry v Peek* would be liable for negligent misrepresentation.) There are two categories of negligent misrepresentation:

- *At common law*

  Prior to 1963, the law recognised no such concept as negligent misrepresentation. The possibility of liability in negligence for misstatements arose from *Hedley Byrne and Co v Heller* (1964). In *Hedley Byrne and Co v Heller*, however, the parties were not in a contractual or a pre-contractual relationship, so there could not have been an action for misrepresentation. But, in *Esso Petroleum v Mardon* (1976), Mardon succeeded in an action for negligent misstatement, on the basis that he had been wrongly advised as to the amount of petrol he could expect to sell from a garage.

- *Under the Misrepresentation Act (MA) 1967*

  Although it might still be necessary, or beneficial, to sue at common law, it is more likely that such actions would now be taken under the statute. The reason for this is that s 2(1) of the MA 1967 reverses the normal burden of proof. In an action in negligence, the burden of proof is on the party raising the action to show that the other party acted in a negligent manner. However, where a misrepresentation has been made, then, under s 2(1) of the MA 1967, it is up to the party who made the statement to show that they had reasonable grounds for believing it to be true.

Innocent misrepresentation

Innocent misrepresentation occurs where the false statement is made by a person who not only believes it to be true, but also has reasonable grounds for that belief.

Remedies for misrepresentation

For fraudulent misrepresentation, the remedies are rescission, and/or damages for any loss sustained. Rescission is an equitable remedy which is designed to return the parties to their original position. The action for damages is in the tort of deceit. In *Doyle v Olby (Ironmongers) Ltd* (1969), it was decided that, where a contract was induced by a fraudulent misrepresentation, the measure of damages was not merely what was foreseeable but all damages which directly resulted as a consequence of the aggrieved party having entered into the contract. An example of this principle can be seen in *Smith and New Court Securities Ltd v Scrimgeour Vickers (Asset Management) Ltd* (1996), in which the plaintiffs were induced to buy 28 million shares in Ferranti plc on the basis of a fraudulently made claim about the shares. They had been told falsely that two other companies had already bid for the package of shares and this led them to offer and pay 82.25 pence per share, a total of £23,141,424. Without the false representation, they would not have offered more than 78 pence per share and, as the defendants would not have sold at that price, Smith New Court would not have acquired any shares in Ferranti. When it transpired that Ferranti had been subject to a completely unrelated fraud, its share price fell considerably and, although the plaintiffs managed to sell their shareholding at prices ranging from 30 to 44 pence, they suffered an overall loss of £11,353,220. The question to be decided was as to the amount the defendants owed in damages. Was it the difference between the market value of the shares and the price actually paid at the time, a matter of 4.25 pence per share, or was it the full loss, which was considerably larger? The House of Lords decided that the latter amount was due. The total loss was the direct result of the share purchase which had been induced by the fraudulent statement: the defendants were, therefore, liable for that amount and the foreseeability test in relation to negligence, as stated in *The Wagon Mound (No 1)* (1961), did not apply (see 8.5.6 for a detailed consideration of this test).

For negligent misrepresentation, the remedies are rescission, and/or damages. The action for damages is either in the tort of negligence, at common law or under s 2(1) of the MA 1967. Under the statute, the measure of damages will still be determined as in a tort action (see *Royscot Trust Ltd v Rogerson* (1991) where the Court of Appeal confirmed this approach).

For innocent misrepresentation, the common law remedy is rescission.

Under the MA 1967, however, the court may award damages instead of rescission, in cases where it is considered equitable to do so (s 2(2)).

With regard to s 2(2), it was once thought that the court could only award damages, instead of rescission, where the remedy of rescission was itself available. The implication of that view was that if the right to rescission was lost for some reason, such as the fact that the parties could not be restored to their original positions, then the right to damages under s 2(2) was also lost (*Atlantic Lines and Navigation Co Inc v Hallam* (1992)). However, in *Thomas Witter v TBP Industries* (1996), Jacob J examined and rejected that suggestion. In his opinion, the right to damages under s 2(2) did not depend upon the right to damages still being available but on the fact that the plaintiff had had such a right in the past. Thus, even if the right to rescission was ultimately lost, the plaintiff could still be awarded damages.

The right to rescind can be lost for any one of the following reasons:

• by affirmation, where the innocent party, with full knowledge of the misrepresentation, either expressly states that they intend to go on with the agreement, or does some action from which it can be implied that they intend to go on with the agreement. Affirmation may be implied from lapse of time (see *Leaf v International Galleries* (1950));

• where the parties cannot be restored to their original positions;

• where third parties have acquired rights in the subject matter of the contract (see *Phillips v Brooks* (1919), p 322).

Section 3 of the MA 1967 provides that any exclusion of liability for misrepresentation must comply with the requirement of reasonableness.

The diagram on p 308 shows how statements may be classified and the consequence of such classification.

6.11.3 Duress

Duress is some element of force, either physical or economic, used to override one party's freedom to choose whether or not to enter into a particular contract. Under such circumstances, the contract is voidable at the instance of the innocent party.

Its application used to be restricted to contracts entered into as a consequence of actual physical violence, or the threat of such violence to a person.

In *Barton v Armstrong* (1975), the defendant threatened Barton with death if he did not arrange for his company to buy Armstrong's shares in it. Barton sought to have the agreement set aside. It was found that the threats had been made but that, in addition, Barton thought that the transaction was a favourable one. Barton nonetheless succeeded. The court held that the proper inference was that duress was present, and the burden of proof was on Armstrong to show that the threats had played no part in Barton's decision. He had failed to discharge this burden.

Originally, it was held that threats to a persons goods could not amount to duress, but relatively recently a doctrine of economic duress has been developed by the courts. The germ of the doctrine, that an abuse of economic power can render a contract invalid, can be found in Lord Denning's decision in *D and C Builders Ltd v Rees* (1966), and was developed in later cases such as *The Siboen and The Sibotre* (1976); and *The Atlantic Baron* (1979).

In the latter, fully cited as *North Ocean Shipping Company v Hyundai Construction* (1979), a contract had been entered into for the building of a ship. The builders then stated that they would not complete construction unless the purchasers paid an extra 10%. Without the ship, the buyers would have lost a lucrative contract with a third party, to whom they had already agreed to charter the ship. The buyers paid the extra money and then, at a later date, sued to recover it, on the basis of economic duress, amongst other things. It was held that the threat to terminate the contract did constitute economic duress, which rendered the contract voidable. In the event, the buyers' delay in bringing the action acted as an affirmation of the agreement and they lost their right to rescission.

There is a difficulty in distinguishing ordinary commercial pressure from economic duress (see *Pao On v Lau Yiu Long* (1979)), but the existence of economic duress as a distinct principle of contract law finally received the approval of the House of Lords in *Universe Tankships Inc v ITWF* (1982), the *Universe Sentinel* case. The facts of the case concerned the blacking of the plaintiffs' ship by the defendant trade union which meant that it could not leave the port. As part of negotiations to lift the blacking, the plaintiffs paid money into the unions benevolent fund. They subsequently and successfully reclaimed the money from the union on the basis that it had been induced through economic duress.

In order to benefit from the doctrine, plaintiffs must show the following two things:

• that pressure, which resulted in an absence of choice on their part, was brought to bear on them; and

• that the pressure was of a nature considered illegitimate by the courts.

Only under such circumstances will the court permit rescission of an agreement as can be seen in *Atlas Express v Kafco* (1990). The defendant company had secured a highly-profitable contract with Woolworths, the large retail outlet, and employed the plaintiffs as their carriers. After beginning to perform the contract, Atlas sought to increase their price. Although they protested, Kafco felt they had no option but to agree to the demand rather than break their contract with Woolworths which would have proved economically disastrous for them. When Atlas sued to recover the increased charges, they failed, as it was held that the attempt to increase the charge was a clear case of economic duress. (This should be compared with the situation and outcome of *Williams v Roffey Bros* (1990), see 6.6.4.)

6.11.4 Undue influence

Transactions, either contract or gifts, may be avoided where they have been entered into as a consequence of the undue influence of the person benefiting from them. The effect of undue influence is to make a contract voidable, but delay may bar the right to avoid the agreement. There are two possible situations relating to undue influence.

Special relationships

Where there is a special relationship between the parties, there is a presumption that the transaction is the consequence of undue influence. The burden of proof is on the person receiving the benefit to rebut the presumption.

In *Re Craig* (1971), after the death of his wife, Mr Craig, then aged 84, employed a Mrs Middleton as his secretary-companion. In the course of six years for which she was employed, he gave her money to the extent of some £30,000. An action was taken to have the gifts set aside. The action succeeded as it was held that the circumstances raised the presumption of undue influence, which Mrs Middleton had failed to rebut.

Examples of special relationships are:

- parent and child while still a minor;

- guardian and ward;

- religious adviser and follower;

- doctor and patient;

- solicitor and client.

The list is not a closed one, however, and other relationships may be included within the scope of the special relationship (as in *Re Craig*).

Where a special relationship exists, then an important way in which the presumption of undue influence can be rebutted is to show that independent advice was taken by the other party, although all that is necessary is to show that the other party exercised their will freely.

Even where a special relationship exists, a transaction will not be set aside unless it is shown to be manifestly disadvantageous.

In *National Westminster Bank v Morgan* (1985), when a couple named Morgan fell into financial difficulties, the plaintiff bank made financial arrangements which permitted them to remain in their house. The refinancing transaction secured against the house was arranged by a bank manager who called at their home. Mrs Morgan had no independent legal advice. When the husband died, the bank obtained a possession order against the house in respect of outstanding debts. Mrs Morgan sought to have the refinancing arrangement set aside, on the grounds of undue influence. The action failed on the grounds that the doctrine of undue influence had no place in agreements which did not involve any manifest disadvantage, and Mrs Morgan had actually benefited from the transaction by being able to remain in her home for a longer period.

The key element in deciding whether a relationship was a special one or not was whether one party was in a position of dominance over the other. *National Westminster Bank v Morgan* also decided that a normal relationship between a bank manager and his client is not a special relationship.

No special relationship

Where no special relationship exists between the parties, the burden of proof is on the party claiming the protection of the undue influence doctrine. It is of interest to note that relationships which are not included as special relationships include the relationships of husband and wife and bank and customer yet these are precisely the relationships that are likely to generate the most problems.

The rule relating to manifest disadvantage, considered above in relation to special relationships, does not apply in the case where no such special relationship applies.

In *CIBC Mortgages plc v Pitt* (1993), Mrs Pitt sought to set aside a mortgage she had signed against her home in favour of the plaintiffs on the basis that her husband had exerted undue influence over her. Whereas the Court of Appeal had rejected her plea on the grounds that the agreement was not to her manifest disadvantage, the House of Lords declared that such a principle did not apply in cases where undue influence was actual rather than presumed. They did, however, recognise the validity of the mortgage on the grounds that the creditor had no knowledge, either actual or constructive, of the exercise of undue influence in relation to the transaction.

It is of interest to note in relation to this last case that the House of Lords, in *Barclays Bank plc v O'Brien* (1993), referred to an implied duty on creditors, in particular circumstances which certainly included a marital relationship, to ensure that parties had not entered into agreements on the basis of misrepresentation or undue influence. In that particular case, the bank were held to have constructive notice of the undue influence wielded by the husband, that is, they should have known, whether they actually did or not. For that reason the bank was not permitted to enforce the agreement entered into on the basis of that undue influence.

Inequality of bargaining power

It has been suggested that undue influence and duress are simply examples of a wider principle, based on inequality of bargaining power. The existence of such a principle was suggested in a number of decisions involving Lord Denning. It was intended to provide protection for those who suffered as a consequence of being forced into particular agreements due to their lack of bargaining power. This doctrine, however, was considered, and firmly rejected by the House of Lords in *National Westminster Bank v Morgan*. It could be suggested that the very idea of inequality of bargaining power is incompatible with the reality of today's economic structure with its domination by large scale, if not monopolistic, organisations. It should be recognised, however, that, as considered in 6.10.5, the idea of inequality of bargaining power has found a place in determining how the Unfair Contract Terms Act 1977 is to operate.

6.11.5 Contracts and public policy

It is evident that some agreements will tend to be contrary to public policy. The fact that some are considered more serious than others is reflected in the distinction drawn between those which are said to be illegal and those which are simply void.

Illegal contracts

A contract which breaks the law is illegal. The general rule is that no action can be brought by a party to an illegal contract. The contract may be expressly prohibited by statute, or implicitly prohibited by the common law. The following is a list of illegal contracts:

- contracts prohibited by statute;

- contracts to defraud the Inland Revenue;

- contracts involving the commission of a crime or a tort;

- contracts with a sexually immoral element, although contemporary attitudes may have changed in this respect (see *Armhouse Lee Ltd v Chappell* (1996));

- contracts against the interest of the UK or a friendly State;

- contracts leading to corruption in public life;

- contracts which interfere with the course of justice.

Void contracts

A void contract does not give rise to any rights or obligations. The contract is only void so far as it is contrary to public policy, thus the whole agreement may not be void. Severance is the procedure whereby the void part of a contract is excised, permitting the remainder to be enforced. Contracts may be void under statute or at common law.

Contracts void by statute

Wagering contracts

A wagering contract is an agreement that, upon the happening of some uncertain event, one party shall give something of value to the other, the party who has to pay being dependent on the outcome of the event. Such contracts are governed by the Gaming Acts (1968 being the most recent).

Restrictive trading agreements

Certain restrictive trading agreements are subject to registration and investigation under the Restrictive Trade Practices Act 1976. If the agreements cannot be justified by the parties to them, as required under s 10 of the Restrictive Trade Practices Act 1967, then they are void and unenforceable.

Resale price maintenance agreements

Agreements which seek to enforce minimum prices for goods through resale price maintenance agreements are void, and the enforcement of such agreements is prohibited under the Resale Prices Act 1976. It is possible, however, for particular classes of goods to qualify for exemption from the provisions of the Resale Prices Act.

Contracts void at common law

Contracts to oust the jurisdiction of the court

Any contractual agreement which seeks to deny the parties the right to submit questions of law to the courts are void, as being contrary to public policy. Agreements which provide for compulsory arbitration are enforceable.

Contracts prejudicial to the status of marriage

It is considered a matter of public policy that the institution of marriage be maintained. Hence, any contract which seeks to restrain a person's freedom to marry, or undermines the institution in any way, will be considered void.

Contracts in restraint of trade

One area of particular importance subject to the control of the common law are contracts in restraint of trade. A contract in restraint of trade is an agreement whereby one party restricts their future freedom to engage in their trade, business, or profession. The general rule is that such agreements are *prima facie* void but they may be valid if it can be shown that they meet the following requirements:

- the person who imposes the restrictions has a legitimate interest to protect;

- the restriction is reasonable as between the parties;

- the restriction is not contrary to the public interest.

The doctrine of restraint of trade is flexible in its application, and may be applied to new situations when they arise. Bearing this in mind, however, it is usual to classify the branches of the doctrine as follows.

Restraints on employees

Employers cannot protect themselves against competition from an ex-employee, except where they have a legitimate interest to protect. The only legitimate interests recognised by the law are trade secrets and trade connection.

Even in protecting those interests, the restraint must be of a reasonable nature. What constitutes reasonable in this context depends on the circumstances of the case.

In *Lamson Pneumatic Tube Co v Phillips* (1904), the plaintiffs manufactured specialised equipment for use in shops. The defendants contract of employment stated that, on ceasing to work for the plaintiffs, he would not engage in a similar business, for a period of five years, anywhere in the Eastern hemisphere. It was held that such a restriction was reasonable, bearing in mind the nature of the plaintiffs business.

This has to be compared with *Empire Meat Co Ltd v Patrick* (1939), where Patrick had been employed as manager of the company's butchers business in Mill Road, Cambridge. The company sought to enforce the defendants promise that he would not establish a rival business within five miles of their shop. In this situation, it was held that the restraint was too wide and could not be enforced.

The longer the period of time covered by the restraint the more likely it is to be struck down, but, in *Fitch v Dewes* (1921), it was held that a life long restriction placed on a solicitor was valid.

Restraints on vendors of business

The interest to be protected in this category is the goodwill of the business, that is, its profitability. Restrictions may legitimately be placed on previous owners to prevent them from competing, in the future, with new owners. Again, the restraint should not be greater than is necessary to protect that interest.

In *British Reinforced Concrete Engineering Co Ltd v Schelff* (1921), the plaintiffs sought to enforce a promise given by the defendant, on the sale of his business to them, that he would not compete with them in the manufacturing of road reinforcements. It was held that given the small size and restricted nature of the business sold, the restraint was too wide to be enforceable.

However, in *Nordenfelt v Maxim Nordenfelt Guns and Ammunition Co* (1894), a worldwide restraint on competition was held to be enforceable, given the nature of the business sold.

Restraints on distributors/solus agreements

This category of restraint of trade is usually concerned with solus agreements between petrol companies and garage proprietors, by which a petrol company seeks to prevent the retailer from selling its competitors petrol. It is recognised that petrol companies have a legitimate interest to protect, and the outcome depends on whether the restraint obtained in protection of that interest is reasonable.

In *Esso Petroleum v Harpers Garage* (1968), the parties had entered into an agreement whereby Harper undertook to buy all of the petrol to be sold from his two garages from Esso. In return, Esso lent him £7,000, secured by way of a mortgage over one of the garages. The monopoly right in regard to one garage was to last for four and a half years, and in regard to the other garage for 21 years. When Harper broke his undertaking, Esso sued to enforce it. It was held that the agreements in respect of both garages were in restraint of trade. But whereas the agreement which lasted for four and a half years was reasonable, the one which lasted for 21 years was unreasonable and void.

Until fairly recently, it was thought that *Esso v Harper* had set down a rule that any solus agreement involving a restriction which was to last longer than five years would be void, as being in restraint of trade. In *Alec Lobb (Garages) Ltd v Total Oil Ltd* (1985), however, the Court of Appeal made it clear that the outcome of each case depended on its own particular circumstances, and in that case approved a solus agreement extending over a period of 21 years.

Exclusive service contracts

This category relates to contracts which are specifically structured to exploit one of the parties by controlling and limiting their output, rather than assisting them. The most famous cases involve musicians.

In *Schroeder Music Publishing Co v Macauley* (1974), an unknown songwriter, Macauley, entered into a five year agreement with Schroeder. Under it, he had to assign any music he wrote to them, but they were under no obligation to publish it. The agreement provided for automatic extension of the agreement if it yielded £5,000 in royalties but the publishers could terminate it at any time with one months notice. It was decided that the agreement was so one-sided as to amount to an unreasonable restraint of trade, and hence was void.

Since the above case, numerous artists have made use of this ground for avoiding their contracts.

6.12 Discharge of contract

Discharge of contract means that the parties to an agreement are freed from their contractual obligations. A contract is discharged in one of four ways:

(a) agreement;

(b) performance;

(c) frustration;

(d) breach.

6.12.1 Discharge by agreement

Emphasis has been placed on the consensual nature of contract law, and it follows that what has been made by agreement can be ended by agreement. The contract itself may contain provision for its discharge, by either the passage of a fixed period of time, or the occurrence of a particular event. Alternatively, it may provide, either expressly or by implication, that one or other of the parties can bring it to an end, as in a contract of employment.

Where there is no such provision in a contract, another contract would be required to cancel it before all of the obligations have been met. There are two possible situations:

(a) where the contract is executory, the mutual exchange of promises to release one another from future performance will be sufficient consideration;

(b) where the contract is executed, that is, one party has performed, or partly performed, their obligations, the other party must provide consideration in order to be released from performing their part of the contract (unless the release is made under seal). The provision of this consideration discharges the original contract, and there is said to be accord and satisfaction.

6.12.2 Discharge by performance

This occurs where the parties to a contract perform their obligations under it. It is the normal way in which contracts are discharged. As a general rule, discharge requires complete and exact performance of the obligations in the contract.

In *Cutter v Powell* (1795), Cutter was employed as second mate on a ship sailing from Jamaica to Liverpool. The agreement was that he was to receive 30 guineas when the journey was completed. Before the ship reached Liverpool, Cutter died and his widow sued Powell, the ship's master, to recover a proportion of the wages due to her husband. It was held that the widow was entitled to nothing as the contract required complete performance.

There are four exceptions to the general rule requiring complete performance:

(a) Where the contract is divisible

In an ordinary contract of employment, where it is usual for payment to be made periodically, the harshness of the outcome of *Cutter v Powell* is avoided.

In *Bolton v Mahadeva* (1972), the plaintiff had contracted to install central heating for the defendant for £560. It turned out to be defective and required a further £179 to put right. It was held that Bolton could not claim any of the money as he had failed to perform the contract. An agreement to supply a bathroom suite was divisible from the overall agreement, however, and had to be paid for.

(b) Where the contract is capable of being fulfiled by substantial performance

This occurs where the essential element of an agreement has been performed, but some minor part remains to be done, or some minor fault remains to be remedied. The party who performed the act can claim the contract price, although they remain liable for any deduction for the work outstanding.

In *Hoenig v Isaacs* (1952), Hoenig was employed by Isaacs to decorate his flat. The contract price was £750, to be paid as the work progressed. Isaacs paid a total of £400, but refused to pay the remainder as he objected to the quality of the work carried out. Hoenig sued for the outstanding £350. It was held that Isaacs had to pay the outstanding money less the cost of putting right the defects in performance. These latter costs amounted to just under £56.

This should be compared with *Bolton v Mahadeva*, above, in which no payment was allowed for work done in a totally unsatisfactory manner.

(c) Where performance has been prevented by the other party

Under such circumstances, the party prevented from performance can sue for breach of contract, or on a *quantum meruit* basis (see 6.12.5).

(d) Where partial performance has been accepted by the other party

This occurs in the following circumstances: A orders a case of 12 bottles of wine from B. B only has 10, and delivers those to A. A is at liberty to reject the 10 bottles if he or she wants to, but once the goods are accepted he or she must pay a proportionate price for them.

Tender of performance

Tender of performance simply means an offer to perform the contractual obligations. For example, if a buyer refuses to accept the goods offered, but later sues for breach of contract, the seller can rely on the fact that they tendered performance as discharging their liability under the contract. The seller would also be entitled to claim for breach of contract.

In *Macdonald v Startup* (1843), Macdonald promised to deliver 10 tons of oil to the defendant within the last 14 days of March. He tried to deliver on Saturday, 31 March at 8.30 pm, and Startup refused to accept the oil. It was held that the tender of performance was equivalent to actual performance, and Macdonald was entitled to claim damages for breach of contract.

Section 29(5) of the SoGA 1979 now provides that tender is ineffectual unless made at a reasonable hour. It is unlikely that 8.30 pm on a Saturday evening would be considered reasonable.

6.12.3 Discharge by frustration

Where it is impossible to perform an obligation from the outset, no contract can come into existence. Early cases held that subsequent impossibility was no excuse for non-performance. In the 19th century, however, the doctrine of frustration was developed to permit a party to a contract, in some circumstances, to be excused performance on the grounds of impossibility arising subsequently to the formation of the contract.

A contract will be discharged by reason of frustration in the following circumstances:

- *Where destruction of the subject matter of the contract has occurred*

  In *Taylor v Caldwell* (1863), Caldwell had agreed to let a hall to the plaintiff for a number of concerts. Before the day of the first concert, the hall was destroyed by fire. Taylor sued for breach of contract. It was held that the destruction of the hall had made performance impossible and, therefore, the defendant was not liable under the contract.

- *Where government interference, or supervening illegality, prevents performance*

  The performance of the contract may be made illegal by a change in the law. The outbreak of war, making the other party an enemy alien, will have a similar effect.

  In *Re Shipton, Anderson and Co, etc* (1915), a contract was made for the sale of wheat stored in a warehouse in Liverpool. Before the seller could deliver, it was requisitioned by the government, under wartime emergency powers. It was held that the seller was excused from performance. Due to the requisition, it was no longer possible to lawfully deliver the wheat.

- *Where a particular event, which is the sole reason for the contract, fails to take place*

  In *Krell v Henry* (1903), Krell let a room to the defendant for the purpose of viewing the coronation procession of Edward VII. When the procession was cancelled due to the King's ill health, Krell sued Henry for the due rent. It was held that the contract was discharged by frustration, since its purpose could no longer be achieved.

This only applies where the cancelled event was the sole purpose of the contract.

In *Herne Bay Steamboat Co v Hutton* (1903), a naval review, which had been arranged as part of Edward VII's coronation celebrations, also had to be cancelled due to illness. Hutton had contracted to hire a boat from the plaintiffs for the purpose of seeing the review. It was held that Hutton was liable for breach of contract. The sole foundation of the contract was not lost as the ship could still have been used to view the assembled fleet.

- *Where the commercial purpose of the contract is defeated*

This applies where the circumstances have so changed that to hold a party to their promise would require them to do something which, although not impossible, would be radically different from the original agreement.

In *Jackson v Union Marine Insurance Co* (1874), the plaintiff's ship was chartered to proceed to Newport to load a cargo bound for San Francisco. On the way, it ran aground. It could not be refloated for over a month, and needed repairs. The charterers hired another ship and the plaintiff claimed under an insurance policy he had taken out to cover the eventuality of his failure to carry out the contract. The insurance company denied responsibility on the basis that the plaintiff could claim against the charterer for breach of contract. The court decided, however, that the delay had put an end to the commercial sense of the contract. As a consequence, the charterers had been released from their obligations under the contract and were entitled to hire another ship.

- *Where, in the case of a contract of personal service, the party dies or becomes otherwise incapacitated*

In *Condor v Barron Knights* (1966), Condor contracted to be the drummer in a pop group. After he became ill, he was medically advised that he could only play on four nights per week, not every night as required. It was decided that the contract was discharged by the failure in the plaintiff's health preventing him from performing his duties under it, and thus any contractual obligations were unenforceable.

Situations in which doctrine of frustration does not apply

In *Tsakiroglou and Co v Noblee and Thorl* (1960), it was stated that frustration is a doctrine only too often invoked by a party to a contract who finds performance difficult or unprofitable, but it is very rarely relied on with success. It is, in fact, a kind of last resort, and it is a conclusion which should be reached rarely and with reluctance. A contract will not be discharged by reason of frustration in the following circumstances:

- *Where the parties have made express provision in the contract for the event which has occurred*

In this case, the provision in the contract will be applied.

- *Where the frustrating event is self-induced*

An example of such a situation is the case of *Maritime National Fish Ltd v Ocean Trawlers Ltd* (1935). Maritime were charterers of a ship, equipped for otter trawling, owned by Ocean Trawlers. Permits were required for otter trawling, and Maritime, who owned four ships of their own, applied for five permits. They were only granted three permits, however, and they assigned those permits to their own ships. They claimed that their contract with Ocean Trawlers was frustrated, on the basis that they could not lawfully use the ship. It was held, however, that the frustrating event was a result of their action in assigning the permits to their own ships and, therefore, they could not rely on it as discharging their contractual obligations.

- *Where an alternative method of performance is still possible*

In such a situation, the person performing the contract will be expected to use the available alternative method.

In *Tsakiroglou and Co v Noblee and Thorl* (1962), a contract was entered into to supply 300 tons of Sudanese groundnuts CIF Hamburg. It had been intended that the cargo should go via the Suez canal, and the appellants refused to deliver the nuts when the canal was closed. It was argued that the contract was frustrated, as to use the Cape of Good Hope route would make the contract commercially and fundamentally different from that which was agreed. The court decided that the contract was not fundamentally altered by the closure of the canal and, therefore, was not discharged by frustration. The appellants therefore were liable for breach of contract.

- *Where the contract simply becomes more expensive to perform*

In such circumstances, the court will not allow frustration to be used as a means of escaping from a bad bargain.

In *Davis Contractors v Fareham UDC* (1956), the plaintiffs contracted to build 78 houses in eight months, at a total cost of £94,000. Due to shortage of labour, it actually took 22 months to build the houses, at a cost of £115,000. They sought to have the contract set aside as frustrated, and to claim on a *quantum meruit* basis. The court determined that the contract had not been frustrated by the shortage of labour, and the plaintiffs were thus bound by their contractual undertaking with regard to the price.

The effect of frustration

At common law, the effect of frustration was to make the contract void as from the time of the frustrating event. It did not make the contract void *ab initio*, that is, from the beginning. The effect of this was that each party had to perform any obligation which had become due before the frustrating event, and was only excused from obligations which would arise after that event. On occasion, this could lead to injustice. For example, in *Krell v Henry*, the plaintiff could not claim the rent, as it was not due to be paid until after the coronation event had been cancelled. The outcome was different in a similar case, however, where the rent had to be paid immediately on the making of the contract.

In *Chandler v Webster* (1904), the plaintiff had already paid £100 of the total rent of L141 15s for a room from which to watch the coronation procession, before it was cancelled. He sued to recover his money. It was decided that not only could he not recover the £100, but he also had to pay the outstanding L41 15s as the rent had fallen due before the frustrating event had taken place.

Law Reform (Frustrated Contracts) Act 1943

Statute intervened to remedy the potential injustice of the common law in 1943 with the introduction of Law Reform (Frustrated Contracts) Act 1943. The position is now as follows:

- any money paid is recoverable;

- any money due to be paid ceases to be payable;

- the parties may be permitted, at the discretion of the court, to retain expenses incurred from any money received; or recover those expenses from money due to be paid before the frustrating event. If no money was paid, or was due to be paid, before the event, then nothing can be retained or recovered.

The Law Reform (Frustrated Contracts) Act does not apply to the following types of contract:

(a) contracts for the carriage of goods by sea;

(b) contracts of insurance;

(c) contracts for perishable goods.

6.12.4 Discharge by breach

Breach of a contract occurs where one of the parties to the agreement fails to comply, either completely or satisfactorily, with their obligations under it. A breach of contract may occur in three ways:

- where a party, prior to the time of performance, states that they will not fulfil their contractual obligation;

- where a party fails to perform their contractual obligation;

- where a party performs their obligation in a defective manner.

Any breach will result in the innocent party being able to sue for damages. In addition, however, some breaches will permit the innocent party to treat the contract as discharged. In this situation, they can refuse either to perform their part of the contract, or to accept further performance from the party in breach. The right to treat a contract as discharged arises in the following instances:

- where the other party has repudiated the contract before performance is due, or before he has completed performance;

- where the other party has committed a fundamental breach of contract. As has already been pointed out in 6.10.2 there are two methods of determining whether a breach is fundamental or not; one relying on the distinction between conditions and warranties, the other relying on the seriousness of the consequences that flow from the breach.

Anticipatory breach

Anticipatory breach arises where one party, prior to the actual due date of performance, demonstrates an intention not to perform their contractual obligations. The intention not to fulfil the contract can be either express or implied:

- *Express*

  This occurs where a party actually states that they will not perform their contractual obligations.

  In *Hochster v De La Tour* (1853), De La Tour engaged Hochster, in April, to act as courier on his European tour, starting on 1 June. On 11 May, De La Tour wrote to Hochster stating that he would no longer be needing his services. The plaintiff started proceedings for breach of contract on 22 May, and the defendant claimed that there could be no cause of action until 1 June. It was held, however, that the plaintiff was entitled to start his action as soon as the anticipatory breach occurred (that is, when De La Tour stated he would not need Hochster's services).

- *Implied*

  This occurs where a party carries out some act which makes performance impossible.

  In *Omnium Enterprises v Sutherland* (1919), the defendant had agreed to let a ship to the plaintiff. Prior to the actual time for performance, he sold the ship to another party. It was held that the sale of the ship amounted to repudiation of the contract and the plaintiff could sue from that date.

With regard to anticipatory breach, the innocent party can sue for damages immediately, as in *Hochster v De La Tour*. Alternatively, they can wait until the actual time for performance before taking action. In the latter instance, they are entitled to make preparations for performance, and claim the agreed contract price, even though this apparently conflicts with the duty to mitigate losses (see 6.12.5).

In *White and Carter (Councils) v McGregor* (1961), McGregor contracted with the plaintiffs to have advertisements placed on litter bins which were supplied to local authorities. The defendant wrote to the plaintiffs asking them to cancel the contract. The plaintiffs refused to cancel, and produced, and displayed, the adverts as required under the contract. They then claimed payment. It was held that the plaintiffs were not obliged to accept the defendant's repudiation. They were entitled to perform the contract and claim the agreed price.

Where the innocent party elects to wait for the time of performance, they take the risk of the contract being discharged for some other reason, such as frustration, and thus of losing their right to sue.

In *Avery v Bowden* (1955), Bowden chartered the plaintiffs ship in order to load grain at Odessa within a period of 45 days. Although Bowden later told the ship's captain that he no longer intended to load the grain, the ship stayed in Odessa in the hope that he would change his mind. Before the end of the 45 days, the Crimean War started and thus the contract was discharged by frustration. Avery then sued for breach of contract. It was held that the action failed. Bowden had committed anticipatory breach, but the captain had waived the right to discharge the contract on that basis. The contract continued and was brought to an end by frustration, not by breach.

A relatively recent case sheds some light on the operation and effect of anticipatory breach. In *Vitol SA v Norelf Ltd* (1996), the parties entered into a contract for the purchase of a cargo of propane gas by the plaintiff. The contract was made on 11 February, but on 8 March, Vitol sent a telex to Norelf which purported to repudiate the agreement on the basis of an alleged breach by the latter party. As the allegation of breach on the part of Norelf subsequently turned out to be unfounded, the telex of 8 March was itself an anticipatory breach of the contract on the part of Vitol. Norelf did not communicate with Vitol but sold the cargo to another party on 15 March. In arbitration, it was decided that this subsequent sale effectively represented Norelf's acceptance of the anticipatory breach and left Vitol with no action in relation to the cargo. In the Court of Appeal, however, it was held that Norelf should have indicated their acceptance of the anticipatory breach in a clear and unequivocal manner, and that silence could not amount to such acceptance. In restoring the decision of the arbitrator, the House of Lords decided that the fact that Norelf had not taken the next step in the contract by delivering a bill of lading was sufficient notification that they had accepted Vitol's repudiatory breach. In so doing, they set out three principles that govern the acceptance of repudiatory breach:

- in the event of repudiatory breach, the other party has the right either to accept the repudiation or affirm the contract;

- the aggrieved party does not specifically have to inform the other party of their acceptance of the anticipatory breach, and conduct which clearly indicates that the injured party is treating the contract as at an end is sufficient;

- the aggrieved party need not personally notify the other of the decision to accept the repudiation and it is sufficient that they learn from some other party.

6.12.5 Remedies for breach of contract

The principle remedies for breach of contract are:

- damages;

- *quantum meruit*;

- specific performance;

- injunction.

Damages

According to Lord Diplock, in *Photo Productions Ltd v Securicor Transport Ltd* (1980):

> Every failure to perform a primary obligation is a breach of contract. The secondary obligation on the part of the contract-breaker to which it gives rise by implication of the common law is to pay monetary compensation to the other party for the loss sustained by him in consequence of the breach.

Such monetary compensation for breach of contract are damages. The estimation of what damages are to be paid by a party in breach of contract can be divided into two parts: remoteness and measure.

Remoteness of damage

What kind of damage can the innocent party claim? This involves a consideration of causation, and the remoteness of cause from effect, in order to determine how far down a chain of events a defendant is liable. The rule in *Hadley v Baxendale* (1845) states that damages will only be awarded in respect of losses which arise naturally, that is, in the natural course of things; or which both parties may reasonably be supposed to have contemplated, when the contract was made, as a probable result of its breach.

In *Hadley v Baxendale*, Hadley, a miller at Gloucester, had engaged the defendant to take a broken mill-shaft to Greenwich so that it could be used as a pattern for a new one. The defendant delayed in delivering the shaft, thus causing the mill to be out of action for longer than it would otherwise have been. Hadley sued for loss of profit during that period of additional delay. It was held that it was not a natural consequence of the delay in delivering the shaft that the mill should be out of action. The mill might, for example, have had a spare shaft. So the first part of the rule stated above did not apply. In addition, Baxendale was unaware that the mill would be out of action during the period of delay, so the second part of the rule did not apply, either. Baxendale, therefore, although liable for breach of contract was not liable for the loss of profit caused by the delay.

The effect of the first part of the rule in *Hadley v Baxendale* is that the party in breach is deemed to expect the normal consequences of the breach, whether they actually expected them or not.

Under the second part of the rule, however, the party in breach can only be held liable for abnormal consequences where they have actual knowledge that the abnormal consequences might follow.

In *Victoria Laundry Ltd v Newham Industries Ltd* (1949), the defendants contracted to deliver a new boiler to the plaintiffs, but delayed in delivery. The plaintiffs claimed for normal loss of profit during the period of delay, and also for the loss of abnormal profits from a highly lucrative contract which they could have undertaken, had the boiler been delivered on time. In this case, it was decided that damages could be recovered in regard to the normal profits, as that loss was a natural consequence of the delay. The second claim failed, however, on the grounds that the loss was not a normal one, but was a consequence of an especially lucrative contract, about which the defendant knew nothing.

The decision in the *Victoria Laundry* case was confirmed by the House of Lords in *The Heron II (Czarnikow v Koufos)* (1967), although the actual test for remoteness was reformulated in terms of whether the consequence should have been within the reasonable contemplation of the parties at the time of the contract.

In *The Heron II*, the defendants contracted to carry sugar from Constanza to Basra. They knew that the plaintiffs were sugar merchants, but did not know that they intended to sell the sugar as soon as it reached Basra. During a period when the ship was delayed, the market price of sugar fell. The plaintiffs claimed damages for the loss from the defendants. It was held that the plaintiffs could recover. It was common knowledge that the market value of such commodities could fluctuate, therefore, the loss was within the reasonable contemplation of the parties.

As a consequence of the test for remoteness, a party may be liable for consequences which, although within the reasonable contemplation of the parties, are much more serious in effect than would be expected of them.

In *H Parsons (Livestock) Ltd v Uttley Ingham and Co* (1978), the plaintiffs, who were pig farmers, bought a large food hopper from the defendants. While erecting it, the plaintiffs failed to unseal a ventilator on the top of the hopper. Because of lack of ventilation, the pig food stored in the hopper became mouldy. The pigs which ate the mouldy food contracted a rare intestinal disease and died. It was held that the defendants were liable for the loss of the pigs. The food affected by bad storage caused the illness as a natural consequence of the breach, and the death from such illness was not too remote.

Measure of damages

Damages in contract are intended to compensate an injured party for any financial loss sustained as a consequence of another party's breach. The object is not to punish the party in breach, so the amount of damages awarded can never be greater than the actual loss suffered. The aim is to put the injured party in the same position they would have been in had the contract been properly performed. There are a number of procedures which seek to achieve this end:

- *The market rule*

  Where the breach relates to a contract for the sale of goods, damages are usually assessed in line with the market rule. This means that, if goods are not delivered under a contract, the buyer is entitled to go into the market and buy similar goods, and pay the market price prevailing at the time. They can then claim the difference in price between what they paid and the original contract price as damages. Conversely, if a buyer refuses to accept goods under a contract, the seller can sell the goods in the market, and accept the prevailing market price. Any difference between the price they receive and the contract price can be claimed in damages.

- *The duty to mitigate losses*

  The injured party is under a duty to take all reasonable steps to minimise their loss. So, in the above examples, the buyer of goods which are not delivered has to buy the replacements as cheaply as possible; and the seller of goods which are not accepted has to try to get as good a price as they can when they sell them.

  In *Payzu v Saunders* (1919), the parties entered into a contract for the sale of fabric, which was to be delivered and paid for in instalments. When the purchaser, Payzu, failed to pay for the first instalment on time, Saunders refused to make any further deliveries unless Payzu agreed to pay cash on delivery. The plaintiff refused to accept this and sued for breach of contract. The court decided that the delay in payment had not given the defendant the right to repudiate the contract. As a consequence, he had breached the contract by refusing further delivery. The buyer, however, should have mitigated his loss by accepting the offer of cash on delivery terms. His damages were restricted, therefore, to what he would have lost under those terms, namely, interest over the repayment period.

A recent case highlights the problems that can arise in relation to both the market rule and the duty to mitigate losses.

In *Western Web Offset Printers Ltd v Independent Media Ltd* (1995), the parties had entered into a contract under which the plaintiff was to publish 48 issues of a weekly newspaper for the defendant. In the action which followed the defendant's repudiation of the contract, the only issue in question, was the extent of damages to be awarded. The plaintiff argued that damages should be decided on the basis of gross profits, merely subtracting direct expenses such as paper and ink, but not labour costs and other overheads: this would result in a total claim of some £177,000. The defendant argued that damages should be on the basis of net profits with labour and other overheads being taken into account: this would result in a claim of some £38,000. Although the trial judge awarded the lesser sum, the Court of Appeal decided that he had drawn an incorrect analogy from cases involving sale of goods. In this situation, it was not simply a matter of working out the difference in cost price from selling price in order to reach a nominal profit. The plaintiff had been unable to replace the work due to the recession in the economy and, therefore, had not been able to mitigate the loss, and in the circumstances was entitled to receive the full amount that would have been due in order to allow it to defray the expenses it would have had to pay during the period the contract should have lasted.

- *Non-pecuniary loss*

At one time, damages could not be recovered where the loss sustained through breach of contract was of a non-financial nature. The modern position is that such non-pecuniary damages can be recovered.

In *Jarvis v Swan Tours Ltd* (1973), the defendants brochure stated that various facilities were available at a particular ski resort. The facilities available were in fact much inferior to those advertised. The plaintiff sued for breach of contract. The court decided that Jarvis was entitled to recover, not just the financial loss he suffered, which was not substantial, but also for loss of entertainment and enjoyment. The Court of Appeal stated that damages could be recovered for mental distress in appropriate cases, and this was one of them.

Particular problems arise in relation to estimating the damages liable in relation to construction contracts. Where a builder either has not carried out work required, or has carried it out inadequately, he or she will be in breach of contract and the aggrieved party will be entitled to claim damages. The usual measure of such damages is the cost of carrying out the work or repairing the faulty work. However, this may not be the case where the costs of remedying the defects are disproportionate to the difference in value between what was supplied and what was ordered.

In *Ruxley Electronics and Construction Ltd v Forsyth* (1995), the parties had entered into a contract for the construction of a swimming pool and surrounding building. Although the contract stated that the pool was to be 7ft 6in deep at one end, the actual depth of the pool was only 6ft 9in. The total contract price was £70,000. Fixing the error would have required a partial reconstruction and would have cost £20,000. The trial judge decided that the measure of damages for the plaintiffs breach was the difference between the value of the pool actually provided and the value of the pool contracted for. He decided that the difference was nil but awarded the defendant £2,500 for loss of amenity. On appeal, the Court of Appeal overturned that award, holding that Forsyth was entitled to the full cost of reconstruction. On further appeal, the House of Lords reinstated the decision of the trial judge. They considered that, in building contracts, there were two possible ways of determining damages; either the difference in value, as used by the trial judge, or the cost of reinstatement, as preferred by the Court of Appeal. As the costs of reinstatement would have been out of all proportion to benefit gained, the House of Lords awarded the difference in value. According to Lord Jauncey: 'Damages are designed to compensate for an established loss and not to provide a gratuity to the aggrieved party.'

It should be noted that such construction contracts are evidently to be treated differently from contracts for the sale of goods, for purchasers of goods can reject them under s 13 of the SoGA 1979 where they do not match their description, even if they are otherwise fit for the purpose for which they were bought.

Liquidated damages and penalties

It is possible, and common in business contracts, for the parties to an agreement to make provisions for possible breach by stating in advance the amount of damages that will have to be paid in the event of any breach occurring. Damages under such a provision are known as liquidated damages. They will only be recognised by the court if they represent a genuine pre-estimate of loss, and are not intended to operate as a penalty against the party in breach. If the court considers the provision to be a penalty, it will not give it effect, but will award damages in the normal way.

In *Dunlop v New Garage and Motor Co* (1915), the plaintiffs supplied the defendants with tyres, under a contract designed to achieve resale price maintenance. The contract provided that the defendants had to pay Dunlop £5 for every tyre they sold in breach of the resale price agreement. When the garage sold tyres at less than the agreed minimum price, they resisted Dunlop's claim for £5 per tyre, on the grounds that it represented a penalty clause. On the facts of the situation, the court decided that the provision was a genuine attempt to fix damages, and was not a penalty. It was, therefore, enforceable.

In deciding the legality of such clauses, the courts will consider the effect, rather than the form, of the clause as is seen in *Cellulose Acetate Silk Co Ltd v Widnes Foundry (1925) Ltd* (1933). In that case, the contract expressly stated that damages for late payment would be paid by way of penalty at the rate of £20 per week. In fact, the sum of £20 pounds was in no way excessive and represented a reasonable estimate of the likely loss. On that basis, the House of Lords enforced the clause in spite of its actual wording.

The whole question of penalty clauses is a fraught one. It is obviously advantageous, in a business context, for the parties to a contract to know with certainty what the financial consequences of any breach of the contract will be, so as to allow them to manage their risk properly. However, the possibility of the courts subsequently holding a damages clause to be punitive introduces the very uncertainty that the clause was designed to avoid.

In any case, why should businesses not be bound by clauses as long as they have been freely negotiated? This point leads to a comparison between liquidated damages clauses and limitation and exclusion clauses. Usually, penalty clauses are thought of as overestimating the damages but it should be considered that such a pre-estimation may be much lower than the damages suffered, in which case the clause will effectively operate as a limitation clause. It would surely be better all round if the liquidated damages/penalties clause question was subject to a similar regime as regulates exclusion/limitation clauses under the UCTA 1977. The courts would then be required to examine whether the clause was the product of truly free negotiation and not the outcome of an abuse of power, in which case it would be effective; or alternatively, whether it was imposed on one of the parties against their wishes, in which case it would be inoperative.

Quantum meruit

Quantum meruit means that a party should be awarded as much as he had earned, and such an award can be either contractual or quasi-contractual (see below) in nature. If the parties enter into a contractual agreement without determining the reward that is to be provided for performance, then in the event of any dispute, the court will award a reasonable sum.

Payment may also be claimed on the basis of *quantum meruit*, where a party has carried out work in respect of a void contract.

In *Craven-Ellis v Canons Ltd* (1936), the plaintiff had acted as the managing director of a company under a deed of contract. However, since he had not acquired any shares in the company, as required by its articles, his appointment was void. He sued to recover remuneration for the service he had provided prior to his removal. The court decided that, although he could not claim under contract, he was entitled to recover a reasonable sum on the basis of *quantum meruit*.

Specific performance

It will sometimes suit a party to break their contractual obligations, and pay damages; but, through an order for specific performance, the party in breach may be instructed to complete their part of the contract. The following rules govern the award of such a remedy:

- An order of specific performance will only be granted in cases where the common law remedy of damages is inadequate. It is not usually applied to contracts concerning the sale of goods where replacements are readily available. It is most commonly granted in cases involving the sale of land, where the subject matter of the contract is unique.

- Specific performance will not be granted where the court cannot supervise its enforcement. For this reason, it will not be available in respect of contracts of employment or personal service.

  In *Ryan v Mutual Tontine Westminster Chambers Association* (1893), the landlords of a flat undertook to provide a porter, who was to be constantly in attendance to provide services such as cleaning the common passages and stairs, and delivering letters. The person appointed spent much of his time working as a chef at a nearby club. During his absence, his duties were performed by a cleaner or by various boys. The plaintiff sought to enforce the contractual undertaking. It was held that, although the landlords were in breach of their contract, the court would not award an order of specific performance. The only remedy available was an action for damages.

- Specific performance is an equitable remedy which the court grants at its discretion. It will not be granted where the plaintiff has not acted properly on their part. Nor will it be granted where mutuality is lacking; thus, a minor will not be granted specific performance, because no such order would be awarded against them.

Injunction

This is also an equitable order of the court, which directs a person not to break their contract. It can have the effect of indirectly enforcing contracts for personal service.

In *Warner Bros v Nelson* (1937), the defendant, the actress Bette Davis, had entered a contract which stipulated that she was to work exclusively for the plaintiffs for a period of one year. When she came to England, the plaintiffs applied for an injunction to prevent her from working for someone else. The court granted the order to Warner Bros. In doing so, the court rejected Nelson's argument that granting it would force her either to work for the plaintiffs, or not to work at all.

An injunction will only be granted to enforce negative covenants within the agreement, and cannot be used to enforce positive obligations.

In *Whitwood Chemical Co v Hardman* (1891), the defendant had contracted to give the whole of his time to the plaintiffs, who were his employers, but he occasionally worked for others. The plaintiffs applied for an injunction to prevent him working for anyone else. No injunction was granted; Hardman had said what he would do, not what he would not do; and, therefore, there was no negative promise to enforce.

Quasi-contractual remedies

Quasi-contractual remedies are based on the assumption that a person should not receive any undue advantage from the fact that there is no contractual remedy to force them to account for it. An important quasi-contractual remedy is an action for money paid and received.

If no contract comes into existence for reason of a total failure of consideration, then under this action, any goods or money received will have to be returned to the party who supplied them.

THE LAW OF CONTRACT

The formation of a contract

In order to create a contract, the following factors have to be present.

Offer

An offer is a promise, which is capable of acceptance, to be bound on particular terms.

An offer may be made to a particular person or to a group of people or to the world at large. If the offer is restricted, then only the people to whom it is addressed may accept it; but if the offer is made to the public at large, it can be accepted by anyone.

A person cannot accept an offer that they do not know about.

An offer may be revoked at any time before acceptance but cannot be revoked after acceptance.

An offer must be distinguished from an invitation to treat which is an invitation to others to make offers. The person extending the invitation is not bound to accept any offers made to them. Examples are goods in windows and goods on the shelves of supermarkets.

Acceptance

In order to form a binding agreement, the acceptance must correspond with the terms of the offer.

The general rule is that acceptance must be communicated to the offeror. Exceptions are where; the offeror has waived the right to receive communication, or acceptance is through the postal service.

Consideration

English law does not enforce gratuitous promises unless they are made by deed. Consideration consists of some benefit to the promisor or detriment to the promisee.

Consideration is provided either at the time of the creation of a contract (executed) or at a later date (executory). Past consideration, performed before the promise it seeks to bind, is normally not sufficient, although there are specific exceptions to this where the action was requested by the promisor and payment was expected by the promisee.

Consideration must be sufficient but need not be adequate. The courts will not inquire into the economics of a transaction as long as some consideration is provided.

It generally has been accepted that performance of an existing duty does not provide valid consideration, however, the authority of *Williams v Roffey* (1990) has indicated a contrary possibility. The situation would now seem to be that the performance of an existing contractual duty can amount to consideration for a new promise in circumstances where there is no question of fraud or duress, and where practical benefits accrue to the promisor.

Promissory estoppel

The equitable doctrine of promissory estoppel can sometimes be relied upon to prevent promisors from going back on their promises.

Promissory estoppel does not apply to the formation of contract and therefore it does not avoid the need for consideration to establish a contract in the first instance. It only varies or discharges of rights within a contract. It normally only suspends rights. The promise relied upon must be given voluntarily.

Privity

The Contracts (Rights of Third Parties) Act 1999 establishes the circumstances in which third parties can enforce terms of contracts. The requirement is that, in order for the third party to gain rights of enforcement, the contract in question must, either, expressly confer such a right on the third party or, alternatively, it must have been clearly made for their benefit.

Capacity

People under the age of 18 have only a limited capacity to enter into binding agreements. Contracts can be enforced against minors where they relate to contracts for necessaries or beneficial contracts of service. Other commercial contracts are unenforceable against a minor.

Voidable contracts are binding on a minor, unless they are repudiated during the period of minority or within a reasonable time after reaching the age of majority.

As a consequence of the Minors Contracts Act 1987, unenforceable, as well as voidable, contracts may be ratified on the minor attaining the age of majority.

The courts will not permit a party to enforce a contract indirectly by substituting an action in tort, or quasi-contract, for an action in contract.

A contract by a person who is of unsound mind or under the influence of drink or drugs is *prima facie* valid. The person claiming incapacity must show that they were incapable of understanding the nature of their action and that the other party was aware of this. Nonetheless, they must pay a reasonable price for necessaries sold to them.

Intention to create legal relations

The courts will only enforce those agreements which the parties intended to have legal effect.

In social and domestic agreements, there is a rebuttable presumption that the parties do not intend to create legal relations.

In commercial and business agreements, there is a rebuttable presumption that the parties intend to create legal relations.

Agreements between employers and trade unions, although commercial in nature, are presumed not to give rise to legal relations.

Letters of comfort usually amount to statements of present intention and do not amount to offers capable of acceptance.

Contents of a contract

Contract terms and mere representations

There are four tests for distinguishing a contractual term from a mere representation:

- Where the statement is of such major importance that the promisee would not have entered into the agreement without it, then it will be construed as a term.

- Where there is a time gap between the statement and the making of the contract, then the statement will most likely be treated as a representation.

- Where the statement is oral, and the agreement is subsequently drawn up in written form, then the exclusion from the written document will suggest that the statement was not meant to be a contractual term.

- Where one of the parties to an agreement has special knowledge or skill, then statements made by them will be terms, but statements made to them will not.

Terms

Terms can be classified as one of three types:

- A condition is a fundamental part of the agreement it is something which goes to the root of the contract.

- A warranty is a subsidiary obligation which is not vital to the overall agreement, and does not totally destroy its efficacy.

- In the case of an innominate term, if the innocent party is deprived of substantially the whole benefit of the contract, then the right to repudiate will be permitted even if the term might otherwise appear to be a mere warranty.

Express terms

Express terms are the terms which the parties themselves state are to be in the contract.

Implied terms

Implied terms are terms which are not expressly stated but which are nonetheless treated as part of the contractual agreement.

Terms may be implied by:

- statute;

- custom;

- the courts.

The parol evidence rule

If all the terms of a contract are in writing, then there is a strong presumption that no evidence supporting a different oral agreement will be permitted to vary those terms.

Exemption or exclusion clauses

An exemption clause is a term in a contract which tries to exempt, or limit, the liability of a party in breach of the agreement.

The following questions should always be asked with regard to exclusion clauses:

- has the exclusion clause been incorporated into the contract?;

- does the exclusion clause effectively cover the breach?;

- what effect does the UCTA 1977 have on the exclusion clause?

There are three ways in which such a term may be inserted into a contractual agreement:

- by signature;

- by notice;
- by custom.

The judiciary have developed rules of construction which operate to restrict the effectiveness of exclusion clauses. Foremost amongst these is the *contra proferentem* rule.

The Unfair Contract Terms Act 1977

The controls under the UCTA 1977 relate to two areas:

- there is an absolute prohibition on exemption clauses in relation to liability in negligence resulting in death or injury;
- any exclusion clause which seeks to avoid liability for breach of contract is only valid to the extent that it complies with the requirement of reasonableness.

The first Unfair Terms in Consumer Contracts Regulations (1994) were introduced to implement the European Unfair Contract Terms Directive (93/13/EEC). Those original regulations were repealed and replaced by the current regulations (SI 1999/2083), which came into effect on 1 October 1999.

They operate in addition to the UCTA and strike out terms which are unfair as being not entered into in good faith. They also introduce a requirement that contracts should be made in plain intelligible language and give the Director General of Fair Trading, and other qualifying bodies, the power to take out injunctions against unfair terms.

Vitiating factors

Mistake

Operative mistake renders a contract void *ab initio*. There are three kinds of operative mistake:

- *Common mistake*

  Where both parties to an agreement share the same error about the circumstances surrounding the transaction. Examples usually involve either res sua or res extincta.

- *Mutual mistake*

  This occurs where the parties believe different versions of the facts of the situation, but they do not realise it. In order for mutual mistake to be operative, it must comply with an objective test.

- *Unilateral mistake*

  This occurs where only one of the parties to the agreement is mistaken as to the circumstances of the contract, and the other party is aware of that fact. Where parties enter into a contract face to face, it is generally presumed that the seller intends to deal with the person before them and, therefore, they cannot rely on unilateral mistake to avoid the contract.

Mistake in respect of documents

There are two mechanisms for dealing with mistakes in written contracts.

- *Rectification*

  This allows the contract to be altered where it does not accurately represent the intentions of the parties.

- Non est factum

  This may operate where someone, without carelessness, signs a document under a misapprehension as to its true nature or content. If the document is fundamentally different from what they thought they were signing, they may avoid its effect.

Misrepresentation

Misrepresentation can be defined as a false statement of fact, made by one party before or at the time of the contract which induces the other party to enter into the contract.

Some statements will not amount to a representation, that is, sales puffs, statements of opinion, statements of law. The statement must actually induce the contract.

Types of misrepresentation

In fraudulent misrepresentation, the statement is made, knowing it to be false, or believing it to be false, or recklessly careless whether it is true or false.

In negligent misrepresentation, the false statement is made in the belief that it is true, but without reasonable grounds for that belief. There are two categories of negligent misrepresentation:

- at common law;

- under the MA 1967.

The latter is preferable in most cases as it reverses the burden of proof.

Innocent misrepresentation occurs where the false statement is made by a person who not only believes it to be true, but also has reasonable grounds for that belief.

Remedies for misrepresentation

Initially, rescission was the main remedy for misrepresentation. Damages were only available for fraud.

The possibility of damages in negligence was opened after *Hedley Byrne v Heller* (1963).

The MA provides the possibility of damages under s 2(1) for negligent misrepresentation and under s 2(2) for innocent misrepresentation.

Duress

Duress is some element of force used to override a party's freedom to choose whether or not to enter into a particular contract. Duress renders a contract voidable at the instance of the innocent party. This concept used to be restricted to contracts entered into as a consequence of actual physical violence, or the threat of such violence to a person, but has been extended so far as to include economic duress.

In order to benefit from the doctrine of economic duress, plaintiffs must show the following two things:

- that pressure, which resulted in an absence of choice on their part, was brought to bear on them; and

- that the pressure was of a nature considered illegitimate by the courts (*Atlas Express v Kafco* (1990)).

Undue influence

The effect of undue influence is to make a contract voidable, but delay may bar the right to avoid the agreement.

Where there is a special relationship between the parties, there is a presumption that the transaction is the consequence of undue influence. The presumption is open to rebuttal.

Examples of special relationships are:

- parent and child while still a minor;

- guardian and ward;

- religious adviser and follower;

- doctor and patient;
- solicitor and client.

The above list is not a closed one.

Where no special relationship exists between the parties, the burden of proof is on the party claiming the protection of the undue influence doctrine.

Contracts and public policy

A contract which breaks the law is illegal. Contracts may be expressly prohibited by statute, or implicitly prohibited by the common law. The general rule is that no action can be brought by a party to an illegal contract.

A void contract does not give rise to any rights or obligations. Contracts are only void so far as they are contrary to public policy.

Severance is the process whereby the void part of a contract is excised, permitting the remainder to be enforced.

Contracts void by statute

- Wagering contracts.
- Restrictive trading agreements.
- Resale price maintenance agreements.

Contracts void at common law

- Contracts to oust the jurisdiction of the court.
- Contracts prejudicial to the status of marriage.

Contracts in restraint of trade

The general rule is that such agreements are *prima facie* void but they may be valid if it can be shown that they meet the following requirements:

- the person who imposes the restrictions has a legitimate interest to protect;
- the restriction is reasonable as between the parties;
- the restriction is not contrary to the public interest.

There are four distinct areas in relation to restraint of trade and the application of the law differs in each:

- restraints on employees;
- restraints on vendors of business;
- restraints on distributors/solus agreements;
- exclusive service contracts.

Discharge of a contract

Discharge by agreement

Where the contract is executory, the mutual exchange of promises to release one another from future performance will be sufficient consideration.

Where the contract is executed, the other party must provide consideration in order to be released from performing their part of the contract: this amounts to accord and satisfaction.

Discharge by performance

As a general rule, discharge by performance requires complete and exact performance of the obligations in the contract. Except where:

- the contract is divisible;
- the contract is capable of being fulfiled by substantial performance;
- performance has been prevented by the other party;
- partial performance has been accepted by the other party.

Tender of performance

Tender of performance simply means an offer to perform the contractual obligations. Acceptable tender of performance discharges liability under a contract.

Discharge by frustration

A contract will be discharged by reason of frustration in the following circumstances where:

- destruction of the subject matter of the contract has occurred;
- government interference, or supervening illegality, prevents performance;
- a particular event, which is the sole reason for the contract, fails to take place;
- the commercial purpose of the contract is defeated;

- in the case of a contract of personal service, the party dies or becomes otherwise incapacitated.

Frustration will not apply where:

- the parties have made express provision in the contract for the event which has occurred;

- the frustrating event is self-induced;

- an alternative method of performance is still possible;

- the contract simply becomes more expensive to perform.

At common law, the effect of frustration was to make the contract void as from the time of the frustrating event. Under the Law Reform (Frustrated Contracts) Act 1943:

- money paid is recoverable;

- money due to be paid ceases to be payable;

- the parties may be permitted, at the discretion of the court, to retain expenses incurred from any money received; or recover those expenses from money due to be paid before the frustrating event;

- where a party has gained a valuable benefit under the contract he or she may, at the discretion of the court, be required to pay a reasonable sum in respect of it.

Discharge by breach

A breach of contract may occur in three ways:

- where a party, prior to the time of performance, states that they will not fulfil their contractual obligation;

- where a party fails to perform their contractual obligation;

- where a party performs their obligation in a defective manner.

Any breach will result in the innocent party being able to sue for damages.

Where a breach gives the right to treat the agreement as discharged, the innocent party can refuse either to perform their part of the contract, or to accept further performance from the party in breach.

Anticipatory breach

Anticipatory breach arises where one party, prior to the actual due date of performance, demonstrates an intention not to perform their contractual obligations. Anticipatory breach may be express or implied.

The innocent party can sue for damages immediately or wait until the actual time for performance before taking action.

Damages

The estimation of what damages are to be paid by a party in breach of contract can be divided into two parts: remoteness and measure.

Remoteness of damage

The rule in *Hadley v Baxendale* (1845) states that damages will only be awarded in respect of losses which arise naturally or which both parties may reasonably be supposed to have contemplated, when the contract was made, as a probable result of its breach.

Measure of damages

The aim of damages is to put the injured party in the same position they would have been in had the contract been properly performed.

There are a number of procedures which seek to achieve this end:

- the market rule;
- the duty to mitigate losses.

The parties to an agreement may make provisions for the amount of damages that will have to be paid in the event of any breach occurring. The court will only enforce the terms where they represent a genuine pre-estimate of loss, and not a penalty against the party in breach.

Quantum meruit

If the parties enter into a contractual agreement without determining the reward that is to be provided for performance, then in the event of any dispute, the court will award a reasonable sum.

Specific performance

Through an order for specific performance, a party in breach may be instructed to complete their part of the contract:

- an order of specific performance will only be granted in cases where the common law remedy of damages is inadequate;
- specific performance will not be granted where the court cannot supervise its enforcement;

- specific performance is an equitable remedy which the court grants at its discretion.

Injunction

This is also an equitable order of the court, which directs a person not to break their contract.

Quasi-contractual remedies

These are based on the assumption that a person should not receive any undue advantage from the fact that there is no contractual remedy to force them to account for it.

CHAPTER 7

CONSUMER PROTECTION

Introduction to consumer protection

The previous chapter has focused on what has been described as the 'Classical Model of Contract Law'. The assumptions underlying such a model are based on the appearances of a competitive, free market, system, in which the parties to contracts are truly free to determine their own economic/market relationships. It has to be recognised, however, that this competitive market model of contractual relationships is no longer an accurate representation of what actually takes place in the contemporary market place. We now live in economies that are dominated by huge economic organisations which wield extensive economic power. In such situations of oligopolistic, if not monopolistic, power it is simply nonsensical to think in terms of consumer sovereignty, or its legal equivalent, equality of bargaining power. It would be a misrepresentation of reality, for example, to suggest that individual consumers negotiate the terms of their individual purchases in supermarkets in the way that is assumed in the invitation to treat-offer-acceptance description portrayed in cases such as *Pharmaceutical Society of Great Britain v Boots* (1953). In reality, consumers are faced with the simple, single, choice; take it or leave it, and go elsewhere to be met by the same conditions.

With the collapse of the notion of equality of bargaining power, the modern state has intervened to protect individual consumers who would otherwise be left at the mercy of those who might abuse the market relationship. The introduction of consumer protection legislation, of course, has also been aimed at safeguarding the individual from the depredations of the mere crooked and criminal trader. Given the nature of this book, it is impossible to do justice to all the aspects of consumer protection, and it is recognised that extremely important areas, such as the product liability and the consumer protection legislation, cannot be covered in the limited space available. It is hoped, however, that what is dealt with in this chapter will follow on from, and build upon, the previous chapter of contract law, whilst providing an indication of the role of consumer protection. The areas to be dealt with are:

- Sale of Goods Act 1979;
- Consumer Protection Act 1987;
- Trade Descriptions Act 1968;
- Consumer Credit Act 1974.

7.1 Sale of goods

Contracts for the sale and supply of goods are probably the most common form of contract found in business. For the main part, the Sale of Goods Acts have merely codified the business practice, but, in so doing, they also introduced elements that are now certainly considered to be aspects of consumer protection law. Although widespread in its general application, the Sale of Goods Act (SoGA) 1979 specifically protects consumers by ensuring that certain terms are to be included in consumer contracts as a matter of implication.

7.1.1 Implied terms

There are some terms which are implied into every contract for the sale of goods by the SoGA 1979 (as amended). It is important to understand the legal effect of such terms as the remedy in the event of a breach may differ. The most important implied terms are conditions. A condition is a fundamental term of the contract, any breach of which will allow the injured party to treat the contract as repudiated. This means that the parties are returned to their original positions (see 6.10 for details on the limitations of the right to repudiate). The buyer may bring an action for damages instead of repudiating the contract, and, if he or she has been deemed to have accepted the goods, he or she will have no choice but to sue for damages rather than repudiate the contract.

A warranty is a lesser term of the contract and is not seen as being as important as a condition. A breach of warranty will allow the buyer to claim damages, but not to reject the goods. Apart from the implied terms which stipulate the nature of the term, whether any other term is a condition or warranty will depend on the construction of the contract and the intentions of the parties. As a general rule, terms relating to the time of payment are not regarded as conditions whereas terms relating to the time of delivery are to be treated as conditions. A term which is not a condition or warranty is an innominate term, a breach of which may result in repudiation if it goes to the root of the contract. Further information can be found in 6.10.2.

The terms implied under the SoGA are as follows:

- the seller must give a good title to the goods (s 12);

- the goods must correspond with any description applied to them (s 13);

- the goods must be of satisfactory quality (s 14);

- the goods must be reasonably fit for their normal purpose or for a purpose which was specified by the buyer (s 14);

- if the sale is a sale by sample, the goods must correspond with the sample shown (s 15).

7.1.2 Title (s 12)

There is an implied condition that the seller has the right to sell the goods and the ability to transfer a good title to the buyer.

In *Niblett Ltd v Confectioners Materials Co* (1921), the labels on a number of tins containing condensed milk infringed Nestlé's trademark. These tins were being imported from America and were seized by customs and not released to the buyer. It was held that, although the American company had a right to transfer title in these goods, the goods were not what they purported to be. The buyer could, therefore, claim damages and breach of condition, as he or she would not be obtaining a trouble-free title to the goods, that is, what the law calls quiet enjoyment of the goods. His or her title would clearly be challenged as sale of the goods infringed Nestlé's trademark.

In cases brought under s 12, the buyer can recover the full purchase price, even though the buyer may have used the goods for some time, as if a good title to the goods is not received there is deemed to be a total failure of consideration. In *Rowland v Divall* (1923), the buyer had used a car for four months. The title to the car had not been transferred to him. It was held that, since he had not received what he had bargained for, he could recover the full price paid.

There are also implied warranties that the goods are free from any charge or encumbrance not disclosed or known to the buyer before the contract is made and that the buyer will have quiet possession of the goods (s 12(2)).

In *Microbeads AC v Vinhurst Road Markings* (1975), the seller sold some road marking machines to the buyers. Unknown to the seller at the time of the sale, another firm was in the process of patenting this type of equipment, although rights to enforce the patent did not commence until after the contract between the seller and buyer was made. A patent action was subsequently brought against the buyer who then claimed that the seller was in breach of the implied condition as he had no right to sell and was in breach of the warranty of quiet possession. It was held that, at the time of sale, the seller had every right to sell the goods, but was in breach of the warranty of quiet possession, because that amounted to an undertaking as to the future.

The rule *nemo dat quod non habet* means that a person cannot give what he or she has not got, so that, in general, ownership is protected. The general rule is that, where goods are sold by a person who is not the owner, the buyer acquires no better title than the seller (s 21 of the SoGA 1979). However, there are exceptions and the law may often have to choose between the rights of two innocent parties; the innocent purchaser and the real owner of the goods. Generally, the buyer will have to return the goods to the true owner, usually without any recompense, although where the goods have been improved the buyer may be entitled to some reimbursement.

7.1.3   Description (s 13)

Where the sale of goods is by description, the goods must accord with any description applied to them. Goods are sold by description either where the buyer does not see the goods but relies on a description of them, or where the buyer sees the goods, but relies on terms describing features of the goods or self-description. It must be proved that there was such a description and that the buyer relied on it (*Harlingdon and Leinster Enterprises v Christopher Hull Fine Art* (1991)). It can then be determined whether the goods complied with it. A contractual description consists of any words, oral or written, which can be relied upon as identification of the goods that are being bought.

In *Beale v Taylor* (1967), the buyer read an advertisement offering for sale a Herald convertible 1961. He went to see the car. On the back of the vehicle was a plate which stated 1200. He bought the car and later discovered that it was the back half of a 1961 model welded to the front half of an earlier model. It was held that since the buyer bought the car with reference to the description he was entitled to damages for breach of the implied condition under s 13.

The description may be very simple, as in the case of *Grant v Australian Knitting Mills* (1970), in which underpants was held to be a contractual description as it was the way in which the buyer identified the item he was purchasing. Not all the words used by the seller will be part of the contractual description.

In *Ashington Piggeries v Christopher Hill Ltd* (1972), there was a written contract which stated that the sellers would make a vitamin-fortified mink food to be called King Size. The food was made up to a formula specified by the buyers which was also in the contract. It was stated that the formula was the description which specified what the buyers wanted. One of the ingredients was herring meal which was contaminated, but which was still identifiable as herring meal. It was held that the sellers had made up the food correctly so that there was no breach relating to the description of the goods. As we shall see, however, there may be potentially more than one breach of the implied terms.

Section 13 may be breached even if the goods themselves are of satisfactory quality and fit for the purpose (*Arcos v Ronaasen* (1933)) and the implied condition extends to the packaging of the goods if that is part of the description, as illustrated in *Re Moore and Co and Landauer and Co* (1921), in which the buyer was allowed to reject the goods because he had bought tinned fruit in cases containing 30 tins and the seller delivered the correct tinned fruit in cases some of which contained 30 tins and some 24 tins. It was held that as the goods delivered did not correspond with those ordered, the whole consignment could be rejected. This would now be subject to s 15A and s 15(2A) as inserted by the Sale and Supply of Goods Act (SSGA) 1994 which respectively removes the right of rejection for breach of a condition in non-consumer sales where the breach is so slight that it would be unreasonable to reject the goods, and specifically removes the right to reject the goods, and specifically removes the right to reject the whole consignment where the seller delivers a quantity of goods less or larger than contracted to sell if the shortfall or excess is so slight that it would be unreasonable to do so. Section 35A of the SoGA 1979 as amended which now provides the buyer with a right of partial rejection must be read subject to s 15.

Where the sale of goods is by sample, the goods must correspond to the description as well as the sample. If there is no reliance on the description, then s 13 is inapplicable (*Harlingdon and Leinster Enterprises Ltd v Christopher Hull Fine Art Ltd* (1991)).

7.1.4 Satisfactory quality (s 14(2))

There is an implied term that the goods shall be of satisfactory quality according to s 14(2) of the SoGA 1979 (as amended). While the new s 14(2) uses the word 'term', it is clear from the new s 14(6) that the term is a condition. Unlike s 13, s 14 does not apply to private sales, that is, the goods must be sold in the course of a business, The term 'sale in the course of a business' is not defined in the SoGA 1979 but is used in other legislation, such as the Trade Descriptions Act 1968, Unfair Contract Terms Act (UCTA) 1977 and the Supply of Goods and Services Act (SGSA) 1982.

Until recently, it was apparent from the case law relating to this legislation that any sale had to form an integral part of the business or, where it was incidental to the business, such transactions had to be on a sufficiently regular basis to bring them within the scope of the section (*Davies v Sumner* (1984) and *R and B Custom Brokers Ltd v United Dominions Trust Co* (1988)). However, in *Stevenson v Rogers* (1999), the Court of Appeal held that a fisherman who sold the boat he had used in his business was potentially liable under s 14(2), in that he had sold the boat in the course of his business. In reaching its decision and extending the application of the law to cover one-off transactions, the Court of Appeal distinguished the earlier precedents, although not without some difficulty, especially as regards the decision in *R and B Custom Brokers Ltd v United Dominions Trust Co.*

Section 14(2C) states that the term does not extend to any matter making the quality of goods unsatisfactory:

- which is specifically drawn to the buyers attention before the contract is made;

- where the buyer examines the goods before the contract is made, which that examination ought to reveal; or

- in the case of a contract for sale by sample, which would have been apparent on reasonable examination of the sample.

These exceptions are essentially the same as those found previously in the SoGA 1979, although the seller may be able to invoke the exception by not pointing out the actual defect (as per the SoGA 1979), but merely indicating the matter which may lead to the quality of the goods being unsatisfactory, that is, are the matter and the defect the same thing for the purposes of the SSGA 1994?

It should be remembered that the buyer is under no obligation to carry out an examination. If, however, the buyer chooses to carry out an examination, then defects which that examination actually or ought to have revealed will be excluded from s 14(2).

The goods which come within s 14(2) include not only goods sold in the normal course of business but also goods sold as part of a business to the consumer, for example, the sale of a van which has been used in a grocery business.

The SSGA 1994 introduces a definition of the term 'satisfactory quality'. First, s 14(2A) states that goods are of satisfactory quality if they meet the standard that a reasonable person would regard as satisfactory, taking account of any description of the goods, the price (if relevant) and all the other relevant circumstances. This section must then be read subject to s 14(2B). This states that the quality of the goods includes their state and condition and the following (among others) are in appropriate cases aspects of the quality of goods:

- fitness for all the purposes for which goods of the kind in question are commonly supplied;

- appearance and finish;

- freedom from minor defects;

- safety; and

- durability.

The SSGA, in replacing s 14(6) of the SoGA 1979, attempts to clarify the meaning of satisfactory quality. An objective test based on the reasonable man is introduced as well as statutory recognition that second hand goods may have some acceptable minor defects. The factors are to be regarded as a non-exhaustive list and failure to comply with one of the factors will not necessarily result in goods being classified as unsatisfactory quality. Existing case law may still be relevant in interpreting both s 14(2A) and s 14(2B). For example, the price of the goods may be extremely relevant in the case of second hand goods (*Business Application Specialists Ltd v Nationwide Credit Ltd* (1988)).

In *Rogers v Parish (Scarborough) Ltd* (1987), the buyer bought a Range Rover for £16,000. It transpired that it had a defective engine, gear box and bodywork, all of which were below the standard normally expected of a vehicle costing that much. It was held that the vehicle was not of merchantable quality (under the earlier s 14). The fact that it was driveable and repairable did not satisfy s 14 of the SoGA 1979 as this could only be judged by considering whether it was of a reasonable standard for a vehicle of its type. As a result, the buyers rejection was valid and he was entitled to recover the purchase price and damages.

With regard to new cars, in *Bernstein v Pamson Motors (Golders Green) Ltd* (1987), the buyer purchased a new Nissan car for £8,000. He drove it for three weeks (approximately), covering some 140 miles. The engine then seized and had to undergo extensive repairs. The buyer rejected the car and refused to take it back after it had been repaired. The court felt that the buyer of a new car was entitled to expect more than the buyer of a second hand car, although how much more was dependent upon the nature of the defect, length of time of repairs and the price of the vehicle. The court distinguished between the merest cosmetic blemish on a new Rolls Royce which might render it unmerchantable whereas on a humbler car it might not. However, whilst at the time of delivery the car was unmerchantable, it was further held that a period of three weeks and 140 miles was a reasonable time to examine and try out the goods. The buyer was therefore deemed to have accepted the goods within the meaning of s 35 and could, therefore, only claim for breach of warranty.

It is unlikely that the decisions in *Rogers* and *Bernstein* would have been different in the light of the new definition. However, the goods have to be suitable for all their common purposes under s 14(2B) which is an extension of the s 14(6) definition. As a result, *Aswan Engineering Establishment v Lupdine* (1987) may need to be reconsidered, although the decisions would probably stand in *Kendall (Henry) and Sons v William Lillico and Sons Ltd* (1968) and *Brown and Sons Ltd v Craiks Ltd* (1970).

The factors now specifically include appearance and finish as well as freedom from minor defects. The former clearly refer to cosmetic defects which may or may not affect the quality of the goods by reference to the type of goods, price, etc. The same is true of minor defects, for example, a scratch on a Rolls Royce may affect quality whereas a scratch on a second hand Ford Escort may not.

Safety is now a specific factor in assessing satisfactory quality and it would appear that any matter which results in the goods being unsafe would be within the SSGA 1994.

Finally, durability of the goods also has to be considered. This raises the contentious issue of the length of time which a buyer can expect goods to remain of satisfactory quality. However, the test to be applied is that of the reasonable man, that is, an objective one. Again, an assessment of durability can only be made by reference to description, purpose, price, etc. Indeed, it would appear that there will only be rare situations where these factors are considered in isolation of each other. Only the buyer may use the remedies of repudiation and damages as the rules relating to privity of contract apply.

7.1.5 Reasonable fitness for the purpose

There is an implied condition in a contract for the sale of goods that the goods supplied are reasonably fit for any purpose expressly or impliedly made known to the seller under s 14(3) of the SoGA 1979. A breach of this section is to be treated as a breach of a condition. Where goods have a normal purpose, the law implies that you buy those goods for that purpose, for example, in the case of *Grant v Australian Knitting Mills* where the purpose of underpants was to be worn and *Godley v Perry* (1960) where in purchasing a toy catapult the buyer did not have to state specifically the purpose. If the purpose or use is unusual or the goods have several normal but distinct uses, for example, timber for paper or for furniture, then the purpose must be made known expressly that is it must be spelt out clearly either verbally or in writing to the seller before the buyer can rely on this section. An example of this is illustrated by the case of *Ashington Piggeries v Hill,* where the buyers made it clear to the seller that the end product would be fed to mink, even though they supplied the formula.

The question of whether goods are reasonably fit for the purpose is a question of fact. In *Griffiths v Peter Conway Ltd* (1939), the buyer bought a Harris tweed coat. It transpired that she was allergic to the fabric. It was held that there was no breach of s 14(3) as the coat was fit for wear by any normal person and she had failed to make any reference to her condition or sensitivity when she made her purchase.

It is clear that this condition does not apply where the buyer does not rely on the seller's skill and judgment, for example, if a brand is chosen other than that recommended by the seller or where it is unreasonable for the buyer to have relied on that skill and judgment if, for example, he or she had greater expertise.

7.1.6 Sale by sample (s 15)

Section 15 of the SoGA 1979 imposes an implied condition that where goods are sold by sample, they will comply with that sample. Furthermore, such goods will be free from any defect, making their quality unsatisfactory, which would not be apparent on reasonable examination of the sample.

This section applies only if there is a term of the contract which states that it is a contract of sale by sample. This could be an oral term, but if it is in writing, then the term about sale by sample must be written into the contract. The mere act of showing a sample of the goods during negotiations does not make the sale one of sale by sample unless the parties agree to do so. In *Drummond v Van Ingen* (1887), Lord MacNaughten explained the function of a sample in stating that:

> ... the office of a sample is to present to the eye the real meaning and intention of the parties with regard to the subject matter of the contract, which, owing to

the imperfection of language, it may be difficult or impossible to express in words. The sample speaks for itself.

It is no defence under s 15(2) to say that the bulk can easily be made to correspond with the sample.

In *E and S Ruben Ltd v Faire Bros and Co Ltd* (1949), a material known as Linatex was sold which was crinkly, whereas the sample had been soft and smooth. The seller argued that by a simple process of warming, the bulk could have been made as soft as the sample. It was held that there had been a breach of s 15(2) and the sellers were therefore liable to pay damages to the buyer.

A buyer may not be able to claim damages under s 15(2) for defects he could reasonably have discovered upon examination of the goods. He may still have an action under s 14(2) and (3). It is important to remember that the implied conditions under s 15 are:

• that the bulk shall correspond with the sample;

• that the buyer shall have a reasonable opportunity to compare the goods with the sample;

• that the goods will be free from any defect rendering them unsatisfactory which would not be apparent on reasonable examination of the sample.

7.1.7 Exclusion clauses

The effect of exclusion clauses on the operation of the SoGA 1979 is limited not only by the Act itself, but also by UCTA 1977. The limitations are as follows:

• Section 12 of the SoGA cannot be excluded, that is, the seller must pass on a good title.

• In the case of a consumer purchaser (that is, where the purchaser is a private individual dealing with a trader, for example, an individual in a shop), it is impossible to exclude liability under ss 13–15 of the SoGA.

• In the case of a non-consumer contract (that is, where the buyer is not a private individual and/or the seller is not acting in the course of business as, for example, in a private sale), it is possible to exclude liability under ss 13–15 of the SoGA, but only if the exclusion clause satisfies the test of reasonableness.

• By virtue of the Consumer Transactions (Restrictions on Statements) Order 1976 (SI 1976/1813), it is a criminal offence to include in a contract a term, or to display a notice, which purports to exclude the statutory implied terms or restrict liability for their breach as against a person who deals as a consumer.

• Any other liability for breach of contract can be excluded or restricted only to the extent that it is reasonable.

- Exclusion of liability for death and personal injury is prohibited.

- It is possible to exclude liability for other loss or damage arising from negligence or misrepresentation only to the extent that the clause is deemed to be reasonable.

The requirement of reasonableness means that the exclusion clause shall be a fair and reasonable one to be included, having regard to the circumstances which were or ought to have been known to or in the contemplation of the parties when the contract was made (Sched 2 to the UCTA 1977).

In addition, the Unfair Terms in Consumer Contracts Regulations 1999 which implement EC Directive 93/13 provide further protection with respect to exclusion or other unfair terms in consumer contracts where the term has not been individually negotiated, such as may be found in a standard form contract. (See 6.10.6 for a detailed consideration of these provisions.)

7.2 Supply of Goods and Services Act 1982

The SGSA 1982 provides protection in respect of agreements which do not fulfil the definition of the SoGA 1979 but under which goods are supplied, usually along with a service. The SGSA 1982 itself mirrors the SoGA 1979 in that it implies conditions with respect to goods supplied. These implied conditions are contained in ss 2–5 and are very similar to ss 12–15 of the SoGA 1979, that is, there is an implied condition re title, description, quality and fitness for the purpose as well as sample. The SGSA 1982 also applies to contracts of hire in that ss 6–10 imply in hire contracts terms similar to those implied by ss 12–15 of the SoGA 1979 in sale of goods contracts. The SGSA 1982 is also subject to similar amendments introduced by the SSGA 1994. These amendments can be found in Sched 2.

Furthermore, the SSGA 1982 provides protection for the victims of poor quality workmanship, including the time it takes to provide services and the price for such services. The SSGA 1982 applies to all contracts where a person agrees to carry out a service in the course of a business. The implied terms as to services can be found in ss 13–15.

Section 13 states that there is an implied term that, where the supplier is acting in the course of a business, the supplier will carry out the service with reasonable skill and care.

Section 14 states that, where the supplier is acting within the course of a business and the time for the service to be carried out is not fixed by the contract or determined by a course of dealings between the parties, the supplier will carry out the service within a reasonable time.

Section 15 states that, where the consideration is not determined by a contract or in a manner agreed in the contract or by the course of dealing between the parties, the party contracting with the supplier will pay a reasonable price.

7.2.1 Exclusion clauses

These are governed by the UCTA 1977 with respect to contracts for the supply of goods and services.

Title cannot be excluded and any attempt to exclude renders the clause void. In consumer sales, any attempt to exclude the terms contained in ss 2–5 will render the clause void. If the buyer does not deal as a consumer, any attempt to exclude these terms will be subject to the test of reasonableness.

However, where there is a contract of hire, the terms as to title and quiet possession can be excluded or restricted by an exemption clause, subject to the test of reasonableness.

Where an exclusion clause relates to s 13, it must satisfy the test of reasonableness. Liability for death or personal injury cannot be excluded.

7.3 Product liability

The Consumer Protection Act (CPA) 1987 was passed to implement the EC Directive on product liability. The CPA 1987 provides a means of redress for a consumer against the manufacturer of a product for injury caused by that product. Although a consumer would have had an action against the manufacturer in negligence (*Donoghue v Stevenson* (1932)), this would involve establishing fault; the CPA 1987 does not require such evidence in order to establish liability.

In order to succeed in a claim, the plaintiff must show that:

- the product contained a defect;
- the plaintiff suffered damage;
- the damage was caused by the defect;
- the defendant was a producer, own brander, or importer of the product.

A producer of a product is defined as including the manufacturer of a finished product or of a component; any person who won or abstracted the product; where goods are not manufactured or abstracted, any person responsible for an industrial or other process to which any essential characteristic of the product is attributable, for example, a person who processes agricultural produce (s 1(2)(a)).

Although a supplier of a defective product does not have primary liability, the supplier will be liable if he or she fails to identify the producer or importer when requested to do so (s 2(2)).

A person may be deemed to be a producer of a defective product if that person claims to be a producer by putting his name or trade mark on the product.

7.3.1 Defective product

A product will be defective within the meaning of s 3 of the CPA if the safety of the product is not such as persons generally are entitled to expect, taking all circumstances into account, including the marketing of the product, the presentation of the product including instructions and warnings, the use to which it might reasonably be expected to be put, and the time when it was supplied, that is, the state of the art at the time of supply.

A product is anything which has undergone an industrial process and it must be moveable.

7.3.2 Defences

Although the CPA 1987 imposes strict liability, there are a number of defences provided by s 4.

Any person has a defence if it can be shown that:

- the defect is attributable to compliance with a domestic or EC enactment;
- the person was not at any time the supplier of the product;
- the supply was not in the course of business;
- the defect did not exist in the product at the time it was supplied;
- the state of scientific and technical knowledge at the relevant time was not such that the producer might be expected to have discovered the defect;
- the defect was in a product in which the product in question had been comprised and was wholly attributable to the design of the subsequent product;
- more than 10 years has elapsed since the product was first supplied.

The development risks defence allows the producer to show that the defect was not discoverable at the time of supplying the product. What is required of a producer for this defence to operate is an area of contention awaiting clarification by the courts. Should the producer make sure he or she is aware of all available knowledge related to the product and then ensure it is applied or will it suffice to do limited research bearing in mind the cost of development and the potentially small risk to the consumer?

7.3.3   Liability cannot be excluded or limited (s 7)

Any person injured by the product can claim; this includes personal injury or damage to private property, the latter cannot be brought where the amount claimed is less than £275. No claim can be made for pure economic loss or for damage to the product itself.

There is a three year limitation period for claims, the date of which runs from the date of the injury. Where the damage is not apparent, the date runs from the time the plaintiff knew or could reasonably have known of the claim.

7.4   Consumer safety

The CPA 1987 also provides protection for the public from unsafe consumer goods. This part of the statute imposes criminal liability rather than civil liability. It enables the Secretary of State to make safety regulations, which has been done with respect to certain products such flammable materials in furniture, children's nightclothes, etc.

It creates a criminal offence of supplying consumer goods which are not reasonably safe (s 10). It allows the Secretary of State to serve a prohibition notice on a supplier, prohibiting him from supplying goods which are unsafe or a notice to warn which requires the supplier to publish warnings about the unsafe goods.

A consumer may have a civil action for breach of statutory duty against the supplier of unsafe goods under this part of CPA 1987.

In addition to the CPA 1987, the General Product Safety Regulations (GPSR) 1994 impose safety requirements on producers and distributors of products. The GPSR 1994 arose out of EC Directive 92/59 which requires Member States to introduce general product safety requirements and develop and implement procedures for the notification and exchange of information relating to dangerous products. The new Regulations apply to all manufacturers and producers within the EC. If the manufacturer/producer does not have a base within the EC, the onus will fall on the distributor/importer (reg 2). The main requirement which in effect displaces s 10 of the CPA 1987 states that no producer shall place a product on the market unless the product is a safe product (reg 7).

The GPSR 1994 apply to any product intended for, or likely to be used by, consumers. Product has a wider meaning than that found in the CPA 1987, for example, tobacco was specifically excluded from the CPA but is covered by the GPSR 1994.

A safe product is further defined as:

> ... any product which, under normal or reasonably foreseeable conditions of use, including duration, does not present any risk or only the minimum risks compatible with the products use, considered as acceptable and consistent with

a high level of protection for the safety and health of persons, taking into account in particular:

- the characteristics of the product, including its composition, packaging, instructions for assembly and maintenance;

- the effect on other products, where it is reasonably foreseeable that it will be used with other products;

- the presentation of the product, the labelling, any instructions for its use and disposal and any other indication or information provided by the producer; and,

- the categories of consumers at risk when using the product, in particular children.

Clearly, the packaging itself or misleading or inadequate instructions can render a product unsafe and result in a breach of the Regulations.

Where the producer or distributor is accused of an offence under the GPSR 1994, the due diligence defence may be raised (reg 14), that is, it can be shown that all reasonable steps were taken and all due diligence was exercised to avoid committing the offence.

On conviction of an offence under the GPSR, the penalty may either be imprisonment for up to three months and/or a fine.

7.4.1 Misleading indications about price

The CPA 1987 (s 20) provides that a person is guilty of an offence if, in the course of a business, consumers are given a misleading indication as to the price at which any goods, services, accommodation or facilities are available. Evidence of an offence is provided by compliance or non-compliance with the Code of Practice published by the Office of Fair Trading.

A number of defences are provided. The defendant must prove that all reasonable precautions were taken and exercised all due diligence to avoid the commission of an offence; or that he or she was an innocent publisher/advertiser who was unaware and who had no ground for suspecting that the advertisement contained a misleading price indication.

7.5 Trade Descriptions Act (TDA) 1968

The Trade Descriptions Act (TDA) 1968 provides criminal sanctions for offences relating to the sale of goods, involving the use of false or misleading descriptions as well as misleading statements about services. It also provides facilities for the court to make a compensation order for the consumer who has suffered loss.

Under the TDA 1968, it is a criminal offence to apply, in the course of a trade or business, a false description to goods or to sell goods where such a description is applied. Private sales are outside the remit of the TDA 1968. The professions also fall within the scope of the TDA 1968. For example, in *Roberts v Leonard* (1995), a veterinary surgeon was held to be carrying on a trade or business. False means false to a material degree, therefore, in effect, any deviation from the description must be significant. The meaning of trade description is indicated in s 2(1) as including statements about quantity, size, method of manufacture, fitness for purpose, other physical characteristics, testing and the results of such tests, approvals by any person, place, date and name of manufacturer, producer or processor and any history, including ownership and use.

A watch described by the maker as a divers watch and inscribed waterproof, filled with water and stopped on its first immersion. The defendant was found guilty of a breach of s 1 of the TDA 1968 in supplying goods to which a false description had been applied by another person (*Sherratt v Geralds the American Jewellers Ltd* (1970)).

The TDA 1968 not only makes it unlawful for the trader to apply a false trade description to goods but extends to supplying goods, exposing goods for supply or having goods in his possession for the purposes of supply (s 6). In *Yugo Tours Ltd v Wadsley* (1988), a tour operator advertised a holiday on board a three-masted schooner under full sail and included a photograph. It was held that the tour operator was in breach of the TDA 1968 as customers having relied on the brochure to book their holiday, then found themselves on a two-masted schooner without sails.

A person may be guilty of an offence even where the description is technically correct where it is likely to mislead a customer without specialist knowledge, although this is subject to the general provision that the description must be false or misleading to a material degree. For example, to describe a car as beautiful when it is, may be a false description to a material degree (*Robertson v Dicicco* (1972)).

In *Lewin v Rothersthorpe Road Garage* (1984), the defendant raised the s 24 defence by establishing that he was a member of the Motor Agents Association and had adopted the code of practice drawn up by the Association as approved by the Office of Fair Trading. This was sufficient for the court to accept that the defendant had taken reasonable precautions to avoid commission of an offence by his employee.

The TDA 1968 provides two defences (s 24):

- that the misdescription was due to a mistake or to reliance on information supplied by a third party or to the act or default of a third party or some other cause beyond the control of the defendant;

- that all reasonable precautions were taken and due diligence exercised to avoid the commission of an offence.

It is also open to a trader who is supplying goods to issue a disclaimer. This will provide a defence as long as it is sufficiently bold to equal that of the description supplied (*Norman v Bennett* (1974)). Such a disclaimer is not available where the trader is actually applying the trade description himself (see *Newham LBC v Singh* (1988)).

7.6 Consumer credit

As the developed market economy has led to an increase in the use of credit, the need for greater control and more protection for the individual borrower has become of paramount importance. The Consumer Credit Act (CCA) 1974 attempts to rectify, and regulate, the imbalance in the bargaining position of the respective parties.

The Consumer Credit Act (CCA) 1974 was passed following the *Report of the Committee on Consumer Credit* (Cmnd No 4569, 1971) (Crowther Committee Report). It offered greater protection to persons buying on credit, removing the distinction between purchases on credit, hire purchase and cash. It also repealed and replaced, for the most part, the Hire Purchase Act 1965. A wide variety of transactions are now within the remit of the CCA 1974, for example, loans, credit card agreements, bank overdrafts, credit sale agreements, hire purchase agreements, etc, which are the most common form of credit agreement.

The CCA 1974 only applies to regulated agreements. Fortunately, the CCA 1974 provides a clear definition of what amounts to such an agreement.

It also introduced a wide range of terminology which needs to be explained before other aspects of the legislation can be considered.

7.6.1 The terminology

Creditor   The person/body who supplies the credit/finance.

Debtor   The customer, borrower/the person who is obliged to repay the finance.

Credit   Includes a cash loan or any other form of financial accommodation (s 9(1)).

The definition of credit is extremely wide in a bid to encompass all existing forms of consumer credit as well as any new ones. Credit is confined to the principal sum advanced. As a result, any charge for credit should be ignored in determining whether the agreement falls within the current statutory limit. This prevents circumvention of the CCA 1974 by, for example, credit brokers, who may include their fees as part of the total charge for credit and as a result appear to exceed the £15,000 limit. However, when such charges are deducted, if the sum falls below £15,000 it will be regulated by the Act. In *Huntpast Ltd v Leadbetter* (1993), the first premium of an insurance policy on mortgaged property subject to the agreement was deducted from the brokers fee which at the time did not form part of the total charge for credit. It was held by the Court of Appeal that the insurance premium was part of the total charge for credit, as a result when the premium was deducted from the sum advanced, the agreement fell within the financial limit of £15,000 or less.

First, a regulated consumer credit agreement is defined as:

> ... an agreement by which the creditor provides an individual (the debtor) with credit not exceeding a specified figure (at present £15,000). Obviously, where the debtor is a company or other body corporate an agreement is not a consumer credit agreement [s 8].

However, a partnership is to be regarded as an individual. Secondly, a regulated consumer hire agreement is defined as:

> ... an agreement made between a person and the hirer under which goods are hired, leased bailed which is capable of lasting more than three months and does not require the hirer to make payments exceeding £15,000 [s 15].

Credit-token agreements may also be regulated agreements within s 14 of the CCA 1974. A credit-token is defined as a card, check, voucher, coupon, stamp, form, booklet or other document or thing given to an individual by a person carrying on a consumer credit business, who undertakes:

- that on the production of it ... he or she will supply cash, goods and services on credit; or

- that where, on production of it to a third party ... the third party supplies, cash, goods and services, he or she will pay the third party for them ... in return for payment to him or her by the individual.

This definition covers in-house credit cards where the creditor is also the supplier as well as situations where the issuer is a separate party who undertakes to pay the supplier. It should be noted that cheque guarantee cards are outside the definition as was decided in *Metropolitan Police Commissioner v Charles* (1977) as the bank is merely guaranteeing to honour the cheque. However where the card holder is authorised to obtain credit on the card, a regulated agreement is formed.

Debtor-creditor-supplier agreements

Debtor-creditor-supplier agreements are restricted use consumer credit agreements where the creditor and supplier are either the same person, for example, retailer financing purchase by customer, or there are pre-existing arrangements between the creditor and supplier, for example, credit card transactions; in addition, there can be unrestricted use debtor-creditor-supplier agreements where the creditor has pre-existing arrangements between himself and the supplier, with a view to financing transactions between the debtor and the supplier.

In debtor-credit-supplier agreements, the debtor will have an action against the creditor for any misrepresentation or breach of contract on the part of the supplier (s 75 of the CCA 1974). Whilst in theory this appears to place quite a burden on the creditor, if the debtor pursues a claim against the creditor, the creditor can claim an indemnity from the supplier presuming he or she is still in existence. There are limitations on the use of s 75 in that it does nor apply to a non-commercial agreement, not does it apply to a claim in respect of any item where the cash price does not exceed £100 or is more than £30,000. However, in these circumstances, the debtor could still take action against the supplier.

The application of s 75 has not proved to be straightforward, particularly where credit card holders have used the section to pursue claims against banks. First, it does not apply to credit card agreements made before 1 July 1977; secondly, where there is a main card holder and a second authorised user, only the main card holder has the right to use s 75 which means that, if defective goods are purchased by the second user, s 75 may not operate and, thirdly, where the card has been used abroad, the banks are keen to avoid liability on the basis that the law of the country in which the purchase is made should apply.

Debtor-creditor agreements

Any agreement not falling within the above category are debtor-creditor agreements. In some circumstances where an agreement falls within more than one category as defined by the CCA 1974, it will be known as a multiple agreement and each divisible part will be regulated accordingly (s 18(1)(a)). The distinction between this type of consumer credit agreement and a debtor-creditor-supplier agreement is based on the existence of a business connection between the creditor and supplier which may result in both the creditor and supplier being liable to the debtor for defects in the goods.

Restricted-use credit agreement

A restricted-use credit agreement is an agreement whereby the debtor has no control over the use to which the credit is put.

Unrestricted-use credit agreement

An unrestricted-use credit agreement is an agreement whereby the debtor has control over the use of the finance even where the contract itself states that the money must be used for a specific purpose (s 11(3) of the CCA 1974).

Fixed-sum credit

Fixed-sum credit is where the actual amount of the loan is fixed from the start of the agreement subject to the statutory limit for regulated agreements. The relevant figure is the actual amount of the sum being loaned excluding the amount payable as interest or deposit. It is irrelevant that it may be repaid or received by instalments.

Running-account credit

Running-account credit is where credit is fixed up to an agreed limit, for example, credit card agreements, bank overdrafts. Again such agreements will be regulated agreements within the CCA 1974 as long as the credit limit does not exceed the current specified figure (s 10).

Regulated agreements defined

Again an agreement where the hirer is a body corporate is outside the CCA 1974 because the hirer must be an individual. Furthermore, a hire purchase agreement is not within the definition since this type of agreement falls within the definition of a consumer credit agreement.

Small agreement

A small agreement is either a regulated consumer credit agreement or a regulated consumer hire agreement where, with respect to the former, the amount of credit does not exceed £50 and with respect to the latter, the hire/rental charge does not exceed £50. The rules for determining whether the credit exceeds the limit are explained above by reference to fixed-sum and running-account credit.

Small agreements are exempt from some but not all of the provisions of the CCA 1974. However the main provisions contained in Pt IV relating to seeking business, the requirement on the creditor to supply information on request and the provisions restricting remedies on default will apply.

Exempt agreements

Even though agreements may fall with the definitions provided by the CCA 1974, they may be exempt by virtue of s 16. For example, secured loans relating to the purchase of land or dwellings entered into by local authorities are generally exempt, as are similar loans provided by building societies and other authorised institutions, such as banks. The exemption only applies to loans for the original purpose and therefore such transactions as second mortgages are not exempt. The Office of Fair Trading keep regular checks on the exempt categories and as with all exempt agreements the Exempt Agreements Order 1989 (SI 1989/869) must be satisfied as to the criteria laid down.

Other agreements are exempted because of the nature of the agreement. For example fixed sum debtor-creditor-supplier agreements which involve no more than four payments in 12 months are specifically exempted. The CCA

1974 and the Order also exempt three categories of low-cost credit agreement; and certain agreements that involve a connection with a non-UK country; for example, where the agreement is in connection with trade in goods and services between the UK and a non-UK country or within a country or between countries outside the UK or where the agreement is between a creditor listed in Part IV, such as the Federal Credit Union and a member of the US armed forces not habitually resident in the UK.

Non-commercial agreements are also exempt from some of the provisions of the CCA 1974. Such agreements are made by a creditor not in the course of a business carried on by him (s 189(1)), even where providing credit is purely ancillary to the main business, it will not fall within the definition of a non-commercial agreement. In practical terms, the granting of credit would have to be on an occasional basis for it to amount to a non-commercial agreement (*Hare v Schurek* (1993)). Non-commercial agreements are exempt from formal documentary requirements, cancellation rights, cooling-off periods, the provisions relating to the duty to supply information, licensing provisions, etc.

Linked transactions

This is an agreement entered into by the debtor with the creditor or a third party in relation to the regulated agreement but which does not form any part of the regulated agreement. Linked transactions take three forms:

• *Compulsory*

  That is, it has to be entered into as part of the principal agreement, for example, a maintenance agreement on the purchase of a cooker.

• *Financial*

  Where the agreement is a debitor-creditor-supplier agreement and the transaction is financed by the principal agreement, for example, a credit card transaction.

• *Suggested linked transaction*

  For example, where the debtor or the creditor is induced to enter the principal loan agreement.

The significance of a linked transaction is that they are affected by action taken in respect of the principal agreement. For example, the cancellation of the principal agreement under s 69 or early settlement of the principal agreement will discharge the linked transaction.

7.6.2 Licensing

Businesses which provide facilities for regulated agreements must be licensed by the Office of Fair Trading. These include not only businesses where their main activity is the supply of credit, but also businesses where credit is ancillary to its main activity, for example, debt-collecting, debt-counselling, credit reference agencies, credit brokerage. If the licence is refused, then an appeal may be made to the Secretary of State for Trade and Industry. Unlicensed trading is an offence under the CCA 1974 (s 39) and the unlicensed trader will have no legal means of enforcing his agreement (s 40). In addition, licences may be withdrawn, varied or suspended.

The licensing provisions do not apply to local authorities or to businesses which only provide credit in excess of £15,000 or provide credit only to companies.

There are two types of licence which may be issued by the Office of Fair Trading: a standard licence which is granted to a named individual for specific activities and a group licence which is granted to an identifiable group if the Office of Fair Trading feels that it is in the public interest to do so. Standard licences last for a period of five years; group licences for 15 years.

The issue of licences is subject to specific criteria which if met must result in the licence being granted, that is, there is no discretion to refuse. Applicants must satisfy the Director General as to their fitness to be engaged in a licensed activity. The Director General will take into account convictions for fraud, theft, criminal offenses under consumer law, such as breaches of the Trade Descriptions Act 1968. He will also ensure that the applicant is not applying to trade under a name which is misleading and in these circumstances the Director General has the power to reject such names. In *Hunter-Jaap v Hampshire Credit Consultants Ltd* (1986), it was held that a trader may be prevented from using a name (even where it is his own name) which, with intent to deceive, might mislead the public into thinking that it is someone else's business. The fact that a trader has a valid licence in that name is no defence to an action in damages for passing-off.

A register is kept of all licence applications, licences granted, refused and revoked. The register is open to inspection for a fee.

Trading without a licence may result on conviction of a fine of up to £5,000 and/or two years imprisonment, as may a conviction for trading under a different name to that on a licence (s 167).

7.6.3 Advertising and canvassing

The Consumer Credit (Advertisements) Regulations 1980 provide for control over the form and content of advertisements for credit. The spirit of the regulations is that any advertisement should contain a fair and reasonably comprehensive indication of the nature of the credit and hire facilities offered and their true cost or, at the very least, indicate that such information is available. Failure to comply with the Regulations is a criminal offence.

Additionally, it is an offence to advertise goods or services on credit where they are not available for cash (s 45).

Further offences include sending someone under the age of 18 years a document inviting him to seek information about credit or to obtain credit (s 50); issuing an unsolicited credit-token other than as a renewal or replacement; infringing regulations as to the content and form of a quotation of credit terms; such quotations must include prominent reference to the annual percentage rate (APR) (s 52); failing to comply with regulations as to information to be displayed at the premises of credit businesses (s 53).

Specific exemptions from the regulation of advertising are provided in reg 43(5) of the Consumer Credit (Exempt Advertisements) Order 1985 (SI 1985/621).

An offence against the advertising provisions does not in itself affect the validity or enforceability of an agreement (s 170).

Specific offences have also been created concerning canvassing debtor-creditor agreements off trade premises; this is illegal unless the canvasser is responding to a written request (s 49). However, it is not unlawful to canvass debtor-creditor-supplier agreements provided that the creditor has a licence to trade in this manner. Note that canvassing involves making oral representations about the agreements, that is, trying to verbally persuade people to enter into the agreements by making comments about it.

7.6.4 Form of the regulated agreement

There are certain rules affecting regulated agreements which if they are not complied with prevent the creditor or owner from enforcing the agreement (ss 60–65):

- the terms of the agreement must be in writing and must be legible (s 61);

- the cash price of the goods must be stated in the agreement;

- the agreement must provide for payment of equal instalments at equal intervals and must include reference to the method of payment;

- the agreement must include a description of the goods sufficient to identify them;

- the agreement must contain certain statutory notices for example, rights to terminate or cancel the agreement where that is applicable (s 64), plus rights over protected goods;

- there are certain regulations about the written format of the agreement, for example, it must be typewritten and the hirer/debtor must sign in a box outlined in red which has a printed warning that the hirer/debtor must only sign this if he intends to be legally bound by it; the creditor/owner must also sign the agreement. Contravention of these provisions results in an agreement becoming unenforceable.

The hirer/debtor is entitled to copies of the agreement. If the creditor or finance company signs at the same time as the hirer/debtor, then the hirer/debtor must receive a copy immediately (s 62). If, however, there is a time lag and the dealer/supplier has to send the forms off to a finance company for agreement, then the hirer/debtor must receive:

• a copy of his offer on the spot (known as the first statutory copy);

• a subsequent copy of the concluded agreement within seven days (known as the second statutory copy (s 63)).

This is to ensure that debtors/hirers have an opportunity to consider the terms and conditions of the proposed agreement at the offer stage and are informed of their rights to withdraw from or cancel agreements as well as being supplied with copies of the final agreement so that they are fully conversant with their rights, liabilities and obligations.

In *National Guardian Mortgage Corp v Wilkes* (1993), the plaintiff failed to send an advance copy of a prospective regulated secured agreement to a customer and had, therefore, failed to give the defendant the requisite seven days under s 58 before requesting signature of the agreement. This led to the defendant signing an agreement at a high APR. It was held that the agreement could be enforced, but only on the condition that the defendant be compensated under s 127 for the prejudice caused by the non-compliance. The defendant should have had the time and therefore the opportunity to obtain a loan at a lower rate of interest.

7.6.5 Breach of the regulations relating to formation

All copies must comply with the regulations as to form and content. Any breach will render the agreement improperly executed so that, in effect, it is unenforceable except through a court order. The courts can grant an enforcement order and, in so doing, can vary the terms of the original agreement. However, the courts tend not to do this if the agreement does not comply with the regulations or the correct notices were not served or copies given. The correct copies must be given to the hirer or debtor before the court proceedings. If the agreement does not give notice of cancellation rights where they are appropriate, the courts will not issue an enforcement order.

7.6.6 Cancellation

If the agreement is signed off trade premises (for example, on the front doorstep), it is cancellable and there must be a notice in the agreement about the right of cancellation and how it can be exercised, including the names and addresses of persons to whom cancellation can be sent (ss 67–73). The purpose of these requirements is to allow the customer a cooling off period so that he has an opportunity to think about whether he actually wants to enter into the transaction. An essential element must be personal contact between the debtor/hirer and the salesman including antecedent negotiations which include oral representations made by the creditor or owner in the presence of the customer.

The cooling off period commences when the customer signs the agreement and lasts until the fifth clear day after he receives the second copy (s 68). To cancel the agreement, the customer must give written notice within this period to the creditor/owner or dealer.

Where the agreement is a debtor-creditor-supplier agreement for restricted-use credit or a consumer hire agreement, the customer is entitled to recover any payment he has made. He must, however, return the goods although this allows him to await collection of the goods by the creditor/owner/dealer (s 72). He must take reasonable care of the goods for 21 days after serving the notice cancelling the agreement.

Where the agreement is a debtor-creditor agreement for unrestricted-use credit, the debtor must repay any credit received with interest, although he does not have to pay interest on credit which he repays within one month of cancellation (s 71).

In addition, the Consumer Protection (Cancellation of Contracts concluded away from Business Premises) Regulations 1987 provide that any agreement by a consumer to buy goods or services from a trader during an unsolicited visit to their home or place of work shall be subject to a seven day cooling off period, during which agreements covered by the Regulations can be cancelled without any penalty to the consumer.

Effect of cancellation

The effect of cancellation is as follows:

- the agreement is erased and there is no liability under it;

- all sums cease to be payable and all sums paid out are recoverable;

- the hirer is not obliged to return the goods but must hand them over if the owner calls at a reasonable time;

- the hirer has a duty to take care of the goods for 21 days after notice of cancellation;

- the hirer has a lien on the goods for the repayment of sums paid under the agreement;

- any part-exchange goods can be recovered within 10 days or a part-exchange allowance must be given to the hirer.

Section 94 of the CCA 1974 provides for early settlement of the debt. In these circumstances, the debtor must give written notice of the intention to the creditor and provide full payment of the sums due under the agreement. A rebate is then calculated in accordance with the Consumer Credit (Rebate on Early Settlement) Regulations 1983.

7.6.7 Default

Default occurs where the debtor or hirer fails to meet the repayments. The goods would normally be repossessed. This is, however, subject to the rules for protected goods.

Protected goods

Where there is a hire purchase or conditional sale agreement, the hirer or debtor is protected from repossession of the goods after he has paid one third or more of the price of the goods. Section 90 of the CCA 1974 specifies three requirements for the goods to become protected goods:

- a debtor is in breach of a regulated hire purchase or conditional sale agreement relating to the goods;

- the debtor has paid to the creditor one third or more of the total price of the goods;

- the property in the goods remains with the creditor.

Under s 90, the owner of the goods which are protected (normally, the finance company) cannot enforce his right to repossess the goods, other than by action in the courts. This normally means obtaining a court order even though the creditor may wish to terminate the agreement because of the hirers default.

This section does not apply if the hirer wishes to terminate the agreement himself and probably does not apply if the hirer has disposed of or abandoned the goods.

In *Bentinck Ltd v Cromwell Engineering* (1971), a car was the subject of a hire purchase agreement. The car was involved in an accident. The hirer took the car to a garage for repair; he then failed to pay any more hire purchase instalments or to collect the car. The finance company traced the car and repossessed it. They sold the car and sought to recover depreciation costs from the hirer. He claimed that they had repossessed the car without consent. It was held that when a hirer has abandoned goods and his rights to them show that he no longer has any interest in them, then the owner has a right to repossess even if the goods had been protected goods. The defendants were found to be liable for damages.

Effect of repossession without a court order

If the owner does try to repossess the goods without a court order after the goods have become protected, the following will ensue:

- the hire purchase agreement is terminated;

- the hirers responsibility is at an end and he can claim back anything he has paid under the agreement;

- any guarantor/indemnifier is released from liability and entitled to recover any security given.

Note: a guarantor is someone who guarantees that the creditor will receive payment due to him or her from the hirer/debtor. It is a secondary responsibility based solely on the responsibility of the hirer to pay. An indemnity is a promise to pay the creditor for any loss suffered on the contract and is a primary responsibility to indemnify loss suffered by the creditor as a result of his contract with the hirer. Thus, an indemnity may have to be paid when the hirer could avoid responsibility, whereas a guarantor can only be asked to pay where the hirer should have paid.

In *Capital Finance Co Ltd v Bray* (1964), Bray acquired a car under a hire purchase agreement. He fell behind with the repayments and an agent of the finance company repossessed the car without obtaining Bray's consent or a court order. The finance company realised it had made a mistake and the car was duly returned to Bray. Unfortunately, Bray continued to default on the repayments and the company sued for repossession. It was held, on granting a repossession order, that Bray was entitled to recover all the money he had previously paid to the finance company.

Action to recover possession of protected goods

The CCA 1974 gives the county court exclusive jurisdiction over all actions relating to hire purchase contracts within the Act, that is, personal credit agreements under £15,000. All parties concerned including any guarantor or indemnifier must be made party to the court action and the court can make various orders:

- *Return order*

  The hirer is asked to return the goods to the owner/creditor. If the hirer fails to return the goods, the only fall-back position is to send in the bailiffs.

- *Suspended return order*

  This is awarded when the hirer has a reasonable excuse for default for example, redundancy or ill health. The court can vary the terms of the original agreement to enable the hirer to meet his obligations. It can reduce the amount of each instalment and extend the period of time to pay if this is deemed necessary. These are known as time orders. The effect of a suspended order can therefore be summarised as follows:

  (a) the agreement continues but with a variation in terms;

  (b) the owner cannot claim extra interest for the longer period of time;

(c) if the hirer breaks any terms as specified in the agreement it is possible for the court to make an order that the creditor can repossess without going back to court that is, implement the suspended order;

(d) the court can vary the time order upon application from the hirer or the owner, if the hirers financial circumstances get better or worse;

(e) the hirer may avoid the suspended order by paying off the unpaid balance and becoming the owner of the goods.

- *Transfer order*

This order gives part of the goods back to the owner and allows the hirer to retain part of the goods and become owner of them. The hire purchase agreement is at an end.

Notice of default

Whenever the owner/creditor on the default of the hirer/debtor wishes to terminate the agreement, repossess the goods, etc, he must serve a default notice (s 87). The notice must give the hirer/debtor seven days to pay or remedy the default, state the total amount due plus the consequences of non-payment that is, termination and how the breach can be rectified if at all possible. If the hirer/debtor pays in time, the contract will continue as if there has been no default. Notices of default must be issued whenever the debtor/hirer is in breach of any term of the agreement, before the agreement can be terminated.

Default notices must be in the form prescribed by the Consumer Credit (Enforcement, Default and Termination) Regulations 1983. A breach of s 87 resulting in goods being seized by the creditor, etc, may allow the debtor to sue for damages, recover the goods or obtain an injunction to prevent unlawful enforcement.

Where a default notice is complied with, the creditor will not be able to enforce the agreement the breach is treated as not having occurred.

Time order

The debtor/hirer, having been served with a default notice or in the event of any other action being taken to enforce a regulated agreement, may apply to the court for a time order allowing him extra time to make payments or rectify the breach. Such orders can be varied, extended or revoked by the court (s 129 of the CCA 1974).

The terms of a time order will depend on the debtor's circumstances. The court will also consider what is just bearing in mind the creditors position and the debtors future prospects. During the period of the time order, the creditor cannot take any action to terminate the agreement, recover possession of any land or goods or remove or vary any rights of the debtor (s 130). Following the decision in *Southern District Finance v Barnes* (1995), where a default notice has been served, the court will have the power under s 129 to rewrite the agreement resulting in the rescheduling of the whole of the outstanding balance under the loan and if necessary, where it is just, vary the rate of interest.

The dealer as agent of the finance company

The dealer/supplier is often regarded by statute as the agent of the finance company. He or she is agent in the following circumstances:

- for notice of cancellation;
- to receive the goods;
- to receive notice of withdrawal of offers;
- to receive notice of the rescission of the contract;
- to receive notice of termination.

Also, by virtue of s 56(2) of the CCA 1974, the dealer is to be treated as the agent of the creditor in antecedent negotiations.

Termination of a regulated agreement

Where there is a regulated hire purchase or conditional sale agreement, the debtor can terminate at any time provided notice is given to the finance company or its agent. He or she may be required to pay up to 50% of the price of the goods (or less if specified in the contract) as well as all sums due. The debtor will be liable for any damage caused by failure to take reasonable care of the goods (ss 99–100 of the CCA 1974).

The creditor cannot terminate for any breach of contract without serving a seven day notice of default (above).

A consumer credit agreement may contain an acceleration clause providing for immediate payment of the whole of the outstanding balance on default of payment. This is valid, provided it is not capable of being interpreted as a penalty clause. (*Note*: this can be achieved by providing for an appropriate rebate on early payment.) Such an acceleration clause cannot be operated without at least seven days notice in writing.

It should also be noted that s 101 of the CCA 1974 provides for termination in consumer hire agreements. The hirer must give written notice which is subject to a minimum period. The agreement must have run for at least 18 months before the right to terminate can operate.

Extortionate credit bargains

The CCA 1974 gives the court power to reopen a credit agreement and take action if it finds that a credit agreement is extortionate (ss 137–40). A bargain is defined as extortionate when payments imposed on the debtor are grossly exorbitant or grossly contravene the ordinary principles of fair dealing. The court will take into account the prevailing interest, the age, capacity and experience of the hirer/debtor. In considering whether the agreement is extortionate, the courts must also consider the degree of risk accepted by the creditor and the nature and value of the security. The court can rewrite the agreement or set aside the contract. They can, however, seem to be reluctant to intervene on some occasions.

In *Ketley v Scott* (1981), Mr Scott had negotiated a loan for which he was paying interest at the rate of 48% per annum. He had an overdraft at the bank and the loan was negotiated in a hurry without full inquiries being made. He defaulted on the loan and the plaintiffs sued him. Mr Scott claimed the interest rate was extortionate. It was held that there was a high degree of risk involved in the loaning of money and therefore the interest charged was not disproportionately high.

Lawyers have speculated that the courts would be reluctant to intervene using this section of the CCA 1974. Perhaps the *caveat emptor* principle has left its mark on the judiciary.

Credit reference agencies

To reflect the growth in the number of credit reference agencies and to provide protection and redress for those persons who are incorrectly rated as to their creditworthiness, ss 157–59 allow someone who has been refused credit to request the name and address of the credit reference agency from the creditor/owner. The customer is then entitled to make a written request to the agency for a copy of his file (subject to a small fee). The customer can then take the necessary steps to have the file amended if necessary (s 159).

It should be noted that a report by the Director General of Fair Trading *Consumer Credit Deregulation* (a review of the scope and operation of the Consumer Credit Act 1974) has recommended a number of amendments to the current system of regulation, including increasing the upper limit for regulated agreements, simplifying the regulations relating to advertising, etc.

CONSUMER PROTECTION

Sale of goods

Although widespread in its general application, the Sale of Goods Act (SoGA) 1979 specifically protects consumers by ensuring that certain terms are to be included in consumer contracts as a matter of implication.

Implied terms

The most important implied terms are conditions. A condition is a fundamental term of the contract, any breach of which will allow the injured party to treat the contract as repudiated. This means that the parties are returned to their original positions

A warranty is a lesser term of the contract and is not seen as being as important as a condition. A breach of warranty will allow the buyer to claim damages, but not to reject the goods.

Title (s 12)

There is an implied condition that the seller has the right to sell the goods (*Niblett Ltd v Confectioners Materials Co* (1921)); and an implied warranty of quiet possession and that the goods are free from any charge or encumbrance (*Microbeads AC v Vinhurst Road Markings* (1975)).

The rule *nemo dat quod non habet* means that a person cannot give what he or she has not got, so that, in general, ownership is protected. The general rule is that, where goods are sold by a person who is not the owner, the buyer acquires no better title than the seller (s 21 of the SoGA 1979). However, there are exceptions.

Description (s 13)

There is an implied condition that goods will correspond with the description applied to them:

- *Beale v Taylor* (1967);
- *Ashington Piggeries v Christopher Hill Ltd* (1972);
- *Re Moore and Co and Landauer and Co* (1921).

Satisfactory quality (s 14(2))

There is an implied condition that goods shall be of satisfactory quality as defined (s 14(2A)), subject to defects specifically brought to the buyers attention and defects revealed by examination:

- *Rogers v Parish (Scarborough) Ltd* (1987);
- *Kendall (Henry) and Sons v William Lillico and Sons Ltd* (1968);
- *Brown and Sons Ltd v Craiks Ltd* (1970).

Fitness for the purpose (s 14(3))

There is an implied condition in a contract for the sale of goods that the goods supplied are reasonably fit for any purpose expressly or impliedly made known to the seller:

- *Griffiths v Peter Conway Ltd* (1939).

Sale by sample (s 15)

There is an implied condition that, where goods are sold by sample, they will comply with that sample:

- *E and S Ruben Ltd v Faire Bros and Co Ltd* (1949).

Exclusion of liability for breach of the implied terms

The effect of exclusion clauses on the operation of the SoGA 1979 is limited not only by the Act itself, but also by UCTA 1977. The limitations are as follows:

- Section 12 of the SoGA cannot be excluded.
- Section 13–15 of the SoGA cannot be excluded in consumer sales.

- Sections 13–15 of the SoGA can only be excluded in non-consumer sales if the test of reasonableness is satisfied.

- Liability for death or personal injury cannot be excluded (UCTA 1977).

- Any other loss can only be excluded subject to the test of reasonableness.

- Any terms may now be subject to the Unfair Terms in Consumer Contract Regulations 1999.

Supply of Goods and Services Act 1982

The SGSA 1982 provides protection in respect of agreements which do not fulfil the definition of the SoGA 1979 but under which goods are supplied, usually along with a service. The SGSA 1982 itself mirrors the SoGA 1979 in that it implies conditions with respect to goods supplied.

Furthermore, the SSGA 1982 provides protection for the victims of poor quality workmanship, including the time it takes to provide services and the price for such services. The SSGA 1982 applies to all contracts where a person agrees to carry out a service in the course of a business. The implied terms as to services can be found in ss 13–15.

Product liability

The CPA 1987 provides a means of redress for a consumer against the manufacturer of a product for injury caused by that product. The CPA 1987 does not require evidence of fault in order to establish liability. All that has to be shown is:

- the product contained a defect;

- the plaintiff suffered damage;

- the damage was caused by the defect;

- the defendant was a producer, own brander, or importer of the product.

The CPA 1987 imposes strict liability, subject to a number of defences.

Consumer safety

The CPA 1987 also provides protection for the public from unsafe consumer goods. This part of the statute imposes criminal liability rather than civil liability. It enables the Secretary of State to make safety regulations, which has been done with respect to certain products such flammable materials in furniture, children's nightclothes, etc.

In addition to the CPA 1987, the General Product Safety Regulations (GPSR) 1994 impose safety requirements on producers and distributors of products. The GPSR 1994 arose out of EC Directive 92/59 which requires Member States to introduce general product safety requirements and develop and implement procedures for the notification and exchange of information relating to dangerous products. The new Regulations apply to all manufacturers and producers within the EC.

Trade Descriptions Act 1968

The TDA 1968 provides criminal sanctions for offences relating to the sale of goods, involving the use of false or misleading descriptions as well as misleading statements about services. It also provides facilities for the court to make a compensation order for the consumer who has suffered loss.

Consumer credit

A wide variety of transactions are now within the remit of the CCA 1974, for example, loans, credit card agreements, bank overdrafts, credit sale agreements, hire purchase agreements, etc, which are the most common form of credit agreement.

The CCA 1974 only applies to regulated agreements, that is, personal credit agreements under £15,000.

Businesses which provide facilities for regulated agreements must be licensed by the Office of Fair Trading.

The Consumer Credit (Advertisements) Regulations 1980 provide for control over the form and content of advertisements for credit. The spirit of the regulations is that any advertisement should contain a fair and reasonably comprehensive indication of the nature of the credit and hire facilities offered and their true cost or, at the very least, indicate that such information is available. Failure to comply with the Regulations is a criminal offence.

There are certain rules affecting regulated agreements which if they are not complied with prevent the creditor or owner from enforcing the agreement (ss 60–65).

Failure to comply with the rules will render the agreement improperly executed so that, in effect, it is unenforceable except through a court order.

The CCA 1974 gives the court power to reopen a credit agreement and take action if it finds that a credit agreement is extortionate (ss 137–40). A bargain is defined as extortionate when payments imposed on the debtor are grossly exorbitant or grossly contravene the ordinary principles of fair dealing.

CHAPTER 8

THE TORT OF NEGLIGENCE

8.1 Introduction

A tort is a wrongful act against an individual, or body corporate, or their property, which gives rise to a civil action (usually for damages, although other remedies are available). It is possible, however, for the same action to provide grounds for a criminal action as well as a giving rise to a civil action. Thus, for example, assault and/or battery are torts as well as crimes, and may give rise to a civil case as well as, or in place of a criminal case. Liability in tort is based on fault, although there are exceptions, for example, the tort of *Rylands v Fletcher* (1868) in which a person may be held liable for harm resulting from the non-natural use of land, breach of statutory duty, vicarious liability. The motive of the defendant in committing the tort is generally irrelevant There are a number of torts, such as negligence, trespass, nuisance defamation, but this chapter will focus on the most important of these, negligence (the tort of employer's liability will be considered separately in 8.8).

Negligence is the most important of all the torts, not only because an understanding of it is vital to the comprehension of other torts, such as employers liability and occupier's liability, but also because it is the one tort which is constantly developing in the light of social and economic change. This can be seen by reference to product liability, professional negligence and economic loss, all of which were originally only compensated if there was in existence a valid contract; in other words, no contract, no claim. After a period of continual development in the scope and application of this tort, the signs are that the courts are beginning to be more cautious. They are aware of the economic implications on the public and private sector if they continue to extend the scope of actions in negligence. Whether this should be an issue for the courts is always open to debate, but if the courts are to be pragmatic, then they may have no choice but to be restrained in the current economic climate.

The prime object of the tort of negligence is to provide compensation for the injured person. It has also been suggested that liability in tort provides a deterrent and that negligence is no exception, that is, it helps to define what is or is not acceptable conduct and, therefore, sets the boundaries of such behaviour. Unfortunately, people rarely act by reference to the civil law and the only real deterrent is through market forces, that is, the economic impact being passed on to those who have a higher risk of causing injury. Alternative compensation systems have been considered as this would largely eradicate the need of the injured party to pursue legal action. The alternatives on offer are no fault compensation schemes (see the Pearson Commission, *Report on*

Civil Liability and Compensation for Personal Injury (Cmnd 7054, 1978)) and extending public and private insurance schemes.

8.2 Elements of the tort of negligence

There are specific elements of the tort of negligence which have to be established in the correct order if a claim by an injured party is to succeed. The burden of proof is on the claimant, to show on a balance of probabilities that the following elements exist.

8.2.1 Duty of care

A person is not automatically liable for every negligent act he or she commits. The need to establish the essentials and, in particular, duty of care sets a legal limit on who can bring an action as a duty is not owed to the world at large. The onus is on the claimant to establish that the defendant owes him a duty of care. Unless this first hurdle is crossed, no liability can arise. The test for establishing whether a duty of care exists arises out of the case of *Donoghue v Stevenson* (1932). Prior to this case, the duty of care was only owed in limited circumstances. Now, it is said that the categories of negligence are never closed, in that the law can change to take into account new circumstances and social or technical change. Where, therefore, there is unintentional damage, there is, potentially, an action in negligence.

In *Donoghue v Stevenson*, a lady went into a cafe with her friend who bought her a bottle of ginger beer. After she had drunk half from the bottle, she poured the remainder into a glass. She then saw the remains of a decomposed snail at the bottom. She suffered nervous shock. She sued the manufacturer as the snail must have got into the bottle at the manufacturer's premises since the bottle top was securely sealed when her friend bought it. It was held that a manufacturer owes a duty of care to the ultimate consumer of his goods. He or she must, therefore, exercise reasonable care to prevent injury to the consumer. The fact that there is no contractual relationship between the manufacturer and the consumer is irrelevant to this action.

The most important aspect of this case is the test laid down by Lord Atkin. He stated that:

> You must take reasonable care to avoid acts and omissions which you could reasonably foresee would be likely to injure your neighbour. Who then in law is my neighbour? ... any person so closely and directly affected by my act that I ought reasonably to have them in contemplation as being so affected when I am directing my mind to the acts and omissions which are called in question.

This test forms the basis for deciding the existence of a duty. It follows that, if a duty of care is to exist, the question for the court is somewhat hypothetical in that the court does not look at the subjective reality (that is, did you contemplate the effect on the injured party of your actions?) but looks at the situation objectively (that is should you have contemplated the effect on the injured party of your actions?). This does not require specific identity of the injured person, merely of the class of person, for example, pedestrians, children, etc.

The test in *Donoghue v Stevenson* was qualified in *Anns v Merton LBC* (1978). Lord Wilberforce in this case introduced the two stage test for establishing the existence of a duty:

(a) is there between the alleged wrongdoer and the person who has suffered damage a sufficient relationship of proximity or neighbourhood such that, in the reasonable contemplation of the former, carelessness on his part may be likely to cause damage to the latter?

(b) if (a) is answered in the affirmative, are there then any considerations which ought to negate, reduce or limit the scope of the duty or the class of persons to whom it is owed or the damages to which a breach of duty may give rise?

The first question clearly corresponds with the neighbour test in *Donoghue v Stevenson*, although it is referred to as the proximity test. The second question introduces the consideration of public policy issues which may be grounds for limiting the situations where a duty of care is found to exist. As far as new situations are concerned, the following are some of the policy arguments which, if justified, may prevent a duty of care from being actionable:

- the floodgates argument, that is, will an extension of duty to cover this situation lead to a flood of litigation?;

- will it lead to an increase in the number of fraudulent claims either against insurance companies or in the courts?;

- what are the financial or commercial consequences of extending the duty?

The impact of *Anns* resulted in the expansion of negligence as the policy reasons only acted to limit liability once a duty had been found to exist as opposed to limiting the existence of a duty. This was illustrated in the case of *Junior Books Ltd v Veitchi Co Ltd* (1983) in which the House of Lords extended the duty of care because of the close proximity between the parties in that their relationship was quasi-contractual. As a result, the defendants were found to be liable for pure economic loss resulting from their negligent actions. However, it should be noted that the decision in *Junior Books* has come to be regarded as a special case, providing a narrow exception to the rule that in general there can be no liability in negligence for pure economic loss. However, there was gradual criticism of and retraction from the approach taken by Lord Wilberforce, as can be seen in *Peabody Donation Fund v Sir Lindsay Parkinson and Co Ltd* (1984) in which the court stressed that the proximity test had to be satisfied before a duty of care could be found to exist and *Leigh and Sullivan Ltd v Aliakmon Shipping Co Ltd* (1986) (known as *The Aliakmon*) in which Lord Brandon stated that when Lord Wilberforce laid down the two stage test in *Anns* he was:

> ... dealing with the approach to the questions of existence and scope of duty of care in a novel type of factual situation which was not analogous to any factual situation in which the existence of such a duty had already been held to exist. He was not suggesting that the same approach should be adopted to the existence of a duty of care in a factual situation in which the existence of such a duty had repeatedly been held not to exist.

This further limitation was developed in *Yuen Kun Yeu v AG of Hong Kong* (1987) in which Lord Keith stated that Lord Wilberforce's approach had been elevated to a degree of importance greater than it merits and greater perhaps than its author intended. Finally, the decision in *Anns* was overruled by *Murphy v Brentwood DC* (1990) in which it was held that local authorities owed a duty of care to a building owner to avoid damage to the building which would create a danger to the health and safety of the occupants. The duty arose out of the local authority's powers to require compliance with building regulations. However, as the damage was held to be pure economic loss it was irrecoverable.

The present position, following this rapid retraction from *Anns*, appears to be that in establishing the existence of a duty of care in negligence an incremental approach must be taken.

The claimant must show that the defendant foresaw that damage would occur to the claimant, that is, there was sufficient proximity in time, space and relationship between the claimant and the defendant (see *Bourhill v Young* (1943), 8.2.2). In practical terms, in many personal injury cases, foreseeability of damage will determine proximity. The courts will then, where appropriate, consider whether it is just and reasonable to impose a duty and whether there are any policy reasons for denying or limiting the existence of a duty, for example, floodgates argument. The courts will not necessarily consider these in all cases.

The final retraction from *Anns* and support for the incremental approach was seen in *Caparo Industries plc v Dickman* (1990), which recommended application of a three stage test for establishing a duty of care. This requires consideration of the following questions:

(a) was the harm caused reasonably foreseeable?;

(b) was there a relationship of proximity between the defendant and the claimant?;

(c) in all the circumstances, is it just, fair and reasonable to impose a duty of care?

This decision has since been followed in *Marc Rich and Co AG v Bishop Rock Marine Co Ltd, The Nicholas H* (1994). The Court of Appeal in this case held that a duty of care would only be imposed if the three parts of the test expounded in *Caparo* could be satisfied. These would have to be applied irrespective of the type of loss suffered. If anything, this takes the retraction from *Anns* one step further, as in the past it could always be argued that *Anns* applied to new duty situations as opposed to all situations.

A clear application of policy reasons limiting the existence of a duty of care can be seen in *Hill v Chief Constable of West Yorkshire* (1990) in which Hill's daughter was the last victim of the Yorkshire Ripper. She alleged that the police had failed to take reasonable care in apprehending the murderer as they had interviewed him but not arrested him prior to her daughter's unlawful killing. The House of Lords had to determine whether she was owed a duty of care by the police. While confirming the need to establish foresight and proximity, the court went on to state that there were policy reasons for not allowing the existence of a duty in this case; the reason being that any other result may lead to police discretion being limited and exercised in a defensive frame of mind. This may in turn distract the police from their most important function, the suppression of crime.

A further illustration of public policy influences on whether there is a duty of care owed by the police can be seen in *Alexandrou v Oxford* (1993), in which it was held that there was no duty owed by the police to the owners of premises with a burglar alarm system connected to a police station to protect the owners from theft.

8.2.2 Nervous shock

Nervous shock, or post-traumatic stress disorder to give it its medical name, is a form of personal injury which may give rise to an action for damages. If damages are to be recoverable, nervous shock must take the form of a recognised mental illness; mental suffering such as grief is not recoverable. No physical injury need be suffered. The basis of liability for nervous shock depends on whether this type of injury was reasonably foreseeable and whether there was sufficient proximity between the claimant and the defendant.

In *Bourhill v Young* (1943), the plaintiff heard a motor accident as she alighted from a tram. A little while later she saw some blood on the road. She was pregnant and she alleged that as a result of seeing the aftermath of the accident she suffered nervous shock leading to a miscarriage. It was held that the plaintiff did not fall within the class of person to whom it could be reasonably foreseen that harm might occur.

Indeed, it was made clear in this case that one could expect passers-by to have the necessary phlegm and fortitude not to suffer nervous shock as a result of seeing the aftermath of an accident. As a result, the abnormally sensitive claimant will not recover for nervous shock unless the person with normal phlegm and fortitude would have sustained shock in those circumstances as illustrated in *Jaensch v Coffrey* (1984).

At present, the courts appear to be treating the professional rescuer as a bystander for the purposes of nervous shock claims and expecting them to have the requisite phlegm and fortitude described in *Bourhill v Young*.

As far as the courts are concerned persons claiming for nervous shock fall into distinct categories:

- *The claimant experiences shock and illness after fearing for his or her own safety*

  In *Dulieu v White* (1901), a pregnant woman was serving in a public house when the defendant's employee negligently drove the van into the front of the building. The plaintiff was not physically injured but suffered severe shock leading to illness. It was held that she was allowed to recover damages as the shock and illness arose out of fear of immediate personal injury to herself.

  Recent application of the decision in *Dulieu* can be seen in *Page v Smith* (1995), in which the House of Lords held that foreseeability of physical injury was sufficient to enable the plaintiff who was directly involved in an accident to recover damages for nervous shock, even though in the event he had not been physically hurt. Interestingly, Lord Keith in a dissenting judgment felt that the plaintiff's claim for nervous shock should be defeated on the basis of remoteness of damage, that is, the class of injury was unforeseen.

- *Where the claimant fears for the personal injury of a close relative*

  In *Hambrook v Stokes Bros* (1925), a lorry began to roll down a hill, out of control. A mother had just left her children when she saw the lorry go out of control. She could not see her children but heard the crash. She was told that a child with glasses had been hurt and one of her children wore glasses. She suffered shock which was so severe it eventually led to her death. It was held that her estate could recover damages even though her illness caused by fear for her children, not for herself. The defendant should have foreseen that his negligence might put someone in such fear of bodily injury, that is, that they would suffer nervous shock and that this could be extended to cover fear for one's children.

  In *McLoughlin v O'Brian* (1982), a mother was told in her home that her family had been injured in a road accident two miles away. She suffered psychiatric illness caused by the shock of hearing this news and later seeing her family in hospital before they had received any treatment and were in a particular bloody state; one child had been killed. It was held that she should recover damages as the shock was a foreseeable consequence of the defendant's negligence. The court felt that the proximity of the claimant to the accident was relevant. However, proximity here meant closeness in time and space. Furthermore, the shock must be caused by the sight or hearing of the event or its immediate aftermath.

The essential elements for establishing duty in similar cases arises out of Lord Wilberforce's *dictum* in *McLoughlin*, which is that, in addition to foresight, the claimant must show that there was a close relationship between him or her and the person suffering injury; second, that there was sufficient proximity between the claimant and the accident in terms of time and space; finally, it was concluded that being told about the accident by a third party was outside the scope of the duty. The application of Lord Wilberforce's *dictum* was seen in *Alcock and Others v Chief Constable of South Yorkshire* (1991). This case arose out of the accident at Hillsborough stadium in Sheffield, involving Liverpool supporters who were crushed as a result of a surge of supporters being allowed into the ground by the police. The nervous shock claim was made by those friends and relatives who witnessed the scenes on television or heard them described on the radio or were at the ground. The House of Lords repeated the requirements for establishing duty of care in cases of nervous shock. There should be:

o   a close and loving relationship with the victim if reasonable foresight is to be established;

o   proximity in time and space to the accident or its aftermath;

o   nervous shock resulting from seeing or hearing the accident or its immediate aftermath.

It is still open to debate whether viewing simultaneous television is equivalent to seeing the accident. It is generally considered not to be, because broadcasting guidelines prevent the showing of suffering by recognisable individuals. Furthermore, any such transmission may be regarded as a *novus actus interveniens*.

- *Where the claimant suffers nervous shock through seeing injury to others, even though he or she is in no danger himself*

In *Dooley v Cammell Laird and Co* (1951), a faulty rope was being used on a crane to secure a load which was being loaded into the hold of a ship. The rope broke causing the load to fall into the hold where people were working. The crane driver suffered shock arising out of a fear for the safety of his fellow employees. It was held that the crane driver could recover damages as it was foreseeable that he was likely to be affected if the rope broke.

It would appear that the decision in *Dooley* is confined to situations where the employee making the claim has been directly involved in the incident rather than a mere bystander. In *Robertson and Rough v Forth Road Bridge Joint Board* (1995), two employees claimed damages for nervous shock after witnessing another colleague who was working alongside them on the Forth Road bridge fall to his death. It was held that their claim would fail as they were, in effect, mere bystanders and their illness was not, therefore, reasonably foreseeable.

This was confirmed in *Hegarty v EE Caledonia Ltd* (1996) in which the plaintiff who was on one of the support vessels and witnessed at close range the Piper Alpha oil rig disaster in which over 150 men died. He claimed nervous shock but was found to be a person of normal fortitude who as a mere bystander was close to the danger but not actually in danger himself. Although it could now be argued that psychiatric harm suffered by an employee witnessing the event and being in danger himself may be recoverable following the decision in *Young v Charles Church (Southern) Ltd* (1996).

In *Chadwick v British Railways Board* (1967), Chadwick took part in the rescue operations after a train crash. He suffered a severe mental condition as a result of the horrific scenes. He had a previous history of mental illness. It was held that BRB were liable. It was reasonably foreseeable that in the event of an accident someone other than the defendants employees would intervene and suffer injury. Injury by shock to a rescuer was reasonably foreseeable even if he suffered no physical injury.

In *Frost v Chief Constable of South Yorkshire* (1997), a number of policemen involved in the Hillsborough stadium disaster in which 95 football supporters were crushed to death brought claims for psychiatric damage attributable to witnessing the events. It was held by the Court of Appeal that the police who attended on the scene in the immediate aftermath of the incident were rescuers and were entitled to recover on that basis. It was further held that a rescuer, whether a policeman or layman, may recover against a tortfeasor for physical or psychiatric injury sustained during a rescue. Among the factors to be considered in determining whether a particular person is a rescuer are the character and extent of the initial incident caused by the tortfeasor; whether that incident has finished or is continuing; whether there is any danger, continuing or otherwise, to the victim or to the claimant; the character of the claimant's conduct, in itself and in relation to the victim; and how proximate, in time and place, the claimant's conduct is to the incident.

It is certainly possible for an extension to the law in this area. For example, in *Attia v British Gas* (1987), the claimant was able to recover damages for nervous shock resulting from the sight of her house being burned down as a result of the defendant's negligence.

8.2.3 Economic loss

There are two categories of economic loss which may form the basis of a claim in negligence. First, there is economic loss arising out of physical injury or damage to property and, second, there is what is known as pure economic loss which is the sole loss sustained, unconnected with physical damage. Following recent developments, only the former is now recoverable and the law has reverted to the decision in the following case for defining the extent of liability for economic loss.

In *Spartan Steel and Alloys Ltd v Martin and Co* (1973), the plaintiffs manufactured steel alloys 24 hours a day. This required continuous power. The defendants' employees damaged a power cable which resulted in a lack of power for 14 hours. There was a danger of damage to the furnace so this had to be shut down and the products in the process of manufacture removed, thereby reducing their value. The plaintiffs also suffered loss of profits. It was held that the defendants were liable for physical damage to the products and the loss of profit arising out of this. There was, however, no liability for economic loss unconnected with the physical damage.

The rule that economic loss was only recoverable where it was directly the consequence of physical damage was challenged in *Junior Books Ltd v Veitchi Ltd* (1983) (see 8.2.1) in which a claim for pure economic loss was allowed on the basis of there being sufficiently close proximity between the plaintiffs and the sub-contractor who had carried out the work for the main contractor. However, following this case there was a gradual retraction from recovery for pure economic loss, see *Muirhead v Industrial Tank Specialities Ltd* (1986), where it was held that there was insufficient proximity between the purchaser of goods and the manufacturer of the goods with respect to a claim for economic loss. This was reinforced in the cases of *Simaan General Contracting Co v Pilkington Glass Ltd* (1988) and *Greater Nottingham Co-operative Society Ltd v Cementation Piling and Foundations Ltd* (1988), where the courts refused to find sufficient proximity in tripartite business relationships, although the decision in *Junior Books* appears to stand at least for the moment.

The expansion of the law in this area was seen to result from Lord Wilberforce's two stage test in *Anns v Merton LBC*. As the gradual withdrawal from that decision grew apace, it was inevitable that a final blow would be dealt to this test. First, in *D and F Estates Ltd v Church Commissioners for England* (1988), it was held that a builder was not liable in negligence to the owner for defects in quality, only for personal injury or damage to other property, thereby bringing back the distinction between actions in tort and contract. Additionally, it was held that pure economic loss could only be recovered in an action for negligent misstatement or where the circumstances fell within *Junior Books*. Secondly, in *Murphy v Brentwood DC* (1990), in which the decision in *Anns* was overruled, it was made clear that liability for pure economic loss could only be sustained in an action for negligent misstatement based on *Hedley Byrne and Co v Heller and Partners* (1964).

8.2.4   Negligent misstatements

The importance of the neighbour or proximity test can be seen in the extension of the duty of care to cover negligent misstatements which result in economic loss. Indeed, as we have seen, this is the only heading under which pure economic loss can be claimed. This expansion of the duty arose out of the case of *Hedley Byrne and Co v Heller and Partners* (1964). Prior to this case, there was only liability for negligent misstatements causing physical damage; intentionally dishonest or fraudulent statements or where there was a fiduciary or contractual relationship between the parties (*Derry v Peek* (1889)).

In *Hedley Byrne and Co v Heller and Partners* (1964), Hedley Byrne asked their bank to make inquiries into the financial position of one of their clients. The bank made inquiries of Hellers Bank, who gave a favourable reply about the client's financial position, adding the words 'without responsibility'. Hedley Byrne relied on this advice and lost a lot of money when their client went into liquidation. However, they lost their action against the bank because of the exclusion clause which at that time was held to be valid. The importance of the case is the *dictum* on negligent misstatements. It was held that a duty of care exists where:

> ... one party seeking information and advice was trusting the other to exercise such a degree of care as the circumstances required, where it was reasonable for him to do that, and where the other party gave the information or advice when he knew or ought to have known the inquirer was relying on him.

Liability for negligent misstatements is based on the existence of a special relationship, that is, the defendant must hold himself out in some way as having specialised knowledge, knowing that any information he or she gives will be relied upon by the claimant. Interestingly, it has recently been decided that there may be concurrent liability in tort and contract so that the claimant may choose which cause of action provides him or her with the best remedy. This is illustrated in *Henderson v Merrett Syndicates Ltd* (1994), in which it was held that an assumption of responsibility by a person providing professional or quasi-professional services coupled with reliance by the person for whom the services were provided could give rise to tortious liability irrespective of whether there was a contractual relationship between the parties. Obviously, lawyers, accountants, bankers, surveyors, etc, come within this special relationship. Although, as the law has developed, some attempts to limit liability can be found in the case law. For example, in *Mutual Life and Citizens Assurance Co v Evatt* (1971), it was held that the defendant should be in the business of giving such advice, although the minority in this case required the claimant to make it clear to the defendant that he was seeking advice which he may then rely on. There is in general no liability for information given on a purely social occasion, but advice from friends on other occasions may result in liability as can be seen in *Chaudry v Prabhakar* (1988). Silence or inaction can rarely amount to misstatement unless there was a duty on the defendant to disclose or take action. The courts have recognised that it is possible for there to be a voluntary assumption of responsibility by the defendant and reliance by the claimant on that assumption (*La Banque Financière de la Cité v Westgate Insurance Co Ltd* (1990)). Any attempt at excluding liability may be subject to the Unfair Contract Terms Act (UCTA) 1977 and would then have to satisfy the test of reasonableness laid down in s 2(2). It should also be noted that any attempt to exclude liability for death or personal injury is not permitted by virtue of s 2 of the UCTA 1977.

8.3 Professional negligence

A professional person, such as an auditor, accountant, lawyer or doctor may find themselves in a non-contractual relationship with another who will have little choice but to pursue an action in negligence if they are injured as a result of professional malpractice. Indeed, to cover potential actions in negligence and contract, many professional bodies require, as part of membership approval and the issue of practising certificates, that their members take out insurance cover which will be sufficient to meet such claims, usually a minimum amount of cover is stipulated for an individual claim. This is known as professional indemnity insurance.

In considering whether a duty of care is owed by the defendant to the claimant, it is necessary to consider the particular position of the professional person who, through the nature of his or her job, will be giving advice or carrying out acts which may leave them open to an action in negligence.

8.3.1 Accountants and auditors

While there may be a contractual relationship between an accountant and his client on which the client can sue, the contentious legal area arises in respect of other people who may rely on reports made or advice given in a non-contractual capacity. Indeed, in many situations, the potential plaintiff may be unknown to the accountant. Whether there is liability appears to depend upon the purpose for which reports are made or accounts prepared.

In *JEB Fasteners v Marks, Bloom and Co* (1983), the defendants – who were accountants – negligently overstated the value of stock in preparing accounts for their client. At the time of preparation, the accountants were aware that their client was in financial difficulties and actively seeking financial assistance. After seeing the accounts, the plaintiffs decided to take over the company. They then discovered the true financial position and sued the accountants for negligent misstatement. It was held that a duty of care was owed by the accountants as it was foreseeable that someone contemplating a takeover might rely on the accuracy of the accounts, but that they were not liable as their negligence had not caused the loss to the plaintiffs. The evidence revealed that, when they took over the company, they were not interested in the value of the stock but in acquiring the expertise of the directors, so, although they relied on the accounts, the accounts were not the cause of the loss as they would have taken over the company in any respect.

The case of *Caparo Industries plc v Dickman* (1990) served to limit the potential liability of auditors in auditing company accounts. Accounts were audited in accordance with the Companies Act 1985. The respondents who already owned shares in the company, decided to purchase more shares and takeover the company after seeing the accounts. They then incurred a loss which they blamed on the negligently audited accounts which were inaccurate. It was held that when the accounts were prepared, a duty of care was owed to members of the company, that is, the shareholders, but only so far as to allow them to exercise proper control over the company. This duty did not extend to members as individuals and potential purchasers of shares. The onus was clearly on the appellants in these circumstances to make their own independent enquiries as it was unreasonable to rely on the auditors.

However, where express representations are made about the accounts and the financial state of the company by directors or financial advisers of that company, with the intention that the person interested in the takeover will rely on them, a duty of care is owed (*Morgan Crucible Co plc v Hill Samuel Bank Ltd* (1991)).

8.3.2 Lawyers

Solicitors are usually in a contractual relationship with their client; however, there may be circumstances outside this relationship where they are liable in tort for negligent misstatements. The definitive position was stated in *Ross v Caunters* (1980), in which the defendant solicitors prepared a will under which the plaintiff was a beneficiary. The solicitors sent the will to the person instructing them but failed to warn him that it should not be witnessed by the spouse of a beneficiary. When the will was returned to them, they failed to notice that one of the witnesses was the plaintiff's spouse. As a result, the plaintiff lost her benefit under the will. It was held that a solicitor may be liable in negligence to persons who are not his clients on the basis of the principle in either *Hedley Byrne* or *Donoghue v Stevenson* which was specifically applied in this case; the claimant being someone so closely and directly affected by the solicitor's acts that it was reasonably foreseeable that they were likely to be injured by any act or omission.

The decision in *Ross v Caunters* is further supported by the decision of the House of Lords in *White v Jones* (1995), in which the plaintiff was cut out of his father's will. The father then instructed his solicitors to reinstate him. Unfortunately, the solicitors delayed some six weeks in carrying out the change and in the meantime the father died. It was held that the solicitors owed a duty of care to the son as a potential beneficiary. The loss to the plaintiff was reasonably foreseeable and the duty of care was broken by their omission to act promptly. Barristers are in the position of not being in a contractual relationship with the client, that is, the person they are representing, nor are they liable in tort for the way in which they conduct a case in court. There are policy reasons for this as the duty to the court is higher than the duty to the client and must be put first, as can be seen *Rondel v Worsley* (1969). In *Saif Ali v Sidney Mitchell* (1980), it was confirmed that a barrister was not liable for conduct of the case in court nor was he liable for pre-trial work connected with the conduct of the case in court. However, he would be liable in tort for negligent opinions, that is, written advice where there was no error on the part of the solicitor briefing him.

8.3.3 Surveyors

A duty of care is owed by surveyors, builders, architects, etc, to the client with whom they are generally in a contractual relationship. However, there may be liability in tort as a result of *Hedley Byrne*, although this hinges on the question of reasonable reliance by the third party and whether the defendant ought to have foreseen such reliance.

In *Yianni v Edwin Evans and Sons* (1982), surveyors acting for the building society valued a house at £15,000 and as a result the plaintiffs were able to secure a mortgage of £12,000. The house was in fact suffering from severe structural damage and repairs were estimated at £18,000. The basis of the plaintiff's claim was not only the surveyors' negligence but that he ought reasonably to have contemplated that the statement would be passed on by the building society to the plaintiff and that they would rely on it, which they did. It was held that a duty of care was owed by the defendants. An important factor was that the price of the house indicated that the plaintiff was of modest means and would not be expected to obtain an independent valuation and would in all probability rely on the defendants' survey which was communicated to them by the building society. The court was also confident that the defendants knew that the building society would pass the survey to the purchasers and that they would rely on it.

The decision in *Yianni* was approved in *Smith v Eric Bush* (1989) and *Harris v Wyre Forest District Council* (1989). The facts of the former case are very similar to *Yianni* in that the plaintiff was sent a copy of the surveyors' report by the building society. This report stated that no essential repairs were necessary and, although it contained a recommendation on obtaining independent advice, the plaintiff chose to rely on the report. In fact, the property had defective chimneys. In *Harris*, the plaintiffs did not see the surveyors' report as it was stated on the mortgage application that the valuation was confidential and that no responsibility would be accepted for the valuation. However, the plaintiff paid the valuation fee and accepted the 95% mortgage on offer. When they attempted to sell the house three years later, structural defects were revealed and the property was deemed to be uninhabitable and unsaleable. It was held, in both cases, that there was sufficient proximity between the surveyor and the purchaser and that it was foreseeable that the plaintiff was likely to suffer damage as a result of the negligent advice. It was felt that, in general, surveyors knew that 90% of purchasers relied on their valuation for the building society; it was therefore just and reasonable for a duty to be imposed. The limitation on this decision is that it does not extend protection to subsequent purchasers, nor where the property is of a high value (although this will need to be determined on the facts of each case). The attempt to exclude liability in this case was seen as an attempt to exclude the existence of a duty of care which it was felt was not within the spirit of the UCTA 1977 and could not be permitted.

The decision in *Murphy v Brentwood DC* (1990) has seriously limited the potential liability of builders, architects and quantity surveyors in respect of claims arising out of defective buildings. Where the defect is discovered prior to any injury to person or health or damage to property, other than the defective premises itself, this is to be regarded as pure economic loss, not physical damage to property, and is not, therefore, recoverable in negligence.

8.4 Breach of duty of care

Once the claimant has established that the defendant owes him a duty of care, the claimant must establish that the defendant is in breach of this duty. The test for establishing breach of duty was laid down in *Blyth v Birmingham Waterworks Co* (1856). A breach of duty occurs if the defendant:

> ... fails to do something which a reasonable man guided upon those considerations which ordinarily regulate the conduct of human affairs would do, or does something which a prudent and reasonable man would not do.

The test is an objective test, judged through the eyes of the reasonable man. The fact that the defendant has acted less skillfully than the reasonable man would expect will usually result in breach being established. This is the case even where the defendant is inexperienced in his particular trade or activity. One cannot condone the incompetence of such defendants. For example, a learner driver must drive in the manner of a driver of skill, experience and care (*Nettleship v Weston* (1971)). However, the degree or standard of care to be exercised by such a person will vary as there are factors such as the age of the claimant which can increase the standard of care to be exercised by the defendant. The test is therefore flexible. The following factors are relevant.

8.4.1 The likelihood of injury

In deciding whether the defendant has failed to act as the reasonable man would act, the degree of care must be balanced against the degree of risk involved if the defendant fails in his duty. It follows, therefore, that the greater the risk of injury or the more likely it is to occur, the more the defendant will have to do to fulfil his duty.

In *Bolton v Stone* (1951), a cricket ground was surrounded by a 17 foot wall and the pitch was situated some way from the road. A batsman hit the ball exceptionally hard driving it over the wall where it struck the plaintiff who was standing on the highway. It was held that the plaintiff could not succeed in his action as the likelihood of such injury occurring was small, as was the risk involved. The slight risk was outweighed by the height of the wall and the fact that a ball had only been hit out of the ground six times in 30 years.

8.4.2 Egg-shell skull rule

The degree of care to be exercised by the defendant may be increased if the claimant is very young, old or less able-bodied in some way. The rule is that you must take your victim as you find him. This is illustrated in *Haley v London Electricity Board* (1965), in which the defendants, in order to carry out repairs, had made a hole in the pavement. Haley, who was blind, often walked along this stretch of pavement. He was normally able to avoid obstacles by using his white stick. The precautions taken by the Electricity Board would have prevented a sighted person from injuring himself, but not a blind person. As a result, Haley fell, striking his head on the pavement, and became deaf as a consequence. It was held that the Electricity Board were in breach of their duty of care to pedestrians. They had failed to ensure that the excavation was safe for all pedestrians, not just sighted persons. It was clearly not reasonably safe for blind persons, yet it was foreseeable that they may use this pavement.

There are other cases which you might wish to refer to in this field, for example: *Gough v Thorne* (1966) concerning young children; *Daly v Liverpool Corporation* (1939) concerning old people; and *Paris v Stepney BC* (1951) concerning disability.

8.4.3 Cost and practicability

Another factor in deciding whether the defendant is in breach of his duty to the claimant is the cost and practicability of overcoming the risk. The foreseeable risk has to be balanced against the measures necessary to eliminate it. If the cost of these measures far outweighs the risk, the defendant will probably not be in breach of duty for failing to carry out these measures. This is illustrated by the case of *Latimer v AEC Ltd* (1952). A factory belonging to AEC became flooded after an abnormally heavy rainstorm. The rain mixed with oily deposits on the floor making the floor very slippery. Sawdust was spread on the floor but there was insufficient to cover the whole area most of the floor was covered. Latimer, an employee, slipped on a part of the floor to which sawdust had not been applied. It was held that AEC Ltd was not in breach of their duty to the plaintiff. It had taken all reasonable precautions and had eliminated the risk as far as it practicably could without going so far as to close the factory. There was no evidence to suggest that the reasonably prudent employer would have closed down the factory and as far as the court was concerned the cost of doing that far out weighed the risk to the employees.

Compare this case with *Haley v London Electricity Board* where the provision of two foot barriers around excavations in the pavement was practicable and would have eliminated the risk to blind people.

8.4.4 Social utility

The degree of risk has to be balanced against the social utility and importance of the defendants activity. If the activity is of particular importance to the community, then in the circumstances the taking of greater risks may be justified.

In *Watt v Hertfordshire CC* (1954), the plaintiff, a fireman, was called out to rescue a woman trapped beneath a lorry. The lifting jack had to be carried on an ordinary lorry as a suitable vehicle was unavailable. The jack slipped, injuring the plaintiff. It was held that the employer was not in breach of duty. The importance of the activity and the fact that it was an emergency was found to justify the risk involved.

8.4.5 Common practice

If the defendant can show that what he or she has done is common practice, then this is evidence that a proper standard of care has been exercised. However, if the common practice is in itself negligent, then his or her actions in conforming to such a practice will be actionable, as can be seen in *Paris v Stepney BC* (1951) in which the common practice of not wearing safety glasses could not be condoned as it was in itself inherently negligent.

8.4.6 Skilled persons

The standard of care to be exercised by people professing to have a particular skill is not be judged on the basis of the reasonable man. The actions of a skilled person must be judged by what the ordinary skilled man in that job or profession would have done, for example, the reasonable doctor, plumber, engineer, etc. Such a person is judged on the standard of knowledge possessed by the profession at the time the accident occurred. Obviously, there is an onus on the skilled person to keep himself abreast of changes and improvements in technology.

In *Roe v Minister of Health* (1954), a patient was paralysed after being given a spinal injection. This occurred because the fluid being injected had become contaminated with the storage liquid which had seeped through minute cracks in the phials. It was held that there was no breach of duty since the doctor who administered the injection had no way of detecting the contamination at that time.

Furthermore, the common practice of the profession may, if this is followed, prevent liability. This can be seen in *Bolam v Friern Hospital Management Committee* (1957). Bolam broke his pelvis whilst undergoing electro-convulsive therapy treatment at the defendants' hospital. He alleged that the doctor had not warned him of the risks, nor had he been given relaxant drugs prior to treatment and no one had held him down during treatment. It was held that the doctor was not in breach of duty (and there was therefore no vicarious liability) because this form of treatment was accepted at that time by a certain body of the medical profession.

8.4.7 *Res ipsa loquitur*

The burden of proof in establishing breach of duty normally rests on the claimant. In certain circumstances, the inference of negligence may be drawn from the facts. If this can be done, the claimant is relieved of the burden which moves to the defendant to rebut the presumption of negligence. This is known as *res ipsa loquitur*, that is, the thing speaks for itself. It can only be used where the only explanation for what happened is the negligence of the defendant, yet the claimant has insufficient evidence to establish the defendant's negligence in the normal way. There are three criteria for the maxim to apply:

(a) *Sole management or control*

It must be shown that the damage was caused by something under the sole management or control of the defendant, or by someone for whom he or she is responsible or whom he or she has a right to control (*Gee v Metropolitan Railway* (1873)).

(b) *The occurrence cannot have happened without negligence*

This depends on the facts of each case. If there are other possible explanations as to how the incident occurred, *res ipsa loquitur* will fail. In *Mahon v Osborne* (1939), a patient died after a swab was left in her body after an operation. No one could explain how this had happened, therefore, *res ipsa loquitur* applied.

(c) *The cause of the occurrence is unknown*

If the defendant can put forward a satisfactory explanation of how the accident occurred which shows no negligence on his part, then the maxim is inapplicable. In *Pearson v NW Gas Board* (1968), the plaintiff's husband was killed and her house destroyed when a gas main fractured. She pleaded *res ipsa loquitur*. However, the Gas Board put forward the explanation that the gas main could have fractured due to earth movement after a heavy frost. This explanation was plausible and as it showed no negligence on their part, they were not liable.

If the defendant can rebut the presumption of negligence by giving a satisfactory explanation, it is open to the claimant to establish negligence in the normal way. In practice, he or she is unlikely to succeed as, if sufficient evidence were available in the first place, *res ipsa loquitur* would not have been pleaded.

8.5   Resultant damage

The claimant must show that he or she has suffered some injury, not necessarily physical. Furthermore, he or she must show that this injury was caused by the defendants negligence. This is known as causation in fact. The but for test is used to establish whether the defendant's negligence was the cause of the injury to the plaintiff.

8.5.1   The but for test

In order to satisfy the test, the plaintiff must show that but for the defendant's actions the damage would not have occurred. If the damage would have occurred irrespective of a breach of duty on the part of the defendant, then the breach is not the cause.

In *Cutler v Vauxhall Motors Ltd* (1971), the plaintiff suffered a grazed ankle while at work due to the defendant's negligence. The graze became ulcerated because of existing varicose veins and the plaintiff had to undergo an immediate operation for the removal of the veins. It was held that the plaintiff could not recover damages for the operation because the evidence was that he would have to undergo the operation within five years irrespective of the accident at work.

If the same result would have occurred regardless of the breach, then the courts are unlikely to find that the breach caused the injury. This is illustrated in *Barnett v Chelsea and Kensington Hospital Management Committee* (1969), in which a doctor in a casualty department sent home a patient without treating him, telling him to go and see his own doctor. The patient died from arsenic poisoning. Whilst it was held that the doctor was negligent, the evidence indicated that the patient would have died anyway. The doctor's conduct did not therefore cause his death. This is further supported by the case of *Robinson v Post Office* (1974) in which a doctor failed to test for an allergic reaction before giving an anti-tetanus injection. However, it was held that the doctor would not be liable for the reaction of the patient because the test would not have revealed the allergy in time.

Recent case law has not been sympathetic to the claimant where there have been a number of potential causes of the injury. The onus is on the claimant to show that the defendant's breach was a material contributory cause of his or her injury.

Where there are a number of possible causes, establishing causation may prove difficult, particularly in medical negligence cases. In *Wilsher v Essex Area Health Authority* (1988), the plaintiff was born three months prematurely. He suffered almost total blindness as a result of a condition known as retrolental fibroplasia. It was claimed on behalf of the plaintiff that this was caused by the negligence of the doctor who had failed to notice that the device for measuring oxygen to the blood had been wrongly attached, resulting in an excessive dose of oxygen. However, medical evidence showed at least six potential causes of the plaintiff's blindness, the majority of which were inherent in premature babies. It was held by the House of Lords there was insufficient evidence to show which of the six caused the injury to the plaintiff.

The case of *Hotson v East Berkshire Area Health Authority* (1987) considered whether the defendant could be liable for loss of a chance. The facts of Hotson are that a boy fell from a tree and injured his hip. At the hospital, his injury was misdiagnosed and by the time the mistake was discovered he was left with a permanent disability. It was held that as 75% of such cases were inoperable, there was no lost chance and, therefore, the plaintiff could not recover. There can also be problems, where there are two or more independent tortfeasors, in establishing how far each one is responsible for the damage caused.

In *Baker v Willoughby* (1970), the plaintiff injured his leg through the defendant's negligence, leaving him partially disabled. Subsequently, the plaintiff was shot in the same leg by another person and as a result the leg had to be amputated. It was likely that the leg would have had to have been amputated as a result of the shooting anyway. It was held that the first defendant was liable for the plaintiff's disability (not the amputation) for the rest of his life. Irrespective of the amputation, it would have been a continuing disability and this was reflected in the responsibility imposed on the defendant. The liability for the existing disability did not cease when the second incident took place.

The but for test cannot solve all questions of factual causation. Indeed, where there has been an omission to act or there has been an act which does not in itself have physical consequences, it may not be an appropriate test. In *Joyce v Merton, Sutton and Wandsworth Health Authority* (1996), the plaintiff underwent an operation which resulted in a partially blocked artery which in turn some three months later resulted in total paralysis. The procedure itself was not necessarily negligent, however, it was concluded that the immediate after-care was in that the plaintiff was discharged from hospital without proper instructions and advice. The plaintiff should have been seen by a vascular surgeon within the first 48 hours and he should have operated to deal with the blockage. To succeed on the point of causation, it was held that the claimant would have to prove either that, had the vascular surgeon been summoned, he would have operated or that it would have been negligent for him not to do so. The correct test in these circumstances was to satisfy one of two questions. Either what steps would have been taken if proper care had been taken. Or what would have been the outcome of any further steps that ought to have been taken? In this case, the plaintiff was able to satisfy the first question, by establishing that his injuries would have been avoided if proper care had been taken.

The but for test can be used to establish causation on the facts. However, once this has been established, it does not mean that the defendant will be liable for all of the damage to the claimant. There must be causation in law. This can be seen through the maxim *novus actus interveniens* (a new intervening act).

8.5.2 *Novus actus interveniens*

Where there is a break in the chain of causation, the defendant will not be liable for damage caused after the break. The issue is whether the whole sequence of events is the probable consequence of the defendant's actions and whether it is reasonably foreseeable that these events may happen. The break in the chain is caused by an intervening act and the law recognises that such acts fall into three categories.

8.5.3 A natural event

A natural event does not automatically break the chain of causation. If the defendant's breach has placed the claimant in the position where the natural event can add to that damage, the chain will not be broken unless the natural event was totally unforeseeable.

In *Carslogie Steamship Co Ltd v Royal Norwegian Government* (1952), a ship owned by Carslogie had been damaged in a collision caused by the defendants negligence. The ship was sent for repair and on this voyage suffered extra damage caused by the severe weather conditions. This resulted in the repairs taking 40 days longer than anticipated. It was held that the bad weather acted as a new intervening act for which the defendant was not liable. The effect of the new act in this case prevented the plaintiff from recovering compensation for the time it would have taken to repair the vessel in respect of the collision damage as the ship would have been out of use due to the damage caused by the weather.

8.5.4 Act of a third party

Where the act of a third party following the breach of the defendant causes further damage to the claimant, such act may be deemed to be a *novus*; the defendant would not then be liable for damage occurring after the third party's act.

In *Lamb v Camden LBC* (1981), due to the defendants' negligence, a water main was damaged causing the plaintiff's house to be damaged and the house vacated until it had been repaired. While the house was empty, squatters moved in and caused further damage to the property. It was held that the defendant was not liable for the squatters' damage. Although it was a reasonably foreseeable risk, it was not a likely event. Furthermore, it was not the duty of the Council to keep the squatters out.

The third party's act need not be negligent in itself to break the chain of causation, although the courts take the view that a negligent act is more likely to break the chain than one that is not negligent, as can be seen in *Knightley v Johns* (1982).

8.5.5 Act of the claimant himself

In *McKew v Holland, Hannen and Cubbitts (Scotland) Ltd* (1969), the plaintiff was injured at work. As a result, his leg, on occasions, gave way without warning. He was coming downstairs when his leg gave way, so he jumped, rather than fall head first, and badly injured his ankle. It was held that the defendants were not liable for this additional injury. The plaintiff had not acted reasonably in attempting to negotiate the stairs without assistance and his actions amounted to a *novus actus interveniens*.

Where it is the act of the claimant that breaks the chain, it is not a question of foresight but of unreasonable conduct.

8.5.6 Remoteness of damage

It must be understood that, even where causation is established, the defendant will not necessarily be liable for all of the damage resulting from the breach. This was not always the case and the way in which the law has developed must be considered.

In *Re Polemis and Furness, Withy and Co* (1921), the plaintiff's ship was destroyed by fire when one of the employees of the company to whom the ship had been chartered negligently knocked a plank into the hold. The hold was full of petrol vapour. The fall of the plank caused a spark as it struck the side and this ignited the vapour. It was held that the defendants were liable for the loss of the ship, even though the presence of petrol vapour and the causing of the spark were unforeseen. The fire was the direct result of the breach of duty and the defendant was liable for the full extent of the damage even where the manner in which it took place was unforeseen.

The case of *Re Polemis* is no longer regarded as the current test for remoteness of damage, even though it has not been distinguished or overruled.

The test currently used arose out of *The Wagon Mound (No 1)* (1961). The defendants negligently allowed furnace oil to spill from a ship into Sidney Harbour. The oil spread and came to lie beneath a wharf owned by the plaintiffs. The plaintiffs had been carrying out welding operations and on seeing the oil they stopped welding in order to ascertain whether it was safe. They were assured that the oil would not catch fire and so resumed welding. Cotton waste which had fallen into the oil caught fire. This in turn ignited the oil and this fire spread to the plaintiffs' wharf. It was held that the defendants were in breach of duty. However, they were only liable for the damage caused to the wharf and slipway through the fouling of the oil. They were not liable for the damage caused by fire because damage by fire was at that time unforeseeable. This particular oil had a high ignition point and it could not be foreseen that it would ignite on water. The court refused to apply the rule in *Re Polemis*.

The test of reasonable foresight arising out of *The Wagon Mound* clearly takes into account such things as scientific knowledge at the time of the negligent act. The question to be asked in determining the extent of liability is: is the damage of such a kind as the reasonable man should have foreseen? This does not mean that the defendant should have foreseen precisely the sequence or nature of the events. Lord Denning in *Stewart v West African Air Terminals* (1964) said:

> It is not necessary that the precise concatenation of circumstances should be envisaged. If the consequence was one which was within the general range which any reasonable person might foresee (and was not of an entirely different kind which no one would anticipate), then it is within the rule that a person who has been guilty of negligence is liable for the consequences.

This is illustrated in the case of *Hughes v Lord Advocate* (1963), where employees of the Post Office who were working down a manhole, left it without a cover but with a tent over it and lamps around it. A child picked up a lamp and went into the tent. He tripped over the lamp knocking it into the hole. An explosion occurred in which the child was burned. The risk of the child being burned by the lamp was foreseeable. However, the vapourisation of the paraffin in the lamp and its ignition were not foreseeable. It was held that the defendants were liable for the injury to the plaintiff. It was foreseeable that the child might be burned and it was immaterial that neither the extent of his injury nor the precise chain of events leading to it was foreseeable.

The test of remoteness is not easy to apply. The cases themselves highlight the uncertainty of the courts. For example, in *Doughty v Turner Manufacturing Co Ltd* (1964), an asbestos cover was knocked into a bath of molten metal. This led to a chemical reaction which was at that time unforeseeable. The molten metal erupted and burned the plaintiff who was standing nearby. It was held that only burning by splashing was foreseeable and the burning by an unforeseen chemical reaction was not a variant on this. It could be argued that the proper question in this case should have been was burning foreseeable as this was the question asked in *Hughes*.

A similar issue surrounding the questions asked to establish whether the harm is foreseeable can be seen in *Tremain v Pike* (1969), in which a farmhand contracted a rare disease transmitted by rats' urine. It was foreseeable that the plaintiff may sustain injury from rat bites or from contaminated food, but not from the contraction of this disease. Once again, this case raises the issue of whether the correct question was asked, see *Robinson v Post Office* (1974) which was considered earlier (see 8.5.1).

8.6 Defences

The extent of the liability of the defendant may be reduced or limited by one of the defences commonly pleaded in negligence actions.

8.6.1 Contributory negligence

Where the claimant is found in some way to have contributed through his own fault to his injury, the amount awarded as damages will be reduced accordingly (Law Reform (Contributory Negligence) Act 1945). The onus is on the defendant to show that the claimant was at fault and that this contributed to his injury.

The court, if satisfied that the claimant is at fault, will reduce the amount of damages by an amount which is just and reasonable, depending on the claimant's share of the blame. For example, damages may be reduced by anything from 10% to 75%. However, a 100% reduction was made in *Jayes v IMI (Kynoch) Ltd* (1985).

8.6.2 *Volenti non fit injuria*

Volenti, or consent as it applies to negligent acts, is a defence to future conduct of the defendant which involves the risk of a tort being committed. *Volenti* may arise from the express agreement of the claimant and defendant or it may be implied from the claimant's conduct.

In *ICI v Shatwell* (1965), the plaintiff and his brother ignored the safety precautions issued by their employer and breached the regulations in testing detonators. As a result, the plaintiff was injured in an explosion. The action against the employer was based on vicarious liability and breach of statutory duty on the part of the plaintiff's brother. It was held that the defence of *volenti* would succeed. The plaintiff not only consented to each act of negligence and breach of statute on the part of his brother, but also participated in it quite willingly.

It must be stressed that this particular case highlights extreme circumstances where *volenti* is likely to succeed. However, if the defence is to succeed, it must be shown that the claimant was fully informed of the risks when he gave his consent.

In *Dann v Hamilton* (1939), a girl accepted a lift in the car of a driver whom she knew to be drunk. She could have used alternative transport. She was injured as a result of his negligent driving. It was held that, although she knew of the risk, this was insufficient to support the defence of *volenti*. It was necessary to show that she had consented to the risk, which could not be established. She therefore succeeded in her action against the driver.

Following this case, it is unlikely that this defence will succeed where the implied consent is given before the negligent act occurs. In practice, the courts do not look favourably on this defence in respect of negligent actions and therefore it is not usually pleaded.

Finally, there is a limitation period for commencing an action in tort. The Limitation Act 1980 states that generally an action must be brought within six years from the date on which it occurred. If the action is for personal injury, the period is three years from the date on which it occurred, or the date of knowledge of the injury, whichever is later.

8.7   Vicarious liability

As a general rule, vicarious liability only arises out of the employer/employee relationship, although it can be found in the principal/agent relationship and, as an exceptional case, in the employer/independent contractor relationship. It is dependent upon this type of special relationship being established.

8.7.1   Meaning of vicarious liability

Vicarious liability is not a tort; it is a concept which is used to impose strict liability on a person who does not have primary liability, that is, is not personally at fault. Literally, it means that one person is liable for the torts of another. The employer is, therefore, liable for the torts of his employee. This liability only arises while the employee is acting within the course of his or her employment. The concept has found favour with the courts and claimants alike, because, realistically, the employer is likely to have the money to pay for any claim for damages, whereas the main tortfeasor, the employee, will not. This does not mean that the employee will escape liability. The employer can insist that he or she is joined in any action or, if the employer is found to be vicariously liable, he or she may insist on an indemnity from his or her employee. The effect of this is that the employee will have to pay towards the damages imposed on the employer (see the Civil Liability (Contribution) Act 1978 which provides for this).

It must not be forgotten that this concept depends on the primary liability of the employee being established, that is, the employee must have committed a tort. Once this is done, the claimant has the option to sue the employer, the employee or both.

8.7.2   Employer/employee relationship

The claimant must establish that there is in existence an employer/employee relationship (or in less common situations a principal/agent relationship), that is, a contract of service as opposed to a contract for services. In the majority of cases, this may not be an issue, but just because the word employee is used in the contract, it does not automatically follow that it is a contract of service (or employment). There are tests for establishing this relationship which are considered in depth in 9.4.1 and to which reference should be made.

8.7.3 Scope of vicarious liability

Once it is established that there is in existence a contract of service and that the employee has committed a tort, that is, has primary liability, the consideration of whether the employer should be vicariously liable can take place. This stage is important because the employer will only be liable if the employee is acting within the course of his employment when the tort is committed. It is, therefore, essential to consider what is meant by this in law. If the employee is outside the scope of his or her employment, the injured person has no choice but to sue the employee who may not be in a financial position to pay compensation.

8.7.4 Course of employment

The interpretation given by the courts is wide as in the past they have favoured making the employer liable, if it is at all possible to do so. The onus is on the claimant to show that the employee is a servant and that the tortious act was committed whilst was going about his or her employer's business. Once this is established, the onus moves to the employer who must show that the tortious act was one for which he or she was not responsible. As a general rule, to be within the course of employment, one of the following must be established:

- the act must be incidental to the job the employee was employed to do;

- the act should have been authorised by the employer, either expressly or impliedly;

- the authorised act has been carried out in a wrongful, negligent or unauthorised manner.

These can best be illustrated through the case law which shows how far the courts are prepared to go in holding an employer vicariously liable. The following cases relate to situations where the employee was found to be within the course of his employment.

In *Century Insurance Co Ltd v Northern Ireland Road Transport Board* (1942), Davison was employed as a tanker driver for the NIRTB. He was delivering petrol at a garage. Whilst the underground storage tank was being filled with petrol, Davison lit a cigarette and threw away the lighted match. The petrol vapour ignited resulting in an explosion. The employer's insurance company claimed that the driver's actions regarding the cigarette were outside the course of his employment as being wholly unauthorised; thereby avoiding liability on the part of the employer and payment of compensation by the insurance company. It was held that the employer was vicariously liable for the negligent act of the employee. The lighting of the cigarette was an act of convenience on the part of the employee and, although it was not necessarily for the employer's benefit, it did not prevent them from being made liable. It was the time and place at which the employee struck the match which was negligent. The employee was seen to be carrying out the job he was employed to do in a negligent manner.

From this case, it can been seen that such acts as taking a tea-break, having a cigarette, going to the washroom, etc, are all acts which are incidental to the main job, although it is still necessary to consider all the facts of the case at the time of the tortious act; of course, the question as to whether, in the present climate of no smoking policies, the smoking of a cigarette would be seen as incidental to one's employment is debatable. The next case is regarded as the leading authority with respect to actions which are specifically prohibited by the employer.

In *Rose v Plenty* (1976), Plenty was employed as a milkman by the Co-operative Dairy. A notice had been posted up in the depot which prohibited all milkmen from using young children to deliver milk and from giving lifts to them on the milk float. Plenty ignored this notice and engaged the assistance of Rose, a 13 year old boy. Rose was injured whilst riding on the milk float through the negligent driving of Plenty. It was held that, applying the decision in *Limpus v London General Omnibus Co* (1862), since the prohibited act was being done for the purpose of the employers business and not for the employees own benefit or purpose, Plenty was within the course of his employment and, therefore, the employer was vicariously liable.

Obviously, where the employee carries out a prohibited act all the circumstances will have to be considered to see if the employee remains within the course of his or her employment. However, the key to establishing vicarious liability in such cases is to ask the question: who is the intended beneficiary of the prohibited action? In *Rose v Plenty*, Lord Denning applied his own earlier judgment in *Young v Edward Box and Co Ltd* (1951) in which he said:

> In every case where it is sought to make the master liable for the conduct of his servant, the first question is to see whether the servant was liable. If the answer is yes, the second question is to see whether the employer must shoulder the servants liability.

This approach gives little weight to the issue of the course of employment by adopting the view that, generally, it is the employer who will have the money to pay the compensation because of insurance cover and, therefore, if it is at all possible to do so, the employer should be made responsible for an employee's tortious acts. It should not be forgotten that the concept of vicarious liability may also enable an employee who has been injured by a fellow employee to recover compensation, even though a claim for employer's liability would fail. In *Harrison v Michelin Tyre Co Ltd* (1985), Harrison was injured when a fellow employee, Smith, deliberately tipped up the duck-board on which he was standing at his machine. The employer contended that Smith, who caused the injury, was on a frolic of his own when he caused the injury. However, the court held that although it was an unauthorised act, Smith was going about his job when he committed the act, which was so closely connected with his employment, he remained within the course of his employment, thereby resulting in the employer being vicariously liable. Some doubt about the decision in *Harrison* was expressed in *Aldred v Nacanco* (1987). Vicarious liability extends to acts which may be crimes as well as torts, for example, assault, fraud. Where force or violence is used by the employee, the courts will look closely at the circumstances surrounding its use and question whether it was necessary or excessive. Early case law illustrates that the use of force may result in the employer being vicariously liable. In *Poland v Parr and Sons* (1927), an employee saw some boys whom he believed to be stealing from his employers wagon. He struck one of them who fell and was run over. The employer was held to be vicariously liable as the servant was legitimately protecting his employers property. Although as the social climate has changed so has the attitude of the courts. This is illustrated in *Keppel Bus Co Ltd v Saad bin Ahmad* (1974), in which the employer was found not to be vicariously liable for an assault carried out by a bus conductor on a passenger. Whether the employee has an implied authority to use force in a given situation, such as protecting his employer's property, and why and how that force is used are key issues.

The following cases consider the position where the employee is put in a position of trust and abuses that position so that a crime or tort is committed.

In *Morris v Martin and Sons Ltd* (1966), Morris's mink stole was sent by her furrier to Martins to be cleaned. Whilst there, an employee of Martin and Sons who had been entrusted with the cleaning of the fur, stole it (tort of conversion). It was held that the employer was liable for the act of conversion of their employee. Martin and Sons were bailees for reward of the fur and were, therefore, under a duty to take reasonable care of it. It was then entrusted to an employee to do an act which was within the course of his employment, that is, clean it. What the employee did in stealing the fur was merely an abuse of his job.

A critical element in this case was the fact that Martin and Sons had become bailees of the fur and would, therefore, probably have been liable for anything happening to it. There is a further limitation on the application of the rule in *Morris v Martin and Sons*; it can only serve to make the employer vicariously liable where the goods come into the employees possession as part of his or her job. If, for example, an employee not involved in the cleaning of the fur had stolen it, the employer would not have been vicariously liable. The courts have reinforced the limit on the application of the decision in the *Morris* case by requiring a nexus between the criminal act and the circumstances of the employment. In *Heasmans v Clarity Cleaning Co Ltd* (1987), an employee of a firm contracted to clean offices, whose job involved the cleaning of telephones, dishonestly made use of the telephones to make private calls. It was held that the telephone calls were outside the purpose for which the man was employed. For an employer to be liable for the criminal acts of his employees, there must be some nexus between the criminal act of the employee and the circumstances of his employment. In this case, the requirement to dust the telephones merely provided the employee with an opportunity to commit the crime access to the premises was an insufficient nexus. How far the question of nexus is becoming an issue in all cases of vicarious liability can be seen in *Irving v Post Office* (1987) and *Aldred v Nacanco* (1987). Where an employee is involved in a fraud, the fact that the employer has placed the employee in a position to perpetrate the fraud may result in the employer being vicariously liable.

In *Lloyd v Grace, Smith and Co* (1912), Lloyd went to the defendant solicitors to discuss some properties she had for investment purposes. She saw their managing clerk who persuaded her to sell the properties and to sign some documents which, unbeknown to her, transferred the properties to him. He then disposed of them for his own benefit. It was held that the solicitors were liable for the fraudulent act of their employee, even though they did not benefit from the fraud. They had placed him in a position of responsibility which enabled him to carry out the fraud. Also, as far as the general public was concerned he was in a position of trust and appeared to have the authority for his actions.

The facts of *Lloyd* are rather special and the decision is based on the special relationship between solicitor and client which is one of trust. The court did not regard benefit to the employer as an issue. In reality there can be no set formula for deciding whether an employer should be vicariously liable. The fact that in many of the cases it appears that justice was seen to be done, probably justifies Lord Denning's stance in *Young v Edward Box and Co Ltd*.

8.7.5 Outside the course of employment

In considering those cases in which the employee has been held to be outside the course of employment, a significant issue has been the deviation of the employee from the job employed to do. Once again, there is no set criteria for judging this issue; it remains a question of fact in each case, based on the nature of the job and the actions of the employee. The standard is laid down in *Hilton v Thomas Burton (Rhodes) Ltd* (1961). Four workmen were allowed to use their employer's van as they were working on a demolition site in the country. At lunchtime, they decided to go to a cafe some seven miles away. Before reaching the cafe, they changed their minds and set off to return to the site. On the return journey, one of them was killed through the negligent driving of the van driver. It was held that the employer was not vicariously liable. By travelling such a distance to take a break, they were no longer doing something incidental to their main employment; nor were they doing anything for the purpose of their employer's business. As far as the court was concerned, they were on a frolic of their own.

Following this case, it is pertinent to ask how far the employee has deviated from his course of employment. This is a question of degree which depends on the facts of each case. There are cases dealing with prohibited acts which have reached the decision that the employee is outside the course of his employment. It should be noted that many of these decisions were made before *Rose v Plenty* which is seen as the watershed for such cases. It could, therefore, be argued that the decision in *Twine v Beans Express Ltd* (1946) in which the employer was not liable for the injuries to a hitchhiker who had been given a lift contrary to the express instructions of the employer would be different today as the reasoning that no duty was owed because he was a trespasser is doubtful in the light of the decision in *Rose*. However, the problem of tortious acts which are also crimes has not been totally resolved, although it is possible to distinguish the case law on its facts.

In *Warren v Henlys Ltd* (1948), a petrol pump attendant employed by Henlys used verbal abuse when wrongly accusing Warren, a customer, of trying to drive away without paying for petrol. Warren called the police and told the attendant that he would be reported to his employer. This so enraged the attendant that he physically assaulted Warren. It was held that the employer was not liable. The act of violence was not connected in any way to the discharge of the pump attendants duties. When he assaulted Warren, he was not doing what he was employed to do but was acting in an unauthorised manner. The act was done in relation to a personal matter affecting his personal interests, not in respect of the protection of his employers property as in *Poland v Parr* (1927).

Finally, both the Sex Discrimination Act 1975 and the Race Relations Act 1976 recognise a statutory form of vicarious liability which results in the employer being liable for acts of discrimination carried out by his or her employees. Whether the employer is so liable will depend on whether the employee is acting within the course of his or her employment when he commits the act. In *Irving v Post Office* (1987), a postman took the opportunity whilst sorting mail to write racist remarks on post addressed to his neighbour. It was held that the employer would not be liable for such actions since the employee had gone beyond what he was employed to do as the only authorised act in these circumstances would have been an amendment to the address.

The test was considered in *Tower Boot Co Ltd v Jones* (1997), where the complainant was subjected to deliberate branding with a screw driver and whipping as well as racial taunts by fellow employees. It was held by the Court of Appeal that the Employment Appeal Tribunal (EAT) had erred in apply the common law test in interpreting the statutory provision contained in s 32 of the Race Relations Act. The words in the course of employment for the purposes of s 32 of the Race Relations Act and s 41 of the Sex Discrimination Act should be interpreted in the sense in which they are employed in everyday speech and not restrictively by reference to the principles laid down by case law for establishing an employer's vicarious liability for the torts committed by an employee. If the common law approach were to be taken, this would result in employers avoiding liability for particularly heinous acts of discrimination.

Both statutes recognise that an employer may escape being vicariously liable if it can be shown that all reasonably practicable steps were taken to prevent or stop the act of discrimination.

8.7.6   Principal and agent

The rules relating to the vicarious liability of a principal for the tortious acts of his or her agent operate in the same way as those for the employer/employee. However, the key to the principal's liability will be based on whether the agent has exceeded the authority. As can be seen in 9.1, an agent's authority can be extremely wide in that it can be express, implied, ostensible and usual. There is, therefore, more scope for making the principal vicariously liable, even though in *Lloyd v Grace, Smith and Co Ltd* (1912) the employee had only intended to benefit himself.

8.7.7   Employer and independent contractor

As a general rule, the employer is not liable for the torts of any independent contractor he or she chooses to employ. However, he or she may be made a joint tortfeasor with the independent contractor where the employer has:

* ratified or authorised the tortious act;

* contributed to the commission of the tort by the independent contractor, either by the way in which the work was directed or by interfering with the work;

* been negligent in the selection of his independent contractor

In *Balfour v Barty-King* (1957), Barty-King's water pipes were frozen. She asked two men at a nearby building site to help unfreeze them. They did this by using a blowlamp, rather than a heated brick, on the lagged pipes in her loft. The lagging caught fire and the fire spread to the adjoining premises. It was held that Barty-King was jointly liable for the negligence of the contractor. She had chosen them, invited them onto her premises and then left them to do the job. She should have exercised more care, not only in her selection, but also in overseeing their work:

* a non-delegable duty, for example, under the Factory Act 1961 and related statutes (see *Wilsons and Clyde Coal v English* (1938));

* asked the independent contractor to carry out work which is particularly hazardous, or is situated on the highway.

In *Salsbury v Woodland* (1970), the independent contractor was contracted to fell a tree in his client's garden close to the highway. He was an experienced tree-feller but was negligent in felling the tree. Telephone lines were brought down and the plaintiff, whilst attempting to move the wires from the highway, was struck by a car. It was held that the person employing the independent contractor was not liable. The work was not being carried out on the highway and near to the highway is not the same thing. Furthermore, this work would only be regarded as extra-hazardous if it had been carried out on the highway. The independent contractor must bear sole responsibility.

The criteria for judging whether work is particularly hazardous involves looking at where the work is to be carried out, whether members of the public are at risk and what the dangers are (see *Honeywell and Stein Ltd v Larkin Bros Ltd* (1934)).

8.8   The tort of employer's liability

This particular aspect of the general tort of negligence arises out of the duty on an employer to take reasonable care for the safety of his or her employees whilst they are at work. It gives the employee the right to sue the employer when injured at work for negligent acts by the employer arising out of the course of his or her employment. In order to ensure that the employer can pay any award of damages, the Employers' Liability (Compulsory Insurance) Act 1969 imposes a duty on the employer to take out the necessary insurance cover.

It should also be noted that, if an action for employers' liability is unavailable, the injured employee may have the same rights as any other individual injured by another employee, that is, to pursue an action for vicarious liability (see 8.7).

It was not until the late 19th century that employees were able to proceed with such claims. The courts originally took the view that the doctrine of common employment precluded an action against the employer where the employee had been injured by the actions of a fellow employee (*Priestley v Fowler* (1837)); the rationale for this being that the employee had impliedly agreed to accept any risks incidental to his contract of employment. There was also concern expressed for the possible financial burden placed on employers having to pay compensation for industrial accidents if such actions were allowed to proceed. In addition, the defences of *volenti* and contributory negligence removed any chance of success in such claims, as *volenti* in particular was freely available to the employer. Gradually, the doctrine of common employment was removed and limitations placed on the use of *volenti* as a defence (*Smith v Baker and Sons* (1891)); as a result, the tort of employer's liability was allowed to develop.

8.8.1 Employer's duty of care

The general nature of the duty requires employers to take reasonable care in the way they conduct their operations so as not to subject their employees to unnecessary risks (*Smith v Baker and Son* (1891)).

The employer's duty of care is owed to each individual employee and, as it is a personal duty, it cannot be delegated by the employer to anyone else. This was made quite clear in *Wilsons and Clyde Coal Co v English* (1938), where the day to day responsibility for the mine was delegated to a mine manager as required by statute. However, the court concluded that the ultimate responsibility for health and safety remained with the employer.

The duty is only owed whilst the employee is acting within the course of his employment, that is, is doing something reasonably incidental to the employee's main job. In *Davidson v Handley-Page Ltd* (1945), the plaintiff was washing his teacup in the sink at his place of work when he slipped and hurt his leg whilst standing on a duck-board. The duck-board had become slippery because water was constantly splashed upon it. It was held that the employer was in breach of his duty because the employee was carrying out a task which was reasonably incidental to his job; tea-breaks were an accepted part of working life.

As a general rule, employees are not acting within the course of their employment whilst travelling to and from work. The exception to this was recognised in *Smith v Stages and Darlington Insulation Co Ltd* (1989), which offers some protection to peripatetic workers or any employee who may have to work away from his main base. Where employees are paid their normal wage for this travelling time, they will be within the course of their employment.

As the duty is of a personal nature, the standard of care will vary with the individual needs of each employee. It follows, therefore, that special regard must be had for the old, young, inexperienced and less able-bodied.

8.8.2 Scope of the employer's duty

This was defined in *Wilsons and Clyde Coal Co v English* (1938). Following this case, the employer's duty has been determined as extending to the provision of:

- competent fellow employees;
- safe plant and appliances;
- safe place of work;
- safe system of work.

However, it has been recognised that there is an overlap between the duties owed at common law and the duties implied into the contract of employment, a breach of which would allow the employee to pursue either cause of action. An example of this can be seen in *Johnstone v Bloomsbury Health Authority* (1991), where it was concluded that requiring junior hospital doctors to work excessive hours may be a breach of the employer's implied duty, although the implied contractual duty to take reasonable care for the safety of employees would have to be read subject to the express terms in the contract of employment.

The remit of the employer's duty is open to expansion through the case law. In *McFarlane v EE Caledonia* (1993), a claim was made that an employer owed a duty to prevent psychiatric injury. The Court of Appeal concluded that as the plaintiff was not directly involved in the accident and did not fall within the recognised categories of plaintiffs who can recover as outlined in *Alcock v Chief Constable of South Yorkshire* (1991), the employer cannot be liable.

It was further held in *Frost v Chief Constable of South Yorkshire* (1997) that an employer owed a duty of care to avoid exposing an employee to unnecessary risk of physical or psychiatric injury. Although the standard of care in discharging the duty will vary from case to case according to the nature of the job and the degree of fortitude to be expected of the employee. As a result, police officers who were at the ground in the course of their duty, within the area of risk of physical and psychiatric injury, dealing with the dead and dying and who were thus exposed, by their employers' negligence, to the exceptionally horrific events which occurred could recover damages.

However, the risks from passive smoking may well be within the remit of the employer's duty. As a result, a reasonable employer would be expected to produce and implement a no-smoking policy (*Bland v Stockport County Council* (1992)).

Competent fellow employees

The employer must ensure that all his staff are competent to do the job which they have been employed to do. The employer must, therefore, make sure that they have the necessary experience and qualifications, and where necessary, must be prepared to train them accordingly. If an employee is injured as a result of the incompetence of a fellow employee, then the employer may be liable. The word incompetence covers a range of ineptitude; many of the cases arising out of practical jokes. In this situation, whether the employer is liable will depend on the depth of knowledge about the incompetent employee. If, for example, the employer has been put on warning or given notice that the employee is capable of committing an incompetent act, such as a practical joke, the employer will be liable.

In *O'Reilly v National Rail and Tramway Appliances Ltd* (1966), O'Reilly was employed with three others to break up scrap from railways. His colleagues persuaded him to hit, with his sledge-hammer, a shell case embedded between the railway sleepers. When he did this, the shell exploded. It was held that the employer was not in breach of his duty because he had no previous knowledge that these workmen played practical jokes or were capable of encouraging such an act. He had not, therefore, failed to employ competent fellow employees.

The previous conduct of the incompetent employee is therefore extremely relevant. Where the employer has been given notice, he should take suitable action to ensure that such conduct does not result in something more serious; failure to take action will leave the employer open to a claim in the event of an accident arising out of the employee's incompetence. Depending on the nature of the previous conduct, dismissal of the incompetent employee may be justified.

In *Hudson v Ridge Manufacturing Co Ltd* (1957), Hudson was on his way to the sick room when a fellow employee tripped him up and broke his wrist. This employee was known as a practical joker and had been warned by his employer to stop fooling about. It was held that the employer was in breach of his duty because he was aware of his employee's tendency to fool around. He should have done more to curb this employee even if this meant dismissal.

Safe plant and appliances

The employer must not only provide his employees with the necessary plant and equipment to do the job safely, but must also ensure that such plant and equipment is safe, that is, properly maintained. For example, guards must be provided on dangerous machinery to protect the employee from injury and these guards must be inspected regularly to ensure that they are securely in position and are not damaged in any way.

In *Bradford v Robinson Rentals Ltd* (1967), Bradford was employed as a driver. He was required to drive over 400 miles in extremely cold weather in a van with a broken window and a heater which did not work. He suffered severe frost bite. It was held that the van was not safe and, therefore, the employer had failed in his duty to provide safe plant and equipment. Although the conditions were extreme, it was foreseeable that the employee would suffer some injury if sent out on a long journey in a van in that condition. A further illustration of this duty can be seen in *Taylor v Rover Car Co Ltd* (1966). Taylor was using a hammer and chisel when a piece of metal flew off the chisel and blinded him in one eye. This batch of chisels was in a defective state when supplied by the manufacturers. It was held that Taylor's employer was liable because a similar incident had occurred four weeks previously without any one being injured. This meant that the employer should have known of the likelihood of such an accident occurring. To avoid this, the chisels should have been taken out of use and returned to the manufacturer.

If the previous incident in *Taylor* had not occurred, Taylor's only remedy at that time would have been against the manufacturer. However, the Employer's Liability (Defective Equipment) Act 1969 provides that where an employee is injured at work as a consequence of defective equipment supplied by his employer and the defect is the fault of a third party, for example, the manufacturer, the employer will be deemed to be negligent and, therefore, responsible for the injury. This statute removes the need to establish foresight on the part of the employer in cases like *Taylor*.

Safe place of work

The employer must ensure that his employees are not exposed to any dangers arising out of the place where they are expected to work. This covers any place under the control of the employer including access and egress and may extend to the premises of a third party, although, in the latter case, the employer may not reasonably be expected to go to the same lengths as he or she would on his own premises, although, as can be seen in *Wilson v Tyneside Window Cleaning Co* (1958), at the very least it may be necessary to warn employees of the dangers when visiting/working on the premises of a third party.

In *Smith v Vange Scaffolding and Engineering Co Ltd* (1970), Smith was employed on a building site by Vange. There were other contractors on site. As Smith returned to the changing hut at the end of the working day, he tripped over the cable of a welding machine which had been left there by a contractor. Vange were aware of the obstructions on site which made access to and from the place of work difficult and dangerous, but they had not complained to the other contractors. It was held that the employer had failed in his duty to his employee, because, being aware of the situation, he should have made the necessary complaints to the main contractor. It was foreseeable that such an accident might occur and reasonable precautions should have been taken.

The remit of this duty extends to consideration of the nature of the place and the potential risks involved, the work to be carried out, the experience of the employee and the degree of control or supervision which the employer can reasonably exercise. There may be situations where a safe place of work overlaps with the employer's duty to provide a safe system of work. Finally, the duty may apply where the employer sends employees overseas to work. However, whether there has been a breach of duty will depend on whether the employer acted reasonably in the circumstances of that particular case.

In *Cook v Square* (1992), an employee was sent to Saudi Arabia on a two month contract. His employer was satisfied that the site occupiers and the contractors were reliable companies and had a good health and safety record. In these circumstances, it was held that the employer could not be held to be responsible for the day to day running of the site, nor undertake safety inspections. However, the situation may be different if a number of employees were required to work there for long periods.

Safe system of work

The duty of the employer to provide a safe system of work extends to a consideration of the following by the employer: the physical layout of the job, safety notices, special procedures, protective clothing, training and supervision.

In order to fulfil this duty, the employer must take into account all foreseeable eventualities including the actions of any employees. Any system, to be safe, must reduce the risks to the employee to a minimum; it is accepted that not all risks can be eliminated. Furthermore, the employer must do more than introduce a safe system of work, it must be ensured that it is observed by the employees. The case law highlights the breadth of this duty.

For example, it can extend to preventing staff being exposed to risk of violence if this is a foreseeable risk, as in *Charlton v Forrest Printing Ink Co Ltd* (1980). This aspect of the duty will also cover claims for compensation for work-related upper-limb disorder (WRULD/RSI) as in (*Bettany v Royal Doulton (UK) Ltd* (1993)). This is now further supported by the decision in *Pickford v Imperial Chemical Industries plc* (1996), in which the plaintiff contracted repetitive strain injury as a result of her employment as secretary which involved in excessive typing for prolonged periods without proper breaks or rest pauses. This had come about because they did not give her the same instructions as they gave their typists working in the accounts department who carried out typing for most of the day. Those who were liable to do a great deal of typing should be told that they must take breaks and rest pauses. It was also advisable to explain why this was necessary.

Stress at work also falls within the remit of the employer's liability. In *Walker v Northumberland County Council* (1994), Walker was employed as an area social services officer with responsibility for four teams of field workers. As the volume of work increased, Walker wrote reports and memoranda regarding the increased workload and the need for urgency in redistributing staff to assist. Nothing was done about this and, one year later, Walker suffered a nervous breakdown. Before returning to work, Walker's superior agreed to provide him with assistance. However, one month after he returned to work, assistance was withdrawn and, in September 1987, he suffered a second nervous breakdown. In 1988, he was dismissed on grounds of permanent ill health. It was held that the defendants were in breach of the duty of care owed to the plaintiff in respect of the second nervous breakdown which he suffered as a result of stress and anxiety occasioned by his job.

The contentious issue surrounds instruction and supervision. Is it sufficient to order an employee to take safety precautions or should they be supervised as well if the duty is to be satisfied? The answer depends on the degree of risk and the experience of the employee concerned, including how far the employee has been warned of the risks. It is, however, quite clear from the decision in *Pape v Cumbria County Council* (1991) that merely providing protective clothing without warning of the risks may not be sufficient to discharge the duty.

Constant supervision is, on the whole, not necessary where the employees have the necessary experience and have been trained or instructed accordingly. However, the degree of supervision is commensurate to the severity of the risk.

In *Bux v Slough Metals Ltd* (1974), Bux's job involved the removal of molten metal from a furnace and the pouring of this metal into a die-casting machine. Goggles were supplied and Bux was made aware of the risks. He refused to wear the safety goggles because they misted up and he complained to the supervisor who informed him that no other goggles were available. He was injured when molten metal splashed into his eye. It was held that the employer was liable because, where the work was of a particularly hazardous nature, he should do more than merely provide safety equipment. He should constantly urge his employees to use or wear it.

8.8.3 Breach of the employer's duty

Once duty is established, the remaining essentials are judged on the same basis as any action in negligence. The burden is on the employee to show that the employer is in breach of his or her duty. The employee must prove fault on the part of the employer, that is, has the employer failed to act as a reasonable employer, or alternatively can *res ipsa loquitur* be established? If the employer has taken all reasonable precautions considering all the circumstances of the case, then he or she will not be liable (see *Latimer v AEC Ltd* (1953)).

The standard of care will vary with respect to the individual needs of each employee. The employer must have special regard for the old, young, inexperienced and employees with special disabilities, that is, the standard of care will be increased.

Having established duty and breach, the employee must show that injury has been suffered as a result of the employer's breach of duty. Injury is not confined to physical injury but includes damage to personal property, loss of earnings, etc. The test for establishing liability is the one used in negligence, that is, the but for test. The question which has to be answered by the court is therefore: but for the employer's breach of duty would the employee have been injured? If the answer is no, causation is established.

Even after causation has been established, the employer is not necessarily liable for all the damage to his employee. The employer will only be liable for foreseeable damage. This does not mean that the precise nature or extent of the injury has to be foreseen, only that some harm will result from the breach of duty. Applying the rule in *The Wagon Mound (No 1)* (1961), the employer will only be liable for the foreseeable consequences of his breach, that is, not the unexpected.

There are no defences which are unique to this particular tort. In general, the main ones pleaded are contributory negligence and *volenti*; the former may result in a reduction in the amount of damages payable. The latter is rarely accepted by the courts in actions founded in employer's liability.

The principal remedy available for employer's liability is compensation for personal injury; the object being to put the plaintiff in the position he or she would have been in if the accident had never occurred. The limitation period for bringing such an action is three years from the date on which the cause of action arose or the date of knowledge, whichever is the later (Limitation Act 1980).

THE TORT OF NEGLIGENCE

A tort is a wrongful act against an individual, or body corporate, or their property, which gives rise to a civil action. The tort of negligence imposes a duty to take reasonable care to prevent harm or loss occurring from ones actions.

The elements of the tort which must be established by the claimant are:

- duty of care;
- breach of duty;
- resultant damage.

Duty of care

The test for establishing duty is the neighbour test as expounded by Lord Atkin in *Donoghue v Stevenson* (1932).

There is therefore a duty to take reasonable care to avoid acts or omissions which you could reasonably foresee may injure your neighbour. In deciding who falls within the remit of the word 'neighbour', the courts apply the proximity test not only referred to by Lord Atkin, but also seen in *Peabody Donation Fund v Sir Lindsay Parkinson and Co Ltd* (1984) and *Leigh and Sillivan Ltd v Aliakmon Shipping Co Ltd* (1986).

It is also clear from the decision in *Anns v Merton LBC* (1978) that public policy issues may be used to restrict the existence of a duty of care. Whilst one argument was that the decision in *Anns* was restricted to new duty situations, this has to be considered in the light of *Caparo Industries plc v Dickman* (1990), which introduced a three stage test for establishing the existence of a duty of care. This test appears to apply to all situations.

The test is incremental, requiring consideration of the following:

- foresight;
- proximity;
- just and reasonable.

It was approved in *Marc Rich and Co AG v Bishop Rock Marine Co Ltd, The Nicholas H* (1994).

Nervous shock

The tort of negligence also recognises liability for nervous shock, sometimes known as post-traumatic stress disorder. However, establishing duty of care in respect of such loss may not be easy. The claimant must show that he or she has suffered a recognised medical condition which goes beyond grief and distress. Foresight and proximity must also be established.

The courts clearly distinguish between fearing for one's own safety – as in *Dulieu v White* (1901) – and merely being a passing witness to an accident – as in *Bourhill v Young* (1943) and *Hegarty v EE Caledonia Ltd* (1996). A further contentious issue arises where the claimant who witnesses the accident or its immediate aftermath has a close relationship with the victim. Where there is a close loving relationship and proximity to the accident in terms of time and space, then as can be seen in *Hambrook v Stokes Bros* (1925) and *McLoughlin v O'Brian* (1982) the claimant is likely to recover damages. The limits of the establishing liability can be seen in *Alcock and Others v Chief Constable of South Yorkshire Police* (1991), where claims by friends and relatives who witnessed the events at Hillsborough via the television or radio in general failed because of the lack of proximity in time and space.

Rescuers are in general treated as a special case, particularly where they are not professional rescuers (*Chadwick v British Railways Board* (1967)). Although the courts have opened the debate on who may in law qualify as a rescuer by the decision in *Frost v Chief Constable of South Yorkshire* (1997).

Economic loss

Liability for economic loss arising out of physical injury or damage to property may be compensated in negligence; however, liability for pure economic loss cannot, in general, be compensated.

The limit of liability for this type of loss is illustrated in *Spartan Steel and Alloys Ltd v Martin and Co* (1973). Although there had been some expansion of liability through the cases, particularly *Junior Books Ltd v Veitchi Ltd* (1983). In the latter case, the extremely close proximity in terms of the quasi-contractual relationship of the parties was clearly a feature in allowing recovery for pure economic loss. There has been a clear retraction from the position in *Junior Books* which is to be regarded as a special case decided on its facts and, as can be seen in *Murphy v Brentwood District Council* (1990), liability for pure economic loss will in general only be upheld where negligent misstatement is proven.

Pure economic loss arising from negligent misstatements is the exception to the general rule and such loss can, therefore, be compensated.

The watershed for such liability was *Hedley Byrne and Co Ltd v Heller and Partners* (1964). Where a special relationship is found to exist between the parties, falling short of contract, the defendant may be liable for giving negligent advice. This is particularly true where the defendant holds himself out as being in the business or competent to give such advice and it is reasonable in the circumstances for the claimant to rely on it (*Mutual Life and Citizens Assurance Co v Evatt* (1971) and *Chaudry v Prabhakar* (1988)).

Many professions have been deemed to owe a duty of care to persons other than their clients and may therefore be liable for economic loss arising from their negligent statements.

Such professionals will be deemed to be in a special relationship with the claimant and, where it is found that reliance on the advice or actions is reasonable, liability will ensue. Accountants and auditors may be particularly vulnerable, although as can be seen in *JEB Fasteners v Marks Bloom and Co* (1983) the claimant will have to show that they actually relied on the advice. Furthermore, in *Caparo Industries plc v Dickman* (1990), the extent of the duty may be limited so that the claimant does not fall within its scope. Other professionals may also find themselves liable, although following the decision in *White v Jones* (1995), this may be based on the test in *Donoghue v Stevenson* (1932).

Breach of duty

Once the claimant has established a duty of care, breach of duty must be proven. The test for establishing breach of duty is whether the defendant has acted as a reasonable man in all the circumstances of the case. The courts will take into account the:

- likelihood of harm occurring (*Bolton v Stone* (1951));

- thin skull rule (*Haley v London Electricity Board* (1965); *Paris v Stepney BC* (1951));

- cost and practicability of taking precautions (*Latimer v AEC* (1952));

- social utility of the act (*Watt v Hertfordshire CC* (1954));

- common practice (*Roe v Minister of Health* (1954)).

In certain circumstances, the claimant may rely on the maxim *res ipsa loquitur* in order to establish breach. However, the following must be shown:

- sole management or control on the part of the defendant;

- the occurrence could not have happened without negligence;

- the cause of the occurrence is unknown.

Resultant damage

Finally, the claimant must show that the breach of duty on the part of the defendant was the cause of his or her loss. The test for establishing causation in fact is the but for test, that is, but for the defendant's actions the damage would not have occurred.

The cases clearly illustrate that, if there is another acceptable explanation for the injury, causation may not be proven as in *Cutler v Vauxhall Motors Ltd* (1971). This is particularly true in medical negligence claims where there may be a number of potential causes of injury but the onus rests on the claimant to show that the defendant's breach was a material contributory cause, as in *Wilsher v Essex Area Health Authority* (1988) and *Hotson v East Berkshire Area Health Authority* (1987).

The extent of the defendant's liability may be further limited by the rules for determining remoteness of damage.

Where the cause and extent of the harm is unforeseen, the loss will not be recoverable. The test for establishing remoteness is that of reasonable foresight as expounded in the *Wagon Mound (No 1)* (1961), where damage was limited to the fouling of the wharf by oil, and did not extend to the damage caused by the fire as, at the time of the accident, it could not be foreseen that the oil would ignite on water.

As a general rule, it is not necessary to foresee the exact cause of the harm as long as it is within the general range which any reasonable person might foresee (*Stewart v West African Air Terminals* (1964) and *Hughes v Lord Advocate* (1963)). Although not all the cases are easy to reconcile (see *Doughty v Turner Manufacturing Co Ltd* (1964) and *Tremain v Pike* (1969)).

Defences

Damages may be reduced by the plaintiff contributory negligence (Law Reform (Contributory Negligence) Act 1945).

The defence of *volenti* or consent may operate as a complete defence (*ICI v Shatwell* (1965); *Dann v Hamilton* (1939)).

Vicarious liability

An employer is, in general, liable for torts committed by his or her employees whilst they are acting within the course of their employment. Whilst the employee has primary liability for the tort and can be sued personally, if the plaintiff pursues an action against the employer, the employee may be joined in the action or his or her employer may, where a claim is unsuccessfully defended, seek an indemnity from his or her employee:

- There must be in existence an employer/employee relationship. The test for determining this can be found in 9.4.1.

- The employee must be acting within the course of his or her employment. This may be doing something incidental to his or her job or carrying out an authorised act in a wrongful, negligent or unauthorised manner.

- Cases which illustrate within the course of employment extend to smoking a cigarette whilst unloading a petrol tanker (*Century Insurance Co Ltd v Northern Ireland Road Transport Board* (1942)); carrying out a prohibited act for the purpose of the employer's business (*Rose v Plenty* (1976)); carrying out an unauthorised act which was closely connected with the main employment (*Harrison v Michelin Tyre Co Ltd* (1985)); using force to protect the employer's property (*Poland v Parr and Sons* (1927)); using one's employment to carry out an unauthorised task (*Morris v Martin and Sons Ltd* (1966) and *Lloyd v Grace Smith and Co* (1912)).

- Cases which illustrate outside the course of employment extend to deviating so far from one's employment so as to be on a frolic of ones own (*Hilton v Thomas Burton (Rhodes) Ltd* (1961)); use of excessive violence (*Warren v Henlys Ltd* (1948)); doing an act at work which is unconnected with the actual employment (*Aldred v Nacanco* (1987)); carrying out a criminal act for which there is no nexus between the job and the act (*Heasmans v Clarity Cleaning Co Ltd* (1987) and *Irving v Post Office* (1987)).

The concept of vicarious liability arises where there is in existence a special relationship. It can, therefore, also arise between principal and agent and in limited circumstances between employer and independent contractor:

- *Balfour v Barty-King* (1957);

- *Salsbury v Woodland* (1970);

- *Honeywell and Stein Ltd v Larkin Bros Ltd* (1934).

Employer's liability

An employer is under a duty to take reasonable care in respect of the health and safety of his or her employees. This duty is personal in that it is owed to each individual employee and cannot be delegated.

The duty is owed whilst the employee is acting within the course of his or her employment.

The course of employment extends to the carrying out of tasks reasonably incidental to ones job as in *Davidson v Handley-Page Ltd* (1945).

The scope of the duty is four-fold:

- to provide competent fellow employees;
- to provide safe plant and appliances;
- to provide a safe place of work;
- to provide a safe system of work.

CHAPTER 9

BUSINESS AND CORPORATE LAW

This chapter introduces some of the essential elements of the law relating to business activity and, in particular, focuses on the structure of the business enterprise (see the following diagram):

Business forms in the UK

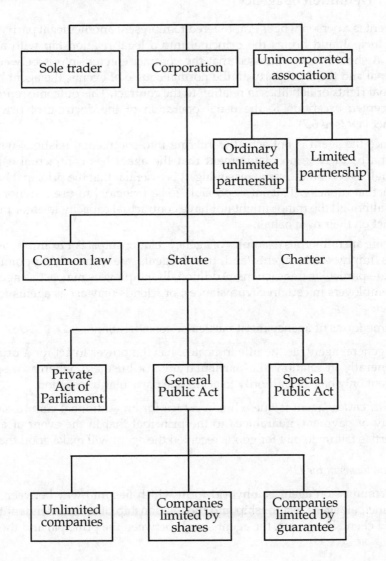

445

9.1 Agency

The general assumption is that individuals engaging in business activity carry on that business by themselves on their own behalf, but it is not uncommon for such individuals to engage others to represent them and negotiate business deals on their behalf. Indeed, the role of the middleman is a commonplace one in business and commerce. The legal relationship between such a representative, or middleman, and the business person making use of them is governed by the law of agency.

9.1.1 Definition of agency

An agent is a person who is empowered to represent another legal party, called the principal, and brings the principal into a legal relationship with a third party. It should be emphasised that the contract entered into is between the principal and the third party. In the normal course of events, the agent has no personal rights or liabilities in relation to the contract. This outcome represents an accepted exception to the usual operation of the doctrine of privity in contract law (see 6.7).

Since the agent is not actually entering into contractual relations with the third party, there is no requirement that the agent has contractual capacity although, based on the same reasoning, it is essential that the principal has full contractual capacity. Thus, it is possible for a principal to use a minor as an agent although the minor might not have contractual capacity to enter into the contract on their own behalf.

There are numerous examples of agency relationships. For example, as their names imply, estate agents and travel agents are expressly appointed to facilitate particular transactions. Additionally, employees may act as agents of their employers in certain circumstances; or friends may act as agents for one another.

Some forms of agency merit particular consideration:

- A general agent, as the title indicates, has the power to act for a principal generally in relation to a particular area of business, whereas a special agent only has the authority to act in one particular transaction.

- A *del credere* agent is one who, in return for an additional commission by way of payment, guarantees to the principal that in the event of a third party's failure to pay for goods received the agent will make good the loss.

Business forms in the UK

- A commission agent is a hybrid form which lies mid-way between a full principal/agent relationship and the relationship of an independent trader and client. In essence, the agent stands between the principal and the third party and establishes no contract between those two parties. The effect is that, although the commission agent owes the duties of an agent to his or her principle, he or she contracts with the third party as a principal in his or her own right. The effectiveness of this procedure is undermined by the normal operation of the agency rule relating to an undisclosed principal.

- The position of a mercantile agent/factor is defined in the Factors Act 1889 as an agent:

  ... having in the customary course of his business as such agent authority either to sell goods, or to consign goods for the purpose of sale, or to buy goods, or to raise money on the security of goods.

However, of perhaps more contemporary importance are marketing agents, distribution agents and the question of franchising.

Marketing agents only have a limited authority. They can only introduce potential customers to their principals and do not have the authority either to negotiate or enter into contracts on behalf of their principals.

Distribution agents are appointed by suppliers to arrange the distribution of their products within a particular area. The distributors ordinarily cannot bind the supplier, except where they have expressly been given the authority to do so.

Franchising arrangements arise where the original developer of a business decides, for whatever reason, to allow others to use their goodwill to conduct an independent business whilst continuing to use the original name of the business. Examples of such arrangements are McDonalds, The Body Shop and Sock Shop. It is essential to emphasise that any such relationship does not arise from or give rise to a relationship of principal and agent. Indeed, it is commonplace, if not universal, that franchise agreements include an express clause to the effect that no such relationship is to be established.

Commercial agents are specifically covered by the Commercial Agents (Council Directive) Regulations 1993, which were enacted in order to comply with European Community Directive 86/653. The Regulations define a commercial agent as a self-employed intermediary who has continuing authority to negotiate the sale or purchase of goods on behalf of another person or to negotiate and conclude such transactions on behalf of that person. Although intended to harmonise the operation and effect of agency law within the European Union, the Regulations do not introduce any major substantive changes into UK agency law. The effect of the Regulations will be considered in more detail below:

- A power of attorney arises where an agency is specifically created by way of a deed.

9.1.2 Creation of agency

No one can act as an agent without the consent of the principal, although consent need not be expressly stated.

In *White v Lucas* (1887), a firm of estate agents claimed to act on behalf of the owner of a particular property although that person had denied them permission to act on his behalf. When the owner sold the property to a third party introduced through the estate agents, they claimed their commission. It was held that the estate agents had no entitlement to commission as the property owner had not agreed to their acting as his agent.

The principal/agent relationship can be created in a number of ways. It may arise as the outcome of a distinct contract, which may be made either orally or in writing, or it may be established purely gratuitously where some person simply agrees to act for another. The relationship may also arise from the action of the parties.

It is usual to consider the creation of the principal/agency relationship under four distinct categories.

Express appointment

This is the most common manner in which a principal/agent relationship comes into existence. In this situation, the agent is specifically appointed by the principal to carry out a particular task or to undertake some general function. In most situations, the appointment of the agent will itself involve the establishment of a contractual relationship between the principal and the agent but need not necessarily depend upon a contract between those parties.

For the most part, there are no formal requirements for the appointment of an agent, although, where the agent is to be given the power to execute deeds in the principal's name, they must themselves be appointed by way of a deed (that is, they are given power of attorney).

Ratification

An agency is created by ratification when a person who has no authority purports to contract with a third party on behalf of a principal. Ratification is the express acceptance of the contract by the principal. Where the principal elects to ratify the contract, it gives retrospective validity to the action of the purported agent. There are, however, certain conditions which have to be fully complied with before the principal can effectively adopt the contract:

- *The principal must have been in existence at the time when the agent entered into the contract*

  Thus, for example, in *Kelner v Baxter* (1866), where the promoters attempted to enter into a contract on behalf of the, as yet unformed, company, it was held that the company could not ratify the contract after it was created and that the promoters, as agents, were personally liable on the contract (this is now given statutory effect under s 36(C) of the Companies Act 1985).

- *The principal must have had legal capacity to enter into the contract when it was made*

  When the capacity of companies to enter into a business transaction was limited by the operation of the doctrine of *ultra vires* (see 9.3), it was clearly established that they could not ratify any such *ultra vires* contracts. Similarly, it is not possible for minors to ratify a contract even though it was made in their name.

- *An undisclosed principal cannot ratify a contract*

  The agent must have declared that he or she was acting for the principal. If the agent appeared to be acting on his or her own account, then the principal cannot later adopt the contact (see *Keighley, Maxsted and Co v Durant* (1901)).

- *The principal must adopt the whole of the contract*

  It is not open to the principal to pick and choose which parts of the contract to adopt – he or she must accept all of its terms.

- *Ratification must take place within a reasonable time*

  It is not possible to state with certainty what will be considered as a reasonable time in any particular case. Where, however, the third party with whom the agent contracted becomes aware that the agent had acted without authority, a time limit can be set within which the principal must indicate their adoption of the contract for it to be effective.

Implication

This form of agency arises from the relationship that exists between the principal and the agent and from which it is assumed that the principal has given authority to the other person to act as his or her agent. Thus, it is implied from the particular position held by individuals that they have the authority to enter into contractual relations on behalf of their principal. Thus, whether an employee has the actual authority to contract on behalf of his or her employer depends on the position held by the employee; and, for example, it was decided in *Panorama Developments v Fidelis Furnishing Fabrics Ltd* (1971) that a company secretary had the implied authority to make contracts in the company's name relating to the day to day running of the company.

Problems most often occur in relation to the implied extent of a person's authority rather than their actual appointment (but see *Hely-Hutchinson v Brayhead Ltd* (1967) as an example of the latter).

Necessity

Agency by necessity occurs under circumstances where, although there is no agreement between the parties, an emergency requires that an agent take particular action in order to protect the interests of the principal. The usual situation which gives rise to agency by necessity occurs where the agent is in possession of the principal's property and, due to some unforeseen emergency, the agent has to take action to safeguard that property:

- *In order for agency by necessity to arise, there needs to be a genuine emergency*

  In *Great Northern Railway Co v Swaffield* (1874), the railway company transported the defendant's horse and, when no one arrived to collect it at its destination, it was placed in a livery stable. It was held that the company was entitled to recover the cost of stabling as necessity had forced them to act as they had done, as the defendant's agents.

- *There must also be no practical way of obtaining further instructions from the principal*

  In *Springer v Great Western Railway Co* (1921), a consignment of tomatoes arrived at port after a delayed journey due to storms. A railway strike would have caused further delay in getting the tomatoes to their destination, so the railway company decided to sell the tomatoes locally. It was held that the railway company was responsible to the plaintiff for the difference between the price achieved and the market price in London. The defence of agency of necessity was not available as the railway company could have contacted the plaintiff to seek his further instructions.

- *The person seeking to establish the agency by necessity must have acted* bona fide *in the interests of the principal*

  See *Sachs v Miklos* (1948).

Estoppel

This form of agency is also known as 'agency by holding out' and arises where the principal has led other parties to believe that a person has the authority to represent him. (The authority possessed by the agent is referred to as apparent authority: see 9.1.3.) In such circumstances, even though no principal/agency relationship actually exists in fact, the principal is prevented (estopped) from denying the existence of the agency relationship and is bound by the action of his or her purported agent as regards any third party who acted in the belief of its existence:

- *To rely on agency by estoppel, there must have been a representation by the principal as to the authority of the agent*

  In *Freeman and Lockyer v Buckhurst Park Properties Ltd* (1964), a property company had four directors but one director effectively controlled the company and made contracts as if he were the managing director even though he had never actually been appointed to that position and, therefore, as an individual, had no authority to bind the company. The other directors, however, were aware of this activity and acquiesced in it. When the company was sued in relation to one of the contracts entered into by the unauthorised director, it was held that it was liable as the board which had the actual authority to bind the company had held out the individual director as having the necessary authority to enter such contracts. It was, therefore, a case of agency by estoppel.

- *As with estoppel generally, the party seeking to rely on it must have relied on the representation*

  In *Overbrooke Estates Ltd v Glencombe Properties Ltd* (1974), a notice which expressly denied the authority of an auctioneer to make such statements as actually turned out to be false was successfully relied on as a defence by the auctioneer's employers.

9.1.3 The authority of an agent

In order to bind a principal, any contract entered into must be within the limits of the authority extended to the agent. The authority of an agent can be either actual or apparent.

Actual authority

Actual authority can arise in two ways:

(a) *Express actual authority*

  This is explicitly granted by the principal to the agent. The agent is instructed as to what particular tasks he or she is required to perform and is informed of the precise powers given in order to fulfil those tasks.

(b) *Implied actual authority*

  This refers to the way in which the scope of express authority may be increased. Third parties are entitled to assume that agents holding a particular position have all the powers that are usually provided to such an agent. Without actual knowledge to the contrary, they may safely assume that the agent has the usual authority that goes with their position. (This has been referred to above in relation to implied agency.)

  In *Watteau v Fenwick* (1893), the new owners of a hotel continued to employ the previous owner as its manager. They expressly forbade him to buy certain articles, including cigars. The manager, however, bought cigars from a third party who later sued the owners for payment as the manager's principal. It was held that the purchase of cigars was within the usual authority of a manager of such an establishment and that, for a limitation on such usual authority to be effective, it must be communicated to any third party.

Apparent authority

Apparent authority is an aspect of agency by estoppel considered above. It can arise in two distinct ways:

(a) Where a person makes a representation to third parties that a particular person has the authority to act as their agent without actually appointing the agent.

In such a case, the person making the representation is bound by the actions of the apparent agent (see *Freeman and Lockyer v Buckhurst Park Properties Ltd* (1964)). The principal is also liable for the actions of the agent where it is known that the agent claims to be his or her agent and yet does nothing to correct that impression.

(b) Where a principal has previously represented to a third party that an agent has the authority to act on their behalf.

Even if the principal has subsequently revoked the agent's authority, they may still be liable for the actions of the former agent unless they have informed third parties who had previously dealt with the agent about the new situation (see *Willis Faber and Co Ltd v Joyce* (1911)).

Warrant of authority

If an agent contracts with a third party on behalf of a principal, the agent impliedly guarantees that the principal exists and has contractual capacity. The agent also implies that he or she has the authority to make contracts on behalf of that principal. If any of these implied warranties prove to be untrue, then the third party may sue the agent in quasi-contract for breach of warrant of authority. Such an action may arise even though the agent was genuinely unaware of any lack of authority.

In *Yonge v Toynbee* (1910), a firm of solicitors was instructed to institute proceedings against a third party. Without their knowledge, their client was certified insane and, although this automatically ended the agency relationship, they continued with the proceedings. The third party successfully recovered damages for breach of warrant of authority since the solicitors were no longer acting for their former client.

9.1.4 The relationship of principal and agent

The following considers the reciprocal rights and duties which principal and agent owe each other.

9.1.5 The duties of agent to principal

The agent owes a number of duties, both express and implied, to the principal. These duties are as follows.

To perform the agreed undertaking according to the instructions of the principal

A failure to carry out instructions will leave the agent open to an action for breach of contract. This, of course, does not apply in the case of gratuitous agencies where there is no obligation whatsoever on the agent to perform the agreed task. See *Turpin v Bilton* (1843), where an agent was held liable for the loss sustained by his failure to insure his principal's ship prior to its sinking.

To exercise due care and skill

An agent will owe a duty to act with reasonable care and skill, regardless of whether the agency relationship is contractual or gratuitous. The level of skill to be exercised, however, should be that appropriate to the agent's professional capacity and this may introduce a distinction in the levels expected of different agents. For example, a solicitor would be expected to show the level of care and skill that would not be expected of a competent member of that profession whereas a layperson acting in a gratuitous capacity would only be expected to perform with such degree of care and skill as a reasonable person would exercise in the conduct of their own affairs (see *Keppel v Wheeler* (1927), where the defendant estate agents were held liable for failing to secure the maximum possible price for a property).

To carry out instructions personally

Unless expressly or impliedly authorised to delegate the work, an agent owes a duty to the principal to act personally in the completion of the task. The right to delegate may be agreed expressly by the principal or it may be implied from customary practice or arise as a matter of necessity. In any such case, the agent remains liable to the principal for the proper performance of the agreed contract.

To account

There is an implied duty that the agent keep proper accounts of all transactions entered into on behalf of the principal. The agent is required to account for all money and other property received on the principal's behalf and should keep his or her own property separate from that of the principal.

In addition to these contractual duties, there are general equitable duties which flow from the fact that the agency relationship is a fiduciary one, that is, it is one based on trust. These general fiduciary duties are as follows.

Not to permit a conflict of interest to arise

An agent must not allow the possibility of personal interest to conflict with the interests of his or her principal without disclosing that possibility to the principal. Upon full disclosure, it is up to the principal to decide whether or not to proceed with the particular transaction. If there is a breach of this duty the principal may set aside the contract so affected and claim any profit which might have been made by the agent.

In *McPherson v Watt* (1877), a solicitor used his brother as a nominee to purchase property which he was engaged to sell. It was held that, since the solicitor had allowed a conflict of interest to arise, the sale could be set aside. It was immaterial that a fair price was offered for the property.

The corollary to the above case is that the agent must not sell his or her own property to the principal without fully disclosing the fact (see *Harrods v Lemon* (1931)). This leads into the next duty which is:

Not to make a secret profit or misuse confidential information

An agent who uses his or her position as an agent to secure financial advantage for him or herself, without full disclosure to his principal, is in breach of fiduciary duty. Upon disclosure, the principal may authorise the agents profit but full disclosure is a necessary precondition (see *Hippisley v Knee Bros* (1905) for a clear cut case). An example of the strictness with which this principle is enforced may be seen in the case of *Boardman v Phipps* (1967), in which agents were held to account for profits made from information which they had gained from their position as agents, even though their action also benefited the company they were acting for.

Not to take a bribe

This duty may be seen as merely a particular aspect of the general duty not to make a secret profit but it goes so much to the root of the agency relationship that it is usually treated as a distinct heading in its own right. Again, for a clear cut case, see *Mahesan v Malaysian Government Officers Co-operative Housing Society* (1978) where the plaintiff received a bribe to permit a third party to profit at his principal's expense.

Where it is found that an agent has taken a bribe, the following civil remedies are open to the principal:

- to repudiate the contract with the third party;

- to dismiss the agent without notice;

- to refuse to pay any monies owed to the agent or to recover such monies already paid;

- to claim the amount of the bribe;

- to claim damages in the tort of deceit for any loss sustained as a result of the payment of the bribe.

The payment of the bribe may also have constituted a breach of criminal law.

9.1.6 The rights of an agent

The Commercial Agents (Council Directive) Regulations 1993, reg 3, provides that agents must act dutifully and in good faith in the interests of their principal. The agents must negotiate in a proper manner, execute the contracts they are contracted to undertake, communicate all necessary information to, and comply with all reasonable instructions from, their principal. Regulation 22 states that any agreements in restraint of trade in agency contracts are only effective if they are in writing. Such restraints must relate solely to the type of goods dealt with under the agency agreement and must be limited to the geographical area, or the particular customer group, allocated to the agent. In any case, such restraints may only be valid for a maximum period of two years.

It is a simple matter of fact that the law does not generally provide agents with as many rights as it imposes duties on them. The agent, however, does benefit from the clear establishment of three general rights. These rights are:

(a) *To claim remuneration for services performed*

It is usual in agency agreements for the amount of payment to be stated, either in the form of wages, or commission, or indeed both. Where a commercial agreement is silent on the matter of payment, the court will imply a term into the agreement requiring the payment of a reasonable remuneration. Such a term will not be implied in contradiction of the express terms of the agreement. See *Re Richmond Gate Property Co Ltd* (1965), where it was held that no remuneration could be claimed where an agreement stated that payment would be determined by the directors of the company but they had not actually decided on any payment.

(b) *To claim indemnity against the principal for all expenses legitimately incurred in the performance of services*

Both contractual and non-contractual agents are entitled to recover money spent in the course of performing their agreed task. In the case of the former, the remedy is based on an implied contractual term and, in the case of a gratuitous agent, it is based on the remedy of restitution. Money can, of course, only be claimed where the agent has been acting within his actual authority.

(c) *To exercise a lien over property owned by the principal*

This is a right to retain the principal's goods, where they have lawfully come into the agent's possession, and hold them against any debts outstanding to him as a result of the agency agreement. The nature of the lien is usually a particular one relating to specific goods which are subject to the agreement and not a general one which entitles the agent to retain any of the principal's goods even where no money is owed in relation to those specific goods. The general lien is only recognised on the basis of an express term in the contract or as a result of judicially recognised custom, as in banking.

The Commercial Agents (Council Directive) Regulations 1993 provide that agents are entitled to notice of termination (reg 14), and are entitled to indemnity or compensation on termination of the agency agreement (reg 17). In addition, reg 4 introduces duties on the principal. These duties are reciprocal to those owed by the agent to the principal under reg 3, thus, the principal is required to act dutifully and in good faith towards the agent. Additionally, the principal must provide the agent with the necessary information and documentation to allow the proper performance of the agent's contract. Moreover, the principal has to inform the agent if there is any reason to expect that there will be a significantly lower volume of business than would normally be expected and has to inform the agent if a third party has declined to confirm a deal set up by the agent.

9.1.7 Relations with third parties

In the words of Wright J in *Montgomerie v UK Mutual Steamship Association* (1891), once an agent creates a contract between the principal and a third party, *prima facie* at common law the only person who can sue is the principal and the only person who can be sued is the principal. In other words, the agent has no further responsibility. This general rule is, however, subject to the following particular exceptions which in turn tend to depend upon whether the agent has actually disclosed the existence of the principal or not.

Where the principal's existence is disclosed

Although the actual identity of the principal need not be mentioned, where the agent indicates that he is acting as an agent, the general rule is as stated above; only the principal and the third party have rights and obligations under the contract. Exceptionally, however, the agent may be held liable as a party to the contract. This can occur:

- *At third party insistence*

  Where the agent has expressly accepted liability with the principal in order to induce the third party to enter the contract.

- *By implication*

  Where the agent has signed the contractual agreement in his or her own name without clearly stating that he or she is merely acting as a representative of the principal, he or she will most likely be liable on it.

- *In relation to bills of exchange*

  As in the previous situation, where an agent signs a bill of exchange without sufficiently indicating that he or she is merely acting as the agent of a named principal he or she will become personally liable on it.

- *In relation to the execution a deed*

  Where the agent signs the deed, other than under a power of attorney, he will be personally liable on it.

- *Where the principal's existence is not disclosed*

  Even in the case of an undisclosed principal, where the agent has authority but has failed to disclose that he or she is acting for a principal, the general rule is still that a contract exists between the principal and the third party which can be enforced by either of them. The following, however, are some modifications to this general rule:

  o the third party is entitled to enforce the contract against the agent and, in turn, the agent can enforce the contract against the third party. In both cases, the principal can intervene to enforce or defend the action on his or her own behalf;

  o as stated previously, an undisclosed principal cannot ratify any contract made outside of the agent's actual authority;

  o where the third party had a special reason to contract with the agent, the principal may be excluded from the contract. This will certainly apply in relation to personal contracts such as contracts of employment and, possibly, on the authority of *Greer v Downs Supply Co* (1927), where the third party has a right to set off debts against the agent;

  o authority exists in *Said v Butt* (1920) (where a theatre critic employed someone to get him a ticket for a performance he would not have been allowed into) for claiming that an undisclosed principal will not be permitted to enforce a contract where particular reasons exist as to why the third party would not wish to deal with him. This decision appears to run contrary to normal commercial practice and is of doubtful merit.

It is certain, however, that where the agent actually misrepresents the identity of the principal, knowing that the third party would not otherwise enter into the contract, the principal will not be permitted to enforce the contract (see *Archer v Stone* (1898)).

Payment by means of an agent

Payment by means of an agent can take two forms:

(a) *Payment by the third party to the agent to pass on to the principal*

In this situation, if the principal is undisclosed, then the third party has discharged liability on the contract and is not responsible if the agent absconds with the money. However, if the principal is disclosed then any payment to the agent only discharges the third party's responsibility if it can be shown that the agent had authority, either express or implied, to receive money.

(b) *Payment by the principal to the agent to pass on to the third party*

In this situation, the general rule is that if the agent does not pay the third party, the principal remains liable. This remains the case in the situation of an undisclosed principal (see *Irvine and Co v Watson and Sons* (1880)).

Breach of warrant of authority

As has been stated (see 9.1.3), where an agent purports to act for a principal without actually having the necessary authority, the agent is said to have breached his warrant of authority. In such circumstances, the third party may take action against the purported agent.

Liability in tort

An agent is liable to be sued in tort for any damages thus caused. However, the agent's right to indemnity extends to tortious acts done in the performance of his actual authority. In addition, the principal may have action taken against him directly, on the basis of vicarious liability (see 8.7).

9.1.8 Termination of agency

The principal/agent relationship can come to end in two distinct ways: either by the acts of the parties themselves either jointly or unilaterally, or as an effect of the operation of law.

Termination by the parties

There are a number of ways in which the parties can bring an agency agreement to an end:

- *By mutual agreement*

  Where the agency agreement is a continuing one, the parties may simply agree to bring the agency relationship to an end on such terms as they wish. Where the agency was established for a particular purpose, then it will automatically come to an end when that purpose has been achieved. Equally, where the agency was only intended to last for a definite period of time, then the end of that period will bring the agency to an end.

- *By the unilateral action of one of the parties*

  Because of the essentially consensual nature of the principal/agency relationship, it is possible for either of the parties to bring it to an end simply by giving notice of termination of the agreement. Although the agency relationship will be ended by such unilateral action, in situations where the principal has formed a contractual relationship with the agent, such unilateral termination may leave the principal open to an action for damages in breach of contract.

- *Irrevocable agreements*

  In some circumstances, it is not possible to revoke an agency agreement. This situation arises where the agent has authority coupled with an interest. Such an irrevocable agency might arise where a principal owes money to the agent and the payment of the debt was the reason for the formation of the agency relationship. For example, where in order to raise the money to pay off his debt the principal appoints his creditor as his agent to sell some particular piece of property, the principal may not be at liberty to bring the agency to an end until the sale has taken place and the debt paid off.

Termination by operation of law

This refers to the fact that an agency relationship will be brought to an end by:

- *Frustration*

  Contracts of agency are subject to discharge by frustration in the same way as ordinary contracts are (see 6.12.3 for the general operation of the doctrine of frustration).

- *The death of either party*

  Death of the agent clearly brings the agreement to an end as does the death of the principal. The latter situation may, however, give rise to problems where the agent is unaware of the death and continues to act in the capacity of agent. In such circumstances, the agent will be in breach of his warrant of authority and will be personally liable to third parties.

- *Insanity of either party*

  As in the previous situation, the insanity of either party will bring the agency to an end and agents similarly will have to be careful so as not to breach their warrant of authority by continuing to act after the insanity of the principal (see *Yonge v Toynbee* (1910) in 9.1.3).

- *Bankruptcy*

  The bankruptcy of the principal generally will end the agency agreement, but the bankruptcy of the agent will only bring it to an end where it renders him unfit to continue to act as an agent.

9.2 Partnership

The partnership is a fundamental form of a business/commercial organisation. Historically, the partnership predated the registered limited company as a means for uniting the capital of separate individuals and it was of the utmost importance in financing the Industrial Revolution in the UK in the 18th and 19th centuries.

As an economic form, the partnership is still important. However, since the last quarter of the 19th century, as unlimited partnerships have transformed themselves into private limited companies, partnership law has given way to the control of company law as a form of legal regulation. This shift goes some of the way to explaining why partnership case authorities tend to be so old. It could be argued that nowadays the important partnership cases take place in the Companies Court. The continued relevance of partnership law should not be underestimated, however, since it remains the essential form of organisation within the sphere of such professional activity as the law, accountancy and medicine, where there is either no wish, or need, for limited liability.

9.2.1 The Partnership Acts

The legal regulation of partnerships is mainly to be found in the Partnership Act (PA) 1890. The PA recognised the existing business and commercial practice and at least some of the previous decisions of common law and equity as they affected partnerships.

In line with the consensual nature of partnership undertakings, the PA did not seek to achieve a complete codification of the law but merely to establish a basic framework, whilst leaving open the possibility for partners to establish their own terms. The limited nature of the PA means that reference has to be made to cases decided by the courts both before and after the PA in order to understand the full scope of partnership law (s 46 expressly maintains all the rules of the common law and equity except where they are inconsistent with the provisions of the PA).

A key attribute of the partnership is the fact that its members are liable to the full extent of their personal wealth for the debts of the business. The Limited Partnership Act 1907, however, allows for the formation of limited partnerships. For members of a partnership to gain the benefit of limited liability under this legislation, the following rules apply:

- limited partners are not liable for partnership debts beyond the extent of their capital contribution, but in the ordinary course of events they are not permitted to remove their capital;

- one or more of the partners must retain full, that is, unlimited, liability for the debts of the partnership;

- a partner with limited liability is not permitted to take part in the management of the business enterprise and cannot usually bind the partnership in any transaction (contravention of this rule will result in the loss of limited liability);

- the partnership must be registered with the Companies Registry.

9.2.2 Definition of partnership

Section 1 of the PA 1890 states that partnership is the relationship which subsists between persons carrying on a business in common with a view to profit.

In relation to this definition, it should be noted that:

- the section expressly excludes companies registered under the Companies legislation;

- the nature of the relationship is a contractual one;

  Partners enter into the agreement on the terms that they themselves have negotiated and acceded to. As a consequence, they are contractually bound by those terms, as long as they do not conflict with the express provisions of the PA and they may be enforced by the law in the same way as other contractual terms;

- it is a requirement that a business be carried on.

  The term 'business' includes any trade, occupation or profession. The mere fact that individuals jointly own property does not necessarily mean that they are partners if the property is not being used by them to pursue some collective business activity. See, also, *Britton v Commissioners of Customs and Excise* (1986), where it was held that the fact that a wife received a share of the profits of her husband's business did not make her a partner in the business since this was a purely domestic arrangement;

- partnerships may be created for the purposes of a single venture.

  It is usually the case that partnerships continue over an extended period of time but this is not necessarily the case;

- the business must be carried on with a view to profit.

  An immediate result of this provision is that neither charitable nor mutual benefit schemes are to be considered as partnerships.

It used to be the case that the mere receipt of a share of profit was enough to make a person a partner and responsible for partnership debts (see *Waugh v Carver* (1793)). Nowadays, although the receipt of a share of profits may be *prima facie* evidence of a partnership relationship, it is not conclusive.

Section 2(2) of the PA 1890 expressly states that the sharing of gross returns does not in itself indicate the existence of a partnership agreement, since such an arrangement may simply represent a form of payment for the individual concerned. Thus, by way of example, the authors of this book will receive a percentage of the total sales value of the book. That, however, does not make them partners of the publishers, so, if publication of the book results in massive losses for the publishers, third parties cannot look to the authors for any money owed.

Even receiving a share of net profits does not necessarily indicate a partnership. For example, a person would not be treated as a partner where they received payment of a debt by instalments made from business profits; or where they received wages in the form of a share of profit; or received interest on a loan to a business the rate of which varied in relation to the level of the business profits. (See, also, *Britton v Commissioners of Customs and Excise* (1986).)

9.2.3 Types of partners

It is sometimes thought necessary to distinguish between different types of partners but in reality such a division is of most use in pointing out particular dangers inherent in a failure to adopt an active, if only a supervisory, role in a partnership enterprise. Thus, a general partner is the typical member of a partnership. The term is actually used in the Limited Partnership Act to distinguish that usual type from the unusual limited partner. The general partner is one who is actively engaged in the day to day running of the business enterprise whereas the limited partner is actually precluded from participating in the management of the enterprise.

Section 24(5) of the PA provides that every partner is entitled to take part in the management of the partnership business. The partnership agreement may place limitations on the actual authority of any such person but, unless an outsider is aware of the limitation, the partnership is responsible for any business transaction entered into by a partner within his usual authority. (For further consideration of these types of authority, see 9.1.3).

A dormant or sleeping partner is a person who merely invests money in a partnership enterprise but, apart from receiving a return on capital invested, takes no active part in the day to day running of the business. The limited partner in a limited partnership may be seen as a dormant partner. The term is used more generally, however, to refer to people who simply put money into partnership enterprises without taking an active part in the business and yet do not comply with the formalities required for establishing a limited partnership. The essential point that has to be emphasised in this regard is that, in so doing, such people place themselves at great risk. The law will consider them as general partners in the enterprise and will hold them personally and fully liable for the debts of the partnership to the extent of their ability to pay. By remaining outside the day to day operation of the business, such people merely surrender their personal unlimited liability into the control of the active parties in the partnership.

9.2.4 The legal status of a partnership

A partnership is an organisation established by individuals to pursue some business activity. Although the law is permissive in relation to the establishment of such enterprises, there are particular ways in which the law impinges on and controls, not just the operation of partnerships, but their very formation and existence.

Legal personality

The definition of a partnership expressly states that it is a relationship between persons. The corollary of this is that the partnership has no existence outside of, or apart from, that relationship. In other words, the partnership has no separate legal personality apart from its members as does a joint-stock company.

Although Scottish law does grant corporate personality to the partnership without the benefit of limited liability, in English law, a partnership is no more than a group of individuals collectively involved in a business activity. Section 4 of the PA 1890, however, does recognise an element of unity within the partnership organisation to the extent that it permits the partnership to be known collectively as a firm and permits the business to be carried out under the firm's name. In addition, the RSC Ord 81, provides that legal action may be taken by, and against, the partners in the firms name, although any award against the partnership may be executed against any of the individual partners.

Illegal partnerships

A partnership is illegal if it is formed to carry out an illegal purpose or to carry out a legal purpose in an illegal manner. In such circumstances, the courts will not recognise any partnership rights between the persons involved but will permit innocent third parties, who have no knowledge of any illegality, to recover against them.

Partnerships are generally not lawful if they consist of more than 20 persons as provided by s 716 of the Companies Act 1985. However, certain professional partnerships, such as solicitors, accountants and surveyors, etc, are exempt from this maximum limit.

Capacity

There are two distinct aspects relating to capacity:

(a) *Capacity of individuals to join a partnership*

The general common law rules relating to capacity to enter into contracts apply in the particular case of the membership of a partnership. Thus, any partnership agreement entered into by a minor is voidable during that person's minority and for a reasonable time after they have reached the age of majority. If the former minor does not repudiate the partnership agreement within a reasonable time of reaching the age of majority, then they will be liable for any debts as a *de facto* partner. Third parties cannot recover against partners who are minors but they can recover against any other adult partners.

Mental incapacity does not necessarily prevent someone from entering into a partnership, but subsequent mental incapacity of a partner may be grounds for the dissolution of a partnership.

(b) *Capacity of the partnership*

A particular consequence of the fact that the partnership is, at least in the perception of the law, no more than a relationship between individuals is that there are no specific rules controlling the contractual capacity of partnerships, other than those general rules which constrain individuals' capacity to enter into contracts.

Section 5 of the PA 1890 provides that each partner is the agent of the firm and the other partners for the purpose of the business of the partnership, but, as that purpose is determined by the members and is not fixed by law, it can be changed by the unanimous agreement of those members (see below.)

9.2.5 Formation of a partnership

There are no specific legal requirements governing the formation of a partnership. Partnerships arise from the agreement of the parties involved and are governed by the general principles of contract law. An agreement to enter into a partnership, therefore, may be made by deed, or in writing, or by word of mouth. Such agreement may even be implied from the conduct of the parties.

The partnership agreement

It is usual for the terms of the partnership to be set out in written form. The document produced is known as the articles of partnership. The parties involved, no doubt after some negotiation, decide what they wish to be specifically included in the articles. Any gaps in the articles will be filled in by reference to the PA 1890 or the existing common law and equitable rules relating to partnerships but it is necessary for the future partners to provide for any unusual or specialised terms to be included in the articles.

The detailed provisions in articles of partnership usually refer to such matters as: the nature of the business to be transacted; the name of the firm; the capital contributions to be made by the individual partners; the drawing up of the business accounts; the method of determining and sharing profits; and the dissolution of the partnership. It is also usual for there to be a provision for disputes between partners to be referred to arbitration for solution.

The partnership agreement is an internal document and, although it has effect between the partners, it does not necessarily affect the rights of third parties. Thus, where the agreement seeks to place limitations on the usual authority of a partner, it is effective with regard to the internal relations of the partners but does not have any effect as regards an outsider who deals with the partner without knowledge of the limitation.

In *Mercantile Credit v Garrod* (1962), two people, Parkin and Garrod, were partners in a garage business mainly concerned with letting garages and repairing cars. The partnership agreement expressly excluded the sale of cars. After Parkin had sold a car to which he had no title to the plaintiffs, they claimed back the money they had paid from Garrod.

It was held that, since selling cars was within the usual scope of a garage business, it was within the usual authority of a partner in such a business. Parkin, therefore, had acted within his implied authority and the partnership was responsible for his actions. The plaintiffs had no knowledge of the limitation contained within the articles and could not be subject to it.

Alteration of partnership agreement

Just as the consensual nature of the partnership relationship allows the parties to make the agreement in such terms as they wish, so are they equally free to alter those terms at a later date. Section 19 of the PA, however, enacts the common law rule that any decision to alter the terms of partnership articles must be made unanimously. Consent does not have to be expressed but may be inferred from the conduct of the partners.

In *Pilling v Pilling* (1887), the articles of partnership entered into between a father and his two sons stated that the business was to be financed by the fathers capital and that such capital was to remain his personal property and not be treated as the partnership property. The articles also stated that the father should receive interest on his capital. In practice, however, the sons as well as the father received interest on the partnership capital. It was held that the capital originally provided by the father was partnership property and that the conduct of the parties in treating it as such had amounted to a valid alteration of the written agreement.

The firm's name

Partnerships may use the words 'and Company' or its alternative form '& Co' in their name, for example, a firm of solicitors may call itself Brown, Smith and Co. This merely indicates that the names of all the partners are not included in the firm's name. As has been seen above, it in no way indicates that the partnership has any existence apart from its constituent members or that those members have the benefit of limited liability. Even in the case of limited partnerships, someone must accept full liability for partnership debts. Section 34 of the Companies Act 1985 consequently makes it a criminal offence for a partnership to use the word 'limited' or the abbreviation 'Ltd' in its name.

A partnership may trade under the names of the individual partners or it may trade under a collective name. Any name must comply with both the Business Names Act (BNA) 1985 and the common law provisions relating to the tort of passing off.

Business Names Act 1985

Section 4 of the BNA requires that, where a partnership does not trade under the names of all of its members, the names of individuals must be displayed on the business premises and on the firm's business documents. Where the partnership is a large one with more than 20 members, the individual names do not have to be listed on business documents but a list of all partners must be available for inspection at the firm's principal place of business. Any failure to comply with this requirement may result in the person in breach not being able to enforce a claim against another party who was disadvantaged by the breach.

There is no longer any requirement that business names be registered as such but the BNA requires the approval of the Secretary of State for Trade and Industry before certain names can be used. Such names may imply that the business is related in some way to the Crown, the government, local authorities or other official bodies.

Passing off

The BNA 1985 does not prevent one business from using the same or a very similar name as another business. However, the tort of passing off prevents one person from using any name which is likely to divert business their way by suggesting that the business is actually that of some other person, or is connected in any way with that other business. It thus enables people to protect the goodwill they have built up in relation to their business activity. See *Ewing v Buttercup Margarine Company Ltd* (1917), where the plaintiff successfully prevented the use by the defendants of a name that suggested a link with his existing dairy company. For a more up to date and less serious case, see *Stringfellow v McCain Foods GB Ltd* (1984), in which the owner of the famous Stringfellows nightclub failed to prevent a manufacturer of long thin oven chips from calling their product by the same name.

9.2.6 Arbitration clauses

The consensual nature of the relationship on which any partnership is based has been repeatedly emphasised. It should always be remembered, however, that even the best of friends can fall out and, when they are engaged in a joint business venture, any such conflict may be disastrous for the business. In an attempt to forestall such an eventuality, and to avoid the cost, delay and publicity involved in court procedure, it is standard practice for partnership articles to contain a clause referring disputes to arbitration for solution.

The actual procedure of arbitration will be considered in Chapter 12 but it should be recognised that arbitration, although relatively cheaper than the court system, is not cheap in absolute terms. Nor can it deal with situations where the partners have reached the stage where their continued conflict prevents the effective operation of the business. In such circumstances, it is probably wiser if the partnership is wound up on just and equitable grounds under s 35 of the PA (see 9.3.9; *Re Yenidje Tobacco Co Ltd* (1916) as an example where the partnership principle was extended to a quasi-partnership company).

9.2.7 The relation of partners to one another

The partnership agreement is contractual in nature – the partnership also involves a principal/agency relationship, but is complicated by the fact that partners are, at one and the same time, both agents of the firm and their fellow partners, and principals as regards those other partners. Partners are equally subject to the equitable rights and duties that derive from their being in a fiduciary position in relation to one another. Thus, the legal nature of the partnership involves a complicated mixture of elements of contract, agency and equity.

Duties of partners

The fiduciary nature of the partnership relationship imports the usual duties that derive from such a relationship, which can be summed up under the general heading of a duty to act in good faith. In addition to these general fiduciary duties, ss 28–30 of the PA 1890 lay down specific duties as follows:

- *The duty of disclosure*

    Section 28 provides that partners must render true accounts and full information in relation to all things affecting the partnership to the other partners or their legal representatives.

    In *Law v Law* (1905), one partner accepted an offer from the other to buy his share of the firm. He only later discovered that certain partnership assets had not been disclosed to him and sought to have the contract set aside. The court decided that, as the purchasing partner had breached the duty of disclosure, the agreement could have been set aside. In actual fact, the parties had come to an arrangement so it was not necessary for such an order to be granted.

- *The duty to account*

  Section 29 provides that partners must account to the firm for any benefit obtained, without consent, from any transaction concerning: the partnership; its property, including information derived from membership of the partnership; its name; or its business connection. As with fiduciary duties generally, such profit is only open to challenge where it is undisclosed. Full disclosure is necessary and sufficient to justify the making of an individual profit from a partnership position.

  In *Bentley v Craven* (1853), Craven was in partnership with the plaintiff in a sugar refinery business. He bought sugar on his own account and later sold it to the partnership at a profit, without declaring his interest to the other partners. It was held that the partnership was entitled to recover the profit from the defendant.

- *The duty not to compete*

  Section 30 provides that, where a partner competes with the partnership business, without the consent of the other partners, then that person shall be liable to account to the partnership for any profits made in the course of that business. Once again, it is essential to note that full disclosure is necessary to validate any such profits made in competition with the partnership. (See *Trimble v Goldberg* (1906) for a case where the court declined to recognise competition in relation to a partnership; but the likely severity of the courts' approach can be surmised from the company law case of *Industrial Development Consultants v Cooley* (1972).)

Rights of partners

Subject to express provision to the contrary in the partnership agreement, and remembering the consensual nature of the partnership which allows the parties to avoid the provisions of the Act, s 24 of the PA sets out the rights of partners. Amongst the most important of these are the rights:

- *To share equally in the capital and profits of the business*

  Even where the partnership agreement is silent on the matter, s 24 does not mean that someone who has contributed all, or the greater part, of the capital of a firm must share it equally with the other partners. In such circumstances, it would most likely be decided that the facts of the case provided evidence of such contrary intention as to rebut the statement in the PA 1890. What the section does mean is that, even in the same circumstances, the partners will share profits equally, although it is not unusual to find clauses in agreements which recognise differences in capital input by providing for profits to be shared on an unequal basis. The same effect can be achieved by permitting interest to be paid on capital before profits are determined and it should also be noted that, where partners advance additional capital to the firm, they are entitled to interest at 5%.

The corollary of this right is the duty to contribute equally to any losses of capital even where no capital was originally brought into the business. For example, if A and B enter into a partnership, with A providing all of the capital £10,000 but sharing the profits equally, and if, upon winding up, the business has accrued a loss of £2,000, then both parties are required to contribute to the loss. In effect, B will have to contribute £1,000 and A will only receive a return of £9,000

- *To be indemnified by the firm for any liabilities incurred or payments made in the course of the firm's business*

This may be seen as merely an express declaration of the usual right of an agent to indemnity. The right of an agent to act outside their authority in the case of necessity is also expressly set out in s 24.

- *To take part in the management of the business*

The unlimited nature of the ordinary partnership means that involvement in such a business brings with it the risk of one's personal wealth. It is essential under such circumstances, therefore, that partners are able to protect their interests by taking an active part in the operation of the business in order to assess and control the level of their risk. It is for this reason that the right to take part in the management of the business is stated expressly. In the case of quasi-partnership companies, the courts will imply such a right.

A partner is generally not entitled to receive any salary for acting in the partnership business but it is not unusual for the agreement effectively to provide for the payment of a salary to particular partners before the determination of net profit.

- *To have access to the firm's books*

This right follows from, and is based on, the same reasoning as the previous provision. The books are normally kept at the firm's principal place of business.

- *To prevent the admission of a new partner or prevent any change in the nature of the partnership business*

Any differences relating to the partnership business can be decided by the majority but unanimity is required to change the nature of the business. Again, this reflects the need for individual partners to accept risk voluntarily. They have only accepted existing business risks and cannot be forced to alter or increase that risk.

Similarly, as principals, they have agreed to give their authority to bind them and make them liable for partnership debts to particular individuals. They cannot be forced to extend that authority against their wishes.

In addition to the above rights, s 25 provides that no majority can expel another partner, unless such power is contained in the partnership agreement. Even where such a power is included, it must be exercised in good faith. See *Blisset v Daniel* (1853), where the majority attempted to expel a partner in order to acquire his share of the business cheaply; and *Green v Howell* (1910), where a partner was properly expelled for a flagrant breach of his duties. For more recent cases, see *Kerr v Morris* (1987) and *Walters v Bingham* (1988).

Partnership property

Property may be owned collectively by all of the partners and thus amount to partnership property. Alternatively, it is possible for property to be used by the partnership as a whole, yet remain the personal property of only one of the partners.

Section 20 of the PA 1890 states that partnership property consists of all property brought into the partnership stock or acquired on account for the purposes of the firm. Section 21 further states that any property bought with money belonging to the firm is deemed to have been bought on account of the firm.

Whether any particular item of property belongs to the firm or not is always a matter of fact to be determined in relation to the particular circumstances of any case. If there is no express agreement that property is to be brought into the firm as partnership property, the court will only imply such a term to the extent required to make the partnership agreement effective.

In *Miles v Clarke* (1953), Clarke had carried on a photography business for sometime before taking Miles into partnership. The partnership agreement merely provided that the profits should be divided equally. When the partners fell out, a dispute arose as to who owned the assets used by the partnership. It was held that only the consumable stock-in-trade could be considered as partnership property. The leases of the business premises and other plant and equipment remained the personal property of the partner who introduced them into the business.

It is important to distinguish between partnership property and personal property for the following reasons:

• *Partnership property must be used exclusively for partnership purposes (s 20)*

This may been seen as a statement of the general duty not to make a personal profit from a fiduciary position without full disclosure. Thus, partners are not supposed to use partnership property for their own personal benefit or gain and, if they were to do so, they would be liable to account to the partnership for any profit made.

It also makes it clear that partners do not own the firm's assets directly. All they have, under s 30, is the partnership lien over those assets which entitles them on dissolution to participate in any surplus after their realised value has been used to pay off partnership debts.

- *Any increase in the value of partnership property belongs to the partnership*

    As a consequence, the increased value when realised will be divided amongst all of the partners.

- *Any increase in the value of personal property belongs to the person who owns the property*

    Consequently, the increased value will not have to be shared with the other partners.

- *On the dissolution of the firm, partnership property is used to pay debts before personal property*

    This is clearly stated in s 39 which has been considered above in relation to the nature of the partnership lien.

- *Partnership and personal property are treated differently in the satisfaction of claims made by partnership creditors as opposed to personal creditors*

    Under s 23, a writ of execution can only be issued against partnership property in respect of a judgment against the partnership. A personal creditor of a partner may not, therefore, take action against partnership property. They can, however, apply for a charging order against that partner's share in the partnership which would entitle them to receive the partner's share of profits, or assets on dissolution, to the extent of the debt and interest. The other partners may redeem the charge at any time by paying off the debt, in which case, the charge becomes vested in them.

- *On the death of a partner, any interest in partnership land will pass as personalty, whereas land owned personally will pass as realty*

    In effect, this means that the interest may pass to different people depending on whether the party has made an appropriate will or not.

    In relation specifically to land, s 22 enacts the equitable doctrine of conversion by providing that any such partnership property is to be treated as personal property.

Assignment of a share in a partnership

Unless the partnership agreement states otherwise, partners are at liberty to mortgage or assign absolutely their shares in partnerships to outsiders. The assignee is, however, only entitled to the share of profits due to the partner assigning the shares or, on dissolution, to the appropriate share of partnership assets. Section 31 makes it clear that any such assignee does not become a partner and has no right whatsoever to get involved in the management of the business. In *Garwood v Paynter* (1903), Garwood charged his shares to a trust, of which his wife was one of the beneficiaries. When the other partners began to pay themselves salaries, Mrs Garwood objected on the grounds that such payment reduced the net profit of the firm and hence indirectly the income to the trust. It was held that the payment of salaries was an internal management matter and therefore the trustees, who were assignees, by virtue of s 31 could not interfere in the absence of fraud.

The assignee does not take over responsibility for partnership debts. These remain the liability of the assignor. Where, however, the assignment is absolute, the assignee must indemnify the assignor in respect of future liabilities arising from the business.

9.2.8   The relation of partners to outsiders

Of equal importance to the internal relationships of the partnership is the relationship of the members of the partnership to outsiders who deal with the partnership and, in particular, the extent to which the partnership, and hence the partners, are liable for the actions of the individual partners.

The authority of partners to bind the firm

As stated in s 5 of the PA 1890, every partner is an agent of the firm and of the other partners. Each partner, therefore, has the power to bind co-partners and make them liable on business transactions. The partnership agreement may, however, expressly seek to limit the powers of particular members. The effect of such limitations depends on the circumstances of each case. They do not apply where the other partners have effectively countermanded the restriction.

This can occur in two ways:

- if the other partners give their prior approval for a partner to exceed his actual authority, then the partner in question has express actual authority and the firm is bound by his action;

- if the other partners give their approval after the event, then they have ratified the transaction and the partnership is again liable.

The firm may also be liable, even where the other partners have not expressly approved the action in excess of authority, as long as the partner has acted within his implied powers, that is, within the usual scope of a partner in the particular business concerned (see *Mercantile Credit v Garrod* (1962)). If, however, the outsider had actual knowledge of the partner's lack of authority then the partnership is not bound by the transaction.

Every partner, other than a limited partner, is presumed to have the implied authority to enter into the following transactions:

- to sell the firm's goods;

- to buy goods of a kind normally required by the firm;

- to engage employees;

- to employ a solicitor to act for the firm in defence of an action or in pursuit of a debt.

The above implied powers apply equally to trading and non-trading partnerships. Partners in trading firms, those which essentially buy and sell goods, have the following additional implied powers:

- to accept, draw, issue or endorse bills of exchange or other negotiable instruments on behalf of the firm;

- to borrow money on the credit of the firm;

- to pledge the firm's goods as security for borrowed money.

The nature of partner's liability

Every partner is responsible for the full amount of the firm's liability. Outsiders have the choice of taking action against the firm collectively or against the individual partners. Where damages are recovered from one partner only, the other partners are under a duty to contribute equally to the amount paid.

- *Liability on debts and contracts*

  Under s 9 of the PA 1890, the liability of partners as regards debts or contracts is joint. The effect of joint liability used to be that, although the partners were collectively responsible, a person who took action against one of the partners could take no further action against the other partners, even if they had not recovered all that was owing to them.

  That situation was remedied by the Civil Liability (Contributions Act) 1978, which effectively provided that a judgment against one partner does bar a subsequent action against the other partners.

- *Liability for torts*

  Under s 10 of the PA 1890, the liability of partners with regard to torts or other wrongs committed in the ordinary course of the partnership business is joint and several. In such a situation, there is no bar on taking successive actions against partners in order to recover all that is due.

  It should be emphasised that, in order for the partnership to be responsible, the wrong sued on must have been committed in the ordinary course of partnership business or with the express approval of all the partners. If a tort is committed outside this scope, then the partner responsible is personally liable.

In *Hamlyn v Houston and Co* (1815), one of the partners in Houston and Co bribed a clerk employed by the plaintiff in order to get information about their rival's business. Hamlyn sued the defendant partnership to recover the loss he claimed to have suffered as a consequence. It was held that the defendant firm were liable for the wrongful act of the individual partner as he had acted within the usual scope of his authority, although he had used illegal methods in doing so.

But, see *Arbuckle v Taylor* (1815), where the partnership was not liable because the individual partner had gone beyond the general scope of the partnership business.

The liability of incoming and outgoing partners

A person who is admitted into an existing firm is not liable to creditors of the firm for anything done before they became a partner (see s 17 of the PA 1890). The new partner can, however, assume such responsibility by way of the device known as novation. This is the process whereby a retiring partner is discharged from existing liability and the newly constituted partnership takes the liability on themselves. Novation is essentially a tripartite contract involving the retiring partner, the new firm and the existing creditors. As creditors effectively give up rights against the retiring partner, their approval is required. Such approval may be express or it may be implied from the course of dealing between the creditor and the firm.

In *Thompson v Percival* (1834), Charles Thompson and James Percival had been in partnership until Thompson retired. The plaintiff creditors, on applying for payment, were informed that Percival alone would be responsible for payment as Thompson had retired. As a consequence, they drew a bill for payment against Percival alone. It was held subsequently that they no longer had a right of action against Thompson since their action showed that they had accepted his discharge from his liability.

Creditors do not have to accept a novation. A creditor may still hold the retired partner responsible for any debts due at the time of retirement. The newly constituted firm may, however, agree to indemnify the retiring partner against any such claims.

Apart from novation, a retired partner remains liable for any debts or obligations incurred by the partnership prior to retirement. The date of any contract determines responsibility: if the person was a partner when the contract was entered into, then they are responsible, even if the goods under the contract are delivered after they have left the firm. The estate of a deceased person is only liable for those debts or obligations arising before death.

Where someone deals with a partnership after a change in membership, they are entitled to treat all the apparent members of the old firm as still being members until they receive notice of any change in the membership. In order to avoid liability for future contracts, a retiring partner must take the following action:

- ensure that individual notice is given to existing customers of the partnership; and

- advertise the retirement in the *London Gazette*. This serves as general notice to people who were not customers of the firm prior to the partner's retirement, but knew that that person had been a partner in the business. Such an advert is effective whether or not it comes to the attention of third parties.

A retired partner owes no responsibility to someone who had neither dealings with the partnership nor previous knowledge of his membership.

In *Tower Cabinet Co Ltd v Ingram* (1949), Ingram and Christmas had been partners in a firm known as Merrys. After it was dissolved by mutual agreement, Christmas carried on trading under the firm's name. Notice was given to those dealing with the firm that Ingram was no longer connected with the business, but no notice was placed in the *London Gazette*. New notepaper was printed without Ingram's name. However, the plaintiffs, who had no previous dealings with the partnership, received an order on old notepaper on which Ingram's name was included. When Tower Cabinet sought to enforce a judgment against Ingram, it was held that he was not liable since he had not represented himself as being a partner, nor had the plaintiffs been aware of his membership prior to dissolution.

Partnership by estoppel

Failure to give notice of retirement is one way in which liability arises on the basis of estoppel or holding out. Alternatively, anyone who represents themselves, or knowingly permits themselves to be represented, as a partner is liable to any person who gives the partnership credit on the basis of that representation. Although they may become liable for partnership debts, they are not, however, partners in any other sense. (In *Tower Cabinet Co Ltd v Ingram*, the defendant was not affected by partnership by estoppel since he was never actually aware that he had been represented as being a partner.)

9.2.9 Dissolution and winding up of the partnership

There are a number of possible reasons for bringing a partnership to an end. It may have been established for a particular purpose and that purpose has been achieved, or one of the partners might wish to retire from the business, or the good relationship between the members, which is essential to the operation of a partnership, may have broken down. In all such cases, the existing partnership is dissolved, although in the second case a new partnership may be established to take over the old business.

Grounds for dissolution

As has been repeatedly emphasised, the partnership is based on agreement. It is created by agreement and it may be brought to an end in the same way. However, subject to any provision to the contrary in the partnership agreement, the PA 1890 provides for the dissolution of a partnership on the following grounds:

- *The expiry of a fixed term or the completion of a specified enterprise (s 32(a) and (b))*

  If the partnership continues after the pre-set limit, it is known as a partnership at will and it can be ended at any time thereafter at the wish of any of the partners.

- *The giving of notice (s 32(c))*

  If the partnership is of indefinite duration, then it can be brought to an end by any one of the partners giving notice of an intention to dissolve the partnership.

- *The death or bankruptcy of any partner (s 33(1))*

  Although the occurrence of either of these events will bring the partnership to an end, it is usual for partnership agreements to provide for the continuation of the business under the control of the remaining/solvent partners. The dead partner's interest will be valued and paid to his or her personal representative, and the bankrupt's interest will be paid to his or her trustee in bankruptcy.

- *Where a partner's share becomes subject to a charge under s 23 (s 33(2))*

  Under such circumstances, dissolution is not automatic but it is open to the other partners to dissolve the partnership.

- *Illegality (s 34)*

  The occurrence of events making the continuation of the partnership illegal will bring it to an end. An obvious case would be where the continuation of the partnership would result in trading with the enemy (see *R v Kupfer* (1915)). The principle applied equally, however, in a more recent, and perhaps more relevant, case: *Hudgell, Yeates and Co v Watson* (1978). Practising solicitors are legally required to have a practice certificate. However, one of the members of a three-person partnership forgot to renew his practice certificate and thus was not legally entitled to act as a solicitor. It was held that the failure to renew the practice certificate brought the partnership to an end; although a new partnership continued between the other two members of the old partnership.

In addition to the provisions listed above, the court may, mainly by virtue of s 35 of the PA 1890, order the dissolution of the partnership under the following circumstances:

- *Where a partner becomes a patient under the Mental Health Act 1983*

  The procedure is no longer taken under s 35 of the PA 1890, but, where the person is no longer able to manage their affairs because of mental incapacity, the Court of Protection may dissolve a partnership at the request of the person's receiver or the other partners.

- *Where a partner suffers some other permanent incapacity*

  This provision is analogous to the previous one. It should be noted that it is for the other partners to apply for dissolution and that the incapacity alleged as the basis of dissolution must be permanent. It is not unusual for partnerships to include specific clauses in their agreement in order to permit dissolution on the basis of extended absence from the business. (See *Peyton v Mindham* (1971), where a clause in a partnership covering medical practice provided for termination after nine months continuous absence or a total of 300 days in any period of 24 months.)

- *Where a partner engages in activity prejudicial to the business*

  Such activity may be directly related to the business, such as the misappropriation of funds. Alternatively, it may take place outside the business but operate to its detriment. An example might be a criminal conviction for fraud.

- *Where a partner persistently breaches the partnership agreement*

  This provision also relates to conduct which makes it unreasonable for the other partners to carry on in business with the party at fault.

- *Where the business can only be carried on at a loss*

  This provision is a corollary of the very first section of the PA 1890 in which the pursuit of profit is part of the definition of the partnership form. If such profit cannot be achieved, then the partners are entitled to avoid loss by bringing the partnership to an end.

- *Where it is just and equitable to do so*

  The courts have wide discretion in relation to the implementation of this power. A similar provision operates within company legislation and the two provisions come together in the cases involving quasi-partnerships. On occasion, courts have wound up companies on the grounds that they would have been wound up had the business assumed the legal form of a partnership. For examples of this approach, see *Re Yenidje Tobacco Co Ltd* (1916) and *Ebrahimi v Westbourne Galleries Ltd* (1973).

After dissolution, the authority of each partner to bind the firm continues so far as is necessary to wind up the firms affairs and complete transactions that have begun but are unfinished at the time of dissolution (s 38). Partners cannot, however, enter into new contracts.

Winding up

Since the introduction of the Insolvency Act (IA) 1986, partnerships as such are not subject to bankruptcy although the individual partners may be open to such procedure. Partnerships may be wound up as unregistered companies, under Pt V of the IA 1986, where they are unable to pay their debts.

Treatment of assets on dissolution

On dissolution, the value of the partnership property is realised and the proceeds are applied in the following order:

- in paying debts to outsiders;

- in paying to the partners any advance made to the firm beyond their capital contribution;

- in paying the capital contribution of the individual partners.

Any residue is divided between the partners in the same proportion as they shared in profits (s 44 of the PA).

If the assets are insufficient to meet debts, partners advances and capital repayments, then the deficiency has to be made good out of any profits held back from previous years, or out of partner's capital, or by the partners individually in the proportion to which they were entitled to share in profits.

An example will clarify this procedure. Partners A, B and C contributed £5,000, £3,000 and £1,000 respectively. In addition, A made an advance to the firm of £1,000. On dissolution, the assets realised £8,000, and the firm had outstanding debts amounting to £2,500. The procedure is as follows.

First, the creditors are paid what is due to them from the realised value of the assets. Thus, £8,000 less £2,500 = £5,500.

Secondly, A's advance of £1,000 is paid back, leaving £4,500.

Assuming that there was no agreement to the contrary, profits and losses will be shared equally. The actual loss is determined as follows:

Original capital	£9,000
Minus money left	£4,500
Total	£4,500

This loss of £4,500 has to be shared equally in this case. Each partner has to provide £1,500 to make good the shortfall in capital. In the case of A and B, this is a paper transaction as the payment due is simply subtracted from their original capital contribution. C, however, actually has to make a contribution of £500 from his personal wealth as his due payment exceeds his original capital. The outcome is as follows:

A's share of net assets is £5,000 less £1,500 = £3,500

B's share of net assets is £3,000 less £1,500 = £1,500

C's share of net assets is £1,000 less £1,500 = – £500

A provision in the partnership agreement for profits to be shared in proportion to capital contribution, that is, in the ratio 5:3:1, would have the following effect:

A would contribute five-ninths of the £4,500 loss, that is, £2,500

B would contribute three-ninths of the £4,500 loss, that is, £1,500

C would contribute one-ninth of the £4,500 loss, that is, £500

Their shares in net assets would, therefore, be as follows:

A: (£5,000 – £2,500) = £2,500

B: (£3,000 – £1,500) = £1,500

C: (£1,000 – £500)   =   £500

Bankruptcy of partners

Where a partner is bankrupt, on the dissolution of a firm, the partnership assets are still used to pay partnership debts. It is only after the payment of partnership debts that any surplus due to that partner is made available for the payment of the partner's personal debts.

Where one partner is insolvent and there is a deficiency of partnership assets to repay the firm's creditors and any advances, the burden of making good the shortfall has to be borne by the solvent partners in the proportion to their share in profits. If, however, the shortfall only relates to capital then the situation is governed by the rule in *Garner v Murray* (1904). This rule means that, in any such situation, the solvent partners are not required to make good the capital deficiency due to the insolvency of their co-partner. But, as a consequence, there will be a shortfall in the capital fund which has to be borne by the solvent partners in proportion to their capitals.

To return to the original example, the net assets were £4,500 and the capital deficiency was £4,500. All three partners were to contribute £1,500. In effect, C was the only one actually to pay out any money since A and B merely suffered an abatement in the capital returned to them. However, if it is now assumed that C is insolvent and can make no contribution the situation is as follows.

C loses his right of repayment so this reduces the capital fund required to pay back partners contributions to £8,000.

As previously, A and B contribute their portion of the total loss taking the available capital fund up to £7,500 (that is, £4,500 + (2 x £1,500)).

There still remains a shortfall of £500. This is borne by A and B in proportion to their capital contribution. Thus, A suffers a loss of five-eighths of £500; and B suffers a loss of three-eighths of £500.

So, from the capital fund of £7,500:

A receives £5,000 − (5/8 x £500) = £4,687.50 (in reality, he or she simply receives £3,187.50).

B receives £3,000 − (3/8 x £500) = £2,812.50 (in reality, he or she simply receives £1,312.50).

9.3   Company law

9.3.1   Introduction

This section deals with the formation and regulation of a common alternative form of business association to the partnership, namely, the registered company. The flexibility of the company form of organisation is shown by the fact that it is used by businesses of widely different sizes and needs; from the one-man business to the transnational corporation.

9.3.2   Corporations and their legal characteristics

Companies differ from partnerships in that they are bodies corporate, or corporations.

Types of corporation

Corporations can be created in one of three ways:

(a) By grant of royal charter

Such corporations are governed mainly by the common law. Although the very earliest trading companies were created by royal charter in order to secure monopoly privileges, nowadays, this method of incorporation tends to be restricted to professional, educational and charitable institutions and is not used in relation to business enterprises.

(b) By special Act of Parliament

Such bodies are known as statutory corporations. Although this method of incorporation was common during the 19th century, particularly in relation to railway and public utility companies, it is not greatly used nowadays, and certainly not by ordinary trading companies.

(c) By registration under the Companies Acts

Since 1844, companies have been permitted to acquire the status of a corporation simply by complying with the requirements for registration set out in general Acts of Parliament. This is the method by which the great majority of trading enterprises are incorporated. The current legislation is the Companies Act 1985, as subsequently amended by the Companies Act 1989.

The doctrine of separate personality

Whereas English law treats a partnership as simply a group of individuals trading collectively, the effect of incorporation is that a company once formed has its own distinct legal personality, separate from its members.

The doctrine of separate or corporate personality is an ancient one and an early application of it can be seen in *Salmon v The Hamborough Co* (1671). The usual case cited in relation to separate personality is *Salomon v Salomon and Co* (1897). Salomon had been in the boot and leather trade for some time. Together with other members of his family, he formed a limited company and sold his previous business to it. Payment was in the form of cash, shares and debentures (the latter is loan stock which gives the holder priority over unsecured creditors if the company is wound up). When the company was eventually wound up, it was argued that Salomon and the company were the same and, as he could not be his own creditor, his debentures should have no effect. Although previous courts had decided against Salomon, the House of Lords held that under the circumstances, in the absence of fraud, his debentures were valid. The company had been properly constituted and consequently it was, in law, a distinct legal person, completely separate from Salomon.

It is important to note that, contrary to what some, if not most, textbooks state, the *Salomon* case did not establish the doctrine of separate personality. It merely permitted its application to one-man companies.

Following the European Community Twelfth Directive on Company Law (89/667/EC) which was enacted in the UK in the form of the Companies (Single Member Private Limited Companies) Regulations 1992, provision has been made for the establishment of true one-man companies. These Regulations permit the incorporation of private limited companies by one person and with only one member. Thus, there is no longer any need for any pretence in the registration of sole traders as companies. (It should be noted, as a matter of related interest, that the Law Commission is currently engaged in examining the whole question of limited liability as it applies, or should be applied, to economic partnerships.)

The effects of incorporation

A number of consequences flow from the fact that corporations are treated as having legal personality in their own right:

• *Limited liability*

No one is responsible for anyone else's debts unless they agree to accept such responsibility. Similarly, at common law, members of a corporation are not responsible for its debts without agreement. However, registered companies, that is, those formed under the Companies Acts 1985 and 1989, are not permitted unless the shareholders agree to accept liability for their company's debts. In return for this agreement, the extent of their liability is set at a fixed amount. In the case of a company limited by shares, the level of liability is the amount remaining unpaid on the nominal value of the shares held. In the case of a company limited by guarantee, it is the amount that shareholders have agreed to pay on the event of the company being wound up.

- *Perpetual succession*

  As the corporation exists in its own right, changes in its membership have no effect on its status or existence. Members may die, be declared bankrupt or insane, or transfer their shares without any effect on the company. As an abstract legal person the company cannot die, although its existence can be brought to an end through the winding up procedure (see 9.3.10).

- *Business property is owned by the company*

  Any business assets are owned by the company itself and not the shareholders. This is normally a major advantage in that the company's assets are not subject to claims based on the ownership rights of its members. It can, however, cause unforeseen problems.

  In *Macaura v Northern Assurance* (1925), the plaintiff had owned a timber estate. He later formed a one-man company and transferred the estate to it. He continued to insure the estate in his own name. When the timber was lost in a fire, it was held that Macaura could not claim on the insurance since he had no personal interest in the timber which belonged to the company.

  What the member owns is so many shares in the company and the precise nature of the share will be considered below (see 9.3.6).

- The company has contractual capacity in its own right and can sue and be sued in its own name.

  The nature and extent of a company's contractual capacity will be considered in detail later (see 9.3.5), but for the moment it should be noted that contracts are entered into in the company's name and it is liable on any such contracts. The extent of the company's liability, as opposed to the members' liability, is unlimited and all its assets may be used to pay off debts.

  The board of directors are the agents of the company. Members as such are not agents of the company; they have no right to be involved in the day to day operation of the business and they cannot bind the company in any way.

- The rule in *Foss v Harbottle* (1843)

  This states that, where a company suffers an injury, it is for the company, acting through the majority of the members, to take the appropriate remedial action. Perhaps of more importance is the corollary of the rule which is that an individual cannot raise an action in response to a wrong suffered by the company.

Lifting the veil of incorporation

There are a number of occasions, both statutory and at common law, when the doctrine of separate personality will not be followed. On these occasions, it is said that the veil of incorporation, which separates the company from its members, is pierced, lifted or drawn aside. Such situations arise:

- *Under the companies legislation*

  Section 24 of the Companies Act 1985 provides for personal liability of the member where a company carries on trading with fewer than two members; and s 229 requires consolidated accounts to be prepared by a group of related companies.

  Section 213 of the IA 1986 provides for personal liability in relation to fraudulent trading and s 214 does the same in relation to wrongful trading.

- *At common law*

  As in most areas of law that are based on the application of policy decisions, it is difficult to predict when the courts will ignore separate personality. What is certain is that the courts will not permit the corporate form to be used for a clearly fraudulent purpose or to evade a legal duty.

In *Gilford Motor Co Ltd v Horne* (1933), an employee had covenanted not to solicit his former employer's customers. After he left their employment, he formed a company to solicit those customers. It was held that the company was a sham and the court would not permit it to be used to avoid the prior contract.

As would be expected, the courts are prepared to ignore separate personality in times of war to defeat the activity of shareholders who might be enemy aliens. See *Daimler Co Ltd v Continental Tyre and Rubber Co (GB) Ltd* (1917).

Where groups of companies have been set up for particular business ends, the courts will not usually ignore the separate existence of the various companies unless they are being used for fraud. There is authority for treating separate companies as a single group as in *DHN Food Distributors Ltd v Borough of Tower Hamlets* (1976) but later authorities have cast extreme doubt on this decision (see *Woolfson v Strathclyde RC* (1978) and *National Dock Labour Board v Pinn and Wheeler* (1989)).

9.3.3 Types of companies

Although the distinction between public and private companies is probably the most important, there are a number of ways in which companies can be classified.

Limited and unlimited companies

One of the major advantages of forming a company is limited liability, but companies can be formed without limited liability. Such companies receive all the benefits that flow from incorporation except limited liability, but in return they do not have to submit their accounts and make them available for public inspection.

The great majority of companies, however, are limited liability companies. This means, as explained above, that the maximum liability of shareholders is fixed and cannot be increased without their agreement. There are two ways of establishing limited liability:

(a) *By shares*

This is the most common procedure. It limits liability to the amount remaining unpaid on shares held. If the shareholder has paid the full nominal value of the shares to the company, then that is the end of responsibility with regard to company debts.

(b) *By guarantee*

This type of limited liability is usually restricted to non-trading enterprises such as charities and professional and educational bodies. It limits liability to an agreed amount which is only called on if the company cannot pay its debts on being wound up. In reality, the sum guaranteed is usually a nominal sum, so no real risk is involved on the part of the guarantor.

Public and private companies

The essential difference between these two forms is an economic one, although different legal rules have been developed to apply to each of them:

• *Private companies*

Private companies tend to be small scale enterprises owned and operated by a small number of individuals who are actively involved in the day to day running of the enterprise. Many such companies are sole traders or partnerships which have registered as companies in order to take advantage of limited liability. Outsiders do not invest in such companies and, indeed, they are precluded from offering their shares to the public at large. Their shares are not quoted on any share market and in practice tend not to be freely transferable. The legal validity of such private companies was clearly established in the *Salomon* case (see 9.3.2) and, since then, the courts and legislation have developed specific rules governing their operation.

- *Public limited companies*

  Public companies, on the other hand, tend to be large, and to be controlled by directors and managers rather than owners. They are essentially a source of investment and have freely transferable shares which are quoted on the Stock Exchange.

As a consequence of the difference with regard to ownership and control, many of the provisions of the companies legislation, designed to protect the interests of shareholders in public companies, are not applicable to private companies. In his leading text on company law, Professor John Farrar lists some 18 differences in the way in which the legislation operates as between public and private companies. The most important of these are as follows:

- public companies must have at least two directors whereas private companies need only have one. This recognises the reality of the true one-man business. It is important to note that the Companies (Single Member Private Limited Companies) Regulations 1992 provide for the formation of a limited company with only one member. These Regulations are in line with the European Community Twelfth Company Law Directive;

- the requirement to keep accounting records is shorter for private companies: three years, as opposed to six years for public companies;

- the controls over distribution of dividend payments is relaxed in relation to private companies;

- private companies may purchase their own shares out of capital whereas public companies are strictly forbidden from doing so;

- private companies can provide financial assistance for the purchase of their own shares where public companies cannot;

- there are fewer and looser controls over directors of private companies with regard to their financial relationships with their companies;

- in a private company, anything that might be done by way of a resolution of a general meeting or a meeting of a class of members may instead be achieved by a resolution in writing signed by all the members of the company without the need to convene any such meeting;

- private companies may pass an elective resolution dispensing with the need to appoint auditors annually, to lay accounts before an annual general meeting or, indeed, to hold annual general meetings at all. An elective resolution also permits private companies to reduce the majority needed to call meetings at short notice from 95% to 90%.

It may also be suggested that, in cases involving private limited companies which the courts view as quasi-partnerships, other general company law principles are applied less rigorously or not at all. See, for example, *Ebrahimi v Westbourne Galleries Ltd* (1973), where the court seemed to play down the effect of separate personality in such instances. Consider also *Clemens v Clemens Bros Ltd* (1976) over which much ink has been spilled in trying to establish a general rule concerning the duties owed by majority to minority shareholders. The reality is that there was no general principle that could be applied: the case merely reflects the courts' willingness to treat what they see as quasi-partnerships in an equitable manner. What is certain about the *Clemens* case is that it would find no application in public limited companies.

There is much to be said for the suggestion that private limited companies should be removed from the ambit of the general companies legislation and be given their own particular legislation. It is apparent that they are not the same as public companies and cannot be expected to submit to the same regulatory regime as applies to the latter. In practice, the law recognises this but only in a roundabout way by treating them as exceptions to the general law relating to public companies. The argument, however, is that they are not exceptions; they are completely different, and this difference should be clearly recognised by treating them as a legal form *sui generis*. It is to be hoped that the current review of the possibility of extending limited liability to the partnership form currently being carried out by the Law Commission will deal with the general anomalies of the current situation.

Parent and subsidiary companies

This description of companies relates to the way in which large business enterprises tend to operate through a linked structure of distinct companies. Each of these companies exists as a separate corporate entity in its own right but the group is required to be treated as a single entity in relation to the group accounting provisions under s 229 of the Companies Act 1985.

The Companies Act 1989 changed the definition of holding and subsidiary companies in s 736 of the Companies Act 1985. The new section states that one company, S, is a subsidiary of another company, H, its holding company, in any of the following circumstances:

- where H holds a majority of voting rights in S;

- where H is a member of S and has a right to appoint or remove a majority of its board of directors;

- where H is a member of S and controls a majority of the voting rights in it;

- where S is a subsidiary of a company which is in turn a subsidiary of H.

Section 258 defines the relationship of parent and subsidiary companies in a similar way but introduces the idea of the parent exercising a dominant influence over the subsidiary company.

Small, medium and large companies

Companies can be categorised in relation to their size. Small- and medium-sized companies are subjected to relaxation in relation to the submission of accounts under s 246. Which category a company fits into depends on its turnover, balance sheet valuation and number of employees.

A small company must satisfy two of the following requirements:

Turnover	not more than £2.8 million
Balance sheet	not more than £1.4 million
Employees	not more than 50

A medium-sized company must satisfy two of the following requirements:

Turnover	not more than £11.2 million
Balance sheet	not more than £5.6 million
Employees	not more than 250

9.3.4 Formation of companies

The Companies Act 1985 establishes a strict procedure with which companies have to comply before they can operate legally. The procedure, which in the case of public companies involves two stages, is as follows.

Registration

A registered company is incorporated when particular documents are delivered to the registrar of companies (s 10). On registration of these documents, the registrar issues a certificate of incorporation (s 13). The documents required under s 10 are:

- a memorandum of association;

- articles of association (unless Table A articles are to apply: see below);

- a statement detailing the first directors and secretary of the company with their written consent and the address of the company's registered office.

In addition, a statutory declaration that the necessary requirements of the Companies Act 1985 have been complied with must be submitted under s 12.

Commencement of business

A private company may start its business and use its borrowing powers as soon as the certificate of registration is issued. A public company, however, cannot start a business or borrow money until it has obtained an additional certificate from the registrar under s 117. In relation to public companies, there is a requirement that they have a minimum allotted share capital, at present, £50,000 (s 11), and the second certificate confirms that the company has met that requirement.

9.3.5   The constitution of the company

The constitution of a company is established by two documents; the memorandum of association, and the articles of association. If there is any conflict between the two documents, the contents of the memorandum prevail over anything to the contrary contained in the articles; although provisions in the articles may be used to clarify particular uncertainties in the memorandum.

As will be seen, there is a large measure of freedom as to what is actually included in such documents but this latitude is extended within a clearly-established framework of statutory and common law rules. Model memorandums and articles of association are set out in the Companies (Tables A to F) Regulations 1985, although companies may alter the models to suit their particular circumstances and requirements.

The memorandum of association

The memorandum of association mainly governs the company's external affairs. It represents the company to the outside world, stating its capital structure, its powers and its objects. The document submitted to the registrar of companies must be signed by at least two subscribers from amongst the company's first shareholders. Every memorandum must contain the following clauses:

• *The name clause*

Except in relation to specifically exempted companies, such as those involved in charitable work, companies are required to indicate that they are operating on the basis of limited liability. Thus, private companies are required to end their names either with the word 'Limited' or the abbreviation 'Ltd'; and public companies must end their names with the words 'public limited company' or the abbreviation 'plc'. Welsh companies may use the Welsh language equivalents (ss 25 and 27). Equally, it amounts to a criminal offence to use the words 'public limited company' or 'Limited' in an improper manner (ss 33 and 34).

A further aspect of this requirement for publicity is that companies display their names outside their business premises, on business documents and on their seal. In addition to committing a criminal offence, any person who fails to use a company's full name on any document will be personally liable for any default. See *Penrose v Martyr* (1858), where a company secretary was held personally liable when he failed to indicate that the company against which he had drawn a bill of exchange was in fact a limited company.

A company's name must not be the same as any already registered, nor should it constitute a criminal offence, be offensive, or suggest unauthorised connection with the government or any local authority (s 26). A passing off action may be taken against a company as previously considered in relation to partnership law (see 9.2.5).

The name of a company can be changed by a special resolution of the company (s 28).

- *The registered office clause*

This is the company's legal address. It is the place where legal documents such as writs or summonses can be served on the company. It is also the place where particular documents and statutory registers such as the register of members (s 353), the register of directors' interests in shares (s 325), the register of debenture holders (s 190), and the register of charges held against the company's property (s 407) are required to be kept available for inspection. The memorandum does not state the actual address of the registered office, but only the country within which the company is registered, whether Scotland or England and Wales. The precise location of the registered office, however, has to be stated on all business correspondence (s 351). It is not necessary that the registered office be the company's main place of business and, indeed, it is not unusual for a company's registered office to be the address of its accountant or lawyer.

- *The objects clause*

Companies registered under the various Companies Acts are not corporations in the same way as common law corporations are. It was established in *Ashbury Railway Carriage and Iron Co Ltd v Riche* (1875) that such companies were established only to pursue particular purposes. Those purposes were stated in the objects clause of the company's memorandum of association and any attempt to contract outside of that limited authority was said to be *ultra vires* and, as a consequence, void.

It was felt for a long time that the operation of the *ultra vires* doctrine operated unfairly on outsiders and various attempts were made to reduce the scope of its application. Since the introduction of the Companies Act 1989, it is fortunately no longer necessary to enter into a detailed consideration of the history and operation of the doctrine of *ultra vires*. After the Companies Act 1989, *ultra vires* has been effectively reduced to an internal matter and does not affect outsiders; and, even as a means of limiting the actions of directors, it has been considerably weakened (see ss 35, 35A and 35B).

Whereas, in the past, companies used to register extended objects clauses to provide for unforeseen eventualities, now, under the new legislation they can simply register as a general commercial company which will empower them to carry on any trade or business whatsoever and to do all such things as are incidental or conducive to the carrying on of any trade or business (s 3A).

Companies can alter their objects clause by passing a special resolution, by virtue of s 4, although such procedure is subject to a right of appeal to the courts within 21 days by the holders of 15% of the issued capital of the company. However, given the effect of the Companies Act 1989, this element of control will only have indirect effect on the external relations of the company to the extent that members may bring proceedings to prevent directors from acting beyond the stated objects of the company (s 35(2)).

- *The limited liability clause*

This clause simply states that the liability of the members is limited. It must be included even where the company has permission not to use the word 'Limited' in its name.

- *The authorised share capital clause*

This states the maximum amount of share capital that a company is authorised to issue. The capital has to be divided into shares of a fixed monetary amount as no-fixed-value shares are not permissible in UK law.

- *The association clause*

This states that the subscribers to the memorandum wish to form a company and agree to take the number of shares placed opposite their names.

It should also be recalled that the memorandum of public companies must contain a clause stating that they are public companies.

The articles of association

The articles primarily regulate the internal working of the company. They govern the rights and relations of the members to the company and vice versa, and the relations of the members between themselves. As provided in s 14 of the Companies Act 1989, the articles are to be treated as an enforceable contract; although it has to be stated that it is a peculiar contract, in that its terms can be altered by the majority of the members without the consent of each member.

The articles deal with such matters as the allotment and transfer of shares, the rights attaching to particular shares, the rules relating to the holding of meetings and the powers of directors.

A company is at liberty to draw up its own articles but regulations made under the Companies Act 1989 provide a set of model articles known as Table

A. Companies do not have to submit their own articles and, if they do not, then Table A applies automatically. The provisions contained in Table A also apply to the extent that they have not been expressly excluded by the company's particular articles. Usually, companies adopt Table A with appropriate modifications fitting to their own situation.

Articles can be altered by the passing of a special resolution. Any such alteration has to be made '*bona fide* in the interest of the company as a whole', but the exact meaning of this phrase is not altogether clear. It is evident that it involves a subjective element in that those deciding the alteration must actually believe they are acting in the interest of the company. There is additionally, however, an objective element. In *Greenhalgh v Arderne Cinemas Ltd* (1951), it was stated that any alteration had to be in the interest of the individual hypothetical member; thus, the alteration that took a pre-emptive right from a particular member was held to be to the advantage of such a hypothetical member, although it severely reduced the rights of a real member. Such distinction between concrete and hypothetical benefits is a matter of fine distinction although it can be justified. In any case, persons suffering from substantive injustice are now at liberty to make an application under s 459 for an order to remedy any unfairly prejudicial conduct (see 9.3.9).

The following two cases may demonstrate the difference between the legitimate use and the abuse of the provision for altering articles: each of them relates to circumstances where existing shareholders' rights were removed.

In *Brown v British Abrasive Wheel Co* (1919), an alteration to the articles of the company was proposed to give the majority shareholders the right to buy shares of the minority. It was held under the circumstances of the case that the alteration was invalid since it would benefit the majority shareholders rather than the company as a whole.

In *Sidebottom v Kershaw Leese and Co* (1920), the alteration to the articles gave the directors the power to require any shareholder who entered into competition with the company to transfer their shares to nominees of the directors at a fair price. It was held that under these circumstances the alteration permitting the expropriation of members' interests was valid since it would benefit the company as a whole.

9.3.6 Capital

There are many different definitions of capital. The way in which a company raises such money as it needs takes the form of either share capital or loan capital.

Share capital

A share has been defined as the interest of the shareholder in the company measured by a sum of money, for the purposes of liability in the first place and of interest in the second, but also consisting of a series of mutual covenants entered into by all the shareholders (*Borland's Trustees v Steel* (1901)).

On the basis of this definition, it may be taken that:

- the nominal value of the share normally fixes the amount which the shareholder is required to contribute to the assets of the company;

- the share represents a proportionate interest in the business. This right is, however, no more than the contingent rights to receive a dividend payment and attend and vote at general meetings of the company. As has been seen above in considering separate personality, the concrete capital assets of the business are the property of the company and there is no direct link between the shareholder and those assets. Shareholders merely have the right to participate in the profit generated by concrete assets while the company continues to operate, and only have a claim against the assets when the company is wound up.

Section 182 of the Companies Act 1985 provides that shares are personal property and are transferable in the manner provided for in the company's articles of association. Although the articles of private limited companies tend to restrict the transfer of shares within a close group of people, it is an essential aspect of shares in public limited companies that the investment they represent is open to immediate realisation and to that end they are made freely transferable, subject to following the appropriate procedures.

Types of share capital

The word 'capital' is used in a number of different ways in relation to shares:

- *Nominal or authorised capital*

  This is the figure stated in the company's memorandum of association. It sets the maximum number of shares that the company can issue together with the value of each share. There is no requirement that companies issue shares to the full extent of their authorised capital.

- *Issued or allotted capital*

  This represents the nominal value of the shares actually issued by the company. It is more important than authorised capital as a true measure of the substance of the company. If a company is willing to pay the registration fee, it can register with an authorised capital of £1 million yet only actually issue two £1 shares. Public companies must have a minimum issued capital of £50,000 (s 11 of the Companies Act 1985).

- *Paid up capital*

  This is the proportion of the nominal value of the issued capital actually paid by the shareholder. It may be the full nominal value, in which case it fulfils the shareholder's responsibility to outsiders; or it can be a mere part payment, in which case the company has an outstanding claim against the shareholder. Shares in public companies must be paid up to the extent of at least a quarter of their nominal value (s 101 of the Companies Act 1985).

- *Called and uncalled capital*

  Where a company has issued shares as not fully paid up it can, at a later time, make a call on those shares. This means that the shareholders are required to provide more capital, up to the amount remaining unpaid on the nominal value of their shares. Called capital should equal paid up capital: uncalled capital is the amount remaining unpaid on issued capital.

- *Reserve capital*

  This arises where a company passes a resolution that it will not make a call on any unpaid capital. The unpaid capital then becomes a reserve, only to be called upon if the company cannot pay its debts from existing assets in the event of its liquidation.

Types of shares

Companies can issue shares of different value, with different rights attached to them. Such classes of shares can be distinguished and categorised as follows:

- *Ordinary shares*

  These shares are sometimes referred to as equity in the company. Of all the types of shares they carry the greatest risk but in recompense receive the greatest return. The nominal value of shares is fixed but the exchange value of the shares in the stock market fluctuates in relation to the performance of the company and the perception of those dealing in The Stock Exchange. It is perhaps a matter of regret that the typical shareholder, and that includes the institutional investor, relates more to the performance of their shares in the market than to the actual performance of their company in productive terms.

- *Preference shares*

  These shares involve less of a risk than ordinary shares. They may have priority over ordinary shares in two respects; dividends and repayment. They carry a fixed rate of dividend which has to be paid before any payment can be made to ordinary shareholders. Such rights are cumulative unless otherwise provided. This means that a failure to pay a dividend in any one year has to be made good in subsequent years.

  As regards repayment of capital, preference shares do not have priority, unless, as is usually the case, this is specifically provided for. Also, without specific provision, preference shares have the same rights as ordinary shares; but it is usual for their voting rights to be restricted. Preference shareholders are entitled to vote at class meetings convened to consider any alteration to their particular rights, but apart from that they are usually restricted to voting in general meetings when their dividends are in arrears.

• *Deferred shares*

This type of share postpones the rights of its holder to dividends until after the ordinary shareholders have received a fixed return. In effect, the ordinary shares are treated as preference shares and the deferred shares as ordinary shares. It is no longer a common form of organisation.

• *Redeemable shares*

These are shares issued on the understanding that they may be bought back by the company (s 159). Redemption may be at the option of either the company or the shareholder, depending on the terms of issue. Companies, in any case, now have the right, subject to conditions, to purchase their own shares, and, therefore, are no longer restricted to buying redeemable shares (s 162).

Loan capital

Companies usually acquire the capital they need to engage in their particular business through the issue of shares. It is, however, also common practice for companies to borrow additional money to finance their operation. Such borrowing does not give the lender any interest in the company but represents a claim against the company. The relationship between company and the provider of loan capital is the ordinary relationship of debtor/creditor, although specific mechanisms exist to facilitate the borrowing of companies and secure the interests of their creditors.

Debentures

A debenture is a document which acknowledges the fact that a company has borrowed money. The use of the term debenture, however, is extended to cover the loan itself. A debenture may be issued to a single creditor. Alternatively, it may signify the company's indebtedness to a large number of people, in which case each of the creditors has a proportionate claim against the total debenture stock. With regard to repayment, debts rank in order of creation, so earlier debentures have to be paid before those created later. It is usual, however, for debentures to be issued in a series. In such circumstances a *pari passu* clause is introduced into the document expressing the debt. This has the effect that all of the loans made within the series rank equally with regard to repayment.

Debentures may be issued as redeemable or irredeemable under s 193 of the Companies Act 1985. In addition, they may carry the right to convert into ordinary shares at some later time. Debentures may be transferred from the current holder to another party subject to the proper procedure under s 183 of the Companies Act 1985.

Debentures differ from shares in the following respects:

- debenture holders are creditors of the company; they are not members as shareholders are;

- as creditors, they receive interest on their loans; they do not receive dividends as shareholders do;

- they are entitled to receive interest whether the company is profitable or not, even if the payment is made out of the company's capital; shareholders' dividends must not be paid out of capital;

- debentures may be issued at a discount, that is, at less than their nominal value; whereas shares must not be issued at a discount and the company must receive the equivalent to the shares' nominal value.

Company charges

Debentures which have no security are referred to as unsecured loan stock, although it is usual for debentures to provide security for the amount loaned. Security means that, in the event of the company being wound up, the creditor with a secured debt will have priority as regards repayment over any unsecured creditor.

There are two types of security for company loans:

- *Fixed charge*

  In this case, a specific asset of the company is made subject to a charge in order to secure a debt. The company cannot thereafter dispose of the property without the consent of the debenture holders. If the company fails to honour its commitments, then the debenture holders can sell the asset to recover the money owed. The asset most commonly subject to fixed charges is land, although any other long term capital asset may also be charged, as may such intangible assets as book debts. It would not be appropriate to place a fixed charge against stock in trade as the company would be prevented from freely dealing with it without the prior approval of the debenture holders. This would obviously frustrate the business purpose of the enterprise.

- *Floating charge*

  This category of charge does not attach to any specific property of the company until it crystallises through the company committing some act or default. On the occurrence of such an event, the floating charge becomes a fixed equitable charge over the assets detailed, the value of which may be realised in order to pay the debt owed to the floating charge holder.

The floating charge is most commonly made in relation to the undertaking and assets of a company. In such a situation, the security is provided by all the property owned by the company, some of which may be continuously changing, such as stock in trade. The use of the floating charge permits the company to deal with its property without the need to seek the approval of the debenture holders.

Registration of charges

All charges, including both fixed and floating, have to be registered with the Companies Registry within 21 days of their creation. If they are not registered, then the charge is void, that is, ineffective, against any other creditor or the liquidator of the company; but it is still valid against the company. Effectively, this means that the charge holder loses priority as against other creditors.

In addition to registration at the Companies Registry, companies are required to maintain a register of all charges on their property. Although a failure to comply with this requirement constitutes an offence, it does not invalidate the charge.

Priority of charges

In relation to properly registered charges of the same type, charges take priority according to their date of creation. However, with regard to charges of different types, a fixed charge takes priority over a floating charge even though it was created after it.

Generally, there is nothing to prevent the creation of a fixed charge after the issuing of a floating charge and, as a legal charge against specific property, that fixed charge will still take priority over the earlier floating charge. It is possible, however, for the debenture creating the original floating charge to include a provision to prevent the creation of a later fixed charge taking priority over that floating charge.

9.3.7 Directors

Shareholders in public limited companies typically remain external to the actual operation of the enterprise in which they have invested. They also tend to assess the performance of their investment in relation to the level of dividend payment and the related short term movement of share prices on the stock exchange rather than in relation to any long term business strategy. These factors have led to the emergence of what is known as the separation of ownership and control. As suggested, this idea refers to the fact that those who provide a company's capital are not actually concerned in determining how that capital is used within the specific business enterprise. In effect, the day to day operation of the business enterprise is left in the hands of a small number of company directors, whilst the large majority of shareholders remain powerless to participate in the actual business from which they derive their dividend payments.

In theory, the shareholders exercise ultimate control over the directors through the mechanism of the general meeting. The separation of ownership and control, however, has resulted in the concentration of power in the hands of the directors and has given rise to the possibility that directors might operate as a self-perpetuating oligarchy who seek to run the company in their own interests rather than in the interests of the majority of shareholders. In the light of the lack of fit between theory and practice, statute law has intervened to place a number of specific controls on the way in which directors act.

The position of directors

It is a feature of the companies legislation that it tends to define terms in a tautological way, using the term to be defined as part of the definition. Thus, s 741 of the Companies Act 1989 defines the term 'director' to include any person occupying the position of director, by whatever name called. The point of this definition is that it emphasises the fact that it is the function the person performs rather than the title given to them that determines whether they are directors or not. Section 741 also introduces the concept of the shadow director. This is a person who, although not actually appointed to the board, instructs the directors of a company as to how to act. The point is that such a person is subject to all the controls and liabilities that the ordinary directors are subject to.

The actual position of a director may be described in a number of ways:

- they are officers of the company (s 744);

- the board of directors is the agent of the company and, under Table A, Art 84, the board may appoint one or more managing directors. They are, therefore, able to bind the company without incurring personal liability. It should be noted that directors are not the agents of the shareholders (see below in relation to the powers of directors);

- directors are in a fiduciary relationship with their company. This means that they are in a position similar to trustees. The importance of this lies in the nature of the duties it imposes on directors (see below);

- directors are not employees of their companies *per se*. They may, however, be employed by the company, in which case they will usually have a distinct service contract detailing their duties and remuneration. Apart from service contracts, the articles usually provide for the remuneration of directors in the exercise of their general duties.

Appointment of directors

The first directors are usually named in the articles or memorandum. Subsequent directors are appointed under the procedure stated in the articles.

The usual procedure is for the company in annual general meeting (AGM) to elect the directors by an ordinary resolution.

Casual vacancies are usually filled by the board of directors co-opting someone to act as director. That person then serves until the next AGM when they must stand for election in the usual manner.

Removal of directors

There are a number of ways in which a person may be obliged to give up their position as a director:

• *Rotation*

Table A provides that one-third of the directors shall retire at each AGM, being those with longest service. They are, however, open to re-election and, in practice, are usually re-elected.

• *Retirement*

Directors of public companies are required to retire at the first AGM after they have reached the age of 70. They may retire at any time before then.

• *Removal*

A director can be removed at any time by the passing of an ordinary resolution of the company (s 303). The company must be given special notice (28 days) of the intention to propose such a resolution.

The power to remove a director under s 303 cannot be removed or restricted by any provision in the company's documents or any external contract. It is possible, however, for the effect of the section to be avoided in private companies by the use of weighted voting rights.

In *Bushell v Faith* (1969), the articles of association of a company, which had three equal shareholders each of whom was a director, provided that, on a vote to remove a director, that person's shares would carry three votes as against its usual one. The effect of this was that a s 303 resolution could never be passed. The House of Lords held that such a procedure was legitimate, although it has to be recognised that it is unlikely that such a decision would be extended to public limited companies.

As regards private/quasi-partnership companies, it has been held, in *Re Bird Precision Bellows Ltd* (1984), that exclusion from the right to participate in management provides a ground for an action for a court order to remedy unfairly prejudicial conduct under s 459 of the Companies Act 1989 (see 9.3.9).

• *Disqualification*

The articles of association usually provide for the disqualification of directors on the occurrence of certain circumstances: bankruptcy; mental illness; or prolonged absence from board meetings.

In addition, individuals can be disqualified from acting as directors up to a maximum period of 15 years under the Company Directors Disqualification Act 1986. The Company Directors Disqualification Act was introduced in an attempt to prevent the misuse of the company form. One of its specific aims was the control of what are described as 'phoenix companies'. These are companies which trade until they get into financial trouble and accrue extensive debts. Upon this eventuality, the company ceases trading only for the person behind the company to set up another company to carry on essentially the same business, but with no liability to the creditors of the former company. Such behaviour is reprehensible and clearly an abuse of limited liability. The Company Directors Disqualification Act seeks to remedy this practice by preventing certain individuals from acting as a company director.

Grounds for disqualification include:

(a) persistent breach of the companies legislation;

(b) committing offences in relation to companies;

(c) fraudulent trading;

(d) general unfitness.

Power of directors as a board

Article 70 of Table A provides that the directors of a company may exercise all the powers of the company. It is important to note that this power is given to the board as a whole and not to individual directors, although Art 72 does allow for the delegation of the board's powers to one or more directors.

Article 70 gives the board of directors general power but the articles may seek to restrict the authority of the board within limits expressly stated in the company's constitutional documents. The effectiveness of such restrictions has been greatly reduced by the operation of s 35 of the Companies Act 1985, as amended by the Companies Act 1989. As a consequence of s 35, as it now is, not only can the power of a company not be challenged on the grounds of lack of capacity, but neither can the actions of its directors be challenged on the basis of any limitation contained in the company's documents. This provision is subject to the requirement that any third party must act in good faith, although such good faith is presumed subject to proof to the contrary.

The power of individual directors

There are three ways in which the power of the board of directors may be extended to individual directors. These ways are, however, simply particular applications of the general law of agency considered previously in 9.1.3.

(a) Express actual authority

This category is unproblematic in that it arises from the express conferral by the board of a particular authority onto an individual director. For example, it is possible for the board to specifically authorise an individual director to negotiate and bind the company to a particular transaction.

(b) Implied actual authority

In this situation, the person's authority flows from their position. Article 84 provides for the board of directors to appoint a managing director. The board of directors may confer any of their powers on the managing director as they see fit. The mere fact of appointment, however, will mean that the person so appointed will have the implied authority to bind the company in the same way as the board, whose delegate he or she is. Outsiders, therefore, can safely assume that a person appointed as managing director has all the powers usually exercised by a person acting as a managing director.

Implied actual authority to bind a company may also arise as a consequence of the appointment of an individual to a position other than that of managing director.

In *Hely-Hutchinson v Brayhead Ltd* (1968), although the chairman and chief executive of a company acted as its *de facto* managing director, he had never been formally appointed to that position. Nevertheless, he purported to bind the company to a particular transaction. When the other party to the agreement sought to enforce it, the company claimed that the chairman had no authority to bind it. It was held that, although the director derived no authority from his position as chairman of the board, he did acquire such authority from his position as chief executive and thus the company was bound by the contract he had entered into on its behalf.

(c) Apparent or ostensible authority/agency by estoppel

This arises where an individual director has neither express nor implied authority. Nonetheless, the director is held out by the other members of the board of directors as having the authority to bind the company. If a third party acts on such a representation, then the company will be estopped from denying its truth.

Problems tend to arise where someone acts as a managing director without having been properly appointed to that position. In such a situation, although the individual concerned may not have the actual authority to bind the company, he or she may still have apparent authority and the company may be estopped from denying his or her power to bind the company to particular transactions.

In *Freeman and Lockyer v Buckhurst Park Properties (Mangal) Ltd* (1964), although a particular director had never been appointed as managing director, he acted as such with the clear knowledge of the other directors and entered into a contract with the plaintiffs on behalf of the company. When the plaintiffs sought to recover fees due to them under that contract, it was held that the company was liable: a properly appointed managing director would have been able to enter into such a contract and the third party was entitled to rely on the representation of the other directors that the person in question had been properly appointed to that position.

Directors' duties

At common law, the duties owed by directors to their company and the shareholders, employees and creditors of that company were at worst non-existent or at best notoriously lax. Statute has, by necessity, been forced to intervene to increase such duties in order to provide a measure of protection for those concerned.

As fiduciaries, directors owe the following duties to their company (it is imperative to note that the duty is owed to the company as a distinct legal person and not the shareholders of the company, so the rule in *Foss v Harbottle* applies, see 9.3.2):

• *The duty to act* bona fide *in the interests of the company*

  In effect, this means that directors are under an obligation to act in what they genuinely believe to be the interest of the company.

• *The duty not to act for any collateral purpose*

  This may be seen as a corollary of the preceding duty in that directors cannot be said to be acting *bona fide* if they use their powers for some ulterior or collateral purpose. For example, directors should not issue shares to particular individuals in order merely to facilitate, or indeed prevent, a prospective take-over bid (see *Howard Smith v Ampol Petroleum* (1974) and *Hogg v Cramphorn* (1967)). The breach of such a fiduciary duty is, however, subject to *post hoc* ratification (see *Bamford v Bamford* (1970)).

• *The duty not to permit a conflict of interest and duty to arise*

  This equitable rule is strictly applied by the courts and the effect of its operations may be seen in *Regal (Hastings) v Gulliver* (1942) where the directors of a company owning one cinema provided money for the creation of a subsidiary company to purchase two other cinemas. After the parent and subsidiary companies had been sold at a later date, the directors were required to repay the profit they had made on the sale of their shares in the subsidiary company on the grounds that they had only been in the position to make that profit because of their positions as directors of the parent company. (The profits made went back to the parent company which was by then in the hands of the person who had paid the money to the directors in the first place.)

Duty of care and skill

Common law did not place any great burden on directors in this regard. Damages could be recovered against directors for losses caused by their negligence but the level of such negligence was high. As was stated in *Lagunas Nitrate Co v Lagunas Syndicate* (1989), the negligence must be in a business sense 'culpable or gross'. The classic statement is to be found in *Re City Equitable Fire Assurance Co* (1925) which established three points:

- First, in determining the degree of skill to be expected, the common law applied a subjective test and established no minimum standard. A director was expected to show the degree of skill which might reasonably be expected of a person of their knowledge and experience. As a result, if they were particularly experienced and skilled in the affairs of their business, then they would be expected to perform in line with such skills. On the other hand, however, if the director was a complete incompetent, they would only be expected to perform to the level of a complete incompetent. The reasoning behind this seemed to be that the courts left it to the shareholders to elect and control the directors as their representatives. If the shareholders elected incompetents, then that was a matter for them and the courts would not interfere.

- Secondly, the duties of directors were held to be of no intermittent nature and consequently directors were not required to give continuous attention to the affairs of their company. In *Re Cardiff Savings Bank (the Marquis of Bute's case)* (1892), it emerged that the Marquis had inherited his position as president of the bank at the age of six months and, in the course of 38 years, he only ever attended one board meeting.

- Thirdly, in the absence of any grounds for suspicion, directors were entitled to leave the day to day operation of the company's business in the hands of managers and to trust them to perform their tasks honestly.

The laxity of the situation at common law has been much tightened by statute and particularly by the development of the offence of wrongful trading introduced by s 214 of the IA 1986. Section 214 applies where a company is being wound up and it appears that, at some time before the start of the winding up, a director knew, or ought to have known, that there was no reasonable chance of the company avoiding insolvent liquidation. In such circumstances, then, unless directors took every reasonable step to minimise the potential loss to the company's creditors, they may be liable to contribute such money to the assets of the company as the court thinks proper. In deciding what directors ought to have known, the court will apply an objective test as well as a subjective one. As in common law, if the director is particularly well qualified, they will be expected to perform in line with those standards. Additionally, however, s 214 establishes a minimum standard by applying an objective test which requires directors to have the general knowledge, skill and experience which may reasonably be expected of a person carrying out the same functions as are carried out by that director in relation to the company.

The manner in which incompetent directors will become liable to contribute the assets of their companies was shown in *Re Produce Marketing Consortium Ltd* (1989), in which two directors were held liable to pay compensation from the time they ought to have known that their company could not avoid insolvent liquidation rather than the later time when they did actually realise that fact.

It should also be recalled, as considered previously, that directors may be disqualified from holding office for a period of up to 15 years under the provisions of the Company Directors Disqualification Act 1986.

Company secretary

Section 744 of the Companies Act 1989 includes the company secretary among the officers of a company. Every company must have a company secretary and, although there are no specific qualifications required to perform such a role in a private company, s 286 of the Companies Act 1985 requires that the directors of public company must ensure that the company secretary has the requisite knowledge and experience to discharge their functions. Section 286(2) sets out a list of professional bodies, membership of which enables a person to act as a company secretary.

Although old authorities, such as *Houghton and Co v Northard Lowe and Wills* (1928), suggest that company secretaries have extremely limited authority to bind their company, later cases have recognised the reality of the contemporary situation and have extended to company secretaries potentially significant powers to bind their companies. As an example, consider *Panorama Developments Ltd v Fidelis Furnishing Fabrics Ltd* (1971). In this case, the Court of Appeal held that a company secretary was entitled:

> ... to sign contracts connected with the administrative side of a company's affairs, such as employing staff and ordering cars and so forth. All such matters now come within the ostensible authority of a company's secretary.

Company auditor

Section 384 of the Companies Act 1985 requires all companies to appoint an auditor whose duty it is under s 235 of the Companies Act 1985 to report to the company's members whether or not the company's accounts have been properly prepared and to consider whether the directors report is consistent with those accounts.

In the case of a newly registered company, the first auditors are appointed by the directors until the first general meeting at which they may be reappointed by the members of the company. Thereafter, auditors are appointed annually at AGMs at which accounts are laid (s 385). It should be recalled that private companies may, by means of an elective resolution, dispense with the requirement to appoint auditors annually. In such circumstances, the existing auditor is deemed to be reappointed for each succeeding year (s 386). The Secretary of State has the power to appoint an auditor where the company has not appointed one (s 387).

Section 389 provides that a person can only be appointed as an auditor where they are members of a recognised supervisory body such as the Institute of Certified Accountants or the Chartered Association of Certified Accountants. A person cannot be appointed where they are officers or employees of the company in question.

Auditors are appointed to ensure that the company is being run on a proper basis. They represent the interests of the shareholders and report to them. They are, however, employed by the company and owe their contractual duty to the company rather than the shareholders. As partnerships may now be appointed as auditors (s 26 of the CA 1989), there has been some concern expressed that the large accountancy firms might offer auditor services as a loss leader in order to acquire more lucrative accountancy deals with the company. The concern is that this might lead to a conflict of interest between the accountancy firm's role as auditor and its other roles in relation to the company.

Auditors are required to make a report on all annual accounts laid before the company in AGMs during their tenure of office (s 235(1)). The report must state the names of the auditors and must be signed by them (s 236(1), (3)).

The auditors are required to report (s 235(2)): whether the accounts have been properly prepared in accordance with the Companies Act 1989; and whether the individual and group accounts show a true and fair view of the profit or loss and state of affairs of the company and of the group, so far as concerns the members of the company.

Auditors are required to make the necessary investigations and consider the following, which need only be reported on if there are deficiencies: whether the company has kept proper accounting records and obtained proper accounting returns from branches (s 237(1) and (2)); whether the accounts are in agreement with the records (s 237(1) and (2)); whether they have obtained all the information and explanations that they considered necessary (s 237(3)); whether the requirements of Sched 6 concerning disclosure of information about directors' and officers' remuneration, loans and other transactions have been met; whether the information in the directors' report is consistent with the accounts (s 235(3)).

Where the company circulates a summary financial statement, the auditors are required to give a report on whether the summary statement is consistent with the company's annual accounts and directors' report and whether it complies with the requirements of the Companies Act 1985 and regulations in relation to this statement (s 251(4)(b)).

If the auditor's report does not state that, in their unqualified opinion, the accounts have been properly prepared in accordance with the relevant legislation governing the relevant undertakings accounts (s 262(1)), then the accounts are said to be qualified.

An auditor may be removed by an ordinary resolution of the company. Where auditors resign they are required to submit a statement setting out any circumstances that should be brought to the attention of the members of the company. A resigning auditor can require the company to call an extraordinary general meeting to consider any such statement (s 392A).

The tortious liability of auditors has been considered in 8.3.1.

9.3.8 Company meetings

In theory, the ultimate control over a company's business lies with the members in the general meeting. In practice, however, the residual powers of the membership are restricted to their ultimate control over the company's memorandum and articles of association, although this control has been reduced by the introduction of the new s 35 of the Companies Act 1985, as amended by the Companies Act 1989, together with their control of the composition of the board of directors. The reality of such limited theoretical powers are further constrained by the practicalities involved with the operation of company meetings.

In line with this approach, some powers are specifically reserved to the members by statute, such as the right to petition for voluntary winding up; and Art 70 of Table A provides that the shareholders, by passing a special resolution, can instruct the directors to act in a particular way. In reality, the ideal-typical shareholder tends to either not be bothered about taking an active part in the conduct of company meetings or else uses his or her vote in a way directed by the board of directors.

One would obviously conclude that a meeting involved more than one member and indeed there is authority to that effect in *Sharp v Dawes* (1876), in which a meeting between a lone member and the company secretary was held not to be validly constituted. It is possible, however, for a meeting of only one member to take place in the following circumstances:

- in the case of a meeting of a particular class of shareholders and all the shares of that class are owned by the one member;

- by virtue of s 371 of the Companies Act 1985, the court may order the holding of a general meeting at which the quorum is to be one member. This eventuality might arise in a quasi-partnership where a recalcitrant member of a two person company refused to attend any meetings thus preventing the continuation of the enterprise.

Types of meetings

There are three types of meeting:

(a) The AGM

By virtue of s 366 of the Companies Act 1985, every company is required to hold an AGM every calendar year; subject to a maximum period of 15 months. This means that, if a company holds its AGM on 1 January 1995, then it must hold its next AGM by 31 March 1996 at the latest.

In line with the recognised distinction between public and private companies, the Companies Act 1989 introduced a provision in the form of a new s 366A, which permitted private companies, subject to approval by a unanimous vote, to dispense with the holding of an AGM.

If a company fails to hold an AGM, then any member may apply to the Secretary of State, under s 367, to call a meeting in default.

(b) The extraordinary general meeting

An extraordinary general meeting (EGM) is any meeting other than an AGM. EGMs are usually called by the directors, although members holding 10% of the voting shares may requisition such a meeting.

(c) The class meeting

This refers to the meeting of a particular class of shareholder, that is, those who hold a type of share providing particular rights, such as preference shares considered in 9.3.6).

Under s 381A of the Companies Act 1985, it is no longer necessary for a private company to convene a general meeting where the members have unanimously signed a written resolution setting out a particular course of action.

Calling meetings

Meetings may be convened in a number of ways by various people:

- by the directors of the company under Art 37 of Table A. Apart from this usual power, directors of public limited companies are required, under s 142 of the Companies Act 1985, to call meetings where there has been a serious loss of capital, defined as the assets falling to half or less than the nominal value of the called up share capital;

- by the members using the power to requisition a meeting under s 368 of the Companies Act 1985. To require the convening of a company meeting, any shareholders must hold at least one-10th of the share capital carrying voting rights. If the directors fail to convene a meeting as required within 21 days of the deposit of the requisition, although the actual date of the meeting may be within eight weeks of the date of requisition, then the requisitionists may themselves convene a meeting and recover any expenses from the company;

- by the auditor of a company under s 392A which provides for a resigning auditor to require the directors to convene a meeting in order to explain the reason for the auditor's resignation;

- the Secretary of State may under s 367, on the application of any member, call a meeting of a company where it has failed to hold an AGM as required by s 366;

- the court may order a meeting under s 371 where it is impracticable otherwise to call a meeting.

Notice of meetings

Proper and adequate notice must be sent to all those who are entitled to attend any meeting, although the precise nature of the notice is governed by the articles of association:

- *Time*

  This is set out in s 369 of the Companies Act 1985. The minimum period of notice is 21 clear days for an AGM and 14 clear days for all other meetings, except those called to consider a special resolution, which also require 21 clear days notice. Shorter notice is permissible in the case of an AGM where all the members entitled to attend agree and in the case of any other meeting where holders of 95% of the nominal value of the voting shares agree. Private companies, by means of an elective resolution, may reduce this latter requirement to 90%.

- *Content*

  Adequate notice of the content of any resolution must be sent to members so that they can decide whether to attend the meeting or to appoint a proxy to vote in line with their instructions.

Agenda

It is usually the prerogative of the directors to decide which motions will be put to the company in the general meeting. Members, however, may set the agenda where they have requisitioned an EGM under the procedure established in s 368. In relation to an AGM, s 376 provides a procedure whereby a minority of members, amounting to one-20th of the total voting rights or 100 members holding an average of £100 worth of shares, may have a motion considered.

This mechanism is complicated and expensive and the practicalities of trying to use it, especially in large public companies, means that it is not often used.

The difficulties involved in ordinary members getting issues onto the agenda also extend to resolutions to remove directors. Although s 303 provides for the removal of directors on the passing of an ordinary resolution, it was held in *Pedley v Inland Waterways Association Ltd* (1977) that a disgruntled member could only get such a resolution onto the agenda if he or she satisfied the requirements of s 376.

Types of resolutions

There are essentially three types of resolution:

(a) An ordinary resolution

This requires a simple majority of those voting. Members who do not attend or appoint a proxy, or who attend but do not vote, are disregarded.

Notice in relation to an ordinary resolution depends on the type of meeting at which it is proposed, 21 days for an AGM and 14 days for an EGM, although in relation to an ordinary resolution to remove a director under s 303, the company must be given special notice of 28 days. It should be noted that in this latter case the notice is given to the company, whereas usually it is the company that is required to give notice to the members.

(b) An extraordinary resolution

This requires a majority of not less than three-quarters of those voting. An extraordinary resolution requires a minimum of 14 days notice, but, if it is to be voted on at an AGM, notice of 21 days will be required.

(c) A special resolution

This requires a majority of not less than three-quarters but, in all circumstances, members must be given 21 days' notice of its contents.

In considering types of resolutions it should be recalled that private companies, by virtue of s 381A, can function on the basis of written resolutions. The effect of this is that anything that can be done by means of passing a resolution at a general meeting can be done by all of the members signing the resolution without the need to convene a meeting.

It should also be recalled that private companies, by virtue of s 379A, can pass elective resolutions as a means of dispensing with particular requirements of the Companies Act 1985. The formalities that can be avoided relate to:

- the duration of directors' authority to allot shares;
- the need to lay accounts and reports before general meetings;

- the majority required to sanction the holding of meetings at short notice;
- the need to hold AGMs;
- the need to appoint auditors on an annual basis.

It was the case that elective resolutions required 21 days' notice, however, under the Deregulation (Resolutions of Private Companies) Order 1996, SI 1996/1471, itself made under the Deregulation and Contracting Out Act 1994, that requirement has been removed and such a resolution is effective notwithstanding that less than 21 days' notice was given. It is still the case that unanimity is required both to pass the resolution and to accept the shorter notice. So, all those entitled to attend and vote at a meeting must approve of the resolution, but it should also be noted that elective resolutions can themselves be passed using the procedure for passing written resolutions.

Quorum

This is the minimum number of persons whose presence is required for the transaction of business at any meeting. The precise details are set out in the articles of association, although s 370 and Art 41 of Table A sets the minimum at two who must be continuously present at the meeting.

Votes

A resolution is initially decided upon by a show of hands unless a poll is demanded. On a show of hands, every member has one vote. In a poll, it is usual for each share to carry a vote and thus for the outcome of the poll to reflect the concentration of interest in the company (for exceptions to this, see *Bushell v Faith* in 9.3.7).

Article 41 of Table A enables any two members or the chairman to call for a poll.

Proxies

Section 372 of the Companies Act 1985 provides that any member of a company who is entitled to attend and vote at a meeting may appoint another person as their proxy, that is, to act as his or her agent in exercising the member's voting right. Every notice of a meeting must state the member's right to appoint a proxy and, although the articles may require notice of the appointment of a proxy to be given to the company, they may not require more than 48 hours' notice. Proxies need not be members of the company. They have no right to speak at meetings of public companies but may speak in private companies. They are not allowed to vote on a show of hands but only in regard to a poll vote.

Chairman

Although s 370 provides that any member may act as chair, Art 43 states that the chairman of the board of directors shall preside. The chairman conducts the meeting and must preserve order and ensure that it complies with the provisions of the companies legislation and the company's articles. He or she may adjourn it with the consent of, or where instructed to do so by, the meeting. The chairman has a casting vote in the case of equality. He or she is under a general duty at all times to act *bona fide* in the interests of the company as a whole and thus must use his or her vote appropriately.

Minutes

Section 382 requires that minutes of all general meetings and directors' meetings must be kept and are regarded as evidence of the proceedings when signed by the chairman.

9.3.9   Majority rule and minority protection

It has been seen how the day to day operation of a company's business is left in the hands of its directors and managers, with shareholders having no direct input into business decisions. Even when the members convene in general meetings, the individual shareholder is subject to the wishes of the majority as expressed in the passing of appropriate resolutions. In normal circumstances, the minority has no grounds to complain, even though the effect of majority rule may place them in a situation they do not agree with. Even where the minority shareholders suspect that some wrong has been done to the company, it is not normally open to them to take action. This situation is encapsulated in what is known as the rule in *Foss v Harbottle* (1843) (see 9.3.2). In this case, individual members were not permitted to institute proceedings against the directors of their company. It was held that, if any wrong had been committed, it had been committed against the company and that it was for the company acting through the majority to decide to institute proceedings.

It is important to distinguish the various ways in which one or more minority shareholders may take action against the company, the directors or the majority shareholders.

In a personal action, shareholders sue in their own name, to enforce a personal right. An example might be where the individual's voting rights are denied, as in *Pender v Lushington* (1877).

A representative action is a collective action taken where the rights of other shareholders have been affected by the alleged wrongdoing. Once again, if the rights in question are membership rights, the rule in *Foss v Harbottle* does not apply.

A derivative action is the usual form of action where minority shareholders sue under the fraud on the minority exception to the rule in *Foss v Harbottle* (see below). The plaintiffs sue in their own name, usually in representative form, on behalf of themselves and all the other shareholders except those who are named as defendants. The defendants in the action are, first, the alleged wrongdoers and, secondly, the company itself. As the plaintiff shareholders are seeking to redress a corporate wrong, they are actually seeking a remedy on the company's behalf. As a result, if the action is successful, the judgment takes the form of an order against the first defendants and in favour of the company as second defendant.

Particular problems may arise where those in effective control of a company use their power in such a way as either to benefit themselves or cause a detriment to the minority shareholders. In the light of such a possibility, the law has intervened to offer protection to minority shareholders. The source of the protection may be considered in three areas.

Common law

At common law, it has long been established that those controlling the majority of shares are not to be allowed to use their position of control to perpetrate what is known as a fraud on the minority. In such circumstances, the individual shareholder will be able to take legal action in order to remedy their situation.

In *Cook v Deeks* (1916), directors, who were also the majority shareholders of a company, negotiated a contract on its behalf. They then took the contract for themselves and used their majority voting power to pass a resolution declaring that the company had no interest in the contract. On an action by the minority shareholder in the company, it was held that the majority could not use their votes to ratify what was a fraud on the minority. The contract belonged to the company in equity and the directors had to account to the company for the profits they made on it. Thus, the minority shareholder was not excluded from benefiting from the contract.

Statutory protection

In circumstances where the minority shareholders disagree with the actions of the majority, but without that action amounting to fraud on the minority, one remedy is simply to leave the company. In a listed public limited company, this procedure is easily achieved by selling the shares held, but things are more difficult in the case of small private companies. In these quasi-partnership cases, an alternative to bringing a derivative action in the name of the company is to petition to have the company wound up or to apply to the court for an order to remedy any unfairly prejudicial conduct.

- *Just and equitable winding up*

   Section 122(g) of the IA 1986 gives the court the power to wind up a company if it considers it just and equitable to do so. Such an order may be applied for where there is evidence of a lack of probity on the part of some of the members. It may also be used in small private companies to provide a remedy where there is either deadlock on the board, or a member is removed from the board altogether or refused a part in the management of the business.

In *Re Yenidje Tobacco Co Ltd* (1916), the company only had two shareholders who also acted as its directors. After quarrelling, the two directors refused to communicate with one another except through the company secretary. It was held that the company was essentially a partnership and that, as a partnership would have been wound up in this eventuality, the company should be wound up as well.

In *Re Westbourne Galleries*, also known as *Ebrahimi v Westbourne Galleries* (1973), a business which two parties had carried on previously as a partnership was transformed into a private limited company. After a time, one of the two original partners was removed from the board of directors of the company. It was held that the removal from the board, and the consequential loss of the right to participate in the management of the business, was ground for winding up the company.

- *Unfairly prejudicial conduct*

Use of the procedure under s 122 of the IA 1986 is likely to have extremely serious consequences for the business. Indeed, the fact that the company has to be wound up will probably result in losses for all the parties concerned. It is much better if some less mutually destructive process can be used to resolve disputes between members of private companies.

Under s 459 of the Companies Act 1985, any member may petition the court for an order on the grounds that the affairs of the company are being conducted in a way that is unfairly prejudicial to the interests of some of the members or the members generally. Section 461 gives the court general discretion as to the precise nature and content of any order it makes to remedy the situation. The following case demonstrates the operation and scope of the procedure.

In *Re London School of Electronics* (1986), the petitioner held 25% of the shares in the company LSE. The remaining 75% were held by another company, CTC. Two directors of LSE, who were also directors and the principal shareholders in CTC, diverted students from LSE to CTC. The petitioner claimed that such action deprived him of his share in the potential profit to be derived from those students. It was held that the action was unfairly prejudicial and the court instructed CTC to purchase the petitioner's shares in LSE at a value which was to be calculated as if the students had never been transferred.

In *Re Ringtower Holdings plc* (1989), Gibson J made the following four points in relation to the operation of s 459:

(1) the relevant conduct (of commission or omission) must relate to the affairs of the company of which the petitioners are members;

(2) the conduct must be both prejudicial (in the sense of causing prejudice or harm) to the relevant interests and also unfairly so: conduct may be unfair without being prejudicial or prejudicial without being unfair and in neither case would the section be satisfied;

(3) the test is of unfair prejudice, not of unlawfulness, and conduct may be lawful but unfairly prejudicial;

(4) the relevant interests are the interests of members (including the petitioners) as members, but such interests are not necessarily limited to strict legal rights under the company's constitution, and the court may take into account wider equitable considerations, such as any legitimate expectation which a member has which goes beyond his or her legal rights.

The s 459 procedure has also been used in cases where a member has been excluded from exercising a legitimate expectation to participate in the management of a company business (see *Re Bird Precision Bellows Ltd* (1984)).

And, in *Re Sam Weller and Sons Ltd* (1990), the court decided that the failure to pay dividends may amount to unfairly prejudicial conduct.

In *Re Elgindata Ltd* (1991), it was held that, depending on the circumstances of the case, serious mismanagement could constitute unfairly prejudicial conduct, although normally the court would be reluctant to make such a finding. On the facts of that case, evidence of mismanagement was found together with a lack of managerial purposefulness, but this was not sufficient to amount to unfairly prejudicial conduct.

Section 459 is an extremely active area of company law and has probably replaced s 122 of the IA 1986 as the most appropriate mechanism for alleviating the distress suffered by minority shareholders. It is essential, however, to note that the cases considered above all involved economic partnerships which had merely assumed the company legal form as a matter of internal and external convenience. The same outcomes would not be forthcoming in relation to public limited companies. The statutory protections still apply in the case of public companies but it is extremely unlikely that they would be used as freely or as widely as they are in quasi-partnership cases. As evidence of this claim, see *Re A Company* (1986), in which the exclusion of a party from management was held not to be unfairly prejudicial as the business had not been established on a quasi-partnership basis.

Investigations

In order for minority shareholders to complain, they must know what is going on in their company. It is part of their position as minority shareholders, however, that they do not have access to all the information that is available to the directors of the company. As a possible means of remedying this lack of information, and thus as a means of supporting minority protection, the Department of Trade and Industry has been given extremely wide powers to conduct investigations into the general affairs of companies, their membership, and dealings in their securities. Such powers are framed extremely widely and the courts have accepted the need for such wide powers; but this theoretical power is much limited, in practice, by a reluctance on the part of government to finance their use and by those given the powers to use them adequately.

Bearing in mind the foregoing caveats, the Secretary of State has the power, under s 431 of the Companies Act 1985, to appoint inspectors to investigate the affairs of a company on application by the following:

- the company itself after passing an ordinary resolution;

- members holding 10% of the company's issued share capital;

- 200 or more members.

Under s 432, the Secretary of State may order such an investigation where:

- the company's affairs have been conducted with intent to defraud creditors, or for an unlawful or fraudulent purpose;

- the company's affairs have been conducted in a manner unfairly prejudicial to some part of the members;

- the promoters or managers have been found guilty of fraud;

- the shareholders have not been supplied with proper information.

In addition, under s 442, the Secretary of State has the power to appoint inspectors to investigate the ownership and control of companies. Investigations may also be instigated into directors' share dealings under s 446 of the Companies Act 1985, and into insider dealing under s 177 of the Financial Services Act 1986.

Once appointed, the investigators have very wide powers under s 433 to examine the affairs of related companies; and under s 434 to require the officers of the company to attend for interview and to produce documents as required.

Consequent upon an investigation, the Secretary of State may take any of the following actions:

- petition to have the company wound up under s 124 of the IA 1986;

- petition for an order under s 459;

- bring a civil action in the name of the company against any party;

- apply to the courts to have any director disqualified from acting as a director in future under s 8 of the Company Directors Disqualification Act 1986.

Given the extent of the powers given to the Secretary of State and the investigators appointed by him or her, it is a little ironic, if not symptomatic of the failures in the system of company investigations, that some of the most famous cases of the early 1970s, that is, *Re Pergamon Press Ltd* (1971) and *Maxwell v Dept of Trade and Industry* (1974), involved the late, and generally unlamented, publishing mogul Robert Maxwell. Maxwell's death in 1991 revealed the corruption and criminal illegality on which his business empire had been based and sustained. The blameworthy part of the Maxwell saga was, however, that his corrupt behaviour was an open secret that should have been investigated before it reached its inevitable disastrous conclusion.

9.3.10 Winding up and administration orders

Winding up and administrative orders are alternative mechanisms for dealing with companies whose business activity is in a state of potentially terminal decline.

Winding up

Winding up, or liquidation, is the process whereby the life of the company is terminated. It is the formal and strictly regulated procedure whereby the business is brought to an end and the company's assets are realised and distributed to its creditors and members. The procedure is governed by the IA 1986 and may be divided into three distinct categories:

(a) *Compulsory winding up*

This is a winding up ordered by the court under s 122 of the IA 1986. Although there are seven distinct grounds for such a winding up, one of which, depending upon just and equitable grounds, has already been considered, the most common reason for the winding up of a company is its inability to pay its debts. Section 123 provides that, if a company with a debt exceeding £750 fails to pay it within three weeks of receiving a written demand, then it is deemed unable to pay its debts.

(b) *Members' voluntary winding up*

This takes place when the directors of a company are of the opinion that the company is solvent, that is, capable of paying off its creditors. The directors are required to make a statutory declaration to that effect and the actual liquidation process is initiated by a special resolution of the company.

(c) Creditors' voluntary winding up

This occurs when the directors of the company do not believe that it will be able to pay off its debts and thus do not make the necessary declaration required for a members' voluntary winding up. The creditors may form a committee of inspection which oversees the actions of the liquidator. Again, the liquidation is initiated by a special resolution of the company.

Administration orders

Administration is a relatively new procedure having been introduced in line with the recommendations of the Cork Report of 1982. The aim of the administration order is to save the business as a going concern by taking control of the company out of the hands of its directors and placing it in the hands of an administrator. Alternatively, the procedure is aimed at maximising the realised value of the business assets.

The rules are set out in the IA 1986. Section 8 of the IA provides that, where the court is satisfied that the company is, or is likely to become, unable to pay its debts, it may issue an administrative order to achieve one or more of the following purposes:

- the survival of the whole or part of the business as a going concern;

- the approval of a voluntary arrangement under Pt 1 of the IA by which the creditors reach an agreement between themselves and the company as to the satisfaction of their debts;

- the sanctioning of a compromise or arrangement under s 425 of the Companies Act 1985;

- a more advantageous realisation of the assets of the company than would be effected on the winding up of the company.

Once an administration order has been issued, it is no longer possible to commence winding up proceedings against the company or enforce charges, retention of title clauses or even hire purchase agreements against the company. This major advantage is in no small way undermined by the fact that an administration order cannot be made after a company has entered the liquidation process. Since companies are required to inform any person who is entitled to appoint a receiver of the fact that the company is applying for an administration order, it is open to any secured creditor to enforce their rights and to forestall the administration procedure. This would cause the secured creditor no harm, since their debt would more than likely be covered by the security, but it could well lead to the end of the company as a going concern.

9.3.11 Insider dealing

One of the most important attributes of a share is the right to participate in the profit generated by a company, although, for the purposes of company law, the value of a share is fixed at its nominal value.

However, the exchange value of the share, that is, the amount of money that can be realised by selling the share, which essentially reflects the value of the share as a source of income, changes in line with the profitability of the company. This fluctuation in the exchange value of shares in listed public limited companies is readily apparent in the constantly changing value of shares on the Stock Exchange. It is, of course, the fact that share prices fluctuate in this way that provides the possibility of individuals making large profits, or losses, in speculating in shares. It also, however, provides other people with the opportunity to take advantage of their close relationship with particular companies in order to make profits from illegal share dealing. Such illegal trading in shares is known as insider dealing and is now governed by Pt V of the Criminal Justice Act 1993 which repeals and replaces the Company Securities (Insider Dealings) Act 1985.

Section 52 of the CJA states that an individual who has information as an insider is guilty of insider dealing if they deal in securities that are price affected securities in relation to the information. They are also guilty of an offence if they encourage others to deal in securities that are linked with this information, or if they disclose the information otherwise than in the proper performance of their employment, office or profession.

Section 56 makes it clear that securities are price affected in relation to inside information if the information, made public, would be likely to have a significant effect on the price of those securities.

Section 57 defines an insider as a person who knows that they have inside information and knows that they have the information from an inside source. This section also states that 'inside source' refers to information acquired through being a director, employee or shareholder of an issuer of securities, or having access to information by virtue of their employment. Additionally, and importantly, it also treats as insiders those who acquire their information from those primary insiders previously mentioned.

There are a number of defences to a charge of insider dealing. For example, s 53 makes it clear that no person can be so charged if they did not expect the dealing to result in any profit or the avoidance of any loss.

On summary conviction, an individual found guilty of insider dealing is liable to a fine not exceeding the statutory maximum and/or a maximum of six months' imprisonment. On indictment, the penalty is an unlimited fine and/or a maximum of seven years' imprisonment.

9.4   Employment law

Most businesses employ a workforce of some size, no matter how limited. This section examines the nature of the employment relationship.

9.4.1   Contract of employment

The relationship between the employee and the employer is governed by the contract of employment which forms the basis of the employee's employment rights. It is, therefore, important to comprehend the meaning of this term. Employees are employed under a contract of employment or contract of service, whereas self-employed persons, that is, independent contractors, are employed under a contract for services. There are tests which enable the courts to distinguish between the two types of contract, particularly where there are disputes. The following example assists in distinguishing between employees and independent contractors.

If you employ a plumber to install your washing machine, you do not become an employer as the plumber is an independent contractor, although he or she may be employed by a firm of plumbers. If you were to employ a nanny, as a general rule, he or she would become your employee and you would, therefore, be responsible for deductions from his or her salary, for example, tax, national insurance, etc.

The distinction between a contract of service and a contract for services must be appreciated because, where a person is employed under the former, that person is afforded a certain amount of statutory and common law protection, whereas a person employed under the latter is not, although limited exceptions can be found in the Equal Pay Act 1970, the Sex Discrimination Act 1975 and the Race Relations Act 1976.

Employee v independent contractor

Employee is defined in the Employment Rights Act (ERA) 1996 as an individual who has entered into or works under (or, where the employment has ceased, worked under) a contract of employment (s 230(1)); a contract of employment means a contract of service or apprenticeship, whether express or implied, and (if it is express) whether oral or in writing (s 230(2)).

Although for the majority of people at work there is no problem in deciding whether they are employees or independent contractors, there may be occasions where the distinction is not clear cut. Over the years, the courts have devised tests for establishing employee status. These tests will be considered in chronological order since, although the early tests are still of relevance, the multiple test and the mutuality of obligations test are now at the forefront should the question of employment status arise.

Control test

In applying the control test, the question to be asked is, does the person who is to be regarded as the employer control the employee or servant? Control extends to not just what the employee does but how it is done. If the answer is in the affirmative, there is an employer/employee relationship. The reasoning behind this question was that an independent contractor may be told what to do, but probably had a discretion as to how to do the work. However, in the modern workplace, this question has become a little unreal and therefore this test has fallen into decline as the sole test applied by the courts, although it is still a vital element in the multiple test.

In *Walker v Crystal Palace Football Club* (1910), Walker was employed as a professional footballer with the defendant club. It became necessary to decide whether he was employed under a contract of service or a contract for services. It was held that he was employed under a contract of service or employment because he was subject to the control of his master in the form of training, discipline and method of play.

One of the problems in applying the control test was that, if interpreted strictly, it resulted in skilled and professional people being categorised as independent contractors, which, at a time when there were limited employment rights, was not a problem for them, but proved to be a problem for persons injured as a result of their negligence at work who would be unable to rely on the principle of vicarious liability to claim against the employer. As a result, the courts saw fit to develop another test which would reflect this development in the workplace by recognising that skilled and professional people could also be employees.

Integration test

This test was developed to counter the deficiencies of the control test. In applying the integration test, the question to be asked is how far is the servant/employee integrated into the employer's business? If it can be shown that the employee is fully integrated into the employer's business, then there is in existence a contract of employment. It is clear that an independent contractor does not become part of the employer's business. The use of this test was confirmed in *Stevenson Jordan and Harrison Ltd v MacDonald and Evans* (1952), in which Lord Denning expressed the following view:

> One feature which seems to run through the instances is that, under a contract of service, a man is employed as part of the business and his work is done as an integral part of the business; whereas, under a contract for services, his work, although done for the business, is not integrated into it but is only accessory to it.

In *Whittaker v Minister of Pensions and National Insurance* (1967), Whittaker was employed as a trapeze artist in a circus. She claimed industrial injuries benefit as a result of an accident sustained at work. Initially, this was refused on the basis that she was not an employee of the circus. She was, however, able to show that for at least half of her working day she was expected to undertake general duties other than trapeze work, such as acting as usherette and working in the ticket office. It was held that her general duties showed that she was an integral part of the business of running a circus and was, therefore, employed under a contract of employment.

Although this test developed due to the impracticalities of the control test, it never gained popularity with the courts. It was successfully used in cases, such as *Cassidy v Ministry of Health* (1951), to establish that highly skilled workers, such as doctors and engineers, can be employed under a contract of employment and may even have a type of dual employment where they are to be regarded, in some circumstances, as employees and, in others, as self-employed. The control test was clearly inapplicable to these situations. The need to develop a test which would suit all circumstances became of paramount importance. Employers were able to avoid various aspects of the statutory provisions by categorising employees as self-employed when in reality this was not necessarily the case, but at that time there was no test to cover these situations, for example, an employer could avoid tax and national insurance provisions as well as liability for accidents caused by these persons whilst going about their jobs. As a result, the multiple test was developed.

Multiple test

The multiple test is by definition much wider than both the control test and the integration test. It requires numerous factors to be taken into account in deciding whether a person is employed under a contract of service or a contract for services. It arose out of the case of *Ready Mixed Concrete (South East) Ltd v Minister of Pensions and National Insurance* (1968). RMC previously employed a number of lorry drivers under a contract of employment. The company then decided to dismiss the drivers as employees. However, it allowed them to purchase their vehicles, which had to be painted in RMC's colours. The contract between the drivers and the company stated that the drivers were independent contractors. This was disputed by the minister who believed the drivers were employees and therefore RMC were liable for national insurance contributions. There were a number of stipulations under the contract. The drivers had to wear the company's uniform and the company could require repairs to be carried out to the vehicles at the drivers' expense. The vehicle could only be used for carrying RMC's product for a fixed period and the drivers were told where and when to deliver their loads, although if a driver was ill a substitute driver could be used. It was held by MacKenna J that a contract of service exists if three conditions are fulfiled:

(a) the servant agrees that, in consideration of a wage or other remuneration, he will provide his own work and skill in the performance of some service for his master;

(b) he agrees, expressly or impliedly, that in the performance of that service he will be subject to the other's control in a sufficient degree to make that other master;

(c) the other provisions of the contract are consistent with its being a contract of service.

In this case, it was decided that the drivers were independent contractors as there were factors which were inconsistent with the existence of a contract of employment, for example, the ability to provide a replacement driver if the need arose.

This test has proved to be most adaptable in that it only requires evaluation of the factors which are inconsistent with the existence of a contract of employment. It is important to appreciate that there is no exhaustive list of inconsistent factors. The courts will ask questions such as: who pays the wages? Who pays income tax and national insurance? Is the person employed entitled to holiday pay?

It will treat as irrelevant the fact that there is a contract in which someone is termed 'independent contractor' when the other factors point to him being an employee. This is illustrated in *Market Investigations Ltd v Minister of Social Security* (1969) in which Market Investigations employed Mrs Irving as an interviewer on an occasional basis. If she was selected from the pool of interviewers maintained by the firm, she was not obliged to accept the work. However, if she accepted, she was given precise instructions on the methods to be used in carrying out the market research and the time in which the work had to be completed. She could, however, choose the hours she wanted to work and do other work at the same time as long as she met Market Investigation's deadlines. It was held that she was an employee of the company every time she decided to undertake work for them. It was felt that the question to be asked is whether the person who has engaged himself to perform these services is performing them as a person in business on his own account. If so, then there is a contract for services, while if not, there is a contract of service.

A further illustration of the problem of defining status and the implications for the individual can be seen in *Lane v Shire Roofing Co (Oxford) Ltd* (1995). The plaintiff was a roofer who traded as a one-man firm and was categorised as self-employed for tax purposes. In 1986, he was hired by the defendants, a newly established roofing business, which had not wanted to take on direct labour and so had taken on the plaintiff on a payment-by-job basis. While re-roofing a porch of a house, he fell off a ladder, suffering serious injuries. It was held initially that the defendants did not owe the plaintiff a duty of care as he was not an employee. However, on appeal, the Court of Appeal found for the plaintiff. They concluded, in recognition of greater flexibility in employment patterns, that many factors had to be taken into account in determining status. First, control and provision of materials were relevant but not decisive factors;

secondly, the question might have to be broadened to whose business was it? Finally, these questions must be asked in the context of who is responsible for the overall safety of the men doing the work in question.

Obviously, as in the *RMC* case, there are other factors which may have to be taken into account, although the courts are reluctant to state what other factors should be considered, except an element of control. It is important that the multiple test is flexible so that it can adapt with changes in the labour environment. Unfortunately, these tests have tended to result in the atypical worker being categorised as self-employed. This is particularly true of casual or seasonal workers, even though, in practical terms, they may see themselves as tied to a particular firm and, therefore, have an obligation to that business. There have, however, been some developments in this area which provide possible redress for such workers. The test which has developed is known as the mutuality of obligations test. This arose out of the case of *O'Kelly v Trusthouse Forte plc* (1983). O'Kelly and his fellow appellants worked on a casual basis as wine waiters at the Grosvenor House Hotel. They were regarded as regular casuals in that they were given preference in the work rota over other casual staff. They had no other employment. They sought to be classified as employees so that they could pursue an action for unfair dismissal. They argued that, if they were to be classified as employees, then each independent period of work for THF could be added together and the qualifying period of employment under the Employment Protection (Consolidation) Act 1978 would be met. It was held that the regular casuals in this case were self-employed as there was no mutuality of obligation, on the part of either party, in that THF was not obliged to offer work nor were O'Kelly and his colleagues obliged to accept it when it was offered. The preferential rota system was not a contractual promise. The court made it clear that an important factor in determining whether there is a contract of service in this type of situation is the custom and practice of the particular industry.

The case of *Wickens v Champion Employment* (1984) supports the decision in *O'Kelly*. However, a more liberal approach was taken in *Nethermore (St Neots) v Gardiner and Taverna* (1984), in which home workers making clothes on a piecework basis were accorded employee status on the basis that a mutuality of obligation arose out of an irreducible minimum obligation to work for that company by the regular giving and taking of work over periods of a year or more.

Finally, it was held in *McMeecham v Secretary of State for Employment* (1995) that previous authorities did not establish any principle that those working through employment agencies are not employees:

> The furthest they go is to state the general legal principles applicable to the question whether a contract of employment exists and then proceed to decide the individual case on the basis of the actual terms and conditions.

Loaning or hiring out of employees

One area of contention involves the loaning or hiring out of an employee; the issue being whose is the employee? This is particularly important in respect of who should be vicariously liable for the employee's torts. As can be seen in *Mersey Docks and Harbour Board v Coggins and Griffiths (Liverpool) Ltd* (1947), there is a rebuttable presumption that, when an employee is loaned out, he or she remains the employee of the first/original employer. In *Mersey Docks*, a crane and its driver were hired out to C and G to assist in the loading of a ship. C and G paid the driver's wages. While the crane driver was doing this work, he negligently injured an employee of the stevedores, C and G. The issue to be decided by the courts was whether the Harbour Board or C and G were vicariously liable for the crane driver's negligence. It was held that the Harbour Board remained the employer of the crane driver. He was under their ultimate control as to the work he should do, even though he was under the temporary direction of the stevedores, that is, the original employer retained the right to hire, dismiss and decide on his work, even though day to day control passed to the stevedores.

The courts are reluctant to find that there has been a transfer of employment where employees are loaned or hired out, unless there is consent on the part of the employee or there is an agreement which clearly states the position in the event of liability accruing. There may, however, be exceptional circumstances where the courts may declare that *pro hac vice* (for that one occasion), a loaned or hired employee has become the employee of the second employer as in *Sime v Sutcliffe Catering* (1990).

9.4.2 Terms of the contract of employment

In general terms, there are no formalities involved in the formation of a contract of employment. The contract itself may be oral or in writing, with the exception of apprenticeship deeds and articles for merchant seamen which, obviously, by their nature have to be in writing.

Express terms are those agreed upon by the employer and employee on entering into the contract of employment. They may be oral or in writing and will cover such things as the point on the salary scale at which the employee will commence employment. However, oral terms may be open to dispute and it is in the interests of both parties to have such terms in writing, for example, a restraint of trade clause is unlikely to be enforceable unless it is in writing. Disputes about oral terms may result in the employee pursuing an action for clarification before an employment tribunal. A breach of an express term of the contract may result in the dismissal of the employee and, if it is a breach by the employer, may enable the employee to resign and bring an action for constructive dismissal. A collective agreement made between the employer and a trade union may be expressly incorporated into the contract of employment. Such agreements usually provide a comprehensive set of terms and conditions for particular types of employees and, where they are expressly incorporated into the employment contract, they will bind the employer and the employee.

9.4.3 Implied terms

Implied terms may arise out of the custom and practice of a particular industry, for example, deductions from wages for bad workmanship were accepted as a term of contracts in the cotton industry. The courts may be the final arbiter as to whether an implied term is incorporated into the contract and, as can be seen in *Quinn v Calder Industrial Materials* (1996), such claims are not always successful. Collective agreements may become implied terms of the contract, even if there is no reference to the agreement in the written particulars. However, such incorporation will depend on knowledge by the employee and some form of acceptance by his local union representatives.

Implied terms generally have to be read subject to any express terms which may be to the contrary. Although where the implied term is necessary to give efficacy to the contract, the implied term will take precedence over the express term. This is illustrated in *Johnstone v Bloomsbury Health Authority* (1991), which was considered in 8.8.2.

A hospital doctor was obliged to work a stipulated number of hours under his contract, plus additional hours if required. As a result, the doctor found himself working, on average, over 80 hours per week and, as a result, he became ill. It was held that the express term regarding the additional hours had to be read subject to the implied term of care and safety. The implied term in this case was necessary to give efficacy to the contract.

In addition, a number of standard implied terms have developed in respect of the employer/employee relationship. These take the form of duties imposed on the respective parties. A breach by the employee may result in disciplinary action or even dismissal; a breach by the employer may result in legal proceedings before a tribunal.

9.4.4 Duties imposed on the employer

Duties imposed on the employer are to provide work; pay wages; indemnify the employee; hold in mutual respect; and provide for the care and safety of the employee.

To provide work

An employer will not be in breach of the implied duty to provide work as long as he or she continues to pay his or her employees even though there may be no work available. Although, in certain situations, the employer may be liable for failing to provide work, for example, if a reduction in the employee's earnings occurs. This is most likely to affect those employees on piece-work or commission. For example, in *Devonald v Rosser and Sons* (1906), Devonald's employers found that they could no longer run the works at a profit, so they gave Devonald, a piece-worker, a month's notice but closed the factory immediately. Devonald claimed damages for the wages he lost during this period, arguing that there was an implied term that he would be provided with work during the notice period. It was held that the necessary implication from the contract was that the master will find a reasonable amount of work up to the expiration of the notice. Furthermore, if the employee needs to work in order to maintain particular skills, then to deny him this right may also be a breach of this duty.

In *Collier v Sunday Referee Publishing Co Ltd* (1940), Collier was employed as a sub-editor with the defendant's newspaper. The defendant sold the newspaper and continued to pay the plaintiff although he was not provided with any work. Collier claimed the company was under a duty to supply work. It was held that there was a breach of the duty to provide work in this case as the plaintiff had been appointed to a particular job which had been destroyed on the sale of the newspaper. However, Asquith J stated:

> It is true that a contract of employment does not necessarily, or perhaps normally, oblige the master to provide the servant with work. Provided I pay my cook her wages regularly, she cannot complain if I choose to eat all my meals out.

Interestingly, the courts took this duty one step further in *Langston v Amalgamated Union of Engineering Workers* (1974), in which Langston refused to join the trade union. As a result of union pressure, his employers were forced to suspend him from work on full pay. It was said (*obiter*) that, where a person employs a skilled employee who needs practice to maintain or develop those skills, there may be an obligation to provide a reasonable amount of work.

To pay wages

As a general rule, the employer must pay his employees their wages even if there is no work available. In relation to piece-workers, this means that they should be given the opportunity to earn their pay. However, it is possible for the employer to exclude or vary this implied term by providing that there will be no pay where there is no work available.

To indemnify the employee

Where the employee in the course of his or her employment necessarily incurs expenses on behalf of the employer, the employee is entitled to be reimbursed. This extends to such things as postage, parking fees, damage to property, etc.

Mutual respect

The employer is under a duty to treat any employee with respect. The basis of the employment relationship is mutuality of respect, trust and confidence. In deciding whether there has been a breach of this term, the actions of the employer are of great importance.

In *Donovan v Invicta Airways Ltd* (1970), Donovan, an airline pilot, was subjected to abusive conduct by his employer on a number of occasions. As a result, Donovan resigned. It was held that in this particular case the incidents were not substantial enough to treat the contract as broken.

It is clear that there is now a duty under which all of the parties to the contract of employment must treat each other with due consideration and courtesy. In *Isle of Wight Tourist Board v Coombes* (1976), a director was heard to describe his personal secretary as an 'intolerable bitch on a Monday morning'. This was held to be a breach of the duty of mutual respect and was conduct which entitled her to resign.

Failure to investigate grievances in certain specific instances has in the past been regarded as a breach of the obligation of trust and confidence on the part of the employer. This is illustrated in *Bracebridge Engineering v Darby* (1990), where a complaint of sexual harassment against a manager was not investigated. More recently, the Employment Appeals Tribunal (EAT) has held in *WA Goold (Pearmak) Ltd v McConnell and Another* (1995) that there is a general implied term that employers will reasonably and promptly afford a reasonable opportunity to their employees to obtain redress of any grievance they may have.

Although there is no requirement that the employer provide a reference for an outgoing or former employee, if one is provided, the employer must ensure that the reference is a fair and accurate reflection of the employees capabilities, etc. Following the decision in *Spring v Guardian Assurance plc* (1994), the employer may be liable in defamation, subject to the defence of qualified privilege and/or negligent misstatement where he provides an inaccurate or misleading reference. The House of Lords in *Spring* held that an employer who supplies a reference is under a duty to take reasonable care in compiling it.

9.4.5   Duties imposed on the employee

There are a number of duties imposed on the employee, many of which are tied to the idea of trust and confidence, underpinned by the concept that the employee owes a degree of loyalty to the employer.

To obey lawful and reasonable orders

If an order given by the employer is reasonable and lawful, it must be obeyed. Indeed, failure to obey may give the employer the right to dismiss the employee. Whether an order is lawful and reasonable is a question of fact in each case depending upon the nature of the job.

In *Pepper v Webb* (1969), an employer instructed his gardener to carry out certain planting work in the garden. The gardener swore at his employer and indicated that he was not prepared to obey the instructions. It was held that the employee was in breach of his implied duty as the orders were not only lawful but reasonable in the circumstances.

Any dismissal for failing to follow an illegal order, that is, to commit a criminal offence, is unlawful and the employee will be able to pursue an action for unfair or wrongful dismissal (see *Morrish v Henlys (Folkestone) Ltd* (1973), where a refusal to falsify the accounts did not amount to a breach of contract on the part of the employee). Further protection is provided by the Trade Union Reform and Employment Rights Act (TURERA) 1993 in respect of dismissals in connection with health and safety. If an employee is dismissed for refusing to work where there is a serious and imminent danger, the dismissal is automatically unfair.

To act faithfully

This duty is fundamental to the relationship of the employer and employee. The employee's first loyalty must be to the employer. The duty encompasses such things as confidentiality, not competing with the employer, etc.

In *Faccenda Chicken Ltd v Fowler* (1986), Fowler was employed as a sales manager by Faccenda Chicken. He resigned with a number of other employees and set up in competition with his previous employer selling chickens. Although there was no restraint of trade clause in the contract, the plaintiff alleged that the duty of confidentiality had been broken as information, such as lists of customers, had been copied and used by the defendant. It was held that, as the scope of the duty to act faithfully varied according to the nature of the contract of employment, it was necessary to consider all the circumstances of the case, in particular, the nature of the employment and the information obtained and used, that is, was it the type of information which was a trade secret and therefore highly confidential? It was held that the employer's claim would be rejected, as the information was not so confidential that it could be covered by an implied prohibition on its use.

This case limits the protection afforded to the employer with respect to confidential information, since the only information which will be protected is that which could be legitimately protected by a restraint of trade clause and does not appear to cover information recalled by the employee as opposed to that copied or memorised.

Working for another employer while still in the employ of the original employer may also be a breach of the duty to act faithfully. Generally, this will only amount to a breach where the second employer is in competition with the first employer or where the nature of the contract is one of exclusivity or there is a conflict of interest. In all other circumstances, the courts will not seek to curb an employee's legitimate spare time activities. If, for example, an employee was a car mechanic by day and worked in a public house at night, there would be no breach (see *Nova Plastics Ltd v Froggatt* (1982), in which it was held that, even where an employee worked for a competitor in his spare time, there had to be some evidence of potential harm).

In *Hivac Ltd v Park Royal Scientific Instruments Ltd* (1946), employees of the plaintiff company were found to be working in their spare time for a company which was in direct competition with their employer. The employees concerned were doing the same job at both establishments. It was held that the employees were under a duty not to work for a competitor of their employer where this work would conflict with their duty of fidelity and might inflict harm on their employer's business. The duty to act faithfully was found to have been breached in *Adamson v B and L Cleaning Services Ltd* (1995), where an employee put in a tender for the future business of his employer's customers.

The employer may prevent his or her employees either working for rival firms or setting up a business in competition with him or her, after they have left his or her employment, by including in the contract of employment an express term which restricts the employee's future employment in some way. Such clauses are known as covenants in restraint of trade. Many professional people, such as solicitors, accountants, etc, will have this type of clause in their contracts. Restraint of trade clauses are only valid if they are reasonable in all the circumstances of the case, that is, the protection afforded the employer must not be excessive. Furthermore, the interests of the public must be considered, this being particularly relevant with respect to trade secrets, inventions, etc. Such clauses will also be subject to rules of construction and severance which may result in part of a clause being struck out.

In *Home Counties Dairies Ltd v Skilton* (1970), Skilton was a milkman. His contract of employment contained a clause which provided that, for a period of one year after the termination of his contract with Home Counties Dairies, he would not sell milk or dairy produce to any person who had been a customer of the dairy for the last six months of his contract and whom he had served. Soon after leaving his employment, he set up his own milk round in the same area as the one in which he had worked for the dairy company. It was held that the former employer should be awarded an injunction to prevent Skilton from working in this area. The clause in his contract was valid as the time limit was reasonable in order to protect the interests of the dairy.

Under the heading of fidelity, the employee must not disclose confidential information which has been acquired in the course of his or her employment. The duty extends to trade secrets, the financial state of the company, new designs, etc.

In *Cranleigh Precision Engineering Co Ltd v Bryant* (1965), Bryant was the managing director of a firm which designed swimming pools. He left the company and started his own business using information which he had gained from his previous employment. It was held that Bryant was in breach of the implied term in his contract of employment as he could only have gained this information from his previous employment. He had made improper use of information gained in confidence to the detriment of his former employer.

To use skill and care

The employee is under a duty to use reasonable skill and care in the performance of the job. If he does so and incurs loss or damage, the employer will indemnify him. However, should the employee be grossly incompetent, the employer may have grounds to dismiss him. The duty extends to taking proper care of the employer's property, as is illustrated by the decision in *Superlux v Plaisted* (1958), in which an employee was held liable for allowing his employer's goods to be stolen whilst in his care.

In *Lister v Romford Ice and Cold Storage Co Ltd* (1957), Lister, a lorry driver employed by Romford Ice, negligently reversed his lorry, seriously injuring a fellow employee. The company claimed an indemnity from Lister on the grounds that he had broken the implied term of skill and care in his contract of employment. It was held that the employer was entitled to an indemnity because the employee had failed to use reasonable skill and care as required by the implied terms. Lister was, therefore, liable for the damages awarded to his fellow employee.

See, also, *Janata Bank v Ahmed* (1981), in which a bank manager, who failed to check adequately customers' creditworthiness before giving them loans and arranging credit, was held to be personally responsible for failing to use sufficient skill and care.

Not to take bribes or make a secret profit

While this duty is part and parcel of the general duty of fidelity, it extends to accounting for any monies or gifts received which may compromise an employee. A breach of this duty by an employee is an abuse of position and may result in a fair dismissal. This is illustrated in *Sinclair v Neighbour* (1967), in which a clerk in a betting shop took £15 from the till without the permission of his employer whom he knew would refuse. The clerk intended to replace it the next day. However, in the interim, the employer discovered what the clerk had done and dismissed him. It was held that the clerk had not acted honestly in attempting to deceive his employer and therefore the employer was entitled to dismiss him.

In *Reading v Attorney General* (1951), Reading, who was a sergeant in the British Army based in Egypt, used his position to accompany lorries containing illicit spirits, so that they would not be stopped by the police. Over a period of time, Reading received £20,000 for his services. When his role was finally discovered, he was arrested and the army authorities confiscated his money. When he was released from prison, he brought an action for the return of the money. It was held that Reading was in breach of the implied duty not to take bribes or make secret profits. He had misused his position of trust and had therefore to account for those profits to his employer. He was not entitled to have any of the money returned to him.

In *British Syphon Co Ltd v Homewood* (1956), Homewood was employed as chief technician by the plaintiff company in the design and development department. During his employment, he designed a new type of soda syphon. He did not disclose his invention to his employers. He then left his employment and applied for letters patent in respect of his invention. It was held that the invention and the profits from it belonged to his employer. The invention was clearly related to his employer's business and they were therefore entitled to the benefits from it.

The common law position regarding employee's inventions has been qualified by ss 39–41 of the Patents Act 1977 and s 11 of the Copyright, Designs and Patents Act 1988. In such cases, the invention or design will only belong to the employer if:

- it is made in the course of normal duties or duties specifically assigned and the invention could reasonably be expected to derive from that work;

- it is made in the normal course of duties and, at the time of the invention, there is a special obligation to further the employer's business interests.

Whilst the employer is under a duty to pay wages, deductions from wages are regulated by Pt II of the ERA 1996, formerly, the Wages Act 1986. First, the mode of payment is as agreed between the employer and employee, for example, directly into a bank account. Every employee is entitled to an itemised pay statement showing gross salary or wages, deductions, net salary or wages, variable deductions and fixed deductions and the purpose for which they are made. Failure to provide this may result in a reference to an industrial tribunal.

Furthermore, there is a general rule that no deductions can be made unless the deduction falls within one of the following: it is required or authorised by statute, such as PAYE; it is authorised by a provision in the employee's contract, for example, contributions to occupational pension schemes; the employee has agreed in advance in writing to the deduction being made. There are exceptions which allow for deductions in respect of overpayment of wages, etc. There are also specific provisions relating to the retail industry which provide that it is permissible to make deductions in respect of cash shortages and stock deficiencies. However, the right to deduct must be included in the contract of employment and any deductions should not exceed 10% of the gross wages payable on the day in question.

Any contravention allows the employee to complain to an employment tribunal within three months of the deduction being made.

BUSINESS AND CORPORATE LAW

Agency

Definition

An agent is a person who is empowered to represent another legal party, called the principal, and brings the principal into a legal relationship with a third party.

Agency agreements may be either contractual or gratuitous.

Creation of agency

Agency requires the consent of the principal but such consent may be implied from circumstances.

Agency may arise expressly, by ratification, by implication, by necessity or by estoppel.

Nature of agent's authority

Actual authority may be divided into express actual authority and implied actual authority.

Apparent authority is based on estoppel and operates in such a way as to make the principal responsible for their action or inaction as regards someone who is known to purport to be the agent. Particular problems arise in relation to ex-employees and ex-agents generally.

Warrant of authority

If an agent contracts with a third party on behalf of a principal, the agent impliedly guarantees that the principal exists and has contractual capacity and that he or she has that person's authority to act as his or her agent. If this is not the case, the agent is personally liable to third parties for breach of warrant of authority.

The duties of agent to principal

The duties of agent to principal are:

* to perform the undertaking according to instructions;

* to exercise due care and skill;

- to carry out instructions personally;
- to account;
- not to permit a conflict of interest to arise;
- not to make a secret profit or misuse confidential information;
- not to take a bribe.

The rights of an agent

The rights of an agent are:

- to claim remuneration for services performed;
- to claim indemnity for all expenses legitimately incurred in the performance of services;
- to exercise a lien over property owned by the principal.

Relations with third parties

Where the agent indicates that he is acting as an agent, the general rule is that only the principal and the third party have rights and obligations under the contract.

Exceptions can occur:

- at the insistence of the third party;
- by implication;
- in relation to bills of exchange;
- in relation to deeds.

Where the principal's existence is not disclosed:

- the agent can enforce the contract against the third party;
- the principal can enforce the contract against the third party;
- the third party can choose to enforce the contract against the agent or the principal;
- an undisclosed principal cannot ratify any contract made outside of the agent's actual authority.

Where the third party had a special reason to contract with the agent, the principal may be excluded from the contract.

Where the agent misrepresents the identity of the principal, the third party may not be bound by the contract.

Payment by means of an agent

If the agent does not pay the third party, the principal remains liable.

If the agent absconds with money paid by the third party, then, if the principal is undisclosed, the third party sustains the loss. If, however, the principal is disclosed, the agent must have had authority to accept money or else the third party is liable.

Termination of agency

Agreements may end:

- by mutual agreement;
- by the unilateral action of one of the parties;
- through frustration;
- due to the death, insanity or bankruptcy of either of the parties.

Partnership law

Definition of partnership

Section 1 of the Partnership Act 1890 states that partnership is the relation which subsists between persons carrying on a business in common with a view to profit.

Simply receiving a payment from profits is not sufficient automatically to make a person a partner in a business concern.

The legal status of a partnership

A partnership has no separate legal personality apart from its members as does a joint-stock company.

Partnerships are generally limited to 20 members, however, certain professional partnerships are exempt from this maximum limit.

Formation of a partnership

There are no specific legal requirements governing the formation of a partnership. Partnerships arise from the agreement of the parties involved and are governed by the general principles of contract law.

The partnership agreement is an internal document and although it has effect between the partners it does not necessarily affect the rights of third parties.

Duties of partners

In addition to the usual general fiduciary duties, ss 28–30 of the Partnership Act (PA) 1890 lay down the specific duties of disclosure; to account; not to compete.

Rights of partners

Subject to express provision to the contrary in the partnership agreement, s 24 of the PA 1890 sets out the rights of partners. Amongst the most important of these are the rights:

- to share equally in the capital and profits of the business;
- to be indemnified by the firm for any liabilities incurred or payments made in the course of the firm's business;
- to take part in the management of the business;
- to have access to the firm's books;
- to prevent the admission of a new partner;
- to prevent any change in the nature of the partnership business.

Partnership property

It is important to distinguish between partnership property and personal property for the following reasons:

- partnership property must be used exclusively for partnership purposes;
- any increase in the value of partnership property belongs to the partnership;
- any increase in the value of personal property belongs to the person who owns the property;
- on the dissolution of the firm, partnership property is used to pay debts before personal property;
- partnership and personal property are treated differently in the satisfaction of claims made by partnership creditors as opposed to personal creditors;
- on the death of a partner, any interest in partnership land will pass as personalty, whereas land owned personally will pass as realty.

The authority of partners to bind the firm

Authority can be actual or implied on the basis of the usual authority possessed by a partner in the particular line of business carried out by the firm.

Partner's liability on debts

Every partner is responsible for the full amount of the firm's liability. Outsiders have the choice of taking action against the firm collectively, or against the individual partners. Where damages are recovered from one partner only, the other partners are under a duty to contribute equally to the amount paid.

Partners may be liable for debts, contracts and torts.

Partnership by estoppel

Failure to give notice of retirement is one way in which liability arises on the basis of estoppel or holding out. Alternatively, anyone who represents themselves, or knowingly permits themselves to be represented, as a partner is liable to any person who gives the partnership credit on the basis of that representation.

Dissolution

Grounds for dissolution are:

- the expiry of a fixed term or the completion of a specified enterprise;
- the giving of notice;
- the death or bankruptcy of any partner;
- where a partner's share becomes subject to a charge;
- illegality;
- where a partner becomes a patient under the Mental Health Act 1983;
- where a partner suffers some other permanent incapacity;
- where a partner engages in activity prejudicial to the business;
- where a partner persistently breaches the partnership agreement;
- where the business can only be carried on at a loss;
- where it is just and equitable to do so.

Winding up

Since the introduction of the Insolvency Act (IA) 1986, partnerships as such are not subject to bankruptcy. Partnerships may be wound up as unregistered companies under Pt V of the IA.

Treatment of assets on dissolution

On dissolution, the value of the partnership property is applied in the following order:

- in paying debts to outsiders;
- in paying to the partners any advance made to the firm beyond their capital contribution;
- in paying the capital contribution of the individual partners.

Any residue is divided between the partners in the same proportion as they shared in profits.

Company law

The effects of incorporation

Separate personality is where the company exists as a legal person in its own right, completely distinct from the members who own shares in it.

Limited liability refers to the fact that the potential liability of shareholders is fixed at a maximum level equal to the nominal value of the shares held.

Perpetual succession refers to the fact that the company continues to exist irrespective of any change in its membership. The company only ceases to exist when it is formally wound up.

The company owns the business property in its own right – shareholders own shares; they do not own the assets of the business they have invested in.

The company has contractual capacity in its own right and can sue and be sued in its own name. Members, as such, are not able to bind the company.

Lifting the veil of incorporation

The courts will, on occasion, ignore separate personality. Examples can be given in relation to statutory provisions, and the use of the company form as a mechanism for perpetrating fraud. It is difficult, however, to provide a general rule to predict when the courts will take this approach, other than to see it as depending on judicial views as to public policy.

Public and private companies

This is an essential distinction which causes/explains the need for different legal provisions to be applied to the two forms. The essential difference is to be found in the fact that the private company is really an economic partnership seeking the protection of limited liability.

The company's documents

The memorandum of association governs the company's external affairs. It represents the company to the outside world, stating its capital structure, its powers and its objects.

The articles of association regulate the internal working of the company.

If there is any conflict between the two documents, the contents of the memorandum prevail over anything to the contrary contained in the articles; although provisions in the articles may be used to clarify particular uncertainties in the memorandum.

Share capital

A share has been defined as the interest of the shareholder in the company measured by a sum of money, for the purposes of liability in the first place and of interest in the second, but also consisting of a series of mutual covenants entered into by all the shareholders (*Borlands Trustees v Steel* (1901)).

The main ways of categorising shares is in terms of: nominal or authorised capital; issued or allotted capital; paid up and unpaid capital; called and uncalled capital.

Types of shares

Shares can be divided into: ordinary; preference; deferred; and redeemable shares, each of which carries particular and distinct rights.

Loan capital

The term debenture refers to the document which acknowledges the fact that a company has borrowed money and also refers to the actual debt.

In the case of a fixed charge, a specific asset of the company is made subject to a charge in order to secure a debt.

A floating charge does not attach to any specific property of the company until it crystallises through the company committing some act or default.

All charges, both fixed and floating, have to be registered with the Companies Registry within 21 days of their creation.

In relation to properly registered charges of the same type, they take priority according to their date of creation. As regards charges of different types, a fixed charge takes priority over a floating charge even though it was created after it.

Directors

The board of directors is the agent of the company and may exercise all the powers of the company. Individual directors may be described as being in a fiduciary relationship with their companies.

A director can be removed at any time by the passing of an ordinary resolution of the company (s 303 of the Companies Act 1985).

Individuals can be disqualified from acting as directors up to a maximum period of 15 years under the Company Directors Disqualification Act 1986.

As fiduciaries, directors owe the following duties to their company:

• to act *bona fide* in the interests of the company;

• not to act for a collateral purpose; and

• not to permit a conflict of interest to arise.

They also owe the company a duty of care and skill. This has been enhanced by s 214 of the IA 1986.

Meetings

In theory, the ultimate control over a company's business lies with the members in general meeting. In practice, however, the residual powers of the membership are extremely limited.

There are three types of meeting: the annual general meeting; the extraordinary general meeting; and the class meeting.

Proper and adequate notice must be sent to all those who are entitled to attend any meeting, although the precise nature of the notice is governed by the articles of association.

There are three types of resolution: the ordinary resolution; the extraordinary resolution; and the special resolution.

Voting is by a show of hands or according to the shareholding on a poll. Proxies may exercise voting rights if properly appointed.

Majority rule and minority protection

The majority usually dictate the action of a company and the minority is usually bound by the decisions of the majority. Problems may arise where those in effective control of a company use their power in such a way as to benefit themselves or to cause a detriment to the minority shareholders.

Three remedies are available to minority shareholders:

• the minority may seek court action to prevent the majority from committing a fraud on the minority;

- an order to have the company wound up on just and equitable grounds may be applied for where there is evidence of a lack of probity on the part of some of the members. It may also be used in small private companies to provide a remedy where there is either deadlock on the board, or a member is removed from the board altogether or refused a part in the management of the business;

- under s 459 of the Companies Act 1985, any member may petition the court for an order on the grounds that the affairs of the company are being conducted in a way that is unfairly prejudicial to the interests of some of the members.

In addition to the above remedies, the Secretary of State has the power under s 431 of the Companies Act 1985 to appoint inspectors to investigate the affairs of a company.

Winding up

Liquidation is the process whereby the life of the company is brought to an end.

There are three possible procedures: compulsory winding up; members' voluntary winding up; and creditors' voluntary winding up.

Administration

This is a relatively new procedure aimed at saving the business as a going concern by taking control of the company out of the hands of its directors and placing it in the hands of an of an administrator. Alternatively, the procedure is aimed at maximising the realised value of the business assets.

Once an administration order has been issued, it is no longer possible to commence winding up proceedings against the company or enforce charges, retention of title clauses or even hire purchase agreements against the company.

Employment Law

Insider dealing

Insider dealing is now governed by Pt V of the Criminal Justice Act (CJA) 1993 which repeals and replaces the Company Securities (Insider Dealings) Act 1985. The legislation is aimed at dealing with those who trade in shares on the basis of inside information which is not available to others. It is a criminal offence for an individual who has information as an insider to deal in price affected securities in relation to the information. It is also an offence if they encourage others to deal in securities that are linked with the information.

Contract of employment

An employee is employed under a contract of employment (or contract of service), whereas an independent contractor is employed under a contract for services. The distinction is important because many employment rights only accrue in an employer/employee relationship.

The tests which have developed for establishing the employer/employee relationship are:

- the control test which extends not just to what the employee does, but how it is done. As a single definitive test, the use of control is now rather limited;

- the integration test which considers how far or to what extent the employee is integrated into the employer's business. This has not proved to be a popular test but, as with the control test, may be used as part of the multiple test;

- the multiple test was developed in the case of *Ready Mixed Concrete (South East) Ltd v Minister of Pensions and National Insurance* (1968). The key factors are the provision of own work or labour in return for remuneration, a degree of control and all other terms being consistent with the existence of a contract of service.

Express terms

Express terms are agreed between the employer and employee. Implied terms must be read subject to any express terms in the contract.

Implied terms

Implied terms arise out of custom and practice or through the courts who will determine whether an implied term is part of the contract (*Johnstone v Bloomsbury Health Authority* (1991)).

Once a contract of service is found to exist, there are a number of duties imposed by the common law on the employer and the employee.

The duties imposed on the employer are as follows:

- to provide work (*Collier v Sunday Referee Publishing Co Ltd* (1940));
- to provide wages;
- to indemnify his employees;
- to have mutual respect (*Donovan v Invicta Airways Ltd* (1970));
- to provide for the safety of his employees.

The duties imposed on the employee are:

- to obey lawful and reasonable orders (*Pepper v Webb* (1969));

- to act with loyalty (*Faccenda Chicken Ltd v Fowler* (1986); *Hivac Ltd v Park Royal Scientific Instruments Ltd* (1946); *Home Counties Dairies Ltd v Skilton* (1970); *Cranleigh Precision Engineering Co Ltd v Bryant* (1965));

- to act with skill and care (*Lister v Romford Ice and Cold Storage Co Ltd* (1957));

- not to take bribes or secret profits (*Reading v Attorney General* (1951); *British Syphon Co Ltd v Homewood* (1956)).

CHAPTER 10

THE LAW OF EQUITY AND TRUSTS

10.1 Introduction

In this chapter, we look at the trust, a curious feature of English law. The trust is the relationship existing between a person who holds property for another and that other person. It is the legal relationship (originally recognised as an equitable relationship) between the parties who are called the trustee and the beneficiary. The key scenario is where A hands property to B telling him to hold it on trust for C. In this situation, A is the donor or 'settlor' if he makes a formal settlement or gives property by will, B is the trustee and C is the beneficiary. In order to properly understand this area of law, it is necessary to have an understanding of the basic principles of Equity and how this peculiar feature of English law developed historically.

The branch of law known as Equity developed in England and Wales in the Middle Ages in circumstances where the ordinary common law had failed to give proper redress. Many legal actions, for example, were commenced by the issue of a writ (basically a form in today's general language, or a claim in modern civil law) but the slightest error on the writ would invalidate the whole action. Another deficiency in the ordinary common law concerned the fact that the only remedy was damages (that is, compensation) – thus, court orders did not exist to require people to do something or to desist from some conduct, for example, sell a piece of land according to an agreement made or stop using a particular title.

Dissatisfied litigants often chose to petition the King for him to intervene in a particular case – the courts were, after all, the King's courts. These petitions for justice were dealt with by the King's Chancellor who decided each case according to his own discretion. Over the years, the decisions made by the Lord Chancellor became known as the rules of equity (derived from the Latin aequitas meaning levelling). These new rules came to be applied in a special court, the Chancellor's Court, which became known as the Court of Chancery. Thus equity is law although sometimes, rather confusingly, lawyers distinguish 'equity' from 'law'. The significance of this distinction lies in the fact that it is sometimes important to know whether the origin of a rule was in the ordinary common law as it was evolved by judges in the ordinary law courts or from the Court of Chancery. Different principles concerning how a rule should be enforced and applied come into play accordingly to whether a rule comes from 'equity' or 'law', for example, an equitable remedy of specific performance is discretionary so the court could refuse to give one to a claimant even if the other side had technically broken a rule of trust law, whereas the remedy of damages is a legal remedy and must be granted to a claimant by the court where a legal rule has been broken by the other side.

Probably the most important branch of equity is the law of trusts although equitable remedies like specific performance and the injunction are also widely used today. The order of specific performance allows the High Court to command a recalcitrant party to carry out his side of a contract, and the injunction is a court order which can be used to require someone to refrain from acting in a particular way or to require some sort of positive conduct. Where there is a case of conflict or variance between the rules of common law and the rules of equity, equity will prevail. Historically, there were often battles in a particular case where a litigant who had received satisfaction through the ordinary common law courts could then find himself taken to the Court of Chancery where a different judge would come to a different conclusion on the basis of different principles. This rather odd state of affairs continued until 1875, when the Judicature Act 1873 came into effect and allowed all courts to administer the principles of both equity and law.

Consider the following case (which we take from Glanville Williams, *Learning the Law*, 11th edn, p 28). One of the principles of equity is that 'he who comes to equity must come with clean hands'. This rule applies whenever a claimant is relying on an equitable right but not when he is relying on a common law right. In the case, a landlord brought an action against his tenant, Mr Isaacson, for ejectment. Mr Isaacson had what is known as an equitable lease of the premises, that is not a formal lease under seal but an informal lease valid only in equity. For nearly all practical purposes, these equitable leases were just as good as legal leases even though they were technically void at law. This particular tenant, however, had broken a term of his equitable lease as just after receiving it he had assigned it to a company by the name of Saxon Ltd, and there was in fact a covenant in the lease not to assign. Mr Isaacson awkwardly explained to the court that he did not act improperly because the company was his own creation and 'Saxon' was none other than the latter part of his name. Mr Isaacson's real defence however was that although he might be liable to pay damages for having broken his covenant not to assign, that was not any reason for his being ejected altogether from the premises. If the document had been a legal lease, the defence would have been a good one, for the lease did not contain a proviso for re-entry on breach of covenant. But, unfortunately for the tenant, it was an equitable lease, and so by breaking an important term of it he had soiled his hands and therefore he lost his lease.

The trust developed historically from the 'use'. The 'use' arose in the Middle Ages where a person conveyed property of any sort to another on the understanding that the other was to become seised of it on behalf of the donor or behalf of some third party (*cestui que use*). The person thus trusted with the property (a feoffee to uses) was in a position of confidence, which could easily be abused. Consequently, the rights of the *cestui que* use required protection. The ordinary common law courts did not recognise such uses and therefore did nothing to provide protection but at an early date the Court of Chancery acting as a court of conscience intervened to force the feoffee to uses to administer the property for the benefit of the *cestui que* use according to the terms of the grant. Thus over time, and accumulation of a great many decisions by the Court of Chancery, the *cestui que* use came to have a special interest in the property which could be enforced by the Court of Chancery. This interest was known as an equitable interest. Eventually, the *cestui que* use became a *cestui que* trust (that is, beneficiary) and the feoffee to uses became a trustee.

A modern definition of the trust was formulated and included in Art 12 of the Hague Convention on the Registration of Trusts enacted in the Registration of Trusts Act 1987. This provides that:

> ... the term 'trust' refers to the legal relationship created – '*inter vivos*' or on death – by a person, the settlor, when assets have been placed under the control of a trustee for the benefit of a beneficiary or for a specified purpose.

> A trust has the following characteristics:

> (a) the assets constitute a separate fund and one not a part of the trustee's own estate;

> (b) title to the trust assets stands in the name of the trustee or in the name of another person on behalf of the trustee;

> (c) the trustee has the power and the duty, in respect of which he is accountable, to manage, employ or dispose of the assets in accordance with the terms of the trust and the special duties imposed on him by law.

> The reservation by the settlor of certain rights and powers, and the fact that the trustee may himself have rights as a beneficiary are not necessarily inconsistent with the existence of a trust.

In general, trusts enable people to take the benefit of property where they are for one reason or another unable to hold the legal ownership themselves. Groups or aggregations of people such as unincorporated associations can enjoy the benefit of property held in trust even though the law would not recognise the legal personality (that is, individual status) of their group. In this book, we examine the current law governing the creation of trusts including secret trusts and constructive trusts, the nature of charitable trusts, the appointment and retirement and removal of trustees, the duties and powers of trustees, and the variance of trusts.

10.2 Express trusts

Here, we examine the resulting trust (where the court will imply a trust); the constructive trust (created by the court to satisfy the demands of justice); and the charitable trust (a public trust designed to benefit the public). We start, though, by looking at the express trust.

10.2.1 Creation of an express trust

A settlor is a person who makes a settlement of his land or personal property. A settlement is a deed (a legal document, signed, sealed and delivered) by which property is subjected to a string of limitations. A settlor who wishes to create an express trust is required to adopt either of the following methods:

- a self-declaration of trust; or

- a transfer of property to the trustees subject to a direction to hold upon trust for the beneficiaries.

This is known as the rule in *Milroy v Lord* (1862):

(a) *self-declaration*. A settlor may declare that he holds property on trust for a beneficiary. Generally, no special form is required, so long as the intention of the settlor is sufficiently clear so as to constitute himself a trustee, for 'equity looks at the intent rather than the form'. Thus, the declaration may be in writing or be evidenced by conduct, or may take the form of a verbal statement. It can also be a combination of these (see *Paul v Constance* (1977); contrast *Jones v Lock* (1865). For an interesting case, see *Re Kayford* (1975)). What is required from the settlor is a firm commitment on his part to undertake the duties of trusteeship in respect of the relevant property, on behalf of the specified beneficiaries (see 10.3). In this respect, there is no obligation to inform the beneficiaries that a trust has been created in their favour. The effect of this mode of creation is to alter the status of the settlor from beneficial owner to that of trustee. For example, S, the absolute owner of 50,000 shares in BP plc, declares that henceforth he holds the entire portfolio of shares upon trust for B, his son, absolutely. In these circumstances, an express trust is created. S retains the legal title to the shares, but B acquires the entire equitable interest in the shares;

(b) *transfer to the trustees*. A settlor may create a trust by transferring the property to another person (or persons), subject to a valid declaration of trust. In this context, the settlor must comply with two requirements, namely, a transfer of the relevant property or interest to the trustees, complemented by a declaration of the terms of the trust (see 10.3). If the settlor intends to create a trust by this method, and declares the terms of the trust but fails to transfer the property to the intended trustees, it is clear that no express trust is created. The ineffective transaction will amount to a conditional declaration of trust but without the condition (the transfer) being satisfied. For example, S, a settlor, nominates T1 and T2 to hold 50,000 BT plc shares upon trust for A for life with remainder to B absolutely (the declaration of trust). In addition, S is required to transfer the title to the shares to T1 and T2. The declaration of trust on its own, without the transfer, is of no effect.

The formal requirements (if any) for the transfer of the legal title to property vary with the nature of the property involved. Thus, in order to transfer legal title to registered land, the settlor is required to execute the prescribed transfer form and register the transfer in the names of the trustees at the appropriate Land Registry. The transfer of tangible moveable property requires that the settlor delivers the property to the trustees and has the appropriate intention to donate. The transfer of the legal title to shares in a private company involves the execution of the appropriate transfer form and registration of the transfer in the company's share register.

If, as stated above, a settlor manifests an intention to create a trust by naming another as trustee and setting out the terms of the trust, but fails to deliver the property to the named trustees, the purported trust will not be effective or constituted. In this event, the court will not imply a self-declaration of trust (which would make the settlor the trustee) because this would mean that all imperfect trusts would become perfect. (See *Milroy v Lord* (1862) – ineffective transfer of the legal title to the trustees.)

However, it appears that, if the settlor intends to transfer the legal title to property and has done everything which is necessary for him to do to effect the transfer, but the last act remaining to be done is required to be done by a third party (this being outside the control of the settlor), the transfer or conveyance *will* be effective in equity. In other words, the transfer of the equitable title may be effective even though the transfer of the legal title has not yet taken place (see *Re Rose* (1952) and *Mascall v Mascall* (1985); contrast *Re Fry* (1946)).

No trust of future property

A trust may only be created in respect of existing property. Accordingly, no trust is created in respect of an 'expectancy' or 'future property', such as an anticipated interest under a will during the lifetime of the testator, the reason being that there is no property actually capable of being subject to the protection of equity. The anticipated property may or may not be acquired by the settlor in the future; in the meantime, there is only a hope of acquiring the same. (See *Re Ellenborough* (1903); *Re Cook's Settlement Trust* (1965).)

Trust of a chose in action

A *'chose in action'* is a right that exists in intangible personal property, such as the right to be paid royalties (copyright), the right to receive dividends (shares), the creditor's right to have a loan repaid, etc. The *chose* may be assigned to the trustees, in accordance with the intention of the settlor. Accordingly, the *chose* is capable of being the subject matter of a trust. In *Don King Productions Inc v Warren* (1998), the court decided that the benefit of promotion and management agreements created by boxing promoters was capable of being the subject matter of a trust. Likewise, a trust may be created in respect of the 'benefit of a covenant', which is a *chose in action*. In *Fletcher v Fletcher* (1844), the court decided that, on the execution of the covenant between the settlor and the trustees, the benefit of the covenant was transferred to the trustees and the trust was perfect. However, in *Re Cook's Settlement Trust*, the court distinguished *Fletcher v Fletcher* on the ground that, in the former case, the underlying property intended as the subject matter of the trust (the proceeds of a possible sale of paintings) did not exist and was thus incapable of being trust property.

Effect of a perfect trust

On the creation of an express trust, the beneficiaries are given a recognisable interest in the property. They are entitled to protect their interest against anyone, except the *bona fide* purchaser of the legal estate for value without notice. The beneficiaries are entitled to sue directly for either the common law remedy of damages or, in appropriate cases, an equitable remedy, irrespective of whether they have provided consideration or not (see *Fletcher v Fletcher*, above). In any event, the trustees (as representatives of the trust) are entitled to bring or defend an action on behalf of the trust. Of course, this can only be the case if the trust is perfect.

If the trust is imperfect, the intended beneficiaries may only commence an action if they have provided consideration, that is, if they are non-volunteers (see below). In other words, a non-volunteer of an imperfect trust is placed in almost the same position as that of a beneficiary under a trust. The non-volunteer of an imperfect trust may force the intended trustee to bring or defend an action concerning the relevant property. Similarly, the non-volunteer may bring an action to enforce rights in respect of the property (see *Pullan v Koe* (1913)).

A 'volunteer' is a person who has not provided valuable consideration. 'Valuable consideration' refers to either common law consideration in money or money's worth or marriage consideration. Common law consideration is the price contemplated by each party to an agreement. Marriage consideration takes the form of an ante-nuptial settlement made in consideration of marriage or a post-nuptial settlement made in pursuance of an ante-nuptial agreement. A post-nuptial settlement *simpliciter* is not within the marriage consideration. An ante-nuptial agreement is one made before or at the time of a marriage, on condition that the marriage takes place, or on the occasion of the marriage, for the purpose of facilitating the marriage (see *Re Park (Deceased) (No 2)* (1972)). The persons who are treated as providing marriage consideration are the parties to the marriage and the issue of the marriage, including remoter issue. Any other children affiliated to the parties to the marriage are volunteers. Thus, illegitimate, legitimated and adopted children, as well as children of a subsequent marriage, are volunteers.

Effect of an imperfect trust

The imperfect trust operates as an agreement to create a trust and, in accordance with contractual principles, a party is entitled to sue for breach of contract. This is subject to the limitation that he must have provided valuable consideration for the promise, for 'equity will not assist a volunteer' and 'equity will not perfect an imperfect gift'. For example, A voluntarily promises to transfer 10,000 BP plc shares to B to hold on trust for C, a volunteer and non-party, absolutely. A fails to transfer the shares to B. The trust is, therefore, imperfect. Since B and C are volunteers, neither may bring an action against A to enforce the promise.

The general rule, that only persons who have provided consideration may claim rights under a promise to create a trust, is subject to one limitation, namely that a party to a voluntary covenant (deed) may claim a remedy of damages for breach of covenant. The rule at common law is that in a 'specialty' contract (deed), the absence of consideration does not prevent a party from enforcing the contract at law by claiming damages. In this respect, 'equity follows the law' and does not prevent the party from enforcing his legal rights. At the same time, the volunteer is not entitled to claim equitable assistance. In the above example, if the voluntary promise between A and B is incorporated in a deed for the benefit of C, B, in theory, is entitled to claim damages at common law for breach of contract, even though B and C are volunteers. (See *Re Cavendish Browne's Settlement Trust* (1916) (substantial damages were awarded); contrast *Re Kay's Settlement* (1939) (B was prevented from bringing an action for damages on behalf of C).) The quantum of damages may sometimes pose a problem. But, if C is also a party to the covenant, he will be entitled to claim damages in his own right. In the above example, neither B nor C claims equitable assistance (see *Cannon v Hartley* (1949)). Under the Contracts (Rights of Third Parties) Act 1999, the decision in *Re Kay* is reversed. Under s 1 of the Act, a third party to a contract is entitled in his own right to enforce a term of the contract if, *inter alia*, a 'term of the contract purports to confer a benefit on him'. This is clearly covered by a contract, albeit voluntary, to create a trust for the benefit of C. Today, C would be entitled to claim substantial damages from A, even though he is not a party to the contract. Notwithstanding the reforms enacted in the 1999 Act, C, a volunteer, will not be entitled to an equitable remedy of specific performance. Such a remedy would not have been available to him even if he had been a party to the contract, for 'equity will not assist a volunteer'.

10.2.2 Exceptions to the rule that 'equity will not assist a volunteer'

There are a number of occasions when, although a gift or trust is imperfect, equity would give assistance to volunteers and force the defendant to complete the intended gift or trust.

The rule in Strong v Bird

The rule in *Strong v Bird* (1874) is that, if an *inter vivos* gift is imperfect by reason only of the fact that the transfer to the intended donee is incomplete, the gift will become perfect when the donee acquires the property in the capacity of executor of the donor's estate. In probate law, a deceased's estate devolves to his executor as appointed in his will. The executor is treated in law as the *alter ego* of the deceased. The intended donee/executor will take the property beneficially, in accordance with the intention of the donor, even though he acquires the asset in a different capacity. In short, the defective gift will be cured by operation of law. In *Strong v Bird*, a loan without consideration was effectively eliminated in favour of the debtor/executor.

The donor's intention is of paramount importance. The donor is required to manifest a present, continuous intention to make an *inter vivos* gift. This rule has been extended to imperfect transfers to trustees (see *Re Ralli* (1964)). However, the test will not be satisfied if the donor declares an intention to transfer the property to the donee in the future (see *Re Freeland* (1952)). If the donor changes his mind at any time before death, the test will not be satisfied (*Re Wale* (1956)). In *Re James* (1935), the principle was extended to the acquisition of property by the next of kin on an intestate succession.

Donatio mortis causa *(DMC)*

A DMC is an *inter vivos* delivery of property by a person contemplating death, subject to the condition that the gift will take effect only on the donor's death. The effect is that, on the donor's death, the conditional transfer becomes complete and the donee (volunteer) is entitled to retain the property or compel the personal representatives of the deceased to transfer the property to him. For example, T, by his will, appoints A as his executor and disposes of all his property to B. On his death bed, T gives C his watch and his building society passbook showing a credit balance of £1,000. These transfers were made conditional on death. On T's death, the gift of the watch becomes complete. The transfer of the building society funds is incomplete, but C will be entitled to compel A to perfect the intended gift.

Proprietary estoppel

Proprietary estoppel is a right given to a volunteer whenever a landowner stands by and permits a volunteer to incur expenditure in order to improve his (the landowner's) property, on the promise or assumption that there will be a transfer of an interest to him. The principle may be used as a cause of action entitling the volunteer to acquire an interest in land. The landowner and his successors in title will be estopped from denying the interest in land acquired by the volunteer. The court will decide the nature of the interest that may be acquired by the volunteer. The test today is: having regard to all the circumstances of the case, would it be unconscionable to deny the promisee an interest or right in the land? For example, L, a landowner, encourages his son,

S, to build a house on his farm. No conveyance is made to S. On L's death, S is entitled to claim that the house be conveyed to him (*Dillwyn v Llewellyn* (1862)).

10.3 The three certainties

An established test to determine whether a valid declaration of trust has been effected is the 'three certainties test'. These certainties are certainty of intention, subject matter and objects. The declaration of trust may take effect as a self-declaration by the settlor, or may complement a transfer of property to the trustees.

10.3.1 Certainty of intention

The issue here is to identify whether the settlor has manifested a 'present irrevocable intention' to create a trust. This is a subjective question, and the focus of attention is on the spoken or written words of the settlor and his conduct. In the event of a dispute, the question is decided by the court. An intention to benefit another *simpliciter* is distinct from the narrow question of whether the settlor intended to create a trust obligation (see *Jones v Lock*).

Use of the expressions 'trust' and 'trustees', although desirable, is not obligatory. Substitute expressions vary in the degree of precision insisted on by the court in order to create a trust. A testator who intends to create a trust should avoid the use of 'precatory' words. Such words express a 'hope', 'recommendation', 'desire', 'confidence', etc, that the transferee of property will deal with the property in a particular way. Precatory words impose a moral obligation on the transferee to accomplish the stated result, but whether they create a trust obligation will depend on the facts of each case. Unless the document and the surrounding circumstances establish the existence of an obligation to hold the property upon trust, the transferee will be entitled to take the property beneficially. (See *Re Adams and the Kensington Vestry* (1884); contrast *Comiskey v Bowring-Hanbury* (1905).)

10.3.2 Certainty of subject matter

It is obvious that an express trust cannot be created if the subject matter is uncertain. The property (including the appropriate interest) which is intended to be subject to the trust is required to be ascertainable, to such an extent that the court may impose an order in respect of the property. Assuming that the property can be identified, its type and nature is irrelevant. All kinds of property, whether legal, equitable, real or personal, are capable of being the subject matter of a trust. If the property cannot be identified with certainty, then there can be no trust and the transferee may take the property beneficially. In this respect, uncertainty in identifying the property creates a 'reflex action on the words of the settlor and creates doubt as to his intention' (*Missoorie Bank v*

Raynor (1882), *per* Hobhouse J). Examples of failure of a trust for uncertainty of subject matter include directions regarding 'the bulk of my estate' (*Palmer v Simmonds* (1854)); 'the remaining part of what is left that he does not want for his own use to be equally divided between A, B and C' (*Sprange v Barnard* (1789)); where a claimant argued he was entitled to a number of bottles of wine from a wine company, but where the claim failed because it could not be shown which bottles of wine the claimant was entitled to, nor had it appropriated any (*Re London Wine Co* (1986)); and shares and debentures in the 'blue chip' category (*Re Kolb's Will Trust* (1961)). On the other hand, trusts were created in respect of declarations of '5% of the issued share capital' of a company (*Hunter v Moss* (1994)) and 'reasonable income from my properties' *(Re Golay* (1965)).

If the beneficial interest (as opposed to the property) is uncertain, the trust will not be void *ab initio* but the transferee (trustee) will hold the property on resulting trust for the settlor. Failure to exercise a personal obligation to select one property from two trust properties resulted in failure of the express trust in *Boyce v Boyce* (1849).

10.3.3 Certainty of objects

No express trust can be created if it is unclear in whose favour the trust was intended to be created. The settlor has a duty to identify the beneficiaries with sufficient clarity. The effect of uncertainty of objects (assuming that there is certainty of intention and subject matter) is that the intended express trust fails and a resulting trust is set up in favour of the settlor or his estate.

The test for certainty of objects varies with the nature of the trust. If the trust is 'fixed', the test is whether the trustees are capable of identifying all the members of the class. In other words, the test is whether the trustees are capable of drawing up a comprehensive list of all the beneficiaries (see *IRC v Broadway Cottages Ltd* (1955)). A 'fixed' trust is one where the trustees are required to distribute the property among all the beneficiaries in the shares specified (fixed) by the settlor, for example, £20,000 to be divided equally by the trustees among four named beneficiaries. On the other hand, a trust is 'discretionary' if the trustees are obliged to exercise their discretion to distribute the property (subject to the terms of the trust) among such of the objects, and in such proportions, as the trustees may decide in their discretion. An example of this is a direction to distribute 'the income from £50,000, held by the trustees, for 10 years, in favour of such of my relatives and on such terms as the trustees may decide in their absolute discretion. Subject thereto, the property is to be held upon trust in favour of a named charity'.

The test for certainty of objects in the context of discretionary trusts was laid down in *McPhail v Doulton* (1971). The test is whether the trustees may say with certainty that any given individual is or is not a member of a class of objects. Thus, there is no need to identify all the objects, but the class (or classes) of objects is required to be clearly defined so that the trustees are able to say who comes within or falls outside the class. In the example above, the trustees are required to be aware of and apply the legal definition of 'relatives'. In so doing, the trustees are capable of deciding whether X or Y is a relative. It is unnecessary to identify all the relatives of the settlor. The expression, 'relatives' was defined by the Court of Appeal in *Re Baden (No 2)* (1972) as anyone who can prove a common ancestry with the relevant person (the settlor).

10.4 Formalities

In addition to the tests stated above, in order to create an express trust, a settlor is required to comply with any formal statutory requirements. These formalities vary with the subject matter of the trust (for example, land or personalty), the nature of the interest involved (for example, a legal or equitable interest and the mode of creation (*inter vivos* or by will).

10.4.1 *Inter vivos* declarations of trusts of land

Section 53(1)(b) of the Law of Property Act 1925 provides that 'a declaration of trust concerning land or any interest therein must be manifested and proved by some writing, signed by some person who is able to declare the same or by his will'.

This sub-section concerns the creation of an express trust of realty. It is not applicable to personalty. The declaration of trust is not required to be created in writing, but must be proved in writing. Failure to comply with the sub-section leads to the trust being unenforceable, but not void. The writing may be supplied subsequently, and the trust will then be enforceable.

Resulting and constructive trusts are exempt from the above formal requirement, because s 53(2) of the Law of Property Act 1925 provides that: 'This section shall not affect the creation or operation of implied, resulting and constructive trusts.' Accordingly, a resulting trust of land may arise without the terms being reduced into writing. (See *Hodgson v Marks* (1971).)

Inter vivos *dispositions of equitable interests*

Section 53(1)(c) of the Law of Property Act 1925 provides that:

> ... a disposition of an equitable interest or trust subsisting at the time of
> disposition must be in writing, signed by the person disposing of the same or
> by his agent thereunto lawfully authorised in writing or by his will.

The policy of the sub-section is to prevent oral hidden transfers of equitable interests which exist under trusts. The wording of the sub-section, as opposed to that of s 53(1)(b), is mandatory in effect. Accordingly, non-compliance with the provision results in the purported disposition being void, subject to limited exceptions. The sub-section is applicable to transactions concerning interests in both realty and personalty subsisting under a trust. The provision is not applicable in relation to the original creation of a trust. For example, on day one, S creates a trust by transferring shares to T, a trustee, on trust for B, a beneficiary. This transaction does not come within s 53(1)(c). On day two, B verbally declares himself a trustee of his interest for C. This arrangement falls within s 53(1)(c) and, as the transaction is not in writing, it is void.

The key feature of s 53(1)(c) is the meaning of the term 'disposition'. This has not been defined in the statute. But the term 'conveyance' has been defined in s 205(1)(ii) of the Law of Property Act 1925 as including a disposition. However, Romer LJ, in *Timpson's Executors v Yerbury* (1936), went some way to defining what a disposition is when he classified four types of disposition that can be made by a beneficiary under a trust:

- an assignment to a third party;

- a direction to the trustees to hold on trust for a third party;

- a contract for valuable consideration to assign the equitable interest; and

- a self-declaration by the beneficiary under a trust in favour of another.

In *Grey v IRC* (1960), the House of Lords decided that an oral direction by an equitable owner to the trustees to hold upon trust for another was void for non-compliance with s 53(1)(c).

In *Vandervell v IRC* (1967), the House of Lords held that s 53(1)(c) has no application where the equitable owner under a trust directs the legal owner to transfer his title to a third party and where, in the same transaction, the equitable owner, in the absence of writing, transfers his interest to the same third party. In other words, the sub-section is not applicable where the equitable owner terminates the trust by a transfer of both equitable and legal title in favour of a third party.

In *Neville v Wilson* (1996), the Court of Appeal held that s 53(2) restricts the operation of s 53(1)(c) by exempting constructive trusts from the operation of the sub-section. In *Re Vandervell Trusts (No 2)* (1974), the Court of Appeal decided that equitable estoppel was excepted from the provision. The same court decided in *Re Paradise Motor Co* (1968) that a disclaimer of an equitable interest under a trust was not a disposition; and in *Re Danish Bacon Staff Pension Fund* (1971), the High Court held that nominations by staff pension fund holders are outside the provision.

It appears that a self-declaration of trust of part of an equitable interest in favour of another is outside the operation of s 53(1)(c). The reason for this is that such an arrangement operates as the creation of a new trust. For example, T, a trustee, holds the legal title to 50,000 BT plc shares upon trust for B, a beneficiary. B subsequently orally declares himself trustee of his interest for himself for life with remainder to C. Since B has active duties to perform, he does not drop out of the picture and his self-declaration of trust is outside sub-s (c).

10.4.2 Contracts for the sale of land

Section 2 of the Law of Property (Miscellaneous Provisions) Act 1989 declares that a contract for the sale or other disposition of land or an interest in land must be in writing. The need for writing is mandatory; informal transactions concerning land, such as mortgages and options, which fail to comply with the section are treated as void. Excluded from the provision are constructive and resulting trusts.

10.4.3 Testamentary dispositions

Any donation of property (including a gift by way of a trust) must be made by will if the property is intended to take effect on the death of the donor, but is revocable by him until death. The will must comply with the provisions of s 9 of the Wills Act 1837, as amended by s 17 of the Administration of Justice Act 1982. Broadly, the formalities are threefold: the will must be in writing, signed by the testator, and his signature must be witnessed by two witnesses, who are also required to sign. Failure to fulfil any of these requirements renders the purported will void and the deceased's property will be distributed on an intestacy. Excepted from these provisions are secret trusts. These are considered below.

10.5 Secret trusts

A secret trust is an equitable obligation, communicated to an intended trustee during the testator's lifetime, but which is intended to attach to a gift arising under the testator's will.

On a testator's death, his will becomes a public document. But the testator may wish to make provision for what he considers to be an embarrassing object, such as a mistress or an illegitimate child. To avoid adverse publicity, he may make an apparent gift by will to an intended trustee, subject to an understanding created outside the will that the trustee will hold the property for the benefit of the secret beneficiary.

In enforcing such trusts, equity does not contradict s 9 of the Wills Act 1837, as amended, because the trust operates outside (*dehors*) this Act. Indeed, the secret trust complements the will, in that a valid will is assumed, but it is recognised that the will on its own does not reflect the true intention of the testator. The bare minimum requirements are a validly executed will which transfers property to the trustees, whether or not named as such under the will, and the *inter vivos* acceptance by the trustees of an equitable obligation. It is immaterial that one of the intended beneficiaries under the trust, as distinct from the will, witnesses the will. Section 15 of the Wills Act 1837 is not applicable in this context (see *Re Young* (1951)).

There are two types of secret trusts – fully and half secret trusts.

10.5.1 Fully secret trusts

These trusts are fully concealed on the face of the will. The testator (a person who makes a will) transfers property by will to the trustees apparently beneficially, but subject to an understanding created outside the will that they will hold on trust for beneficiaries when they acquire the property. For example, T, a testator, transfers '50,000 BT plc shares by will to my legatee, L'. Prior to his death, T orally informs L that he wishes him to hold the shares on trust for B, the secret beneficiary, absolutely. L becomes a trustee for B on T's death and is not allowed to take the property beneficially.

The following conditions need to be fulfilled in order to create a fully secret trust:

- it is essential that, during his lifetime, the testator communicates the terms of the intended trust to the trustee (legatee or devisee). This requirement reflects the distinction between a gift on trust and an absolute gift to the legatee. It follows that, if the legatee or devisee only hears of the trust after the testator's death, no secret trust is created and the legatee or devisee may take beneficially. Section 9 of the Wills Act 1837 may be used as a defence by the legatee or devisee (see *Wallgrave v Tebbs* (1865));

- if the testator communicates to the legatee the fact that he is to hold the legacy on trust, but fails to disclose the terms of the trust before his death, the intended secret trust fails. The legatee will not take the property beneficially, but will instead hold the property on resulting trust for the testator's estate or next of kin (see *Re Boyes* (1884));

- the communication of the terms of the trust may be made before or after the execution of the will, provided that it is made during the lifetime of the testator. Communication may either be made directly with the legatee or be effected constructively, that is, the testator may deliver a sealed envelope to the legatee, marked with a direction such as 'Not to be opened before my death'. Once the legatee is aware that the contents of the envelope are connected with a transfer of property by will, the communication is effective. The communication is deemed to be made on the date of the delivery of the envelope (see *Re Keen* (1937));

- the legatee may 'expressly' or 'impliedly' accept the obligation imposed by the testator. An 'implied' acceptance is signified by silence or acquiescence on the part of the legatee. Thus, if the legatee does not wish to become a trustee, it is incumbent on him to inform the testator during his lifetime. Failure to do so amounts to an acceptance of the obligation by the legatee;

- the fully secret trust obligation may take the form of the trustee holding the property on trust for the secret beneficiary absolutely. Alternatively, the obligation may require the legatee to execute a will in favour of the secret beneficiary. In this event, the legatee may enjoy the property beneficially during his lifetime (see *Ottoway v Norman* (1972));

- where a testator leaves property to two or more legatees but informs one or some of them (but not all of them) of the terms of the trust, the issue arises as to whether the uninformed legatees are bound by the communication to the informed legatees. The solution here depends on the timing of the communication and the status of the legatees. If: (a) the communication is made to the legatees before or at the time of the execution of the will; and (b) they take as joint tenants, the uninformed legatees are bound to hold for the purposes communicated to the informed legatees. The justification commonly ascribed to this principle is that no one is allowed to take property beneficially under a fraud committed by another. If any of the above conditions is not satisfied, the uninformed legatees are entitled to take the property beneficially (see *Re Stead* (1900)).

10.5.2 Half secret trusts

This classification arises where the legatee or devisee takes as trustee on the face of the will, but the terms of the trust are not specified in the will. For example, T, a testator, transfers property to L, a legatee, to 'hold upon trust for purposes that have been communicated to him'. The will acknowledges the existence of the trust, but the terms have been concealed.

The following points are relevant in order to establish a half secret trust:

- the will is irrevocable on the death of the testator. Thus, evidence is not admissible to contradict the terms of the will. To adduce such evidence would perpetrate a fraud. For example, if the will points to a past communication (that is, a communication of the terms of the trust before the will was made), evidence is not admissible to prove a future communication. Similarly, since the will names the legatee as trustee, evidence is not admissible to prove that he is a beneficiary (see *Re Rees* (1950));

- where the communication of the terms of the trust is made before or at the time of the execution of the will, evidence may be adduced to prove the terms of the trust (see *Blackwell v Blackwell* (1929));

- if the communication of the terms of the trust is made after the execution of the will, but during the lifetime of the testator, the courts have ruled that such communication is inadmissible. The justification commonly given for this principle is that a testator is prohibited from making a future unattested disposition by naming a trustee in the will and supplying the purposes subsequently (see *Blackwell v Blackwell*; *Re Keen* (1937)). This principle is not without its critics;

- the persons named as trustees on the face of the will are not entitled to take any part of the property beneficially. For these purposes, it is immaterial that the testator made such an arrangement (see *Re Rees*). Likewise, on a failure, whole or in part, of the secret trust, the trustee holds the property on resulting trust for the testator's estate or next of kin.

10.6 Resulting trusts

A resulting trust, unlike an express trust, is implied by the court in favour of the settlor/transferor (or his estate if he is dead). Such trusts arise by virtue of the unexpressed or implied intention of the settlor or testator. The settlor (or his estate) becomes the beneficial owner under the resulting trust. The trust is created as a result of defective drafting. The expression 'resulting trust' derives from the Latin verb *'resultare'*, meaning to spring back (in effect, the trust 'springs back' to the original owner). Examples are the transfer of property subject to a condition precedent which cannot be achieved, and the creation of an express trust which becomes void.

In *Re Vandervell's Trusts (No 2)* (1974), Megarry J classified resulting trusts into two categories, namely, 'automatic' and 'presumed'.

10.6.1 Automatic resulting trusts

Sometimes, legal title to property has been transferred but the destination of the beneficial interest remains unclear. Automatic resulting trusts arise in order to fill a gap in ownership. This type of resulting trust arises in a variety of situations, as follows:

- on the failure of an express trust (see *Re Ames* (1946), where a purported marriage settlement was void);

- on the transfer of property to trustees where the terms of the trust have not been specified (see *Vandervell v IRC* (1967), where there was vagueness as to the destination of the equitable interest in a share option scheme);

- on the transfer of property subject to a condition precedent which has not been achieved (see *Barclays Bank v Quistclose* (1970), where a loan created for a specific purpose was not fulfilled);

- where the trust exhausts only some of the trust property. The surplus may be held on resulting trust (see *Re Abbott* (1900)). By way of contrast, the court may decide, on construction of the instrument, that the ulterior purpose of the settlor/transferor may be achieved by permitting the transferee to retain the property beneficially. In these circumstances, there is no room for a resulting trust (see *Re Osoba* (1979)).

10.6.2 Presumed resulting trusts

A presumed resulting trust is, *prima facie*, a rule of evidence that creates a rebuttable presumption of law. Where (a) there is a purchase of property in the name of another or the voluntary transfer of property to another; and (b) there is no definitive evidence in the first place concerning the transferor's real intention, equity *prima facie* considers that the transferee is a trustee for the transferor. In short, the transferor is presumed to have retained the equitable title and the transferee is presumed to obtain a nominal interest in the property. The rule is arbitrary, but the presumption has the advantage of determining the ownership of the beneficial interest, subject to evidence of the contrary.

There are two occasions when the presumption arises, namely:

- a purchase of property in the name of another; and

- a voluntary conveyance of property in the name of another.

Purchase in the name of another

The rule is that, where a purchaser contracts with a vendor to acquire real or personal property, but directs the vendor to transfer the legal title in the name of another, the transferee is presumed to hold the property on trust for the purchaser. Parol evidence is admissible in order to identify the purchaser.

Thus, if A purchases shares in the name of B (that is, B becomes the legal owner), the latter is presumed to hold the shares on trust for A. B is a mere nominee for A until he rebuts the presumption.

Similarly, where A and B jointly purchase a house and have it conveyed in the name of B, so that B becomes the legal owner of the house, B is presumed to hold the house on trust for both A and B in proportion to the contribution made by each of them. If A provides four-fifths and B provides one-fifth of the purchase monies, B is presumed to hold the house for himself beneficially as to one-fifth and to hold the remainder on trust for A (see *Bull v Bull* (1955)).

Voluntary transfer in the name of another

Another state of affairs which gives rise to a presumed resulting trust is the occasion of a voluntary transfer of personal property in the name of another. No consideration is provided by the person in whose favour the transfer is made.

For example, if A transfers the legal title to shares in the name of B, a resulting trust is presumed in favour of A (see *Re Vinogradoff* (1935)).

By virtue of s 60(3) of the Law of Property Act 1925, this principle does not extend to realty. Nevertheless, the circumstances may give rise to a presumption of resulting trust (see *Hodgson v Marks* (1971)).

10.6.3 Presumption of advancement

A presumption of advancement, unlike a presumption of a resulting trust, is a presumption of a gift in favour of the transferee. Where there is a 'special relationship' between the transferor and transferee, a purchase or voluntary transfer of property in the name of the transferee gives rise to a presumption of a gift. In short, the transferee is presumed to own both the legal and equitable interests. This presumption, like the presumption of a resulting trust, may be rebutted by evidence of the intention of the transferor.

The courts have, in the past, recognised the 'special relationship' as giving rise to a moral obligation on the part of the transferor to benefit the transferee.

These are occasions where:

• the transferee is the wife of the transferor. This presumption has been considerably weakened with regard to the family home (see later);

• there is a transfer by a father to his legitimate child (see *Shephard v Cartwright* (1955));

• the transferor stands in the shoes of the male parent *(loco parentis patris)* towards the child (see *Re Paradise Motor Co* (1968)).

10.6.4 Rebuttal of the presumptions

The presumptions of resulting trust and advancement are, in a sense, artificial rules adopted for deciding the intention of the transferor or purchaser and may give way to the real intention of the parties. Although the weight of the presumptions depends on the circumstances of each case, the courts will consider all the surrounding facts and decide whether the presumptions have been rebutted or not. The quality of the rebutting evidence varies from case to case. Much depends on the relationship between the parties, their conduct and any statements made by them. For example, strong evidence will be needed to rebut the presumption of a resulting trust where a transfer of the legal title to property is made by a client to his solicitor. On the other hand, less evidence will be needed to rebut the presumption where a transfer is made by an uncle to his favourite nephew.

Recently, the courts have considered the position of a transferor who disposes of property to another in pursuance of a fraudulent or illegal purpose, but subsequently repents and withdraws from the illegal purpose, wishing to recover the property from the transferee. The law was reviewed by the House of Lords in *Tinsley v Milligan* (1994). It was decided that, if a party does not rely on the illegality in order to establish a claim to an equitable interest, the illegality is no bar to a successful action. In other words, if the claimant enjoys an equitable interest by way of a resulting trust, his subsequent illegality is not decisive. On the other hand, in the different context of the presumption of advancement, the transferor is generally prevented from establishing his equitable interest by virtue of his fraudulent conduct. The principle here is, 'he who comes to equity must come with clean hands' (see *Tinker v Tinker* (1970)). However, in *Tribe v Tribe* (1995), the Court of Appeal decided that the claimant was entitled to rebut the presumption on the ground that he had withdrawn from the unlawful venture.

10.7 Constructive trusts

A constructive trust is fundamentally different from an express or resulting trust. The constructive trust is not created in accordance with the express or implied intention of the settlor. It is a device adopted by the courts in the interests of justice and good conscience. The constructive trust is a residual category of trust which is called into play whenever the court desires to impose a trust and no other category of trust is suitable. The courts reserve the power to interpret a transaction as giving rise to a constructive trust.

For example, T1 and T2 hold property on trust but, in breach of trust, purport to sell the property to X, a third party, who has knowledge of the breach of trust. Although T1 and T2 are already express trustees and are liable to the beneficiaries for breach of trust, they will become constructive trustees of any unauthorised profit made from their office as trustees, such as the proceeds of sale received from X. By virtue of X's participation in the breach with knowledge of the facts, he will be treated as a constructive trustee.

Thus, constructive trusts may be imposed on express trustees and other 'fiduciaries' in respect of any unauthorised benefits received by them. In addition, strangers or third parties who have misconducted themselves with knowledge that their actions constitute an unwarranted interference with the interest of the beneficiary will become constructive trustees.

The effect of a constructive trust is similar in many ways to any other type of trust, in that the beneficiary retains a proprietary interest in the subject matter of the trust. In the event of the constructive trustee becoming bankrupt, the trust property is granted in favour of the beneficiaries who take precedence over the trustee's creditors. If the trustee disposes of the assets, the beneficiary is entitled to 'trace' his property in the hands of a third party, not being a *bona fide* transferee of the legal estate for value without notice.

The courts have adopted a pragmatic, broad based approach towards constructive trusts which, although classifiable into various categories, remain subject to extension and development.

Per Edmund-Davies LJ in *Carl Zeiss Stiftung v Herbert Smith and Co* (1969):

> English law provides no clear and all-embracing definition of a constructive trust. Its boundaries have been left perhaps deliberately vague, so as not to restrict the court by technicalities in deciding what the justice of a particular case may demand.

10.7.1 Categories of constructive trusts

Trustee or fiduciary making an unauthorised profit

The rule is that a person occupying a position of confidence (such as a trustee or fiduciary) is prohibited from deriving any personal benefit from the property in the absence of authority from the beneficiaries, the trust instrument or the court. In other words, the trustee or fiduciary should not place himself in a position where his duty may conflict with his personal interest. If such a conflict occurs and the trustee obtains a benefit or profit, the advantage is held on constructive trust for the beneficiary. In particular, a trustee, without specific authority to the contrary, is not entitled to purchase trust property for his own benefit. The position remains the same even if the purchase appears to be fair. If such a purchase takes place, the transaction is treated as voidable, that is, valid until avoided. In *Keech v Sandford* (1726), an unauthorised renewal of a lease (trust property) by a trustee for his own benefit was treated as voidable.

The rule in *Keech v Sandford* (as it is sometimes called) has been extended to other fiduciary relationships, including: agents acting on behalf of principals; directors in favour of companies; partners vis à vis co-partners; and solicitors in respect of clients. A 'fiduciary' is an individual who is aware that his judgment and confidence is, and has been, relied on by the claimant. Apart from the traditional categories of fiduciaries, the existence of such a relationship is a question for the court to decide.

In claims concerning breach of fiduciary duties, the claimant is required to establish each of the following three complementary propositions:

- the defendant holds a fiduciary position towards the claimant; and

- the defendant obtained a benefit; and

- there is a causal connection between the relationship and the benefit.

In *Holder v Holder* (1968), the plaintiff failed to establish that the defendant held a fiduciary position. Normally, trustees cannot purchase trust property because they cannot be both vendors and purchasers. The circumstances of this case, however, were special. The trustee in question took no part in instructing the valuer or in the preparations for the auction. He never assumed the duties of an executor.

In *English v Dedham Vale Properties* (1978), the prospective purchasers of land were held to be fiduciaries when they obtained planning permission without the vendor's authority. In *Boardman v Phipps* (1967), the House of Lords held that a solicitor was a fiduciary when, acting on behalf of the trust, he obtained confidential information and made an unauthorised profit therefrom.

In *AG v Blake* (1998), the Court of Appeal decided that a former member of the Secret Service was no longer a fiduciary in respect of non-confidential information, but he was accountable in respect of profits earned from his memoirs.

In accordance with the rule in *Keech v Sandford*, a trustee is not entitled to receive any remuneration or benefit for his services as trustee without appropriate authority (see *Williams v Barton* (1927)). But the trustee may be reimbursed in respect of expenditure properly incurred in connection with his trusteeship (s 30(2) of the Trustee Act 1925). Similarly, where a fiduciary accepts a bribe in breach of his fiduciary duty, the bribe, including property representing the unauthorised profit, is held upon trust for the persons to whom the duty is owed (see *AG for Hong Kong v Reid* (1993)).

Likewise, trustees who are appointed directors of a company by virtue of their trust shareholding are accountable to the trust for their remuneration (see *Re Macadam* (1946)).

Occasions when a trustee may be paid

The general rule, as illustrated in *Williams v Barton*, is subject to the following four exceptions.

Authority in the trust instrument

The settlor may authorise the trustees to be paid from the trust funds, but such a power is required to be expressed in the trust instrument. Professional trustees normally insist on an adequate charging clause before they undertake the duties of trusteeship.

However, in the event of any ambiguity, charging clauses are strictly construed against the trustees. Furthermore, trustees may only charge a reasonable amount which would vary with the circumstances of each case.

Authority of the court

The court will only authorise reasonable remuneration for services performed by trustees which are of exceptional benefit to the trust (see *Boardman v Phipps* (1967)).

Agreement with all the beneficiaries

Where the beneficiaries are all *sui juris* and absolutely entitled to the trust property, they may make an agreement with the trustees for the latter to be remunerated. This is an application of the *Saunders v Vautier* rule.

The rule in **Cradock v Piper** (1850)

A solicitor/trustee may charge his usual fees for acting on behalf of his co-trustees in litigation concerning the trust, but is not permitted fees for representing himself.

Company directors stand in a fiduciary relationship to the company and are subject to the rigours of the trust principle. If a director places himself in a position where his duty to the company conflicts with his personal interest, any benefits obtained in consequence are accountable to the company. In *Regal*

(Hastings) Ltd v Gulliver (1942), the unauthorised purchase by directors of shares in a subsidiary company gave rise to a constructive trust.

Contracts for the sale of land

Once a specifically enforceable contract for the sale of land is made, the purchaser becomes the equitable owner of the property. Thus, on the date of the exchange of contracts, the vendor becomes a constructive trustee for the purchaser until the date of the completion of the sale (see *Lysaght v Edwards* (1876)).

Equity will not allow a statute to be used as an engine for fraud

Acts of Parliament are binding on all courts, even a court of equity. However, if a strict compliance with a statutory provision (for example, in the case of formalities) has the incidental effect of perpetrating a fraud, the court is entitled to suspend such a provision (see *Rochefoucauld v Boustead* (1897)).

Strangers to the trust

The general rule is that third parties or persons who have not been appointed trustees (such as agents of trustees, for example, accountants and solicitors) are not constructive trustees if they merely act in breach of their duties. Instead, they may be personally liable in damages for breach of contract or tort. Provided that the agent acts within the limits of his authority, does not receive the trust property for his own benefit, and is unaware that he is acting in a manner inconsistent with the terms of the trust, he does not become a constructive trustee (see *Barnes v Addy* (1874), where a solicitor to a trust was not a constructive trustee when he gave the sole trustee sound advice which was disregarded and resulted in loss to the trust):

However, there are three occasions when a stranger to a trust may become a constructive trustee:

- *The stranger becomes a trustee* de son tort *(that is, a trustee of his own wrong)* To fall within this category, the stranger is required to undertake acts that are characteristic of trusteeship, and act on behalf of the trust and not for his own benefit. In short, this type of constructive trustee is one who, by mistake, believes that he was properly appointed to act on behalf of the trust (see *Boardman v Phipps* (1967) and *James v Williams* (1999)).

- *The stranger knowingly receives trust property for his benefit*
  The rationale for liability under this head is that a stranger who knows that trust property has been transferred to him in breach of trust cannot take possession of the property for his own benefit, but is subject to the claims of the trust. He is not a bona fide transferee of the legal estate for value without notice.

  The contest in this context is based on the assertion of proprietary rights. The trust sues the stranger claiming that he/it has better title to the property. Equity is entitled to make the most strenuous efforts in order to protect the beneficiary's interest under the trust. In the majority of cases, the view is that any form of knowledge on the part of the trustee, subjective or objective, will be sufficient to make him liable under this head (see Belmont Finance Corp Williams Furniture (No 2) (1980)). On the other hand, in Re Montagu (1987), the court advocated the view that only subjective knowledge is relevant to make the stranger liable under this head.

- *The stranger knowingly assists in a fraudulent transaction*
  Under this head of liability, a stranger to a trust becomes a constructive trustee (a form of personal liability) if he knowingly assists in a fraudulent scheme devised by another (perhaps the settlement trustee). This is the position even though the stranger does not receive the trust property. In effect, the stranger acts as an accomplice to the principal fraudulent trustee or other party.

The following four elements must be established in order to attach liability to the stranger: (a) the existence of the trust (or a fiduciary relationship); (b) the existence of a dishonest or fraudulent design; (c) the assistance by the stranger in that design; and (d) the knowledge of that stranger. Since the benchmark of liability is dishonesty, the type of knowledge involved is subjective (see *Agip v Jackson* (1991)).

The family home

The family home is regarded by the majority of families as their most valuable asset. The legal title may be vested in the joint names of the partners or, as is sometimes the case, one partner acquires the legal title. There is an issue concerning the principles of property law applicable in this context in order to ascertain ownership of the home. The following principles emerge from the case and statute law:

(a) The presumptions of resulting trusts and advancement are regarded as outmoded principles, better suited to a different society (see *Pettit v Pettit* (1970)).

(b) The same common law principles are applicable to married and unmarried partners.

(c) If the parties have expressly declared their beneficial interests in writing, then, in the absence of fraud or mistake, this will be conclusive as to their interests (see *Goodman v Gallant* (1986)).

(d) If the express intention of the parties is not declared in writing, the intention becomes unenforceable for non-compliance with s 53(1)(b) of the Law of Property Act 1925.

(e) The court may infer the intention of the parties based on all the circumstances of the case under s 53(2) of the Law of Property Act 1925 (that is, resulting and constructive trusts). The overriding consideration in creating such trusts is not primarily to achieve justice between the parties, but to give effect to their intentions.

(f) The two governing principles are that, at any time prior to the acquisition (or exceptionally afterwards), there is:

- evidence of an agreement, arrangement or understanding reached between the parties, based on express discussion between them, concerning the beneficial interest in the property. In addition, the claimant has acted to his or her detriment in reliance on such agreement; or

- evidence of the conduct of the parties which gives rise to a constructive trust, such as direct contributions (including mortgage payments) to the purchase price of the home (see *Lloyds Bank v Rosset* (1990)).

(g) Ordinary domestic services, such as looking after the children, without more, are insufficient to create an interest in the home (see *Burns v Burns* (1984)).

(h) With regard to married couples, in addition to the principles as outlined above, ss 23–25 of the Matrimonial Causes Act 1973 give the court wide discretionary powers to declare or vary the interests of spouses in family assets on a divorce, decree of nullity or judicial separation.

(i) Under s 37 of the Matrimonial Proceedings and Property Act 1970, spouses (but not unmarried couples) who contribute in a substantial way in money or money's worth to the improvement of real (or personal) property may enjoy a share or enlarged share in the asset. The court decides whether a contribution is substantial or not by having regard to all the circumstances of the case.

(j) Once the claimant has established an interest in the property, the value of that interest is quantified at the time the property is sold. Accordingly, any increases or decreases in the value of the property are taken into consideration.

(k) The claimant is entitled to apply to the court, under s 14 of the Trusts of Land and Appointment of Trustees Act 1996, for an order of sale.

10.8 Purpose trusts

A purpose trust is designed to promote a purpose as an end in itself, such as the discovery of an alphabet of 40 letters, to provide a cup for a yacht race or the boarding up of certain rooms in a house. Such intended trusts are void, for the court cannot give effect to a trust which it cannot supervise. There is no beneficiary with a *locus standi* capable of enforcing such trust. In *Re Astor's Settlement Trust* (1952), a gift on trust for 'the maintenance of good understanding between nations and the preservation of the independence and integrity of newspapers' was void.

This general rule is subject to a number of exceptions:

- charitable trusts (see 10.9);

- gifts for the care of animals are generally charitable, but trusts for the care of specific animals, such as pets, are treated as private purpose trusts (see *Pettingall v Pettingall* (1842));

- a trust for the building of a memorial or monument for an individual is not charitable, but may exist as a valid private purpose trust if the trustees express a desire to perform the trust. In *Re Hooper* (1932), a gift for the maintenance of particular graves 'for as long as the law allows' was valid as a private purpose trust;

- the '*Denley* approach': it is a question of construction for the court to ascertain whether a gift or trust is for the promotion of a purpose *simpliciter* (within the *Astor* principle), which is void, or, alternatively, whether the trust is for the benefit of persons who are capable of enforcing the trust. The settlor may, in form, create what appears to be a purpose trust but, in substance, the trust may be construed as being for the benefit of human beneficiaries (see *Re Denley's Trust Deed* (1969), where land was conveyed on trust for use as a sports ground;

- a trust for the promotion of fox hunting was held to be valid in *Re Thompson* (1934). A trust for the saying of masses in private is not charitable, but may create a valid private trust (*Bourne v Keane* (1919)). In *Khoo Cheng Teow* (1932), a trust for the performance of non-Christian ceremonies was upheld.

10.8.1 The rule against perpetuities

The grant of future interests is void unless the property vests within the perpetuity period. At common law, the perpetuity period is a life or lives in being and/or 21 years from the date that the instrument creating the gift takes effect. Only human lives are taken into consideration (including an embryonic child (*en ventre sa mère*)). A life or lives in being, whether connected with the gift or not, may be chosen expressly by the donor or settlor, or may be implied. A life is implied if it is so related to the gift that it is capable of being used to measure the date of the vesting of the interest. A group of lives may be selected by the settlor, provided that it is possible to say when the last member of the group dies. Indeed, the settlor may select persons who have no connection with the settlement, such as royal lives, for example, 'the lineal descendants of Queen Elizabeth II living at my death'. If no lives are selected or implied, the perpetuity period at common law is 21 years.

In substance, the perpetuity rule not only requires a future interest to vest within the perpetuity period, but also stipulates the maximum period of duration in which such an interest may be enjoyed following the vesting of the interest. On analysis, the rule may be classified into two categories, namely:

• the rule against remote vesting; and

• the rule against excessive duration.

The rule against remote vesting

This rule stipulates the maximum period of time in which the vesting of a future interest may be postponed. Before 1964, if there was a possibility, however slight, that a future interest may vest outside the perpetuity period, the gift was void. The Perpetuities and Accumulations Act 1964 introduced three major reforms to the law. Under the Act, a future interest is no longer void on the ground that it 'might' vest outside the perpetuity period. It is void if, in the circumstances, the interest does not vest within the perpetuity period. In the meantime, the court will 'wait and see' whether or not the gift vests. Secondly, the Act introduced a certain and fixed period not exceeding 80 years which the grantor may nominate as the perpetuity period. Thirdly, s 3(5) of the Act introduced a variety of persons who may be treated as a 'statutory life'. These are: the grantor; the beneficiary or potential beneficiary; the donee of a power, option or other right; parents and grandparents of the grantor; and any person entitled in default. Where there are no lives within any of these categories, the wait and see period is 21 years from the date the instrument takes effect.

The rule against excessive duration

Closely related to the rule against remote vesting is the rule against the inalienability of property. This rule renders void any trust or interest which is required to be enjoyed for longer than the perpetuity period. Charitable trusts are exempt from this principle (see 10.9). The issue here is not whether the property or interest is, in reality, tied up forever, but whether the owner is capable of disposing of the same within the perpetuity period. Thus, property may be owned perpetually by persons, companies or unincorporated associations if these bodies are entitled to dispose of the same at any time but have refrained from exercising the right of disposal.

Unincorporated associations

In *Conservative and Union Central Office v Burrell* (1982), Lawton LJ defined an unincorporated association as follows:

> ... two or more persons bound together for one or more common purposes, not being business purposes, by mutual undertakings, each having mutual duties and obligations, in an organisation which has rules which identify in whom control of it and its funds rests and on what terms and which can be joined or left at will.

The difficulty concerning unincorporated associations is that they are not separate legal persons. They are bodies with labels which identify their members. Such bodies may only act through their members or officers. Accordingly, such associations cannot hold property, except through their officers, and likewise, gifts cannot be made to such organisations *per se*. The following solutions have been adopted from time to time by the courts in respect of gifts to unincorporated associations:

(a) a donor may make a gift to an association which, on a true construction, is a gift to the members of that body who take as joint tenants free from any contractual fetter. Any member is entitled to sever his share. In these circumstances, the association is used as a label or definition of the class which is intended to take (see *Cocks v Manners* (1871), where a gift by will to the Dominican Convent at Carisbrooke 'payable to the supervisor for the time being' was treated as a gift to the members of the community;

(b) more frequently, a gift to an association may be construed as a gift to the members of the association, not beneficially, but as an accretion to the funds of the society regulated by the contract (evidenced by the rules of the association) that was made by the members *inter se*. A member who leaves the association by death or resignation will have no claim to the property in the absence of any rules to the contrary. In *Re Recher* (1972), a gift to the London and Provincial Anti-Vivisection Society was held to be a gift to the members as an addition to the funds of the society, but subject to contract of the members, as set out in the rules;

(c) a gift to an association may be construed by the court as a gift to both present and future members of the association. In coming to this conclusion, the courts are required to consider the rules of the association and its function, in addition to the intention of the donor. But, if the members of the society (in accordance with its constitution) are incapable of disposing of the assets of the society or are incapable of altering the rules of the association, the gift may fail for infringing the perpetuity rule. In *Re Grant's Will Trust* (1980), a gift to the Chertsey Labour Party was void for infringing the perpetuity rule. The members did not have the power to change the rules of the association. Such control was vested in the National Executive Committee of the Labour Party;

(d) a transfer of property to an association may be construed as a transfer on trust for the function or operation of the society and not for its members. If this construction is adopted, the court may decide that the trust fails under the *Astor* principle, owing to the intention to promote a purpose. Such a construction would be exceptional. Moreover, if the intention of the settlor is to set up an endowment in favour of the beneficiary (that is, the association), the gift may fail on the separate ground of the infringement of the perpetuity rule. In *Leahy v AG for New South Wales* (1959), a gift of a sheep station for 'such order of nuns of the Catholic Church or the Christian brothers as my trustees shall select' was construed as an intended gift on trust to promote a purpose, and thus failed. The gift also failed on the separate ground of infringing the perpetuity rule, as the capital could not be spent;

(e) a gift of property to an association may be construed as a transfer on trust for the current members of the association and not on trust for purposes. In this event, provided that the rules of the association empower the members to liquidate and distribute the assets, the perpetuity rule will not be infringed and the trust will be valid. The position remains the same even though the settlor specifies a purpose for which the fund may be used. Such a stipulation may be construed as insufficient to prevent the members (beneficiaries) disposing of the property in any way they consider appropriate within the rules of the society. In *Re Lipinski* (1977), a testator bequeathed half of his residuary estate on trust for an association to be used 'solely' in constructing or maintaining the association's buildings. This transfer was valid as a gift to the members, subject to the contract between them as members.

Dissolution of unincorporated associations

The issue here concerns the occasions when the rules are silent as to the destination of assets following a dissolution of an unincorporated association. In effect, there are a number of issues involved, namely, whether the members of the association are entitled to the assets on a distribution (and if so, whether only members on the date of dissolution or all members, past and present), or whether the Crown should be entitled as *bona vacantia*. If the members are entitled, how much ought they to claim? In short, the question is: on what basis should a distribution of assets of a society be made?

So far, the courts have adopted the following three approaches to this question:

(1) *The resulting trust*

This was the original remedy adopted and it represents, in theory, a solution to the problem, although the more recent cases have considered this basis of distribution with disfavour. The approach was adopted in *Re Printers and Transferrers Society* (1899). On a dissolution of a trade union society, the court decided that the surplus was acquired by the subsisting members at the time of the dissolution. This approach was followed (with some adaptation) in *Re Printers and Transferrers Society* (1899). In this case, the surplus funds were held on resulting trust for everyone who contributed, past and present, in proportion to their contribution, but with a reduction for any benefits received from the fund.

(2) *Bona vacantia*

A second solution adopted by the courts is to assume that the members of a society who make their contributions for the benefit of others do not expect the return of their subscriptions or assets of the society on the date of liquidation. The members parted 'out and out' with their subscriptions. Accordingly, the assets of the society may be taken by the Crown as *bona vacantia*. This solution is adopted only as a last resort when the settlor and beneficiary, and no one else, is entitled to claim the property. The property being ownerless, the Crown steps in to fill the gap. In *Cunnack v Edwards* (1896), a society was formed to raise funds to provide annuities for the widows of deceased members. The personal representatives of the last widow unsuccessfully claimed the surplus funds.

A similar result was reached by the court in *Re West Sussex Constabulary's Widows, Children and Benevolent Fund Trusts* (1971). A fund was established for providing payments to widows of deceased members of the West Sussex Constabulary. Receipts were derived from four classes of contributors, namely: (a) identifiable donations and legacies; (b) members' subscriptions; (c) collecting boxes; and (d) proceeds of entertainment, sweepstakes and raffles. In 1968, the Constabulary was amalgamated with other police forces and the purpose came to an end, leaving a surplus of funds. It was held that, with the exception of contributors in category (a) (a resulting trust was set up for these contributors), the balance of the fund passed to the Crown as *bona vacantia*. The contributors within category (b) got what they bargained for, following *Cunnack v Edwards*. In any event, members' contributions were received by way of contract and not trust. The contributors in category (c) were treated as parting with their money 'out and out'. Contributors in category (d) received what they were contractually entitled to.

(3) Contractual basis

In *Cunnack v Edwards* (1896) and *Re West Sussex* (1971), the courts adopted the notion that members contributed to the society on a contractual basis, but decided on the facts that such contributions were taken by the Crown as *bona vacantia*. In more recent cases, the courts have decided that subsisting members of the association are entitled to participate in the distribution of the society's funds. Their contributions are made as an accretion to the funds of the association, by reference to the contract made *inter se*, in accordance with the rules of the society. The members control the association, subject to the constitution of the society. Equally, the subsisting members alone are entitled to the surplus funds on a dissolution, in the absence of any agreement between members to the contrary. In *Re Bucks Constabulary Widows' and Orphans' Fund Friendly Society (No 2)* (1979), the fund was established for purposes similar to those in *Re West Sussex*, but the court decided that the fund belonged to the subsisting members of the association. At all times, the members could have altered the rules and obtained the funds.

Date of dissolution

In the ordinary course of events, the date of the dissolution of an association will not be in dispute. This will be the date when a formal resolution is passed to wind up the association. But, exceptionally, an association may become inactive for an exceptionally long period of time, and the formal resolution to wind up the body may not, in itself, reflect the true state of affairs concerning the date of termination of operations. In these circumstances, the extraordinarily prolonged period of inactivity may offer strong evidence of spontaneous dissolution. The court will decide, on the facts, the precise date of dissolution. The subsisting members of the association will then be entitled to participate in the distribution of the assets. But mere inactivity, by itself, is insufficient to constitute spontaneous dissolution. The association may be treated as going through a dormant period (see *GKN Bolts and Nuts Ltd Sports and Social Club* (1982)).

10.9   Charitable trusts

A charitable trust is a trust set up to benefit society as a whole or a sufficiently large section of society.

10.9.1 Characteristics of charitable trusts

Donations for charitable purposes have always been recognised as sentiments to be encouraged, as a matter of public policy. Generally, charitable trusts are subject to the same rules as private trusts but, as a result of the public nature of such bodies, they enjoy a number of advantages over private trusts in respect of certainty of objects, the perpetuity rule, the *cy-près* rule and fiscal privileges.

Certainty of objects

A charitable trust is subject to a unique test for certainty of objects, namely, whether the objects are exclusively charitable. In other words, if the trust funds may be used solely for charitable purposes, the test will be satisfied. Indeed, it is unnecessary for the settlor or testator to specify the charitable objects. A gift 'on trust for charitable purposes' will satisfy this test. The Charity Commissioners and the courts have the jurisdiction to establish a scheme for application of the funds. In *Moggridge v Thackwell* (1807), a bequest 'to such charities as the trustee sees fit' was valid as a gift for charitable purposes.

On the other hand, if the trust funds are capable of being devoted for both charitable and non-charitable purposes, the gift may be construed as being non-charitable for these purposes. In *IRC v City of Glasgow Police Athletic Association* (1953), the association promoted both a charitable purpose (efficiency of the police force) and a non-charitable purpose (promotion of sport). The court decided that the association was not charitable.

In two circumstances, an objects clause which seeks to benefit both charitable and non-charitable purposes will not fail as a charity if:

- the non charitable purpose is construed as being incidental to the main charitable purpose. This involves a question of construction for the courts to evaluate the importance of each class of objects (see *Re Coxen* (1948)); and

- the court is able to sever the fund and devote the charitable portion of the fund for charitable purposes. This is the case where only part of the fund is payable for charitable purposes and the rest is for non-charitable purposes. In the absence of circumstances requiring a different division, the court will apply the maxim 'equality is equity' and order an equal division of the fund. In *Salusbury v Denton* (1857), severance was permitted where an unspecified part of a fund was made for charitable purposes (the relief of poverty) and the remainder for a private purpose (testator's relatives).

Perpetuity

Charities are not subject to the rule against excessive duration. But charitable gifts, like private gifts, are subject to the rule against remote vesting, that is, the subject matter of the gift is required to vest in the charity within the perpetuity period.

Cy-près doctrine

When a charitable trust fails to vest in the relevant association, the funds may be applied *cy-près* (to the nearest alternative).

Fiscal advantages

A variety of tax reliefs are enjoyed by both charitable bodies and members of the public (including companies) who donate funds for charitable purposes. A detailed analysis of such concessions is outside the scope of this book.

10.9.2 Charitable purposes

There is no statutory or judicial definition of a charity. It has been recognised that a definition of charities would have the undesirable effect of restricting the flexibility which currently exists in permitting the law to keep abreast of the changing needs of society. Most charitable bodies are required to be registered with the Charity Commissioners under s 3(2) of the Charities Act 1993. The effect of registration creates a conclusive presumption of charitable status. (See s 4(1) of the Charities Act.)

Ever since the passing of the Charitable Uses Act 1601 (sometimes referred to as the Statute of Elizabeth I), the courts developed the practice of referring to its Preamble for guidance as to charitable purposes. The preamble contained a catalogue of purposes which, at that time, were regarded as charitable. It was not intended to constitute a definition of charities. The Preamble has been expressly preserved by the s 38(4) of the Charities Act 1960.

Lord MacNaghten, in *IRC v Pemsel* (1891), classified charitable purposes into four categories: trusts for relief of poverty; trusts for the advancement of education; trusts for the advancement of religion; and trusts for other purposes beneficial to the community. An additional requirement for charitable status is that the trust exists for the public benefit, that is, the institution is required to confer some tangible benefit on the public at large or a sufficiently large section of the public. Trusts for the relief of poverty are exempt from this requirement.

The extent to which the benefit will be required to benefit the public varies according to the type of charitable purpose in question. Judges must rely on their own subjective views. The test will not be satisfied if there is a personal nexus, in blood or contract, between the donor and the beneficiaries or between the beneficiaries themselves. In *Re Compton* (1945), the test was not satisfied where the gift was on trust for the education of the children of three named relatives. In *Oppenheim v Tobacco Securities Trust Co Ltd* (1951), a gift for the education of employees and ex-employees of a company did not satisfy the public element test. The majority of their Lordships decided that, to constitute a section of the public, the beneficiaries must neither be numerically negligible nor be subject to a personal nexus. In *Gilmour v Coats* (1949), a community of 20 cloistered nuns did not satisfy this test. On the other hand, in *Neville Estates v Madden* (1962), the members of the Catford Synagogue satisfied the public element test.

Classification of charitable purposes

Relief of poverty
'Poverty' connotes that the beneficiaries are in straitened circumstances and unable to maintain a modest standard of living (determined objectively). The beneficiaries need not be destitute but must suffer from a standard of living lower than that generally enjoyed in the community. Relief may take many forms, as, for example, direct payments to the poor (*Pemsel's* case (1891)), the funding of soup kitchens (*Biscoe v Jackson* (1887)), and the provision of rest homes or flats let out at below commercial rents (*Re Cottam* (1955)). The practice of the courts has always been to exclude such trusts from the public element test. At the same time, the courts have drawn a subtle distinction between private trusts for the relief of poverty and public trusts for the same purpose. For example, a gift for the settlor's 'poor relations, A, B and C', may not be charitable but may exist as a private trust, whereas a gift for the benefit of the settlor's 'poor relations', without identifying them, may be charitable. It appears that the distinction between the two types of trust lies in the degree of precision with which the objects have been identified. The more precise the language used by the settlor in identifying the poor relations, the stronger the risk of failure as a charitable trust. This is a question of degree. In *Re Scarisbrick*

(1951), a bequest was made on trust 'for such relations of my said son and daughters as in the opinion of the survivor shall be in needy circumstances'. The court held that the gift was charitable.

The advancement of education

'Education' has been interpreted generously and is not restricted to the classroom mode of disseminating knowledge, but it does require some element of instruction or supervision. Research is capable of being construed as providing education if: (a) the subject matter is a useful object of study; (b) the knowledge acquired from the research will be disseminated to others; and (c) the public element test is satisfied (see Slade J in *McGovern v AG* (1981)). Examples of the provision of education are: gifts for the provision of scholarships and academic prizes; donations to specific educational institutions, such as universities or museums; the publication of law reports which record the development of judge made law; the promotion of artistic and cultural activities of value to the community; and the promotion of concerts and choral works of renowned composers. Expert evidence is admissible as to the value of the activity (see *Re Pinion* (1965)).

The advancement of religion

The advancement of religion was described by Donovan J in *United Grand Lodge of Freemasons in England and Wales v Holborn Borough Council* (1957):

> To advance religion means to promote it, to spread its message ever wider among mankind ... It should include religious instruction, a programme for the persuasion of unbelievers, and religious supervision to see that its members remain active and constant in the various religions they may profess.

Religion may be advanced in a variety of ways, such as: the maintenance of places of worship, including the upkeep of churchyards; gifts for the clergy; the provision of an organ or maintenance of a choir; and the active spread of religion at home and abroad. A gift for 'parish work' will be void for including many objects which are not charitable (see *Farley v Westminster Bank* (1939)). On the other hand, in *Re South Place Ethical Society* (1980), it was decided that the study and dissemination of ethical principles which did not involve faith in a deity could not constitute religion. The society was charitable on the ground of advancement of education.

Unlike trusts for the advancement of education, the courts do not evaluate the merit of one religion as opposed to another or, indeed, the benefit of religious instruction to the public. Provided that the religious gift is not subversive of all morality, the gift will be charitable.

A gift for the saying of masses in public is charitable, for the gift promotes an integral part of religion, namely, the saying of prayers. The *prima facie* assumption is that prayers are assumed to be said in public, until the contrary is established (see *Re Hetherington* (1989)).

Other purposes beneficial to the community

The approach of the courts under this head is to treat the examples stated in the Preamble as a means of guidance for deciding on the validity of the relevant purpose. Two approaches have been adopted by the courts:

- *Reasoning by analogy*

  The approach here is to ascertain whether a purpose has some resemblance to an example stated in the Preamble or to an earlier decided case which was considered charitable. For example, the provision of a crematorium was considered charitable by analogy with 'the repair of churches' as stated in the Preamble in *Scottish Burial Reform and Cremation Society v City of Glasgow Corporation* (1968). In that case, a crematorium was found to be a charitable body.

- *The spirit and intendment of the Preamble*

  This approach is much wider than the previous approach. The courts decide if the purpose of the organisation is 'within the spirit and intendment' or 'within the equity' of the statute, unhindered by the specific purposes as stated in the Preamble (see *Incorporated Council of Law Reporting v AG* (1972): law reporting was a charitable activity).

Illustrations of charitable purposes under this head

Animals

A trust which promotes the welfare of animals generally, as opposed to benefiting specific animals, is charitable because it promotes public morality (see *Re Wedgewood* (1915)).

It is essential to establish that the welfare of the animals provide some benefit to mankind, albeit indirect. Failure to establish such a benefit was fatal in *National Anti-Vivisection Society v IRC* (1948).

The relief of the aged and impotent

The Preamble specifically refers to 'the relief of the aged, impotent and poor people'. The words have been construed disjunctively and objects need not qualify on all three grounds. (See *Joseph Rowntree Memorial Trust Housing Association v AG* (1983)). In this case, a scheme of dwelling houses for the elderly (males aged at least 65 and females aged 60 and over) was charitable.

Recreational facilities

The promotion of sport *simpliciter* is not charitable, as such an activity is not within the Preamble or the spirit and intendment of the Preamble (see *IRC v City of Glasgow Police Athletic Association* (1953) (sport within the police force)). However, with appropriate drafting, sport within a school may be treated as charitable for the advancement of education (see *IRC v McMullen* (1981), which concerned the encouragement of the playing of football in schools).

In *IRC v Baddeley* (1955), the House of Lords was in doubt as to whether the provision of recreational facilities was charitable. The Recreational Charities Act 1958 was passed in order to clarify the law. The Act stipulates that the provision of recreational facilities shall be charitable if two criteria are fulfilled: the public benefit test; and the test of 'social welfare'.

Under the Act, the 'social welfare' test will be satisfied if two conditions are complied with. The first requirement is that the facilities are provided with the object of improving the conditions of life of the beneficiaries (s 1(2)(a)). The second requirement may be satisfied in alternative ways, by proving either that the facilities are available to a limited class of objects who have a need for such facilities by virtue of one or more of the factors enumerated within s 1(2)(b)(i) (such as a youth club or an organised outing for orphaned children) or that the facilities are available to 'the entire public' (such as a public swimming pool or a public park) or 'female members of the public' (women's institutes, etc).

In *Guild v IRC* (1992), the House of Lords decided that the material issue concerns the nature of the facilities rather than the status of the participants. *Per* Lord Keith: 'Hyde Park improves the conditions of life for residents in Mayfair and Belgravia as much as those in Pimlico or the Portobello Road.' In this case, a devise of land by will for use as a sports centre in North Berwick gained charitable status.

Miscellaneous examples

Other charitable purposes decided under Lord MacNaghten's fourth heading include: the encouragement and advancement of choral singing (*Royal Choral Society v IRC* (1943)); gifts for the promotion of the defence of the UK (*Re Good* (1905)); gifts for the production of better organists and better organ music (*Re Levien* (1955)); a gift to provide a local fire brigade (*Re Wokingham Fire Brigade Trusts* (1951)); a trust to relieve hardship and suffering by the local people as a result of a disaster (*Re North Devon and West Somerset Relief Fund Trusts* (1953)) (but it is imperative that the size of the class of beneficiaries be sufficiently large to satisfy the public element test); the promotion of industry, commerce and art (*Crystal Palace Trustees v Minister of Town and Country Planning* (1950)); the general improvement of agriculture (*IRC v Yorkshire Agricultural Society* (1928)); a gift to the inhabitants of a town or village (*Goodman v Saltash Corporation* (1882)); a gift 'to my country, England' (*Re Smith* (1932); and a gift 'to the Queen's Chancellor of the Exchequer' (*Nightingale v Goulburn* (1849)).

Political purposes

Political purposes include attempts to change the law and gifts to further the objects of political parties. A trust for political purposes is incapable of subsisting as a charity because the court may not stultify itself by deciding that it is in the public good for the law to be changed (see *National Anti-Vivisection Society v IRC* and *McGovern v IRC* (1948)).

Cy-près *doctrine*

Where property is donated for charitable purposes but the purposes cannot be carried out (initially or subsequently), the trust objectives will not necessarily fail. The *cy-près* doctrine enables the court and the Charity Commissioners to make a scheme for the application of the funds for other charitable purposes as closely as possible (*cy-près*) to those intended by the donor.

There are only two conditions to be satisfied for a *cy-près* application:

- the impossibility or impracticality of carrying out the original charitable purpose or the existence of a surplus of funds after the charitable purpose has been fulfiled; and

- the manifestation of a general charitable intention by the donor, as opposed to a specific charitable intention.

Impossibility

Section 13 of the Charities Act 1993 (which re-enacts s 13 of the Charities Act 1960) consolidates to some extent and substantially extends the powers of the Charity Commissioners and the courts to apply property *cy-près*. The circumstances when the purposes of the charity will become impractical or impossible are enacted in s 13(1)(a)–(e) of the Charities Act 1993:

> 13(1)(a) ... where the original purposes wholly or partly have been as far as may be fulfilled, or cannot be carried out according to the directions given and to the spirit of the gift.

This sub-section gives the court the jurisdiction to decide that the original purposes of the gift have been fulfilled or have become impractical. The only restriction on the discretion of the court is in regard to the construction of the expression 'spirit of the gift'. This phrase has been interpreted by Pennycuick VC, in *Re Lepton's Charity* (1972), as meaning 'the basic intention underlying the gift, as ascertained from its terms in the light of admissible evidence'. In this case, a testator who died in 1716 devised specific property to trustees on trust to pay an annual sum of £3 to the Protestant Minister in Pudsey, and the surplus income to the poor and aged people of Pudsey. In 1716, the total income was £5. On the date of the application to the court, that income was £790 per annum. The court held that, on a construction of the will, the minister was not entitled to three-fifths of the annual income but only a fixed sum of £3 per annum. However, having regard to the spirit of the gift, a *cy-près* scheme would be approved, entitling the minister to £100 per annum:

> 13(1)(b) ...where the original purposes provide a use for part only of the property available by virtue of the gift.

The approval of the court may be granted under this paragraph where a surplus of funds are left over after the original charitable purposes have been carried out. This paragraph merely declares the law that existed before 1960 (see *Re North Devon and West Somerset Relief Fund* (1953)):

> 13(1)(c) ... where the property available by virtue of the gift and other property applicable for similar purposes can be more effectively used in conjunction with property held for common purposes, regard being had to the spirit of the gift.

This provision enables a number of small charities with common purposes to be amalgamated in order to create larger funds (see *Re Faraker* (1912)):

> 13(1)(d) ... where the original purposes were laid down by reference to an area which has ceased to be a unit, or by reference to a class of persons or to an area which has ceased to be suitable or practicable, regard being had to the spirit of the gift.

Under this sub-section, the court is entitled to consider that the original class of beneficiaries has become difficult to identify or that the class of beneficiaries has dwindled over the years. See *AG v City of London* (1790), where a fund for the advancement of the Christian religion among infidels in Virginia was applied *cy-près*:

> 13(1)(e) ... where the original purposes, in whole or in part, have, since they were laid down:
>
> (i) been adequately provided for by other reasons; or
>
> (ii) ceased, as being useless or harmful to the community, or, for other reasons, to be in law charitable; or
>
> (iii) ceased in any other way to provide a suitable and effective method of using the property given, regard being had to the spirit of the gift.

Sub-section (e)(i) empowers the court to modify the original purposes as stated by the donor, in view of the charitable purposes being provided for by other bodies.

Sub-section (e)(ii) will rarely be used. It assumes that a purpose was once charitable but, owing to changed circumstances, the purpose ceases to be charitable. An example of this is the Anti-Vivisection Society.

Sub-section (e)(iii) enacts a wide ranging provision giving the courts the power to consider whether the original purposes selected by the donor represent an effective method of using the property. In *Re Lepton's Charity* (1972), the court assumed jurisdiction under, *inter alia*, s 13(1)(e)(iii) to sanction the scheme.

General charitable intention

This is the second condition which is required to be fulfilled before the charitable funds may be applied *cy-près*.

Subsequent failure

The courts have dispensed with the need to prove a general charitable intention when the charitable body exists at the appropriate date of vesting but which ceases to exist subsequently. In *Re Wright* (1954), a remainder interest by will to found and maintain a convalescent home for needy women was viable on the date of the testatrix's death but impracticable on the subsequent death of the life tenant. The court decided that the fund was applied *cy-près*.

Initial failure

In the event of an initial failure of the charitable institution, it is essential to prove a general charitable intention before the funds are applied *cy-près*. The intention of the donor is essentially a question of fact. The courts are required to consider all the circumstances in order to determine whether the donor intended to benefit a charitable 'purpose' *simpliciter*, identified by reference to a charitable institution (paramount charitable intention), or whether the settlor's intention was to benefit a specifically identified charitable body.

The court adopted a broad approach to this question in *Re Lysaght* (1966), where a bequest by will was made to the Royal College of Surgeons (the trustees) to apply the income in establishing studentships, subject to a religious bar. The college declined to accept the gift with the religious bar. The court decided that, in accordance with the paramount charitable intention of the testatrix (to make the college a trustee), the religious bar would be deleted.

Form and substance

A gift may appear, in form, to provide for a particular purpose but, on construction, the court may decide that the paramount intention of the donor in substance is to promote a general charitable intention. *Re Lysaght* (above) is an example of this principle. Alternatively, the donor may make a gift which, in both form and substance, promotes a specific charitable intention. In the latter type of case, there is no room for the application of the *cy-près* principle. In *Re Good* (1950), the provision of a detailed scheme for the provision of rest home in Hull proved impracticable. This was evidence of a specific charitable intention.

Non-existent charitable bodies

The identification by the donor of a named charitable institution which had never existed may be construed as a reference to a purpose for which the donor intended to devote his funds. This is evidence of a general charitable intention. In *Re Harwood* (1936), a donation to a non-existent body referred to as the 'Peace Society of Belfast' was construed a general charitable intention to promote peace in Belfast.

Incorporated and unincorporated associations

An incorporated association, as distinct from an unincorporated association, has an independent legal existence distinct from its members. In *Re Vernon's Will Trust* (1972), Buckley J expressed the view that a gift to a corporate charity is *prima facie* intended to take effect as a beneficial gift to the named body and will lapse if the charity ceases to exist before the testator's death. On the other hand, a gift to an unincorporated association *prima facie* takes effect for the purposes of the association. The named unincorporated association is treated as the trustee in order to carry out the charitable purpose. Accordingly, if the association ceases to exist, the court is entitled to use its inherent jurisdiction to ensure that the trust will not fail for want of a trustee, and may appoint new trustees to continue the charitable purposes. (This *prima facie* rule may be rebutted by evidence which shows that the gift was dependent upon the continued existence of the particular trustees.) In *Re Finger's Will Trust* (1972), a testatrix left shares of her residuary estate to various charities, two of which had ceased to exist by the date of her death. One of these was an unincorporated association. It was held that the gift was for charitable purposes and, as such purposes were still sought, a *cy-près* scheme was ordered. The other charity was a corporation and, *prima facie,* the gift was to the corporation itself and not for its purposes. However, on the facts, it was possible to find a general charitable intention.

Section 14 of the Charities Act 1993 (re-enacting s 14 of the Charities Act 1960)

The general rule, as detailed above, is that property given for a specific charitable purpose which fails from the outset cannot be applied *cy-près* if no general charitable intention can be imputed to the donor. Such property will be held on resulting trust for the donor.

By way of exception to that general rule, s 14 of the Charities Act 1993 enacts that property given for specific charitable purposes which fail shall be applicable *cy-près* as if given for charitable purposes generally. This is generally the case where the property belongs to a donor who cannot be identified or found after reasonable inquiries and advertisements have been made or who disclaims his right to the property in writing.

10.10 Appointment, retirement and removal of trustees

There are only two occasions when it may be necessary to appoint trustees:

- on the creation of a new trust – whether *inter vivos* or by will; and

- during the continuance of an existing trust, either in replacement of a trustee or as an additional trustee.

10.10.1   Creation of a new trust

Where, in the purported creation of a trust *inter vivos*, the settlor fails to nominate trustees, the intended trust will be imperfect.

Where a trust is created by will but the testator does not name trustees in his will, or the trustees named are unwilling or unable to act, a replacement trustee will be appointed as on a continuance of the trust (see 10.10.2). The principle applied here is that 'equity will not allow a trust to fail for want of a trustee'.

10.10.2   Continuance of the trust

When a trust is created (whether *inter vivos* or by will), the trust property (real or personal) vests in all the trustees as joint tenants. The effect is that, on the death of a trustee, the property devolves on the survivors (see s 18(1) of the Trustee Act 1925).

On the death of the sole or surviving trustee, the property vests in his personal representatives, subject to the trust, until replacement trustees are appointed (see s 18(2) of the Trustee Act 1925).

The authority to appoint replacement trustees is derived from three sources:

- express power;
- statutory power;
- the courts.

In *Re Higginbottom* (1892), the majority of the beneficiaries under a trust were not able to prevent the sole executrix of the sole surviving trustee from appointing new trustees.

Express power

The trust instrument may confer the authority to appoint a trustee. This is exceptional, for the statutory power to appoint is generally regarded as adequate. The express authority may be 'general' or 'special'. A general authority is one which confers an authority to appoint trustees in any circumstances. If the authority is special (that is, exercisable in limited circumstances), it would be strictly construed by the courts. In *Re Wheeler and De Rochow* (1896), a nominee was entitled to appoint trustees in specified circumstances, including the occasion when a trustee became 'incapable' of acting. One of the trustees became bankrupt. The court decided that this made him 'unfit' but not incapable of acting as a trustee. Thus, the nominee did not have the authority to appoint.

Statutory power (s 36 of the Trustee Act 1925)

The statutory power to appoint trustees is contained in s 36 of the Trustee Act 1925 (replacing the Trustee Act 1893). The occasions giving rise to the need to appoint trustees are enacted in s 36(1) (replacement trustees) and s 36(6) (additional trustees).

10.10.3 Replacement trustees (s 36(1))

There are seven circumstances listed in s 36(1) when a replacement trustee may be appointed. These are:

(1) Where a trustee is dead. Under s 36(8), this includes the person nominated as trustee under a will but predeceasing the testator.

(2) Where a trustee remains outside the UK for a continuous period of 12 months or more. The motive for remaining outside the UK is irrelevant, so this condition will be satisfied even if the trustee remains outside the UK against his will.

(3) Where a trustee desires to be discharged from all or any of the trusts or powers reposed in or conferred on him. Thus, a trustee may retire from part only of the trust.

(4) Where a trustee refuses to act. This includes the occasion when the trustee disclaims his office. It is advisable that the disclaimer be executed by deed.

(5) Where a trustee is unfit to act. Unfitness refers to some defect in the character of the trustee which creates an element of risk in leaving the property in the hands of the individual. For example, a conviction for an offence involving dishonesty or bankruptcy (see *Re Wheeler and De Rochow* (1896)).

(6) Where a trustee is incapable of acting. Incapacity refers to some physical or mental inability to adequately administer the trust, but does not include bankruptcy (see *Re Wheeler and De Rochow* (1896)).

(7) Where the trustee is an infant, that is, under the age of 18. Such a person may become a trustee under an implied trust (resulting or constructive).

Persons who may exercise the statutory power

Section 36(1) of the Trustee Act lists, in chronological order, the persons who are entitled to exercise the statutory power of appointing replacement trustees. These are:

(a) the person or persons nominated in the trust instrument for the purpose of appointing new trustees (see 10.10.2);

(b) the surviving or continuing trustee, if willing to act. Section 36(1) was enacted to empower a sole retiring trustee to appoint his successor. It enables a 'retiring' or 'refusing' trustee to participate with the surviving trustees in appointing a successor (sub-ss (6), (8) of the Trustee Act 1925);

(c) the personal representatives of the last surviving or continuing trustee.

10.10.4 Additional trustees (s 36(6))

Section 36(6) authorises the appointment of additional trustees, although no trustee needs to be replaced when:

...

(a) the person or persons nominated for the purpose of appointing new trustees by the instrument, if any, creating the trust; or

(b) if there is no such person, or no such person able and willing to act, then the trustee or trustees for the time being,

may, by writing, appoint another person or other persons to be an additional trustee or additional trustees ...

This sub-section is self-explanatory, but it may be observed that a trust corporation (corporate professional trustee, such as a bank or an insurance company) has the power of two or more individual trustees. No power exists under s 36(6) to increase the number of trustees beyond four.

10.10.5 Direction of the beneficiaries

Sections 19–21 of the Trusts of Land and Appointment of Trustees Act (TLATA) 1996 have invested new powers in the beneficiaries to direct a retirement and/or appoint trustees. These provisions relate to trusts of all types of property (whether land or personalty). But the provisions may be excluded in whole or in part by the trust.

Section 19 applies where there is no person nominated under the trust instrument to appoint new trustees, and all the beneficiaries are of full age and capacity and collectively are absolutely entitled to the trust property. The beneficiaries have either one or both of the following rights: a right to direct in writing that one or more of the trustees shall retire from the trust; and/or a right that a named person or persons be appointed, in writing, as new trustee or trustees. The direction may be by way of substitution for a trustee or trustees directed to retire or as an additional trustee or trustees.

Section 20 of TLATA 1996 enacts a similar provision where the trustee becomes mentally incapable of exercising his functions.

Section 36(7) of the Trustee Act 1925 (as amended by TLATA) enacts that the effect of an appointment under s 36 or ss 19 or 20 of TLATA shall have the same consequences 'as if he had been originally appointed a trustee by the instrument, if any, creating the trust'.

10.10.6   The number of trustees

Realty

Section 34 of the Trustee Act (as amended by TLATA) provides that, where land is held on trust, there may not be more than four trustees. If the instrument purports to appoint more than four trustees, only the first four named as trustees will take the property.

On the other hand, while a sole trusteeship is not forbidden, s 14(2) of the Trustee Act enacts that a sole trustee (other than a trust corporation) may not give a valid receipt for the proceeds of sale.

Personalty

In theory, there is no restriction on the number of persons who may be appointed trustees of personalty. The office of trusteeship requires unanimous approval of all the trustees (charities are treated as an exception).

In practice, it may be inconvenient and cumbersome to have too many trustees. But the law does not recognise a 'sleeping' or inactive trustee. A breach may be committed by a 'sleeping' trustee in failing to oppose a decision taken by his colleagues (see *Bahin v Hughes* (1886)).

There are rarely more than four trustees and, if the appointment is made under s 36 of the Trustee Act, there will be not more than four trustees.

On the other hand, a sole trustee is most unsatisfactory because of the danger or risks of fraud or misconduct in administering the trust.

10.10.7   Vesting of trust property in trustees

On an appointment of replacement or additional trustees, the trust property is required to be vested in the new trustee or trustees to enable him or them to carry out his or their duties. Trustees hold the property as joint tenants so that the right of survivorship applies.

The vesting of the property in new trustees may be effected in one of two ways:

- by a conveyance or transfer effective to vest the property in the transferee; or

- under s 40(1) and (2) of the Trustee Act 1925, which create short form and inexpensive methods of vesting the trust property in the new trustee or trustees. Under s 40(1)(a), if the deed merely declares that the property vests in the new trustee, this would be sufficient without a conveyance, etc. Section 40(1)(b) enacts that, if the deed of appointment omits to include a vesting declaration, it will be treated as if it had contained one.

However, s 40(4) of the Trustee Act 1925 excludes certain types of properties from the general provisions in s 40(1) and (2). These include land held by trustees on a mortgage, certain leases, and stocks and shares.

These properties are required to be transferred in accordance with the appropriate formalities for that type of property.

10.10.8   Appointment by the court

Section 41 gives the court the sweeping power to appoint new trustees, either as replacement or additional trustees:

> The court may, whenever it is expedient to appoint a new trustee or new trustees, and it is found inexpedient, difficult or impracticable so to do without the assistance of the court, make an order appointing a new trustee or new trustees either in substitution for or in addition to any existing trustee or trustees, or although there is no existing trustee ...

The court will only exercise its power to appoint trustees when all other avenues have been exhausted. The most popular occasions when this power may be exercised are: where a sole surviving trustee dies intestate; where an appointor is incapable of making an appointment because he is an infant; where all the trustees of a testamentary trust predecease the testator; or where there is friction between the trustees.

In exercising its discretion under s 41, the court will have regard to the wishes of the settlor, the interests of the beneficiaries and the efficient administration of the trust. In *Re Tempest* (1866), the court decided that a nominated person was unsuitable to be appointed as trustee, in order to avoid family dissension.

10.10.9   Retirement

A trustee may retire from the trust in one of five ways:

(1) by taking advantage of a power in the trust instrument;

(2) by taking advantage of a statutory power under:
   - s 36(1) of the Trustee Act 1925 when a new trustee is appointed; or
   - s 39 of the Trustee Act 1925 where no new trustee is appointed;

(3) by obtaining the consent of all the beneficiaries who are *sui juris* and absolutely entitled to the trust property under the *Saunders v Vautier* principle;

(4) by direction from the relevant beneficiaries under s 19 of TLATA 1996; or

(5) by obtaining the authority of the court.

Unlike a retirement under s 36(1), a trustee is not allowed to retire from part of a trust under s 39. The procedure for retirement under s 39 is as follows:

- at least two individuals will continue to act as trustees or a trust corporation;

- the remaining trustees (or trustee) and other persons empowered to appoint trustees consent to the retirement by deed; and

- the retiring trustee makes such a declaration by deed.

It should be noted that a retiring trustee remains liable for breaches of trust committed whilst he was a trustee. He is absolved from liability in respect of subsequent breaches, unless he retired in order to facilitate a breach of trust (see *Head v Gould* (1898)).

Retirement under a court order

Generally speaking, the court will not discharge a trustee under its statutory jurisdiction under s 41 unless it appoints a replacement trustee. However, the court has an inherent jurisdiction to discharge a trustee without replacement, in accordance with its responsibility to administer the trust. This will be the position when s 39 is not applicable because the appropriate consent cannot be obtained.

10.10.10 Removal of trustees

A trustee may be removed from office in one of the following four ways:

- by virtue of a power contained in the trust instrument. This is highly unusual and requires construction of the trust instrument;

- under s 36 of the Trustee Act 1925. This involves the removal of and appointment of a replacement trustee in circumstances laid down in s 36(1) (see 10.10.3);

- in the circumstances specified in ss 19 and 20 of TLATA 1996;

- under a court order under s 41 of the Trustee Act or under the inherent jurisdiction of the court.

Court order

Under s 41 of the Trustee Act, the court has the jurisdiction to remove an existing trustee and appoint a replacement trustee (see above).

Under its inherent jurisdiction to secure the proper administration of the trust, the court has the power to remove a trustee without appointing a replacement trustee. In *Letterstedt v Broers* (1884), the Privy Council declared that the court has a general duty to ensure that the trusts were properly executed and their main guide was the welfare of the beneficiaries.

Accordingly, friction and hostility between the trustees and beneficiaries which is likely to prejudice the proper administration of the trust may be a ground for the removal of trustees.

10.11   Duties and powers of trustees

The duties of a trustee are varied and extremely onerous. They are required to be executed with the utmost diligence and good faith. Otherwise, he will be liable for breach of trust. The primary duty of the trustee is to comply with the terms of the trust and, subject thereto, to act in the best interests of the beneficiaries. In order to carry out these duties, the trustee is invested with a variety of powers and discretions which are required to be exercised for the benefit of the beneficiaries.

10.11.1   The duty and standard of care

Throughout the administration of the trust, the trustees are required to exhibit an objective standard of skill as would be expected from an ordinary prudent man of business (see *Learoyd v Whiteley* (1887)).

In the case of a power of investment, the duty must be exercised so as to yield the best return for all the beneficiaries, judged in relation to the risks inherent in the investments, the prospects of the yield of income and capital appreciation.

The courts will have regard to all the circumstances of each case in order to ascertain whether the trustees' conduct fell below the standard expected of such persons.

In considering the investment policy of the trust, the trustees are required to put their own personal interests and views on one side. They may have strong social or political views. They may be firmly opposed to any investments in companies connected with alcohol, tobacco, armaments or many other things. In the conduct of their own affairs, trustees are free to abstain from making any such investments. However, in performance of their fiduciary duties, if investments of the morally reprehensible type would be more beneficial to the beneficiaries than other investments, the trustees must not refrain from making the investments by reason of the views that they hold. Trustees may even act dishonourably (though not illegally) if the interests of their beneficiaries require it, as in *Buttle v Saunders* (1950). Here, trustees struck a bargain for the sale of trust property, but the bargain was not legally binding. The court held that the trustees were under a duty to consider and explore a better offer received by them. Similarly, in *Cowan v Scargill and Others* (1984), the defendants were trustees of the Mineworkers Pension Scheme who raised an objection to a new investment plan of trust funds in competing forms of energy. The court decided that the plan would yield the best return for the beneficiaries and refused the application.

In an action for breach of trust, the claimant is required to establish that the trust has suffered a loss which is attributable to the conduct or omission of the trustees. If the trustees' conduct or omission fell below the required standard imposed on trustees, they become personally liable, whether they acted in good faith or not. In *Re Lucking's Will Trust* (1968), a trustee-director of a company was liable to the trust when he allowed the managing director to appropriate £15,000 of the company funds through the delivery of blank cheques to the managing director which were signed by the trustee.

With regard to professional trustees, such as banks and insurance companies, the standard of care imposed on such bodies is higher than the degree of diligence expected from a non-professional trustee. The professional trustee is required to administer the trust with such a degree of expertise as would be expected from a specialist in trust administration. This objective standard is applied by the courts after due consideration of the facts of each case.

In *Bartlett v Barclays Bank* (1980), a trust corporation, in managing a property development company, did not actively participate in the company's deliberations, nor was it provided with regular information concerning the company's activities, but was content to rely on the annual balance sheet and profit and loss account. One of the schemes pursued by the company proved to be disastrous. In an action brought against the trustee, the court held that the trustee was liable, because it (the trust corporation) had not acted reasonably in the administration of the trust.

On the other hand, the claimant failed in her action in *Nestle v National Westminster Bank* (1993) on the ground that she failed to prove positively that the defendant's action or inaction resulted in a loss to the trust.

10.11.2 Duty to act unanimously

Trustees are required to act unanimously. The settlor has given all of his trustees the responsibility to act on behalf of the trust. Subject to provisions to the contrary in the trust instrument, the acts and decisions of some of the trustees (even a majority of trustees) are not binding on the others. Thus, once a trust decision is made, the trustees become jointly and severally liable to the beneficiaries in the event of a breach of trust. In *Bahin v Hughes* (1886), 'passive' trustees were liable to the beneficiaries for breach of trust along with an 'active' trustee.

A claim by one trustee against his co-trustee is now subject to the Civil Liability (Contribution) Act 1978. A trustee who is sued for breach of trust may claim a contribution from his co-trustee. The court has a discretion to make a contribution order if it 'is just and equitable, having regard to the extent of the (co-trustee's) responsibility for the damage in question'.

10.11.3 Duty to act personally

Generally speaking, a trustee is appointed by a settlor because of his personal qualities. It is expected that the trustee will act personally in the execution of his duties. The general rule is *delegatus non potest delegare.*

However, in the current commercial climate, it is unrealistic to expect trustees to act personally in all matters relating to the trust. Accordingly, trustees are entitled to appoint agents to perform acts in respect of the trust.

Under s 23(1) of the Trustee Act 1925 (consolidating previous provisions), trustees may appoint agents to transact trust business, even if the trustees themselves could have properly conducted the transaction. Of course, the trustees are required to exercise care in making the appointment and are entitled to pay the agent for his services.

In *Fry v Tapson* (1884), trustees were liable for loss in failing to exercise care in appointing an agent.

But s 23(1) declares that the trustee 'shall not be responsible for the default of such agent if employed in good faith'. Furthermore, s 30(1) of the Trustee Act enacts that the trustee is answerable for his own acts, receipts, neglects or defaults and not for those of other persons 'unless the same happens through his own wilful default'. The question in issue is, to what extent may a trustee be liable for the acts of an agent if the latter was appointed in good faith? In other words, what is meant by the phrase 'wilful default'?

In the leading case of *Re Vickery* (1931), the expression was described as involving 'a consciousness of negligence or breach of duty or recklessness'. In this case, the defendant, an executor, appointed a solicitor to wind up an estate. The solicitor ultimately absconded with moneys belonging to the estate. In the ensuing action, the court held that the defendant was not liable for wilful default because he did not act with the intention to commit a breach, nor did he act recklessly in the sense of not caring whether his act constituted a breach or not.

Although the *Vickery* test has been subjected to severe criticism, in *Re Lucking*, Cross J decided that the trustee retains his duty of care and may be liable for breach of trust if he does not act like a prudent man of business in supervising the actions of the agent.

10.11.4 Delegation under the Trusts of Land and Appointment of Trustees Act 1996

Section 9 of TLATA 1996 enacts that trustees of land may delegate any of their powers in relation to the land by a power of attorney to adult beneficiaries who are currently entitled to interests in possession. The powers of trustees are 'all the powers of an absolute owner' (s 6). In exercising their powers, trustees may not favour or prejudice the interest of any beneficiary. It should be noted that the powers included in s 6 relate only to a trust of land and not to any personal property. In addition, the s 6 powers may be amended or excluded by the settlement, or made subject to obtaining the consent of any person (s 8). Thus, the settlor may prevent any dealing with the land (although this could be challenged under s 14 (see 10.7.1). In the case of charitable trusts, the trustees' powers may not be amended or excluded, but they may be made subject to obtaining consent.

10.11.5   Protection of purchasers from delegate

In respect of land, it is presumed that the trustees were entitled to delegate to a certain person, unless the purchaser had knowledge at the time of the transaction that the trustees were not entitled to delegate to that person (s 9(2)). 'Knowledge' for these purposes has not been defined in the legislation, but it is submitted that, since we are concerned here with a proprietary interest, any type of cognisance will suffice for these purposes, even constructive knowledge.

10.11.6   Exclusion clauses

Exclusion clauses which are validly inserted into trust instruments may have the effect of limiting the liability of trustees. Such clauses are not, without more, void on public policy grounds. Moreover, provided the clause does not purport to exclude the basic minimum duties ordinarily imposed on trustees, it may be valid. Some of the minimum duties which cannot be excluded are the duties of honesty, good faith and acting for the benefit of the beneficiaries (see *Armitage v Nurse* (1997)). Much depends on the wording of such clauses. *Prima facie*, any ambiguities are construed against the trustees. See *Wight v Olswang* (1999). In this case, a trust settlement incorporated two conflicting exemption clauses, one protecting all trustees from liability for breach of trust (a general exemption clause) and the other applied only to unpaid trustees. The court decided that the paid trustees could not rely on the general exemption clause.

10.11.7   Duty to provide accounts and information

Owing to the nature of the fiduciary character of trustees, a duty is imposed on them to keep proper accounts for the trust. In pursuance of this objective, the trustees may employ an agent (an accountant) to draw up the trust accounts. The beneficiaries are entitled to inspect the accounts, but if they need copies they are required to pay for these from their own resources.

In addition, the beneficiaries are entitled to inspect documents created in the course of the administration of the trust. These are trust documents and are *prima facie* the property of the beneficiaries. Indeed, 'trust documents' were described by Salmon LJ in *Re Marquess of Londonderry's Settlement* (1965) as possessing the following characteristics:

- they are documents in the possession of the trustees as trustees;

- they contain information about the trust which the beneficiaries are entitled to know; and

- the beneficiaries have a proprietary interest in the documents and, accordingly, are entitled to see them.

10.11.8   Powers of investment

Trustees have an obligation to maintain the real value of trust funds and may need to consider investing the trust property. An 'investment' for these purposes refers to property which will produce an income yield (see *Re Wragg* (1918–19)). The trustees are required to consider the investment policy of the trust with the standard of care expected from an ordinary prudent man of business. The powers of investment may exist in the trust instrument or may be implied by statute, or the court may enlarge the power of the trustees.

Express power

A prudent settlor will include a wide investment clause in the trust instrument, in order to give the trustees the maximum flexibility in the selection of investments. The modern approach of the courts is to construe investment clauses liberally (see *Re Harari's Settlement* (1949)).

10.11.9   Statutory power under the Trustee Investments Act 1961

The Trustee Investments Act 1961 structures investments into three categories, namely, Pts I and II ('narrow range' investments) and Pt III ('wider range' investments).

The investments detailed in Pt I include defence bonds and National Savings Certificates, and may be described as 'small savings' investments. There is no obligation on the trustees to seek advice before investing. The capital value of these investments do not fluctuate. Part II investments include debentures in UK companies which comply with a number of conditions and fixed interest investments issued by local or public companies. The trustees are required to seek written advice (s 6(5)) from a person whom the trustees reasonably believe to be qualified to give it by reason of ability and experience. The wider range investments created by Pt III of Sched 1 to the Act include unit trusts, shares in certain UK companies and shares in building societies.

An authorised investment in shares and debentures in UK companies is required to satisfy the following conditions laid down in para (3) of Pt IV of Sched 1:

- the shares are quoted on the stock exchange;

- the shares are fully paid up or are issued on terms that they will be fully paid up within nine months from the date of issue;

- the company has a total issued and has paid share capital of at least £1 million;

- the company is required to have paid a dividend in each of the preceding five years on all of its shares.

Division of the fund (s 2(1))

The scheme of the Act requires the trustees who wish to invest in wider range investments to value the fund and divide it into two unequal parts (25% and 75%), the narrower and wider range parts respectively. This division is permanent and the two parts are kept distinct. After a division of the fund, there is no obligation on the trustees to invest the wider range part of the fund entirely in wider range investments, provided a portion of the fund is so used. The remainder of the fund may only be invested in narrower range investments. Moreover, if property is transferred from either part of the fund to the other part, a 'compensating transfer' in the opposite direction is required to be made. Thus, if property from the narrower range part of the fund is transferred to the wider range part, a compensating transfer to the narrower range part is required to be made as soon as possible.

Accruals

If property accrues to the trustees, as owners of property, comprised in either part of the fund, it shall be treated as belonging to that fund. For example, a bonus issue of shares will belong to the fund which comprised the shares.

Withdrawals

Generally speaking, s 2(4) provides that a withdrawal of funds in the exercise of any power or duty of the trustees may be made from either part of the fund at the discretion of the trustees. This provision has the effect of abrogating the '25/75% rule', but was inserted into the Act in order to give the trustees a greater latitude in performing their powers.

However, if the trustees wish to withdraw funds in order to form a separate trust, the withdrawal may be made at the trustees' discretion. The division of the fund of the new trust need not be on a 25/75% basis (assuming the trustees of the new trust wish to invest in wider range investments) but may be effected in the form of one of the following alternative modes:

- 25/75%; or

- in the same proportion to each other as the two corresponding parts of the original fund bore at the time of the appropriation; or

- in some intermediate proportion (see s 4(3)).

Special range investments

Section 3(1) declares that, if property is acquired as a result of additional powers conferred on the trustees by the trust instrument or by the court, such property will comprise a 'special range' part of the fund.

Special duty of diversification

In addition to the general duty of care imposed on trustees, the Act imposes a special duty on the trustees to have regard to the need for securing 'diversification' of the investments and to consider the suitability to the trust of the investments proposed (s 6(1)).

Mortgages of land

Under s 8 of the Trustee Act 1925, which consolidated previous statutory provisions, trustees are authorised to lend trust moneys by way of a mortgage, provided that the following conditions are satisfied:

- the trustees are required to act on a report as to the value of the property made out by a person whom they reasonably believed to be an able practical surveyor or valuer, instructed and employed independently of any owner of the property;

- the amount of the loan must not exceed two-thirds of the value of the property as stated in the report. This is the upper limit. If the loan exceeds the upper limit but is otherwise proper in the circumstances, the trustees may be liable for breach of trust in respect of the excess amount (see s 9 of the Trustee Act 1925 (which replaced s 8 of the Trustee Act 1893) and *Shaw v Cates* (1909));

- the loan is made on the advice of the surveyor or valuer as expressed in the report.

Subject to the above conditions, a loan secured on the mortgage of land is an authorised investment under the Trustee Investments Act 1961, falling within the narrower range investments requiring advice (Pt II of Sched 1), if it is made on a mortgage of freehold land in the UK or a leasehold which has more than 60 years to run.

Purchase of land

The Trustee Investments Act 1961 does not treat the purchase of land as an authorised investment, but, under the Settled Land Act 1925, trust moneys may be invested in freehold land or leasehold property with not less than 60 years to run. The settlor may authorise the purchase of land in the trust instrument.

Moreover, under s 6 of TLATA 1996, trustees of land have the 'powers of an absolute owner'. These include the power to buy a legal estate in land as an investment for the trust or for occupation by any beneficiary (including the right to impose conditions on such beneficiaries), or for any other reason (s 6(4)). Where the land is leasehold, the restriction under the Settled Land Act 1925 with respect to leases with at least 60 years unexpired will not apply. The trustees of land have unlimited power to mortgage or lease the land. These powers of the trustees may be excluded or varied by the trust deed.

10.11.10   The right of beneficiaries to occupy land

Section 12 of TLATA 1996 confers on a beneficiary entitled to an interest in possession under a trust of land the right to occupy the land. But this right does not apply where the land is not available or is unsuitable for occupation by the beneficiary.

10.11.11   Enlargement of investment powers

Trustees are entitled to apply to the court under either s 57 of the Trustee Act 1925 or the Variation of Trusts Act 1958 in order to widen these investment powers. The approach of the courts has been encouraging in granting approval in order to update the investment policy of trusts beyond the scope of the Trustee Investments Act 1961. In *Mason v Farbrother* (1983), the court approved a scheme to widen the investment powers of trustees of the employees of the Co-operative Society's pension fund owing to the effects of inflation and the size of the funds (some £127 million).

10.11.12   Powers of maintenance and advancement

Power of maintenance

A power of maintenance is a discretion granted to the trustees to pay or apply income for the benefit of an infant beneficiary at a time prior to the beneficiary acquiring a right to the income or capital of the trust. Maintenance payments are expenditure incurred out of the income of a fund for routine recurring purposes, such as food, clothing, rent and education.

The issues that are required to be considered by the trustees are:

- whether they have a power to maintain an infant beneficiary;
- whether there is any income available for maintenance;
- whether the trustees are prepared to exercise their discretion to maintain the beneficiary.

Express power

A settlor may expressly include a power of maintenance in the trust instrument. Most professionally drafted settlements will include this power. If this is the case, the trustees' duties will be encapsulated in the clause.

Inherent power

The court has an inherent power to authorise the trustees to maintain beneficiaries. The underlying unexpressed intention of the settlor must have been consistent with the maintenance payments in favour of infant beneficiaries.

Statutory power

Section 31 of the Trustee Act 1925 authorises the trustees, in their discretion, to pay the whole or part of the income from the trust to the parent or guardian of an infant beneficiary, or otherwise apply the relevant amount towards the maintenance, education or benefit of the infant beneficiary during his infancy or until his interest fails.

This statutory power may be modified or excluded by the settlor in the trust instrument (see s 69(2) of the Trustee Act 1925). An exclusion of the power may be express or implied in the settlement. Section 31 is intended to be implied into every settlement, subject to any contrary intention expressed by the terms of the instrument. A contrary intention will be established if the settlor has specifically disposed of the income, for example, a payment of the income to another or a direction to accumulate income.

Availability of income

The issue here is whether the income of the trust is available to maintain the infant beneficiary. The effect of complex rules of case law, s 175 of the Law of Property Act 1925 and s 31(3) of the Trustee Act 1925 is that a vested interest carries the intermediate income, unless someone else is entitled to it or the income is required to be accumulated. Contingent interests created *inter vivos* or by will carry the intermediate income (save insofar as the settlor or testator has otherwise disposed of the income). A contingent pecuniary legacy does not carry the income, except where the gift was made by the infant's father or a person standing *in loco parentis*, and the contingencies are attaining the age of majority and that no other fund is set aside for the maintenance of the legatee.

Exercise of power during infancy

The trustees have a discretion to maintain infant beneficiaries. This discretion is required to be exercised responsibly and objectively, as ordinary prudent men of business. Thus, trustees who applied the income automatically to the infant's father, without consciously exercising their discretion, were liable to the beneficiaries for breach of trust when the father used the sums for his own benefit (see *Wilson v Turner* (1883)).

Under the proviso to s 31(1) of the Trustee Act 1925, the trustees are required to take a number of factors into account, such as the age and requirements of the infant, whether other income is applicable for the same purpose and, generally, all the surrounding circumstances. The exercise of the power will vary with the facts of each case.

Accumulations

The trustees may accumulate the income instead of maintaining the infant with the fund. Such accumulations (or capitalised income) will produce further income if invested in authorised investments. The additional income, as well as accumulations of income, become available for the maintenance of the infant beneficiary in the future, should the need arise (proviso to s 31(2)).

Attaining the age of majority

If the beneficiary attains the age of majority without attaining a vested interest under the terms of the trust, the trustees are required to pay the income to the beneficiary until he acquires a vested interest, dies or his interest fails (s 31(1)(ii)). The payment includes accumulated income. Accordingly, a beneficiary acquires a vested interest in the income of the trust by statute on attaining the age of majority even though, under the trust, he does not enjoy a vested interest. Take, for example, a gift 'on trust for A, provided he attains the age of 25'. On attaining the age of 18, A becomes entitled to an interest in possession.

However, this provision is subject to any contrary intention stipulated by the settlor. Such contrary intention may be manifested by the settlor directing the income to be accumulated beyond the age of majority (see *Re Turner's Will Trust* (1937)).

Power of advancement

An advancement is a payment from the capital funds of a trust to, or on behalf of, a beneficiary in respect of some long term commitment, such as the purchase of a house or establishment of a business. A potential beneficiary may be in need of capital from the trust fund prior to his becoming entitled, as of right, to the capital from the fund. In such a case, the trustees may be entitled to accelerate the enjoyment of his interest by an advance payment of capital.

For example, S transfers £50,000 to T1 and T2 on trust for B, contingent on B's attaining the age of 25. While B is only 14 years old, a legitimate need for capital arises. But for special provisions to the contrary, the trustees would be prevented from making an advancement to B on the grounds that the contingency entitling B to the capital has not taken place, and in any event B, as a minor, is incapable of giving a valid receipt for the payment of capital. If, on the other hand, the trustees validly exercise their power of advancement, capital may be released in favour of B before the satisfaction of the contingency and B will be prevented from claiming the capital a second time.

Authority to advance

The authority to exercise a power of advancement may originate from a variety of sources such as the trust instrument, the inherent jurisdiction of the courts or statutory power. Only the statutory power is considered below.

Statutory power

Section 32 of the Trustee Act creates a statutory power of advancement, which is not limited to minors, but empowers the trustees with a discretion to distribute an amount not exceeding one half of the beneficiary's presumptive share capital in favour of any beneficiary, who may become entitled to the whole or part of the capital in the future.

However, this statutory power may be excluded expressly or impliedly by the settlor. An implied exclusion involves any power of advancement which is inconsistent with the statutory power, such as an express power which exceeds the statutory maximum amount (see *IRC v Bernstein* (1961)).

Advancement or benefit

Under s 32, the trustees are entitled to pay or apply capital in their discretion for the 'advancement or benefit' of a beneficiary. This expression has been interpreted widely by the courts, and 'benefit' was interpreted by Viscount Radcliffe in *Pilkington v IRC* (1964) as extending the wide ambit of 'advancement':

> The word 'advancement' itself means ... the establishment in life of the beneficiary ... The expression ['benefit'] means any use of the money which will improve the material situation of the beneficiary.

Thus, the phrase includes the use of money not only for the immediate personal benefit of the beneficiary but also for an indirect benefit, such as a moral obligation to give to a charity (see *Re Clore's Settlement* (1966)). Similarly, in *Re Kershaw* (1868), the power was exercised, with the intention of benefiting the object under a trust, by making a loan to the beneficiary's husband to help him set up a business in England in order to keep the family together.

Scope of s 32

The policy of s 32 is to invest trustees with a discretion to appoint up to one half of the presumptive share of the capital of the beneficiary for his advancement or benefit. The value of the presumptive share of the beneficiary is measured on the date of the advancement. If the ceiling concerning the statutory power of advancement has been reached (that is, 50% of the presumptive share of capital), the statutory power of advancement would be exhausted even if the value of the capital increases subsequently (see *Marquess of Abergavenny v Ram* (1981)).

The settlor may expressly increase the ceiling of sums which may be advanced. The sum advanced is credited to the prospective share of the beneficiary so that, if he becomes absolutely entitled to a share as of right, the sum advanced is taken into account (s 32(1)(b)).

Prior interests

If a beneficiary is entitled to a prior interest (life interest), whether vested or contingent, his consent in writing must be obtained prior to the exercise of the power of advancement. The reason for this is that an advancement reduces the income available to other beneficiaries (s 32(1)(c)).

Trustees' duties

The trustees are required to exercise their power of advancement in a fiduciary manner. The exercise will not be *bona fide* and will be void if the trustees advance funds to a beneficiary on condition that the sum is used to repay a loan made by one of the trustees (*Molyneux v Fletcher* (1898)). Moreover, the trustees may transfer the capital to the beneficiary directly if they reasonably believe that he can be trusted with the money. If the trustees specify a particular purpose which they reasonably believe the beneficiary is capable of fulfilling, they (the trustees) may pay the fund over to him. But the trustees are under an obligation to ensure that the beneficiary, the recipient of the fund, expends the sum for the specific purpose (see *Re Pauling Settlement Trust* (1964)).

10.12 Variation of trusts

Trustees are required to administer the trust in accordance with its terms. They have a primary duty to obey the instructions as detailed by the settlor or as implied by law. Any deviation from the terms of the trust is a breach, making the trustees personally liable, irrespective of how well intentioned they may have been. But circumstances may have arisen since the setting up of the trust which indicate that the trust may be more advantageously administered if the terms were altered.

In these circumstances, the trustees are in need of some mechanism whereby authority may be conferred on them to depart from or vary the terms of the trust. Such authority may be conferred in a variety of ways. Under the rule in *Saunders v Vautier* (1841), where the beneficiaries are of full age and of sound mind and are absolutely entitled to the trust property, they may deal with the equitable interest in any way they wish. They may sell, exchange or gift away their interest. As a corollary to this rule, such beneficiaries acting in unison are entitled to terminate the trust.

10.12.1 Management and administration

Inherent jurisdiction of the court

The court has an inherent jurisdiction to depart from the terms of a trust in the case of an 'emergency', that is, on an occasion when no provision was made in the trust instrument and the event could not have been foreseen by the settlor.

This power is very narrow and arises in order to 'salvage' the trust property, for example, to order essential repairs to buildings (see *Re New* (1901)).

Section 57 of the Trustee Act 1925

This section is drafted in fairly wide terms and empowers the court to confer authority on the trustees to perform functions whenever it is 'expedient' to do so. The policy of s 57 is to ensure that the trust property is managed as advantageously as possible in the interests of the beneficiaries and to authorise specific dealings with the trust property that are outside the scope of the inherent jurisdiction of the court. It may not be possible to establish that the situation is an emergency or that the settlor could not reasonably have foreseen the circumstances which have arisen. In these circumstances, the court may sanction the scheme presented.

Under this provision, the courts have sanctioned schemes for the following: partitioning of land (*Re Thomas* (1939)); a sale of land where the necessary consent could not be obtained (*Re Beale's Settlement Trust* (1932)); the sale of a reversionary interest which the trustees had no power to sell until it fell into possession (*Re Heyworth's Contingent Reversionary Interest* (1956)); two charitable trusts blended into one (*Re Shipwrecked Fishermen's and Mariners' Benevolent Fund* (1959)); extended investment powers of pension fund trustees (*Mason v Farbrother* (1983)); a power created to invest abroad (*Trustees of the British Museum v AG* (1984)); and a power created to invest as if the trustees were beneficial owners, subject to certain guidelines (*Steel v Wellcome Custodian Trustee* (1988)).

Variation of beneficial interest

The courts have the jurisdiction both to approve schemes which go beyond an alteration of the management powers of trustees and to effect arrangements which vary the beneficial interests under a trust.

Section 53 of the Trustee Act 1925

Where an infant is beneficially entitled to real or personal property and the property does not produce income which may be used for the infant's maintenance, education or benefit, the court may adopt a proposal authorising a 'conveyance' of the infant's interest, with a view to the application of the capital or income for the maintenance, education or benefit of the infant.

Section 64 of the Settled Land Act 1925

The jurisdiction of the courts under s 64 is much wider than their jurisdiction under s 57. Section 64 not only entitles the courts to sanction schemes connected with the management and administration of the trust; they are also entitled to alter beneficial interests under the settlement.

Compromise

The court has the jurisdiction to approve compromise arrangements governing the rights of beneficiaries, including infants and unborn persons under trusts. The House of Lords in *Chapman v Chapman* (1954) clarified the meaning of the expression 'compromise' by deciding that its jurisdiction concerned cases of genuine disputes about the existence of rights.

Variation of Trusts Act 1958

The Variation of Trusts Act 1958 was passed in order to reverse the decision of the House of Lords in *Chapman v Chapman* and to introduce sweeping changes in the law.

The court is entitled, at its discretion, to sanction 'any arrangement varying or revoking all or any trusts or enlarging the powers of the trustees of managing or administering any of the property subject to the trusts', provided that the beneficiary (actual or potential) falls within at least one of the following categories as enumerated in s 1(1) of the Act:

(a) any person having, directly or indirectly, an interest, whether vested or contingent, under the trusts who by reason of infancy or other incapacity is incapable of assenting; or

(b) any person (whether ascertained or not) who may become entitled, directly or indirectly, to an interest at a future date or on the happening of a future event, a person of any specified description or a member of any specified class of persons, but not including any person who would be of that description or a member of that class if the said date had fallen or the said event had happened at the date of the application to the court; or

(c) any person unborn; or

(d) any person in respect of any discretionary interest of his under protective trusts where the interest of the principal beneficiary has not failed or determined,

provided that, with the exception of para (d) above, the arrangement was carried out for the benefit of that person.

The purpose of the Act is to permit the court to approve arrangements on behalf of beneficiaries who cannot give their consent by reason of infancy or other incapacity or because their identity is unascertained, for example, a future spouse. It follows, therefore, that the court has no jurisdiction to approve arrangements on behalf of beneficiaries who are *sui juris*, adult and ascertained. Thus, the consent of all adult, ascertained beneficiaries must be obtained before a court grants its approval to a scheme.

The only exception to the above rule is to be found in s 1(1)(d) of the Act. The court may consent on behalf of an adult 'beneficiary' who may become entitled to an interest on the failure of the principal beneficiary's interest under a protective trust.

Settlor's intention

In deciding whether to approve an arrangement or not, the intention of the settlor (if relevant) or testator is only a factor to be taken into consideration by the court. But the settlor's or testator's intention is certainly not an overriding factor, nor is it even a weighty consideration in determining how the discretion of the court is to be exercised. The role of the court is not to act as a representative of the settlor or testator in varying the trusts. Thus, the court approved a scheme, despite the contradiction of the clear intention of the testatrix, in *Goulding v James* (1997).

Benefit

The notion of benefit is not restricted to financial benefits, though variations have been made to avoid tax. In *Re Weston's Settlement* (1969), the Court of Appeal refused to approve a scheme because, despite being financially advantageous, it would have been morally and socially detrimental to the beneficiaries. In appropriate cases, the court may have regard to the financial instability of an infant beneficiary and approve a scheme by postponing the vesting of such beneficiary's interest in capital (see *Re T's Settlement* (1964)). Likewise, the court may approve an arrangement if its effect would be to prevent real or potential conflict within a family (*Re Remnant's Settlement Trust* (1970)).

10.13   Breach of trust

A trustee is liable for a breach of trust if he fails to perform his duties, either by omitting to do any act which he ought to have done, or by doing an act which he ought not to have done. The beneficiary is required to establish a causal connection between the breach of trust and the loss suffered either directly or indirectly by the trust. Indeed, even if the trust suffers no loss, the beneficiary is entitled to claim any profit accruing to the trustees as a result of a breach.

10.13.1   Measure of liability

Trustees' liability for breach of trust is based on principles of restitution to the trust estate. The trustee in default is required to restore the trust property, or its equivalent, to the trust estate. In respect of a breach of trust claim, the basic right of the beneficiary is to have the trust duly administered in accordance with the trust instrument and general law. In this regard, the common law rules on remoteness of damage and causation are not applied strictly, but there still has to be some causal link between the breach of trust and loss to the estate. Once the trust fund is 'reconstituted', the defaulting trustee becomes a bare trustee for the claimant and will have no answer to a claim by him for the payment of the moneys in the 'reconstituted' fund.

The fact that there is an accrued cause of action as soon as the breach is committed does not mean that the quantum of the compensation payable is ultimately fixed as at the date when the breach occurred. The quantum is fixed at the date of judgment, according to circumstances which would put the beneficiary back into the position he would have been, but for the breach. The plaintiff's actual loss is assessed with the full benefit of hindsight. In *Target Holdings v Redfern* (1995), the court rejected the claim of the plaintiffs that the loss is to be measured at the time of the breach. This would have entitled the plaintiffs to obtain compensation of an amount which exceeded its loss and would not have reflected the basic principles of equitable compensation.

Interest

As a general rule, the court is entitled to award simple interest under s 35A of the Supreme Court Act 1981. There is no consistent view as to the rate of interest. In recent years, some courts have taken the view that the rate is 1% above the minimum lending rate (see *Belmont Finance Corp v Williams Furniture Ltd (No 2)* (1980)). Other courts have suggested that the appropriate rate is that allowed from time to time on the court's short term investment account (see *Bartlett v Barclays Bank (No 2)* (1980)).

The court has a discretion to award compound interest against trustees. The principle here stems from the policy of preventing the trustees from profiting from their breach. Their Lordships in *Westdeutsche Landesbank Girozentrale v Islington BC* (1996) decided that, in the absence of fraud, this jurisdiction is exercised against a defendant who is a trustee or otherwise stands in a fiduciary position and makes an unauthorised profit, or is assumed to have made such profit. The majority of their Lordships decided that, since the defendant local authority did not owe fiduciary duties to the bank, compound interest would not be awarded against it.

Contribution and indemnity between trustees

Trustees are under a duty to act jointly and unanimously. In principle, the liability of the trustees is joint and several. The innocent beneficiary may sue one or more or all of the trustees.

If a successful action is brought against one trustee, he has a right of contribution from his co-trustees, with the effect that each trustee will contribute equally to the damages awarded in favour of the plaintiff, unless the court decides otherwise. The position today is that the right of contribution is governed by the Civil Liability (Contribution) Act 1978. The court has a discretion concerning the amount of the contribution which may be recoverable from any other person liable in respect of the same damage.

The Act does not apply to an indemnity which is governed entirely by case law. There are three circumstances when a trustee is required to indemnify his co-trustees in respect of their liability to the beneficiaries:

- where one trustee has fraudulently obtained a benefit from a breach of trust (see *Bahin v Hughes* (1886));

- where the breach of trust was committed on the advice of a solicitor-trustee (see *Re Partington* (1887)). In *Head v Gould* (1898), the claim for an indemnity against a solicitor-trustee failed because the co-trustee actively encouraged the solicitor-trustee to commit the breach of trust. The mere fact that the co-trustee is a solicitor is insufficient to establish the claim;

- the rule in *Chillingworth v Chambers* (1896): where a trustee is also a beneficiary (whether he receives a benefit or not is immaterial) and the trustees are liable for breach of trust, the beneficiary/trustee is required to indemnify his co-trustee to the extent of his beneficial interest. If the loss exceeds the beneficial interest, the trustees will share the surplus loss equally, insofar as it exceeds the beneficial interest.

Defences to an action for breach of trust

In pursuance of an action against trustees for breach of trust, there are a number of defences which the trustees are entitled to raise. These are as follows.

Knowledge and consent of the beneficiaries

A beneficiary who has freely consented to or concurred in a breach of trust is not entitled to renege on his promise and sue the trustees.

In order to be prevented from bringing an action against the trustees, the beneficiary is required to be of full age and sound mind, with full knowledge of all the relevant facts, and must exercise an independent judgment. The burden of proof will be on the trustees to establish these elements (see *Nail v Punter* (1832)).

Impounding the interest of a beneficiary

Under the inherent jurisdiction of the court, a beneficiary who instigated a breach of trust may be required to indemnify the trustees. The rule of equity was extended in s 62 of the Trustee Act 1925. Under that section, the court has a discretion which it will not exercise if the beneficiary was not aware of the full facts. Section 62 is applicable irrespective of whether the beneficiary has an intention to receive a personal benefit or not. The beneficiary's consent is required to be in writing.

Relief under s 61 of the Trustee Act 1925

Section 61 of the Trustee Act 1925 provides three main ingredients for granting relief. The trustee: (a) must have acted honestly; (b) must have acted reasonably; and (c) ought fairly to be excused in respect of the breach. The trustee bears the burden of proof.

The expression 'honestly' means that the trustee acted in good faith. This is a question of fact. The word 'reasonably' indicates that the trustee acted prudently. If these two criteria are satisfied, the court has a discretion to excuse the trustee. The test in exercising the discretion is to have regard to both the interests of the trustees and the beneficiaries and to decide whether the breach of trust ought to be forgiven in whole or in part. In the absence of special circumstances, a trustee who has acted honestly and reasonably ought to be relieved.

In *Perrins v Bellamy* (1899), the trustees of a settlement, acting on the erroneous advice of their solicitor, executed a sale of leaseholds, thereby diminishing the income of the plaintiff (who was a tenant for life). In an action for breach of trust, the trustees successfully claimed relief under the predecessor to s 61 of the Trustee Act 1925.

But each case is decided on its own facts. A factor which is capable of influencing the court is whether or not the trustee is a professional. In *Bartlett v Barclays Bank* (1980), the professional trustee company was refused relief under s 61 of the Trustee Act 1925 because it acted unreasonably in failing to keep abreast or informed of the changes in the activities of the investment company.

Limitation and laches

The limitation periods concern the time limits during which a beneficiary is required to pursue a cause of action in respect of trust property:

- *Six year limitation period*: under s 21(3) of the Limitation Act 1980, the general rule concerning the limitation period for actions for breach of trust is six years from the date on which the cause of action accrued. A cause of action does not accrue in respect of future interests (remainders and reversions) until the interest falls into possession. In addition, time does not begin to run against a beneficiary suffering from a disability (infancy or mental incapacity) at the time of the breach until the disability ends. For these purposes, a 'trustee' includes a personal representative, and no distinction is drawn between express, implied or constructive trustees.

- *Exceptions*: under s 21(1), where a beneficiary brings an action in respect of any fraud by the trustee or to recover trust property or the proceeds of sale from trust property (that is, actions *in rem* (see below)), the limitation period fixed shall not apply. A transferee is in the same position as the trustee unless he is a *bona fide* transferee of the legal estate for value without notice.

  Where the right of action has been concealed by fraud or where the action is for relief from the consequences of a mistake, time does not begin to run until the plaintiff discovers the fraud or mistake or ought, with reasonable diligence, to have discovered it (s 32).

- *Laches:* where no period of limitation has been specified under the Act (see s 21(1)), the doctrine of laches will apply to equitable claims. Section 36(2) of the Limitation Act 1980 states that 'nothing in the Act shall affect any equitable jurisdiction to refuse relief on the grounds of acquiescence or otherwise'.

The doctrine of laches consists of a substantial lapse of time coupled with the existence of circumstances which make it inequitable to enforce the claimant's claim. The doctrine is summarised in the maxim 'equity aids the vigilant and not the indolent'. It may be treated as inequitable to enforce the claimant's claim where the delay has led the defendant to change his position to his detriment, in the reasonable belief that the claimant's claim has been abandoned, where the delay has led to the loss of evidence which might assist the defence, or where the claim is related to a business (because the claimant should not be allowed to wait and see if it prospers).

In order to raise a successful defence, the defendant is required to establish the following three elements, as laid down in *Nelson v Rye* (1996):

- there has been unreasonable delay in bringing the action by the claimant;

- there has been consequential substantial prejudice or detriment to the defendant; and

- the balance of justice requires the claimant's action to be withheld.

Proprietary remedies

A beneficiary is entitled to 'trace' the trust assets in the hands of the trustees or third parties (not being *bona fide* transferees of the legal estate for value without notice) and recover such property, or obtain a charging order in priority over the trustees' creditors. This is known as a proprietary remedy, or a claim *in rem* or tracing order.

A tracing order is a process whereby the claimant establishes and protects his title to assets that are in the hands of another. The remedy is 'proprietary' in the sense that the order is attached to specific property under the control of another or may take the form of a charging order, thereby treating the claimant as a secured creditor. The remedies at common law and equity are mainly 'personal', in the sense that they are remedies which force the defendant to do or refrain from doing something in order to compensate the claimant for the wrong suffered. But the proprietary remedy exists as a right to proceed against a particular asset in the hands of the defendant.

Advantages of the proprietary remedy over personal remedies

The proprietary remedy has a number of advantages over the personal remedy, namely:

- the claimant's action is not dependant on the solvency of the defendant. Indeed, the claimant's claim is based on an assertion of ownership of the asset in question;

- the claimant may be able to take advantage of increases in the value of the property in appropriate cases; and

- on a proprietary claim, interest accrues from the date the property was acquired by the defendant, while claims *in personam* carry interest only from the date of the judgment.

Tracing at common law

The approach at common law is that, provided the claimant's property is 'identifiable', the process of tracing may continue through any number of transformations. The main restriction to the common law right to trace is that the property ceases to be 'identifiable' when it becomes comprised in a mixed fund or when the asset ceases to be wholly owned by the claimant (see *Taylor v Plumer* (1815)). In *Lipkin Gorman v Karpnale* (1991), a partner in a firm of solicitors fraudulently misappropriated some of the firm's funds, part of which were lost at a casino. Although the plaintiff had not sought a tracing order, Lord Goff considered that such a claim may have had a reasonable chance of success. The relationship of banker and customer created a *chose in action* in favour of the plaintiff. The customer (plaintiff) was entitled to trace his property in its unconverted form.

Tracing in equity

Equity had conceived the notion that, once property was identifiable, recognition of the claimant's right could be given by:

- attaching an order to specific property; or

- by charging the asset for the amount of the claim.

Unmixed fund

Equity followed the common law and declared that, where the trust property has been transformed into property of a different form by the trustees and has been kept separate and distinct from the trustees' resources, the beneficiary may take the proceeds. If the proceeds of sale have been used to acquire further property, the beneficiary may elect:

- to take the property which has been acquired wholly with the trust property; or

- to charge the property for the amount belonging to the trust.

See *Banque Belge pour l'Estrange v Hambrouck* (1921).

Mixed fund

Where the trustee or fiduciary mixes his funds with that of the beneficiary or purchases further property with the mixed fund, the beneficiary loses his right to elect to take the property acquired. The reason for this is that the property would not have been bought with the beneficiary's money, pure and simple, but with the mixed fund. However, in the exercise of the exclusive jurisdiction of equity, the beneficiary would be entitled to have the property charged for the amount of the trust money (see *Re Hallett's Estate* (1880)).

The rule in *Re Hallett's Estate* seems to be that, if a trustee or fiduciary mixes trust monies with his own:

- the beneficiary is entitled in the first place to a charge on the amalgam of the fund in order to satisfy his claim; and

- if the trustee or fiduciary withdraws moneys for his own purposes, he is deemed to draw out his own moneys, so that the beneficiary may claim the balance of the fund as against the trustee's general creditors.

Assets purchased

Since the beneficiaries are entitled to trace their property (including a charge) into a mixed fund, it follows that that right (to trace) may extend to property (assets) acquired with the mixed fund. Accordingly, if a part of the fund is used to purchase an asset which is identifiable and the remainder of the fund has been exhausted (the right to trace against the fund becoming otiose), the beneficiary may claim to trace against the asset acquired by the trustees.

In short, from the point of view of the beneficiary, the trustee and his successors in title are prevented from denying the interest deemed to be acquired with the mixed fund. In *Re Oatway* (1903), the trustees mixed their funds with trust moneys and bought shares with part of the fund. The remaining funds in the account were exhausted. The court held that the beneficiaries were entitled to claim the proceeds of sale of the shares.

Lowest intermediate balance

If the funds in the account fall below the amount of the trust funds originally paid in, that part of the trust fund (the depreciation) is presumed to have been spent. The right to trace into the balance held in the bank account will be depreciated to the extent of the lowest balance in the account. The lowest intermediate balance is presumed to be the trust property (see *Re Goldcorp Exchange Ltd* (1994)). Subsequent payments are not *prima facie* treated as repayments to the trust fund in order to repair the breach, unless the trustee earmarks such repayments as having that effect.

Rule in Clayton's Case

The rule in *Clayton's Case* (1816) is a rule of banking law and one of convenience which had been adopted in the early part of the 19th century to ascertain the respective interests in a bank account of two innocent parties *inter se*. Where a trustee mixes trust funds subsisting in an active current bank account belonging to two beneficiaries, the amount of the balance in the account is determined by attributing withdrawals in the order of sums paid into the account. This is referred to as 'first in first out' (FIFO).

The rule is applied as between beneficiaries (or innocent parties) *inter se* in order to:

- ascertain ownership of the balance of the fund; and

- ascertain ownership of specific items bought from funds withdrawn from the account.

The basis of the rule lies in the fact that, as between the beneficiaries (or innocent parties), the 'equities are equal'. That is, there is no need to give one beneficiary any special treatment over the other (see *Clayton's Case; Devaynes v Noble* (1816)). But it is worth noting that, as between the trustee and beneficiary, the rule in *Re Hallett*, not *Clayton's Case*, applies. The wrongdoer may never take advantage of the FIFO rule.

However, *Clayton's Case* was distinguished in *Barlow Clowes International Ltd v Vaughan* (1992). The rule in *Clayton's Case* was considered to be impractical, unjust, and contrary to the intention of the investors. Accordingly, the court was entitled to refuse to apply it, provided that an alternative method of distribution was available.

Limitations

The Court of Appeal, in *Re Diplock* (1948), enunciated the limits surrounding the right to trace. The principles discerned are as follows:

- The equitable remedy does not affect rights obtained by a *bona fide* transferee of the legal estate for value without notice. All equitable claims are extinguished against such persons.

- Tracing will not be permitted if the result will produce inequity, for 'he who comes to equity must do equity'. Accordingly, if an innocent volunteer spends money improving his land, there can be no declaration of charge because the method of enforcing the charge would be by way of sale, thus forcing the volunteer to convert his property. In *Lipkin Gorman (A Firm) v Karpnale* (1991), Lord Goff advocated a defence of change of position which ought to be adopted in English law in respect of restitution claims. This defence is to be developed on a case by case basis.

- The right to trace is extinguished if the claimant's property is no longer identifiable, for example, if the trust monies have been spent on a dinner or a cruise or in paying off a loan (see *Re Diplock*).

- It is essential that the claimant proves that the property was held by another on his behalf in a fiduciary or quasi-fiduciary capacity in order to attract the jurisdiction of equity. This fiduciary need not be the person who mixes the funds or the assets. The mixture may be effected by an innocent volunteer, as was the case in *Re Diplock*. In *Chase Manhattan Bank v Israel-British Bank* (1979), the court decided that a payment by mistake of funds from the claimant bank to the defendant bank affected the conscience of the latter to such an extent that the defendant bank became subject to a fiduciary duty to repay the fund to the plaintiff.

THE LAW OF EQUITY AND TRUSTS

Express trusts

An *express* trust is created when the settlor either:

- vests the legal title to the trust property in the trustee(s), subject to the terms of the trust; or

- declares himself a trustee and sets out the terms of the trust.

A principle for deciding whether the terms of the trust have been validly declared is 'the three certainties' test, that is, certainties of intention, subject matter and objects.

The creation of an express trust has the following consequences:

- the settlor, in his capacity as settlor, cannot change his mind and recover the property;

- the trustees are required to deal with the property in accordance with the terms of the trust and the general law;

- the beneficiaries acquire equitable interests and are entitled to protect these against anyone except a *bona fide* transferee of the legal estate for value without notice.

An express trust may be classified as 'fixed' or 'discretionary'.

Alternatively, if the intended trust is not perfectly created, the arrangement involving the intended settlor operates as an agreement to create a trust. The claimant is required to establish that he has furnished consideration, for 'equity will not assist a volunteer' or 'equity will not perfect an imperfect gift'. Exceptionally, equity will assist a volunteer under any of the following principles, the *Strong v Bird* rule, *donatio mortis causa* or proprietary estoppel.

Resulting trusts

A *resulting* trust is a device, which is implied by the court, whereby the equitable interest in property is returned to the settlor or transferor. The trust is created in order to fill a gap in ownership. These trusts may be classified into two categories namely, automatic and presumed. The automatic resulting trust arises in a variety of situations. Examples are a failure of an express trust, or a transfer of property subject to a condition precedent which has not been achieved or when a surplus of funds is left over after the purpose has been fulfilled. The presumed resulting trust is created when property is bought or transferred in the name of another. This presumption may be rebutted by evidence which establishes that the settlor or transferor did not intend to retain a beneficial interest.

Constructive trusts

A *constructive* trust is created by the court in order to satisfy the demands of justice and good conscience without reference to the express or presumed intention of the parties. The categories of constructive trusts are never closed because the occasions when there is a need to maintain a balance between the trustees and the beneficiaries are limitless. Instances are a conflict of fiduciary duty and interest, specifically enforceable contracts of sale, proprietary rights in the family home, the frustration of fraudulent or unfair conduct. In addition, a constructive trust arises whenever a stranger to a trust intermeddles with trust property.

Charitable trusts

A *charitable* trust is distinctive in that it is a public trust designed to benefit society as a whole or a sufficiently large section of society. This type of trust enjoys a number of privileges not accorded to other trusts. Charitable purposes are schemes which relieve poverty, advance education or religion, and promote other purposes which are beneficial to the community.

Breach of trusts

Generally, the duties of trustees, in respect of all types of trusts, are primarily to comply with the terms of the trust and the general law. Subject thereto, the trustees are required to act in the best interests of the beneficiaries. Failure to perform his or her duties exposes the trustee to liability for breach of trust. A disappointed beneficiary is entitled to bring a personal action against the trustee or an action *in rem* to recover the trust property.

CHAPTER 11

THE CIVIL PROCESS

Bleak House, Charles Dickens:

> Jarndyce [v] Jarndyce drones on. This scarecrow of a suit has, in the course of time, become so complicated that no man alive knows what it means. The parties to it understand it least; but it has been observed that no two Chancery lawyers can talk about it for five minutes without coming to a total disagreement as to all the premises. Innumerable children have been born into the cause; innumerable young people have married into it; innumerable old people have died out of it. Scores of persons have deliriously found themselves made parties in Jarndyce and Jarndyce, without knowing how or why; whole families have inherited legendary hatreds with the suit. The little plaintiff or defendant, who was promised a new rocking horse when Jarndyce and Jarndyce should be settled, has grown up, possessed himself of a real horse, and trotted away into the other world. Fair wards of court have faded into grandmothers; a long procession of Chancellors has come in and gone out ... there are not three Jarndyces left upon the earth perhaps, since old Tom Jarndyce in despair blew his brains out at a coffee-house in Chancery Lane; but Jarndyce and Jarndyce still drags its dreary length before the Court, perennially hopeless.
>
> ......
>
> Many critics believe that the adversarial system has run into the sand, in that, today, delay and costs are too often disproportionate to the difficulty of the issue and the amount at stake. The solution now being followed to that problem requires a more interventionist judiciary: the trial judge as the trial manager [LJ Henry in *Thermawear v Linton* (1995), CA].

The extent of delay, complication and therefore expense of civil litigation may have changed since the time of Dickens' observations about the old Court of Chancery but how far the civil process is as efficient as it might be is a matter of some debate.

A survey by the National Consumer Council in 1995 found that three out of four people in serious legal disputes were dissatisfied with the civil justice system (*Seeking Civil Justice: A Survey of People's Needs and Experiences*, 1995, NCC). Of the 1,019 respondents, 77% claimed the system was too slow, 74% said it was too complicated, and 73% said that it was unwelcoming and outdated.

According to the Civil Justice Review (CJR) 1988, delay in litigation 'causes continuing personal stress, anxiety and financial hardship to ordinary people and their families. It may induce economically weaker parties to accept unfair settlements. It also frustrates the efficient conduct of commerce and industry'.

Despite some of the innovations in the five years following that CJR, the problems continued. In 1994, the Lord Chancellor set up the Woolf Inquiry to look at ways of improving the speed and accessibility of civil proceedings, and of reducing their cost.

The Heilbron Hodge Report, *Civil Justice on Trial: The Case for Change* (1993), recommended many changes in civil procedure. The Report resulted from an independent working party set up in 1992 by the Bar Council and The Law Society. The 39 member working party was chaired by Hilary Heilbron QC; its vice chair was solicitor Henry Hodge OBE. The report called for a 'radical reappraisal of the approach to litigation from all its participants'.

The Report painted a depressing picture of the civil justice system where delays are endemic and often contrived and procedures are inflexible, rule ridden and often incomprehensible to the client. It noted that incongruously for a multi-million pound operation, technology scarcely featured. All High Court and county court records, for example, were kept manually. The main plank of the report was concerned with making the operation of the courts more 'litigant-friendly'. It said that judges, lawyers and administrators should develop a culture of service to the litigant. The report made 72 recommendations for change.

11.1   The 1999 Woolf reforms – an overview

When Lord Woolf began his examination of the civil law process, the problems facing those who used the system were many and varied. His Interim Report, published in June 1995, identified these problems. He noted, for example, that:

> ... the key problems facing civil justice today are cost, delay and complexity. These three are interrelated and stem from the uncontrolled nature of the litigation process. In particular, there is no clear judicial responsibility for managing individual cases or for the overall administration of the civil courts. Just as the problems are interrelated, so too the solutions, which I propose, are interdependent. In many instances, the failure of previous attempts to address the problem stems not from the solutions proposed but from their partial rather than their complete implementation [*Access to Justice*, Interim Report, 1995].

In the system that Lord Woolf examined, the main responsibility for the initiation and conduct of proceedings rested with the parties to each individual case, and it was normally the plaintiff (now claimant) who set the pace. Thus, Lord Woolf also noted:

> Without effective judicial control ... the adversarial process is likely to encourage an adversarial cultural and to degenerate into an environment in which the litigation process is too often seen as a battlefield where no rules apply. In this environment, questions of expense, delay, compromise and fairness have only a low priority. The consequence is that the expense is often excessive, disproportionate and unpredictable; and delay is frequently unreasonable [*Access to Justice*, Interim Report, 1995, p 7].

The system has degenerated in a number of other respects. Witness statements, a sensible innovation aimed at a 'cards on the table' began after a very short time to follow the same route as pleadings, with the draftsman skill often used to obscure the original words of the witness.

The use of expert evidence under the old system left a lot to be desired:

> The approach to expert evidence also shows the characteristic range of difficulties: instead of the expert assisting the court to resolve technical problems, delay is caused by the unreasonable insistence on going to unduly eminent members of the profession and evidence is undermined by the partisan pressure to which party experts are subjected.

Historically, change has come very slowly and gradually to the legal system. The report of the CJR was largely ignored and, with the exception of a shift in the balance of work from the High Court to the county court (under CLSA 1990), no major changes came from its recommendations. The whole process began again with the Woolf Review of the Civil Justice System. In March 1994, Lord Woolf was invited by the government to review the work of the civil courts in England and Wales. He began from the proposition that the system was 'in a state of crisis ... a crisis for the government, the judiciary and the profession'. The recommendations he formulated – after extensive consultation in the UK and in many other jurisdictions – form the basis of major changes to the system that came into effect in April 1999. David Gladwell, head of the Civil Justice Division of the Lord Chancellor's Department, stated (*Civil Litigation Reform*, 1999, LCD, p 1) that these changes represent 'the greatest change the civil courts have seen in over a century'.

Following the Civil Procedure Act 1997, the changes are effected through the new Civil Procedure Rules 1998. These have been supplemented by new practice directions and pre-action protocols. The principal parts of all of these new rules and guidelines are examined below. Thus, 'rule 4.1' refers to r 4.1 of the Civil Procedure Rules.

Leaving aside for the moment the pervasive theme of the reforms – to simplify procedure – there are three main aspects to the reforms:

Judicial case management

The judge is a case manager in the new regime. The new system allocates cases to one of three 'tracks' depending upon the complexity and value of the dispute. The small claims track deals with the simplest cases; the fast track deals with more weighty disputes; and the multi-track system allows a court to use a variety of procedures (see 11.6–11.8). He or she will be centre stage for the whole action, not just in David Gladwell's phrase, 'someone who is brought in for the final triumphal scene'. Litigation proceeds on a court controlled timetable. Parties can no longer agree extensions with each other. Previously, lawyers from either side were permitted to wrangle almost endlessly with each other about who should disclose what information and documents to whom and at what stage. Now, the judge is under an obligation to 'actively' manage cases. This includes:

- encouraging parties to co-operate with each other;

- identifying issues in the dispute at an early stage;

- disposing of summary issues which do not need full investigation;

- helping the parties to settle the whole or part of the case;

- fixing timetables for the case hearing and controlling the progress of the case; and

- considering whether the benefits of a particular way of hearing the dispute justify its costs.

If the parties refuse to comply with the new rules, the practice directions or the protocols, the judge will be able to exercise disciplinary powers. These include:

(a) using costs sanctions against parties (that is, refusing to allow the lawyers who have violated the rules to recover their costs from their client or the other side of the dispute);

(b) 'unless' orders;

(c) striking-out;

(d) refusal to grant extensions of time; and

(e) refusal to allow documents not previously disclosed to the court and the other side to be relied upon.

One of the greatest changes, however, will concern the spirit of the law. The new style of procedure which is intended to be brisk will be of paramount importance. The courts will become allergic to delay or any of the old, ponderous, long-winded techniques previously used by many lawyers. David Gladwell (*Civil Litigation Reform*, 1999, LCD, p 2) has noted that 'Strict observance of the black letter of the rules, so beloved of procedural lawyers, will no longer be enough. The courts will be adopting a more creative approach'.

Pre-action protocols

Part of the problem in the past has arisen from the fact that the courts can only start to exercise control over the progress of a case, and the way it is handled, once proceedings have been issued. Before that stage, lawyers were at liberty to take inordinate time to do things related to the case, to write to lawyers on the other side to the dispute and so forth. Now, a mechanism allows new pre-action requirements to be enforced. Two protocols have been drawn up, to apply in the largest areas of litigation: clinical negligence (including actions against doctors, nurses, dentists, hospitals, health authorities, etc); and personal injury (road accidents, work accidents, etc).

The object of the protocols is:

- to encourage greater contact between the parties at the earliest opportunity;

- to encourage a better exchange of information;

- to encourage better pre-action investigation;

- to put parties in a position to settle cases fairly and early; and

- to reduce the need for the case going all the way to court.

Alternatives to going to court

Rule 4.1 requires the court as a part of its 'active case management' to encourage and facilitate the use of Alternative Dispute Resolution (ADR) (which is examined in Chapter 12), and r 26.4 allows the court to stay proceedings (that is, halt them) to allow the parties to go to ADR either where the parties themselves request it or where the court 'of its own initiative' considers it appropriate. The Commercial Court already uses this policy with notable success. It often acts to send cases to ADR, for example, where one side applies for a lengthy extension of time for the case to be heard.

11.2 The cost of litigation – the pre-1999 problems

Many potential litigants are deterred from taking action by the high costs. It is also relevant to remember that whichever party loses the action must pay for his or her own expenses and those of the other side; a combined sum which will, in many cases, be more than the sum in issue. An appeal to the Court of Appeal will increase the costs even further (in effect, fees and expenses for another action) and the same may be true again if the case is taken to the House of Lords. There is in such a system a great pressure for parties to settle their claims. The CJR found that 90–95% of cases were settled by the parties before the trial.

The cost of taking legal action in the civil courts has been gigantic. Two cases cited by Adrian Zuckerman in an address to Lord Woolf's Inquiry illustrate the point. In one, a successful action by a supplier of fitted kitchens to stop a £10,000 a year employee from taking up a job with a competitor cost the employer £100,000, even though judgment was obtained in under five weeks from the start of the proceedings. The expense of this case was in fact double the stated amount when the cost of the legal aid fund's bill for the employee's defence is added to the total. In another case, a divorced wife had to pay £34,000 in costs for a judgment which awarded her £52,000 of the value of the family home.

It was the spiralling costs of civil litigation, to a large extent borne by the taxpayer through legal aid, which has prompted the Lord Chancellor to move to cap the legal aid fund. The legal aid budget rose from £426 million in 1987–88 to £1,526 million in 1997–98.

The system of civil procedure entails a variety of devices. Very complex cases may require the full use of many of these devices but most cases could be tried without parties utilising all the procedures. Exorbitant costs and long delays often resulted from unduly complicated procedures being used by lawyers acting for parties to litigation. Zuckerman has argued that this problem arose from the fact that the legal system was evolved principally by lawyers with no concern for cost efficiency. In both the High Court and the county court, the system allowed parties to quarrel as much over procedural matters as the actual merits of the substantive dispute. In one case, for example, the issue of whether a writ had been properly served on the other side had to be considered by a Master (the High Court judicial officer empowered to deal with procedural matters) and then, on appeal, by a judge, and then, on another appeal, by the Court of Appeal. Thus, cost and delay could build up before the parties even arrived at the stage of having their real argument heard. If a claim or defence was amended, the fate of the amendment could take two appeal hearings to finally resolve. The pre-trial proceedings often degenerated into an intricate legal contest separate from the substantive issue.

The CJR 1988 recommended unification of the county courts and the High Court. It accepted the need for different levels of judiciary but argued that having different levels of courts was inefficient. This recommendation carried what Roger Smith, then director of the Legal Action Group, called an 'unspoken sting', namely, that a divided legal profession could hardly survive a unified court. The Bar rebelled and the judiciary was solidly opposed to such change. The recommendation was not legislated.

The CLSA 1990, following other recommendations in the CJR, legislated for large numbers of cases in the High Court being sent down to the county courts to expedite their progress. No extra resources were given to the county courts to cope with the influx of cases and so, not surprisingly, there has been a growing backlog of cases and a poorer quality of service in the county courts. This problem may well worsen rather than be helped by the introduction of the Civil Procedure Rules as more cases will be heard in the county courts.

There were tactical reasons why parties were tempted to use the full panoply of procedural rules. The rule that 'costs follow success' (that is, the losing side usually has to pay the legal costs of the other side) can operate to encourage the building up of expense. Wealthy litigants could employ protracted procedures in an effort to worry poorer opponents to settle on terms determined by the former. Conditional fee arrangements (see 16.5) have made very little impact on the system, so lawyers who are paid by the hour regardless of success are unlikely to be especially anxious about the speed and efficiency of their work.

Zuckerman has argued for the introduction of a more efficient system like the one used in Germany. There, legal fees are determined by law. A lawyer is paid for litigation in units that represent a small proportion of the value of the claim. Payment is in three stages. The first is made at the commencement of the action; the second when representation begins at a hearing; here, the judge will attempt to procure a settlement. If this fails, he will give directions for the preparation of evidence. The third payment will be made if the case goes to a full hearing. Since lawyers earn only a fixed fee, there is no systemic incentive for them to prolong any stage of the litigation; on the contrary, they have an incentive to work as expeditiously as possible so as to maximise their rate of pay at any given stage (that is, to get a reasonable return per hour). There was evidence, however, that this system encourages some lawyers to go to the final stage even where there might have been a reasonable chance of settlement at the second stage. To overcome that difficulty, it has now been regulated that a lawyer can get a full three-part fee even if the case is settled at the second stage.

In January 1995, instructions to judges from Lord Taylor, the then Lord Chief Justice, and Sir Nicholas Scott, the Vice Chancellor, may well have an effect on the length and therefore cost of High Court cases. Judges have been instructed to use their discretion to set strict time limits to lawyers' speeches and cross-examination, to limit the issues in cases and the documents to be disclosed ahead of trial, and to curb reading aloud from documents and case reports (*Practice Direction, Civil Litigation: Case Management* (1995)). Lawyers who violate these instructions will stand to lose some of their fees as the direction states that: failure by practitioners to conduct cases economically will be visited by appropriate orders for costs, including wasted costs orders (that is, some of the costs incurred will not be recoverable). Now, lawyers are no longer allowed to examine their own witnesses in court (examination-in-chief) without the express permission of the judge. These new rules apply to actions in the Queen's Bench Division and Chancery Division of the High Court and the county courts, and are modelled on those which have been used for some time in the Commercial Court where cases are dealt with most expeditiously.

In a statement to launch the new rules (24 January 1995), the Lord Chief Justice said that:

> The aim is to try and change the whole culture, the ethos, applying in the field of civil litigation. We have over the years been too ready to allow those who are litigating to dictate the pace at which cases proceed. Time is money, and wasted time in court means higher charges for litigants and for the taxpayer. It also means that everyone else in the queue has to wait longer for justice.

For this system to operate well, however, there is a need for judges to be better assisted with researchers and assistant lawyers so that they can be properly briefed on the contents and significance of witness statements, and so forth. So far, there has been little improvement in the provision of such services for judges.

The CJR recommended that more cases should be devolved from the county court to arbitration in the small claims procedure. Such a policy was facilitated by changes to the rule in 1992, and 1996, which raised the limit of the value of claims with which the county court small claims procedure can adjudicate to £1,000 and £3,000, respectively (now, the limit is £5,000; see 11.6). Cases in the small claims procedure are heard without the ordinary formal rules of evidence and procedure, the consequential informality being seen as conducive to quicker settlement of issues. The full width of jurisdiction of the court has been confirmed by the Court of Appeal's decision in *Afzal and Others v Ford Motor Company Ltd* (1994). The court gave guidance on the approach to be adopted by county court judges when deciding whether small claims involving amounts below £1,000 should be tried in court instead of being automatically referred to arbitration under Ord 19 r 3 of the County Court (Amendment No 2) Rules 1992 (SI 1992/1965). The court allowed an appeal by Ford against the decision of a judge who had declined to refer to arbitration 16 employees' claims for damages for personal injuries sustained in the workplace. The employees were supported by their trade union, and the employer's case was handled by its insurer.

The employees had argued that compulsory arbitration was unsuitable for their claims and that the issues of liability involved were too complex for summary resolution. Moreover, it was argued that the denial of the right to recover the cost of legal advice and representation at arbitration would deter trade unions from assisting claimants, who would be at a disadvantage in negotiating compensation settlements out of court. In a submission to the Woolf Inquiry in 1995, Marlene Winfield of the National Consumer Council argued that companies and insurance firms are the real beneficiaries of this law. As neither legal aid nor costs are generally available for arbitrated disputes, many people who suffer relatively minor injuries now no longer go to law because they cannot afford to get the assistance of a lawyer. How far the new system for small claims (see 11.6) is able to ensure greater fairness remains to be judged, but the limited costs regime in the new system and absence of legal aid do not provide for much optimism.

When Lord Woolf came to examine the system, small claims hearings played a very important part in the resolution of disputes. He noted that:

> ... in 1994, 24,219 cases where disposed of by full trial [in the county courts] while the number of small claims hearings was 87,885 [*Access to Justice*, Interim Report, 1995, p 102].

What had began life in 1973 as a new system, designed to facilitate ordinary individuals using the law, had degenerated by 1995 into a system which business and organisations played the major part. Lord Woolf noted:

> ... in a sample [by RDA Bowles] of 134 county court cases, in one court including a hundred small claims, only 12% of the cases were brought by private

individuals, although individuals formed a large proportion of defendants. More recently, Professor John Baldwin of the University of Birmingham found that some 40% of the 109 plaintiffs in his 1994 research for the Office of Fair Trading were individuals [*Access to Justice*, Interim Report, 1995, p 106].

Professor Baldwin's research also identified some fundamental differences among district judges in the way in which they dealt with evidence and applied the substantive law to small claims. Additionally, Woolf found a real problem in the way that ordinary citizens were expected to present their cases in court (see *Access to Justice*, Interim Report, 1995, pp 102–10).

11.3 The pressure to settle claims

Most civil disputes are settled out of court. Fewer than 10% of cases where a claim form is issued actually go to court and, even of those which go to trial, many are settled before judgment. Evidence presented by the London Passenger Transport Board to the Winn Committee on Personal Injury Litigation (1968), for example, showed that, of about 5,000 claims made against it a year, about 4,900 were settled without proceedings. Of the 100 or so cases which were commenced, only about one-quarter were taken to full judgment.

The largest study of this sort was conducted by the Oxford Centre for Socio-Legal Studies (Harris *et al*, *Compensation and Support for Illness and Injury* (1984)) which examined a random sample of 1,711 accident victims who had been incapacitated for a minimum of two weeks. Of this group, only 26% had considered claiming damages, only 14% had consulted a solicitor and only 12% were awarded damages. The study looked at the level of damages obtained by the small group (8%) who gained them without the use of solicitors, and concluded that these people appeared to be under-compensated. In the 182 cases (from 1,711 in the sample) in which damages were obtained, the claimant accepted the first offer made in 104 cases. See Genn, *Hard Bargaining: Out of Court Settlement in Personal Injury Claims* (1987).

11.3.1 Costs

Many factors combine to persuade disputants to settle out of court and the fear of prohibitive costs can be a serious deterrent to taking proceedings. This is particularly so when it is remembered that the basic rule is that 'costs follow the event', that is, the successful party can expect the judge to order the loser to pay some or all of his or her solicitor's bill. Costs, however, are a discretionary matter so the whole process is beset with uncertainties. Another gamble the claimant is faced with is the procedure of 'payment into court' (now known as a 'Pt 36 payment'; see 11.12, below) where, at any stage after the commencement of proceedings, the defendant may make a payment into court in satisfaction of the claimant's claim. The claimant may accept the payment or continue the action. If the latter and the damages obtained are not greater than the amount paid in by the defendant, the claimant will be liable for the defendant's taxed costs from the time of payment in even though he or she has won the action. When the judge makes an award of damages, he will not know the amount of any payment into court, so he cannot influence the matter of whether the claimant has to suffer under the rule.

There were 80 cases in the Oxford study which involved abandoned claims and, of these, 16% were abandoned because of fear of legal expenses. Where a claimant is not legally aided, the lawyer may try to persuade him or her to accept a settlement offer plus costs rather than risk a legal action which could fail. This is better for the lawyer as it assures the payment of costs but arguably not in the best interest of many claimants because settlement awards are generally lower than damages awarded by courts for the same types of case.

A study of High Court personal injury cases by Zander ((1975) 72 Law Soc Gazette 680) showed that, while costs were a relatively low proportion of damages in large claims, they were proportionately very high in small claims. Where the damages were under £1,000, 86% of cases had claimed costs for one side amounting to three-fifths of the damages or more. In 33% of cases, the total costs of both sides amounted to more than the amount in dispute. The CJR found that the average cost to the claimant in High Court personal injury actions in 1984 was £6,830 in London and £2,480 outside London. In the county court, costs were an average of 99% of the claimant's damages recovered, as opposed to about one-quarter in the High Court. When the costs of both sides were combined, it was estimated that in the county court they amounted to 125% of damages and between 50 and 75% in the High Court. Research conducted for the Woolf Report on the civil justice system threw further light on this area. The Final Report (*Access to Justice*, 1996) includes a survey of Supreme Court Taxing Office taxed bills conducted by Professor Hazel Genn of University College, London. Genn found alarming data on costs. Her findings indicate the average costs among the lowest value claims consistently represented more than 100% of the claim value. They also showed that, in cases worth between £12,500 and £25,000, average costs ranged from 40% to 95% of the value of the claim. The system provided higher benefits to lawyers than to their clients.

11.3.2 Delay

In the Oxford study, delay was another significant factor influencing people to discontinue claims; 6% of those who abandoned their actions cited it as affecting their decision. Cane (*Atiyah's Accidents, Compensation and the Law* (1993)) has shown evidence that delay and its attendant anxiety can cause a recognisable state of 'litigation neurosis', a complaint which ceases upon the resolution of the dispute. Delay generally assists the defendant and is sometimes used as a deliberate tactic against weaker opponents or to alleviate the cash flow problems of the smaller insurance companies.

11.3.3 Uncertainty

Another factor putting pressure on litigants to settle is that of the risks and uncertainties entailed in the claim. If the case goes to trial then the claimant will, to succeed, have to prove his or her case on the balance of probabilities. The process is beset with legal uncertainties. Is the defendant liable at law for the claimant's loss or injury? Even where the law is clear, there may be evidential difficulties. Genn (*Hard Bargaining: Out of Court Settlement in Personal Injury Claims* (1987)) has presented material to suggest that, in many cases, a claimant's solicitor either does not have sufficient resources to undertake proper factual investigations or does not seek out all available reports. It is also very difficult to contact all relevant witnesses and to assess how persuasive their courtroom evidence would be. Defendants, including or assisted by insurance companies, will often have resources which place them in a good position to fully investigate the circumstances of accidents. Assessing the quantum of damages is another very problematic part of litigation. In an American experiment, 20 pairs of practising lawyers negotiated on identical information about a case and were instructed to negotiate a settlement. Their resultant settlements ranged from the highest of US$95,000 to the lowest of US$15,000 with an average of just over US$47,000.

11.3.4 Other factors

The Oxford study found that many other factors contributed to the discontinuation of claims, including the fear of affecting a continuing relationship and arguments that the victim's own fault caused the accident. The most cited reason (mentioned by 45% of respondents) was problems over obtaining evidence. There have been some legal changes since the Oxford study in 1984 and it will be interesting to see if future studies detect any significant consequential changes in claimants' behaviour.

The Lord Chancellor's Department committed itself (in the CJR's *General Issues Paper*) to the use of new technology, especially for improving the system of county court debt business. The Production Centre has operated since early 1990 since when, relying on new technology, it has issued over 1.5 million summonses. Dealing more expeditiously with this sort of work could free the courts, and thus reduce delays, for other types of case.

The courts have made some progress in this area since 1996, although the challenges in the UK are considerable. Lord Justice Brooke, a leading proponent of the use of information and communications technology (ICT) in the courts, has made the following observation:

> In England, we do not have a Ministry of Justice, with masses of resources at its command. The Lord Chancellor's Department, which supports the courts, is a small department, and, over the last 10 years, its credibility with the Treasury was damaged because of the way that unbudgeted Legal Aid expenditure went on soaring. I believe that expenditure on IT suffered as a result. We have certainly not seen any of the imaginative forward investment in IT which other comparable countries have experienced. In America, for instance, the federal judiciary run the federal courts, and, in 1990, the Senate voted them US$70 million to undertake a programme of computerisation in the court process [Lord Justice Brooke, Keynote Speech to the 13th Bileta Conference: The Changing Jurisdiction, 'IT and the English and Welsh Courts: the Next 10 Years', Dublin, 28 March 1998].

There are only about 60 judges using computers in court, but the government is committed to achieving the transaction of 25% of all dealings with the public through ICT by 2000 (Geoff Hoon MP, then Minister of State at the Lord Chancellor's Department, Speech to the Society for Computers and the Law, The Law Society, London, 25 January 1999).

11.4 The new civil process

The new Civil Procedure Rules (CPR) will be the same for the county court and the High Court. They apply to all cases except (Pt 2) to insolvency proceedings, family proceedings, and non-contentious probate proceedings. The vocabulary will be more user friendly, so, for example, what used to be called a 'writ' will be a 'claim form' and a *guardian ad litem* will be a 'litigation friend'.

Although, in some ways, all the fuss about the new CPR being so far reaching creates the impression that the future will see a sharp rise in litigation, the truth may be different. It seems likely that a fall off in litigation in the 1990s will continue. Judge John Frenkel ('On the road to reform' (1998) 95(48) Law Soc Gazette 33) has pointed to the data. Queen's Bench Division writs were down from 50,295 in 1993–94 to 22,483 in 1997–98, and county court summonses from 2,577,704 to 1,959,958. During the same period, the number of district judges increased from 289 to 337.

11.4.1 The overriding objective

The overriding objective of the new CPR is to enable the court to deal justly with cases. The first rule reads:

> 1.1(1) These rules are a new procedural code with the overriding objective of enabling the court to deal with cases justly.

This objective will include ensuring that the parties are on an equal footing, and saving expense. When exercising any discretion given by the CPR, the court must, according to r 1.2, have regard to the overriding objective, and a checklist of factors, including the amount of money involved, the complexity of the issue, the parties' financial positions, how the case can be dealt with expeditiously and by allotting an appropriate share of the court's resources while taking into account the needs of others. In future, as Judge John Frenkel observes, 'the decisions of the Court of Appeal are more likely to illustrate the application of the new rules to the facts of a particular case as opposed to being interpretative authorities that define the meaning of the rules'.

11.4.2 Practice directions

Practice directions (official statements of interpretative guidance) play an important role in the new civil process. In general, they supplement the CPRs, giving the latter fine detail. They tell parties and their representatives what the court will expect of them, in respect of documents to be filed in court for a particular purpose, and how they must co-operate with the other parties to their action. They also tell the parties what they can expect of the court. For example, they explain what sort of sanction a court is likely to impose if a particular court order or request is not complied with. Almost every part of the new rules has a corresponding practice direction. They supersede all previous practice directions in relation to civil process.

11.4.3 Case control

Judges will receive support from court staff in carrying out their case management role. The court will monitor case progress by using a computerised diary monitoring system which will:

- record certain requests, or orders made by the court;

- identify the particular case, or cases to which these orders/requests refer, and the dates by which a response should be made; and

- check on the due date whether the request or order has been complied with.

Whether there has been compliance or not, the court staff will pass the relevant files to a procedural judge (a Master in the Royal Courts of Justice, a district judge in the county court) who will decide if either side should have a sanction imposed on him or her.

In the new system, the litigants will have much less control over the pace of the case than in the past. They will not be able to draw out proceedings or delay in the way that they once could have done because the case will be subject to a timetable. Once a defence is filed, the parties will get a timetable order that includes the prospective trial date. The need for pre-issue preparation is increased, and this will probably benefit litigants because, as Genn's research has shown (*Hard Bargaining: Out of Court Settlement in Personal Injury Claims* (1987)), in settled personal injury actions, 60% of costs were incurred before proceedings. The court now has a positive duty to manage cases. Rule 1.4(1) states that 'The court must further the overriding objective by actively managing cases'. The rule goes on to explain what this management involves:

1.4(2) Active case management includes:

    (a) encouraging the parties to co-operate with each other in the conduct of the proceedings;

    (b) identifying the issues at an early stage;

    (c) deciding promptly which issues need full investigation and trial and accordingly disposing summarily of the others;

    (d) deciding the order in which issues are to be resolved;

    (e) encouraging the parties to use an alternative dispute resolution procedure if the court considers that appropriate ...;

    (f) helping the parties to settle the whole or part of the case;

    (g) fixing timetables or otherwise controlling the progress of the case;

    (h) considering whether the likely benefits of taking a particular step justify the cost of taking it;

    (i) dealing with as many aspects of the case as it can on the same occasion;

    (j) dealing with the case without the parties needing to attend court;

    (k) making use of technology; and

    (l) giving directions to ensure that the trial of a case proceeds quickly and efficiently.

We shall have to wait and see how judges use these rules and principles in practice but it is clear that what Lord Woolf identified as the misuse of rules by some lawyers (with unjust results) will be much less likely in the new environment. It is worth noting here that district judges and deputy district judges have had extensive Woolf training to promote a common approach (see 4.8.3). Training is being taken very seriously by the judiciary. District judges now occupy a pivotal position in the civil process.

Part 3 of the CPR gives the court a wide range of substantial powers. The court can, for instance, extend or shorten the time for compliance with any rule, practice direction or court order, even if an application for an extension is made after the time for compliance has expired. It can also hold a hearing and receive evidence by telephone or 'by using any other method of direct oral communication'.

Part 3 of the CPR also gives the court powers to:

- strike out a statement of case;

- impose sanctions for non-payment of certain fees;

- impose sanctions for non-compliance with rules and practice directions;

- give relief from sanctions.

There is, though, a certain flexibility built into the rules. A failure to comply with a rule or practice direction will not necessarily be fatal to a case. Part 3.10 of the CPR states:

> Where there has been an error of procedure such as a failure to comply with a rule or practice direction:
>
> (a) the error does not invalidate any step taken in the proceedings unless the court so orders; and
>
> (b) the court may make an order to remedy the error.

The intention of imposing a sanction will always be to put the parties back into the position they would have been in if one of them had not failed to meet a deadline. For example, the court could order that a party carries out a task (like producing some sort of documentary evidence) within a very short time (for example, two days) in order that the existing trial dates can be met.

11.4.4 Court allocation

The new civil system works on the basis of the court, upon receipt of the claim (accompanied by duly filled-in forms giving all the relevant details of the claim including how much it is for, and an indication of its factual and legal complexity) allocating the case to one of three tracks for a hearing. These are: (a) small claims; (b) fast track; and (c) multi-track.

The new small claims limit will be £5,000, although personal injury and housing disrepair claims for over £1,000, illegal eviction and harassment claims will be excluded from the small claims procedure (for detail, see 11.6). The limit for cases going into the fast track system will be £15,000, and only claims for over £15,000 can be issued in the Royal Courts of Justice. Applications to move cases 'up' a track on grounds of complexity will have to be made on the new allocation questionnaire (see below).

11.4.5 Pre-action protocols

The pre-action protocols (PAPs) are an important feature of the reforms. They exist for cases of *clinical negligence* (formerly called medical negligence but now extended to cover claims against dentists, radiologists *et al*) and *personal injury* cases, and are likely to be followed, over time, with similar protocols for cases involving other specialisms like debt.

In the *Final Report on Access to Justice* (1996), Lord Woolf stated (Chapter 10) that PAPs are intended to 'build on and increase the benefits of early but well informed settlements'. The purposes of the PAPs, he said, are:

(a) to focus the attention of litigants on the desirability of resolving disputes without litigation;

(b) to enable them to obtain the information they reasonably need in order to enter into an appropriate settlement ...;

(d) if a pre-action settlement is not achievable, to lay the ground for expeditious
    . conduct of proceedings.

The protocols were drafted with the assistance of The Law Society, the Clinical Disputes Forum, the Association of Personal Injury Lawyers, and the Forum of Insurance Lawyers. Most clients in personal injury and medical negligence claims want their cases settled as quickly and as economically as possible. The new spirit of co-operation fostered by the Woolf reforms should mean that, in future, fewer cases are pushed through the courts. The PAPs are intended to improve pre-action contact between the parties and to facilitate better exchange of information and fuller investigation of a claim at an earlier stage. Both clinical negligence and personal injury PAPs recommend:

- The claimant sending a reasonably detailed letter of claim to the proposed defendant, including details of the accident/medical treatment, a brief explanation of why the defendant is being held responsible, a description of the injury, and an outline of the defendant's losses. Unlike a 'pleading' in the old system (which could not be moved away from by the claimant), there will be no sanctions applied if the proceedings differ from the letter of claim. However, as Gordon Exall has observed ('Civil litigation brief' (1999) 144 SJ 32), letters of claim should be drafted with care because any variance between them and the claim made in court will give the defendant's lawyers a fruitful opportunity for cross-examination.

- The defendant should acknowledge the letter within 21 days, identifying insurers if applicable. The defendant then has a maximum of three months to investigate and tell the claimant whether liability is admitted. If it is denied, reasons must be given.

- Within that three month period or on denial of liability, the parties should organise disclosure of key documents. For personal injury cases, the protocol lists the main types of defendant's documents for different types of cases. If the defendant denies liability, then he should disclose all the relevant documents in his possession which are likely to be ordered to be disclosed by the court. In clinical negligence claims, the key documents will usually be the claimant's medical records, and the protocol includes a pro-forma application to obtain these.

- The personal injury PAP also includes a framework for the parties to agree on the use of expert evidence, particularly in respect of a condition and prognosis report from a medical expert. Before any prospective party instructs an expert, he should give the other party a list of names of one or more experts in the relevant specialty which he considers are suitable to instruct. Within 14 days, the other party may indicate an objection to one or more of the experts, the first party should then instruct a mutually acceptable expert. Only if all suggested experts are objected to can the sides instruct experts of their own. The aim, here, is to allow the claimant to get the defendant to agree to one report being prepared by a mutually agreeable non-partisan expert. The clinical negligence PAP encourages the parties to consider sharing expert evidence, especially with regard to quantum (that is, the amount of damages payable).

- Both PAPs encourage the parties to use ADR or negotiation to settle the dispute during the pre-action period.

At the early stage of proceedings, when a case is being allocated to a track (that is, small claims, fast track) after the defence has been filed, parties will be asked whether they have complied with a relevant protocol, and, if not, why not. The court will then be able to take the answers into account when deciding whether, for example, an extension of time should be granted. The court will also be able to penalise poor conduct by one side through costs sanctions – an order that the party at fault pay the costs of the proceedings or part of them.

11.4.6 Jurisdiction for the start of proceedings

Part 7 of the CPR sets out the rules for starting proceedings. A new restriction is placed on which cases may be begun in the High Court. The county courts retain an unlimited jurisdiction for handling contract and tort claims (that is, negligence cases, nuisance cases). Issuing proceedings in the High Court is now limited to:

- personal injury claims with a value of £50,000 or more;

- other claims with a value of more than £15,000;

- claims where an Act of Parliament requires an action to start in the High Court; or

- specialist High Court claims which need to go to one of the specialist 'lists', like the Commercial List, the Technology List, and the Construction List.

11.5 Proceedings – the CPR Pt 7 claim

One of the main aims of the Woolf reforms is to simplify court forms. Under the old system, there were various forms that needed to be completed at the outset of an action – different types including summonses, originating applications, writs and petitions. Under the new system, most claims will be begun by using a Pt 7 claim form – a form which has been designed for multi-purpose use. It can be used if the claim is for a *specified* amount of money (the old term was *liquidated* damages) or an *unspecified* amount (replacing the term *unliquidated* damages). The form can also be used for non-monetary claims, for example, where the claimant just wants a court order, not money. The person issuing the claim form is called a claimant (plaintiff, in old vocabulary) and the person at whom it is directed will continue to be known as a defendant.

Under the new rules, the court can grant any remedy to which the claimant is entitled even if the claimant does not specify which one he or she wants. It is, though, as Gordon Exall has observed ((1999) 144 SJ 162), dangerous to start an action without having a clear idea of the remedy you want. The defendant might be able to persuade the court not to allow the claimant a certain part of his or her costs if he (the defendant) finds himself having to consider a remedy which had not been mentioned prior to the trial.

How far these plainer forms simplify matters remains to be seen. In the longer term, it seems clear that a set of plain language forms designed all at one time, as a part of one coherent system, will provide a more efficient system than that afforded by a collection of outdated forms which had been generated reactively over a long period. Nonetheless, it might take a while for the new system to become fully operational in an efficient way. Around 75% of the matters received for issue at Bristol County Court in the week following the implementation of the reforms were returned, as solicitors were using either the old forms or the new ones wrongly completed ('Claims tumble in first week of Woolf as forms stymie solicitors' (1999) 96(18) Law Soc Gazette 3). Similarly, a spokesperson for Manchester County Court said 'almost all' forms were sent back to solicitors in the week following the introduction of the new rules. Only 74 claims were received by that court that week, as opposed to a weekly average prior to the reforms of 550 claims.

11.5.1 Value

The 'value' of a claim is the amount a claimant reasonably expects to recover. Unless the amount being claimed is a specified amount, a claimant will be expected (CPR Pt 16) to state the value band into which the claim is likely to fall. The value bands reflect the values for the different tracks (for example, £1 to £5,000 for small claims). Value is calculated as the amount a claimant expects to recover, ignoring any interest, costs, contributory negligence or the fact that a defendant may make a counterclaim, or include a set-off in the defence. If a claimant is not able to put a value on the claim, the reasons for this must be given.

11.5.2 Particulars of claim

Particulars of claim, may be included in the claim form, attached to it, or may be served (that is, given or sent to a party by a method allowed by the rules) separately from it. Where they are served separately, they must be served within 14 days of the claim form being served. The time for a defendant to respond begins to run from the time the particulars of claim are served.

CPR Pt 16 is entitled *Statements of Case* (replacing the term *pleadings*). Statements of case include documents from both sides: claim forms, particulars of claims, defences, counterclaims, replies to defences and counterclaims, Pt 20 (third party) claims and any *further information* provided under CPR Pt 18 (replacing the term *further and better particulars*). Part 16 of the rules also sets out what both particulars of claim and defences should contain.

The particulars of claim must contain:

• a concise statement of facts on which the claimant relies;

• details of any interest claimed; and

• specific details if exemplary, provisional and aggravated damages are claimed.

The Woolf Report was against obliging the claimant to state the legal nature of the claim as this would prejudice unrepresented defendants. If the nature of the claim is uncertain, then the court can take its own steps to clarify the matter.

Where a claimant is going to rely on the fact that the defendant has been convicted for a crime arising out of the same circumstances for which the claimant is now suing, then the particulars of claim must contain details of the conviction, the court which made it and exactly how it is relevant to the claimant's arguments.

It is optional for the claimant to also mention any point of law on which the claim is based, and the names of any witnesses which he or she proposes to call.

All statements of case must also contain a statement of truth.

11.5.3 Statements of truth

A statement of truth is a statement that a party believes that the facts or allegations set out in a document which they put forward are true. It is required in statements of case, witness statements, and expert reports. Any document which contains a statement of truth may be used in evidence. This will avoid the previous need to swear affidavits in support of various statements made as part of the claim.

Any document with a signed statement of truth which contains false information given deliberately, that is, without an honest belief in its truth, will constitute a contempt of court (a punishable criminal offence) by the person who provided the information. Solicitors may sign statements of truth on behalf of clients, but on the understanding that it is done with the clients' authority, and with clients knowing the consequences of any false statement will be personal to them.

11.5.4 Response pack

When a claim form is served, it will be served with a response pack. The response pack will contain an acknowledgment of service, a form of admission and a form of defence and counterclaim. The response pack will be served with a claim form containing the particulars of claim or which are attached to it, or, where particulars of claim are served after the claim form, with the particulars. A defendant must respond within 14 days of service of the particulars of claim. If a defendant ignores the claim, the claimant may obtain judgment for the defendant to pay the amount claimed. A defendant may:

- pay the claim;
- admit the claim, or partly admit it;
- file an acknowledgment of service; or
- file a defence.

New requirements have now also been introduced regarding the content of a defence. A defence which is a simple denial is no longer acceptable and runs the risk of being struck out by the court (that is, deleted so that it may no longer be relied upon). A defendant must state in any defence:

- which of the allegations in the particulars of claim are denied, giving reasons for doing so;
- which the defendant is not able to admit or deny but which the claimant is required to prove;
- which allegations are admitted; and
- if the defendant disputes the claimant's statement of value, the reasons for doing so and if possible, stating an alternate value.

These rules mark a significant change of culture from the old civil procedure rules. Under the old rules, a defendant could, in his defence, raise a 'non-admission' or a 'denial'. The first meant that the defendant was putting the plaintiff (now claimant) to proof, that is, challenging him to prove his case on the balance of probabilities. The second meant that the defendant was raising a specific defence, for example, a 'development risks defence' under the Product Liability Act 1987. Defendants were allowed under the old rules to keep as many avenues of defence available for as long as possible. Under the new rules, the defendant must respond according to the choices in the four options (above). According to r 16.5(5), if the defendant does not deal specifically with each allegation, then it will be deemed to be admitted.

Writing just before the new CPR came into effect, barrister Gordon Exall observed that:

> In theory, this should lead to an enormous change in culture. In personal injury cases, for example, the defendant often denies the existence of various statutory duties owed. Often, nothing will induce the defendant to cease this denial up to the morning of the trial when the defendant's counsel, sensibly, concedes that the various duties are owed [(1999) 144 SJ 270].

11.5.5 Part 8 claims (CPR Pt 8)

Part 8 of the new rules introduces the *alternative procedure for claims*. This procedure is commenced by the issue of a Pt 8 claim form. It is intended to provide a speedy resolution of claims which are not likely to involve a substantial dispute of fact, for example, applications for approval of infant settlements, or for orders enforcing a statutory right such as a right to have access to medical records (under the Access to Health Records Act 1990).

The main differences between this and the Pt 7 procedure are as follows:

- a hearing may be given on issue or at same later stage if required;
- only an acknowledgment of service is served with the claim form by way of a response document:
- a defendant must file an acknowledgment of service to be able to take part in any hearing;
- a defendant must serve a copy of the acknowledgment on the other parties, as well as filing it with the court;
- no defence is required;
- default judgment is not available to the claimant; the court must hear the case;
- there are automatic directions for the exchange of evidence (in this case, in the form of witness statements);
- Pt 8 claims are not formally allocated to a track; they are automatically multi-track cases.

11.5.6 Default judgment (CPR Pt 12)

If a defendant (to a Pt 7 claim) files an acknowledgment stating an intention to defend the claim, this extends the period for filing a defence from 14 to 28 days from the date of service of the particulars. Failure to file an acknowledgment or, later, failure to file a defence can result in default judgment, that is, the court will find for the claimant so the defendant will lose the case.

If the defendant does not to reply to the claim, a claimant may apply for default judgment for the amount claimed if the amount claimed is a specified amount, or on liability, if the amount claimed is unspecified, after the 14 day period from service has elapsed.

There are a number of cases in which it is not possible to obtain judgment in default, notably, in claims for delivery of goods subject to an agreement controlled by the Consumer Credit Act 1974.

11.5.7 Service (CPR Pt 6)

Where the court is to serve any document (not just claim forms), it is for the court to decide the method of service. This will generally be by first class post. The deemed date of service is two days after the day of posting for all defendants, including limited companies. Where a claim form originally served by post is returned by the Post Office, the court will send a notice of non-service to the claimant. The notice will tell the claimant that the court will not make any further attempts at service. Service, therefore, becomes a matter for claimants. The court will return the copies of the claim form, response pack, etc, for claimants to amend as necessary, and re-serve.

Claimants may serve claim forms, having told the court in writing that they wish to do so, either personally, by post, by fax, by document exchange (a private courier service operated between law firms) or by email or other electronic means. A claimant who serves a document must file a certificate of service within seven days of service with a copy of the document served attached.

11.5.8 Admissions and part admissions

The possibility of admitting liability for a claim for a specific amount and making an offer to pay by instalments, or at a later date, applies to both county court and High Court cases. Where the claim is for a specific amount, the admission will be sent direct to the claimant. However, if a claimant objects to the rate of payment offered, there are changes which affect the determination process, that is, the process by which a member of a court's staff, or a judge, decides the rate of payment.

Cases involving a specific amount where the balance outstanding, including any costs, is less than £50,000 will be determined by a court officer. Those where the balance is £50,000 or more, or for an unspecified amount of any value, must be determined by a Master or district judge. The Master, or judge, has the option of dealing with the determination on the papers without a hearing, or at a hearing.

A defendant in a claim for an unspecified amount of money (damages) will be able to make an offer of a specific sum of money in satisfaction of a claim which does not have to be supported by a payment into court. A claimant can accept the admission and rate of payment offered as if the claim had originally been for a specific amount. The determination procedure described above will apply where a claimant accepts the amount offered but not the rate of payment proposed.

If a claimant does not accept the amount offered, a request that judgment be entered for liability on the strength of the defendant's admission may be made to the court. In the new system, this is referred to as *judgment for an amount and costs to be decided by the court* (replacing *interlocutory judgment for damages to be assessed*). Where judgment is entered in this way, the court will at the same time give case management directions for dealing with the case.

Where a request for such a judgment is received, the court file will be passed to a procedural judge. The judge may allocate the case to the small claims track and give directions if it is of appropriate value; ask that the case be set down for a *disposal* hearing, or, where the amount is likely to be heavily disputed, order a trial. Directions will be given as appropriate. A disposal hearing in these circumstances may either be a hearing at which the court gives directions, or at which the amount and costs are decided.

11.5.9 Defence and automatic transfer (CPR Pt 15)

Claims for specified amounts will be transferred automatically to the defendant's 'home court' where the defendant is an individual who has filed a defence. The defendant's home court will be 'the court or district registry, including the Royal Courts of Justice, for the district in which the defendant's address for service as shown on the defence is situated'. This means that, where the defendant is represented by a solicitor, this will be the defendant's solicitor's business address.

Where there is more than one defendant, it is the first defendant to file a defence who dictates whether or not automatic transfer will take place. For example, if there are two defendants to a claim, one an individual and one a limited company, there would be no automatic transfer if the limited company was the first defendant to file a defence.

11.5.10 Allocation questionnaire

The purpose of this document is to enable to court to judge in which track the case should be heard. When a defence is filed, the issuing court will send out a copy of the defence to all other parties to the claim together with an allocation questionnaire, a notice setting out the date for returning it and the name and address of the court (or district registry or the Royal Courts of Justice (that is, High Court), as appropriate) to which the completed allocation questionnaire must be returned. A notice of transfer will also be sent if the case is being automatically transferred.

When the allocation questionnaire is returned, or at the end of the period for returning it, and whether or not only some, or none, of the questionnaires (if there is more than one defendant) have been filed, the court file will be passed to a procedural judge for directions and allocation to track. If there is sufficient information, the judge will allocate the case to a track and a notice of allocation and directions will be sent out to each party. Where only one party has filed a questionnaire or there is insufficient information, the judge may make an order requesting further information, or order an allocation hearing. Where none of the parties has filed a questionnaire, the judge may also decide to impose a sanction, for example, ordering that a statement, or statements, of case be struck out unless a completed questionnaire is filed within three days of service of the order.

The questionnaire asks a number of questions, for example:

- Do you wish there to be a one month stay to attempt to settle this case?

- Which track do you consider most suitable for your case (small claims, fast track, or multi-track)? A party wishing a case to be dealt with on a track which is not the obviously suitable track must give reasons.

- At this stage, you are asked whether you have complied with any relevant protocols, and, if not, why not and the extent of the non-compliance.

- You are asked for an estimate of costs to date and the overall costs up to trial.

- You are asked if you wish to use expert evidence at the trial, whether expert reports have been copied to the other side, who the expert is, and, if the parties have not agreed upon a common expert, why not.

The purpose of this questionnaire is to make both sides have a clear overview of the case at an early stage so it becomes very difficult for lawyers to bumble along buffeted by developments in a case. To reduce delays and therefore costs, it is desirable that a lawyer should be able to purposefully stride through a case along a planned route.

11.5.11 Applications to be made when claims come before a judge

The overriding objective in Pt 1 requires the court to deal with as many aspects of the case as possible on the same occasion. The filing of an allocation questionnaire is one such occasion. Parties should, wherever possible, issue any application they may wish to make, such as an application for summary judgment (CPR Pt 24), or to add a third party (CPR Pt 20), at the same time as they file their questionnaire. Any hearing set to deal with the application will also serve as an allocation hearing if allocation remains appropriate.

11.5.12 Summary judgment (CPR Pt 24)

Summary judgment is available to both claimants and defendants. Where either party feels that the other does not have a valid claim or defence, they can apply to the court for the claim or defence to be struck out and for judgment to be entered in their favour. The applicant, either claimant or defendant, must prove to the court's satisfaction, that the other party has 'no real prospect of success' and that 'there is no other reason why the case or issue should be dealt with at trial'.

Application for summary judgment cannot be made without the court's permission (replacing the term leave), before an acknowledgment of service has been filed. Where an application is made by the claimant before a defendant files a defence, the defendant against whom it is made need not file a defence. If a claimant's application is unsuccessful, the court will give directions for the filing of a defence.

11.5.13 Allocation to track (CPR Pt 26)

Allocation will be to one of three tracks: the *small claims track*, the *fast track* and the *multi-track*. Each of the tracks offers a different degree of case management.

Directions (instructions about what to do to prepare the case for trial or hearing) will be proportionate to the value of the claim, its importance, complexity, and so on. Each track requires a different degree of case monitoring, that is, the more complex the claim, the more milestone events there are likely to be (that is, important points in the process, like the date by which the allocation questionnaire should be returned). Time for carrying out directions, no matter which track, may be extended or shortened by agreement between parties but must not, as a result, affect any of the milestones relevant to that track. The time for carrying out directions will be expressed as calendar dates rather than periods of days or weeks. Directions will include the court's directions concerning the use of expert evidence.

11.6 The small claims track (CPR Pt 27)

There is no longer any 'automatic reference' to the small claims track. Claims are allocated to this track in exactly the same way as to the fast or multi-tracks. The concept of an *'arbitration'* therefore disappears and is replaced by a *small claims hearing*. Aspects of the old small claims procedure which are retained, include their informality, the interventionist approach adopted by the judiciary, the limited costs regime and the limited grounds for appeal (misconduct of the district judge or an error of law made by the court).

Changes to the handling of small claims are:

- *an increase in the jurisdiction from £3,000 to no more than £5,000* (with the exception of claims for personal injury where the damages claimed for pain and suffering and loss of amenity do not exceed £1,000 and the financial value of the whole claim does not exceed £5,000; and for housing disrepair where the claim for repairs and other work do not exceed £1,000 and the financial value of any other claim for damages is not more than £1,000);

- *hearings to be generally public hearings* – but subject to some exceptions (CPR Pt 39);

- *paper adjudication, if parties consent* – where a judge thinks that paper adjudication may be appropriate, parties will be asked to say whether or not they have any objections within a given time period. If a party does object, the matter will be given a hearing in the normal way;

- *parties need not attend the hearing* – a party not wishing to attend a hearing will be able to give the court and the other party, or parties, written notice that they will not be attending. The notice must be filed with the court seven days before the start of the hearing. This will guarantee that the court will take into account any written evidence that party has sent to the court. A consequence of this is that the judge must give reasons for the decision reached which will be included in the judgment;

- *the introduction of tailored directions* – to be given for some of the most common small claims, for example, spoiled holidays, or wedding videos, road traffic accidents, building disputes.

Parties can consent to use the small claims track even if the value of their claim exceeds the normal value for that track, but subject to the court's approval. The limited cost regime will not apply to these claims. But, costs will be limited to the costs that might have been awarded if the claim had been dealt with in the fast track. Parties will also be restricted to a maximum one day hearing.

The milestone events for the small claims track are the *date for the return of the allocation questionnaire and the date of the hearing*.

The right to appeal under the CPR is governed by new principles. You can appeal on the basis that:

(a) there was a serious irregularity affecting the proceedings; or

(b) the court made a mistake of law.

An example of (a) (see Paul McGrath (1999) 149 NLJ 748) would be where an arbitrator fails to allow submissions on any crucial point upon which he hangs his judgment.

11.7   The fast track (CPR Pt 28)

In accordance with one of the main principles of the Woolf reforms, the purpose of the fast track is to provide a streamlined procedure for the handling of moderately-valued cases – *those with a value of more than £5,000 but less than £15,000* – in a way which will ensure that the costs remain proportionate to the amount in dispute. The features of the procedure which aim to achieve this are:

- standard directions for trial preparation which avoid complex procedures and multiple experts, with minimum case management intervention by the court;

- a limited period between directions and the start of the trial, or trial period, of around 30 weeks;

- a maximum of one day (five hours) for trial;

- trial period must not exceed three weeks and parties must be given 21 days notice of the date fixed for trial;

- normally, no oral expert evidence is to be given at trial; and costs allowed for the trial are fixed and which vary depending on the level of advocate.

Directions given to the parties by the judge will normally include a date by which parties must file a listing questionnaire. As with allocation questionnaires, the procedural judge may impose a sanction where a listing questionnaire is not returned by the due date. Listing questionnaires will include information about witnesses, confirm the time needed for trial, parties' availability and the level of advocate for the trial.

The milestone events for the fast track are *the date for the return of allocation* and *listing questionnaires* and the *date for the start of the trial, or trial period*.

11.8   The multi-track (CPR Pt 29)

The multi-track is intended to provide a flexible regime for the handling of the higher value, more complex claims, that is, those with a *value of over £15,000*.

This track does not provide any standard procedure, such as those for small claims or claims in the fast track. Instead, it offers a range of case management tools – *standard directions, case management conferences* and *pre-trial reviews* – which can be used in a 'mix and match' way – to suit the needs of individual cases. Whichever of these is used to manage the case, the principle of setting a date for trial, or a trial period at the earliest possible time, no matter that it is some way away, will remain paramount.

Where a trial period is given for a multi-track case, this will be one week. Parties will be told initially that their trial will begin on a day within the given week. The rules and practice direction do not set any time period for giving notice to the parties of the date fixed for trial.

11.9 Public and private hearings (CPR Pt 39)

In the new rules, the distinction between 'public' and 'private' hearings is not whether a claim, or application, is heard in a court room or the judge's room (formerly called *chambers*), but whether members of the public are allowed to sit in on the hearing wherever it takes place.

Courts are not required to make any special arrangements to accommodate members of the public, for example, if the judge's room is too small to accommodate more than those directly concerned with the claim. However, where a hearing is 'public', anyone may obtain a copy of the order made upon payment of the appropriate fee.

11.10 Case management conferences

Case management conferences may be regarded as an opportunity to 'take stock'. There is no limit to the number of case management conferences which may be held during the life of a case, although the cost of attendance at such hearings against the benefits obtained will always be a consideration in making the decision. They will be used, among other things, to consider:

- giving directions, including a specific date for the return of a listing questionnaire;

- whether the claim, or defence, are sufficiently clear for the other party to understand the claim they have to meet;

- whether any amendments should be made to statements of case;

- what documents, if any each party needs to show the other;

- what factual evidence should be given;

- what expert evidence should be sought and how it should be sought and disclosed; and

- whether it would save costs to order a separate trial of one or more issues.

11.11 Pre-trial reviews

Pre-trial reviews will normally take place after the filing of listing questionnaires, and before the start of the trial. Their main purpose is to decide a timetable for the trial itself, including the evidence to be allowed and whether this should be given orally, instructions about the content of any trial bundles (bundles of documents including evidence, such as written statements, for the judge to read) and confirming a realistic time estimate for the trial itself.

Rules require that, where a party is represented, a representative 'familiar with the case and with sufficient authority to deal with any issues likely to arise must attend every case management conference or pre-trial review'.

11.12 Stays for settlement (CPR Pt 26) and settlements (Pt 36)

Under the new CPR, there is a greater incentive for parties to settle their differences.

The court will take into account any pre-action offers to settle when making an order for costs. Thus, a side which has refused an reasonable offer to settle will be treated less generously in the issue of how far the court will order their costs to be paid by the other side. For this to happen, the offer, though, must be one which is made to be open to the other side for at least 21 days after receipt (to stop any undue pressure being put on someone with the phrase: 'take it or leave it, it is only open for one day then I shall withdraw the offer'). Also, if the offer is made by the defendant, it must be an offer to pay compensation and to pay the claimant's costs

Several aspects of the new rules encourage litigants to settle rather than take risks in order (as a claimant) to hold out for unreasonably large sums of compensation, or try to get away (as a defendant) with paying nothing rather than some compensation. The system of Pt 36 payments or offers does not apply to small claims but, for other cases, it seems bound to have a significant effect. Thus, if at the trial a claimant does not get more damages than a sum offered by the defendant in what is called a 'Pt 36' payment (that is, an offer to settle or a payment into the court), or obtain a judgment more favourable than a Pt 36 offer, the court will order the claimant to pay any costs incurred by the defendant after the latest date for accepting the payment or offer. The court now has a discretion to make a different order for costs than the normal order. District Judge Frenkel has given the following example:

> Claim, £150,000 – judgment, £51,000 – £50,000 paid into court. The without prejudice correspondence shows that the claimant would consider nothing short of £150,000. The claimant may be in trouble. The defendant will ask the judge to consider overriding principles of Pt 1 'Was it proportional to incur the further costs of trial to secure an additional £1,000?'. Part 44.3 confirms the general rule that the loser pays but allows the court to make a different order to take into account offers to settle, payment into court, the parties, conduct including pre-action conduct and exaggeration of the claim [(1999) 149 NLJ 458].

Similarly, where, at trial, a defendant is held liable to the claimant for more money than the proposals contained in a claimant's Pt 36 offer (that is, where the claimant has made an offer to settle), the court may order the defendant to pay interest on the award at a rate not exceeding 10% above the base rate for some or all of the period starting with the date on which the defendant could have accepted the offer.

Active case management imposes a duty on the courts to help parties settle their disputes. A 'stay' is a temporary halt in proceedings, and an opportunity for the court to order such a pause arises at the stage when the defence to a claim has been filed. Parties can indicate that they have agreed on a stay to attempt to settle the case and, provided the court agrees, can have an initial period of one month to try to settle the case. In order to avoid the stay being used as a delaying tactic, the order granting the stay will require the parties to report back to the court within 14 days of the end of the period of the stay to:

- inform the court if the matter has been settled either wholly or partly; or

- asking for more time for settlement; or

- reporting that the attempt to settle has failed, so that the process of allocation of court track can take place.

The court will always give the final decision about whether to grant the parties more time to use a mediator, or arbitrator, or expert to settle, even if the parties are agreed they wish to have more time. A stay will never be granted for an indefinite period.

11.13 Witness statements

In the *Final Report on Access to Justice,* Lord Woolf recognised the importance of witness statements in cases but observed that they had become problematic because lawyers had made them excessively long and detailed in order to protect against leaving out something which later proved to be relevant. He said 'witness statements have ceased to be the authentic account of the lay witness; instead they have become an elaborate, costly branch of legal drafting' (para 55).

Under the new rules, witness statements must contain the evidence that the witness will give at trial but they should be briefer than those drafted under the previous rules: they should be drafted in lay language and should not discuss legal propositions. Witnesses will be allowed to amplify on the statement or deal with matters that have arisen since the report was served, although this is not an automatic right and a 'good reason' for the admission of new evidence will have to be established.

11.14 Court fees

A new fee structure will be introduced to take account of the different procedures, a movement towards a 'pay as you go' fees regime and the need for full cost recovery. Pay as you go means that parties will be expected to contribute more in fees, the more court and judicial time they use, for example, if they do not settle and carry on to trial.

Courts will be pro-active in collecting fees, in particular, those which are payable at allocation and listing stages, but *without interrupting* a case's progress. There will be sanctions for non-payment of allocation and listing questionnaire fees which could lead to a party's statement of case being struck out.

11.15 Experts (CPR Pt 35)

New rules place a clear duty on the court to ensure that 'expert evidence is restricted to that which is reasonably required to resolve the proceedings'. That is to say that expert evidence will only be allowed either by way of written report, or orally, where the court gives permission. Equally important is the rules' statement about experts' duties. They state that it is the clear duty of experts to help the *court* on matters within their expertise, bearing in mind that this duty overrides any obligation to the person from whom they have received instructions or by whom they are paid.

There will be greater emphasis in the future on using the opinion of a single expert. Experts will only be called to give oral evidence at a trial or hearing if the court gives permission. Experts' written reports must contain a statement that they understand and have complied with their duty to the court. Instructions to experts will no longer be privileged and their substance, whether written or oral, must be set out in the expert's report. Thus, either side can insist, through the court, on seeing how the other side phrased its request to an expert.

11.16 Costs

11.16.1 Fixed costs (CPR Pt 45)

There are new rates for the fixed costs allowed on issue of a claim and on entry of judgment where a party is represented by a solicitor.

11.16.2 Assessment (CPR Pt 47)

The terms *taxed* costs and *taxation* become redundant and are replaced by assessment. Costs will either be assessed summarily, that is, there and then, or there will be a *detailed assessment* at some later stage where one party has been ordered to pay another's costs.

Summary assessment

Judges will normally summarily assess costs at the end of hearings, both interim and final, and particularly at the end of fast track trials. Parties will be expected to bring any necessary documentation to the hearing for this purpose. In this way, the need for detailed assessment of costs is avoided so far as possible.

11.17 What will the new system achieve?

The positive answer, self-evidently, is that it will achieve all or most of the reforms whose spirit is captured in Lord Woolf's *Final Report*. The new system, clearly though, will not be without its problems, some minor and others more troubling.

Professor Michael Zander QC has made substantial criticisms of the new civil procedure reforms. At the heart of the Woolf reforms is the mechanism of 'judicial case management'. Looking at the results of an American study about how the system operates in the United States, Zander raises serious questions about whether the Woolf reforms would be subject to similar problems (see 'How does judicial case management work?' (1997) 147 NLJ 353). The major official study that Zander examined was published by the Institute of Civil Justice at the Rand Corporation in California. The study was based on 10,000 cases in Federal Courts drawn from 16 States. It appears that a range of judicial case management techniques introduced in America had little effect on the time it took to deal with cases, litigation costs, and lawyer satisfaction. There was evidence that early judicial case management is associated with significantly increased costs to litigants because lawyer work increases in such circumstances. Zander notes that interviews with judges and lawyers in the American study suggested some reasons why tracking cases (the American divisions were Expedited/Standard/Complex) had proved problematic. One of the problems was the difficulty of deciding the correct track assignment for most civil cases using data available at or soon after the filing of the case. This would perhaps not be such a problem in the English model, as assignment to cases comes at a later stage when a defence has been entered so it is easy to evaluate the potential complexity of the case. Additionally, though, the American study showed that judges often wished to tailor case management to the needs of the case and to their style of management rather than having the track assignment provide the management structure of cases. This could equally apply to English judges.

The Rand Report explains that case management tends to increase rather than reduce costs because it generates more work by lawyer:

> ... lawyer work may increase as a result of earlier management because lawyers need to respond to a courts management – for example, talking to the litigant and to the other lawyers in advance of a conference with the judge, travelling

and spending time at the court house, meeting with the judge and updating the file after conference [Zander (1997) 147 NLJ 353, p 354].

Zander has taken the view that the reasons for delay in civil legal process are not primarily to do with the adversarial nature of civil litigation. The only serious empirical study of the reasons for delay, argues Zander, is that done by KPMG Peat Marwick for the Lord Chancellors Department in 1994 ('Study on causes of delay in the High Court and county courts', 1994). The study was based on scrutiny of the court records in a 150 High Court personal injury cases and a 188 county court personal injury cases in nine out of London courts. The researchers also interview solicitors for both parties in 26 High Court cases and 40 county court cases from the sample. Zander has regretted that Lord Woolf did not at any time either in his Report or since cite any evidence for his view that the chief cause of delay is the way that the adversary system is played by the lawyers ('Woolf on Zander' (1997) 147 NLJ 768). The KPMG Report identified seven causes of delay:

- the nature of the case;

- delay caused by the parties;

- delay caused by their representatives;

- external factors such as the difficulty of getting experts' reports;

- the judiciary;

- court procedures; and

- court administration.

How the lawyers play the adversary game was not one of these factors. KPMG considered the relative important of the seven factors and found that the two factors that gave rise to the most significant delay were first, delay caused by lawyers, mainly due to pressure of work and inexperience or inefficiency in the handling of the case by the parties' solicitors, and, secondly the time taken to obtain medical or other expert reports. Zander observes:

> KMPG thought that the delay due to solicitors' inefficiency was partly remediable by better office management systems. Maybe timetabled deadlines will help some firms to brace up – but it seems improbable that the imposition of sanctions for failure to meet timetabling requirements will do much to reduce the pressure of work or the inexperience of staff which so often caused firms delay.

Zander further argues ((1997) 147 NLJ 768, p 769) that the enterprise of setting detailed procedural timetables, such as operate for the fast track, is doomed to failure because a huge proportion of firms, including inefficient firms, will for all sorts of reasons – some good, some bad – fail to keep to the prescribed timetables. He writes: '... if I am right, that will lead to enforcement procedures and sanctions on a vast scale, which in turn will lead to innumerable appeals.

It will also lead to the imposition of sanctions that are disproportionate and therefore unjust and that will often work great injustice to clients for the failings of the lawyers'.

Many barristers have been following the same intricate procedures, and using the same argot for three or four decades in the civil courts. It will not be easy for them to suddenly adapt to the fundamental changes introduced by the CPR. The following opening to a report from Frances Gibb in (1999) *The Times*, 27 April is worth noting. Writing about the first day in which the new CPR were applicable in court (26 April 1999), she reported:

> Within hours of the start of new reforms, part of the biggest shake-up in civil justice this century, some had already fallen foul of the rules. Michael Tillet QC, opening his case, told Mr Justice Turner: 'My Lord, I appear for the plaintiff in this action.' 'No you don't' came the judge's swift rebuke, 'You appear for the claimant'.

The following letter from Professor IR Scott, of the Faculty of Law at the University of Birmingham, appeared in (1999) *The Times*, 26 April, the day the new rules came into effect. It is worth quoting in full:

From Professor IR Scott

Sir, on 26 April, the Civil Procedure Rules 1998, implementing the reforms to the administration of justice recommended by Lord Woolf, come into force. Doubtless, the Lord Chancellor's publicity machine will be putting out a considerable amount of information extolling the virtues of the new system and emphasising in particular that it will provide faster and cheaper justice.

I doubt whether one will find any hint that the implementation of the new scheme is turning out to be a shambles.

It has been asserted that the Civil Procedure Rules (CPR) constitute a 'new procedural code', written in plain English and that they will be readily understood by lawyer and lay-person alike. The truth is that, in many respects, the rules and their supplementing Practice Directions are an impenetrable mess. Errors abound. Additions and changes have been made from week to week as 'Woolf day' approached. Many appear to be very important. I say 'appear to be' because some of the material put out recently is incomprehensible. Indeed, the further supplementing Practice Direction to Pt 8 of the CPR (produced during the first week of this month) is one of the worst examples of procedural drafting I have seen.

As a result of the mismanaged implementation of the new scheme, judges, lawyers, court staff and litigants in person have been placed in an impossible position and recriminations are likely to be fierce. The civil justice system faces a long period of 'muddling through', during which much time, effort and money will be spent on trying to operate and manage a procedural system that ought to have been got right well in advance of Woolf day.

Not everyone involved in the civil process will accept the view of Professor Scott. Moreover, even for those who share his pessimism, quite how long a period of 'muddling through' will have to be undergone is unclear.

For another useful and engaging overview of the reforms, we can turn to Anthony Scrivener QC. Writing in (1999) *The Independent*, 26 April, Mr Scrivener argued thus:

> The new procedures are more 'consumer friendly', to use the parlance of the day. The old procedures deterred litigants conducting their own cases. Before they could gather up their papers, they had failed to comply with some rule they had never heard of or, if they had, which they would not have understood. Under the new rules, this may be less likely to happen. The ability of a litigant to conduct a case personally has become more important now that the present Government is abolishing legal aid. It is rather like encouraging self-treatment under the National Health Service ...
>
> ... Non-compliance with time limits could have disastrous consequences for the litigant. The new procedures tend to move away from the more liberal attitude that pertained under the old regime towards dismissing a claim for non-compliance. It is said that, if you have broken the time limits, you are delaying other litigants. However, it does seem wrong to penalise the litigant for the errors of his lawyers: surely, a better consequence would have been to penalise the lawyers personally in costs but leave the action to proceed and be tried on the merits.

On the subject of the new CPR's preference for a single expert, Mr Scrivener was equally sceptical:

> Under the new system, the parties are to agree before trial on a joint expert. The idea of solicitors for the injured workman and the solicitors for the insurance company amicably agreeing on an expert whose opinion will probably determine the outcome of the case seems a little remote from reality. Litigators are resourceful and unlikely to allow, without a fight, some expert to be appointed who is likely to find against their client, and so they will obtain their own expert to advise them as to which expert should be appointed. There will then have to be a determination as to who should be the anointed expert. No doubt this will be fiercely fought since the outcome of the case may depend on it. Not only is the procedure bizarre, but it hardly advances the interest of justice, which should be directed towards getting the correct result rather than finding the most expeditious way of disposing of a case.

Another criticism of the reforms is that they will, paradoxically, complicate the legal system and cost clients money. This view has been expressed by James Diamond, a legal costs expert.

Mr Diamond, managing director of Legal Costs Services, a company which prepares figures in court costs disputes, argues that the CPR invite abuse from wealthy groups to the detriment of the less well off. The requirement that a party must pay the other side's costs 14 days after losing an interim hearing – even if it has a good chance of winning the case overall – instead of being able to set them off against final judgment winnings will, says Diamond, lead to 'a summons by warfare'.

Diamond contends that:

> Big insurance companies will just issue claim after claim, because, even if they know they're likely to lose the case, they may still win a claim on a certain point. This could leave a deserving opponent facing a £5,000 bill which they have to pay in a fortnight. Some people won't be able to afford that ['Woolf reforms hike costs' (1999) *The Lawyer*, 11 January, p 2].

The abolition of the punitive percentage fee is also open to abuse, in Diamond's view. He says that, under the old law, if a company wished to appeal, it had to pay 7.4% of the disputed figure up front. But, the reforms have introduced a fixed fee figure of £100 plus interest, so 'parties will have nothing to lose by appealing'. Even without such abuses, he asserts, appeals are likely to increase by up to 100-fold due to the need to assess every interim claim. He predicts that, in 2000, it may take up to 18 months to set a date for costs assessments. Diamond argues that the 'draconian' new time limits that require a paying party to file its objections to the receiving party's costs within 21 days will mean outfits, such as his, will have to accept fewer clients because preparing the schedule for each hearing would be so time consuming. Moreover, he observes that, since the provisions allow clients to be charged for preparation of bills of costs, they too will be out of pocket. One final point we can make here concerns the levelness of the playing field under the new system. Access to justice will, in some ways, be as unequal as it was under the old system. Those who can afford to pay for the best QC with 40 years' experience at the Bar will perhaps be given a better service than those whose purse can only run to the most junior, inexperienced and recently qualified barrister. 'There won't be an equal playing field in my case', one claimant, Dulce Maltez, insisted, 'I will be represented at trial by a junior counsel of seven years' call. My opponent will be instructing leading counsel of considerably greater call and experience. Debar him from instructing leading counsel or senior counsel'. This argument was rejected by Neuberger J in *Maltez v Lewis* (1999). There are, however, as District Judge Stephen Gold has observed, some ways in which the new CPR can help the poorer party ((1999) 149 NLJ 718). Where the representatives could be said to be unequal, the new rules could be applied to ensure that one side was not unfairly subject to excessive costs because the other party had instructed unreasonably expensive advisers. It would also be possible to allow more time to the side engaging the smaller firm.

11.18 Appeals

The appeal system is covered in Chapter 3. The important procedural points are as follows.

From the county court, appeal lies to the Court of Appeal (Civil Division). In almost all cases, permission is needed in order to appeal.

Appeals from the three Divisions of the High Court, and from the Divisional Courts also go to the Court of Appeal (Civil Division). Appeals are not re-trials with witnesses being called again. The appellant is limited to arguing only the narrow points of law, or law and fact, on which the appeal has been granted. The parties have four weeks from the judge's judgment in which to give notice of appeal. There are usually eight or nine courts sitting during term.

Appeals from the Court of Appeal lie to the House of Lords but the appellant must be granted leave either by the Court of Appeal or by the House of Lords. Only cases involving points of public importance reach the House of Lords and there are usually fewer than 50 civil appeals heard by the Lords each year. It is possible, under the Administration of Justice Act 1969, for the House of Lords to hear an appeal direct from the High Court, 'leapfrogging' the Court of Appeal. The agreement of both parties and the High Court judge are required. Such cases must concern a point of statutory interpretation (including the construction of a Statutory Instrument) which has been fully explored by the High Court judge or concerns a point on which he was bound by precedent to follow.

11.19 The division of work between the High Court and county courts after the Woolf reforms

In *A Programme for the Future*, the Lord Chancellor's Department's strategic plan for 1993/94–1995/96, a number of aims are set out in relation to the civil process. One of its objectives is stated to be the need: 'To match fora [that is, each type of court being a different forum] and resources to different types and levels of cases.' The problem of allocating the right sort and volume of cases to the appropriate courts is a long running challenge. It is a matter of debate how far the problems highlighted by the CJR and tackled by the CLSA 1990 have been significantly reduced.

The differences in procedure between the High Court and the county court were considerable and applied from the inception of litigation until the enforcement of court judgments. The arguments for a single court were rehearsed over many years, beginning not long after the establishment of the county courts (1846) when the Judicature Commission considered the proposal in 1869. The Law Society supported the idea in 1980, arguing that: 'A one court system would lead to the expedition, standardisation and simplification of proceedings and to a saving in judicial time.'

A merger of the High Court and county court was considered by the Beeching Royal Commission in 1969, but was rejected. Instead, it recommended a more flexible use of the judiciary. Some judges are more experienced and expert than others. Clearly, it makes sense for the judges with greater expertise to preside in the more important cases, but how is 'importance' to be judged? The sum involved may not be very large but the legal point in issue may be of enormous significance. Conversely, a case where the sum claimed is very great may not raise any particularly difficult or consequential point of law. Beeching recommended that the allocation of cases to the different tiers of judges should be determined to some extent by judges rather than by simply looking at the sum claimed. Now, because there is just one set of rules (the CPR) governing both the High Court and the county courts, the courts in one sense have been unified. We now have a single procedural system.

11.20 Do we need two sorts of court after Woolf?

The introduction of the Woolf reforms in 1999 adds new impetus to the case for having only one type of civil court. With a unified set of forms and procedures applicable to both the High Court and the county courts, the question is raised as to why we need to have two sorts of venue. In an article entitled 'Why have two types of civil court?' ((1999) 149 NLJ 65), Richard Harrison has argued for unification.

Lord Woolf came close to recommending that the two sorts of court be merged but stopped short of that because such a suggested merger would have involved Lord Woolf in dealing with matters beyond his remit. There are three main issues:

- the need to preserve the special status of High Court judges;

- the existence of inherently specialist jurisdictions in each court;

- the problem with rights of audience.

Harrison presents cogent arguments against all three points being raised as obstacles to change. He argues:

- under the new system, cases could be allocated simply to judges 'at the right level' without levels being characterised by special conditions of service and the trappings of prestige. Now, a High Court judge is given a knighthood or a damehood and his or her tenure is under letters patent, with removal from office being only theoretically possible under address by both Houses of Parliament. Her Majesty's judges are the fount of the common law as opposed to being creatures of statute like circuit judges and district judges. Harrison states that: 'I do not think it is possible to argue sensibly that there should be a distinction between levels of the judiciary with increased prestige, respect and remuneration being afforded to an elite band';

- resistance to change relies on the view that High Court judges should not have to deal with small claims and that county court judges should not be able to judge in cases like those involving judicial review. Harrison says that specialist judges (from the High Court) could carry on, as at present, dealing with highly complex or sensitive cases without having a separate rank;

- in future, rights of audience will depend upon fitness and qualification, not on whether one is a solicitor or barrister or practising in the High Court or county court. In these circumstances, it does not appear, argues Harrison, that this will present any problem for a unified court.

Harrison recognises that unification of the civil court structure may be some time away. He therefore proposes an interim practical solution – ignoring the distinction in procedural terms. Cases could be headed 'Before the Civil Courts ...' without worrying the claimant about through which type of court his or her case is going. Case management decisions on allocation could then be made in accordance with the spirit of the Woolf reforms.

THE CIVIL PROCESS

The Woolf Inquiry into the civil justice system was set up by the government in 1994 to examine why civil litigation was generally very costly, protracted, complicated and subject to long delays.

The Inquiry published its final report in 1996 and its proposals resulted in the Civil Procedure Act 1997, and the Civil Procedure Rules 1998. The new Civil Procedure Rules (CPR) will be the same for the county court and the High Court. They apply to all cases except (Pt 2) to insolvency proceedings, family proceedings, and non-contentious probate proceedings.

The overriding objective

The overriding objective of the new CPR is to enable the court to deal justly with cases. The first rule states:

> 1.1(1) These rules are a new procedural code with the overriding objective of enabling the court to deal with cases justly.

Practice directions

Practice directions (official statements of interpretative guidance) play an important role in the new civil process. In general, they supplement the CPRs, giving the latter fine detail. They tell parties and their representatives what the court will expect of them, in respect of documents to be filed in court for a particular purpose, and how they must co-operate with the other parties to their action. They also tell the parties what they can expect of the court.

Case control

Judges will receive support from court staff in carrying out their case management role. The court will monitor case progress by using a computerised diary monitoring system.

Active case management includes:

(a) encouraging the parties to co-operate with each other in the conduct of the proceedings;

(b) identifying the issues at an early stage;

(c) deciding promptly which issues need full investigation and trial and, accordingly, disposing summarily of the others;

(d) deciding the order in which issues are to be resolved.

Court allocation

The new civil system works on the basis of the court, upon receipt of the claim (accompanied by duly filled-in forms giving all the relevant details of the claim, including how much it is for, and an indication of its factual and legal complexity), allocating the case to one of three tracks for a hearing. These are:

- small claims;

- fast track;

- multi-track.

The new small claims limit will be £5,000, although personal injury and housing disrepair claims for over £1,000, illegal eviction and harassment claims will be excluded from the small claims court. The limit for cases going into the fast track system will be £15,000, and only claims for over £15,000 can be issued in the Royal Courts of Justice. Applications to move cases 'up' a track on grounds of complexity will have to be made on the new allocation questionnaire (see below).

Pre-action protocols

The pre-action protocols (PAPs) are an important feature of the reforms. They exist for cases of clinical negligence and personal injury cases, and are likely to be followed, over time, with similar protocols for cases involving other specialisms like debt.

Jurisdiction for the start of proceedings

Part 7 of the CPR sets out the rules for starting proceedings. A new restriction is placed on which cases may be begun in the High Court. The county courts retain an unlimited jurisdiction for handling contract and tort claims (that is, negligence cases, nuisance cases). Issuing proceedings in the High Court is now limited to:

- personal injury claims with a value of £50,000 or more;

- other claims with a value of more than £15,000;

- claims where an Act of Parliament requires an action to start in the High Court; or

- specialist High Court claims which need to go to one of the specialist 'lists', like the Commercial List, the Technology List, and the Construction List.

Particulars of claim

Particulars of claim may be included in the claim form, attached to it, or may be served (that is, given or sent to a party by a method allowed by the rules) separately from it. Where they are served separately, they must be served within 14 days of the claim form being served. The time for a defendant to respond begins to run from the time the particulars of claim are served.

Part 16 of the CPR is entitled 'statements of case' (replacing the word 'pleadings'). Statements of case include documents from both sides: claim forms, particulars of claims, defences, counterclaims, replies to defences and counterclaims, Pt 20 (third party) claims and any further information provided under Pt 18 of the CPR (replacing the term 'further and better particulars'). Part 16 of the rules also sets out what both particulars of claim and defences should contain.

Statements of truth

A statement of truth is a statement that a party believes that the facts or allegations set out in a document which they put forward are true. It is required in statements of case, witness statements, and expert reports. Any document which contains a statement of truth may be used in evidence. This will avoid the previous need to swear affidavits in support of various statements made as part of the claim.

Part 8 Claims (CPR Pt 8)

Part 8 of the new rules introduces the alternative procedure for claims. This procedure is commenced by the issue of a Pt 8 claim form. It is intended to provide a speedy resolution of claims which are not likely to involve a substantial dispute of fact, for example, applications for approval of infant settlements, or for orders enforcing a statutory right such as a right to have access to medical records (under the Access to Health Records Act 1990).

Default judgment (CPR Pt 12)

If a defendant (to a Pt 7 claim) files an acknowledgment stating an intention to defend the claim, this extends the period for filing a defence from 14 to 28 days from the date of service of the particulars. Failure to file an acknowledgment or, later, failure to file a defence, can result in default judgment, that is, the court will find for the claimant so the defendant will lose the case.

Defence and automatic transfer (CPR Pt 15)

Claims for specified amounts will be transferred automatically to the defendant's 'home court' where the defendant is an individual who has filed a defence. The defendant's home court will be 'the court or district registry, including the Royal Courts of Justice, for the district in which the defendant's address for service as shown on the defence is situated'. This means that, where the defendant is represented by a solicitor, this will be the defendant's solicitor's business address.

Where there is more than one defendant, it is the first defendant to file a defence who dictates whether or not automatic transfer will take place. For example, if there are two defendants to a claim, one an individual and one a limited company, there would be no automatic transfer if the limited company was the first defendant to file a defence.

Allocation questionnaire

The purpose of this document is to enable to court to judge in which track the case should be heard. When a defence is filed, the issuing court will send out a copy of the defence to all other parties to the claim together with an allocation questionnaire, a notice setting out the date for returning it and the name and address of the court (or district registry or the Royal Courts of Justice – that is, High Court – as appropriate), to which the completed allocation questionnaire must be returned. A notice of transfer will also be sent if the case is being automatically transferred.

When the allocation questionnaire is returned, or at the end of the period for returning it, and whether or not only some, or none, of the questionnaires (if there is more than one defendant) have been filed, the court file will be passed to a procedural judge for directions and allocation to track. If there is sufficient information, the judge will allocate the case to a track and a notice of allocation and directions will be sent out to each party. Where only one party has filed a questionnaire or there is insufficient information, the judge may make an order requesting further information, or order an allocation hearing. Where none of the parties has filed a questionnaire, the judge may also decide to impose a sanction, for example, ordering that a statement, or statements, of case be struck out unless a completed questionnaire is filed within three days of service of the order.

Case management conferences

Case management conferences may be regarded as an opportunity to 'take stock'. There is no limit to the number of case management conferences which may be held during the life of a case, although the cost of attendance at such hearings against the benefits obtained will always be a consideration in making the decision.

Pre-trial reviews

Pre-trial reviews will normally take place after the filing of listing questionnaires, and before the start of the trial. Their main purpose is to decide a timetable for the trial itself (including the evidence to be allowed and whether this should be given orally), instructions about the content of any trial bundles (bundles of documents including evidence such as written statements, for the judge to read) and confirming a realistic time estimate for the trial itself.

Rules require that, where a party is represented, a representative 'familiar with the case and with sufficient authority to deal with any issues likely to arise must attend every case management conference or pre-trial review'.

Settlements

Under the new CPR, there is a greater incentive for parties to settle their differences.

The court will take into account any pre-action offers to settle when making an order for costs. Thus, a side which has refused a reasonable offer to settle will be treated less generously in the issue of how far the court will order their costs to be paid by the other side. For this to happen, the offer, though, must be one which is made open to the other side for at least 21 days after receipt (to stop any undue pressure being put on someone with the phrase: 'take it or leave it; it is only open for one day, then I shall withdraw the offer'). Also, if the offer is made by the defendant, it must be an offer to pay compensation and to pay the claimant's costs.

Witness statements

Under the new rules, witness statements must contain the evidence that the witness will give at trial but they should be briefer than those drafted under the previous rules; they should be drafted in lay language and should not discuss legal propositions. Witnesses will be allowed to amplify on the statement or deal with matters that have arisen since the report was served, although this is not an automatic right and a 'good reason' for the admission of new evidence will have to be established.

Court fees

A new fee structure will be introduced to take account of the different procedures, a movement towards a 'pay as you go' fees regime and the need for full cost recovery. Pay as you go means that parties will be expected to contribute more in fees, the more court and judicial time they use, for example, if they do not settle and carry on to trial.

Experts (CPR Pt 35)

New rules place a clear duty on the court to ensure that 'expert evidence is restricted to that which is reasonably required to resolve the proceedings'. That is to say, expert evidence will only be allowed either by way of written report or orally, where the court gives permission. Equally important is the rules' statement about experts' duties. They state that it is the clear duty of experts to help the court on matters within their expertise, bearing in mind that this duty overrides any obligation to the person from whom they have received instructions or by whom they are paid.

CHAPTER 12

ARBITRATION, TRIBUNAL ADJUDICATION AND ALTERNATIVE DISPUTE RESOLUTION

12.1 Introduction

Law is one method of resolving disputes when, as is inevitable, they emerge. All societies have mechanisms for dealing with such problems but the forms of dispute resolution tend to differ from society to society. In small scale societies, based on mutual co-operation and interdependency, the means of solving disputes tend to be informal and focus on the need for mutual concessions and compromise to maintain social stability. In some such societies, the whole of the social group may become involved in settling a problem; whereas in others particular individuals may be recognised as intermediaries, whose function it is to act as a go-between to bring the parties to a mutually recognised solution. The common factor remains the emphasis on solidarity and the need to maintain social cohesion. With social, as well as the geographical, distance, disputes become more difficult to deal with.

It should not be thought that this reference to anthropological material is out of place in a book of this nature. It is sometimes suggested that law itself is a function of the increase in social complexity and the corresponding decrease in social solidarity; the oppositional, adversarial nature of law being seen as a reflection of the atomistic structure of contemporary society. Law as a *formal* dispute resolution mechanism is seen to emerge because *informal* mechanisms no longer exist or no longer have the power to deal with the problems that arise in a highly individualistic and competitive society. That is not to suggest that the types of mechanisms mentioned previously do not have their place in our own society: the bulk of family disputes, for example, are resolved through internal informal mechanisms without recourse to legal formality. It is generally recognised, however, that the very form of law makes it inappropriate to deal adequately with certain areas, family matters being the most obvious example. Equally, it is recognised that the formal and rather intimidatory atmosphere of the ordinary courts is not necessarily the most appropriate one in which to decide such matters, even where the dispute cannot be resolved internally. In recognition of this fact, various alternatives have been developed specifically to avoid the perceived shortcomings of the formal structure of law and court procedure.

The increased importance of alternative dispute resolution (ADR) mechanisms has been signalled in both legislation and court procedures. For example, the Commercial Court issued a practice statement in 1993, stating that it wished to encourage ADR, and followed this, in 1996, with a further direction allowing judges to consider whether a case is suitable for ADR at its outset, and to invite the parties to attempt a neutral non-court settlement of their dispute. In cases in the Court of Appeal, the Master of the Rolls now writes to the parties, urging them to consider ADR, and asking them for their reasons for declining to use it. Also, as part of the civil justice reforms, r 26.4 of the Civil Procedure Rules 1998 enables judges, either on their own account, or at the agreement of both parties, to stop court proceedings where they consider the dispute to be better suited to solution by some alternative procedure, such as arbitration or mediation.

In particular, the Family Law Act 1996, which aimed to reform the operation of divorce law, emphasises the importance of mediation in this area and provides for the possibility of legal aid to finance it in appropriate instances. This will be considered further in 12.5.

More generally, Lord Mackay, the former Lord Chancellor, considered various ADR mechanisms in the fourth of his Hamlyn Lectures, expressing the view that:

> ... the need seems to be not for further law based processes outside the courts ... but ... for processes which broaden the issues and available outcomes beyond those based in law.

The current Lord Chancellor has continued to look favourably on ADR, as is evident in his Inaugural Lecture to the Faculty of Mediation and ADR, in which he said:

> ADR has many supporters. But they, too, have a responsibility to proceed with care. ADR is not a panacea, nor is it cost free. But, I do believe that it can play a vital part in the opening of access to justice [www.open-gov.uk./lcd/speeches/1999/27-1-99.htm].

12.2 Arbitration

The first and oldest of these alternative procedures is arbitration. This is the procedure whereby parties in dispute refer the issue to a third party for resolution, rather than take the case to the ordinary law courts. Studies have shown a reluctance on the part of commercial undertakings to have recourse to the law to resolve their disputes. At first sight, this appears paradoxical. The development of contract law can, to a great extent, be explained as the law's response to the need for regulation in relation to business activity, yet business declines to make use of its procedures. To some degree, questions of speed and cost explain this peculiar phenomenon, but it can be explained more fully by reference to the introduction to this chapter. It was stated there that informal procedures tend to be most effective where there is a high degree of mutuality and interdependency, and that is precisely the case in most business relationships. Businesses seek to establish and maintain long term relationships with other concerns. The problem with the law is that the court case tends to terminally rupture such relationships. It is not suggested that, in the final analysis, where the stakes are sufficiently high, that recourse will not be had to law; but such action does not represent the first or indeed the preferred option. In contemporary business practice, it is common, if not standard, practice for commercial contracts to contain express clauses referring any future disputes to arbitration. This practice is well established and its legal effectiveness has long been recognised by the law.

12.2.1 Procedure

The Arbitration Act (AA) 1996 repeals Pt 1 of the Arbitration Act 1950 and the whole of the Arbitration Acts of 1975 and 1979. As the Act is a relatively new piece of legislation, it is necessary to consider it in some detail.

Section 1 of the Act 1996 states that it is founded on the following principles:

(a) the object of arbitration is to obtain the fair resolution of disputes by an impartial tribunal without necessary delay or expense;

(b) the parties should be free to agree how their disputes are resolved, subject only to such safeguards as are necessary in the public interest;

(c) in matters governed by this part of the Act the court should not intervene except as provided by this part.

This provision of general principles, which should inform the reading of the later detailed provisions of the Act, is unusual for UK legislation, but may be seen as reflecting the purposes behind the new Act, one major one of which was the wish to ensure that London did not lose its place as a leading centre for international arbitration. As a consequence of the demand driven nature of the new legislation, it would seem that court interference in the arbitration process has had to be reduced to a minimum and replaced by party autonomy. Under the new Act, the role of the arbitrator has been increased and that of the court has been reduced to the residual level of intervention where the arbitration process either requires legal assistance or else is seen to be failing to provide a just settlement.

The Act follows the Model Arbitration Law adopted in 1985 by the United Nations Commission on International Trade Law (UNICTRAL).

Whilst it is possible for there to be an oral arbitration agreement at common law, s 5 provides that Pt 1 of the new Act only applies to agreements in writing. What this means in practice, however, has been extended by s 5(3) which provides that, where the parties agree to an arbitration procedure which is in writing, that procedure will be operative, even although the agreement between the parties is not itself in writing. An example of such a situation would be where a salvage operation was negotiated between two vessels on the basis of Lloyd's standard salvage terms. It would be unlikely that the actual agreement would be reduced to written form, but, nonetheless, the arbitration element in those terms would be effective.

In analysing the AA, it is useful to consider it in three distinct parts: autonomy of the parties; powers of the court; and appellate rights:

- *Autonomy*

  It is significant that most of the provisions set out in the AA 1996 are not compulsory. As is clearly stated in s 1, it is up to the parties to an arbitration agreement to agree what procedures to adopt. The main purpose of the Act is to empower the parties to the dispute and to allow them to decide how it is to be decided. In pursuit of this aim, the mandatory parts of the Act only take effect where the parties involved do not agree otherwise. It is actually possible for the parties to agree that the dispute should not be decided in line with the strict legal rules but rather in line with commercial fairness, which might be a completely different thing altogether.

- *Powers of the arbitrator*

  Section 30 provides that, unless the parties agree otherwise, the arbitrator can rule on questions relating to jurisdiction, that is, in relation to:

  (a) whether there actually is a valid arbitration agreement;

  (b) whether the arbitration tribunal is properly constituted;

  (c) what matters have been submitted to arbitration in accordance with the agreement.

  Section 32 allows any of the parties to raise preliminary objections to the substantive jurisdiction of the arbitration tribunal in court, but provides that they may only do so on limited grounds which require either: the agreement of the parties concerned; the permission of the arbitration tribunal; or the agreement of the court. Leave to appeal will only be granted where the court is satisfied that the question involves a point of law of general importance.

  Section 28 expressly provides that the parties the proceedings are jointly and severally liable to pay the arbitrators such reasonable fees and expenses as appropriate. Previously, this was only an implied term.

  Section 29 provides that arbitrators are not liable for anything done or omitted in the discharge of their functions unless the act or omission was done in bad faith.

  Section 33 provides that the tribunal has a general duty:

  (a) to act fairly and impartially between the parties, giving each a reasonable opportunity to state their case; and

  (b) to adopt procedures suitable for the circumstance of the case, avoiding unnecessary delay or expense.

Section 35 provides that, subject to the parties agreeing to the contrary, the tribunal shall have the following powers:

(a) to order parties to provide security for costs (previously a power reserved to the courts);

(b) to give directions in relation to property subject to the arbitration;

(c) to direct that a party or witness be examined on oath, and to administer the oath.

The parties may also empower the arbitrator to make provisional orders (s 39).

- *Powers of the court*

Where one party seeks to start a court action, contrary to a valid arbitration agreement to the contrary, then the other party may request the court to stay the litigation in favour of the arbitration agreement under ss 9–11 of the AA 1996. Where, however, both parties agree to ignore the arbitration agreement and seek recourse to litigation then, following the party consensual nature of the Act, the agreement may be ignored.

The courts may order a party to comply with an order of the tribunal and may also order parties and witnesses to attend and to give oral evidence before tribunals (s 43).

The court has power to revoke the appointment of an arbitrator on application of any of the parties, where there has been a failure in the appointment procedure under s 18, but it also has powers to revoke authority under s 24. This power comes into play on the application of one of the parties in circumstances where the arbitrator:

(a) has not acted impartially;

(b) does not possess the required qualifications;

(c) does not have either the physical or mental capacity to deal with the proceedings;

(d) has refused or failed: (i) to properly conduct the proceedings; or (ii) has been dilatory in dealing with the proceedings or, in making an award, to the extent that it will cause substantial injustice to the party applying for their removal.

Under s 45, the court may on application by one of the parties, decide any preliminary question of law arising in the course of the proceedings.

Arbitrators

The arbitration tribunal may consist of a single arbitrator, or a panel as the parties decide (s 15). If one party fails to appoint an arbitrator, then the other party's nominee may act as sole arbitrator (s 17). Under s 20(4), where there is a panel and it fails to reach a majority decision, the decision of the chair shall prevail.

The tribunal is required to fairly and impartially adopt procedures which are suitable to the circumstances of each case. It is also for the tribunal to decide all procedural and evidential matters. Parties may be represented by a lawyer or any other person, and the tribunal may appoint experts or legal advisors to report to it.

Arbitrators will be immune from action being taken against them except in situations where they have been acted in bad faith.

- *Appeal*

  Once the decision has been made, there are limited grounds for appeal. The first ground arises under s 67 of the AA 1996 in relation to the substantive jurisdiction of the Arbitral panel, although the right to appeal on this ground may be lost if the party attempting to make use of it, took part in the arbitration proceedings without objecting to the alleged lack of jurisdiction. The second ground for appeal to the courts is on procedural grounds, under s 68, on the basis that some serious irregularity affected the operation of the tribunal. By serious irregularity is meant:

  (a) failure to comply with the general duty set out in s 33;

  (b) failure to conduct the tribunal as agreed by the parties;

  (c) uncertainty or ambiguity as to the effect of the award;

  (d) failure to comply with the requirement as to the form of the award.

Parties may also appeal on a point of law arising from the award under s 69. However, the parties can agree beforehand to preclude such a possibility and, where they agree to the arbitral panel making a decision without providing a reasoned justification for it, they will also lose the right to appeal.

12.2.2 Relationship to ordinary courts

In general terms, the courts have no objection to individuals settling their disputes on a voluntary basis, but, at the same time, they are careful to maintain their supervisory role in such procedures. Arbitration agreements are no different from other terms of a contract, and, in line with the normal rules of contract law, courts will strike out any attempt to oust their ultimate jurisdiction, as being contrary to public policy. Thus, as has been stated previously, arbitration proceedings are open to challenge through judicial review, on the grounds that they were not conducted in a judicial manner.

The AA 1950 allowed for either party to the proceedings to have questions of law authoritatively determined by the High Court through the procedure of *case stated*. The High Court could also set aside the decision of the arbitrator on grounds of fact, law or procedure. Whereas the arbitration process was supposed to provide a quick and relatively cheap method of deciding disputes, the availability of the appeals procedures meant that parties could delay the final decision and in so doing increase the costs. In such circumstances, arbitration became the precursor to a court case rather than replacing it. The AA 1979 abolished the case stated procedure and curtailed the right to appeal and, as has been seen, the AA 1996 has reduced the grounds for appeal to the court system even further.

12.2.3 Advantages

There are numerous advantages to be gained from using arbitration rather than the court system:

- *Privacy*. Arbitration tends to be a private procedure. This has the twofold advantage that outsiders do not get access to any potentially sensitive information and the parties to the arbitration do not run the risk of any damaging publicity arising out of reports of the proceedings.

- *Informality*. The proceedings are less formal than a court case and they can be scheduled more flexibly than court proceedings.

- *Speed*. Arbitration is generally much quicker than taking a case through the courts. Where, however, one of the parties makes use of the available grounds to challenge an arbitration award the prior costs of the arbitration will have been largely wasted.

- *Cost*. Arbitration is generally a much cheaper procedure than taking a case to the normal courts. Nonetheless, the costs of arbitration and the use of specialist arbitrators should not be underestimated.

- *Expertise*. The use of a specialist arbitrator ensures that the person deciding the case has expert knowledge of the actual practice within the area under consideration and can form their conclusion in line with accepted practice.

It can be argued that arbitration represents a privatisation of the judicial process. It may be assumed, therefore, that of all its virtues, perhaps the greatest, at least as far as the government is concerned, is the potential reduction in costs for the State in providing the legal framework within which disputes are resolved.

12.2.4 Small claims procedure in the county court

Since 1973, an arbitration service has been available within the county court specifically for the settlement of relatively small claims. This small claims procedure, known as arbitration, is operated by county court district judges.

Under the Civil Justice Reforms, reference to arbitration will normally be automatic in cases involving sums of money up to £5,000, and arbitration proceedings may be used in situations involving more than £5,000 where the parties concerned agree. The limit with regard to personal injury cases remains at £1,000. The district judge can refuse to deal with the case in arbitration and may refer it for trial in the county court. The grounds for this action depend on:

- the case involving a difficult point of law or fact, or involving a charge of fraud;

- the agreement of the parties;

- whether the district judge considers that it would be unreasonable to decide the case in arbitration on the basis of the subject matter, or the circumstances of the parties, or the interests of any person likely to be affected by any award made. For example, in *Pepper v Healey* (1982), it was decided that it was legitimate for a registrar to use the discretion to decide that a case should be heard before the court rather than arbitration because the plaintiff required to be legally represented, as the defendant was, and could not have recovered costs in arbitration, although such cost could have been recovered in court proceedings.

In *Afzal and Others v Ford Motor Co Ltd* (1993), the Court of Appeal held that claims from employees against their employer for personal injury damages of less than £1,000 could be suitable for decision under the county court arbitration scheme. The district judge had accepted that the case should be heard in the county court, on the basis of representations that: first, the issues of liability involved in such compensation cases were too complex for resolution in arbitration; and, secondly, the denial of the right to recover the costs of legal advice and representation at arbitration would deter trade unions from assisting claimants who would consequently be disadvantaged. In rejecting both of these grounds for not making use of the arbitration system, the Court of Appeal also considered the possibility of claimants inflating their claims above the £1,000 figure in order to avoid its operation. It stated that such action would be a misuse of process and that, in determining the financial limit, the test should be the amount that the plaintiff could reasonably expect to be awarded: if that did not exceed £1,000, then the case should be decided by arbitration procedure.

12.2.5 Procedure

Arbitration proceedings begin with an individual filing a *statements of case* at the county court. This document details the grounds of their dispute and requests the other party to be summonsed to appear. There may be *preliminary hearings* at which the issues involved are clarified, but it is possible for the dispute to be settled at such hearings. If no compromise can be reached at this stage, a date is set for the hearing of the arbitration.

Arbitration hearings are usually heard by the district judge, although the parties to the dispute may request that it be referred to the circuit judge or even an outside arbitrator. The arbitrator hearing the case may at any time before or after the hearing, with the agreement of the parties, consult an expert on the matter under consideration and, again with the approval of the parties, may invite an expert to sit on the arbitration in the role of *assessor*.

If one of the parties fails to appear at the hearing, the dispute can be decided in their absence. Alternatively, the parties may agree to the case being decided by the arbitrator, solely on the basis of documents and written statements.

The arbitration procedure is intended to be a less formal forum than that provided by the ordinary courts and to that end the county court rules provide that the strict rules of evidence shall not be applied. Parties are encouraged to represent themselves rather than make use of the services of professional lawyers although they may be legally represented if they wish.

The county court rules give arbitrators wide discretion to adopt any procedure they consider helpful to ensure that the parties have an equal opportunity to put their case. This discretion is not limitless, however, and it does not remove the normal principles of legal procedure, such as the right of direct cross-examination of one of the parties by the legal representative of the other party (see *Chilton v Saga Holidays plc* (1986), where the Court of Appeal held that a registrar was wrong to have refused to allow solicitors for the defendant in the case to cross-examine the plaintiff on the grounds that that person was not also legally represented).

On the basis of the information provided, the arbitrator decides the case and, if the plaintiff is successful, makes an award for appropriate compensation. A no-costs rule operates to ensure that the costs of legal representation cannot be recovered, although the losing party may be instructed to pay court fees and the expenses of witnesses. Judgments are legally enforceable.

12.2.6 Evaluation

Problems have become evident in the operation of the arbitration procedure, particularly in cases where one party has been represented whilst the other has not. In spite of the clear intention to facilitate the resolution of disputes cheaply, and without the need for legal practitioners, some individuals, particularly large business enterprises, insisted on their right of legal representation. As legal aid is not available in respect of such actions, most individuals cannot afford to be legally represented and therefore find themselves at a distinct disadvantage when opposed by professional lawyers.

One solution to this difficulty would have been to make legal aid available in the case of arbitration. Such a proposal is very unlikely ever to come to fruition, first on economic grounds, but also on the grounds that the use of professional lawyers in such cases would contradict the spirit and the whole purpose of the procedure.

Alternatively, it might have been provided that no party could be legally represented in arbitration procedures; but to introduce such a measure would have been a denial of an important civil right.

The actual method chosen to deal with the problem was to lift the restrictions on the rights of audience in small debt proceedings. Parties to the proceedings were entitled to be accompanied by a *McKenzie friend* to give them advice but such people had no right of audience and thus had no right actually to represent their friend in any arbitration (see *McKenzie v McKenzie* (1970)). In October 1992, under the Courts and Legal Services Act 1990, the Lord Chancellor extended the right of audience to lay representatives in small claims courts. This decision has the effect of allowing individuals access to non-professional, but expert, advice and advocacy. Members of such organisations as Citizens Advice Bureaux and Legal Advice Centres will now be permitted to represent their clients, although they will still not be permitted to issue proceedings. In cases involving claims of more than £1,000, they may even charge a fee.

The increase in the maximum amount to be claimed to £5,000 introduces two particular difficulties with regard to representation. The first, and by far the more serious, is the fact that the raising of the ceiling to what is a not inconsiderable sum of money, means that individuals will lose legal aid to fund their claims in such cases, and, therefore, may not have access to the best possible legal advice with respect to their case. The second, and apparently contradictory, point is that the number of lawyers appearing in small claims proceedings may actually increase as a result of the rise in the limit. Whereas it might not have been worth paying for legal representation in a £3,000 claim, it might make more economic sense to pay for professional help if the sum being claimed is that much higher. Which alternative actually happens, remains to be seen.

Perhaps the major difficulty in regard to small claims procedures is the fact that the mere winning of a case and the awarding of compensation does not actually mean that the successful party will receive any recompense if the other party chooses simply to ignore the award. A recent study concluded that 36% of those successful in the small claims procedure actually received nothing by way of recompense awarded (*Handling Small Claims in the County Courts* (1996)). More stringent and efficient mechanisms for enforcing judgments, even in relation to the comparatively small awards as are made under the arbitration procedure, is a necessity.

In evaluating the small claims arbitration procedure, regard has to be had to the Civil Justice Review of 1996 which specifically considered the arbitration procedure and concluded that it generally works in a satisfactory way to produce a relatively quick, cheap, and informal mechanism for resolving many smaller cases without the need to overburden the county courts.

The small claims procedure has not gone uncriticised. A research report from the National Consumer Council (NCC) in 1993 concluded that the civil courts were 'far from user-friendly'. It asked 819 people using 35 county courts in England and Wales about their experience. Of 12% in the survey who wanted to complain about their experience, 76% did not know there was a complaints procedure. It found that many standards in the charter were designed to assist business users rather than ordinary citizens. The 1994 report of the NCC on the courts is even more damning. It concludes that performance indicators issued by the Lord Chancellor's Department (LCD) paint a 'rosy picture' of the courts but 'do not seem to bear any relation to the experiences of court users'.

FH Pedley ((1994) 144 NLJ 1217), who was a magistrate for 12 years, contended that district judges are not sufficiently specialist in the areas of law they have to deal with. This would not matter so much in the ordinary courts but here, where the parties are encouraged to be unrepresented (there is no legal aid or costs for lawyers), it is critical because the judge is supposed to be active in applying his knowledge of the law.

12.2.7 Arbitration under codes of conduct

When it was first established in 1973, the small claims procedure was seen as a mechanism through which consumers could enforce their rights against recalcitrant traders. In reality, the arbitration procedure has proved to be just as useful for, and to have been used just as much by, traders and businesses, as consumers. There remains one area of arbitration, however, that is specifically focused on the consumer: arbitration schemes run under the auspices of particular trade associations. As part of the regulation of trade practices and in the pursuit of effective measures of consumer protection, the Office of Fair Trading has encouraged the establishment of voluntary codes of practice within particular areas. It is usual to find that such codes of practice provide arbitration schemes to resolve particularly intractable problems between individual consumers and particular members of the association. Such schemes are never compulsory and do not seek to replace the consumer's legal rights but they do provide a relatively inexpensive mechanism for dealing with problems without the need even to bother the county court. Such schemes are numerous; the most famous one is probably the travel industry scheme operated under the auspices of the Association of British Travel Agents, but other associations run similar schemes in such areas as car sales, shoe retailing, dry-cleaning, and many other areas. Again, the point of such schemes is to provide a quick, cheap means of dealing with problems without running the risk of completely alienating the consumer from the trade in question.

Although many of the trade arbitration schemes offered consumers distinct advantages, some did not and, in order to remedy any abuses, the Consumer Arbitration Act 1988 was introduced. This statute provides that, in the case of consumer contracts, no prior agreement between the parties that subsequent disputes have to be referred to arbitration can be enforced. However, consumers will be bound by arbitration procedures where they have already entered into them as a consequence of a prior agreement, or have agreed to them subsequently.

12.3   Administrative tribunals

Although attention tends to be focused on the operation of the courts as the forum within which legal decisions are taken, it is no longer the case that the bulk of legal and quasi-legal questions are determined within that court structure. There are, as an alternative to the court system, a large number of tribunals which have been set up under various Acts of Parliament to rule on the operation of the particular schemes established under those Acts. There are at least 60 different types of administrative tribunal, and within each type there may well be hundreds of individual tribunals operating locally all over the country to hear particular cases. Over a quarter of a million cases are dealt with by tribunals each year, and, as the Royal Commission on Legal Services (Cmnd 7648) pointed out in 1979, the number of cases then being heard by tribunals was six times greater than the number of contested civil cases dealt with by the High Court and county court combined. It is evident, therefore, that tribunals are of major significance as alternatives to traditional courts in dealing with disputes.

The generally accepted explanation for the establishment and growth of tribunals in Britain since 1945 was the need to provide a specialist forum to deal with cases involving conflicts between an increasingly interventionist welfare state, its functionaries, and the rights of private citizens. It is certainly true that, since 1945, the Welfare State has intervened more and more in every aspect of people's lives. The intention may have been to extend various social benefits to a wider constituency, but in so doing the machinery of the Welfare State, and in reality those who operate that machinery, have been granted powers to control access to its benefits, and as a consequence have been given the power to interfere in and control the lives of individual subjects of the State. By its nature, welfare provision tends to be discretionary and dependent upon the particular circumstance of a given case. As a consequence, State functionaries were extended discretionary power over the supply/withdrawal of welfare benefits. As the interventionist State replaced the completely free market as the source of welfare for many people, so access to the provisions made by the State became a matter of fundamental importance, and a focus for potential contention, especially given the discretionary nature of its provision. At the same time as Welfare State provisions were being extended, the view was articulated that such provisions and projects should not be under the purview and control of the ordinary courts. It was felt that the judiciary reflected a culture which tended to favour a more market-centred, individualistic approach to the provision of rights and welfare and that their, essentially formalistic, approach to the resolution of disputes would not fit with the operation of the new projects.

12.3.1 Tribunals and courts

There is some debate as to whether tribunals are merely part of the machinery of administration of particular projects or whether their function is the distinct one of adjudication. The Franks Committee (Cmnd 218, 1957) favoured the latter view, but others have disagreed and have emphasised the administrative role of such bodies. Parliament initiated various projects and schemes, and included within those projects specialist tribunals to deal with the problems that they inevitably generated. On that basis, it is suggested that tribunals are merely adjuncts to the parent project and that this therefore defines their role as more administrative than adjudicatory.

If the foregoing has suggested the theoretical possibility of distinguishing courts and tribunals in relation to their administrative or adjudicatory role, in practice it is difficult to implement such a distinction for the reason that the members of tribunals may be, and usually are, acting in a judicial capacity (see *Pickering v Liverpool Daily Post and Echo Newspapers* (1991) in which it was held that a Mental Health Review tribunal was a court whose proceedings were subject to the law of contempt. Although a newspaper was entitled to publish the fact that a named person had made an application to the tribunal together with the date of the hearing and its decision, it was not allowed to publish the reasons for the decision or any conditions applied).

If the precise distinction between tribunals and courts is a matter of uncertainty, what is certain is that tribunals are inferior to the normal courts. One of the main purposes of the tribunal system is to prevent the ordinary courts of law from being overburdened by cases, but tribunals are still subject to judicial review on the basis of breach of natural justice or where it acts in an *ultra vires* manner or indeed where it goes wrong in relation to the application of the law when deciding cases.

In addition to the control of the courts, tribunals are also subject to the supervision of the Council on Tribunals originally established under the Tribunals and Inquiries Act 1958, as subsequently amended by the Tribunals and Inquiries Acts 1971 and 1992 which is the current legislation. Members of the Council are appointed by the Lord Chancellor and its role is to keep the general operation of the system under review.

The Annual Report of the Council of Tribunals for 1995–96 (HC 114) contained some surprisingly sharp comments aimed at the way in which the government has attempted to introduce economic imperatives into the operation of the tribunal system, as it has in all other aspects of the judicial system. As the report stated:

> We draw attention to ... a number of instances where the continued pressure on public resources is seriously eroding the quality of service which tribunals are able to deliver to the public and, in some cases, impinging on the proper exercise of the tribunal's judicial task [para 1.2],

and, later, the Council stated that their:

> ... major concern ... is the movement in the direction of fuller cost recovery. We believe that this trend is inimical to the administration of justice in tribunals [para 1.21].

The concern expressed by the Council was in relation to the introduction of fees in cases before leasehold valuation tribunals which were designed to recover the full cost of the operation. The Council, through the offices of its chair Lord Archer of Sandwell in the House of Lords, secured a reduction in the maximum fees payable to £500 for the present, but subject to alteration in the future. Equally it was concerned by the increase in fees payable for cases dealt with by the lands tribunal. The report also expressed concern at the reluctance of the government to increase the availability of legal aid in relation to tribunal hearings beyond the areas already covered which are; the land tribunal, employment appeals tribunals; the Commons Commissioners, and mental health review tribunals (para 2.85).

12.3.2 Composition of tribunals

Tribunals are usually made up of three members, only one of whom, the chair, is expected to be legally qualified. The other two members are lay representatives. The lack of legal training is not considered a drawback, given the technical, administrative, as opposed to specifically legal, nature of the provisions they have to consider. Indeed, the fact of there being two lay representatives on tribunals provides them with one of their perceived advantages over courts. The non-legal members may provide specialist knowledge and thus they may enable the tribunal to base its decision on actual practice as opposed to abstract legal theory or mere legal formalism. An example of this can be seen with regard to the tribunals having responsibility or determining issues relating to employment, which usually have a trade union representative and an employers' representative sitting on the panel, and are therefore able to consider the immediate problem from both sides of the employment relationship.

The procedure for nominating tribunal members is set out in the parent statute but generally it is the Minister of State with responsibility for the operation of the statute in question who ultimately decides the membership of the tribunal. As tribunals are established to deal largely with conflicts between the general public and government departments, this raises, at least the possibility of, suspicion that the members of tribunals are not truly neutral. In response to such doubts, the 1957 Franks Committee recommended that the appointment of the chairmen of tribunals should become the prerogative of the Lord Chancellor and that the appointment of the other members should become the responsibility of a Council on Tribunals. This recommendation was not implemented and ministers, by and large, still retain the power to appoint tribunal members. As a compromise, however, the minister selects the chairperson from a panel appointed by the Lord Chancellor.

12.3.3 Statutory tribunals

There are a number of tribunals which have considerable power in their areas of operation and it is necessary to have some detailed knowledge of a selection of the most important of these. Examples of such tribunals are:

- *Employment tribunals*

  These are governed by the Employment Tribunals Act 1996 which sets out their composition, major areas of competence and procedure. In practice, such tribunals are normally made up of a legally qualified chairperson, a representative chosen from a panel representing employers and another representative chosen from a panel representing the interests of employees.

  Employment tribunals have jurisdiction in relation to a number of statutory provisions relating to employment issues. The majority of issues arise in relation to such matters as disputes over the meaning and operation of particular terms of employment, disputes relating to redundancy payments, disputes involving issues of unfair dismissal, and disputes as to the provision of maternity pay.

  They also have authority in other areas under different legislation. Thus they deal with complaints about racial discrimination in the employment field under the Race Relations Act 1976; complaints about sexual discrimination in employment under the Sex Discrimination Act 1975; complaints about equal pay under the Equal Pay Act 1970 as amended by the Sex Discrimination Act 1975; complaints under the Disability Discrimination Act 1995; complaints about unlawful deductions from wages under the Wages Act 1986; and appeals against the imposition of improvement notices under the Health and Safety at Work Act 1974. There are, in addition, various ancillary matters relating to trade union membership and activities that industrial tribunals have to deal with.

• *Social security appeal tribunal*

Various Social Security Acts have provided for safety net provisions for the disadvantaged in society to ensure that they at least enjoy a basic standard of living. In the pursuit of this general goal, various State functionaries have been delegated the task of implementing the very complex provisions contained in the legislation and have been granted considerable discretionary power in the implementation of those provisions. The function of the social security tribunals is to ensure that such discretion is not abused and that the aims of the legislation are being met generally. The tribunals, of which there are some 200 in England and Wales, are charged with the duty of hearing and deciding upon the correctness of decisions made by adjudication officers, who are the people who actually determine the level of benefit individuals are entitled to receive.

• *Mental health review tribunals*

These operate under the Mental Health Act 1983. The tribunals have wide powers to decide whether individuals should be detained for the purposes of compulsory treatment. They can also dispose of the property of such individuals. Given the particular area within which the mental health review tribunal operates, it is essential that there are medical experts present to decide on medical issues. This latter requirement also applies in respect of social security issues relating to the state of the individual claimant's health.

• *The Lands Tribunal*

Established under the Lands Tribunal Act 1949, its essential function is to determine the legality of, and the levels of compensation in relation to, compulsory purchase orders over land. It also considers matters relating to planning applications.

• *Rent Assessment Committee*

This committee deals with matters specifically relating to the rent charged for property. It resolves disputes between landlords and tenants of private accommodation, hears appeals from decisions of rent officers and has the power to fix rent in relation to furnished and unfurnished residential tenancies.

12.3.4 Domestic tribunals

The foregoing has focused on public administrative tribunals set up under particular legislative provisions to deal with matters of public relevance. The term tribunal, however, is also used in relation to the internal, disciplinary procedures of particular institutions. Whether these institutions are created under legislation or not is immaterial; the point is that domestic tribunals relate mainly to matters of private rather than public concern although at times the two can overlap. Examples of domestic tribunals are the disciplinary committees of professional institutions such as the Bar, The Law Society or the British Medical Association; trade unions; and universities. The power that each of these tribunals has is very great and it is controlled by the ordinary courts through ensuring that the rules of natural justice are complied with and that the tribunal does not act *ultra vires*, that is, beyond its powers. Matters relating to trade union membership and discipline are additionally regulated by the Employment Rights Act 1996.

12.3.5 Advantages of tribunals

Advantages of tribunals over courts relate to such matters as:

* *Speed*

  The ordinary court system is notoriously dilatory in hearing and deciding cases. Tribunals are much quicker to hear cases. A related advantage of the tribunal system is the certainty that it will be heard on a specific date and not subject to the vagaries of the court system. This being said, there have been reports that the tribunal system is coming under increased pressure and is falling behind in relation to its caseload. Thus, in 1993, in relation to the industrial tribunal, Fraser Youlson, the Vice Chair of the Employment Lawyers Association, complained that cases which had previously taken three to five months to be heard could now take over 18 months to be heard.

* *Cost*

  Tribunals are a much cheaper way of deciding cases than using the ordinary court system. One factor that leads to a reduction in cost is the fact that no specialised court building is required to hear the cases. Also the fact that those deciding the cases are less expensive to employ than judges, together with the fact that complainants do not have to rely on legal representation, makes the tribunal procedure considerably less expensive than using the traditional court system. These reductions are further enhanced by the additional facts that there are no court fees involved in relation to tribunal proceedings and that costs are not normally awarded against the loser.

* *Informality*

  Tribunals are supposed to be informal in order to make them less intimidating than full blown court cases. The strict rules relating to evidence, pleading and procedure, which apply in courts, are not binding in tribunal proceedings. The lack of formality is strengthened by the fact that proceedings tend not to be inquisitorial or accusatorial but are intended to try to encourage and help participants to express their views of the situation before the tribunal. Informality should not, however, be mistaken for a lack of order and the Franks Committee Report itself emphasised the need for clear rules of procedure. The provision of this informal situation and procedure tends to suggest that complainants do not need to be represented by a lawyer in order to present their grievance. They may represent themselves or be represented by a more knowledgeable associate such as a trade union representative or some other friend. This contentious point will be considered further below.

• *Flexibility*

Tribunals are not bound by the strict rules of precedent although some pay more regard to previous decisions than others. It should be remembered that, as tribunals are inferior and subject to the courts, they are governed by the precedents made in the courts.

• *Expertise*

Reference has already been made to the advantages to be gained from the particular expertise that is provided by the laymembers of tribunals as against the more general legal expertise of the chairperson.

• *Accessibility*

The aim of tribunals is to provide individuals with a readily accessible forum in which to air their grievances, and gaining access to tribunals is certainly not as difficult as getting a case into the ordinary courts.

• *Privacy*

The final advantage is the fact that proceedings can be taken before a tribunal without triggering the publicity that might follow from a court case.

12.3.6 Disadvantages of tribunals

It is important that the supposed advantages of tribunals are not simply taken at face value. They represent significant improvements over the operation of the ordinary court system; but it is at least arguable that some of them are not as advantageous as they appear at first sight, and that others represent potential, if not actual weaknesses, in the tribunal system.

Tribunals are cheap, quick, flexible and informal; but their operation should not be viewed with complacency. These so called advantages could be seen as representing an attack on general legal standards; and the tribunal system could be portrayed as providing a second rate system of justice for those who cannot afford to pay to gain access to 'real law' in the court system. Vigilance is required on the part of the general community to ensure that such does not become an accurate representation of the tribunal system.

In addition to this general point, there are particular weaknesses in the system of tribunal adjudication. Some of these relate to:

- *Appeals procedures*

There is ground for confusion in lack of uniformity in relation to appeals from tribunals. Rights of appeal from decisions of tribunals and the route of such appeals depend on the provision of the statute under which a particular tribunal operates. Where such rights exist, they may be exercised variously, to a further tribunal, a minister or a court of law. A measure of coherence would not come amiss in this procedure.

Prior to the Report of the Franks Committee, tribunals were not required to provide reasons for their decisions and this prevented appeals in most cases. Subsequent to the report, however, most tribunals, although still not all of them, are required to provide reasons for their decisions under s 10 of the Tribunals and Inquiries Act 1992. The importance of this provision is that, in cases where a tribunal has erred in its application of the law, the claimant can appeal to the High Court for an application for judicial review to have the decision of the tribunal set aside for error of law on the face of the record. All tribunals should be required to provide reasons for their decisions.

- *Publicity*

It was stated above that lack of publicity in relation to tribunal proceedings was a potential advantage of the system. A lack of publicity, however, may be a distinct disadvantage because it has the effect that cases involving issues of general public importance are not given the publicity and consideration that they might merit.

- *The provision of legal aid*

It was claimed previously that one of the major advantages of the tribunal system is its lack of formality and non-legal atmosphere. Research has shown, however, that individual complainants fare better where they are represented by lawyers. Additionally, as a consequence of the Franks' recommendations, the fact that chairpersons have to be legally qualified has led to an increase in the formality of tribunal proceedings. As a consequence, non-law experts find it increasingly difficult, in practice, to represent themselves effectively. This difficulty is compounded when the body which is the object of the complaint is itself legally represented; for, although the parties to hearings do not have to be legally represented, there is nothing to prevent them from being so represented.

This leads to a consideration of the major weakness in the operation of tribunals: the fact that, except for lands tribunal, employment appeals tribunals, mental health tribunals and the Commons Commissioners, legal aid is not available to people pursuing cases at tribunals. They may be entitled to legal advice and assistance under the 'green form' system but such limited assistance is unlikely to provide potential complainants with sufficient help to permit them to pursue their case with any confidence of achieving a satisfactory conclusion.

Although former Lord Chancellor Lord Mackay did not consider the operation of tribunals in his Hamlyn Lecture on ADR, he did make a comment that perhaps should be considered in this context. In justifying his refusal to provide legal aid for ADR generally, he stated that:

> Legal aid presupposes that there is a need, so undeniable that the taxpayer should support it, for legal advice or legal services relating to legal issues.

It is suggested that the operation of the tribunal system fits within these strictures and that, on the basis of the former Lord Chancellor's own reasoning, legal aid should be available to all of those involved in and subject to the adjudication of tribunals. If tribunals are becoming increasingly important in determining individual rights and are, at the same time, becoming formalistic, then the refusal of legal aid to those seeking to use tribunals is tantamount to refusing them access to justice. The Council on Tribunals has consistently advocated the proposal that the provision of legal aid should be extended to all tribunals. Their case is unarguable on the grounds of justice; unfortunately it appears to be defensible on the grounds of economics. Unfortunately, it would appear unlikely in the extreme that the current Lord Chancellor, Lord Irvine, will disagree with his predecessor.

12.4 Ombudsman

As with tribunals, so the institution of the ombudsman reflects the increased activity of the contemporary State. As the State became more engaged in everyday social activity, it increasingly impinged on, and on occasion conflicted with, the individual citizen. Courts and tribunals were available to deal with substantive breaches of particular rules and procedures but there remained some disquiet as to the possibility of the adverse effect of the implementation of general state policy on individuals. If tribunals may be categorised as an ADR procedure to the ordinary court system in relation to *decisions taken in breach of rules*, the institution of ombudsman represents a procedure for the redress of complaints about *the way in which those decisions have been taken*. It has to be admitted, however, that the two categories overlap to a considerable degree. The ombudsman procedure, however, is not just an alternative to the court and tribunal system; it is based upon a distinctly different approach to dealing with disputes. Indeed, the Parliamentary Commissioner Act 1967, which established the position of the first ombudsman, provides that complainants with rights to pursue their complaints in either of those forums will be precluded from making use of the ombudsman procedure. (Such a prohibition is subject to the discretion of the ombudsman who tends to interpret it in a generous manner in favour of the complainant.)

The concept of the ombudsman is Scandinavian in origin, and the function of the office holder is to investigate complaints of *maladministration*; that is, situations where the performance of a government department has fallen below acceptable standards of administration. The first ombudsman, appointed under the 1967 legislation, operated, and the present ombudsman still operates, under the title of the Parliamentary Commissioner for Administration (PCA) and was empowered to consider central government processes only. Since that date, a number of other ombudsmen have been appointed to oversee the administration of local government in England and Wales, under the Local Government Act 1974. Scotland and Northern Ireland have their own local government ombudsmen fulfilling the same task. There are also Health Service Commissioners for England, Wales and Scotland, whose duty it is to investigate the administration and provision of services in the health service, and, in October 1994, Sir Peter Woodhead was appointed as the first Prisons Ombudsman. The ombudsman system has also spread beyond the realm of government administration and there are ombudsmen overseeing the operation of, amongst other things, legal services, banking, and insurance. Some schemes, such as the legal services scheme, have been established by statute but many others have been established by industry as a means of self-regulation; as regards this latter type, the newspaper ombudsman does not appear to have been a great success and it has been rumoured that it will be disbanded.

The European Parliament appointed an ombudsman under the powers extended to it by the Treaty Establishing the European Community (EC Treaty) (Art 195, formerly 138(e)). The European ombudsman has the function of investigating maladministration in all of Community institutions, including the non-judicial operation of the European Court of Justice.

12.4.1 Procedure

Although maladministration is not defined in the Parliamentary Commissioner Act 1967, it has been taken to refer to an error in the way a decision was reached rather than an error in the actual decision itself. Indeed, s 12(3) of the Parliamentary Commissioner Act 1967 expressly precludes the PCA from questioning the merits of particular decisions taken without maladministration. Maladministration, therefore, can be seen to refer to procedure used to reach a result rather than the result itself. In an illuminating, and much quoted, speech introducing the Act, Richard Crossman, the then leader of the House of Commons, gave an indicative, if non-definitive, list of what might be included within the term maladministration, and included within it: bias, neglect, inattention, delay, incompetence, ineptitude, perversity, turpitude and arbitrariness.

Members of the public do not have the right to complain directly to the PCA but must channel any such complaint through a member of Parliament. Complainants do not have to provide precise details of any maladministration. They simply have to indicate the difficulties they have experienced as a result of dealing with an agency of central government. It is the function of the PCA to discover whether the problem arose as a result of maladministration. There is a 12 month time limit for raising complaints but the PCA has discretion to ignore this.

The powers of the PCA to investigate complaints are similar to those of a High Court judge to require the attendance of witnesses and the production of documents; and wilful obstruction of the investigation is treated as contempt of court.

On conclusion of an investigation, the PCA submits reports to the member of Parliament who the raised complaint, and to the principal of the government office which was subject to the investigation. The ombudsman has no enforcement powers but, if his recommendations are ignored, and existing practices involving maladministration are not altered, he may submit a further report to both Houses of Parliament in order to highlight the continued bad practice. The assumption is that on the submission of such a report, members of Parliament will exert pressure on the appropriate Minister of State to ensure that any changes needed in procedure are made.

Annual reports are laid before Parliament and a Parliamentary Select Committee exists to oversee the operation of the PCA. The operation of the Parliamentary Commissioner for Administration is subject to judicial review (*R v Parliamentary Commissioner for Administration ex p Balchin* (1997)); however, the Parliamentary Commissioner for Public Standards, established after the Nolan Inquiry into cash for questions in Parliament, is not open to judicial review (*R v Parliamentary Commissioner for Standards ex p Al Fayed* (1997)) (see 1.3.2).

The relationship between the PCA and the government is highlighted by three case studies:

(a) *Barlow Clowes*

The first of these concerned the Barlow Clowes group of companies. In 1988, Peter Clowes, and three others were arrested and charged with offences in connection with the Prevention of Fraud (Investments) Act 1958 and theft. The prosecution alleged an investment fraud said to have been over £115 million. The main allegation was that members of the public were induced to deposit their moneys in the belief that they would be invested in gilt-edged securities; but that only £1.9 million was in fact so invested. The rest was misappropriated by the defendants. Clowes alone faced charges of theft totalling some £62 million. The PCA received hundreds of complaints from investors who had lost their money in relation to the Barlow Clowes affair; all alleging maladministration on the part of the Department of Trade and Industry, which had responsibility for licensing such investment companies. The PCA made five findings of maladministration against the DTI and recommended that compensation should be paid to those who had suffered as a result of it. Surprisingly, the government initially denied any responsibility for providing compensation. Subsequently, after the PCA had expressed his regret at the government's initial stance, the government agreed to pay the recommended compensation payments, amounting to £150 million; but with the rider that it still accepted no legal liability.

(b) *Child Support Agency*

The much criticised Child Support Agency (CSA) had been established in an endeavour to ensure that absent parents, essentially fathers, would have to accept financial responsibility for the maintenance of their children as determined by the Agency. The PCA's report followed complaints referred to him by 95 members of Parliament covering the time from the Agency started its operations in April 1994 until the end of 1995. Although the PCA investigated 70 complaints, the report focused on seven of those as being representative of the whole. These complaints highlighted a number of failures on the part of the CSA: mistakes as to the identity of individuals subjects to the determinations of the CSA; failure to answer correspondence; delay in assessing and reviewing maintenance assessments and delays in actually securing payments due; and the provision of incorrect or misleading advice. The conclusion of the PCA was that the CSA was liable for maladministration, inexcusable delays and slipshod service. In response to the report, the chief executive of the CSA wrote to the PCA informing him that steps were being taken to deal with the problems highlighted in the report. Such changes in the way the CSA operated has not staved off its proposed replacement by a more sympathetic, and efficient, organisation.

(c) *Channel Tunnel Rail Link*

As a consequence of the four year delay on the part of the Department of Transport in deciding on a route for the Channel Tunnel Rail Link, the owners of properties along the various possible routes found the value of their properties blighted, not to say unsaleable. The situation was not finalised until the Department announced its final selection in 1994.

According to the PCA:

The effect of the Department of Transport's policy was to put the project in limbo, keeping it alive when it could not be funded.

As a consequence, he held that the Department:

... had a responsibility to consider the position of such persons suffering exceptional or extreme hardship and to provide redress where appropriate. They undertook no such considerations. That merits my criticism.

The unusual thing about this case, however, was the reaction of the Department of Transport, which rejected the findings of the PCA and refused to provide any compensation. The refusal of the Department of Transport led the PCA to lay a special report before Parliament, consequent upon a situation where an 'injustice has been found which has not or will not be remedied' (s 10(3) of the Parliamentary Commissioner Act 1967). Even in the face of the implementation of this extremely rare form of censure, the government maintained its original policy that it was not liable for the consequences of either general, or particular, blight. The matter was then taken up by the Select Committee on the Parliamentary Commissioner for Administration, which supported the conclusions of the PCA and recommended that:

... the Department of Transport reconsider its response to the Ombudsman's findings, accept his conclusions that maladministration had occurred ... It would be most regrettable if the department were to remain obdurate. In such an event, we recommend that as a matter of urgency a debate on this matter be held on the floor of the House on a substantive motion in government time [Sixth Report of PCA].

Such a demonstration of solidarity between the PCA and the Committee had the desired effect; leading to the government's climb down, and payments of £5,000 to those property owners who had suffered as a consequence of the housing blight.

12.4.2 Evaluation

All in all, the system appears to operate fairly well within its restricted sphere of operation, but there are major areas where it could be improved. The more important of the criticisms levelled at the PCA relate to:

- the retention of members of Parliament as filters of complaints. It is generally accepted that there is no need for such a filter mechanism. At one level, it represents a sop to the idea of parliamentary representation and control. Yet, at the practical level, PCAs have referred complaints made to them directly, to the constituent's member of Parliament in order to have them referred back to them in the appropriate form. It is suggested that there is no longer any need or justification for this farce;

- the restrictive nature of the definition of maladministration. It is possible to argue that any procedure that leads to an unreasonable decision must involve an element of maladministration and that, therefore, the definition as currently stated is not overly restrictive. However, even if such reverse reasoning is valid, it would still be preferable for the definition of the scope of the PCA's investigations to be clearly stated, and be stated in wider terms than at present;

- the jurisdiction of the PCA. This criticism tends to resolve itself into the view that there are many areas that should be covered by the PCA but which are not. For example, as presently constituted, the ombudsman can only investigate the *operation* of general law. It could be claimed, and not without some justification, that the process of *making* law, in the form of delegated legislation, could equally do with investigation;

- the lack of publicity given to complaints. It is sometimes suggested that sufficient publicity is not given either to the existence of the various ombudsmen or to the results of their investigations. The argument is that if more people were aware of the procedure and what it could achieve, then more people would make use of it leading to an overall improvement in the administration of governmental policies;

- the reactive role of the ombudsman. This criticism refers to the fact that the ombudsmen are dependent upon receiving complaints before they can initiate investigations. It is suggested that a more *pro-active* role under which the ombudsmen would be empowered to initiate investigation on their own authority would lead to an improvement in general administration as well as increase the effectiveness of the activity of the ombudsmen. This criticism is related to the way in which the role of the ombudsmen is viewed. If they are simply a problem solving dispute resolution institution, then a *reactive* role is sufficient; if, however, they are seen as the means of improving general administrative performance, then a more *pro-active* role is called for.

In his Hamlyn Lecture, the former Lord Chancellor, Lord Mackay, approvingly categorised the ombudsman as:

> Popularly representing justice for the small against the great – justice that is quick, inexpensive and unfettered by legalistic procedures – acceptance of the institution of ombudsman now extends well beyond central and local government administration. The concept is widely viewed as a desirable, and even necessary, avenue to fairness wherever the individual is perceived to be at the mercy of an impenetrable administrative system.

12.5 Mediation and conciliation

The final alternative dispute mechanisms to be considered, mediation and conciliation, are the most informal of all.

12.5.1 Mediation

Mediation is the process whereby a third party acts as the conduit through which two disputing parties communicate and negotiate in an attempt to reach a common resolution of a problem. The mediator may move between the parties, communicating their opinions without their having to meet, or alternatively the mediator may operate in the presence of the parties, but, in either situation, the emphasis is on the parties themselves working out a shared agreement as to how the dispute in question is to be settled.

In his Hamlyn Lecture, Lord Mackay considered three alternative systems of mediation and examined the possibility of annexing such schemes to the existing court system. One, involving lawyers advising parties as to the legal strengths of their relative positions, he rejected on the grounds that it merely duplicated, without replacing or extending, what was already available in the courts. A second, based on judges adopting the role of mediators, he rejected on the ground that it might be seen as undermining the traditional impartiality of the judiciary. The third type, and the one that found most favour with him, broadened the issues beyond the legal, to explore solutions that were not available to the court. His approval, however, did not extend to financing such a system; the implication being that public money should, and does, finance the civil justice system and that any benefits that flow from a different system should be financed privately.

In March 1998, the Lord Chancellor's Department reported that take up of the voluntary mediation procedure offered in the pilot schemes had been fairly low. As regards the pilot scheme established in the Central London County Court, a monitoring report found that only 5% of cases referred to the ADR scheme actually took it up. However, in a more positive mode, the report did find that, in cases that did go to mediation, 62% settled during the process without going on to court. The conclusion of the report was that mediation was capable of dealing with a wider range of cases than might have been expected, including personal injury cases. It also found that those who participate found the process satisfying and led to outcomes that the parties generally found acceptable.

12.5.2 Mediation in divorce

... in government, we have continued to encourage the use of mediation, most notably in the area of family law, where it is a central tent of divorce law reform. The importance of mediation and ADR in family law cases can scarcely be understated, given the high incidence of family breakdown and the appalling social consequences which result [Lord Chancellor Irvine, Speech to Faculty of Mediators, 1999].

Mediation has an important part to play in family matters, where it is felt that the adversarial approach of the traditional legal system has tended to emphasise, if not increase, existing differences of view between individuals and has not been conducive to amicable settlements. Thus, in divorce cases, mediation has traditionally been used to enable the parties themselves to work out an agreed settlement rather than having one imposed on them from outside by the courts.

This emphasis on mediation was strengthened in the Family Law Act 1996, but it is important to realise there are potential problems with mediation. The assumption that the parties freely negotiate the terms of their final agreement in a less than hostile manner may be deeply flawed to the extent that it assumes equality of bargaining power and knowledge between the parties to the negotiation. Mediation may well ease pain, but, unless the mediation procedure is carefully and critically monitored, it may gloss over and perpetuate a previously exploitative relationship, allowing the more powerful participant to manipulate and dominate the more vulnerable, and force an inequitable agreement. Establishing entitlements on the basis of clear legal advice may be preferable to apparently negotiating those entitlements away in the non-confrontational, therapeutic, atmosphere of mediation.

Under the Divorce Reform Act 1969, the concept of 'no fault' divorce was introduced for those couples who had been separated for two years, and it was assumed that this would provide the main grounds for divorce applications. This has not proved to be the case and it is commonly accepted that, because of the two year delay involved, 75% of those seeking divorces still apply on the basis of adultery or unreasonable behaviour, permitting them to complete the procedure in between three and six months.

The Family Law Act proposed to introduce real 'no fault' divorce by abolishing the grounds of adultery and unreasonable behaviour, but couples will have to wait a minimum of 12 months before their divorce was confirmed. Instead of filing a divorce petition, the person seeking to be divorced is merely required to submit a statement certifying that their marriage has broken down. The process of divorce will require that the parties attend an informal meeting three months before they make their statement of marital breakdown. They will then have to wait a further nine months for their divorce, during which time they should reflect on whether the marriage could be saved, have an opportunity for reconciliation, and consider arrangements relating to finance, property and children. The Act encourages the use of mediation in appropriate cases, and allows the court, after it has received a statement of marital breakdown, to direct the parties to attend a meeting with a mediator for an explanation of the mediation process. The role of the mediator is restricted to sorting out the aspects of the divorce relating to finance and children, and should refer the case to an appropriate counsellor if it appears that the parties to the marriage might be open to reconciliation. During the 'cooling off period', State funding would be available for meetings with marriage guidance counsellors for those eligible for legal aid, and others would be encouraged to take advantage of such marriage support services.

Although the Family Law Act was passed in 1996, the proposed reforms were not implemented immediately, and trials were conducted as to the appropriateness of the new procedures. Also, the fact that the Family Law Act was passed under the previous Conservative administration, and as a consequence of the strenuous endeavours of the then Lord Chancellor, Lord Mackay, did not prevent the incoming Labour administration's continued support for the proposed reforms. As Lord Chancellor Irvine stated:

> ... in government, we have continued to encourage the use of mediation, most notably in the area of family law, where it is a central tenet of divorce law reform. The importance of mediation and ADR in family law cases can scarcely be understated, given the high incidence of family breakdown and the appalling social consequences which result [Lord Chancellor Irvine, Speech to Faculty of Mediators, 1999].

However, in June 1999, Lord Irvine announced that the government would not be implementing the new proposals in the Family Law Act in the year 2000 as had been previously intended. It has to be said that much academic, and legal practitioner, opinion was dubious, if not hostile, to the way in which the mediation procedure would operate. It was accepted generally that mediation might work in relation to children, but it was thought less likely to work where money was concerned and, in those circumstances, it was suggested that people would still be likely to look for their own personal legal representative rather than submit to mediation. It would appear that the results of the trials support such scepticism. Lord Irvine stated that the results of the mediation pilot schemes were disappointing, in that fewer than 10% of divorcing couples in the pilot areas were willing to make use of the preliminary information meetings, which would become compulsory under the Family Law Act proposals. Of those attending the meetings; only 7% were successfully encouraged to opt for mediation, and only 13% took up the offer to see a marriage counsellor. Almost 40% of those attending the meetings stated that they were more convinced of the need to see an independent lawyer to protect their legal rights.

Lord Irvine's announcement was merely as to the postponement of the implementation of the divorce law reforms. Many, however, believe that this postponement is merely a precursor to their future abandonment.

In March 1998, the Lord Chancellor's Department reported that take up of the voluntary mediation procedure offered in the pilot schemes had been fairly low, at least as regards the pilot scheme established in the Central London

County Court (see above). A monitoring report found that only 5% of cases referred to the ADR scheme, actually took it up. However, in a more positive mode, the report did find that in cases that did go to mediation, 62% settled during the process without going on to court. The conclusion of the report was that mediation was capable of dealing with a wider range of cases than might have been expected, including personal injury cases. It also found that those who participate found the process satisfying and led to outcomes that the parties generally found acceptable. It has to be stated, however that at least, with specific reference to the provisions of the Family Law Act, which will be fully implemented in 1999, much academic and legal practitioner opinion remains dubious, if not hostile, to the way in which the mediation procedure will operate. It is accepted that mediation may work in relation to children, but it is thought less likely to work where money is concerned, and in those circumstances, people are still likely to look for their own personal legal representative rather than submit to mediation.

In a speech at The UK Family Law Conference in London on 25 June 1999, Lord Irvine recognised that his decision to postpone the implementation of Pt 2 of the Family Law Act raised a question mark over its future, but he went on to say that the final decision depended on the outcome of the current and future research into the area (www.open-gov.uk/lcd/speeches/1999/25-6-99.htm).

12.5.3 Conciliation

Conciliation takes mediation a step further and gives the mediator the power to suggest grounds for compromise and the possible basis for a conclusive agreement. Both mediation and conciliation have been available in relation to industrial disputes under the auspices of the government funded Advisory Conciliation and Arbitration Service (ACAS). One of the statutory functions of ACAS is to try to resolve industrial disputes by means of discussion and negotiation or, if the parties agree, the Service might take a more active part as arbitrator in relation to a particular dispute.

The essential weakness in the procedures of mediation and conciliation lies in the fact that, although they *may* lead to the resolution of a dispute, they do not *necessarily* achieve that end. Where they operate successfully, they are excellent methods of dealing with problems, as essentially the parties to the dispute determine their own solutions and therefore feel committed to the outcome. The problem is that they have no binding power and do not always lead to an outcome. As the Heilbron Report emphasises, even if the civil law procedure is reformed to make it more litigant-friendly, ADR mechanisms will still have a very important part to play in dealing with problems in certain delicate areas that are not susceptible to resolution by the ordinary court system. Lord Mackay has recognised this in his proposal for divorce reform but he has also resisted the call to fund a wider use of mediation on the basis that for the State to fund it would lead to its use becoming compulsory and yet it is the very lack of compulsion in the procedure that makes it work successfully.

ARBITRATION, TRIBUNAL ADJUDICATION AND ALTERNATIVE DISPUTE RESOLUTION

Alternative dispute resolution

ADR has many features that make it preferable to the ordinary court system in many areas.

Its main advantage is that it is less antagonistic than the ordinary legal system, and is designed to achieve agreement between the parties involved.

Arbitration

This is the procedure whereby parties in dispute refer the issue to a third party for resolution, rather than take the case to the ordinary law courts. Arbitration procedures can be contained in the original contract or agreed after a dispute arises. The procedure is governed by the Arbitration Act 1996. The Act follows the Model Arbitration Law adopted by the United Nations Commission on International Trade Law (UNICTRAL). Arbitration awards are enforceable in the ordinary courts. They must be carried out in a judicial manner and are subject to judicial review.

Advantages over the ordinary court system are: privacy; informality; speed; lower cost; expertise; and it is less antagonistic.

Small claims procedure in the county court is a distinct process, although referred to as arbitration. Although still called small claims, the upper limit for such proceedings is the not inconsiderable sum of £5,000. This has raised some doubts as to the future operation of the system.

Administrative tribunals

These deal with cases involving conflicts between the State, its functionaries, and private citizens. Domestic tribunals deal with private internal matters within institutions. Tribunals may be seen as administrative but they are also adjudicative in that they have to act judicially when deciding particular cases. Tribunals are subject to the supervision of the Council on Tribunals but are subservient to and under the control of the ordinary courts.

Usually, only the chair of a tribunal is legally qualified.

Examples of tribunals are: industrial tribunal; social security appeals tribunal; mental health review tribunal; lands tribunal; Rent Assessment Committee.

Advantages of tribunals over ordinary courts relate to: speed; cost; informality; flexibility; expertise; accessibility; privacy.

Disadvantages relate to: appeals procedure; lack of publicity; the lack of legal aid in most cases.

Ombudsmen

The role of ombudsmen is to investigate complaints of maladministration in various areas of State activity. Members of the public must channel complaints through a Member of Parliament.

The powers of the PCA to investigate complaints are similar to those of a High Court judge. The ombudsman has no direct enforcement powers as such.

On conclusion of an investigation, he submits reports to the member of Parliament who raised complaint, and to the principal of the government office which was subject to the investigation. He can also report to Parliament.

Shortcomings in the procedure: the member of Parliament filter; uncertain if not narrow jurisdiction; lack of publicity; the reactive rather than proactive nature of the role.

Mediation and conciliation

Mediation: the third party only acts as a go-between. The Family Law Act 1996 proposed a greater role for mediation in relation to divorce. This proposal has been brought into doubt by the recent announcement of its postponement by the Lord Chancellor, in the light of the results of a pilot study.

Conciliation: the third party is more active in facilitating a reconciliation or agreement between the parties.

CHAPTER 13

THE CRIMINAL PROCESS:
(1) THE INVESTIGATION OF CRIME

13.1 General introduction to the criminal process

13.1.1 The criminal justice system in the 21st century

The criminal justice system has recently been the subject of widespread heated debate in Parliament, the broadcast media and the print media and in academic and professional journals. The British Crime Survey (BCS) (Home Office Statistical Bulletin, issue 21/98) estimates that there were nearly 16,500,000 crimes against adults living in households in 1997. The long term trend shows that the gradual rise in BCS crime during the 1980s and the steeper rise during the early 1990s have now been reversed. Even so, the number of crimes counted by the BCS has increased by 49% since 1981.

This chapter, and the following one, refers to the 'criminal justice system'. This has been, for many years, an accepted descriptive term used by social scientists, journalists and, occasionally, lawyers. Officially, however, there is no such thing as the 'criminal justice system'. Governmental responsibilities, for example, overlap in this area. The Home Secretary is responsible for the Metropolitan Police, criminal statistics, the Probation Service, and the Crown Prosecution Service (and, more broadly, for 'law and order'), while the Lord Chancellor is responsible for all the criminal law courts, the appointment of magistrates, and the judges. Nonetheless, in recent times, there has been increasing governmental recognition of something called the 'criminal justice system'. On 30 December 1998, for example, a single official statement entitled 'Joint Press Release on the Criminal Justice System Public Service Agreement' was issued on behalf of the Home Office, the Lord Chancellor's Department, and the Attorney General's Office. It stated:

> The overarching aims, objectives and performance measures for the criminal justice system have been published for the first time in a cross departmental Public Service Agreement. The three Departments, and their respective services, will be working more closely than ever before to ensure that the criminal justice system protects the public and delivers justice. Inter-agency co-operation will be promoted at regional, local, as well as at the national level. Ministers believe that these arrangements are a good example of 'joined-up government' in practice [www.nds.coi.gov.uk/coi/coipress.ns].

The significance of such a pronouncement is that it reveals an attempt to make co-ordinated policy in respect of each of these branches of operation. In fact, the statement goes on to become quite explicit:

The three ministers have set two overarching aims to provide a strategic direction for the system as a whole. They have made clear that every part of the criminal justice system (including the police, courts, Crown Prosecution Service, prison and probation services) should work together so as to best serve and protect the public.

The two overarching aims are:

- to reduce crime and the fear of crime and their social and economic costs; and

- to dispense justice fairly and efficiently and to promote confidence in the rule of law.

Supporting the aims are the following eight objectives.

In support of the first aim:

(1) to reduce the level of actual crime and disorder;

(2) to reduce the adverse impact of crime and disorder on people's lives;

(3) to reduce the economic costs of crime.

In support of the second aim:

(4) to ensure just processes and just and effective outcomes;

(5) to deal with cases throughout the criminal justice process with appropriate speed;

(6) to meet the needs of victims, witnesses and jurors within the system;

(7) to respect the rights of defendants and to treat them fairly;

(8) to promote confidence in the criminal justice system.

13.2   Mistrust of the system

On the one hand, there has been an apparently growing public mistrust of the criminal justice system as a system which can convict the innocent. The number of exposed miscarriages of justice involving malpractice and disastrous errors by agencies of the criminal justice system has grown rapidly. On 19 March 1991, the day the Birmingham Six were released from prison having wrongly served 16 years in jail, the Home Secretary announced a Royal Commission on Criminal Justice to examine the system with a view to reducing the chances of wrongful conviction. The Commission published its report with 352 recommendations in July 1993. Although some of these recommendations have been implemented in subsequent legislation (like the establishment of the Criminal Cases Review Commission by the Criminal Appeal Act (CAA) 1995), great concern has been expressed by pressure groups about the government's rejection of the Royal Commission's findings in relation to the so called 'right to silence'. This right was effectively undermined by ss 34–37 of the Criminal Justice and Public Order Act (CJPOA) 1994, and this change will, arguably, increase the chances of miscarriages occurring rather than reduce them. Confidence in the criminal justice system appears to be in decline. In a national survey for the 1962 Royal Commission on the Police (Cmnd 1728, 1962), 83% of respondents indicated that they had 'a great deal of respect' for the way the police operated. In a national poll in 1993 conducted by MORI for *The Sunday Times* and the Police Federation, under 50% of respondents indicated that they had 'a great deal of respect' for the way the police operated. The poll also showed that one in six adults (7 million people) actually distrust the police ((1993) *The Sunday Times*, 25 July). In another nationwide poll ((1993) *The Independent*, 21 June), 28% of respondents indicated that they would be 'concerned at what might be going to happen' if stopped by the police, with only 36% of respondents indicating they would be confident that they would be treated fairly.

Public confidence in the police continued to fall in the late 1990s (see, for example, 'Lack of trust at heart of attitude problem' (1999) *The Guardian*, 25 February; 'One in four say police racist' (1999) *The Guardian*, 9 February). This drop in confidence plummeted with particular sharpness after the publication of the Macpherson Report into the racist killing of the black London teenager, Stephen Lawrence. The Report identified various fundamental operational failings of the police and, more significantly, 'institutional racism'.

13.2.1 The Macpherson Report

Following the stabbing of Stephen Lawrence, a black teenager from South London, by a group of racist thugs in 1993, defects in several aspects of the English legal system failed to bring his killers to justice. There was a catalogue of profoundly incompetent errors in the way the police handled events. These included: the failure to administer proper first aid at the scene of the attack; a failure to properly search for evidence and suspects; a failure to properly log and investigate tip-offs about the identity of the killers; and a failure to treat the family of Stephen Lawrence with proper respect and sensitivity. A judicial inquiry headed by a former High Court judge, Sir William Macpherson, was set up by the government in 1997 and its report was published in February 1999 (The Stationery Office, Cm 4262-I, 1999).

The Report accuses the Metropolitan Police (in London) of 'institutional racism'. It recommends that the police and several other public services should now be brought fully within the Race Relations Act 1976 which deals with racism in the private employment sector. At present, the Act can be used only where police are operating in a service capacity but not in the course of their operational duties. For example, there is not presently any legal remedy under the Act if a black person believes he or she has been stopped in the street for reasons of racial prejudice.

Another recommendation in the report would, if enacted, end the ancient principle against 'double jeopardy' whereby a person cannot be tried more than once for the same, or substantially the same, crime. This arose from one twist in the developments in the Lawrence case in which three suspects were sent for trial at Crown Court after a private prosecution brought by Stephen's father. The trial was stopped by the judge who ruled that there was insufficient evidence to proceed and ordered the jury to acquit the defendants. The rule of double jeopardy (*autrefois acquit* – the person has been otherwise acquitted) will now prevent any further prosecution being brought against the main suspects even if strong evidence against them is subsequently found. The feeling that the guilty have got away with such a serious and repulsive crime is widespread. One national newspaper, beneath the banner headline 'Murderers', put the names and photographs of the five chief suspects of the killings.

The report recommends (Recommendation 38) that the Court of Appeal should have the power to permit prosecution after acquittal 'where fresh and viable evidence is presented'. The Home Secretary has said that he will refer the matter to the Law Commission. There is, arguably, a good case for change here. The rule which prevents anyone from being charged more than once in respect of the same crime arose in an ancient era when there existed none of today's multifarious checks and balances against the abuse of official power (committal proceedings, independent magistrates and judges, random juries, stringent laws of evidence; see Chapter 14). At the time of the origin of the rule against double jeopardy, powerful aristocrats could, effectively, terrorise individual enemies with the threat of repeated prosecutions. By contrast, in today's setting, provided some form of high level and independent authorisation were to be required (Macpherson recommends the Court of Appeal) before a second prosecution could be brought, there would be no real risk that the threat of re-prosecution would constantly hang over an acquitted defendant's head. Only those fearful of new, viable incriminating evidence for serious crimes would have reason to worry.

The report's other recommendations are summarised in the numbered sections below and are followed by the authors' brief comment:

(1) That a ministerial priority be established for all police services 'to increase trust and confidence in policing among minority ethnic communities'.

Comment: Unfortunately, only days after this report was published, it came to light that a special report commissioned 15 months ago showed that 17 out of the 43 police forces of England and Wales did not have any community and race relations policy, despite having been urged to establish one ((1999) *The Times*, 2 March).

(9) That a Freedom of Information Act should apply to all areas of policing, subject only to a 'substantial harm' test for withholding information.

Comment: Both during the investigation and at various stages after the failed public prosecution, the friends and relatives of Stephen Lawrence found it impossible to get clear and accurate information from the police about how the case had been handled and was being taken forward. The more open and transparent a system, the more likely it is to carry public confidence.

(11) That the Race Relations Acts should apply to police officers and that Chief Constables should be vicariously liable for the acts and omissions of their officers in this area.

Comment: This proposal would help focus police attention on what might otherwise be unconscious or unintended racist behaviour.

(33) That the Crown Prosecution Service (CPS) should, in deciding whether to prosecute a racist crime, consider that, once the 'evidential test' is satisfied (that is, that there is a 'realistic prospect of conviction'), there is a rebuttable presumption that the public interest test is in favour of prosecution.

Comment: Racism in a crime is currently a factor which should strengthen the chances of a prosecution according to the Code for Crown Prosecutors; the change would make a prosecution more certain in such circumstances.

(34) That the police and CPS should take particular care to recognise and to include any evidence of a racial motivation in a crime. The CPS should take care to ensure that any such motivation is referred to at trial and in the sentencing process. No plea bargaining should ever exclude such evidence.

Comment: This highlights that racism is a serious aggravating factor in any crime, as it shows that the innocent victim has been specially and vindictively selected for a reason that is irrational, and, therefore, especially terrifying.

(41) That consideration be given to the proposition that victims or victims' families should be allowed to become 'civil parties' to criminal proceedings, to facilitate and to ensure the provision of all relevant information to victims and their families.

Comment: Unlike civil litigation, it is the State that prosecutes where there has been a crime; the victim neither determines whether to prosecute nor, if someone is convicted, can the victim influence the sentence for the crime. Recommendation 41 is therefore a controversial proposal, as there has traditionally been great resistance to permitting citizens to participate in the prosecution of crimes. The essentially communicative role, suggested here, however, is arguably different from an influential role.

(42) That there should be advance disclosure of evidence and documents as of right to parties who have leave from a coroner to appear at an inquest.

Comment: Presently, relatives often only discover the terrible details of the death of their loved ones at the inquest in open court as some coroners will not release any information even to bereaved next of kin before the hearing.

(43) That consideration be given to the provision of legal aid to victims or the families of victims to cover representation at an inquest in appropriate cases.

Comment: This is a recommendation that has been made for many years by various bodies and committees. There is a very strong case for bereaved people *in extremis*, who cannot afford to have representation at the inquest of their loved one, to receive legal aid.

Britain is a multi-cultural and ethnically diverse community. Its policing is based on consent rather than sheer strength: there are 60 million citizens and only 130,000 police, so it can only work on consent. At the heart of the debate about policing, the law, and the criminal justice system in the wake of the Macpherson Report is the question of whether ethnic minorities, especially visible minorities, can quickly be made to feel confident about the way they are treated by the English legal system.

A recent report produced by the Metropolitan Police Service (MPS) entitled *Stop and Search: Reviewing the Tactic* (1999) and two Home Office research papers *Entry into the Criminal Justice System: A Survey of Police Arrests and their Outcomes* (1998) and *Statistics on Race and the Criminal Justice System* (1998) recognise the disproportionate use of stop and search powers against black people (see Cragg, 'Stop and search powers: research and extension' (1999) *Legal Action* 3, February). Cragg argues that:

> ... with the figures already showing that almost 90% of those stopped are not arrested (and, therefore, the implication must be that there were, in fact, no grounds to stop and search these people), the training and management strategy proposed by the MPS 'to manage the tactic more fairly and effectively' must be rigorously imposed and monitored if it is to have any chance of success.

The exercise of stop and search powers by the police is governed by the revised Code of Practice A (see 13.3.14) which states that it is important these powers are used responsibly and sparingly. It warns, 'misuse of the powers is likely to be harmful to the police effort in the long run and can lead to mistrust of police in the community'.

13.2.2 Lack of confidence in the system

The rise in crime, especially certain types of offence like domestic burglary, taking and driving away (joyriding) offences, and theft of, and from, vehicles has greatly vexed large sections of the population. These crimes account for over two-thirds of all crime recorded in the Annual Criminal Statistics (1998).

In the 12 months ending March 1998, the police in England and Wales recorded a total of 4.5 million offences (Home Office Statistical Bulletin, Notifiable Offences, issue 22/98). Certain types of offence like domestic burglary, theft of, and from, vehicles and vandalism against vehicles and other household and personal property has greatly vexed large sections of the population. These offences accounted for 91% of all recorded crimes during this period. However, a large proportion of crime is unrecorded, as many offences are not reported to the police. The number of offences committed in England and Wales is double the recorded figure according to a MORI poll conducted in 1997 ((1997) *The Times*, 15 March). The poll found that 44% of victims had failed to report incidents to police because they had no confidence the offenders would be caught, or felt that the offences were too trivial or that the police would not investigate.

The survey showed that 47% of people had been a victim of crime in 1996. Of BCS crimes that can be compared to recorded offences, just a quarter ended up in police records. This is because less than half were reported to the police, and only about half of those that were reported were recorded (issue 21/98, section 4).

13.2.3 A contradiction

There is a friction between the sort of policies that these two concerns generate, that is, people seem to want the police to have greater powers to combat crime, and yet, contradictorily, want greater controls on the police and evidence so as to avoid more miscarriages of justice. It is argued that, if we wish to avoid unjust convictions like those of the Winchester Three, the Guildford Four, the Birmingham Six, the Maguire Seven, the Tottenham Three, Stefan Kiszko, Judith Ward and the Bridgewater Three ((1997) *The Guardian*, 21, 22 February), we should tighten the rules of evidence and procedure that govern the investigation and prosecution of crime. Against this, it has been argued (for example, by Charles Pollard, Chief Constable of the Thames Valley Police, letter (1995) *The Times*, 12 April; article (1995) *The Sunday Times*, 9 July) that the police should have greater powers and that the trial process should be tilted less in favour of the defendant. The rules on disclosure of evidence in criminal trials, for example, have been radically changed by the Criminal Procedure and Investigations Act 1996. In particular, the material the prosecution has to disclose to the defence is now staged and brought within a more restrictive framework and since, for the first time, the defence has a duty to disclose its case in advance of trial.

One problem, therefore, in this area of the English legal system is that as the growing problems of crime, and the fear of crime, become more important concerns of government, there are emerging two lobbies for change, lobbies which are diametrically opposed.

The criminal process is examined here in two chapters. This chapter considers the law relating to important pre-trial matters up to and including the admissibility of confession evidence in court. Chapter 14 looks at institutional and procedural aspects of prosecution and matters relating to bail, the classification of offences, trials, plea bargaining and the jury. In examining all these topics, it is important to keep in mind the various aims of the criminal justice system and the extent to which the existing law serves these aims. Amongst the aims to be borne in mind are the following:

- to detect crime and convict those who have committed it;

- to have rules relating to arrest, search, questioning, interrogation and admissibility of evidence which do not expose suspects to unfair treatment likely to lead to unjust convictions;

- to have rules as above which do not unnecessarily impede the proper investigation of crime;

- to ensure that innocent persons are not convicted;

- to maintain public order;

- to maintain public confidence in the criminal justice system;

- to properly balance considerations of justice and fair procedure with those of efficiency and funding.

13.2.4 Contemporary issues

The criminal justice system is bearing signs of strain as it tries to cope with a society in the throes of major transitions: changes in the pattern of family life, changes in the nature of employment expectations, and a revolution in information and communications technology.

In 1999, there are 67,000 people in prison with official predictions putting the figure at 83,000 at the beginning of the next century. Violent crime rose by 8% over the last year and, now that s 34 of the Crime and Disorder Act 1998 has brought 10–14 year olds within the criminal law (by abolishing the rebuttable presumption of *doli incapax* for that age range), the number of offences processed by the authorities will be likely to rise significantly over the next several years.

The Police and Magistrates' Courts Act 1994 amended the Police Act 1964, permitting Home Secretaries now to 'determine objectives for the policing of all of the areas of all police authorities'. Under this power, a new police mission statement was announced earlier this year. The purpose of the police, according to this, is 'to help secure a safe and just society in which the rights and responsibilities of individuals, families and communities are properly balanced'. This raises many contentious issues, as the determination of, for example, what is a 'just society' becomes something which is more overtly a matter for policing policy than in previous times when the police role was more simply (in the words of Robert Peel, the 19th century founder of modern policing) to 'prevent and detect crime'.

Yet, can 130,00 police officers do well enough to retain credibility in a society of 56 million people undergoing all sorts of social upheavals? In 1998, the police had to respond to 17.8 million incidents and 7.5 million 999 calls. The racist canteen culture revealed in the wake of the Stephen Lawrence Inquiry, (see 13.2.1) and the recognition in 1998 by the Commissioner for the Metropolitan police that he probably has 250 corrupt officers on his force did not help raise public confidence.

It is not clear yet what is the main thrust of governmental policy in relation to the criminal justice system. Thus far, we have seen an unusual cocktail consisting of several privatisation measures and a good dose of centralisation.

Criminal justice has, historically, been regarded by government as, *par excellence*, a matter for the State. Recently, however, first under the Conservative government in the early 1990s and now under Labour, various parts of the system have been privatised. Such moves have not generally been seen as runaway successes. In November 1998, there was public scandal at the extent of injury to prison officers and trainers and damage to the premises of the country's leading private institution for young offenders. It was revealed that over £100,000 of damage had been wrought by wild 12–14 year olds at the Medway Secure Training Centre in Kent. After more than one fiasco, privatised prison escort services have come in for severe criticism, and a provision of the CJPOA 1994 allowing for private sponsorship of police equipment has been a boon for satirical cartoonists.

By contrast, there are several ways in which aspects of the criminal justice system, historically, all independent from each other and detached from governmental control, have been drawn within the influence of central government. It has, for example, been a hallowed precept of the British constitution that police forces are local and not governmental agencies. Yet, under Conservative legislation, the Home Secretary became allowed to 'determine objectives for the policing of the areas of all police authorities'.

More worryingly, there has been a notable governmental move to integrate different organisational functions. The Crown Prosecution Service (CPS) has been re-structured so that its erstwhile 13 regions are turned into 42 to match the 43 police forces of England and Wales. This is a remarkable swerve from previous policy. Close and often cosy relations between police officers and the lawyers who used to prosecute their cases (sometimes with atrocious malpractice) was the very reason for the establishment of the CPS.

But, moves towards criminal justice system unification go further than this. The Lord Chancellor announced in 1997 (Ministerial Statement to the House of Lords, 29 October 1997) that the 96 Magistrates' Courts Committees (which administer the courts dealing with 95% of all criminal cases) should enjoy much greater alignment with the police and the CPS.

Most disturbingly of all, for some, are the foundations for the Criminal Defence Service (CDS) (laid in the Access to Justice Act 1999) which will give the government greater control over legal representation. The Law Society has pointed out that campaigning lawyers like Gareth Pierce, who represented the Guildford Four, and Jim Nicol, who represented the appellants in the Carl Bridgewater case, could be avoided by the new body.

There is also reason for disquiet about the law, contained in the Criminal Justice (Terrorism and Conspiracy) Act 1998, which makes the opinion of a police officer admissible evidence in court – proof of membership of a proscribed organisation may be based upon the opinion of a senior police officer. In the wake of considerable evidence (from miscarriage of justice cases, especially those involving suspects of terrorism from Northern Ireland) that some police officers were apparently prepared to lie and falsify evidence to secure convictions, the new law has caused some people to become alarmed at the prospect that a person could be convicted of a serious offence on evidence taken mainly from the opinion of a police officer.

Other threats to the criminal justice system include plans to allow crown prosecutors to present cases in the higher courts and a public defender system, like the one being piloted in Scotland, in which defence lawyers are employed by the State.

Taken together, such moves could be seen to pose a risk to the British justice system, in which top advocates defend and prosecute in the criminal courts and appear for both sides in the civil courts; this would be lost for good were the State to take over control of all advocacy in the prosecution and defence of crimes.

Heather Hallett QC, Chair of the Bar Council, has said:

> We still have a system whereby some of the best advocates in the world can be seen day in, day out, in our criminal and civil courts ... acting for the State and for the ordinary man and woman in the street, prosecuting one day, defending the next, acting for the injured plaintiff one week, the insurance company the next [(1998) *The Times*, 5 October].

She has expressed fears about increased State involvement in the criminal courts, through allowing crown prosecutors into the higher courts, and the creation of public defenders, and has said she was astonished by claims from the Scottish Legal Aid Board, which is running the pilot on public defenders, that other jurisdictions operated such a scheme successfully:

> I wonder if they have spoken to the New Orleans Public Defender, Rick Tessier, who sued himself because he was being forced to take on three times more cases each year than the recommended maximum.

Many have asked why the English Bar was so concerned about the proposed changes – the answer is that the Bar does not wish to move to a system where, as in most countries, top lawyers specialised only in commercial work.

The Bar does not wish to became a small cadre of highly specialist commercial practitioners available to just the few. It has expressed a wish to remain as a body of specialist advocates and advisers available to all.

The question now is whether the peculiar current mix of privatisation and centralisation policies will satisfy some of the people some of the time or none of the people all of the time.

13.3 Arrest

Before considering the rights of the citizen and the law governing arrest and detention, what happens in the police station and what evidence is admissible in court, it is appropriate to look first at what the citizen can do if those rights are violated.

13.3.1 Remedies for unlawful arrest

Like other areas of law where the liberty of the subject is at stake, the law relating to arrest is founded upon the principle of *justification*. If challenged, the person who has attempted to make an arrest must justify his or her actions and show that the arrest was lawful. Failing this, the arrest will be regarded as unlawful.

There are three possible remedies:

- The person, or someone on his or her behalf, can bring proceedings of habeas corpus. This ancient prerogative writ used to begin with the words 'habeas corpus', meaning 'You must have the body'. It is addressed to the detainer and asks him to bring the detainee in question before the court at a specified date and time. The remedy protects the freedom of those who have been unlawfully detained in prison, hospital, police station or private custody. The writ is applied for from a judge in chambers and can, in emergencies, be made over the telephone. It must be issued if there is *prima facie* evidence that the detention is unlawful. As every detention is unlawful, the burden of proof is on the detainer to justify his conduct. If issued, the writ frees the detainee and thus allows him to seek other remedies (below) against the detainer.

- To use the illegality of the detention to argue that any subsequent prosecution should fail. This type of argument is very rarely successful as illegally obtained evidence is not, *ipso facto*, automatically rendered inadmissible. The House of Lords ruled in *R v Sang* (1979) that no discretion existed to exclude evidence simply because it had been illegally or improperly obtained. A court could only exclude relevant evidence where its effect would be 'unduly prejudicial'. This is reflected in s 78(1) of the Police and Criminal Evidence Act (PACE) 1984. This perhaps surprising rule was supported by the Royal Commission on Criminal Justice (although the argument there was chiefly focused on the admissibility of confession evidence). Professor Zander, however, in a note of dissent, contested the idea that a conviction could be upheld despite serious misconduct by the prosecution if there is other evidence against the convicted person. He states: 'I cannot agree. The moral foundation of the criminal justice system requires that, if the prosecution has employed foul means, the defendant must go free if he is plainly guilty ... the conviction should be quashed as an expression of the system's repugnance.'

- An action for damages for false imprisonment. In some cases, the damages for such an action would be likely to be nominal if the violation by the detainer does not have much impact on the detainee. Consider cases under this heading like *Christie v Leachinsky* (1947). Damages can, however, be considerable. In *Reynolds v Commissioner of Police for the Metropolis* (1982), a jury awarded £12,000 damages to the plaintiff. She had been arrested in the early hours in connection with charges of arson for gain, that is, that insured houses which had been set alight deliberately would be the subject of 'accidental fire' insurance claims. She was taken by car to a police station, a journey which took two and a half hours. She was detained until about 8 pm when she was told there was no evidence against her. She arrived home about 11 pm. The judge, Caulfield J, ruled that the police had no reasonable grounds for suspecting the plaintiff of having committed an arrestable offence and he directed the jury in relation to damages. The jury awarded £12,000 and the defendant's appeal against this sum, as excessive, was dismissed.

In a review of recent trends in actions against the police, Sadiq Khan and Mathew Ryder ((1998) *Legal Action*, 16 September) comment on two recent cases in relation to damages. In *Goswell v Commissioner of Police for the Metropolis* (1998), CA, a jury awarded damages totalling £302,000 to Mr Goswell, comprising of £120,000 for assault, £12,000 for false imprisonment and £170,000 exemplary damages. On appeal, Simon Brown

LJ held that £100 was an appropriate award for basic damages for false imprisonment for 20 minutes. He allowed for the fact that the unlawfulness of the detention was a consequence of a breach of s 28 of PACE 1984 and expressed the opinion that the case 'does not in the fullest sense involve a wrongful deprivation of liberty'. Basic damages were assessed at £22,500, aggravated damages at £10,000 and £15,000 for exemplary damages. Overall, the figure was reduced from £302,000 to £47,500. In a second case against the police, *Commissioner of Police of the Metropolis v Gerald* (1998), CA, an initial award by a jury of £125,000 for assault, false imprisonment and malicious prosecution was reduced to £50,000 on appeal by the commissioner.

Apart from the question of civil remedies, it is important to remember:

- If the arrest is not lawful, there is the right to use reasonable force to resist it. This is a remedy, however, of doubtful advisability as the legality of the arrest will only be properly tested after the event in a law court. If a police officer was engaged in what the courts decide was a lawful arrest or conduct, then anyone who uses force against the officer might have been guilty of an offence of assaulting an officer in the execution of his duty, contrary to s 51 of the Police Act 1964.

- That, for our purposes in considering the consequences for an unlawfully arrested person faced with prosecution, s 78 of PACE 1984 states:

  78(1) In any proceedings, the court may refuse to allow evidence on which the prosecution proposes to rely to be given if it appears to the court that, having regard to all the circumstances, including the circumstances in which the evidence was obtained, the admission of the evidence would have such an adverse effect on the fairness of the proceedings that the court ought not to admit it.

13.3.2 General powers of arrest

In *Spicer v Holt* (1977), Lord Dilhorne stated:

Whether or not a person has been arrested depends not upon the legality of the arrest, but on whether he has been deprived of his liberty to go where he pleases.

So, a person detained by the police against his will is arrested. Whether this arrest is lawful will depend on whether the conditions for a lawful arrest have been satisfied.

Lawful arrests are those (1) under warrant; (2) without warrant at common law; or (3) without warrant under legislation.

13.3.3 Arrest under warrant

The police lay a written information on oath before a magistrate that a person 'has, or is suspected of having, committed an offence' (s 1 of the Magistrates' Courts Act 1980). The Criminal Justice Act (CJA) 1967 provides that warrants should not be issued unless the offence in question is indictable or is punishable with imprisonment.

13.3.4 Common law arrests

The only power to arrest at common law is where a breach of the peace has been committed and there are reasonable grounds for believing that it will be continued or renewed or where a breach of the peace is reasonably apprehended. Essentially, it requires *conduct* related to violence, real or threatened. A simple disturbance does not, in itself, constitute the offence unless it results from violence, real or threatened.

In 1981, two cases decided within months of each other offered definitions of a breach of the peace in an attempt to bring some clarification to an area of law that previously was in doubt. In *R v Howell* (1981), the defendant was arrested after being involved in a disturbance at a street party in the early hours of the morning. Watkins LJ who delivered the judgment of the court observed that there was a power of arrest for anticipated breach of the peace provided the arrestor had been witness to the earlier shouting and swearing of H, and therefore had reasonable grounds for belief, and did believe at the time, that the defendant's conduct, either alone or as part of a general disturbance, was likely to lead to the use of violence by the defendant or someone else in the officer's presence.

The court adopted the following definition of 'breach of the peace'. It occurs:

> Wherever harm is actually done or is likely to be done to a person or in his presence his property or a person is in fear of being so harmed through an assault, an affray, a riot, unlawful assembly or other disturbance.

In the second of the two cases, *R v Chief Constable of the Devon and Cornwall Constabulary ex p Central Electricity Generating Board* (1981), Lord Denning MR suggested that breach of the peace might be considerably wider than this. This case involved a group of protesters who had occupied private land in order to prevent CEGB employees from carrying out a survey to assess its suitability for a nuclear power station. The protest was intended to be peaceful and non-violent. Lord Denning MR suggested that:

> There is a breach of the peace whenever a person who is lawfully carrying out his work is unlawfully and physically prevented by another from doing it ... If anyone unlawfully and physically obstructs the worker, by lying down or chaining himself to a rig or the like, he is guilty of a breach of the peace.

He appears to have been saying (Feldman, *Civil Liberties and Human Rights in England and Wales*, 1993, pp 788–89) not that a breach of the peace is automatic in such circumstances but that, in the context of the *Central Electricity Generating Board* case, any obstruction or unlawful *resistance* by the trespasser could give the police a reasonable apprehension of a breach of the peace, in the sense of violence.

However, in cases that have followed (such as *Parkin v Norman* (1982); *Percy v DPP* (1995); and *Foulkes v Chief Constable of Merseyside Police* (1998), CA), it is the definition in *R v Howell* that has been preferred. Despite earlier doubts, argues Parpworth ('Breach of the peace: breach of human rights?' (1998) 152 JP 6, 7 November), the recent decision of the European Court of Human Rights in *Steel and Others v United Kingdom* (1998) brings clear and authoritative clarification to this area of law. This case represents 'a clear indorsement by a court largely unfamiliar with the common law concept of a breach of the peace that such a concept is in accordance with the terms of the European Convention on Human Rights'.

At common law, a constable may arrest a person for conduct which he genuinely suspects might be likely to cause a breach of the peace even on private premises where no member of the public is present: *McConnell v Chief Constable of Manchester* (1990). Although mere shouting and swearing alone will not constitute a breach of the peace, it is an offence under s 28 of the Town Police Causes Act 1847 and could lead to an arrest under s 25 of PACE 1984 (general arrest conditions). If it causes harassment, alarm or distress to a member of the public, it may constitute an offence under s 5 of the Public Order Act 1986.

13.3.5 Arrest under legislation

The right to arrest is generally governed by s 24 of PACE 1984 (as amended by s 85 of the CJPOA 1994). This provides that the police may arrest without a warrant for 'arrestable offences' and certain other offences. An arrestable offence is one for which the sentence is fixed by law (there are very few of these, life imprisonment for murder being the most common); any offence for which a person could be liable to a sentence of five years imprisonment or more; any one of the offences listed in s 24(2); any attempt to commit any of the above. The offences listed in s 24(2) involve Customs and Excise, the Official Secrets Acts, indecent assaults on women and taking a motor vehicle without authority and going equipped for stealing, and, since 1995, certain offences relating to obscenity and indecent photographs and pseudo-photographs of children.

There are differences between the powers of arrest given by PACE 1984 to police constables and ordinary citizens:

24(4)   Any person may arrest without a warrant:

    (a)   anyone who is in the act of committing an arrestable offence;

    (b)   anyone whom he has reasonable grounds for suspecting to be committing such an offence.

(5)   Where an arrestable offence has been committed, any person may arrest without a warrant:

    (a)   anyone who is guilty of the offence;

    (b)   anyone whom he has reasonable grounds for suspecting to be guilty of it.

(6)   Where a constable has reasonable grounds for suspecting that an arrestable offence has been committed, he may arrest without a warrant anyone whom he has reasonable grounds for suspecting to be guilty of the offence.

(7)   A constable may arrest without a warrant:

    (a)   anyone who is about to commit an arrestable offence;

    (b)   anyone whom he has reasonable grounds for suspecting to be about to commit an arrestable offence.

A police officer is given additional powers under s 25 which states:

25(1)   Where a constable has reasonable grounds for suspecting that an offence which is not an arrestable offence has been committed or attempted, or is being committed or attempted, he may arrest the relevant person if it appears to him that service of a summons is impracticable or inappropriate because any of the general arrest conditions is satisfied.

The general arrest conditions are specified in s 25(3). They are that the officer does not know and cannot find out the suspect's name and address (or he has reasonable grounds to think that he has been given a false name or address), or has reasonable grounds for believing that an arrest is necessary to prevent someone causing physical harm to himself or someone else; or loss of or damage to property; or an offence against public decency; or an obstruction of the highway.

13.3.6 *G v DPP* (1989)

In *G v DPP* (1989), the appellant (G) with other juveniles, including a co-accused Gill, went to a police station to complain about being ejected from a public service vehicle. On being asked for their names and addresses by the officer, G, the appellant, refused to do so; some of the others gave false particulars but Gill gave his real name and address. The officer did not accept that Gill's particulars were correct because in his experience people who committed offences did not give correct details (even though the juveniles had only gone to the police station to complain about the way they had been treated on the bus). The juveniles would not accept the officers advice about their complaint and became threatening and abusive. Gill was arrested for 'disorderly behaviour in a police station' and he struggled and resisted; the appellant joined in, punching the officer and causing him to lose hold of Gill. Both Gill and G were convicted of assaulting a police officer in the execution of his duty. The Divisional Court quashed their convictions. The offence of 'violent behaviour' or 'disorderly behaviour' under the Town Police Causes Act 1847 was not an arrestable offence. The only power the officer therefore had to arrest Gill was under s 25(3) of PACE 1984 if there were genuine doubts about Gill's name and address. But, the ground given by the officer – about people who commit offences not giving their proper name, etc – was not a proper ground because there was no evidence that the youths had committed any offences; they had gone to the police simply to complain. Therefore, in purporting to arrest Gill, the officer had not been acting in the execution of his duty and the appellant could not, therefore, have been guilty of obstructing him in the performance of such duty.

It should be noted in particular that, under s 24(6), no offence need actually have been committed. All that is required is that the police officer reasonably believes that an arrestable offence has been committed.

The differences in the powers of arrest in s 24 are based on whether an offence:

- *is being* committed: anyone may make the arrest – see s 24(4);

- *has been* committed: anyone may make the arrest – see s 24(5) or the wider powers of the police, s 24(6), who can arrest where they 'have reasonable grounds for suspecting that an arrestable offence has been committed' whether one has in fact been committed or not;

- is *about to be* committed: only a police officer may act here – see s 24(7).

PACE 1984 preserves an old common law distinction in respect of the powers of constables and private individuals when making such arrests. Where an arrest is being made *after* an offence is thought to have been committed, then PACE 1984 confers narrower rights upon the private individual than on the police officer.

13.3.7 *Walters v WH Smith & Son Ltd* (1914)

In *Walters v WH Smith & Son Ltd* (1914), the defendants had reasonably suspected that Walters had stolen books from a station bookstall. At his trial, Walters was acquitted as the jury believed his statement that he had intended to pay for the books. No crime had therefore been committed in respect of any of the books. Walters sued the defendants, *inter alia*, for false imprisonment, a tort which involves the wrongful deprivation of personal liberty in any form, as he had been arrested for a crime which had not in fact been committed. The Court of Appeal held that, to justify the arrest, a private individual had to show not only reasonable suspicion but also that the offence for which the arrested person was given over into custody had in fact been committed, even if by someone else. A police officer making an arrest in the same circumstances could legally justify the arrest by showing 'reasonable suspicion' alone without having to show that an offence was, in fact, committed.

This principle is now incorporated in s 24 of PACE 1984. It is worthy of note that the less prudent arrestor who acts against a suspect when the latter is suspected of being in the act of committing an arrestable offence (s 24(4)) can justify his or her conduct simply by showing that there were 'reasonable grounds' on which to base the suspicion. They need not show that an offence was in fact being committed. If the arrestor waits until he or she thinks the crime has been committed, then, whereas a police officer will only have to show 'reasonable grounds for suspecting that an arrestable offence has been committed' (s 24(6)), a citizen can only justify his behaviour if an offence 'has been committed' (s 24(5)).

13.3.8 *R v Self* (1992)

This analysis is supported by the decision of *R v Self* (1992). The defendant was seen by a store detective in Woolworths to pick up a bar of chocolate and leave the store without paying. The detective followed him out into the street and, with the assistance of a member of the public, she arrested the suspect under the powers of s 24(5) of PACE 1984. The suspect resisted the arrest and assaulted both his arrestors. He was subsequently charged with theft of the chocolate and with offences of assault with intent to resist lawful apprehension or detainer, contrary to s 38 of the Offences Against the Person Act 1861. At his trial, he was acquitted of theft (apparently for lack of *mens rea*) but convicted of the assaults. These convictions were quashed by the Court of Appeal on the grounds that, as the arrest had not been lawful, he was entitled to resist it. The power of arrest conferred upon a citizen (s 24(5)) in circumstances where an offence is thought to *have been committed*, only applies when an offence *has* been committed, and as the jury decided that Mr Self had not committed any offence, there was no power to arrest him.

13.3.9 *John Lewis & Co v Tims* (1952)

In *John Lewis & Co v Tims* (1952), Mrs Tims and her daughter were arrested by store detectives for shoplifting four calendars from the appellant's Oxford Street store. It was a regulation of the store that only a managing director or a general manager was authorised to institute any prosecution. After being arrested, Mrs Tims and her daughter were taken to the office of the chief store detective. They were detained there until a chief detective and a manager arrived to give instructions whether to prosecute. They were eventually handed over to police custody within an hour of arrest. In a claim by Mrs Tims for false imprisonment, she alleged that the detectives were obliged to give her into the custody of the police immediately upon arrest. The House of Lords held that the delay was reasonable in the circumstances as there were advantages in refusing to give private detectives a 'free hand' and leaving the determination of such an important question as whether to prosecute to a superior official.

13.3.10   What is the meaning of 'reasonable grounds for suspecting'?

Many of the powers of the police in relation to arrest, search and seizure are founded upon the presence of reasonable 'suspicion', 'cause' or 'belief' in a state of affairs, usually that a suspect is involved actually or potentially in a crime.

In *Castorina v Chief Constable of Surrey* (1988), detectives reasonably concluded that the burglary of a company's premises was an 'inside job'. The managing director told them that she had recently dismissed someone (the plaintiff) although she did not think it would have been her, and that the documents taken would be useful to someone with a grudge. The detectives interviewed the plaintiff, having found out that she had no criminal record, and arrested her under s 2(4) of the Criminal Law Act 1967 (which has now been replaced by s 24(6) of PACE 1984). She was detained at the police station for almost four hours, interrogated and then released without charge. On a claim for damages for wrongful arrest and detention, a jury awarded her £4,500. The trial judge held that the officers had had a *prima facie* case for suspicion but that the arrest was premature. He had defined 'reasonable cause' (which the officers would have needed to show they had when they arrested the plaintiff) as 'honest belief founded upon reasonable suspicion leading an ordinary cautious man to the conclusion that the person arrested was guilty of the offence'. He said an ordinary man would have sought more information from the suspect, including an explanation for any grudge on her part. In this, he relied on the *dicta* of Scott LJ in *Dumbell v Roberts* (1944), that the principle that every man was presumed innocent until proved guilty also applied to arrests. The Court of Appeal allowed an appeal by the chief constable. The court held that the trial judge had used too severe a test in judging the officer's conduct.

Purchas LJ said that the test of 'reasonable cause' was objective and, therefore, the trial judge was wrong to have focused attention on whether the officers had 'an honest belief'. The question was whether the officer had had reasonable grounds to suspect the woman of the offence. There was sufficient evidence that the officer had had sufficient reason to suspect her.

Woolf LJ thought there were three things to consider in cases where an arrest is alleged to be unlawful:

- did the arresting officer suspect that the person who was arrested had committed the offence? This was a matter of fact about the officer's state of mind;

- if the answer to the first question is yes, then was there reasonable proof of that suspicion? This is a simple objective matter to be determined by the judge;

- if the answers to the first two questions are both yes, then the officer did have a discretion to arrest and the question then was whether he had exercised his discretion according to *Wednesbury* principles of reasonableness.

This case hinged on the second point and, on the facts, the Chief Constable should succeed on the appeal.

Note: The *Wednesbury* principles come from *Associated Provincial Picture Houses Ltd v Wednesbury Corporation* (1948). Lord Greene MR laid down principles to determine when the decision made by a public authority could be regarded as so perverse or unreasonable that the courts would be justified in overturning that decision. The case actually concerned whether a condition imposed by a local authority on cinemas operating on Sundays was reasonable. Lord Greene MR said:

> ... a person entrusted with a discretion must, so to speak, direct himself properly in law. He must call his own attention to matters which he is bound to consider. He must exclude from his consideration matters which are irrelevant to what he has to consider. If he does not obey those rules, he may be truly said, and often is said, to be acting 'unreasonably'.

Sir Frederick Lawton, the third judge in the Court of Appeal in *Castorina*, agreed. The facts on which 'reasonable cause' was said to have been founded did not have to be such as to lead an ordinary cautious man to conclude that the person arrested *was* guilty of the offence. It was enough if they could lead an ordinary person to *suspect* that he was guilty.

This allows quite a latitude to the police. Additionally, the House of Lords has decided in *Holgate-Mohammed v Duke* (1984) that, where a police officer reasonably suspects an individual of having committed an arrestable offence, he may arrest that person with a view to questioning her at the police station. His decision can only be challenged on *Wednesbury* principles if he acted improperly by taking something irrelevant into account. The police arrested a former lodger for theft of jewellery from the house where she had lived in order to question her at the police station. The trial judge awarded her £1,000 damages for false imprisonment. The Court of Appeal set aside the award and the decision was upheld by the House of Lords. The following passage from a judgment in the Court of Appeal in *Holgate-Mohammed* was approved in the House of Lords:

> As to the proposition that there were other things which [the police officer] might have done. No doubt there were other things which he might have done first. He might have obtained a statement from her otherwise than under arrest to see how far he could get. He might have obtained a specimen of her handwriting and sent that off for forensic examination against a specimen of the writing of the person who had obtained the money by selling the stolen jewellery, which happened to exist in the case. All those things he might have done. He might have carried out finger print investigations if he had first obtained a print from the plaintiff. But, the fact that there were other things which he might have done does not, in my judgment, make that which he did do into an unreasonable exercise of the power of arrest if what he did do, namely, to arrest, was within the range of reasonable choices open to him.

It has been forcefully contended, however, that, in some circumstances, a failure to make inquiries before making an arrest could show that there were insufficient grounds for the arrest. See Clayton and Tomlinson, 'Arrest and reasonable grounds for suspicion' (1988) 85(32) Law Soc Gazette 22.

Note, however, that the powers are discretionary. See *Simpson v Chief Constable of South Yorkshire Police* (1991).

13.3.11 Detention short of arrest

For there to be an arrest, the arrestor must regard his action as an arrest. If he simply detains someone to question him without any thought of arrest, the action will be unlawful. It is often reported in criminal investigations that a person is 'helping police with their inquiries'. In *R v Lemsatef* (1977), Lawton LJ said:

> It must be clearly understood that neither customs officers nor police officers have any right to detain somebody for the purposes of getting them to help with their inquiries.

There is no police power (except under the Prevention of Terrorism (Temporary Provisions) Act 1989) to detain someone against his or her will in order to make inquiries about that person. See, also, *Franchiosy* (1979). This is confirmed by s 29 of PACE 1984 which states that, where someone attends a police station 'for the purpose of assisting with an investigation', he is entitled to leave at any time unless placed under arrest. He must be informed at once that he is under arrest 'if a decision is taken by a constable to prevent him from leaving at will'. There is, however, no legal duty on the police to inform anyone whom they invite to the station to help with their inquiries that he or she may go.

13.3.12   Suspects stopped in the street

In *Kenlin v Gardiner* (1967), a police officer took hold of the arm of a boy he wanted to question about the latter's suspicious conduct. The boy did not believe the man was a policeman, despite having been shown a warrant card, and punched the officer in order to escape. The other boy behaved similarly and their convictions for assaulting an officer in the execution of his duty were quashed by the Divisional Court. The court held that the boys were entitled to act as they did in self-defence as the officer's conduct in trying to physically apprehend them had not been legal. There is no legal power of detention short of arrest. As Lawton LJ observed in *R v Lemsatef* (1977) (see 13.3.11), the police do not have any powers to detain somebody 'for the purposes of getting them to help with their inquiries'.

It is important, however, to examine the precise circumstances of the detaining officer's conduct because there are cases to suggest that if what the officer does amounts to only a *de minimis* interference with the citizen's liberty, then forceful 'self-defence' by the citizen will not be justified. In *Donnelly v Jackman* (1970), an officer approached a suspect to ask some questions. The suspect ignored the request and walked away from the officer. The officer followed and made further requests for the suspect to stop and talk. He tapped the suspect on the shoulder and the suspect reciprocated by tapping the officer on the shoulder and saying 'Now we are even, copper'. The officer tapped the suspect on the shoulder again which was replied to with a forceful punch. Mr Donnelly's conviction was upheld and the decision in *Kenlin v Gardiner* was distinguished as, in the earlier case, the officers had actually taken hold of the boys and detained them. The court stated that 'it is not every trivial interference with a citizen's liberty that amounts to a course of conduct sufficient to take the officer out of the course of his duties'.

In *Bentley v Brudzinski* (1982), the facts were very close to those in question. A constable stopped two men who had been running barefoot down a street in the early hours. He questioned them about a stolen vehicle, as they fitted the description of suspects in an earlier incident. They waited for about 10 minutes while the officer checked their details over a radio and then they began to leave. Another constable, who had just arrived on the scene, then said 'Just a minute' and put his hand on the defendant's shoulder. The defendant then punched that officer in the face. Unlike the decision in *Donnelly v Jackman*, the Divisional Court held, here, that the officer's conduct was more than a trivial interference with the citizen's liberty and amounted to an unlawful attempt to stop and detain him. The respondent was thus not guilty of assaulting an officer in the execution of his duty.

Note, also, that a person may be arrested for being silent or misleading under s 25 of PACE 1984 if the officer has reasonable doubts about the suspect's name and address or whether the summons procedure can be used at the address given.

13.3.13 Stop and search

PACE 1984 gives the police power to search 'any person or vehicle' and to detain either for the purpose of such a search (s 1(2)). A constable may not conduct such a search 'unless he has reasonable grounds for suspecting that he will find stolen or prohibited articles' (s 1(3)). Any such item found during the search can be seized (s 1(6)). An article is 'prohibited' if it is either an offensive weapon or it is 'made or adapted for use in the course of or in connection with burglary, theft, taking a motor vehicle without authority or obtaining property by deception or is intended by the person having it with him for such use by him or by some other person' (s 1(7)). An offensive weapon is defined as meaning 'any article made or adapted for use for causing injury to persons or intended by the person having it with him for such use by him or by some other person' (s 1(9)). This definition is taken from the Prevention of Crime Act 1953. It has two categories: things that are offensive weapons *per se* (that is, in themselves), like a baton with a nail through the end or knuckle-dusters, and things that are not offensive weapons, like a spanner, but which are intended to be used as such. If the item is in the first category, then the prosecution need prove only that the defendant had it with him to put the onus onto the accused to show that he had a lawful excuse. Stop and search powers can now also be exercised under s 8A to items covered by s 139 of the CJA 1988. These items are any article which has a blade or is sharply pointed except folding pocket knives with a blade of less than three inches. It is an offence to possess such items without good reason or lawful authority, the onus of proof being on the defendant. The courts will not accept the carrying of offensive weapons for generalised self-defence unless there is some immediate, identifiable threat (Broadbent, 'Offensive weapons and the Criminal Justice Act' (1989) 86(27) Law Soc Gazette, pp 23–25).

Under s 2 of PACE 1984, a police officer who proposes to carry out a stop and search must state his name and police station, and the purpose of the search. A plain clothes officer must also produce documentary evidence that he is a police officer. The officer must also give the grounds for the search. Such street searches must be limited to outer clothing; the searched person cannot be required to remove any article of clothing other than a jacket, outer clothes or gloves. The officer is required to make a record of the search immediately, or as soon as is reasonably practicable afterwards (s 3). The record of the search should include the object of the search, the grounds of the search and its result (s 3). A failure to give grounds as required by s 2(3)(c) will render the search unlawful (*R v Fennelley* (1989)).

13.3.14 The Code of Practice for the exercise of statutory powers of stop and search

In view of the wide powers vested in the police in the exercise of stop and search, Code A has been revised to reflect the new legislation and to clarify how searches under stop and search powers are to be conducted. The revised Code came into effect on 1 March 1999 and supersedes the edition of Code A which came into effect on 15 May 1997.

The Code (1AA) restates the guidance under the previous edition and emphasises:

> It is important to ensure that the powers of stop and search are used responsibly by those who exercise them and those who authorise their use ... It is also particularly important to ensure that any person searched is treated courteously and considerately.

A person can be stopped and questioned prior to a search to discover whether the suspicion that a search is required is well founded but a person cannot be stopped in order to find grounds for a search (Code A, para 2.1). There must be a suspicion that the suspect was carrying 'articles unlawfully obtained or possessed' (para 1.5). The reasonable suspicion must be based on objective grounds (para 1.6):

> Whether reasonable grounds for suspicion exist will depend on the circumstances in each case, but there must be some objective basis for it. An officer will need to consider the nature of the article suspected of being carried in the context of other factors, such as, the time and place, and the behaviour of the person concerned or those with him.

The Code goes on to say that reasonable suspicion may exist where information has been received like a description of an article being carried or where a person is seen acting 'covertly or warily or attempting to hide something' or where a person is seen carrying something at an unusual time or in a place where a number of burglaries or thefts are known to have taken place recently.

Reasonable suspicion can never be supported on the basis of personal factors alone. For example, 'a person's colour, age hairstyle or manner of dress, or the fact that he is known to have a previous conviction for possession of an unlawful article, cannot be used alone or in combination with each other as the sole basis on which to search that person (para 1.7). The Code was amended in 1997 to provide some clarification of police powers in relation to groups and gangs who habitually carry knives or weapons or controlled drugs. The additional section (now para 1.7AA), states that, 'where there is reliable information or intelligence that members of a group or gang who habitually carry knives unlawfully or weapons or controlled drugs and wear a distinctive item of clothing or other means of identification to indicate membership of it, the members may be identified by means of that distinctive item of clothing or other means of identification'. Other means of identification might include jewellery, insignias, tattoos or other features which are known to identify members of the particular gang or group (Note 1H).

It is important to note that PACE 1984 does not apply to 'voluntary searches'. If this is given a wide interpretation, then many of the safeguards in the Act are rendered useless. Research by Dixon, Coleman and Bottomley ((1990) 17 JLS 345) has shown that the safeguards are being undermined by many police forces. If the police can get the suspect to *consent* to the search, then the search is not being made under a power but merely by agreement. Hence, if the search is not made by virtue of s 1 of PACE 1984, then Code A does not apply. The Act and, therefore, the Code would only apply if the suspect did not consent to the search so that the officer had to resort to his powers under the Act by telling the suspect that, despite the lack of consent, the officer was empowered by PACE 1984 to search the suspect. Some of the researchers' observations are controversial; they state, for instance:

> 'Consent', here, frequently consists of acquiescence based on ignorance. Many people assume that the officer who says 'What have you got in your pockets?' or 'Let's have a look in your bag' has a power to search. We asked officers how often people whom they searched knew their rights: 79% said rarely or never. Such a lack of knowledge must mean that their 'consent' has little substance. Familiar strategies are used to deal with those who do raise questions about the authority to search. As a sergeant put it: 'A lot of people are not quite certain that they have the right to say no. And then we, sort of, bamboozle them into allowing us to search.' Such 'bamboozling' is done by appealing to the willingness of the innocent to be searched, by threatening arrest, or by claiming the authority of fictional powers [see 'Consent and legal regulation of policing' (1990) 17 JLS 345].

Code A states, in relation to the ability of an officer to search a person in the street with his consent where no search power exists, that:

> In these circumstances, an officer should always make it clear that he is seeking the consent of the person concerned to the search being carried out by telling the person that he need not consent and that, without his consent, he will not be searched [para 1D(b)].

The new Code, in addition to clarifying the procedural requirements and conduct of all searches, makes important restrictions regarding searches of non-arrested suspects in police vans. It prohibits searches in police vans that involve exposure of intimate parts of the body. Any search involving the removal of more than an outer coat, jacket, gloves, headgear or footwear, or any other item concealing identity, may only be made by an officer of the same sex as the person searched and may not be made in the presence of anyone of the opposite sex unless the person being searched specifically requests it. All searches involving exposure of intimate parts of the body shall be conducted in accordance with para 11 of Annex A to Code C (para 3.5). Every reasonable effort must be made to reduce to the minimum the embarrassment that a person being searched may experience (para 3.1).

The revised Code A includes instructions and guidance where there may be religious sensitivities about asking someone to remove a face covering using s 60 (as amended by s 25 of the Crime and Disorder Act 1998). For example, in the case of a Muslim woman wearing a face covering for religious purposes, the officer should permit the item to be removed out of public view. Where practicable, the item should be removed in the presence of an officer of the same sex as the person and out of sight of anyone of the opposite sex. In all cases, the officer must reasonably believe that the person is wearing the item in question *wholly or mainly* to conceal his or her identity (para 1AA).

Where there may be religious sensitivities about asking someone to remove headgear using a power under s 13A or 13B of the Prevention of Terrorism (Temporary Provisions) Act 1989, the police officer should offer to carry out the search out of public view (for example, in a police van or police station if there is one nearby) (para 3C).

13.3.15 Search of arrested persons

The power to search after arrest somewhere other than at the police station is governed by s 32 of PACE 1984 (searches of detained persons are dealt with by s 54 and Code C, para 4). Section 32(1) allows the police to search someone arrested where there are grounds for believing that he may present a danger to himself or to others; s 32(2) allows a search for anything that might be used to effect an escape or which might be evidence relating to any offence. Additionally, s 32(2)(b) gives the police power to enter and search premises in which he was when arrested, or immediately before he was arrested, for evidence relating to the offence for which he was arrested. Unlike the power to search under s 18, this is not limited to arrestable offences, nor do the searched premises need to be occupied or controlled by him. Such searches, however, are only lawful where there are reasonable grounds for believing that the search might find something for which a search is permitted under s 18(5) and (6). Random or automatic searching is not lawful. Section 32(4) states that a person searched in public cannot be required to take off more than outer garments like coats, jackets and gloves.

13.3.16 Search on detention

Section 54 of PACE 1984 and Code C, para 4.1 require the custody officer (a particular officer with special responsibilities in police stations) to take charge of the process of searching detainees. He must make sure a record is made of all the suspect's property unless he is to be detained for only a short time and not put in a cell. The person detained can be searched to enable this to happen but the custody officer needs to believe it to be necessary; it is not an automatic right (s 54(6)). Anything the suspect has can be seized and retained although clothes and personal effects can only be kept if the custody officer *believes* that the detained person *may* use them to escape, interfere with evidence, or cause damage or injury to himself, to others or to property. The police are not permitted, however, to retain anything protected by legal professional privilege, that is, private legal communications between the suspect and his or her legal adviser. The police can also seize things they *reasonably believe* to be evidence of an offence. A search must be carried out by a constable and only one who is the same sex as the person to be searched. Strip searches can only be made where the custody officer thinks it necessary to get some item that the suspect would not be allowed to keep; the officer must make a record of the reason for the search and its result.

13.3.17   Procedure on arrest

At common law (that is, before PACE 1984), it was necessary for the arrestor to make it clear to the arrestee that he was under compulsion either (a) by physical means, such as, taking him by the arm, or (b) by telling him, orally, that he was under compulsion. There was a danger, where words alone were used, that they might not be clear enough. Consider *Alderson v Booth* (1969). Following a positive breathalyser test, the officer said to the defendant: 'I shall have to ask you to come back to the station for further tests.' D did accompany the officer to the station. Lawful arrest was a condition precedent to anyone being convicted of driving with excess alcohol in their blood. At his trial, the defendant said he had not been arrested. He was acquitted and the prosecution appeal failed. Compulsion is a necessary element of arrest and the magistrates were not convinced that it was present in this case. The Divisional Court was not prepared to contradict the factual finding of the magistrates.

Additionally, where words alone were used, it was necessary for the arrestee to accede to the detention. There was no arrest where the arrestor said 'I arrest you' and the arrestee ran off before he could be touched (see *Sandon v Jervis* (1859)).

These principles remain good law after PACE 1984; see, for example, *Nichols v Bulman* (1985).

According to s 28(3) of PACE 1984, no arrest is lawful unless the arrestee is informed of the ground for the arrest at the time of, or as soon as reasonably practicable after, the arrest. Where a person is arrested by a constable, this applies (s 28(4)) regardless of whether the ground for the arrest is obvious.

The reasons for this rule were well put by Viscount Simon in *Christie v Leachinsky* (1947):

> ... a person is *prima facie* entitled to personal freedom [and] should know why for the time being his personal freedom is being interfered with ... No one, I think, would approve of a situation in which when the person arrested asked for the reason, the policeman replied 'that has nothing to do with you: come

along with me' ... And there are practical considerations ... If the charge ... is then and there made known to him, he has the opportunity of giving an explanation of any misunderstanding or of calling attention to other persons for whom he may have been mistaken, with the result that further inquiries may save him from the consequences of false accusation ...

An arrest, however, becomes lawful once the ground is given. In *Lewis v Chief Constable of the South Wales Constabulary* (1991), the officers had told the plaintiffs of the fact of arrest but delayed telling them the grounds for 10 minutes in one case and 23 minutes in the other. The Court of Appeal said that arrest was not a legal concept but arose factually from the deprivation of a person's liberty. It was also a continuing act and therefore what had begun as an unlawful arrest could become a lawful arrest. The remedy for the plaintiffs was the damages they had been awarded for the 10 minutes and 23 minutes of illegality: £200 each.

In *DPP v Hawkins* (1988), the Divisional Court held that an exception to the rule requiring information to be given to the arrestee exists where the defendant makes it impossible (for example, by his violent conduct) for the officer to communicate the reasons for the arrest to him. In that situation, the arrest is lawful, and remains lawful until such a time as the reasons should have been given. The fact that the reasons were not given then does not invalidate the original arrest. The arrest would only become unlawful from the moment when the reasons for it should have been given to the arrested person.

In *R v Telfer* (1976), a police officer knew that the defendant was wanted for questioning about certain burglaries. The officer checked that the suspect was wanted but not for which particular burglaries. He then stopped the defendant and asked him to come back to the station; when the defendant refused, he was arrested 'on suspicion of burglary'. The arrest was held to be unlawful. The person arrested was entitled to know the particular burglary of which he was suspected.

In *Nicholas v Parsonage* (1987), N was seen riding a bicycle without holding the handlebars by two police officers. They told him twice to hold the bars and then he did so. When they drove off, N raised two fingers. They then stopped N and PC Parsonage asked him for his name, telling him it was required as he had been riding his bicycle in a dangerous manner. N refused. P then informed him of his powers under PACE 1984 and requested N's name and address. N again refused. P then arrested him for failing to give his name and address. N attempted to ride off and a struggle ensued. N was subsequently convicted of, *inter alia*, assaulting a police officer in the execution of his duty contrary to s 51(1) of the Police Act 1964. His appeal was dismissed by the Divisional Court which held that the arrest under s 25 of PACE 1984 had been lawful as a constable exercising power under s 25(3) was not required to say why he wanted the suspect's name and address. Nicholas had been adequately informed of the ground of arrest under s 28(3) of PACE 1984. N was not arrested for failing to give his name and address, he was arrested because, having committed the minor offence of 'riding in a dangerous manner', it then became necessary to arrest him because the conditions in s 25(3)(a) and (c) were satisfied, namely, that an arrest for a minor offence is possible where the officer believes that the service of a summons is impracticable because he has not been given a proper name and address.

As to the extent of the explanation that has to be given on arrest under s 28 of PACE 1984, *Christie v Leachinsky* (above) was considered in *R v Chalkley and Jeffries* (1998), CA. In this case, an arrest for an alleged credit card fraud was made for an ulterior motive, namely, to place recording equipment in the arrested defendant's house in order to record the defendants' discussions about planned robberies. The Court of Appeal held that, as there were reasonable grounds for suspecting the arrested defendant's involvement in the credit card frauds, and given that the police had informed him of this, the trial judge had been correct to rule that the arrest was lawful notwithstanding the ulterior motive.

Is it necessary for an arrestor to indicate to the arrestee the grounds on which his 'reasonable suspicion' was based? In *Geldberg v Miller* (1961), the appellant parked his car outside a restaurant in London while he had a meal. He was asked by police officers to move the car. He refused, preferring to finish his meal first. On being told that the police would remove the car, he removed the rotor arm from the distributor mechanism. He also refused to give his name and address or show his driving licence and certificate of insurance. He was arrested by one of the officers for 'obstructing him in the execution of his duty by refusing to move his car and refusing his name and address'. There was no power to arrest for obstruction of the police as no actual or apprehended breach of the peace was involved. The court held, however, that the arrest was valid for 'obstructing the thoroughfare', an offence under s 56(6) of the Metropolitan Police Act 1839, an offence the officer had not mentioned. Lord Parker CJ said:

> In my judgment, what the appellant knew and what he was told was ample to fulfil the obligation as to what should be done at the time of an arrest without warrant.

An arrest will be unlawful, however, where the reasons given point to an offence for which there is no power of arrest (or for which there is only qualified power of arrest) and it is clear that no other reasons were present to the mind of the officer: *Edwards v DPP* (1993), DC. This principle was confirmed in *Mullady v DPP* (1997), DC. A police officer arrested M for 'obstruction', an offence with the power of arrest only if the defendant's conduct amounted to a breach of the peace (for which there is a common law power of arrest) or if one of the general arrest conditions as set out in s 25 is satisfied. The police argued that the officer could have arrested M for a breach of the peace and merely gave the wrong reason. The Divisional Court held that the officer had acted unlawfully and that it would be wrong for the justices to go behind the reason given and infer that the reason for the arrest was another lawful reason.

In some circumstances, the court may infer a lawful reason for an arrest if the circumstantial evidence points clearly to a lawful reason (*Brookman v DPP* (1997), DC). However, if there is insufficient evidence to determine whether a lawful or unlawful reason was given for the arrest, then the police will fail to show that the arrest was lawful (*Clarke v DPP* (1998), DC). The issue seems to be what degree of evidence is necessary to allow the court to infer a lawful reason for arrest (see, further, Khan and Ryder (1998) *Legal Action*, 16 September).

13.3.18 Police powers under s 60 of the Criminal Justice and Public Order Act 1994

Section 60 of the CJPOA 1994 provides for a new stop and search power in anticipation of violence, and was introduced to deal with violent conduct, especially by groups of young men. The section provides that, where authorisation for its use has been granted, a constable in uniform may:

60 (4) (a) stop any pedestrian and search him or anything carried by him for offensive weapons or dangerous instruments;

(b) stop any vehicle and search it, its driver and any passenger for offensive weapons or dangerous instruments.

(5) A constable may, in the exercise of those powers, stop any person or vehicle and make any search he thinks fit whether or not he has any grounds for suspecting that the person or vehicle is carrying any weapons or articles of that kind.

(6) If, in the course of such a search under this section, a constable discovers a dangerous instrument or an article which he has reasonable grounds for suspecting to be an offensive weapon, he may seize it.

The authorisation required by s 60 must be given by a police officer of, or above, the rank of superintendent (or a chief inspector or inspector where such an officer reasonably believes that incidents involving serious violence are imminent and no superintendent is available). The authorising officer must reasonably believe that:

(a) incidents involving serious violence may take place in any locality in his area; and

(b) it is expedient to grant an authorisation to prevent their occurrence.

Such an authorisation, which must be in writing, will permit the exercise of stop and search powers within that locality for a period up to 24 hours. The authorisation could conceivably be given in fear of a single incident, even though the CJPOA 1994 requires fear of 'incidents'. This is because s 6 of the Interpretation Act 1978 states that the plural includes the singular unless a contrary intention is shown.

There are several aspects of this section which have been drafted in what appears to be a deliberately vague way. We shall therefore have to wait and see how the courts interpret certain words in the CJPOA 1994. 'Serious violence' is not defined and this will be very much within the judgment of the senior officer concerned, provided, of course, that his view is based upon reasonable belief. Richard Card and Richard Ward, in a commentary on the Act (*The Criminal Justice and Public Order Act 1994*, 1994), have noted that the dictionary includes 'force against property' as within the definition of violence, and this may well become an important matter for decision by the courts.

The word 'locality' is left undefined in the CJPOA 1994. It could be an area outside a particular club or pub, or it might extend to a large estate. The courts have the power to declare an authorisation invalid because of an over expansive geographical area; they are unlikely to substitute their own view for that of the operational officer.

13.3.19 Other aspects of s 60 of the Criminal Justice and Public Order Act 1994

'Offensive weapon' (s 60(4), (11)) means the same as for s 1(9) of PACE 1984. It is: (a) any article made or adapted for use for causing injury to persons; or (b) intended by the person having it with him for such use by him or some other person. There is no provision for reasonable excuse for the possession of such weapons.

'Dangerous instruments' (s 60(4)) will often be caught within the definition of offensive weapons but the definition extends to cover instruments which have a blade or are sharply pointed (s 60(11)).

The authorising officer must reasonably believe that it is 'expedient' to give an authorisation in order to prevent the occurrence of incidents of serious violence. Thus, the authorisation need not be the only way in which such incidents may be prevented. Various policing factors may have to be balanced including the ability of the police force to remain effective and efficient if it were to use other methods.

There is no specification about where the stop and search power may be exercised (unlike s 1 of PACE 1984) but a draft annex to Code of Practice A suggests that the power is exercisable wherever there is public access even of just a practical (rather than legal) nature. Thus, someone could not evade the powers being exercised on himself by jumping off the highway into a front garden.

There is no power to detain especially conferred on officers by s 60 in order to carry out the search but it does make failure to stop a summary offence. As it stands, there is nothing in s 60 which would permit an officer to use any force to conduct a non-consensual search. It is possible that the courts will imply such a power. When conducting the search, the officer must give the suspect his or her name, the police station to which he or she is attached, the authorisation for the search, and the reason for the search. It seems that failure to comply with these conditions will make the search unlawful (see *Fennelley* (1989), a case where the defendant was not told why he was stopped, searched and arrested in the street. Evidence from the search, some jewellery, was excluded at the trial. Evidence of drugs found on him at the police station was also excluded).

The scope of s 60 and police powers to stop and search are being incrementally extended through various Acts of Parliament. They include the following. Section 8 of the Knives Act 1997 amended s 60 to allow *initial* authorisations by an inspector or above thus obviating the need for an officer of at least the rank of superintendent; s 60(1)(b) extends the criteria under which an authorising officer may invoke this power to include reasonable belief that incidents involving serious violence may take place or that such instruments of weapons are being carried in a particular area; and s 60(3) provides that authorisations may be extended up to 24 hours instead of six although only an officer of the rank of superintendent or above may do this. A new sub-s 11A was inserted under s 60 by s 8 of the Knives Act 1997 and states that, 'for the purposes of this section, a person carries a dangerous instrument or an offensive weapon if he has it in his possession'.

'Offensive weapon' means the same as for s 1(9) of PACE 1984 (see 13.3.13). 'Dangerous instruments' means instruments which have a blade or are sharply pointed.

These amendments are intended to deal with anticipated violence in situations where gangs or persons may be 'tooled-up' and travelling through various police areas en route to an intended scene of confrontation. Thus, the power may be invoked even where the actual anticipated violence is believed may occur in another police jurisdiction, for example, by football hooligans travelling to and from matches.

Further amendments to s 60 have recently been made under the Crime and Disorder Act (CDA) 1998. This is mainly to deal with the problem of troublemakers deliberately wearing facial coverings to conceal their identities especially when the police are using CCTV cameras. Section 25 of the CDA 1998 inserts a new sub-s 4A under s 60 which confers a power on any constable in uniform to demand the removal of, or seize, face coverings where an authority has been given under s 60 if the officer reasonably believes that the face covering is being worn or is intended to be used to conceal a person's identity. Section 25 also extends s 60(8) and makes it a summary offence if a person fails to stop or to stop a vehicle or to remove an item worn by him when required by the police in the exercise of their powers under s 60. This is punishable by a term of imprisonment not exceeding one month and/or a maximum fine of £1,000. Section 60A inserted by s 26 of the CDA 1998 provides that things seized under s 60 may be retained in accordance with regulations made by the Secretary of State. (See Jason-Lloyd (1998) 162 JP 836.)

13.3.20 Accountability and s 60 of the Criminal Justice and Public Order Act 1994

There are dangers that the powers under s 60 could be misused, as no reasonable suspicion is required and the requirements for authorisation are rather nebulous.

The safeguards against misuse include the fact that the admissibility of evidence gained through the use of a dubious stop and search event may be in doubt if there are serious breaches of the revised Code A. Someone charged with obstructing a police officer in the exercise of duty may raise breaches of the Code in defence. Unlawful search or seizure may also provide a basis for an application for exclusion of evidence thus obtained under s 78 of PACE 1984.

As the police have a common law power to take whatever action is necessary in order to prevent an imminent breach of the peace (*Moss v Mclachlan* (1985)), then, even if a challenge to the use of a s 60 power is technically successful, the police conduct in question may often be thus justified.

13.3.21 Section 81 of the Criminal Justice and Public Order Act 1994

Section 81 of CJPOA 1994 creates a new power of stop and search of persons and vehicles where it is expedient to do so to prevent certain acts of terrorism. This was a response to various acts of terrorism involving concealed bombs, and car bombs in 1993. The section inserts a new section (s 13A) into the Prevention of Terrorism (Temporary Provisions) Act 1989.

Any officer of, or above, the rank of commander or assistant chief constable may authorise a stop and search where 'it appears to him to be expedient to do so' in order to prevent acts of terrorism connected with Northern Ireland or international terrorism. There is no requirement for reasonable suspicion.

If authorisation is granted, the powers of stop and search are exercisable at any place within the area of the senior officer's force, or within a locality.

If authorisation is given, pursuant to s 13A, it confers on any police officer in uniform the power:

(a) to stop any vehicle;

(b) to search any vehicle, its driver or any passenger for articles of any kind which could be used for a purpose connected with the commission, preparation or instigation of acts of terrorism connected with the affairs of Northern Ireland or acts of international terrorism;

(c) to stop any pedestrian and search anything carried by him [but not him] for articles of a kind which could be so used.

This is thus a very wide power, and is subject to few restraints. The search could be for virtually anything, and it need not be based upon a reasonable suspicion. This power was given in the face of progressively more devastating acts of terrorism and an apparent inability of the State to deal with the threat. Any vehicle may be stopped under the section, whether or not the officer has grounds for suspecting that it contains items to be used in terrorism. It is thus unlike the power conferred under s 1 of PACE 1984 which does, to be valid, require a reasonable suspicion that the vehicle contains a proscribed item.

The powers of stop and search can only be exercised for a period specified in the authorisation, and this can be as long as 28 days (s 13A(1)). A person failing to stop for such a check, or who wilfully obstructs an officer in the exercise of these powers, is guilty of an offence (s 13A(6)).

13.3.22 The use of force to effect an arrest

The use of force by a member of the public when arresting someone is governed by the Criminal Law Act 1967. This states:

3   Use of force in making an arrest, etc

     (1)   A person may use such force as is reasonable in the circumstances in the prevention of crime, or in effecting or assisting in the lawful arrest of offenders or suspected offenders or of persons unlawfully at large.

Reasonable force will generally mean the minimum necessary to effect an arrest.

The use of force by police officers is governed by PACE 1984. This states:

117   Power of constable to use reasonable force

     Where any provision of this Act:

    (a)   confers a power on a constable; and

    (b)   does not provide that the power may only be exercised with the consent of some person, other than a police officer,

the officer may use reasonable force, if necessary, in the exercise of the power.

13.3.23 Duties after arrest

A person arrested by a constable, or handed over to one, must be taken to a police station as soon as is 'practicable', unless his presence elsewhere is 'necessary in order to carry out such investigations as is reasonable to carry out immediately' (s 30(1), (10)). Where a citizen makes an arrest, he 'must, as soon as he reasonably can, hand the man over to a constable or take him to the police station or take him before a magistrate', *per* Lord Denning in *Dallison v Caffery* (1965). There is no requirement, however, that this be carried out immediately: *John Lewis & Co v Tims* (1952) (see 13.3.9).

13.4 Entry, search and seizure

A number of statutes give police officers the powers to stop and search people and vehicles where no arrest has been made. See, for example, s 23(2) of the Misuse of Drugs Act 1971. Here, we shall concentrate on the powers given under ss 1 and 2 of PACE 1984 which relate to stolen goods, offensive weapons and articles for use in Theft Act offences. These provisions are supplemented by two new ones in s 81(1) of the CJPOA 1994 and s 60 of the 1994 Act (as amended by s 8 of the Knives Act 1997 and ss 25–27 of the Crime and Disorder Act 1998). All are, in turn, supplemented by provisions in the new Code of Practice A issued under PACE 1984, effective from 1 March 1999.

Note: PACE 1984 came into force on 1 January 1986. The Act was accompanied by four Codes of Practice: Code A on Stop and Search; Code B on Search of Premises; Code C on Detention, Questioning and Treatment of Persons in Custody; and Code D on Identification. A fifth, Code E on Tape-recording of Interviews, was added later. The Codes were produced after consultation with a wide range of interested groups and people and were debated and approved by both Houses of Parliament before being promulgated. Revised versions of these Codes came into force in 1991. The Codes are not technically law and s 67(10) of PACE 1984 states that a breach of them can lead to neither an action for damages nor a criminal prosecution against police officers. A breach of the Codes is, though, automatically a disciplinary offence (s 67(8)).

The chief significance of a breach of the Codes is that a judge may exclude otherwise relevant evidence if it has been obtained in such a way and an appeal court may quash a conviction where a trial judge has not excluded such evidence (s 67(7)).

13.4.1 Entry of premises under the common law

Premises can be searched by consent. Here, the constable must get written consent from the occupier of the premises on a special 'Notice of Powers and Rights' form before the search takes place. The officer must make inquiries to ensure that the person concerned is in a position to give that consent. Before seeking the consent, the officer in charge must state the purpose of the proposed search and inform the person concerned that he is not obliged to consent, that anything seized may be produced in evidence, and, if such is the case, that he is not suspected of any offence. These propositions come from the governing Code of Practice B for the Searching of Premises by Police Officers and the Seizure of Property found by Police Officers on Persons or Premises. An officer cannot enter and search, or continue to search premises by consent, if the consent is given under duress or is withdrawn before the search is completed (Code B, para 4.3). Consent need not be sought if this would cause disproportionate inconvenience to the occupiers of premises, for example, where the police wish to briefly check a number of gardens on a suspected escape route.

Police officers may enter premises with permission or under implied permission but then must leave when required unless remaining under some particular power. In *Davis v Lisle* (1936), Sidney Davis was a member of a firm that occupied a railway arch as a garage. Two police officers entered the garage to ask about a lorry that had been obstructing the highway. The lorry had since been moved into the garage. D, using obscene language and abuse, told the officers to leave. L was in the act of producing his warrant card when D struck him in the chest and stomach, damaging his tunic. The convictions of D for assaulting and obstructing a police officer in the execution of his duty were quashed by the Divisional Court. Lord Hewart CJ held that the officers were not acting in the course of their duty once they had remained on premises having been told in forthright terms by the occupiers to leave: 'From that moment on, while the officers remained where they were, it seems to me that they were trespassers.'

13.4.2 Entry of premises to prevent an offence being committed

There is a common law right for police officers to enter a building to deal with or prevent a breach of the peace. In *Thomas v Sawkins* (1935), the Divisional Court held that police officers were entitled to enter and remain on premises, despite being asked by the occupiers to leave, in circumstances where the officers believed that certain offences (seditious speeches, incitements to violence) would be committed if they were not present. Lord Hewart CJ said:

> I am not at all prepared to accept the doctrine that it is only where an offence has been, or is being, committed, that the police are entitled to enter and remain on premises. On the contrary, it seems to me that a police officer has, *ex virtute officii*, full right so to act when he has reasonable grounds for believing that an offence is imminent or is likely to be committed.

Section 17(5) and (6) of PACE 1984 abolishes all common law powers of entry except to deal with or prevent a breach of the peace.

Note, however, that a licensee must be given a reasonable time to leave premises before his continued presence on the land constitutes a trespass, unless he makes it clear that he will not leave voluntarily (*Robson v Hallet* (1967)).

The power has even extended to private homes. In *McGowan v Chief Constable of Kingston upon Hull* (1968), the Divisional Court held that the police were entitled to enter and remain in a private dwelling where they feared there would be a breach of the peace arising out of a private quarrel.

13.4.3 Entry and search of premises to make an arrest

This is governed by s 17 of PACE 1984 which says that a constable may enter and search premises for the purposes of arresting someone for an arrestable offence or under warrant, recapturing a person unlawfully at large whom he is pursuing; saving life or limb or preventing serious damage to property. This power can only be exercised if the constable has 'reasonable grounds' for believing that the person whom he is seeking is on the premises.

A police officer exercising his power to enter premises by the use of reasonable force to arrest a person for an arrestable offence (pursuant to ss 17 and 117 of PACE 1984) should, unless circumstances make it impossible, impracticable or undesirable, announce to the occupier the reason why he is exercising that power. In *O'Loughlin v Chief Constable of Essex* (1998), a police officer who had a lawful right to enter premises but failed to announce why he was entering when it was practicable and possible to do so was held to be acting unlawfully. In such circumstances, the occupier is entitled to use reasonable force to prevent the entry.

The relevant powers here are those discussed below under ss 18 and 32 of PACE 1984. In practice, the police act routinely under s 18 and rarely under s 32.

Section 18 of PACE 1984 gives the police power to enter and search:

> ... any premises occupied or controlled by a person who is under arrest for an arrestable offence, if he has reasonable grounds for suspecting that there is on the premises evidence other than items subject to legal privilege that relates (a) to the offence; or (b) to some other arrestable offence which is connected with or similar to that offence.

If, therefore, the police suspect that evidence of other unconnected offences is to be found at the address, then they must get a search warrant or seek the householder's consent to the search. The search of someone's address after they have been arrested normally requires the written permission from an officer of the rank of inspector or above (s 18(4)). Section 18(5) makes an exception when the arrested person is taken straight to the address rather than the police station. A search must not go beyond what is normally required to find the particular item(s) being sought; no general search is permitted (s 18(3)). The time constraint when the police use s 32 (the search has to be made at the time of the arrest) (see below) does not appear to apply to a s 18 search (see *R v Badham* (1987) (see below)). It is perhaps because of this and the comparative narrowness of s 32 in respect of searches of premises (see below) that s 18 is much more frequently used by police. Research by Ken Lidstone, for example, found that, in a survey of two city forces, s 18 accounted for 75% of searches compared with 2% for s 32: 'Entry, search and seizure' (1989) 40 NILQ 333, p 355, n 67.

Section 32(2)(b) gives the police power to enter and search premises in which the suspect was when arrested, or immediately before he was arrested, for *evidence relating to the offence for which he was arrested*. Unlike the power to search under s 18, this is not limited to arrestable offences, nor do the searched premises need to be occupied or controlled by him. Such searches, however, are only lawful where there are reasonable grounds for believing that the search might find something for which a search is permitted under s 32(5) and (6). Random or automatic searching is not lawful.

Section 32(7) states that, where a person is arrested in premises consisting of two or more separate dwellings, only the premises in which he was arrested or was in immediately beforehand and any common parts (like stairways and common corridors) can be searched.

The powers here are narrower than those given under s 18 to enter and search the premises of an arrested person. Under s 18, the police may enter and search for evidence of the offence for which the person was arrested or *any* offence which is 'connected with or similar to that offence'. Section 32 only covers searches for evidence relating to the actual offence for which the suspect was arrested. The police can, however, under s 32, search the person himself for evidence of any offence. It was held in *R v Badham* (1987) that s 32 only applies to a search made at the time of the arrest. It does not permit the police to return to the premises several hours after the arrest.

In *R v Churchill* (1989), the defendant was arrested on suspicion of burglary and placed in a police car. The police asked him to hand over the keys to the car he had been in so that they could lock it, thus keeping it safe for a later scientific examination. C was convicted of assault when, after refusing to hand over the keys, a struggle ensued and he hit an officer. On appeal, he contended that the police had no power to take the keys since they had no evidence of any crime. The court quashed the conviction, saying that the case could have been argued on the basis of the officer's duty to preserve the property but the prosecution had not used that argument. The police could, alternatively, have searched the car under s 32 as that section confers a power to search any 'premises' the defendant was in immediately before arrest and this includes a vehicle (s 23(a)).

13.4.4 Seizure of articles from searches

Seizure of articles from searches is controlled by s 19 and Code B, para 6. These state that where a constable is searching premises under statutory powers or by consent, he may seize anything on the premises (except things exempted from seizure) if he reasonably believes that it is evidence in relation to an offence which he is investigating or *any other offence* and that it is necessary to seize it in order to prevent it from being concealed, lost, altered or destroyed (s 19(3)(b)) or that it has been obtained in consequence of the commission of an offence. Items exempted from seizure are those reasonably believed to be subject to legal professional privilege (s 19(6)). The scope of the seizure rights is therefore quite wide and Zander has argued that the insistence since *Entick v Carrington* (1765) that general warrants are unlawful must now be qualified by the knowledge that, once the police have entered premises lawfully, it is difficult to hold them to a search restricted to the specific purpose of the search. The only serious restraint is the requirement in s 16(8) that a search under warrant must be carried out in a manner consistent with the items being looked for and in Code B, para 5.9 which states that 'premises may be searched only to the extent necessary to achieve the object of the search having regard to the size and nature of whatever is sought'.

13.4.5 Search warrants and safeguards

Section 8 of PACE 1984 provides for the issue of warrants by magistrates to enter and search premises for evidence of serious arrestable offences. This gives justices of the peace the power, on written application from a constable, to issue a search warrant where he or she is satisfied that there are reasonable grounds for believing that a 'serious arrestable offence' has been committed. A 'serious arrestable offence' (as distinct from an 'arrestable offence' defined by s 24) is defined by s 116 and Sched 5 of PACE 1984). The definition divides offences into two categories. One category comprises offences so serious that they are always 'serious arrestable offences'; they are listed in Sched 5 and include treason, murder, manslaughter, rape, kidnapping, incest and possession of firearms with intent to injure and attempts or conspiracies are treated as if they were completed. Any other arrestable offence is serious only if its commission has led, or is likely to lead, to any of the consequences specified in s 116(6), namely: (a) serious harm to the security of the State or public order; (b) serious interference with the administration of justice or with the investigation of offences; (c) the death of anyone; (d) serious injury to anyone; (e) substantial financial gain to anyone; (f) serious financial loss to anyone in the sense that, having regard to all the circumstances, it is serious, for the person suffering loss (the seriousness of the loss is therefore to be measured by the financial position of the potential loser).

The magistrate must also be satisfied that:

- there is material on the premises likely to be of substantial value to the investigation (s 8(1)(b));

- that it is likely to be relevant evidence (s 8(1)(c));

- that it does not include 'excluded material' (for example, human tissue taken for medical diagnosis and held in confidence); journalistic material held in confidence (see s 11), or 'special procedure material' (for example, confidential business/professional material, see s 14); or material subject to legal privilege (s 10); and

- that any of the conditions in s 8(3) applies. These are, essentially, that it is not practicable to gain entry to the premises in question without a search warrant or that the reasons for the search would be frustrated if the constable did not gain immediate entry upon arrival.

Section 15 incorporates proposals made by the Philips Royal Commission on Criminal Procedure (Cmnd 8092, 1981, HMSO) to protect against warrants being too easily obtained. Clearly, it is highly contentious at what point there is the correct, desirable balance between the State's concern to prevent and detect crime and the interests of the public at large in having the civil liberty of freedom from speculative entry into their homes by the police. If police officers could legally enter any home at any time without permission from anyone, then the detection of crime would arguably be easier than now but there would be a significant price to pay in the consequential public resentment against the police and the probably profound loss of faith in the legal and political system.

An application for a search warrant must now state the grounds for making the application, the statutory authority under which the claim is made and the object of the proposed search in as much detail as possible. Research by Lidstone (see 13.4.3) has shown a tendency for informations (the applications) and warrants to use very generalised terms like 'electrical goods' which he argues is not desirable. The applications are normally made *ex parte* (that is, from one side, the police, without the presence of the person whose premises are to be searched) and the information must be made in writing by an officer who must answer any questions (from the magistrate) under oath. Lidstone's research also suggests that, both before and after PACE 1984, there is evidence of reliance on formulaic informations, for example, 'As a result of information received from a previously reliable source ...', and a lack of any probative questioning by magistrates on such informations. The warrant may only be used to gain entry on one occasion; if the police find nothing relevant and wish to return, they must apply for another warrant. On each search, the occupier must be given a copy of the warrant authorising entry.

One part of s 15 has caused some difficulty for the courts. It relates to the word 'it' in s 15(1) which states that 'an entry on or search of premises under warrant is unlawful unless it complies with this section and s 16 below'.

What must comply – the warrant or the whole entry and search? In *R v Longman* (1988), Lord Lane CJ said, *obiter*:

With some hesitation, we are inclined to think it probably refers to the warrant, but the real probability is that the intention of the framers of the Act was to provide that the warrant should comply with the terms of s 25 and the entry and search should comply with s 16. But, unhappily, that is not what it says. So, we leave that problem unresolved.

Section 16 and Code B govern the actual search of premises and seek to ensure that warrants are executed in a proper and reasonable manner. It states that any constable, not just the one named in the warrant, may execute that warrant (s 16(1)) and it must be carried out within one month of its date of issue (s 16(3)). The search must be at a 'reasonable hour' unless 'it appears to the constable executing it that the purpose of a search may be frustrated on an entry at a reasonable hour' (s 16(4)). Notice that, here, the test is subjective, it is what 'appears to the constable' which is critical, not whether such a belief is reasonable or not. If the occupier is present, he must be given a copy of the warrant (s 16(5)); if he is not there, then a copy must be left in a prominent place (s 16(7)). A constable executing a warrant must identify himself and, if he is not in uniform, he must produce documentary evidence that he is a constable, even if he is not asked (s 16(5)).

In *R v Longman* (above), a plain clothes police officer posed as a delivery girl from Interflora to gain entry to premises without alerting the occupants. She had come to the premises with other officers with a warrant to search for drugs. It was not the first time that the premises had been searched and the officers knew that entry would be very difficult. When the door was opened, the officers burst in. They did not, therefore, properly identify themselves as officers according to s 16(5), nor had they shown the householder their search warrant as required by Code B (para 5.5). The Court of Appeal held that force or subterfuge could lawfully be used for the purposes of gaining entry with a search warrant. The warrant was 'produced' for the purposes of s 16(5) when the occupier was given the opportunity of inspecting it. In this case, the occupier had not attempted to look at the warrant, he had shouted a warning to others on the premises and then tried to stab the officers with a knife. The court held that it would be prepared to overlook failures to comply with the precise provisions of ss 15 and 16 regarding production of the warrant whenever circumstances made it wholly inappropriate, such as a search for drugs or in a terrorism case. In any event, it was not necessary that the formalities set out in s 16(a)–(c), on identification of the searcher as a police officer and production of the warrant, be carried out before *entry* but only before the search begins. The revised Code B states that the officer shall first attempt to get access by asking the occupier unless (Code B, para 5.4(iii)):

> ... there are reasonable grounds for believing that to alert the occupier or any other person entitled to grant access by attempting to communicate with him would frustrate the object of the search or endanger the officers concerned or other persons.

A search under a warrant 'may only be a search to the extent required for the purpose of which the warrant was issued' (s 16(8)). In *Chief Constable of the Warwickshire Constabulary ex p Fitzpatrick* (1998), the Divisional Court disapproved of the police practice of using a warrant phrased in broad terms to seize every possible item that could broadly fall within those terms. They should ensure both that the material seized falls within the terms of the warrant and, because such a warrant is granted to search for material of evidential value, that there are reasonable grounds for believing so and to be likely to be of substantial value in the investigation. In this case, in relation to one of the warrants, the police officers went on a 'fishing expedition' and seized a large selection of documents, not on their face related to the offence under investigation. In doing so, they exceeded the ambit of the warrant. Thus, the entire search was a trespass and unlawful under ss 16(8) and 15(1) of PACE (see, further, Khan and Ryder, 'Police and the law' (1998) *Legal Action*, 16 September, p 21).

A search warrant does not entitle the executing officers to search persons on the premises. Such persons may only be searched if arrested or if there is a specific power in the warrant, for example, as in warrants issued under s 23 of the Misuse of Drugs Act 1971 (Home Office Circular on PACE 1984, 1985, issue 88/1855).

13.5 Interrogation, confession and admissibility of evidence

Before moving into the specific provisions of PACE 1984 and the Codes of Practice, it is important to be aware of the general issues at stake in this area of law. Are the rights of suspects being interrogated by the police sufficiently protected by law? Is there scope for abuse of power by the police? Are the police burdened by too many legal requirements when trying to induce a suspect to confess to a crime? What effects are likely to flow from the undermining of the right to silence (see ss 34–37 of the CJPOA 1994, 13.5.17)?

13.5.1 Time limits on detention without charge

Under s 42 of PACE 1984, a suspect can be held without being charged for 24 hours before any further authorisation needs to be given. At this point, the situation must be reviewed and further detention must be authorised by an officer of at least the rank of superintendent. The period is measured from arrival at the police station. If he is arrested by another force, the time runs from his arrival at the station of the area where he is wanted. If further detention is authorised, this can continue for up to the 36 hour point. After 36 hours from the beginning of the detention, there must be a full hearing in a magistrates' court with the suspect and, if he wishes, legal representation (s 43). The magistrates can grant a warrant of further detention for up to a further 60 hours – making a total of 96 hours (ss 43 and 44). However, the police could not be granted the 60 hour period as a whole because the maximum extension that a magistrates' court can grant at one time is 36 hours (ss 43(12), 44). The magistrates can only grant such extensions if the offence being investigated is a serious arrestable offence (s 116), is being investigated diligently and expeditiously and provided that the further detention is necessary to secure or preserve evidence relating to an offence for which the suspect is under arrest or to obtain such evidence by questioning him (s 43(4)).

Section 38 states that, *after being charged*, the arrested person must be released, with or without bail, unless:

- it is necessary to hold him so that his name and address can be obtained; or

- the custody officer reasonably thinks that it is necessary to hold him for his own protection or to prevent him from causing physical injury to anyone or from causing loss of or damage to property; or

- the custody officer reasonably thinks that he needs to be held because he would otherwise fail to answer bail or to prevent him from interfering with witnesses or otherwise obstructing the course of justice; or

- if he is a juvenile and ought to be held 'in his own interests'.

If the suspect is charged and not released, he will have to be brought before a magistrates' court 'as soon as practicable', and not later than the first sitting after being charged (s 46(2)).

13.5.2 Searches of detained persons

Searches of people detained at police stations are governed by s 54 and Code C. PACE 1984 has been amended by the CJPOA 1994 (ss 54–59). The rules governing the taking of intimate and non-intimate body samples have been changed. The new Act also allows 'speculative searches' in which fingerprints, samples, or information in respect thereof, can be checked against other similar data held by the police. The changes follow recommendations of the Runciman Commission Report which recommends the establishment of a national DNA database.

A person may only be searched if the custody officer considers this necessary in order to make a complete list of his property (s 54(6)). There is no automatic right to search all suspects as a matter of routine. The police can, however, search anyone to ascertain whether he has with him anything which he could use to cause physical injury, damage property, interfere with evidence or assist him to escape (s 55, as amended). Section 65 deals with intimate searches. The CJPOA 1994 repeals the old s 118 of PACE 1984 (which defined 'body orifice', including anus, vagina, mouth, nostrils and ears) and s 54(1) inserts a new definition into s 65 of PACE 1984. Section 65 of PACE 1984 now defines an intimate search as:

... a search which consists of the physical examination of a person's body orifices other than the mouth.

A physical examination of the mouth is therefore allowed in the circumstances where a non-intimate search of the person may occur, subject to the ordinary safeguards (Code of Practice A, para 3; Code C, para 4). A search of the mouth for drugs is not the taking of a sample as defined by s 65 of PACE 1984, so the restrictions which apply to the taking of samples do not apply here. A search of an arrested person's mouth may thus be carried out by a police officer at the station, subject to the safeguards in Code C. The officer carrying out the search must be of the same sex as the arrested person (s 54(9)). Nonetheless, an officer of either sex may search the arrested person's mouth at the time of the arrest if he has reasonable grounds to believe that the arrested person is concealing therein evidence related to the offence (s 32(2)(b)).

These searches must be authorised by an officer of the rank of superintendent or above on the basis of reasonable belief that the arrested person in police detention has concealed on him anything which could be used to cause physical injury to himself or to others and that he might so use it. Intimate searches for weapons can, if a doctor or registered nurse is not available, be carried out by a police officer of the same sex as the suspect. If the search is for drugs, it can only be carried out by a doctor or registered nurse and it cannot be carried out at a police station (s 55(4)). Intimate searches for drugs are limited to those for hard drugs, defined as Class A drugs in Sched 2 to the Misuse of Drugs Act 1971.

13.5.3 The right to have someone informed when arrested

The effect of s 56 and Code C is that, when a suspect is under arrest and is being held in custody in a police station, he is entitled, if he so requests, to have 'one friend or relative or other person who is known to him or who is likely to take an interest in his welfare' to be told as soon as practicable that he is under arrest and his whereabouts (s 56(1), Code C, para 5.1). If such a person cannot be contacted, the Code allows for two alternates to be nominated, following which any further alternates can be called at the discretion of the custody officer. Delay is only permissible in the case of a 'serious arrestable offence' (see s 116) and only if authorised by an officer of at least the rank of superintendent. The grounds for delaying appear in Annex B. They are, essentially, that there are reasonable grounds for believing that telling the named person of the arrest will lead to interference with, or harm to, evidence of witnesses or the alerting of others involved in such an offence; or will hinder the recovery of property obtained as a result of the offence. No one, however, may be prevented from notifying someone outside the police station for longer than 36 hours after 'the relevant time' (s 41(2)), usually the time that he or she arrived at the station. Unless the reasons for a lawful delay (see Annex B) exist, Code C states that the detainee should be allowed to speak on the telephone 'for a reasonable time to one person' (para 5.6) and that this privilege is in addition to the right to phone someone under para 5.1 to inform him or her of the arrest or under para 6.1 to obtain legal advice. Children and young persons are afforded additional rights by s 57; the section says that the police should contact a person 'responsible for his welfare' to inform the person about the arrest.

13.5.4 The right to consult a solicitor

Section 58(1) of PACE 1984 states that: 'A person who is in police detention shall be entitled, if he so requests, to consult a solicitor privately at any time.' The rules relating to persons held under suspicion of terrorist offences are different and will not be covered here. Where the detained person is a juvenile or is mentally handicapped or disordered, then 'the appropriate adult' (see Code C, para 3) may exercise the right to ask for legal advice.

Where the suspect has been allowed to consult a solicitor, and the solicitor is available, the solicitor must be allowed to sit in on any interview the police give the suspect (Code C, para 6.8). Normally, the request must be allowed as soon as practicable (s 58(4)).

13.5.5 Notifying the suspect of the right to free legal advice

There is clearly the danger that a person's right to legal advice can be effectively curtailed if they are not aware of it. Code C therefore goes to some lengths to ensure the suspect is aware of the right. The custody officer is required (para 3.5), when he authorises a person's detention in the police station, to make sure that the suspect signs the custody record signifying whether he wishes to have legal advice at that point. The revised Code adds the following:

> The custody officer is responsible for ensuring that the person signs the custody record in the correct place to give effect to his decision.

The Code stipulates that police stations must advertise the right to free legal advice in posters 'prominently displayed in the charging area of every police station' (para 6.3). The Code also gives precise rules concerning at what point and in what form a person should be notified of the right to get free legal advice. For example, a person who comes to the station *under arrest* must be told immediately both orally and in writing (paras 3.1, 3.2). A person who comes to the police station voluntarily (that is, someone who is helping the police with their inquiries) is to be given a leaflet if he or she requests information but, strangely, there is no police duty to notify if that person does not ask.

A person who asks for legal advice should be given the opportunity to consult a specific solicitor (for example, his or her own) or the duty solicitor (see 13.5.6). Alternatively, he or she should be given an opportunity to chose one from a list of those available to give advice. Ultimately, the custody officer has discretion to allow further requests if the others are unsuccessful. The revised Code C carries the provision that 'No attempt should be made to dissuade the suspect from obtaining legal advice' (para 6.4) and that reminders of the right to consult legal advice should be given at specified times, for example, on commencement and re-commencement of interviews.

The revised Code also states (para 6.15) that, if a solicitor arrives at the station to see a particular person, that person must (unless Annex B, above, applies) be informed of the solicitor's arrival and asked whether he would like to see him. This applies even if the person concerned has already declined legal advice. This would be important, for example, where the lawyer had been sent by a friend or family member.

Until the revision of Code C (effective from 1991), there was evidence that the way most police stations informed suspects of their right to legal advice meant that suspects did not realise the advice would be free and that this might well have acted as a deterrent against accepting such advice. Now, suspects must be told that 'independent legal advice is available free of charge' (para 3.1(ii)). The solicitor is paid under the legal aid scheme. At his or her discretion, a solicitor may give the advice over the telephone. The Law Society advises the solicitor when he or she is considering whether the telephone is a suitable medium to have regard to certain issues, for example, would the suspect be likely to be inhibited from speaking freely by fear of being overheard and whether the suspect has already been charged and no further police interview is proposed.

There has been notable judicial concern that the suspect's rights to be informed about the availability of legal advice is enforced. In *R v Absolam* (1989), the Court of Appeal quashed a conviction for the supply of cannabis and substituted one for simple possession because the defendant had not been informed of his right to see a solicitor before he had been questioned. The trial judge had held that the series of preliminary questions and answers did not amount to an 'interview', but the Court of Appeal disagreed; the questions were an 'interview' within the meaning of the Code because they were directed at a suspect with the aim of obtaining admissions on which a prosecution could be based. The reference in s 58(4) to seeing a solicitor 'as soon as practicable' was not relevant to the suspect's right to be informed of his right to legal advice from the outset of his detention.

Note: The Runciman Royal Commission Report on Criminal Justice 1993 recommends (para 38):

The definition of an interview in Code C Note for Guidance 11A should be clarified to remove the apparent confusion as to what constitutes an interview for the purposes of the Code.

In *R v Beycan* (1990), the defendant was arrested in connection with a charge of supplying heroin. He was taken to a police station where he was asked 'Are you happy to be interviewed in the normal way we conduct these interviews without a solicitor, friend or representative?'. The Court of Appeal held that this did not amount to informing him of his right to legal advice and it quashed his conviction which was based on his subsequent confession.

13.5.6 Duty solicitors

The duty solicitor schemes at police stations and magistrates' courts are run locally but organised under the auspices of the Legal Aid Board which was set up by the Legal Aid Act (LAdA) 1988. At police stations, the duty solicitor is contacted through a special national telephone network provided by a company, Air Call plc. When a suspect asks for a duty solicitor (at any time of the day or night), a call is made to Air Call who then contact either the rota duty solicitor or telephone duty solicitors on the panel until, in the latter case, one is found who is able and willing to attend. In rota schemes, there is always (in theory) someone on duty; in panel schemes, the panellists are called one after the other on a list beginning with the name after the last solicitor to have come out. One area of concern (which has arisen from several recent cases involving poor advice to suspects in police stations) is the extent to which advice is regularly given to suspects by people who are not fully qualified solicitors but solicitor's clerks or trainee solicitors whom the duty solicitor is allowed to send as his or her 'representative'. This is permitted by the current Duty Solicitor Arrangements, Pt VI. The local committee which can approve such representation must be satisfied that the representative is in full or part time employment and has had 'experience of providing advice at a police station on behalf of the duty solicitor' on the basis of experience depending on the person's status, for example, a solicitor's clerk should have at least three years' experience of criminal defence work.

The Runciman Royal Commission on Criminal Justice noted the problem of inadequate professional advice in some cases, stating in its report (para 69) that:

> The Legal Aid Board should commission occasional empirical research as a means of checking on the quality of performance of legal advisers at police stations.

The inadequacy of much legal advice given to suspects was highlighted when Stephen Millar, one of the Cardiff Three, had his conviction quashed on appeal ((1992) *The Times*, 11 December). In his judgment, the Lord Chief Justice criticised the defence solicitor for not intervening to halt the questioning. In his research for the Royal Commission on Criminal Justice, Professor John Baldwin analysed 600 police interviews (see 13.5.25) and found that, in 66.5% of them, the advisor said nothing at all ((1993) 33 Brit J Crim 3).

13.5.7 Delaying access to legal advice

The police have no right to delay a suspect's access to legal advice except in the case of a serious arrestable offence (Annex B to Code C). Code C (para 6.2) states that 'the custody officer must act without delay to secure the provision of such advice to the person concerned'. If the suspect is being held in connection with a serious arrestable offence (s 116), he or she can be delayed access to legal advice but the delay must be authorised by an officer of the rank of superintendent and only where he has reasonable grounds for believing that the exercise of the right:

- will lead to interference with, or harm to, evidence connected with a serious arrestable offence or interference with or physical harm to other persons; or

- will lead to the alerting of other persons suspected of having committed such an offence but not yet arrested for it; or

- will hinder the recovery of any property obtained as a result of such an offence.

If a delay is authorised, the suspect must be told the reason for it and the reason must be recorded in the custody record. The maximum period of delay is 36 hours (Annex B, para 4).

13.5.8 *R v Samuel* (1988)

In *R v Samuel* (1988), the defendant was arrested on suspicion of robbery and taken to a police station. During that day and the following day, he was interviewed several times about the robbery and other offences. He asked for a solicitor during the second interview. His request was refused by a superintendent on the grounds that two of the offences under investigation were serious arrestable offences and there would be a danger of accomplices being inadvertently alerted. At the fourth interview, Samuel confessed to two burglaries. A little later, a solicitor instructed by the family was notified of the charges but he was refused access to the suspect. Shortly after that, Samuel confessed to the robbery charge. The trial judge admitted evidence of the last interview, Samuel was convicted of robbery and sentenced to 10 years' imprisonment. The Court of Appeal quashed the conviction. Two important issues were clarified:

- The police were not entitled to deny a suspect access to a solicitor after he has been charged, even if other charges are still being investigated. This follows from the plain and natural meaning of Annex B (para 1) which states the right to legal advice can be delayed where:

  > ... the person is in police detention in connection with a serious arrestable offence, has not yet been charged with an offence and an officer of the rank of superintendent or above has reasonable grounds for believing ...

- The right of access to a solicitor was a 'fundamental right of a citizen' and if the police sought to justify refusing that right, they must do so by reference to specific aspects of the case; it was insufficient to suppose that giving the suspect access to a solicitor *might* lead to the alerting of accomplices. The officer had to believe that it probably would and that the solicitor would either commit the criminal offence of alerting other suspects or would be hoodwinked into doing so inadvertently or unwillingly. Either belief could only be genuinely held by an officer on rare occasions. The belief that a solicitor would commit the criminal offence had to be based on knowledge of that particular solicitor. It could not be advanced successfully in relation to solicitors generally. As to the other point, Hodgson J observed (p 626):

  > But, what is said is that the detained person will be able to bring about one or more of the happenings (a) to (c) [in Annex B] by causing the solicitor to pass on unwittingly some form of coded message. Whether there is any evidence that this has or may have happened in the past we have no way of knowing. Solicitors are intelligent, professional people; persons detained by the police are frequently not very clever and the expectation that one of (a) to (c) will be brought about in this way seems to contemplate a degree of intelligence and sophistication in persons detained, and perhaps a naïveté and lack of common sense in solicitors which we doubt often occurs.

This is not perhaps a view of offenders and solicitors which would be immediately agreed with by all those whose work brings them into contact with either group. Hodgson J said there were two tests. First, did the officer have the belief? This was a subjective question. Secondly, was that belief reasonable? This is an objective matter. In this case, the solicitor was well known and highly respected. He was unlikely to be hoodwinked by a 24 year old. The suspect's mother had been informed of her son's arrest hours before the solicitor was refused access to the son. If anyone was to have been alerted, it could easily have been done already. The solicitor would have advised his client to have said nothing at that stage. Samuel would not have made his admission having been denied his 'fundamental freedom' to consult with a solicitor. The evidence of the admission should, therefore, have been excluded under s 78.

13.5.9   *R v Alladice* (1988)

In *R v Alladice* (1988), the Court of Appeal allowed the evidence of an admission made during an interview where the suspect had had access to a solicitor delayed. The decision has been regarded as based on the narrow facts of the case. Alladice had made admissions of involvement in an armed robbery and was convicted but argued on appeal that the evidence should have been excluded because there had been no valid reason for delaying his access to a solicitor. He argued that the real reason for the delay was that the police believed that a solicitor would have advised him to remain silent and that, as the Code and *Samuel* showed, this was not a valid reason. The court found that, on the facts, there had been a breach of s 58 but that this did not mean that the evidence obtained in breach of the section should automatically be excluded. There was no suggestion of oppression nor was there evidence of bad faith on the part of the police. The court took the view that it would be wrong to regard the admission has having resulted from the refusal to grant access to a solicitor. Alladice had stated that he understood the caution, that he was aware of his rights and that he was able to cope with the interview. He argued that the alleged admissions had not been made although that argument was rejected by the judge. In any event, it seemed to the Court of Appeal that the presence of a solicitor would not have made any difference to the suspect's knowledge of his rights. There was no causal link between the absence of Alladice's solicitor and the admission.

13.5.10   *R v Davidson* (1988)

In *R v Davidson* (1988), the trial judge stated that *Samuel* meant that, in order for the police to validly delay access to advice, they had to be 'nearly certain' that the solicitor granted access to a suspect would warn an accomplice or get rid of the proceeds of the crime. Davidson had been arrested for handling a stolen ring, the fruit of an armed robbery. The power to delay access to a solicitor could not be exercised until D had nominated a particular lawyer. As this had not been done when the superintendent came to consider the matter, he could not have had a reasonable fear that the lawyer would pass a message to another person involved in the crime. The suspect had already spoken to his wife twice, so the reality of the police fears that he would use the lawyer as a messenger had to be doubted. The court excluded the crucial confessions and the prosecution's case collapsed.

13.5.11   *R v Parris* (1989)

In *R v Parris* (1989), the court quashed a conviction for armed robbery because of breaches of s 58. The police arrested Parris for armed robbery and took him to the station where he was kept incommunicado (under s 56). He asked to see a solicitor at his first interview and was refused. He refused to answer any questions. During his second interview, he agreed to answer some questions provided nothing was written down. He then allegedly made oral admissions although, at trial, he denied these took place. The Crown did not deny that there had been a breach of s 58(8) as there had been no valid reason for refusing access to a solicitor; the incommunicado order under s 56 was wrongly assumed to also exclude access to a solicitor under s 58. Had there been a solicitor present at the second interview, he would probably have advised Parris not to speak; at the least, he would have discouraged the alleged fabrication of admissions. The appeal succeeded.

Code C, Annex B, B4 states:

> ... the officer may authorise delaying access to a solicitor only if he has reasonable grounds to believe that the specific solicitor will, inadvertently or otherwise, pass on a message from the detained person which will lead to any of the three results in para 1 coming about. In these circumstances, the officer should offer the detained person access to a solicitor on the Duty Solicitor Scheme.

13.5.12   Interviewing before solicitor arrives

The police have a right to start questioning suspects before a solicitor has arrived at the police station if the situation is an emergency or the solicitor is not likely to arrive for a considerable period. The power is governed by Code C (para 6.6). This says that a person who asks for legal advice may not be interviewed or continue to be interviewed until he has received it unless Annex B applies (advice delayed by superintendent, etc) or an officer of at least the rank of superintendent has reasonable grounds for believing that a delay in questioning will involve an immediate risk of harm to persons or serious loss of, or damage to, property; or where a solicitor has been contacted and is on his way but waiting 'would cause unreasonable delay to the process of investigation'. It will not normally be appropriate to begin an interview if the solicitor has said he is on his way (para 6A). Another exception is where the solicitor cannot be contacted or declines to attend and the suspect, having been told about the Duty Solicitor Scheme, declines to ask for the duty solicitor or the duty solicitor is unavailable.

13.5.13   Answering police questions and the right to silence

The police are free to ask anyone any questions. The only restriction is that all questioning is supposed to cease once a suspect has been charged. Code C, para 16.5 states that questions relating to an offence 'may not be put to a person after he has been charged with that offence, or informed that he might be prosecuted for it, unless they are necessary for the purpose of preventing or minimising harm or loss to some other person ...' or where it is in the interests of justice that the person should be given an opportunity to comment on new information which has come to light since he was charged.

Note: The Runciman Royal Commission Report 1993 recommends (para 22):

> The questioning of suspects after charge should be permissible provided that the usual caution is repeated, and that the person charged has the usual opportunity of consulting a solicitor free of charge before any interview and of having that solicitor present at the interview.

Note that this would affect the current Code C, para 16.5 (see 13.5.5) and 11.4.

For a good examination of the circumstances in which police questioning of a suspect may amount to a breach of Code C, see Cape, 'Police interrogation and interruption' (1994) 144 NLJ 120.

There is no obligation on a citizen to answer police questions. A person cannot be charged, for example, with obstructing the police in the execution of their duty simply by failing to answer questions, nor can the judge or prosecutor suggest to the jury that such silence is evidence of guilt.

In *Rice v Connolly* (1966), the appellant was seen by officers in the early hours of the morning behaving suspiciously in an area where house breaking had taken place on the same evening. On being questioned, he refused to say where he was going or where he had come from. He refused to give his full name and address, though he did give a name and the name of a road which were not untrue. He refused to accompany the officer to a police box for identification purposes, saying: 'If you want me, you'll have to arrest me.' He was arrested and charged with wilfully obstructing a police officer contrary to s 51(3) of the Police Act 1964.

His appeal against conviction succeeded. Lord Parker CJ noted that the police officer was acting within his duty in inquiring about the appellant and that what the appellant did was obstructive. The critical question though was whether the appellant's conduct was 'wilful' within the meaning of s 51. Lord Parker CJ, in the Divisional Court, took that word to mean 'intentional [and] without lawful excuse'. He continued:

> It seems to me quite clear that, though every citizen has a moral duty or, if you like, a social duty to assist the police, there is no legal duty to that effect, and, indeed, the whole basis of the common law is the right of the individual to refuse to answer questions put to him by persons in authority, and to refuse to accompany those in authority to any particular place; short, of course, of arrest.

The court was unanimous although one judge, James J, cautioned that he would not go as far as to say that silence coupled with conduct could not amount to obstruction. It would depend on the particular facts of any given case.

In *Ricketts v Cox* (1982), two police officers who were looking for youths responsible for a serious assault, approached the defendant and another man in the early hours of the morning. The justices found that the officers acted in a proper manner in putting questions to the men. The defendant was abusive, unco-operative and possibly hostile to the officers, using obscene language calculated to provoke and antagonise the officers and tried to walk away. The justices were satisfied that this conduct amounted to an obstruction for the purposes of a charge under s 51(3) of the Police Act 1964. The defendant's appeal was dismissed by the Divisional Court which found that the case raised the point reserved by James J in *Rice v Connolly* – the combination of silence and hostility without lawful excuse. As Zander has observed, the state of the law here is now unclear.

13.5.14 Duties to answer

There are certain circumstances where the citizen is under a duty to answer police questions. Where a constable has reasonable grounds for believing that a vehicle has been involved in an accident and he seeks the particulars of the driver, he may arrest that person if the information is not given. With the Home Secretary's consent, and on the authority of a chief constable, coercive questioning (that is, where a suspect's silence can be used in evidence against him or her) can be used in matters under s 11 (as amended) of the Official Secrets Act 1911. There are also wide powers under the Companies Act 1985 to require officers and agents of companies to assist inspectors appointed to investigate the company. Refusal to answer questions can be sanctioned as a contempt of court (s 431) and as a criminal offence (s 447). A person can also be required to answer questions put to him or her by a liquidator of a company (*Bishopsgate Management Ltd v Maxwell Mirror Group Newspapers* (1993)).

Under s 2 of the CJA 1987, the Director of the Serious Fraud Office (SFO) (dealing with frauds worth over £5 million) can require anyone whom he has reason to think has relevant information to attend to answer questions and to provide information including documents and books. Such statements, however, cannot be used in evidence against the persons who make them unless they go into the witness box and give inconsistent testimony. Even this power, though, does not require the breach of legal professional privilege. Failure to comply with s 2 requests is a criminal offence and can result in an application for a magistrates' search warrant. These powers have been widely used. The SFO Annual Report for 1991–92 reveals that a total of 793 notices had been given during that year. In *R v Director of the Serious Fraud Office ex p Smith* (1993), the House of Lords held that the SFO could compel a person to answer questions relating to an offence with which he had already been charged. It followed that in relation to such questions the suspect did not have to be further cautioned.

Other powers to compel answers on pain of penalties for refusal exist under the Prevention of Terrorism (Temporary Provisions) Act 1989, and refusal to answer certain allegations from the prosecutor can be treated as acceptances of them under the Drug Trafficking Offences Act 1986.

The closest English law comes to creating a duty to give one's name and address is the power given to the police under s 25(3) of PACE 1984. This is the power to arrest for a non-arrestable offence where the officer cannot find out the suspect's particulars for the purpose of serving a summons on him.

There is no duty to offer information about crime to the police. However, s 11 of the Prevention of Terrorism (Temporary Provisions) Act 1989 makes it an offence for a person who has information which he knows or believes might be of material assistance in preventing an act of terrorism or to secure the arrest of anyone involved in terrorism 'to fail, without reasonable cause, to disclose that information as soon as reasonably practicable'. Additionally, s 5 of the Criminal Law Act 1967 creates the offence of accepting money or other consideration for not disclosing information that would lead to the prosecution of an arrestable offence. The House of Lords has also held that it is the duty of every citizen in whose presence a breach of the peace is being committed to attempt to stop it if necessary by detaining the person responsible. It is, however, except in the case of a citizen who is a police officer, 'a duty of imperfect obligation' (*Albert v Lavin* (1982), *per* Lord Diplock).

13.5.15 What can be said in court about silence in the face of police questioning

There is an established common law rule that neither the prosecution nor the judge should make adverse comment on the defendant's silence in the face of questions. The dividing line, however, between proper and improper judicial comment was a matter of great debate. There are many reasons why a suspect might remain silent when questioned (for example, fear, confusion, reluctance to incriminate another person) and the 'right of silence' enjoyed the status of a long established general principle in English law. Thus, in *R v Davis* (1959), a judge was ruled on appeal to have misdirected the jury when he told them that '... a man is not obliged to say anything but you are entitled to use your common sense ... can you imagine an innocent man who had behaved like that not saying anything to the police ... He said nothing'.

An exception, though, was that some degree of adverse suggestion was permitted where two people were speaking on equal terms and one refused to comment on the accusation made against him by the other. In *R v Parkes* (1976), the Privy Council ruled that a judge could invite the jury to consider the possibility of drawing adverse inferences from silence from a tenant who had been accused by a landlady of murdering her daughter. The landlady and tenant for the purposes of this encounter were regarded as having a parity of status unlike a person faced with questions from the police. It was held in *R v Chandler* (1976) that the suspect was on equal terms with the police officer where the former was in the company of his solicitor. Chandler had refused to answer some of the questions he had been asked by the police officer before the caution and the judge told the jury that they should decide whether the defendant's silence was attributable to his wish to exercise his common law right or because he might incriminate himself. The Court of Appeal quashed Chandler's conviction since the judge had gone too far in suggesting that silence before a caution could be evidence of guilt.

It was proper for the judge to make some comment on a defendant's reticence before being cautioned provided that the jury were directed that the issue had to be dealt with in two stages: (i) was the defendant's silence an acceptance of the officer's allegations? And, if so, (ii) could guilt of the offence charged be reasonably inferred from what the defendant had implicitly accepted? The court said that it did not accept that a police officer always had an advantage over a suspect. Everything depended on the circumstances. In an inquiry into local government corruption, for example, a young officer might be at a distinct disadvantage when questioning a local dignitary. That type of interview was very different from a 'tearful housewife' being accused of shoplifting.

The Court of Appeal decision in *Chandler* asserted that silence might only be taken as acquiescence to police allegations before a caution. The court excluded silence after the caution as being something from which anything adverse can be inferred because a suspect could not be criticised for remaining silent having been specifically told of that right. This, however, seemed like an irrational dichotomy. If the suspect did, in fact, have a legal right to silence whether or not he or she has been cautioned, it is very odd that full enjoyment of the right could only be effective from the moment of it being announced by the police. Additionally, any questioning of a suspect at a police station prior to a caution being given is probably in contravention of Code C, para 10 which requires a caution to be given at the beginning of each session of questioning. Violation of the Code affords grounds for an appeal under s 78 of PACE 1984. Cautions need not be given according to para 10.1:

> ... if questions are put for other purposes, for example, to establish his identity or his ownership of any vehicle or the need to search him in the exercise of powers of stop and search.

13.5.16   Right to silence in courts

Since 1988, the right to silence was effectively abolished in Northern Ireland. It is possible for a court to draw adverse inferences from a defendant's silence when he was arrested. Adverse inferences can also be drawn from the defendant's failure to provide an explanation for any 'object, substance or mark' on his clothing, footwear or in his possession which the arresting officer found suspicious and questioned the suspect about (Criminal Evidence (Northern Ireland) Order 1988).

Similar recommendations were made by the Home Office Working Group on the Right to Silence in 1989. This question was also considered by the Runciman Royal Commission on Criminal Justice. It had to decide whether to adopt a practice like the Northern Ireland system and the one recommended by the Home Office or whether to retain the right to silence as the Philips Royal Commission on Criminal Procedure had recommended in 1981. In evidence to the Runciman Royal Commission, the proposal to retain the right to silence was supported by The Law Society, the Bar Council and the Magistrates' Association. It was opposed by the police, the Crown Prosecution Service, HM Council of Circuit Judges and senior judges.

Professor Michael Zander's research on this issue has suggested that the role of the right to silence in the real workings of the criminal justice system is in fact not as significant as is often argued. In one of his studies, 'Investigation of crime' [1979] Crim LR 211, he looked at 150 cases randomly drawn from those heard at the Old Bailey. According to police statements, of the 286 defendants (in many cases, there was more than one defendant), only 12 were said to have relied on their right of silence when confronted by police accusations. Of these, nine were convicted. Zander has also made the following points:

- most defendants plead guilty, so the right to silence is unimportant in such a context;

- common law rules permit the judge to *mention* the defendant's silence and in some limited circumstances, to comment on it;

- in any event, the jury may draw adverse conclusions about the defendant's silence to police questions, that is, whether the judge is permitted to comment on this or not.

In a study commissioned by the Lord Chancellor's Department, only 2% of 527 suspects exercised their right to silence, see Sanders *et al*, *Advice and Assistance at Police Stations and the 24 Hour Duty Solicitor Scheme*, 1989.

In a study by Stephen Motson, Geoffrey Stephenson and Tom Williamson ((1992) 32 Br J Crim 23, pp 23–40), the researchers looked at 1,067 CID interviews carried out in nine London police stations in 1989. By carefully matching cases where the right to silence had been exercised with like cases where it had not and then comparing the outcomes, the researchers found that decisions as to whether to prosecute were based on factors like the strength of the evidence against the suspect and the seriousness of the offence; they were not correlated with whether the suspect responded to questions or not. There was no evidence that silence at the police station gave the suspect any advantage at court. They commented:

The high proportion of silence cases who ultimately plead guilty might be taken to suggest that the use of silence is a ploy – adopted for the most part by previously convicted offenders, [it] is abandoned in favour of a guilty plea when prosecution, probable conviction and (especially) sentencing are nigh.

The Runciman Royal Commission eventually decided to recommend retaining the right to silence. Its Report (1993) states (para 82):

The majority of us believe that adverse inferences should not be drawn from silence at the police station and recommend retaining the present caution and trial direction.

The Commission did, however, recommend (para 84) the retention of the current law regarding silence in investigations of serious and complex fraud under which adverse consequences can follow from silence (see 13.5.14). The Report notes that a large proportion of those who use the right to silence later plead guilty. The majority of the commission felt that the possibility of an increase in convicting the guilty by abolishing the right would be outweighed by the considerable extra pressure on innocent suspects in police stations. The commission did, however, meet the police and CPS concern about 'ambush defences' where a defence is entered late in a trial thus leaving the prosecution no time to check and rebut the defence. The Commission recommends that if the defence introduces a late change or departs from the strategy it has disclosed in advance to the prosecution, then it should face adverse comment (para 136). Zander, however, issued a note of dissent that the principle must remain that the burden of proof always lies with the prosecution. He states:

The fundamental issue at stake is that the burden of proof throughout lies with the prosecution. Defence disclosure is designed to be helpful to the prosecution and, more generally, to the system. But, it is not the job of the defendant to be helpful either to the prosecution or the system.

13.5.17   Effective abolition of the right to silence

The government ignored the recommendations of the Runciman Commission and, in ss 34–37 of the CJPOA 1994, effectively abolished the right to silence. 'Abolished' may be too strong a word because everyone still has the right to remain silent in the same circumstances as they did before the CJPOA 1994; what has changed is the entitlement of a judge or prosecuting counsel to make adverse comment on such a silence.

Notwithstanding the new Act, therefore, any person may refuse to answer questions put to him or her out of court. There are only a few exceptions to this (as with s 2 of the CJA 1987 which concerns the investigation of serious fraud, and requires certain questions to be answered under pain of punishment for refusal) and they existed before the new Act. The CJPOA 1994 does not alter the position of the accused person as a witness – he or she remains a competent but not compellable witness in their own defence (s 35), although, now, the prosecution as well as the judge may comment upon such a failure to give evidence (s 168).

Except in so far as the new law makes changes, the old law still applies.

In enacting ss 34–37 of the CJPOA 1994, the government was adopting a particular policy. The general purpose of the Act was to assist in the fight against crime. The government took the view that the balance in the criminal justice system had become tilted too far in favour of the criminal and against the public in general and victims in particular. The alleged advantage of the change in law is that it helps convict criminals who, under the old law, used to be acquitted because they took advantage of the right to keep quiet when questioned without the court or prosecution being able to comment adversely upon that silence. Introducing the legislation, the Home Secretary said that change in law was desirable because 'it is professional criminals, hardened criminals and terrorists who disproportionately take advantage of and abuse the present system'.

Section 34 states that where anyone is questioned under caution by a police officer, or charged with an offence, then a failure to mention a fact at that time which he later relies on in his defence will allow a court to draw such inferences as appear proper about that failure. Inferences may only be drawn if, in the circumstances, a suspect could reasonably have been expected to mention the fact when he was questioned. The inferences which can be drawn can be used in determining whether the accused is guilty as charged. The section, however, permits adverse inferences to be drawn from silence in situations that do not amount to 'interviews' as defined by Code C of PACE 1984, and thus which are not subject to the safeguards of access to legal advice and of contemporaneous recording which exist where a suspect is interviewed at the police station. The newly amended draft caution to be administered by police officers will read as follows (with appropriate variants for ss 36 and 37):

> You do not have to say anything. But, it may harm your defence if you do not mention when questioned something which you later rely on in court.

As Card and Ward have warned in a commentary on the CJPOA 1994 (*The Criminal Justice and Public Order Act 1994*, 1994), a temptation may arise for police officers to give this caution at the earliest possible stage in any situation in which they are talking to someone in connection with a crime, given that the caution may be understood (incorrectly) by some suspects as creating an obligation to speak.

The CJPOA 1994 does not affect earlier law on alibi defences. Under s 11 of the Criminal Justice Act 1967, the defence at trial on indictment cannot adduce evidence in support of an alibi defence (that is, where the accused claims to have been away from the crime at the time of its occurrence) unless notice of the details of that defence have been served on the prosecution within seven days of the transfer for trial. Nevertheless, this rule does not prevent an adverse inference being drawn by a court from a failure to have disclosed that alibi at an earlier stage (when, for instance, the accused was arrested).

Section 35 allows a court or jury to infer what appears proper from the refusal of an accused person, aged 14 or over, to testify in his own defence, or from a refusal without good cause to answer any question at trial. In the *Practice Direction (Procedure in Crown Court Trials – Right to Silence)* (1995), the Lord Chief Justice indicated that, where the accused is legally represented, the following should be said by the judge to the accused's lawyer at the end of the prosecution case if the accused is not to give evidence:

> Have you advised your client that the stage has now been reached at which he may give evidence and, if he chooses not to do so or, having been sworn, without good cause refuses to answer any question, the jury may draw such inferences as appear proper from his failure to do so?

If the lawyer replies to the judge that the accused has been so advised, then the case will proceed. If the accused is not represented, and still chooses not to give evidence or answer a question, the judge must give him a similar warning, ending: '... the jury may draw such inferences as appear proper. That means they may hold it against you.'

Section 36 permits inferences to be drawn from the failure or refusal of a person under arrest to account for any object, substances or mark in his possession, on his person, in or on his clothing or footwear, or in any place at which he is at the time of arrest. Section 37 permits inferences to be drawn from the failure of an arrested person to account for his presence at a particular place where he is found.

Thus, as the late Lord Taylor, the then Lord Chief Justice, observed, the legal changes do not, strictly speaking, abolish the right to silence:

> If a defendant maintains his silence from first till last, and does not rely on any particular fact by way of defence, but simply puts the prosecution to proof, then [ss 34–37] would not bite at all.

This is, of course, correct, but it ignores the change in the general structure of proofs. Article 6 of the European Convention on Human Rights aims to protect the rights of a suspect to a fair trial. It states that:

> Everyone charged with a criminal offence shall be presumed innocent until proved guilty in accordance with law.

The European Commission on Human Rights has already ruled as admissible a complaint that provisions in the law of Northern Ireland equivalent to those in ss 34–37 infringe Art 6. The English provisions will also be taken to Strasbourg.

Since the abolition of the court of Star Chamber in 1641, no English court has had the power to use torture or force to exact confessions from suspects. The so called 'right to silence' really meant that a suspect could remain silent when questioned by police or in court without prosecution counsel or the judge being allowed to make adverse comment to the jury about such a silence. Traditionally, silence could not be used in court as evidence of guilt.

In support of the old rule, it could be said, that:

- people are innocent until proven guilty of a crime by the State;

- people should never be under force to condemn themselves;

- there are several reasons other than genuine guilt why someone may wish to remain silent in the face of serious accusations – he or she might be terrified, confused, retarded, wish to protect someone else or fear that the truth would get them in some other type of trouble. The 11th Report of the Criminal Law Revision Committee (1972) gives several examples. The accused might be so shocked at an accusation that he forgets a vital fact which would acquit him of blame; his excuse might be embarrassing like being in the company of a prostitute; or he may fear reprisals from another party.

The 'right' is widely protected in other aspects of society: the police, for example, when facing internal disciplinary charges, are not bound to answer questions or allegations put to them.

The change has been widely and strongly opposed by lawyers, judges and legal campaign groups. Liberty, for example, has said that drawing adverse inferences from silence would undermine the presumption of innocence. Silence is an important safeguard against oppressive questioning by the police, particularly for the weak and vulnerable.

John Alderson, former chief constable of Devon and Cornwall (1973–82) and a respected writer on constitutional aspects of policing, has written of the impending danger when police are able to 'exert legal and psychological pressure on individuals held in the loneliness of their cells'. He states ((1995) *The Independent*, 1 February) that:

> History tells us that, when an individual has to stand up against the entire apparatus of the modern State, he or she is very vulnerable. That is why, in criminal cases, the burden of proof has always rested on the State rather than on the accused. The Founding Fathers of America amended their constitution to that effect in 1791.

Another opponent of the change is the leading criminal law barrister and editor of the authoritative practitioners' text *Archbold on Criminal Evidence, Pleading and Practice*. He has described the CJPOA as 'an ill thought-out package of expedients'. (Richardson, 'Preface', in *Archbold*, 1995, p vii.)

Undermining the right to silence may constitute a significant constitutional change in the relationship between the individual and the State. It may be doubted whether the majority of suspects should be put under greater intimidation by the system because of the conduct of a few 'hardened criminals' – the justification for the legislation given by the Home Secretary when he introduced the legislation.

Two points should be noted, however, to put the debate in its proper historical context. First, it should not be forgotten that there were, prior to the Act, several instances in English law where there was already a legal obligation for a suspect to answer questions. These included the obligation to speak under s 2 of the CJA 1987 (see above); the obligations under ss 431–41 of the Companies Act 1985 (concerning investigations in respect of company officers and agents whose companies are being investigated by the Department of Trade and Industry); the obligations under ss 22 and 131 of the Insolvency Act 1986 (concerning inquiries upon the winding up of companies); s 18 of the Prevention of Terrorism (Temporary Provisions) Act 1989 (concerning information relating to terrorism); and the law under s 11 (as amended) of the Official Secrets Act 1911.

Secondly, in the few cases where the right to silence was used under the pre-CJPOA law, we need to ask how far juries were genuinely sympathetic to the judge's directions that they could not assume guilt from silence. Juries convicted in half of such cases so there is evidence that jurors were suspicious and sceptical about people who exercise the right, just as they may be today where someone exercises the right (that is, remains silent from arrest until the jury retires without relying on any fact he could have mentioned earlier).

13.5.18   Directions to the jury on silent defendants

Following the enactment of the CJPOA 1994, there has been a steady stream of case law as to correct judicial practice when directing the jury about the drawing of adverse inferences under s 34 and s 35.

In *R v Cowan* (1995), the Court of Appeal considered what should be said in the summing up if the defendant decides not to testify. The jury must be directed that (as provided by s 38(3) of the CJPOA 1994) an inference from failure to give evidence could not on its own prove guilty. The jury had to be satisfied (on the basis of the evidence called by the prosecution) that the prosecution had established a case to answer before inferences could be drawn from the accused's silence. The jury could only draw an adverse inference from the accused's silence if it concluded that the silence could only be sensibly attributed to the accused having no answer to the charge or none that could stand up to cross-examination.

The difficult issue as to correct judicial practice when the accused remains silent during interview on the advice of his solicitor was considered in *R v Condron* (1997) and *R v Argent* (1997). These cases make it clear that such advice was only one factor to be taken into consideration along with all the other circumstances, in any jury determination as to whether adverse inferences could be drawn from a 'no comment' interview. In *Condron*, the Court of

Appeal considered the guidelines set out in *Cowan* (above) and concluded that they were equally applicable to failure to answer questions (s 34) and failure to testify (s 35). The Court of Appeal approved the Judicial Studies Board specimen direction which states:

> If he failed to mention when he was questioned [a fact which he relied on in his defence], decide whether, in the circumstances which existed at the time, it was a fact he could have reasonably be expected then to mention.

> The law is that you may draw such inferences as appear proper from his failure to mention it at that time. You do not have to hold it against him. It is for you to decide whether it is proper to do so.

> Failure to mention such a fact at that time cannot, on its own, prove guilt, but, depending on the circumstances, you may hold that failure against him in deciding whether he is guilty, that is, take into account as some additional support for the prosecution's case. It is for you to decide if it is fair to do so.

Stuart-Smith LJ, giving the judgment of the court, went on to say that, in addition to the Judicial Studies Board direction, it was desirable to direct the jury that if, despite any evidence relied upon to explain the failure (to answer questions), or, in the absence of such evidence, they concluded that the failure could only sensibly be attributed to the accused having fabricated the evidence subsequently, they might draw an adverse inference.

More detailed guidance was given in *Argent* where Lord Bingham set out the conditions that had to be met before s 34 could operate. They include:

(a) the failure to answer had to occur before the defendant was charged;

(b) the alleged failure must occur during questioning under caution;

(c) the questioning must be directed at trying to discover whether and by whom the offence has been committed;

(d) the failure must be a failure to mention any fact relied on in the person's defence;

(e) the fact the defendant failed to mention had to be one which this particular defendant could reasonably be expected to have mentioned when being questioned, taking account of all the circumstances existing at that time (for example, the time of day, the defendant's age, experience, mental capacity, state of health, sobriety, personality and access to legal advice).

The Court of Appeal in *Argent* took a similar view to that of the Judicial Studies Board (JSB) as regards the relevance of legal advice to remain silent. This, of course, puts the solicitor who attends the interview under some difficulty, especially as The Law Society's guidelines suggest that to remain silent is inappropriate when the police have made less than full disclosure of the evidence available. However, Lord Bingham in *Argent* (1997) added that the jury is not concerned with the correctness of the solicitor's advice, nor with whether it complies with The Law Society's guidelines, but with the reasonableness of the defendant's conduct in all circumstances.

The court approved the trial judge's direction to the jury:

> You should consider whether or not he is able to decide for himself what he should do or having asked for a solicitor to advise him he would not challenge that advice [p 34].

Finally, in *R v Daniel (Anthony Junior)* (1998), CA, it was held that the *dicta* of Stuart-Smith LJ in *Condron* (1997) need not be confined to a subsequent fabrication. In addition to the JSB specimen direction, it is desirable for the judge in an appropriate case to include a passage to the effect that, if the jury conclude that the accused's reticence could only sensibly be attributed to his unwillingness to be subjected to further questioning, or that he had not thought about all the facts, or that he did not have an innocent explanation to give, they might draw an adverse inference. This was upheld soon after by the Court of Appeal in *R v Beckles and Montague* (1999) when the defendant gave a 'no comment' interview on legal advice. It was held that the proper inference under s 34 was not limited to recent fabrication.

Where, however, a judge concludes that the requirements of s 34 have not been satisfied and, therefore, that it is not open to him to leave to the jury the possibility of drawing adverse inferences, he must direct the jury in terms that that they should not in any way hold against the accused the fact that he did not answer questions in interview (*R v McGarry* (1998)).

For a critical examination of the current law on the nature of inferences that may be drawn under s 34, see Turner, 'Inferences under s 34 of the Criminal Justice and Public Order Act 1994: Part One and Part Two' (1999) 163(17) JP 323, pp 323–25 and pp 924–26.

13.5.19 Tape-recording of interrogations

The police were initially very hostile to the recommendation of the Philips Royal Commission on Criminal Procedure that there should be tape-recording of interviews with suspects. After a while, however, the police became more enthusiastic when it became apparent that the tape-recording of the interrogations increased the proportion of guilty pleas and reduced the challenges to prosecution evidence. Tape-recording of interviews is conducted in accordance with Code of Practice E. The tapes are time-coded so that they cannot be interfered with. It is now compulsory for all police stations to record all interviews with suspects interrogated in connection with indictable offences.

13.5.20 Confessions and the admissibility of evidence

It was long established by the common law that a confession would not be admitted in evidence if it was 'involuntary' in the sense that it was obtained by threat or promise held out by a person in authority. This would include '... even the most gentle, if I may put it that way, threats or slight inducements', *per* Lord Parker CJ in *R v Smith* (1959). In that case, a sergeant major had put the whole company on parade and told them no one would be allowed to move until one of them gave details about which of them had been involved in a fight resulting in a stabbing. A confession resulting from this incident was ruled to have been something that should not have been admitted (although the conviction was not quashed as there was other evidence against the defendant).

In *R v Zavekas* (1970), a conviction was quashed where it had resulted from an improper promise. Z was told that the police were arranging an identification parade and that he would be free to go if he was not picked out. He asked whether he could be allowed to go at once if he made a statement. The officer agreed and then Z made a statement admitting guilt. The admission was given in evidence and Z was convicted. His conviction was quashed even though the inducement had not been proffered by the police. Similarly, the Court of Appeal regarded it a 'fatal inducement' for a police officer to have agreed to a request by the defendant, in *R v Northam* (1967), for a second offence to be taken into account at a forthcoming trial rather than tried as a separate matter.

Apart from threats and promises, 'oppression' leading to a confession would render such a statement inadmissible. The Judges' Rules were a set of guidelines made by Divisional Court judges for excluding unreliable evidence but they left it as discretionary whether violation of the rules should result in the exclusion of any resultant evidence.

There had been a significant change in the approach of the courts by the 1980s. The new approach was to ask, even where there had been promises or threats, as a matter of fact and causation, had there been an involuntary confession? In *R v Rennie* (1985), Lord Lane CJ stated that, even where a confession was made 'with a hope that an admission may lead to an earlier release or a lighter sentence' and the hopes were prompted by something said or done by a person in authority, the confession would not automatically be regarded as involuntary. The same applied where, as in the present case, a confession was prompted by a fear that otherwise the police would interview and perhaps charge the defendant's sister and mother. The judge should apply his 'common sense' and assume that voluntary meant 'of one's own free will'.

This approach was much criticised as it was often impossible for even trained psychologists to realise which pressures on a suspect being questioned were the ones that prompted him or her to confess.

The law is now contained in s 76 of PACE 1984 which renders inadmissible any confession obtained as a result of oppression (s 76(2)(a)) or which was obtained in consequence of something 'likely in the circumstances to render unreliable any confession which might be made by the accused in consequence thereof' (s 76(2)(b)). 'Oppression' is defined by s 76(8) to include 'torture, inhuman or degrading treatment, and the use or threat of violence'.

13.5.21 Oppression

The judge rules on whether evidence is admissible on these lines; if it is admitted, then the jury decides whether to believe it. There should be a 'trial within a trial' – without the jury – to determine whether the evidence is admissible (*R v Liverpool Juvenile Court ex p R* (1988)).

The courts have not found much evidence of 'oppression' in police questioning. In *Miller* (1986), a paranoid schizophrenic had confessed to killing his girlfriend. He had admitted the killing in an interview which contained both reliable and unreliable matter. He later retracted his confession. It was argued for him at trial that the confession should be excluded under s 76(2)(a) – that it had been obtained by 'oppression of the person who made it' as it had come as the result of protracted and oppressive interviews which had caused him to suffer an episode of 'schizophrenic terror'. Medical evidence was given that the style and length of questioning had produced a state of voluntary insanity in which his language reflected hallucinations and delusion. The judge would not exclude the evidence and the defendant was convicted of manslaughter. The Court of Appeal held that the mere fact that questions triggered off hallucinations in the defendant was not evidence of oppression.

In *R v Fulling* (1987), the Court of Appeal held that it was not oppression for the police to tell the defendant that her lover had been having an affair with another woman which so affected her that she made a confession. The word 'oppression', the court held, should be given its ordinary dictionary meaning as stated in the *Oxford English Dictionary*:

> The exercise of authority or power in a burdensome, harsh or wrongful manner; unjust or cruel treatment of subjects, inferiors, etc; the imposition of unreasonable or unjust burdens.

13.5.22 Unreliability

Evidence of a confession can be excluded if it was given:

> ... in consequence of anything said or done which was likely in the circumstances existing at the time, to render unreliable any confession which might be made by him in consequence thereof ... [s 76(2)(b)].

The phrase 'anything said or done' means by someone other than the suspect. In *R v Goldenberg* (1988), G, a heroin addict, was arrested on a charge of conspiracy to supply the diamorphine. He requested an interview five days after his arrest and, during this, he gave information about a man whom he said had supplied him with heroin. It was argued for G at trial that he had given the statement to get bail and thus to be able to feed his addiction; that the words 'in consequence of anything said or done ...' included things said or done by the suspect and that the critical thing here was the things G had said and done: namely, requested the interview and given any statement that would be likely to get him out of the station. G was convicted and his appeal was dismissed. Neill LJ stated:

> In our judgment, the words 'said or done' in s 76(2)(b) of the 1984 Act do not extend so as to include anything said or done by the person making the confession. It is clear from the wording of the section and the use of the words 'in consequence' that a causal link must be shown between what was said or done and the subsequent confession. In our view, it necessarily follows that 'anything said or done' is limited to something external to the person making the confession and to something which is likely to have some influence on him.

The reasoning in cases like *Zavekas* (1970) (see 13.5.20) has now clearly been rejected. This view is confirmed by Code C that, if a suspect asks an officer what action will be taken in the event of his answering questions, making a statement or refusing to do either, the officer may inform him what action he proposes to take in that event 'provided that the action is itself proper and warranted' (para 11.3).

13.5.23   *R v Heaton* (1993)

In *R v Heaton* (1993), the appellant was convicted of manslaughter of his 26 day old son. The evidence of the mother, who was of limited intelligence, was that the appellant had shaken the child hard to quieten him and that he subsequently went limp and breathless. She had also said that she had given the child Calpol (a children's medicine containing paracetamol).

Due to difficulties in contacting the appellant's solicitor, he had been in custody overnight for some 15 and a half hours by the time he was able to see a solicitor. As he said he had been ill, he was examined by a doctor who said he was fit to be interviewed. He was interviewed for about 75 minutes in the presence of the solicitor and the interview was tape-recorded. The first part of the interview dealt with his background details. When asked about the events leading up to the child's death, he at first denied that he had held the child. Later, he admitted holding the child but denied holding him up in the air. Under further questioning, he admitted holding the child up in the air and finally conceded that he had shaken the child about four times to and fro to keep him quiet and that the child's head was flopping.

The defence case was that the death could have been caused solely by the administration of the wrong drug by the mother; although she claimed to have given the child Calpol, which contained paracetamol, no evidence of any paracetamol was found in the child's body on post-mortem; however, promethazine was found in the blood and was the active ingredient of Phenergen, a drug which the mother also had in the house for the older children. In his evidence, the appellant said that he come downstairs to find the baby purplish in the face and breathless and had seen the mother giving him some medicine, following which she became hysterical and shook the baby. In the interview, he had been upset and, as the police would not believe what he was saying, in the end, he had told them that he had shaken the child. He denied that he had done so violently or in order to quieten the child.

On the *voir dire* (the trial within a trial where the judge, having asked the jury to go out, decides a dispute between counsel as to whether certain evidence is admissible), the defence sought to exclude the evidence of the appellant's interview under ss 76 and 78 of PACE 1984. An application was made to call a psychiatrist, Dr Z, on the *voir dire*. The trial judge ruled against admitting Dr Z's evidence and that the interview should be admitted.

On appeal, it was argued on the appellant's behalf: that the trial judge was wrong to exclude the evidence of Dr Z; that the trial judge should have excluded the interview because the officers concerned had applied pressure to the appellant, raising their voices and repeating their questions.

13.5.24 The Court of Appeal's decision

The Court of Appeal dismissed the appeal, holding:

- The trial judge had considered Dr Z's report, which was based upon a single interview with the appellant, sight of the case papers, hearing of the interview tapes and a conversation with the probation officer. Dr Z had noted in particular: 'My impression is that he is not exceptionally bright and is possibly of dull normal intelligence and is very suggestible.' In *R v Turner* (1975), Lawton LJ said (p 83):

  ... an expert's opinion is admissible to furnish the court with scientific information which is likely to be outside the experience and knowledge of a judge or jury. If, on the proven facts, a judge or jury can form their own conclusions without help, then the opinion of an expert is unnecessary. In such a case, if it is given dressed up in scientific jargon, it may make judgment more difficult. The fact that an expert witness has impressive scientific qualifications does not, by that fact alone, make his opinion on matters of human nature or behaviour within the limits of normality any more helpful than that of the jurors themselves; but there is a danger that they may think it does.

  In the more recent case of *R v Raghip, Silcott and Braithwaite* (1991), the Court of Appeal had drawn a distinction between psychiatric or psychological evidence going to *mens rea* and such evidence going to the reliability of a confession, but had not criticised the general principle laid down in *Turner*. The court had rejected a 'judge for yourself' approach by the judge in respect of the jury and, it would seem, in respect of his own task on a *voir dire*, where there was expert evidence which would have been of assistance in assessing the defendant's mental condition. In that case, Alliott J said:

> ... the state of the psychological evidence before us ... is such that the jury would have been assisted in assessing the mental condition of Raghip and the consequent reliability of the alleged confessions. Notwithstanding that Raghip's IQ was at 74 just in the borderline range, a man chronologically aged 19 years seven months at the date of the interview with a level of functioning equivalent to that of a child of nine years, and the reading capacity of a child of six years, cannot be said to be normal. It would be impossible for the layman to divide that data from Raghip's performance in the witness box, still less the abnormal suggestibility of which [the expert witness] spoke.

- There was, in *Heaton*, no suggestion of mental handicap or retardation; the appellant was within the normal range of intelligence albeit towards the duller end of it. There was nothing more than Dr Z's bare impression that the appellant was very suggestible; there was no data on which to found that assertion nor was it clear that 'very suggestible' was outside the normal range. The judge expressly indicated that he should be told if there was anything more to Dr Z's evidence than was contained in his report and he was not informed of anything else. In those circumstances, he concluded that there was nothing in the doctor's impression which complied with the tests laid down in *Turner* and illustrated by *Raghip*; in the court's judgment, he was justified in ruling as he did. Unless the medical evidence sought to be introduced on an issue of this kind was truly based on some scientific data or expert analysis outside the experience of judge and jury, a mere impression, even of a highly qualified doctor, that the defendant 'is not exceptionally bright' or was 'very suggestible' was not admissible for the reasons set out by Lawton LJ.

- The court had read the transcript of the interview and heard the tape-recordings. The appellant had a full opportunity to consult with a solicitor before the interview and the solicitor was present throughout. A doctor had examined the appellant and pronounced him fit to be interviewed. The questioning lasted in all only some 75 minutes and much of the first two tapes was concerned merely with taking the appellant's history. Voices were slightly raised but there was no shouting and no oppressive hostility; the pace of the interview was slow and the appellant was given time to consider his replies. Some questions were repeated several times but not inappropriately. In *R v Paris, Abdullahi and Miller* (1992), where similar arguments were raised, the court said:

> Of course, it is perfectly legitimate for officers to pursue their interrogation of their suspect with a view to eliciting his account or gaining admissions. They

are not required to give up after the first denial or even after a number of denials.

In that case, the questioning had continued for some 13 hours and the tapes had shown hostility and bullying on the part of the interviewing officers. In the present case, the situation was wholly different, with the appellant changing his story gradually over a comparatively short period and providing further details without the police putting them in. The judge had been right to conclude that the prosecution had discharged the burden upon them to exclude oppression and the possibility that the circumstances might have rendered the admission unreliable.

In a commentary on *Heaton* in the *Criminal Law Review*, it is pointed out that the law on confessions is developing in a number of ways to prevent, as far as is possible, the conviction of weak minded and suggestible persons on the basis of their own unreliable statements. In addition to the exclusionary rule in s 76(2)(b) of PACE 1984 and the discretion in s 78, defendants labouring under a 'significant degree of mental handicap' are protected by the rule in *McKenzie* (1992), which requires an unconvincing case based solely on confessions to be withdrawn from the jury.

13.5.25 Research findings

In an interesting study of police interview techniques ('Police interview techniques: establishing truth or proof?' (1993) 33 Brit J Crim 3), John Baldwin analysed 400 videoed police interviews with suspects – 100 from each of four police stations – and 200 audio-taped interviews taken from two busy stations. As he observes, an interrogation leading to a confession can be of great importance to the police as it can provide an alternative to a time consuming investigation of the crime. Baldwin did not find much evidence of oppression but rather of deficiency in questioning technique:

> … coercion or belligerence in police interviews strike the observer much less frequently than feebleness and ineptitude. Instances of heavy handedness were much less common than unduly timorous questioning. It must, nonetheless, be acknowledged that the boundaries between officers acting, say, upon an assumption of guilt, or failing adequately to listen to suspects' responses, and exerting undue pressures to induce a confession, are thoroughly blurred.

Baldwin concludes that, evaluated as a search for 'the truth', most police interviews are 'thoroughly deficient'. But such a judgment would be to miss the point of interrogation, a central feature of which is concerned with the future rather than past events. Interrogations are, he argues, conducted with an eye to any subsequent trial:

> A main purpose of the interrogation is thus to seek to limit, close down, or pre-empt the future options available to the subject. It will be very difficult for

suspects to claim in court that, say, goods were taken by accident or that they were not at the scene when precisely the opposite was established in an earlier taped interview.

13.5.26 Evidence illegally or improperly obtained

There is an overlap between the subject of this discussion and that above because, sometimes, the illegally or improperly obtained evidence will be a confession, in which case the rules above will also apply.

There was for a long time a judicial discretion to exclude otherwise admissible evidence on the basis that it would be unfair to the defendant. The *dictum* of Lord Goddard CJ on this was often cited. He said: 'If, for instance, some admission or piece of evidence, for example, a document, had been obtained from a defendant by a trick, no doubt the judge might properly rule it out.' (See *Kuruma Son of Kaniu v R* (1955), a Privy Council case dealing with an appeal from Kenya. It held that, if evidence was relevant, it did not matter how it was obtained.)

In *R v Sang* (1979), the House of Lords took a very restrictive view of the discretion, holding that it could not be used to exclude evidence merely on the basis that it was given by an agent provocateur. The defendant claimed he had been induced to commit an offence by an informer acting on the instructions of the police. All the judges ruled that there was no defence of entrapment in English law. They were also unanimous in ruling that (except for confessions or issues of self-incrimination) no discretion existed to exclude evidence simply on the basis that it had been improperly or illegally obtained. Such illegality might lead to civil proceedings or disciplinary action within the police but not for excluding evidence. The only basis for excluding relevant evidence was if its prejudicial effect outweighed its probative value. This reasoning has been reconfirmed by the Court of Appeal in *R v Spurthwaite and Gill* (1993).

The approach of s 78 of PACE 1984 is to widen the discretion. It does not go so far as the system in the United States where improperly obtained evidence is inadmissible – the doctrine that the fruit of the poisoned tree should not be eaten. It states that the court *may* refuse to allow evidence on which the prosecution proposes to rely:

> ... if it appears to the court that, having regard to all the circumstances, including the circumstances in which the evidence was obtained, the admission of the evidence would have such an adverse effect on the fairness of the proceedings that the court ought not to admit it.

The courts have been persuaded on many occasions to exclude evidence using this section. In fact, Zander has suggested that 'the judges have forged the somewhat ambiguous words of s 78 into a powerful weapon to hold the police accountable for breaches of the law and the Codes of Practice'. Most cases have involved access to solicitors or the law relating to interrogations. In *R v Absolam* (1989), the Court of Appeal quashed a conviction for supplying cannabis where A, in contravention of the Code, had not been told of his right to a solicitor and rules about the tape-recording of interviews were broken.

Unlike the rule applying to s 76 (see 13.5.22), there does not need to be a trial within a trial under s 78 to determine whether the evidence is admissible. The admissibility of a confession can be opposed under both s 76 and s 78. The court will be less willing to exclude evidence where there were technical breaches but the defendant had experience of police stations. In *R v Dunford* (1991), the Court of Appeal refused to quash a conviction in spite of a serious breach of s 58 (see 13.5.4) because D, who had several previous convictions, answered 'No comment' to awkward questions of the police and refused to sign a record of the interview. The court thought it was extremely doubtful 'whether the solicitor's advice would have added anything to [his] knowledge of his rights'.

13.5.27 Runciman Royal Commission proposals

The Commission's recommendations in this area are of particular interest as it was set up in the wake of a number of grave miscarriages of justice in which people had been wrongly convicted on the basis of subsequently discredited confession evidence. The Commission was announced on the day the Birmingham Six were released from jail having served 16 years for crimes which later scientific evidence showed they could not have confessed to in the way the police alleged.

13.5.28 Confession evidence

The Commission said:

- (para 85) when PACE 1984 is next revisited, attention should be given to the fact that s 77 (judge's duty to caution the jury of the need for care in cases where mentally handicapped people have made confessions without independent witnesses) is limited to the 'mentally handicapped' and does not include the 'mentally ill' or other categories of the 'mentally disordered';

- (para 86) the law should be changed so that a judge may stop any case if the prosecution evidence is demonstrably unsafe or unsatisfactory or too weak to be allowed to go to the jury;

- (para 87) wherever a confession has allegedly been made to the police outside the police station, whether tape-recorded or not, it should be put to the suspect at the beginning of the first tape-recorded interview at the station. Failure to do this may render the alleged confession inadmissible, but, if the suspect does not confirm the confession on the tape, it should not automatically be inadmissible;

- (para 88) an alleged confession to an investigating official should be allowed to go before the jury even if not tape-recorded, provided it meets the tests contained in PACE 1984 and the judge believes the jury could safely consider it.

13.5.29 Corroboration of confessions

- (para 89) there should be a judicial warning in cases where confession evidence is involved. The precise terms of the warning should depend on the circumstances of the case. If it remains possible for a confession to be admitted without other supporting evidence, the jury should be warned that great care is needed before convicting on the basis of the confession alone;

- (para 90) the majority of the commission believed that, where a confession is credible, and has passed the tests laid down in PACE 1984, the jury should be able to consider it even in the absence of other evidence. The judge should in all such cases give a strong warning to the jury. The other evidence which the jury should be advised to look for should be supporting evidence (that is, of a different kind) in the *R v Turnbull* (1977) sense.

There was considerable disquiet among defence lawyers and civil liberty groups that the Commission had not recommended the automatic inadmissibility of uncorroborated confessions. (See, for example, (1993) *The Guardian*, 7 July.) Consider, for example, the case of the Guildford Four. Three men and a woman were jailed for life in 1975 after being convicted of bombing pubs in 1974 which killed five people. The evidence against them amounted to confessions they were alleged to have made. Fourteen years after conviction, a rough set of typed notes was discovered with handwritten addenda which matched one of the men's supposedly contemporaneously recorded interview. The Lord Chief Justice, Lord Lane, concluded that the police officers involved must have lied. The three former officers, however, were acquitted later on charges of attempting to pervert the course of justice. Alistair Logan, solicitor for two of the men, has pointed out that the men would not necessarily have been saved by Runciman's recommendations because these accept the possibility of uncorroborated confessions going to the jury.

The Commission's report notes that it is now generally accepted that people do on occasion confess to crimes they have not committed, perhaps due to a desire for notoriety, to protect somebody else, or for immediate advantage like wanting to get out of the police station. The long held belief that people will not make false statements against themselves can no longer be sustained. The report advocates the introduction of continuous video-recording of all police custody suites at a cost of about £9 million. The report states (para 50):

> Continuous video-recording (including sound track) of all the activities in the custody office, the passages and stairways leading from the custody office to the cells and, if feasible, the cell passage and the doors of individual cells of all police stations designated under PACE 1984 as suitable for detaining suspects should be introduced as soon as practicable.

John Baldwin has argued ('Power and police interviews' (1993) 143 NLJ 1194, 14 August) that the Royal Commission's report was sadly lacking in not providing recommendations for a better legal regulation of police questioning of suspects. He says in the report:

> There is little new thinking or analysis; rather, the emphasis is upon re-working old ideas and offering encouragement to those professional groups which are striving to improve their own procedures.

The problem needing to be addressed, argues Baldwin, is basically one of power:

> Legal advisers and their clients are bound to be relatively powerless in a situation in which it is police officers who decide when an interview takes place, how it is to be conducted and for how long. Interviews take place on police territory and on police terms. Police officers can even determine who sits where in the interview room and they may deliberately prevent eye contact between legal representatives and their clients by physically bolting the chairs to the floor. Their power to eject troublesome advisers from the interview room [Code of Practice C, para 6.9], though very infrequently exercised, underlines still further who is in charge.

It would still be open to the Home Secretary to enact changes that were not contained in the Runciman Report.

THE CRIMINAL PROCESS:
(1) THE INVESTIGATION OF CRIME

At the end of the 20th century, we can see the first governmental recognition of something of something called a 'criminal justice system'. The police, the probation service, the prison service, the magistracy, the Crown Courts and other elements have all been grouped within the system. This means that rules or policy relating to one element can be evaluated in terms of their impact in relation to another part of the system. Conflicting public desires arise in this area. On the one hand, there is a general mistrust of certain sorts of policing, and a desire for more protective civil liberties law, while, on the other hand, there is a desire for more offenders to be captured and punished, and the belief that, in order for this to succeed, civil liberties need to be reduced. The Macpherson Report following the stabbing of Stephen Lawrence has given a significant impetus for reform of the law relating to policing.

Remedies

Remedies for unlawful arrest include: (1) an action for habeas corpus; (2) that any subsequent prosecution arising from the arrest should fail – s 78 of PACE 1984; and (3) an action for damages for false imprisonment. If the arrest is not lawful then reasonable force may be used to resist it.

Arrest

Arrest can be: (1) under police warrant; (2) under common law for breach of the peace; or (3) under legislation, principally, PACE 1984. The details in ss 24 and 25 of PACE 1984 and connected cases are very important.

Detention

Detention short of arrest does not exist except under the Prevention of Terrorism (Temporary Provisions) Act 1989. Note this confirmation by s 29 of PACE 1984.

Suspects stopped in the street

Suspects stopped in the street are not legally obliged to help police with enquiries. Note the distinction between *Kenlin v Gardiner* (1967) and *Donnelly v Jackman* (1970). Note also that a person may be arrested for being silent or misleading under s 25 if the officer has reasonable doubts about the suspect's name and address or whether the summons procedure can be used at the address given. Note the newly enlarged powers of stop and search under s 60 and s 81 of the Criminal Justice and Public Order Act 1994.

Procedure on arrest

Procedure on arrest involves the arrestor having to inform the suspect of the grounds for arrest (s 28(3)). Note, though, that an arrest becomes lawful from when the information is given. The extent of the required information to the suspect is important (see *Geldberg v Miller* (1961); *R v Telfer* (1976)).

The use of force

The use of force to effect an arrest must be 'reasonable in all the circumstances' (s 3 of the Criminal Law Act 1967 (citizens); s 117 of PACE 1984 (police officers)).

Stop and search

Stop and search is governed by s 1 and Code A of PACE 1984. The judge can exclude evidence obtained in breach of the Codes (s 67(7) of PACE 1984). There are legal obligations on an officer conducting a search (ss 2 and 3 of PACE 1984). Note the Code is quite specific about what indices can be grounds for reasonable suspicion and which, individually or combined, may not.

Section 60 of the CJPOA 1994 has provided a new stop and search power in anticipation of violence. Under it, with authorisation, an officer can stop any pedestrian and search him or her for offence weapons or dangerous instruments, or even stop vehicles. The authorising officer must reasonably believe that incidents involving serious violence may take place in the area. Section 81 of the same Act creates a new power of stop and search of people and vehicles where it is expedient to do so to prevent certain acts of terrorism.

Search of arrested persons

Search of arrested persons is governed by s 32 of PACE 1984. The person arrested cannot be required to take off more than outer garments. The place where he or she was arrested, or where he or she was immediately before can also be searched under s 32. Note the differences between this power and those of s 18 regarding premises.

Search on detention

Search on detention is governed by s 54 of PACE 1984 and Code C, para 4.1 which require the custody officer to take charge of the process of searching the detained person.

Premises

Premises can be entered by police (1) with permission; or (2) to prevent a breach of the peace; or (3) pursuant to s 18 or s 32 of PACE 1984. The differences between these provisions are important. They are:

	Section 18 (entry and search after arrest)	Section 32 (Search of premises has to be at time of arrest)
Search of person:	(only s 32)	for weapons, means to escape, evidence relating to 'an offence', that is, any offence
Search of premises:	The police may enter and search the arrestee's premises to look for evidence relating to the offence for which the person was arrested or some other arrestable offence connected with that or similar to that offence for which he was arrested.	To enter and search premises where D was when or immediately before arrest for evidence relating to *the offence for which the person was arrested.* They need not be his premises but the power must be based on reasonable belief that the officer will find something for which a search is permitted.

Seizure of articles from searches

Seizure of articles from searches under s 19 and Code B, s 6 are quite wide, including items from any offence. The exemptions, like items under legal professional privilege, are important.

Search warrants and safeguards

Search warrants and safeguards issued under s 8 of PACE 1984 require the magistrate to be satisfied of four things. Note the difficulty of balancing the interests of effective policing with those of civil liberties. Note the ambiguity in s 15 and the way it was resolved in *R v Longman* (1988).

Interrogation, confession and admissibility of evidence

The main problem here is for the law to strike the proper balance between giving the police sufficient power to interrogate and protecting the interests of suspects. Too few rules governing how the police can conduct an interrogation and too few rules restricting the sort of evidence that can be put to a jury, might easily lead to oppressive behaviour by the police interviewing suspects. Too many restrictive rules, conversely, will thwart the police in their endeavours to prosecute offenders successfully.

The right to have someone informed

The right to have someone informed after arrest is given (s 56(1) and Code C, para 5.1) to all suspects after arrest. It can be delayed, however, under s 116. The case must involve a 'serious arrestable offence' and it must be authorised by a superintendent on certain grounds, for example, the arrested person would alert others involved in a crime.

Access to legal advice

Access to legal advice is provided for under s 58 and Code C. The notification must accord with details set out in Code C. Note the criticisms of the Duty Solicitor scheme. Is it adequately staffed? Note also the circumstances in which legal advice can be delayed under s 116 and Code C, Annex B. In an emergency, questioning can begin before the suspect's legal advisor arrives (Code C, para 6.6).

Time limits

Time limits before and after charges note ss 42 and 38 of PACE 1984. Delayed access to legal advice is possible in cases of serious arrestable offences. A suspect can be held for up to 24 hours without being charged; longer with authorisation from the superintendent and up to 96 hours with magistrates' permission.

The right to silence

The right to silence means that a person cannot be charged with obstructing the police in the execution of their duty simply by failing to answer questions. Note the important difference between *Rice v Connolly* (1966) and *Ricketts v Cox* (1982). There are some circumstances where the suspect does have to answer on pain of penalty (s 2 of the CJA 1987).

What could be said in court, before April 1995, about the defendant's silence, varied according to whether the questions were put by an officer or someone on equal terms to the questioned person. Generally, no adverse inferences could be invited although the judge could comment on reticence prior to cautioning. Most defendants did not use the right and of those who did few seemed, according to research, to benefit from it.

Now, after ss 34–37 of the CJPOA 1994, certain adverse inferences may be drawn from a suspect's failure to answer police questions, or his failure to answer them in court.

Confessions

Confessions must be voluntary and given without oppression being used to extract them; they must also not come from any circumstances likely to make them unreliable (s 76).

Evidence illegally obtained

Evidence illegally or improperly obtained is not automatically inadmissible but it may be excluded under s 78 if it appears to a court that in all the circumstances the admission of the evidence 'would have such an adverse effect on the fairness of the proceedings that the court ought not to admit it'.

Runciman Royal Commission recommendations

The Runciman Royal Commission recommendations included:

- that the law should be changed so that a judge may stop any case if the prosecution evidence is demonstrably unsafe or unsatisfactory or too weak to be allowed to go to the jury;

- that wherever a confession has allegedly been made to the police outside the police station, whether tape-recorded or not, it should be put to the suspect at the beginning of the first tape-recorded interview at the station. Failure to do this may render the alleged confession inadmissible, but if the suspect does not confirm the confession on the tape, it should not automatically be inadmissible;

- that there should be a judicial warning in cases where confession evidence is involved. The precise terms of the warning should depend on the circumstances of the case. If it remains possible for a confession to be admitted without other supporting evidence, the jury should be warned that great care is needed before convicting on the basis of the confession alone;

- that where a confession is credible, and has passed the tests laid down in PACE 1984, the jury should be able to consider it even in the absence of other evidence. The judge should in all such cases give a strong warning to the jury. The other evidence which the jury should be advised to look for should be supporting evidence of a different kind.

CHAPTER 14

THE CRIMINAL PROCESS:
(2) THE PROSECUTION

The classification of offences, and matters relating to transfers for trial, summary trial and trial on indictment are dealt with in Chapter 3.

Until 1986, England was one of only a few countries which allowed the police to prosecute rather than hand over this task to a State agency like the district attorney in the United States. The Crown Prosecution Service (CPS) was established by the Prosecution of Offences Act (POA) 1985 and the police now play no part in prosecutions beyond the stage of charging the suspect.

There have been many problems with the new system and some writers, like Michael Zander, have argued that the change could represent a considerable setback for the criminal justice system (Zander, *Cases and Materials on the English Legal System* (1996)). There used to be five different forms of prosecution, those by:

- the police, who prosecuted most offences;

- the Attorney General/Solicitor General whose permission is needed to prosecute for many serious crimes and who can enter a *nolle prosequi* to stop certain prosecutions or give a *fiat* to disallow them to begin;

- the Director of Public Prosecutions (DPP) who prosecutes in very serious cases and cases brought to him by the government;

- public bodies, like local authorities. These used to amount to about 25% of all prosecutions, most being by the Post Office for television licence offences;

- private prosecutions, which involve having to persuade a magistrate of the propriety in issuing a summons. The Attorney General and the DPP both have the power to take over a private prosecution and then drop it for reasons of public policy. Private bodies like stores and the RSPCA most regularly bring prosecutions. A study in 1980 showed that only 2.4% of prosecutions were private (Lidstone, *Prosecutions by Private Individuals and Non-Police Agencies*, 1980).

14.1 The Crown Prosecution Service

The move to establish a CPS was precipitated by a report from JUSTICE, the British section of the International Commission of Jurists, in its 1970 report, *The Prosecution Process in England and Wales*. It argued that the police were not best suited to be prosecutors because they would often have a commitment to winning a case even where the evidence was weak. They were also not best placed to consider the public policy aspects of the discretion not to prosecute. The police were firmly opposed to such a change. They argued that statistics showed that the police were not given to pursuing cases in a way which led to a high rate of acquittal. They also showed that in cases involving miscarriages of justice, the decision to prosecute had been taken by a lawyer.

The question was referred to the Philips Royal Commission on Criminal Procedure which judged the then existing system according to its fairness, openness and accountability. It proposed a new system based on several distinct features including:

- that the initial decision to charge a suspect should rest with the police;

- that thereafter all decisions as to whether to proceed, alter or drop the charges should rest with another State prosecuting agency;

- this agency would provide advocates for all cases in the magistrates' courts apart from guilty pleas by post. It should also provide legal advice to the police and instruct counsel in all cases tried on indictment.

The Crown Prosecution Act 1985 established a national prosecution service under the general direction of the DPP. The 1985 Act gives to the DPP and the CPS as a whole the right to institute and conduct any criminal proceedings where the importance or difficulty of the case make that appropriate (s 3(2)(b)). This applies to cases that could also be started by the police or other bodies like local authorities. It can also, in appropriate circumstances, take over and then discontinue cases. The CPS relies on the police for the resources and machinery of investigation.

In the period following its launch, the CPS experienced severe problems of staff shortage related to the general funding of the service. This improved over the years, and by March 1993 the full lawyer staff establishment had almost been met. It was apparently difficult to recruit staff of an adequate standard for the available pay and there has been considerable use of agents, that is, lawyers in private practice working for the CPS on a fee-for-case basis. The 1992–93 Annual Report of the CPS stated that:

> In the absence of CPS rights of audience, the presentation of all cases in the Crown Court and higher courts continues to be undertaken by counsel in private practice. In 1992–93, total expenditure was £68.5 million. The average payment in the Crown Court was £460.

The eighth annual report of the CPS (June 1994) brought much new information into the debate about how well this controversial organisation is doing its job. The new Code for Crown Prosecutors, published at the same time, makes some contentious changes to the criteria used to decide whether a prosecution should be brought.

Since its inception, the CPS has been criticised for a variety of alleged faults, principally that it is inefficient and has a low success rate in prosecutions. Many police officers have expressed doubts about the rigour with which cases are handled by the CPS, and have dubbed it the 'Criminal Prosecution Society'. The Bar Council passed a motion in 1993 condemning the service for being too ready to abandon cases 'fearing defeat or cost'.

The former Director of Prosecutions, Barbara Mills QC, who headed the CPS until April 1998, laid much of the responsibility for poor conviction rates at the door of the police. In one public statement, she blamed lack of proper preparation by the police for two-fifths of the 185,824 cases dropped in the magistrates' court in 1992–93. Another 8,046 were dropped at the Crown Court. Mrs Mills claimed that in a quarter of cases that had to be dropped, CPS lawyers had no option because witnesses were missing or refused to give evidence or because the case was being considered elsewhere in the justice system so the 'double jeopardy' rule applied. Between 1994 and 1997, crime figures fell but arrest rates remained static reflecting what police claim was increasing success against offenders but the percentage of magistrate-level cases discontinued by the CPS crept up. Again, the reasoning for dropping or downgrading cases was found wanting.

To answer criticism, the CPS commissioned an analysis sample 10,000 cases that it had to drop in 1992–93. The results show that 43% were abandoned on the ground of insufficient evidence to provide a realistic prospect of conviction. In 31% of cases, prosecutors abandoned them because it was 'not in the public interest' to proceed, for example, where the defendant had already been convicted and sentenced on another matter (9%) or only a nominal penalty was likely (6%). Much criticism of the CPS has come from police officers who object to the CPS continuing not to pursue cases for these very reasons.

A highly critical report published by a review body headed by Sir Iain Glidewell in June 1998, concluded that the CPS failed to achieve the expected improvements in the prosecution system since it was set up in 1986 and became bureaucratic and over-centralised. The report depicts a service where charges are thought to be 'inappropriately downgraded' and a disproportionately large number of serious violent crimes not prosecuted. Proposals for a complete overhaul of the CPS were strongly backed by many in the criminal justice system ((1998) *The Times*, 2 June).

As a result of the Glidewell Report, the CPS underwent a major structural re-organisation in 1999. Its operation was decentralised so as to realign the CPS areas to match the boundaries of police forces – there were previously 13 CPS areas and now there are 42 to match the 43 police forces of England and Wales (there are two police forces for London, the Metropolitan Police and the City of London police). New Chief Crown Prosecutors (CCPs) for the 42 areas were appointed in 1999. As its casework load is so large, London has three CCPs. The new DPP, David Calvert-Smith QC, stated that:

The new postholders will, in effect, be local DPPs with the power to act on their own initiative and to take their own decisions. They will be placing a priority on prosecution work which will benefit the local communities they serve [Crown Prosecution Service Official Statement, issue 109/99, 8 March 1999].

The Codes for Crown Prosecution will be accountable to their local communities, and the CPS contends that a localised service will enable good working relationships with the other agencies in the criminal justice system, including the police, the courts, and the judiciary (Crown Prosecution Service Official Statement, issue 113/99, 12 April 1999).

In its 1997–98 Annual Report, the CPS states that, in the year under review, it dealt with more than 1.4 million cases in the magistrates' courts and around 128,000 in the Crown Court. The organisation is clearly under a certain pressure as only 50.6% of committal papers were delivered to the defence within agreed timescales. The report notes that, in the magistrates' courts, the overall conviction rate was 98.1% (compared with 98.0% in 1996–97). The conviction rate in the Crown Court was 90.6% compared with 90.8% in 1996–97. These figures, though, represent cases which end up in court and they include guilty pleas. The number of discontinuances in both sorts of court is high. Discontinuances occur where witnesses fail to attend or attend and change their evidence. In 1997–98, there were 164,438 cases discontinued by the CPS in the magistrates' courts (12% of all cases brought – the same as the year before), and 8,130 cases not proceeded with in the Crown Court (7.7% of all cases brought, 1,504 more abandoned cases than the year before).

The document *Judicial Statistics 1997* (1998, LCD) notes that, of the 91,110 cases being brought to trial at Crown Court in 1997 (p 61), only 11,510 defendants who pleaded not guilty to all or some the charges against them were convicted by juries (p 65).

According to the Judicial Statistics (1994), the chances of being acquitted in the Crown Court seem quite high. Statistically, a defendant has three chances out of five of being acquitted if he or she pleads not guilty. Roger Smith ((1994) 144 NLJ 1088) has pointed to the fact that, given the choice (which they are not), defendants would be best advised to opt for trial in Newcastle, rather than Cardiff. Trial on the North East circuit, rather than Wales and Chester, increased the chance of acquittal from 55 to 65% in 1994.

According to the figures released in 1995, there was a 9% fall in the number of discontinued cases in the Crown Courts. The CPS attributed this change to a better understanding amongst police officers of tests applied by the CPS to decide whether to prosecute. In 1994, the CPS finalised 1,462,967 cases, of which 11.7% (159,803) were discontinued, compared to 12.8% in 1993.

The CPS Annual Report 1999 notes that, during the year under review, the CPS dealt with proportionally more serious crime with indictable only cases – the most serious – rising to 30% of the total Crown Court caseload.

The report shows the proportion of indictable only offences in the Crown Court rose from 18.2% in 1991–92 to 26% in 1997–98 and 30% in 1998–99. The rise has been influenced by the plea before venue procedure for either way cases, which means such cases are not unnecessarily committed to the Crown Court.

In the magistrates' courts, indictable and either way cases rose by 1.8%. The total number of cases dealt with by the CPS in 1998–99 was 1,423,200 in magistrates' courts and 124,781 in the Crown Court. In magistrates' courts, 98.3% of hearings ended in conviction and in the Crown Court the figure was 89.1%.

Pilot schemes aimed at reducing delays in criminal courts have led to more efficient and speedier justice, with more cases dealt with at the first hearing; cases which go to trial being heard more quickly and a reduction in bureaucracy.

The CPS shares key performance targets for the criminal justice system with the Home Office and Lord Chancellor's Department. These include halving the time from arrest to sentence for persistent young offenders from 142 to 71 days by 31 March 2002.

14.1.1 The Code for Crown Prosecutors

The CPS Code for Crown Prosecutors (1994) is issued under s 10 of the Prosecution of Offences Act 1985. It explains the principles used by the CPS in its work. It says that 'police officers should take account of the principles of the Code when they are deciding whether to charge a defendant with an offence'.

14.1.2 The discretion to prosecute

The police have a very significant discretion as to what to do when a crime has possibly been committed. They could turn a blind eye, caution the suspect or charge the suspect in which latter case they must decide for what. As is very cogently argued by McConville, Sanders and Leng in *The Case for the Prosecution*, 1991, prosecution cases are constructed from the evidence and testimony of many people including lay witnesses, victims, the police, CPS lawyers and expert witnesses. Each of these parties is fallible and prone to perceive events in line with their own sorts of experience. The net result of this is that the prosecution case is normally nothing more than an approximation to 'the truth'. The most influential role is that of the police, as it is they who ultimately decide whether to charge anyone, if so whom and for what. Once these discretions have been exercised, there is a relatively narrow band of data on which the CPS can work.

In 1951, the Attorney General, Lord Shawcross, noted that:

It has never been the rule in this country – I hope it never will be – that suspected criminal offences must automatically be the subject of prosecution [HC Deb Vol 483 Col 681, 29 January 1951].

This *dictum* has been almost universally accepted within the criminal justice system.

There is evidence, however, that the police do (for operational or social reasons) tend to focus their attention on particular types of conduct. Research, for example, by Andrew Sanders has shown a tendency for there to be a bias in favour of prosecuting working class offenders as opposed to middle class offenders. He compared the police response to offences with that of the Factory Inspectorate's response to violation of the Health and Safety laws and found that the police were much more prone to initiate prosecutions against working class suspects than were the factory inspectors against businesses and business executives. For the police there was an institutional bias in favour of prosecution reflected in the principle 'let the court decide', whereas with the factory inspectorate prosecution was only a last resort after an attempt at negotiated compliance had failed. In 1980, there were 22,000 serious cases of tax evasion but only one in 122 cases was prosecuted. By contrast, there were 107,000 social security frauds, of which one in four were prosecuted. Tax evasion resulted in a loss to the public purse 30 times larger than that caused by social security fraud yet there was more state money spent on prosecuting people for social security fraud. See Sanders, 'Class bias in prosecutions' (1985) 24 Howard J 176.

14.1.3 Police cautioning of offenders and CPS guidelines

During 1992–93, there was a sharp increase in the number of offenders whom police chose to caution rather than prosecute (Criminal Statistics, 1992). The Home Office has encouraged cautioning noting that, especially in the case of juveniles, 'there may be a positive advantage to society as well as for the individual in using prosecution as a last resort' (Home Office Circular, issue 14/1985). The current criteria for cautioning are: the nature of the offence; the likely penalty; the offender's age and health; and his or her criminal record and attitude towards the offence. There is a presumption against prosecuting offenders with no record to show who are juvenile, young adults or elderly. The 1994 guidelines say that (at para 6.9):

Crown prosecutors should tell the police if they think that a caution would be more suitable than a prosecution.

The Code for Crown Prosecutors (promulgated on behalf of the DPP) sets out the official criteria governing the discretion to prosecute.

The Code, the second to be issued, retains the two previous tests which determine whether a prosecution should be brought: there must be a 'realistic prospect of conviction' (the evidential test) and the prosecution must be 'in the public interest'.

The evidential test remains the same, requiring prosecutors to predict what a jury, or bench, properly directed, would be likely to decide. The guidelines require prosecutors to assess the reliability of evidence, not just its admissibility. Thus, the question (para 5.3b): 'Is it likely that a confession is unreliable, for example, because of the defendant's age, intelligence or lack of understanding?'

As Glanville Williams ([1985] Crim LR 115) and Andrew Sanders ((1994) 144 NLJ 946) have argued, this test favours people who are well respected in society like police officers and businessmen – in whose favour juries and magistrates might be biased. It also disfavours the sort of victims who are unlikely to make good witnesses. Sanders proposes a better test: whether, on the evidence, a jury or bench ought (on the balance of probabilities) to convict.

The public interest must be considered in each case where there is enough evidence to provide a realistic prospect of conviction. In cases of any seriousness, a prosecution will usually take place unless there are public interest factors tending against prosecution which clearly outweigh those tending in favour.

One innovation in the new Code is the listing of some 'public interest factors in favour of prosecution' (para 6.4) and some against (para 6.5). The former include cases where:

- a conviction is likely to result in a significant sentence;

- a weapon was used or violence was threatened during the commission of the offence;

- the offence was committed against a person serving the public, like a police officer or a nurse;

- the offence, although not serious in itself, is widespread in the area where it was committed;

- there is evidence that the offence was carried out by a group;

- the offence was motivated by any form of discrimination against the victim's ethnic or national origin, sex, religious beliefs, political views, or sexual preference.

A prosecution is less likely to proceed, we are told, where:

- the court is likely to impose a very small or nominal penalty;

- the offence was committed as a result of a genuine mistake or misunderstanding (judged against the seriousness of the offence);

- the loss or harm can be described as minor and was the result of a single incident, particularly if it was caused by a misjudgment;

- a prosecution is likely to have a very bad effect on the victim's physical or mental health, always bearing in mind the seriousness of the offence;

- details could be made public that could harm sources of information, international relations or national security.

Crown prosecutors must balance factors for and against prosecution carefully and fairly. Deciding on the public interest is, the Code says (para 6.6) 'not simply a matter of adding up the number of factors on each side'.

Barbara Mills has stated that the Attorney General has commended the Code to other prosecutors. This may help to correct inconsistent approaches between the police and CPS on the one hand and, on the other, prosecutors like the Inland Revenue, and Health and Safety Executive. As Sanders (see above) has observed, if you illegally gain a fortune or maim someone, you will probably be treated more leniently than ordinary disposals for such offences if the crimes are, technically, tax evasion and operating an unsafe workplace.

14.1.4 CPS independence from the police

The CPS is institutionally separate from the police. The police are no longer in a client-lawyer relationship with the prosecutor, able to give instructions about how to proceed. The police are still, however, in the most influential position as it is only once they have taken the decision to charge a suspect that the CPS will be called on to look at the case. The CPS in practice exercises no supervisory role over the police investigation of cases; it simply acts on the file presented after the investigation by the police. The power of the CPS to discontinue prosecutions (under s 23 of the POA 1985) or the continuing power to withdraw or offer no evidence is an important feature of its independence. An argument that 'The system is dominated throughout its stages by the interests and values of the police, with the CPS playing an essentially subordinate and reactive role' is put by McConville (ed) in *The Case for the Prosecution*, 1991.

The Report of the Runciman Royal Commission on Criminal Justice (1993) recommends the CPS plays a greater role in the investigative process. It states (para 93):

> The police should seek the advice of the CPS at the investigation stage in appropriate cases in accordance with guidelines to be agreed between the two services.

The report also states (para 95):

> Where a chief officer of police is reluctant to comply with a request from the CPS to investigate further before a decision on discontinuance is taken, HM Chief Inspector of Constabulary in conjunction with the Director of Public Prosecutions should bring about a resolution of the dispute.

Oddly, however, the rationale underlying the establishment of the CPS (independence from the police) appears to have been undermined since 1998 when many police stations have has CPS liaison officers working in the stations themselves.

The following letter to *The Times* (6 August 1999) raises several noteworthy points on the other side of the argument:

From His Honour Judge Barrington Black

Sir, You report (3 August) that staff from the Crown Prosecution Service are to work with police officers in police stations to speed justice, and save £20 million a year.

Twenty years, and many millions of pounds ago, prior to the creation of the CPS, in the city where I practised, and throughout the country, the county prosecutor and his staff occupied an office above police headquarters.

They were available for consultations with police officers at any time, and they knew about the details of a case as it progressed. The police officer was responsible for the main papers and ensuing witness attendance. Defence solicitors also had direct contact with someone who could make decisions.

The words 'plea bargaining' are now forbidden but, in those days, a calculated assessment of the evidence and an indictment appropriate to that evidence were often determined to the benefit of the victim, the defendant, the public purse and justice.

I am delighted to hear that a system which was tried, tested and worked is to be revived.

Yours truly,

BARRINGTON BLACK

Harrow Crown Court

There may, however, be serious problems in developing too cosy a relationship between the police and the prosecuting authorities as, sometimes, the former have to come under the professional consideration of the latter. In August 1999, the CPS came under severe criticism in an official report into decisions not to prosecute police officers in circumstances where people had died in police custody. The report, *Inquiry into Crown Prosecution Service Decision Making in relation to Deaths in Custody and Related Matters by His Honour Judge Gerald Butler QC*, states that the way the CPS responded to such cases was 'inefficient and fundamentally unsound'. It lead to a 'thoroughly unsatisfactory situation' which needed to be urgently rectified. Following the criticisms in the Butler Report and further analysis by the CPS Inspectorate, the relevant decision making processes are being revised.

14.1.5 Judicial control of prosecution policy

There is a very limited way in which the courts can control the exercise of prosecutorial discretion by the police. Lord Denning MR gave the example in one case of a chief constable issuing a directive to his men that no person should be prosecuted for stealing goods worth less than £100 (over £1,000 in 1993 prices) and said 'I should have thought the court could countermand it. He would be failing in his duty to enforce the law'. More generally, the courts had no control, *per* Lord Denning MR, *R v Metropolitan Police Commissioner ex p Blackburn* (1968):

> For instance, it is for the Commissioner of Police of the Metropolis, or the chief constable, as the case may be, to decide in any particular case whether inquiries should be pursued, or whether an arrest should be made or a prosecution brought. It must be for him to decide on the disposition of his force and the concentration of his resources on any particular crime or area. No court can or should give him directions on such a matter.

Apart from this, there is the doctrine of constabulary independence, see *Fisher v Oldham Corporation* (1930), which regards the constable as an independent office holder under the Crown who cannot be instructed by organisational superiors or by governmental agency about how to exercise his or her powers. The constable is accountable only to law.

An interesting instance of the courts being used to attack a use of police discretion is *R v Coxhead* (1986). The appellant was a police sergeant in charge of a police station. A young man was brought into the station to be breathalysed and the sergeant recognised him as the son of a police inspector at that station. The sergeant knew the inspector to be suffering from a bad heart condition. In order not to exacerbate this condition, the sergeant did not administer the test and allowed the motorist to go free. The sergeant was prosecuted and convicted for conduct tending and intended to pervert the course of justice. The sergeant's defence was that his decision came within the legitimate scope of discretion exercised by a police officer. The trial judge said the matter should be left for the jury to determine; they must decide the extent of any police discretion in accordance with the facts. The jury convicted the sergeant and this was upheld by the Court of Appeal. In minor cases, the police had a very wide discretion whether to prosecute but in major cases they had no discretion or virtually none. Thus, in a serious case like drink driving, there was no discretion which the sergeant could have been exercising legitimately. It is odd, however, that this is left for the jury to decide after the event rather than be subject to clear rules.

It is a matter of contention how far the changes proposed in the Sheehy Report on the Police (Cmnd 2280, 1993) will entail constitutional changes to the accountability of the police. Reiner has argued ('Responsibilities and reforms' (1993) 143 NLJ 1096) of the proposed change that:

It will devolve responsibility downwards to local police commanders, but power will be concentrated more than ever in the hands of central government. Central government will 'set the key objectives which it expects the police to secure'.

14.1.6 State prosecutors in the Crown Courts

Much concern has been expressed about the government's plans to allow Crown Prosecution Service lawyers to conduct prosecutions in the Crown Courts (see 'Modernising justice' (1999) 26 SLR 31). The basis of the worry is that, as full time salaried lawyers working for an organisation, CPS lawyers will sometimes be tempted to get convictions using dubious tactics or ethics because their own status as employees and prospects of promotion will depend on conviction success rates. Where, as now, barristers from the independent Bar are used by the CPS to prosecute, there is (it is argued) a greater likelihood of the courtroom lawyer dropping a morally unsustainable case.

Section 42 of the Access to Justice Act 1999 tries to overcome the possible difficulties with a provision (amending s 27 of the Courts and Legal Services Act 1990) that every advocate 'has a duty to the court to act with independence in the interests of justice', in other words, a duty which overrides any inconsistent duty, for example, one to an employer. Professor Michael Zander QC has contended, however, that these are 'mere words'. He has said (letter to *The Times*, 29 December 1998) they are unlikely to exercise much sway over CPS lawyer employees concerned with performance targets set by their line managers, and that:

> The CPS as an organisation is constantly under pressure in regard to the proportion of discontinuances, acquittal and conviction rates. These are factors in the day to day work of any CPS lawyer. It is disingenuous to imagine they will not have a powerful effect on decision making.

The Bar is also very wary of this change, an editorial in *Counsel* (the journal of the Bar of England and Wales) says:

> ... we are gravely concerned about the extent to which prosecutions will be done in-house by the CPS when the need for independent prosecutors is so well established in our democracy [(1999) *Counsel*, February, p 3].

Whichever point of view you have on this, it is important when writing on the subject to set the argument in a wider context. What are the social, economic or political debates surrounding this issue of how best to run a system of courtroom prosecutors? The change to having Crown Court prosecutions carried out by salaried CPS lawyers will be more *efficient* (as the whole prosecution can be handled in-house without engaging the external service of an independent barrister), and will, ultimately, cost the State less than is currently spent on prosecutions. Some will argue that justice is being sacrificed to the deity of cost cutting. On the other hand, you could argue that justice and efficiency are not mutually exclusive phenomena.

14.2 Bail

Bail is the release from custody, pending a criminal trial, of an accused on the promise that money will be paid if he absconds. All decisions on whether to grant bail therefore involve delicate questions of balancing interests. A person is presumed innocent of a criminal charge unless he or she is proved guilty of it; this implies that no one should ever be detained unless he or she has been found guilty. For several reasons, however, it can be regarded as undesirable to allow some accused people to go back to society before the case against them is tried in a criminal court.

To refuse bail to an accused might involve depriving liberty to someone who is subsequently found not guilty or convicted but given a non-custodial sentence. Such a person will probably have been kept in a police cell or in a prison cell for 23 hours per day. Unlike the jurisdictions in The Netherlands, Germany and France, no compensation is payable in these circumstances. On the other hand, to allow liberty to the accused pending trial might be to allow him or her to abscond, commit further offences, interfere with witnesses and obstruct the course of justice. The difficulties involved in finding the proper balance have recently been highlighted by several recent cases of serious assault and rape being committed by persons who were on bail and the fleeing of Asil Nadir to Northern Cyprus in May 1993. Mr Nadir skipped his £3.5 million bail to travel to a jurisdiction which would not extradite him to England. He claimed that he would not be given a fair trial for the offences of theft and false accounting with which he was charged and went on the public record as saying that his sureties would not suffer hardship as he would repay those who had put up bail for him.

The basic way in which the law currently seeks to find the right balance in such matters is by operating a general presumption in favour of bail, a presumption which can be overturned if one or more of a number of indices of suspicion exist in respect of a particular defendant. Even where bail is granted, it may be subject to certain conditions to promote public safety and the interests of justice.

14.2.1 The Criminal Justice and Public Order Act 1994

Over recent years, the government took the view that bail was too easily granted and that too many crimes were being committed by those on bail who deserved to be in custody while awaiting trial. The Bail (Amendment) Act 1993 and the CJPOA 1994 (ss 25–30) emanate from that philosophy, their aim being to restrict the granting of bail. A case which caught public sympathy for this view involved a young man who had many convictions for car crime and joyriding. Whilst on bail, he was joyriding in a vehicle when he smashed into a schoolgirl. She clung to the bonnet but he shook her off and thus killed her. The Home Secretary commented publicly that the new legislative measures would prevent such terrible events.

Each year (prior to the Acts), about 50,000 offences are committed by people on bail. A study by the Metropolitan police in 1988 indicated that 16% of those charged by that force were already on bail for another offence. Another study, in 1993, from the same force, showed that of 537 suspects arrested in one week during a clamp-down on burglary, 40% were on bail. Some had been bailed 10 or 15 times during the preceding year. (Figures from Robert Maclennan MP, HC Committee Col 295, 1994.)

In the criminal process, the first stage at which bail is raised as an issue is at the police station. If a person is arrested on a warrant, this will indicate whether he or she is to be held in custody or released on bail. If the suspect is arrested without a warrant, then the police will have to decide whether to release the suspect after he or she has been charged. After a person has been charged, s 38(1)(a) of the Police and Criminal Evidence Act (PACE) 1984 states that a person must be released unless: (a) his name and address are not known; or (b) the custody officer reasonably thinks that his detention is necessary for his own protection; or (c) to prevent him from injuring someone or damaging property or because he might abscond or interfere with the course of justice. Most arrested people are bailed by the police. In 1990, 83% of those arrested in connection with indictable offences and 88% of those arrested for summary offences (other than motoring offences) were released. This area has been amended by s 28 of the CJPOA 1994. A custody officer can now, in the case of an imprisonable offence, refuse to release an arrested person after charge if the officer has reasonable grounds for believing that the detention of that person is necessary to prevent him from committing any offence. Previously, many cases were caught by (b) (above) but some likely conduct, for example, drink driving, was not.

Section 27 of the CJPOA 1994 amends the PACE 1984 (ss 38, 47) so as to allow the police to grant conditional bail to persons charged. The conditions can be whatever is required to ensure that the person surrenders to custody, does not commit an offence while on bail, or does not interfere with witnesses or otherwise obstruct the course of justice. The new powers of the custody officer, however, do not include a power to impose a requirement to reside in a bail hostel. By amending Pt IV of PACE 1984, s 29 of the CJPOA 1994 gives the police power to arrest without warrant a person who, having been granted conditional police bail, has failed to attend at a police station at the appointed time.

The Bail Act (BA) 1976 created a statutory presumption of bail. It states (s 4) that, subject to Sched 1, bail *shall* be granted to a person accused of an offence in a magistrates' court or a Crown Court and convicted people who are being remanded for reports to be made. The court must therefore grant bail (unless one of the exceptions apply) even if the defendant does not make an application. Schedule 1 provides that a court need not grant bail to a person charged with an offence punishable with imprisonment if it is satisfied that there are substantial grounds for believing that, if released on bail, the defendant would:

- fail to surrender to custody;

- commit an offence while on bail; or

- interfere with witnesses or otherwise obstruct the course of justice.

The court can also refuse bail if it believes that the defendant ought to stay in custody for his or her own protection or if it has not been practicable for want of time to obtain sufficient information to enable the court to make its decision on bail or he has previously failed to answer to bail (Pt 1, paras 2–6).

When the court is considering the grounds stated above, all relevant factors must be taken into account, including the nature and seriousness of the offence, the character, antecedents, associations and community ties of the defendant, and his record for satisfying his obligations under previous grants of bail.

If the defendant is charged with an offence not punishable with imprisonment, Sched 1 provides that bail may only be withheld if he or she has previously failed to surrender on bail and if the court believes that, in view of that failure, he or she will fail again to surrender if released on bail.

Section 25 of the CJPOA 1994 provides that in some circumstances a person who has been charged with or convicted of murder, attempted murder, manslaughter, rape or attempted rape must not be granted bail. The circumstances are simply that the conviction must have been within the UK, and that, in the case of a manslaughter conviction, it must have been dealt with by way of a custodial sentence. The word 'conviction' is given a wide meaning and includes anyone found 'not guilty by way of insanity'.

There was debate about whether the changes wrought by s 25 are justifiable. A Home Office Minister defending the section stated that it would be worth the risk if it prevented just one murder or rape even though there might be a few 'hard cases', that is, people eventually acquitted of crime, who were remanded in custody pending trial. (David Maclean MP, Minister of State, Home Office, HC Committee Col 282, 1994.) As Card and Ward have remarked in a commentary on the CJPOA 1994, the government when pushed was unable to cite a single case where a person released on bail in the circumstances covered by s 25 re-offended in a similar way. There is no time limit on the previous conviction and there is no requirement of any connection between the previous offence and the one in question. Card and Ward suggest that there is a world of difference between a person who was convicted of manslaughter 30 years ago on the grounds of complicity in a suicide pact and who is now charged with attempted rape (of which he must be presumed innocent), and the person who was convicted of rape eight years ago and now faces another rape charge. The first person is not an obvious risk to society and it is, they argue, regrettable that bail will be denied to him. There is also argument to be had with the contents of the s 25 list. Why should some clearly dangerous and prevalent crimes like robbery be omitted from it? In any case, it may have been better had the offences in the list raised a strong presumption against bail as opposed to an absolute ban, as the former could be rebutted in cases where there was on the facts no risk.

Parliament has now made a concession on s 25. By s 56 of the Crime and Disorder Act 1998, s 25 of the 1994 Act is amended. Now, bail can be granted to people with convictions for rape or murder, but only if the court or constable considering the grant of bail 'is satisfied that there are exceptional circumstances which justify it'.

Bail can be granted as conditional or unconditional. Where it is unconditional, the accused must simply surrender to the court at the appointed date. Failure to appear without reasonable cause is an offence under the BA 1976 (s 6) and can result, if tried in a Crown Court, in a sentence of up to 12 months' imprisonment or a fine. Conditions can be attached to the granting of bail where the court thinks that it is necessary to ensure that the accused surrenders at the right time, does not interfere with witnesses or commit further offences. There is no statutory limit to the conditions the court may impose and the most common include requirements that the accused reports daily or weekly to a police station, resides at a particular address, surrenders his or her passport or does not go to particular places or associate with particular people.

Section 7 of the BA 1976 gives the police power to arrest anyone on conditional bail whom they reasonably suspect is likely to break the conditions or that he has already done so. Anyone arrested in these circumstances must be brought before a magistrate within 24 hours. The magistrate may then reconsider the question of bail.

Personal recognisances by which the suspect agreed to pay a sum if he failed to surrender to the court were abolished by the BA 1976 (s 3(2)) except in cases where it is believed that he or she might try to flee abroad. The Act did retain the court's right to ask for sureties as a condition of bail. By putting sureties in a position where they can have large sums of money 'estreated' if the suspect does not surrender to the court, a significant pressure (not using the resources of the criminal justice system) is put on the accused. The proportion of those who do not answer to bail is very small – consistently about 4% of those given bail. Section 9 of the BA 1976 strengthens the surety principle by making it a criminal offence to agree to indemnify a surety. This sort of thing could happen, for example, if the accused agreed to reimburse the surety in the event that the accused skipped bail and the surety was requested to pay.

The Crime and Disorder Act 1998 makes further changes to the law relating to bail. Section 54 provides for increased powers to require security or impose conditions (by taking away the requirement that the defendant must appear unlikely to remain in Great Britain). The 1998 Act also allows courts to be able to require defendants to attend interview with a legal representative as a condition of bail.

14.2.2 Appeals and reapplications

The rules which govern how someone who has been refused bail might re-apply and appeal have also been framed with a view to balancing the interests of the accused with those of the public and justice. The original refusal should not be absolute and final but, on the other hand, it is seen as necessary that the refusals are not reversed too easily.

If the court decides not to grant the defendant bail, then s 154 of the Criminal Justice Act (CJA) 1988 provides that it is the court's duty to consider whether the defendant ought to be granted bail at each subsequent hearing. At the first hearing after the one at which bail was first refused, he or she may support an application for bail with any arguments but at subsequent hearings the court need not hear arguments as to fact or law which it has heard before. The CJA 1982 enables a court to remand an accused in his or her absence for up to three successive one week remand hearings provided that he or she consents and is legally represented. Such repeated visits are costly to the State and can be unsettling for the accused, especially if he or she has to spend most of the day in a police cell only to be told the case has been adjourned again without bail. If someone does not consent, they are prevented from applying for bail on each successive visit if the only supporting arguments are those that have been heard by the court before (*R v Nottingham Justices ex p Davies* (1980)).

To avoid unproductive hearings, that is, to promote courts being able to adjourn a case for a period within which reasonable progress can be made on a case, s 155 of the CJA 1988 allows for adjournments for up to 28 days provided the court sets the date for when the next stage of the proceedings should take place. What began as an experiment under this section has now by statutory order (SI 1991/2667) been extended to all courts.

The interests of the accused are also served by the variety of appeals he or she may make if bail has been refused. If bail has been refused by magistrates, then, in limited circumstances, an application may be made to another bench of magistrates. Applications for reconsideration can also be made to a judge in chambers (through a legal representative) or to the Official Solicitor (in writing). Appeal can also be made to a Crown Court in respect of bail for both pre-committal remands and where a defendant has been committed for trial or sentence at the Crown Court.

Section 3 of the BA 1976 allows for an application to vary the conditions of court bail to be made by the person bailed, or the prosecutor or a police officer.

Application may also be made for the imposition of conditions on unconditional court bail. As amended by the CJPOA 1994, s 3 of the BA 1976 now allows for the same thing in relation to police bail, although the new provisions do not allow the prosecutor to seek reconsideration of the decision to grant bail itself. Under the Bail (Amendment) Act 1993, however, the prosecution does now have a right to appeal against the grant of bail by a court. This right applies to offences which carry a maximum sentence of imprisonment of five years or more, and to offences of taking a vehicle without consent (joyriding). When this right of appeal is exercised, the defendant will remain in custody until the appeal is heard by a crown court judge who will decide whether to grant bail or remand the defendant in custody within 48 hours of the magistrate's decision. Parliament was concerned that this power could be abused and has stated that it should be reserved 'for cases of greatest concern, when there is a serious risk of harm to the public' or where there are 'other significant public interest grounds' for an appeal.

Section 67(1) of the CJA 1967 states that time spent in custody pre-trial or pre-sentence can generally be deducted from the ultimate sentence. No compensation, however, is paid to people who have been remanded in custody but are subsequently found not guilty. Several European countries like France and Germany will sometimes offer compensation in similar circumstances.

Although this area of law was subject to a comprehensive revision after a Home Office special working party reported in 1974, and has been legislatively debated and modified twice since the BA 1976, it is still a matter of serious concern both by those civil libertarians who consider the law too tilted against the accused and by the police and commentators who believe it too lenient in many respects. This criticism of the law from both sides to the debate might indicate a desirable state of balance reached by the current regulatory framework.

Opposition to the current arrangements – civil libertarian perspective

It is a cause for concern that, in the 1990s, of those dealt with summarily after being remanded in custody, about 50% received non-custodial sentences and a further 25% were acquitted.

There are wide variations in the local policies of different courts; one study has shown, for instance, that the number of indictable custodial remands per 1,000 indictable proceedings was 111 in Brighton as against 313 in Bournemouth (Gibson, B, 'Why Bournemouth?' (1987) 151 JP 520, 15 August).

The last decade has seen a disturbing rise in the remand prison population. In 1980, it accounted for 15% of the average prison population. By 1990, it had risen to over 10,000 prisoners, 22% of the average prison population.

Opposition to the current arrangements – a police/public perspective

There are arguments which point to the numbers of people who commit offences whilst out on bail. A study conducted in Bristol, for example, showed that over one-third of all defendants charged with burglary were on bail for another offence at the time of their arrest. Following some dreadful cases of serious offences being committed whilst the perpetrator was on bail, s 153 of the CJA 1988 required magistrates to give reasons if they decided to grant bail against police objections in cases of murder, manslaughter or rape.

The percentage of people who skip bail is too high, especially for the more minor offences. *Note*: the annual figure, however, of those who do not answer to bail is consistently under 4%.

Positive developments in recent years have been the use of Bail Information Schemes (BIS) for courts (about 100 courts now operate such schemes) and government concern to increase the number of bail hostels. The BIS resulted from pilot schemes organised by the Vera Institute of Justice of New York. They give courts verified information from the probation service about defendants' accommodation or community ties. The evidence suggests that the courts using such schemes make greater use of bail than those which do not have the schemes.

14.3   Plea bargaining

'Plea bargaining' has been defined as 'the practice whereby the accused enters a plea of guilty in return for which he will be given some consideration that results in a sentence concession' (Baldwin and McConville, *Negotiated Justice: Pressures on Defendants to Plead Guilty*, 1977). In practice, this can refer to:

- a situation either where there has been a plea arrangement for the accused to plead guilty to a lesser charge than the one with which he or she is charged (for example, charged with murder, agrees to plead guilty to manslaughter). This is sometimes called 'charge bargaining'; or

- where there is simply a sentencing discount available on a plea of guilty by the accused. This is sometimes called a 'sentence bargain'.

14.3.1   *R v Turner* (1970)

A plea of guilty by the accused must be made freely. The accused must only be advised to plead guilty if he or she has committed the crime in question. In Turner (1970), Lord Parker CJ set out guidelines on plea bargaining. He stated that: (1) it may sometimes be the duty of counsel to give strong advice to the accused that a plea of guilty with remorse is a mitigating factor which might enable the court to give a lesser sentence; (2) the accused must ultimately make up his or her own mind as to how to plead; (3) there should be open access to the trial judge and counsel for both sides should attend each meeting, preferably in open court; and (4) the judge should never indicate the sentence which he is minded to impose, nor should he ever indicate that on a plea of guilty he would impose one sentence but that on a conviction following a plea of not guilty he would impose a severer sentence. The judge could say what sentence he would impose on a plea of guilty (where, for example, he has read the depositions and antecedents) but without mentioning what he would do if the accused were convicted after pleading not guilty. Even this would be wrong, however, as the accused might take the judge to be intimating that a severer sentence would follow upon conviction after a guilty plea. The only exception to this rule is where a judge says that the sentence will take a particular form, following conviction, whether there has been a plea of guilty or not guilty.

14.3.2 Court of Appeal *Practice Direction*

The above guidelines were subsequently embodied in a Court of Appeal *Practice Direction* (1976). A number of difficulties have been experienced in applying them however. Perhaps the greatest problem has resulted from the fact that, although the principles state (No 4) that a judge should never say that a sentence passed after a conviction would be more severe than one passed after a guilty plea, it is a generally known rule that guilty pleas lead to lesser sentences. In *R v Cain* (1976), it was stressed that, in general, defendants should realise that guilty pleas attract lesser sentences. Lord Widgery said: 'Any accused person who does not know about it should know about it.' The difficulty is that the trial judge must not mention it, otherwise he or she could be construed as exerting pressure on the accused to plead guilty.

In *R v Turner*, the defendant pleaded not guilty on a charge of theft. He had previous convictions and during an adjournment he was advised by counsel in strong terms to change his plea; after having spoken with the judge, which the defendant knew, counsel advised that in his opinion a plea of guilty would result in a non-custodial sentence, whereas, if he persisted with a not guilty plea and thereby attacked police witnesses, there was a real possibility of receiving a custodial sentence. The defendant changed his plea to guilty and then appealed on the ground that he did not have a free choice in changing his plea. His appeal was allowed on the basis that he might have formed the impression that the views being expressed to him by his counsel were those of the judge, particularly as it was known by the accused that counsel had just returned from seeing the judge when he gave his advice to the accused.

The advantages for the prosecution in gaining a guilty plea are obvious but, as the Code for Crown Prosecutors notes, 'Administrative convenience in the form of a rapid guilty plea should not take precedence over the interests of justice' (1992–93 para 11). Justice demands that the court should be able to pass a proper sentence consistent with the gravity of the accused's actions and if a plea is accepted then the defendant can only be sentenced on the basis of the crime that he or she has admitted. It is noteworthy that the judge is not bound to accept a plea arrangement made between the sides. The Farquharson Committee on the Role of Prosecuting Counsel thought that there is a general right for the prosecution to offer no evidence in respect of any particular charge but that where the judge's opinion is sought on whether it is desirable to reassure the public at large that the right course is being taken, counsel must abide by the judge's decision. Where the judge thinks that counsel's view to proceed is wrong, the trial can be halted until the DPP has been consulted and given the judge's comments. In the notorious case of *R v Sutcliffe* (1981), the 'Yorkshire Ripper' case, the prosecution and defence had agreed that Sutcliffe would plead guilty to manslaughter on the grounds of diminished responsibility but the trial judge rejected that agreement and, after consultations with the DPP, Sutcliffe was eventually found guilty of murder.

14.3.3 *R v Pitman* (1991)

The extent of the difficulties in framing rules on plea bargaining which achieve clarity and fairness can be judged by the remark of Lord Lane CJ in the case of *R v Pitman* (1991):

> There seems to be a steady flow of appeals to this court arising from visits by counsel to the judge in his private room. No amount of criticism and no amount of warnings and no amount of exhortation seems to be able to prevent this from happening.

In this case, on counsel's advice, the appellant pleaded not guilty to causing death by reckless driving. On Cup Final Day in 1989, he had driven, having been drinking all afternoon, in a car without a rear view mirror. He had crashed into another car, killing one of its passengers, whilst having double the permitted level of alcohol in his blood.

During the trial, the judge called both counsel to his room and stated that he did not think there was a defence to the charge. Counsel for the appellant explained that although the appellant had admitted that his carelessness caused the accident the advice to plead not guilty was based on the fact that the prosecution might not be able to prove the necessary recklessness. The trial judge replied that the appellant's plea was a matter for the appellant himself and not counsel and that if the appellant accepted responsibility for the accident he ought to plead guilty and if he did so he would receive 'substantial credit' when it came to sentencing.

Counsel for the appellant then discussed this with the appellant who changed his plea to guilty and was sentenced to nine months imprisonment and was disqualified from driving for four years. His appeal was allowed as the judge had put undue pressure on the appellant and his counsel to change his plea to guilty as the remarks suggested that his chances of acquittal were slight if he pleaded not guilty and that if he was found guilty he would certainly be sentenced to imprisonment. Lord Lane CJ emphasised that a judge should not initiate discussions in private and that where, at the behest of counsel, they are absolutely necessary, they should be recorded by shorthand or on a recording device.

Another problem here concerns making the guidelines sufficiently permissive to allow counsel access to the judge in his private room in deserving cases, while avoiding the problems of confidentiality. As Mustill LJ said in *R v Harper-Taylor and Barker* (1988): 'The need to solve an immediate practical problem may combine with the more relaxed atmosphere of the private room to blur the formal outlines of the trial.' There is a risk that counsel and solicitors may hear something said to the judge which they would rather not hear, putting them into a state of conflict between their duties to their clients and their obligations to maintain the confidentiality of the private room. Reviewing the current state of the law, Curran has written that the effect of cases like *R v Bird* (1977) and *R v Agar* (1990) (the latter not a plea bargaining case but one which hinged on a judge's ruling in his private room as complied with by counsel to the appellant's detriment) is that defence counsel has a duty to disclose to his client any observations made by the judge in his room which significantly affect the client's case, whether or not the judge expresses them to be made confidentially.

The difficulties in this area of law stem, largely, not from deficient rules but rather from the wish that the rules should achieve diverse aims. As Zander has observed, the fundamental problem is that the Court of Appeal wants to have it both ways: 'On the one hand, it wants defendants to appreciate that, if they plead guilty, they will receive a lesser sentence. On the other hand, it does not want judges to provide defendants with solid information as to how great the discount will be.'

14.3.4 Royal Commission recommendations

A more open system of plea bargaining was advocated by the Runciman Royal Commission on Criminal Justice (para 156). The report argues that this would do much to alleviate the problem of 'cracked trials' in which defendants do not plead guilty until the last moment, wasting the time of witnesses, the police, the CPS and the court. In a system where the vast majority of cases in the Crown Court and magistrates' courts result in guilty pleas (79% and 81.5%, respectively), the operation of the plea bargain becomes very important.

The Commission research indicated that 'cracked trials' accounted for more than one-quarter of all cases. The Commission also noted that sentence discounts of between 25% and 30% for guilty pleas have been long established practice in the Crown Court. The Commission suggested that higher discounts should be available for those who plead guilty earlier in the process. The report states:

> The most common reason for defendants delaying a plea of guilty until the last minute is a reluctance to face the facts until they are at the door of the court. It is often said too that a defendant has a considerable incentive to behave in this way. The longer the delay, the more the likelihood of witnesses becoming intimidated or forgetting to turn up or disappearing.

It recommends (para 157):

> At the request of defence counsel on instructions from the defendant, judges should be able to indicate the highest sentence that they would impose at that point on the basis of the facts as put to them.

On the issue of charges, it recommends (para 161):

> Discussions on the level of charge (charge bargaining) should take place as early as possible in order to minimise the need for cases to be listed as contested trials.

Requests made to the judge could be made at a preparatory hearing, at a hearing called specially for the purpose, or at the trial itself. The Report denies that such a system is at all near the American scheme which is widely regarded as promoting injustice as it acts as a wholesale plea bargaining system in which the prosecution can suggest the appropriate sentence. Lord Runciman states that: 'We agree that to face defendants with a choice between what they might get on an immediate plea of guilty and what they might get if found guilty by the jury does amount to unacceptable pressure.'

Research conducted by Professor Zander for the Royal Commission on Criminal Justice (Zander and Henderson, *The Crown Court Study*, Royal Commission on Criminal Justice Study 19, 1993, p 145) found that, in a study of 900 Crown Court cases, 90% of barristers and two-thirds of judges were in favour of formalising plea bargaining based on sentence discounts. The study suggests that 11% of those who pleaded guilty in fact maintained their innocence but wanted to secure a reduction in sentence.

The Court of Appeal has consistently indicated that the information should not be given to defendants because that might put undue pressure on them to plead guilty, but sentence discounts are legally recognised: in Thomas (ed), *Current Sentencing Practice*, para A8 2(b) says: '... a guilty plea attracts a lighter sentence, the extent of the reduction is usually between one-quarter and one-third of what would have otherwise been the sentence.' Moreover, Lord Widgery has stated (see 14.3.2) that defendants should know about them. The pressure could scarcely be increased by informing a defendant with details rather than leave it to his or her general knowledge. If anything, Zander has argued, it would diminish the pressure by making it clear that the defendant's fears about the penalty for pleading not guilty are exaggerated.

In a detailed research report on this issue, the reform group JUSTICE has cast serious doubt on many aspects of the system which could soon be adopted if the Runciman Royal Commission proposals are enacted. In *Negotiated Justice: A Closer Look at the Implications of Plea Bargaining* (1993), it is argued that, although favoured in some form by 90% of barristers and 60% of judges, plea bargaining can not only lead to unjust convictions but also inaccurate and unfair sentences. The latter occur because when the trial judge is making an offer of a reduced penalty, the defendant is still at that stage formally protesting his innocence so it is extremely difficult for his lawyer to present a plea in mitigation of sentence.

The reform body JUSTICE argues that the earlier withdrawal of weak prosecution cases; better liaison between defence and prosecution; and earlier contact between defendant and barrister would result in greater efficiency and fairness.

There is, though, reason for anxiety with such a call for more openness. Sanders and Young ((1994) 144 NLJ 1200) regard it as 'an idealistic notion' that one can improve the effectiveness of the system in convicting the guilty without also increasing its effectiveness in convicting the innocent. They say that one simply has to make a 'value choice' about the weight to be given to protecting the innocent relative to other important values such as repressing crime, and economy in the use of scarce resources. In one Home Office Study (*Magistrates' Court or Crown Court? Mode of Trial Decisions and Sentencing*, Home Office Study No 125, 1992), Hedderman and Moxon found that 65% of those pleading guilty in Crown Court cases said that their decision had been influenced by the prospect of receiving a discount in sentence, and nearly one-third claim to have pleaded guilty as a direct result of a charge bargain. Even the Royal Commission recognised that not all those pleading guilty are, in fact, guilty; some may have just capitulated to the pressure of taking the reduced sentence rather than run the risk of the full sentence. As Sanders and Young contend, this issue goes to the heart of constitutional principles. Only if the State acts properly in collecting and presenting evidence can punishment be justified according to commonly accepted principles. Even the guilty are entitled to due process of law. A system of plea bargaining may undermine such principles as it allows the state to secure convictions based on unproven allegations.

14.4 The jury

It is generally accepted that the jury of '12 good men and true' lies at the heart of the British legal system. The implicit assumption is that the presence of 12 ordinary lay persons, randomly introduced into the trial procedure to be the arbiters of the facts of the case, strengthens the legitimacy of the legal system. It supposedly achieves this end by introducing a democratic humanising element into the abstract impersonal trial process, thereby reducing the exclusive power of the legal professionals who would otherwise command the legal stage and control the legal procedure without reference to the opinion of the lay majority.

According to EP Thompson:

> The English common law rests upon a bargain between the law and the people. The jury box is where the people come into the court; the judge watches them and the jury watches back. A jury is the place where the bargain is struck. A jury attends in judgement not only upon the accused but also upon the justice and humanity of the law [*Writing by Candlelight*].

Few people have taken this traditional view to task but, in a thought-provoking article in the *Criminal Law Review* ([1991] Crim LR 740), Penny Darbyshire did just that. In her view, the jury system has attracted the most praise and the least theoretical analysis of any component of the criminal justice system. As she correctly pointed out, and as will be shown below, juries are far from being either a random or a representative section of the general population. In fact, Darbyshire goes so far as to characterise the jury as 'an anti-democratic, irrational and haphazard legislator, whose erratic and secret decisions run counter to the rule of law'. She concedes that while the 20th century lay justices are not representative of the community as a whole, neither is the jury. She points out that jury equity, by which is meant the way in which the jury ignores the law in pursuit of justice, is a double-edged sword which may also convict the innocent; and counters examples such as the *Clive Ponting* case with the series of miscarriages of justice relating to suspected terrorists in which juries were also involved.

Darbyshire is certainly correct in taking to task those who would simply endorse the jury system in an unthinking, purely emotional, manner. With equal justification, she criticises those academic writers who focus attention on the *mystery* of the jury to the exclusion of the hard reality of the magistrates court. It is arguable, however, that she goes to the other extreme. Underlying her analysis and conclusions is the idea that 'the jury trial is primarily ideological' and that 'its symbolic significance is magnified beyond its practical significance by the media, as well as academics, thus unwittingly misleading the public'. Whilst one might not wish to contradict the suggestion that the jury system operates as a very powerful ideological symbol, supposedly grounding the criminal legal system within a framework of participative democracy and justifying it on that basis, it is simply inadequate to reject the practical operation of the procedure on that basis alone. Ideologies do not exist purely in the realm of ideas, they have real concrete manifestations and effects; and, in relation to the jury system, those manifestations operate in a such a way as to offer at least a vestige of protection to defendants. In regard to the comparison between juries and the summary procedure of the magistrates' courts, Darbyshire puts two related questions. First, she asks whether the jury system is more likely to do justice and get the verdict right than the magistrates' courts;

then, she goes on to ask why the majority of defendants are processed through the magistrates' courts. These questions are highly pertinent; it is doubtful, however, whether her response to them is as equally pertinent. Her answers would likely be that the jury does not perform any better than the magistrates and, therefore, it is immaterial that the magistrates deal with the bulk of cases. Her whole approach would seem to be concentrated on denigrating the performance of the jury system. A not untypical passage from her article admits that, in relation to the suspect terrorist miscarriages of justice, juries 'were not to blame for these wrongful convictions' but then goes on in the same sentence to accuse the juries of failing 'to remedy the lack of due process at the pre-trial stage', and thus blames them for not providing 'the brake on oppressive state activity claimed for the jury by its defenders'.

Although there is most certainly scope for less a romantic view of how the jury system actually operates in practice, Darbyshire's argument seems to be that the magistrates are not very good but then neither are the juries; and as they only operate in a small minority of cases anyway, the implication would seem to be that their loss would be no great disadvantage. Others, however, would maintain that the jury system does achieve concrete benefits in particular circumstances and would argue further that these benefits should not be readily given up. Amongst the latter is Michael Mansfield QC who, in an article in response to the Runciman Report, claimed that the jury 'is the most democratic element of our judicial system' and the one which 'poses the biggest threat to the authorities'.

(These questions will be considered further in relation to the Report of the Runciman Commission.)

Having defended the institution of the jury generally, it has to be recognised that there are particular instances which tend to bring the jury system into disrepute. For example, in October 1994, the Court of Appeal ordered the re-trial of a man convicted of double murder on the grounds that four of the jurors had attempted to contact the murder victims using a Ouija board in what was described as a 'drunken experiment'. A second convicted murderer appealed against his conviction on the grounds of irregularities in the manner in which the jury performed its functions. Amongst the allegations levelled at the jury is the claim that they clubbed together and spent £150 on drink when they were sent to a hotel after failing to reach a verdict. It is alleged that some of the jurors discussed the case against the express instructions of the judge and that on the following day the jury foreman had to be replaced because she was too hung-over to act. One female juror is alleged to have ended up in bed with another hotel guest.

Another example of the possible criticisms to be levelled against the misuse of juries occurred in Stoke on Trent, where the son of a court usher, and another six individuals, were found to have served on a number of criminal trial juries. Whilst one could praise the public spirited nature of this dedication to the justice process, especially given the difficulty in getting members of jury panels (see 14.6 and 14.7), it might be more appropriate to condemn the possibility of the emergence of a professional juror system connected to court officials. Certainly, the Court of Appeal was less than happy with the situation, and overturned a conviction, when the Stoke practice was revealed to it.

14.5 The role of the jury

It is generally accepted that the function of the jury is to decide on *matters of fact*, and that *matters of law* are the province of the judge. Such may be the ideal case, but most of the time the jury's decision is based on a consideration of a mixture of fact and law. The jury determines whether a person is guilty on the basis of their understanding of the law as explained to them by the judge.

The oath taken by each juror states that they 'will faithfully try the defendant and give a true verdict according to the evidence', and it is contempt of court for a juror, subsequent to being sworn in, to refuse to come to a decision. In 1997, Judge Anura Cooray, sentenced two women jurors to 30 days in prison for contempt of court for their failure to deliver a verdict. One of the women, who had been the jury foreman, claimed that the case, involving an allegation of fraud, had been too complicated to understand, and the other had claimed that she could not ethically judge anyone. Judge Cooray was quoted as justifying his decision to imprison them on the grounds that:

> I had to order a re-trial at very great expense. Jurors must recognise that they have a responsibility to fulfil their duties in accordance with their oath.

The women only spent one night in jail before the uproar caused by Cooray's action led to their release and the subsequent overturning of his sentence on them.

14.5.1 The jury's function in trials

Judges have the power to direct juries to acquit the accused where there is insufficient evidence to convict them, and this is the main safeguard against juries finding defendants guilty in spite of either the absence, or the insufficiency, of the evidence. There is, however, no corresponding judicial power to instruct juries to convict (*DPP v Stonehouse* (1978)). There is nothing to prevent the judge summing up in such a way as to make it evident to the jury that there is only one decision that can reasonably be made, and that it would be perverse to reach any other verdict but guilty.

What judges must not do is, overtly, put pressure on juries to reach guilty verdicts. Finding of any such pressure will result in the overturning of any conviction so obtained. The classic example of such a case is *R v McKenna* (1960) in which the judge told the jury, after they had spent all of two and a quarter hours deliberating on the issue, that, if they did not come up with a verdict in the following 10 minutes, they would be locked up for the night. Not surprisingly, the jury returned a verdict; unfortunately for the defendant, it was a guilty verdict; even more unfortunately for the judicial process, the conviction had to be quashed on appeal, for clear interference with the jury.

In the words of Cassels J:

> It is a cardinal principle of our criminal law that in considering their verdict, concerning, as it does, the liberty of the subject, a jury shall deliberate in complete freedom, uninfluenced by any promise, unintimidated by any threat. They stand between the Crown and the subject, and they are still one of the main defences of personal liberty. To say to such a tribunal in the course of its deliberations that it must reach a conclusion ... is a disservice to the cause of justice ... [*R v McKenna* (1960)].

Judges do have the right, and indeed the duty, to advise the jury as to the proper understanding and application of the law that they are considering. Even when the jury is considering its verdict, they may seek the advice of the judge. The essential point, however, is that any such response on the part of the judge must be given in open court, so as to obviate any allegation of misconduct (*R v Townsend* (1982)).

In criminal cases, even perversity of decision does not provide grounds for appeal against acquittal. There have been occasions where juries have been subjected to the invective of a judge when they have delivered a verdict with which he disagreed. Nonetheless, the fact is that juries collectively, and individual jurors, do not have to justify, explain, or even give reasons for their decisions. Indeed, under s 8 of the Contempt of Court Act 1981, it would be a contempt of court to try to elicit such information from a jury member in either a criminal or a civil law case. (See below for the Runciman Commission's proposal to amend s 8.)

These factors place the jury in a very strong position to take decisions that are 'unjustifiable' in accordance with the law, for the simple reason that they do not have to justify the decisions. Thus, juries have been able to deliver what can only be described as perverse decisions. In *R v Clive Ponting* (1985), the judge made clear beyond doubt that the defendant was guilty, under the Official Secrets Act 1911, of the offence with which he was charged: the jury still returned a not-guilty verdict. Similarly, in the case of *Pat Pottle and Michael Randall* (1991), who had openly admitted their part in the escape of the spy George Blake, the jury reached a not guilty verdict in open defiance of the law.

In *R v Kronlid* (1996), three protestors were charged with committing criminal damage, and another was charged with conspiracy to cause criminal damage, in relation to an attack on Hawk Jet aeroplanes that were about to be sent to Indonesia. The damage to the planes allegedly amounted to £1.5

million, and they did not deny their responsibility for it. They rested their defence on the fact that the planes were to be delivered to the Indonesian State, to be used in its allegedly genocidal campaign against the people of East Timor. On those grounds, they claimed that they were, in fact, acting to prevent the crime of genocide. The prosecution cited assurances, given by the Indonesian government, that the planes would not be used against the East Timorese, and pointed out that the UK government had granted an export licence for the planes. As the protestors did not deny what they had done, it was apparently a mere matter of course that they would be convicted as charged. The jury, however, decided that all four of the accused were innocent of the charges laid against them. A government Treasury Minister, Michael Jack, subsequently stated his disbelief at the verdict of the jury. As he stated:

> I, and I am sure many others, find this jury's decision difficult to understand. It would appear there is little question about who did this damage. For whatever reason that damage was done, it was just plain wrong [(1996) *The Independent*, 1 August].

It is perhaps just such a lack of understanding, together with the desire to save money on the operation of the legal system, that has motivated the government's expressed wish to replace jury trials in relation to either way offences (see 14.8.6).

A non-political example of this type of case can be seen in the jury's refusal to find Stephen Owen guilty of any offence after he had discharged a shotgun at the driver of a lorry that had killed his child. The tendency of the jury occasionally to ignore legal formality in favour of substantive justice is one of the major points in favour of its retention, according to its proponents.

14.5.2 Appeals from decisions of the jury

In criminal law, it is an absolute rule that there can be no appeal against a jury's decision to acquit a person of the charges laid against him.

Although there is no appeal as such against acquittal, there does exist the possibility of the Attorney General referring the case to the Court of Appeal to seek its advice on points of law raised in criminal cases in which the defendant has been acquitted. This procedure was provided for under s 36 of the CJA 1972 although it is not commonly resorted to. It must be stressed that there is no possibility of the actual case being reheard or the acquittal decision being reversed, but the procedure can highlight mistakes in law made in the course of Crown Court trial and permits the Court of Appeal to remedy the defect for the future. (See *Attorney General's Reference (No 1 of 1988)* (1988) for an example of this procedure in the area of insider dealing in relation to shares on the Stock Exchange. This case is also interesting in relation to statutory interpretation.)

In civil law cases, the possibility of the jury's verdict being overturned on appeal does exist, but only in circumstances where the original verdict was perverse, that is, no reasonable jury properly directed could have made such a decision.

14.5.3 Majority verdicts

The possibility of a jury deciding a case on the basis of a majority decision was introduced by the CJA 1967. Prior to this, the requirement was that jury decisions had to be unanimous. Such decisions are acceptable where there are:

- not less than 11 jurors and 10 of them agree; or

- there are 10 jurors and nine of them agree.

Where a jury has reached a guilty verdict on the basis of a majority decision, s 17(3) of the Juries Act (JA) 1974 requires the foreman of the jury to state in open court the number of jurors who agreed and the number who disagreed with the verdict. See *R v Barry* (1975), where failure to declare the details of the voting split resulted in the conviction of the defendant being overturned. In *R v Pigg* (1983), the House of Lords held that it was unnecessary to state the number who voted against where the foreman stated the number in favour of the verdict and thus the determination of the minority was a matter of simple arithmetic. There is no such requirement in respect of a not guilty verdict.

14.5.4 Discharge of jurors or the jury

The trial judge may discharge the whole jury if certain irregularities occur. These would include the situation where the defendant's previous convictions are revealed inadvertently during the trial. Such a disclosure would be prejudicial to the defendant. In such a case, the trial would be ordered to commence again with a different jury. Individual jurors may be discharged by the judge if they are incapable of continuing to act through illness 'or for any other reason' (s 16(1) of the JA 1974). Where this happens the jury must not fall below nine members.

14.6 The selection of the jury

In theory, jury service is a public duty that citizens should readily undertake. In practice, it is made compulsory, and failure to perform one's civic responsibility is subject to the sanction of a £1,000 fine.

14.6.1 Liability to serve

The JA 1974, as amended by the CJA 1988, sets out the law relating to juries. Prior to the JA, there was a property qualification in respect to jury service which skewed jury membership towards middle class men. Now, the legislation provides that any person between the ages of 18 and 70 who is on the electoral register and who has lived in the UK for at least five years is qualified to serve as a juror.

The procedure for establishing a jury is a threefold process:

- an officer of the court summons a randomly selected number of qualified individuals from the electoral register;

- from that group, panels of potential jurors for various cases are drawn up;

- the actual jurors are then randomly selected by means of a ballot in open court.

As has been pointed out, however, even if the selection procedure were truly random, randomness does not equal representation. Random juries, by definition, could be: all male, all female, all white, all black, all Conservative or all members of the Raving Loony Party. Such is the nature of the random process; the question that arises from the process is whether such randomness is necessarily a good thing in itself, and whether the summoning officer should take steps to avoid the potential disadvantages that can result from random selection.

As regards the actual random nature of the selection process, a number of problems arise from the use of electoral registers to determine and locate jurors:

- electoral registers tend to be inaccurate. Generally, they mis-report the number of younger people who are in an area simply because younger people tend to move about more than older people and therefore tend not to appear on the electoral role of the place they currently live in;

- electoral registers tend to under-report the number of members of ethnic minorities in a community. The problem is that some members of the ethnic communities, for a variety of reasons, simply do not notify the authorities of their existence;

- the problem of non-registration mentioned above was compounded by the disappearance of a great many people from electoral registers in order to try to avoid payment of the former poll tax. It is a matter of some doubt whether such people have registered with the passing of that particular tax or whether they will simply cease to exist for the purpose of jury service. The Runciman Commission, not surprisingly, suggested that every endeavour should be made to ensure that electoral registers are accurate.

14.6.2 Exceptions, excusals and disqualifications

The general qualification for serving as a juror is subject to a number of exceptions.

A number of people are deemed to be *ineligible* to serve on juries on the basis of their employment or vocation. Amongst this category are judges; justices of the peace; members of the legal profession; police and probation officers; and members of the clergy or religious orders. The reason for excluding those involved in the administration of justice is understandable, but less so is the exclusion of clergy. The Runciman Report recommends that the clergy and members of religious orders should be eligible to serve on juries, but that members of such orders which have beliefs that are incompatible with jury service should be excused. The latter recommendation was introduced by s 42 of the CJA 1994.

In an endeavour to maintain the unquestioned probity of the jury system, certain categories of persons are *disqualified* from serving as jurors. Amongst these is anyone who has been sentenced to a term of imprisonment, or youth custody, of five years or more. In addition, anyone who, in the past 10 years, has served a sentence, or has had a suspended sentence imposed on them, or has had a community service order made against them, is also disqualified. Finally, with respect to people with criminal records, anyone who has been placed on probation within the previous five years is also disqualified. Those on bail in criminal proceedings are disqualified from serving as a juror in the Crown Court. (See the recommendations of the Runciman Commission, below.) The final category of people disqualified from serving as jurors are the mentally ill.

Certain people are *excused as of right* from serving as jurors on account of their jobs. Amongst these are members of the medical professions, members of Parliament and members of the armed forces. Others may be excused from current jury service on the basis of past service. There is additionally a *discretionary power* given to the court to release a person from jury service, or alternatively to defer their service to some time in the future, if they show grounds for such treatment. Grounds for such excusal or deferral are supposed to be made only on the basis of good reason but there is at least a measure of doubt as to the rigour with which such rules are applied.

Practice Note (Jury: Juror Excuse) (1988) stated that applications for excusal should be treated sympathetically and listed the following as good grounds for excusal:

(a) personal involvement in the case;

(b) close connection with a party or a witness in the case;

(c) personal hardship;

(d) conscientious objection to jury service.

14.6.3 Physical disability and jury service

It is to be hoped that the situation of people with disabilities has been altered for the better by the CJPOA 1994 which introduced a new section, 9B, into the JA 1974. Previously, it was all too common for judges to discharge jurors with disabilities, including deafness, on the assumption that they will not be capable of undertaking the duties of a juror. One notorious case occurred in January 1994 when Judge John Binns discharged a deaf woman from jury service in King's Lynn Crown Court even though there were interpreting facilities in the court.

Under the new provision, where it appears doubtful that a person summoned for jury service is capable of serving on account of some physical disability, that person, as previously, may be brought before the judge. The new s 9B, however, introduces a presumption that people should serve and provides that the judge must affirm the jury summons unless he or she is of the opinion that the person will not be able to act effectively. Whether such a presumption is sufficient to displace preconceptions remains to be seen.

14.6.4 Challenges to jury membership

That juries can be 'self-selecting' provides grounds for concern as to the random nature of the jury; but the traditional view of the jury is further, and perhaps even more fundamentally, undermined by the way in which both prosecution and defence seek to influence their constitution.

Under s 12(6) of the JA 1974, both prosecution and defence have a right to challenge the array where the summonsing officer has acted improperly in bringing the whole panel together. Such challenges are rare, although an unsuccessful action was raised in *R v Danvers* (1982) where the defendant tried to challenge the racial composition of the group of potential jurors.

14.6.5 Challenge by the defence

Until the CJA 1988, there were two ways in which the defence could challenge potential jurors:

- *Peremptory challenge*

  The defence could object to any potential jury members, up to a maximum number of three, without having to show any reason or justification for the challenge. Defence counsel used this procedure in an attempt to shape the composition of the jury in a way they thought might best suit their client, although it has to be said that it was an extremely inexact process, and one that could upset or antagonise rejected jurors. In spite of arguments for its retention on a civil liberties basis, the majority of the Roskill Committee on Fraud Trials (January 1986) recommended that the right be abolished, and abolition was provided for in the CJA 1988.

- *Challenge for cause*

The defence retains the power to challenge any number of potential jurors *for cause*, that is to say that there is a substantial reason why a particular person should not serve on the jury to decide a particular defendant's case. A simple example would be where the potential juror has had previous dealings with the defendant or has been involved in the case in some way. There may be less obvious grounds for objection, however, which may be based on the particular juror's attitudes, or indeed political beliefs. The question arises whether such factors provide grounds for challenge. In what is known as *The Angry Brigade* case in 1972 (see (1971) *The Times*, 10–11 December; (1972) *The Times*, 12–15 December), a group of people were charged with carrying out a bombing campaign against prominent members of the Conservative government. In the process of empanelling a jury, the judge asked potential jurors to exclude themselves on a variety of socio-political grounds, including active membership of the Conservative Party. As a consequence of the procedure adopted in that case, the Lord Chief Justice issued *Practice Direction (Juries)* (1973) in which he made it clear that potential jurors were not to be excluded on account of race, religion, politics or occupation. Since that Practice Direction, it is clear that the challenge for cause can only be used within a restricted sphere, and this makes it less useful to the defence than it might otherwise be if it were to operate in a more general way.

It has been argued that the desire of civil libertarians to retain the right of the defence to select a jury that might be more sympathetic to its case is contradictory, because although in theory they usually rely on the random nature of the jury to ensure the appearance of justice, in practice they seek to influence its composition. When, however, the shortcomings in the establishment of panels for juries is recalled it might be countered that the defence is attempting to do no more than counter the in-built bias that ensues from the use of unbalanced electoral registers.

14.6.6 Challenge by the prosecution

If the defence attempts to ensure that any jury will not be prejudiced against its case, if not predisposed towards it, the same is true of the prosecution. However, the prosecution has a greater scope to achieve such an aim. Whilst the prosecution has the same right as the defence to challenge for cause, it has the additional option of excluding potential jury members by simply asking them to *stand by* until a jury has been empanelled. The request for the potential juror to stand by is only a provisional challenge and, in theory, the person stood by can at a later time take their place on the jury if there are no other suitable candidates. In practice, of course, it is unlikely in the extreme for there not to be sufficient alternative candidates, to whom the prosecution do not object, and prefer to the person stood by.

When the Roskill Committee recommended the removal of the defence's right to pre-emptive challenge, it recognised that, in order to retain an equitable situation, the right of the Crown to ask potential jurors to stand by should also be withdrawn. Unfortunately, although the government of the day saw fit to follow the committee's recommendation in relation to the curtailment of the defence rights, it did not feel under the same obligation to follow its corresponding recommendation to curtail the rights of the prosecution. Thus, the CJA 1988 made no reference to the procedure and, in failing to do so, established a distinct advantage in favour of the prosecution in regard to selecting what it considered to be suitable juries.

The manifest unreasonableness of this procedure led to the Attorney General issuing a Practice Note (1988) to the effect that the Crown should only exercise its power to stand by potential jurors in the following two circumstances:

- to prevent the empanelment of a 'manifestly unsuitable' juror, with the agreement of the defence. The example given of manifest unsuitability is an illiterate person asked to sit in a highly complex case. It is reasonable to doubt the ability of such a person to follow the process of the case involving a number of documents, and on that basis they should be stood by;

- in circumstances where the Attorney General has approved the vetting of the potential jury members and that process has revealed that the particular juror in question might be a security risk. In this situation, the Attorney General is also required to approve the use of the 'stand by' procedure.

14.6.7 Jury vetting

Jury vetting is the process in which the Crown checks the background of potential jurors to assess their suitability to decide particular cases. The procedure is clearly contrary to the ideal of the jury being based on a random selection of people; but it is justified on the basis that it is necessary to ensure that jury members are not likely to divulge any secrets made open to them in the course of a sensitive trial, or, alternatively, on the ground that jurors with extreme political views should not be permitted the opportunity to express those views in a situation where they might influence the outcome of a case.

The practice of vetting potential jurors developed after the *Angry Brigade* trial in 1972 but it did not become public until 1978. In that year, as a result of an Official Secrets Act case, known by the initials of the three defendants as the ABC trial, it became apparent that the list of potential jurors had been checked to establish their 'soundness'. As a consequence of that case, the Attorney General published the current guidelines for vetting jury panels. Since that date, the guidelines have been updated and the most recent guidelines were published in 1988. These guidelines maintain the general propositions that jury members should normally be selected at random from the panel and should be disqualified only on the grounds set out in the JA 1974. The guidelines do, however, make reference to exceptional cases of public importance where potential jury members might properly be vetted. Such cases are broadly identified as those involving national security, where part of the evidence may be heard in camera, and terrorist cases.

Vetting is a twofold process. An initial check into police criminal records and police Special Branch records should be sufficient to reveal whether a further investigation by the security services in required. Any further investigation requires the prior approval of the Attorney General.

In addition to vetting, properly so called, the Court of Appeal in *R v Mason* (1980) approved the checking of criminal records to establish whether potential jurors had been convicted of criminal offences in the past and therefore were not eligible to serve as jurors. The Runciman Commission recommended that this process of checking on those who should be disqualified on the basis of previous criminal conviction should be regularised when the collection and storage of criminal records is centralised.

14.6.8 The racial mix of the jury

In *R v Danvers* (1982), the defence had sought to challenge the array on the basis that a black defendant could not have complete confidence in the impartiality of an all white jury. And the question of the racial mix of a jury has exercised the courts on a number of occasions. In *R v Ford* (1989), the trial judge's refusal to accept the defendant's application for a racially mixed jury was supported by the Court of Appeal, on the grounds that 'fairness is achieved by the principle of random selection' as regards the make up of a jury, and that to insist on a racially balanced jury would be contrary to that principle, and would be to imply that particular jurors were incapable of impartiality. A similar point was made in *R v Tarrant* (1997), in which a person accused of drug related offences was convicted by a jury that had had been selected from outside the normal catchment area for the court. The aim of the judge had been to minimise potential jury intimidation, but, nonetheless, the Court of Appeal overturned the conviction on the grounds that the judge had deprived the defendant of a randomly selected jury.

To deny people of colour the right to have their cases heard by representatives of their own race, on the basis of a refusal to recognise the existence of racial discriminatory attitudes, cannot but give the appearance of a society where such racist attitudes are institutionalised. This has particular resonance given the findings of the Macpherson Inquiry that the police force were 'institutionally racist'. Without suggesting that juries as presently constituted are biased, it remains arguable that if, in order to achieve the undoubted appearance of fairness, jury selection has to be manipulated to ensure a racial mix then it should at least be considered.

An interesting case study in this respect is the trial in 1994 of Lakhbir Deol, an Asian who was accused of the murder of a white youth in Stoke on Trent in 1993. Mr Deol's lawyers sought to have the case moved from Stafford to Birmingham Crown Court on the grounds that Stafford has an almost completely white population whereas Birmingham has an approximately 25% ethnic minority population. Mr Justice McKinnon repeatedly refused the request and the trial was heard in Stafford as scheduled. Mr Deol was acquitted, so his fears were proved groundless but, surely, the worrying fact is that he had those fears in the first place.

It is heartening to note that the Runciman Commission fully endorsed the views expressed above and recommended that either the prosecution or the defence can insist that up to three jury members be from ethnic minorities, and that at least one of those should be from the same ethnic minority as the accused or the victim. (This will be considered in more detail immediately below.)

It is of interest, if not concern, to note that the former Lord Chief Justice, Lord Taylor, whilst recognising that the criminal justice system was:

> ... failing blacks and Asians, by tolerating racist attitudes and allowing ethnic minorities to believe that they were beyond the protection of the law ...,

was equally sure that proposals for ethnically balanced juries, and, indeed, the new offence of racially-motivated attacks, were:

> ... Attractive sounding, but deeply flawed proposals.

He went on to criticise the Runciman proposals as:

> ... the thin edge of a particularly insidious wedge ...,

and, somewhat ironically, given subsequent proposals by the current Home Secretary, he asserted that:

> We must on no account introduce measures which allow the State to start nibbling away at the principle of random selection of juries [Speech to NACRO (1999)].

14.7   The decline of the jury trial

The resistance to the Runciman proposal to reduce the scope of jury trials (see 3.18.5) has to be placed within the context of the general decline in the use of jury trials that has occurred in the fairly recent past. Perhaps the heat engendered in the current debate is a consequence of the fact that the continued existence of the jury as it is presently constituted cannot be taken for granted.

14.7.1   The jury trial in civil procedure

Under s 69 of the Supreme Court Act 1981, the right to a jury trial is limited to only four areas: fraud; defamation; malicious prosecution; false imprisonment. (Similar provisions are contained in the County Courts Act 1984.)

Even in these areas, the right is not absolute and can be denied by a judge under s 69(i) where the case involves 'any prolonged examination of documents or accounts or any scientific or local investigation which cannot conveniently be made with a jury'. (See *Beta Construction Ltd v Channel Four TV Co Ltd* (1990) for an indication of the factors that the judge will take into consideration in deciding whether a case should be decided by a jury or not.)

The question of whether or not juries should be used in libel cases gained wider consideration in the case involving McDonalds, the fast-food empire, and two environmentalists, Dave Morris and Helen Steel. McDonalds claimed that their reputation was damaged by an allegedly libellous leaflet issued by members of an organisation called London Greenpeace including Morris and Steel, which linked McDonalds' products to heart disease and cancer as well as the despoliation of the environment and the exploitation of the Third World. In a preliminary hearing, later confirmed by the Court of Appeal, it was decided that the evidence to be presented would be of such scientific complexity that it would be beyond the understanding of a jury (see (1997) *The Times*, 10 June).

The right to jury trial in defamation cases has been the object of particular criticism. In 1975, the Faulks Committee on the Law of Defamation recommended that the availability of jury trial in that area should be subject to the same judicial discretion as all other civil cases. In its conclusions, the Faulks Report shared the uncertainty of the Court of Appeal in *Ward v James* (1965) as to the suitability of juries to determine the level of damages that should be awarded. Support for these views has been provided by a number of defamation cases decided since then, such as *Sutcliffe v Pressdram Ltd* (1990), in which the wife of a convicted serial killer was awarded damages of £600,000. She eventually settled for £60,000 after the Court of Appeal stated that it would re-assess the award. In *Aldington v Watts and Tolstoy* (1989), damages of £1.5 million were awarded.

This huge award was subsequently held by the European Court of Human Rights to be so disproportionate as to amount to a violation of Tolstoy's right to freedom of expression under Art 10 of the Convention (*Tolstoy Miloslavsky v UK* (1995). Domestic law has also sought to deal with what could only be seen as excessive awards of damages in defamation cases, even prior to the Human Rights Act 1998 which makes the ECHR *Tolstoy* decision, and Art 10 of the Convention, binding in UK law.

Section 8 of the Courts and Legal Services Act 1990 gave appeal courts the power to alter damages awards made by juries to a level that they felt to be 'proper'. Nonetheless, the question of what actually constitutes a proper level of damages continued to present problems for juries, which continued to award very high damages. The problem arose from the limited guidance that judges could give juries in making their awards. In *Rantzen v Mirror Group Newspapers* (1993), the Court of Appeal stated that judges should advise juries, in making their awards, to consider the purchasing power of the award, and its proportionality to the damage suffered to the reputation of the claimant, and should refer to awards made by he courts under s 8 of the CLSA (Rantzen's original award of £250,000 was reduced to £110,000). Still, extremely large awards continued to be made, and, in *John v MGN Ltd* (1996), the Court of Appeal stated that past practice should be altered to allow juries to refer to personal injury cases to decided the level of award and that the judge could indicate what sort of level would be appropriate (John's awards of £350,000 for the libel and £275,000 in exemplary damages were reduced to £75,000 and £50,000 respectively).

In 1996, statute law intervened in the form of the Defamation Act, which was designed to simplify the procedure of defamation cases. The main provisions of the Act are:

(a) a new one year limitation period for defamation actions;

(b) a new statutory defence based on responsibility for publication. This replaces the common law defence of innocent dissemination;

(c) an updating of defences in relation to privilege; that is, reporting on the proceedings and publications of, for example, the courts and government;

(d) a new streamlined procedure for dealing with a defendant who has offered to make amends. This would involve paying compensation, assessed by a judge, and publishing an appropriate correction and apology.

(e) new powers for judges to deal with cases without a jury. Under this provision, the judge can dismiss a claim if he considers it has no realistic prospect of success. Alternatively, if he considers there to be no realistic defence to the claim, he can award summary relief. Such relief can take the form of a declaration of the falsity of the statement; an order to print an apology; an order to refrain from repeating the statement; and damages of up to £10,000.

Although enacted in July 1996, the procedure relating to the new defence of making amends and the, more controversial, summary disposal of claim procedure have not yet been implemented. In April 1999, the Lord Chancellor's Department announced its intention to issue a consultation paper before bringing all the rules into effect on 1 January 2000.

It is a matter of constitutional interest that s 13 of the Defamation Act 1996 altering the operation of s 9 of the Bill of Rights 1689, was specially introduced to allow the former Conservative MP, Neil Hamilton, to take a defamation action against the *Guardian* newspaper, which had accused him of accepting money for asking question in the House of Commons. The Bill of Rights had granted qualified privilege to MPs, but the *Guardian* had successfully argued that, as they could not sue Hamilton in regard to parliamentary matters, he, in turn, could not sue them. Unusually, as Law Lords are not supposed to involve themselves in party political matters, s 13 of the Defamation Act, which allowed MPs to waive their privilege, was moved by Lord Hoffman, apparently at the behest of the then Lord Chancellor, Lord Mackay. Hamilton's action against the *Guardian* subsequently collapsed and he lost his parliamentary seat in the 1997 election. Lord Hoffman went on to demonstrate his lack of political grasp in the infamous *Pinochet* case (see Chapter 4).

If the extent of damages has been a particular problem in relation to defamation actions, especially when they are compared to the much smaller awards made in relation to personal injury, it should also be noted that legal aid is not normally available in defamation cases, although it is available in relation to malicious falsehood. This effectively has made defamation a rich person's action. As a consequence, people without the necessary wealth to finance a legal action find it extremely difficult to gain redress when they have suffered from what subsequently turns out to be false and damaging press coverage of their affairs. It is to be hoped that the new summary procedure, under the Defamation Act 1996, will redress this situation. But of equal concern is the way some wealthy people were able and allowed to abuse the system. One example was the late, and notorious publisher, Robert Maxwell who often used libel proceedings or the threat of them to silence critics. As it turned out, much of what Mr Maxwell sought to prevent from becoming public knowledge was, in fact, illegal and harmful business conduct.

In all other civil cases, there is a presumption against trial by jury although, under s 69(3), the judge has the discretion to order a trial by jury. (See *Ward v James* (1965), where the court decided that a jury should be used in civil cases only in 'exceptional circumstances', although no exhaustive list as to what amounted to exceptional circumstances was provided.)

14.7.2 Criminal juries

This issue was central to the Runciman Report and detailed consideration will be postponed till later. It has to be borne in mind, however, that the criminal jury trial is essentially the creature of the Crown Court, and that the magistrates' courts deal with 97% of criminal cases. In practice, juries determine the outcome of less than 1% of the total of criminal cases for the reason that, of all the cases that are decided in the Crown Court, 72% of defendants plead guilty on all counts and therefore have no need of jury trial, and a further 2% plead guilty to some counts. In all, there were only a total of 26,117 contested cases in the Crown Court in 1990 (Judicial Statistics, Cmnd 1573, 1990). It can be seen, therefore, that, in absolute and proportional terms, the jury does not play a significant part in the determination of criminal cases.

If trial by jury is not statistically significant, it cannot be denied that it is of major significance in the determination of the most serious cases. Even this role, however, has not gone without scrutiny and, in 1986, the Roskill Committee on Fraud Trials critically examined the operation of the jury in complex criminal fraud cases. Its report recommended the abolition of trial by jury in such cases. The Roskill Committee did not go as far as to recommend that all fraud cases should be taken away from juries, only the most complex, of which it was estimated that there were about two dozen or so every year. It was suggested that these cases would be better decided by a judge assisted by two lay persons drawn from a panel with specialist expertise. The government declined to implement the recommendations of the Roskill Committee and, instead, introduced procedures designed to make it easier to follow the proceedings in complex fraud cases. It is interesting to note, given the controversy relating to the accusation that the Runciman Report represented an attack on the jury system, that it did not follow Roskill in its recommendations.

After being found not guilty of a £19 million fraud charge, George Walker, the former chief executive of Brent Walker, said: 'Thank God for the jury. It would be madness to lose the jury system.' This enthusiastic endorsement of the jury system is in no little way undercut, however, by the fact that Walker is reported as going on to state that he was sure the jury had not properly understood much of the highly detailed material in the trial, as he admitted: 'I didn't understand a lot of it, so I can't see how they could.'

Mr Walker's enthusiasm perhaps was not shared by his co-accused, Wilfred Aquilina, who was found guilty, on a majority verdict, of false accounting.

In February 1998, the Home Office issued a Green Paper entitled *Juries in Serious Fraud Trials*. The consultation paper suggested the need for a new procedure in relation to complex fraud trials, due to the fact that 'the detection, investigation and trial of serious criminal fraud offences have presented certain difficulties not commonly found amongst other types of offences'. A variety of possible alternatives were put forward:

- *special juries*: these would be made up of qualified people and might be drawn from a special pool of potential jurors. Alternatively, ordinary jurors would have to be assessed as to their competency to sit on the case;

- *judge run trials*: specially trained judges, either singly or in a panel, and possibly with the help of lay experts;

- *fraud tribunals*: following Roskill, these would be made up of a judge and qualified lay members with the power to question witnesses;

- *verdict-only juries*: in this situation the judge would hear the evidence and sum up the facts leaving the jury simply to vote on guilt or innocence;

- *a special juror*: here, 11 of the jury would be selected as normal, but the 12th would be specially qualified in order to be able to assist the others on complex points.

With respect to these alternatives, the government stated that it had no particular preference.

Under the proposals, a judge would decide at a pre-trial hearing if the case would be heard by an ordinary jury, or under whichever of the possible new procedures is finally selected. The Green Paper estimated that, at most, 85 cases per year would be subject to the new procedure, but, significantly, it was also estimated that costs of adopting the new procedures would cut costs by up to 25%.

Subsequently, in April 1998, the Home Secretary requested the Law Commission to carry out a review of fraud trials focusing particularly on whether the existing law is:

- readily comprehensible to juries;

- adequate for effective prosecution;

- fair to defendants; and

- able to cope with changes in technology.

It should not be forgotten that the right to jury trial has been abolished in Northern Ireland since 1973. In response to the problem of the intimidation of jury members, the Report of the Commission to Consider Legal Procedures to Deal with Terrorist Activities in Northern Ireland, headed by Lord Diplock, recommended that cases be decided without juries in particular situations. The so called Diplock courts operate in relation to certain 'scheduled offences', particularly, but not exclusively, associated with terrorism.

14.8 The Runciman Commission

The Report of the Royal Commission on Criminal Justice made numerous recommendations relating to juries. Indeed, the very first recommendation made by it was that s 8 of the Contempt of Court Act 1981 should be repealed to enable research to be conducted into juries' reasons for their verdicts. At present, s 8 makes it an offence to obtain, disclose or solicit any particulars of statements made, opinion, expressed, arguments advanced or votes cast by members of a jury in the course of their deliberations in any legal proceedings.

In *Attorney General v Associated Newspapers* (1994), the House of Lords held that it was contempt of court for a newspaper to publish disclosures by jurors of what took place in the jury room while they were considering their verdict, unless the publication amounted to no more than a republication of facts already known. It was decided that the word 'disclose' in s 8(1) applied not just to jurors but to any others who published their revelations.

14.8.1 General points about jury selection

In relation specifically to the selection of juries, the Commission addressed itself to many of the problems that were considered above and made the following recommendations:

- *Every endeavour should be made to ensure that the electoral rolls are comprehensive and include everybody who ought to be included*

    Such a recommendation is certainly worthy, but it is difficult to see how electoral registration officers will succeed in overcoming the problems, considered previously, of people's failure to appear on the register through conscious design or mere accident.

- *Clergymen and members of religious orders should be eligible; but practising members of religious sects which object to jury service should be excluded*

    Alterations should be made to the list of people liable to serve on juries. This sensible measure to increase the pool of potential jurors was enacted by s 92 of the CJA 1989.

- *Potential jurors should be given alternative dates if they cannot sit on the date originally suggested*

    This recommendation is aimed at accommodating people who have difficulty attending for jury service at a particular time, whilst at the same time it does not simply let them disappear if they cannot make that date. It thus aims at preventing certain individuals from opting out of the duty to serve on juries.

- *The rates of financial allowances for those on jury service should be reviewed as a matter of urgency*

    This is a clear recognition of the fact that it costs people money to serve on juries and that, as a consequence, people try to avoid their social and legal duty to serve. The Commission is clearly of the opinion that this should not be the case and that to avoid this occurrence, the levels of allowance should be raised.

- *Jury-summoning officers should try to make sure that potential jury members do not know each other or the accused*

Clearly, such occurrences, but especially the latter one, are to be avoided wherever possible.

14.8.2 Disqualification

The Commission made some recommendations designed to improve the operation of the existing disqualification procedure, and as such no great exception can be taken to them:

- when the national criminal record system is fully operational courts should arrange for that agency to screen jurors on a routine basis to discover any disqualifying convictions they might have;

- jurors should be required to positively affirm that they have no disqualifying convictions, and should be open to conviction if they provide false information.

There are, however, some recommendations that are less obviously justified or needed and which give some cause to suspect the underlying purpose of the Commission's report in general. These are:

- *People currently on bail should be disqualified from serving*

One is immediately prompted to ask why such people should be disqualified. By definition, they have not been convicted of the offence of which they stand charged, and may not be. Is disqualifying them, on no other ground than they have been charged with an offence, not tantamount to pre-judging the case against them? It may be argued that if such people are later found guilty of the offence in relation to which they were granted bail, then their previous disqualification was clearly justified; and if they are later found innocent then they would not have been in the right frame of mind to decide any cases they would have been involved in an objective manner. The former argument is at best a *post hoc* justification for an action that has no inherent justification; the latter is even more objectionable in that it assumes that objectivity cannot encompass scepticism of the case presented by the prosecution with its underlying assumption that the purpose of the trial process is simply to convict the accused.

In any case, the proposal was effected by s 40 of the CJA 1994 and consequently any person on bail in criminal proceedings is disqualified from serving as a juror in the Crown Court. The disqualification does not cover service in civil proceedings.

- *Once s 8 of the Contempt of Court Act is repealed, it is recommended that research be carried out into the possible influence of jurors with criminal records on the decisions of juries*

It would appear to be an implicit assumption that such people have a deleterious effect on the operation of juries. The further implication is that such research would be conducted to prove the point, as the first step to disqualifying them as potential jurors. Thus, the apparently praiseworthy procedure of opening up the jury process to investigation may have the ulterior motive of intending to discredit its operation.

14.8.3 The ethnic origin of jurors

The Runciman Commission addressed the difficulties looked at above (see 14.6.8) and made the following recommendations:

- in exceptional cases, it should be possible for either the prosecution or the defence to apply to the trial judge to have the jury selected in such a way as to ensure that it contains three people from ethnic minority communities;

- it should also be open for the prosecution or defence to argue the need that one of these three be of the same ethnic minority as the defendant or the victim.

It should be noted that these two measures would not just operate in cases where the accused was a member of an ethnic minority but could also be used in relation to trials involving white accused, perhaps charged with racist offences. In either situation, the intention would be to provide a signal indication of the impartiality of the procedure.

14.8.4 The conduct of trials

Most of the proposals made in this section relate to ensuring that jurors are fully aware of what is going on in the court and what is expected of them. There are a couple of recommendations that are worthy of closer consideration:

- Every effort should be made to protect jurors from intimidation. Guidance should be given to jurors on what to do if they feel intimidated and in sensitive cases the public gallery should be sited in such a way as to preclude the possibility of intimidation of the jury.

In the context of this chapter, it is worth noting that claims about intimidation have been used to justify the removal of jury trials in

Northern Ireland. This proposal, however, appears to be a reasonable and practical suggestion designed to curtail the problem without undermining the jury system. Section 51 of the CJPOA 1994 introduced the offence of jury intimidation in furtherance of this aim.

- In long trials lasting weeks or months, judges should consider staggering the courts' normal hours to enable jurors to keep in touch with their employment. Once again, this is a sensible proposal recognising and attempting in some way to deal with one of the problems that arise for jurors from involvement in long trials.

With specific regard to fraud trials, it is recommended that:

- Section 10(3) of the CJA 1988 should be amended to permit judges to put the issues before the jury at the outset of the trial.

    This proposal recognises the particular difficulties faced by jurors in fraud trials but, in the light of the controversy considered below in cases triable 'either way', it is interesting to note that the Commission does not suggest the removal of the jury from such cases.

14.8.5 The rights to jury trial

The general proposals of the Runciman Commission in relation to juries were not without an element of controversy but it was, without doubt, the Commission's proposal to limit the role of the jury in the criminal process that generated the most controversy. This particular recommendation, number 114 out of a total 352, stimulated more response than any other single proposal; and, by and large, that response was hostile.

In order to understand the full implications of the recommendation, it is necessary to reconsider points that have been discussed previously in Chapters 3 and 4.

It is essential to appreciate the distinction, established in the Criminal Law Act 1977, between offences to be tried *only* by summary procedure, offences to be tried *only* on indictment and offences triable *'either way'*. Summary offences are those which are triable only in the magistrates' courts and cases which, as has been noted previously, magistrates decide on their own without the assistance of a jury. There are literally hundreds of summary offences; given the limitations on the sentencing powers of magistrates, they are by necessity the least serious of criminal acts, such as road traffic offences, and minor assault. The most serious offences, such as major theft, serious assault, rape, manslaughter and murder have to be tried on indictment before a jury in the Crown Court. There is, however, a third category, offences triable 'either way' which, as the name suggests, may be tried either summarily or on indictment. It was the Runciman Commission's recommendation in relation to this third category that gave rise to most controversy.

The current way of determining how an offence triable 'either way' is actually heard is set out in the Magistrates' Courts Act (MCA) 1980. Under s 19 of that Act, the magistrates' court has to decide whether the offence is more suitable for summary trial or trial on indictment. In reaching that decision, the magistrates must take into account the nature of the case, its seriousness, and whether the penalty they could impose would be adequate, and any other circumstances which appear to the court to make it more suitable for the offence to be tried one way rather than the other. (Guidelines are set out in *Practice Note (Offences Triable Either Way: Mode of Trial)* (1990).) If the magistrates decide that the case is suitable for summary hearing, they are required by s 20 of the MCA 1980 to inform the defendant of their decision and also to inform him that, if he is found guilty on the summary hearing, he may still be committed to the Crown Court for sentencing if the magistrates are of the opinion that their powers of sentencing are inadequate. If the accused agrees to a summary hearing, the trial goes ahead in the magistrates' court. If, however, the defendant objects to the summary procedure, the case goes on indictment to the Crown Court and the magistrates merely act as examining justices. It is this latter right, the right of the defendant in cases triable 'either way' to elect for/insist on a trial by jury, that the Runciman Commission recommended should be removed. It is not inappropriate to cite the recommendation in full:

> In cases involving 'either way' offences, the defendant should no longer have the right to insist on a trial by jury. Where the CPS (the Crown Prosecution Service) and the defendant agree that the case is suitable for summary trial, it should proceed to trial in a magistrates' court. The case should go to the Crown Court for trial if both the prosecution and defence agree that it should be tried on indictment. Where the defence do not agree with the CPS's proposal on which court should try the case, the matter should be referred to the magistrates for a decision [Royal Commission, *Report on the Criminal Justice System*, Cm 2263, 1993].

This recommendation supports the view of the former Director of Public Prosecution, Barbara Mills, who, in an interview in (1993) *The Times*, 21 April, suggested that the right to opt for trial by jury should be removed from a greater number of defendants who should be dealt with in a summary manner. If accepted, according to the report it would affect more than 35,000 cases per year.

The declared aim of the recommendation is the achievement of 'a more rational division of "either way" cases between the magistrates' courts and the Crown Court' (see para 6.13 of the report) and it is claimed that this rationalisation would bring about 'significant benefits for the overall efficiency of the criminal justice system ... without the quality of justice being diminished thereby' (see para 6.15 of the report). If efficiency is defined in relation to the parameter of economic cost then the first half of this claim may well be true, for as the Commission itself pointed out 'A trial in a magistrates' court is many times cheaper than a trial at the Crown Court'. It is greatly to be doubted, however, if the second part of that claim is as accurate; and it is on the need to maintain the quality of justice that much of the attack on Runciman focused.

In support of its recommendation, the Runciman Commission cited statistics drawn from various research projects and although some of the statistics did not actually support the argument of the Commission, the main problem with its recommendation was that there was a fundamental flaw at the heart of its apparent logic. As pointed out in Chapter 4 of this book, the Commission referred to empirical research that found that for offences that could be tried 'either way', the chances of acquittal were substantially higher in the Crown Court with a jury (57%) than in the magistrates' courts without a jury (30%). The Commission commented, with what can only be taken as irony, on the fact that, although most defendants opt for the Crown Court on the basis of an expectation of an acquittal, by the time their trial comes on, 70% of them plead guilty to all charges and a further 13% plead guilty to at least some of the charges of which they are accused. The Commission, however, also provided the answer for this apparent paradox in the conclusions of another research project. This one found that, of a sample of defendants who elected to have their case decided in the Crown Court, 50% did so in the belief that, even if the jury decided they were guilty, their sentence would be lighter in the Crown Court than it would have been in the magistrates' court. The same research proved the fallacy of that belief, for it found that in practice, in matched cases, judges were three times more likely to impose immediate custody and their sentences were on average two and a half times longer than those delivered by magistrates. That latter finding in no way undermines the former point relating to the defendants' subjective perception of the two courts; indeed it strengthens it. A further point in relation to subjective opinions about the operation of the Crown Court is provided by a research study produced for the Commission. It was stated that the police and the Crown Prosecution Service found nearly half of all jury acquittals surprising; but as Michael Mansfield QC has suggested such an opinion might well be predicated on an arrogant assumption that they know best who is guilty in the first place.

The Commission's report stated that defendants should not 'be able to choose their court of trial solely on the basis that they think that they will get a fairer hearing at one level than another' (see para 6.18 of the report). The conclusion of the Commission seems to be that because defendants do not trust the magistrates' court, and there is some justification for this in respect of the rates of acquittal, and do have more faith in the Crown Court than is warranted in terms of sentencing, then they should be *forced* to use the magistrates' court. As the report stated: 'Magistrates' courts conduct over 93% of all criminal cases and should be trusted to try cases fairly' (see para 6.18 of the report). It is at least arguable that in this conclusion the Commission is missing the point. Put starkly, the evidence supports the conclusion that defendants do not trust magistrates' courts. Indeed, the evidence as to the number of people changing their plea to guilty in the Crown Court would seem to support the conclusion, not so much that defendants trust juries but more that they do not trust magistrates. This lack of trust in the magistracy is further highlighted by the fact that those who do not plead guilty would rather have their guilt or innocence determined by a jury.

Simply forcing such people to use the magistrates' courts does not address the underlying problem let alone solve it.

It would have been possible for the Commission to have achieved its end by simply recommending that particular offences, that are defined as triable 'either way' at present, should be re-categorised as offences only open to summary procedure. That it did not do so further indicates the weakness of the underlying logic of its case for removing the right to insist on trial on indictment. The Commission rejected the reclassification of offences partly because of the difficulty and uncertainty inherent in the task. Additionally, and more importantly, however, it rejected this approach because it wished to leave available the possibility of the defendant successfully insisting on trial on indictment in the case of first offenders, where the consequences of loss of reputation would be significant. In the words of the Commission: 'Loss of reputation is a different matter, since jury trial has long been regarded as appropriate for cases involving that issue. But, it should only be one of the factors to be taken into account and will often be relevant only to first offenders' (see para 6.18 of the report).

There are two assumptions in this proposal. First, there is the, surely objectionable, assumption that the reputation of anyone with a previous conviction is not important. But, of even more concern is the fact that it is recognised that in the cases of first offenders they *should* be permitted access to the jury. The question has to be asked: why should this be the case if juries do no more than magistrates do? It appears that in the instance of first offenders it is recognised that juries *do* offer more protection than magistrates. Again, this demands the question: why should the extra protection not be open to all? Thus, once more, the economic imperative that motivated the Commission comes into question, and once again the pursuit of lower cost takes over from the need *to be clearly seen to provide justice*.

It has been claimed that this proposal comes dangerously close to advocating a two-tier system of criminal justice, with the cheaper version being reserved for the punishment of the 'criminal classes'. Opposition to it has been voluble and former Lord Chief Justice Taylor stated his personal disapprobation. Also, the Vice President of The Law Society, Charles Elly, stated the Society's strong opposition to this particular proposal and expressed the view that it 'can only have been based on the interests of cost-cutting, not of justice'. The then Chairman of the Criminal Bar, whilst approving of the rest of the report, was equally outspoken about this proposal. As he saw it, the abolition of the right to jury trial in such cases was: '... likely to involve unequal treatment of defendants, favouring those whom society views as more respectable than others'. Or, as Michael Mansfield QC put the matter: 'If the Commission has its way we are racing towards middle class justice.'

14.8.6 Proposals for change

In May 1999, the government announced its intention to introduce legislation to curb the right to jury trial. In essence, it wishes, in cases triable either way, to disallow a defendant from insisting upon trial by jury in circumstances where magistrates believe that they are well suited to hear the case ((1999) *The Times*, 19 May). More than 18,500 defendants a year would lose their right to trial by jury under these plans. The plans were advanced by the government to, according to its own contentions, speed up the hearing of criminal cases. The proposed reform was widely condemned by civil rights groups, the Bar and other lawyers.

The Home Secretary, Mr Straw, decided to push ahead with the change after finding that many people who opt in the early stages of their cases for trial by jury change their plea to guilty before the trial is heard. Home Office research shows that more than 70% of those who opt for jury trial plead guilty by the day their Crown Court case opens. The average cost of a jury trial is £13,500, compared with £2,500 for a hearing by magistrates. Mr Straw has been convinced of the need for change in spite of opposing a similar plan when it was floated by Michael Howard, as Conservative Home Secretary. Mr Straw attacked the idea then as 'unfair, short-sighted and likely to prove ineffective' ((1999) *The Times*, 19 May).

One Home Office paper (*Jury Trials*, 1998) suggested that defendants elect for trial by jury at the Crown Court in an attempt to put pressure on the Crown Prosecution Service to accept a plea to a less serious charge; to make it more likely that witnesses do not turn up or be vague in their recollections; or simply to put off the day of conviction and sentence.

One problem for those who support such a change is that if, for serious crimes, you support the rigmarole of jury trials because so much is at stake for the defendant, how then can you justify removal of the defendant's right to a jury trail in cases which manifestly threaten life-ruining results for a defendant? Offences like indecent assault and theft are cases in point.

In earlier times, judges would often fine or imprison jurors who persisted in returning verdicts at variance with the preference of the Bench. In 1671, *Bushell's Case* established that juries should be immune from punishment for their verdicts. Such meddling, however, might be seen by some as of modest significance in contrast to a plan to rule out the right to jury trial for several types of serious offence.

14.8.7 Conclusion

It has been repeatedly suggested by those in favour of abolishing, or at least severely curtailing, the role of the jury in the criminal justice system that the general perception of the jury is romanticised and has little foundation in reality. Runciman did not actually make this point explicitly but it is implicit in his assessment of the jury system as against the magistrates' courts. Others have been more explicit; thus, the Roskill Committee expressed the view that:

> Society appears to have an attachment to jury trial which is emotional or sentimental rather than logical [para 8.21].

A similar point had been made previously by the Faulks Committee, but that report also recognised the source of the public's opinion and was careful not to dismiss it as unimportant:

> Much of the support for jury trials is emotional and derives from the undoubted value of juries in serious criminal cases where they stand between the prosecuting authority and the citizen [para 496].

The ideological power of the jury system should not be underestimated. It represents the ordinary person's input into the legal system and it is at least arguable that in that way it provides the whole legal system with a sense of legitimacy. It is argued by some civil libertarians that the existence of the non-jury Diplock Courts in Northern Ireland brings the whole of the legal system in that province into disrepute.

As Lord Devlin noted (*Trial By Jury*, 1966):

> The first object of any tyrant in Whitehall would be to make Parliament utterly subservient to his will; and the next to overthrow or diminish trial by jury, for no tyrant could afford to leave a subject's freedom in the hands of 12 of his countrymen.

THE CRIMINAL PROCESS:
(2) THE PROSECUTION

The Crown Prosecution Service

The Crown Prosecution Service (CPS) was introduced in 1986 and it is important to understand the five types of prosecution which existed before this time and how the CPS was supposed to improve the old system's criticisms. What sort of biases can occur in the use of prosecutorial discretion and why? Why were the police regarded as not the most suitable agency to exercise the prosecutorial discretion? What were the police defences to those criticisms? The police argued that conviction rates vindicated the way they exercised their discretion. The new Code for Crown Prosecutors (1994) introduces factors which should weigh for and against a prosecution.

Cautioning offenders

Cautioning offenders has recently increased as a proportion of the ways police respond to crime. Why is this? The CPS guidelines on prosecution require a 'realistic prospect of conviction' and that the 'public interest' is served by any prosecution. What difficulties are entailed by such formulae?

Judicial control

Judicial control of prosecution policy is very limited and amounts to being able to correct only flagrantly irrational decisions by senior officers (*R v Metropolitan Police Commissioner ex p Blackburn* (1968)).

Bail

Bail is the release from custody, pending a criminal trial, of an accused on the promise that money will be paid if he or she absconds. The important issue raised here is how best the regulations should be framed so as to balance the conflicting interests of public safety and civil liberty. Public safety would perhaps be best served by keeping in custody everyone accused of a crime until their trial; this, though, would clearly be unnecessarily draconian. Conversely, civil liberty might be best served by allowing every suspect to remain free however heinous the crime they have been accused of and whatever their past record. The important statutory provisions are s 38 of PACE 1984 and ss 3, 4, 6 and Sched 1 of the BA 1976. Changes made by the Bail (Amendment) Act 1993, and the Criminal Justice and Public Order Act 1994, allow prosecutors to appeal against the granting of bail, restrict some aspects of it being granted, and afford greater opportunities for police bail.

Plea bargaining

Plea bargaining is the practice where the accused enters a plea of guilty in return for which he will be given a sentence concession. It can also refer to 'plea arrangements' where the accused agrees to plead guilty to a lesser charge than the one with which he or she is or is to be charged. Note the recommendation of the Runciman Commission to introduce sentence discounting as a means to avoid 'cracked trials'. Dangers arising from such procedures include innocent persons being pressurised to 'take a plea' and serious offenders being processed for minor offences. In a system where the vast majority of cases in the Crown Court and magistrates' courts result in guilty pleas (79% and 81.5%, respectively), the operation of the plea bargain becomes very important.

The jury

The jury has come under close public scrutiny since the Runciman Commission's recommendation to curtail the right to jury trial. It is important to know the standard arguments in favour of the jury and also the arguments showing it to be not truly random and representative. The detail of the jury's function in a trial and the extent to which its verdict can be appealed against are important. In what ways can the membership of the jury be challenged? What arguments were adopted by the Runciman Commission when recommending fewer jury trials? Juries lie at the heart of the English criminal justice system. There is debate about whether juries provide any better justice than magistrates' courts or whether the role is purely symbolic.

The role of the jury

To decide matters of fact – judges decide matters of law. Judges can instruct juries to acquit but not to convict. Juries do not have to give reasons for their decision. There is no appeal against an acquittal verdict, although points of law may be clarified by an Attorney General's reference. Civil cases can be overturned if perverse – but not criminal cases. Verdicts can be delivered on the basis of majority decisions. The use of juries has declined in relation to criminal and civil law.

Selection of juries

Random in theory – selective in practice. All on the electoral register are liable to serve but the registers tend to be inaccurate. Service is subject to exemption, excusal and disqualification. Defence and prosecution can challenge for cause. Prosecution can ask jurors to stand by. Jury vetting is checking that jurors are suitable to hear sensitive cases. If Runciman is followed, juries may be required to have a racial mix.

The Runciman Report

Section 8 of the Contempt of Court Act 1981 should be amended. Attempts should be made to improve the representative nature of juries. The operation of disqualification procedures should be tightened and extended to those on bail. The ethnic mix of a jury should be open to adjustment. In complex fraud trials, judges should be permitted to explain the matters involved at the outset of the trial. Magistrates should have the final say in where offences triable 'either way' are heard.

CHAPTER 15

LEGAL SERVICES

15.1 Introduction

We are concerned here with a number of issues related to the provision and organisation of legal services, and the problem of access to legal services. This is a period of great change for all of these matters. The legal profession has undergone a series of major changes as a result of the Courts and Legal Services Act (CLSA) 1990. The provision of legal aid, advice and assistance has been drastically altered as a result of changes introduced in 1999. The introduction of the 'conditional fee arrangement' in 1995 was another contentious issue in this area.

The former Lord Chancellor, Lord Mackay, saw his primary objective as improving access to justice by making the environment of legal services more competitive. He was also very concerned at the costs of providing free and subsidised legal aid, advice and assistance. Speaking in October 1992 at The Law Society Conference, Lord Mackay said:

> My task is to secure a balance between my responsibilities to the public to provide the means for reasonable access to justice and my responsibility to the public as taxpayers in controlling what is now a very high level of expenditure [then over £1.1 billion gross]. That task is not an easy one, but I am convinced that I can achieve it. To do so, however, will involve some radical re-thinking of some elements of the present system. In the short term, it may involve measures which will be uncomfortable and, perhaps to some of you, unwelcome. But, if the future of the legal aid scheme is to be put on a firm base ... changes are inevitable.

It is important when considering all the elements of this chapter to ask yourself questions about the aims of all the systems and proposed changes to them. What is their immediate aim? Is such an immediate aim part of a wider legal or social objective? How does the funding of any given component operate and what do its critics say is wrong or undesirable about it or the way it works?

15.2 The legal profession

The English legal system is one of only three in the world to have a divided legal profession where a lawyer is either a solicitor or a barrister. Each branch has its own separate traditions, training requirements and customs of practice. It is important to remember that not only lawyers regularly perform legal work. As one text notes (Bailey and Gunn, *Smith & Bailey on the Modern English Legal System*, 1991, p 105):

> ... many non-lawyers perform legal tasks, some of them full time. For example, accountants may specialise in revenue law, trade union officials may appear regularly before industrial tribunals on behalf of their members, and solicitors may delegate work to legal executives. Conversely, many of the tasks performed by lawyers are not strictly 'legal'.

15.3 Solicitors

The solicitor can be characterised as a general practitioner: a lawyer who deals with clients direct and when a particular specialism or litigation is required will engage the services of counsel, that is, a barrister. Looking at the solicitor as a legal GP and the barrister as a specialist, however, can be misleading. Most solicitors, especially those in large practices, are experts in particular areas of law. They may restrict their regular work to litigation or commercial conveyancing or revenue work. Many barristers on the other hand might have a quite wide range of work including criminal, family matters and a variety of common law areas like tort and contract cases. The origins of the solicitor go back to the *attornatus*, or later the 'attorney', a medieval officer of the court whose main function was to assist the client in the initial stages of the case. One group of people practising in the Court of Chancery came to be known as 'solicitors'. Originally, they performed a variety of miscellaneous clerical tasks for employers such as land owners and attorneys. Their name was derived from their function of 'soliciting' or prosecuting actions in courts of which they were not officers or attorneys. Eventually, neither of these groups were admitted to the Inns of Court (where barristers worked); they merged and organised themselves as a distinct profession.

It was not, however, until 1831 that 'The Society of Attorneys Solicitors Proctors and Others not being Barristers Practising in the Courts of Law and Equity in the United Kingdom' was given its Royal Charter. This body emerged as the governing body of solicitors, the term 'attorney' falling from general use.

According to the latest Law Society figures available (June 1999), there are 95,521 solicitors on the Roll, an annual increase of 4.1% on the previous year. Of these, 75,072 had practising certificates. Of those holding practising certificates, Law Society statistics (*Trends in the Solicitors' Profession*, Annual Statistical Report 1998) show that 81% work in private practice. The remaining 19% work in commerce, industry or the public sector. Of those currently holding practising certificates, 33.9% are women and 52% are aged under 40. Overall, membership of The Law Society has increased by 230% since 1968.

One very significant area of development and concern for solicitors at the beginning of the 21st century is the extent to which their monopolies of certain sorts of practice have been eroded. They have already lost their monopoly on conveyancing (although only a solicitor is authorised to give final endorsement to such work if carried out by a licensed conveyancer). Then, in 1999, the Access to Justice Act (see Chapter 16) introduced the provision that the Lord Chancellor will in future be able to authorise bodies other than The Law Society to approve of their members carrying out litigation. This, however, should be seen in the wider context of the policy to break down the historical monopolies of both branches of the legal profession. Thus, we can note the growth, since the CLSA 1990, of solicitors rights of audience in court, and a corresponding anxiety at the Bar when these rights were granted.

The 1999 Act provides that every barrister and every solicitor has a right of audience before every court in relation to all proceedings. The right, however, is not unconditional. In order to exercise it, solicitors and barristers must obey the rules of conduct of the professional bodies and must have met any training requirements that have been prescribed like the requirement to have completed pupillage in the case of the Bar, or to have obtained a higher courts advocacy qualification in the case of solicitors who wish to appear in the higher courts.

15.3.1 Training

The standard route to qualification is a law degree followed by a one year Legal Practice Course (LPC) and then a term as a trainee solicitor which, like the barrister's pupillage, is essentially an apprenticeship. Non-law graduates can complete the Common Professional Examination in one year and then proceed as a law graduate. All newly admitted solicitors must now undergo regular continuing education which means attendance at non-examined legal courses designed to update knowledge and improve expertise. After completion of the LPC and traineeship, a trainee solicitor may apply to The Law Society to be 'admitted' to the profession. The Master of the Rolls will add the names of the newly qualified to the roll of officers of the Supreme Court. To practise, a solicitor will also require a practising certificate (in February 2000, £430) issued by The Law Society and will be required to make a contribution to the compensation fund run by The Law Society to pay clients who have suffered loss through the misconduct of a solicitor. Additionally, solicitors have to pay an annual premium for indemnity insurance.

15.3.2 The Law Society

This is the profession's governing body controlled by a council of elected members and an annually elected President. Its powers and duties are derived from the Solicitors Act 1974. Complaints against solicitors used to be dealt with by the Solicitors' Complaints Bureau and the Solicitors' Disciplinary Tribunal, the latter having power to strike from the rolls the name of an offending solicitor. It had been sometimes seen as worrying that the Society combined two roles with a possible conflict of interests: maintenance of professional standards for the protection of the public and as the main professional association to promote the interests of solicitors. Consider a rather basic example. Acting for its members, The Law Society should perhaps try to ensure that insurance policies against claims for negligence are always available for solicitors even if they have been sued for this several times. For such insurance to be granted to someone with such a questionable professional record is, however, clearly not in the best interests of the public who use solicitors.

Office for the Supervision of Solicitors

From 1 September 1996, the solicitors' disciplinary tribunal continued to work as before, but the Office for the Supervision of Solicitors (OSS) took over the work of the Solicitors' Complaints Bureau, and the old organisation was abolished. The new organisation, based in Leamington Spa, has more than 200 staff and employs solicitors, accountants, qualified mediators and administrative support staff. The Office is divided into two parts, one of which deals with client-related matters and the other with regulation. All new cases are examined upon arrival and directed to one or other of them. Staff work in small teams, and one member of staff will follow a complaint through from start to finish.

A Remuneration Certificate Department carries out free reviews of solicitors' bills to ensure that they are fair and reasonable. The Office for Professional Regulation (a part of OSS) ensures that solicitors comply with the regulations that govern them like the Solicitors' Investment Business Rules.

The Compensation Fund was set up in 1941 by The Law Society to protect the clients of dishonest solicitors. The fund is supervised by the OSS. In matters of professional misconduct, OSS can either impose an internal disciplinary sanction or prosecute the most serious cases before the solicitors' disciplinary tribunal. In cases of inadequate professional service, the OSS can order compensation of up to £1,000. The mission statement of the OSS states that 'our aim is to work for excellence and fairness in guarding the standards of the solicitors' profession'. How far that aim is achieved must be judged in the light of developments over the next couple of years.

Members of the public with criticisms about solicitors' work will receive an initial response within 24 hours under the new practice of OSS. Staff have been asked to be more open with the public, make greater use of telephones in contacting complainants and to write letters in plain English rather than in legalistic language. Advertisements were placed in the media for 10 lay people to join a committee dealing with the supervision of the profession.

The major problem for OSS is delay in responding to complaints (*Annual Report 1997–98*) – a point which irks many solicitors as the complaint against them often involves allegations of delay (Editorial, 'Best practice and the OSS' (1999) 149 NLJ 589). According to the 1997–98 Report, the extent of complaints against solicitors is considerable. Approximately 950 firms out of the 8,500 practices in England and Wales are responsible for 80% of the problems brought to OSS.

A new strategy to deal with complaints was announced in 1999 by Philip Hamer, Chairman of the OSS Review Task Force ((1999) 149 NLJ 959).

It followed publication by The Law Society of an independent review of its complaints handling. The review, conducted by management consultants Ernst and Young, outlined a series of steps that must be taken if the OSS is to clear its backlog and end the delays which have beset the organisation for so long. The Report has concentrated on client complaints, currently rising at 16% per year, although, of course, other regulatory matters are also dealt with by the OSS.

Mr Hamer said:

> The problems at the OSS are well known and often repeated. There are unacceptable delays in resolving cases and those delays have led to a growing backlog of untouched complaints. This is causing serious damage to the credibility of the profession and, unless something radical is done, the situation can only get worse [(1999) 149 NLJ 959].

The report by Ernst and Young indicates that the necessary improvements needed – to establish an efficient and effective complaints handling system, clear the backlog of 17,000 complaints, and to deal with all complaints within three months – are achievable by December 2000.

The Review recommends improved systems of management and case filtering, and that an extra 23 permanent and 82 temporary caseworkers be recruited by OSS, together with support and supervisory staff, as well as an increase in the number of additional senior management posts. Estimates of likely costs, excluding overheads, are expected to be in the region of £1.4 million for 1999 and a further £4.3 million in 2000. This sum needs to be considered in context, since the Society has already invested some £5 million in a new computer system for the OSS, which went live at the end of 1998.

OSS is, however, funded by The Law Society, so a serious question arises as to whether the new body will be seen as sufficiently independent by the public.

In *Wood v Law Society* (1995), the plaintiff (W) alleged that she was the victim of continuing misconduct by a firm of solicitors. She complained that H, a partner in a law firm, wrongly acted for both sides when arranging a series of loans for W on the security of W's home, and that H failed to disclose that H's husband was a director of one of the lenders. H's firm acted for the lenders in issuing court proceedings and obtained possession of the cottage for them. After many complaints to them by W, The Law Society conceded, after much delay, that it had been 'unwise' for H's firm to act for the lenders and that this was 'conduct unbefitting a solicitor'. The Society issued a formal rebuke. W sought damages from The Law Society, arguing that as a result of the Society's incompetence and delay, she lost the chance of avoiding repossession of her home and suffered anxiety and distress.

The Court of Appeal held that if there was a duty owed to W by the Society it did not include a duty to provide peace of mind or freedom from distress. Even though the Society appeared not to have lived up to the standards reasonably to be expected of it, there was no prospect of establishing that its failure properly or timeously to investigate her complaints could have any sounding in damages. The loss suffered by W was not directly caused by The Law Society's incompetence and delay.

Another recent case dealing with the liability of solicitors is *White v Jones* (1995). This decision arguably widens the liability of solicitors. The House of Lords decided that a solicitor owes a duty of care to the intended beneficiary of a will when instructed by the testator to draw up that will. A firm of solicitors had been instructed by a client to change his will so that his daughters (whom he had previously cut out of an inheritance) should each receive £9,000. The firm did not act promptly on these instructions and the father eventually died before the will had been changed. Thus the daughters received nothing. The person actually acting in the matter was a legal executive, not a solicitor, but it was the liability of the firm which was in issue. The Court of Appeal allowed an appeal by the plaintiffs, and granted that they should be awarded damages from the firm of solicitors to cover the loss, that is, the amounts they would have inherited had the firm acted professionally. The House of Lords upheld this decision.

The case is an interesting illustration of the judicial development of the common law. There was no obvious way in which the plaintiffs had an action. They could not sue the firm in contract because they had made no contract with the firm; only their father had done so. The daughters were outside of the arrangements between their father and his solicitors; they were third parties and the law does not recognise a *ius quaesitum tertio* (a contractual right for the benefit of a third party). The precedents in the tort of negligence did not provide much assistance because unlike the facts of those cases, the daughters here were not people who had relied upon the firm (as in a case like *Ross v Caunters* (1979)).

The leading opinion was given by Lord Goff who decided that there was a need to give people like the plaintiffs a remedy in this sort of situation, a remedy which was not available according to technical rules of law. He thus favoured 'practical justice', recognising that:

> ... cases such as these call for an appropriate remedy and that the common law is not so sterile as to be incapable of supplying that remedy when it is required [p 777].

By a majority of three to two, the Lords extended the duty of care owed by professionals as it had been expressed in *Hedley Byrne v Heller* (1963). They said that, where the loss suffered by the victim was purely economic, it would be possible to bring an action not only where the professional had given negligent advice or made negligent statements, but it extended to the general principle that the provider of professional services could be liable for pure economic loss where his or her skills were being relied upon.

15.3.3 The Institute of Legal Executives

The Institute of Legal Executives represents senior persons employed in solicitors' offices. There are currently over 20,000 legal executives. They are legally trained (the Institute runs its own examinations) and carry out much of the routine legal work which is a feature of most practices. Changes made to the law by the Access to Justice Act 1999 (see 15.8.3) mean that the Institute will apply for limited rights of audience for those of its members who pass certain examinations.

15.3.4 British Standard 5750

The Law Society has launched a scheme whereby firms of solicitors can prove the quality of the services they offer by the award to the firm of British Standard 5750. Applicant firms are judged on their administrative and legal systems and the efficiency and professionalism with which their clients are handled.

15.4 Barristers

The barrister is often thought of as primarily a court advocate although many spend more time on drafting, pleadings and writing advices for solicitors. Professional barristers are technically competent to perform all advocacy for the prosecution or defence in criminal cases and for a plaintiff or defendant in a civil action. More generally, however, established barristers tend to specialise in particular areas of work. Over 60% of practising barristers work in London.

According to the latest figures (General Council of the Bar, *Annual Report 1998*, 1999), there were 9,698 barristers in independent practice in England and Wales in 1998, of whom 7,288 were men and 2,410 were women. There were 1,006 Queen's Counsel (QCs), of whom 974 were men and 72 women.

The Bar had been organised as an association of the members of the Inns of Court by the 14th century. Today, there are four Inns of Court (Inner and Middle Temples, Lincoln's Inn and Gray's Inn) although there were originally more, including Inns of Chancery and Sergeants' Inns, the latter being an association of the King's most senior lawyers. Until the CLSA 1990, the barrister had a virtual monopoly on advocacy in all the superior courts (in some cases, solicitors could act as advocates in the Crown Court). Barristers, known as 'counsel' when acting in the course of their profession, number about 8,935, of whom 2,115 are women. They cannot deal direct with clients but must be engaged by solicitors.

15.4.1 Training

Entry to the Bar is now restricted to graduates and mature students. An aspirant barrister must register with one of the four Inns of Court in London. Commonly, a barrister will have a law degree and then undertake professional training for one year leading to the Bar Examinations. Alternatively, a non-law graduate can study for the Common Professional Examination for one year and, if successful in the examinations, proceed to the Bar Examinations. The successful student is then called to the Bar by his or her Inn of Court. It is also a requirement of being called that, during study for the vocational course, the student attends his or her Inn to become familiar with the customs of the Bar. A Bar student must attend to eat a certain number of dinners over the course. The student then undertakes a pupillage, essentially, an apprenticeship to a junior counsel. Note that all barristers, however senior in years and experience, are still 'junior counsel' unless they have 'taken silk' and become QCs. Barristers who do not intend to practise do not have to complete the pupillage.

15.4.2 The Inns of Court

The Inns of Court are administered by their senior members (QCs and judges) who are called Benchers. The Inns administer the dining system and are responsible for calling the students to the Bar.

15.4.3 The General Council of the Bar

The General Council of the Bar of England and Wales and of the Inns of Court (the Bar Council) is the profession's governing body. It is run by elected officials. It is responsible for the Bar's Code of Conduct, disciplinary matters and representing the interests of the Bar to external bodies like the Lord Chancellor's Department, the government and The Law Society. According to its own literature, this Council:

> ... fulfils the function of what might be called a 'trade union', pursuing the interests of the Bar and expanding the market for the Bar's services and is also a watchdog regulating its practices and activities.

15.4.4 The Council of Legal Education

The Council of Legal Education is responsible for the educational programme of prospective barristers, their examination and admission.

15.4.5 Queen's Counsel

QCs are senior barristers of special merit. There are currently over 1,006 QCs in practice, the status being conferred on about 45 barristers each year. They are given this status (known as 'taking silk', as a part of the robe they are entitled to wear is silk) by the Queen on the advice of the Lord Chancellor. There are annual invitations from the Lord Chancellor for barristers to apply for this title. Applicants need to show at least 10 years successful practice at the Bar. If appointed, the barrister will become known as a 'Leader' and he or she will often appear in cases with a junior. The old 'Two Counsel Rule' under which a QC always had to appear with a junior counsel, whether one was really required or not, was abolished in 1977. He or she will be restricted to high level work (of which there is less available in some types of practice) so appointment can be financially difficult but in most cases it has good results for the QC as he or she will be able to considerably increase fee levels.

15.4.6 The barrister's chambers

Barristers are not permitted to form partnerships (except with lawyers from other countries); they work in sets of offices called chambers. Most chambers are run by barrister's clerks who act as business managers, allocating work to the various barristers and negotiating their fees. Imagine the situation where a solicitor wishes to engage a particular barrister for a case on a certain date and that barrister is already booked to be in another court three days before that date. The clerk cannot be sure whether the first case will have ended in time for the barrister to be free to appear in the second case. The first case might be adjourned after a day or, through unexpected evidential arguments in the early stages in the trial, it might last for four days. If the barrister is detained, then his brief for the second case will have to be passed to another barrister in his chambers very close to the actual trial. This is known as a late brief. Who will be asked to take the brief and at what point is a matter for the clerk. The role of the barrister's clerk is thus a most influential one.

15.5 Professional etiquette

The CLSA 1990 introduced a statutory committee with responsibilities in the regulation of both branches of the profession. It is the Lord Chancellor's

Advisory Committee on Legal Education and Conduct and comprises a chairman and 16 members appointed by the Lord Chancellor. The chairman is to be a Lord of Appeal or judge of the Supreme Court. The membership must comprise another judge, two practising barristers; two practising solicitors; two law teachers and nine lay members. The committee is under a general duty (s 20) of 'assisting in the maintenance and development of standards in the education, training and conduct of those offering legal services'. It has some specific functions, including giving advice to the General Council of the Bar and The Law Society on all aspects of their qualification regulations and rules of conduct.

The Law Society and the Bar Council exercise tight control over the professional conduct of their members. Barristers can only meet the client when the solicitor or his or her representative is present. This is supposed to promote the barrister's detachment from the client and his or her case and thus lend greater objectivity to counsel's judgment. Barristers and solicitors must dress formally for court appearances although solicitors, when appearing in the Crown, county or High Court, are required to wear robes but not wigs. A barrister not wearing a wig and robe cannot be 'seen' or 'heard' by the judge.

Traditionally, lawyers were not permitted to advertise their services although this area has been subject to some deregulation in the light of recent trends to expose the provision of legal services to ordinary market forces. Solicitors can, subject to some regulations, advertise their services in print and on broadcast media.

15.5.1 Immunity from negligence claims

Barristers cannot be sued by their clients for negligent performance in court or for work which was preparatory to court work (*Rondel v Worsley* (1969)); this immunity has also been extended to solicitors who act as advocates (*Saif Ali v Sidney Mitchell* (1980)). The client of the other side, however, may sue for breach of duty (*Kelly v London Transport Executive* (1982)).

The immunity is justified on the grounds that advocacy could not be executed to the desired standards if its practitioners were always worried about being sued for negligence. Their performance would be impaired by such anxiety and this could lead to too many decisions prompted by a desire to play things safely rather than as well as they might be played. There are also public policy considerations. Lord Wilberforce addressed this problem in *Saif Ali*. He said the immunity was justified:

> ... mainly on the grounds that a barrister owes a duty to the court as well as to his client and should not be inhibited through fear of an action by his client, from performing it; partly on the undesirability of relitigation as between barrister and client of what was litigated between the client and his opponent.

The immunity has been extended to other advocates under s 62 of the CLSA 1990. It has never extended, however, to negligent advice. In *Saif Ali*, the House of Lords held that the immunity only extended to pre-trial work which was:

> ... so intimately connected with the conduct of the cause in court that it can fairly be said to be a preliminary decision affecting the way that cause is to be conducted when it comes to a hearing.

In *Saif Ali*, it was alleged that a barrister had given negligent advice which led to the wrong person being joined as defendant in an action. The House of Lords held that the immunity did not apply here as the decision in question had effectively prevented the plaintiff's claim from coming to court.

Bailey and Gunn (*Smith & Bailey on the Modern English Legal System*, 1991) have characterised the arguments by which the immunity is defended as follows:

- the barrister's duty to the court transcends the duty to the client so the necessary confidence between the Bar and Bench would be undermined if barristers were afraid of being sued;

- rules should promote openness in court and the administration of justice would be badly affected if participants in cases could be sued;

- the 'cab rank rule' (by which barristers are obliged to take the next case irrespective of its desirability in their opinion; the same rule applies to cab drivers picking up passengers) would be difficult to apply properly if barristers had to take on clients who could pursue actions against them;

- that relitigation of cases is undesirable and the correct method of challenge is *via* an appeal.

It could be argued that rules, very protective as they are to barristers, have been contrived by judges (senior barristers who have spent their working lives in that profession) with a particular sympathy for the work, worries and economic interests of advocates. The judges who have been responsible for framing the law in cases like *Rondel v Worsley* and *Saif Ali v Sidney Mitchell* have been in an unusual position. Surgeons and plumbers do not make the law concerning the circumstances in which they can and cannot be sued. Barristers do (if one accepts that a judge, whilst no longer practising as counsel, is by training, custom company and working life a barrister) have a say.

Zander has argued against the immunity. He has doubted whether barristers would be influenced to do their work much differently by the thought that they might be sued for negligence; he has contended that re-opening a case is not necessarily a bad thing, for example, if someone has been wrongly imprisoned because of a lawyer's negligence; and that there is little prospect of a huge wave of litigation in view of the other existing barriers facing a potential litigant. See *Legal Services for the Community*, 1978.

There would not be a barrage of litigation if the immunity was abolished, nor is there any evidence that the performance of barristers would weaken as alleged. There is, though, every good reason to believe that their performances would improve (JUSTICE, *Professional Negligence and the Quality of Legal Services – An Economic Perspective*, 1983). The studies mentioned above also show the significance of the rule that barristers are only liable for negligence, not errors of judgment. If the immunity rule were abolished, it would not entail aggrieved litigants being able to successfully sue their barristers for any error made in the course of handling their cases. It would have to be the sort of mistake that no reasonably competent barrister would have made in identical circumstances.

The immunity was, however, supported by the Benson Royal Commission on Legal Services in 1979 and is preserved by s 62 of the CLSA 1990.

A new system of dealing with complaints against barristers was introduced in 1997. It is operated by the Professional Conduct and Complaints Committee (PCCC), and a Complaints Commissioner, who is not a lawyer. The Commissioner oversees the investigation of complaints. Conduct which is not serious enough to amount to professional misconduct is judged against a concept of 'inadequate professional service'. If there is a *prima facie* case of such wrong then the Commissioner will refer the matter to the PCCC. Panels, summary hearings and disciplinary tribunals are now able to require barristers to repay fees or, in certain circumstances, pay compensation up to £2,000 to a lay client in cases involving inadequate professional service. The Commissioner is able to encourage barristers and complainants to resolve their differences by means of conciliation in appropriate cases. Powers to disbar or suspend a barrister will remain with the Disciplinary Tribunals of the four Inns of Court. The new system meets criticisms of the earlier model of insufficient lay involvement, lack of opportunity for conciliation, and redress for inadequate service.

15.6 Fusion

The division of the legal profession into two branches can be seen as problematic in some respects. Even before the changes wrought by the CLSA 1990, solicitors did a reasonable amount of advocacy in the lower courts and in tribunals. On the other hand, barristers quite often give advice to clients, albeit through solicitors. Both barristers and solicitors do pleadings and drafting work. One article contends that 'solicitors and barristers are now seeing the lines of distinction between them blurred' (see MacErlean (1993) 7 *The Lawyer* 30, 27 July). For many years, there was a strong movement for fusion of the two branches. Submissions made to the Benson Royal Commission on Legal Services argued that the necessity of a member of the public employing a barrister as well as a solicitor for certain work (for example, litigation) was like insisting on a taxi traveller hiring two taxis at once when one would be sufficient to get him to his destination. The legal need to hire two lawyers when one will do causes inefficiency (failures in communication, delay, return of briefs by barristers who are fully booked), damages the client's confidence in the legal process as barristers are regarded as too remote and often insufficiently prepared, and is more expensive than simply engaging a single lawyer.

Fusion was strongly opposed by The Law Society and the Senate of the Inns of Court (now the Bar Council) in their submissions to the Benson Commission. It was argued that fusion would lead to a fall in the quality of advocacy. The leading barristers in a single-profession environment would simply join the major law firms and thus be unavailable for general engagement. Smaller firms would be unlikely to generate enough litigation to keep a barrister as a partner and then find it increasingly challenging to brief counsel of equal standing with that of an opponent. This would create an overall pattern of larger firms expanding and smaller ones – those serving small towns, etc – going out of business.

There would be a reduced number of specialist advocates because whereas with the divided profession a specialist barrister could 'sell' his specialism to a queue of solicitors from different firms, under the fused profession he would be pressured into working at one firm. Another opposition hinges on two features of the English court process: orality and single, continuous hearings designed to make the best use of judicial time but at the expense of practitioners. It has been argued that barristers are better placed organisationally to meet both such requirements.

Additionally, unlike the American system, judges do not have researchers or much time to prepare themselves for cases. The judge relies on the parties to present the case thoroughly. In such circumstances, it is argued, there is a critical need for the judge to have confidence in the competency of the advocates appearing in the case. This can only be properly achieved in the system which cultivates the barrister as a separate professional branch.

The Benson Royal Commission on Legal Services unanimously rejected the idea of fusion. The report concedes that fusion might lead to some saving but only in the smaller cases and in larger cases the expense could be even greater. Using two lawyers did not necessarily entail duplicated work.

It is arguable now that fusion has effectively been organised covertly and gradually. Solicitors' monopolies over conveyancing and the right to conduct litigation have been technically removed (by the CLSA 1990, and the Access to Justice Act 1999, respectively), and the Bar's monopoly over rights of audience, even in the higher courts, has also been removed (by the same legislation, see below). Specialism thus becomes a *de facto* matter more than an automatic function of one branch of the profession. We begin the new century with specialist criminal law solicitor advocates operating from dedicated offices in some cities (a sort of solicitors 'chambers'), and barristers who are effectively working as in-house lawyers in companies doing work which seems very like the traditional work of solicitors.

15.7 The Courts and Legal Services Act 1990

In December 1983, a second reading was given to the House Buyers Bill, a Private Members' Bill introduced by Austin Mitchell MP. It proposed the introduction of a system of licensed conveyancers who would be permitted to undertake the conveyancing of houses with registered title. This was hitting at the solicitors' cherished monopoly of this type of work. They had sometimes even justified the high fees charged for such work as their 'bread and butter' money which enabled them to undertake the more unusual types of work from most high streets. The government responded by indicating its intention to introduce legislation establishing a system of licensed conveyancers and to allow solicitors employed by building societies and banks to undertake conveyancing for their employers' clients whether the land was registered or not. The government wanted to engender more competition and to reduce prices. The Administration of Justice Act (AJA) 1985 went some way to these ends but the government was persuaded by The Law Society that the banks and building societies could not offer the conveyancing if they were the lending institution; to allow otherwise might be to cause conflicts of interest. The provisions, however, were never brought into effect.

The Law Society was alarmed by the potential loss to its members if the mainstay of revenue for many practices (conveyancing) was to become something which non-solicitors could also perform. In attempts to increase business opportunities for its members it quickly relaxed the rules on solicitors being able to advertise; it also revived its opposition to the Bar's monopoly on High Court advocacy. As Zander has charted (*A Matter of Justice*, 1989), there then followed an acrimonious dispute between the two branches. The Marre Committee was established to look into the extent to which the needs and demands of the public were being met by the current structure of the legal profession. It was asked to examine how the services of the profession could be made readily available to meet public needs and those areas where changes in the education, structure and practices of the legal profession might be in the public interest. The Committee's 1988 report offered no radical remedies and largely supported the *status quo*. Significant change became more likely with the appointment of Lord Mackay of Clashfern as Lord Chancellor. He came to the position from the Scottish Bar and with a particular enthusiasm for opening up the legal process to market forces.

On 25 January 1989, Lord Mackay published three Green Papers: *The Work and Organisation of the Legal Profession; Contingency Fees;* and *Conveyancing by Authorised Practitioners*. The first paper contained a statement of the government's overall objective (para 1.1):

... to see that the public has the best possible access to legal services and that those services are of the right quality for the particular needs of the client.

These, it stated, would be best achieved by ensuring that:

- a market providing legal services operates freely and efficiently so as to give clients the widest possible choice of cost effective services; and

- the public can be certain that those services are being supplied by people who have the necessary expertise to provide a service in the area in question.

After a four month consultation period, the Lord Chancellor published a White Paper, *Legal Services: A Framework for the Future*, which took up many of the proposals from the 1987 Civil Justice Review. This formed the basis of the CLSA 1990. The main changes of Pts II to IV of the Act are:

- the establishment of the Lord Chancellor's Advisory Committee on Education and Conduct;

- the establishment of the Legal Services Ombudsman;

- the extension of rights of audience, rights to conduct litigation and undertake probate work to suitably qualified persons, even to non-lawyers;

- the removal of the restriction preventing banks and building societies offering conveyancing services to borrowers, subject to safeguards like the Conveyancing Ombudsman Scheme;

- new regulations and codes setting qualification standards and practice requirements for advocacy and litigation;

- the ending of restrictions on multi-disciplinary and multi-national partnerships;

- changes in rules of eligibility for judicial appointment to reflect the enjoyment of advocacy rights rather than status as barrister or solicitor.

15.8 The effects of the CLSA 1990

Both branches of the legal profession have traditionally enjoyed monopolies in the provision of certain legal services. The Lord Chancellor argued that these monopolies did not best serve the users of legal services as they entailed unnecessarily limited choice and artificially high prices.

Two principal questions examined by the Benson Royal Commission on Legal Services (1979) were: (1) whether barristers should retain their monopoly of the right of audience in the higher courts; and (2) whether solicitors should retain their monopoly over conveyancing work. The Commission recommended in favour of the status quo on each point.

The government at first accepted these proposals but later changed its mind and in the AJA 1985, it broke the solicitors' conveyancing monopoly in allowing licensed conveyancers to practise (above). There was, initially, evidence that this increased competition resulted in benefits to the consumer. From 1985, The Law Society permitted solicitors to sell property, like estate agents, so as to promote 'one-stop' conveyancing. The Consumers' Association estimated that solicitors' conveyancing prices fell by a margin of 25–33% before licensed conveyancers actually began to practise.

Under the CLSA 1990, apart from allowing the Bar Council and The Law Society to grant members rights of audience as before, The Law Society is able to seek to widen the category of those who have such rights. Applications are made to the Lord Chancellor who refers the matter to his Advisory Committee. If the Committee favours the application it must also be approved by four senior judges (including the Master of the Rolls and the Lord Chief Justice) each of whom can exercise a veto. The Director General of the Office of Fair Trading must also be consulted by the Lord Chancellor. All those who consider applications for extended rights of audience or the right to conduct litigation, must act in accordance with the 'general principle' in s 17.

15.8.1 Section 17

The principle in s 17 states that the question whether a person should be granted a right of audience or to conduct litigation is to be determined only by reference to the following four questions:

- is the applicant properly qualified in accordance with the educational and training requirements appropriate to the court or proceedings?

- are applicants members of a professional or other body with proper and enforced rules of conduct?

- do such rules have the necessary equivalent of the Bar's 'cab rank rule', that is, satisfactory provision requiring its members not to withhold their services on the ground that the nature of the case is objectionable to him or her or any section of the public; on the ground that the conduct, opinions or beliefs of the prospective client are unacceptable to him or her or to any section of the public; on any ground relating to the prospective client's source of financial support (for example, legal aid)?

- are the body's rules of conduct 'appropriate in the interests of the proper and efficient administration of justice'?

Subject to the above, those who consider applications must also abide by s 17's 'statutory objective' of 'new and better ways of providing such services and a wider choice of persons providing them, while maintaining the proper and efficient administration of justice'.

Applications have been made by The Law Society, the Head of the Government Legal Service and the Director of Public Prosecutions (DPP). The Advisory Committee, whilst rejecting the idea of an automatic extension of solicitors' rights of audience upon qualification (for example, guilty plea cases in Crown Courts), accepted the principle that they should qualify for enlarged rights after a course of advocacy training. The Committee rejected the idea that employed lawyers like those in the Crown Prosecution Service (CPS) should be granted extended rights of audience. It was thought that such employed lawyers would not have the necessary detachment and objectivity to carry out the work properly and, in any event, the CPS was still experiencing difficulties in coping with its current workload.

Non-lawyers can also apply for rights of audience in the courts. The Chartered Institute of Patent Agents is applying for rights to conduct litigation in the High Court. Under s 11 of the CLSA 1990, the Lord Chancellor will use his power to enable lay representatives to be used in cases involving debt and housing matters in small claims procedures. Similarly, under ss 28 and 29 of the CLSA 1990, the right to conduct litigation is thrown open to members of any body which can persuade the Advisory Committee, the Lord Chancellor and the four senior judges that its application should be granted as the criteria set out in s 17 (above) are satisfied.

The historic monopoly of barristers to appear for clients in the higher courts was formally ended in 1994 when the Lord Chancellor approved The Law Society's proposals on how to certify its members in private practice as competent advocates. The innovation is likely to generate significant change in the delivery of legal services, especially in the fields of commercial and criminal cases. The prospective battle between solicitors and barristers for advocacy work can be simply characterised. The 1995 figures show that there are 63,600 solicitors with practising certificates, and about 7,000 barristers. To the extent that solicitors qualify as certified advocates (solicitor advocates) and take up work in the magistrates' courts, Crown Courts, county courts and the High Court, barristers will be forced out of work, as most cannot survive on opinion and non-contentious work alone. One Bar Council member estimates that up to 50% of practising barristers may be casualties of such a change. The results for the consumers of legal services may be a cheaper, more efficient service. On the other hand, the quality of advocacy work might deteriorate. It is important to be aware of the brief history of developments leading to this change.

15.8.2 Employed solicitors' rights of audience

In February 1997, the Lord Chancellor, Lord Mackay, and the four designated judges (Lord Bingham, Lord Woolf, Sir Stephen Brown, and Sir Richard Scott; see s 17 of the CLSA 1990) approved The Law Society's application for rights of audience in the higher courts for employed solicitors, but subject to certain restrictions.

Following the approval (see 15.8.1) for solicitors in private practice to apply for rights of audience in the higher courts, there are (1 February 2000) 999 solicitors in private practice with such rights. The number of employed solicitors expected to apply is likely to be greater. Although the new right has been granted to a category of solicitor, solicitors will, individually, have to apply to be granted the rights of audience. They will have to take the established tests and show relevant court experience (see below).

Under Law Society proposals now approved by the Lord Chancellor's Department, some solicitors (those who are also barristers or part time judges) will be granted exemption from the new tests of qualification for advocacy. Others will need to apply for the grant of higher courts qualifications, either in civil proceedings, criminal proceedings or in both. A holder of the higher courts (criminal proceedings) qualification will have rights of audience in the Crown Court in all proceedings (including its civil jurisdiction) and in other courts in all criminal proceedings. A holder of the higher courts (civil proceedings) may appear in the High Court in all proceedings and in other courts in all civil proceedings. Applicants for these qualifications must have practised as a solicitor for at least three years. The qualifying scheme is designed only for solicitors who are already lower court advocates. The three elements which must be demonstrated by an applicant are:

- two years' experience of advocacy in the lower courts and experience of the procedures of the relevant higher court;

- competency in a written test on evidence and procedure; and

- satisfactory completion of an advocacy training course.

Large, city firms of solicitors are already having their litigation lawyers trained to qualify for advocacy in the High Court. Three of the biggest commercial firms in England and Wales have held a one week course for partners and fee earners, run by the National Institute of Trial Advocacy, an American body with a good reputation for its methods of training. Investment in training is heavy – one major firm estimated the cost of the course, which trained 24 lawyers, at about £100,000 – but the rewards to be reaped in future are potentially great if solicitors can offer a one-stop service in major commercial work. Continental and American clients are often perplexed by the need to brief an outside barrister.

One problem, however, for these large firms is that they will find it very difficult for their applicants (for audience rights) to meet The Law Society's requirement for county court advocacy experience. Although the expansion of this court's jurisdiction under the CLSA 1990 (in particular, commercial litigation involving sums up to £50,000) has given more county court work to large firms, they generally do very little of this. Large firms are worried that they will have to take on perhaps hundreds of county court cases just to get the ones that will go to trial, and even then these would only be a means to an end, namely the qualification to appear in the High Court.

One benefit for law firms is that those which offer advocacy training are likely to attract the best graduates. Julian Wilson, a litigation partner in Herbert Smith, has said that this is a major worry for the commercial Bar, as graduates will see articles with advocacy as a better option than the insecure Bar pupillage. The Bar is determined that it will not lose any significant ground in the face of this new competition. Its representatives claim that solicitors will not be able to compete with barristers because of their much higher overheads. Peter Goldsmith QC, former Vice Chairman of the Bar Council, has stated that: 'Barristers will remain the pre-eminent advocates. They are the only professionals who are fully trained for advocacy and practise it full time.' Solicitors have replied that their fees are now much more competitive because of the recession, and that cost savings will be made because time will not be spent briefing barristers.

The take-up rate for solicitors opting to try and qualify for rights of audience has, so far, not been high. There are now 170 solicitor advocates with rights of audience in the higher courts. In the first generation of those seeking qualification (that is, those who had not been granted exemption) only 34 out of 72 passed the criminal and civil evidence and procedure tests. Nevertheless, the phenomenon of the solicitor advocate may well expand significantly. An eight-strong solicitor advocate chambers in Birmingham called Midlands Solicitor Chambers is already a model for such developments elsewhere. The larger firms may soon find it propitious to create general or specialist advocacy units, a point whose significance is best seen when the influence of the large firms is appreciated. There are currently 8,524 solicitor firms of which no more than 420 have 10 or more partners, yet this small group of firms employ the vast majority of the workforce: 34% of all principals, and 56% of all assistant solicitors.

Many barristers are very worried about the threat to their traditional work. In 1994, a the Bar Council rejected a proposal to allow its members to deal directly with the public. If it had succeeded, the change would have put those barristers specialising in criminal, family, personal injury, and commercial work in a better position to compete with solicitor advocates. Neil Addison, a member of the Bar Council, has argued that an exclusively referral Bar is only practicable if the Bar becomes, in effect, a branch of the solicitors' profession as in Australia and New Zealand. If the Bar wishes to remain totally independent with separate recruiting and training, it must act accordingly. Young barristers will now be in open competition with solicitor advocates and, Addison argues, it is unrealistic to expect them to fare well in such competition while they remain completely dependent on solicitors for their work. They must, therefore, he argues, be allowed direct access to the public, and be allowed to form partnerships with each other and with solicitors.

15.8.3 The Access to Justice Act 1999 and rights of audience

Lawyers' rights of audience before the courts are covered in Pt III of the Access to Justice Act 1999. It replaces the Lord Chancellor's Advisory Committee on Legal Education and Conduct with a new Legal Services Consultative Panel and:

- provides that, in principle, all lawyers should have full rights of audience before any court, subject only to meeting reasonable training requirements;

- reforms the procedures for authorising further professional bodies to grant rights of audience or rights to conduct litigation to their members; and for approving changes to professional rules of conduct relating to the exercise of these rights.

The Act also contains sections which:

- simplify procedures for approving changes to rules and the designation of new authorised bodies;

- give the Lord Chancellor power, with the approval of Parliament, to change rules which do not meet the statutory criteria set out in the CLSA 1990 as amended by these sections;

- establish the principle that all barristers and solicitors should enjoy full rights of audience; and

- establish the primacy of an advocate's ethical duties over any other civil law obligations.

The legislation enables employed advocates, including Crown Prosecutors, to appear as advocates in the higher courts if otherwise qualified to do so, regardless of any professional rules designed to prevent their doing so because of their status as employed advocates.

Background

The background to these proposals is set out in a consultation paper issued by the Lord Chancellor's Department in June 1998, entitled *Rights of Audience and Rights to Conduct Litigation in England and Wales: The Way Ahead*.

Rights to appear as an advocate in court (rights of audience) and rights to do the work involved in preparing cases for court (rights to conduct litigation) are governed by the CLSA 1990. The 1990 Act leaves it to 'authorised bodies' (currently, the Bar Council, The Law Society and the Institute of Legal Executives) to set the rules which govern the rights of their members, subject to a statutory approval process in which new or altered rules must be submitted for the approval of the Lord Chancellor and the four 'designated judges' (the Lord Chief Justice, Master of the Rolls, President of the Family Division and Vice Chancellor). Before making their decisions, the Lord Chancellor and designated judges receive and consider the advice of the Lord

Chancellor's Advisory Committee on Legal Education and Conduct (ACLEC) and of the Director General of Fair Trading. Applications for the designation of new authorised bodies are subject to a similar procedure, but the designation of the new body is made by Order in Council subject to approval by both Houses.

The government argued that the old approval procedures were convoluted and slow, and that rights of audience were too restrictive. Some applications for approvals took several years to be processed, in part, due to the need for applications to meet the approval of several parties. Rights of audience in the higher courts (the House of Lords, Court of Appeal, High Court and Crown Court) remain restricted to barristers and a small number of solicitors in private practice.

The Act simplifies and expedites the approval procedure. ACLEC will be replaced by a smaller and less expensive committee, the Legal Services Consultative Panel. The functions of the new Panel are not prescribed in detail in the statute, and its composition will be left to the Lord Chancellor to determine, although, in appointing members, he will be required to have regard to specified criteria setting out appropriate knowledge and experience. This will enable the Panel to develop flexibly, in response to the matters on which the Lord Chancellor requires expert independent advice, and will leave the Lord Chancellor free to appoint the best candidates to the Panel. The Act will also give the Lord Chancellor a new power to call in and if necessary replace professional rules affecting rights of audience or rights to conduct litigation, which he considers unduly restrict the exercise of those rights. The exercise of this power will be subject to Parliamentary approval.

The Act makes the Bar Council and the Institute of Legal Executives authorised bodies for the purpose of granting rights to conduct litigation to their members. At present, The Law Society is the only body able to grant these rights; so currently only solicitors are able to conduct litigation. It will also put into statutory form the principle that an advocate's or litigator's first duties are to the court to act with independence in the interests of justice, and to his profession's ethical standards and that these duties cannot be overridden by any other civil law obligations, such as a contract of employment.

The Act provides that every barrister and every solicitor has a right of audience before every court in relation to all proceedings. These general rights were not present for solicitors in the 1990 Act. The Act also restates the current position, that all solicitors have rights to conduct litigation before all courts. These rights are not unconditional; in order to exercise them, solicitors and barristers must obey the rules of conduct of the professional bodies and must have met any training requirements that may be prescribed (such as the requirement to complete pupillage in the case of the Bar, or to have obtained a higher courts advocacy qualification in the case of solicitors who wish to appear in the higher courts).

Section 38 of the Access to Justice Act 1999 provides that advocates and litigators employed by the Legal Services Commission can provide their services to members of the public. Without this clause, they might be prevented from doing so by professional rules.

Section 40 of the 1999 Act gives the General Council of the Bar and the Institute of Legal Executives the power to grant their members rights to conduct litigation. There will be no requirement to grant such rights and it would be a matter for the authorised bodies to propose, subject to approval under the provisions contained in Scheds 5 and 6 of the 1999 Act, whether and in what form such rights might be granted.

The new procedures do not contain the old requirement for each of the designated judges to approve an application (for a body to become an authority to grant rights of audience or rights to conduct litigation), although the Lord Chancellor must seek, and have regard to, their advice. An applicant body will first submit its application to the Lord Chancellor. In the case of an application to become an authorised body, the Lord Chancellor must consult the Legal Services Consultative Panel (ACLEC's replacement body, established by s 35), the Director General of Fair Trading (DGFT), and the designated judges.

Schedule 5, cl 17(1) of the 1999 Act confers on the Lord Chancellor a controversial new power to amend the qualification regulations or rules of conduct of an authorised body by order, if he considers that they place unreasonable restrictions on rights of audience or rights to conduct litigation, or the exercise of those rights. He will be required to consult the Panel, the DGFT and the designated judges before doing so; and his order will be subject to Parliamentary approval by the affirmative resolution procedure.

Section 42 of the 1999 Act gives statutory force to the existing professional rules which make it clear that the overriding duties of advocates and litigators are their duty to the court to act with independence in the interests of justice; and their duty to comply with their professional bodies' rules of conduct. Those duties override any other civil law obligation which a person may be under, including the duty to the client or a contractual obligation to an employer or to anyone else. A barrister, solicitor or other authorised advocate or authorised litigator must refuse to do anything required, either by a client or by an employer, that is not in the interests of justice (for example, suppress evidence). The purpose of this clause is to protect the independence of all advocates and litigators.

15.8.4 Accelerating legal argument

In an effort to reduce the cost of High Court cases, a new measure was introduced in 1995 to put limits on the time lawyers spend addressing the judge. Lawyers who are long winded, or call unnecessary witnesses, can be financially penalised by not being awarded their full costs. The *Practice Direction (Civil Litigation)* (1995) allowed judges to use their discretion to set limits for lawyers' speeches and cross-examination, to limit the issues in cases, and to curb the reading aloud of documents and case reports. Lawyers became unable to examine their own witnesses in court without the permission of the judge. Such an 'examination-in-chief' is normally replaced by the courts' acceptance of a written statement. The *Direction* stated that:

> The paramount importance of reducing the cost and delay of civil litigation makes it necessary for judges sitting at first instance to assert greater control over the preparation for and conduct of hearings than has hitherto been customary. Failure by practitioners to conduct cases economically will be visited by appropriate orders for costs, including wasted order costs.

The *Direction* also instructed judges to ensure that the parties have tried and failed with alternative dispute resolution before the case goes to trial.

The *Practice Direction* has now been superseded by the new Civil Procedure Rules 1998 (see Chapter 11), but the principles have been retained within the new Rules.

15.8.5 Partnerships

By virtue of s 66 of the CLSA 1990, solicitors are enabled to form partnerships with non-solicitors (multi-disciplinary partnerships or MDPs) and confirms that barristers are not prevented by the common law from forming such relationships. They are, however, prohibited from doing so (unless with a foreign lawyer) by the Bar. Solicitors are able, under s 89 of the CLSA 1990 (Sched 14) to form multi-national partnerships (MNPs). The arrival of MNPs over the coming years will raise particular problems concerning the maintenance of ethical standards by The Law Society over foreign lawyers. MDPs also raise potentially serious problems as even in arrangements between solicitors and others, it will be likely that certain work (for example, the conduct of litigation) would have to be performed by solicitors.

15.8.6 Monopoly conveyancing rights

Historically, barristers, solicitors, certified notaries and licensed conveyancers enjoyed statutory monopolies making it an offence for any other persons to draw up or prepare documents connected with the transfer of title to property for payment. The CLSA 1990 seeks to break this monopoly by allowing any person or body, not currently authorised, to provide conveyancing services to make an application to the Authorised Conveyancing Practitioners Board (established by s 34) for authorisation under s 37. The Board must be satisfied, before granting authorisation, that the applicant's business is, and will be, carried on by fit and proper persons, and must believe that the applicant will establish or participate in the systems for the protection of the client specified in s 37(7) including, for example, adequate professional indemnity cover and regulations made under s 40 concerning competence and conduct. Banks and building societies are in a privileged position (s 37(8)) since they are already regulated by statute. These institutions did not initially appear enthusiastic to compete with solicitors by establishing in-house lawyers. They have preferred instead to use panels of local practitioners. Because of this lack of interest, the Lord Chancellor has postponed the making of new regulations (under s 40). David Tench, director of legal affairs for the Consumers Association, has stated that it was appropriate for the regulations to be postponed in the current depressed market.

Mr Tench has also observed that the way solicitors have responded to the threat of competition, by becoming more competitive in terms of price and service, has diminished the need to broaden the market. Another factor reducing the urgency of the matter is the change in Law Society rules which allows solicitors to contract with lenders to provide conveyancing for lenders' customers thus, in effect, permitting one-stop house transfer packages.

The solicitors' monopoly on the grant of probate has also been abolished. Under ss 54–55 of the CLSA 1990, probate services were opened to be available from approved bodies of non-lawyers. Grant of probate is the legal proof that a will is valid, which is needed for a person to put the will into effect. New probate practitioners directly compete with solicitors for probate work. The grant of probate is only a small part of the probate process but when it was restricted as business which only a solicitor could perform it effectively prevented others, except some banks, from being involved in probate. The banks seem best placed to take up work in this area as they already have trustee and executor departments. Like the slow take-up to do conveyancing work (there are still only relatively few commercial licensed conveyancers), enthusiasm to break into the probate business has been hard to detect.

In its Green Papers published in 1989, the government stated that the means it favoured to produce the most efficient and effective provision of legal services would be 'the discipline of the market'. This technique, however, has not been without its problems. There was not a rush to use the conveyancing services of solicitors who had made their prices very competitive in the wake of competition from licensed conveyancers. In one survey, The Law Society found that only 8% of clients had opted for cheaper services ((1993) *The Lawyer*, 12 October). More worrying is the allegation that a significant number of those offering 'cut-price' conveyancing are not producing a respectable quality of service. Tony Holland, a former president of The Law Society, has argued that this is a result of a rush of inadequately trained persons to make money from that part of solicitors' erstwhile monopoly which has been thrown open to non-lawyers ((1994) 144 NLJ 192). He notes that, at the time of writing the article, he was engaged in giving expert testimony in no fewer than 19 actions for negligence arising from incompetent conveyancing.

Nevertheless, recent research published by the Department of the Environment, Transport and the Regions showed that conveyancing in England and Wales was the cheapest of the 10 European countries surveyed, even though it was the slowest. It takes an average of six to eight weeks for a contract to be exchanged in England and Wales while, in the USA and South Africa, the average is a week. Even so, while the legal fee for conveyancing on a £60,000 house in England and Wales is about £1,500, the same service in France costs about £3,600 and, in Portugal, it is about £6,000 (see News in Brief, 'Cheap conveyancing' (1998) 148 NLJ 8).

Various reports by consumer associations have attacked aspects of the delivery of legal services in the years following the implementation of the CLSA 1990. In 1994, Dr Neville Harris of the University of Liverpool surveyed 60 firms of solicitors and 301 clients. He found that 40% of privately paying clients were not told at the outset of cases how much they would be likely to have to pay. One in four of the firms did not operate the internal complaints procedure required by The Law Society, and only one firm in 10 said that it actively sought feedback from clients (see National Consumer Council, 'Solicitors and client care: an aspect of professional competence', February 1994).

15.8.7 The Legal Services Ombudsman

This position was created by s 21 of the CLSA 1990 to reinforce the existing system with more effective measures for dealing with complaints. The Legal Services Ombudsman (LSO), currently Ann Abraham, is empowered by s 22 to 'investigate any allegation which is properly made to him and relates to the manner in which a complaint made to a professional body with respect to an authorised advocate, authorised litigator, licensed conveyancer, recognised body or notary who is a member of that professional body; or any employee of such a person, has been dealt with by that professional body'. The LSO cannot normally investigate any complaint whilst it is being investigated by a professional body nor if it has been dealt with by a court or the solicitors' disciplinary tribunal or the disciplinary tribunal of the Council of the Inns of Court, since the procedures in such tribunals satisfy the need for public accountability.

Upon completing an investigation, the LSO must send a copy of his reasoned conclusions to the complainant and the person or body under investigation. The report can make any of the following recommendations:

- that the complaint be reconsidered by the professional body;

- that the professional body should consider its powers in relation to the person who was the subject of complaint;

- that the person complained about, or any person connected to him or her, should pay compensation to the complainant for loss suffered or inconvenience or distress caused;

- that the professional body concerned should pay such compensation;

- that a separate payment be made to the complainant in respect of costs related to the making of the allegation.

The person or body to whom these recommendations are sent must reply within three months explaining what action has been or is proposed to be taken to comply with the recommendation(s) made.

The 1998–99 Annual Report of the Legal Services Ombudsman states that 1998 saw a continuing increase in the number of complaints handled by all the professional bodies – the Office for the Supervision of Solicitors (OSS), the General Council of the Bar, and the Council for Licensed Conveyancers (CLC). Complaints against the Institute of Legal Executives (ILEX) are included for the first time in the annual report (*Modernising Justice ... Modernising Regulation?*, 8th Annual Report of the Legal Services Ombudsman, 1998–99).

The Ombudsman conducted 1,658 investigations in the 15 months from January 1998 to March 1999. In 1998, the Report notes: one complaint was made to the professional body for every 24 practising solicitors, for every 18 practising barristers; and one complaint for every five practising licensed conveyancers. In each case, the figures represent an increase in the number of complaints per lawyer since 1997.

The Ombudsman states in the Report that, in 67% of cases, she was satisfied with the way the complaint had been handled by the professional body, and thus made no formal recommendation or criticism. This, however, represents an overall decrease in the Ombudsman's level of satisfaction with the handling of complaints by the professional bodies since 1997 when the relevant figure was 70%.

The total number of recommendations made was 510. These comprised 192 recommendations that the professional body reconsider; 206 recommendations for payment of compensation by the professional body; and 112 recommendations for payment of compensation by the individual lawyer. Compensation awards for loss ranged from £10 to £6,850.

LEGAL SERVICES

The main area of debate on this theme is the best approach to supplying the highest number and widest range of people with legal services appropriate to what citizens need. How can the legal profession become more user friendly? Have the changes made under the CLSA 1990 to increase competition in the provision of legal services been successful? Have the restrictive professional monopolies been properly broken and if so will the quality of services offered by non-lawyers (for example, conveyancing, probate, litigation) be reduced? Will the exclusion of millions of people from legal aid eligibility have any serious consequences?

The impact of the conditional fee arrangements, the 1995 Green Paper on legal aid and franchising are of special importance, but to deal with these issues properly you need to be familiar with the details of how legal services are delivered in general.

The legal profession

The legal profession, although not fused, comprises solicitors and barristers whose work is becoming increasingly similar in many respects. Additionally, the ending of monopolies on litigation, probate and conveyancing have meant that lawyers' traditional work is increasingly becoming blurred with that of other professionals. The liabilities of lawyers for errors and negligence is a key issue. Another is the way in which complaints are handled by the professions.

The Courts and Legal Services Act 1990

The CLSA 1990 was passed 'to see that the public has the best possible access to legal services and that those services are of the right quality for the particular needs of the client'. The detail by which the Act sought to do this is very important, especially s 17 (general principle, litigation and rights of audience); s 11 (lay representatives); ss 28–29 (right to conduct litigation); s 66 (multi-disciplinary partnerships); s 89 (multi-national partnerships); ss 34–37 (conveyancing); ss 21–26 (the Legal Services Ombudsman); and s 58 (conditional fee arrangements).

The Access to Justice Act 1999

The 1999 Act makes many changes which will have an impact upon the professions. It articulates the principle that all lawyers should have full rights of audience before all courts, provided they have passed the relevant examinations. Also, by reforming the procedures for authorising further professional bodies to grant rights of audience, it signals a widening of those rights in the future.

CHAPTER 16

THE FUNDING OF LEGAL SERVICES

16.1   Introduction

Legal aid was introduced after the second world war to enable people who could not otherwise afford the services of lawyers to be provided with those services by the state. The system grew and extended its reach and range of services enormously over the decades. Costs to the government were gigantic. The system underwent various restrictions and cut-backs during the late 1990s and was almost abolished in 1999. In this chapter, we sometimes refer to the 'current' system of legal aid. This is because parts of the system will still be operational for much of 2000, until it is entirely replaced by the new amendments we describe.

Two factors combined in the early 1990s to cause great change in the way that legal services are funded. The first factor was the spiralling cost of legal aid to the State during a period of recession. The money available to government was insufficient to meet the rising cost of maintaining the level and extent of legal services previously available. The second factor (and some people would directly link these in a causational way) was the professed aim of the government in general and Lord Mackay, the then Lord Chancellor, in particular, to reduce the State's role in the provision of legal services.

Over 10 million people have been taken out of the bracket of legal aid eligibility as a result of governmental changes of the eligibility criteria (see Smith, *Shaping the Future: New Directions in Legal Services*, 1995). To try to compensate for this exclusion of millions of people from the effective right to use the law, other schemes have been promoted and developed. These include the use of 'no win, no fee' arrangements, the use of non-lawyer legal services, and legal services private insurance.

The legal aid budget for 1996–97 was £1.48 billion. It was in this context that the White Paper *Striking the Balance: the Future of Legal Aid in England and Wales* was published in 1996. The paper proposed the most radical changes to the legal aid system since its launch in 1951. The main aims of the White Paper in relation to funding legal services were: (a) to impose cash limits on the legal aid scheme (instead of allowing it to have a demand-led budget); (b) to require some form of payment from all users; and (c) to operate a separate budget for major, expensive cases.

There are several State funded schemes to facilitate the provision of aid and advice. Each scheme has different rules relating to its scope, procedures for application and eligibility. Because of the importance of justice and access to the legal machinery, the idea behind legal aid is to give people who could otherwise not afford professional legal help the same services as more wealthy citizens. This raises important social, political and economic questions. Do poorer people deserve the same quality of legal advice as that which can be afforded by wealthy people? If so, how should such schemes be funded?

16.1.1 A brief historical overview

The legal aid system was introduced under the Legal Aid and Advice Act 1949 by a Labour government after the Second World War to allow poor people to have access to the justice system. Before this time, such people had to rely on charity if they went to court. The system was seen by the government as the 'second arm of the Welfare State' (the first one being the National Health Service). The system expanded throughout the 1950s and 1960s. It moved from just covering the higher courts to covering the lower courts; and from just civil courts to criminal courts.

A number of historical and economic factors combined to reduce the scope of the system from the mid-1970s. By the 1990s, the system applied to a much smaller section of the community than it had done in previous decades. In the 1950s, about 80% of the population was covered by the legal aid system, whereas, by 1998, less than 40% of the population is covered.

The scope of eligibility had expanded quickly in the 1970s. As a result, more lawyers were setting up practices catering for legal aid clients. Divorces were becoming much more common (as the result of social factors and legislation which made divorce easier), and divorce accounts for a very large part of civil legal aid. Alongside all this, the economy was going into recession, and this had two effects: (a) it resulted in there being less money in government funds from which to finance legal aid; and (b) it generated waves of economically related problems (unemployment, family break-ups, welfare problems) which needed legal services for people who could not afford to pay for them.

From the mid-1980s, successive Lord Chancellors have been engaged in a series of measures to try to reduce public expenditure on the legal system. They have been particularly concerned to curb expenditure on legal aid which almost doubled to £1.4 billion over a four year period to 1995. The system of paying lawyers for legal aid work has been changed, the eligibility criteria have been changed to exclude millions of people from the scheme, and control of the funds has been moved from The Law Society to the Legal Aid Board and now much power has been devolved to regional centres and particular firms through 'franchising'.

Since 1950, the system has been 'demand-led'. This meant that a person needing a service could get it, provided that he or she satisfied the appropriate 'means test' and appropriate 'merits test'. From 1996, the then Lord Chancellor, Lord Mackay, proposed that the system will be financially capped, that is, that regional authorities of the Legal Aid Board be given a single lump sum at the beginning of the financial year for expenditure that year and when that sum is spent on legal services, no more becomes available for any applicant, no matter how urgent and deserving his or her case. Lord Mackay said that 'legal aid is not, and cannot be, an unconditional blank cheque from the taxpayer'.

In an address to The Law Society in October 1992, Lord Mackay, the then Lord Chancellor, made the following comment:

> Expenditure on legal aid is now over £1.1 billion gross. That figure is the amount paid from legal aid to the legal profession (including VAT and other outgoings). The net cost to the taxpayer in 1991–92, after allowing for legal aid contributions and costs recovered, was more than £900 million. The net figure ... will exceed £1 billion during [1992–93], more than double what it was a mere four years ago ... This rate of growth, and that's what I'm speaking of, cannot be allowed to continue. Every extra pound for legal aid means a pound less for the NHS, for schools, for social security, or for the infrastructure of the economy.

It is this thinking which prompted major changes in the provision of legal aid in 1993 and 1995. In particular, the financial eligibility criteria were changed so that only the very poorest people qualify for free aid. Additionally, the Lord Chancellor changed the way that solicitors are paid for criminal legal aid and assistance, with the result that the pay will be worse and many practitioners currently offering the service are expected to withdraw from the scheme as they would be losing money by continuing to do such work.

Speaking to the Social Market Foundation in 1995, the Lord Chancellor traced the geometric growth in legal aid expenditure since 1949. The scheme cost £685 million in 1990–91 and, in the year 1995–96, cost around double that sum. The number of people now being assisted is high: around 4.5 million in 1997–98. Nonetheless, as a result of recent significant financial cut-backs and changes in eligibility regulations, it can be argued that the original ideal is now quite remote from current practice.

The cuts were intended by Lord Mackay to make savings of £43 million during 1993–94, £110 million the following year and £170 million during 1995–96. During the financial year 1996–97, the legal aid budget of £1.48 billion was £150 million less than an original government estimate after savings of £240 million over three years.

The last government had been particularly keen to reduce fraud on legal aid funds by the 'apparently wealthy'. Lord MacKay, the former Lord Chancellor, made new regulations changing eligibility following a period of consultation about this problem in 1995. The Civil Legal Aid (Assessment of Resources) (Amendment) Regulations 1996 and the Legal Aid in Criminal and Care Proceedings (General) (Amendment) Regulations 1996 address this issue. The most important change concerns the treatment of an assisted person's dwelling house which has previously been wholly exempt for eligibility purposes. Since June 1996, for both advice and assistance, and legal aid, it has been possible to take into account the market value of the applicant's property in so far as it exceeds £100,000 when calculating the applicant's capital. Where there is equity in the property (that is, the property is worth more than the mortgage), then the equity can count as capital in so far as it exceeds £100,000.

Lord Justice Steyn once observed (*Lwch* (1994)) that 'it is a principle of our law that every citizen has a right of unimpeded access to a court'. Taken with the recent doubling of many civil court fees, the radical reduction of legal aid introduced in 1999 will not, despite the various alternative measures to be established, further the principle enunciated by Lord Steyn. The changes will, if anything, confirm the observation of Mr Justice Darling that 'the law courts of England are open to all men, like the doors of the Ritz Hotel'.

According to one theory of law and government, the justice system has a pre-eminent claim on resources. This is because, however important are social services like health and education, if people do not have the effective citizen's right to take and defend legal action (including actions concerning health and education), then they are not properly incorporated into society. A society without the majority feeling they could, if necessary, participate in the legal process is an unstable society.

Today, however, it is arguable that the principles of ordinary market economics have superseded theories of social incorporation and 'stake holding' in determining who gets access to lawyers and courts.

The dangers of social exclusion

The new systems for allowing citizens to participate in the legal system, and the dramatic reduction in legal aid provision demonstrate that nothing is sacred within the legal system. In a parliamentary debate in 1997, Earl Russell reminded the government of what can happen in societies where people *en masse* are denied access to the courts. He urged that we consider 'the cost of not spending money as well as the cost of spending it'. He was speaking about the obstacles posed to the prospective litigant by high court fees but his observations are equally applicable to debate about dismantling civil legal aid.

16.1.2 Types of legal aid

Although the term 'legal aid' is used to cover a wide range of subsidised or free services, in strict language it only refers to one sort of help: representation in court. Legal Advice and Assistance (also known as the Green Form scheme) covers advice and help with any legal problem; and, in some cases, under what is called 'assistance by way of representation' (ABWOR), it also covers going to court, for example, with the permission of the local Legal Aid Board Director, a solicitor can represent a client in court in most civil proceedings in magistrates' courts. It is available for cases where advice or letter writing has not solved a problem and the matter has to go to court. Civil legal aid is available for many types of action but not, notably, for proceedings in coroners' courts, tribunals (except the lands tribunal and the employment appeal tribunal) nor for proceedings involving libel or slander. Criminal legal aid covers the cost of case preparation and representation in criminal cases. In addition to these schemes, some solicitors are prepared to give a free or fixed-fee interview without giving any means test related to the interviewee's income or capital. Duty Solicitor Schemes are available at most magistrates' courts and police stations. Solicitors can give free legal advice to someone who is being questioned by the police whether or not such a suspect has been arrested; advice and free representation can also be given for someone's first appearance for a particular offence at a magistrates' court.

16.1.3 Legal advice and assistance

Under the Green Form scheme, a solicitor can undertake ordinary legal work (excluding court work) up to a limit, initially, of two hour's worth of work for a client who passes the relevant means test. The amount of work done can be extended with the permission of the local Legal Aid Area Committee. Undefended divorce cases have not been eligible for legal aid since 1977 but the Green Form scheme is available and extends now to a limit of three hours worth of work. The work which a solicitor may undertake includes assistance with certain hearings to which the client may be a party; this is ABWOR. In 1998–99, there were 1,592,722 Green Form acts of assistance and 58,123 acts of Assistance by Way of Representation. Most solicitors participate in this scheme. It is within the solicitor's discretion as to what sort of work he or she undertakes. An argument for presentation in a court or tribunal could be prepared, letters written, documents drafted; negotiation with another party may even be undertaken.

The Green Form scheme and ABWOR were the most widely used of the legal aid schemes prior to the Access to Justice Act. At the beginning of the 1990s, the take-up was stable at around one million acts of assistance per year, but then the scheme began to grow, reaching a peak of 1.6 million acts of assistance in 1993–94. This growth was principally fuelled by increased demand for advice on social and economic matters, such as housing, debt and welfare benefits, although advice on personal injuries, employment and immigration matters also grew during that period (Legal Aid Board, *Annual Report*, 1998–99, section 3, p 117). Since 1996, the volume of Green Form cases paid for by the Legal Aid Board started to rise again. The introduction of standard fees for criminal legal aid in the magistrates' courts in 1993 produced a steady growth in demand for advice and assistance on criminal matters, but, more recently, another factor has been renewed demand for advice on civil, non-matrimonial matters. In 1998, demand in this area reached its 1994 peak. (p 120). The most rapidly growing areas of advice have been immigration and nationality and welfare benefits.

The means test for the applicant is administered by the solicitor. The upper limit for Green Form assistance, from April 1999, is a disposable income of £83 per week and a disposable capital of £1,000 for those without dependants (moving up with each additional dependant, for example, £1,335 for those with one dependant).

ABWOR allows representation to be undertaken without a legal aid certificate. It applies to domestic proceedings in magistrates' courts, proceedings before mental health review tribunals, representations under the Police and Criminal Evidence Act (PACE) 1984 for warrants of further detention and representation in certain child care proceedings. The scheme covers the cost of a solicitor preparing a case and representing a client in most civil cases in magistrates' courts, now known as Family Proceedings Courts. These cases include separation, maintenance (except child maintenance where the Child Support Agency has jurisdiction) residence/contact, paternity and defended adoption proceedings. The income and capital conditions for ABWOR are different from those applying in Legal Advice and Assistance (LAA) cases. Here, applicants will qualify if their weekly disposable income is £172 or less and they have savings of no more than £3,000. The same dependant's allowances apply as for the LAA scheme. Unlike LAA, the applicant might have to make a contribution for ABWOR. If the applicants disposable income is between £72 and £172, he or she will have to make a contribution of one-third of the amount by which the income exceeds £72. Someone, for example, whose disposable income is £102 per week (£30 over the lower limit) will have to pay a contribution of £10 per week, payable to the solicitor.

16.1.4 Civil legal aid

Since 1989, civil legal aid has been run by the Legal Aid Board. An applicant must satisfy two tests. Under the 'merits test', now governed by the Legal Aid Act (LAdA) 1988, the applicant must show the Board that he or she has reasonable grounds for taking, defending or being party to an action (s 15) but the applicant can be refused aid if it appears to the Board unreasonable to grant representation. The *Legal Aid Handbook* (published by the Board) states that, although financial benefit set against the costs of an action will be the normal criterion, there might be cases involving the applicant's status, reputation or dignity (for example, sex or race discrimination) where legal aid would be appropriate even though the financial benefit to be gained from any action was small.

Means test

The other test is a means test. This uses the concepts of 'disposable capital' and 'disposable income'. The former includes savings, jewellery, etc, but not the value of a house nor of a car unless it is especially valuable; the latter involves actual income less income tax, national savings, money for dependants, necessaries, travel to work, etc. From April 1999, to qualify for free legal aid, an applicant must have a disposable income of not more than £2,680 a year and a disposable capital of not more than £3,000. If disposable income is more than £2,680 but less than £7,940 (£8,751 for personal injury cases), or disposable capital is between £3,000 and £6,750 (or £8,560 for personal injury cases), then an applicant can qualify for legal aid subject to a contribution. An applicant with more than £7,940 disposable income (£8,751 in personal injury cases) or disposable capital of more than £6,750 (£8,560 in personal injury cases) will not be eligible for aid. Where applicants have to make a contribution because of their income, it is an ongoing monthly contribution from the applicant's income, and is $\frac{1}{36}$ of the excess over £2,680 for the life of the certificate. A contribution from the applicant's disposable capital (in excess of £3,000) may also be required. Where contributions are payable owing to capital, the payment will be all of the disposable capital over £3,000.

In 1993–94, 359,000 civil legal aid certificates were issued. Over the last two years, this has been the area of most rapid growth within the Legal Aid Board's responsibility. Under s 17 of the LAdA 1988, a legally aided person can, if he or she loses the case, be liable to meet some of the opponent's costs. This is known as the Indemnity Rule. Usually, the legally aided person is asked to pay the same amount again as that already paid in respect of his or her own contribution. When a legally aided party wins the case, the Legal Aid Fund recoups its costs from costs paid by the loser, from the winner's contribution and from any damages awarded to him or her or property won or recovered in the action. Some awards, like maintenance, are exempt from this 'statutory charge'.

There is now much evidence to show that the eligibility for legal aid has fallen dramatically over recent years. Glasser (a solicitor and former consultant to the Lord Chancellor on legal aid) has argued that the numbers eligible for legal aid fell by 13 million between 1979 and 1989 ((1988) 85 Law Soc Gazette 11; (1989) 86 Law Soc Gazette 9). Murphy, a statistician at the London School of Economics, has put the figure closer to 14 million ((1989) *Legal Action*, 7 October). In 1991, in a report on legal aid undertaken for the Lord Chancellor, figures were given which were the basis of the Lord Chancellor's concern to control legal aid expenditure. In the five years to 1990, whilst the number of legal aid certificates had risen by 22%, gross expenditure rose by 120% from £70 million to £153 million and net expenditure (cost to the taxpayer) had risen from £31 million to £76 million.

The review showed a marked decline in eligibility for legal aid: 74% of the population were eligible in 1979 whereas only 66% were eligible in 1990. The review was, however, critical of the notion that a particular proportion of the population 'should' be eligible for legal aid. Such a notion presupposed that the distribution and level of means in the population remained constant in relation to legal costs, that is, that, for example, the poorest 70% of the population would always be too poor to afford legal representation.

16.1.5 Criminal legal aid

The decision as to whether to grant legal aid is made by the court clerk according to criteria in the LAdA 1988. In the event of a refusal, there is a statutory right to criminal legal aid committees run by The Law Society. As with civil legal aid, the applicant must pass a merits and a means test. The merits test is simply whether it would be in the 'interests of justice' (s 21). This is usually satisfied by defendants in the Crown Court – the success rate has been about 98% in recent years. Section 22 of the LAdA 1988 lists some factors to be taken into account by any court which is deciding whether granting legal aid would be in the interests of justice. The factors are: (a) whether the offence is such that if proved it is likely that the court would impose a sentence which would deprive the defendant of his liberty or lead to his loss of livelihood or serious damage to his reputation; (b) the determination of the case may involve consideration of a substantial question of law; (c) where the defendant has linguistic difficulties or other disability; (d) the defence will require expertise like cross-examination; or (e) it is in the interests of another party that the accused be represented.

The means test is normally carried out by court clerks. Until 1982, there was a discretion as to whether the defendant should make any contribution and, if so, how much. Under current Regulations (which came into force on 10 April 1995), the courts question the defendant to determine his or her disposable income and capital. The income limit for free criminal legal aid is £51 a week disposable income. The capital limit for free legal aid is £3,000. The contribution system here requires a person to pay anything above £3,000 disposable capital, and weekly contributions from income of £1 for every £3 or part of £3 by which disposable income exceeds £51. Anyone receiving the State benefits of income support, family credit or disability working allowance is automatically eligible for criminal legal aid without having to make any contribution.

In 1983, an official survey of the granting of criminal legal aid confirmed earlier research in finding a distinct lack of uniformity in the decisions of different courts when refusing aid in similar cases. Research published by the Legal Aid Board (September 1992) also confirms the discrepancies between the approaches of both court clerks and area committees. In dummy applications for aid in a range of typical criminal cases, one court granted 10 out of 12 whilst two courts refused aid in seven cases. The Lord Chancellor referred to these as 'alarming inconsistencies'. Clearly, inadequate training of clerks and committees in this area may have resulted in a number of applicants being refused aid, thus adding to the numbers who have been, in effect, cast out of the system of protection.

16.1.6 Legal franchising

Since October 1993, following a pilot scheme in the Birmingham area, solicitors who meet certain management criteria have been devolved certain administrative powers previously exercised by the Legal Aid Board, thereby reducing the administrative costs to the Board and increasing the speed with which legal aid can be obtained. In return for meeting the management efficiency criteria, the practices receive certain fiscal benefits such as a lump sum payment from the Legal Aid Board on account immediately upon the approval of a case.

The devolved powers the solicitors receive are approval of Green Form extensions and granting of emergency certificates, 'where the interests of justice demand the immediate taking or defending of proceedings' – issued in circumstances such as the urgent need for orders preventing domestic violence. The old system will continue for firms which do not obtain a franchise, that is, applications for aid will still be made to the Board but clearly, in time, franchised firms will obtain a competitive advantage. The Board, soon to be superseded by the Legal Services Commission will then move from being an approving body to a quality control organisation. The fear amongst many lawyers and commentators is that this trend will lead to seriously reduced access to legal services because the smaller firms, which find it too difficult to satisfy the management criteria, will become uncompetitive and a number will go out of business.

Over 2,500 offices were franchised by July 1999, with over 2,000 more applications being processed. The emerging picture of future practice is one in which law firms and advice agencies bid for part of a fixed regional civil legal aid budget. The work to be covered by the franchised firms will include family, housing, debt, employment, welfare benefits, immigration, consumer, and mental health. Personal injury and medical negligence work will be handled by specialist franchised firms.

One real danger here is the expected move away from paying lawyers for the time they take to do the necessary work and towards paying set sums for particular sorts of work. In a strong editorial against such changes, the *New Law Journal* ((1998) 148 NLJ 577, 24 April) reflects The Law Society's view that these changes could 'pave the way to a bureaucratic and inflexible system for rationing legal advice to people on low incomes and that the bureaucrats will pay for what they perceive is needed rather than what is actually required'. The Criminal Law Solicitors' Association and the Legal Aid Practitioners' Group have both expressed fears that the proposals would lead to a breach of a basic principle of practice: that lawyers should be able to provide fearless representation for clients. By entering into contracts with the Legal Aid Board (soon to be superseded by the Legal Services Commission), lawyers might well end up compromising or impairing their independence as they will be under pressure to retain favour with the Board or Commission in order to ensure renewal of the contract.

16.1.7 Modernising justice

The White Paper, *Modernising Justice: the Government's Plans for Reforming Legal Services and the Courts,* was published on 2 December 1998. It proposed the most fundamental changes in the English legal system for over 40 years.

The paper stated:

> A fair and efficient justice system is a vital part of a free society. The criminal justice system exists to help protect us from crime, and to ensure that criminals are punished. The civil justice system is there to help people resolve their disputes fairly and peacefully. This government has a radical programme of reform for the whole country. The justice system cannot be left out. We want a clearer, fairer, better system, that will make justice available to all the people.

The paper asserted that many people are put off getting help with legal problems because the legal system is slow, expensive and difficult to understand. It proposed a new Community Legal Service that will ensure that 'people's needs are properly assessed, and that public money is targeted on the cases that need help most'.

Providing value for money in law is identified as a key aim of reform. The paper argued that taxpayers have, year on year been paying heavily for legal aid, while fewer people have been helped. By introducing contracting for legal services (the franchise system) and abolishing restrictive practices, the government aims to increase competition among lawyers and help keep costs down. It committed itself to create new avenues to justice by extending conditional fees, and modernising court procedures. References to statute sections below are to the Access to Justice Act 1999.

The Community Legal Service

Until recently, about £800 million a year was spent on lawyers' fees under the civil legal aid system. Another £150 million a year from local government, central government, charities and businesses is spent on the voluntary advice sector, including Citizens Advice Bureaux, law centres and other advice centres. The Legal Services Commission (to replace the Legal Aid Board) will take the lead in establishing a Community Legal Service to co-ordinate the provision of legal services in every region (s 1 of the 1999 Act). The plan is to achieve control over the legal aid budget and to gradually change over to a system in which the governmental spending on legal aid and voluntary sector advice is managed from one fund.

The Legal Services Commission will manage the Community Legal Service fund (s 4 of the 1999 Act), which will replace legal aid in civil and family cases.

Why replace civil legal aid?

The government argues as follows. Taxpayers spend £800 million a year through the civil legal aid system on buying legal services from lawyers for those who cannot afford to pay for themselves, and this system now needs radical change:

- it is too heavily biased towards expensive court based solutions to people's problems;

- despite a merits test, legal aid is sometimes used to fund cases that appear to be undeserving;

- it is not possible to control spending effectively. From 1992–93 to 1997–98, spending on civil and family legal aid grew by 35% from £586 million to £793 million; but, at the same time, the number of cases funded actually fell by 31% from 419,861 to 319,432;

- in the ordinary legal aid system, lawyers were paid according to the amount of work claimed for, so there is no incentive to handle cases quickly or work efficiently.

Who will do the work and who will qualify for help?

The Legal Services Commission will buy services for the public under contracts. Only lawyers and other providers with contracts will be able to work under the new scheme. This will enable budgets to be strictly controlled, will help to ensure quality of service, and will provide a basis for competition between different providers. The fund will be targeted at those people who are most in need of help and high-priority cases. There will be no absolute entitlement to help, and the fund will not be spent on cases which could be financed by other means, such as conditional fees (see 16.5). The government does, however, intend to increase the number of people potentially eligible for advice and assistance under the scheme, to bring this into line with eligibility for representation. At the same time, those who can afford to contribute towards their legal expenses will be required to do so.

How will the government help people who do not qualify for help from the Community Legal Service fund?

It is clear that not everyone will benefit from the new scheme. In this context, the government states that it will work with the insurance industry to widen cover (it says that 17 million people are already covered by one sort of legal insurance or another, although this figure includes people entitled to legal services in respect of only one type of situation like a traffic accident or holiday disasters). It is also intended to widen the scope of the conditional fee system.

Criminal Defence Service

The government states that it will maintain the fundamental principle that those facing a criminal trial should not be afraid that lack of resources and proper representation might lead to their wrongful conviction. However, serious weaknesses in the current criminal legal aid system are identified.

The cost has risen from £507 million in 1992–93 to £733 million in 1997–98 – an increase of 44%. At the same time, the number of cases dealt with increased by only 10%. Although standard fees are now paid in many cases, the most expensive cases are paid in the traditional way by calculating the fee after the event. The White Paper, *Modernising Justice,* stated that the system gave lawyers an incentive to boost their fees by dragging cases out, and that such cases took up a disproportionate amount of money. The system for means testing defendants to see whether they should contribute to the costs of their case was seen as a waste of time and money. The test has not stopped some apparently wealthy defendants from receiving free legal aid, and 94% of defendants in the Crown Court pay no contribution.

The government will replace the current criminal legal aid scheme with a new Criminal Defence Service (CDS). To begin with, the CDS will be run, by the Legal Services Commission (LSC), but it will be an entirely separate scheme from the Community Legal Service, with a separate budget. The Commission will develop contracts for different types of criminal defence services and implement them following pilot schemes. All contracts for criminal defence services will include quality requirements, and, wherever possible, prices for the contracts will be fixed in advance. Fixed prices create an incentive to avoid delay, and reward efficient practice. Eventually, contracts with solicitors firms will cover the full range of defence services, from advice at the police station to representation in court. If a case requires the services of a specialist advocate in the Crown Court, this is likely to be covered by a separate contract. Opponents of this move argue that fixed price work is not conducive to justice as such a system of payment encourages corner-cutting and work of an inferior standard.

Very complex and expensive cases – where the trial is expected to last 25 days or more – will not be covered by ordinary contracts. A defendant's choice of solicitor will be limited to firms on a specialist panel, and a separate contract will be agreed in each case.

One key question here was to what extent a defendant's choice of lawyer in a criminal matter would be restricted under the new scheme. Many lawyers expressed worry that if the legislation allowed the government (through the Lord Chancellor's Department) to choose the defendant's lawyer, then famous campaigning lawyers, such as Gareth Peirce (who helped release the Guildford

Four and the Birmingham Six) and Jim Nicol (who acted for the appellants in the Carl Bridgewater case), might be shunned by the Criminal Defence Service ((1998) *The Independent*, 25 November). The right to choose a defence lawyer has historically been regarded as a precious one in the UK. As prosecutions are brought in the name of the Crown, there is an appreciable danger in permitting the Crown (albeit a different branch of government) to have an influence over who represents the defendant. In the end, the Access to Justice Act 1999 offers a compromise in s 15. The section says that, where a defendant has been granted the right to representation, he may choose any representative and the LSC must fund that representation. However, s 15(2) explains that regulations can be made which do restrict the defendant's choices in some ways. In some types of cases, for example, the right might be excluded – the government has mentioned complex fraud trails as an example. The right will not include a right to choose only a lawyer of a particular description, for example, a defendant on a simple theft charge could not insist on representation by a QC. Section 15(4) provides that the regulations made to determine the details of how the system will work 'may not provide that only a person employed by the Commission, or by a body established and maintained by the Commission, may be selected'. Thus, there will always be the right to select a lawyer from the independent field, rather than (as some lawyers feared) a choice only of lawyers employed directly or indirectly by a governmental agency.

Who will decide whether to grant criminal representation, and how? As now, it will be for the court to decide whether to grant a defendant representation at public expense, according to the interests of justice (Sched 3, cl 5(1) of the 1999 Act). But the current requirement for a means test will be abolished. Instead, after a case is over, a judge in the Crown Court will have the power to order a convicted defendant to pay some or all of the costs of his defence. This will mean that assets frozen during criminal proceedings, and any assets which only come to light during proceedings, will be taken into account, so some wealthy criminals will pay much more than they do now.

16.1.8 The Access to Justice Act 1999 – a summary

We address the main provisions of the Act where relevant throughout this chapter. Here, for convenience, we present an overview of the main changes made by the Act and related regulations.

Under the new system, legal aid will no longer be available for:

- those seeking personal injury compensation (except clinical negligence cases);

- disputes about inheritance under a will or an intestacy;

- matters affecting the administration of a trust or the position of a trustee;

- matters relating to the position of directors of companies, restoring a company to the Register or dealing with the position of minority shareholders;

- matters affecting partnerships;

- matters before the Lands Tribunal;

- cases between landowners over a disputed boundary of adjacent property; and

- cases pursued in the course of a business.

The hope is that the extension of conditional fees in these areas will provide increased public access to lawyers.

The government is now committed to:

(a) allowing conditional fee agreements (no-win, no-fee agreements) to be used in all except family and criminal cases;

(b) transferring to conditional fees most money and damages claims currently supported by legal aid;

(c) removing most personal injury actions from the scope of legal aid;

(d) ensuring that medical negligence cases are to be conducted only by practitioners who are experienced in this field of litigation;

(e) the setting up of a limited transitional fund which would provide support in cases where there are high investigative costs in establishing the merits of a case or where the costs of carrying the case are very high.

Since 1995, 45,000 people have taken advantage of conditional fee arrangements (CFAs) to bring personal injury claims. The government has noted that many of these people would have been unable to afford to pursue their claims at all without conditional fees – people only just above the legal aid limit, people who are far from well off. These people, the Lord Chancellor has argued, are the great majority of the population who are in work – with families, mortgages, savings, or other assets, which mean that they are not eligible for legal aid, but who cannot contemplate the open-ended commitment of meeting lawyers' fees.

Lord Irvine stated that the government had been listening carefully to the comments received in relation to medical negligence cases, and accepted that many lawyers practising in this area needed time to modernise the way they run their firms so that they can take cases on regardless of their financial standing. That is why State funding of representation will be retained for the time being. There is currently not a good record of claims in this area. The net cost of medical negligence cases to the taxpayer last year was £27 million. Looking at the cases closed by the Legal Aid Board in 1996–97, 32 cases recovered £500,000 or more. Leaving these cases aside, the average cost of cases was £4,122 to recover average damages of £4,107. In only 17% of cases was £50 or more recovered (and 1996–97 was a good year: closed case data from previous years shows recovery rates between 13% and 17%). Medical negligence cases are a specialist area of litigation. It can be difficult to identify at the outset whether a case has merit, and, even as the medical evidence unfolds, whether the negligence alleged has caused the ailment or injury. The government believes that part of the reasons for the high failure rate is that cases are being pursued by lawyers who are insufficiently experienced in this area of litigation.

The Lord Chancellor stated that:

> The government does not, therefore, propose to remove these cases from the scope of legal aid for the present. We do, however, intend to do what we can to reduce the high failure rate of these cases. It cannot be right that it is only in as few as 17% of all the cases that are supported by a legal aid certificate that more than £50 is recovered in damages. Medical negligence cases should be conducted by practitioners who are experienced in this field of litigation. We cannot any longer allow inexperienced practitioners to take cases. We propose that the Legal Aid Board should establish contracts only with lawyers of sufficient experience. Anyone who is granted legal aid to pursue a medical negligence case will be required to use a lawyer who holds a contract with the Board [Lord Chancellor's Department, Official Statement 57/98, 4 March 1998].

16.2 The Access to Justice Act 1999

16.2.1 Background

The old scheme was contained in the Legal Aid Act (LAdA) 1988.

A common feature of the civil and criminal legal aid schemes was that expenditure on them was demand-led. Any lawyer could do legal aid work for a client who passed the relevant means test (if any), and whose case passed the statutory merits test (in the case of civil legal aid), or the interests of justice test (in the case of criminal legal aid). Lawyers were (and will continue to be under the transitional arrangements) paid on a case by case basis for each individual case or other act of assistance, usually at rates or fees set in regulations, but in some cases on the same basis as a privately funded lawyer.

This, in the government's view, meant that there were few mechanisms or incentives for promoting value for money or assuring the quality of the services provided; and that neither the government nor the Legal Aid Board was able to exert adequate control over expenditure or determine the priorities for that expenditure.

During 1992–1998, expenditure on legal aid overall increased from £620 million in 1991–92 to £1,526 million in 1997–98, a rise of 68%. In comparison,

GDP rose by 18% over the same period. Meanwhile, the number of people helped overall increased by 18% to 3.6 million. In civil and family legal aid, expenditure rose from £330 million to £634 million, an increase of 92%, while the number of people helped fell by almost 10%. Average payments in civil and family cases rose by almost 90%, from £1,598 in 1991–92 to £3,018 in 1997–98. The cost of criminal legal aid rose by 50% between 1991–92 and 1997–98, from £397 million to £597 million, while the numbers helped remained at around 615,000. Over the period average payments to defence lawyers went up by 11% and 66% in the magistrates' courts and the Crown Court respectively.

Since August 1994, the Legal Aid Board operated a voluntary quality assurance scheme, known as franchising. Currently, some 2,500 solicitors' firms have franchises in one or more of the 10 subject categories in which they are awarded (criminal, family, personal injury, housing, etc). A further 2,030 applications for franchises were pending in July 1999. The Board is continuing to develop the franchising scheme, and to introduce new categories, in order to underpin the move to a generally contracted scheme under the reforms in this Act.

In Autumn 1994, the Board set up a pilot scheme which showed that non-profit making advice agencies could provide legally aided advice and assistance which the government argued were to the same standard as those provided by solicitors' firms. In October 1996, a second pilot was established, involving a larger number of agencies, to develop systems for contracting for advice and assistance work.

In November 1996, the Board began to pilot contracts with solicitors' firms to provide advice and assistance in civil matters. A pilot of contracts to provide mediation in family cases under the legal aid scheme commenced in May 1997. A pilot covering advice and assistance in criminal cases began June 1998, and was extended to cover representation in the youth court in February 1999. Since October 1997, the Board has set up a Regional Legal Services Committee in each of its 13 areas to advise it about future priorities for contracting.

In 1999, the government announced that all civil advice and assistance, and all family work will be provided exclusively under contract from January 2000. Only organisations with a relevant franchise will be eligible to bid for these contracts. Also, a new clinical negligence franchise came into effect in February 1999; and from July 1999 only firms with that franchise will be able to take these cases under the legal aid scheme.

16.2.2 The advice sector

There are over 1,500 non-profit making advice agencies in England and Wales. They receive their funding – over £150 million a year in total – from many different sources, mainly local authorities, but also charities, including the National Lottery Charities Board, Central Government, the Legal Aid Board, and business.

The provision of advice services is not spread consistently across the country. Some areas appear to have relatively high levels of both legal practitioners and voluntary outlets, while others have little or none. For example, the Legal Aid Board's South East Area has one Citizens Advice Bureau per 46,000 people, but, in the East Midlands, 138,000 people share a Citizens Advice Bureau. The government believes that the fragmented nature of the advice sector obstructs effective planning, and prevents local needs for legal advice and help from being met as rationally and fully as possible.

16.3 Overview of the Act

The 1999 Act replaces the legal aid system with two new schemes; and makes provisions about rights to supply legal services, appeals (we look at these in Chapter 15) and court procedure (we look at these in Chapter 11), magistrates and magistrates' courts (see Chapter 3).

The provisions in the Act form part of the wide ranging programme of reforms to legal services and the courts, described in the government's White Paper, *Modernising Justice* (1998). Except where noted, the Act only affects England and Wales. There is currently very little literature on the Act as it has only just been promulgated so, aside from our own views and the viewpoints of other commentators, we rely heavily here, for official interpretations, on governmental guidance provided when the legislation was in draft form, that is, a Bill.

16.3.1 Funding of legal services (Pts I and II)

Part I of the 1999 Act provides for two new schemes, replacing the legal aid scheme, to secure the provision of publicly funded legal services for people who need them. It establishes a Legal Services Commission to run the two schemes; and enables the Lord Chancellor to give the Commission orders, directions and guidance about how it should exercise its functions.

It requires the Commission to establish, maintain and develop a Community Legal Service. A new Community Legal Service fund will replace the legal aid fund in civil and family cases. The Commission will use the resources of the fund, in a way that reflects priorities set by the Lord Chancellor and its duty to secure the best possible value for money, to procure or provide a range of legal services. The Commission will also have a duty to liaise with other funders of legal services to facilitate the developments of co-ordinated plans for making the best use of all available resources. The intention is to develop a network of legal service providers of assured quality, offering the widest possible access to information and advice about the law, and assistance with legal problems.

The Commission will also be responsible for running the Criminal Defence Service, which replaces the current legal aid scheme in criminal cases. The new scheme is intended to ensure that people suspected or accused of a crime are properly represented, while securing better value for money than was possible under the legal aid scheme.

Some of Pt III relates to privately funded litigation. It amends the law on conditional fee agreements between lawyers and their clients, and the recovery of insurance premiums as costs between the parties to litigation.

Lawyers' rights of audience before the courts are also covered in Pt III and we look at this in Chapter 15.

Part IV of the Act deals with aspects of reforms for the system for appeals in civil and family cases, and we look at these in Chapter 3.

16.3.2 The Legal Services Commission

Section 1 of the 1999 Act establishes the new Legal Services Commission, and makes provision for appointments to it. The Commission will replace the Legal Aid Board. It was considered necessary to establish a new body to reflect the fundamentally different nature of the Community Legal Service (CLS) compared to civil legal aid. Within the broad framework of priorities set by the Lord Chancellor, the Commission will be responsible for taking detailed decisions about the allocation of resources. It will also be required to liaise with other funders to develop the CLS more widely. The Commission will also have a wider role in respect of the Criminal Defence Service than the Legal Aid Board did in respect of criminal legal aid. The Board had very limited responsibilities for legal aid in the higher criminal courts. Membership of the Commission will differ from that of the old Legal Aid Board, to reflect a shift in focus from the needs of providers to the needs of users of legal services. Also, the Commission is smaller than the Board: 7–12 members rather than 11–17. This is intended to facilitate 'focused decision making'.

Schedule 14 of the 1999 Act makes transitional provisions for the replacement of the Legal Aid Board by the Commission. Briefly, it provides that, on an appointed day (probably some time in 2000), the Commission shall take over all the property, rights and liabilities of the Board. Staff of the Board will automatically become staff of the Commission. The intention is that the provisions of the 1988 Act will remain in force for any cases that have already started when the new schemes come into effect.

Section 2 of the 1999 Act gives the Lord Chancellor the power to replace the Commission with two bodies: one responsible for the Community Legal Service and the other for the Criminal Defence Service. The intention is to allow for the possibility that, because of the different nature and objectives of the two schemes, it may prove more effective in the longer term to administer them separately. It would not be practicable to set up two bodies from the outset.

This is because of the need to retain, in substance, the existing infrastructure and expertise of the Legal Aid Board to manage the transition from legal aid to the two new schemes. This involves both administering existing cases under the old scheme and developing contracting as the principal means of procuring services under the new schemes.

The government indicated in 1999 that it had no definite intention to split the administration of the two schemes in future. Rather, the intention is to review the situation once the new schemes are firmly established, probably after about five years.

16.3.3 The Community Legal Service

The Legal Services Commission will have two main duties in respect of the Community Legal Service:

- First, it will manage a Community Legal Service fund (ss 4–11), which will replace legal aid in civil and family cases. The CLS fund will be used to secure the provision of appropriate legal services, within the resources made available to it, and according to priorities set by the Lord Chancellor and by regional and local assessments of need. A Funding Code, drawn up by the Commission and approved by the Lord Chancellor, will set out the criteria and procedures for deciding whether to fund individual cases. As spending is brought under better control, the government says, it will be possible to expand the scope of the fund over time into areas that are not covered by legal aid. In particular, the intention is to extend the availability of alternatives to lawyers and courts, like mediation and advice agencies. Mediation is already a requirement in family matters (see Pt III of the Family Law Act 1996).

- Secondly, as part of a wider Community Legal Service, the Commission will, in co-operation with local funders and interested bodies, develop local, regional and national plans to match the delivery of legal services to identified needs and priorities.

The development of the Community Legal Service at a local level is dependent in practice on the formation of Community Legal Service Partnerships (CLSPs) in each local authority area. (These do not require specific provisions in the Act.) The CLSP will provide a forum, in each local authority area, for the local authority and the Legal Services Commission, and if possible other significant funders, to come together to co-ordinate funding and planning of local legal and advice services, to ensure that delivery of services better matches local needs. There have, however, been warnings from some lawyers that government plans are so vague as to how the Community Legal Service will work that the credibility of the entire new system is in question. According to the one view, the Community Legal Service is in danger of becoming a 'leafleting service' (News, 'The legal profession and the Community Legal Service' (1999) 145 NLJ 1195).

Even at early stages of the launch of this project, the government's plan has been attacked by sections of the legal community. In May 1999, the Lord Chancellor faced calls for an imposition of a duty on local authorities to fund legal services after a long-awaited consultation paper on the CLS was published (Irvine (Lord), 'Community vision under fire' (1999) 96 Law Soc Gazette 1, p 5). Michael Mathews, the then Law Society President, said it was 'baffling that after so many months there should be such a lack of information on this important service ... Sadly, this Consultation Paper is more government waffle on legal aid'.

The Commission will develop a system of kitemarking, on the basis of common quality criteria. This is designed to reinforce public confidence that the voluntary sector is a provider of good quality legal advice and help.

The Commission and the CLSPs will encourage innovation by the voluntary sector in the delivery of advice through increased use of information technology and mobile 'outreach' services providing help to people in remote communities.

Overall, the intention is to:

- make best use of all the resources available for funding legal services, by facilitating a co-ordinated approach to planning;

- improve value for money through contracting and the development of quality assurance systems;

- establish a flexible system for allocating Central Government funding, in a rational and transparent way within a controlled budget, so as to provide legal services where they are judged to be most needed; and

- ensure that the scheme is capable of adapting to meet changing priorities and opportunities.

Section 4 of the 1999 Act describes the services which may be provided under the Community Legal Service. These range from the provision of basic information about the law and legal services, to providing help towards preventing or resolving disputes and enforcing decisions which have been reached. The scheme will encompass advice, assistance and representation by lawyers (which have long been available under the legal aid scheme), and also the services of non-lawyers. It will extend to other types of service, including, for example, mediation in family or civil cases where appropriate.

Section 4(3) of the 1999 Act provides that the Community Legal Service does not cover services funded as part of the Criminal Defence Service, in order to avoid any overlap between the two schemes. Under Sched 2, also excluded is any help (beyond the provision of general information about the law and the legal system) relating to company matters, defamation and malicious falsehood, conveyancing and the making of wills.

Under s 5 of the 1999 Act, the Community Legal Service fund is established and the mechanisms by which the Lord Chancellor will provide the resources to the fund are defined. Each year, as part of the general public expenditure planning process, the Lord Chancellor will set a budget for the Community Legal Service. This will take account of the receipts from contributions (for example, from local authorities) with the balance of the budget provided by Lord Chancellor from money voted by Parliament. The Community Legal Service fund will therefore not be an open-ended fund, as was the legal aid fund.

The Lord Chancellor will be able to direct the Commission to use specified amounts within the fund to provide services of particular types (s 5(6)). The intention is that the Lord Chancellor will divide the fund into two main budgets, for providing services in (i) family and (ii) other civil cases, while allowing the Commission limited flexibility to switch money between the two areas. The Lord Chancellor may set further requirements within these two budgets, by specifying the amount, or the maximum or minimum amount, that should be spent on, say, services from the voluntary advice sector, mediation, or cases involving a wider public interest. The idea here is that, in this way, it will be possible to ensure that resources are allocated in accordance with the government's priorities.

A duty is placed on the Commission to aim to obtain the best value for money – a combination of price and quality – when using the resources of the fund to provide services.

Section 6(3) of the 1999 Act sets out the ways in which the Commission may use the Community Legal Service fund to provide services. These include making contracts with or grants to service providers, or employing staff to provide services directly to the public. These flexible powers are intended to give effect to one of the principal objectives of the reform of publicly funded legal services: that is the ability to tailor the provision of services, and the means by which services are to be delivered, to the needs of local populations and particular circumstances. They will also allow the Commission to test new forms of service provision through pilot projects.

Schedule 2 of the 1999 Act excludes from the scope of the Community Legal Service fund specified types of service which would otherwise fall within the broad definition of cases covered by the scheme, and says that the Lord Chancellor can make directions bringing other cases within the provisions of the act in exceptional circumstances. For example, the Lord Chancellor may direct that for personal injury cases (which are generally excluded by Sched 2, because most such cases are suitable for conditional fees) funding by the Community Legal Service fund should nonetheless be possible where exceptionally high investigative or overall costs are likely to be necessary, or where issues of wider public interest are involved. The Consultation Paper, *Access to Justice with Conditional Fees* (LCD, 1998), notes (para 3.31) that it will be necessary to decide what should constitute public interest. For example, a test case about a novel point of law might have no more than a 50% chance of success, but the decision could impact on numerous future cases (in the way that recent cases involving sporting injuries have extended the duty of care owed by officials wider than was previously accepted). Or a claim for a relatively small sum in damages might benefit a large number of other people with a similar claim. Examples might be claims arising out of the use of pharmaceutical products, and pollution of water supplies or the atmosphere. Very expensive cases often include this type of public interest aspect: they are expensive because they are novel and complex, or because their wide potential impact means that they are hard fought.

Under Sched 2, people (but not corporate bodies) will be able to receive information on any matters of English law. Schedule 2 provides for restrictions on the more substantial services that will be available in different categories of case. For some categories, a full range of services will be available (subject to priorities). For some others, all services except representation at court by a lawyer will be available. Finally, for some categories, only the provision of information and basic advice will be possible.

The intention is that the scope of the Community Legal Service fund should initially mirror the previous scope of civil legal aid; but that it may change over time. In particular:

- as conditional fees, legal expenses insurance and other forms of funding develop more widely, it may be possible to exclude further categories which can generally be funded privately;

- as resources become available through the greater control of spending and value for money provided by the new scheme and the development of private alternatives, it may be possible to extend the scheme's scope to cover services that are excluded now because, although they would command some priority, they are unaffordable.

The following changes to the scope of the legal aid scheme were given immediate effect. In future, subject to any exceptions that the Lord Chancellor may make by direction, only basic information and advice will be available for:

- disputes involving allegations of negligent damage to property or the person ('personal injury'), apart from those about clinical negligence. These cases are generally considered suitable for conditional fees;

- allegations of defamation or malicious falsehood. Generally, legal aid was not currently available for representation in defamation, but it was sometimes possible to get legal aid by categorising the case as one of malicious falsehood. The government's view is that these cases do not command sufficient priority to justify public funding; and, in any event, they may often be suitable for a conditional fee;

- disputes arising in the course of business. Legal aid was not available for firms and companies, but a sole trader could get legal aid to pursue a business dispute. Businessmen have the option of insuring against the possibility of having to take or defend legal action. The government does not believe that the taxpayer should meet the legal costs of sole traders who fail to do so;

- matters concerned with the law relating to companies or partnerships; matters concerned with the law of trusts or trustees; boundary disputes. The government does not consider that these command sufficient priority to justify public funding. In addition, funding for representation at proceedings before the Lands Tribunal or Commons Commissioners will no longer be available. Other services, including assistance with preparing a case, will continue to be available.

Section 7 of the 1999 Act allows the Lord Chancellor, using regulations, to set financial eligibility limits for people to receive services funded by the Community Legal Service fund. It allows him to set different conditions, or no conditions, for different circumstances or types of case or service.

There are, however, no immediate plans to make any substantive changes to the present financial eligibility limits, although the government has stated it will continue to uprate them each spring as it did with the legal aid eligibility criteria. The government has said that, in due course, it intends to expand the availability of advice and assistance to people who can afford to make a contribution.

The Commission will, under s 8, prepare a Code setting out the criteria for determining whether services funded by the Community Legal Service fund should be provided in a particular case, and if so what services it is appropriate to provide. The Code will also set out the procedures for making applications.

The funding assessment under the Code will replace the merits test for civil legal aid. Section 8 (its first three sub-sections) of the 1999 Act is the relevant provision. It says:

8 (1) The Commission shall prepare a Code setting out the criteria according to which it is to decide whether to fund (or continue to fund) services as part of the Community Legal Service for an individual ... and ... what services are to be funded for him.

   (2) In settling the criteria to be set out in the Code, the Commission shall consider the extent to which they ought to reflect the following factors:

      (a) the likely cost of funding the services and the benefit which may be obtained by there being provided;

(b) the availability of sums in the Community Legal Service Fund for funding the services and (having regard to the present and likely future demands on that Fund) the appropriateness of applying them to fund the services;

(c) the importance of the matters in relation to which the services would be provided for the individual;

(d) the availability to the individual of services not funded by the Commission and the likelihood of his being able to avail himself of them;

(e) if the services are sought by the individual in relation to a dispute, the prospects of his success in the dispute;

(f) the conduct of the individual in connection with services funded as part of the Community Legal Service (or an application for funding) or in, or in connection with, any legal proceedings;

(g) the public interest; and

(h) such other factors as the Lord Chancellor may by order require the Commission to consider.

(3) The criteria set out in the code shall reflect the principle that, in many family disputes, mediation will be more appropriate than court proceedings.

The new assessment is intended to be more flexible than the existing merits test. It will be possible to apply different criteria in different categories according to their priority. It will also be possible to take account of factors, such as a wider public interest, which attach to particular cases, rather than those whole categories of case for which contracts might be let. The reform of the merits test, which regulates the demand that qualifies for help, is said by the government to complement the reforms of the supply of services – with the intention of creating a flexible system for deploying resources to meet a range of priorities within a controlled budget.

The criteria for funding the various types of service in different categories of case will be defined by considering these factors. The Code will define which factors are relevant in a given category, how they should be taken into account, and what weight should be given to them. For example, prospects of success will not be a relevant factor in cases about whether a child should be taken into local authority care.

The Code is required to reflect the principle that in many family disputes mediation is more appropriate than court proceedings. This is intended to reinforce the development, under the Family Law Act 1996, of mediation as a means of resolving private law family disputes in a way that promotes as good a continuing relationship between the parties concerned as is possible in the circumstances. The government has argued that mediation is more constructive than adversarial court proceedings, and that litigation in these cases usually serves only to reinforce already entrenched positions and further damage the relationship between the parties. In addition, the cost of court proceedings is higher than that of mediation, and additional costs have to borne by the property of the family, reducing the amount available to the parties and their children in future. The credibility of mediation as an appropriate forum for family matters in general took a blow in 1999, when the government abandoned plans to introduce the scheme related to divorce after pilot studies failed to produce good results.

Sections 7 and 8 of the 1999 Act enables the Lord Chancellor to set financial conditions to apply to people receiving services funded by the Community Legal Service fund. Subject to two additions, the effect of the Act is generally to replicate the provisions of the old LAdA 1988.

As before, it will be possible to make regulations requiring people to contribute towards the cost of the services they receive by way of flat rate fees, contributions related to disposable income and capital, and from any property recovered or preserved as a result of the help given. In general, the intention is to replicate the old regulations.

The 1999 Act, though, extends the potential scope of financial conditions in two ways, although there are no immediate plans to use either of these powers:

- It will be possible to make the provision of services in some types of cases subject to the assisted person agreeing to repay an amount in excess of the cost of the services provided in the event that their case is successful (s 10(2)). This might make it possible to fund certain types of case on a self-financing basis, with the additional payments from successful litigants applied to meet the cost of unsuccessful cases. It would also be possible to mix public funding with a private conditional fee arrangement, subject to the same conditions about the uplift to the costs in the event of a successful outcome. The government has suggested that this might be appropriate, for example, where a case could not be taken under a wholly private arrangement, because the solicitors' firm was not large enough to bear the risk of the very high costs likely to be involved.

- It will be possible (s 10(3), (4)) to require the assisted person to repay, over time and with interest, the full cost of the service provided (for example, through continuing contributions from income). This will make it possible to provide services in some categories of case in the form of a loan scheme.

Section 11 of the 1999 Act establishes limits on the liability of the person receiving funded services to pay costs to the unassisted party. The costs he must pay cannot go above what is 'reasonable' (s 11(1)), taking into account the financial resources of all parties. It also provides that regulations may specify the principles that are to be applied in determining the amount of any costs awarded against the party receiving funded services and the circumstances in which a costs order may be enforced against the person receiving funded services.

Henceforward, those regulations which limit the circumstances in which the costs order may be enforced against the person receiving funded services, or the liability of the Commission to meet any costs order on behalf of the person receiving funded services, will be made on a more flexible basis. Previously, protection from costs was seen by governments to create too great an advantage in litigation for the person receiving legal aid.

16.3.4 The Criminal Defence Service

The purpose of the CDS is to secure the provision of advice, assistance and representation, according to the interests of justice, to people suspected of a criminal offence or facing criminal proceedings (s 12).

The Commission will be empowered to secure these services through contracts with lawyers in private practice, or by providing them through salaried defenders, employed by non-profit making organisations. All contractors will be expected to meet quality assurance standards and contracts will, where possible, cover the full range of services from arrest until the case is completed. (The old arrangements for criminal legal aid were widely seen as fragmented: a person could receive assistance in respect of the same alleged offence under several separate schemes, each resulting in a separate payment for the lawyers involved.)

There will be a transitional period while contracts are developed and extended to cover the full range of services. The Commission will therefore be able to pay lawyers on a case by case basis for representation provided on a non-contractual basis, according to remuneration scales set in regulations (that is, broadly on the same basis as the current criminal legal aid scheme).

As under the old system, the courts will grant representation under the scheme to defendants according to 'the interests of justice'. However, the courts will no longer have to conduct a means test as well before granting representation. Instead, at the end of a case in the Crown Court, the trial judge will have power to order a defendant to pay some or all of the cost of his or her defence. The Commission may investigate the defendant's means in order to assist the judge. The intention is to abolish the system of means testing every defendant, which the government considers an ineffective and wasteful aspect of the current scheme, while ensuring that in the more expensive cases defendants continue to pay towards the cost of their defence when they can afford to do so.

Section 12(2) of the 1999 Act defines 'criminal proceedings'. These include criminal trials, appeals and sentencing hearings, extradition hearings, binding over proceedings, appeals on behalf of a convicted person who has died, and proceedings for contempt in the face of any court. The Act allows the Lord

Chancellor to add further categories by regulation. This power will be used, for example, to prescribe Parole Board reviews of discretionary life sentences.

The Legal Services Commission will gradually take over the functions currently undertaken by the higher courts in respect of criminal legal aid. At first, Court Service staff will continue to determine costs in many Crown Court cases but the numbers will diminish as the Commission increases the proportion of cases covered by contracts. Staff at the Court of Appeal (Criminal Division) and the House of Lords will continue to determine costs in cases before those courts, although the scope for the Commission to contract for these cases as well will be considered in due course.

Section 13(1) of the 1999 Act places the Legal Services Commission under a duty to provide such advice and assistance as it considers appropriate in the interests of justice for individuals who are arrested and held in custody, and in other circumstances to be prescribed by the Lord Chancellor in regulations.

Initially, it is intended that regulations will provide for advice and assistance in broadly the categories for which it is currently available to people subject to criminal investigations or proceedings. These categories include advice and assistance provided by duty solicitors at a magistrates' court, at a solicitor's office, and to a 'volunteer' at a police station.

Section 13(2) also enables the Commission to comply with this duty by securing advice and assistance through entering into contracts; by making payments to persons or bodies; by making grants or loans to persons or bodies; by establishing and maintaining bodies; by making grants to individuals; or by doing anything else which the Commission considers appropriate for funding advice and assistance except providing it itself. It also enables the Commission to secure the provision of advice and assistance by different means in different areas in England and Wales and in relation to different descriptions of cases.

The aim of this part of the Act is to provide the Commission with a range of options for securing advice and assistance in criminal matters. Contracting with quality assured suppliers, the government contends, should provide greater control over both expenditure and the quality of the service provided; and better value for money.

Section 13(2)(f) of the 1999 Act also contains powers to enable the Commission to provide services through lawyers in its own employment. These powers are intended to provide flexibility if, for example, there is limited coverage by private lawyers in rural areas. Using employed lawyers should also, the government has argued, provide the Commission with better information about the real costs of providing these services.

Section 14 places a duty on the Commission to fund representation for individuals granted a right to representation. It enables the Commission to comply with this duty in the same ways as for advice and assistance. The power to make direct case by case payments to representatives will allow the Commission to continue to pay non-contracted lawyers to provide representation during the transitional period while contracting develops; and possibly thereafter where that proves to be the best means of securing the necessary services.

The legislation provides that defendants granted a right of representation can choose their representative, restricted only as provided in regulations (s 15). In due course, it is intended that regulations will, in particular, provide that a defendant's choice of representatives is limited to those holding contracts with the Commission. In time, the Commission will provide all, or nearly all, representation exclusively through contracted representatives, who it will require to meet defined quality standards.

In certain types of cases – such as serious fraud trials – defendants' choice may be further limited to representatives from a panel of firms or individual advocates who specialise in a particular type of case. Membership of a panel will depend on meeting pre-determined criteria. In this way, the Commission can ensure that defendants facing charges in these exceptional cases are represented by those with the necessary expertise, experience and resources.

Section 15(2)(a) of the 1999 Act enables the Lord Chancellor to make regulations defining circumstances where a defendant will not have a right to a choice of representative, but will instead have a representative assigned to them. This power might be used, for example, to assign an advocate to a previously unrepresented defendant charged with serious sexual offences where the victim/witness is a child. (Unrepresented defendants may not cross-examine child witnesses directly when charged with violent or sexual offences.)

Schedule 3 deals with the grant of a right to representation and, in particular:

- the individuals to whom a right of representation may be granted;

- the extent of the right;

- which courts and other bodies are competent to grant representation;

- appeals against the refusal of a right to representation; and

- the criteria for granting the right.

Schedule 3 of the 1999 Act provides for rights to representation to be granted to defendants or appellants in criminal proceedings where the interests of justice require it. The factors to be considered in assessing the interests of justice mirror s 22(2) of the LAdA 1988. Other provisions in the Schedule also reflect provisions in the 1988 Act.

Section 16 of the 1999 Act will ensure that salaried defenders employed by the Legal Services Commission – are subject to a code guaranteeing minimum standards of professional behaviour. The Code is to include duties: to avoid discrimination; to protect the interests of the individuals for whom services are provided; to the court; to avoid conflicts of interest; and of confidentiality.

Before preparing or revising the Code, the Commission is required to consult. The Code will be approved by a resolution of each House of Parliament, and published.

The Act enables the Lord Chancellor to make regulations setting out how the new power should be applied.

Under the criminal legal aid scheme, most defendants (about 95%) were not required to make a contribution to their defence costs. Those who did contribute and were acquitted usually had their contributions returned. The cost of means testing and enforcing contribution orders was high in relation to the contributions recovered. In 1997–98, criminal legal aid contributions totalled £6.2 million, while the direct cost of administering the system was about £5 million. Means testing also led to delays in cases being brought to court, because cases had to be adjourned when the evidence required to conduct the test was not produced.

The new law (s 18) requires the Lord Chancellor to provide the necessary funding of criminal defence services secured by the Commission. As a result, like legal aid, the Criminal Defence Service will be a demand-led scheme. The Act also enables the Lord Chancellor to determine the timing and way in which this money should be paid to the Commission, and requires the Commission to seek to secure the best possible value for money in funding the Criminal Defence Service.

16.3.5 Conditional fees

We look at conditional fees more fully at the end of this chapter. For now, it is enough to observe that the Act (ss 27–31) reforms the law relating to conditional fees to enable the court to order a losing party to pay, in addition to the other party's normal legal costs, the uplift on the successful party's lawyers' fees; and in any case where a litigant has insured against facing an order for the other side's costs, any premium paid by the successful party for that insurance. The intention is to:

- ensure that the compensation awarded to a successful party is not eroded by any uplift or premium. The party in the wrong will bear the full burden of costs;

- make conditional fees more attractive, in particular to defendants and to claimants seeking non-monetary redress (these litigants can rarely use conditional fees now, because they cannot rely on the prospect of recovering damages to meet the cost of the uplift and premium);

- discourage weak cases and encourage settlements;

- provide a mechanism for regulating the uplifts that solicitors charge. In future, unsuccessful litigants will be able to challenge unreasonably high uplifts when the court comes to assess costs.

16.4   Unmet legal need

Since the early 1970s, there have been many published research papers and texts which cast doubt on how effectively the legal profession provides for the needs of the whole community. It has been argued that, whilst presenting itself as available to give service to everyone on the full range of matters which are capable of being effectively resolved by law, the truth is that lawyers are generally only used by a narrow social group for a narrow range of services. Many problems people suffer which are susceptible of legal resolution are not taken to lawyers for their advice and assistance. The reasons for this appear to be multifarious but are broadly to do with: (a) the inaccessibility of lawyers; (b) the failure of sufferers to perceive their problem as something a lawyer could help to solve; (c) the failure of lawyers to market themselves as being able to help with as wide a range of problems as the law could help solve; and (d) financial barriers (real or apparent).

Early American research by Mayhew and Reiss ('The social organisation of legal contacts' (1969) 34 American Sociological Rev 311) surveyed American residents and found that while seven out of 10 had seen a lawyer at least once, and one in four had visited one in the last five years, only 39% had ever sought advice on a matter other than property. They concluded:

> The association between income and legal contacts is in part an organisational effect. The legal profession is organised to serve business and property interests. The social organisation of business and property is highly legalised. Out of this convergence emerges a pattern of citizen contact with attorneys that is heavily orientated to property ...

The results of a mass observation study in England in which the legal experiences of 2,004 people were examined showed similar results to the Detroit study. Eighty one per cent of respondents said they had never come into contact with a solicitor. Of those who did consult solicitors, 45% went about a property matter (see Zander, 'Who goes to solicitors?' (1969) 16 Law Soc Gazette 174).

It is appropriate first to consider the nature of a 'legal' problem. The basic premise of pioneering research on this subject is that it is wrong to define as 'legal problems' simply those predicaments which are usually taken to lawyers to solve. Such a definition excludes problems which could be solved by legal means but are not dealt with by lawyers. Solicitors have been criticised for the restricted view they have of their work but there is evidence to suggest that the public has an even narrower perception of the sort of thing a solicitor could help them with than do solicitors themselves (Morris, White and Lewis, 1973). As far as the solicitors themselves are concerned, some of their narrow-minded approaches might be attributable to their legal education. Subjects like welfare law, for example, are only optional and are not widely available to undergraduates. In any event, the subjects which offer more lucrative career paths, like revenue law or company law, have always been more popular than welfare subjects. The Marre Report on the future of the legal profession (*A Time for Change*, 1988) made a specific call for a better response from lawyers to problems involving housing and immigration law.

The largest survey of what lawyers do and for whom was conducted for the Benson Royal Commission on Legal Services (*Survey of Users and Non-users of Legal Services in England and Wales*, Vol 2). The sample was based on 2,026 consultations in 1977 which involved 1,770 people out of 7,941 households interviewed. It found that some 15% of adults used a lawyer's service in 1977. It also found that of 27 categories of work used by the survey, just seven accounted for over 80% of all the work taken to solicitors: domestic conveyancing, probate, wills, divorce and matrimonial, motoring and other offences, personal injury cases and property matters. A survey conducted for The Law Society in 1989 confirmed this general pattern.

There has been much debate as to the true significance of these research findings. Do they reflect a restricted public perception of what solicitors deal with or simply a failure to approach solicitors for other reasons like, for example, perceived costs? The Commission found that, during 1977, a solicitor was used by 25% of the professional class, 21% of employers and managers but only 10% of unskilled workers. Professor Michael Zander has argued that the results of the survey demonstrate that the use of lawyers is 'problem connected' even more than it is 'type-of-person connected'; that is, that, although people from different socio-economic backgrounds use solicitors to a different extent, it is not simply their background that provides the best explanation. In fields of work involving property (for example, conveyancing, probate), those with property use lawyers much more than those who do not. As this is the largest single source of work for the solicitors' profession, it explains why lawyer-use appears to reflect the differences between classes. Zander has argued that this impression is misleading: 'If one looks at non-property types of work, the use of lawyers is relatively even as between members of different socio-economic backgrounds.'

One main reason for people not using solicitors is ignorance that the lawyer could be useful. Genn ('Who claims compensation', in Harris *et al*, *Compensation and Support for Illness and Injury*, 1984) has shown how many people fail to pursue proper claims because their first line of inquiry to another body (for example, employers, police, trade union) gives misleading advice. Apathy in prospective litigants is also a significant factor. The rules permitting solicitors to advertise, made in 1983, and their further relaxation in 1987, will perhaps bring more people into solicitors' offices. This will only help, however, to the extent that the apathy is not as a result of fear of costs. All research on the matter, including that of Genn (1984) and the Marre Committee (1988) has demonstrated that costs have a deterrent effect on seeking legal advice. Widespread ignorance of the legal aid schemes must also be relevant to this point.

The image of lawyers has sometimes been identified as a barrier to a greater range of customers. The Marre Committee focused on the facts that most solicitors' offices are inaccessible and unwelcoming and they do not cater for many needs like those of linguistic minorities. The results of the most recent population census, published in 1992, show that 5.5% of the population is from ethnic minorities (Office for National Statistics, *Britain 1998*, 1998, p 39) and whilst that figure does not represent those who are not conversant in English, it suggests that there might be a real problem for many people – who are perhaps likely to have problems that lawyers could help to solve. The Law Society survey (1989) found that the image of solicitors amongst the general public is 'good but not outstanding'. Compared with bank managers, accountants, NHS doctors and estate agents, although they were found to be easier to talk to than all the others bar doctors, solicitors were regarded as 'after your money' only less than estate agents. In 1999, it found its image was poor enough in the public eye to warrant spending £60,000 on a public relations exercise to improve the way lawyers are perceived.

In *Rethinking Legal Need: The Case of Criminal Justice* (1991), Paul Robertshaw rejects normative definitions of need, arguing that these rely too heavily on the assumptions of whoever is doing the defining; tend to be lawyer orientated and result in other people's problems being re-defined by experts. He also rejects self-defined notions of 'legal need' as it is too uncertain and subject to methodological difficulties. Instead, he uses a concept of comparative need and tries to establish a negative definition of need by comparing outcomes: '... if those in receipt of the [legal] service are not significantly better off than those without them, there can be no need.' He analyses existing research data on the outcomes of legally aided representation and non-legally aided cases and concludes that the general assumption that people assisted by representation need it because they get a better outcome by using it is not proven. There are several problems with such reasoning, as Ed Cape has demonstrated in 'The right to silence: defending at the police station under the new regime' (1995) *Legal Action*, 12 April. Basically, Robertshaw equates the provision of legal services with 'representation', whereas in fact representation is only a part of any legal service. If one just measures the outcome of representation as opposed to the whole legal service, the result is likely to be very misleading. A suspect may well need legal advice at a police station, and such advice may well result in the police deciding not to charge the suspect.

16.4.1 Does it matter if such needs remain unmet?

In the Dimbleby Lecture 1992, the late Lord Chief Justice Taylor observed that there may be very serious social problems even resulting in 'unrest' if the law did not become more accessible.

The true extent of unmet need might be less than is apparent simply by asking questionnaire respondents whether they have consulted solicitors about certain matters. This is because people might be making use of other sources of advice, for example, Citizens Advice Bureaux, accountants, building societies, licensed conveyancers, in circumstances where they might otherwise have consulted lawyers.

The greater the level of unmet need the worse the social implications. It is, though, notoriously difficult to ascertain the extent of the unmet need. Similar problems affect different people to different degrees. When does a person *need* legal advice? The pioneering research by Abel-Smith, Zander and Brooke adopted a partly subjective test of 'need'. They used a test of what would constitute 'a risk of substantial loss or disadvantage which would be important for the individual concerned'. This standard differed for each category of problem. Zander, writing five years later, acknowledged that these tests for need were highly artificial.

On the whole, poor people use lawyers much less than rich people do. Although, as Zander has argued, the current picture of unmet need has come from researchers who have concentrated on the poor, not the whole population; and Genn has found that people from the higher socio-economic groups are less likely to make a claim consequent upon personal injury (Genn, 1984), it is not difficult to see that the poor are legally disadvantaged by their lack of legal awareness, influence and resources like energy and time.

16.4.2 Law Centres

There are 52 Law Centres in England and Wales, staffed by salaried solicitors, trainee solicitors and non-lawyer experts in other areas like debt management. They are funded by local and central government and charity. They have 'shop front' access and aim to be user-friendly and unintimidating. They are managed by committees and represented by the Law Centres Federation. The report of the Rushcliffe Committee on Legal Aid and Advice (1945) had recommended a nationwide network of State salaried lawyers providing advice for a low, fixed fee. There was provision in the Legal Aid and Advice Act 1949 for this but it was never implemented. The first centre was established in England in North Kensington in July 1970 in the face of great opposition from The Law Society. Since then, the Society has developed a more tolerant stance to the centres as it acknowledges that they can confer benefits to local law firms through the referrals of clients.

Law Centres take on individual cases, providing, for example, advice on landlord and tenant matters and representing people at tribunals. Some centres also take on group work since quite often the problems of one client are part of a wider problem. This sort of work is controversial.

How far is it correct for lawyers to become involved in socio-legal problems in an effort to combat the disadvantages of the poor? In 1974, in a collective statement of purpose, the Law Centres supported American statements such as one which claimed that effective solution of the problems of the poor may require the lawyer '... to direct his attention away from the particular claim or grievance to the broader interests and policies at stake ...'. Such campaigns could deal, for example, with slum clearance or matters concerning roads and pavements. The Benson Commission rejected this sort of work for its proposed Citizens' Law Centres (CLCs), taking the view that community action tends to involve only one section of the community and that the independence of a centre can be compromised if it becomes a base for campaigns.

The commission's proposed CLCs seemed to be an attempt to win back for private practitioners the large number of clients who were being assisted by Law Centres, as the CLCs would have been operated under the control of The Law Society and Bar Council and users would pay on the same basis as legally aided clients of private practitioners. This would have increased the burden on the legal aid fund, though, when the government was keen to make retrenchments, so the proposal was rejected.

16.4.3 Other voluntary advice

There are now 709 Citizens Advice Bureaux with 1,313 outlets in total. They deal with a high number of cases (over six million a year) and a very wide range of problems of which between one third and one half are legal problems. There are, however, very few trained lawyers working for the bureaux.

The Bar Council supports a Free Representation Unit for clients at a variety of tribunals for which legal aid is not available. Most of the representation is carried out by Bar students supported and advised by full time case workers. A special Bar unit based in London was formed in 1996 through which more senior barristers provide representation.

Some colleges and universities also offer advice. For example, The College of Law in London operates a free advice service in which vocational students give advice on such matters as personal injury cases and employment law.

16.5 Conditional fee arrangements

As part of the scheme to expose the provision of legal services to the full rigour of market forces, the then Lord Chancellor chose to devote an entire Green Paper in 1989 to contingency fees. Following a recommendation from the Civil Justice Review, the paper had sought opinion on the funding of litigation on a contingent fee basis. This provides that litigation is funded by the claimant only if he or she wins, in which event the lawyer claims fees as a portion of the damages payable to the claimant. The response to this idea was largely hostile although there was a reasonable support for a system based on the Scottish model of the 'speculative fee' whereby the solicitor can agree with his client that he would be paid his ordinary taxed costs only if he won the case. Section 58 of the Courts and Legal Services Act (CLSA) 1990 permitted the Lord Chancellor to introduce conditional fee arrangements, although these cannot apply to criminal cases, family cases or those involving children (s 58(10)). Conditional fees can be based on an 'uplift' from the level of fee the lawyer would normally charge for the sort of work in question. Originally, the maximum uplift was to be 20% in order to induce lawyers to take on potentially difficult cases and to help finance the lawyers' unsuccessful conditional fee cases. This would have meant they could charge the fee that they would normally charge for a given type of case, plus an additional fifth.

In August 1993, after a long process of negotiation with the profession, Lord Mackay, the then Lord Chancellor, finally announced that he would allow the conditional fee to operate on a 100% uplift. Thus, solicitors receive no fee if they lose a case but double what they would normally charge if they win the case. The Law Society had campaigned vigorously against the proposed 20% uplift, arguing that such risks as the no-win, no-fee arrangement entailed would not be regarded as worth taking by many solicitors simply on the incentive that their fee for winning the case would be 20% more than they would normally charge for such a case. The Lord Chancellor's Department originally decided to restrict the scheme to cases involving personal injury, insolvency and the European Court of Human Rights.

The system came into effect in June 1995. Such agreements are legal now, provided that they comply with any requirements imposed by the Lord Chancellor and are not 'contentious business agreements'. These are defined under s 59 of the Solicitors Act 1974 as agreements between a solicitor and his client made in writing by which the solicitor is to be remunerated by a gross sum, or a salary, at agreed hourly rates or otherwise, and whether higher or lower than that at which he would normally be remunerated.

The traditional opposition to contingency fees in the English legal system was that they were 'maintenance' (the financial support of another's litigation) and 'champerty' (taking a financial interest in another's litigation). Champerty occurs when the person maintaining another takes as his reward a portion of the property in dispute. It taints an agreement with illegality and renders it void (for a recent discussion of the principle, see *Grovewood Holding plc v James Capel & Co Ltd* (1995)). Section 14 of the Criminal Justice Act 1967 abolished maintenance and champerty as crimes and torts but kept the rules making such arrangements improper for solicitors.

English litigation uses the Indemnity Rule by which the loser pays the costs of the winner and thus puts him, more or less, in the position he enjoyed before the damage was done. Objectors to contingency fee agreements pointed out that such things were incompatible with the Indemnity Rule because although the winner's costs would be paid for him by the other side, he would still have to pay for his lawyer from his damages (calculated to put him in the position he would have enjoyed if no wrong had been done to him) so he would not really be 'made whole' by his award. The position is different in the United States where contingency agreements are common in personal injury cases because there each side bears his own costs.

It was further contended by objectors to the contingency fee that the legal aid system adequately catered for those who were too poor to afford an ordinary private action. Even if there were people who were just above the legal aid financial thresholds, but still too poor to pay for an action, this should be dealt with simply by changing the threshold.

The Green Paper indicated that the government favoured some form of deregulation. Two forms of contingency fee were rejected during the consultation period as being unsuitable. The first was a restricted contingency fee system in which the fee payable in the event of a successful action would be a *percentage of the damages* but where the actual levels of recovery would be governed by rules. The second was an unrestricted contingency arrangement, similarly based on a percentage of damages, but at uncontrolled levels. These plans were rejected because it was thought that to give the lawyer a stake in the claimant's damages would be likely to create an unacceptable degree of conflict of interests.

16.5.1 The Conditional Fees Order 1998

The right to use no-win, no-fee agreements to pursue civil law claims was extended by the Conditional Fees Order 1998 which came into effect on 30 July.

The Order allows lawyers to offer conditional fee agreements to their clients in all civil cases excluding family cases. Speaking in the House of Lords on 23 July, the Lord Chancellor, Lord Irvine, said:

> These agreements will result in a huge expansion of access to justice. Today, only the very rich or the very poor can afford to litigate. In future, everyone with a really strong case will be able to secure his rights free of the fear of ruin if he loses. They will bring the majority of our people into access to justice.

Conditional fees have been the means by which at least 45,000 personal injury cases have been brought, and many, in all likelihood, would not have been brought but for the existence of conditional fees. The new Order retains the old rule that the maximum uplift on the fees lawyers can charge is 100%, that is, a lawyer may take on an action against an allegedly negligent employer whose carelessness has resulted in the client being injured. The lawyer, who might normally charge £2,000 for such a case, can say 'I shall do this work for nothing if we lose, but £3,000 if we win'. In fact, as the price uplift can be up to 100% of the normal fee, he or she can stipulate for up to £4,000 in this example. The Law Society has recommended an additional voluntary cap of 25% of damages, and this has been widely accepted in practice over the last two years.

The real problems here continue to be:

(a) that the new system, designed really to help the millions who have been regulated out of the legal aid system, does not help people whose cases stand only a limited chance of success – as lawyers will not take their cases; and

(b) the difficulties of a claimant getting insurance to cover the costs that he will have to pay, if he loses the action, for the other side's lawyers. Where a personal injury action arises from a road traffic incident, it is almost always clear to a solicitor where blame and legal liability probably lie. Risks are therefore calculable by insurance companies so one can presently insure against having to pay the other side's costs in the event of losing an action on an insolvency case for about £100 in a no-win, no-fee arrangement. There are, however, many areas, and medical negligence cases are good examples, where the chances of success are notoriously difficult to predict. Thus, insurance against having to pay the other side's costs is prohibitively high, running into many thousands of pounds in some cases. It is quite unrealistic to assume that all such cases arising often from highly distressing circumstances, will be dealt with in future on a no-win, no-fee basis. Lawyers will generally not want to take on such cases on such a basis, and, even where they do, clients will often not be able to afford the necessary insurance. As insurance to cover client costs in medical no-win, no-fee cases has proven so expensive, the government has decided for the time being not to end legal aid for such cases.

In its response to the 1998 Lord Chancellor's consultation paper *Access to Justice with Conditional Fees*, The Law Society made several interesting points. The Lord Chancellor had proposed that insurance premiums supporting conditional fee arrangements should be recoverable between the parties. The Legal Aid Board was in favour of this change. It said in its response document (para 2.7) that 'this would make conditional fee agreements more viable and more attractive for clients and lawyers without unduly penalising opponents'. There is, though, still a risk of a 'perverse incentive' operating – defendants with meritorious defences might end up paying higher premiums than those with no real defence. This is because an insurance company backing a defendant with a good defence will realise that the case will last longer than one where the defendant only has a mediocre defence. If the defendant then loses after a long case, he or she will have a bigger bill to pay for the other side's costs than in a shorter case. This leads to the paradox that the stronger the case you have as a defendant, the higher the premium you will have to pay, as your case will last longer. Weak defendants get defeated early on in proceedings. If a losing defendant has to pay not only the other side's lawyer's fee but also the other side's insurance premium, the paradox above is worsened because a strong defendant will mean that a claimant's premium will be high, and if the claimant's premium is high, and the defendant might end up having to cover that cost if he loses, then the defendant's premium will also be raised!

'Pursuit' is the name of a legal expenses insurance policy offered by the Royal Sun Alliance. Under the policy, the premium is only paid if the case is won although there is a £200 non-refundable assessment fee. The government has endorsed this policy although The Law Society and the Bar have been more reserved. The Law Society Vice President, Robert Sayer, said: 'No insurance product, this included, will provide a solution to the removal of legal aid' ((1999) 96 Law Soc Gazette 12).

16.5.2 The advantages

For claimants, the advantages can be summarised as being:

- that lawyers acting in any case will be confident (they will have had to weigh carefully the chances of success before taking the case as their fee depends on winning) and determined;
- there will be freedom from the anxiety of having to pay huge fees;
- there will be no need to pay fees in advance; and
- there will be no delays or worries with legal aid applications.

For defendants, there will be advantages too as the contingency fee system will probably reduce the number of spurious claims. In a period where legal aid is being cut-back so drastically, preventing so many people from going to law, this system can be seen as a way of preserving at least some limited access to the legal process. Losing parties will still be liable to pay the other side's costs, so it will be unlikely that people will take action unless they consider they have a good chance of success.

The taxpayer can also be given the advantage in the form of a significant reduction in the funding of the legal aid system. Furthermore, practitioners who are competent to assess and willing to take the risks of litigation, will arguably enjoy a better fee-paying basis, increased fee income and overall business, fewer reasons for delay and more satisfied clients with fewer complaints.

Consider two examples. A middle class couple consult their solicitor about injuries received in a road accident. Their joint income and savings puts them outside the legal aid scheme. The proposed litigation is beset with uncertainties as the other driver's insurers have denied liability. The couple have to worry about their own expenses and the possibility under the Indemnity Rule of paying for the defendant's costs. Again, a young man has been injured at work wants to sue his employer. The case will turn on some difficult health and safety law on which there are currently conflicting decisions. He is eligible for legal aid but he will have to make substantial contributions because of his level of income and if his claim fails he will have to pay the same sum again towards the expenses of his employers. In both cases, the prospective litigants might well drop any plan to litigate. Both cases, however, might proceed expeditiously if they could find a lawyer to act on a no-win, no-fee basis.

16.5.3 The disadvantages

Critics of the system argue that it encourages the sort of speculative actions that occur frequently in the United States, taken up by the so called 'ambulance chasing' lawyers. It can be argued that the system of contingency fees creates a conflict of interest between the lay client and the lawyer, with a consequential risk of exploitation of the client. Where a lawyer's fee depends on the outcome of a case, there is a greater temptation for him or her to act unethically. When the Royal Commission on Legal Services (1979) rejected the idea of contingent fees, it stated that such a scheme might lead to undesirable practices by lawyers including 'the construction of evidence, the improper coaching of witnesses, the use of professionally partisan expert witnesses, especially medical witnesses, improper examination and cross-examination, groundless legal arguments designed to lead the courts into error and competitive touting'. If the case was won, the lawyer claimed a significant part of the damages, but there was also a real danger that lawyers would be pressured to settle too readily to avoid the costs of preparing for a trial that could be lost and therewith the fee. An example would be where an insurance company admits liability but contests the level of damages. The claimant might stand to get substantially higher compensation by contesting the case. Under the new system, however, his solicitor will have a strong interest in advising him to settle. A settlement would guarantee the solicitor's costs and the agreed 'mark up' (up to 100% more than a normal fee for such work), both of which would be completely lost if the case was fought and lost. This would not occur outside of a conditional fee arrangement. Although the conventional system of payment was not without problems, as Walter Merricks, then of The Law Society, has stated:

> ... when a lawyer is being paid by the hour, he may have a financial interest in encouraging his client to go on with an open-and-shut case, increasing his own fees.

The Law Society has argued that the system, if not properly regulated, could promote some of the 'ambulance chasing' like that of American lawyers in the wake of the 1984 Bhopal disaster in which over 2,500 people were killed by escaping gas from a UCC plant in India. American lawyers flew out to act for victims and their relatives and some were reported to be taking fees of 50% of the claimant's damages.

It was argued by some that, by allowing lawyers to *double* their normal fee for certain cases, the Lord Chancellor risked eliminating any benefit speculative fees may bring. If the successful client was not be able to recover the *uplift* from the other side, he would have to fund it himself out of the damages he was been awarded. In effect, this often resulted in his damages being halved. The uplift can now be recovered, subject to taxation (that is, court official approval), following changes made by the Access to Justice Act 1999.

It is not even clear that the main claim made for the system – that it increases access to the courts – is correct. The Scottish experience is that speculative cases do not exceed 1% of the cases in the caseload of the Faculty of Advocates. One firm opponent of the system is Mr Justice Auld. He has argued that the system will eventually endanger the esteem in which lawyers are held by the public. He has doubted whether the scheme will produce greater commitment by lawyers to their cases: 'There is a distinction to be drawn between the lawyer's commitment to the case and his anxiety to recover his fees. The two do not always correspond.'

Opinion within the legal profession about the desirability of the changes is mixed. A useful juxtaposition of opposite views (those of George Pulman QC and Michael Napier) appear in (1995) 92 Law Soc Gazette 1626).

16.5.4 The English system – recent changes

The only major study of the conditional fee system (Yarrow, 1997), commissioned by the Lord Chancellor's Advisory Committee on Legal Education and Conduct, assessed how widely, and in what ways, conditional fees were being used. The research was based on a survey of 120 firms of solicitors and an analysis of 197 conditional fee cases begun in the personal injury field. The research found evidence of considerable inconsistency in the size of the 'success fee' calculated for cases with similar chances of success. Moreover, the fee appeared to be too high in up to six cases in 10 which had 'very good' chances of winning.

Yarrow found that a surprisingly high proportion of cases were regarded as having relatively low chances of success, given that personal injury cases usually have an extremely high success rate. This could indicate that some solicitors could be over estimating the chances of failure and, therefore, charging a higher 'success fee'. Yarrow concludes that such concerns could cast doubt over the entire scheme. Overall, the average 'success fee' charged by solicitors was 43% but, for one in 10 cases, it was close to the maximum of 100%. However, the voluntary 25% cap on the proportion of damages that can be swallowed up by the 'success fee', recommended by The Law Society, is used by almost all solicitors.

Since the introduction of conditional fees, the common law has been developed in two recent decisions by the courts (in *Thai Trading Co (A Firm) v Taylor* (1998) and *Bevan Ashford v Geoff Yeandle (Contractors) Ltd* (1998)). In the first of these cases, the Court of Appeal held that there were no longer public policy grounds to prevent lawyers agreeing to work for less than their normal fees in the event that they were unsuccessful, provided they did not seek to recover more than their normal fees if they were successful. (The latter was only permissible in those proceedings in which conditional fee agreements were allowed.) In *Bevan Ashford*, the Vice Chancellor held that it was also lawful for a conditional fee agreement to apply in a case which was to be resolved by arbitration (under the Arbitration Act 1950), even though these were not court proceedings, provided all the requirements specified by regulations as to the form and content of the agreement were complied with.

There are also available insurance policies which can be taken out when someone is contemplating litigation to cover the costs of the other party and the client's own costs (including, if not a conditional fee case, the client's solicitor's fees) if the case is lost. Some of them were developed to support the use of conditional fee agreements but others are used to meet lawyers' fees charged in the more traditional way. For the same reason that the success fee under a conditional fee is being made recoverable, it is also proposed to make any premium paid for protective insurance recoverable too. The principles behind the government's desire to see an expansion in the use of conditional fee arrangements were set out in a Consultation Paper, *Access to Justice with Conditional Fees* (LCD, 1998).

The Access to Justice Act 1999 further reforms the law on conditional fees (see 16.3.5) to allow the courts to order that a successful litigant should recover the success fee payable under the conditional fee arrangement from the losing party. Section 27 of the 1999 Act does this by inserting a new s 58A(7) into the CLSA 1990. By s 27, the 1999 Act also allows the cost of any insurance against the risk of losing the case to be recovered in the same way, and it makes it easier, by s 28, for membership organisations, such as trade unions or motoring organisations, to underwrite litigation on behalf of their members. These changes are likely to make the conditional fee arrangement a more attractive and practicable option for many prospective claimants.

THE FUNDING OF LEGAL SERVICES

Legal aid

The scheme prior to the Access to Justice Act 1999 was contained in the Legal Aid Act (LAdA) 1988. A common feature of the civil and criminal legal aid schemes was that expenditure on them was demand-led. Any lawyer could do legal aid work for a client who passed the relevant means test (if any), and whose case passed the statutory merits test (in the case of civil legal aid), or the interests of justice test (in the case of criminal legal aid). Lawyers were (and will continue to be under the transitional arrangements) paid on a case by case basis for each individual case or other act of assistance, usually at rates or fees set in regulations, but, in some cases, on the same basis as a privately funded lawyer.

This, in the government's view, meant that there were few mechanisms or incentives for promoting value for money or assuring the quality of the services provided.

The Access to Justice Act 1999

The Act replaces the legal aid system with two new schemes, and makes provisions about rights to supply legal services, appeals, and court procedure, magistrates and magistrates' courts.

The provisions in the Act form part of the wide ranging programme of reforms to legal services and the courts, described in the government's White Paper, *Modernising Justice*, published in 1998.

Funding of legal services

The 1999 Act provides for two new schemes, replacing the legal aid scheme, to secure the provision of publicly funded legal services for people who need them. It establishes a Legal Services Commission to run the two schemes and enables the Lord Chancellor to give the Commission orders, directions and guidance about how it should exercise its functions.

It requires the Commission to establish, maintain and develop a Community Legal Service (CLS). A new CLS fund will replace the legal aid fund in civil and family cases. The Commission will use the resources of the fund, in a way that reflects priorities set by the Lord Chancellor and its duty to secure the best possible value for money, to procure or provide a range of legal services. The Commission will also have a duty to liaise with other funders of legal services to facilitate the developments of co-ordinated plans for making the best use of all available resources. The intention is to develop a network of legal service providers of assured quality, offering the widest possible access to information and advice about the law, and assistance with legal problems.

The Commission will also be responsible for running the Criminal Defence Service, which replaces the current legal aid scheme in criminal cases. The new scheme is intended to ensure that people suspected or accused of a crime are properly represented, while securing better value for money than is possible under the legal aid scheme.

The Legal Services Commission

The 1999 Act establishes the new Legal Services Commission and makes provision for appointments to it. The Commission will replace the Legal Aid Board. It was considered necessary to establish a new body to reflect the fundamentally different nature of the CLS compared to civil legal aid. Within the broad framework of priorities set by the Lord Chancellor, the Commission will be responsible for taking detailed decisions about the allocation of resources.

The Community Legal Service

The Legal Services Commission will have two main duties in respect of the CLS.

First, it will manage a CLS fund, which will replace legal aid in civil and family cases. The CLS fund will be used to secure the provision of appropriate legal services, within the resources made available to it, and according to priorities set by the Lord Chancellor and by regional and local assessments of need. A Funding Code, drawn up by the Commission and approved by the Lord Chancellor, will set out the criteria and procedures for deciding whether to fund individual cases.

Secondly, as part of a wider CLS, the Commission will, in co-operation with local funders and interested bodies, develop local, regional and national plans to match the delivery of legal services to identified needs and priorities.

Overall, the intention is to:

- make best use of all the resources available for funding legal services, by facilitating a co-ordinated approach to planning;

- improve value for money through contracting and the development of quality assurance systems.

The Access to Justice Act 1999 describes the services which may be provided under the CLS. These range from the provision of basic information about the law and legal services, to providing help towards preventing or resolving disputes and enforcing decisions which have been reached. The scheme will encompasses advice, assistance and representation by lawyers (which have long been available under the legal aid scheme) and also the services of non-lawyers. It will extend to other types of service, including, for example, mediation in family or civil cases where appropriate.

This sets out the ways in which the Commission may use the CLS fund to provide services. These include making contracts with or grants to service providers, or employing staff to provide services directly to the public. These flexible powers are intended to give effect to one of the principal objectives of the reform of publicly funded legal services, that is, the ability to tailor the provision of services, and the means by which services are to be delivered to the needs of local populations and particular circumstances. They will also allow the Commission to test new forms of service provision through pilot projects.

In future, subject to any exceptions that the Lord Chancellor may make by direction, only basic information and advice will be available for:

- disputes involving allegations of negligent damage to property or the person ('personal injury'), apart from those about clinical negligence. These cases are generally considered suitable for conditional fees;

- allegations of defamation or malicious falsehood. Generally, legal aid is not currently available for representation in defamation, but it is sometimes possible to get legal aid by categorising the case as one of malicious falsehood. The government's view is that these cases do not command sufficient priority to justify public funding and, in any event, they may often be suitable for a conditional fee.

The 1999 Act allows the Lord Chancellor, using regulations, to set financial eligibility limits for people to receive services funded by the CLS fund. It allows him to set different conditions, or no conditions, for different circumstances or types of case or service.

The funding assessment under the Code will replace the merits test for civil legal aid The new assessment is intended to be more flexible than the existing merits test. It will be possible to apply different criteria in different categories according to their priority.

The Code is required to reflect the principle that, in many family disputes, mediation is more appropriate than court proceedings. This is intended to reinforce the development, under the Family Law Act 1996, of mediation as a means of resolving private law family disputes in a way that promotes as good a continuing relationship between the parties concerned as is possible in the circumstances.

The 1999 Act extends the potential scope of financial conditions in two ways, although there are no immediate plans to use either of these powers:

- it will be possible to make the provision of services in some types of cases subject to the assisted person agreeing to repay an amount in excess of the cost of the services provided in the event that their case is successful. This might make it possible to fund certain types of case on a self-financing basis, with the additional payments from successful litigants applied to meet the cost of unsuccessful cases;

- it will be possible to require the assisted person to repay, over time and with interest, the full cost of the service provided (for example, through continuing contributions from income). This will make it possible to provide services in some categories of case in the form of a loan scheme.

The Act establishes limits on the liability of the person receiving funded services to pay costs to the unassisted party.

The Criminal Defence Service

The purpose of the Criminal Defence Service is to secure the provision of advice, assistance and representation, according to the interests of justice, to people suspected of a criminal offence or facing criminal proceedings.

The Commission will be empowered to secure these services through contracts with lawyers in private practice, or by providing them through salaried defenders, employed by non-profit making organisations. This will necessarily mean that suspects' and defendants' choice of representative is limited to contracted or salaried defenders, although the intention is to maintain an element of choice in all but exceptional cases.

There will be a transitional period while contracts are developed and extended to cover the full range of services. The Commission will therefore be able to pay lawyers on a case by case basis for representation provided on a non-contractual basis, according to remuneration scales set in regulations.

The Access to Justice Act 1999 places a duty on the Commission to fund representation for individuals granted a right to representation. It enables the Commission to comply with this duty in the same ways as for advice and assistance. The power to make direct case by case payments to representatives will allow the Commission to continue to pay non-contracted lawyers to provide representation during the transitional period while contracting develops and, possibly, thereafter where that proves to be the best means of securing the necessary services.

Conditional fees

The Act reforms the law relating to conditional fees to enable the court to order a losing party to pay, in addition to the other party's normal legal costs, the uplift on the successful party's lawyers' fees and, in any case where a litigant has insured facing an order for the other side's costs, any premium paid by the successful party for that insurance. The intention is to ensure that the compensation awarded to a successful party is not eroded by any uplift or premium. The party in the wrong will bear the full burden of costs. It is also the intention to make conditional fees more attractive, in particular, to defendants and to claimants seeking non-monetary redress.

CHAPTER 17

THE EUROPEAN CONTEXT

17.1 Introduction

As was stated in Chapter 2, it is unrealistic and, indeed, impossible for any student of English law and the English legal system, to ignore the UK's membership of the European Union (EU) and European Communities. Nor can the impact of the European Court of Human Rights (ECHR) be ignored, especially now that the Human Rights Act (HRA) 1998 has made the Articles of the European Convention on Human Rights directly applicable in the UK. However, it has to be recognised that placing the English legal system in its European context does make some demands on the individual. For one thing, although the Treaty on European Union 1992 (the Maastricht Treaty) established the Union of its title, it did not dissolve its constituent communities which therefore continue in existence, distinct from that Union. There are said to be three pillars to the European Union:

(a) European Community consisting of not only its treaties but wider aspects relating to citizenship and, indeed, economic and monetary union;

(b) common foreign and security policy;

(b) police and judicial co-operation in judicial matters.

It is particularly important to note, however, that the European Union (EU) does not share the same legal institutional form as the European Community (EC) and that it is, therefore, still appropriate to talk about Community law rather than Union law.

It is also essential to distinguish between the two different courts that operate within the European context: the European Court of Justice (ECJ), which is the court of the EC, sitting in Luxembourg; and the ECHR, which deals with cases relating to the European Convention on Human Rights and sits in Strasbourg.

The long term process leading to the, as yet still to be attained, establishment of an integrated EC was a response to two factors: the disasters of the Second World War; and the emergence of the Soviet Bloc in Eastern Europe. The aim was to link the separate European countries, particularly France and Germany, together in such a manner as to prevent the outbreak of future armed hostilities. The first step in this process was the establishment of a European Coal and Steel Community. The next step towards integration was the formation of the European Economic Community (EEC) under the Treaty of Rome in 1957. The UK joined the EEC in 1973. The Treaty of Rome has subsequently been amended in the further pursuit of integration as the Community has expanded. Thus, the Single European Act (SEA) 1986 established a single economic market within the European Community and widened the use of majority voting in the Council of Ministers. The Maastricht Treaty further accelerated the move towards a federal European supranational State in the extent to which it recognised Europe as a social and political – as well as an economic – community. Previous Conservative governments of the UK have resisted the emergence of the EU as anything other than an economic market and have objected to, and resiled from, various provisions aimed at social as opposed to economic affairs. Thus, the UK was able to opt out of the Social Chapter of the Treaty of Maastricht. The present Labour administration in the UK has had no such reservations and, as a consequence, the Treaty of Amsterdam 1997 incorporated the European Social Charter into the EC Treaty which, of course, applies to the UK. One of the consequences of the Amsterdam Treaty was a renumbering of all the Articles in the various EC Treaties. This book will adopt the new numbering, but list the old numbers in brackets.

As the establishment of the single market within the European Community progressed, it was suggested that its operation would be greatly facilitated by the adoption of a common currency, or at least a more closely integrated monetary system. Thus, in 1979, the European Monetary System (EMS) was established, under which individual national currencies were valued against a nominal currency called the ECU and allocated a fixed rate within which they were allowed to fluctuate to a limited extent. Britain was a member of the EMS until 1992, when financial speculation against the pound forced its withdrawal. Nonetheless, other members of the EC continued to pursue the policy of monetary union, now entitled European Monetary Union (EMU) and January 1999 saw the installation of the new European currency, the euro, against which all currencies within the scheme are allocated fixed values. Thereafter, the newly created European Central Bank will oversee the replacement of national currencies by the euro. The UK did not join the EMU at its inception and the question as to whether or not it should join is one of the most pressing of current political issues.

The general aim of the EU is set out in Art 2 (number unchanged) of the Treaty of Rome, as amended by the Maastricht Treaty, as follows:

> The Community shall have as its task, by establishing a common market and an economic and monetary union and by implementing the common policies or activities referred to in Article 3, to promote throughout the Community a harmonious and balanced development of economic activities, sustainable and non-inflationary growth respecting the environment, a high degree of convergence of economic performance, a high level of employment and of social protection, the raising of the standard of living and quality of life, and economic and social cohesion and solidarity among Member States.

Amongst the policies originally detailed in Art 3 (number unchanged) were included:

- the elimination, between Member States, of custom duties and of quantitative restrictions on the import and export of goods;

- the establishment of a common custom tariff and a common commercial policy towards third countries;

- the abolition, between Member States, of obstacles to the freedom of movement for persons, services and capital;

- the adoption of a common agricultural policy;

- the adoption of a common transport policy;

- the harmonisation of laws of Member States to the extent required to facilitate the proper functioning of the single market;

- the creation of a European Social Fund in order to improve the employment opportunities of workers in the community and to improve their standard of living.

Article 3 has subsequently been extended to cover more social, as opposed to purely economic, matters and now incorporates policies relating to education, health, consumer protection, the environment and culture generally. In 1989, the Community adopted a Charter of Fundamental Social Rights of Workers, although the UK government under the leadership of the then Prime Minister, Margaret Thatcher, declined to sign it, seeing it as representing an unacceptable interference in the free operation of the market. The Treaty on European Union, the Maastricht Treaty, had originally contained a 'Social Chapter', based on the earlier Social Charter, and designed to further the 'promotion of employment, improved living and working conditions, proper social protection, dialogue between management and labour, the development of human resources with a view to lasting high employment and the combating of exclusion'. Once again, the UK government, this time under the leadership of John Major, refused to accede to such provisions, and, in order to save the rest of the Treaty, the Social Chapter had to be removed and appended as a protocol binding on the then other 11 Members of the Community, but not the UK. It is of perhaps signal importance that one of the very first measures taken by the new Labour administration, led by Prime Minister Tony Blair, was to declare its intention to sign up to the Social Chapter.

Consequent upon the agreement of the UK government, the Treaty of Amsterdam 1997 was able to incorporate the European Social Charter into the EC Treaty.

Article 10 (formerly, Art 5) requires:

Member States to take all appropriate measures, whether general or particular, to ensure fulfilment of the obligations arising out of this Treaty or resulting from action taken by the institutions of the Community. They shall facilitate the achievement of the Community's tasks. They shall abstain from any measure which could jeopardise the attainment of the objectives of this Treaty.

This Article effectively means that UK courts are now Community law courts and must be bound by, and give effect to, that law where it is operative. The reasons for the national courts acting in this manner are considered by John Temple Lang, Director in the Competition Directorate General, in an article entitled 'The duties of national courts under Community constitutional law' ([1997] EL Rev 22). As he writes:

> National courts are needed to give companies and individuals remedies which are as prompt, as complete and as immediate as the combined legal system of the Community and of Member States can provide. Only national courts can give injunctions against private parties for breach of Community law rules on, for example, equal pay for men and women, or on restrictive practices. Private parties have no standing to claim injunctions in the Court of Justice against a Member State, they can do so only in a national court. In other words, only a national court could give remedies to individuals and companies for breach of Community law which are as effective as the remedies for breach of national law.

Before the UK joined the EU, its law was just as foreign as law made under any other jurisdiction. On joining the EU, however, the UK and its citizens accepted, and became subject to, EC law. This subjection to European law remains the case even where the parties to any transaction are themselves both UK subjects. In other words, in areas where it is applicable, European law supersedes any existing UK law to the contrary.

An example of EC law invalidating the operation of UK legislation can be found in the *Factortame* case. The Common Fishing Policy established by the EEC had placed limits on the amount of fish that any member country's fishing fleet was permitted to catch. In order to gain access to British fish stocks and quotas, Spanish fishing boat owners formed British companies and re-registered their boats as British. In order to prevent what it saw as an abuse and an encroachment on the rights of indigenous fishermen, the British Government introduced the Merchant Shipping Act 1988, which provided that any fishing company seeking to register as British would have to have its principal place of business in the UK and at least 75% of its shareholders would have to be British nationals. This effectively debarred the Spanish boats from taking up any of the British fishing quota. Some 95 Spanish boat owners applied to the British courts for judicial review of the Merchant Shipping Act on the basis that it was contrary to Community law. The case went from the High Court, through the Court of Appeal, to the House of Lords who referred the case to the ECJ. There, it was decided that the Treaty of Rome required domestic courts to give effect to the directly enforceable provisions of Community law and, in doing so, such courts are required to ignore any national law that runs counter to Community law. The decision gave rise to some heated responses in the UK where it was attacked on the basis that it effectively undermined parliamentary sovereignty.

17.2   Sources of European Community law

Community law, depending on its nature and source, may have direct effect on the domestic laws of its various members; that is, it may be open to individuals to rely on it, without the need for their particular State to have enacted the law within its own legal system (see *Factortame*).

There are two types of direct effect. Vertical direct effect means that the individual can rely on EC law in any action in relation to their government, but cannot use it against other individuals. Horizontal direct effect allows the individual to use the EC provision in an action against other individuals. Other EC provisions only take effect when they have been specifically enacted within the various legal systems within the Community.

The sources of Community law are fourfold:

* internal treaties and protocols;

* international agreements;

* secondary legislation;

* decisions of the ECJ.

17.2.1 Internal treaties

Internal treaties govern the Member States of the EU and anything contained therein supersedes domestic legal provisions. The primary treaty is the Treaty of Rome as amended by such legislation as the SEA 1986; or the Maastricht Treaty on European Union and the Amsterdam Treaty. Upon its joining the Community, the Treaty of Rome was incorporated into UK law by the European Communities Act 1972.

As long as treaties are of a mandatory nature and are stated with sufficient clarity and precision, then they have both vertical and horizontal effect (*NV Algemene Transporten Expeditie Van Genden Loos v Nederlandse Administratie der Belastingen* (1963)).

17.2.2 International treaties

International treaties are negotiated with other nations by the European Commission on behalf of the EU as a whole and are binding on the individual members of the EU.

17.2.3 Secondary legislation

Secondary legislation is provided for under Art 249 (formerly, Art 189) of the Treaty of Rome. It provides for three types of legislation to be introduced by the European Council and Commission. These are:

- *Regulations* apply to, and within, Member States generally without the need for those States to pass their own legislation. They are binding and enforceable from the time of their creation and individual States do not have to pass any legislation to give effect to regulations. Regulations must be published in the *Official Journal* of the EU. The decision as to whether or not a law should be enacted in the form of a regulation is usually left to the Commission, but there are areas where the Treaty of Rome requires that the regulation form must be used. These areas relate to: the rights of workers to remain in Member States of which they are not nationals; the provision of State aid to particular indigenous undertakings or industries; the regulation of EU accounts and budgetary procedures.

- *Directives*, on the other hand, state general goals and leave the precise implementation in the appropriate form to the individual Member States. Directives, however, tend to state the means as well as the ends to which they are aimed and the ECJ will give direct effect to directives which are sufficiently clear and complete. See *Van Duyn v Home Office* (1974). Directives usually provide Member States with a time limit within which they are required to implement the provision within their own national laws. If they fail to do so or implement the directive incompletely, then individuals may be able to cite, and rely on, the directive in their dealings with the State in question. Further, *Francovich v Italy* (1991) has established that individuals who have suffered as a consequence of a Member State's failure to implement Community law may seek damages against that State.

The provisions in the Unfair Terms in Consumer Contracts Regulations 1994 is an example of UK law being introduced in response to EU directives.

- *Decisions* on the operation of European laws and policies are not intended to have general effect but are aimed at particular States or individuals. They have the force of law under Art 249 (formerly, Art 189).

- Additionally, Art 211 (formerly, Art 155) provides for the Commission to issue recommendations and opinions in relation to the operation of Community law. These have no binding force although they may be taken into account in trying to clarify any ambiguities in domestic law.

17.2.4 Judgments of the European Court of Justice

The ECJ is the judicial arm of the EU and, in the field of Community law, its judgments overrule those of national courts. Under Art 234 (formerly, Art 177), national courts have the right to apply to the ECJ for a preliminary ruling on a point of Community law before deciding a case.

The mechanism through which Community law becomes immediately and directly effective in the UK is provided by s 2(1) of the European Communities Act 1972. Section 2(2) gives power to designated ministers or departments to introduce Orders in Council to give effect to other non-directly effective Community law.

17.3   The institutions of the European Union

The major institutions of the EU are: the Council of Ministers; the European Parliament; the European Commission; the ECJ.

17.3.1   The Council of Ministers

The Council is made up of ministerial representatives of each of the 15 Member States of the EU. The actual composition of the Council varies depending on the nature of the matter to be considered. When considering economic matters, the various States will be represented by their finance ministers or, if the matter before the Council relates to agriculture, the various agricultural ministers will attend. The organisation of the various specialist councils falls to the President of the Council and that post is held for six monthly periods in rotation by the individual Member States of the EU. The Presidency of the Council is significant to the extent that the country holding the position can, to a large extent, control the agenda of the Council and thus can focus EU attention on areas that it considers to be of particular importance.

The Council of Ministers is the supreme decision making body of the EU and, as such, it has the final say in deciding upon EU legislation. Although it acts on recommendations and proposals made to it by the Commission, it does have the power to instruct the Commission to undertake particular investigations and to submit detailed proposals for its consideration.

Council decisions are taken on a mixture of voting procedures. Some measures only require a simple majority; in others, a procedure of qualified majority voting is used; and, in yet others, unanimity is required. Qualified majority voting is the procedure in which the votes of the 15 Member countries are weighted in proportion to their population from 10 down to two votes each. There are a total of 87 votes to be cast and, in order to pass a vote on the basis of a qualified majority, a minimum of 62 votes in favour is required. The corollary of this is that it requires a total of 26 votes to block any proposal that can be decided on by qualified majority voting. It can be seen, therefore, that even qualified majority voting requires a substantial degree of agreement across the EU.

Prior to approving the enlargement of the EU, by the accession of Austria, Finland and Sweden on 1 January 1995, both the UK and Spain insisted on what is known as the Ioannina Compromise. The Compromise states that:

> ... if members of the Council representing a total of 23 to 25 votes indicate their intention to oppose the adoption by the Council of a decision by qualified majority, the Council will do all in its power to reach within a reasonable time and without prejudicing obligatory time limits laid down in the Treaties and by secondary law, such as Arts 251 and 252 [formerly, Arts 189B and 189C] of the Treaty establishing the European Community, a satisfactory solution that could be adopted by at least 65 votes.

The effectiveness of this Compromise is a matter of some doubt, especially given the Commission's subsequent declaration that it would call for a vote on the new basis, as soon as it considered that a reasonable time had elapsed.

The SEA (a European Treaty legislated into UK law as the European Communities (Amendment) Act 1986) extended the use of qualified majority voting but unanimity is still required in what can be considered as the more politically sensitive areas, such as those relating to the harmonisation of indirect taxation, or the free movement of individuals. In addition to the need for unanimity in such sensitive areas, there is also the ultimate safeguard of what is known as the Luxembourg Compromise. This procedure, instituted at the behest of the French Government in 1966, permits individual Member States to exercise a right of veto in relation to any proposals which they consider to be contrary to what they consider to be a 'very important interest' of theirs.

As the format of particular council fluctuates, much of its day to day work is delegated to a committee of permanent representatives which operates under the title of COREPER.

Article 2 of the SEA 1986 provided that:

> The European Council shall bring together the Heads of State or of government of the Member States and the President of the Commission of the European Communities. They shall be assisted by the Ministers for Foreign Affairs and by a member of the Commission. The European Council shall meet at least twice a year.

The European Council, now known as the Council of the European Union, can be seen, therefore, as a form of EU summit meeting. It is chaired by the head of government currently holding the presidency of the Council. Although not originally recognised in the Treaty of Rome, the function of the European Council was clarified by Art D of the Treaty on European Union which stated that it 'shall provide the union with the necessary impetus for its development and shall define the general political guidelines thereof'.

17.3.2 The European Parliament

The European Parliament is the directly elected European institution and, to that extent, it can be seen as the body which exercises democratic control over the operation on the EU. As in national Parliaments, members are elected to represent constituencies, the elections being held every five years. There are a total of 626 members divided amongst the 15 members approximately in proportion to the size of their various populations. Members of the European Parliament do not sit in national groups but operate within political groupings.

The European Parliament's general secretariat is based in Luxembourg and, although the Parliament sits in plenary session in Strasbourg for one week in each month, its detailed and preparatory work is carried out through 18 permanent committees which usually meet in Brussels. These permanent committees consider proposals from the Commission and provide the full Parliament with reports of such proposals for discussion.

17.3.3 Powers of the European Parliament

The powers of the European Parliament (the Parliament), however, should not be confused with those of national Parliaments, for the European Parliament is not a legislative institution and, in that respect, it plays a subsidiary role to the Council of Ministers. Originally, its powers were merely advisory and supervisory.

In pursuance of its advisory function, the Parliament always had the right to comment on the proposals of the Commission and, since 1980, the Council has been required to wait for the Parliament's opinion before adopting any law. In its supervisory role, the Parliament scrutinises the activities of the Commission and has the power to remove the Commission by passing a motion of censure against it by a two thirds' majority.

The legislative powers of the Parliament were substantially enhanced by the SEA 1986. Since that enactment, it has had a more influential role to play particularly in relation to the completion of the internal market. It can now negotiate directly with the Council as to any alterations or amendments it wishes to see in proposed legislation. It can also intervene to question and indeed alter any 'joint position' adopted by the Council on proposals put to it by the Commission. If the Council then insists on pursuing its original 'joint position', it can only do so on the basis of unanimity.

The SEA 1986 also required the assent of Parliament to any international agreements to be entered into by the EU. As a consequence, it has ultimate control, not just in relation to trade treaties, but also as regards any future expansion in the EU's membership.

The European Parliament is, together with the Council of Ministers, the budgetary authority of the EU. The budget is drawn up by the Commission and is presented to both the Council and the Parliament. As regards what is known as 'obligatory' expenditure, the Council has the final say but, in relation to 'non-obligatory' expenditure, the Parliament has the final decision whether to approve the budget or not. Such budgetary control places the Parliament in an extremely powerful position to influence EC policy, but perhaps the most draconian power the Parliament wields is the ability to pass a vote of censure against the Commission, requiring it to resign en masse.

The events of 1998–99 saw a significant shift in the relationship between the Parliament and the Commission. In December 1998, as a result of sustained accusations of mismanagement, fraud and cover ups levelled against the Commission, the Parliament voted not to discharge the Commission's accounts for 1996. Such action was, in effect, a declaration that the Community's budget has not been properly handled and was tantamount to a vote of no confidence in the Commission. In January 1999, the Community's Court of Auditors delivered what can only be described as a devastating report on fraud, waste and mismanagement and maladministration on the part of the Commission. It was found that the Commission had understated its financial obligations by £3.3 billion, and was so lax in its control that it had not even noticed that its banks were not paying any interest on huge amounts of money they were holding. The report of the Court of Auditors led to a vote of no confidence in the Commission in early January 1999 and, although the Commission survived the vote by a majority of 293 to 232, it had to accept the setting up of a 'committee of wise persons' to investigate and report on its operation. At the time, the appointment of this committee was thought to be a diplomatic fudge, allowing the Commission to carry on under warning as to its future conduct. However, when the committee submitted its report, it was so damning that it was immediately obvious that the Parliament would certainly use its power to remove the Commission. To forestall this event, the Commission resigned en masse. Somewhat ironically and certainly anti-climactically, however, as this book is being written, the previous President of the Commission, Jacques Santer, has actually gone, to be replaced by Romano Prodi; but the same commissioners, including the ones who were particularly picked out as the objects of blame, are still in place; on a temporary basis of course, simply ensuring the continuing smooth operation of the Commission.

The Europe wide selection of a new Parliament in June 1999 saw the election of a centre-right majority which will have a significant role to play in approving a new Commission.

By the first week of July 1999, a new Commission had been proposed and gained the approval of the European Parliament later that month. In what President Prodi has said was to be a reforming Commission, the senior UK Commissioner, Neil Kinnock, has been appointed as Vice President with the specific remit of reforming the EU.

17.3.4 Economic and Social Committees

If the Parliament represents the directly elected arm of the EU, then the Economic and Social Committee represents a collection of unelected but, nonetheless, influential interest groups throughout the EU. This committee is a consultative institution and its opinion must be sought prior to the adoption by the Council of any Commission proposal. The Economic and Social Committee represents the underlying 'corporatist' nature of the EU to the extent that it seeks to locate and express a commonality of view and opinion on proposals from such divergent interests groups as employers, trade unions and consumers. It is perhaps symptomatic of the attitude of recent British governments to this underlying corporatist, essentially Christian Democratic, strand within the EU that it dispensed with its own similar internal grouping, the National Economic Development Council in 1992.

17.3.5 The European Commission

The European Commission is the executive of the EU and, in that role, it is responsible for the administration of EU policies. There are 20 Commissioners chosen from the various Member States to serve for renewable terms of four years. Commissioners are appointed to head departments with specific responsibility for furthering particular areas of EU policy. Once appointed, Commissioners are expected to act in the general interest of the EU as a whole rather than in the partial interest of their own home country.

In pursuit of EU policy, the Commission is responsible for ensuring that Treaty obligations between the Member States are met, and that Community laws relating to individuals are enforced. In order to fulfil these functions, the Commission has been provided with extensive powers both in relation to the investigation of potential breaches of Community law and the subsequent punishment of offenders. The classic area in which these powers can be seen in operation is in the area of competition law. Under Arts 81 and 82 (formerly, Arts 85 and 86) of the EC Treaty, the Commission has substantial powers to investigate and control potential monopolies and anti-competitive behaviour and it has used these powers to levy what, in the case of private individuals, would amount to huge fines where breaches of Community competition law have been discovered. In February 1993, the Commission imposed fines totalling more than £80 million on 17 steel producers for what was described as 'a very serious, illegal price fixing cartel'. The UK company British Steel suffered the greatest individual imposition of £26.4 million.

The Commission also acts, under instructions from the Council, as the negotiator between the EU and external countries.

In addition to these executive functions, the Commission also has a vital part to play in the EU's legislative process. The Council can only act on proposals put before it by the Commission. The Commission, therefore, has a duty to propose to the Council measures that will advance the achievement of the EU's general policies.

17.3.6 The European Court of Justice

The ECJ is the judicial arm of the EU and, in the field of Community law its judgments overrule those of national courts. It consists of 15 judges, assisted by nine advocates general, and sits in Luxembourg. The role of the advocate general is to investigate the matter submitted to the Court and to produce a report together with a recommendation for the consideration of the Court. The actual Court is free to accept the report or not as it sees fit.

The SEA 1986 provided for a new Court of First Instance to be attached to the existing Court of Justice. The jurisdiction of the Court of First Instance is limited mainly to internal claims by employees of the Community and to claims against fines made by the Commission under Community competition law. The aim is to reduce the burden of work on the Court of Justice but there is a right of appeal, on points of law only, to the full Court of Justice.

The Court of Justice performs two key functions:

(a) it decides whether any measures adopted, or rights denied, by the Commission, Council or any national government are compatible with treaty obligations. Such actions may be raised by any EU institution, government or individual. A Member State may fail to comply with its Treaty obligations in a number of ways. It might fail or, indeed, refuse to comply with a provision of the Treaty or a regulation; or, alternatively, it might refuse to implement a directive within the allotted time provided for. Under such circumstances, the State in question will be brought before the ECJ, either by the Commission or another Member State or, indeed, individuals within the State concerned;

(b) it provides authoritative rulings, at the request of national courts under Art 234 (formerly, Art 177) of the Treaty of Rome, on the interpretation of points of Community law. When an application is made under Art 234, the national proceedings are suspended until such time as the determination of the point in question is delivered by the ECJ. Whilst the case is being decided by the ECJ, the national court is expected to provide appropriate interim relief, even if this involves going against a domestic legal provision, as in the *Factortame* case.

This procedure can take the form of a preliminary ruling where the request precedes the actual determination of a case by the national court.

Article 234 (formerly, Art 177) provides that:

The Court of Justice shall have jurisdiction to give preliminary rulings concerning:

(a) the interpretation of treaties;

(b) the validity and interpretation of acts of the institutions of the Union and of the European Central Bank;

(c) the interpretation of the statutes of bodies established by an act of the Council, where those statutes so provide.

Where such a question is raised before any court or tribunal of a Member State, that court or tribunal may, if it considers that a decision on the question is necessary to enable it to give judgment, request the Court of Justice to give a ruling thereon.

Where any such question is raised in a case pending before a court or tribunal of a Member State against whose decision there is no judicial remedy under national law, that court or tribunal shall bring the matter before the Court of Justice.

It is clear that it is for the national court and not the individual parties concerned to make the reference. Where the national court or tribunal is not the 'final' court or tribunal, the reference to the ECJ is discretionary. Where the national court or tribunal is the 'final' court, then reference is obligatory. However, there are circumstances under which a 'final' court need not make a reference under Art 234 (formerly, Art 177). These are:

- where the question of Community law is not truly relevant to the decision to be made by the national court;

- where there has been a previous interpretation of the provision in question by the ECJ so that its meaning has been clearly determined;

- where the interpretation of the provision is so obvious as to leave no scope for any reasonable doubt as to its meaning. This latter instance has to be used with caution given the nature of Community law; for example, the fact that it is expressed in several languages using legal terms which might have different connotations within different jurisdictions. However, it is apparent that, where the meaning is clear, no reference need be made.

Reference has already been made, in Chapter 5, to the methods of interpretation used by courts in relation to Community law. It will be recalled that, in undertaking such a task, a purposive and contextual approach is mainly adopted, as against the more restrictive methods of interpretation favoured in relation to UK domestic legislation. The clearest statement of this purposive contextualist approach adopted by the ECJ is contained in its judgment in the *CILFIT* case:

Every provision of Community law must be placed in its context and interpreted in the light of the provisions of Community law as a whole, regard being had to the objectives thereof and to its state of evolution at the date on which the provision in question is to be applied.

It can be appreciated that the reservations considered previously in regard to judicial creativity and intervention in policy matters in the UK courts apply *a fortiori* to the decisions of the ECJ.

Another major difference between the ECJ and the court within the English legal system is that the former is not bound by the doctrine of precedent in the same way as the latter is. It is always open to the ECJ to depart from its previous decisions where it considers it appropriate to do so. Although it will endeavour to maintain consistency, it has, on occasion, ignored its own previous decisions, as in *European Parliament v Council* (1990) where it recognised the right of the Parliament to institute an action against the Council.

The manner in which European law operates to control sex discrimination, through the Equal Treatment Directive, is of significant interest and, in *Marshall v Southampton and West Hampshire Area Health Authority* (1993), a number of the points that have been considered above were highlighted. Ms Marshall had originally been required to retire earlier than a man in her situation would have been required to do. She successfully argued before the ECJ that such a practice was discriminatory and contrary to Directive 76/207/EC on the equal treatment of men and women.

The present action related to the level of compensation she was entitled to as a consequence of this breach. UK legislation, the Sex Discrimination Act 1975, had set limits on the level of compensation that could be recovered for acts of sex discrimination. Marshall argued that the imposition of such limits was contrary to the Equal Opportunity Directive and that, in establishing such limits, the UK had failed to comply with the Directive.

The House of Lords referred the case to the ECJ under Art 234 (formerly, Art 177) and the latter determined that the rights set out in relation to compensation under Art 6 of the Directive were directly effective, and that, as the purpose of the Directive was to give effect to the principle of equal treatment, that could only be achieved by either reinstatement or the awarding of adequate compensation. The decision of the ECJ, therefore, overruled the financial limitations placed on sex discrimination awards and effectively overruled the domestic legislation.

P v S and Cornwall County Council (1996) extended the ambit of unlawful sex discrimination under the directive to cover people who have undergone surgical gender reorientation (sex change). However, in *Grant v South West Trains Ltd* (1998), the ECJ declined to extend the directive to cover discrimination on the grounds of sexual orientation (homosexuality), even though the Advocate General had initially supported the extension of the directive to same sex relationships. Whilst *Grant* was in the process of being decided in the ECJ, a second case, *R v Secretary of State for Defence ex p Perkins (No 2)*, had been brought before the English courts arguing a similar point, that discrimination on grounds of sexual orientation was covered by the Equal Treatment Directive. Initially, the High Court had referred the matter, under Art

234 (formerly, Art 177), to the ECJ for decision, but, on the decision in *Grant* being declared, the referral was withdrawn. In withdrawing the reference, Lightman J considered the proposition of counsel for Perkins to the effect that:

> ... there have been a number of occasions where the ECJ has overruled its previous decisions; that the law is not static; and, accordingly, in a dynamic and developing field such as discrimination in employment there must be a prospect that a differently constituted ECJ may depart from the decision in Grant ... But, to justify a reference, the possibility that the ECJ will depart from its previous decision must be more than theoretical: it must be a realistic possibility. The decision in Grant was of the full Court; it is only some four months old; there has been no development in case law or otherwise since the decision which can give cause for the ECJ reconsidering that decision ... I can see no realistic prospect of any change of mind on the part of the ECJ.

It could be pointed out that there could be no change in case law if judges, such as Lightman J, refused to send similar cases to the ECJ; but there may well be sense, if not virtue, in his refusal to refer similar cases to the ECJ within such a short timescale.

17.3.7 The Court of Auditors

Given the part that the Court of Auditors played in the 1998–99 struggle between the Parliament and the Commission, the role of this body should not be underestimated.

As its name suggests, it is responsible for providing an external audit of the Communities' finances. It examines the legality, regularity and soundness of the management of all the Communities' revenue and expenditure. The following passage, from its statement of assurance relating to the budget for the year 1996–97, provides a flavour of its findings:

> ... as in previous years, the incidence of errors affecting the transactions underlying the Commission's payments is too high for the Court to provide assurance about their legality and regularity.
>
> Many of the errors found in the payments provide direct evidence of failure to implement the control mechanisms foreseen in the regulations or to apply requisite checks before payments are made ... there were, again, many formal errors affecting payments. These are, essentially, cases where there was a failure to comply with the applicable regulations ... in many cases, formal errors involve specific systems weaknesses, notably failure to implement the control procedure required to ensure the eligibility of the recipients and the accuracy of the amounts paid [www.eca.eu.int.EN/reports_opinions.htm].

From this passage may well be seen the reason why the Parliament sought to establish some control over the operation of the Commission.

17.4 The European Convention on Human Rights

It has to be established, and emphasised, from the outset that the substance of this section has absolutely nothing to do with the EU as such; the Council of Europe is a completely distinct organisation and, although membership of the two organisations overlap, they are not the same. The Council of Europe is concerned not with economic matters but with the protection of civil rights and freedoms.

It is gratifying, at least to a degree, to recognise that the Convention and its Court (the ECHR) are no longer a matter of mysterious external control; the HRA 1998 having incorporated the European Convention on Human Rights into UK law and placing the ECHR as the supreme court in matters related to its jurisdiction. Much attention was paid to the Convention and the HRA in Chapter 1 (see 1.5), so it only remains to consider the structure and operation of the ECHR.

The Convention originally established two institutions:

(a) the European Commission of Human Rights. This body was charged with the task of examining, and if need be investigating the circumstances of, petitions submitted to it. If the Commission was unable to reach a negotiated solution between the parties concerned, it referred the matter to the Court of Human Rights;

(b) the European Court of Human Rights (ECHR). The European Convention on Human Rights provides that the judgment of the Court shall be final and that parties to it will abide by the decisions of the Court. This body, sitting in Strasbourg, was, and remains, responsible for all matters relating to the interpretation and application of the current Convention.

However, in the 1980s, as the Convention and its Court became more known and popular as a forum for asserting human rights, so its workload increased. This pressure was exacerbated by the break up of the old Communist Eastern Bloc and the fact that the newly independent countries, in both senses of the words, became signatories to the Convention. The statistics support the view of the incipient sclerosis of the original structure.

Applications registered with the Commission

Year	Number of applications registered
1981	404
1993	2,037
1997	4,750

Cases referred to the Court

Year	Number of cases referred
1981	7
1993	52
1997	119

As a consequence of such pressure, it became necessary to streamline the procedure by amalgamating the two previous institutions into one Court. In pursuit of this aim, Protocol 11 of the Convention was introduced in 1994. The new ECHR came into operation on 1 November 1998, although the Commission continued to deal with cases which had already been declared admissible for a further year.

The ECHR consists of 40 judges, representing the number of signatories to the Convention, although they do not have to be chosen from each State and, in any case, sit as individuals rather than representatives of their State. Judges are elected, by the Parliamentary Assembly of the Council of Europe, generally for six years, but arrangements have been put in place so that one half of the membership of the judicial panel will be required to seek renewal every three years.

It has to be recognised that the UK does not have a good record in relation to cases taken against it in the ECHR; in fact, currently, it comes second only to Turkey in the league of offenders. A number of case studies may highlight the way in which the ECHR deals with cases. It must not be forgotten, however, that these previous decisions of the ECHR are now binding precedents in UK law.

In *Malone v UK* (1984), the ECHR decided that telephone tapping by the police, authorised by the UK Government, and condoned under common law powers by the High Court, was in breach of Art 8 of the European Convention on Human Rights which guarantees the right to privacy. The Article holds:

> There shall be no interference by a public authority with the exercise of this right except such as is in accordance with the law and is necessary in a democratic society in the interests of national security ...

The ECHR held that the tapping was against the Convention because it was not 'in accordance with law' but rather governed by an unregulated discretion. It could not be 'necessary in a democratic society' as there were no constitutional safeguards against misuse of the power. The government reacted by introducing legislation to control telephone tapping by the police. The Interception of Communications Act 1985 limits telephone tapping to cases where the Home Secretary has issued a warrant and, to safeguard against arbitrary use, the warrant can only be issued in three specified circumstances, one of which is the prevention of serious crime. Further safeguards are provided by a tribunal to investigate complaints about the use of these powers and by the establishment of a commissioner to review annually how the Home Secretary has exercised his powers.

Another example of the way in which the system operates may be seen in the case of Earnest Saunders, one of the original defendants in the *Guinness* fraud trial of 1990. Prior to his trial, Saunders had been interviewed by Department of Trade and Industry inspectors and was required, under the provisions of the companies legislation, to answer questions without the right to silence. It was claimed that interviews under such conditions, and their subsequent use at the trial leading to his conviction, were in breach of the Convention on Human Rights. In October 1994, the Commission decided in Saunders' favour, and the Court confirmed that decision in 1996, although Saunders was not awarded damages. As a result, the Government has recognised that the powers given to DTI inspectors, breach the Convention, and has declared an intention to alter them, but not in a retrospective way that would benefit Mr Saunders.

Nor should one forget the potentially crucially important decision in *McGonnell v UK* (1995), in which the Commission has placed the situation of the Lord Chancellor in doubt.

In deciding cases before it, the ECHR applies what is known as the 'margin of appreciation'. This means that Member States have a measure of national discretion in the way they give effect to general standards set out in the Convention. An example of this may be seen in the 1996 decision on the ECHR in favour of the UK's decision to ban the film, *Visions of Ecstasy*, under its blasphemy law, in spite of the director's claim that the ban was contrary to his right to freedom of speech. The court decided that such delicate decisions as those relating to issues such as blasphemy should be decided at the local level and should not be imposed centrally. This particular decision may have pleased the UK Government, but it has been less than pleased with a number of other controversial cases in which the decisions have gone against it. Notable amongst these was the decision that the rights of the suspected IRA terrorists had been violated by their summary execution in Gibraltar.

Equally, the concerns of the government cannot but have been strengthened by the recent decision of the High Court to effectively take the impact of the HRA into consideration immediately (see 1.5).

17.5 The European Convention and the European Union

Having started this section by stressing the fundamental distinction between the ECJ and the ECHR, it is necessary to finish it by blurring it and pointing out the various ways in which the EC, and then EU, have expressly recognised the rights provided in the Convention and the decisions made by the ECHR. Thus, in a joint declaration delivered in 1997, the European Parliament, the Council, and the Commission emphasised the prime importance they attached to the protection of fundamental rights:

> ... as derived particularly from the constitution of the Member States and the European Convention for the Protection of Human Rights and Fundamental Freedoms [(1977) OJ C103].

Article 6 (formerly, Art F(2)), which was introduced by the Maastricht Treaty, expressly states that:

> The Union shall respect fundamental rights, as guaranteed by the European Convention for the Protection of Human Rights and Fundamental Freedoms ... as general principles of Community law.

The ECJ, in the same way as English courts, has equally been guided by the Convention where Community law is silent. It still remains possible, however, for cases to be brought to either or both judicial forums. Issues relating to discrimination are an ideal case in point by being potentially both in breach of employment law regulated by the EC, and fundamental human rights regulated by the ECHR. It is also an unfortunate fact that it is possible for at least a degree of incompatibility between the decisions of the two courts in relation to very similar matters (for example, see *SPUC v Grogan* (1991); and *Open Door and Well Women v Ireland* (1992)). Such possibilities would be precluded if, following the recent action of the UK, the EU, as a body, were formally to incorporate the Convention.

THE EUROPEAN CONTEXT

The European Union

UK law is now subject to Community law in particular areas.

In practice, this has led to the curtailment of parliamentary sovereignty in those areas.

Sources of European Community law

The sources of European Community law are:

- internal treaties and protocols;
- international agreements;
- secondary legislation; and
- decisions of the European Court of Justice.

Secondary legislation takes three forms:

- regulations which are directly applicable;
- directives which have to be given statutory form;
- decisions are directly applicable.

Major institutions

The major institutions of the European Union are:

- the Council of Ministers;
- the European Parliament; the Commission; and
- the ECJ.

The European Court of Human Rights

The European Council, the European Commission of Human Rights and the European Court of Human Rights are distinct institutions whose purpose is to regulate the potential abuse of human rights. They are not part of the EU structure.

Since the coming into force (October 2000) of the Human Rights Act 1998, the European Convention on Human Rights is incorporated into UK law. It remains to see what effect this has on domestic UK law but it cannot but be significant.

FURTHER READING

Chapter 1   Introduction to Law

Barnett, H, *Constitutional and Administrative Law*, 2nd edn, 1998, London: Cavendish Publishing

Bradney, A *et al*, *How to Study Law*, 3rd edn, 1995, London: Sweet & Maxwell

Clinch, P, *Using a Law Library*, 1992, London: Blackstone

Fitzpatrick, P (ed), *Dangerous Supplements*, 1991, London: Pluto

Holmes, N and Venebles, D, *Researching the Legal Web*, 1997, London: Butterworths

Social and legal order

Mansell, W and Meteyard, B, *A Critical Introduction to Law*, 2nd edn, 1999, London: Cavendish Publishing

Roberts, S, *Order and Dispute*, 1979, Harmondsworth: Penguin

Legal language

Friedman, L, 'On interpretation of laws' (1988) 11(3) Ratio Juris 252, pp 252–62

Goodrich, P, *Reading the Law*, 1986, Oxford: Basil Blackwell

Jackson, B, *Making Sense in Law*, 1995, London: Deborah Charles

Law, politics and the Rule of Law

Bennion, F, 'A naked usurpation?' (1999) 149 NLJ 421, pp 421–26

Dicey, AV, *Introduction to the Law of the Constitution*, 1897, London: Macmillan

Feldman, D, 'The Human Rights Act and constitutional principles' (1999) 19(2) JLS, June

Fine, R, *Democracy and the Rule of Law*, 1984, London: Pluto

Hill, C, *Liberty Against the Law*, 1996, Harmondsworth: Penguin

Horowitz, MJ, 'The Rule of Law: an unqualified good?' (1977) 86 Yale LJ 561

Kairys, D (ed), *The Politics of Law: A Progressive Critique*, 1990, London: Pantheon

Keating, D, 'Upholding the Rule of Law' (1999) 149 NLJ 533, pp 533–34

Laws, J (Sir), 'Law and democracy' [1995] PL 72

Locke, J, *The Treatises of Government*, 1988, Cambridge: CUP

Raz, J, 'The Rule of Law and its virtue' (1972) 93 LQR 195

Sedley, S (Sir), *Freedom, Law and Justice*, 1998, Hamlyn Lectures, London: Sweet & Maxwell

Sedley, S (Sir), 'Human rights: a 21st century agenda' [1995] PL 386

Steiner, H and Alston, P, *International Human Rights in Context*, 1996, Oxford: Clarendon

Thompson, A, 'Taking the right seriously: the case of FA Hayek', in Fitzpatrick, P (ed), *Dangerous Supplements*, 1991, London: Pluto

Thompson, E, *Whigs and Hunters*, 1977, Harmondsworth: Penguin

von Hayek, F, *The Road to Serfdom*, 1962, London: Routledge

Young, J, 'The politics of the Human Rights Act' (1999) 26(1) JLS 27, pp 27–37

Chapter 2   Sources of Law

Boulton, C (ed), *Erskine May's Treatise on the Law, Privileges, Proceedings and Usage of Parliament*, 1989, London: Butterworths

Cross, R, *Cross, Harris and Hart: Precedent in English Law*, 4th edn, 1991, Oxford: Clarendon

Goodhart, A, 'The *ratio decidendi* of a case' (1959) 22 MLR 117

Holdsworth, W, 'Case law' (1934) 50 LQR 180

Jenkins, C, 'Helping the reader of Bills and Acts' (1999) 149 NLJ 798, pp 798–99

MacCormick, N, *Legal Rules and Legal Reasoning*, 1978, Oxford: Clarendon

Simpson, A, 'The *ratio decidendi* of a case' (1957) 20 MLR 413; (1958) 21 MLR 155

The following are also relevant to the issues in Chapter 4:

Bates, T, 'The contemporary use of legislative history in the United Kingdom' (1995) 54(1) CLJ 127, pp 127–52

Bell, J and Engle, G (Sir), *Cross: Statutory Interpretation*, 3rd edn, 1995, London: Butterworths

Bennion, F, *Statutory Interpretation*, 2nd edn, 1992, London: Butterworths

Bennion, F, 'Statute law: obscurity and drafting parameters' (1978) 5 British JLS 235, pp 235–45

Committee on the Preparation of Legislation, *Renton Committee Report*, 1975, Cmnd 6053, London: HMSO

Eskridge, W, *Dynamic Statutory Interpretation*, 1994, Cambridge, MA: Harvard UP

Friedman, L, 'On interpretation of laws' (1988) 11(3) Ratio Juris 252, pp 252–62

Chapter 3   Civil and Criminal Court Structures

Barnard, D and Houghton, M, *The New Civil Court in Action*, 1993, London: Butterworths

Carlen, P, *Magistrates' Justice*, 1976, Oxford: Martin Robertson

Fage, J and Whitehead, G, *Supreme Court Practice and Procedure*, 1992, London: Fourmat

Fallon, P and Bursell, R, *Crown Court Practice (Trial)*, 1978, London: Butterworths

Greenslade, R, *Civil Court Practice*, 1997, London: Butterworths

Harrison, R, 'Why have two types of civil court?' (1999) 149 NLJ 65, pp 65–70

Judicial Statistics Annual Report 1996, Government Statistical Service, 1997, London: HMSO

Malleson, K, 'The Criminal Cases Review Commission: how will it work?' [1995] Crim LR 928

Matthews, P and Foreman, J (eds), *Jervis: On the Office and Duties of Coroners*, 1993, London: Sweet & Maxwell

Moxon, D and Hedderman, C, 'Mode of trial decisions and sentencing differences between courts' (1994) 33(2) Howard J of Criminal Justice 97, pp 97–103

Pedley, FH, 'The small claims process' (1994) 144 NLJ 1217

Pershad, R, 'Delay, listing and the county court' (1994) *Counsel*, February, p 16

Richardson, PJ (ed), *Archbold on Criminal Pleading, Evidence and Practice*, 1997, London: Sweet & Maxwell

Smith, JC, 'The Criminal Appeal Act 1995: appeals against conviction' [1995] Crim LR 921

Smith, R, 'Judicial statistics' (1995) 145 NLJ 1364

Woolf (Lord), *Access to Justice – Final Report to the Lord Chancellor on the Civil Justice System in England and Wales*, 1996, London: HMSO

Chapter 4   The Judiciary

Baldwin, J, 'The social composition of magistrates' (1976) 16 Br J Crim 171

Bell, J and Engle, G (Sir), *Cross on Statutory Interpretation*, 1995, London: Butterworths

Bennion, F, *Statutory Interpretation*, 1992, London: Butterworths

Bindman, G, 'Lessons of *Pinochet*' (1999) 149 NLJ 1050, pp 1050–51

Browne-Wilkinson, N (Sir), 'The independence of the judiciary in the 1980s' [1988] PL 4

Crawford, L, 'Race awareness training and the judges' (1994) *Counsel*, February, p 11

Denning (Lord), *The Discipline of Law*, 1979, London: Butterworths

Denning (Lord), *Due Process of Law*, 1980, London: Butterworths

Griffith, JAG, *The Politics of the Judiciary*, 5th edn, 1997, London: Fontana

Hailsham (Lord), 'The office of Lord Chancellor and the separation of powers' (1989) 8 Civil Justice Quarterly 308, pp 308–18

Lee, S, *Judging Judges*, 1988, London: Faber & Faber

MacCormick, N, *Legal Rules and Legal Reasoning*, 1978, Oxford: Clarendon

Mackay (Lord), *The Administration of Justice*, 1994, London: Sweet & Maxwell

Malleson, K, *The New Judiciary – The Effect of Expansion and Activism*, 1999, Aldershot: Ashgate

McLachlin, B, 'The role of judges in modern Commonwealth society' (1994) 110 LQR 260, pp 260–69

Pannick, D, *Judges*, 1987, Oxford: OUP

Parker, C, 'Judicial decision making' (1999) 149 NLJ 1142, pp 1142–44

Parker, H *et al*, *Unmasking the Magistrates*, 1989, Milton Keynes: Open UP

Pickles, J, *Straight from the Bench*, 1987, London: Hodder & Stoughton

Reid (Lord), 'The judge as law maker' (1972) 12 JSPTL 22

Royal Commission on Criminal Justice, *Runciman Report*, Cm 2263, 1995, London: HMSO

Rutherford, A, 'Judicial training and autonomy' (1999) 149 NLJ 1120, pp 1120–22

Skordaki, E, *Judicial Appointments*, Law Society Research Study No 5, 1991, London: HMSO

Stevens, R, *The Independence of the Judiciary*, 1993, Oxford: OUP

See, in addition, reading for Chapter 2.

Chapter 5   The Criminal Law

Allen, MJ, *Criminal Law*, 5th edn, 1999, London: Blackstone

Ashworth, A, *Principles of Criminal Law*, 2nd edn, 1995, Oxford: Clarendon

Ashworth, A, 'Reason, logic and criminal liability' (1975) 91 LQR 102

Ashworth, A, 'The elasticity of *mens rea*', in Tapper, C (ed), *Crime, Proof and Punishment*, 1981, London: Butterworths

Ashworth, A, 'The scope of criminal liability for omissions' (1989) 105 LQR 424

Card, R, *Card, Cross and Jones: Criminal Law*, 14th edn, 1998, London: Butterworths

Clarkson, CMV and Keating, HM, *Criminal Law: Text and Materials*, 2nd edn, 1990, London: Sweet & Maxwell

Gunn, M, Birch, D and Ormerod, D, *Criminal Law*, forthcoming 2001, London: Cavendish Publishing

Jefferson, M, *Criminal Law*, 1998, London: Pitman

Lacey, N and Wells, C, *Reconstructing Criminal Law*, 1998, London: Butterworths

Law Commission, *A Criminal Code for England and Wales*, No 177, 1989, London: HMSO, Vols 1 and 2

Law Commission, *Legislating the Criminal Code: Involuntary Manslaughter*, 1996, London: HMSO

Norrie, A, *Crime, Reason and History*, 1993, London: Butterworths

Norrie, A, 'After *Woolin*' [1999] Crim LR 532

Padfield, N, 'Clean water and muddy causation' [1995] Crim LR 683

Slapper, G and Tombs, S, *Corporate Crime*, 1999, London: Longman

Smith, JC, 'Using force in self-defence and the prevention of crime' (1994) 47 CLP 101

Smith, JC and Hogan, B, *Criminal Law*, 9th edn, 1999, London: Butterworths

Williams, G, *Textbook of Criminal Law*, 1983, London: Stevens

Chapter 6 The Law of Contract

Collins, H, *The Law of Contract*, 3rd edn, 1997, London: Butterworths

Koffman, L and McDonald, E, *The Law of Contract*, 3rd edn, 1998, Croydon: Tolley

Oughton, D and Davis, M, *Sourcebook on Contract Law*, 1996, London: Cavendish Publishing

Stone, R, *Principles of Contract Law*, 3rd edn, 1997 (4th edn, forthcoming 2000), London: Cavendish Publishing

Chapter 7   Consumer Protection

Lowe, R and Woodroffe, G, *Consumer Law and Practice*, 4th edn, 1995, London: Sweet & Maxwell

Miller, C, Harvey, B and Parry, D, *Consumer and Trading Law*, 1998, Oxford: OUP

Rose, F, *Statutes on Commercial and Consumer Law*, 8th edn, 1999, London: Blackstone

Chapter 8   The Tort of Negligence

Conaghan, J and Mansell, W, *The Wrongs of Tort*, 2nd edn, 1997, London: Pluto

Harpwood, V, *Principles of Tort Law*, 3rd edn, 1997, London: Cavendish Publishing

Rogers, WVH, *Winfield & Jolocwitz on Tort*, 15th edn, 1999, London: Sweet & Maxwell

Chapter 9   Business and Corporate Law

Billins, R, *Agency Law*, 1994, London: Longman

Butterworths Employment Law Handbook, 8th edn, 1999, London: Butterworths

CCH, *British Companies Legislation*, 1999

Davies, P, *Gower's Principles of Modern Company Law*, 6th edn, 1997, London: Sweet & Maxwell

Farrar, J and Hannigan, B, *Farrar's Company Law*, 4th edn, 1998, London: Butterworths

Goulding, S, *Company Law*, 2nd edn, 1999, London: Cavendish Publishing

Kelly, D and Holmes, A, *Principles of Business Law*, 2nd edn, 1997 (3rd edn, forthcoming 2000), London: Cavendish Publishing

Morse, G, *Partnership Law*, 4th edn, 1998, London: Blackstone

Painter, R, Holmes, A and Migdal, S, *Cases and Materials in Employment Law*, 2000, London: Blackstone

Stone, R, *Law of Agency*, 1996, London: Cavendish Publishing

Chapter 10   The Law of Equity and Trusts

Bartlett, R, 'When is a trust not a trust? The National Health Service' [1996] 60 Conv 186

Birks, P, 'Tracing, subrogation and change of position' (1996) 9 Tru LI 124

Gardner, S, 'Knowing assistance and knowing receipt: taking stock' (1996) 112 LQR 86

Goodhart, W, 'Trust law for the 21st century' (1996) 10(2) Tru LI 38

Green, B, 'Grey, Oughtred and Vandervell: a contextual reappraisal' (1984) 47 MLR 385

Hayton, DJ, *Commentary and Cases on the Law of Trusts and Equitable Remedies*, 10th edn, 1996, London: Sweet & Maxwell

Hudson, A, *Principles of Equity and Trusts*, 1999, London: Cavendish Publishing

Martin, J, *Hanbury and Martin: Modern Equity*, 15th edn, 1997, London: Sweet & Maxwell

Mason, A, 'The place of equity and equitable remedies in contemporary society' (1994) 110 LQR 238

McKay, L, 'Trusts for purposes' [1973] Conv 420

Millett, P, 'The *Quistclose* trust: who can enforce it?' (1985) 101 LQR 269

Millett, P, 'Equity's place in the law of commerce' (1998) 114 LQR 214

Milner, M, 'Pension trust: a new trust form?' [1997] Conv 89

Nicholls (Lord), 'Trustees and their broader community: where duty, morality and ethics converge' (1995) 9 Tru LI 71

Oakley, AJ, *Parker and Mellows: Modern Law of Trusts*, 7th edn, 1999, London: Sweet & Maxwell

Pettit, P, *Equity and the Law of Trusts*, 8th edn, 1997, London: Butterworths

Ramjohn, M, *Sourcebook on Trusts Law*, 2nd edn, 1998, London: Cavendish Publishing

Rickett, R, 'Unincorporated associations and their dissolution' (1980) 39 CLJ 88

Swadling, W, 'A new role for resulting trusts' (1996) 16 LS 110

Todd, P, *Textbook on Trusts*, 4th edn, 1996, London: Blackstone

Worthington, S, 'Sorting out ownership interests in a bulk: gifts, sales and trusts' [1999] JBL 1

Chapter 11   The Civil Process

Baldwin, J, *The Small Claims Procedure and the Consumer*, 1995, London: Office of Fair Trading

Genn, H, *Hard Bargaining: Out of Court Settlements in Personal Injury Claims*, 1987, Oxford: OUP

Grainger, I and Fealy, M, *An Introduction to the New Civil Procedure Rules*, 1999, London: Cavendish Publishing

Harrison, R, 'Cry Woolf' (1999) 149 NLJ 1011, pp 1011–13

Lawton, F, 'Court experts' (1995) 140 SJ 793

Miller, F, 'The adversarial myth' (1995) 145 NLJ 743

Thompson, P (ed), *The Civil Court Practice*, 1999, London: Butterworths

Trent, M, 'ADR and the new Civil Procedure Rules' (1999) 149 NLJ 410, pp 410–11

Woolf (Lord), *Access to Justice – Final Report to the Lord Chancellor on the Civil Justice System in England and Wales*, 1996, London: HMSO

Zander, M, 'Are there any clothes for the emperor to wear?' (1995) 145 NLJ 154

Zander, M, 'The trouble with fast track fixed costs' (1997) 147 NLJ 1125

Zander, M, 'The Woolf Report: forwards or backwards for the new Lord Chancellor' (1997) 16 Civil Justice Quarterly 208, pp 208–27

Zuckerman, AAS, 'A reform of civil procedure – rationing procedure rather than access to justice' (1995) 22 JLS 156

Chapter 12 Arbitration, Tribunal Adjudication, and Alternative Dispute Resolution

Abel, R, 'The comparative study of dispute institutions in society' (1973) 8 Law and Society Rev 217

Baldwin, J, *The Small Claims Procedure and the Consumer*, 1995, London: Office of Fair Trading

Beale, H and Dugdale, T, 'Contracts between businessmen: planning and the use of contractual remedies' (1975) 2 British JLS 45

Committee on Administrative Tribunals and Inquiries, *Franks Report*, Cmnd 218, 1957, London: HMSO

Genn, H and Genn, Y, *The Effectiveness of Representation at Tribunals*, 1989, London: LCD

JUSTICE, *Industrial Tribunals*, 1987, London: JUSTICE

Mackay (Lord), *The Administration of Justice*, 1994, London: Sweet & Maxwell

Payne, R, 'To counsel, not confront: the law on ADR' (1999) *Counsel*, February, pp 30–32

Pedley, FH, 'The small claims process' (1994) 144 NLJ 1217

The Annual Report of the Council on Tribunals, 1995–96, London: HMSO

The Annual Report of the Council on Tribunals, 1996–97, London: HMSO

Chapter 13 The Criminal Process: (1) The Investigation of Crime

Baldwin, J, *The Conduct of Police Investigation*, 1992, London: HMSO

Baldwin, J and McConville, M, *Jury Trials*, 1979, Oxford: Clarendon

Bevan, V and Lidstone, K, *The Investigation of Crime*, 2nd edn, 1996, London: Butterworths

Brown, D, Ellis, T and Larcombe, K, *Changing the Code: Police Detention under the revised PACE Codes of Practice*, Home Office Research Study No 129, 1993, London: HMSO

Burrow, J, 'Pre-committal custody time limits' (1999) 149 NLJ 330, pp 330–32

Committee on Fraud Trials, *Roskill Report*, 1986, London: HMSO

Darbyshire, P, 'The lamp that shows that freedom lives – is it worth the candle?' [1991] Crim LR 740

Dennis, I, 'The Criminal Justice and Public Order Act 1994: the evidence provisions' [1995] Crim LR 4

Devlin, P, *Trial by Jury*, 1956, London: Stevens

Dixon, D, Coleman, C and Bottomley, K, 'PACE in practice' (1991) 141 NLJ 1586

Doran, S and Jackson, J, 'The case for jury waiver' [1997] 155 Crim LR

Findlay, M and Duff, P, *The Jury Under Attack*, 1988, London: Butterworths

Greer, S, 'The right to silence: defence disclosure and confession evidence' (1994) 21 JLS 103

Herbert, P, 'Racism, impartiality and juries' (1995) 145 NLJ 146

Royal Commission on Criminal Justice, *Runciman Report*, Cm 2263, 1995, London: HMSO

Wadham, J and Arkinstall, J, 'Human rights and crime' (1999) 149 NLJ 703, pp 703–06

Wolchover, D and Heaton-Armstrong, A, 'Jailing psychopaths and prison cell confessions' (1999) 149 NLJ 285, pp 285–314

Zander, M, *The Police and Criminal Evidence Act 1994*, 3rd edn, 1995, London: Sweet & Maxwell

Chapter 14   The Criminal Process: (2) The Prosecution

Ashworth, A and Fionda, J, 'The new Code for Crown Prosecutors: prosecution, accountability and the public interest' [1994] Crim LR 894

Baldwin, J and McConville, M, *Negotiated Justice: Pressures on Defendants to Plead Guilty*, 1977, Oxford: Martin Robertson

Bindaman, D, 'Crown duals' (1999) 96(13) Law Soc Gazette 22, pp 22–28

Cockburn, JS and Green, TA, *Twelve Good Men and True*, 1988, Guilford: Princeton UP

CPS, *The Code for Crown Prosecutors*, rev edn, June 1994, London: CPS

Devlin, P, *Trial by Jury*, 1956, London: Stevens

Griffiths, C, 'Jury trial' (1999) *Counsel*, April, pp 14–16

Henderson, P and Nicholas, T, *Offending While on Bail*, Home Office Research Bulletin 32, 1992, London: Home Office Research Unit

Hucklesby, A, 'The use and abuse of conditional bail' (1994) 33 Howard J 258

Findlay, M and Duff, P, *The Jury Under Attack*, 1988, London: Butterworths

Mills, B, 'The prosecution code' (1994) 139 SJ 709

Rutherford, A, 'Preserving a robust independence' (1999) 149 NLJ 908, pp 908–10

Rose, D, *In the Name of the Law – The Collapse of Criminal Justice*, 1996, London: Jonathan Cape

Sanders, A, 'Class bias in prosecutions' (1985) 24 Howard J 176

Thompson, EP, *Writing by Candlelight*, 1980, London: Merlin

Watson, A, 'The right to elect trial by jury: the issue re-appears' (1998) 163 JP 636, pp 636–40

Chapter 15   Legal Services

Abel, R, *The Legal Profession in England and Wales*, 1988, Oxford: Basil Blackwell

Barnard, M, 'All bar none' (1999) 96(26) Law Soc Gazette 20, pp 20–24

Boxer, C, 'Conditional fees: lawyers courting disaster' (1995) 145 NLJ 1069

Cocks, R, *Foundations of the Modern Bar*, 1983, London: Sweet & Maxwell

Editorial, 'Rights of audience' (1998) 162 JP 193, pp 193–95

Genn, H and Genn, Y, *The Effectiveness of Representation at Tribunals*, 1989, London: LCD

Holland, A, 'Cut price conveyancing' (1994) 144 NLJ 192

Jackson, R, 'Disappointed litigants and doubtful actions'(1995) *Counsel*, May, p 16

Law Society Consultation Paper, *Supervision of Solicitors – The Next Decade*, July 1995

Money-Kyrle, R, 'Advocates' immunity after *Osman*' (1999) 149 NLJ 945, pp 945–50 and 981–82

Powell, JL, 'Barristers' immunity – time to go' (1995) *Counsel*, March, p 11

St Luce, S, 'Cutting the lifeline' (1999) 149 NLJ 398, pp 398–99

Verkaik, R, 'Opinions on counsel' (1998) 95(4) Law Soc Gazette 22

Chapter 16   The Funding of Legal Services

Bean, D, 'Surveying the new landscape' (1999) *Counsel*, June, pp 8–10

Knafler, S, 'Litigation for the poor' (1994) 139 SJ 256

Law Commission Consultation Paper, *Legal Aid – Targeting Need: The Future of Publicly Funded Help in Solving Legal Problems and Disputes in England and Wales*, Cm 2854, London: HMSO

Morris, P *et al*, *Social Needs and Legal Action*, 1973, Oxford: Martin Robertson

Peysner, J and Balen, P, 'Conditional fees' (1995) 92 Law Soc Gazette 20; (1995) 92 Law Soc Gazette 16

Zander, M, 'Access to justice and legal aid: 12 reasons for rejecting the Legal Aid Green Paper' (1995) 145 NLJ 1098

Zander, M, *Legal Services for the Community*, 1978, London: Temple Smith

Chapter 17   The European Context

Benoetvea, J, *The Legal Reasoning of the European Court of Justice: Towards a European Jurisprudence*, 1993, Oxford: Clarendon

Borgsmit, K, 'The Advocate General at the European Court of Justice: a comparative study' (1988) 13 EL Rev 106

Craig, P and de Búrca, G, *EU Law: Text, Cases and Materials*, 2nd edn, 1998, Oxford: OUP

Dickson, B, *Human Rights and the European Convention,* 1997, London: Sweet & Maxwell

Foster, N, *EC Legislation*, 9th edn, 1998, London: Blackstone

Harris, DJ *et al, Law of the European Convention on Human Rights*, 1995, London: Butterworths

Kennedy, T, *Learning European Law: A Primer and* Vade-mecum, 1998, London: Sweet & Maxwell

Lasok, D, *Law and Institutions of the European Union*, 6th edn, 1994, London: Butterworths

Neville Brown, L and Kennedy, T, *The Court of Justice of the European Communities*, 4th edn, 1994, London: Sweet & Maxwell

Shaw, J, *European Community Law,* 2nd edn, 1996, London: Macmillan

Ward, I, *A Critical Introduction to European Law*, 1996, London: Butterworths

Weatherill, S and Beamont, P, *EC Law*, 1993, London: Penguin

INDEX

Index

Index